The State, Identity, and the National Question in China and Japan

The State, Identity, and the National Question in China and Japan

• GERMAINE A. HOSTON •

PRINCETON UNIVERSITY PRESS

PRINCETON, NEW JERSEY

Library of Congress Cataloging-in-Publication Data

Hoston, Germaine A., [date]
The State, identity, and the national question in China and Japan / Germaine A. Hoston.
p.   cm.
Includes bibliographical references and index.
ISBN 0-691-07873-4 — ISBN 0-691-02334-4 (pbk.)
1. China—Politics and government—1912–1949.   2. Communism—China.   3. Japan—
Politics and government—1926–1945.   4. Communism—Japan.   5. Communism—
Asia.   I. Title.
DS775.7.H67   1994   951.04—dc20   93-50669   cip

This book has been composed in Times Roman
Princeton University Press books are printed on acid-free paper and meet the guidelines for
permanence and durability of the Committee on Production Guidelines for Book
Longevity of the Council on Library Resources

Printed in the United States of America

1   3   5   7   9   10   8   6   4   2

1   3   5   7   9   10   8   6   4   2
(Pbk.)

• *TO VERETTA, MARCIA, IAN,* •

AND THE

MEMORY OF WALTER

· C O N T E N T S ·

FOR THE SCHOLAR, to write is to learn, to gain a deeper understanding of the world and of one's own relation to it. For me, it has been an extended voyage of self-discovery. The rather idiosyncratic approach in this book to Chinese and Japanese radical thought in the twentieth century arose from the synergistic combination of the internal logic of its own emergence with previously unarticulated personal questions of my own concerning individual and group identity in a society of ethnic/national minorities. Certainly, since the victory of the Chinese Communist party over the Guomindang nationalists in 1949 proclaimed the firm implantation of Marxist thought beyond its West European birthplace, others have studied Asian revolutionary movements and their adaptations of Marxism to the strategic requirements of their situations. Pioneering studies by Benjamin Schwartz and Maurice Meisner on Chinese Marxism and by Robert A. Scalapino, George Beckmann, and Okubo Genji on the Japanese Marxist movement have enlightened observers on the challenges of adapting Marxism as revolutionary strategy to the conditions of revolutionary praxis in the concrete situations of East Asia. The object of my concerns, however, went beyond these matters. I wished to unravel the deeper mysteries of the intellectual accommodation to non-Western national identities of an understanding of human history and commitment to revolutionary change that were based on the West European developmental experience. Thus, this volume is as much an inquiry into how national identity was refracted through indigenous radical thought as it is an analysis of the intellectual solutions that Chinese and Japanese Marxists crafted to conventional theoretical issues concerning the state and nationalism.

Many will find perplexing the decision to treat China and Japan comparatively here; these are societies that differ dramatically on the surface. They have traced widely divergent political and economic trajectories during the twentieth century, the one experiencing the drive to victory of a revolutionary movement claiming the Marxist mantle and the other a society to which Marxism itself would seem to be of little consequence. I hope that the latter set of doubts—those concerning the significance and impact of Marxism for Japan—have been allayed by my extended treatment in *Marxism and the Crisis of Development in Prewar Japan* (1986). That earlier work demonstrated that if Marxism failed to prevail organizationally as a revolutionary movement in Japan, it has been at the forefront of developments in Marxist economic theory internationally in the postwar period. More importantly, it is precisely the failure of Marxism as a revolutionary movement in Japan, along with other striking contrasts with China, that holds the key to the articulation of the broadest theoretical concerns of this work. Initially, this project was conceptualized in terms of the problem of the state in Chinese Marxism. I wanted to understand how Chinese Marxists reconciled their attraction to Marxism as an advanced Western philosophical system cum revolutionary strategy that might help to save China, the nation, from the ravages of Western national states with the requirements of the doctrine itself. Their mission on behalf of China would seem to require that they seek to build and strengthen the very accoutrements of state power of which Marxism's internationalist communism mandated the destruction.

The introduction of the comparison with Japan, the primary channel through which Marxist thought was imported into China, however, transformed the study by deepening its *problématique*—a matter that constitutes the nodal point of a set of philosophical issues. The powerful identification of the emperor at the apex of the state with the individual in Japan and its effect—to diminish the appeal of Marxism—in that context recalled the preoccupation with national identity that had hampered Chinese leaders who would fashion a Meiji-style Restoration to "save China" from the Western threat and would continue to be reflected through the Marxist discourse of Li Dazhao and Mao Zedong. This commonality compels the recognition that in wrestling with the present and future of their national states, Chinese and Japanese radical thinkers—first anarchists and then Marxists—were confronting fundamental issues concerning their own national identities. Sharing the dilemmas associated with this issue, these thinkers were much more similarly situated than the tremendous differences between the two societies and their developmental circumstances would seem to indicate. Although their predicament was, no doubt, also addressed by thinkers throughout Asia, Africa, and Latin America, it seemed reasonable that understanding how it was resolved might begin with the two East Asian societies in which Marxian thought was most fully developed and in which enough was shared in cultural and philosophic roots to make comparison feasible. The legitimacy of the comparison is emphasized by the fact that the short but crucial period of the first several decades of the twentieth century saw Chinese and Japanese radical thinkers—in many cases influenced by one another—confronting precisely the same issues.

Thus, in the hope that it might also stimulate similar studies in radical thought elsewhere, this book was conceived with two major objectives: first, to understand what Marxism, and, specifically, the national question therein came to mean in a context substantially different from that of their origin; second, through treatment of the national question, to identify the intellectual and personal dilemmas of individuals who sought to understand and transform their own peoples and societies on the basis of a theoretical perspective concerning humanity, society, and history that took the Western historical experience as the standard and despised the value and contributions of non-Western civilizations. What did it mean to their identities as Chinese and Japanese to be Marxists? How was this impact reflected in their efforts to indigenize Marxism in theory and practice? The significance of the first objective is evidenced in the continuing urgency of conflicts concerning nationality and assertions of nationhood through stateness worldwide. That of the second rests on the observation that issues concerning individual and collective identity are at the heart of what human beings do in their personal as well as political lives. The two themes converge in the recognition that ideas change as they travel across social contexts that embody varying human experiences: Marxism, like liberalism and even apparently unitary religious systems, has undergone change as it has crossed national and ethnic boundaries. Whatever may be the ultimate fate of Marxism as theory and practice in the post–cold war era, the examination of how its comprehensive philosophical perspective responded to challenges proffered by differing cultural contexts will remain suggestive of how other philosophical systems are transformed from context to context.

This project originated as a doctoral dissertation, and over the years since its completion for the degree it has matured. Certain analyses and conclusions have been modified as my knowledge of Eastern and Western political thought expanded, as I was immersed further in China and Japan, and as I shared insights with those who study other regions of the world. Fundamentally, however, the principal concerns of this book and my conviction of their significance have been strengthened rather than contested by new international developments and new knowledge, even if some of its findings have had to be rearticulated with fresh nuances.

Over the years, so many people have contributed to the fruition of this project that the task of thanking them inspires the fear that someone might be forgotten. It is customary to end with one's family, but I feel that I must begin with mine, for it is difficult to express adequately my appreciation of their encouragement of my intellectual preoccupations and support of the travel, research, and writing necessary for this book. The members of my family have endured for years my absorption in the concerns explored here during times I might otherwise have devoted more fully to them. While I was an undergraduate at Princeton, inspiring teachers, including Leo Ou-fan Lee, Edward L. Morse, and Richard H. Ullman, convinced me by their example that my inclination to abandon early ambitions in law for academe were sound. Their standards were reinforced at Harvard by Benjamin I. Schwartz, John D. Montgomery, and Joel S. Migdal, all of whom offered valuable guidance. Professor Schwartz in particular, with his encyclopedic knowledge of Eastern and Western thought and politics was an influence the strength of which I appreciated more deeply as I became immersed in my research and writing. To the now deceased and fondly missed Dita Shklar, as well as Professor Schwartz, I owe a special debt for the steady intensification of my enthusiasm for political philosophy.

As I embarked on the dissertation, Gail Lee Bernstein, Atsuko Hirai, Terry MacDougall, Ezra Vogel, and Theda Skocpol offered conceptual and bibliographical assistance. Stephen F. Cohen offered valuable insights on Soviet approaches to the issues addressed in this study; and Professor Oka Toshirō of Hokkaidō University provided useful advice on the study of Japanese Marxism and the imperial institution during a visiting appointment at Harvard. Others who have offered valuable comments and criticisms on various parts of this book include Baba Hiroji, Lucien Bianco, Yves Chevrier, Doi Takako, Paul Drake, Etō Shinkichi, Fukushima Shingo, Hayashi Takehisa, Ichiko Chūzō, Ichiko Kenji, Ikumi Takuichi, Ishida Takeshi, Ishikawa Tadao, Itō Makoto, Yunghwan Jo, Maruyama Masao, Moriya Fumio, Nakamura Takafusa, Noguchi Takehiko, Onabe Teruhiko, T. J. Pempel, Takahashi Masao, Tracy Strong, George Oakley Totten III, Cecil H. Uyehara, and Yamada Tatsuo. Special thanks are due Edward Friedman and David A. Titus for their careful readings and detailed comments on the manuscript and to my editor, Margaret Case, for her enthusiastic support. In Japan, special hospitality was extended by the Horiguchi Minoru family and Ukai Nobushige and Nobuko, and in Paris the same was offered by Georges Tan Eng Bok and Pierre-Yves Le Priol. At Johns Hopkins, colleagues, including Kristin Bumiller, Matthew Crenson, Steven R. David, Richard E. Flathman, Richard S. Katz, and Katherine E. Verdery, all contributed much through patient conversation and encouragement. Joseph S. Hall and Steven Muller of Johns Hopkins as well as Clements Heller of the Maison des Sciences de l'Homme helped with essential institutional arrangements. Of course, access to archival materials was critical to this project. Eugene Wu of the Harvard Yenching Library, Tsukagoshi Tsutako of the Library of the Institute for Social Science at the University of Tokyo, staff at the Tōyō Bunko, the Tōyō Bunka Kenkyūjo, the National Diet Library, and the Ōhara Shakai Mondai Kenkyūjo in Tokyo, Fumi Norcia of the Library of Congress, the Interlibrary Loan Department at Johns Hopkins University, Emiko Moffitt and Ramon Myers of the Hoover Institution, M. Quinn, Mimi Lam, and Judy Sun of the Fungpingshan Library at the University of Hong Kong, John Dolfin of the Universities Service Center, and the staff of the Centre Chine of the Ecole des Hautes Etudes en Sciences Sociales in Paris all assisted in providing access to invaluable research materials. Research assistance was provided by Maureen C. Feeley, Lise-Ann Shea, Constance Rosemont, Deborah Kravitz, Kevin McNeelege, Li-Shing Wang, Elizabeth A. Peterson, Yun Wang, Crystal Canaan, and Sharon F. Schwartz. Finally, before I could express fully my appreciation to them for their kindnesses, Arahata Kanson, Hirano Yoshitarō, George Armstrong Kelly, Minobe Ryōkichi, Sakisaka Itsurō, and, especially, Ukai Nobushige passed on. To many of these individuals I owe particularly heavy debts of gratitude for guidance and support.

Of course, a project of this magnitude could not have been completed without generous financial assistance. As a Ph.D. candidate, I received support from Harvard University, the National Science Foundation, the Foreign Language and Area Studies Fellowship, and the American Association of University Women. The Northeast Asia Council of the Association for Asian Studies and the Social Science Research Council, Johns Hopkins University, the Maison des Sciences de l'Homme, and the International Federation of University Women helped to support visits to distant research collections. The National Endowment for the Humanities and the Rockefeller Foundation provided essential time off for research and writing. I owe great debts of gratitude to these institutions as well as to the individuals listed. The ultimate responsibility for the interpretations that are offered here, however, remains my own.

The State, Identity, and the National Question in China and Japan

IDENTITY, THE NATIONAL QUESTION, AND

REVOLUTIONARY CHANGE IN CHINA AND JAPAN

Behold my servant, whom I uphold,

my chosen, in whom my soul delights;

I have put my Spirit upon him,

he will bring forth justice to the nations.

—Isaiah 42: 1

The emancipation of Germany is the emancipation of man. The head of this emancipation is philosophy, its heart is the proletariat. Philosophy cannot be actualized without the abolition [*Aufhebung*] of the proletariat; the proletariat cannot be abolished without the actualization of philosophy.

When all the intrinsic conditions are fulfilled, the day of German resurrection will be announced by the crowing of the Gallic cock. (Karl Marx)[1] *Critique of Hegel's Phil of Right*

FROM THE TIME that Karl Marx and Friedrich Engels declared that "the workingman has no country," the Marxist revolutionary movement has struggled with a tension between the aspiration to socialist internationalism and the persistence of fierce nationalist sentiment among its activists and constituents. The resurgence of nationalist animosities dating back to the pre-Communist period in the defunct Soviet Union and the former Communist states of Eastern Europe underscores the power that nationalism continues to wield even after decades of suppression by self-styled "internationalist" regimes. Here, as in the time during which Marx and Engels wrote, nationalities exist that seek recognition as nations with the right to protect and nurture themselves with the secure administrative and military apparatuses of nation(al)-states. The presence of such nationalities, contesting imperial dominion and one another for self-determination, in Marx's and Engels's time provoked concern early in the history of the socialist movement that nationalist claims might overshadow the shared aspirations of the world's workers. The Marxian revolutionary impulse spread eastward, and concomitantly these concerns were heightened, when the nationalistic sentiments of Germans, Jews, and other Western European nationalities were exacerbated, as the disintegrative tendencies of the great Hapsburg, Ottoman, and Russian empires entailed new conflicts among the nationalities that comprised them.

How does one understand the true significance of the abiding potency of nation-

alist passions at the end of the twentieth century? The task is complicated by
ambiguities in the popular usage of the term *nationalism* to describe promotion of
the interests of both the state and its constituent peoples. Among scholars, the term
nationalism, like *nation* and *nationality*, has been defined variously, Peter Alter
has noted, "reflect[ing] the multiformity that nationalism has assumed in historical
and political reality since the late eighteenth century."[2] A major difficulty arises
from the anglophone conflation of the notions of nation/state and nation/people
within the single term *nation*. In an effort to separate the two notions, some
analysts have preferred the term *ethnonationalism*, underscoring the importance of
a shared sense of roots in the notion of nationalism.[3] The ancient Greek notion of
the εθνος (*ethnos*) referred to a people of common descent. This concept was
clearly distinguished from the administrative organization of the state, or κρατος
(*kratos*), which in antiquity took the form of the πολις (*polis*), the centralized city-
state.[4] Similarly, the Latin *natio*, the root of the ambiguous term *nation*, referred
not to a political unit but to a breed or stock of people. Thus, as used here,
nationalities are ethnic peoples with shared histories, languages, cultures, and
consciousness thereof, usually sharing a given territorial space. A nationality sees
itself as a distinct ethnic group; it is frequently a minority; and it often attains
consciousness of itself as a *nation* seeking recognition as such by others in opposition to hostile majorities.[5]

This definition of nationality is less restrictive than others, such as Stalin's
classic Marxist definition of the nation as "a historically evolved, stable community of language, territory, economic life, and psychological makeup manifested in
a community of culture."[6] The broader definition is necessitated by the complications introduced by dispersions of ethnic groups—such as the historic Jewish and
black diasporas.[7] It declines to deny to groups that might once have shared a
specific territory but were dispersed by enslavement or other misfortune the legitimate claim to nationalist sentiments. Nevertheless, Stalin's recognition of the
importance the territorial component may assume remains useful, for it helps to
highlight the historic relationship between the birth and evolution of nationalism
and the locus of sovereignty in the state. The term *state* refers to an administrative
apparatus of centralized power, the key elements of which Marx identified in the
early nation-state (or national state) as "the standing army, police, bureaucracy,
clergy, and judicature."[8] The first three of these institutions—those that would be
emphasized by V. I. Lenin subsequently[9]—perform the essential functions of
protection of the society from external enemies, the maintenance of order to
protect citizens from one another, and administration, respectively.

The relationship between the state and nationalism is complex and highly contested. As it is treated here, nationalism is an integrative ideology that, in the
words of Ernest Gellner, is "primarily a principle which holds that the political and
national unit should be congruent."[10] In other words, it values nationality and
usually aspires to create or protect a sovereign state power of which the nation is
constitutive, that is a nation-state. Recently, John Breuilly has maintained that
nationalism arises in opposition to, rather than for, such a state. In this view,
nationalism emerges as an ideology and movement as the product of an effort to

create a common sense of identity in order to mobilize popular support against an oppressive state structure.[11] It is true, as Gellner contends, that "Nations as a natural, God-given way of classifying men, as an inherent . . . political destiny, are a myth." Rather, "nationalism . . . sometimes takes pre-existing cultures and turns them into nations, sometimes invents them, and often obliterates pre-existing cultures."[12] Nationalism frequently addresses its appeal across the boundaries of national states as it did into Roumania, Yugoslavia, Cyprus, Turkey, and the Ukraine when Greek nationalists sought to gather members of the Greek ethnos into its historic homeland.[13] But Breuilly's interpretation does not adequately interpret the French Revolution as the harbinger of nationalism as a world-historical force. To be sure, the Revolution was in part precipitated by suspicion of treachery on the part of the king in collusion with German peoples with whom the French saw themselves at war. But at the same time, it was an effort to make the *nation, le peuple*, constitutive of the state against the assertion by Louis XIV that "*L'Etat, c'est moi.*" In other words, the Revolution was an attempt to redefine the state as the product of popular sovereignty and claim it as a national state, or, in Habermas's terms, an endeavor to redefine what was "public" as pertaining to the people rather than to the private business of the monarch.[14] Likewise, in Marxian terms, as capitalist expansion spread to East Asia, so too did the impulse not only to resist the encroachment of alien state powers but also to build national states in the East that would provide the *nations* of the East the forces essential to the determination of their own destinies.

For many thinkers and activists in East Asia, the desire for national self-determination coincided with the appeal of Marxism as a historical schema that was critical of the Western states by which these thinkers felt their societies to be threatened. Marx and Engels, Lenin, and Rosa Luxemburg had cautioned against the negative impact that the centrifugal forces generated by such nationalistic claims might have on the international socialist movement. It is important to note, however, that in the Marxian paradigm, nationalism per se was emphatically not problematic. On the contrary, the normative value of nationalism was contingent upon the stage in human history of a given society. Indeed, for Marx and Engels, Lenin and Luxemburg, nationalism had in Europe's past played a progressive historical role, contributing to the transition from feudal to capitalist society. In Western Europe, the nationalistic impulses that had fueled the creation of the national state that Marx now sought to transcend had coincided with the rise of the bourgeoisie and the succession of the feudal order by industrial capitalism. In societies undergoing such transitions nationalism had urged the implementation of measures—such as the construction of massive transportation and communications systems and the mobilization of mass military apparatuses to protect more widely flung national borders—that encouraged the creation of integrated national markets, the regularized transport of commodities, and the rapid dissemination of information on market conditions that facilitated the growth of the bourgeoisie.[15] Conversely, for these thinkers, where the bourgeoisie and industrial capital had already achieved ascendancy, nationalism was a regressive force that incited wars in which proletarians died for the benefit of the few as national bourgeoisies competed with one another for global expansion.[16] Indeed, Marx was careful to note that the positive emergence of national consciousness alongside the growth of big industry entailed the seeds of the demise of nationalism itself: because "big industry created everywhere the same relations between the classes of society, [it] thus destroyed the peculiar individuality of the various nationalities."[17] The globe-shrinking technological and economic changes that accompanied the maturation of industrial capitalism would render the ideal and reality of the nation-state and the nationalisms that supported them obsolete.   *German Id.*

Thus, in midnineteenth-century Western Europe, Marx made eschatological claims to supersede nationality by aspiring to the international liberation of the working class to restore men and women to wholeness as "species-beings" after a long prehistory of class struggle.[18] This aspiration collided fiercely with the continued potency of national inequalities and nationalist passions in the nineteenth and twentieth centuries. As a result, within Marxism, historically, a disaccord has arisen within the pursuit of human liberation at three levels: (1) the individual, (2) the individual's nation and membership in an ethnic group through which he or she might find validation of personal value vis-à-vis the Other, and (3) the interests of humanity as a whole transcending national differences. The matter of how to resolve these tensions has come to be characterized as the *national question* in Marxism.[19] More generally, the national question has also come to be acknowledged in the popular and scholarly consciousness outside the Marxist theoretical system as these antinomies have been manifested beyond the bounds of specifically Marxian revolutionary movements.

As this consciousness has become more global in its embrace, the national question has become more compelling than ever as the twentieth century draws to a close. To be sure, the first half of the century saw extreme nationalist divisions,[20] intense conflicts among ethnic groups contesting one another for territorial status as nations and then national states. With respect to the Marxian movement, such tensions engulfed the strongest socialist movements,[21] and they destroyed the Second, Socialist, International during World War I. Consumed by aggressive nationalisms born of the disintegration of the great empires, the 1920s and 1930s saw the rise of the new social formations of fascism and national socialism, movements that made their imprint on East Asia as well as on Europe. Indeed, it is this period that is the primary focus of this work. Events since that time have heightened rather than diminished the significance of these movements. As early as the 1920s and 1930s, in the societies under scrutiny here the national question had begun to entail new dimensions, new philosophicohistorical proportions that dwarfed the old nationalisms. When the national question emerged in Europe, the birthplace of Marxism, the national question appeared simply to be a *nationality* question. It was linked to the treatment of the state in Marx's thought inasmuch as ethnic peoples sought to assert themselves as *nations* by constructing national states. It was, after all, the modern nation-state associated with the consolidation of industrial capitalism that was Marx's own primary focus when he wrote about the state. Marx's original dualistic treatment of nationalism in the context of state building subsequently permitted Lenin to recognize that even while nationalism was regressive in the West, it could still play a legitimate and progressive role in abetting revolution of the bourgeois-national variety in the East where precapitalist production relations continued to prevail.[22] But Lenin approached the exploitation of nationalist sentiments in the East in order to facilitate the export of revolution on the Marxian model from the vantage point of one who saw himself as part of the Europe that had given birth to Marxism itself. Thus, what Lenin did not discern was that once Marxism moved eastward beyond its European birthplace, the national question assumed a much broader significance.

Interestingly, this evolution was presaged in Marx's original treatment of Germany. In his earliest writings, Marx expressed profound disappointment that the German peoples had not achieved politically and economically what Britain and France had. The state of which Hegel had written and which Marx rejected was only a Prussian polity, not a German national state. Yet it was in pondering the prospects for his backward Germany that Marx first seized upon the proletariat as the universal class whose quest for liberation would produce emancipation for all mankind:

> Where, then, is the positive possibility of German emancipation?
>
> Our answer: in the formation of a class with radical chains, a class in civil society that is not of civil society, an estate that is the dissolution of all estates, a sphere of society having a universal character because of its universal suffering and claiming no particular right because no particular wrong but unqualified wrong is perpetrated on it; a sphere that can claim no traditional title but only a human title; a sphere that does not stand partially opposed to the consequences, but totally opposed to the premises of the German political system; a sphere, finally, that cannot emancipate itself without emancipating itself from all the other spheres of society, thereby emancipating them; a sphere, in short, that is the complete loss of humanity and can only redeem itself through the total redemption of humanity. This dissolution of society existing as a particular class is the proletariat.[23] *Critique of Hegel's ---*

For Germany, as for all capitalist societies, Marx envisaged a liberation that would transcend mere "political" liberation: it would embrace the realization of social and economic rights as well as political *Recht*.[24] It would restore to human beings the wholeness that they had lost in the progressive development of the division of labor in class society. Yet, the liberation of the individual could occur only by means of a totalizing[25] emancipation at the level of the collectivity. Ultimately, then, Marx's vision of radical socioeconomic change embraced revolution on a world scale. Nevertheless, the point of departure for the articulation of this vision lay in an Hegelian predisposition to identify Germany with human destiny. As Marx asserted in 1843, "The emancipation of Germany is the emancipation of man."[26]

What, then, was the German problem for Marx? And what is the significance of Marx's treatment of it for those who would find Marxism attractive in other later-industrializing and non-European societies? For Marx, the difficulty lay at once in the failure of German peoples to achieve unification in the form of the nation-state and in their inability, theretofore, to replicate the industrial capitalist order that

Great Britain and France had achieved. Yet Marx's prescription for these features of German backwardness was precisely the same as it was for the evils of the more advanced industrialized societies of France and England. So the pattern has remained as Marxism has moved eastward. In Japan, however, where significant numbers of ethnic minorities did not exist, and in China, where Chinese cultural identity has historically overwhelmed the claims of ethnic minorities, the national question is not primarily a nationalities question. Rather, while retaining the dual problématique of nation- and statehood, it has assumed a new form. The new formulation arises first out of the fact that Marxism was imported into China, Japan, and other later-industrializing societies as a tool, as a model of national development that embraced a critical view of the Western socioeconomic order by which many of their leaders felt victimized. When such thinkers and activists sought to adapt Marxism as a revolutionary strategy to their own societies, they confronted the national question in a new form. This new version of the question retained its dual facets regarding both the national and statist aspects of the original national question. First, these non-Western thinkers embraced Marxism, a thought system that advocated the ultimate dissolution of the state, yet they tended to retain the state as a desideratum for the protection of their peoples from the West. Second, even as Marxism was imported in appreciation of its value as a model of national development, it was based on the West European experience and, thus, existed in these non-Western societies in tension with the desire to assert and affirm their own indigenous cultural contributions to human history.

It is in this sense that although the 1920s and the 1930s comprised an era of ultranationalism and fascism, the national question writ large to embrace postcolonial experiences in Asia, Africa, and Latin America—and even Eastern Europe in its struggle to break free of the Soviet empire—has never been more compelling that it has proved to be at the end of the twentieth century. The year of the two-hundredth anniversary of the great French Revolution was marked dramatically by the spectacle of massive popular uprisings overwhelming heavily armed apparatuses of state power across nearly the whole of Eastern and Central Europe. The 1989 revolutions overturned deeply entrenched bureaucratic elites from gradually reforming Poland and Czechoslovakia to East Germany and Roumania, the two most stubbornly conservative Communist powers in the region. These movements were accompanied by equally dramatic displays outside Europe. The gradual dismantling of the edifice of apartheid and the release of the aged but unbowed Nelson Mandela in South Africa were the product of vehement demands for national self-determination and true democracy by the black majority in the country, bolstered by the pressure of international economic sanctions. Meanwhile, in the Soviet Union, the potential for violent confrontation in the home of the world's first proletarian Marxist-led revolution escalated as Mikhail Gorbachev's *glasnost'* encouraged the assertion of national sovereignty in the Baltic republics against the authority of the center. The irresolution of the Soviet example in the persistence of nationalist tensions and uncertainties about what constitutes modernity has underscored the ambiguity of the outcome of the 1989 crises. Not all popular movements that year issued in victory for those demanding national self-determination and democratization. In China, the most populous Communist power, another anniversary was commemorated in a brutally contrasting fashion. The seventieth anniversary of the nationalistic and democratizing May Fourth movement saw impassioned demonstrations in Tiananmen Square that ended in massacre before a shocked world on June 4. This occurred in the same spring that Round Table talks brought a relatively peaceful end to a rule long viewed as occupation by an alien power in Poland.

These historic junctures bespeak a universal impulse among men and women to assert their identity and self-worth, to demand the "unquestionable right to be free"[27] to determine their own destinies. Beneath the cries for national self-determination across the globe lies a primal impulse to seek authentication of one's being. Collectively, this quest manifests itself in a people's appeal for the space and opportunity to assert its own selfhood vis-à-vis—and without interference from—the Other. Ironically, the collapse of Communist regimes that claimed patrimony in Marxism reveals not the irrelevance or death of Marxism as philosophy but the abiding quality and inherent complexity of some of Karl Marx's earliest insights into the human condition. In the pleas for justice of Vaclav Havel, Jean-Paul Sartre,[28] and Mihaly Vajda,[29] the demand for human freedom has been linked intimately to the aspiration to national liberation. The images of crowds marching before the Brandenburg Gate and in Prague's Wenceslaus Square in the fall of 1989 were as much a reflection of men and women seeking national salvation from external domination as of individuals demanding democratic rights.[30]

From the perspective of the crises of 1989, then, Marxism has long been in competition with the conservative liberalism of advanced capitalist societies as a contender in defining the conditions by which humankind may achieve liberation individually and collectively. Nationalism is cast in a problematic role in both philosophical systems. In liberalism, as in the social contract theory of Jean-Jacques Rousseau, the attribution of higher value to the well-being of the collectivity of the political community may constitute a potential threat to individual liberty. That liberty may be sacrificed to the preeminence of the "general will" in the framework of the national state.[31] In Marxism, the issue arises from the conflict between pursuing human liberation at two levels of the collectivity—the nation, on the one hand, and the interests of humanity as a whole transcending national differences, on the other.

The national question was first posed in Western Europe where Marxism was born. There small nationalities coexisted within a relatively limited space, arousing conflicts for economic, political, and cultural primacy. With the outbreak of World War I, conflict erupted between loyalty to existing national states threatened by war and internationalist class allegiance to the proletarian socialist cause. As Marxism migrated from West to East under the sponsorship of the Soviet Union, reverberations of this sharp schism would echo there as well. By the 1920s and 1930s, the national question would etch deep divisions and arouse heated controversy within the revolutionary movements in China and Japan. These tensions would be reflected strikingly in radical Marxist scholarship, which articulated the issue as it was manifested in the theory and practice of the Marxist movements in the two societies. It would culminate in nationalistic adaptations of the doctrine that would fall on both sides of the demarcation between orthodoxy and heresy. Some of these nationalistic formulations—such as the statist Marxism of Takabatake Motoyuki and Sano Manabu's Marxian national socialism—challenged the legitimacy of Marxist-Leninist orthodoxy itself, whereas others such as Maoism would claim simply to enlarge its frontiers. As these endeavors reveal, the national question itself experienced a metamorphosis in the East as it was interpreted and reformulated in accordance with the new national and international contexts. It came to embrace a broader range of issues than it had encompassed in the West as the diversity of its hosts multiplied and as Eastern Marxists found themselves in problematic relation to the culture that had engendered Marxism itself. These endeavors to define and resolve the national question in China and Japan illuminate profound dilemmas concerning identity, modernity, and human freedom that have become manifest elsewhere in non-European later-industrializing societies.

My purpose in this work is to examine how these endeavors evolved in China and Japan, two among the first non-European societies to which the Soviets sought to export revolution. How did Chinese and Japanese thinkers perceive their positions in the non-European Asiatic world? What were the conceptions and valuations of the national state—a relatively new idea and ideal in East Asia when Marxism was imported into the two societies—that informed their thought, and how did they reconcile their appreciation of its importance for preserving their nations with the internationalist and ultimately stateless ideals of their revolutionary Marxian impulses? The lengthy controversies of the 1910s, 1920s, and 1930s among both Chinese and Japanese radical thinkers on these themes reflect the extent to which those attracted to Marxism were absorbed by this concern. Did early Marxists show reservations in their acceptance of the doctrine as a result of this consciousness of operating outside the European context of Marx's model? What adjustments did they make in Marxism to accommodate this geographical and cultural disparity? Were these adjustments reflected in their conceptions of the nation-state and its role in revolution, and how? The highly nationalist overtones of many Chinese Marxist writings, alongside the phenomenon of *tenkō*—whereby Japanese Communists abandoned their Comintern ties to convert to ultrarightist nationalism—raise additional questions. Was the Chinese or Japanese nation-state perceived to embody a character different from that of the Western body politic so that it could be salvaged after a Marxian revolution? Would or did it reflect classless values so that it might escape Marx's law of the withering away of the state? How did the ideas of Chinese and Japanese Marxist thinkers on these themes compare with one another and with Russian Bolshevik and Menshevik ideas? How might one account for the similarities and differences? Finally, what impact did the political theory that dominated the Marxist movements in each case have on the subsequent course of the movements in China and Japan?

The skeptic might question the utility of a study focusing on the responses of intellectual elites to these issues for the scholar who wishes to understand the dynamics of mass-based revolutionary politics. Of what significance for the fates of the revolutionary Marxist movements in China and Japan could it have been how their leaders and intellectual fellow-travelers *thought* about the state and national identity? Issues concerning the state have received a renewed interest among Western scholars in recent years, but while the state as an analytical concept has enjoyed a resurrection,[32] concern for "ideologies"[33] has declined. A major premise in the present work is that political thought as ideology is a significant force shaping revolutionary movements and that perspectives on the national question were of particular consequence for Marxist revolutionary movements in East Asia whether successful (China) or not (Japan).

It is not the purpose here to undertake to offer a general theory concerning revolutions. Yet a full appreciation of the significance of thought on the national question within indigenous revolutionary movements in China and Japan demands that the social scientific literature on revolutionary change be engaged. In the shadow of the cold war, suspicion and hostility toward the Marxist-Leninist and Maoist theories of revolution that spawned the Communist regimes in the Soviet Union and China reinforced the pejorative connotation of the term *ideology* itself "in prevalent American usage."[34] These factors have produced a widespread tendency to discount the significance of thought in explaining revolutionary change. That is, to articulate an objectively derived "scientifically tenable theory of revolution," as opposed to "ideological" nonscientific theories such as Marxism-Leninism, American social science has purposefully neglected the ideological element in favor of presumably value-free, neutral systems, and equilibrium models of society and social change.[35] In effect, the *creative* element in political action has been excised from the treatments of revolution that have gained ascendancy in the United States.[36]

Yet American political science has long been "drawn into a political contest with revolutionary ideology."[37] This is not surprising, inasmuch as the conflicts among (social) scientific theories or paradigms are essentially political in nature.[38] Nor is this particularly astonishing when the object of study is the rapid, violent change that we call social, including political, revolution.[39] Partisanship urges supporters of revolution to emphasize inevitable historical forces toward change, whereas defenders of the status quo indict revolutionary leaders as deviants or cunning opportunists, seizing upon momentary social disequilibrium (as functionalists argue), and using ideology as a convenient rationalization for psychological frustrations (as aggregate-psychological theorists argue) to divert events from the "normal" course of orderly and incremental human progress.[40]

Ideological theories of revolution, such as Marxism-Leninism, view revolution as constructive, as the fundamental motor force of human history. By contrast, social science theories of political change, such as the dominant functionalist model, have portrayed revolution as primarily destructive. In structural functionalism, "societies are mutually interconnected wholes, every aspect of which impinges upon every other and contributes something to the viability of the whole. Upon this view, societies are units in equilibrium that have a tendency toward inertia and change through the persistent or serious disturbance of any part of their equilibrium."[41] Structural functional analysis allows one to "think in terms of very broad and rapid changes," but most leading structural functionalist studies have been in the "anti-Marxist tradition," stressing "static over dynamic studies," premised on assumptions of "integration rather than conflict, and consequently inertia rather than constant motion, as the 'normal' state of society."[42] This approach has developed as a successor of sorts to the "science of order" of Auguste Comte, Max Weber, and Emile Durkheim. In this literature, one finds "disapproval of revolutionary movements, as well as numerous counsels on how to avoid, prevent, or scotch revolutionary outbreaks," indicating that social scientific studies share with the ideological theorists they denounce "an orientation which is hortatory, activist, and practical, the difference being that the orientation is counter-revolutionary."[43]

Yet the structural-functionalist and aggregate-psychological scientific approaches to revolution have not been alone in their ideological repudiation of ideology as a major factor in understanding revolutions. More recently, compelling new "macroanalytic" sociological approaches to revolution have emerged. Combining analytical concepts from Marx, Weber, and structural-functionalism, these studies seek "to identify and explain the causes and dynamics of large scale structures at the national and transnational level."[44] These studies, which may be termed *neo-structuralist*, are interdisciplinary works drawing upon the most advanced techniques of political science, sociology, and traditional historical and quantitative analysis. They share in common a "non-voluntarist, structural perspective" on the causes and nature of revolutionary change, and they attribute singular importance to the role of the state in impeding or abetting revolutionary change.[45] The neostructuralist argument is that the "purposive image" of revolution necessarily implies a consensus view of social order; contradicts the fact that "in no sense did such [radical] vanguards—let alone vanguards with large, mobilized, and ideologically imbued mass followings—ever create the revolutionary crises they exploited" and is misleading in its implication "that revolutionary processes and outcomes can be understood in terms of the activity and intentions or interests of the key group(s) who launch the revolution in the first place." Pioneers of this approach argue for a "structural perspective on sociohistorical reality"— "focusing simultaneously upon the institutionally determined situations and relations of groups within society and upon the interrelations of societies within world-historically developing international structures"—in analyzing the causes, processes, and outcomes of revolutions.[46] These studies exhibit Marxist perspectives on the importance of social class, the state, and the international political-economic context; but they reject the voluntarism associated with Leninism and Maoism. They tend to reflect a Weberian perspective (as interpreted by Reinhard Bendix rather than Talcott Parsons) on the relationship between state and society but object to its emphasis on ideas and legitimation of authority in isolation from "socio-economic structures."[47] They ostensibly share the structural functionalist emphasis on the role of social structures in relation to their environment but object to its presumption that the existing state of society is the normal, legitimate product of popular consensus as well as to its view of frustration as the locus of the revolutionary impulse arising when social structures are for some reason in disequilibrium. Most importantly, although neostructuralist studies reflect a renewed appreciation of one of the two major themes of this study, the state, they share with other predominant American social-scientific approaches the rejection of the importance of ideology in determining the causes, processes, and outcomes of revolutions.

It should be noted that despite the neostructuralist critique of the significance of the voluntarism in Marxism and Leninism, there is a significant ambiguity, or rather, tension, in most strands of Marxism, including Leninism and Maoism, between voluntarism (or "consciousness") and historical determinism.[48] This dualism is logically implicit in Marx's concept of human history as "a process by which man makes himself fully man."[49] Thus, one may attribute great significance to the role of human consciousness in human history as do "instrumentalist" contemporary Marxist theorists such as Ralph Miliband[50] while the same voluntarist element of consciousness (or "ideology", in the non-Marxist sense) is forsaken by structuralist Marxists. "Consciousness," the structuralists claim, "explains nothing; the point is to explain consciousness through an analysis of the dynamics of the society."[51]

Thus, neostructuralist studies have offered important, penetrating criticisms of other major social scientific approaches to revolution, and they have emphasized in a new way the nature and role of the state and of the international political economic context for the development of revolutions from above and below.[52] Nevertheless, the relationship between revolutionary thought, on the one hand, and the genesis, processes, and outcomes of revolution still lacks satisfactory resolution. The difficulty is that neostructuralism eschews any effort "to decipher the logic of the process or outcomes of a social revolution by adopting the perspective or following the actions of any one class or elite organization—no matter how important its participatory role." Instead, one must seek "the emergence (not 'making') of a revolutionary situation within an old regime" and discern the objective factors that determine the outcome of this process by assuming "an impersonal and nonsubjective viewpoint—one that emphasizes patterns of relationships among groups and societies," one that focuses on objective rather than subjective factors contributing to revolutionary change.[53] This approach has forged a causal link that has been conspicuously absent in structural and aggregate-psychological treatments of revolution. The structural functionalist reference to disequilibrium cannot establish the relationship between individual or group frustrations and their translation into revolutionary movements when the conditions of that change are left unspecified, nor can they establish the degree to which disequilibrium must manifest itself before frustrated individuals can turn it to their revolutionary cause. In this respect, the new structuralism has made crucial contributions to the literature on Marxist-inspired revolutions. Nevertheless, its neglect of the ideas and intentions of revolutionary vanguards has resulted in a serious underestimation of the importance of revolutionary thought in shaping the emergence of revolutionary crisis, the process of revolution itself, and the nature of its outcome. Despite the minor concessions that are made to the role of revolutionary vanguard ideology therein, the new approach threatens to yield a mechanistic image of the revolutionary process, in which conflicting or interacting structures, rather than human beings capable of purposeful and conscious action, are the primary actors.

This problem is not inherent to a structural perspective, an approach that can constitute a meaningful point of departure for understanding revolutions and systems of thought developed in a mutually interactive relationship with the structural realities of the contexts in which revolutions occur. It is valid to assert that the ideologies and intentions of revolutionary vanguards are not a good predictor of revolutionary outcomes, but the dynamic relationship between ideals and reality offers important insights into the origins and consequences of revolutionary change. Ideas are "particularly crucial in political struggles; those who appeal to values, whether as ends in themselves or as ideological cover for their material interests, become constrained by these very values."[54] As cognitive theorists have stressed in applications to international politics and foreign policy-making,[55] perceptions may affect reality just as structural or objective realities condition ideas. This point is acknowledged briefly in Skocpol's analysis of the development of the "mass line" and its impact on the outcome of the Chinese revolution.[56] Yet this analysis limits the appreciation of this factor before the stage of postrevolutionary change although it might also play a pivotal role in the creation of revolutionary crises and the formation of the dynamic of the revolutionary process itself. As Charles Tilly's work suggests, the manner in which revolutionaries think about politics might be of major significance to the emergence of a revolutionary situation at the outset.[57] Even if the thought and actions of revolutionaries alone may not suffice to cause revolutionary crises, the extent to which a revolutionary crisis may be identified as such depends to a large extent upon the ability of revolutionary vanguards, armed with ideology and military weaponry, to exploit the situation and render a merely political or socioeconomic crisis a revolutionary one. The cases of the Russian and Chinese revolutions are instructive on this point. Both anciens régimes collapsed from within precisely because of the combination of "objective" conditions cited in Skocpol's account: increased agrarian disorder, dissolution of central state structures, both aggravated by successive and unsuccessful involvement in wars. One might argue that such conditions might have continued indefinitely—in Russia, under the shifting coalition of struggling political parties, with the residual possibility of a military coup, and, in China, under the decentralized and Republican regimes of local and rural government. Nothing in the confluence of structural conditions in either case made a specifically revolutionary crisis inevitable.

It is helpful to maintain the analytical distinction between the emergence of revolutionary crises and the processes and outcomes of revolutionary state building that Skocpol has made so effectively. This differentiation, however, is not sufficient to dispense with the issue of revolutionary thought.[58] Indeed, as Skocpol's discussion of state building in France as a process that was at least partly dependent upon a "legitimating theme" illustrates, certain key elements of Weber's ideas on legitimation help to underscore this significance of revolutionary thought. This element is even more salient in the central role of the "mass line" in the Chinese

Communist party's new state-building process. If it is indeed correct that "*[t]he more mobilized an interest group for organized political action, the more likely it is to take command of the state in a crisis*,"[59] then legitimation as an aspect of mobilizing ideology appears to be crucial. It plays a significant role in all three stages of revolutionary change: (1) a vanguard's mobilization of support that can transform a political crisis into a revolutionary one or, as in the Chinese case, allow it to mobilize active support for opposing an existing regime; (2) the manner in which the revolutionary struggle is conducted, which in turn may bear important consequences for the postrevolutionary experience; and (3) the state-building process—if there is one—that determines the outcome of the revolution. The Weberian concept of legitimation, then, need not be isolated from the objective structural conditions within which revolutionary mobilization occurs. On the contrary, this legitimacy may be recognized as class based and contingent on a variety of objective socioeconomic forces. This factor accrues additional significance as the distinction (insofar as it concerns revolutionary ideology) between the emergence of crises and the building of new state power breaks down. It might be correct that without the confluence of objective circumstances cited previously, the Bolshevik and Chinese Communist revolutionary vanguards would probably not have succeeded. Scholars of Japan have likewise pointed to the strength of the repressive state apparatus as a major objective factor contributing to the failure of the Japanese Communist movement. Without taking into account the crisis-generating role of the revolutionaries' thought and its translation into practice, and the resistance offered by official, state-nurtured ideology, it is impossible to understand the rise of the Marxist revolutionary movement in China and its aftermath or the collapse of the Communist movement in Shōwa Japan. As the analysis offered here will demonstrate compellingly, revolutionary thought—particularly concerning such crucial matters as national identity and the essential nature and shape of the body politic—must be counted among the circumstances that turn what might begin as mere social and political instability into a revolutionary crisis.

The study of Marxist revolutionary movements is particularly fruitful ground for the examination of such themes in radical theory and practice. If it is generally true that "[m]en's beliefs about power are as crucial as the actual exercise of coercion itself,"[60] then the role of the thought of an "intellectual vanguard" is particularly significant in the Marxist case.[61] Lenin may have overstated this point when he declared, "Without revolutionary theory there can be no revolutionary movement."[62] In the Marxian paradigm, "human acts are governed by specific intentions," but "the result of all these multifarious acts does not reflect the intentions of any one person," as philosopher Leszek Kolakowski has noted. "Human beings and their relations are, nevertheless, the sole reality of the historical process, which ultimately consists of the conscious behavior of individuals."[63] With respect to revolution, Marxism has always flourished in intimate relation to practice. Thus, it is inadequate to analyze Marxian revolutionary thought specifically "as the product of 'frustration' which then somehow finds its appropriate ideological 'rationalization'." As Sheldon Wolin has argued, "In a constitutive relationship action is inseparable from its meaning. An ideology such as Marxism is not only a system of meanings, but one which conceives action as expressive of that system. An actor who is, so to speak, in-formed by that system of meanings understands what he is doing or what is happening to him and others by virtue of a coherent prior understanding of what revolutionary action means."[64] This is precisely what Lenin meant when he argued that "the Communists of every country should quite consciously take into account both the main fundamental tasks of the struggle against opportunism and 'left' doctrinairism and the *specific features* which this struggle assumes and inevitably must assume in each separate country in conformity with the peculiar features of its economics, politics, cultural national composition."[65] " 'Correct revolutionary theory [thus] . . . assumes final shape only in close connection with the practical activity of a truly mass and truly revolutionary movement'."[66]

This is the essence of the problem of adapting Marxism or Marxism-Leninism to Asia, to Chinese and Japanese contexts that differed in many respects from the Western European and Russian settings in which its premises were born and elaborated. The notion of the sinification of Marxism by Mao has long been a common theme in academic writings on Chinese Marxism,[67] and, more recently, it has become evident that the variants of national or state socialism that emerged in the writings of Japanese Marxists during the 1930s and 1940s represented analogous efforts to Japanize Marxism.[68] Clearly, both Chinese and Japanese Marxists made earnest efforts to adapt Marxism to what they perceived as the requirements of their individual national contexts, although these scholar-activists met with varying degrees of success in treating the issues that arose out of such an endeavor. How was one to approach Leninism? If Leninism was merely " 'Russianized' Marxism," as Mao appears to have concluded,[69] how much of Marxist-Leninist theory could be assumed to be directly applicable to the contexts of China and Japan? How much could the form of Marxism be changed in the process of adaptation—particularly in light of issues bearing on national identity—without causing the new emergent theory to lose its special essence as "Marxism"?

There is evidence that the political theory of Marxism was a major inducement for those who joined the Chinese and Japanese Marxist revolutionary movements. As Matsuzawa Hiroaki has noted, the conclusions of Gabriel Almond's survey comparing motivations for participation in communist parties across several American and Western European countries[70] simply did not apply to Japan. Self-related and group-related interests, which in Almond's study accounted for 42 and 44 percent of communist party participation respectively, "were insufficient inducements to enter the party" in Japan. There, where "one could not expect generally that participation in the revolutionary movement could give opportunity for a rise in social status and other benefits to the individual," "faith in Marxist thought . . . played an overwhelming role." Individuals often joined the party as part of a quest for a vehicle for the performance of altruistic service to society, a search that had gone unfulfilled in previous experiences with conventional religious institutions.[71] Similar considerations combined to make philosophical perspectives concerning politics more consequential in the Chinese context as well. The profound sense of "cultural despair" arising from the need to replace the defunct Confucian political philosophy[72] predisposed Chinese intellectuals to seek an alternative Weltanschauung to guide meaningful socioeconomic and political change in their troubled society. In both settings, the endeavor among those attracted to Marxism to articulate and resolve concerns intimately related to their own notions of identity and purpose would hold particular potency for the creation and resolution of revolutionary crises. As discussed here, the national question reflected such concerns in all their dimensions.

In seeking patterns in how Chinese and Japanese addressed the national question in adapting Marxism to their native contexts, I have organized this work in a thematic fashion that coincides with the chronological unfolding of alternative resolutions of the issue. The book begins with an examination of the evolution of the national question in European Marxism. In chapter 1, I trace how the national question underwent transformation as it migrated from West to East by way of the Russian revolution. In chapter 2, I explore the relationship between the national question and outstanding issues in the Marxist theory of the state that would confront Chinese and Japanese Marxists. In chapter 3, I examine the philosophical setting into which Marxist theory and practice were introduced in China and Japan. Here one gains an appreciation of the challenges arising in any effort to combine Marxist perspectives on nation and state with indigenous ideas concerning the polity. Then, the appeal of Marxism as social theory cum revolutionary schema in the early anarcho-socialist movements and the competition between anarchism and Marxism-Leninism in the two societies are examined in chapters 4 and 5. As they absorbed Marxist theory and its implications for understanding the history and political status quo of their own societies, Chinese and Japanese Marxists naturally turned to the task of explicating their own social histories in terms of the Marxist historical schema. In chapters 6 and 7, I analyze the ramifications of these endeavors for the national question. Efforts to resolve the dilemmas exposed in these efforts are investigated in the fullness of their implications for nationalism and statism in the two societies in chapters 8 and 9. Finally, I update these resolutions to the postwar era in a final chapter and seek to draw larger generalities linking Marxism, nationalism, and late industrialization.

Marxism, Revolution, and the National Question

CHINESE AND Japanese responses to the national question were influenced heavily by how the issue had been addressed by the founders of Marxism and by leading Marxists in Europe and the Russian empire. Marx, Engels, Luxemburg, Lenin, and others defined the terms of the discourse on the state and on the relationship between the nation and the state in a Marxian socialist revolution. These terms began to change, and the national question underwent a subtle metamorphosis, however, as the Marxian revolutionary idea reached toward East Asia by way of the October Revolution.

This metamorphosis occurred in three ways. First, when the Bolsheviks sought to transform the defunct tsarist empire into a Union of Soviet Socialist Republics, they not only had to contend with White Russian resistance and foreign invasion but also were compelled to respond to the fervent nationalistic passions of minority non-Russian peoples seeking to establish autonomous national states of their own.[1] Second, the Bolsheviks attempted to extend their socializing revolution beyond the European part of the empire to Central Asian peoples who lacked the essential prerequisities for a Marxist socialist revolution. These peoples resisted (Westernizing) changes that would undermine their historic values, customs, and social structures. Third, there was the matter of foreign policy. The Bolsheviks, alarmed by the failure of a supportive socialist regime to materialize in Western Europe, sought to ignite revolution in the East. Recognizing that the three problems were inextricably linked, the same Russian and non-Russian Marxists who addressed the nationality problem within the USSR and policy in Soviet Central Asia formulated the Comintern's strategy in the East. When Marxism-*Leninism* reached China and Japan, then, the doctrine bore the imprint of the Soviet experience with its own nationalities and with Asia. Embedded in this experience were fundamental issues such as the compatibility and acceptability of Marxism itself as a universal theory of development in cultures with different, non-Western values, some of which were expressed in the institutions that Marxism called them to destroy. The following analysis traces this evolution of the national question from the European context of the founders to early twentieth-century China and Japan.

THE NATIONAL QUESTION FROM MARX TO LENIN

It is not the intention here to reiterate the detailed explications of the national question in Marxism that have already been made, with excellence, by others.[1] Nevertheless, it is essential to establish as a point of departure what conventional treatments of the national question have to offer to an understanding of the role it played in China and Japan. I begin by tracing images of nationality and revolution as they emerged in the birthplace of Marxism before the first experiment in socialist revolution and proletarian statehood in Russia.

As the language from the *Critique of Hegel's "Philosophy of Right"* cited at the outset of the Introduction suggests, Marx's stance on the nation in the revolutionary struggle was decidedly ambiguous.[2] The famous formulation of the *Communist Manifesto*—"The working men have no country"—penned just five years after the *Critique*, is commonly cited as evidence of the primacy of internationalism in the Marxist movement. In the *Manifesto*, Marx and Engels asserted that in the course of its struggle, the proletariat itself would comprise and redefine the nation. "Since the proletariat must first of all acquire political supremacy, must rise to be the leading class of the nation, must constitute itself *the* nation," they wrote, "it is, so far, itself national, though not in the bourgeois sense of the word."[3] As Roman Szporluk has noted, this position on nationalism and nationality was problematic from the outset. The tension between nationalism and internationalism was particularly profound in Marx's consideration of the fate of his own nation, Germany. In the *Manifesto*, while urging "workers of the world" to unite, Marx and Engels were compelled to acknowledge that "the struggle of the proletariat with the bourgeoisie is at first a national struggle. The proletariat of each country must, of course, first of all settle matters with its own bourgeoisie."[4] But what of the fate of Germany? Here was a problem that would be immediately relevant to those in Russia, China, or elsewhere in the East hastening to make a socialist revolution where there was not yet a secure bourgeoisie. Marx called on his native proletariat to rise and save Germany, for its own bourgeoisie was too immature to achieve political domination. "The [German] middle class hardly dares to conceive the idea of emancipation from its own point of view," Marx lamented, "and already the development of social conditions and the progress of political theory, show that this point of view itself is already antiquated, or at least questionable."[5] Here was Marx's effort to resolve the German problem—the set of issues posed by Germany's late industrialization and tardy unification into an effective national state with democratic politics on the model of England and France.[6] In this Marx firmly opposed the vision of Friedrich List (1789–1846), his most formidable rival in addressing the German problem. Marx rejected the notion that a true solution to the German problem might be achieved within the framework of the existing German state. Thus, he identified German liberation with the imminent demise of capitalism itself as a world system.[7]

This view of the future of Germany was consistent with Marx's vision of proletarian revolution as an international movement. Nevertheless, important ambiguities concerning the nation and the state were inherent in this formulation. If the German bourgeoisie had failed to achieve dominion in the form of a bourgeois national state, was it not premature to call for a proletarian socialist revolution? On what basis would the existing state power that Marx attacked in his *Critique* of Hegel be destroyed if it were not a bourgeois state? And what of the achievement of the national political unity and the democratic politics on whose strengths Marx predicated his vision of the transcendence of the limitations of bourgeois freedom and of nationalism by proletarian internationalism? Although nationalism antedated the Industrial Revolution,[8] to a large extent Marx's reflections on the German problem reflected the role that nationalism had come to play in his own time. His position, in turn, both established the basis for Marxism's metamorphosis into an ideology of industrialization and betrayed the weaknesses inherent in Marx's and Engels's internationalist vision of socialist revolution. As Szporluk notes, both Marxism and nationalism became ideologies of late industrialization, contesting one another for adherents among those who would seek modernity in Germany, Italy, and Russia.[9] This phenomenon would render the national question even more significant for Marxism as the doctrine moved from its birthplace in Western Europe to the later-industrializing societies of the East. This would also mean that the national question, as conceived and addressed by Marx's contemporaries and immediate successors—and, indeed, as treated in conventional Western literature on the subject—would have expanded and deepened significance as it journeyed to the East.

Long before it reached the Far East, however, the issue would prove to be deeply divisive within the circles of nineteenth-century European Marxism itself. The dense concentration of small nationalities in Eastern and Central Europe caused the national question to become the focus of heated controversy in the 1880s through the turn of the century. In Germany in particular, the achievement of unification and rapid national strengthening through state-led industrialization under Otto von Bismarck reinforced nationalist sentiments in Germany and in surrounding areas. Consequently, the German Social-Democratic party and associated national parties, such as the Polish Socialist party and the Jewish Bund, become embroiled in conflict over the legitimacy of nationalism as a force supporting the international movement. As the Marxist movement embraced socialists of smaller nationalities sandwiched between the two great powers Germany and Russia, conflict erupted over the question of how the quest for the fulfillment of Polish or Jewish national interests could be incorporated into the pursuit of socialism.

The Polish Jewish socialist in exile Rosa Luxemburg confronted both Polish and Jewish nationalist aspirations in her leadership of the international movement.[10] Arguing that the struggle for socialism must proceed "on a class basis within the framework of existing political entities," Luxemburg vehemently repudiated any effort to meld nationalist aspirations into the movement. In her view, the very concept of the nation "as a homogeneous social and political entity" was merely a "categor[y] of bourgeois ideology" that mystified and veiled the reality of classes with concrete and disparate material interests.[11] Kautsky attempted to remove the veil by describing the forces that had given rise to the idea of the nation-state: first, "the desire of the bourgeoisie to assure for itself an internal or domestic market for its own commodity production; second, the desire for political freedom—democracy; and finally, expansion of the national literature and culture to the populace."[12] Luxemburg revised this formulation slightly to argue that the national state had become the aspiration of the bourgeoisie not only for its material interests, but also for its political independence: its primary political interest was "*state independence*," to enable it to take the offensive vis-à-vis other classes in bourgeois society. Once it had attained this independence, the bourgeoisie then moved to oppress both other classes and other nationalities. Thus, she concluded, the aims of the bourgeoisie in creating the national state could never "be the aims of a conscious proletariat." In this sense, the national state was "national" only inasmuch as it incarnated "the dominance of the bourgeoisie of a certain nationality over the entire mixed population of the state."[13] The model of such a national state was to be found in Germany, Britain, and, especially, the United States, "a state which keeps in its bosom like a gaping wound the oppression of the Negro people, and seeks to conquer the Asiatic peoples."[14] As a result, preoccupation with national self-determination for the individual nationalities held fateful consequences for the international socialist movement, Luxemburg concluded. "The marriage of a utopian pipe-dream for the restoration of Poland with the struggle for Socialism leads the working class astray into the blind alley of nationalism, . . . weakens Socialist action, causes internal dissension and frustration, . . . reduces the moral authority of Socialism, and finally condemns Socialist agitation to complete sterility."[15]

In this early development of Marxist discourse on the national question, Luxemburg joined Kautsky in claiming to define Marxist orthodoxy on the issue. Both voiced principled opposition to nationalist sentiments that threatened to dissolve the movement in cultural separatism during the controversy that culminated at the Congress of the Second International in London in 1896. Yet both recognized the legitimacy of the appeal to freedom of nationalities and accepted the principle of national self-determination. "If we recognize the rights of each nation to self-determination," Luxemburg conceded, "it is obviously a logical conclusion that we must condemn every attempt to place one nation over another, or for one nation to force upon another any form of national existence." She was careful to stress, however, that Social Democracy's "duty to protest and resist national oppression" did not emerge "from any special 'right of nations'." "A 'right of nations' which is valid for all countries and all times is nothing more than a metaphysical cliché" with no grounding in the "*material* social conditions of the environment in a given historical epoch." Both Luxemburg and Kautsky, then, insisted on a practical solution to the problem that would emanate from such material conditions. Such circumstances in Europe at the turn of the twentieth century persuaded the two to accept the restructuring of socialist parties as federations of groups representing disparate national aspirations within the socialist movement.[16] Kautsky's proposal in the *Neue Zeit* the following year, which Luxemburg endorsed, proffered a federative "solution that would prefigure that chosen by the Austrian Social-Democratic Party at its Brünn Congress of 1899."[17]

Given the increasing diversity of the movement, the ambiguities of Marx's and Engels's original formulations, and the contradictions implicit in Kautsky's and Luxemburg's efforts to distinguish legitimate from illegitimate national aspirations, it was predictable that Kautsky's and Luxemburg's claims to orthodoxy would not be the last word on the subject. A new stage in the evolution of the issue opened with the proliferation of pamphlets and articles calling into question their views. The most important of these initiatives was Otto Bauer's 1907 study, *Die Nationalitätenfrage und die Sozialdemokratie* (The Nationalities question and social democracy). Bauer and other Austro-Marxists felt a need to define the Marxist position anew in the age of imperialism driven by capitalist development. In his new and controversial study, Bauer called into question any view that failed to appreciate adequately national differences. The new age, marked by the increasing assimilation of national minorities into empires, threatened to be matched by the internationalization of a revolutionary movement that dissolved the identities of individual nationalities into the whole. Bauer asserted that such tendencies must be resisted, and he insisted on the need to recognize the enduring reality of "national character"—"differences . . . in the basic structure of the national mind, intellectual and aesthetic taste, and reactions to the same; differences of which we become aware when we compare the cultural life of the nations, their science and philosophy, their poetry, music, and arts, their political and social life, their customs and way of life." Bauer's concept of the nation as "a community of character arising out of a community of fate" repudiated "nationalistic conceptions of history," but it required that the international socialist movement allow national diversity to flourish within "international unity."[18] Bauer's piece was immediately attacked by Kautsky in the *Neue Zeit*. The paper immediately became the forum for a debate between what Lenin would call the "psychological cultural" and "historico-economic" conceptions of the nation. Arguing that the nation was merely the product of the expansion of capitalist economies over large territories, Kautsky feared that Bauer's cultural concept implied a permanence of national divisions. By contrast, Kautsky advocated a dialectical appreciation of the issue in the context of his own formalistic historical materialism. In his view, differences among nationalities would disappear with the internationalization of capital and the revolutionary struggle.[19] This position allowed Kautsky to avert the potential statist implications of Bauer's approbation of cultural nationalism.

Clearly, though, Kautsky's and Luxemburg's position was not sufficiently compelling to those Marxists who feared for the very survival of the motherlands in which they hoped to build socialism. On the eve of World War I, nationalistic tendencies flourished within the Austrian Social Democratic and then the Russian Social Democratic Labor party. The Austrian party had become a virtual federation of autonomous parties representing German, Czech, Italian, Polish, Ruthenian, and Southern Slav national interests. Such a situation threatened the Russian party as well; the Jewish Workers' Bund, a socialist group formed in 1897 to represent Polish, Lithuanian, and Latvian Jews, entered the Social Democratic party at its 1898 founding congress, briefly withdrew, and then rejoined in 1906. The Bund thereupon acted as an autonomous party organization, as did the Latvian, Lithuanian, and Polish groups. By 1912, these groups were advocating the Austro-Marxist principle of "national-cultural autonomy" within the Russian movement, spurring Lenin to write in November condemning "'the adaptation of socialism to nationalism'" in his party. In Lenin's view, national separatism would cripple the movement's class-based opposition to tsarism.[20] Lenin, then, undertook to systematize his thinking on the national question in a manner that would accomplish a most delicate task: support the unity of the Social Democratic movement across nationalities without undermining its appeal to national interests. Joseph Stalin, as a Georgian sympathetic to Lenin on the national question, was requested to undertake this task on Lenin's behalf. As early as 1897, Lenin had already begun to recognize the national question as a factor that could benefit the movement against the tsarist state and included "'persecuted'" "'nationalities, religions, and sects'" among those who could fight alongside the working class "'in the democratic struggle'."[21] Thus, as a tactical matter, Lenin had come to support the call for self-determination of national minorities in the Russian empire without specifying any precise future for them. In the meantime, the issue of national separatism had come to the forefront with the idea of cultural autonomy so popular in the Bund spreading to other nationalities in the Social Democratic party, particularly the Ukrainians. Meanwhile, the Bolsheviks' major rivals, the Social Revolutionaries, had accepted the notion of a federal state guaranteeing cultural autonomy to the minorities, and the Mensheviks were approaching the same position.[22]

Commissioned by Lenin to critique the Austro-Marxist position on "national-cultural autonomy" of Otto Bauer and Karl Renner, Stalin produced an article, "Marksizm i natsional'noi vopros" (Marxism and the national question).[23] Stalin defined the nation as a community that was "historically stable" and constituted by four commonalities: language, territory, economic life, and psychological makeup. Following Kautsky's treatment (without attribution), Stalin characterized the nation as a historic entity rather than the "quasi-mystical" one defined by the Austro-Marxists. As for the posture of the socialist movement, Stalin argued that a distinction must be drawn between the demand for democratic rights of the nationalities, on the one hand, and the call for cultural autonomy, on the other. The first was a legitimate demand that was consistent with the objectives of the labor movement and should be supported. The second, however, posited cultural and national differences as permanent and, thus, threatened separatism to the detriment of the polity as a whole. Such a perspective that insisted on cultural "autonomy" would leave not only advanced peoples, such as Ukrainians and Jews, but also so-called primitive cultures in their isolation and fail to assimilate them into the society as a whole. This tendency and the perspective of the Austro-Marxists, therefore, should be opposed strenuously. Stalin argued that such a prescription did not conflict with the Bolsheviks' stance in favor of self-determination, but it did mean that the Social Democratic party should oppose the narrow allegiances of nationalism "just as," in the paraphrase of Robert Tucker, "it ought to agitate against Catholicism, Protestantism, and Orthodoxy while upholding the right of all people to freedom of religious worship. The duty of Social Democracy was to influence the will of nations to arrange their affairs in the manner best corresponding to the interests of the proletariat."[24]

Lenin appears to have been well pleased with Stalin's contribution to the Bolshevik position on the national question. Nevertheless, there were important respects in which Lenin's and Stalin's formulations differed. Stalin drew much more from the Bauer-Renner concept of the nation. For example, the Georgian portrayed the nation as a "stable" community with a common "psychological life," whereas Lenin treated the nation as transitory and ephemeral. Stalin also viewed the nation as a result of historical development that antedated the capitalist stage. Lenin, by contrast, like Kautsky, considered the idea of the nation as a product of capitalist development and firmly repudiated the notion of *national culture* as a bourgeois concept. In any case, Lenin defined his position for himself once Russia's national question became an international national question when World War I erupted. Here, Lenin confronted a situation in which he fundamentally agreed with Luxemburg's and Kautsky's orthodox position but tactically disagreed with Luxemburg on the position the party should take on the national question. Recognizing that the Russian Social-Democratic Labor party needed to rely on minority nationalities as allies in the struggle against tsarism, Lenin adhered to the formula calling for self-determination, but this was reinterpreted to accord with the needs of the proletarian movement.[25] Before the victory of the revolution the national minorities were a valuable ally whose claims to oppression drew them close to the cause of the proletariat.[26] Moreover, Lenin, like Leon Trotsky, recognized Russia's "backwardness" vis-à-vis the West, which meant that nationalities could continue to play a positive role historically as long as Russia was still completing the "bourgeois-democratic" stage of its revolution.[27] Thus, after the revolution, Lenin formally retained his adherence to the notion of national self-determination, indeed opposing all vestiges of Great-Russian chauvinism, including those he detected in Stalin.[28] Yet he remained convinced that the belief in national self-determination must not mean that nationalist passions of small nations should preempt the internationalist cause any more than the majority nationalities of great empires should be allowed to prevail over the less powerful in their territorial domains.

With the outbreak of World War I and the question of whether to vote war credits to their national governments, the national parties that comprised the Second International splintered dramatically. On the eve of the war, a widespread simultaneous recantation across several European countries had occurred, and in the 1920s, in the war's aftermath, individual and group repudiations of Marxism among adherents to the socialist movement ensued in Italy, France, and Germany.[29] Throughout Europe the decision to rally to the support of the homeland explicitly involved rejection of the orthodox Marxist claim that the worker had no country. This reaction to the threat of war was particularly pronounced in Germany where the German problem remained not only unresolved but particularly cumbersome in the wake of the humiliating Treaty of Versailles.[30] The socialist movement experienced a severe setback despite the strenuous efforts of Lenin and radicals in the German Social-Democratic movement, such as Rosa Luxemburg, to maintain internationalist solidarity. After the war, German recanters were succeeded by advocates of National Bolshevism—"a rapprochement between German nationalism and Russian Communism"[31]—but they too rejected the notion of attaining socialism through class conflict within existing national bounds. Ultimately, of course, the radicalism of Luxemburg's orthodoxy was crushed with her slaying after the aborted Spartacus uprising, and social democracy gave way to a national socialism that was opposed to Marxism. In its place would emerge a transmogrification of Marxism into national socialism, which argued that human liberation is achieved solely through the liberation of one's nation (or *Volk*).[32]

Thus, in the late nineteenth and early twentieth centuries, the relationship between Marxism and nationalism became considerably more complex. Lenin's treatment of the issue would comprise the basis for a new strategy for revolution in the East for the Third (Communist) International (Comintern). In Russia, Marxism was adopted by those such as Lenin and his comrades in the labor movement who opposed the *narodnik* (populist) view that Russia's historical destiny diverged fundamentally from that of the West. In *The Development of Capitalism in Russia* (1899), Lenin maintained that although Russia still maintained some of its Asiatic (i.e., backward) attributes, capitalism had come to be firmly rooted in the country and would, thus, inevitably carve the same trajectory as Western Europe. Discouraged by the collapse of the European revolutionary movement in the Paris Commune and the rise of Bismarck, Marx himself had briefly entertained the narodnik notion that Russia's backwardness—the strengthening of serfdom well after its decline had begun in the West—would permit it to bypass the agonies of capitalist industrialization and proceed to build socialism on the remanent primitive peasant commune (*mir* or *obshchina*). Socialism on such a basis could only be realized, however, if it were supported by proletarian revolutions in the advanced industrial societies of Western Europe.[33] Clearly, such a prospect would have undermined Marx's and Engels's claim to the universality of their scientific analysis of the historical progress of human society, and the two men hastily retreated from this position. Thus, Engels admonished the narodnik Pyotr Tkachov, "Only at a certain level of development of the productive forces of society, an even very high level for our modern conditions, does it become possible to raise production to such an extent that the abolition of class distinctions can be a real progress, can be lasting without bringing about stagnation or even decline in the mode of social production. Hence a man who will say that this revolution can be more easily carried out in a country because, *although* it has no proletariat, it has no bourgeoisie *either*, only proves that he has still to learn the ABC of socialism."[34] Lenin's response to the narodniks echoed Marx's and Engels's judgment that its admittedly "Asiatic" characteristics did not exempt Russia from the universal laws they claimed governed human development. These laws would, however, dictate that Russia's tardy start in developing industrial capitalism would permit a proletarian-socialist revolution only after the same had occurred in the more "advanced" national states of Western Europe. Presumably, by then, the nationality question—and the quest for a powerful nation-state—would have been eclipsed in Russia, as in the West, by the urgency of proletarian internationalism.

Yet a Marxist-inspired, proletariat-led revolution did occur first in Russia, and with it the national question accompanied Marxism into the Far East. Not surprisingly, the nationality problem would prove to be no less intractable in the later-industrializing Russia than it remained in the West. As it migrated eastward, the national question would acquire new dimensions, aspects that had been implicit but unarticulated in its West European homeland, because of two separate but related factors: (1) the manner in which it was confronted by the Bolshevik leaders of the world's first socialist state; (2) and the way in which Marxist political philosophy came to have an impact in Asia. Under the influence of these elements, the national question would undergo a transformation as it was adapted by new Marxists in changed cultural, economic, and political circumstances.

THE TRANSFORMATION OF THE NATIONAL QUESTION AFTER OCTOBER 1917

Immediately after the Bolshevik revolution of October 1917, the Bolsheviks confronted the three major issues that contributed to this transformation of the national question: (1) the national question in its conventional sense in the form of the nationalities problem in what was now the Soviet empire; (2) the challenge of spreading the Bolsheviks' socialist revolution to all parts of the former tsarist empire in the face of stubborn obstacles presented by non-European institutions that resisted the framework of Marxian proletarian revolution; and (3) the effort to export their revolution to other non-European societies. In the last endeavor, the Bolsheviks would find it necessary to temper their critique of nationalism to acquire new allies in support of their revolution. Together the three challenges marked the first stage in the transformation of the national question as it migrated from Russia farther east.

The new proletarian state was immediately confronted with the legacy of the very same nationality problem that had faced the tsarist regime: how to handle aspirations to national sovereignty among minority nationalities on the periphery of Russia proper. To some extent, the nationalities problem in these years was of the Bolsheviks' own making. Before the revolution, seeking to unite disgruntled nationalities to overthrow the tsar, Lenin had asserted that his goal was to "unite the workers of all nations living in this state." He insisted that the Bolsheviks "firmly uphold something that is beyond doubt: the right of the Ukraine to form such ['an independent national'] . . . state."[35] On the outbreak of World War I, indeed, Lenin boldly assumed the unpopular position of defeatism for Russia in a manner that maintained, in equally uncompromising fashion, the right of all nations in the tsarist empire, not just the Russian, to sovereignty.[36]

In the ensuing civil war, the national question figured prominently, particularly among opposition forces in the Ukraine.[37] As Tucker has noted, "the non-Communist Transcaucasian regimes were not contesting Bolshevik rule in Russia proper but only exercising that right of national self-determination to which Lenin and his party in theory subscribed."[38] How were the Bolsheviks to deal with such aspirations to national sovereignty now that they themselves were heirs to the hated "center"? The key to resolving this vexatious problem was to acknowledge "'that moral quality which expresses itself in the attempts to harmonize national and all-human interests, to consider all nations'."[39] But what did such a formula mean in terms of practical policy? In accordance with the principle of self-determination that the Bolsheviks had affirmed before the revolution, a decree issued on November 2, 1917, "proclaimed the sovereign equality of all the peoples of Russia, recognized their right to self-determination, including the right to secession, and promised the abolition of all national privileges and restrictions."[40] It was, of course, one thing to make such a blanket pronouncement and quite another to implement it when individual nationalities asserted their right to self-determination against a state that felt itself under dire threat from both internal opposition and outside powers.

In the years of the civil war, in fact, policy concerning the nationalities was made with much inconsistency, the tack taken dependent upon immediate political interests. A major factor that would determine the Bolshevik response to the issue in these years lay in the internationalization of the problem that had begun with the outbreak of World War I. After the revolution, and with the Allied intervention against Bolshevik rule, the empire was in pieces, and the nationalities that de-manded self-determination turned to foreign powers for support.[41] In two cases, Poland and Finland, self-determination was the outcome of a frank recognition on the part of the Bolsheviks that they were helpless to prevent it. Poland's indepen-dence had been made a fait accompli by German policy during Germany's occupa-tion of Poland, and the decree of December 1917 by the Sovnarkom (Council of People's Commissars, of which Lenin was the head) recognized the independent state of Finland. In the latter case, however, the situation was more complex. A strong proletarian movement had emerged in Finland, and if the Bolsheviks were to be consistent in their claim that the wishes of the proletariat had to be attributed primacy over those of the bourgeoisie, they would have to support the demands of the former. Thus, in January 1918, the Red Army supported the Finnish revolu-tion, and the Soviet Union signed a treaty of friendship with the new revolutionary Finnish state in March 1918. The nationalist Mannerheim government that Russia had recognized in the December decree then turned to Germany for help and successfully ejected the new revolutionary government. As Carrère d'Encausse has noted, in this case, as indeed in Poland, independence was gained not as a result of Lenin's analysis of the national question and devotion to the principle of self-determination but as a result of the intervention of an outside power.[42]

The situation was similar in the Baltics. In Lithuania, a pro-German government was installed in February 1918, while in Estonia, the departure of the German army permitted the establishment of a workers' republican commune that was in turn recognized and supported by the Russian Soviet Federal Socialist Republic (RSFSR). Similarly, an independent Latvian workers' republic was proclaimed in December and was, thereupon, supported by the Sovnarkom. Nevertheless, the presence of the English fleet in the Baltic, which sought to bolster bourgeois nationalist governments in the region, prevailed over the Bolsheviks' feeble power. Here, the Bolsheviks had to accept the collapse of the workers' republics and reconcile themselves to the independence of governments that were not to their liking, but they hoped to be able to use them as intermediaries in their troubled relations with the Western capitalist powers. Ultimately, under outside pressure the RSFSR was constrained to recognize the sovereignty of Latvia and Estonia in the peace treaties of February and August of 1920. This sequela was duplicated in the case of Lithuania under circumstances that were even more heavily influenced by international developments. The German-supported government collapsed when Germany lost the war and was replaced by a provisional revolutionary government recognized by the RSFSR in December 1918. In February 1919, a joint Union of Lithuania and Byelorussia was proclaimed, and a close relationship was established with the RSFSR, which had already cultivated federalist ties to Byelorussia. But this federalist relationship was disrupted when Polish troops seized Vilnius in 1920, and when the Poles retreated from their brief occupancy, the RSFSR was obliged to recognize Lithuania's independence in the treaty of July 1920.[43] Conversely, the Ukraine lost its ability to attain independence from the Russian Soviet Republic, when it found no external ally to help it defend the guarantees that it appeared to have won in the Treaty of Brest-Litovsk.[44]

The Bolsheviks had been obliged to handle the Caucasus in a particularly delicate and sensitive fashion lest it be lured to the side of the Western powers that had sent missions against the struggling young Bolshevik regime. As Stalin noted in a *Pravda* interview in 1920, "'The Caucasus' important significance for the Revolution turns not only on its being a source of raw materials, fuel, and food, but also on its position between Europe and Asia, between Russia and Turkey in particular, and on the presence of highly important economic and strategic roads (Batum-Baku, Batum-Tabriz, Batum-Tabriz-Erzerum)'."[45] Likewise, the grain of the Ukraine was a critical resource to be protected against the Polish invasion.[46] Circumstances were diverse across the region, but again external forces were significant. In Azerbaijan, there had been a significant basis of support for Bolshevik ideals in the months following the October Revolution. Local Bolsheviks had successfully established a Baku Commune—recalling its French ancestor of 1871—but the new commune was also short lived under a combination of internal and external (specifically Turkish) pressures.[47] Meanwhile, appreciative of the region for its value vis-à-vis the West, Lenin resisted pressures by more adventurous lieutenants of nationalities policy in the Caucasus, such as Sergo Ordzhonikidze and Stalin, to use force to "sovietize" Georgia. In the Transcaucasus, Georgia was an especially troublesome case. As Tucker has noted, "Unlike Azerbaijan, which was less formed as a nation, and Armenia, whose people perforce saw in Russia a protector against Turkey, Georgia had taken readily to independent existence as a nation-state." It had been led effectively by the Mensheviks after the split of the short-lived Federal Republic of Transcaucasia (February through April 1918), and now Stalin saw in his homeland the need for a "'ruthless struggle against nationalism'."[48] In the ensuing months, the conflict between the Georgian communists, on the one hand, and Stalin and Ordzhonikidze, on the other, resulted in the resignation of the entire Central Committee of the Georgian party organization.

Lenin would subsequently conclude that although he had initially supported Stalin and Ordzhonikidze in this conflict, they had, in fact, been guilty of the very "Great Russian chauvinism" that he so despised. Lenin now worried about the overcentralization of authority in the nascent Soviet Union: Perhaps the Union should be limited to cooperation in military and foreign affairs with autonomy attributed to the individual republics in other matters. The consequences of such autonomy would "be infinitely less," he reasoned, than the harm that could result "if, on the eve of the debut of the East, just as it is awakening, we undermined our prestige with its peoples, even if only by the slightest crudity or injustice towards our own non-Russian nationalities" or if the Soviet leaders were to "lapse, even if only in trifles, into imperialist attitudes towards oppressed nationalities, thus undermining all our principled sincerity, all our principled defence of the struggle against imperialism."[49] With these dangers in mind, and with Japanese forces present in Siberia beginning in 1918, the Bolsheviks were quick to allow the establishment of an independent Far Eastern Republic. The new entity lasted until November 1922, when Japanese forces finally withdrew from the area.[50]

After Germany was defeated and the civil war was won, Allied forces withdrew from the territories of the former Russian empire. Soviet initiative and preferences could now determine the resolution of the national question throughout Russia. Ironically, however, the outcomes that were dictated more by the presence of foreign forces immediately after the revolution benefited the Bolsheviks. These external pressures allowed the party to avoid actions that might have been viewed as imperialistic at a time when the Bolsheviks were wooing support from Asia. The threat of losing the East was an ominous prospect, indeed, because the failure of revolution in Europe made the Bolsheviks all the more dependent on the rich natural resources of the Caucasus and Soviet Central Asia as well as support from sympathetic revolutionary governments in the East.

Thus, Lenin's concerns about the possible negative perceptions of Soviet national policy were influential during the civil war years. But, by December 1922 with the civil war won, plans for the formal creation of a federal union, contemplated for several months, were drafted and approved by the Tenth Congress of the Soviets of the RSFSR. At the end of the year, the completed articles of union were signed by party representatives of the RSFSR and the Ukrainian, Byelorussian, and Transcaucasian republics. Stalin, as head of the Narkomnats (People's Commissariat for Nationalities) since 1917, saw the new union as a means to maintain strict centralized control over potentially difficult republics. The constitution that was approved in July 1923 and ratified by the January 1924 Second All-Union Congress of Soviets formally left to the republics authority only in areas of domestic policy such as agriculture, justice, education, health, and social matters. In fact, of course, the party's pervasive central control over all commissariats nullified the provision for autonomy even in these areas.[51]

At the same time, Lenin had always insisted on equality among peoples, and now he repudiated Great Russian chauvinism, even among his closest colleagues, including Stalin.[52] He hoped to bring economically "backward" areas up to the level of economic development achieved in the heartland of Russia.[53] Some 21 percent of the 130 million Soviet citizens lived in tribal or pastoral socioeconomic formations. Lenin envisioned that industrial development would create an industrial working class, the traditional basis of Bolshevik support, in these societies.[54] By the 1930s, the Bolsheviks had made significant gains in improving the economic and social well-being of the Central Asian republics as well as in terms of such conventional measures as gross national product and communications and transportation facilities.[55] While in the USSR and the RSFSR large-scale industry grew 5.7 times between 1913 and 1935, it expanded 8.5 and 8.3 times in the Kazakh SSR and the Kirghiz SSR, respectively.[56]

In addition, with the party the dominant actor in all national affairs, major efforts were also made to increase the participation of non-Russian national minorities in party activities. Within the first decade of the revolution, positive results were already evident. Great Russians comprised 52.9 percent of the entire population in 1926, and their percentage of party membership declined from 72 to 65 percent from 1922 to 1927. During the same period, the percentages of Central Asians and other minority nationalities in the party increased from 2.5 to 3.5 (40 percent) and from 2.9 to 3.8 (30 percent), respectively. This was, in part, the product of a significant lowering of standards for entry into the party. For example, in 1929, the quota of party members to originate from the working class was fixed at 90 percent in the industrial areas and 70 percent in agrarian areas of the RSFSR proper but only 60 percent in the non-Russian republics.[57] Such compromises were easily justified if one believed, as Lenin did, that although national differences were a fact to be taken seriously in the early years of the union, they would shortly wither away as the forces of production matured. Indeed, in this view, federation itself was but a temporary concession to the reality of national differences. "Federation is a transitional form to the complete unity of the working people of different nations," Lenin wrote in mid-1920. Gradually, he argued, the Soviet federation would involve more and more intimate economic and political ties, as society as a whole moved toward "a single world economy, regulated by the proletariat of all nations as an integral whole and according to a common plan."[58]

Other compromises were also necessary to accommodate other minority nationalities in the young Soviet republic. The most important of these concerned the Jews. The history of Bolshevik policy toward the Jews goes far to explain their status in the Soviet Union in the period following World War II. In fact, the case of Soviet Jewry demonstrates vividly how difficult it was to treat all nationalities equally and, indeed, for Soviet leaders to take any significant action to improve the well-being of one nationality without incurring the hostility and resentment of other nationalities. One of the first efforts taken vis-à-vis the nationality problem was the establishment in October 1917 of the Narkomnats, composed, in 1918, of eight commissariats (*natskom*) and eleven subordinate departments (*natsotdel*). It was not always clear what determined which nationalities were represented by commissariats or by departments.[59] It is noteworthy, however, that there were commissariats of Jewish and Moslem affairs, respectively, even though neither the Jews nor the Moslems technically could be categorized as nationalities by the Bolsheviks.[60] Before 1917, Lenin and Stalin had agreed that the Jews did not constitute a nation by Marxist criteria because they possessed no historic attachment to a given territory nor had they over the centuries come to enjoy a particular mode of economic life as society moved from feudalism to capitalism. They were identified only by their religious culture. Thus, they could constitute a nation in Bauer's sense but not in Lenin's, Kautsky's, or Stalin's usage of the term. After the revolution, however, the Jewish problem cried out for resolution because of the oppression that Jews had suffered under tsarism and internationally. Lenin's solution was inconsistent, if justifiable. "[Lenin] avoided making any pronouncements concerning the future of the Jews, or giving them any particular political status," Carrère d'Encausse explains. "But, at the same time, he recognized the necessity for Jewish representation in the Narkomnats and for a Jewish section within the party (the Evsektsiia) to express and defend the interests of the Jews. If it was not a question of autonomy on whatever basis it might be, the existence of a *cultural* difference was implicitly accepted through the organs that were charged with representing it."[61] At every step, however, the position Jews would gain vis-à-vis the center was opposed by advocates of Byelorussian autonomy. Unlike Ukrainian *indépendentistes*, those in Byelorussia were motivated by deep animosity against "Jewish and Polish cultures" rather than against Russian culture.[62] As a result, any initiatives to accommodate the nationalist aspirations of Poles or Jews were contested by Byelorussians demanding equivalent or superordinate rights.

Despite these difficulties, the Bolshevik search for support from revolutionary movements in the East after 1919 led Lenin to broaden his nationalities policy to the Orient in order to promote what he called "movements of national liberation" from the imperialist activity of Western capitalist societies. Lenin envisioned that such nationalistic anticolonial movements in the East would break the crucial link that enabled West European capitalist economies to thrive on imperialist expansion. Thus, a second aspect of the national question to emerge in the wake of the October Revolution concerned the extent to which Marx's scenario of proletarian socialist revolution might need to be altered to apply to nations outside Western Europe. To some extent, this issue had already emerged long before, when Marx and Engels had contemplated the prospects for socialist revolution in the Russia they considered the bastion of reaction in Europe. The problem was that Russia west of the Urals was surely European, but east of the Urals it was not. Marx and Engels had believed, albeit briefly, that an early socialist revolution was possible in Russia on the basis of the primitive peasant commune, but they had expected such a revolution to survive only if it served as a spark for international revolution among the proletariats of the advanced capitalist societies of Western Europe. Similarly, Lenin believed that given its laggard industrial development Russia could sustain a socialist revolution only if it was supported by immediate proletarian socialist revolutions in Western Europe. When that prospect collapsed with the 1919 Spartacus uprising, Lenin and other Bolsheviks turned to the colonial and semicolonial societies of the East victimized by Western imperialism for revolutionary support. When Lenin and his Bolshevik comrades founded the Third International (Comintern) that year, they turned their attention to insurgent movements of national liberation in the East that would sever the ties between the advanced industrialized societies of Western Europe and the predominantly agrarian societies that they had victimized through their imperialist adventures.

Lenin had made his first theoretical efforts in this direction in 1916 in the midst of World War I. Even before he had completed his analysis of imperialism, Lenin affirmed nationalism in the East as a progressive development: "We cannot say whether Asia will have had time to develop into a system of independent national states, like Europe, before the collapse of capitalism, but it remains an undisputed fact that capitalism, having awakened Asia, has called for national movements everywhere in that continent, too; that the tendency of these movements is towards the creation of national states in Asia; that it is such states that ensure the best conditions for the development of capitalism."[63] Nationalism could play a positive, progressive role for world revolution in the East by disrupting the flow of resources from East to West that was so crucial to the survival of the Western industrial societies, thereby causing economic hardship, labor mobilization, and, finally, proletarian socialist revolution in the West.

Writing in mid-1920, therefore, Lenin grounded his analysis of the national question in lessons to be drawn from imperialism. His views became the basis of Comintern policy in the 1920s in support of the fledgling Marxian socialist movements in China and Japan. With this interpretation of Marxism to apply to revolution in later-industrializing societies, the Comintern formula bore all the complexities of the national question as it had unfolded to date in the Soviet Union. Now, however, Marxism brought with it new complications arising out of the internationalization of the national question beyond the bounds of Western Europe and the Soviet Union. Many such difficulties were foreshadowed by the Soviet experience of trying to extend the Bolsheviks' proletarian revolution to the outer expanses of Soviet Central Asia, which shared little with the milieu that had spawned Marx's historical schema.

Soviet Central Asia was the first scene of a dramatic confrontation between Bolsheviks determined to bring their vision of socialist modernity to what they expected would be a pliant population and a self-contained society equally resolved to maintain its own deeply rooted way of life. The particular form of precapitalist society in the region was divided between self-sufficient sedentary-pastoral and nomadic communities in which kinship units were organized "by and large along patriarchal, patrilineal, and patrilocal lines."[64] The indigenous population was overwhelmingly Turkic with Slavic and Iranian minorities. Ninety percent rural when Russia penetrated the region in the midnineteenth century, their mode of life was based on agriculture and stockbreeding. Moslem religious traditions, other folk customs, and the heavily nomadic influence combined to make Central Asia substantially different from what the Bolsheviks either had experienced firsthand in other areas outside Russia proper or expected to encounter on the basis of Marx's and Engels's writings on precapitalist societies.

This was not greatly significant at the outset of the effort to bring Central Asia under Soviet military and political control from 1918 to 1921. Unlike the strong community and national identities found in the Baltic and the Caucasus, in Central Asia, "the largest (supra-communal)—and hence the most *heterogeneous*—historical subdivisions were on the verge of disintegration, while the smallest—and hence the most *homogeneous*, including clans, extended families, and village communities—were relatively intact."[65] This social structure facilitated the initial extension of Soviet power into the region. But as soon as the Bolsheviks attempted to effect social transformation and genuinely integrate Central Asia into a socialist union, conflict arose. Once Soviet administrative power was instituted over the entire area, the rural populations simply resumed their customary mode of life and maintained traditional values and practices that conflicted fundamentally with what the Bolsheviks aspired to bring them.[66]

In response, the Bolsheviks first tried to remove traditional elites in the belief that by decapitating the traditional organizational structure they would be able to cripple its resistance to modernization. They soon found, however, that these structures were considerably more resilient than anticipated. Local replacements for these elites were recruited immediately, but the Bolsheviks needed to find genuine revolutionaries to act as the vanguard of change in the region. Although there were urban areas with small concentrations of merchants and artisans in the 1920s, clearly, the overwhelmingly rural Central Asian setting lacked a major prerequisite for a socialist revolution in the Marxist historical schema—a proletariat. After studying the culture and social organization of the region, Bolshevik activists devised an innovative solution: where there was no genuine proletariat, they would identify a surrogate. In Soviet Central Asia, the most despised, lowly, and oppressed class was one of the two that Engels had seen as the original classes in the first division of labor in human society—women. The Bolsheviks, therefore, targeted the defense and conversion of women to their cause as the key to undermining the traditional patriarchal social structure of the region. As Massell's insightful study has demonstrated, this strategy yielded mixed results. "For the most part, women may be said to have failed to function as a social class, a stratum with a sense of shared identity, with a distinct, clearly perceived community of experience, interest, purpose, and action."[67] Although the struggle of Soviet adminstrative "socialist" law with the *shariat* (Moslem religious law) and *adat* (customary Central Asian law) achieved some successes, the use of force to support that struggle provoked new forms of resistance. Finally, in the face of a backlash that threatened the very groups they were attempting to protect, the Bolsheviks were forced to retreat from their endeavor to undertake a cultural revolution alongside a massive economic reconstruction of Central Asia.[68] Moreover, it became apparent that the extension of the administrative power of the revolutionary state could not necessarily guarantee dominance of a new cultural hegemony over the power of traditional, indigenous practices that the Bolsheviks regarded as incompatible with their new socialist order.

The fate of this experiment bore important implications for any effort to export revolution outside the West European context. When the Bolsheviks finally recognized the true depth of the challenge they faced in seeking to transform Central Asia into an industrialized socialist society, they turned to their experts on the East for guidance. G. Safarov, M. Sultan-Galiev, and A. I. Mikoyan alerted the party to the fact that it had neglected "the eastern question." At the party's Tenth Congress in 1921, Mikoyan pleaded for the party to adopt a nuanced approach to the East. Instead of categorizing its varied peoples into a single set of stereotyped images, the party needed to examine individual societies in detail. Yet in tackling Soviet Central Asia, the party relied on a practice that would become standard in its treatment of the East, including China and Japan: they looked to Marx's and Engels's categorizations of precapitalist societies and devised new labels that would enable them to prescribe strategies for these societies as if they fit neatly into the Marxian schema of historical change. Thus, the polyethnic Central Asian social structure was characterized as "patriarchal feudal" and dominated by "semi-feudal lords."[69] Such depictions would be of limited use to activists in the field responding to concrete local realities in implementing policies dictated from above. In this novel context, the national question was no longer simply an issue of the self-determination of individual nations with respect to the creation of independent national states in the context of a socialist revolution. There were cultural issues as well, questions of cultural sovereignty, so to speak, as the effort to engineer social and economic revolution mandated cultural changes premised on attitudes toward Asian cultures that could legitimately be faulted as imperialistic on the part of the Bolsheviks. Although he did not go so far as to suggest this possiblity explicitly, the fear of such a tendency was implicit in Safarov's remarks cautioning the Tenth Party Congress against implementing policies that would issue from "traditional Russian contempt and brutality toward Moslems." Any such measures would constitute " 'unforgivable mistakes' " that could " 'block [the Asian borderlands'] revolutionary development'."[70]

The Bolsheviks in Central Asia experienced additional difficulties in the internationalization of the national question. The region was within Soviet borders, and, thus, the issue differed slightly from what it would become in China and Japan. In Central Asia, the Bolsheviks sought to incorporate peoples with fundamentally different social structures into a socialist revolution that had already occurred from below and was continuing from above in Russia proper. By contrast, as the discussion here will demonstrate, Lenin and his comrades did not envisage immediate *socialist* revolution in other parts of Asia that were not within the boundaries of the Russian empire.

Nevertheless, the Central Asian example helps to illuminate some of the dilemmas that would arise when the national question had to be resolved beyond Soviet borders in the East. Lenin's own formulation, however imaginative, was responsible for many of these new difficulties. The model for Lenin's revolution in the East seemed to be the experience of Russia's own revolution. He condemned the bourgeoisie internationally in the same language with which he had condemned it in Russia. "Under the guise of the equality of the individual in general," Lenin argued before the Second Comintern Congress, "bourgeois democracy proclaims the formal or legal equality of the property-owner and the proletarian, the exploiter and the exploited, thereby grossly deceiving the oppressed classes." This formula would be transferred to an international scale. At Lenin's insistence, Comintern policy would be premised in part on a "clear distinction between the oppressed, dependent and subject nations and the oppressing, exploiting and sovereign nations, in order to counter the bourgeois-democratic lies that play down this colonial and financial enslavement of the vast majority of the world's population by an insignificant minority of the richest and advanced capitalist countries, a feature characteristic of the era of finance capital and imperialism." As a result, Lenin—and Nikolai Bukharin several years later—envisaged a revolutionary alliance of the peasant masses in the "national and colonial liberation movements" with the proletariat of the West. The new combination would mirror the *smychka* (alliance) between peasants and workers in Russia itself in 1905 and 1917.[71]

Lenin's prescription for the national policy of the Comintern, then, was that the international revolutionary body should encourage the "bourgeois-democratic liberation movement" in "the more backward states and nations, in which feudal or patriarchal and patriarchal-peasant relations predominate."

> The Communist parties must consistently expose that constant violation of the equality of nations and of the guaranteed rights of national minorities which is to be seen in all capitalist countries, despite their "democratic" constitutions. It is also necessary, first, constantly to explain that only the Soviet system is capable of ensuring genuine equality of nations, by uniting first the proletarians and then the whole mass of the working population in the struggle of the bourgeoisie; and, second, that all Communist parties should render direct aid to the revolutionary movements among the dependent and under-privileged nations (for example, Ireland, the American Negroes, etc.) and in the colonies.[72]

Herein lay the kernel of the new difficulties that would confront those in Asia in the national question after Lenin, for Lenin's own prescription was fraught with internal contradictions. The Communist parties of the Communist International would support movements of national liberation in the East, but what was to be the essential character of these movements? They were "bourgeois" movements, in Lenin's view, seeking to attain what the bourgeoisie had historically achieved in Western Europe: unified, independent national states, within which national bourgeoisie could flourish. As in Soviet Central Asia, the ideal and reality of the national state had arrived only recently in the East, and in Marxist theory the path to socialist revolution passed through the maturation of capitalism within the national framework. Thus, Lenin officially blessed the nationalistic aspirations of the bourgeoisie in these societies. Yet in the same breath he asserted that this nationalism must be subordinated consistently to "proletarian internationalism": "[P]etty-bourgeois nationalism preserves national self-interest intact, whereas proletarian internationalism demands, first, that the interests of the proletarian struggle in any one country should be subordinated to the interests of that struggle on a world-wide scale, and, second, that a nation which is achieving victory over the bourgeoisie should be able and willing to make the greatest national sacrifices for the overthrow of international capital." There was much ambiguity and mischief to be made in this formulation. Struggles for national liberation were "bourgeois," targeting "the clergy and other influential reactionary and medieval elements in backward countries," but at the same time, they were to be directed against the international and national bourgeoisie.[73] Who was to be at the head of the struggle? The proletarian communist parties in the respective countries would lead it, just as, when the Russian bourgeoisie abdicated its historical responsibilities, the Russian proletariat had had to take the lead in its stead, in temporary alliance with the peasantry.[74] Yet, unlike the Russian example, these new revolutionary movements in the East were not destined to culminate in proletarian socialist revolutions in the near term. In response to a Japanese journalist asking about the relative prospects for communist revolution in the East and the West, Lenin asserted with confidence, " 'Real communism can . . . have success only in the West'."[75]

It is clear, then, that Lenin's conception of nationalist movements in the East was purely instrumental: they were a tool to provoke the economic collapse and, thereby, the proletarian socialist revolutions in the West that he so eagerly awaited. Indeed, Lenin warned emphatically that the Comintern should make "a determined struggle against attempts to give a communist colouring to bourgeois-democratic liberation trends in the backward countries."[76] It is doubtful, however, that such a limited conception of the potential for revolution in Asian societies would have been shared by those who risked prison and, indeed, their very lives to form communist parties in China, Japan, and elsewhere in East Asia. Herein lay the seeds of future discord between the Comintern and the national communist parties of the East. To what extent should such parties be expected to subordinate what they saw as the legitimate "interests of the proletarian struggle" in their own societies "to the interests of that struggle on a world-wide scale"? How willing could the Comintern expect its allies in the national bourgeoisie to be "to make the greatest national sacrifices for the overthrow of international capital"?[77]

The Bolsheviks had acknowledged, and even found virtue in, Russia's backwardness. In both theory and practice they had telescoped the completion of the bourgeois-democratic and proletarian revolutions into what Trotsky depicted as a single "uninterrupted" revolution.[78] Nonetheless, Lenin and his colleagues in the Comintern were not equally sanguine about revolution in the East, which, like Marx, they saw with condescension as considerably less "advanced" socioeconomically than Russia had been in 1905. Thus, at least three separate but interrelated questions arose from Lenin's prescription for the revolution in the Orient. First, nationalism was legitimate in the context of "backward" nations, but at what point in the capitalist development of a later industrializing society did it become illegitimate? As the concerns of Japan's Marxists with their society's disadvantages in the international system would illustrate, this would not be a clearcut matter. Second, unlike Comintern leaders, native Marxists were disposed to see their societies as following the Russian path, that is, impelling their bourgeois-democratic revolutions to grow over into proletarian socialist revolutions. What would be the legitimate bounds for their own "adaptations" of the Bolshevik model to the concrete circumstances of their disparate national settings? As discussed before, in Soviet Central Asia, the Bolsheviks had had to adjust their policies to the fact that these societies simply had no proletariats. What social classes would comprise revolutionary vanguards if Asian societies lacked socioeconomic structures that fit neatly into the categories of the orthodox Marxist model of bourgeois and proletarian revolutions? Again, to what extent might accommodations be made legitimately without threatening the right of such reformulations to the appellation *Marxist*? As nationalist sentiments grew in the more industrially advanced Japan as well as in economically lagging China, such questions would come to discommode indigenous Asian thinkers and revolutionaries who felt compelled to be creative in applying Marxism to their societies, and the same issues would dominate efforts by Marxists and non-Marxists to assess the contributions of such thinkers to the Marxist canon.

Nationalism, of course, was intimately linked to the question of the nature and role of the state. As observed here, Marxist perspectives on the character of the nation-state were by no means monomorphic. The state came to figure in the national question after 1917 in two ways. First was the issue of the value and role of the state in the struggle for human liberation. That problem was particularly acute where the precise stage of the revolutionary struggle was unclear, and at the bourgeois-democratic stage, the Marxist stance toward the state was ambivalent at best. On the one hand, the centralized state was a desideratum of the bourgeoisie, a set of institutions that could be crafted and wielded to protect indigenous bourgeoisie against the encroachments of outside powers. At the same time, the notion of this revolution as bourgeois *democratic* carried ambivalent implications concerning the relationship among the state, society, and the individual. In the Lockean liberal paradigm that animated one model of bourgeois democracy, although the state was the product of consent, it also had to be prevented from prevailing over the rights of individual citizens and the desires of those who comprised the civil society that had conceived it. Moreover, the Lockean paradigm as political myth implied that the bourgeois state served the interests of all its citizens, not only those of the bourgeoisie. Exposing this myth, Lenin, in *State and Revolution*, wrote that the liberal, bourgeois state must be destroyed in the course of a proletarian socialist revolution. Herein lay a second complication concerning the role and nature of the state in revolution. Lenin's "Preliminary Draft Theses on the National and Colonial Questions" left unclear whether the formation of nation-states in the East genuinely served the interests of all their various peoples. If so, then nationalism was a positive force that nurtured the creation of progressive, independent, and assertive national states. But what would be the posture of such states vis-à-vis the tasks of the proletariat once they were instituted? How long would the bourgeois-democratic stage last, if it was not to be expected that the "backward" societies of the East could move directly into the proletarian-socialist stage of the revolution as Russia had done?

The Bolshevik experience in the tumultuous years after 1917 suggested that even if Lenin had found Asian societies capable of emulating the Russian example, the answer to these questions would have been no more readily evident. Lenin had written that the state with its pillars in the army, the bureaucracy, and the police must be destroyed and replaced by a quasi-state that would effectuate the transition to stateless communism. As Engels had written, the "working class must, on the one hand, do away with all the old machinery of oppression previously used against it itself, and, on the other, safeguard itself against its own deputies and officials, by declaring them all, without exception, subject to recall at any time."[79] Nonetheless, pressed by the exigencies of the civil war, the new Bolshevik leaders were compelled to rely on former bureaucrats, managers, and military officers who had served under the tsarist regime to manage their enormous country; and to save the revolution itself, they felt they had to resurrect the secret police. Both the scope and the complexity of the tasks the Bolsheviks were called upon to accomplish were considerably greater than what Lenin had initially thought necessary. In large part, this was so because a Marxist-inspired socialist revolution had been made where the conditions Marx had deemed necessary for its fruition had not yet ripened. Where capitalism had not developed fully, the new leaders had to complete the tasks of the bourgeoisie. Thus, the new state was compelled to appropriate much broader powers to perform the tasks of industrialization in addition to suppressing counterrevolutionary remnants. Furthermore, as Richard Pipes has noted, the tsarist legacy of militarist bureaucratism and the pervasiveness of the secret police might have influenced the measures the Bolsheviks would take.[80] In any case, the statist outcome of 1917 was undeniable. By 1923, Bukharin, who had advocated statization in many respects immediately after the revolution, was warning against the resurgence of official *proizvol*, or bureaucratic arbitrariness, of the sort that had been associated with the old tsarist bureaucracy.[81]

This emergence of a powerful state in the Soviet Union would raise additional issues with respect to the national question among Marxists in Asia. Perhaps, Marx's treatment of the state did not account adequately for the nature of the polity in their own late-industrializing societies. Perhaps the state in their own societies—such as the imperial institution in Japan—held intrinsic, class- and time-transcending value and should not be overthrown. Perhaps, if their societies were still more backward than that of Russia in 1905, they would require a substantial and effective bureaucratic state even more than the Bolsheviks did to propel the revolution forward. Here the limits of the universality of the Marxian doctrine as a whole were revealed as Chinese and Japanese Marxists confronted the peculiarities of their own revolutionary dilemmas.

MARXISM AND THE NATIONAL QUESTION IN EAST ASIA

By the time the national question arrived in the later industrializing societies of East Asia, with Comintern prescriptions to draw them into the international socialist movement, Chinese and Japanese intellectuals had already begun to confront it in terms that were much more expansive than those in the Comintern formula. For them, the national question emerged at the outset from the fact that, paradoxically, Western political thought, including Marxism, was imported into China and Japan to strengthen those societies against Western intrusion. Even before Marx looked eastward to Russia in the 1870s as a possibility for his socialist revolution, Chinese and Japanese intellectuals and political leaders in the two societies were launching massive reforms to resolve the confusion and disorder in their societies occasioned by internal threats coupled with external pressures to open their doors to economic and political intercourse with the West. The two endeavors would meet with widely disparate consequences: the Tongzhi Restoration in China, founded upon the dichotomy between an alleged essence (*ti*) of Chinese society and the mere utility (*yong*) of Western technology, met with frustration even though it succeeded in achieving some of the accoutrements of Western "modernity"—railroads, telegraphs, and foreign language schools among them.[82] By contrast, the Meiji Restoration in Japan established the requisites for the tremendous economic growth that enabled Japan to defeat China and then the sprawling Russian empire in the decade between 1894 and 1905.

Despite these differences, the national question would be no less central to the fate of Marxism in the Japanese context than in the Chinese setting. The extension of Marxism into Asia required an appreciation of the importance of national variations in historical experience. Marx himself had retained much of Hegel's imagery of progressively higher political development moving westward from the despotism characteristic of "strictly the beginning of world History" lingering in stagnant "China and India, exhibiting as it were the dull half-conscious brooding of Spirit" to the free modern state in contemporary Europe.[83] The chronological expansion of the Marxian theory of revolution further entailed the incorporation into Marxism of new observations made by Bukharin, Trotsky, and others concerning the expansive, increasingly powerful capitalist nation-state, a reality that was impressed deeply on the minds of intellectuals in China and Japan. By the 1920s and 1930s, new state forms, most notably fascism, emerged in Italy and Germany, and these examples were beginning to appeal to Shōwa Restorationists and even to China's Guomindang.[84] These new developments made the issue of the state even more urgent to Marxists in the 1920s and 1930s. Attracted to Marxism for its promise of progress based on scientific truth, Chinese and Japanese Marxists were compelled to resolve the national question with respect to the state and the nation in such a manner that these realities and the theory fit neatly together. Otherwise, their radical socialism would lose its scientific validity and be indistinguishable from the utopian socialism so vehemently denounced by Marx and Engels.[85] If the facts could not be reinterpreted to fit the theory, then it remained to interpret, or even remold, the theory to suit the uncomfortable realities. This was precisely the alternative adopted by many who became national or state socialists in response to what appeared to be the enduring character of the modern state.

The theory of the state as such never became a dominant issue in the work of Chinese and Japanese Marxists. Yet, it constituted a thread that ran through much of their writing on the nature of their societies, their pasts, and the promise offered for the future by the Marxian schema of revolutionary change. It is possible to identify at least four themes in their analyses of the national question: (1) the place of Asia in human history; (2) the role of nationalism in the changed international and non-European contexts; (3) the question of what alterations might be needed to make the theory of Marxism-Leninism accommodate the changing international context; and, finally, (4) how Marxist theory might be adapted to accommodate national differences in indigenous values and political thought as the non-European world was brought into the orbit of the international communist movement.

The first issue arose from a concern that the Marxian historical schema born in Western Europe might not be readily transplanted to the Asian context. This question drew Chinese and Japanese Marxists to investigate in depth Marx's notion of the Asiatic mode of production, which was described both as one of the major universal historical stages through which human society passed and as a pattern of economic and social development that was geographically specific. Since the term *Asiatic* was associated with the phenomenon of "oriental despotism" in the writings of Marx, as in those of his philosophical predecessors in the West, the struggle to resolve the question of whether history exhibited a unilinear or at least dual pattern of evolution also involved an effort to comprehend Asia's political past and the implications of that past for its political future in Marxian revolution.

In part, this effort was prompted by Western imperialism. Since Marx first wrote on Asia, a more mature and expansive international capitalist system had emerged. Lenin and Bukharin undertook to update Marxism to accommodate these changes, but for Chinese and Japanese thinkers this new world would appear dramatically different from their vantage point at the bottom of the international system. What were the implications of the emergence of the new international order for the theory of the capitalist state and for the role of the national state in Marxist-inspired revolutions that began as movements of national liberation outside Western Europe? What was the legacy of what Marx had identified as "Asiatic despotism" for these struggles and their efforts to achieve self-liberation? What did the changing international context bode for the historical relationship between the nation and the state? What did it imply for the role of nationalism and national identity in the East that the *Manifesto* had condemned as progressive phenomena only in the past?

The extension of Marxism to Asia thus brought with it new questions about the universality of Marx's, Engels's, and, indeed, Lenin's observations concerning the character and endurance of the state. These concerns were intimately linked to issues concerning national identity. Were all states universally the same in character, or, to quote Solomon Bloom, was there "room for variety in the world, even if its economic systems should approach uniformity?"[86] Marx's empirical and historical description of contemporary states suggested that "[t]he forms of the state varied from country to country and to age to age in the same country"[87] and that these forms would be reflected accordingly in variations in political ideas. Should not they also be reflected in national adaptations of Marxist thought? This question, in turn, raised additional issues concerning the role of indigenous political perspectives in the adaptation of Marxism to the national contexts of non-European societies. If nationality could be accommodated to Marxist revolutionary theory, might aspirations concerning the state be accommodated as well? If the nation or national identity would not or should not wither away, perhaps domestic and international conditions would indicate that the state could remain as well. It was certainly possible that in China and Japan, as in other non-European cultural contexts, the state might embody transcendent values, that it might have a character that was not tied to the existence of class or other social phenomena that might or might not be characteristic of these contexts. How might such a state be incorporated into the Marxist vision of socialist revolution? Indeed, how much change in the process of adaptation to national peculiarities could be accommodated in general within Marxism without the resulting system losing its "Marxian" character?

In confronting matters such as these, Marxists in China and Japan found themselves on the horns of a dilemma. On the one hand, particularly because of Marx's few and generally negative comments on Asia, Chinese and Japanese Marxists needed to emphasize the universalities that their historical experiences shared with Marx's scenario of progress. They needed to place themselves and their societies squarely within the mainstream of the flow of human history so that revolution would seem not only viable but scientifically necessary and justified. Yet, ironically, in so doing, Marxists in each case found themselves tempted to stress their national peculiarities: in Japan, the coexistence of an autocratic imperial system and "feudal" elements with an imperialism that seemed of a piece with the phenomenon Lenin and Bukharin described as the product of a highly developed capitalism, and in China, the coincidence of a fledgling, if fragile, form of republican government with much less impressive indigenous capitalist economic development. The periodization of Chinese and Japanese history was undertaken to fit the universal categories of Marxist theory, yet underlying particularities were often invoked to demonstrate a complete fit. Finally, with regard to the continuing need to promote and preserve the national state, the example of the development of the Bolshevik state and pressures exercised by the Western powers on China and Japan further challenged the doctrine of the withering away of the state and strengthened this impulse to particularism.

In China, the combination of particularism and Marxism would be explored by academic Marxists and, finally, yield the new doctrine of Mao Zedong thought, which would emerge at the forefront of the Chinese revolution with contradictions of its own concerning the national question. In Japan, there would be no such successful revolutionary movement, but the endeavor to reconcile national identity with Marxian universalism would be no less significant. Because Japan was a society that had developed industrial capitalism far beyond that of China—and because it threatened the new Soviet state—strict limits were imposed by the Communist International on Marxist theorizing within the confines of the Japanese Communist party (JCP). This requires that one look beyond the official record of JCP doctrine to the work of revolutionary Marxist scholars and independent activists to find the full range of efforts to resolve the national question in Japan. Whether these impulses culminated in new Marxian theoretical endeavors that fell within or beyond the realm of what was considered to be Marxist-Leninist orthodoxy, however, their common point of departure was the Marxist theory of the state.

PART ONE

The National Question and the Political Theory of Marxism in Asia

The National Question and Problems in the Marxist Theory of the State

CHINESE and Japanese intellectuals and revolutionists confronting the national question in Marxism would find in the work of Marx and his successors a complex combination of ideas concerning the body politic. These concepts were treated social-scientifically and normatively—if not always consistently—in ways that differed dramatically from the treatment of the polity in their indigenous pre-Marxian systems of political thought.[1] In Marxism, the national question has embraced issues having to do with both the nation and the state. The value attributed to the nation and the state has varied from one historical epoch to another, and it has not always been clear how the concept of the state is related to the idea of the nation. Yet the West European historical experience out of which Marxism emerged presumed a certain positive relationship between the articulation of the idea of the nation and identification with it, on the one hand, and the historic birth of centralized states, on the other. The alleged coincidence of the borders of modern nation-states with peoples of common ethnic and linguistic heritages defined the difference between this modern form of the polity and the historical succession of city-states, sprawling empires of Greece and Rome, and then much smaller feudal fiefdoms.

This experience contributed to a Western philosophical discourse on the state dating at least to the time of Niccolò Machiavelli that, in turn, delineated the terms with which Marx, Engels, and their Western Marxist heirs defined and approached the problem of the state. When Marx and Engels treated the state in their own philosophical system, they were contesting its liberal and conservative conceptualizations as impartial "arbiter" of social conflict and "supplier of public goods"[2] as well as its Hegelian formulation as a suprahistorical realization of a disembodied *Geist* (spirit). Similarly, their handling of nationhood reflected a revolutionary aspiration to overturn what they perceived as formerly progressive impulses that now imposed important limitations on man's self-realization. These European philosophical and cultural traditions did not bear equally great significance for Chinese and Japanese Marxists seeking to resolve the national question in their own contexts. These thinkers shared varying degrees of familiarity with these Western traditions, and they had indigenous perspectives of their own that would influence how they would resolve the various components of the national question. Nevertheless, the manner in which Chinese and Japanese Marxists would treat the state within the context of Marxism clearly depended upon how the state and nation had been conceptualized within the Marxian philosophical system itself. There they would confront the Western discourse in a different form as they sought to apply Marxian perspectives to their own revolutionary circumstances.

In the West, this discourse evolved as the state grew historically in Europe. Beginning in the sixteenth century, the characteristics of statehood, or what J. P. Nettl has called "stateness" came increasingly into evidence.[3] Historically, stateness was the product of a process by which "an organization which controls the population occupying a defined territory" comes to be "differentiated from other organizations operating in the same territory" and is "autonomous" and "centralized." Organizationally, "its divisions are formally coordinated with one another."[4] As Nettl notes, "the real development of the historical tradition [of this stateness, broadly conceived] took place in France; it is the French state, and idea of state, that provide the basic European model—even though the philosophical and intellectual tradition of ideas about the state reached the fullness of universality and precision in German hands from the beginning of the nineteenth century onward."[5] By the time that Marx wrote, the French state made its imprint boldly on Marx's view of the state in both real and philosophical terms. Thus, the intellectual and historical development of stateness were closely intertwined.

Just as the idea saw fruition at different times, first in France and only subsequently in Germany, so also varied the pace of state building throughout Europe as a whole.[6] "[T]he sixteenth century was a time of significantly rising stateness, the later seventeenth century a frenzy of state-making, the eighteenth century (outside) and in the East a period of consolidation, the nineteenth century and early twentieth century an age of convergence among governments which were significantly different from each other in 1800."[7] This development depended on several conditions, including: "(1) the availability of extractible resources; (2) a relatively protected position in time and space; (3) a continuous supply of political entrepreneurs; (4) success in war; (5) homogeneity (initial or created) of the subject population; (6) strong coalitions of the central power with major segments of the landed elite." In Europe, these factors combined with others to determine the rate and manner in which each nation-state was constructed. Two basic paths of state building have been discernable there: first, the progressive expansion willy-nilly of a political organization "by conquest, alliance, bargaining, chicanery, argument, and administrative encroachment," a process common to France, England, and Spain, and, subsequently, as in Germany and Italy, "the more or less deliberate *creation* of new states by existing states"[8] often in response to external threats from preexisting states that had evolved earlier. Marx's essay into the theory of the state occurred just as state making was moving from one stage to the next. This historic juncture was reflected in some of the most engaging problems in Marx's treatment of the state.

THE DUAL CONCEPTION OF THE STATE IN MARX

The character of the state is the least developed aspect of Marx's philosophy. Marx's notes indicate that he once intended to write a work on the state as part of the larger opus of which the volumes of *Capital* were to form the first three parts.[9] This work never emerged, however, and his *Critique of Hegel's "Philosophy of*

Right" remains the most comprehensive elaboration of his views on the state, supplemented by scattered passages in *On the Jewish Question, The German Ideology, Capital, The Eighteenth Brumaire of Louis Bonaparte,* and *The Communist Manifesto.* To be sure, *Capital* absorbed most of Marx's energies, and illness prevented that work from being completed before his death in 1883. Although politics was ultimately Marx's central concern, "private government in the economic life was for him the primary and decisive realm of the political, and public government—the sphere of the state—was a secondary and subordinate political field"[10] "the understanding of which was to be derived from outside itself."[11] As a result, it has fallen to Marx's successors to systematize a Marxist theory of the state, with Lenin's *State and Revolution* (1917) being the most influential work. Indeed, Lenin's postulation of the modern state as *"the dictatorship of the bourgeoisie"*[12] has been so widely and uncritically accepted that it has dissuaded many from undertaking "a sustained historical analysis of the state, or of the way that dominant classes have exercised power over it."[13]

The difficulty with the simple designation of the state as class dictatorship or in terms of the use of force (in agreement with Max Weber's definition)[14] is that it fails to comprehend the full range of issues that Marx's writings suggest are to be encompassed in a theory of the state. Such questions include the origin and development of the state; its universality and particularity across time and space; the relationship between the state and "civil society" (in the usage that Marx adapted from Hegel); the relationship between the state and social classes; the complexity and variability of the states that may arise on similar economic bases;[15] the state as a realm of alienation of man from himself; the state as the locus of class or supraclass societal value; and the relationship between nation and state. His theory also involved the state as an autonomous force in revolution, "the driving force of history" and, thus, the source of man's self-realization.[16]

Taken together, the writings of Marx and Engels offer several different notions of the state collectively comprising two complementary conceptions. From these have emerged all subsequent developments in Marxist state theory. The first conception, the "critical perspective," considers the relationship between state and society as a whole,[17] whereas the second, the "scientific perspective,"[18] treats the relationship between the state and social classes. These perspectives coincide with two tendencies in scholarship on Marx: (1) the first, emphasizing the importance of the work of the young Marx for understanding the essential unity and continuity of Marx's thought from the early through the "mature" works; (2) the second, "posit[ing] a radical break (*coupure*) between Marx's early and later writings," and drawing on the post-1847 works, which are said to "constitute a valid science of the structures of capitalist society," superseding and rendering irrelevant the writings of the young Marx. The first school regards alienation and the second surplus value "as the nodal point of Marxist theory" in developing their treatments of the state.[19] Despite the apparent conflict between the two approaches, in fact, they are complementary perspectives that together offer a more complete and viable theory of the state than either can yield alone.

The Critical Perspective: Alienation, the State and Civil Society

The point of departure for the critical perspective is the view that Marx was "basically a Hegelian philosopher above all else." Those writings that were most heavily imbued with Marx's Heglianism are said to "constitute the deepest expression of Marx's eternal fascination."[20] These texts include Marx's critiques of Hegel's theory of the state, *The German Ideology* (with Engels), *On the Jewish Question*, and *The Holy Family* (with Engels), all of which were penned before 1847. Treating the state as "a form of alienated life,"[21] these works pursue the issue of the *homme-citoyen* dualism of life in bourgeois society first raised by Rousseau's *Le Contrat social* (The social contract).[22] Premised on the observation that with the full emergence of private property after the Middle Ages, the spheres of public and private life were separated for the first time, this view posits a corresponding schism within man himself: private man versus political man. In Hegel, this distinction was one of *"Burgher-citoyen*, the burgher meaning a man who is active in civil as distinct from political life, or a man who pursues his private and particular interests as distinct from the public and universal interests of the body politic."[23] In *The Philosophy of Right*, Hegel claimed that in the modern state (in constitutional monarchy) this contradiction was resolved in the form of the Estates, or legislature: "[I]n them the subjective moment in universal freedom— the private judgment and private will of the sphere called 'civil society' in this book—comes into existence integrally related to the state." Through the Estates the schism in man produced by the development of bourgeois society was healed because "it is through them that the state enters the subjective consciousness of the people and that the people begins to participate in the state."[24]

The theme of the separation of private from public man, articulated subsequently in terms of "alienation" in *On the Jewish Question* and *The German Ideology*, formed the main thread of Marx's *Critique of Hegel's "Philosophy of Right"* (the *Critique*). Like Hegel, Marx accepted the dichotomy posited by Rousseau between state and civil society, between public or political man and private, egoistic man. Unlike Hegel, however, Marx responded with a resounding "no" to the question of whether "'something right and whole [can] be made of the modern bourgeois'."[25] Two points formed the crux of Marx's argument. First, Marx contended that the organs of the modern state and above all the Estates could not provide the rational solution that Hegel proposed by mediating between the state on one hand and the people on the other. The Estates, part of the state itself, did not represent any necessary harmonization by acting as "a mediating organ" between the people and the executive;[26] on the contrary, "[a]ll the contradictions of modern state-organizations converge in the Estates."[27] Far from resolving the dichotomy, the Estates actually expressed it fully: "The deputies of civil society constitute themselves into an assembly, and only this assembly is the actual political existence and will of civil society. The separation of the political state from civil society appears as the separation of the deputies from their mandators."[28] Marx then ridiculed Hegel's designation of the state bureaucracy as the universal class, that social class whose interests were identical with those of society as a whole and, thus, with man as a whole species-being. On the contrary, Marx claimed, bureaucratic officialdom came to regard the state as "its private property"[29] thereby becoming a kind of "closed corporation, a kind of civil society within the state, which transforms the universal aims of the state into another form of private interests."[30] The role of the universal class, Marx averred, could only be played by the proletariat because of the universality of its misery.[31] Finally, the crown, the hereditary monarch that Hegel favored, epitomized for Marx the absurdity of Hegel's claim that his state, which, Marx asserted, was merely the real actual state, could represent the rational essence of the state. Hegel envisaged the accession of a monarch to the throne by birthright as the means to avoid his being subjected to the caprice of bureaucratic infighting, but in so doing made the quality and skills of the monarch the product of the accident of birth.[32] The blame for all these contradictions in Hegel's theory of the state, Marx declared, was not to be laid at Hegel's feet. They merely represented the contradictions inherent in bourgeois society and the existing state. Hegel's work offered the "most logical, profound and complete expression of the German philosophy of right and its realization in the modern bourgeois state," which had developed in Europe outside of the lagging Germany.[33] Hegel could not resolve these difficulties because they remained unresolved in the actual state. Hence, Hegel's "claim that the rational is actual is contradicted precisely by an irrational actuality, which everywhere is the contrary of what it asserts and asserts the contrary of what it is."[34] Above all, Hegel's greatest offense was his "uncritical spirit" compounded by his sin of "mystification."

Marx had shared much with the early Hegel, including Hegel's "instinct to transcend the given state."[35] At the time of the French Revolution, Hegel had claimed that " 'there is no idea of the state; for the state is something mechanical. Only that which is an object of freedom may be called an idea. We must, therefore, transcend the state. For every state is bound to treat free men as cogs in a machine. . . . Hence the state must perish'."[36] But this radical, critical sentiment had faded into oblivion in the *Philosophy of Right* (1821), and to the mature Hegel's acceptance of the actual state Marx objected violently. On the premise that human beings are naturally social beings, Marx did share Hegel's aversion to the atomistic individualism of bourgeois society. Hegel's opposition to this consisted in the following formula directed against social contract theory:

> If the state is confused with civil society, and if its specific end is laid down as the security and protection of property and personal freedom, then the interest of the individuals as such becomes the ultimate end of their association, and it follows that membership of the state is something optional. But the state's relation to the individual is quite different from this. Since the state is mind objectified, it is only as one of its members that the individual himself has objectivity, genuine individuality, whose supreme duty is to be a member of the state.[37]

Hegel's solution was repugnant to Marx precisely because it constituted no solution and expressed most fully the mystification that had come to pervade Hegel's work. First, no distinction was made between what is and what ought to be: Hegel declared the two to be identical and proved the rationality of the state by asserting that the state was the expression of some absolute and intangible spirit rather than the product of human efforts. Secondly, Marx contended that Hegel's philosophy was but a secular religion, false consciousness, a reflection of man's alienation from himself. This theme he developed most fully in *The German Ideology* after the "Contribution to the *Critique*."[38] Philosophy must "unmask human self-alienation in all its secular forms, once its sacred form [religion] has been unmasked," Marx argued.[39] In this case, the secular form was the theory of the state articulated by Hegel. This "bourgeois idea of the state rests on illusion," an illusion shared by both those in authority and those ruled, and an illusion that is "necessary to the functioning of the state."[40] The illusion was that the division between civil society and the state was overcome and that man's freedom as a species-being was attained in the form of the modern state.[41]

Marx himself was content to resolve this problem in the 1843 *Critique* by transcending the "political state" through a vaguely defined form of political democracy based on universal suffrage.[42] Yet, writing subsequently in *On the Jewish Question*, Marx seemed to abandon this position, arguing that "even the most highly developed state—a democratic republican state—is the incarnation of a religious principle."[43] "The limits of political emancipation," he asserted, "appear at once in the fact that the *state* can liberate itself from a constraint [such as religion] without man himself being *really* liberated."[44] Thus, even the democratic state was merely an illusory community of alienated individuals whose class and other material differences remained in the separate sphere of civil society. "*Political* emancipation certainly represents a great progress," Marx conceded, but it was not "the final form of human emancipation"; it constituted only "the final form of human emancipation within the framework of the prevailing social order." True freedom would be achieved only by "'socialized humanity'" after the social order that produced alienation had been transcended.[45]

Scientific Materialism: The State and Social Classes

Hegel's state could not achieve the human emancipation that Marx envisaged, for it was conceived in a mystifying idealist fashion, conceptually isolated from the social context of men and women themselves. As seen here, "the individual appears in Hegelian philosophy only after the construction of the state has already been accomplished and perfected, as if 'state' and 'individual' could be discussed separately."[46] For Marx, by contrast, a state so conceived was purely illusory; for Marx, as for Ludwig Feuerbach before him, man was subject, not object. It was the state that was the object of human activity, at once the product and reflection of class and individual conflicts among egoistic men as well as the vehicle that "maintain[ed] the cohesion of a society deeply undermined by the contradictions inherent in the relations of production" and prevented it from being rent apart by those conflicts.[47] Here Marx asserted a materialist interpretation of the state in protest against Hegel's abstract idealism, a "scientific" perspective focusing on the relationship of the state to the socioeconomic classes that constituted society.

The fundamental compatibility of the scientific with the critical perspective is suggested by Marx's rejection of Hegel's idealism, his acknowledgment of the basis of the state in private property, and his suggestion in the *Critique of Hegel's "Philosophy of Right"* that beneath the institutional structure of the state remained the material conflicts of civil society. The key linking the two perspectives is the theme of alienation and its sources in bourgeois society, as analyzed in "The Economic and Philosophic Manuscripts of 1844," *The Holy Family* (1845), and other works.[48] Here the connection between alienation and socioeconomic class has been crucial. In the words of John Plamenatz, "the division of labour that produces alienation also gives rise to classes and makes possible the exploitation of some classes by others. . . . The fact . . . that both alienation and class exploitation are effects of a certain kind of division of labour does not entail that the state is a symptom of alienation, that in the activities which constitute it the alienated condition of human beings is manifested. Nevertheless, Marx had his reasons for speaking of the state in this way."[49]

These remarks suggest that Marx held two ideas concerning the relationship between the state and social classes that can be separated analytically but are more often confused. The first conceptualizes of the state as an instrument of class rule, whereas the second treats the state as a condition enabling the exploitation of one class by another. As Plamenatz argues, "to call the state a condition of class exploitation," "is not to imply that any one class governs it, either directly or through representatives; it is to imply that, if there were no state, no class would be in a position to exploit another." As for Marx and Engels, "though they sometimes spoke as if the state's being an instrument of class rule were a definite characteristic of it, [they] quite often admitted, when speaking of some particular state, that no class was in control of it."[50] Neither Marx nor Engels ever suggested that the state does not always accompany class exploitation. Nevertheless, Engels in *Anti-Dühring* and, subsequently, Lenin in *State and Revolution* advanced the idea of the necessary "withering away" of the state after the demise of capitalist society.[51] By contrast, Marx's "hostility to the state was held in check by a decidedly authoritarian doctrine of political rule during the transition period."[52] His dictatorship of the proletariat would play an important role in the "revolutionary transformation" of capitalist into communist society.[53] Marx's anarchist opponents, under Bakunin's leadership, would argue that such a function could not exist because the demise of authority could not issue from authority itself. The state must be abolished at once. Marx's concept of the transitional state—"[t]he political form at last discovered under which to work out the economic emancipation of labor," best represented in the Paris Commune[54]—was too Hegelian, too dialectical for those who repudiated any state as an inherently authoritarian structure.

Thus, Marx's conception of the state in relation to social class is far more complex than the simple Leninist definition of the state as a class dictatorship would indicate. Indeed, there are those who have argued that it was Engels, in *Anti-Dühring* and *Origin of the Family*, and not Marx who produced a Marxian theory of the state, yet its inconsistencies must ultimately be attributed to Marx himself because "the ideas that [Engels] tries to fit together into it are as much Marx's as his own, and quite often they do not fit."[55] These inconsistencies are glaring in the two accounts of the origin of the state found in Engels's writings. In the earlier work, *Anti-Dühring*, the state appears to precede class rule; originally it was not a vehicle for class exploitation but only attained that character at a subsequent point in its development. In this Rousseauean construct, the state is produced by the community to protect "certain common interests" by assuming specific functions: "the adjudication of disputes; repression of encroachments by individuals on the rights of others; control of water supplies, especially in hot countries; and finally, when conditions were absolutely primitive, religious functions."[56] The state might then become exploitative in one of two ways. On the one hand, with the emergence of "class differences" in society, the state, "first arrived at only for safeguarding . . . common interests (such as irrigation in the East) and providing protection against external enemies, from this stage onwards acquires just as much the function of maintaining by force the economic and political position of the ruling class against the subject class."[57] In this instance, the state undertook activities that were "political" in the same sense in which Marx spoke of the political state in the *Critique*: they occured amid, and were reflective of, fundamental conflicts of interest in a society. The state might become oppressive, however, when its functionaries came to identify themselves as a group with interests distinct from those of society as a whole and, thus, came to act politically. In this case, the state's agents became an authority outside of the originally "self-governing" community: the state's organs "soon make themselves even more independent . . . until . . . [the state has] developed into domination over society."[58]

This idea of the origin of the state before class differences and class exploitation disappeared from Engels's subsequent, more systematic treatment of the state in *Origin of the Family*. In tracing the development and dissolution of the gentile (tribal) constitution among the Greeks, Romans, and Germans, Engels argued that the state arose to perform functions that the gentes could not perform. The emphasis in this argument was placed on the emergence of new social conflicts that could not be handled by the traditional gens organization, "which had grown out of a society which knew no internal contradictions . . . [,] was only adapted to such a society . . . [and, thus,] possessed no means of coercion except public opinion."[59] Nevertheless, Engels's presentation here was not wholly consistent, for it was unclear whether the emergence of (private) property or social classes was ultimately responsible for this development. The more persistent argument stressed the emergence of classes per se. The rise of the state was "the admission that this society has involved itself in insoluble self-contradiction and is cleft into irreconcilable antagonisms which it is powerless to exorcise," Engels wrote. "But in order that these antagonisms, classes with conflicting economic interests, shall not consume themselves and society in fruitless struggle, a power apparently standing above society, has become necessary to moderate the conflict and keep it within the bounds of 'order'; and this power, arisen out of society but placing itself above it and increasingly alienating itself from it is the state." This new power was characterized by territorial rather than kinship-based organization, the establishment of a public force, and taxation so that the state could maintain itself.[60]

The role of private property was problematic in this account. In this treatment, private property was but one of many new economic conditions that combined to produce cleavages within gentile society.[61] Yet earlier in the same work, Engels placed far greater emphasis on the role of private property in the rise of the state:[62]

Only one thing was wanting: an institution which not only secured the newly acquired riches of individuals against the communistic traditions of the gentile order, which not only sanctified the private property formerly so little valued and declared this sanctification to be the highest purpose of human society; but an institution which set the seal of general social recognition on each new method of acquiring property and thus amassing wealth at continually increasing speed; an institution which perpetuated not only this growing cleavage of society into classes but also the right of the possessing class to exploit the non-possessing, and the rule of the former over the latter. And this institution came. The *state* was invented.[63]

This question of the relative significance of class conflict and private property in the origin of the state illuminates a major problem in the Marxist theory of classes and of the class state. In Marxian usage, the "modern state" generally refers to the bourgeois state, the national or nation-state and, thus, cannot antedate the birth of capitalism. This raises the issue of the universality of the concepts of class and state in Marxism and of their relationship to the emergence of private, as opposed to communal, property in land or in any other form. In *German Ideology*, Marx and Engels implied a fairly narrow concept of class in contradistinction with the medieval estates when they spoke of "'the emergence of class'" as "'itself a product of the bourgeoisie'."[64] Nevertheless, more dominant, particularly in the later works such as *Capital*, was Marx's and Engels's tendency to use the terms *class* and *state* in a broader sense to apply to all postcommunal (class) social formations.[65] Most scholars have accepted this looser connotation of the term *state* to "assume that each successive epoch in the social history of mankind, each dominant socioeconomic formation . . . has its own characteristic form of statehood."[66] This usage suggests that if the state were a realm of human alienation, then alienation was also possible in precapitalist society, arising out of the division of labor (and private property), the emergence of classes, and the tendency of the state and its functionaries to elevate themselves above and apart from the society that produced it.[67]

It would seem, then, that the illusory character of the state in bourgeois society, with its need to maintain itself through the myth that its existence serves the interests of the entire community, was not peculiar only to bourgeois society in Marx's and Engels's view. But this observation raises the question of the relationship between this general alienation and the alienation Marx discussed in the *Critique* as inherent in the schism between the state and civil society. For civil society in Marx's conception appeared only with the firm establishment of private property, with the passing of the Middle Ages. One is, thus, left with no real solution to the question of the relationship among Marx's state, classes, and private property. To assert simply that the state came into existence as a condition of class oppression in Marx's and Engels's view would be a misreading of *Capital*, *Origin of the Family*, and the *Grundrisse*.[68] Finally, even if one grants that a particular state form arises within each mode of production, precapitalist or capitalist, by Marx's own admission, identifying the form of the economic base alone is necessary but by no means sufficient "for analyzing the political structure of a specific historical instance of class rule."[69] His formulation did "not prevent the same economic basis—the same from the standpoint of its main conditions—due to innumerable different empirical circumstances, natural environment, racial relations, external historical influences, etc., from showing infinite variations and gradations in appearance."[70] If state forms could vary so greatly, what uniformities remained within this rich diversity on the basis of which one might generalize about the nature of the state in each mode of production?

Marx wrote very little in response to this issue concerning precapitalist political structures, but in the great deal that he wrote about the state in capitalist society, he asserted forcefully that the state was "an instrumentality of class struggle," "a repressive force."[71] It is here that the state was most closely identified with class society so that with the demise of class society, Marx argued, the need for the state would disappear, although a temporary state in the form of the dictatorship of the proletariat would be necessary . "[T]he working class cannot simply lay hold of the ready-made state machinery, and wield it for its own purposes";[72] but the newly formed proletarian state would not only conduct "administrative functions necessary for the management of production." Its raison d'être was to eliminate the last vestiges of class exploitation, and it would thus continue to be essentially repressive in character.[73]

Marx was fundamentally consistent in stressing that the bourgeois state was an instrument of class rule, its "executive" "'but a committee for managing the common affairs of the bourgeoisie'."[74] Nonetheless, notable uncertainty remained in Marx concerning the relationship of the state to social classes. Noting that the "ambivalence of class relationships in English politics extends back as far as 1688," for example, Marx observed that "the political representatives of a class may very often not in fact be of that class."[75] As one scholar has noted, Marx's writings revealed at least "three possible relations" between the state and the economically dominant class. "In the first place, [the state] can be *servile*, in that it serves the bourgeoisie's interests. In the second place it can be *dominant*, in that it imposes its will on society (including the bourgeoisie). In the third, in a situation where it cannot in fact be dominant, because of power held by the bourgeoisie, it can nevertheless refuse to be meekly servile, and try to be dominant: in that case, it is *pretentious*."[76] The "dominant" model of the state raises the possibility that the state can be relatively autonomous of class and society, a notion that has aroused much heated discussion among contemporary Marxists. It also converges with the suggestion in many of Marx's and Engels's writings that the origin of the state has, in many cases at least, been independent of the emergence of social class. This common thread bears such clear implications for the notion of the state as modernizer—a theme particularly salient for Chinese and Japanese Marxists in the twentieth century—that it warrants separate consideration.

The Potential Autonomy of the State

The discussion above distinguished two conceptions of the state in Marx and Engels, one treating the relationship between the state and society as a whole, the other pertaining to the relationship between the state and classes within society. The former appeared primarily in the work of the young Marx and the latter in his so-called mature writings, respectively, although a certain overall unity of Marx's thought on the state is indicated by the persistence of the theme of alienation into Marx's later work on, for example, the division of labor, class conflict, and private property.

This fundamental continuity in Marx's thought on the state is reflected in yet another way. The notion of the "relative autonomy," or independence, of the state,[77] as it has come to be called in contemporary Western Marxist circles, can refer equally to the position of the state vis-à-vis society as a whole and to the state's position in relation to the dominant economic class in a given society. Far from comprising merely an unsuccessful "partial solution" offered by Engels to a conflict between these two conceptions of the state, the notion of the relative autonomy of the state emerged repeatedly in Marx's and Engels's writings on the state. It further suggests that although a "tension" may indeed exist between the broad and narrow conceptions of the state in Marxism,[78] Marx always conceptualized the state as a sphere of alienation, its illusions inevitably victimizing even the ruling class itself.[79]

The controversy over the notion of state autonomy, however, first arose out of Engels's contention in *Origin of the Family* that although the state helps to make the economically dominant class politically supreme, there are exceptions. "Exceptional periods . . . occur," Engels wrote, "when the warring classes are so nearly equal in forces that the state power, as apparent mediator, acquires for the moment a certain independence in relation to both. This applies to the absolute monarchy of the 11th and 18th centuries, which balanced the nobility and the bourgeoisie against one another, and to the Bonapartism of the First and particularly of the Second French empire, which played off the proletariat against the bourgeoisie and the bourgeoisie against the proletariat. The latest achievement in this line," he concluded, "is the new German Empire of the Bismarckian nation; here the capitalists and the workers are balanced against one another and both of them fleeced for the benefit of the decayed Prussian cabbage Junkers."[80] This passage suggests that although the state may represent the ruling class in a society, it could also "succeed in establishing a considerable degree of independence" when class conflict yielded not a dominant class but a balance among classes or an interregnum between one mode of production and class rule and another.[81] Besides the obvious conceptual difficulties that this possibility poses for a narrowly defined concept of the state as the organ of class rule, an additional problem exists. There appears to be a conflict between Marx's adherence to a narrow doctrine of class rule in his mature works, on the one hand, and Engels's more flexible amenability to historical instances in which the identity between the state and the interests of an economically superordinate class is obscure at best, on the other.

Marx's hesitancy to acknowledge the potential for state autonomy was "best illustrated by his interpretation of the rule of Louis Bonaparte":[82] "Only under the second Bonaparte does the state seem to have made itself completely independent. . . . The political influence of the small peasants . . . finds its final expression in the executive power subordinating society to itself." [83]

Because Marx and Engels coauthored the *Manifesto*, from which the instrumentalist formula was derived, the alleged conflict here between Marx and Engels may be more apparent than real. It is Engels rather than Marx, after all, who is generally credited with the narrowly instrumental and mechanistic conception of the state associated with "vulgar Marxism." Indeed, if there is a real contradiction here, it lies in the greater subtlety of Marx's interpretation rather than the more mechanical balance of forces notion in Engels's writings. This is not to say that there is no difficulty within the Marxist theory of the state concerning the relationships between state and class and between state and society. What it does mean is that uncertainty about how much real rather than merely apparent independence the state might have runs throughout, from Marx's *Critique* of Hegel through the systematization of state theory presented in Engels's *Origin of the Family*. In the *Critique*, Marx's earliest work on the state, he noted the tendency of any state to arrogate to itself powers beyond those originally delegated to it by the society that created it. Here the state already possessed the potential for autonomy from both economic classes and society ("civil society" in the *Critique*). Engels subsequently observed this inherent tendency for the state to be transformed from the mere instrumentality of society into its lord in every historical instance: "Society had created its own organs to look after its common interests, originally through simple division of labour. But these organs, at whose head was the state power, had in the course of time, in pursuance of their own special interest, transformed themselves from the servants of society into the masters of society." This phenomenon was prevalent, Engels insisted, in democracies as well as in hereditary monarchies.[84]

Thus, there appeared to be a dual division of labor in Marx's and Engels's writings: one among economic classes in society and another between society and its rulers (the state versus civil society). While the state reflected the economic struggles of class society and was ultimately repressive—"nothing but a machine for the oppression of one class by another"[85]—the individuals involved in the two divisions of labor did not necessarily coincide. Writing on Britain, Marx made this point when he argued that the political representatives of a particular class in the state need not necessarily be of that class; and he reiterated that point when he contended that Bonapartism represented the interests of the French small peasantry. This observation did not vitiate the fact that the state indeed acted in the interests of a particular class, that is, that the state's interests coincided with those of a particular class, even if in performing an ideological function the state might appear to serve society as a whole. Such a situation might be most apparent in the modern bourgeois state, which claims to be a political democracy. In this view, while professing to represent and act in the interests of the public good, the state in fact serves to maintain the social order in which the bourgeoisie is supreme.[86] It would seem, then, that Marx's remarks in the "Eighteenth Brumaire" are best taken as a protest against a simple "great man" theory of history and as a firm assertion that even individual dictatorships reflect in some way the character of their socioeconomic bases. At the same time, his argument weakens the validity of any effort to analyze the state simply by looking at the class(es) from which those holding office come. In short, one can no more infer the nature of the economic base directly from the character of individuals in the political superstructure than can one comprehend fully the nature of the state merely by determining the character of its economic base.

In Marx's and Engels's view, however, the state's potential for autonomy might be greater under some historical circumstances than others. This potential might peak not only during periods of transition from one historical epoch to another, as from feudalism to capitalism; it could also flourish in certain geographic and cultural conditions. Writing in the *Grundrisse*, for example, Marx described the extraordinary preponderance of the state over society under oriental despotism. The Asiatic state, an "*all-embracing unity* which stands above all these small common bodies [communities] may appear as the higher or *sole proprietor*, the real communities only as *hereditary* possessors. . . . The despot here appears as the father of all the numerous lesser communities, thus realizing the common unity of all. It therefore followed that the surplus product . . . belongs to this highest unity."[87] Such a state produced "a legal absence of property,"[88] Marx argued, a characteristic that alone was sufficient to imply the stagnancy that he, like Hegel, attributed to such societies. At the very least, it meant that such societies lacked the internal impetus necessary to evolve to the bourgeois mode of production based on private property. In the notion of Asiatic despotism, pursued in more detail later, was a powerful indicator of Marx's belief in the potential autonomy of the state and its organs.

The possibility that the state could act autonomously held the prospect of revolutions from above, such as occurred in Japan's Meiji Restoration and in other later industrializing societies such as those in Egypt and Peru.[89] Such state efforts have encouraged later Marxian scholars to reexamine Marx's and Engels's views on state power to highlight the pivotal role of the state in social revolutions, thus challenging what has become the prevailing Marxist interpretation of the state as dominated by the leading socioeconomic class. Japanese Marxists used such implications in the Marxist theory of the state to reinterpret the Meiji Restoration and to construct indigenous theories of state and national socialism. It was also potentially important for Chinese Marxists who were concerned with developing a revolutionary state that would enable China to complete its socialist revolution without first enduring the painful consequences of industrial capitalism. In both cases, the precedent of a strong Soviet state after a Marxian socialist revolution that had occurred when industrial capitalism had barely matured reinforced Chinese and Japanese interest in the notion of the autonomy of the state. Engels had argued in *Anti-Dühring* that once the state had achieved relative independence from society, it might seek to facilitate or obstruct economic progress. On the one hand, Engels maintained that when seeking to abet economic development it would succeed. On the other hand, Engels also claimed, with true Enlightenment conviction, that any effort by the state to arrest the "normal" course of economic development was destined to fail. Conquest by barbarians might retard socioeconomic progress, but it could do so only temporarily.[90]

If this interpretation did not support Marx's view that oriental despotism per se prevented the emergence of private property and economic progress to industrial capitalism, it bolstered the sanguine view that Western imperialism was essential for the progressive development of allegedly stagnant Asiatic societies.[91] It also lent support to a positive appreciation of the role of revolutions in advancing human socioeconomic progress whether propelled from above or from below. Engels pointedly condemned the application of the term *state socialism* indiscriminately to justify any form of intervention from above.[92] Yet it is apparent that the overall impact of his work, along with the reality of the Bolshevik state, would be to encourage analyses of revolution from above, especially those that would justify the activism of a postrevolutionary state in constructing socialism. The absence of the critique of the Hegelian state, the omission of Marx's own anarchist strain from the Marxism that was imported into China and Japan, greatly facilitated such theoretical developments under the banner of revolutionary Marxism.

THE THEORY OF THE STATE AFTER MARX AND ENGELS

Bolshevik State Theory and the Omission of the Critique of the Hegelian State

The Marxist theory of the state as it was developed by the Bolsheviks constituted an essential link in the articulation of Chinese and Japanese Marxist views on the subject. It was in Soviet Russia that the notion of the autonomy of the state came to full fruition first in theory and then in practice, and that experience was transmitted to Chinese and Japanese revolutionists through the Comintern and through Soviet theoretical writings on the state, nationalism, and revolution in the East. Despite commonalities rooted in the Russian historical experience, the theoretical interpretations of the state component of the national question offered by V. I. Lenin, Nikolai Bukharin, Leon Trotsky, and Joseph Stalin differed from one another, reflecting dissimilarities in personality, political position, and the stages of the Russian Revolution in which each developed. All were based, however, on the need to take up where Marx had left off—to articulate a theory of the state in the context of an international capitalist state system that had not emerged fully in Marx's time; to fulfill the requirement for a theory of the postrevolutionary state about which Marx had said very little; and finally, to respond to the need for a theory of the state after a revolution in Russia that had not been echoed in the West as Marx and Lenin had envisaged but instead had established a single "socialism in one country" surrounded by hostile capitalist forces.

In responding to these demands, none of the Bolshevik theorists was able to incorporate the young Marx's critical perspective on the Hegelian state into their work. When they first encountered Marxism, Lenin and his colleagues in Russia lacked access to such works as Marx's *Critique of Hegel's "Philosophy of Right,"*

The German Ideology, and "The Economic and Philosophic Manuscripts of 1844,"[93]—all works that were critical of the tendency for the state to assert its independence from society. This omission tended to result in Bolshevik adherence (with the notable exception of Stalin) to the narrow class conception of the state, and this Bolshevik pattern deeply influenced Chinese and Japanese Marxists. The new Soviet state in both theory and reality also exercised a direct and significant impact on the adaptation of Marx's theory of the state by Chinese and Japanese Marxists.

It may be argued that the direction of Russian Marxism after the 1917 revolution represented a multifaceted divergence from the mainstream of Marxist theory, which had been dominated by Germany and Austria until 1914.[94] For the Bolsheviks, the October Revolution marked a new era. With the collapse of the socialist movement in Germany, Lenin and Bukharin could no longer turn to Germany "for theoretical and political leadership." As a result, as Lichtheim has observed, the theory arising out of the Bolshevik experience in Russia "lent an East European imprint to what had hitherto been a Western, or at most a German, doctrine." The shift from the German to the Russian arena "rekindled those long dormant elements of the original Marxian synthesis [from circa the 1848 revolutions] which went all the way to French utopian Socialism and further to the French Revolution itself."[95]

Lenin's conception of the vanguard party leading the proletariat in battle against the bourgeoisie in *What Is to Be Done?* (1902) offered the nucleus of the new Bolshevik synthesis, combining the idea of the vanguard party with a narrow class conception of the state. The product was the "Leninist notion of the communist party-state as a force for social change, an instrumentality of a long-range revolutionary transformation of society from above." This constituted "a serious modification of Marxist theory and represent[ed] one of the significant points of divergence between classical and communist [Soviet] Marxism."[96] Marx had repudiated the vanguard concept when he attacked the Blanquism of 1871. Nurtured "in the school of conspiracy, and held together by the strict discipline which went with it, [the followers of Louis Auguste Blanqui] started out from the viewpoint that a relatively small number of resolute well-organized men would be able, at a given favourable moment, not only to seize the helm of state, but also by a display of great, ruthless energy, to maintain power until they succeeded in sweeping the mass of the people into the revolution and ranging them round the small band of leaders. This involved, above all [Engels later observed], the strictest, dictatorial centralisation of all power in the hands of the new revolutionary government."[97] This approach, with its lack of regard for ordinary workers, whom Blanqui swept aside "under the comprehensive label of 'the people',"[98] was discredited in Marx's view by the demise of the Paris Commune. Clearly the vanguard party in both its Blanquist and Leninist incarnations implied the possibility of an enduring state, monopolized by such a party elite, alienating itself from the people, a possibility that Marx had deplored in the *Critique*. Engels saw this happening in the pre-1871 French state, and Trotsky and Milovan Djilas would subsequently condemn this in the new Soviet state.[99] In retrospect, the emergence

of a revolutionary party-state in Russia with major long-term constructive responsibilities appears to have been the necessary consequence of a revolution that had
occurred before the material conditions for its success had ripened and then had to
survive in a hostile international environment. Perhaps the task of creating a "new
Soviet man"—a new socialist psychology—would have been a prerequisite for
achieving Marxian socialism in any national context.[100] In any event, the development of the Soviet party-state was not a simple monochronic process. Instead,
from the very outset, the evolution of Bolshevik theory on the state incorporated,
in a most dialectical fashion, many of the same ambiguities and uncertainties
concerning the relationship between state and society identified here in Marx's
original views.[101]

This dialectic is readily apparent in Lenin's most influential work on this subject, *State and Revolution*, which has been interpreted variously as both anar-
chistically utopian and fundamentally authoritarian in character. The work seemed
to mark a major deviation in the basic trajectory of Lenin's thought, if that thought
is associated with the notion of the vanguard party, because, as Robert V. Daniels
has noted, the party is only mentioned in the work, indirectly, "exactly *once*."
Indeed, Daniels also identifies the theory of the state as a new object of analysis
for Lenin, one to which he turned only under the influence of Bukharin.[102] In
1916, Bukharin had penned an article entitled "K teorii imperialisticheskogo gosudarstva" (Toward a theory of the imperialist state), which treated the character of
the capitalist state and its fate during and after a socialist revolution. Lenin refused
to publish the piece in *Social-Democrat* because of its alleged "semi-anarchist
errors";[103] but the work's emphasis on the need to destroy the old state machinery
made its way into Lenin's *State and Revolution*. Written in the rising crescendo of
revolution between February and October the following year, the pamphlet harshly
repudiated the moderate provisional government, paralyzed by its inability to
respond effectively to the increasingly radical demands of workers, peasants, and
soldiers. As the dictatorship of the bourgeoisie, this regime had to be smashed,
Lenin maintained. Furthermore, in outlining his postrevolutionary vision, Lenin
harkened back to Marx's depiction of the short-lived Paris Commune as the ideal
postrevolutionary state and eschewed all institutional arrangements conventionally associated with state power. Yet, not surprisingly, after the October Revolution, the Bolsheviks moved swiftly to consolidate state power in the face of the
combined pressures of civil war, famine, and the need to build anew after the
economic and social devastation of World War I. It would be improper to argue,
however, that the anarchistic strains of *State and Revolution* were abandoned
immediately after the revolution simply for the sake of base political motivations.
Rather, the book had never been wholly antistatist in flavor. Although the role of
the party was not emphasized here, the need for a postrevolutionary proletarian
dictatorship was staunchly defended throughout, imbuing the work with its dialectical and ultimately unsatisfying character.

Although the work is more theoretical than Lenin's other writings, *State and
Revolution*, too, grew out of Lenin's characteristic preoccupation with practical
questions. Suddenly confronted with the prospect of a successful revolution, Lenin

produced this work to elaborate upon the postrevolutionary state on which Marx's works provided so little guidance. Lenin's close textual analysis was based on the so-called "classic texts" of mature Marxism such as the *Manifesto* and *The Poverty of Philosophy*; historical works such as "The Eighteenth Brumaire," "The Civil War in France," "The Critique of the Gotha Program," and "Germany: Revolution and Counterrevolution" (1851–1852); and Engels's *Origin of the Family* and *Anti-Dühring*.[104] The premise of Lenin's work was, thus, the narrow class definition of the state as a class dictatorship that predominated in these texts.[105] The inherently oppressive nature of the bourgeois state, which he saw in Russia's provisional government, necessitated its destruction. But it was here that the matter became more complex, however simple the basic formula. When discussing the dictatorship of the proletariat, Lenin found himself confronting complications previously mentioned here in the dual conception of the state in Marx and Engels. If the state existed as a product of "irreconcilable class antagonism," then once classes were eliminated with the last form of class society, bourgeois society, the state would lose its raison d'être and, ultimately, its very existence. Yet Marx and Engels had called for a dictatorship of the proletariat to precede the final withering away of the state. Here there was a disjuncture in Lenin's treatment between the claim that the state qua state would cease to exist with the replacement of army, police, and the bureaucracy by a people's militia, guardians of the whole people, and a minimal apparatus for the day-to-day administration of things, on the one hand, and the requirement that the dictatorship of the proletariat retain the essential attribute of the modern state in serving as an instrument of class domination over prospective counterrevolutionaries, on the other. Convinced that tremendous growth in the forces of production would render the tasks necessary to address the common needs of society simple enough for any individual to perform, Lenin maintained that all administrative functions could be accomplished by anyone. All such functions would be rotated, and because everyone would be a bureaucrat, no one would be a professional bureaucrat.[106] Lenin would not be impressed by the claims of contemporaries, such as Max Weber, that bureaucracy was necessary, even desirable, as a sign of rationality, of modernity, and he seemed oblivious to the reality that Russia's lagging industrial development, the immaturity of its industrial capitalist economy, made his rationale for a nonstate state unsuitable for Russia. Although these concerns were enhanced by the need for the Bolsheviks to complete what Russia's bourgeoisie had not in industrializing their society, they could apply universally to all postproletarian revolutionary societies. What would be the nature of the dictatorship of the proletariat? What would distinguish it from previous forms of state? What would assure that it would indeed wither away? Was it conceivable that the state, in fact, had a broader relationship to society as a whole? Might or must some form of the state continue to exist to perform administrative services for the benefit of all society rather than for a single social class, even after classes had disappeared? Was the possibility of its autonomy from society inherent in the very nature of the state? If so, then perhaps Marx's and Engels's views on the nature and origins of the state—at least Lenin's understanding of them—had erred from the outset.

Attempting to respond to such concerns, Lenin stressed that the state would be eliminated in a two-staged process. The violent proletarian revolution would destroy the bourgeois state, but would then replace it with a revolutionary proletarian dictatorship modeled on the Paris Commune. Necessitated by the resistance of vestiges of "bourgeois right," the proletarian dictatorship would resemble other states in acting as an instrument of class rule. Nonetheless, it would exist only as a temporary "semi-state," for during the transition from capitalism to communism, "the state must inevitably be a state that is democratic *in a new way* (for the proletariat and propertyless in general) and dictatorial *in a new way* (against the bourgeoisie)."[107] Once a sufficiently high level of industrial capitalist development had been attained for the achievement of communism, Lenin wrote, there would be "the *preconditions* that *enable* really 'all' to take part in the administration of the state." At this point, the state qua state could disappear because "[w]hen the more important functions of the state are reduced to such accounting and control by the workers themselves, it will cease to be a 'political state' and 'public functions will lose their political character and become mere administrative functions'." In the absence of classes, such a state would no longer constitute a "proper state." Yet this left unresolved the problem observed earlier (though Lenin did not see it) posed in Marx's *Critique of Hegel's "Philosophy of Right"* —the tendency for the state to acquire its own raison d'être and arrogate to itself powers as master over society. Lenin spoke of removing "capitalists and bureaucrats," but could the solution whereby "[a]ll citizens are transformed into hired employees of the state" prevent the reemergence of a new bureaucratic elite?[108] The complexity of advanced industrialized societies alone suggests a negative response to this question. When the role of the vanguard party as midwife of revolutionary change is reintroduced into the model, such a resolution appears even more dubious. It was this dilemma that Bukharin and Trotsky addressed.

Concern with the state becoming dangerously autonomous from, even dominant over, society grew out of other, broader concerns about future forms of the state in Bukharin's work, whereas for Trotsky, it was linked more intimately to his own political misfortunes. As the party's leading theoretician in the estimation of Lenin himself, Bukharin wrote extensively on the state.[109] As discussed, although Lenin rejected it for publication, he was influenced by Bukharin's article on the imperialist state. The subsequent *Historical Materialism* (1921), which subordinated the state to the mechanical equilibrium model of human development that dominates the work, was less suggestive than Bukharin's early work. Drawing on *Capital* and the passages on base and superstructure in the preface to Marx's "Contribution to the Critique of Political Economy" that have caused such deterministic mischief in the history of Marxist philosophy, *Historical Materialism* offered a simple formula on the state. "[A]mong all the varied production relations," Bukharin wrote, "one type of such relations stands foremost, namely, the type that is expressive of the relations between the classes which hold the principal means of production in their hands, and the other classes which hold either subsidiary means or no such means at all. The class that is dominant in economy will also be dominant in politics and will *politically fortify* the specific type of production relations which will give security to the process of exploitation operating in favor of this class."[110]

In contrast to the simplicity of this formulation, the notions of "state capitalism" and "state capitalist trust" presented in *Imperialism and World Economy* and then in "K teorii imperialisticheskogo gosudarstva" (Toward a theory of the imperialist state) offered the germ of "a radical reinterpretation of the Marxist view of the state"[111] that Bukharin would develop further in the mid-1920s. Here, Bukharin pursued a concern that was left unelaborated in *State and Revolution*: the possibility of the emergence of an autonomous and oppressive new bureaucracy within the postrevolutionary state. "The workers did not destroy the old official-ridden state with the intention of allowing it to grow up again from new roots," Bukharin wrote in *The ABC of Communism* in 1919.[112] Then, during the civil war period, Bukharin was very statist in his views, emphasizing the need to consolidate power. Yet he remained optimistic that after the need for "war communism" had passed, the state could indeed begin to wither away. Not surprisingly, he would be disappointed in this expectation, for the state had still had not begun to "wither away" by 1925. Although Bukharin was deeply involved in the 1923–1924 condemnation of Trotsky and his "deviations" and would never allow that he held any common theoretical ground with Trotsky, in fact, he shortly found himself echoing the fear that would become Trotsky's firm conviction by the 1930s, namely, that the new Soviet bureaucracy was becoming a "new class."[113] In the mid-1920s, Bukharin warned repeatedly against the continued growth in power and autonomy of the young Soviet state. Although he distinguished carefully between "evil 'bureaucratism' and bureaucracy as an organizational necessity," Bukharin feared the rebirth of the official "arbitrariness" (*proizvol*) and an oppressive state apparatus that nineteenth-century Russian radicals had castigated as characteristic of tsarist rule.[114]

On this point, Bukharin came no closer than Lenin to any solution to this possibility. With respect to two other issues, however, Bukharin's work on the state was more fruitful, innovative, and of special interest to Marxists in China and Japan. The first concerned the concepts of state capitalism, organized capitalism, and state capitalist trust that would be censured by Stalin after his defeat of Bukharin in 1929. The second was the related possibility of the resurgence or stabilization of capitalism through the emergence of new, more powerful, forms of the state in postcapitalist society, forms other than socialism, arising out of a world capitalist order that had developed beyond Marx's expectations. These ideas originated in Bukharin's *Imperialism and World Economy*. Drawing on Hilferding's *Finance Capital* and the example of Germany in his time, Bukharin argued that in advanced capitalist societies the state and the economy were more closely linked than ever before. "The stronger state secures for its industries the most advantageous trade treaties, and establishes high tariffs that are disadvantageous for the competitors. It helps its finance capital to monopolise the sales markets, the markets for raw materials, and particularly the spheres of capital investment." Ultimately, there emerged what Bukharin labeled "state capitalist trusts" which were compelled to embark on imperialist policies to ensure their own survival in violent competition with one another.[115]

After World War I, Bukharin applied this analysis to define the "third period" of capitalism and its implications for international revolution. In the wake of the failure of revolution in Western Europe, despair among Marxists in Russia and elsewhere led Lenin to turn toward Asia and nationalist uprisings against world imperialism in colonial areas as the new hope for revolutions that could sustain the lone Bolshevik state. Initially, in his wartime article on the imperialist state, Bukharin disparaged nationalism, arguing that the international character of capitalism had rendered nationalism obsolete. After the war, however, Bukharin changed his views to coincide with Lenin's appreciation of nationalism in societies victimized by imperialism. Criticizing the narrow view of the proletarian revolution as exclusively a European scenario and the pessimism accompanying it, Bukharin argued that "[t]he ultimate destruction of world capitalism (imperialism) would come about through an eventual global *smychka* [alliance] between proletarian insurrections in the 'metropolises' and 'the colonial movement, in which the peasantry plays a large role,' in the East."[116] This turn eastward was written into Comintern policy during Bukharin's leadership of that organization, until his power was undermined in 1928 and 1929.[117] In China and Japan, this Eastern orientation was explicitly associated with Bukharin and helped to reinforce his prestige as a theorist.

Meanwhile, Bukharin also argued that the tremendous economic difficulties experienced by the capitalist world after the war did not indicate, as some assumed, that world capitalism was on the brink of economic ruin resulting from insoluble internal contradictions. Rather, "capitalism's 'third period' witnessed not internal breakdowns but further stabilization on a high technological and organization level." Because of this stabilization, the *smychka* of Western proletarian and Eastern colonial-nationalist insurrections was crucial, for the impetus for revolution in the capitalist system would arise not from within but from " 'external crises'."[118] Militarization had motored the statization of economic life in the capitalist state, but now, after the war, the state was being fused with the economy "from below." Previously, military-related economic interests had been dependent on the state's demand for armaments. Now "the state was becoming 'directly dependent on large and powerful concerns or combinations of these concerns'" in a process of "trustification" of state power that culminated in the formation of a *state capitalism* where " 'the state power controls and develops capitalism'."[119] Such a statization of capitalism was occurring on the basis of a higher level of technological development than ever before attained, uniting the state and capitalist management into a single formidable organization capable of rationalizing and regulating not only the economy but the whole of society as well.

This concept of state capitalism also implied the possibility of a new nonsocialist, postcapitalist form of the state in terms of the organization of the Soviet proletarian dictatorship itself. Bukharin first raised this issue when he criticized Mikhail Tugan-Baranovsky's work on economic crisis. Tugan-Baranovsky, whose work was widely cited by Kawakami Hajime and other Japanese Marxists in the early 1920s, was a "revisionist" economic theorist who had argued that the growth of production and capital accumulation need not be dependent on the social consumption of the populace. Industry could itself provide the demand for its own production. In 1924, Bukharin attacked this view, making the normative argument that production *must* always be directed toward the satisfaction of social needs.[120] At the time, when the New Economic Policy (NEP) had restored the Soviet economy from the ravages of the civil war, Bukharin feared the heavy costs to the Russian peasantry—the vast majority of the consuming public—that would be levied by the rapid industrialization program focusing on heavy industry advocated by Yevgeny Preobrazhensky, Trotsky, and the Bolshevik Left.[121] His opposition to Tugan-Baranovsky's argument notwithstanding, Bukharin's own theory of state capitalism held important similarities to it. In his writings on militaristic state capitalism during the war, the possibility of the state's becoming both the largest producer and the greatest consumer of its own economic output loomed large. The same possibility seemed to be present in the postrevolutionary Soviet state if economic activity was to be determined by central planning rather than by consumer demand.

Understandably, Bukharin's work on the role of the state in hindering or abetting revolution from above and below would hold a certain fascination for Marxists in China and Japan. The repressive and economically centralized Japanese state, like Germany and Italy, seemed to furnish evidence for Bukharin's notion of state capitalist trusts. As the relationship between the state and capitalist industrialists grew increasingly intimate and Japan's imperialist policies toward China became more aggressive, Bukharin's views on state capitalism appeared increasingly relevant to the Japanese experience. In China, however, Bukharin's affirmation of a central role for nationalist anticolonial movements helped to assure Marxists there that they, too, played a major role in the world revolution. The differences between socioeconomic developments in China and Japan coincided with the two strands in Bukharin's thought, making the nation-state a focal point for both Chinese and Japanese Marxists.

Yet it was the reality of growing state power and national chauvinism in Soviet Russia that would lend the single greatest source of support to the theoretical endeavors of those who would fashion of Marxism a national or state socialism. Although his works were not widely published, translated, and read in China and Japan until the early 1930s, it was Joseph Stalin who codified this reality into theoretical terms. Arguing that, under conditions of "hostile capitalist encirclement," the strength of the Soviet party-state was justified because by definition "socialism in one country" served society as a whole, Stalin's work marked a devious return to the broad conception of the state.[122] Needless to say, this perspective shared very little with Marx's discussion in the *Critique*, which was preoccupied with the notion of alienation. Stalin's view did not attribute a sinister character to centralization or bureaucratism but claimed to serve all members of society by containing tensions, providing for defense, and building the Soviet economy.

Although this view was evident in scattered statements from Stalin in the late

1920s and 1930s, he did not present a comprehensive theoretical statement on the state until the Eighteenth Party Congress of the Communist Party of the Soviet Union (CPSU) in 1939. There, Stalin "undertook to correct the doctrine of the withering away of the State as formulated by Engels. He contended that Engels had reasoned in abstraction from the international context, with his assumption of the simultaneous victory of socialism in most or all states."[123] Engels's premise had been invalidated, in Stalin's view, by the position of the Soviet Union as a lone socialist state in which the remnants of bourgeois society needed to be eradicated. Defending the state from bourgeois enemies within and without demanded a powerful state. As Tucker has argued, this interpretation as offered by Stalin fused certain Russian traditions with Bolshevism. Stalin borrowed from the tsarist "model of forced national development for creating a strong military state in a hostile international encirclement"—of revolution from above. The ultimate extension of this tendency affected Chinese and Japanese Marxian revolutionaries when "the international communist revolution was equated with the aggrandizement of the Soviet Russian state."[124] Under Stalin's uncompromising domination in the Soviet and the international movement, his was the last word on Soviet state theory at least until Nikita Khrushchev launched de-Stalinization with trenchant criticism of the late leader at the Twentieth Party Congress in 1956.[125] His justifications of "socialism in one country" in the Soviet Union bolstered Chinese and Japanese conceptions of a strong autonomous state that propelled the international proletarian socialist revolution forward.

The Problem of the State in Contemporary Western Marxism

In the years since Lenin penned *State and Revolution*, there have been important new developments in the Marxist theory of the state. These are significant for this study because they help to delineate the range of possibilities for new theoretical work among Chinese and Japanese Marxists who were influenced by Leninism but felt compelled to revise it for adaptation to their own societies. The developments also illuminate the impact of excluding the work of the younger Marx on both Eastern and Western treatments of the state. As demonstrated in the chapters to follow, many of the questions that have bedeviled Western Marxists since Lenin's time also emerged in Chinese and Japanese discussions. In many instances, East Asian thinkers took approaches that were strikingly similar to those devised in the West. In others—where circumstances posed new problems, or where satisfactory answers could not be found in the absence of most of the more humanistic early writings of Marx and Engels—Chinese and Japanese Marxists would supplement the Marxism-Leninism they knew with indigenous philosophical perspectives. In either case, examining the issues and solutions that post-Leninist Marxists have posed in the West will contribute to an appreciation of those questions that were especially problematic for Marxists in the Far East and the universality or particularity of their responses.

The post-Lenin era in the West has produced two major approaches to the state. So-called critical or Hegelian Marxists have sought to bridge Hegelian idealism with Marx's materialist perspectives on the state. This endeavor is best represented in the work of the Hungarian Marxist Georgy Lukács and the German emigré Herbert Marcuse. More recent efforts, however, have focused on the workings of the advanced capitalist state in terms of its functional and its structural relationships to society as a whole. In many respects, this latter work is properly regarded as an outgrowth of critical Marxism, but it eschews much of the Frankfurt school's preoccupation with the more abstract psychological, metaphysical, and humanistic dimensions of Marxist philosophy. The contrast between the two approaches highlights the disparity between an understanding of Marxism that takes as its point of departure the humanism of the young Marx and Engels and one that does not. The two approaches are not unrelated, however. They are linked at the outset of their development by the idealist tendencies in the work of the cofounder of the Italian Communist party Antonio Gramsci and today converge in the provocative contributions of Jürgen Habermas.

Gramsci, like Lenin and his fellow Bolshevik theorists, did not have access to the earliest writings of Marx. Nevertheless, relying heavily on Marx's "Theses on Feuerbach" and the 1859 *Preface to the Critique of Political Economy*, Gramsci was able to formulate an approach to the state that echoed many of the Hegelian elements of Marx's thought. Gramsci's theory developed as a mediation between vulgar historical materialism, as explicated in Bukharin's book on the subject, and the idealism of Benedetto Croce. He accomplished this by injecting a powerful subjectivist component into his Marxism. Lenin had already made an important step in this direction by articulating his notion of the vanguard party. Stressing that the subjective conditions for revolutionary change are as indispensable as the objective factors, Lenin had argued in *What Is to Be Done?* (1902) that revolutionary "class political consciousness can be brought to the workers *only from without*." The vanguard party of professional revolutionaries, formed around a core of socialist intellectuals, would help to bring that consciousness that was essential for a socialist revolution to the proletariat.[126] Lenin's argument was cast in terms that would apply to all societies, but this issue of subjective conditions was particularly important for Russia, where both industrial capitalism and the urban working class were immature, and it would be echoed as Marxism moved farther East.

In the meantime, in the West, Gramsci, leading the Italian socialist movement in the early-1920s, was also concerned with the presence of the subjective, as well as the material, conditions for revolutionary change. The world, in his view, was not objectively real but was created actively by human subjects. Men and women transformed the material world collectively on the basis of their shared interests and consciousness.[127] Unlike Lenin, Gramsci did not see the knowledge of totality that was essential to the revolutionary movement as coming only from outside the proletariat. Nevertheless, he saw in the state and associated elements of civil society, particularly in advanced capitalist societies, important barriers to that consciousness. Schools, churches, and the ideological hegemony of the economically dominant classes that they inculcated and perpetuated inhibited the formation of revolutionary consciousness. Thus, in Gramsci's often confusing conception, the two levels of superstructure, the state and civil society, were absorbed within one another: "[I]n actual reality," he wrote, "civil society and State are one and the same."[128] The ability of the institutions generally associated with civil society to inhibit revolutionary change peaked in capitalist societies, where they had the ability to elicit consent from the subaltern classes. Thus, Gramsci averred, although the tsarist state in Russia, unsupported even by an illusion among the workers and peasants that it served their interests, collapsed readily when attacked, revolution in advanced capitalist societies was likely to be prolonged, like a military "war of position" as opposed to a "war of movement" or "maneuver."[129]

Gramsci was a revolutionary strategist as well as a theoretician, and, writing the greatest volume of theoretical work while imprisoned from 1926 to 1933, Gramsci made his theoretical contributions in isolation from those who would found the critical movement. By contrast, among the critical Marxists who worked within the bounds of the Hegelian Marxist approach on the basis of the increasingly available early Marxist texts, relatively less development has occurred to link philosophical with empirical observations. The critical Marxist approach to the state emerged from a revulsion against crude positivist and vulgar tendencies of Marxism presented as historical materialism. In their view, the critical theorists of the Frankfurt school were returning to Marx's aspiration to the *"ruthless criticism of everything existing."*[130] Like Gramsci, Georgy Lukács and his successors in the movement articulated an approach to the state comprised of an admixture of Marx's scientism with Hegelian idealism. Rejecting what had become conventional bourgeois antinomies between fact and value, phenomena (appearances) and noumena (things in themselves), subject and object, free will and necessity, and *Sein* (what is) and *Sollen* (ought), Lukács forged a return to Marx's approach to philosophy as thoroughgoing criticism. A major aspect of Lukács's work was his concept of "reification," by which he "meant the petrification of living processes into dead things, which appeared as an alien 'second nature'."[131] Reification was a manifestation of human alienation, and it was this notion of alienation, extracted from the writings of the young Marx, that would constitute the central strand linking all critical Marxist work on the state. As in the young Marx, man's return to himself, through the totalizing universal class of the proletariat, would also constitute the abolition and transcendence of the reification that was the state.[132]

Similarly, Herbert Marcuse, especially in *One-Dimensional Man*, focused on the critique of ideology as the most repressive aspect of the political superstructure. Here again, as in Gramsci, the notion of the state was expanded to embrace aspects of the society itself, which Marcuse saw as permeated by a repressive ideology. The result, in Marcuse's view, was a unidimensionality of human existence in advanced industrial societies—capitalist or Communist—that were dominated by technology, "the great vehicle of *reification*."[133] Thus, in returning to the neo-Hegelianism of the young Marx, Marcuse was able to offer a basis for not only transcending but repudiating the new repressive incarnation of the state that had appeared in the wake of the world's first proletarian socialist revolution. Ultimately, their critical stance led Hegelian Marxists to conclude that the Soviet, and especially the Stalinist, outcome by no means accurately or necessarily represented the essence of Marxian socialism. The Soviet bureaucratic state, in their view, incarnated a *statist myth of socialism*. As the Yugoslav philosopher Svetozar Stojanović argued, "A new class-system—statism—developed with the degeneration of the October Revolution, a system that still successfully legitimizes itself as socialism. True Marxists have the duty to pierce this mythical veil and unmask the statist reality which lies behind it. Its paradigm is Stalinist society."[134]

The critical Marxist movement, then, produced powerful critiques of both capitalist society and the first experiment in Marxian socialism, but its conclusions did not signal optimism for man's extrication of himself from them. Ultimately, in the 1960s, then, Marcuse's representation of modern society as a wholly manipulated society gave way to a more sanguine perspective on man in society and the state in the work of Habermas. Like Gramsci and other critical theorists, Habermas found the state spreading beyond the bounds that had been identified by Marx— the apparatuses of authority in the police, the army, and the bureaucracy. Indeed, Habermas's criticism of Marx himself for excessive materialism and, thus, for failing to foresee the expansion of the capitalist state into formerly nonpolitical realms affecting ideology and consciousness rendered Habermas's status as a Marxist problematic.[135]

His and other treatments drawing on Marx's Hegelian tendencies complemented and challenged the work of Bolshevik theorists based on the narrow class conception of the state and helped to elicit a more complete understanding of Marx's views on the subject. They did not, however, deal with the economic structural context of the state or class relations, nor did they consider empirical evidence from historical developments since Marx's time in order to refine or revise these views. The Hegelian approach has tended to treat the state in general and abstract terms, shunning analyses of particular kinds of state structures. For Hegelian Marxists, "[t]he key question appears to be, '*What* is the state?' The basic answer is that the state is a mystification, a concrete institution which serves the interests of the dominant class, but which seeks to portray itself as serving the nation as a whole, thereby obscuring the basic lines of class antagonism. Thus, the state represents a universality, but a false one, an 'illusory community'."[136] Characteristically, then, Hegelian Marxist theorists have relegated the relationship between class antagonisms and the state to a secondary position, following Marx's *Critique*. Work on the state in this Hegelian-Marxist tradition was not available to Chinese and Japanese Marxists in the prewar period, but such contributions do help to elucidate what many might have felt was missing from the account of society and the state offered to them.

Contemporary Marxists who have taken the more restricted class conception— the "scientific" approach—as their point of departure have not hesitated to propose clarifications on Marx's views in light of the nature of actual advanced capitalist states. Scientific Marxists have begun with the premise that to understand the nature of the (bourgeois) state, one must comprehend the nature of capitalist society, its contradictions and class conflicts. *Capital*, then, is the basic text of this school. The renowned, often obfuscatory contributions of the French structuralist school pioneered by Louis Althusser notwithstanding, the approach of such theorists is straightforward: from the analysis of historical developments in economic and state forms since Marx's time, they move from the empirical and the specific to integrate their observations into a more abstract and general theory of the capitalist state.

One may find limited traces of the Hegelian themes of Marx's early writings in this work, most notably in the treatment of ideological functions of the state by Althusser, his disciple Nicos Poulantzas, and Claus Offe.[137] More often, however, a balanced meshing of the themes of the early works with those of the mature works of Marx is not achieved. Indeed, the motivator of Althusser's endeavor was to assault not only Stalinism in the wake of the Twentieth Party Congress but also an allegedly excessive reliance on Hegelian Marxist humanism to purge the movement of Stalinist influence. Thus, Althusser embarked on a rereading of Marx, using scientific Marxism as a method to guide the rereading. Ideology played a central role in this reformulation. For Althusser, ideology was a relation that individuals experience. It manifested a "unity of the real relation and the imaginary relation between [individuals] and the real conditions of existence."[138] In treating ideology, like Gramsci, Althusser developed an expanded appreciation of the state: Ideological State Apparatuses (ISAs) were to be found in institutions, such as schools, churches, the family, and trade unions, that have conventionally been identified as part of civil society, independent of the state.[139] This apparent link to Hegelian Marxism came to an abrupt end in Althusser, however, when he defined Marxism as science and, thus, allied himself firmly with the scientific approach to Marxism. This perspective sees its truth in the works of the mature Marx, those penned between 1857 and 1883, marking a decisive "epistemological break" with the Hegelian Marxist problématique.[140] Thus, in treating the state, Althusser and others of the contemporary scientific Marxist school have interpreted the state on the basis of the narrow class conception thereof. This conception poses two issues: "'*Why* does the state serve the interests of the capitalist class? And 'How does the state function to maintain and expand the capitalist system?'"[141] Because this approach has focused on the state in capitalist society, difficulties arise when one endeavors to extend its analyses of the bourgeois state to states in the abstract and to other particular historical forms of the state.[142] A brief examination of the state theory of this scientific school is instructive, however, for one may expect to find difficulties similar to those encountered in the efforts of Chinese and Japanese Marxists unacquainted with Marx's early writings to extend his views on the state in *Capital* geographically and temporally to apply to the historical development of states in East Asia. It is, perhaps, for this very reason that Engels's *Origin of the Family* and *Anti-Dühring*, which did treat precapitalist forms, became such important reference works in China and Japan in the prewar period.

Despite their common point of departure in the works of the mature Marx, theorists of the contemporary Western scientific school exhibit divergences that may be categorized in terms of two approaches to the state: (1) the structuralist, or constraint, approach and (2) the instrumentalist, or influence, interpretation. The latter is the older of the two, and with Lenin's *State and Revolution* and Bukharin's notion of the state capitalist trust as its most influential representatives, instrumentalism generally is associated with vulgar or orthodox Marxism. Instrumentalist theorists such as Ralph Miliband[143] see the state as "an *instrument* of the ruling classes" "in the service of accumulation interests."[144] In this view, the state serves the economically dominant class because it is controlled by a self-conscious ruling elite, and instrumentalists proceed from here to examine "the nature of the class which rules, the mechanisms which tie this class to the state, and the concrete relationships between state policies and class interests." Instrumentalist Marxist studies involve as often empirical analyses on the basis of an implicit theory of the state as efforts to formulate or clarify that theory in formal terms. Thus, they include sociological studies of the capitalist class, "in the first instance simply to show that it exists," and political studies of the linkages between the bourgeoisie and the state structure and how they interact in the policy-making process.[145]

The main burden of the instrumentalist argument is placed on the political and social ties between capitalists and the state. Some have claimed, for example, that the United States Senate serves the interests of capital because its members are of bourgeois origin, hold stock in major companies, and travel in the same social circles with capitalists. Miliband concedes the possibility that such ties might be weak, obscure, or impossible to find at all, in which case, he argues that the state's policies are constrained by its economic environment and state elites by their "ideological commitments."[146] To disarm his critics, Miliband stresses that his interpretation does not take the *Manifesto*'s description of the state as "a committee for managing the common affairs of the whole bourgeoisie" to mean, as vulgar Marxists would have it, that the state acts not only on behalf of the bourgeoisie but at its "behest." Marx had qualified the *Manifesto*'s definition by noting in his studies of France and England that often "it is not the ruling class as a whole, but a fraction of it, that controls the state, and that those who actually run the state may well belong to a class which is not the economically dominant class." Marx had also noted, Miliband adds, the potential autonomy of the state as "an intrinsic part" of the nature of the state deriving from and resting on the fragmented nature of the ruling class, as in the phenomenon of Bonapartism.[147]

These important qualifications to diminish the voluntarism of his account notwithstanding, the main thrust of Miliband's work remains firmly instrumentalist. Even in the case of Bonapartism, he stresses, Marx had recognized that "'the state power is not suspended in mid-air'" but represented small peasants. Thus, "the Bonapartist state, however independent it may have been *politically* from any given class, remains, and cannot in a class society but remain, the protector of an economically and socially dominant class."[148] The state is ultimately an instrument that can be discerned as such with close scrutiny. Whatever qualifications Marx made to the *Manifesto* formulation, for Miliband and other instrumentalists, it is axiomatic that Marx and Engels "never departed from the view that in capitalist society the state was above all the coercive instrument of a ruling class."[149]

Poulantzas contested this view in the structuralist tradition of his mentor Althusser and was quickly drawn into argument with Miliband over the pivotal notion of the potential autonomy of the state. As discussed, this issue arose from the recognition that "important realms of state-related activity . . . are clearly not manipulated by specific capitalists or coalitions, such as culture, ideology and legitimacy."[150] The structuralist emphasis on the state's potential autonomy from the ruling classes reflects dissatisfaction with the assumption of "capitalist rationality" that seems to be inherent in the instrumentalist approach to the state.[151] Instrumentalists tend to posit a self-conscious ruling class that purposively pursues policies advantageous to itself through the state apparatus. As Marx observed, however, people's consciousness is conditioned and limited by the material conditions in which they live.[152] One can "expect the degree of rationality of politically implemented strategies certainly to be restricted and marked by 'false consciousness'."[153] Thus, structuralist or constraint theorists argue "that the institutions of the political system cannot effectively become the instrument of *any non-capitalist interest* whatsoever." Indeed, some have suggested that "the common interests of the ruling class are most accurately expressed in those legislative and administrative strategies of the State apparatus which are *not* initiated by articulated interests, that is 'from outside,' but which arise from the State organizations' own routines and formal structures."[154]

Hence, structuralists commonly assert that "the functions of the state are broadly determined by the structures of society rather than by the people who occupy positions of state power."[155] It is not class consciousness or purposive rationality that is important here but the larger constraints of the society that delimit the activity of the state and its functionaries. These constraints derive from "the systematic functional interrelationships among" "the concrete social institutions that make up a society." Class consciousness, in other words, is even more bounded by the material constraints of objective conditions of human existence in the view of structuralists than it is in the treatment of instrumentalists. In capitalist society, the structural interrelationships that both bound consciousness and constrain the activity of the state involve economic and class contradictions into which the state must intervene and resolve "in order to reproduce capitalist society as a whole."[156] The state serves to maintain the entire society, and it appears to exercise this function as a class-neutral organization, but, in fact, it ultimately serves those who dominate the capitalist system that it helps to reproduce. Indeed, the state is compelled "to execute its *class-bound functions under the pretext of class-neutrality* and provide its particular exercise of power with the alibi of the general interest." The dilemma for the state, then, is that it "*must at the same time practise its class character* and keep it concealed."[157] If the state does not perform this ideological function effectively, its underlying class character will be exposed and subjected to the violent onslaught of the exploited classes.[158] The state must also act to prevent the exacerbation (and the manifestation thereof) of the conflict between the social quality of production and the private appropriation that is characteristic of capitalism.[159] As a result, the state is caught in a dilemma: "If . . . the capitalist system is *not* able to survive *without* bourgeois democratic forms of organizations of political power, the contradiction between the economic and the legitimation [or ideological] functions of the capitalist State points on the other hand to an irreversible politicization of class-conflicts, that is, to the fact that it cannot live *with* them either."[160]

In this account, the state maintains a degree of autonomy in two respects, one illusory and the other real. It maintains an illusory autonomy in its pretext of serving the interests of society as a whole, but it maintains actual autonomy because, structuralists argue against the instrumentalist view, it is not merely subject to direct manipulation of the state organs. In discussing the state's role in supporting the reproduction of capitalism,[161] however, the structuralist view also suggests a second actual form of state autonomy—the ability of the state to develop its own self-interest distinct from those of the ruling class and of society as a whole. The functionaries of the state act to reproduce the existing social mode of production because "their continued power rests on the maintenance of political and economic order." Thus, they will act, often with greater insight than the individual capitalist might have, to support the long-term interests of capital.[162] "A state which [is] . . . the tool of one capitalist grouping would be utterly incapable of accomplishing this."[163]

Despite the obvious strengths of this structuralist analysis, there are many difficulties in the work of both instrumentalists and structuralists, some of which arise from shared perspectives on Marx and the state. Despite their differences, both schools subscribe to the view of the state found in the mature Marx, the class conception observed in Lenin, and, firmly, they repudiate the usefulness of the early works in which the role of consciousness was even less bounded by "objective material conditions" of members of various classes in society.[164] As a result, both structuralists and instrumentalists tend to underestimate the potential autonomy of the state from social classes. Whatever the weaknesses of Marx's and Engels's original scattered formulations, the consequence of omitting fully half of what Marx wrote on the state is the inconsistency exemplified in the conflicting interpretations of the structuralist and instrumentalist schools. If the instrumentalist view "has tended toward voluntarism to explain state activities, the structuralists have almost entirely eliminated conscious action from their analysis"[165] producing "a kind of structural determinism."[166] Consciousness, that dominant theme in the Hegelian Marxist perspective, is the unresolved issue for these scientific Marxists. In rejecting the premise of class-consciousness implicit in the instrumentalist view, the structuralists hasten to disallow any meaningful role for consciousness in comprehending the state. As a result, Poulantzas's work is weak in explaining how in the absence of ruling-class consciousness, "social mechanisms regulate [the] . . . various functional relationships" that govern the structuralist state.[167] In those works that do endeavor to meld theoretical with empirical analysis, consciousness and the "dialectic" of Hegelian Marxism are reintroduced through the back door, so to speak. The work of James O'Connor and Claus Offe are the best examples of this: Offe extends the tentative steps toward invoking consciousness made by Althusser and Poulantzas in their treatment of ideology to describe the problem of bourgeois ideology in the Hegelian Marxist terms of the continuing schism between civil society and the state.[168]

Finally, again because their work is grounded strictly in the late writings of Marx, the conception of the potential autonomy of the state remains undeveloped among both structuralists and instrumentalists. Poulantzas does develop further Marx's observation of the tendency for the state's organs to develop into a power of their own and to pursue their own interests. Yet it is here that the economic determinist tendency of the structuralist approach becomes manifest. The state is ultimately constrained by the need to act in the long-range general interests of capital, the dominant factor in the capitalist mode of production. This argument seems to preclude the possibility of a genuine revolution from above, the "possibility . . . that state organizations might under certain circumstances act *against* the long-run economic interests of a dominant class, or act to create a new mode of production."[169] Such a view implies, on the contrary, that state effectiveness vis-à-vis economic development not only is constrained, as Engels argued in *Anti-Dühring*, when it acts to impede economic progress, but is also prohibited from abetting that development, if to do so, it would have to act against the long-term interests of the dominant class to promote those of an ascendant class in the transition to a new production mode. This and related issues concerning the relationship between the state in general and society were of tremendous importance to Marxists in interwar China and Japan. For there was much in Marx's and Engels's writings on precapitalist development to suggest that the problem of an autonomous and powerful state would plague their societies and obstruct human liberation more than it could in the West.

THE ASIATIC MODE OF PRODUCTION AND THE STATE IN ORIENTAL SOCIETY

Chinese and Japanese Marxists exhibited considerable ambivalence concerning the twin concepts of oriental society and the Asiatic mode of production in Marx's thought. On the one hand, the notion of an "Asiatic" mode of production that was peculiar to the East caused discomfort among radical activitists who were initially attracted to Marxism because of its universalist claims that socialist revolution was inevitable. On the other hand, the apparent ability of the state to arise independently of class forces and to impede the further economic development of society in the East seemed to suggest an Asian exceptionalism that would vitiate such claims. The consequence was that in upholding or repudiating the Asiatic mode of production idea with reference to their own and neighboring societies, East Asian Marxists devoted considerable intellectual and emotional resources to it. Marx's view of the East held a fascination for these thinker-activists, and the twin dimensions of the national question—the state and national identity—were at its core.

The crux of the problem derived from the profound lack of knowledge concerning non-Western societies that undergirded Marx's writings on the East. As E. J. Hobsbawm has noted, in writing about the East, Marx "combined profound insight with mistaken assumptions."[170] Like his Western philosophical forebears, Marx treated the East in the same "Orientalist" fashion[171] that has characterized Western thought since the time of Plato. In Hegel's thought, the Orient functioned as a stagnant, passive antipole of the assertive, progressive culmination of human history in the dynamic West.[172] Marx shared Hegel's depiction of the Orient as a world now bypassed by history. Its only hope lay in the expansion of Western capitalism through imperialism:

> English interference having placed the spinner in Lancashire and the weaver in Bengal, or sweeping away both Hindoo spinner and weaver, dissolved these small semi-barbarian, semi-civilised communities, by blowing up their economic basis, and thus produced the greatest, and, to speak the truth, the only *social* revolution ever heard of in Asia.
>
> Now, sickening as it must be to human feeling to witness those myriads of industrious patriarchal and inoffensive social organisations disorganized and dissolved into their units, thrown into a sea of woes, and their individual members losing at the same time their ancient form of civilisation, and their hereditary means of subsistence, we must not forget that these idyllic village communities, inoffensive though they may appear, had always been the solid foundation of Oriental despotism, that they restrained the human mind within the smallest possible compass, making it the unresisting tool of superstition, enslaving it beneath traditional rules, depriving it of all grandeur and historical energies. . . . We must not forget that this undignified, stagnatory, and vegetative life, that this passive sort of existence evoked on the other part, in contradistinction, wild, aimless, unbounded forces of destruction and rendered murder itself a religious rite in Hindostan. . . .
>
> England, it is true, in causing a social revolution in Hindostan, was actuated only by the vilest interests, and was stupid in her manner of enforcing them. But that is not the question. The question is, can mankind fulfill its destiny without a fundamental revolution in the social state of Asia? If not, whatever may have been the crimes of England she was the unconscious tool of history in bringing about that revolution.[173]

In Marx's portrayal, societies such as China and India had held nothing of lasting humanistic value. Only the dissolution of these societies under the impact of Western economic domination could restore them to the mainstream of human history. Thus, the achievement of Marx's dream of a postexploitative communist society rested on the negation of what Asian society and culture had been for millennia. For Chinese and Japanese activist thinkers drawn to Marxism, this contention would pose major issues concerning nationality and identity in the revolutionary transition to socialist and then communist society. The nature and role of the state in Marx's assessment of the East played a decisive role in defining these issues.

The difficulties are evident in the problematic relationship between the two key concepts in Marx's treatment of the East. There was an apparent conflict between Marx's normative assessment of what he referred to as *oriental society*, on the one hand, and his claim to offer a scientific analysis of the Asiatic along with the "ancient, feudal and modern bourgeois modes of production" that he described in the preface to *A Contribution to the Critique of Political Economy* (1859) as "progressive epochs in the economic formation of society."[174] Oriental society was the product of the dominance of an Asiatic mode of production in which small-scale agriculture was carried out on the basis of communally owned land and cooperation. This was a society characterized by small, self-contained, scattered village communities, the absence of private property, and despotic rule. It is clear why the twin concepts of oriental society and the Asiatic mode of production should have been so problematic for Marx's successors. To be sure, Marx's systematic analysis of the capitalist mode of production was accompanied, even driven by an ambivalent normative judgment concerning the merits of capitalism in enabling man to achieve the material requisites for communist society and its brutality towards those whose labor provided the conditions for those accomplishments. Even if capitalism was the first truly universalizing mode of production in Marx's schema, his categories were to be applied to any social formation in any given society. Yet, the Asiatic society concept was problematic because it was devised "to account for a type of society outside the mainline of western development."[175] Thus, there was an apparent contradiction between Marx's delineation of man's historical modes of production as universal categories of dynamic socioeconomic change, on the one hand, and the view of oriental societies as geographically specific, static, passive entities without any internal dynamic of change. Not surprisingly, as the international socialist movement turned its attention toward colonized and semicolonial societies in Asia in the 1920s, the concepts of the Asiatic mode of production and oriental society aroused heightened interest and heated controversy. This conflict peaked circa 1930, was quashed without resolution under Stalin's dictatorship, and then was revived after World War II, when the Chinese Communist party's victory and the rapid collapse of empire in Asia, Latin America, and Africa seemed to herald new possibilities for revolutionary change without the dominance of Western imperialism in the non-Western world.

A good many valid reasons existed for the concept's exclusion from Stalinist orthodoxy at the Leningrad Conference of 1931.[176] The notion of the Asiatic mode of production seemed to challenge the presumption of the fundamental uniformity in the social development of all humankind that was implicit in Marx's presumably universally valid theory of history. Moreover, the alleged role of geographical factors countradicted the premise of the "primacy of technology over natural conditions." Finally, if Asian societies were plagued with stagnation, then the notion of the "inevitability of progress" would also collapse. Together, such implications might suggest that "the doctrine applied only to Western Europe and that capitalism itself was an accident."[177] Nor were these the only difficulties posed by Marx's and Engels's writings on the East. More specific problems concerned the nature of the state and the normative dilemmas that confronted Asian Marxists in the notion of an Asiatic mode of production. These were not easily ignored by Marxists in China and Japan. The inconsistencies seemed to herald real difficulties, particularly for Chinese revolutionists who needed to believe that Marx's historical schema premised on each mode of production's having its own internal dynamic of change was, indeed, universally valid. In Japan, Marx's admission that Japan was a feudal society and his extension of the concept to apply to Peruvian and Mexican societies seemed to indicate that "[t]he idea of 'Asiatic society' [was] a socio-historical rather than a geographic concept,"[178] and Japan's remarkable success in surpassing even Russia in its capitalist industrial development would seem likely to defuse the issue for Marxists there. Nevertheless, Japan's Marxists found it difficult to ignore the potential significance of the concept of Asiatic society for the trajectory of Japanese development even after 1868. Japan had achieved its outstanding economic success under the leadership of a powerful state, and as late as the 1920s and 1930s, despite the adoption of Western-style democratic institutions, Japanese radicals felt compelled to offer a cogent analysis of their society's past to explain the persistent pattern of autocratic imperial rule and popular passivity that firmly resisted democratic impulses. Thus, they turned to the notion of oriental society to explain not only China's stagnancy but also the possible long-term implications for Japan of the alleged tendency for earlier Asian development to have been limited and dominated by despotism.

The concept of oriental society took shape first in Marx's writings in the New York *Daily Tribune* on "Revolution in China and Europe" (June 14, 1853) and "The British Rule in India" (June 25, 1853) quoted previously. He and Engels subsequently elaborated on the concept in the *Grundrisse*, the three volumes of *Capital*, and *Anti-Dühring*. Because these treatments occur in fragmented passages, Donald Lowe has argued that there are three different versions of the Asiatic mode of production. The 1853 writings stressed the presence of "self-enclosed village communities" and "governmental control of water works," reflecting the influence of the "political economy" of Adam Smith, Richard Jones, J. S. Mill, and François Bernier; the description in *Capital* (vol. 1, chap. 1, sec. 4) described the Asiatic as a variant of the ancient mode of production, stressing the self-contained village community and the state's appropriation of surplus value, with less emphasis on waterworks and the lack of private property; and Engels's *Anti-Dühring* stressed the self-enclosed village community to the neglect of waterworks.[179] The common theme here was the isolated village community, which seemed at once to demand the coordinating powers of the despot and to militate against effective collective resistance against one who aspired to wield absolute power.

By the late 1920s, Chinese and Japanese Marxists were acquainted with these aspects of the notions of oriental society and the Asiatic mode of production as presented in the later works of Marx and Engels and transmitted through the writings of George Plekhanov and Lenin. Together these accounts offered them a complete picture of the causative links associated with what Marx depicted as "the current (stagnant) state of oriental society": climatic conditions → the need for irrigation and large-scale waterworks → despotism resting on the basis of dispersed, isolated, self-contained agrarian village communities → the failure of private landownership to emerge and, therefore, the inability to evolve feudal and capitalist modes of production.[180]

By far the two most important aspects of this sequence of causation were the interrelated "absence of [private] property in land"[181] and the nature of the state in oriental society. Marx and Engels argued that the absence of private property became permanent because of the presence of the "oriental despot." Originally, the community, or village commune, in these primitive societies owned the land, and the emergence of the despot represented the classic case that Engels described in *Anti-Dühring* of a state arising out of the need for certain common social functions to be undertaken in the interests of society as a whole. Such authoritative structures could arise in many kinds of primitive communities, including the "oldest German Mark communities" and India in his day. In every such community, the organs of the state "soon make themselves even more important" "until [this independence of social functions] developed into domination over society."[182] In Engels's view, however, extremely arid climatic conditions, such as those found in Egypt and Persia, made such relations of domination particularly despotic, and "only in the form of Oriental despotism did [such] societal dominance based on public function [as opposed to class conflict] spread far and last long."[183] Here, the state preceded class rule rather than arising out of it; and the "exploitation of man by man exists without private property in land."[184] Instead of private property, landownership rested in "an individual representing the community":[185] *"the king is the sole and only proprietor of all the land."*[186]

This despotic state, which effectively prevented the further development of economic forces in the emergence of private property in land, was the single most important feature distinguishing the Asiatic mode of production from the ancient, feudal, and capitalist modes of production. It was the key to the absence of an internal dynamic moving society to higher levels of economic development. There were only two classes in oriental society, the ruler and the ruled, making the mutually supportive relationship between absolute economic domination and political despotism complete. The despot used coercion to extract surplus labor from the populace, which was then applied to the performance of the essential large-scale public works for which purpose the state was originally created.[187] The people, over whom the monarch arrogated to himself these despotic powers, were direct producers and were subordinated directly to the state. There were private (by individuals) and public (by the village community) possession, but no private ownership of land. Because the state was both landlord and sovereign, rent and taxes coincided: "Sovereignty here exists in the ownership of land concentrated on a national scale."[188] Under such despotic rule, private property would never emerge. This was the key to the stasis of oriental society that Marx derived "scientifically" from its economic basis. Oriental society lacked any impetus toward change from within and because of the presence of the despot was exceptionally resistant to change. Even usury, normally a potent agent of change,[189] and the disintegrative impact of British imperialism, in this view, encountered powerful resistance in such societies.[190] These observations on the power of the state, coupled with the influence of geographical and climatic factors, raised serious questions about the extent to which Marx shared the Enlightenment faith that "progress" would always be made, particularly in Asia.[191]

Marx briefly entertained the possibility that the very primitiveness of oriental societies, with their rural agrarian communities, offered a shorter path—obviating the need to experience the painful disharmonies of class differentiation—to a new mode of production that would restore the halcyon communal state of man's earliest social organization. In either case, Marx's and Engels's views of oriental society seemed to suggest that more than one path to "modernity" was possible. Such a divergence was suggested by Marx's treatment of various forms of property[192] in the *Grundrisse*, where the slavonic community appeared as a modified form of oriental communal property.[193] Indeed, it was the slavonic community, the remanence of the traditional peasant commune in nineteenth-century Russia, that inspired Marx and Engels to suggest that Russia could achieve communism more quickly than societies farther west, provided that a revolution in Russia was followed quickly by proletarian socialist revolution in the industrialized societies of Western Europe.[194]

The Russian experience with oriental society was a major theme in the writings of Plekhanov that were passed on to Chinese and Japanese Marxists. As a narodnik early in his career, Plekhanov had stressed differences between Russia and the West while he stridently attacked tsarism as a form of despotism arising on the basis of a "primitive agricultural economy."[195] Plekhanov wrote in 1895, "'Old Muscovite Russia was distinguished by its completely Asiatic character'." It had developed a form of militarized despotic rule, marked, like oriental societies in general, by the state assuming the ownership of all property to meet the financial needs of maintaining a powerful military establishment against external pressures.[196] Like any other oriental society, Russia had a "vegetative, non-developmental character." The result had been stasis, a lack of any internal dynamic promoting change to new modes of production.[197] After his conversion to Marxism and his conviction that Russia was undergoing progressive Europeanization, Plekhanov continued to see Russia as an oriental society that had diverged from the West after the existence of the primitive communal clan system until the impact of external military pressures from Western industrialized societies.[198]

Chinese and Japanese Marxists came to learn of these ideas from Plekhanov's major work, *Fundamental Problems of Marxism*. This book presented four major themes associated with the Asiatic mode of production: (1) the notion of dual paths of Western and Eastern development after the demise of clan or communal society; (2) the importance of geographical factors for socioeconomic change; (3) the causative role of superstructure acting on base; and (4) the ideas of uneven and combined development that officially came to be attributed to Lenin after Plekhanov was denounced by M. N. Pokrovsky in the 1920s.[199] In *Fundamental Problems*, Plekhanov posited geographical conditions as the primary reason that the development of the forces of production had so differed in East and West. The oriental despotism that emerged in the geographical circumstances of the East, in turn, resulted in economic stagnation largely because of its "decisive influence on the entire mentality of social man."[200] As Lenin argued in *Development of Capitalism in Russia*, the emergence of "conditions required for capitalist production"— cultural factors, such as the absence of a predisposition of people to work for hire and acceptance of patriarchal authority[201]—reflected Russia's Asiatic past and continuing semi-Asiatic nature. This quality was the source of its continuing tardiness in developing capitalism. When capitalism finally did appear in Russia, it emerged in hybrid form, primarily as a result of Russia's Asiatic past. In contrast to the West European experience, "[c]apitalist elements began to appear in Russia not after the liquidation of serfdom in the West but while feudal-serf relations were still developing vigorously."[202]

Here emerged a notion of uneven and combined development that Trotsky would articulate in 1906[203] more formally but which has been attributed instead to Lenin. In this concept, "[u]nevenness refers both to Russia's lag behind the West and the differential rates and modes of socioeconomic change in different parts of the vast Russian realm; combined development refers to the blending of old forms with new in distinctive arrangements, particularly as a result of borrowing that was calculated to overcome the lag."[204] This perspective figured heavily in Lenin's account in the *Development of Capitalism in Russia*. There, Lenin stressed that Russia had evolved a "transitional" economic formation combining elements of the corvée labor system and capitalist economics.[205] It is noteworthy, however, that although Lenin emphasized here the impact of Russia's Asiatic features in describing Russia as semi-Asiatic, he was careful to distinguish his own society from fully Asiatic societies such as India, Persia, and China. Unlike these societies, in which the stagnancy portrayed by Marx and Engels appeared completely to stifle the development of private property, feudalism, and capitalism, Russia had, in fact, experienced not only feudalism but a growing, if hybrid, capitalism as well.

In the period after Lenin wrote, Bolshevik work on the Asiatic mode of production was focused on three objectives: the reconciliation of Marx's writings on the subject with the realities of Asian society; the reconciliation of the same with Marx's scientific approach to the ancient, feudal, and capitalist modes of production; and the application of these perspectives to further Soviet goals in the Chinese revolution.[206] Two major schools of Soviet scholarship would come to influence Chinese and Japanese work on the subject. On the one hand were those surrounding the Hungarian émigré economists Eugene S. Varga and his junior Ludwig S. Mad'iar. Varga, an economist who headed the Soviet Institute for the Study of the World Economy and World Politics from 1927 to 1947, had become an established scholar on international economic crises before launching his foray into the study of the Chinese economy and revolution in 1925.[207] Marx's and Engels's views on the East had been compiled by David B. Riazanov, head of the Marx-Engels Institute in 1925 in an article entitled "Introduction to Karl Marx on India and China,"[208] but Varga's prolific scholarship heightened Soviet interest in the issue. Maintaining that Chinese society was dominated by a scholar-bureaucrat ruling class that exercised a major role in managing large-scale waterworks, Varga argued that the state that it dominated had been created to ensure agricultural production and defense. In short, in Varga's view, the Chinese economic elite was such not because of its ownership of private property but because of its management of public resources. This was an oriental society that differed in major respects from feudalism.[209] Mad'iar, who had accompanied Comintern advisor Mikhail Borodin to China in 1926–1927, shared Varga's position that China was an oriental society that continued to be dominated by the Asiatic mode of production.[210] Mad'iar agreed with Varga that the Asiatic mode of production differed from feudalism in that there were neither feudal domains nor feudal lords. In his view, however, the need for the management of public water control and artificial irrigation accounted for this special mode of production. A despotic state thereby emerged atop scattered, isolated agrarian village communities,[211] and although Mad'iar saw classes in this oriental society, the primary class conflict was between this despotic state and the common peasantry.[212]

By 1930, Varga and Mad'iar had come under attack by Mikhail Godes and Yevgeny S. Iolk, and then, subsequently, by Sergei I. Kovalev. Neither Iolk, who had experience as a translator in China in 1925–1927, nor Godes had published significantly on this issue before 1930.[213] Yet, with the support of Stalin, the two men led the assault on the literature on the Asiatic mode of production at the Leningrad "Discussion on the Asiatic Mode of Production." The language in which Godes and others attacked the notion would not support Wittfogel's allegation that the Asiatic mode of production was regarded as dangerous because of its possible application to interpret Soviet politics under Stalin as an Asiatic bureaucratic "restoration."[214] Nevertheless, the political rather than intellectual impetus behind the assault was evident in Iolk's explicit reference to the failures of China policy under the Comintern leadership (presumably, in part because of the fallen Bukharin's influence) culminating in the Shanghai coup of 1927. Iolk asserted that the "superficially perfected theory about a particular Asiatic mode of production" had to be criticized "in order to turn the practical history now being created by the heroic struggle of the exploited masses of China, Indo-China, and India, to the interests of the labouring masses."[215] At this point, Stalin had prevailed upon the Chinese Communist party to eschew talk of China as an Asiatic society and stress the prevalence of feudal relations in rural China.[216] This position helped to expose the weakness of an Asiatic mode of production thesis because it underscored the fact that private property had, in fact, emerged in China as elsewhere in the Orient.[217] To maintain the Varga-Mad'iar thesis in spite of historical inaccuracies and its internal contradictions, Godes and Iolk charged, reflected "well-defined foreign influences" (such as, perhaps, Germany's Wittfogel) and constituted "the wet nurse for the theoretical position of Trotskyism."[218] Instead, Godes maintained, "The Asiatic mode of production is nothing other than feudalism"; there had been no distinct developmental path in the East.[219] Sergei Kovalev similarly repudiated a separate path for the East, although the Soviet authority (*The History of the Ancient World* [1935]) maintained that the Asiatic mode of production was a variant of the ancient rather than the feudal mode of production. Thus, at once, the critics of a separate Asiatic mode of production reduced the special features of Asian societies to insignificance and allowed Marxists in the Comintern to ignore comfortably Marx's embarrassing comments on the positive role of imperialism in the East.

Nevertheless, the cavalier and anti-intellectual manner in which the notion was treated at this conference—like the associated effort to purge all influences of Bukharin, Trotsky, and other defeated opponents of Stalin at this time—failed to persuade Chinese and Japanese Marxists to forsake their own inquiries into the Asiatic mode of production. Their work on Chinese and Japanese development in the 1930s continued to reflect curiosity and concern about the historical veracity of the concept and its implications for the current development of their societies. It raised too many disturbing issues, especially concerning the relationship between economic base and political superstructure in these societies, to be neglected. Lenin's depiction of a hybrid capitalism imbued with Asiatic features in Russia might help to explain the continued repressiveness of the Japanese state and the persistence of certain features such as its special constitutional arrangements concerning the imperial household. Yet, if Marx's schema of oriental society was valid, how had Japan happened to avoid stagnancy? As for China, certainly there the notion of a stagnating oriental society plotting a separate course of development (or nondevelopment) was far less attractive. If oriental societies had followed a separate path of development, was a Marxist inspired revolution still possible? The effort to create a vanguard party to bring about democratic and then socialist revolution rested on the assumption that voluntarism could counter effectively the material forces that Marx and Engels described; and it required some proof that China had taken even a tentative step out of the stasis of its Asiatic-ness and produced feudalism and, eventually, a significant departure from the heritage of the despotic state. Thus, Chinese Marxists in the 1930s would engage in persistent efforts to periodize Chinese history culminating in Mao's formula of a semi-feudal China.[220] In both China and Japan, then, the Asiatic mode of production issue carried with it a set of issues—concerning the normative value of their indigenous cultures and the nature of their polities—that were so compelling that they could not be ignored.

THE THEORY OF THE STATE, NATION, AND REVOLUTION IN CHINA AND JAPAN

These issues and many others arising from the incompleteness and inconsistencies of the Marxist theory of the state animated vigorous political and scholarly debates among Marxist scholars and activists in interwar China and Japan. The international context—in which despite their varying levels of economic development, both China and Japan felt pressure from more highly industrialized Western national states—created an environment that made the national question in their Marxism all the more urgent. Marxism was introduced into Asia as the expanding world system was brutally incorporating Asian and other non-Western states and societies. This, coupled with the emergence of a new isolated Soviet state, suggested the need to revise, or at least reconsider, the Marxist doctrine of the withering away of the state. Such issues with respect to the national question had already embroiled their predecessors in the Second International in intense confrontation. Hilferding, Rosa Luxemburg, Bukharin, and Lenin all had formulated theories of imperialism, world war, and revolution in response to the Marxist controversy at the turn of the century on the course of the international proletarian socialist movement in an era of seemingly increasing world war. As Chinese and Japanese Marxists embarked on their own scholarly and practical pursuit of these issues concerning the fate of the nation and the state, the influence of the works of Lenin and others, introduced in translation between 1925 and 1927, added fuel to the controversy.[221]

When addressing the implications of this work for the circumstances of revolutionary change in their own societies, Chinese and Japanese Marxists were compelled to confront the distinction between state and nation as a locus of value. State building in the East under the leadership of national liberation movements was historically valid in Lenin's argument and then in Comintern policy, but for how long and how far beyond the task of opposing world capitalism? Once a society had achieved a certain degree of economic development, once it was facing the transition from capitalism or bourgeois-democratic revolution to socialism or proletarian revolution, Bukharin and Lenin reasserted the primacy of Marx's original internationalism. In their view, for the Marxian socialist movement, "the choice is not *whether* the proletariat will or will not struggle, but *in whose interest* it should struggle: its own or that of the bourgeoisie. The question history places before the proletariat is *not to choose between war and peace, but between imperialist war and war against this war: civil war*."[222] As for Marx and Engels,[223] for Lenin, Bukharin, and Comintern leaders of the 1920s and 1930s, the boundaries of national states and with them nationalism and statism were rendered obsolete by the very expansion of the international capitalist system that they deplored. For Chinese and Japanese Marxists observing nationalism and even a large measure of racialist orientalism in their Western mentors, however, the resolution of the national question would be far more complex. The Marxist theory of the state with all its ambiguities would constitute the point of departure for undertaking their own efforts to resolve the national question in all its elements for themselves and their compatriots. The contributions of their theoretical predecessors in the Marxist movement alone, however, would not dictate the outcome of their endeavors. Indigenous Chinese and Japanese perspectives on the nation and the state would also render a decisive influence on their judgments.

The Encounter

INDIGENOUS PERSPECTIVES AND THE INTRODUCTION

OF MARXISM

AT THE TURN of the twentieth century, Otto Bauer took note of the various imprints that "national character" had made on Marxism as the doctrine moved through Europe: "Anyone who compares German Marxism, English Laborism, and Russian Bolshevism cannot overlook the fact that the national cultural heritage impresses a national form upon the international socialist ideology. The nearer the working class of a country comes to taking power, the more must it adapt its practices and methods of struggle to the national peculiarities of the battlefield. Similarly, the socialist ideology of the working class becomes more closely linked with the national cultural heritage, as it absorbs more culture."[1] In very general terms, Bauer contrasted the logical, deductive, and abstractionist tendencies of the French with the concrete, practical, and empirical proclivities of the English "national characters." With much more specificity, it is possible to identify the impact of culture as reflected in indigenous frameworks of political thought upon the shape of the Marxist theory of the state and nation as it was transplanted into China and Japan. As Bauer's comments suggest, this impact could have been made both consciously and unconsciously: consciously, as part of the endeavor to render the theory more palatable and more applicable in the new environment, and unconsciously, as indigenous modes of thinking about politics constituted the conceptual lenses through which Chinese and Japanese intellectuals interpreted and reinterpreted Marxist thought.

The great issues posed by the Marxist theory of the state—the relationship between the state and nation, the dual conception of the state in Marx and Engels, and the fate of the nation and state during and after Marxian socialist revolution— left considerable margin for variation in this process of adaptation. The salient differences among the ideas of Marx, Lenin, and Mao on these issues have led scholars of Marxism to different conclusions in response to the question, "How much change and adaptation can be accommodated within the framework of Marxism without the resulting thought system losing its original 'Marxian' character?"[2] Many have construed the bounds of legitimate or "proper" Marxism so narrowly that the innovations made by Russian, Chinese, and Japanese Marxists in adjusting Marxist theory to their own national contexts can only be regarded as illegitimate. Particularly because it might be infected with doubts about the ability of non-European thinkers and activists to "understand" Marxism, such a narrow construction tends to dismiss the contributions that indigenous perspectives might have to offer to socialist thought in general.[3] It also neglects the impacts that national character or political culture has exercised on Marxism in Western Europe itself. The European examples of the nationalistic remolding of Marxian ideas into national- and state-socialist thought in France at the turn of the twentieth century[4] and in Germany and Italy in the 1930s and 1940s[5] demonstrate that the kinds of adaptations that one finds with respect to the nation and the state in non-European Marxist systems are neither unique to these contexts nor mere distortions caused by the inadequate comprehension of their creators.

Rather, the European cases illuminate three major elements that influenced the manner in which Marxists, generally, and Chinese and Japanese Marxists, in particular, have responded to the national question: (1) their concrete historical circumstances domestically and internationally, particularly the timing and circumstances of the emergence of unified centralized states in these societies; (2) the content of the Marxism that was introduced in their societies; and (3) indigenous philosophical traditions, which comprised ingredients that could be integrated into and recombined with aspects of their Marxism. The German case is most suggestive of the significance of the interaction between contextual elements, on the one hand, and pre-Marxist philosophical traditions on the other. The quest to unify all people of German ethnic origin in a single centralized national state centuries after the same had been accomplished by England and France led to the emergence of a heavily antiliberal mode of political thought. This pattern resulted from both the historical origins of German nationalism in reaction against the French Revolution and Bismarck's rapid industrial revolution from above that left many traditional social forms intact.[6] The articulation of Hegel's notion of the state as the height of human development marked the apogee of this tendency early in the nineteenth century. It was followed by the formulation of German theories of state sovereignty that would influence late-nineteenth-century state building in Japan, the emergence of National Bolshevism in the 1910s,[7] and, finally, German National Socialism in the 1930s. Adaptations of Marxism made in the same context of the late nineteenth and early twentieth centuries underscore the significance of domestic and international forces combined on philosophical discourse. In Germany as well as in France, an intense nationalistic reaction emerged against the rationalist Enlightenment tradition that had produced bourgeois democracy, which to many threatened to vitiate the power of nations that needed to be strong.[8]

The international setting for this development, which affected both European and non-European thinkers, was the intensification of nineteenth-century imperialism and the military-cum-economic competitiveness of the international system. This circumstance, particularly in its coincidence with the popularization of social Darwinism, bore momentous implications for the relationship between Marxism and nationalism. Marx himself had been heavily influenced by the English naturalist Charles Darwin's (1809–1882) "epoch-making work on the origin of species"[9] both in his view of history as a dialectical evolutionary process propelled by conflict and in his critique of capitalist society. Darwin's *Origin of the Species* (1859) depicted "natural selection" in the world of plants and animals as the process by which species, in a continuous struggle for existence, exhibited variations that helped them survive. These were passed along to the offspring of the survivors from one generation to the next. In the latter part of the century, Herbert Spencer, who coined the term *survival of the fittest*, and Thomas Huxley applied Darwin's observations to human society and popularized the notion of social Darwinism. For many observing the rise of fierce international competition over the century, the social Darwinist paradigm seemed an apt description of their world. Such a social application of Darwinism had already been evident in Marx's dialectical materialism, particularly as it applied to relations among classes within individual, especially capitalist, societies. But in the Marxism systematized by Engels in the late 1870s and widely disseminated in introductory Marxist pamphlets, the connection between conflict within society and the escalating strife among national states was clear. Competition among capitalists, Engels wrote, "as between whole industries and whole countries," "is the Darwinian struggle for individual existence, transferred from Nature to society with intensified fury." Here, as in nature, "advantages in natural or artificial conditions of production decide life or death."[10] The Darwinian analogy of the violent international order to the continuous struggle for existence in the natural world was attractive to many who felt their own nations threatened with destruction through war. In this setting, national differences came to assert themselves in a manner that contested the preeminence of the class distinctions stressed in Marxist orthodoxy, and they evoked a response characteristic of both Marxists and non- or anti-Marxists. Applying the social Darwinist elements of the Marxian analysis of domestic class struggle to the international sphere, French and German thinkers evolved systems of national and state socialist thought that confounded the distinctions conventionally drawn between left and right on the political spectrum.

This complex relationship between social Darwinism and Marxism—Marx's intellectual debt to Darwin coupled with his critique of the capitalist system that epitomized the notion of the "survival of the fittest"—enhanced the appeal of Marxism in China and Japan. Chinese and Japanese intellectuals became acquainted with Darwinism through translations of the work of Spencer and Huxley during the critical decade between the Sino-Japanese (1894–1895) and Russo-Japanese wars (1904–1905). In radical student circles, social Darwinism soon became the dominant paradigm for understanding the Western international system that now embraced their societies. In China, "traditional xenophobia and Sinocentrism" were combined with "new concepts of nationalism and Darwinian struggle" to produce a "tendency to see the world in racial terms." Determination that China be strong enough to escape enslavement and then extinction at the hands of the Western powers fueled the revolutionary drive to overthrow the alien Manchu dynasty.[11] In Japan, the Darwinist analogy also prevailed. Japan's intermediate position in the international order encouraged both an antistatism repudiating its implications and an aggressive nationalism among Japanese in the left-wing movement.[12] In both instances, the popular attraction to the Darwinist elements of Marxism underlines the significance that indigenous philosophical traditions— some of which conflicted fundamentally with the views of man and nature reflected in social Darwinism and Marxism—held for Chinese and Japanese adaptations of Marxism. These indigenous traditions must be taken into account alongside historical and geographical contexts if one is to comprehend adequately how Chinese and Japanese Marxists addressed the national question in the twentieth century. I begin by examining the philosophical conceptions of men and women as individuals and people in society and the relationships between society and state and between the nation and the state. The presence or absence of these conceptual distinctions in China and Japan before the introduction of Marxist political thought constitutes an important clue to the manner in which Chinese and Japanese Marxists would treat Marx's theory of the state.

NATION AND STATE IN PRE-MARXIAN JAPANESE ORTHODOXY

A coherent body of "traditional"[13] Japanese political thought in the Meiji period can be identified readily because the Meiji leadership articulated an official state philosophy that was disseminated through a universal educational system.[14] Many elements in that philosophy treated the Japanese polity as unique and, therefore, beyond a Marxist critique of the state in class terms. The incompleteness of the Marxism that was introduced into Japan, the perceived vulnerability of Japan's international situation in the 1920s and 1930s, and orthodox philosophical orientations that valued the state and the nation as organic, supraclass entities with world-historical significance together made it difficult for dissenters, themselves schooled in this orthodoxy, to reject the state and at the same time argue that their crusade for socialism in Japan ultimately rested on a concern with the well-being of Japanese as a people.

In Meiji political orthodoxy, the *tennō*, or *mikado* (emperor), was the pivotal concept, and it explicitly conjoined the notions of nation and state into one. The state, the political organization, absorbed the nation, the ethnic community or society in general, in the traditional Japanese elements that were incorporated into this thought. The tennō was at the apex of both, as the patriarchal head of the unique Japanese *kokutai* (national entity, or national body politic) incorporating race, ethnicity, lineage, spirituality, and political order into a single concept, and as the potentate of a constitutional monarchic form of state (*seitai*). Within the context of the militaristic international system to which the Meiji Restoration itself was a response, the tennō was at once "(1) a constitutional monarch, the monarch of an authoritarian state as established by the Meiji Constitution granted by the emperor; (2) the generalissimo (*daigenshi*), . . . [who held supreme] authority over the armed forces, independent from the control of the cabinet; and (3) a monarch of divine right, representing religious or spiritual authority [analogous to] . . . that of the West's Christianity."[15]

This concept of the imperial system as it evolved after the Meiji Restoration was heavily influenced by German constitutional scholars: Rudolf von Gneist, Lorenz von Stein, Albert Mosse, Karl Rudolph, Hermann Roesler, Georg Jellinek, Johann Kaspar Bluntschli, and Hermann Schulze. Roesler was the only one actually to serve in Japan, working with Itō Hirobumi from 1878 to 1893. Gneist, Stein, and Mosse were important inspirations during Itō's study in Europe in 1882, and Inoue

Kowashi (1844–1895) was heavily influenced by the doctrine of state sovereignty of Hermann Schulze.[16] The theory of state sovereignty that came to be so significant in Meiji Japan, however, was first introduced through Katō Hiroyuki's partial translation of Bluntschli's *Allgemeines Staatsrecht* (Universal right of state, translated as *Ippan kokuhō-gaku*). Completed between 1871 and 1875, this was the first translation of German legal theory in Japan. In all, Katō produced three such partial translations, which he viewed as the essence of Bluntschli's thought—"his organic theory of state sovereignty" as "a 'modernistic' theory of constitutional monarchical sovereignty" applicable to Japan's immediate practical political needs.[17] Bluntschli held a psycho-organic conception of the state, in which the state was a masculine body politic analogous to the feminine body of the Christian church. In this idea, Katō saw a humanistic interpretation of the state, a constitutional rather than an absolutist form of monarchy that he adopted as his own. By personifying the state, this combination of a theory of state sovereignty (*kokka-shuken*) with an organic theory permitted the reconciliation of the notions of sovereignty residing in the state and sovereignty residing in the monarch. It thus enabled Meiji leaders to maintain traditional Japanese notions of imperial leadership in an organic body politic to be incorporated into what Meiji leaders regarded as a modern Western conception of the state. Repudiating the dangerous implications of popular sovereignty, this new construction of the state granted the emperor the right to promulgate a constitution,[18] and Article 1 of the new constitution, in turn, defined the emperor as the locus of sovereignty. Other German scholars, including Stein and Gneist, shared this view of strong imperial sovereignty and a weak Diet and party system. It meshed quite comfortably with Gneist's organic conception, which posited the tennō (mikado) as the head of the body politic, the locus of intuition (*ryōchi*), thought (*isō*), and will (*shinshi*), and the people as limbs or appendages.[19]

It was Roesler, however, who exerted the greatest influence in formulating the emperor's position in the Meiji Constitution. For Roesler the emperor was to play a suprapolitical role that would permit him to transcend the schisms and petty infighting of party politics. This was the position defined for the emperor as the supreme ruler to whom sovereignty was ascribed as he was identified in Article 1 of the Meiji Constitution. As Joseph Pittau has argued, however, in fact, "[t]he mythological implications which Roesler did not accept but which were [also] clearly expressed in article one of the constitution were the basis of denying in practice to the emperor all political power and all active involvement in the decision-making powers of government." The emperor had not played an active political role for the preceding three centuries of Japanese history anyway, and because of the mythology of his and his ancestors' divine origins,[20] he could remain a passive legitimizing figure under the provisions of Article 1.

This is but one instance of the divergence between perceptions of German constitutional advisors, on the one hand, and the interpretations by Japanese leaders such as Itō and Inoue, on the other, concerning the nature of the imperial institution and its potential political role. As a practical matter, "Japanese leaders were mainly interested in the *political* theories of the German scholars" rather than in the social reformism that underlay the ideas of men such as Stein[21] and Roesler.[22] Indigenous thought on the imperial institution reinforced a certain conservatism among Japanese theorists and political leaders, who rejected the liberal elements in the thoughts of these influential German constitutional scholars.[23] This was apparent in attitudes among activists in the Japanese civil rights movement (*jiyū minken undō*). Liberal civil rights advocates such as Ueki Emori (1857–1892) contested the "irrationality" of the monarchy and denied the existence of the tennō itself until about 1880. After 1882, however, such arguments gradually disappeared from the pronouncements of these thinkers, and the legitimate existence of the tennō became the premise for their advocacy of "constitutional democracy."[24] This tendency to appreciate the uniqueness of the *kokutai*, albeit more pronounced after the 1880s, was a constant in the thought of the Meiji Enlightenment leader Fukuzawa Yukichi. Fukuzawa "initially subscribed enthusiastically to natural law and rejected the notion that Japan's *kokutai* was somehow unique,"[25] but by the 1880s, his writings nonetheless underscored the centrality of the imperial institution to the Japanese body politic, contending that the imperial institution could "control the world of human feelings and preserve habits of virtue and righteousness" as mere law could not.[26] The Imperial Household was "our country's greatest treasure"; it—no longer Western science (as in his early writings)—was the "center of civilization and enlightenment." For Fukuzawa, the "majesty and sacredness" of the imperial institution would give Japan the strength in national unity it required to prevail over the Western powers.[27]

Influenced by the mystical elements of this tennō idea, Fukuzawa and other Meiji thinkers shared a conception of Japan that collapsed state and nation into one. That which defined orthodoxy is illuminated by those who dissented from it, such as Ueki and Katō Hiroyuki in his early years. Such liberal thinkers, inspired by Western social contract theorists who advocated natural right, distinguished society from the state, and questioned the origins of legitimate rule, challenged orthodoxy by distinguishing the *kokutai* concept from the idea of *seitai*. Whereas in the *kokutai* the emperor was characterized as the locus of sovereignty as well as the symbol of the Japanese ethnos, the seitai, or form of government, was said to represent "the form in which sovereignty is exercised."[28] Such a precise differentiation was not tenable within the framework of the Meiji state orthodoxy, however, for the construal of *kokutai* as monarchical absolutism insisted that the distinctively Japanese conception of the tennō caused *kokutai* to incorporate a specific seitai as well. Only one form of state was possible, and that was prescribed by the *kokutai* notion itself. It is in this sense that the Peace Preservation Law of 1925 came to be directed against those who intended "to alter the *kokutai*" by advocating any—liberal democratic, socialist, or other—alternative set of political arrangements.[29] This *kokutai* idea was systematized vigorously in the late Meiji era and again in the 1930s with the appearance of the *Kokutai no hongi* text for educators in 1937 as part of the effort to unify the country for war.[30]

The concept of the emperor in *kokutai* was not new, however, and, indeed, its spiritual and ethnic elements can be traced back to Tokugawa political thought. During the Edo period, real political power lay with the shogunate rather than with the emperor; but the tennō remained throughout a symbolic figure whose authority was maintained through the Shintō mythology of his divine origins and his position as head of the extended Japanese national (ethnic) family. The Tokugawa complex of Confucian, Shintō, and new scholastic attitudes toward the emperor nurtured the tennō-centered *kokutai*, or family-state, orthodoxy of the Meiji Restoration. This continuity goes far to explain the conceptual unity of the ideas of nation and state in the late Meiji, Taishō, and early Shōwa periods. This congruity was integral to the more authoritarian nationalistic state theory attributing sovereignty to the emperor himself (*tennō shuken ron*) of Uesugi Shinkichi and Kakei Katsuhiko as well as to the liberal state sovereignty theorists such as Minobe Tatsukichi.

The writings of the authoritarian school reflect the relationship between state building and nation building that contemporary scholars have observed in Europe as well. But the roots of *kokutai* thought had already emerged in the Tokugawa era, "which represented a considerable step forward in the generalization and extension of [state] power in Japan, but . . . did not succeed in creating a rationalized and unified power structure such as that of the Meiji Period." The emergence of critical indigenous philosophical bases of Meiji orthodoxy in the Tokugawa era, however, marked the production of a strong Japanese national consciousness. This process would occur through a dialectical relationship between the acceptance of key Chinese Confucian tenets and the assertion of Japaneseness. In Tokugawa feudalism, *kuni* (country) referred to the *han* or feudal domain; and a great deal of political freedom was left to *tozama* (outside lords or non-Tokugawa daimyo).[31] "Ieyasu and his successors were thoroughly convinced of the fact that a despotic Government is only secure when it guards jealously the minds of the rising generation against the adoption of notions calculated to promote the subversion of authority." Thus, in a measure that foreshadowed the Meiji Imperial Rescript on Education, the Tokugawa regime adopted the Shuki (neo-Confucianist, or Zhuxi) philosophy as the country's official philosophy. Under the influence of such scholars as Fujiwara Seika (1561–1619) and Hayashi Razan (1583–1657) it became the ethical basis for early Tokugawa education and law.[32] Like the critical and more practical Yōmei school (of Wang Yangming), this Shuki Confucianism underwent changes in adaptation to the Japanese environment. Japanese Kogakuha (Ancient School of Philosophy) thinkers such as Yamaga Sokō (1622–1685), Itō Jinsai (1627–1705), and Butsu (Ogyū) Sorai (1666–1728) rejected the quietism of the Shuki school in favor of more aggressive activism, whereas the Yōmei school combined Wang Yangming's teaching with native Shintō and "identified itself with State interests."[33] "For the next hundred years the most vital political thought in Japan [the Kokugaku and the Mito schools] would represent a conscious effort to elevate Japanese ideas over Chinese."[34] The Chinese Confucian terms "*shūshin, seika, chikoku, heitenka*"—that rulers should first cultivate their own morality, make their own homes peaceful, govern the kuni, and then govern all under the heavens, in that order—constituted central precepts. Ogyū Sorai's thought illustrates the acute tension between universal and nativist aspects of thought in this period of burgeoning national self-consciousness. He departed dramatically from this emphasis when he pioneered an iconoclastic quest for philosophy of national political unity from mid-Tokugawa.[35] Yet Sorai remained very much within the Chinese tradition, exhibiting an ambivalence tending toward negativism vis-à-vis Japan's peculiarities.[36]

By contrast, the Kokugaku (National Learning) school sought to establish Japanese political unity on the basis of internal "national-ist" (*minzoku-teki*) sentiment.[37] As its appellation would suggest, the Kokugaku school emerged in reaction against the predominance of Chinese learning and endeavored to establish the preeminence of Japan's own indigenous history, literature, and institutions. The school's pioneers, Kada no Azumamaro (1669–1736), Kamo Mabuchi (1697–1769), Motoori Norinaga (1730–1801), and Hirata Atsutane (1776–1843), studied such ancient Japanese manuscripts as the *Man'yōshū* and championed a "pure Shintō" "on the assumption that the Japanese character was naturally pure, requiring only the removal of besmirching foreign influences to permit it once more to shine forth in splendor."[38] It is not surprising that out of such a glorification of things Japanese, a new emphasis on the emperor should emerge in the form of the *sonnō ron* (the injunction to revere the emperor).[39] Similarly, the Mito school, which developed contemporaneously yet independently of the Kokugaku school, shared the Kokugaku appreciation of things specifically Japanese. "The ideal pattern of government ethics, and morality had [always] been the peculiar possession of Japan" in the view of Mito scholars. The eternal Japanese emperor system was superior to other monarchies for Mito scholars, who "criticize[d] the Chinese for changing their dynasties, and Mencius for his advocacy of the so-called right of revolution." Moreover, again like the Kokugaku school, Mito theorists declined to incorporate Buddhism into their political thought,[40] preferring, under the leadership of Tokugawa Mitsukuni (Mito Mitsukuni, or Giko, 1628–1700), to combine Shuki-gaku Confucianism with Shintō. In Mito teachings, "the heart of Chu Hsi's ethical teaching—loyalty resulting from recognition of inherent duty—was reinterpreted in terms of Shintō belief, on the basis of the *shinchoku* of Amaterasu, as demanding undeviating and eternal loyalty to the Heavenly Sun Succession of the imperial house—and this was equated with filial piety. It was in other words, the theory of *kokutai*."[41]

The Mito school and its doctrine of *kokutai* exercised a much greater influence than the Kokugaku school on the subsequent evolution of Japanese political thought. In practical terms, the impact of Mito scholars was tremendous, for its coupling of the *jōi* (expel the barbarians) slogan with its call for *sonnō* contributed directly to the pressures on the Tokugawa shogunate that led to the emperor-centered Meiji Restoration.[42] Its mixture of traditional Confucian values with nativist Shintō ideas formed the kernel of the family-state idea of *kokutai* thought although the latter was fully incorporated only in the late Meiji as a response to Westernizing tendencies that were felt to threaten indigenous Japanese institutions.

In the middle and late Meiji period, two schools of thought evolved from the ideas that influenced the drafting of the Meiji Constitution. It will be recalled that the notion of state sovereignty had been borrowed from German state theory. An effective antidote to notions of popular sovereignty, it was, nonetheless, not uncongenial to other interpretations antithetical to those of Hozumi Yatsuka and Uesugi Shinkichi, constitutional scholars who emphasized the unique nature of Japan's emperor. Thus, following the organic state theories of Bluntschli and his successors, the constitutional scholar Minobe Tatsukichi argued that the Japanese emperor should be treated in constitutional law on the same basis as all national monarchs. Minobe formulated his emperor-organ theory on that premise. The state was sovereign, according to Minobe, and the emperor as a legal person was its highest organ. In this view, the power to rule was shared between the emperor and the Diet.[43] Uesugi articulated a more nationalistic and authoritarian view that sovereignty (*taiken*) resided not in the state but in the emperor.[44] It is noteworthy that this controversy evolved as purely constitutional legal discourse on Article 1 of the Meiji Constitution. Political theory that would question the origins of legitimate rule was not open to discussion during the consolidation of the Meiji national state efforts.[45] Indeed, the similarities between the two major schools illustrate an underlying consensus on the nature of the tennō: neither Minobe nor Uesugi questioned the Shintō mythology of the origins of the emperor's rule. Unlike Western social contract theorists, or even Mencius in the Chinese Confucian tradition, the account of the origin of the state offered in the *kokutai* orthodoxy provided no basis for the legitimate contestation of existing rule, for there was no state separate from society and no society constituted without the state. Thus, even Minobe's more liberal argument proceeded from the imperial institution in its existing form with its mystical power as a given, just as Uesugi's and Hozumi's views did. The difference was that in the orthodoxy of the latter, the absolutism of the imperial authority was natural and positive.[46]

The divergence between Minobe and Uesugi can be explained by the text of the Meiji Constitution itself. The constitutional scholar Ukai Nobushige once noted that Article 1 of the Meiji Constitution granting sovereignty (*tōchiken*) to the emperor, in fact, contained a dual conception of the emperor. The constitution postulated authoritarian monarchic elements—positing the emperor as subject (*shutai*) and the people as objects of governance—that could be construed to interpret, as Uesugi did, the powers of the emperor in the broadest possible sense. At the same time, the constitution did provide for a limited constitutional monarchy, designating the Diet "as an organ representing the people as one of the ruling organs" of the state. The latter allowed a narrower construction of imperial power such as in Minobe's emperor-organ theory.[47] For a time, from roughly the turn of the twentieth century to the early 1930s, Minobe's interpretation gained considerable influence in academic circles and was uncontested by the government.[48] The ease with which the theory and Minobe himself were crushed by a Diet resolution of censure in 1935,[49] however, testifies to the underlying power of the family-state *kokutai* conception in Japanese political thought through the 1920s and 1930s.[50] Indeed, as educational texts indicate, by 1910 something of a reaction against the legalistic national-state of the Western conception had already become evident in Japan. In 1903, school textbooks emphasized the theme of *chūkun-aikoku* (loyalty to the monarch and patriotism toward the state). This was supplanted in 1910 by the theme of the unity of loyalty with filial piety in Japanese sentiment toward the emperor.[51]

Kokutai, then, with its admixture of distinctively Japanese and Confucian elements, may be regarded as the mainstream Meiji orthodoxy, the backdrop against which Marxist ideas were introduced at the turn of the twentieth century. As Ishida Takeshi's classic study described this family conception of the state (*kazoku kokka*), it was an organic theory in which the Japanese nation was conceived to be a natural extension of the family. In an organic conception of the state, the political community exists before its members, who are simply born into it. In this sense, the *kokutai* notion constituted for the Meiji oligarchs the quintessential noble lie as Socrates described it in Plato's *Republic*—"some one noble lie to persuade, in the best case, even the rulers, but if not them, the rest" of the community that they belong to the polity and that the hierarchy of ruler and ruled was legitimate and just. Here the Shintō elements in the concept of the *kokutai* were crucial. The Japanese people, according to these Shintō components, would believe themselves descended, through the emperor, from the Sun Goddess, just as the people of Socrates' putative city-state would believe that at one time "they were under the earth within, being fashioned and reared themselves, and their arms and other tools being crafted. When the job had been completely finished, then the earth, which is their mother, sent them up. And now, as though the land they were in were a mother and a nurse, they must plan for and defend it, if anyone attacks, and they must think of the other citizens as brothers and born of the earth." The organic origin of the Greeks legitimated acceptance of the existing hierarchy of political rule, according to Plato: "The god, in fashioning those of you who are competent to rule, mixed gold in at their birth," whereas others were born with the "admixture of bronze or iron."[52] Similarly, the *kokutai* idea offered a basis for acceptance of the hierarchy of Japanese society that had emerged on the basis of relative proximity to the emperor figure at the apex of the family-nation. This helped to legitimate Japanese feelings of cultural superiority vis-à-vis other Asian peoples.[53]

This analogy is not to gainsay the significance of original Confucian philosophical notions, such as the cultivation of virtue in loyalty to the monarch and filial piety in the properly constituted Confucian family in the *kokutai* formulation.[54] These underwent a subtle but deeply significant transformation in their migration from China to Meiji Japan under the influence of the Shintō elements. In the *kokutai*, these potentially conflicting values reinforced one another. The unity of filial piety and political loyalty in support of the imperial household was described in the Shōwa text, *Kokutai no hongi*, as follows:

> In our country filial piety is a way of the highest importance. Filial piety originates with one's family as its basis, and in its larger sense has the nation for its foundation. Filial piety directly has for its object one's parents but in its relationship toward the Emperor finds a place within loyalty.
>
> Filial piety in our country has its true characteristics in its perfect conformity with our national entity by heightening still further the relationship between morality and

nature. Our country is a great family nation, and the Imperial Household is the head family of the subjects and the nucleus of national life. The subjects revere the Imperial Household, which is the head family, with the tender esteem [they have] for their ancestors; and the Emperor loves his subjects as his very own.[55]

This unity of loyalty to the emperor with filial piety the late Tokugawa thinker Yoshida Shōin argued was uniquely Japanese: "'It is only in our country that sovereign and subject are united, and that loyalty and filial piety converge'."[56]

The communitarian elements of this family concept of the state would seem to make Japanese intellectuals who subscribed to it more receptive to socialism, and, indeed, despite the social hierarchy affirmed in the *kokutai* myth, in the early days of Japanese socialism, many would discern no disharmony between socialism and the communitarian *kokutai*.[57] Nevertheless, the particularism[58] of the *kokutai* idea was incompatible with the universalism of Western socialism. Inoue Tetsujirō, a philosophy professor at Tokyo Imperial University, and "other 'national morality' spokesmen" explicitly contended that the universality of the Western doctrine violated the Japanese *kokutai*.[59] Furthermore, Japanese spokesmen for the *kokutai* idea, such as those who penned the *Kokutai no hongi*, were emphatic on the difference between their Japanese perspective on man and society and Western philosophical views premised on egoistic individualism.

> The individualistic explanation of human beings abstracts only one aspect of an individuality and overlooks the national and historical qualities. Hence, it loses sight of the totality and concreteness of human beings and deviates from the reality of human existence. . . . The nations of the West have now awakened up to these errors ["of individualism, liberalism, and their developments"] and movements have sprung up in order to overcome them. Nevertheless, these ideologies and movements will eventually end in regarding the collections of people as bodies or classes, or at the most in conceiving a conceptual state; so that such things will do no more than provide erroneous ideas to take the place of existing erroneous ideas, and will furnish no true way out or solution.[60]

Marxism, with its emphasis on class and the conceptual state, was clearly one such response to Western individualism. Was this "solution" required where rampant individualism and materialism had not produced the terrible consequences that it had wrought in the West? This was a pressing issue for Japanese who were drawn to Western socialism in its Marxian form. Marxism-Leninism's emphasis on class conflict threatened to destroy the presumed harmony of traditional Japanese society, tearing the *kokutai* itself asunder.

VIEWS OF THE POLITY IN TRADITIONAL CHINESE THOUGHT

I have spoken of the conceptual state in relation to the idea of the nation. In Meiji Japan, such a purely abstract notion of the state was inconceivable, for the *kokutai* notion allowed for no separation of the two. Much later, in the 1930s, *tenkōsha—*

apostates from the Communist party who reaffirmed their loyalty to the motherland—would illustrate vividly the continued vitality of the *kokutai* idea and the profound impact of the sentimental and quasi-religious ties that bound Japanese educated in Meiji orthodoxy to that imagined community.[61] The native Japanese Shintō concept of an organic polity nurtured the conflation of nation and state in Japan, but it was not alone in doing so. The Confucianism that Japanese borrowed from China likewise offered no conceptual distinction between state and society. *Tianxia* (all under Heaven, or *tenka* in Japanese) was a cultural rather than a political abstraction. As a result, in striking contrast to the West, the state existed as a purely political notion in neither China nor Japan until it was introduced forcibly by the interstate system of the Western powers.[62] Despite this basic similarity and shared philosophical influences, however, there were important divergences between the Chinese and Japanese Confucian systems as political doctrines and between the intellectual milieus into which Marxism was introduced early in the twentieth century.

While establishment intellectuals in Meiji Japan endeavored to mobilize nationalistic sentiment around the transcendent value of the *kokutai* to consolidate gains made in Meiji state building, Chinese political thinkers were in complete disarray. Meiji thinkers systematized an effective national myth drawing syncretically on indigenous Shintō, Japanized Confucian, and Western philosophical elements. Chinese Confucian orthodoxy, however, was dissolving under the force of domestic unrest and the Western onslaught. Most crippling in China's troubled new circumstances was indecision about how best to resist the new challenges posed by the postindustrial revolution Western powers. Could the incursion of Western values—chief among them the primacy of material wealth and military power[63]—be met without sacrificing what many establishment scholar gentry saw as the essence of China's superior civilization? Historically, the empire had always absorbed alien "barbarians," supplanting their cultures and ensuring the continuity of the tianxia of Chinese civilization even when conquered militarily. Thus, it was natural that the first recourse of intellectuals of China's governing elite should have been to distinguish firmly between China's ti (essence) and yong (the application of Western technology) to justify using the latter to defend the former. The fragile dichotomy allowed the "self-strengthening" leaders of the Tongzhi Restoration to undertake industrializing reforms to bolster China's national wealth and military strength while preserving Chinese normative philosophy intact. Japanese were certainly sensitive to such a distinction between native and imported contributions to their society, but Japan's historic syncretic experience reassured them that the admixture of Japanese with imported elements could reliably produce a superior product. Chinese intellectuals diverged prominently from this pattern. As I have noted elsewhere, "the very notion that Western technological advances could be emulated without allowing the philosophical perspectives and moral values that undergirded them to disturb the existing pattern of Chinese values also effectively deterred China's reformers from undertaking the kind of creative ideological manipulation that the Meiji oligarchs used so successfully." As a result, when a myriad of technical reforms showed the ti-yong formulation to be untenable, a younger generation of frustrated intellectuals repudiated the entire orthodox Confucian framework in a wave of cultural iconoclasm, and the "legitimacy of the entire Confucian constellation of values came to be challenged."[64]

This challenge emerged first among scholars trained within China's own Confucian tradition. The 1890s reform efforts in China were pioneered by Kang Youwei (1858–1927) and Liang Qichao (1873–1929), both students and purveyors of that tradition. Emphasizing the Confucian ideal of *datong* (the Great Harmony) and the need to cultivate virtue, they elaborated constitutionalist alternatives to bolster the failing Qing dynasty. Kang posited Confucius himself as a reformer who had sought to mitigate human suffering by devising institutions that were suitable for the world of Disorder (*luan*) in his time. Whereas Confucius had been constrained by the environment in which he lived, Kang aspired to extend his insights to develop institutions appropriate for the era of Universal Peace (*taiping*) and the Great Unity to which humankind aspired.[65] Writing in the 1890s, Kang supported his utopian Confucian vision by offering a reinterpretation of Confucianism that would support institutional reforms of the sort that had been inconceivable two decades earlier at the time of the Tongzhi Restoration. It is important to note, however, that as radical as Kang's reinterpretation of Confucianism was, his own initiatives vis-à-vis the government were strictly reformist in a narrowly delimited sense. As his efforts in the 1898 Reform movement indicated, Kang saw values and practices in Western civilization that could be transplanted to China fruitfully, and he envisaged a gradual planned cultural synthesis between Chinese and Western civilizations. Thus, Kang posed a radical alternative to the earlier ti-yong dichotomy, which was being stubbornly maintained in the antiradical treatise *Quan xue pian* (Exhortation to study) published by Tongzhi Restoration leader Zhang Zhidong in 1898 to protest the reforms. Determined to eliminate the corruption and misuse of authority that he felt vitiated the Qing monarchy, Kang was impressed with the utility of Western-style parliaments as a major tool for correcting such abuses, and aside from urging the establishment of Western-style schools, he advocated the implementation of parliamentary government in China.[66] Nevertheless, although it was perceived as radical in 1898, Kang's reformism always remained strictly within the framework of the Qing monarchy, and he so vehemently opposed republicanism that he participated in an effort at "monarchical restoration" as late as 1923.[67]

Almost immediately after the failure of his 1898 Reform movement and his flight to exile in Japan, Kang's reformism was superseded by republican and revolutionary efforts that no longer saw any need to salvage either the Qing or Confucianism itself. Liang Qichao, Kang's more radical student, asserted that Kang's revisionism had helped to undermine Confucianism as a basis for Chinese political activism. As intellectual historian Xiao Gongquan has noted, "In casting doubt on the authenticity of the Old Text classics, [Kang] unintentionally opened wide the door to questioning the validity of the entire Confucian tradition." Liang, thus, took Kang's moderate reformism much further and started a movement for wholesale cultural transformation that called into question the entire value of Confucianism. Unlike Japanese leaders of the Meiji Restoration, Liang saw no merit in preserving indigenous philosophical traditions, asserting that "'there is much in Confucianism that is unsuitable for the new world'."[68] After escaping to Tokyo following the ill-fated 1898 Hundred Days Reform movement, Liang led an increasingly radical effort to establish a republican form of government. His early call for a revolution against the Manchus brought rebuke from Kang but found sympathetic ears among young Chinese thinker-activists such as Sun Yat-sen, Huang Xing, and Zhang Ji inside China and studying abroad in Japan.[69] Soon, Chinese students subscribed to societies such as Huang's Huaxinghui (Society to Revive China) and then Sun's Tongmenghui, which built on anti-Manchu sentiment to advocate revolutionary change that went far beyond Liang's moderate republicanism.

Liang's approach made a synthesis of indigenous and imported values, such as the amalgam in the *kokutai* conception in Japan, nearly impossible. Repudiating the Confucian-Mencian concept of the polity as the product of a heavenly mandate,[70] Liang called to replace the Confucian "old thinking with new learning" to build a new China. Ironically, as Yü-sheng Lin has noted, the "totalistic iconoclasm" of the May Fourth period to which Liang contributed emerged directly out of Confucian perspectives on man in society. In this Weltanschauung, the key to any change lay in the fundamental change of "worldview": Without transforming the "symbols, values, and beliefs" of the Chinese people, in this view, true reform was not possible.[71] Liang drew on this perspective to advocate a new sense of public-mindedness that would support constitutional republican government in China. This project alone would enable China to contest effectively the domination of the West.[72] Other scholars who would become known as the *guocui* (national essence) school, reacted vehemently against what they saw as the increasing vitiation of their national traditions by Kang and then by more radical intellectuals who became apostates from Confucianism. Against their reformist and radical iconoclasm, the guocui school accentuated the transcendent value of China's ancient philosophical tradition and sought its revitalization.[73]

The response of Chinese intellectuals to the Western idea and reality of stateness, then, ranged from a full iconoclastic reaction against Confucianism, which became increasingly pronounced after the demise of the Qing dynasty in 1911, to an effort to combine tradition with Western theories, to an extreme conservative desire to preserve Confucianism as the Chinese cultural or national essence.[74] This Chinese diversity in response to the intellectual and practical dilemmas posed by the Western intrusion shared a kind of historical continuity with the more unified and coherent response in Japan, which combined neo-Confucian with native Shintō and imported legalist components. In Japan, Confucianism was identified with the essence of Chinese political thought, but, in fact, Confucianism constituted only one of at least three separate strands of pre-Marxist Chinese philosophy—Confucianism, Daoism, and Legalism. These offered what Xiao has identified as three accounts of the origins of government in Chinese political thought, embodying approving, disapproving, and compromising attitudes toward political authority. Confucianists, along with Mohists, shared the mandate of Heaven (*tianming*) interpretation that appears to have originated in the *Shijing*

(Book of poetry) and *Shujing* (Book of history). This key notion was passed down
from the Qin (221–206 B.C.) and Han (206 B.C.–A.D. 220) eras. Theorists such as
Dong Zhongshu and Wang Fu argued that a prince arose in accordance with the
dictates of heaven lest evil tendencies and chaos (*luan*) prevail. This account is
comparable in many respects to the divine right of kings doctrine in the West as
developed by Sir Robert Filmer and described in John Neville Figgis's *Divine
Right of Kings*.[75] Unlike Western divine right theorists, however, and, indeed,
unlike the Japanese notion of the divine tennō, the Confucian doctrine never
asserted the extreme argument that a violently evil king was, in fact, legitimately
executing the will of heaven to inflict punishment on his people.[76] On the contrary,
Confucianism, particularly as developed by Mencius, attributed an essential goodness to humankind in general that extended to the commoner as well as to the
monarch. As Lin notes, "Confucius' conception of the highest moral attainment
[*ren*, or benevolence, humanity] consists in the natural and furthest growth of
man's distinctive nature—the perfect cultivation and development, rather than a
generic change, of his nature."[77]

   This premise, in turn, provided the basis for a development analogous to John
Locke's right of revolution, which had emerged as a riposte to the application of
the divine right of kings notion in revolutionary seventeenth-century England.[78]
Like Locke, Mencius (390?–305? B.C.) provided for a limited "right" of revolution when he argued that popular rebellion signaled the withdrawal of the heavenly
mandate from the existing ruler. The elements of Mencius's view never approached the notion of popular sovereignty in the Lockean version of social
contract theory, for the people would never grasp the power to rule and exercise it
themselves. Nor did the elaboration of the antiautocratic Ming-Qing scholar
Huang Zongxi's (1619–1695) arguments that the emperor was bound to serve the
people (on the basis of a passage in the *Li ji* [Book of rites][79] ever become
dominant. Yet Mencius affirmed, "The people are the most important element *in a
nation*; the spirits of the land and grain are the next; the sovereign is the lightest.
Therefore to gain the peasantry is the way to become sovereign."[80] Nevertheless, it
was from Heaven (*tian*) that the king received his mandate or appointment (*ming*)
to rule, Mencius wrote, and Heaven that ultimately made the judgment as to
whether the ruler remained sufficiently virtuous in exercising benevolent rule.[81]
The distinction between the sovereign and the ruled was firm here, and Mencius
insisted that there be a plain division of labor between those who engaged in
physical labor on the one hand, and those who worked with their minds and were
destined to rule like Plato's (427–347 B.C.) philosopher-king, on the other.[82]
Drawing on the *Analects* of Confucius (551–479 B.C.), Mencius averred that the
ends of the emperor's benevolent rule were two-fold: to enable the people to
prosper in their livelihood (agriculture) and to educate them to become virtuous.[83]
The reaction of people to the comportment of the king was the true measure of how
benevolent his rule was and whether he could claim to continue to have the
mandate of Heaven on that basis, Mencius asserted. "Heaven does not speak. It
simply showed its will by [the king's] personal conduct and his conduct of af-

fairs."[84] This will of Heaven was reflected then in the behavior of the monarch's subjects: The result of benevolent rule was that the people drew near to support the throne;[85] while if the sovereign "outrages righteousness" he himself could legitimately be repudiated by his people and slain by his ministers.[86] Such a revolution would reflect the withdrawal of Heaven's mandate to rule from the sovereign.

Mencius's acknowledgment of the fallibility of the ruler and his affirmation of a popular right to rebel stands in stark contrast with the reinterpretations of Confucianism made by the formulators of Japan's new Meiji orthodoxy. The extension of Confucian familial bonds (especially the appeal to *xiao*, filial piety) to the organization of the state (in *zhong*, or loyalty)[87] was never as absolute in the Chinese Confucian tradition as it was in Japan. I have already mentioned the conditionality of the loyalty of the minister to the king in Mencius's thought. By contrast, Japanese Mito scholars denigrated the Mencian theory of revolution in favor of the continuity of their own tennō from generation to generation. The Japanese emperor, as a divine and somewhat mythical figure, could never err or lapse in his benevolent virtue, and popular rebellion was never justified: That the single most important such event—the Meiji Restoration itself—succeeded as an endeavor to restore rule to the tennō underscored this theme. In Japanese Shintō the attribution of divinity, rather than mere divine right, to the emperor resulted in a decisive divergence between the exercise of Confucian values in family and political life in Japan and China. In both societies, the polity was conceptualized as an extension of the family unit. In the words of Feng Youlan, "In traditional Chinese society chung and hsiao were considered the two major values in social relations. A loyal minister and a filial son both commanded universal respect. But this does not mean that hsiao is not the basic moral principle underlying traditional Chinese society. In the transformation mentioned previously [when a man becomes an official in the state] a filial son does not cease to be a filial son. On the contrary, in his new circumstances, this is the only way in which he can continue to be a filial son. . . . [A] son becomes truly filial by being loyal to the sovereign, if that is his duty. So in traditional Chinese society chung or loyalty to the sovereign was considered an extension of hsiao or filial piety, but hsiao could not be considered an extension of chung." Thus, in Confucianism, the Chinese viewed the polity as "'united families'."[88] The Japanese empire, by contrast, was a single strictly hierarchical family. In such a society, no conflict could occur between xiao (*kō*) and zhong (*chū*), for zhong always took precedence: Xiao was simply absorbed within zhong. It may well be suggestive of a more populist tone in the same philosophy in China that such a conflict could indeed occur, and that its resolution must be the opposite: "The point is that, normally, if one chose to join the official rank, one had 'to transform filial piety into loyalty to the sovereign'; but that when these two virtues seriously conflicted it was the duty of the son as a son that should receive first consideration. This is further evidence that the family system was the foundation of traditional Chinese society and filial piety the basis of all its moral principles," wrote Feng.[89] That in China this value placed on the family system could prevail over the loyalty to be shown to the ruler—coupled with the universalist pretensions of Confucian thought—contributed to a philosophical response to the Western threat that weakened the attachment to the imperial state rather than strengthened it, as in Japan.

Confucianism was but one of the three distinct strands of traditional Chinese thought that have been distinguished here. The point is that for Confucius and Mencius, in the original Chinese context, the need for the monarch was divinely mandated by a preexisting "miserable state of nature without order," but that need was tempered by the possibility that the mandate of any given emperor could be revoked. Nevertheless, it is important to stress that this original Confucian view was the most positive attitude toward government among the major three schools of traditional Chinese political thought. The Daoist school of Laozi and Zhuangzi (fourth century B.C.) opposed the negative view of the state of nature held by Confucianists to argue that in antiquity humans had lived in a "pure and honest state of bliss" (*chunpu xiaoyao*).[90] In this Golden Age, "men, like other animals, lived in a state of perfect innocence, without any knowledge of benefit or injury, competition or struggle, lordship or servitude." Human beings were not equal, but invidious distinctions drawn between "the noble and the lowly, the rich and the poor, the ruler and the ruled" did not exist. A natural morality—the *dao* and the *de*—abode among human beings. It was only when kings were established that immorality and human misery arose. As Yuan Ji (210–263) expressed it, "'When kings were instituted, oppression arose; when officials were appointed, robbery began'."[91] Part of the blame for the new state of affairs lay with the sages themselves. "'Annihilation of *Tao* and *Teh* in order to practise benevolence and justice,—this is the error of the sages'," Zhuangzi lamented.[92] How had kings arisen? Here Daoists such as Bao Jingyan (early A.D. fourth century) firmly repudiated the Confucian-Mencian view:

> Confucianists . . . are wont to hold that God created the people and set up kings above them. But did God earnestly declare that He intended to do so? (No, certainly not.) The truth is that among primitive peoples, when the strong dominated over the weak, the latter had to submit to them. When a person with greater cunning played deception on the simple-minded, the latter became his servants. Submission and servitude, these are the conditions under which the relation between ruler and subjects arose. It was the ultimate result of competition by force and wit, and the blue heaven above certainly had nothing to do with it.[93]

Bao and his predecessor Yuan argued that the legendary cruelty of Jie and Zhou of the Xia and Shang dynasties were the fruits of this situation, and for this evil, the self-proclaimed Confucian sages who would simply transfer Heaven's mandate from one individual to another had no remedy.[94] Nor, regrettably, like Rousseau, who much later also mourned the passing of man's blissful state of nature, did these theorists see any recourse out of this dismal state of affairs except to seek to return to the *Dao* themselves through *wuwei* (nonaction).

Between this passive anarchism of the Daoist philosophy and the Mencian account of the mandate of Heaven existed a third alternative. Thinkers such as Guan Zhong (Guanzi) (?–644 B.C.) and Ban Gu (A.D. 32–92) agreed with the

Confucianists that rulers arose out of virtue rather than strength, but in their view, government on the whole was only a necessary evil. It had been devised to preserve the peace when the purity and simplicity of ancient society had disappeared irretrievably. This third notion of the origins of government bears certain similarities to Western social contract theory, for, following the logic of Guanzi and his Legalist predecessors (such as Han Feizi), the Qing reformer Tan Sitong (1865–1898) wrote much later of the popular selection of a prince when society had become complex and people could no longer govern themselves. Like the Legalists, Guanzi placed a much greater emphasis on the ruler than his subjects. For him, the purpose of government was to inhibit misbehavior among the people by regulating their mores through law. Thus, his view of humanity was fundamentally much more pessimistic than that of Confucius and Mencius.[95]

Although Xiao has treated him as a Confucian thinker, Guanzi's advocacy of government by the rule of law as well as the concept of man on which it was based bore a strong resemblance to the thought of the Legalists Han Feizi (280?–233? B.C.) and Xunzi (340?–245? B.C.). They all placed a much greater emphasis on the need for external discipline over men, and their notion of kingship attached less significance to the role of virtue in the making of a benevolent ruler.[96] As Benjamin Schwartz has noted, Xunzi, like Guanzi, was not attentive to the origins of government. He was more concerned with the common people's inability to exercise effective control over their passions through the application of their reason.[97]

> Man's nature is evil; goodness is the result of conscious activity. The nature of man is such that he is born with a fondness for profit. . . . He is born with feelings of envy and hate[,] . . . with the desires of the eyes and ears. . . . Hence, any man who follows his nature and indulges his emotions will inevitably become involved in wrangling and strife, will violate the forms and rules of society, and will end as a criminal. Therefore, man must first be transformed by the instructions of a teacher and guided by ritual principles, and only then will he be able to observe the dictates of courtesy and humility, obey the forms and rules of society, and achieve order. It is obvious from this, then, that man's nature is evil, and that his goodness is the result of conscious activity.[98]

Xunzi's view of human nature rivals Thomas Hobbes's depiction of man in the state of nature—where life was "solitary, poor, nasty, brutish, and short."[99] Xunzi's remedy was as distasteful to the Daoists as was that of Confucius and Mencius—to establish rites and ceremonies to regulate human behavior. Unlike Hobbes, however, Xunzi's account was so negative, that, as Schwartz has argued, it is difficult to imagine the individuals in his society overcoming their passions sufficiently for reason to induce them to conclude a social contract.[100] Xunzi contrasts this human nature—which he defines as "what is accomplished by heaven, . . . something which cannot be learned"—with human artifice (*wei*), " '[t]hat in man of which he can become capable through learning and which he can perfect through application'."[101] Morality, rites, and law—all the products of human artifice—were to be applied strenuously to prevent the strife that would arise if people were left in their natural condition.[102] Because morality did not inhere in men and women by nature, however, Han Feizi argued that without the force of punishment, an appreciable amelioration in the human condition could not be achieved.

> [T]he people will bow naturally to authority, but few of them can be moved by righteousness. Confucius was one of the greatest sages of the world. He perfected his conduct, made clear the way, and traveled throughout the area within the four seas, but in all that area those who rejoiced in his benevolence, admired his righteousness, and were willing to become his disciples numbered only seventy. For to honor benevolence is a rare thing, and to adhere to righteousness is hard. Therefore within the vast area of the world only seventy men became his disciples, and only one man—he himself— was truly benevolent and righteous.[103]

As a Legalist, then, Han Feizi believed that the methods of the Confucian sages were mistaken. "Nowadays, when scholars counsel a ruler," he admonished, "they do not urge him to wield authority, which is the certain way to success, but instead insist that he must practice benevolence and righteousness before he can become a true king. This is, in effect, to demand that the ruler rise to the level of Confucius, and that all the ordinary people of the time be like Confucius' disciples. Such a policy is bound to fail."[104] The Legalist view, in short, was a realist perspective that was incompatible with the idealism of Confucianism. Only law, rigidly applied and strictly enforced, could rescue humanity from its miserable natural circumstances. As elements of this emphasis on order came to be incorporated into Confucianism over the centuries with the actual practice of imperial rule, however, its emphasis on law came to be tempered by the conditionality of the Confucian/Mencian understanding of the relationship between kingship and virtue.

The Legalist, Confucian, and Daoist strains of classical Chinese political thought, were all transmitted together through the Qing period. In all three schools were significant contrasts with Japanese *kokutai* thought. Where Japanese Shintō and the *kokutai* amalgamation of Shintō with Confucianism simply accepted the mythological account of the Japanese emperor as divine and proceeded therefrom, Chinese theorists of all the schools described here inquired into the origins and nature of government in general, producing theories analogous to the ideas of Plato, Filmer, Hobbes, Locke, and Rousseau. Moreover, the primary dissident tendency away from neo-Confucianism in Japan stressed uniquely Japanese elements such as the imperial system. The notion of a unique Japanese tennō that Meiji theorists tended to emphasize did not question the legitimacy of the emperor's position. Indeed, it even denied the possibility of dynastic change in lineage.

By contrast, in China, among dissenters to the Mencian mandate of Heaven, the reasoning operated in precisely the opposite direction of Japanese thinkers who rejected the concept. Japan did not produce significant champions of views that might be compared with the quasi-anarchism of the Daoists. Its primary dissenters from neo-Confucian orthodoxy were Kokugaku and Mito theorists who emphasized the unique divinity of Japan's tennō, undergirding it with a charismatic basis of authority. Meiji *kokutai* theorists would build on this Shintō conception of the mikado and invest it with a basis for individual and collective Japanese (national) identity. China's dissident Legalists, however, advocated the "routinization" of kingship "by freeing rule from charisma and making the emperor's person just a *persona*." As Frederick Wakeman has argued, "[t]he legalists secularized . . . religious nonattachment into the instrument of law."[105] This contrast bore important consequences for the political development of China and Japan in the mid- to late nineteenth century as well as for the theoretical endeavors of their Marxists. The charismatic authority of the Japanese emperor offered opponents of the Tokugawa shogunate a powerful tool with which to galvanize support for their modernizing revolution. At the same time, their inculcation in the *kokutai* thought centered on that emperor created emotional and conceptual difficulties for Japanese intellectuals who tried to apply the Marxist universalist critique to their own state. In China, Confucian orthodoxy offered a basis of legitimate criticism of the emperor, and its dissenters either repudiated government in toto or diminished the charismatic element of imperial rule. For Chinese intellectuals of the late nineteenth and early twentieth centuries schooled in these philosophical traditions, there was no reason to expect that Marxian socialism should have posed the same dilemmas it brought to their counterparts in Japan. Much later, the traditional philosophical triad in China would also lay the groundwork for a much less statist resolution of the national question when Marxism collided with the nationalist claims of waging war.

Three additional factors reinforced the significance of these differences between China and Japan. First, Marxism was introduced into China as the Qing dynasty was falling, not during constructive state building as in Meiji Japan. Moreover, the existing Chinese regime was an alien dynasty, the ouster of which could be demanded along with the positive effort to create a new national Chinese state. In other words, the task of nation building from Tokugawa to Meiji was consistent with the mission of state building around a nativist imperial symbol to defend against the Western powers, but in China, the desire to build a strong China was consistent with an assertion of nationality that demanded the removal of the imperial regime. Finally, the abolition of the examination system in 1905 marked the final disintegration of the old Chinese philosophical orthodoxy and the need to search for new ideas upon which a viable new polity might be based. Little remained from the Confucian philosophical tradition to be blended creatively with Western elements (as in Meiji Japan) to support a new political structure that could claim continuity with the indigenous past.

None of these contrasts between Chinese and Japanese circumstances diminishes, however, the important contradiction between Marxian internationalism and its call to destroy the state per se, on the one hand, and the perceived need in both China and Japan to build and legitimate a nation-state that could resist Western encroachment. While Japanese scholars found it difficult to distinguish state and nation conceptually, and the Chinese concept of tianxia delimited neither nation nor state, Chinese intellectuals faced additional concerns. Where nationalism (as ethnicity) could readily become a potent idea in Japan via the *kokutai* concept even before the Western challenge, nationalism had to be used with more discretion and far less narrowly ethnic content in China where the national boundaries implicit in the term *guo* might embrace not only Han Chinese but a multiplicity of other (albeit small) minority ethnic groups and linguistic dialects. It was with restraint, therefore, that Sun Yat-sen and Zhang Binglin adjured their compatriots to protect the race in their campaign to overthrow the Manchu Qing dynasty. For *Zhongguo* (China), as a cultural rather than a predominantly ethnic concept, traditionally denoted "belief in the pre-eminence of Chinese culture and its universality over and above any concept of the political entity of a 'nation-state'."[106]

The problem for Chinese intellectuals lay in the conception of the nation-state as one political entity among many equal units with sovereign rights. Among the traditional assumptions concerning Zhongguo were its unity and its "right to govern all mankind" deriving "from Heaven's bestowing its mandate on the Chinese emperor because of his superior [moral] cultivation."[107] The moral concept of government within China was part of a total cosmology, a moral conception of the universe. What Liang Qichao condemned as a lack of a concept of the *guojia* in China, then, was the absence of the Western notion of a centralized nation-state, in the modern Western political and philosophical system dating back to Machiavelli. Unlike the classical framework in China, for example, raison d'état appertained to each national unit. Furthermore, the nationhood that had developed along with stateness since before the French Revolution granted citizenship as a combination of active rights and duties and not merely as the passive dutifulness broken by periodic activity connoted by the rescinding of Heaven's mandate as in China. Reformers Liang, Yan Fu, and Kang actively grasped and accepted the Western idea of sovereignty with rights as a characteristic of stateness. Indeed, only then could Chinese intellectuals become genuinely offended at Western encroachments as violations of China's sovereign rights.[108] Only then could the sentiment of nationalism that identified with the nation-state begin to play a prominent role in the development of Chinese political thought and revolutionary movements. Whereas in Japan such nationalism was intimately linked in the notion of *kokutai* with the preservation of the tennō's unique position, in China the move from the traditional universalist implications of the idea of tianxia implied that intellectuals had to relinquish the claim of their emperor (*tianzi*, son of Heaven) to rule all under the heavens. China's emperor would now be treated as a monarch comparable to the rulers of all other nation-states.[109]

This point marks one of the many important divergences in the intellectual and physical environments into which Marxist thought was introduced in China and Japan and evolved through the 1920s and 1930s. The political perspectives of the indigenous cultures of China and Japan discussed here will resurface as I analyze developments in Chinese and Japanese Marxism with respect to the national question in the prewar period. This cannot proceed, however, without a full appreciation of the Marxism that Chinese and Japanese intellectuals in this era encountered.

THE INTRODUCTION OF MARXISM INTO CHINA AND JAPAN

At the turn of the twentieth century, Marxism and other strains of modern Western political thought were very attractive to young Chinese and Japanese intellectuals. As contact with the West came through religious missions and then military and economic imperialism, intellectuals in the two societies were exposed to Western ideas as alternative premises upon which to reorder their own societies. In Japan, where Marxism was introduced first, the Meiji industrializing political and economic revolution from above brought with it a rise in expectations concerning the possibilities for service to the state and then deepening frustration for many as the limits of that participation within the framework of the Meiji Constitution became manifest. This circumstance heightened curiosity about more liberal Western ideas about the organization of the polity than those present in the German scholarship that so heavily influenced the drafting of the Meiji Constitution. In addition, industrialization itself seemed to draw Japan closer to the West as a Japanese society in transition to capitalism began to share the social problems that had accompanied that transition in the West. In China, the circumstances were dramatically different, but they were no less conducive to the exploration of Western philosophical perspectives. As the Confucian consensus gradually disintegrated with the feeble Qing dynasty's repeated failures in internal reform and inability to repel the Western powers, the need for an alternative comprehensive philosophical perspective was felt acutely. Marxism was especially appealing among the strains of Western thought that discontented intellectuals explored because it offered the sort of all-embracing philosophical framework that could supplant Confucianism as a mode of understanding the world and as a guide for action.

First in Japan and, then, in China through Japan,[110] Marxism would draw a committed following for many reasons, not least of which was its claim to be a theory that was based on modern Western science but also offered a critical perspective on Western society itself. As I have argued elsewhere, where intellectuals were chafing under the social and political constraints of their own societies, Marxism, and then Marxism-Leninism, "offered an alternative philosophical basis (buttressed with organizational support) for one to step outside the dominant philosophical and cultural framework [of one's own society] in order to criticize its separate components fully."[111] Other Western perspectives, such as liberalism and, subsequently, pragmatism, proffered less systematic, holistic, critical frameworks for understanding the world to those who would engage in sustained cultural criticism of their own national contexts. Marxism was also appealing to intellectuals in societies under threat from the Western powers because its critical assessment of Western capitalist society offered a prescription for socioeconomic and political transformation while it appeared to make them less vulnerable to the charge of subjecting themselves to the "cultural imperialism" of a Western philosophical system.[112]

The acquaintance with Marxism, with its advocacy of stateless communism, coincided with a new appreciation among Chinese and Japanese intellectuals of the state as their own societies faced Western military, economic, and cultural pressures. At the turn of the twentieth century, they had just discovered the Western concept of the nation-state, and they found it viable and useful for their own ends.[113] In Japan, the adoption and adaptation of the concept were evident first in the Meiji slogan of *fukoku-kyōhei* (enrich the nation, and strengthen the military), in the combination of the Western state idea with traditional Confucian and Shintō mythical beliefs in the *kokutai* notion, and, finally, in the fruition of its more intense elements in the ultranationalism of the 1930s.[114] In China, too, the appreciation of the Western notion of the nation-state began to be evident in the intellectual movements that supported official reform efforts beginning with the Tongzhi Restoration and culminating in the anti-Japanese thrust of the Chinese Communist movement during the Sino-Japanese War in the 1930s and 1940s.[115] Thus, just as in Western Europe, the social Darwinist elements of Marxism, coupled with interpretations of advanced capitalism and imperialism offered by Rudolf Hilferding, Rosa Luxemburg, Nikolai Bukharin, and V. I. Lenin[116] responded to pressing concerns of Chinese and Japanese intellectuals. One such issue was how best to respond to the troubling impact of the Western-dominated international system. If they had indulged in an "extreme concentration on the individual nation, the political system, society *or* state" in their application of Western thought to the analysis of their own situations, the effect would have been to divert "attention away from the international structures of power within which development takes place."[117] The internationalism of Marxism responded to the dilemmas of their societies.

In the meantime, both Chinese and Japanese intellectuals had come to accept many aspects of Western thought in the late nineteenth and early twentieth centuries, including what Hao Chang has called "transformative thought." This embraces "the impulse toward nationalism; the glorification of struggle, and related Faustian-Promethean outlooks; the conception of the people as a collective entity that serves as the motive force of social progress; the view of history as a process of unilinear development and of the future as pregnant with infinite possibilities; and the image of revolution as an abrupt leap into the future accompanied by a total, cataclysmic break with the past."[118] The Western concept of the nation-state became a convenient, even essential, point of departure for Chinese and Japanese intellectuals precisely because these ideas had been introduced with the force of arms borne by European national states. Marxism provided both an account of the rise of this new form of polity and a prescription for its destruction in the West. The appreciation of the importance of the national state was particularly emphasized in China precisely because of Japan's success in resisting the Western force of arms and the resulting appreciation of the importance of the nation-state among Japanese intellectuals who devised or were raised in the new orthodoxy of the *kokutai*. At the same time, Marxism's call for the ultimate demise of the state everywhere collided with these thinkers' new appreciation of the utility of the national state for their own peoples.

The multiple dimensions of this paradox, however, could not be appreciated fully by these intellectuals. They were not acquainted with the writings of the young Marx, such as the *Critique of Hegel's "Philosophy of Right"* that, in turn, formed the basis for Marx's subsequent elaboration of the theme of the state as the sphere of alienation to wither away following the demise of bourgeois society in his "mature" writings. The manner in which the state was conceived and the aspects of the theory of the state that were contained in, or omitted from, the theory of Marxism as it was inherited by Chinese and Japanese intellectuals are crucial here precisely because of the normative value that the cluster of ideas around nation and state came to have first in Japan and then in China.

The historical materialism that was systematized, even revised, some would argue, by Engels as "scientific socialism"[119] comprised the essence of Marxism in Chinese and Japanese perceptions, and this perspective heavily influenced their interpretations of issues concerning the state and revolution. Marxian socialism was first introduced into Japan as one among many varieties of socialism, including the anarcho-utopian thought of Pierre-Joseph Proudhon and Fabianism. Indeed, the main theoretical origins of early Japanese Marxism derived from the social reformist ideas of the Socialist International centered around the German Social-Democratic party.[120]

The most important agent in the propagation of Western socialism in Japan was the magazine *Kokumin no tomo* (The Nation's Friend), launched in 1887. Beginning with its first issue, the magazine published translated essays of Henry George, and because of the repeated use of the term in these writings, the notion of socialism as *shakai-shugi* came to be widely circulated. The *Kokumin no tomo*, which also serialized articles on Russian revolutionary parties, accounts of May Day demonstrations among European socialist parties, and correspondence among them, had every appearance of being the organ of a socialist party. In fact, however, no Socialist party yet existed in Japan, although Sakai Toshihiko reportedly attended the Second Congress of the Socialist International in Brussels in 1891. His article entitled "Shakai mondai" (Social problems), published in the March 1890 issue of the *Kokumin no tomo*, not only served an important function in disseminating information on the Socialist parties of the International and on the relationship between the monarch and the socialist party in Germany,[121] but it also foreshadowed how Meiji socialism, including Marxian socialism, "grew out of a social reformist response to the structural changes in the Meiji state [occurring] in the 1890s and especially [to] the progress of the industrial revolution and capitalism after the Russo-Japanese War."[122]

Throughout the 1890s, social reformist groups proliferated in Japan, uniting budding humanitarian and Christian socialists with "materialist" (Marxian) Socialists to study a wide array of social reformist ideas.[123] What these perspectives shared in common was the view that current social problems ultimately could be traced to a single cause. Whereas in the early Meiji era the intellectual world had been dominated by the spread of the "British school of economics," or "liberal" economics, the critique of British economics and its premise of free competition in the form of this study of socialist thought emerged in the 1890s.[124] Christian socialists, with their humanitarianism and oath of higher loyalty, played a major role in formulating this critique. They assailed the capitalistic industrializing revolution of a Meiji regime that invoked the "self-serving demands of the modern state" and "claims of national interest" at the expense of large segments of the population left to the mercy of "free" and brutal competition for the bare essentials of life. Interestingly, in contrast to some early socialists whose patriotism was intimately linked to their socialism,[125] such Christian socialists were often the source of an antistatist brand of socialism.[126] This divergence was not immediately apparent, however, in the earliest socialist study groups in which Christian and "materialist" socialists combined their efforts.

Such associations mushroomed during the 1890s. In 1896, the Shakai Seisaku Gakkai (Social Policy Study Group) and the Shakai Gakkai (Social Studies Group) were formed, and the year 1897 saw the launching of the *Shakai zasshi* (Society magazine) by the latter, the emergence of the Rōdō Kumiai Kiseikai (Association for the Formation of Labor Unions), the publication of *Rōdō sekai* (Labor world), and the founding of the Shakai Mondai Kenkyūkai (Association for the Study of Social Problems). More important for the propagation of Marxism were the Shakaigaku Kenkyūkai (Association for the Study of Socialism) around persons associated with Tokyo Imperial University. The latter group was formed by Christians meeting at the Unitarian Kyōkai I'itsukan with the avowed intent "to study the principles of socialism and the possibility of applying it to Japan." Among its leaders were Abe Isoo, Katayama Sen, Kōtoku Shūsui, Kawakami Kiyoshi,[127] and Murai Tomoyoshi, and the group studied the socialist thought of Claude Saint-Simon, Charles Fourier, Ferdinand Lassalle, as well as Marx and Engels.[128] In addition to works by Japanese authors on socialism and state socialism as well as translations of Henry George's *Social Problems* and of a work by the American Christian Socialist Richard Ely,[129] several partial translations of Marxist works were published and studied in Japan before 1903. Works unavailable for translation were often read in other languages. Yamakawa Hitoshi, for example, endeavored to read the 1902 English edition of volume 1 of *Capital*, published in the United States, during his imprisonment.[130]

During the Russo-Japanese War, the Heimin-sha (Commoners' Society), organized by Sakai and Kōtoku in November 1903, played the leading role in the translation and publication of Marxist writings. Like its predecessors, the Heimin-sha was eclectic in the beliefs of its members. The declaration appearing in the inaugural issue of the group's *Heimin shinbun* (Commoners' newspaper) in November 1903 proclaimed that the group "repudiated violence" and advocated working for socialism and the ideals of the French Revolution—liberty, equality, and fraternity—within the scope of the law. Thus, the Heimin-sha socialists were dedicated to the parliamentarism of the German Social-Democratic party "that was the mainstream of the socialist movement at the time." In addition to Marx and Engels, Ferdinand Lassalle, August Bebel, Leo Tolstoy, and Peter Kropotkin were included in a six-page group of picture postcards commemorating the *Heimin shinbun*'s one-year anniversary.[131]

Clearly, there was not yet a unified body of Marxian socialist thought at this point in Japan, even within the Heimin-sha. Nevertheless, the Heimin-sha performed two major functions instrumental to the importation of Marxism into Japan. First, it helped to establish Japanese contact with the Russian Social-Democratic Labor party and other socialist parties affiliated with the Second International. The March 13, 1904, issue of the *Heimin shinbun* carried a letter to the Russian party, calling for its unity with Japanese socialists against "patriotism and militarism" during the war; its number 37 published a reply from *Iskra*.[132] It also reported in its forty-sixth issue (in mid-1904) the historic handshake between Katayama and George Plekhanov when the two men represented their respective parties at the Sixth Congress of the Second International in Amsterdam.[133] In his speech to the congress, Plekhanov declared that "Japan was removing one foot of the colossus of Russian autocracy," just as Lenin the following January praised Japan's defeat of "Russian absolutism, not of the people." Finally, the newspaper's last issue of January 29, 1905, carried an account of the 1905 Russian Revolution, and its successor, *Chokugen* (Plain talk) published translations of Russian revolutionary writings prepared by Kōtoku. Information published concerning the Russian movement focused on the narodniki (populists) and the terrorist activities of their successors, the Social Revolutionary party members (SRs): Heimin-sha sympathies clearly lay with the SRs, despite its own cautious espousal of legal means.[134] In addition, Sakai, who later became the first to introduce Lenin's work into Japan, published the first translation of the *Communist Manifesto* in November 1904 in the *Heimin shinbun*'s one-year anniversary issue.[135] When the sale of the weekly *Heimin shinbun* was banned and Sakai resumed publication with *Chokugen*,[136] he published an article on "Marx's theory" (Marukusu no gakusetsu) that ran from its June 4 (no. 18) through July 16 (no. 24) issues. There he analyzed Marx's historical materialism and theory of value in accordance with Ely's work on the history of contemporary socialism and explained changes in modes of production on the basis of a work by British socialist Henry Mayers Hyndman entitled (in Japanese) *Shakai-shugi keizai ron* (The economic theory of socialism).[137]

These themes are highly indicative of the nature of Marxist theory—as scientific socialism—as it was introduced in Japan and, in turn, into China. By the period of the Heimin-sha, two works had already been widely read in English translation: the *Communist Manifesto* and Engels's *Socialism: Utopian and Scientific*. These writings formed the basis of the two most sophisticated presentations of Marxism available in Japanese at this time, both predating the Russo-Japanese War—Katayama Sen's *Waga shakai-shugi* (My socialism) (1903) and Kōtoku Shūsui's *Shakai-shugi shinzui* (The true meaning of socialism) (1903).[138] The two volumes limited themselves to the basic exposition of Marxism, translating and adapting a combination of Engels's *Socialism: Utopian and Scientific* and the social reformism of the Second International.[139] This particular blend reinforced the tendency to interpret Engels's historical materialism as the essence of Marxism.[140] Both works stressed the notions of surplus value (*jōyo kachi ron*), class struggle, and historical materialism to stress the major contradictions of capitalist society.[141] In addition, both texts also linked Marxism with social Darwinism. In accordance with Engels's pamphlet, translated into Japanese as *From Utopia to Science*, Marxism was presented as scientific socialism, as the culmination of the long historical development of socialist thought. Marx's socialism was grasped as evolutionary (*shinka-teki*) socialism; and "the theory of class struggle was . . . understood in connection with the concept of the survival of the fittest."[142]

From the October Revolution until 1920, when the first Japanese translation of volume one of *Capital* (by Takabatake Motoyuki) was published,[143] it was this "scientific socialism" systematized by Engels that constituted the core of the Marxism first introduced into Japan. There is little indication of any direct influence of Russian interpretations in this early period. Nor was Lenin the dominant figure in the first Russian Marxism to be translated into Japanese. It was not until after the February Revolution in Russia that the introduction of Lenin's work commenced with the publication of his "Roshiya no kakumei" (Russian revolution) in the October 1917 issue of *Shin shakai* (New society). Before that time, Lenin was almost unknown among Japanese socialists: As recently as the June 1917 issue of *Shin shakai*, in fact, Sakai had described Lenin as an anarchist.[144] Because the distinctions among the Russian revolutionary parties remained blurred in Japan until the first real contact between the Japanese Communist movement and Comintern leaders occurred at the Far Eastern People's Congress of November 1921,[145] it is not extraordinary that George Plekhanov's *Fundamental Problems of Marxism* became the first complete major work of Russian Marxism to be translated into Japanese and published between the October Revolution and 1921.[146] The direct contact that Japanese Marxists had had with Plekhanov may help account for this; similarly, Bukharin's encounter with Sakai and others in Tokyo in the spring of 1917 may help explain the predominance of Bukharin's influence over that of Lenin in Japan throughout the 1920s.[147]

Indeed, Bukharin's preeminence is helpful in characterizing the nature of early Japanese Marxism. Two of his works, *The ABC of Communism* (coauthored with Yevgeny Preobrazhensky, 1919) and *Historical Materialism: A System of Sociology* (1921) were promptly translated into Japanese by the mid-1920s, were widely read as basic texts of Marxism, and enjoyed even greater theoretical authority than Lenin's works.[148] These works offered a mechanistic presentation of the "scientific materialism" that was emphasized in the earliest Marxist writings introduced into Japan. They did not include the humanistic theoretical works of the young Marx: "The Economic and Philosophic Manuscripts" (1844), *The German Ideology* (1845–1846), Marx's *Critique of Hegel's "Philosophy of Right"* (1843)—which, as seen, formed the basis for Marx's theory of the state—or even the transitional work, the *Grundrisse (der Kritik der Politischen Ökonomie)* (1857–1858). These texts were not available even to Western Marxists until they were published in the late 1920s and 1930s and thereupon occasioned a reevaluation of Marx's thought in the West in light of the philosophical aspects of the young Marx that they revealed.[149]

Until the mid-1920s, aside from the *Communist Manifesto* and *Capital*, only the following texts were available in Japanese: Karl Kautsky's commentary on *Capital* and *Ethics and the Materialist Conception of History*; a serialization of Herman Gorter's explication of historical materialism (published as "Yuibutsu shikan kaisetsu" in *Shin shakai*); Marx's *Wage Labor and Capital*; Engels's *Socialism:*

Utopian and Scientific (part of the larger work, *Anti-Dühring*); a work by Dutch socialist Antonie Pannekoek on Marxism and Darwinism; a biography of Marx by John Spargo; and partial translations of a work entitled *An Outline of Capital* by E. Aveling and Engels's *Origin of the Family, Private Property and the State*.[150] By the end of the 1920s, Japanese Marxists writing on the state were also able to refer to Engels's *Anti-Dühring*, limited excerpts from Marx's contributions to the *Deutsch-Französische Jahrbücher*, and a secretly circulated version of Lenin's *State and Revolution*. By this time, however, other works of Bukharin had also become available in Japanese translation. His *Economics of the Transition Period* (1920), *Imperialism and World Economy* (1917), and *Imperialism and the Accumulation of Capital* (1924–1925)[151] became particularly influential in Japan because they analyzed in new and innovative ways phenomena that were conspicuous in the development of the Japanese state—such as the intimate relationship between capitalists and the state—but had not been so treated in other European and Russian Marxist writings.

The collective influence of these works, taken together with the role of *The ABC of Communism* as "an elementary textbook of communist knowledge," signify that the Marxist theory of the state was present in Japan with but half its essential elements. This is not to say that the relationship between Marx and his predecessor Hegel was wholly unappreciated in Japan. On the contrary, in the early 1920s young students who encountered Marxist ideas through original English and German texts were fascinated with "the theory of dialectics . . . and theories overcoming and sublating Hegel via Marx." György Lukács's *History and Class Consciousness* (1923) and Karl Korsch's *Marxism and Philosophy* drew the most attention in this regard, but these works treated Marxist philosophy in general rather than the Marxian critique of the Hegelian state. Similarly, the popularity of German idealist philosophy in Japan at the turn of the twentieth century revolved around Kant and neo-Kantian studies. This trend reinforced the widespread nationalistic impulse of the times to establish a "Japanist" philosophy,[152] but it did not contribute to an understanding of the centrality of the critique of Hegel's idealist state to Marxist thought. The lack of familiarity with Marx's earlier writings on this subject[153] meant that, for Chinese and Japanese Marxists, as for Lenin and German Social Democrats, "[w]ithout the components concealed in these books, many sides of the Marxian idea of politics were exceedingly difficult to grasp."[154] This limitation encouraged the polarization of Japanese Marxist theorists into two irreconcilable factions whose contributions on the state were impeded, it may be argued, by these constraints on the extent and nature of the Marxist theory as it was introduced into Japan.[155]

Furthermore, this pattern in the introduction of Marxism may have also contributed to the phenomenon of *tenkō* in the 1930s, in which many Japanese Marxists assailed Marxism and Western social and political thought in general for a lack of humanism and oriental "spiritualism."[156] The breach between the Christian socialist and materialist factions of the Heimin-sha immediately after the Russo-Japanese War presaged this massive wave of disaffection. Meiji socialism was motivated by the ideal of socioeconomic equality, a humanitarian response to the effects of Meiji industrialization and the key to the "fierce ethical idealism" of this first generation of Japanese socialists.[157] This sentiment, in turn, was closely linked with patriotism, that is, the fear among civil rights activists that the newly arisen "social problems" of the era, along with the despotic oligarchy that had betrayed what they saw as the original democratic aspirations of the Meiji Constitution, ultimately threatened the well-being, nay the very existence, of the Japanese nation. Meiji Socialists thus tended to see themselves as the legitimate successors to the rule of "a polity that realized the 'true meaning' of this new [Meiji constitutional] state system."[158]

These considerations on the introduction of Marxist thought into Japan apply as well to China. The conceptual relationship between socialism and patriotism is particularly suggestive here. China and Japan early in the twentieth century were ostensibly in very different positions in the international system with respect to the tasks of nation building and state making. Japan had met with tremendous success in building a powerful state apparatus with the Meiji Restoration and in forging a potent national consciousness with the notion of the *kokutai* and the family conception of the state. The Sino-Japanese and Russo-Japanese wars established Japan's military superiority not only to China, long the dominant cultural entity in the region, but also to Russia, which was a semi-Western yet backward country in Japanese perceptions.[159] By contrast, since the Taiping rebellion in the midnineteenth century, Chinese efforts at reform and revolution had been a long, fruitless endeavor to match the Japanese accomplishment. This disparity between the two national experiences has obscured important similarities, such as the close relationship between Marxism and the nationalistic quest for a strong state in Japan as well as in China. In China, the linkage was evidenced dramatically in the May Fourth movement, when the momentum of the young Marxist movement accelerated as intellectuals became disillusioned with the Western powers. The revolutionary vision of Marxism-Leninism that appeared to have brought Russia into modernity appealed as the new key to saving China from divisive internal warlord forces and from Western encroachments. In Japan, even as the Meiji state began to show the first fruits of its reform efforts, Marxism was grasped as the Western philosophy on the cutting edge of history, and Meiji socialists sought in Marxian socialism a means by which to strengthen Japan internally by resolving new social ills arising out of capitalist industrialization. At least until the Russo-Japanese War, Meiji socialists saw no conflict between their attachment to Marxism and their devotion to the *kokutai*. Japanese expansionism in the 1930s and 1940s reflected a continuing effort to build a viable national state in the face of uncomfortable constraints imposed by Japan's limited natural resource base and the brutally competitive nature of the existing international system. In 1941, Japanese expansion beyond Manchuria, Korea, and China and into Southeast Asia "had become essential to the defense of the [expanding] empire,"[160] and Marxists felt compelled to renounce their ties to the international Communist movement and embrace the cause of the war. Thus, the concern for patriotism expressed by Katayama Sen at the turn of the twentieth century remained as relevant to Japanese Marxists as to Chinese Marxists two decades later.

The specifically Asian context for this nationalism was also significant for these Marxists. Beginning with the First Congress of Far Eastern Peoples in 1921 and throughout the life of the Comintern, of course, the leadership of the international Communist movement encouraged, indeed insisted upon, treating the two movements together in both theory and strategy, prompting some Japanese scholars to remark that Comintern policy in Japan was more often inspired by the fortunes of the turbulent revolution in China than by due consideration of the peculiarities of the Japanese situation.[161] This tendency might have been the historical product of a European orientalism that treated Asian nations in terms of their divergences from the West and failed to distinguish carefully among them.[162] More importantly, prominent Marxists in both countries, including Li Dazhao, Kawakami Hajime, and Sano Manabu may have contributed to treating the two as one by participating in a powerful intellectual current that endeavored to distinguish oriental from Western civilization,[163] perceived common threats imposed by the West and its international system, and saw in their shared philosophical past the promise of a shared future on some level. Hence, one notes the pan-Asianism of Japanese Marxists in *tenkō*,[164] the "new Asianism" advocated by Li Dazhao, the concern of Japanese radicals from Kita Ikki[165] to the leadership of the Japanese Communist party (JCP)[166] with the course of the Chinese revolution, the need on the part of both Chinese and Japanese theorists to address the notion of the "Asiatic mode of production,"[167] and numerous other examples of shared concerns having to do with the state, nation, and revolution in the East. Finally, Chinese and Japanese activist leftist thinkers shared the dilemmas arising from the fact that adoption of the Western path to modernity, including the Marxian concept of social revolution conceived on the European model, "implies Westernization . . . [and thus] calls into question the very specificity which has been the most cherished aim for which the non-European peoples have struggled."[168] Aside from the Asian setting, a major factor contributing to these shared concerns was the fact that Marxism had been introduced into China via Japan. This means that radical intellectuals in both societies shared a common interpretive basis of Marxist thought, and the same unanswered questions that arose in the thought of the late Marx for Japanese Marxists also arose among Chinese revolutionary thinker-activists. Mao claimed that the 1905 Russian revolution had inspired Sun's Tongmenghui to advocate social and political revolution together[169] and, thus, that Marxian socialism was introduced into China by way of Russia.[170] In fact, however, Japanese socialists were the primary agents in a process that began as early as 1900. Their influence on Chinese radicals was exercised through a combination of direct contact with Chinese students living in Japan and written works in Japanese—original and translated writings—concerning Western Marxism. As a result, the materialist Marxism that was introduced into Japan was transmitted directly to China, and it was reinforced there through the influence of the writings of Joseph Stalin after he won the struggle to succeed Lenin as the paramount leader of the CPSU in 1929.

Chinese students flocked to Japan to study in tremendous numbers early in the twentieth century—as many as thirteen to fourteen thousand as compared with "only a few hundred in Europe and the United States."[171] Major works of Western socialism were rendered into Chinese on the basis of Japanese translations, and original Japanese works on Western thought were widely translated and circulated among Chinese first in Japan and then on the Chinese mainland through such magazines as *Xin qingnian* (New youth) and *Dongfang zazhi* (The eastern miscellany). Prominent among these works were the writings of Meiji socialists, such as Kōtoku; JCP leaders, such as Yamakawa Hitoshi; and the Kyōtō Imperial University economist Kawakami Hajime, who became "the most translated author" of Marxist works in the mid-1920s and 1930s.[172] As a result, most of the new foreign terminology in the modern Chinese language was coined by the Japanese. By contrast, few Chinese students studied in Russia, and, even in the 1920s, linguistic proficiency remained far greater in Japanese than in Russian among Chinese intellectuals.[173] Finally, and most importantly, Tokyo and Yokohama, where both the reformist followers of Kang and Liang and Sun's revolutionaries were headquartered and issued their major publications, were the center of Chinese radicalism before the 1911 revolution and the nexus of direct influence of Japanese intellectuals on the adoption of Marxism by Chinese students.[174]

Much as Meiji socialists were concerned with "social problems," Chinese intellectuals were first attracted to socialism as a critique of capitalism and the socioeconomic inequality associated with the newly dominant economic system in the Western Europe by which they felt threatened. Both Kang and Yan Fu, as well as Sun Yat-sen, were "sensitive to the widening gap between the rich and poor in the West."[175] Before the 1898 Reform movement, itself inspired by the Meiji example, Kang had some knowledge of socialism and of the labor movements in Europe and America, and he wrote of these in conjunction with an analysis of capitalism in his *Datong shu* (Book of the great harmony) (1902). Although he sympathized with the plight of workers, "arguing that since the datong had not yet arrived there was no way to save them," he feared a violent revolution by the working class.[176] This combination of sympathy for the working class under capitalism with an aversion to revolution continued to be evident in the reformist writings of Liang, a student of Kang, and others in the *Xinmin congbao*'s (The new citizen) celebrated debate with the *Minbao*, the organ of the revolutionary Tongmenghui in the 1905–1907 period.[177] Liang himself had become familiar with socialist thought primarily through Japanese influence, which by 1901 "had grown more marked" during his exile after the abortive 1898 Reform movement. As early as December 1900, Chinese students in Japan had launched the *Yishu huibian* (subtitled in English "A Monthly Magazine of Translated Political Works"), which carried translations of German, French, American, English, and Japanese writings. As a rule, the Chinese translations were based on Japanese translations of the original texts.[178] Liang's own work reflected the influence of these translations and his direct contacts with Japanese intellectuals: "Japanese translations of Western terminology . . . studded his writings, and even his literary style carried a Japanese flavor."[179] In his debate with the revolutionists, Liang cited Kawakami's economic writings, and his work, in turn, became a vehicle for the introduction of Japanese translations of such Western terms as *socialism* (*shakai-shugi*, or *shehui-zhuyi* in Chinese), and *capitalist* (*shihonka*, or *zibenjia* in Chinese) into Chinese.[180]

Liang's familiarity with Marxian socialism was evident as early as 1902. Writing in the *Xinmin congbao*, he described Marx as the founder of socialism, "one of the two great ideologies dominating Germany."[181] Given his increasing reservations about the applicability of socialism to China, Liang was quick to temper his enthusiasm about Marx's contribution. Writing in 1904, he described the "essence" of socialism as "'no more than public ownership of land and capital and the notion that labor is the exclusive source of value of everything.'" These were not new ideas, he noted, "'The well-field system in ancient China was indeed based on the same principle as modern socialism'."[182] He went on to assert that Marx's and Lassalle's view that "'landlords and capitalists without exception, were thieves and robbers'" did not apply to China.[183] In Liang's view, "Western societies had already become polarized before the Industrial Revolution": "Class opposition between the rich and poor [was] . . . an inveterate and endemic feature of Western societies." By contrast, "Chinese society . . . was largely composed of middle-class families and hence was not an economically polarized one" for three reasons: (1) China had no dominant aristocracy monopolizing "social wealth"; (2) China had had an equal inheritance system instead of primogeniture since the Han era; and (3) the burden of state taxation had been far lighter than in Europe. The consequent absence of class conflict, in Liang's view, obviated the need for social revolution.[184] China's problem lay in production rather than in distribution of wealth. To avoid the ill effects of European-style industrialization, Liang advocated that "the future new government . . . raise a large foreign loan to develop large industries and follow the principles of state socialism [*guojia shehui zhuyi* or *kokka shakai shugi*] of Germany and Austria such as nationalization of railways."[185] In short, although Liang did not reject recourse to foreign capital, he recognized the need for the development of the domestic Chinese economy. In view of the danger of foreign economic domination, this process would have to be carried out with emphasis on internal unity rather than on the conflict between labor and capital.

These reservations notwithstanding, Liang made a significant contribution to Chinese knowledge of socialism at the turn of the twentieth century, and the tremendous Japanese influence was evident here as well. He and fellow constitutionalist reformers founded the Guangzhi shuju (Extension of Knowledge Book Company) in Shanghai in 1901.[186] Among the company's impressive list of publications were major works by Meiji socialists, including Fukui Junzō's *Kinsei shakai-shugi* (Modern socialism) (1899, translated by Zhao Bizhen), Murai Tomoyoshi's *Shakai-shugi* (Socialism) (1899, translated by Luo Dawei), and *Shakaitō* (Socialist parties) (1899, translated by Zhou Baigao), an overview of European socialism by the Christian socialist Nishikawa Kōjirō. The writings of Murai and Nishikawa were heavily influenced by American Christian socialists, and stressed evolutionary socialism.[187] In addition to these works, Kōtoku's *Imperialism: The Spectre of the Twentieth Century* was translated by Zhao Bizhen and published by the Tongya Book Company of Shanghai in 1902; a second translation of Murai's *Shakai-shugi* by Hou Taiwan was published by Wenming Book Company in 1903; and Shimada Saburō's *Sekai no daimondai—shakai-shugi hyōron*

(The great problems of the world: A critical discussion of socialism) (1901) was translated into Chinese and published as *Shehui-zhuyi gaiping* by the Zuoxin Company in 1903.[188] Such works circulated widely through these mainland publishing houses, Liang's popular *Xinmin congbao* and *Yinbing shi ziyou shu* (The ice-drinker's studio: The book on liberty), and other papers such as the *Shiwu bao* (Shanghai, 1896–1898), the *Yishu huibian*, and the *Xin shijie xuebao* (New world learned journal).[189]

Following this initial exposure, a second phase of the introduction of Western socialism to Chinese intellectuals occurred during the reformist-revolutionary debate from 1905 through 1907. Hu Hanmin, Feng Ziyou, Zhu Zhixin, and Zhang Binglin supplemented Liang's writings with their own articles in the *Minbao* interpreting Sun Yat-sen's People's Principle of *minsheng* (people's livelihood) as socialism. In an essay entitled "Deyizhi shehui gemingjia xiaozhuan" (Short biographies of German social revolutionaries), Zhu included the first Chinese partial translation of the *Communist Manifesto* and emphasized Marx's departure from earlier varieties of utopian socialism.[190] Similar pieces included an article of Japanese anarchist Ōsugi Sakae translated by Qiang Zhai (pseudonym of Song Jiaoren), which cited the *Manifesto* and its notion of class conflict as the dominant philosophy of all socialist parties; an article distinguishing Christian socialism from Marxian socialism; and yet another article by Meng Diesheng (pen name of Ye Xiasheng) entitled "Wuzhengfudang yu gemingdang zhi shuoming" (An explanation of anarchist parties and revolutionary parties), which expressed a preference for Marxism over anarchism.[191]

Under the impact of these writings and the influence of meetings held by the Japanese Socialist party organized in 1906, Chinese students in Japan established the Shehui-zhuyi Yanjiuhui (Socialist Study Group) in 1907.[192] The new organization offered a forum for the study of revolutionary thought apart from the more activist Tongmenghui. Finally, yet another reflection of Japanese influence appeared in the *Minbao*'s publication of translations of two articles by Miyazaki Tamizō, a Japanese advocate of land nationalization and a close associate of Sun. In "Tudi fuquan tongzhihui zhuyishu" (The program of the Society for the Restoration of Land Rights), Miyazaki argued that equal access to land was a natural right of all humanity, and his "Oumei shehui geming yundong zhi zhonglei ji pinglun" (Classification and evaluation of social revolutionary movements in Europe and America) described Marxian socialism, constructive and destructive anarchism, and the land rights equalization schemes of Henry George and Alfred Wallace.[193]

Indeed it was land policy, particularly land nationalization as a programmatic implication of Sun's minsheng principle, that became the focus of the revolutionists' debate with the reformists. Sun himself had been exposed to socialism as early as 1897–1898 when he was living in Europe. Sun advocated equal land rights or land nationalization on at least three separate occasions: in 1902 when the Xingzhonghui of Vietnam was founded, in the 1903 oath pledged at Sun's Ribenshe Geming Junshi Xuexiao (Revolutionary Military Academy for Chinese Students in Japan), and in 1904 when Sun signed the *zhigongdang xinzhang*. This was what he meant by *minsheng-zhuyi*, or what he saw as the socialism adopted by

American and European socialist parties.[194] This program was adopted by the Tongmenghui to prevent the ills of industrial capitalism rather than as the cure for the same that it was perceived to be in the West. Sun's followers agreed that capitalism had not yet arrived in China, but, unlike Liang and the reformists who felt that the new Chinese state should encourage the development of native Chinese capitalists lest China fall prey to foreign imperialists, the revolutionaries tended to reject the costs of industrial capitalism as it had developed in the West: socioeconomic inequality, the misery of the working class, and, by implication, increasingly violent class conflict. Capitalism was to be avoided, in this perspective, which went on in some Tongmenghui writings to advocate a form of state socialism—after a combined socialist and nationalist democratic revolution.[195]

The principles of George's program of equalization of land rights were dominant in this application of socialist thought to China. Sun himself had returned from Europe enthralled with George's theories, but it was an article by Feng Ziyou, born and educated in Japan, entitled "Minsheng-zhuyi yu Zhongguo zhengzhi geming zhi qiantu" (The principle of *minsheng* and the future course of the Chinese revolution) that specified the desired form of state socialism for China. Citing the examples of German and Japanese industrial development along with improvements in housing and other projects for the public welfare, Feng argued that state socialist policies, such as the nationalization of railroads, forests, and mines, were the key to Chinese economic development without the ills of Western capitalism. It was steadily increasing land rents that ultimately triggered the widening gap between rich and poor in the process of capitalistic industrialization. The nationalization of land, that is, the abolition of private landownership and rents, would allow China to avert this evil. Many aspects of China's historical experience would make such policies more feasible in China than elsewhere. In the past, for example, the Chinese state had owned forests, monopolies (e.g., in salt production), mines, and roads, and the minsheng principle had been evident in the primitive socialism of China's well-field system. In this piece, Feng argued that military rule would be necessary for the implementation of these policies, but similar articles with variations on the basic principle of land nationalization and minsheng-zhuyi were also penned by Hu Hanmin and Zhu Zhixin.[196] Such propositions for a leading role of a new—reformed or revolutionized—state in China's future economic development were quite similar to one another whether advocated by the Tongmenghui or by Liang Qichao; "Liang's [own] economic policy was, as he claimed it to be, very close to the state socialism of Germany and Japan" in that it foresaw nationalization of private industry after a certain level of industrial development had been attained.[197]

Thus, at the outset, those who introduced socialism to China were concerned with economic inequality, de-emphasized class struggle while stressing an activist role for the state, and foresaw for China a slightly different course of political and economic development from that of Western Europe because of the peculiarities of China's domestic and international situation. These themes took precedence over the exploration of dialectics or historical materialism far more than among Japanese radicals. To be sure, Marxism was perceived in China as scientific socialism just as in Japan. Nevertheless, before 1907, the Japanese terms for dialectics (*benshōhō*) and historical materialism (*yuibutsu shikan*) had not yet been adopted and explored by Chinese writers on socialism.[198] Such subordination of the purely philosophical and metaphysical concerns of Marxism to its practical adaptation to the Chinese context persisted in the 1920s, 1930s, and 1940s, even among the Chinese Communist party's most eminent theorists, such as Qu Qiubai and Mao Zedong.[199] Mao's emergence as the party's leading theorist was intimately linked to his uncompromising denunciation of the Russian-returned students who "can only cite odd quotations from Marx, Engels, Lenin and Stalin in a one-sided manner, but are unable to apply the stand, viewpoint and method of Marx, Engels, Lenin and Stalin to the concrete study of China's present conditions and her history or to the concrete analysis and solution of the problems of the Chinese revolution." Accordingly, Mao recommended the (Stalinist) *History of the Communist Party of the Soviet Union (Bolsheviks), Short Course* as the basic text for the study of Marxism-Leninism,[200] and in writings such as "On Practice" and *On New Democracy* stressed his own contribution to the adaption of Marxism to China's specific historical conditions.

This recommendation came in May 1941, more than a decade after Bukharin had been denounced and removed from the Soviet and Comintern leadership by Stalin. In the 1920s, however, the classic for the Chinese Communists was the *ABC of Communism*,[201] just as in Japan. A brief lapse in the translation of Marxist works into Chinese occurred after the initial flurry of activity in 1900–1907; but such publications resumed after the 1911 revolution with Shi Renrong's serialization of the first Chinese translation of Engels's *Socialism: Utopian and Scientific* in the monthly *Xin shijie* in 1912.[202] Following the Bolshevik revolution, this process accelerated from 1921 to 1927, the two most important publishing houses being the Renmin Chuban-she (Canton) and the Xin Qingnian-she (Shanghai and Canton).[203] In 1919, when Li Dazhao explained "Wo de Makesi-zhuyi guan" (My Marxist views), he cited lengthy passages from *The Poverty of Philosophy*, the *Manifesto*, and the *Preface to a Critique of Political Economy*, as well as *Capital* to observe that "the theory of class struggle was like a 'golden thread' binding together the three great principles of Marxism: scientific socialism, political economy, and the materialist conception of history."[204] The early translation of the *Manifesto* by Zhu in the *Minbao* had been but a partial one. A full translation was completed by Chen Fotu (pseudonym of Chen Wangdao) and published in 1919, just one month before Li's essay appeared, by the Shanghai Shehui-zhuyi Yanjiu-she (Socialist Research Company), and it was reprinted at least four times between 1920 and 1938.[205] The translations used by Li in his essay, then, were necessarily based on Japanese translations by Kawakami Hajime.[206] Indeed, with the exception of the *Manifesto*, there is no evidence that any of the other works that Li cited were fully translated into Chinese at all until 1930 although a partial translation of *Capital* from the Japanese was published by the Renmin Chuban-she (People's Publishing House) in 1920.[207] Other major Marxist texts became available in Chinese, however, between 1921 and 1927. These included the following: Marx's *Wage Labor and Capital*, translated by Yuan Rang and published by Renmin

Chuban-she; Lenin's *Laonong zhengfu zhi chenggong yu kunnan* (Successes and difficulties of the workers' and peasants' government), translated by Li Mogeng and published by the Renmin Chuban-she; the "Program of the Russian Communist Party," translated by Zhang Xiwang (pseudonym of Zhang Ximan), published by the Renmin Chuban-she; *Class Struggle* (probably by Kautsky), translated by Yun Daiying in 1920 and published by the Xin Qingnian-she (New Youth Publishing House); Bukharin and Preobrazhenksy's *ABC of Communism*, published by the Xin Qingnian-she; and Stalin's *Foundations of Leninism*, published in 1926 by the Xin Qingnian-she.[208] Notably, in China as in Japan, the writings of the young Marx that laid the foundation for Marx's uncompromising critique of the state were conspicuously absent. Instead, for intellectuals attempting desperately to save China, Marxism was scientific socialism as systematized by Engels and then by Stalin, even as Stalin was seeking not to eliminate but to build a powerful Russian nation-state *after* the revolution.

There is also evidence that Bukharin's *Historical Materialism* was among these translations. Although the original author is not noted, a book entitled *Weiwu shiguan* (Historical materialism) was published by the CCP's publishing house Shanghai Shudian (Shanghai Publishers) between 1921 and 1927. The influence of Bukharin's highly mechanistic and deterministic presentation is further suggested by the publication in March 1927 of a work entitled *Wuchan jieji de zhexue: Weiwulun* (The philosophy of the proletariat: Historical materialism) by the Changjiang Shudian as one in the Xin Qingnian (New youth) series.[209] Thus, although historical materialism might not have achieved as great a theoretical prominence in China as in Japan, Bukharin's influence reinforced the view of Marxian socialism as scientific socialism presented in the basic texts *The ABC of Communism* and Engels's *Socialism: Utopian and Scientific*.

As for the national question, there is no evidence that works by Engels specifically on the state—for example, the complete *Anti-Dühring* and *Origin of the Family*, both available in Japanese in 1920 and 1927, respectively—were translated and accessible in Chinese. Those aspects of the theory of the state that were consistent with this overall presentation of Marxism in China, however, were widely adopted. In the writings of the mature Marx and Engels and in Soviet works on the theory of the state inhered several issues that became particularly problematic for Chinese and Japanese thinkers. Most important was the contradiction within the orthodox Marxist assertion that those who would aspire to socialism must be committed to destroy the state. This mandate collided directly with the aspirations of Chinese to redeem China by building a new Chinese nation and of Japanese whose own identity was intimately linked to the head of the state. In neither case could Marxist thinkers turn to the works of the younger Marx for their unveiling of the mystical appeal of the national state in Marx's own laggard Germany. Thus, problems such as the distinction between the nation and the state, the proper place of the idea of the nation-state as opposed to the state in general in Marxist philosophy, the special historical forms of the state in Asia and elsewhere, nationalism and internationalism within the socialist community and within the larger capitalist international system as a whole—all these issues posed important challenges for Chinese and Japanese Marxist thinkers in the early part of the twentieth century and remain troublesome issues for Marxists today. In China and Japan, adherence to Marxism placed radical intellectuals in a particularly problematic relationship with indigenous philosophical traditions that (with the exception of China's Daoists) held different, transcendent views of the polity and affirmed it as a locus of positive moral and humanistic value. Even after they adopted the alien Marxian system, such intellectuals remained under the influence of such traditions. These would be tapped to fill what Marxist thinkers found to be absent from the orthodox Marxism-Leninism with which they were acquainted.

INDIGENOUS PERSPECTIVES AND THE INTRODUCTION OF MARXISM: ISSUES AND CONSEQUENCES FOR THE NATIONAL QUESTION

The combination of indigenous perspectives concerning the nation and the state with the substance of the Marxism that was introduced into China and Japan bore important consequences for how the national question was posed and addressed by Marxist thinkers and revolutionaries in the two societies. The dominant pre-Marxian philosophical traditions—the *kokutai* family conception of the state in Meiji Japan and the Mencian view of the polity in Confucianism—treated the state and the nation in a manner that conflicted fundamentally with Marxian concepts of the state and nation-state. Both treated the state as a sphere of high moral value, and neither saw in the state either a manifestation of human alienation nor a reflection of class conflicts in society. Indeed, these concepts of the body politic shared no conceptual distinction between state and society or state and nation. The state and society as well as the state and nation were tightly bound together, particularly in the thought of the Meiji scholars who systematized the family conception of the state. The state was an organic entity: the Japanese nation could not exist without it, and there was no society apart from or against it. The individual Japanese would have no identity or being apart from the state. These tendencies were less pronounced in Chinese Confucianism where the political value of loyalty could conflict with the social value of filial piety. Moreover, the Mencian concept of a right to revolution, albeit a weak attribution of that right, did offer the basis for a critical assessment of those who governed in terms of separate popular and governmental interests. Nevertheless, the polity remained a sphere in which virtue was to be cultivated, and the mission of which was, though limited, essential to the physical and moral well-being of its citizens. The body politic would provide the context within which individuals could cultivate their virtue, and if the current emperor should falter in this task, the individual had recourse to revolutionary change that would culminate in the installation of new personnel as the leaders of the state. If such change could not be realized immediately, those who would be virtuous could simply withdraw from political participation, as many Confucian intellectuals did, particularly during eras of alien rule, until a suitable opportunity for effective mass action against the existing leadership materialized.

Radical intellectuals emerging from such traditions might have been able to identify with the young Marx, who struggled against what he saw as the pseudo-radicalism of his fellow Young Hegelians. Hegel, of course, had also treated the state in terms that transcended man's material life and, like Kant, sought a polity in which man could attain moral freedom. Marx was able to expose the identity of Hegel's ideal with the realities of the unfree protobourgeois state of early nineteenth-century Germany and then extended that critique to apply to bourgeois states in general and, finally, to the state as such. As observed previously, however, this segment of Marx's thought was omitted from the accounts of Marxism that would influence Chinese and Japanese radical intellectuals. Their Marxism was historical materialism, and its state was the product of class divisions.[210] Unmediated by the humanistic focus of Marx's early writings, Comintern directives to abolish the tennō in Japan and to oppose the bourgeois state (but not the Guomindang) in China left Chinese and Japanese Marxists without an account of men and women in society and without a view of the state based on the humanistic, almost spiritual, concern of the young Marx for the full realization of man as man. As a result, many would feel compelled to inject into Marxism the humanistic content that they found lacking in the doctrine that they knew and had adopted for its revolutionary program.

Bukharin's authority as a Bolshevik theorist and a Comintern leader on Asian matters contributed to the primacy of Marxism as historical materialism and scientific socialism in China and Japan. But Chinese and Japanese Marxists were not alone in experiencing this influence. As Isaac Deutscher has noted, circumstances were similar in Europe and Russia. "Until the early thirties Russian and European Communists used to draw their arguments from Bukharin's writings rather than from Stalin's. Bukharin's two books, *The ABC of Communism* (written jointly with Preobrazhensky) and his *Historical Materialism*, were the two most important standard books of Communist propaganda."[211] But if the alternative was to rely on Stalin's writings, these could not have resolved for Europeans and Russians, any more than for Chinese and Japanese Marxists, the difficulties posed by the omission of the critical early writings of Marx for a full appreciation of his conception of the state. That conception is exceptionally weak without the elements contributed by those early writings. What is essential here is that in China and Japan, as in Soviet Russia, one finds the predominance of the simple class dictatorship conception of the state and the associated mechanistic base-superstructure problématique. This had originated in a "suggestive" passage of the 1859 *Preface to the Critique of Political Economy* and in the post-Marx era rapidly became "the methodological platform" for scientific Marxist studies of the state.[212] As in Western Marxism the predominance of these elements has yielded the unsatisfactoriness and inconsistency identified here in the conflicting instrumentalist and structuralist interpretations of the state, and an adequate account of the phenomenon of the potential autonomy of the state has remained elusive.

Would Chinese and Japanese Marxists of the 1920s and 1930s, unexposed to Marx's early works and clinging tenaciously to the scientific Marxian socialism of the mature Marx and Engels, follow the same pattern of Bolshevik and contemporary scientific Marxian theorists on the state? If so, one would expect that their analyses would have proceeded from the narrow class definition of the state and that there would have been very little effort to combine the humanistic themes of consciousness, ideology, and alienation in the young Marx with the more mechanistic base/superstructural approach. These themes, as they drew on Rousseau, Hegel, and Enlightenment thought in general, were essential to a full understanding of Marx's view of the state and his conviction that it must be transcended rather than merely maintained in a new form. The European Enlightenment belief in "freedom to be inherent in the very nature of man" made Marx "confident of being able to dissolve all existing structures [including the state], and challenge[d] every traditional authority, by raising the demand that man should be allowed to rule himself."[213] This was the ultimate philosophical basis for Marx's advocacy of the transcendence (*Aufhebung*) of the state, which, in turn, distinguished his view from a "republican radicalism." For Marx, to maintain the state was inconsistent with his vision of communism because "the state is an institutional expression of man's alienation, [and] this alienation cannot be overcome within the state."[214]

That the state must be dissolved, then, was a philosophical and humanistic necessity in the work of the young Marx. Such a requisite no longer existed in the form of the Marxism introduced into China and Japan through the writings of Engels and transmitted "via Plekhanov and Kautsky to Lenin and Bukharin."[215] The widely read *Anti-Dühring*, *Socialism: Utopian and Scientific*, and *Origin of the Family* all represented, in George Lichtheim's words, "the transformation of Marxism into a 'scientific' doctrine emptied of genuine philosophic content."[216] Engels's discussion of history and evolution—historical materialism—was presented in isolation from Marx's broader philosophy of man and society. For Engels, Hegel's philosophy was valued not for its emphasis on "the constitutive activity of mind" but for its "determinism: his ability to make it appear that nature (and history) follow a preordained course." Thus, in the philosophy presented to Chinese and Japanese Marxists, the need to transcend the state became merely a scientific, evolutional, and mechanistic necessity.[217]

This presentation of Marxism, reinforced by the influence of the mechanistic *Historical Materialism*—which contained Bukharin's least sophisticated analysis of the state—would have significant consequences for the resolution of the national question in prewar China and Japan. Coupled with Lenin's class interpretation of the state, Bukharin's account established a basis for Chinese and Japanese Marxist analyses that would prefigure the instrumentalist and structuralist tendencies already noted in "scientific" Marxism in the West. Chinese and Japanese Marxists would find innovation as challenging as would Western Marxists, particularly when they sought to analyze phenomena such as revolutions from above— like Japan's own Meiji Restoration—or the legacy of a powerful bureaucracy in the absence of advanced capitalist development as in China.[218] They would be ill-equipped with a basis for analyzing critically and with subtlety their own philosophical heritage with concepts of *ideology*, *alienation*, and man as a *species-being* that could arm them against the corrosive and seductive power of the nation-state and its less visible hegemony in nonstate social institutions. At the same time, Chinese and Japanese Marxists writing in the late 1920s and 1930s would find that

Bukharin's more sophisticated ideas concerning the state in advanced capitalist society could support creative analyses of capitalism in prewar Japan.

Still, Marxism did not offer in its incarnation as scientific socialism in China and Japan what indigenous pre-Marxian philosophical formulations did: humanistic and spiritual elements; an appreciation of the spiritual and historical significance of nationhood in relation to the state; and recognition of the limitations of universal categories of history combined with a healthy respect for national differences arising from particular historical developments. As Chinese and Japanese Marxists confronted the national question, such indigenous perspectives could be either abandoned or incorporated into Marxist thought to produce innovation from within. Frequently, ideas from the two intellectual systems were, indeed, recombined to yield new syntheses. Chinese and Japanese syntheses would greatly resemble one another because of shared indigenous philosophical perspectives and their common international setting vis-à-vis the West. In Japan, however, Leninist Marxism would ultimately come into conflict with an indigenous tradition that was not in decline as in China but had succeeded in creating a robust national consensus based on a prior synthesis between Japanese and Western ideas concerning the nation and the state. Under the psychological pressures of mobilization for the Pacific war, the massive defections of Japanese Marxists from the Communist party to the national cause would be the result. Some who confronted this dilemma found themselves devising innovative national socialist schemas that allowed them to remain loyal both to their Japanese roots and to their Marxian allegiances. Meanwhile, in China, Li Dazhao, Mao Zedong, and others would seek a way in which to reconcile the concerns voiced in their indigenous philosophical roots with their dedication to Marxian social revolution. The remainder of this work is devoted to the examination of this outcome in Japan, on the one hand, and of equally compelling resolutions of the national question in China, on the other.

PART TWO

Anarchism, Nationalism, and the Challenge of Bolshevism

Anarchism, Populism, and Early Marxian Socialism

Anarchism and the National Question

Every people, however tiny, has its own specific character, style of life, speech, way of thinking and working; and precisely this character, this style of life, constitutes its nationality, which is the sum total of its historic life, aspirations, and circumstances. Every people, like every individual, are perforce what they are and have the incontestable right to be themselves. This constitutes the alleged national right. But if a people or an individual lives in a certain way, it does not by any means give them the right, nor would it be beneficial, to regard this nationality and individuality as absolute, exclusive principles, nor should they be obsessed by them. On the contrary, the less preoccupied they are with themselves and the more they are imbued by the general idea of humanity, the more life-giving, the more purposeful, and the more profound becomes the feeling of nationality and that of individuality. . . .

In all historical epochs we find one universal interest which transcends all exclusively national and purely local boundaries, and those nationalities who have sufficient understanding, passion, and strength to identify themselves wholeheartedly with this universal interest become historical peoples [who play major historical roles]. (Mikhail Bakunin)[1]

Decades before the Communist parties were founded in China and Japan, young radical intellectuals in the two countries were drawn to anarchist varieties of socialism, and much, if not most of what they knew about socialism, came from anarchosocialists such as Mikhail Bakunin, Peter Kropotkin, Pierre-Joseph Proudhon, and Elisée Reclus. Because the core of anarchism lies in the repudiation of the state, one would not expect the views of those who subscribed to anarchism to contribute significantly to an appreciation of the significance of the national question for those who would later become Marxists. Yet anarchists were numerous among the founders of study groups and revolutionary associations that brought Marxism with other currents of Western socialism to China and Japan. Nationality and nationalism posed significant issues for these revolutionaries, who had much to fear from the power that might be given to a state in order to protect and promote the interests of their peoples.

The anarchist Mikhail Bakunin (1814–1876) assessed the significance of nationality and the legitimacy of nationalism in the ambiguous terms cited when he wrote the influential *Statism and Anarchy* in 1873. At that time, following a heated series of exchanges with Karl Marx on Marx's advocacy of a transitional dictatorship of the proletariat and his subsequent expulsion from the First International in

1871, Bakunin denied the permanence and exclusivity of nationality. Neverthe-less, he also invoked the Hegelian category of world-historical peoples, much as Marx did, to attribute to nationalities a definitive role in charting human progress, a view that would seem to affirm the role of the national state in assuring the historic achievements of these nationalities.[2] In this sense, Bakunin's position on the national question was consistent with Marx's and Engels's affirmation of nationalism when it served progressive social interests—as in the transition from feudalism to capitalism—and condemnation of nationalism when it impeded the kind of progress that proletarian socialist revolution promised. But what defined Bakunin as an anarchist was that his repudiation of the state—including both the tsarist empire and the nation-state—was emphatic and complete, not merely his-torically contingent. Anarchism, then, would not only constitute a precursor to Marxism—"both the antithesis and the antecedent of Marxism-Leninism"[3]—in the development of socialist thought in China and Japan, it would also illuminate the antinomies of the "national question" as it would affect Chinese and Japanese Marxists after the October Revolution.

The anarchism of Bakunin, Kropotkin (1842–1921), and Leo Tolstoy (1817–1875) that so heavily influenced Chinese and Japanese socialists was firmly stamped with the imprint of Russia's own national experience. Bakunin's and Kropotkin's anarchism repudiated the oppressive, bureaucratic, and murderous tsarist state,[4] just as the anarchism of Pierre-Joseph Proudhon (1809–1865) and Jean Jacques Elisée Reclus (1830–1905) in France emerged in protest against the authoritarianism of Charles X and the unresponsiveness of Louis Philippe's consti-tutional monarchy in nineteenth-century France. At the same time, as part of the mainstream of the Slavophile movement in nineteenth-century Russia, Russian anarchists (joined briefly by Marx and Engels)[5] celebrated the virtues of their homeland's alleged "backwardness" relative to the competitive politics and eco-nomics of Western Europe's industrial capitalism. Such a provocative mixture of national pride with antistatism would be replicated among Japanese and then Chinese anarchists as well with the result that the dilemmas of nationalism and culturalism versus stateness comprised a persistent theme in the anarchist currents of early Chinese and Japanese socialists. In China, as in Japan, the national question was a set of issues that scholars and thinkers involved in the socialist movements in the two societies were compelled to face as their less-industrialized Asian societies sought to escape the yoke of Western imperialism and promote their interests as nation-states that had legitimate and esteemed positions in the unfolding of human history.

Although the position on political authority differed between Marxists and anarchists, anarchism was consistent with Marxism in its desire to promote the progressive development of humankind. Both philosophical systems, then, could be understood as strategies for social development that sought to transcend the artificial boundaries and limitations that human beings had hitherto imposed upon themselves. Bakunin's paramount concern was to create a social revolution that would realize "*the triumph of humanity, the most complete conquest and establish-ment of personal freedom and development—material, intellectual, and moral—*

for every individual, through the absolutely unrestricted and spontaneous organi-
zation of economic and social solidarity."[6] The specific arrangements of postrevolutionary society remained vague in Bakunin's thought, but his successor,
Kropotkin, systematized an "anarchist communism" built on the principle of
"mutual aid." Yet both agreed on what Bakunin described as "the great principle of
the French Revolution: that every man is entitled to the material and moral means
for the development of his complete humanity." This demanded that men and
women work "*to organize society in such a manner that every individual endowed*
with life, man or woman, may find almost equal means for the development of his
various faculties and for their utilization in his labor; to organize a society which,
while it makes it impossible for any individual whatsoever to exploit the labor of
others, will not allow anyone to share in the enjoyment of social wealth . . . unless
he has himself contributed to its creation with his own labor."[7] Unresolved,
however, was the question of how society would be "organized" so that these
principles might be enforced among those who would take advantage of the
weaker members of society.

All anarchists agreed that Kropotkin's vision was consistent with natural law.
Indeed, Emma Goldman defined natural law itself in anarchist terms: "A natural
law is that factor in man which asserts itself freely and spontaneously without any
external force, in harmony with the requirements of nature."[8] In Goldman's view,
the state served merely to enforce an iniquitous arrangement in which, as
Proudhon wrote, an unjust division of labor undermined the equality among individuals that is "the law of nature as well as of Justice."[9] The nexus between politics
and the role of the state and this economic injustice lay in the institution of private
property. For anarchists, Proudhon's cry "Property is robbery!" was a revolutionary call to arms to restore human natural instinct to cooperation and mutual aid and
to realize the goal of "free production and equitable distribution."[10] The link
between the human instinct for cooperation, on the one hand, and the natural order,
on the other, was, anarchosyndicalists believed, realized in the syndicalist movement. The mushrooming of labor unions linked in national and international labor
federations concretized the anarchist dream to transcend the evil that seemed
inherent in the practice of politics itself, uniting workers to assault directly the
existing exploitative economic organization and substitute for it an anarcho-
communist order.[11] In this respect, many anarchists saw their quest as one that was
nonpolitical, even antipolitical. Politics, the quest for political power, in this view,
sullied men and women by incorporating them into the leviathan itself, fatally
compromising them with the state that was inherently their foe.

It was the conviction that the state was an inherent evil and not merely a
secondary, superstructural product of the economic causes of human dehumaniza-
tion as described by Marx and Engels, that made the followers of Bakunin and
Kropotkin anarchists rather than simply socialists.[12] For Bakunin, " 'The state by
its very nature signifies the enslavement of the masses by a despotic, privileged
minority, whether priestly, feudal, bourgeois, or "scientific" ' ."[13] Much as Jean-
Jacques Rousseau, in his *Second Discourse*, and Marx, in his *Critique of Hegel's*
Philosophy of Right, had contended, Proudhon argued that the emergence of

private property had exacerbated natural inequalities among men and women and given rise to social conflict; the state simply masked and reinforced social disharmony and man's exploitation by man, while it created new inequities and conflicts of its own.[14] In Goldman's words, "In a society where those who always work never have anything, while those who never work enjoy everything, solidarity of interests is non-existent; hence social harmony is but a myth. The only way organized authority meets this grave situation is by extending still greater privileges to those who have already monopolized the earth, and by still further enslaving the disinherited masses."[15] Such moral indignation against the state and its politics would not yield to protests that human nature precluded the natural harmony they sought. "Poor human nature," charged Goldman eloquently, "what horrible crimes have been committed in thy name!" "How can any one speak of [human nature] today, with every soul in a prison, with every heart fettered, wounded, and maimed?" Just as in animals, the nature of man was transformed by its captivity. Only when men and women had regained their freedom from the state could one discover the heights of their true capacities.[16] The *syndicat*, reflecting man's cooperative instinct and his passion to taste fully the creative, fulfilling essence of his labor, stood as the symbol of these suppressed potentialities.

The anarchists repudiated not only the state but also the state system to which, they believed, the existence of even a single state must give rise. Indeed, they maintained, it was on the international level that the truly antihuman essence of the state became most apparent. "It shatters the universal solidarity of all men on the earth," protested Bakunin, "and brings some of them into association only for the purpose of destroying, conquering, and enslaving all the rest." Its cruelty was most fully exposed in its harsh treatment of foreign populations, "which it can plunder, exterminate, or enslave at will." The absence of international law—which "*could never exist in a meaningful and realistic way without undermining to its foundations the very principle of the absolute sovereignty of the State*"—assured that because the state recognized no right outside itself, it would also acknowledge "no duties toward foreign populations."[17] By this reasoning, the alternative to the state and its international system was the organization of men and women into free associations from below rather than from above.[18] A network of such associations would arise at ever higher levels from the local village to the international sphere, culminating in a single free federation.[19]

Yet, even as West European states would seek much later to overcome conflict over competing sovereignties in the drive toward federation, the dissolution of the Soviet Union and other East and Central European societies into their constituent ethnic peoples in the wake of the revolutions of 1989 indicates that Bakunin's vision might be considerably difficult to realize. Once the state's official Marxist-Leninist ideology of proletarian internationalism collapsed in Eastern Europe and the Soviet Union, the inhibitions on nationalism that it had inculcated into the citizenry evaporated immediately. At the turn of the twentieth century, such passionate nationalistic sentiments pervaded the worlds of Chinese and Japanese revolutionists.[20] Ultimately, although it did not figure as a central problématique in the work of Bakunin and his comrades in the European anarchist movement, nationalism was an important issue for his followers in China and Japan, and historically it has consistently asserted itself as both the catalyst to and antagonist of the centralized state. The appeal of anarchism to East Asian revolutionaries, then, compels one to examine the implications of the anarchist vision for the national question in China and Japan.

As observed, the anarchists expanded the Marxist critique of the bourgeois state and the state in general as a product of class conflict and an agent of class oppression to denounce the state as a fundamental evil. The anarchist view of the state, where it diverged from Marxism and, particularly, from Marxism-Leninism, suggests the first aspect of the national question to face Asian socialists—statism.[21] On this aspect of the problem much has been written, but the literature has focused primarily on a single issue, the means to the ultimate goal on which anarchists and Marxists could agree—socialism. This issue was joined over the notion of the dictatorship of the proletariat. Engels wrote, "'It was simply a matter of the proper order of things: the socialists would destroy capitalism first and then the state, whereas the anarchist, blinded by a passionate rejection of authority to every realistic consideration, would do away with the state at once'."[22] Lenin, whose own *State and Revolution* can be read as an anarchist document, similarly asserted that the real issue between anarchists and Marxists was revolutionary means: "'We do not at all disagree with the Anarchists on the question of the abolition of the state as an aim. We maintain that, to achieve this aim, we must temporarily make use of the instruments, resources, and methods of state power against the exploiters'."[23] The anarchist view, however, was that one could not use authority to eliminate authority, because "authority can breed only more authority."[24] Indeed, the anarchists' aversion to authority was so absolute that Bakunin and his successors objected even to its use in organizing and sustaining the revolutionary movement itself.[25] Hence, Bakunin and Kropotkin also rejected in principle the conspiratorial revolutionary party that could claim authority apart from, and potentially against, the interests of those they claimed to liberate. *"The emancipation of the workers can be achieved only by the workers themselves,"* Bakunin insisted.[26]

These issues comprised only part of the statist aspect of the national question for Chinese and Japanese socialists. The deeper issue of their time arose from their nations' recent negative experiences with Western imperialism and the consequent popularity of social Darwinism. The latter they learned from writings of Huxley and T. R. Malthus, which analyzed the brutality of imperialism in scientistic terms. To what degree should one reject, or could one ignore, the social Darwinist principles of the system and survive, with or without internal social revolution? There was some division within the anarchist movement on this issue. Kropotkin, for example, was unconvinced by Bakunin's insistence that the anarchist revolution would of necessity be a violent one.[27] Although anarchists agreed "that struggle is necessary only in order to eliminate the negatively competitive aspects of existing society," they recognized also that "the continued existence of the kind of perpetual struggle posed by the neo-Darwinians would be fatal to a cooperative society." Thus, Kropotkin undertook to refute Huxley and Malthus on this matter in his *Mutual Aid* (1902). The burden of Kropotkin's argument was that the natural

sociability of animal species, including humans, was as crucial to their development as the instinct to struggle for survival. Animals had an instinct to cooperate as
well as to compete, and those species that developed cooperative urges were at a
relatively greater advantage in the struggle for survival. In Kropotkin's view, when
struggle "does exist within a species, it is injurious rather than otherwise, since it
dissipates the advantages gained by sociability. Far from thriving on competition,
natural selection seeks out the means by which it can be avoided."[28]

Yet Bakunin had observed several decades earlier that the nature of the state—
"by its very nature a military State"—was such that,[29] if Kropotkin's observations
did apply to humankind in general, the urge to cooperate rather than to compete
was not characteristic of states. Could leaders of nations such as China and Japan,
victimized by the powerful national states of Western Europe, realistically ignore
the social Darwinist nature of international relations on ethical grounds—simply
because the world *should* not operate on such a basis even if it did in reality—and
expect to survive? Could their socialistically reorganized societies survive the
military onslaught of enemy states such as those that threatened the fragile Bolshevik regime established in 1917? Ultimately, of course, it was a "species" of
humanity in a larger sense—the nationality, the Chinese *minzu* or Japanese
minzoku—that was threatened. Revolutionaries first and foremost wished to ame-
liorate the condition of their compatriots. How could they abandon the enterprise
of state building, which would protect the very existence of their compatriots (and,
perhaps, even their culture) so that they could build socialism? This dilemma
confronting anarchosocialists in China and Japan compels a return to the question
of nationality.

Bakunin's position on the validity of nationalism changed over the decades. In
his later years, Bakunin roundly condemned the Pan-Slavism, along with other
narrow exclusive nationalisms, that he had embraced previously.[30] This shift was
consistent with his adamant, now more systematized, antistatism. Nevertheless,
Bakunin never abandoned the possibility that certain "nationalist" liberation
movements should be supported because they served the more universal aim of the
liberation of all humankind. In the late 1840s, before his anarchist philosophy had
been developed fully, Bakunin had seen in the Russian people, then oppressed by a
backward and oppressive autocracy, the potential not only to rejoin the forward
flow of human history but also to play a pivotal leading role as a world-historical
people. Concerned with the fate of Slavic peoples, Bakunin had envisaged "the
alliance of Poland and the 'real Russia,' as distinguished from 'official Russia'."[31]
This was a populist program for Slavs that had a significant impact on the narodnik
movement in Russia itself. For Bakunin, the social revolution required that the
people struggle against the state above them: "'Above all we must destroy within
the hearts of the people the remains of that unfortunate faith in the Tsar which for
centuries has condemned them to terrible serfdom'."[32] But this nationalist and
populist program for Russia had greater international implications upon which
Bakunin would build his international anarchist movement. "'The reconciliation
of Russia and Poland'," he declared, "'means the liberation of sixty million souls,
the liberation of all the Slav people who groan under a foreign yoke. It means, in a
word, the fall, the irretrievable fall, of despotism in Europe'."[33]

Thus, Bakunin maintained that certain nationalist movements were of great world-historical value by virtue of their leading role in realizing his "vision of a Europe, dominated by Germany, which would find on its fringes (from Spain to Russia) the forces capable of rebelling against Germany and destroying the oppressive and statist conception at its centre."[34] His antipathy toward German authoritarianism, intensified by the Franco-Prussian War, the experience of the Paris Commune, and the emergence of Otto von Bismarck's statism, ensured that this belief would not disappear from Bakunin's writings of the 1870s, even when he was more inclined to reject the exclusivism of Pan-Slavism and other nationalisms. Thus, there remained in Bakunin's mature philosophy the view that at once rejected nationalism as a principle and yet affirmed it as a liberating force. Bakunin wrote in "Federalism, Socialism, Anti-Theologism" in 1867:

> The League [of Peace and Freedom] will recognize *nationality* as a natural fact which has an incontestable right to a free existence and development, but not as a principle, since every principle should have the power of universality, while nationality, a fact of exclusivist tendency, separates. The so-called *principle of nationality*, such as has been declared in our time by the governments of France, Russia, Prussia, and even by many German, Polish, Italian, and Hungarian patriots, is a mere derivative notion born of the reaction against the spirit of revolution. It is aristocratic to the point of despising the folk dialect, spoken by illiterate peoples. It implicitly denies the liberty of provinces and the true autonomy of communes. Its support, in all countries, does not come from the masses, whose real interests it sacrifices to the so-called public good, which is always the good of the privileged classes. It expresses nothing but the alleged historic rights and ambitions of States. The right of nationality can therefore never be considered by the League except as a natural consequence of the supreme principle of liberty; it ceases to be a right as soon as it takes a stand either against liberty or even outside liberty.[35]

This position would suggest that Chinese and Japanese revolutionaries might well have been able to reconcile antistatism with the spirit of nationalism that emerged in East Asia in response to the West. More importantly, given the tensions in the thought of Bakunin and Kropotkin on nationalism and statism, one might expect to see aspects of the national question exacerbated as Asian socialists were increasingly exposed to and attracted to its rival in Marxism. Finally, the decision to become a Marxist-Leninist revolutionary after 1917 or to reject Leninism for anarchism would constitute a resolution of both aspects of the national question along one trajectory or the other.

Anarchism and the National Question in China and Japan

The domestic and international situations in which Chinese and Japanese anarchists found their societies in the first decades of the twentieth century offer valuable clues to the patterns of their thought on the national question and their prospects for dominance over Marxism-Leninism. J. P. Nettl has suggested that one finds greater and more intense anarchist activity where stateness—"the identification of state with nation"—is more highly developed. Thus, he contrasted the emergence of strong anarchist movements in Germany and France, which shared the experience of having strong states identified with the nation, on the one hand, with the relative weakness of such movements in the United States and Great Britain, on the other. "The notion of state accordingly appears to provide a convenient and polarizing means of disidentification as the reverse side of the Hegelian coin of identification with the state."[36]

These observations suggest that anarchism should have struck deeper roots in Japan, where the Meiji regime had attained a high degree of stateness through modernizing industrial and military reforms, than in China, where the crumbling imperial regime left a virtual political vacuum after its demise in 1911. Yet China did have a thriving anarchist movement both on the mainland and in student circles in Paris and Tokyo. It will be important to note whether this anarchism constituted a response to the disintegrating authority of the Manchu state or if it extended to societal structures of authority, such as the oppressive, traditional, patriarchal family—as would be depicted in popular fiction such as Ba Jin's *Jia* trilogy— against which so many young Chinese rebelled in the first decades of the twentieth century. If the latter is the case, it would appear that Nettl's hypothesis concerning stateness must be reconsidered to incorporate societal authority in the factors that arouse anarchist responses.

In any event, in Japan what had occurred under the auspices of the Meiji oligarchs in the Restoration to encourage nationalism and the identification of state with nation offers a dramatic contrast with the inability of the alien Qing to nurture and galvanize nationalism in support of their own state. When considering Nettl's hypothesis, it is important to note the scholarly and popular use of the term *hantaisei* (antisystem) to describe movements of political opposition in late nineteenth- and early twentieth-century Japan. The Meiji oligarchs had effectively galvanized nationalist sentiment and mobilized it to support their massive modernization effort. Japanese nationalism became the instrument of the state, and it was wielded effectively for state ends in the official *kokutai* thought and its dissemination through the universal education system. One would also expect to find opposition, or at least indifference, to this nationalism, as a tool of the state, among Japanese revolutionaries. The impulse to engage in oppositionist, even anarchist activity, then, should have been particularly powerful among the educated youth of the 1890s, the second generation of Meiji intellectuals.

By virtue of their Confucian training and the promise of constitutional parliamentary government, they expected legitimate and meaningful opportunities to participate actively in the new regime. Such opportunities to participate within the bounds of the institutional structure of the Meiji Constitution, however, were strictly limited. It will be recalled that Article 1 of the constitution declared that "The Great Empire of Japan shall be reigned over and governed by a line of Emperors unbroken for ages eternal."[37] Constitutional scholars Uesugi Shinkichi and Hozumi Yatsuka interpreted this provision as according absolute power to Japan's "divine and inviolable" emperor.[38] To be sure, civic freedom was severely constricted in Meiji Japan. The right to vote was granted only to those men over twenty-five who could pay a hefty 15-yen national land or income tax, a provision that granted suffrage to only 1.15 percent of the population. As late as 1919, the law still required payment of a 10-yen tax from those who would vote, and even the Hara Kei cabinet's proposal to lower that requirement would have enfranchised only 5.6 percent of the rural population and 3.2 percent of the urban population— less than 2.9 million of a total population of 56 million.[39] The powers of the long-awaited Diet were limited by special provisions that granted "broad constitutional powers" to the Privy Council and the House of Peers "enabling them to reject an act of the House of Representatives." The cabinet was not responsible to the Diet, and the military reserved considerable independence from the House of Representatives as well as from the cabinet.[40] Although the parties accommodated some degree of liberal dissidence, the government relentlessly repressed both the civil rights movement and the political party movement. The Peace Police Law in 1900 banned strikes and the right to organize, and the Social-Democratic party (Shakai Minshutō) was outlawed within twenty-four hours of its founding.[41] Individuals associated with such repressed and frustrated groups increasingly turned to anarchist-dominated socialism. The dissident movement grew, and the anarchist influence within it flourished as government repression intensified, culminating in the high-treason trial and execution (*taigyaku jiken*) of the leading anarchist Kō-toku Shūsui in 1911. Kōtoku's death abruptly halted the growth of the socialist movement, inaugurating its so-called "winter period" (*fuyu no jidai*). Anarcho-syndicalist ideas became "overwhelmingly" predominant in the Japanese socialist movement during this period.[42] As government repression intensified after the Bolshevik victory of October 1917, it would be reasonable to expect anarchism to have continued to have a greater appeal in Japan, even as its resistance to organization for the sake of the revolution would place it at a disadvantage vis-à-vis Marxist-Leninist activists.

Conversely, Nettl's proposition would lead one to expect anarchism to have been far less appealing to Chinese intellectuals. Victimized by the Western-dominated social Darwinist system of international relations (a game at which Japan had quickly become exceedingly adept at Chinese expense), China would be expected to produce a more intense nationalist movement. Such a desire to resist Western and Japanese encroachment should have nurtured a concerted effort to replicate the Meiji precedent of vigorous state building in China. The anarchist vision of international cooperation and harmony might have been particularly tantalizing here, but it would have seemed increasingly unrealistic as more and more of the formerly great Middle Kingdom was partitioned and plundered by the Western powers and Japan.

Yet it was primarily through anarchism that Marxian socialism came to find adherents among dissaffected Chinese thinker-activists, and the vitality of the anarchist movement in China exceeded that of its counterpart in the ponderously statist Japan. Certainly, Chinese intellectuals would have found very attractive Bakunin's romantic imagery of a backward and oppressed nationality making a Promethean leap into the role of a world-historic people. Indeed, Scalapino and Yü have properly noted the affinity that Chinese intellectuals, especially in Europe, felt for Russian *narodism* (populism): "Russia and China were the two sick giants of the early twentieth century."[43] Like Slavophiles and narodniki, Chinese intellectuals would be attracted to the populist anarchism of Bakunin and Kropotkin "because they saw them as ways to prevent the rise of the injustices and immoralities of impending capitalism."[44] In anti-Western reaction, they would see in the Russian revolutionary struggle, and in the successes of 1905 to 1917, not merely a way of opposing but superseding the West but a possibility of emerging at the forefront of world history. The Qing inadvertently further undercut its potential support from young intellectuals when it eliminated the examination system in the first decade of the new century without replacing it with an alternative means to recruit political leadership. Suddenly there was no clear avenue to public service, no new set of guiding principles, offered to a generation of youth that aspired desperately to save China. This elite soon comprised a pool of highly activist, disenchanted intelligentsia prepared to stand against the now *ancien* regime. Here the Japanese socialist movement exercised a major impact (far greater than that of Russia) upon the development of Chinese socialist thought. In this respect, the Qing government's desperate decision to send students to study the institutions and more advanced technologies in practice in Japan and Western Europe was a fateful and ultimately fatal one. In Japan as in France, worker-students quickly fell under the influence of the vigorous anarchist and syndicalist movement. These intellectuals promoted their new revolutionary ideas by publishing their own journals, and, when they returned to China, they brought the anarchist movement back with them. Thus, despite the lower degree of stateness of their own China, the young Chinese socialist movement bore the heavy imprint of anarchist movements in the more statist societies where its adherents were first acquainted with Western socialism. Moreover, the violent imagery of destroying all the repressive institutions of existing society—inside and outside the state—was extremely appealing to increasingly iconoclastic young Chinese intellectuals who saw Chinese tradition itself as the burden that placed China at the mercy of the Western powers and Japan. In the absence of a strong state, Chinese were, nevertheless, oppressed socially and economically as individuals and as a nation by an oppressive web of social institutions and practices. The residual influence of the alternative *wuwei* tradition of Daoism reinforced the urge to eliminate the oppression of such societal institutions and practices, thus strengthening and deepening the appeal of anarchism in China.[45] Wishing to rid China of the entire apparatus of Confucianism, from its worldview to the onerous family system and cruel social practices such as footbinding, radical young Chinese found in the anarchist vision refreshing relief. Yet anarchism did not nurture only this negative dimension of revolutionary élan. Particularly in its syndicalist incarnation, Western anarchism was imbued with a powerful positive dimension of self-assertion (which the indigenous Daoist tradition lacked), promising to consolidate the power of the Chinese nation without crippling it with yet another set of oppressive authoritarian institutions.

Yet, in China as in Japan, crippled by its own individualism and aversion to organizational discipline,[46] the anarchist movement rapidly succumbed to the influence of Bolshevism and Sun Yat-senist or Marxian state socialism by the late 1920s. Nevertheless, the anarchist experience would retain enduring significance for the socialist movements in the two societies. The particular virtue of the anarchists was that they forced their colleagues in the movement to address and seek to resolve the national question explicitly. Decades later, Mao Zedong's Marxism would retain a strong streak of the anarchist rebellion against authority and commitment to revolutionizing the cultural dimensions of traditional Chinese society, reflecting, in particular, the early influence of anarchist Qu Shengbai on Mao.[47] In Japan, the rapid decline of anarchism and the persistent challenges even to Marxism-Leninism mounted by Marxian national socialists underscored the ability of state power to exercise effective hegemony.[48] There, the statist *kokutai* myth would prove so powerful that even revolutionary socialists could not fully escape its influence. Thus, nationalistic statism would either be incorporated into Marxism or adopted in its stead. These implications would emerge most dramatically in the conflict between anarchists and Bolshevists in the wake of the October Revolution in both societies. I examine first, however, what the anarchists in China and Japan had to offer in their own terms.

Anti-Westernism and the Impulse Toward Anarchism in Meiji Japan

In both China and Japan, anarchism was first influential as a relatively undifferentiated strand of Western socialist thought. In neither case did anarchism thrive as a distinctive movement until after the Russian revolution of 1905. Even then, anarchist socialism was not immediately distinguishable from other strands of socialist thought as it was reflected in political organizations or in theoretical literature. This was particularly so in Japan, where the anarchism of Kōtoku Shūsui and Ōsugi Sakae emerged as a branch of the main socialist group in 1906 yet remained intermingled with other socialist groups and their writings until the celebrated *anaboru* (anarchist-bolshevist) debate and split of 1921 (see chap. 5 in this volume). In China, the movement was more distinctive. The first avowedly anarchist Chinese group appeared in Paris under the direct influence of France's anarchosyndicalist movement, which was approaching a peak in its radicalism. Anarchism became increasingly influential as a distinct strain within China proper subsequently, primarily through the efforts of Paris student-worker pioneers such as Li Shizeng, Zhang Jingjiang, Chu Minyi, and Wu Zhihui combined with the impact of anarchism among Chinese in Japan.

Despite the separate appeal of anarchism to overseas Chinese studying in France, Japan was a major source of inspiration for the Chinese movement. Literature on Russian nihilism and narodism and European anarchism as well as other currents of Western socialist thought was imported into China by way of more accessible Japanese translations.[49] This factor increased the tendency for anarchism to be intermixed with other socialist ideas among Chinese intellectuals since this had been the predominant trend in Japan from the outset of Japanese interest in Western socialism. As early as 1898, for example, the Shakai-shugi Kenkyūkai (Society for the Study of Socialism) in Tokyo was founded to " 'study the principles of socialism and whether or not they were applicable to Japan'."[50] For two years, the group examined the works of Claude Henri de Saint-Simon, Charles Fourier, and Proudhon, as well as Marx, and when Kōtoku's classic *Shakai-shugi shinzui* (The essence of socialism) was published in 1903, it referred to Marx as the "father of modern socialism" but drew liberally on other Western socialist thinkers.[51] Similarly, Kōtoku's distinction in 1902 between "two contradictory" categories of socialism—"that which expands the power of the state limitlessly" (such as state socialism) and "that which takes it [socialism] to imply the demise of the state" (such as anarchism)—led him to associate the thought of Marx and Engels with anarchism because of their thesis of the withering away of the state.[52] One means by which this admixing of Marxian and other socialist perspectives with anarchism was transmitted to China was legal scholar Kemuyama Sentarō's book *Kinsei museifu-shugi* (Modern anarchism), published in 1902. This volume was then the authoritative source on Russian populism and heavily influenced anarchists Kōtoku, Miyashita Takichi (1875–1911), and Kanno Suga (1881–1911),[53] and parts of it were translated into Chinese and published in widely read Chinese journals. Kemuyama's book, in turn, inspired several Chinese radical works, including a novel by Luo Pu, *Heroines of Eastern Europe*. A commentary on the novel by Han Wenju illustrates Chinese perceptions of the close link between Russian anarchism (which was associated, in Chinese and Japanese perceptions, with nihilism) and European socialism: " 'The thought of the Russian nihilist party was generated out of the philosophy of the Germans Hegel and Marx, and the Frenchman St. Simon, and is what the Japanese call "socialism." The doctrine is very similar to the idea of the Great Harmony in the *Li-yün*. It is certain to spread over the world in the future'."[54]

Chinese and Japanese intellectuals became acquainted with Western anarchosocialist thought together, and together they were drawn to its intriguing combination of radical individualism and utopian communalism harkening back to a preindustrial past devoid of harsh class conflict and alienation. Yet the impulse to adopt anarchist ideas would appear to have come from almost diametrically opposing directions in the two societies. In Japan, and to some extent among Chinese anarchists who developed their anarchism in Japan (such as Liu Shipei)[55] as well, anarchism emerged out of an anti-Westernism and an aspiration to return to traditional values. By contrast, Chinese anarchists, particularly in Paris, tended toward almost complete cultural iconoclasm to embrace the West in every respect. Nevertheless, in both cases, the appeal of a distant past in their own cultural traditions created a problématique in the national question that was more subtle and more complex than these generalizations would admit. For Chinese anarchists so heavily influenced by the Japanese movement, the manner in which the issues were articulated among Meiji socialists was decisive. It is here that I begin the inquiry.

I have suggested that anarchism should have exercised a significantly stronger appeal among Japanese than among Chinese intellectuals in reaction against the powerful modern nation-state constructed by the Meiji oligarchs. There was much in the initial appeal of anarchism in Japan to confirm this view. Because the Meiji regime had so skillfully combined certain traditional Japanese beliefs concerning the emperor with German *Staatsrecht* theory to formulate its official state orthodoxy of the *kokutai*,[56] one would expect this coupling of statism with nationalism from above to have elicited an anarchist repudiation of both elements. Nevertheless, anarchism in Japan was much more nuanced and complex than this proposition would suggest. To be sure, Japanese anarchist currents as disparate as Kōtoku's syndicalist anarchism and Ōsugi Sakae's creative egoism[57] did, indeed, reflect such hostility to state power. Paradoxically, however, the two men and their anarchist followers accomplished what few other Japanese socialists did, although the *kokutai* notion conflated nation and state, these han-taisei leaders clearly distinguished nationalism from statism. Vehemently rejecting imported German statist elements in the Meiji polity, Kōtoku and his followers also experienced a deep yearning for the restoration of what they believed to be traditional Japanese virtues,[58] many of which were expressed in the *kokutai* notion of the organic community itself.

Here one finds something very much akin to the Slavophilism of Russia's narodniki. The massive importation of Western technology, social organization, and, eventually, capitalist labor practices in Russia in the seventeenth, eighteenth, and nineteenth centuries, as in Meiji Japan almost two centuries later, was perceived to have had a corrosive effect on the indigenous social structure and the values supporting it. Slavophiles strenuously opposed their Westernizer compatriots' determination that the traditional peasant commune (mir, or obshchina) should be sacrificed to the development of capitalism on the West European prototype. On the contrary, Slavophiles believed in the uniqueness and special historical destiny of the Russian people. They saw in the obshchina a kind of natural rural commune on which socialism could be built without condemning Russians to endure the painful ills of capitalism that had developed in England. Although Russian populists were not anti-Western "mystical nationalists," they did share the Slavophiles' faith in the obshchina and in the popular values and traditions supporting it. This instinct to look backward toward traditional Russian mores the populists combined with a belief that Russia could reap the benefits of Western science and technology and produce a more palatable outcome than the tortuous Marxian path to socialism and communism by way of capitalism.[59] This conviction brought the narodniki into conflict with Lenin, who set out to prove that the development of capitalism in Russia was already inevitably so far under way that, however painful it might be, the Marxist revolutionary path looking forward rather than backward was the only sensible course for Russian socialists.

Likewise, Japanese socialists were first attracted to socialism out of concern for the social problems (*shakai mondai*) created by the Meiji state's industrialization effort. As were other intellectuals of their generation who shared a diffuse but profound commitment to public service,[60] the pioneers of Japan's socialist movement were adherents of traditional Confucian and Japanese *shishi* norms, and they were profoundly disquieted by the effect of the Meiji reforms on those values. Kawakami Hajime, a leading Marxist scholar in the 1910s and 1920s, was drawn to socialism precisely in reaction against what he saw as the overwhelmingly egoistic and materialistic essence of capitalist society. As his biographer Gail Bernstein has noted, "Kawakami's . . . strong conviction about the importance of the spiritual as opposed to material side of human life marked his coming of age in a period when, it seemed, material technology and materialistic values dominated men's consciousness. Having survived the threat to its existence as an independent nation, Japan was now being eaten from within: immorality—selfishness—was rampant. The cure had proven as bad as the illness."[61] Such moralistic concern for the fate of the Japanese people under the impact of industrialization was widespread as evidenced by the growth of the socialist movement around publications devoted to "social problems." Such magazines as *Rikugō zasshi*, *Kokumin no tomo* (Friend of the People), *Rōdō sekai* (Labor World), *Shakai zasshi* (Society Magazine), and *Shakai* (Society) addressed labor and social issues and were shortly followed by *Kokumin shinbun* (The People's News) and *Yorozu chōhō* (Everything Useful), which openly advocated socialism. In the magazine *Taiyō* (The Sun) circa 1897, Kawakami Kiyoshi advocated the protection of the welfare of workers, and Katayama Sen contributed a "Biography of [Ferdinand] Lassalle" and a study of "Contemporary British Society."[62]

The moral issue was the crucial link binding Japanese Christian socialists to those who became known as "materialist" socialists because both shared "universalist humanitarian concerns."[63] Meiji intellectuals turned toward socialism late in the 1890s in repudiation of the social Darwinist outlook that had come to dominate intellectual discourse. The principle of "free competition" of the "British school of economics" was purportedly the basis of the Western-style capitalism adopted by the Meiji government (although, in fact, intervention by the state made Meiji capitalism more akin to capitalism under Bismarck than to the idealized laissez-faire model). The laws of free economic competition among men and women within Japanese society placed a premium on "individualism" and "egoism," values alien to Japan's traditional, presumably harmonious social order based on the pursuit of the interests of the community. Thus, "when seen as identical with the 'struggle for survival' . . . , 'free competition' [the capitalist organization of labor] was taken to be 'something in irreconcilable contradiction with morality and religion, . . . animalism'."[64]

This moralism was especially apparent in the evolution of Kōtoku Shūsui first as a socialist and then as an anarchist. Schooled in Confucian shishi morality, Kōtoku rejected Darwinism and social Darwinism for the operation of the Confucian idea of *jin* (in Chinese, ren, benevolent love) as the guiding principle of human relations. Early in his career, Kōtoku had reacted even more strongly than his fellow socialists against Westernism and Westernization. Although Kōtoku (like Katayama, who was a Christian)[65] relied heavily on Christian socialist Richard T. Ely's *Socialism and Social Reform* in writing *Shakai-shugi shinzui* (The essence of socialism), shortly after its publication he broke ranks with the Christian socialists. His rejection of the West was so complete that he distrusted Christianity's attribution of higher priority to the individual over the state and society as yet another manifestation of Western-style individualism. His individualism was that of the shishi, which was concerned more with the obligations than with the rights of the individual vis-à-vis society. Thus, when Kōtoku declared himself a socialist in 1901, it was because he found socialism consistent with his own indigenous Confucian values; it was a way to protect traditional Japanese virtues against wholesale Westernization.[66]

Moral regeneration was an essential part of Kōtoku's vision of socialism, and it was this element that was most emphasized in the work by Thomas Kirkup, *An Inquiry into Socialism* (1888), which Kōtoku cited extensively in his own writings on socialism. Kirkup had asserted, " '[E]specially in its earlier stages the industrial revolution acted without social or ethical control, and being made the instrument of private gain resulted in the excessive enrichment of the few, and the impoverishment and degradation of the working classes. *Unless the material and technical appliances of civilization are subordinate to moral ends and to the promotion of true social well being, we have no guarantee that their influence will be beneficial*' ."[67] This identification of moral regeneration as part of the socialist vision enabled Kōtoku, particularly before the Sino-Japanese War but afterward as well, to reconcile socialism with a certain kind of nationalism by separating the statist and national components of the *kokutai* idea. This was evident as early as the late 1890s when widespread economic distress encouraged Meiji socialists to build a mass-based movement. Then, Kōtoku had rejected legal political means of social reform because he was repelled by the increasing immorality—the Machiavellian amorality—of politics since the Restoration. Many intellectuals of Kōtoku's generation felt that the original goals and high moral values of the Restoration had been betrayed by the *hanbatsu* oligarchy (those associated with the Satsuma and Chōshū domains who had spearheaded the overthrow of the Tokugawa shogunate). This sentiment was intensified, not attenuated, after 1890 when the promised Diet and political party system materialized. The Diet itself was weak, and the orthodoxy that emerged on the basis of Article 1 of the Meiji Constitution attributed supreme authority to rule (*tōchiken*) to the emperor in any case. As for the political parties, which had always been suspect in traditional Confucian thought as means for the pursuit of private rather than public interests,[68] it was argued that they had themselves immediately become part of the Sat-Chō clique's betrayal of the higher social goals of the Restoration, and, thus, they could not be trusted to be the agency of true social reform. Kōtoku lamented in 1899, " 'After all, the cause of today's degeneration and decline can be attributed largely to the whole gang of elder statesmen like Itō. . . . Our restoration-revolution was based on the spirit of liberty, equality, and fraternity. If these great ideas had been properly carried out, extended, and directed it would not have been difficult to bring about a healthy development' ."[69]

Kōtoku shared this disillusionment with his progressive predecessors in the jiyū minken undō (civil rights movement). He and men like Nakae Chōmin opposed the statist elements that the Meiji oligarchy had built into the *kokutai* notion. They "opposed . . . the emergence of the bureaucratic state modeled on the Germany of Bismarck which favored special interest groups and remained under the control of a small privileged minority." They "objected to a state that constantly demanded sacrifices from its people without making any significant effort to improve the average citizen's lot."[70] These criticisms were based on very traditional Confucian criteria in which rule by morality for the benefit of the livelihood of the people was the guiding political principle. While both Kōtoku and Nakae identified these Confucian humanitarian goals with the ambitions of the French Revolution, they shared an element of nationalist sentiment in that both felt that these Confucian values inhered in the traditional society that was at the core of the Japanese *kokutai*. In Kōtoku's view, the high moral ideals of politics that he saw as endemic to traditional Japanese society had been supplanted by alien (Western), amoral political practices. Kōtoku, thus, rejected the statist elements of the *kokutai* on the basis of its nativist, or nationalist, components. For this reason, Kōtoku was more attracted to Western socialist writings that were critical of the West and emphasized ethics—Ely, Kirkup, and Albert E. Shäffle (*The Quintessence of Socialism*)—than to the more purely "scientific" socialism of Marx and Engels.[71] Apparent here long before his actual conversion to anarchism in 1906 with his speech on the doctrine of direct action (*chokusetsu kōdō ron*) were the impulses that attracted Kōtoku to anarchism and particularly to the highly ethical anarchism of Kropotkin when he finally read Kropotkin's autobiography and *Fields, Factories, and Workshops* (1899) in prison in 1905.[72]

Notably, then, Kōtoku saw no necessary conflict between what he defined as the true *kokutai* and socialism. Indeed, until the Sino-Japanese War put Japan firmly on an imperialist path, Kōtoku was able to support nationalism. Like many Japanese progressives, Kōtoku "had supported the war idealistically, . . . had seen in it an opportunity to have 'progress' conquer a 'decadent past'." In Kōtoku's view, Japan, as the most advanced Asian society, was embarking on a war to save the continent from further encroachments by the West. The outcome of this war, which expanded Japanese power to Formosa, the Pescadores, and the Liaodong peninsula, however, led Kōtoku and others to oppose imperialistic nationalism.[73] In pacifist opposition to the Russo-Japanese War a decade later, socialists found themselves in direct conflict with the authority of the Japanese state.

Kōtoku's rejection of imperialist expansion as the proper expression of Japan's national mission in his *Imperialism, The Spectre of the Twentieth Century* (1901) coincided with his explicit adoption of socialism. The center of the socialist movement gradually moved from Katayama and his labor concerns to Kōtoku and those such as Ōsugi and Arahata who would form the Heimin-sha (Commoners' Society) in 1903 calling for democracy, socialism, and pacifism. Yet, even as Kōtoku attacked the new expansionist nationalism, he maintained the compatibility of socialism with the *kokutai* and its tennō. In "Shakai-shugi to kokutai" [Socialism and the national polity], published in *Rikugō zasshi* in November 1902, Kōtoku maintained that the true imperial tradition of the *kokutai* as exemplified in the emperor Nintoku—whose "great concern" was the "well being of the people"—"was in complete agreement with socialism and absolutely in no way contradicted it." The goals of "peace, progress, and prosperity were common to both."[74] The invocation of the imperial institution to support imperialism, "a policy of hatred and contempt, not to mention 'vain pride,' constituted a serious perversion of Japan's 'true' imperial tradition."[75] Thus, early in his intellectual development Kōtoku was able to identify statism as alien to Japan while retaining *kokutai* as the referent for the true mystical moral community of the Japanese nation whose well-being political action should serve. Not only did anarchism pose no contradiction with such a conception of the *kokutai*, but in its ethical concerns, in its assumption of the underlying natural cohesion of the community, and in its faith in the moral integrity and regeneration of humankind, anarchism was fully consonant with Kōtoku's earliest impulses toward socialism. He did not repudiate his faith in the promise of the Japanese moral community as the basis for socialism even as he turned his efforts to anarchosyndicalist tactics against capitalism.

Finally, Kōtoku's nationalistic impulses were consistent with his identification of anarchism with Japanese philosophical traditions. Where he and other Japanese anarchists saw the state as an alien power imported and grafted like a leviathan onto the real *kokutai* (compare the narodnik imagery of "official" versus "real" Russia),[76] they also identified anarchism itself as a doctrine with roots in their own cultural past. Kōtoku contended that "the 'theory' of anarchism 'is virtually the same kind of philosophy as the East's Laozi and Zhuangzi, and . . . that once the systems that control coercively, such as with today's political and military power, are gone the natural tendency of human society is to realize a society of communal life, of self-help united with morality and benevolence, and that in order to perfect our freedom and well being we must proceed following this tendency'."[77] Kōtoku looked backward and inward to the roots of Japanese culture to support his anarchosocialist vision.

In subsequent years, the significance of these themes did not abate as the anarchist movement flourished in Japan and then in China. In Japan, the anarchist movement burgeoned in response to the triumph, albeit limited, of the Russian Revolution of 1905. Given their conviction that Russia was irredeemably backward, the Japanese socialists were duly impressed, indeed shocked, by the events in Russia. Like Chinese revolutionists, the Japanese socialists interpreted the revolution in world historical terms. The revolution "made a deep impression that made our blood boil," recalled Arahata Kanson. For Kōtoku and his followers, 1905 was the "spark" that could ignite revolution throughout the Far East, and it aroused the vision of a similar upheaval in Japan.[78]

Profound, then, was the impact of the 1905 revolution on Kōtoku's conversion, which brought anarchism to the forefront of the Japanese socialist movement and made its impact felt on the Chinese movement in turn. Before his prison term of 1905 and his trip to America later that year, Kōtoku had shared his peers' faith in the utility of parliamentary tactics for achieving socialism. Having met American anarchist Albert Johnson, experienced exhilaration in the massive destruction of civilization evidenced in the San Francisco earthquake, engaged in a brief correspondence with Kropotkin, and read Kropotkin's works and accounts of the Marx-Bakunin debates, Kōtoku returned to Japan in June 1906 and immediately urged upon his colleagues a strategy of "direct action" and the repudiation of parliamentary politics.[79] In February 1907, Kōtoku published an influential article in the new daily *Heimin shinbun* entitled "Yo ga shisō no henka" (My change of thought). The piece offered an account of his conversion to anarchosyndicalism and promptly provoked a schism in the Japanese Socialist party. A protracted debate at the party's Second Congress that year resulted in the rejection of the parliamentary formula advocated by Katayama and Tazoe Tetsuji (which received only two votes), widespread support for Kōtoku's new doctrine (twenty-two votes), and the adoption of a compromise formula by Sakai Toshihiko advocating the use of both direct action and parliamentarism (twenty-eight votes). The party's program was revised to omit the original constraints upon its activity dictated by the law, but the conflict was so divisive that the party simply dissolved into a direct-action faction around Kōtoku (including Yamakawa, Arahata, and Ōsugi) and the Katayama faction, which claimed to be the counterpart of the so-called orthodox Marxist faction led by August Bebel and Karl Kautsky that had come to dominate the German Social-Democratic movement and the Second International.[80]

Aside from the inspiration of the 1905 Russian Revolution, other important factors contributed to the shift to anarchism in the Japanese socialist movement. In prison, Kōtoku found himself increasingly alienated from the tennō that he had previously supported.[81] At about the same time, increased government repression encouraged Sakai and Ōsugi to believe that a policy of parliamentarianism alone was ineffective, draining the energies of the movement with few prospects for success. Many were becoming convinced of the potential for a mass movement using tactics such as the general strike as outbursts of violence spread in Japan in 1905 through 1907: the Hibiya riots against the 1905 peace treaty, the March 1906 citizens' meeting protesting the increase of train fares led by the Socialist party, and the riots at the Ashio mines in February 1907.[82]

In light of these events, Kōtoku's advocacy of anarchosyndicalism was most compelling. The experience of the German Social Democratic party over the past thirty years had demonstrated the futility of parliamentarism, he argued. Indeed, logic alone established that reliance on the Diet was unproductive. The Diet was an instrument for the bourgeoisie's exploitation of the proletariat, in this view. Although it had comprised an appropriate instrument for the bourgeoisie's resistance against the feudal nobility, it could not be expected to overthrow the very class that it represented and serve the working class. Nor was there any need for legislation for the workers to seize what was properly theirs in any case: land, money, and civil rights. At this time, Kōtoku's views embraced many of the elements found in Kropotkin's anarchist communism—the pursuit of economic freedom and political freedom. Yet many components of Kropotkin's thought never found their way into Kōtoku's writings. Kropotkin's "fervent desire for freedom," faith in science as a liberating force, and advocacy of the reorganization and integration of factories with rural agriculture and workshops were all absent from Kōtoku's writings. In any case, the appeal of his direct action doctrine lay not in its vision of postrevolutionary society, but rather in its prospects as a strategy for achieving revolution itself in Japan. Notably, most of those who supported Kōtoku were younger socialists who aspired to be more radical than Katayama and other older party members with whose patient labor union-cum-parliamentarist strategy the younger generation of Meiji socialists had become impatient.[83]

The anarchist current in the movement blossomed with a proliferation of anarchist publications, particularly during the winter period after Kōtoku's execution[84] when no open legal action was possible. In the new circumstances, the tensions among the various levels of liberation sought by socialist revolutionaries— individual, community, and humankind—became increasingly evident. Such tensions were already suggested in the shift in Kōtoku's posture vis-à-vis the tennō as the head of the Japanese body politic. The eruption of the Russo-Japanese War illuminated for him how the promotion of the statist and nationalist components of the highly valued *kokutai* could conflict with the universal aspiration to liberate all humankind. Kōtoku resolved this tension by arguing that Japan's imperialist adventures not only violated the rights of those against whom Japanese were waging war, but also signaled the corruption of the imperial state to pursue aims antithetical to those of Japanese themselves. Then the tension between the needs of the individual consumed with revolutionary élan and the larger community became apparent as the leadership of the anarchist movement shifted to Ōsugi Sakae. Ōsugi shared the moral and anti-Western impulses toward anarchism identified in Kōtoku, but in the highly individualistic yet aggressively nationalistic Ōsugi, the problematical relationships among the three levels of revolutionary commitment became even more apparent. A disciple of Kōtoku in 1907, Ōsugi inherited Kōtoku's mantle as the leading anarchist theorist after 1911. Ōsugi was an even more vehement nationalist than Kōtoku in his early years. As a youth, Ōsugi attended military school (from which he was expelled), aspiring to a military career like that of his father. Ōsugi remained highly nationalistic even after he joined the pacifist Heimin-sha.[85] The key event that turned Ōsugi's fledgling radicalism toward anarchosyndicalism came with his arrest in March 1906. During this first imprisonment, he read widely in philosophy, anthropology, economics, and literature in English, French, German, Italian, and Russian, in addition to his native Japanese. A subsequent imprisonment from 1908 to 1910 (which, ironically, enabled Ōsugi to escape Kōtoku's fate in the High Treason Incident) gave Ōsugi the opportunity to systematize his own ideas on anarchism. On this second occasion, Ōsugi found himself drawn to the scientism of Kropotkin's anarchist vision based on the prevalence of people's natural instinct to cooperate rather than to struggle with one another. This dimension of Kropotkin's thought legitimated anarchism and rejected as spurious any claim that the need for concentrated authority in the form of the state was grounded in natural law. At the same time, however, Ōsugi was also repulsed by the rationalist elements of the West's Enlightenment tradition. This tradition, in Ōsugi's view, undervalued the affective ties that drew men and women into community while it failed to valorize the emotional components of the quest for social justice.

This juxtaposition, together with the manner in which Ōsugi addressed the tension between Western-style individualism and the communitarian impulse undergirding Western socialist thought, are the key to Ōsugi's janus-faced attitude toward the West. Like many in China and Japan who were drawn to Marxism for its claim to a scientific approach to human society, so Ōsugi was drawn to anarchism by its apparent scientific basis. At the same time, those by whom the young revolutionist was most influenced—the anarchists Bakunin, Kropotkin, Reclus,[86] Enrico Malatesta (1858–1932), philosophers Henri Bergson, Friedrich Nietzsche, and Max Stirner, and the controversial French Marxist Georges Sorel—shared a certain antipositivist, antirationalist penchant, and several of them also exhibited strong individualist proclivities in their anarchism. Ōsugi himself departed significantly from Kōtoku's exaltation of the specifically Japanese community in the extremity of his individualism. Where Kōtoku saw his anarchosocialism as consistent with his attachment to the traditional normative values of the Japanese moral community, Ōsugi recklessly flouted the narrow strictures of that community, boldly flaunting his illicit relationships with feminist anarchist Itō Noe and syndicalist reporter Kamichika Ichiko while preserving his first marriage to Hori Yasuko.[87] Nevertheless, he repudiated what he saw as excessive individualism in Nietzsche and Stirner. In his own version of individualism, Ōsugi claimed to mediate the schism between "psychological individualism" on the one hand, which, in his view, was excessively pessimistic and denied the importance of the social realm, and "social individualism" on the other, which he viewed as lacking in "subjective sensitivity" and tending to compromise with existing social institutions.[88] The labor union, or syndicalism, played the critical mediating role between these two forms of individualism and helped to bolster Ōsugi's redefinition of individual virtue to embrace universal, collectivist, humanistic values. As an alternative moral community, the union provided the critical social supports for the individual who was liberated through the progressive expansion of the ego.[89] Indeed, the role of syndicalism in Ōsugi's revolutionary theory and practice was particularly pronounced just as he assumed the leadership of the Japanese anarchosyndicalism movement after Kōtoku's death. In October 1912, he joined Arahata Kanson to found the *Kindai shisō* (Modern thought), a journal of anarchist thought,[90] and circa 1914, Ōsugi launched a Sanjikarizumu Kenkyūkai (Syndicalism Study Society).[91] From then until 1917, Arahata drew closer to Yamakawa and others increasingly influenced by Marxism who would form the Japanese Communist party in 1922. Both the Arahata-Yamakawa group and those associated more closely with Ōsugi during this period directed their energies to a mixture of criticism and encouragement of the struggling labor movement.[92] The limited success of the movement in the wake of the trauma of the High Treason Incident afforded Ōsugi the opportunity to refine his own personal anarchist philosophy in dynamic tension with elements of Western social thought.

Bergson, Sorel, and Kropotkin offered the key ingredients of Ōsugi's problematic relationship with the West. Bergson's antipathy to determinism and affirmation of spiritual values coupled with Sorel's rejection of European rationalism and positivism were the most direct inspirations for the personal philosophy of liberation that Ōsugi would elaborate in a series of three articles penned in mid-1913.[93] Like Rousseau, Ōsugi viewed presocial man as free and man in society as subjugated man. In Ōsugi's view, conquest was the origin of both subjugation and society with the technologically superior people prevailing and creating a society of two classes, the conqueror and the conquered. Virtually all institutions of society—not only government and the accoutrements of the state but also religion, education, philosophy, and morality—should be viewed as instruments of human subjugation.[94] Violence, if not always explicit, was endemic to the daily life of the subjugated class, and, as Sorel wrote, it was important to expose this fact lest parts of the subjugated class accept and collaborate with their oppressors.[95] In particular, Ōsugi detested capitalist society as an especially oppressive social formation.[96]

Interestingly, Ōsugi's problematic relationship with Western individualism and socialism placed him at odds with the rigid, highly conformist structure of Japanese society and, eventually, with the Japanese socialist movement itself. If the history of civilization was a history of subjugation, its antithesis was life, which he aggressively redefined as the expansion of the ego. Human consciousness he viewed as the essence of the expansion of one's own life and that of humanity, and it led men and women to self-liberating action. Like Kropotkin, Ōsugi believed that such liberating action was associated with cooperation rather than competition among men and women. Expansion of the ego in class society merely resulted in the class conflict between subjugator and subjugated and in the corruption of both, he argued, while cooperation in rebellion produced liberation of the individual and of all humanity.

There was a certain irony in this formulation. Ōsugi seemed to articulate it rather unreflectively as he brazenly pursued the steady expansion of his own ego at the expense of the egos of both the women with whom he was involved, of his wife, and of the socialist movement that suffered from his scandalous activity. Yet this disposition reflected the highly individualist terms in which Ōsugi conceived the socialist movement itself. Repudiating conventional socialists' emphasis on articulating a clear final goal for the socialist revolution, Ōsugi stressed that his revolution would focus on "the spiritual dimensions of the individual."[97] It was at this point that Ōsugi's socialism joined that of Kōtoku in taking a decisive turn away from Westernism and Western socialism's "excessive concern for economic progress and for industrial technological progress of the elements of social evolution."[98] Nor did Ōsugi ever repudiate his early nationalism. Rather, he reconciled his opposition to the militarism implicit in the allegiance to the nation-state by simply redefining the minzoku: "Within the Japanese people, as in all so-called peoples, there are two different peoples, the conquering class and the conquered class. To put it more concretely, the bourgeoisie and the proletariat." The subjugated class might successfully be educated to share with their oppressors a common view of their history and culture, Ōsugi observed, but since ultimately the national state arose out of conquest, this view could never be true in reality. Thus, arguing that Japan's long history of warfare and aggressive expansion into Taiwan and Korea did not reflect the shared values that were the essence of the Japanese people, Ōsugi repudiated social democrat Ōyama Ikuo's claim that "nationalism [*minzoku kokka-shugi*, nation-statism], is ultimately democracy."[99] Per contra, Ōsugi insisted that Japan's ignominious history of violence was part of what Marx and Engels had correctly identified in *The Manifesto of the Communist Party* as a pattern of class struggle and subjugation that permeated the entire history of humankind.[100] Instead, for Ōsugi, true democracy advocated "free self-rule and federation among [the subjugated] people who genuinely have a common history, culture, tradition, and sense of honor or are seeking to carve out a new common cultural unit in their shared interests."[101] In short, Ōsugi was able to reconcile his nationalism with his anarchism by redefining the Japanese nation in terms of its subjugated proletariat.

In responding thus to the national question, Ōsugi also transposed the virtue to which men and women should aspire from the values of the shishi narrowly conceived, supporting militant and militarist nationalism, to those of the universal human moral community. Here, Ōsugi's anarchist philosophy reinforced his personal defiance of conventionality, and Ōsugi joined his Chinese counterparts in repudiating the confining strictures of the traditional moral community. Indeed, Ōsugi was convinced that the existing moral consensus in society as a whole was but the product of a process controlled by the superordinate class by means of state and nonstate apparatuses:[102]

> Society progressed. Consequently, the methods of subjugation also developed. The methods of violence and deception were established with increasing ingenuity.
>
> Government! Law! Religion! Education! Morality! The Army! Police! Courts! Parliaments! Science! Philosophy! Art! All other social institutions!
>
> Thus, the men of classes between the two extremes of the conquering class and the subjugated class, just like the sages of the primitive age, either consciously or unconsciously became collaborators or assistants of these organizational [means of] violence and deception.[103]

Ōsugi's anarchism was founded in faith that people, by nature—outside artificial communities enforced by law and other accoutrements of authority—were good. Thus, he and his followers directed their hostility at least as much toward institutions in society as against those of the state itself. All were viewed as agents of human subjugation and corruption. Anarchists in China, too, confronting corruption and impotence among its gentry class and the repressive institution of the patriarchical Confucian family system, shared this determination to carry out a revolution against traditional Chinese society as well as against the state.

CULTURAL ICONOCLASM, NATIONALISM, AND CHINESE ANARCHISM

While Japanese anarchism is readily characterized in terms of an anti-Western impulse and a return to traditional values in reaction against the social and political impact of Meiji reforms, the Chinese case is considerably more complex. The Chinese anarchist movement emerged among students studying abroad in two disparate cultural settings—in Paris and in Tokyo—before flourishing in China proper with the return of many of these students circa the 1911 revolution. Attitudes concerning the relative valuation of Western and indigenous Chinese philosophical perspectives differed markedly from setting to setting. Those who became anarchists in France, where the young worker-students drew close to the French anarchosocialist movement, were more often attracted to anarchism precisely because of its Western elements. Enamored of the West, they rejected Chinese culture as the cause of China's predicament and tended to deny any link between the anarchism of Bakunin and Kropotkin and their own philosophical heritage. By contrast, those in Japan, particularly Liu Shipei, found the roots of anarchism deep in China's own philosophical heritage, and, like the Russian narodniki, they harkened back to a communal, bucolic preindustrial past.

Initially, these differences between the nascent Chinese anarchist movements in Japan and France appear to be profound. On closer examination, however, the disparities diminish, unveiling the intricacy of the national question and its intense significance for the Chinese anarchist movement. Chinese anarchists in Tokyo vacillated on the question of nationalism. In this they were not alone. Even the intensely iconoclastic anarchists in Paris—torn between their new adoration of Western culture and a passionate need for self-authentication as Chinese—exhibited a remarkable penchant to draw from Chinese philosophical traditions to expound their anarchist ideal. In short, in neither Japan nor France did Chinese anarchism's fundamental antipathy toward the state resolve the national question by means of an absolute repudiation of the Chinese nation and its cultural heritage. Thus, in Chinese anarchism, as in Japanese anarchism and in the emerging Marxist movements in both societies, the commitment to offer radical new hope to one's countrymen and women through revolution coupled with their vision of a stateless, classless society posed an acute problem concerning the fate of one's own people as a nation in the revolution: Without the political power of the state, could the nation survive?

Cultural Iconoclasm and the Emergence of Chinese Anarchism in France

These tensions were most dramatically displayed among the Chinese worker-students who founded the anarchist movement in France. These pioneers of Chinese anarchism were attracted to Western anarchist thought for reasons that were dramatically opposed to those that motivated Kōtoku and other Japanese radicals. While the latter readily identified sources of anarchist thought in the Eastern philosophies of Laozi and Zhuangzi, opposing them to the statism of Western thought and practice, the Chinese overseas students in Paris who founded the first Chinese anarchist movement explicitly repudiated any effort to equate modern anarchism with China's own "primitive" ancient philosophies (or the *jingtian*, well-field, system with socialism as certain Tongmenghui members did).[104] The movement in France emerged when a group of twenty students accompanied the Chinese Minister Sun Baoqi to Paris in 1902. Among them was twenty-one-year-old Li Shizeng, a student of agriculture and biochemistry, who established a laboratory and then a Chinese store in Paris, where he employed part-time Chinese worker-students.[105] He was shortly joined by Wu Zhihui, who had been expelled as a foreign student from Japan and had then returned to China to continue his radical activities. When his continued revolutionary activism drew the attention of Chinese authorities, Wu fled to England, where he met Sun Yat-sen and joined the latter's Tongmenghui (Revolutionary Alliance). Although he had been exposed to socialism in Japan, it was in France through his association with Li that Wu was drawn to anarchism.[106] In 1907, with the financial support of Zhang Jingjiang

(1876–1950), Wu, Li, and Chu Minyi launched the anarchist journal *Xin shiji* (The New Century, subtitled in Esperanto *La Novaj Tempoj*). A cosmopolitan journal with a strong scientistic bent, the weekly identified Western anarchism as the key to resolving China's increasingly desperate situation over the three years and one hundred plus issues of its life. Its translations of writings of Bakunin, Kropotkin, Malatesta, and Reclus—works to which Li had first been exposed in Japan— became a major source of radical Western thought for Chinese revolutionaries. In large part as a result of its translations, Western "anarchist literature available in Chinese was unmatched in scope and comprehensiveness by any other social and political philosophy of European origin."[107] Li and Wu quickly became the dominant figures in the Paris movement, Li contributing sophisticated theoretical articles drawing on Kropotkin, Bakunin, and the French geographer-anarchist Reclus while Wu penned acerbic essays attacking the Manchus, the Chinese family system, and other aspects of Chinese tradition.[108]

Li, Wu, Chu, Qu Shengbai, and other Chinese studying in France had gone to the West at least tacitly asserting the obsolescence and inadequacy of traditional Chinese learning; and their adoption of anarchism constituted yet another effort to grasp Western "science." The emphasis that the geologist and anarchist Kropotkin, in particular, placed on the liberating value of modern science and technology was especially appealing to them. Kropotkin, whose *Mutual Aid* became the "bible" of the movement, was from a privileged social background like that of many Chinese students in Paris, and, like them, he was struggling against an antiquated state increasingly mired in a hopeless international position, suffering the same ignominious fate that the Qing regime had endured in 1894–1895 at the hands of Japan. Indeed, like Japanese revolutionists, radical Chinese students both inside and outside China were deeply moved by the 1905 Russian revolution. On the Chinese mainland, anarchism had aroused much interest as early as 1903 because of the example of the Russian "nihilists." One writer of the time described "extreme democracy" (anarchism) and communism as the two main schools of socialism; and he depicted the former as the "'party . . . founded by the Frenchman Proudhon and the Russian Bakunin'" and represented in his own day by the Russian nihilists.[109] The impact of the 1905 revolution was to reinforce the Chinese attraction to anarchism; it "significantly clarified Russia's suitability as a revolutionary model." If there had been doubts about the efficacy of the "nihilist" strategy in producing revolutionary change, these were quickly dispelled by the success, albeit limited, of 1905, which inspired Chinese revolutionaries "by showing how strong the revolutionary movement was, even in the world's most powerful autocracy."[110] Interest in anarchism and terrorism, then, intensified dramatically among Chinese radicals inside and outside China after 1905.

Once in Paris, the young worker-students were directly exposed to the influence of the international anarchist movement around Kropotkin. He and Reclus had moved their organ *Le Révolte* from Geneva to Paris in 1885, and from 1895 to 1914, Jean Grave succeeded them in publishing the journal *Les Temps Nouveaux* in Paris as well.[111] The anarchism of Proudhon, Bakunin, Kropotkin, and Reclus, then, became the predominant influence on the Chinese anarchist circle in Paris. Darwinism was certainly influential, but the Darwinism of the Paris anarchists, their evolutionary scientistic view of anarchism, was Spencer's as conveyed via Kropotkin.[112] With their roots in Chinese thought, they were untroubled by the distinction between revolutionism and evolutionism,[113] and they readily adopted Kropotkin's faith in the human natural instinct to cooperation and his stress on the need for mutual aid. Kropotkin's scientism contributed to a belief among Chinese anarchists that mutual aid issued from the instinct to do good that was the human conscience (*liangxin*), which they in turn "endowed . . . with the status of a universal scientific principle (*gongli*), and set . . . against Darwinian notions of conflict."[114] As opposed to the cannabalistic Darwinian perspective, the anarchists argued that "nineteenth-century science had proven that man was a 'social animal'."[115] Kropotkin's more charitable vision of men and women offered a sanguine counterpoint to the painful domination of the world, in reality as in social philosophy, by social Darwinism. At the same time, his emphasis on the paramount importance of the individual and faith in the individual's propensity to seek association with others freely stood in contrast to the coercive and ultimately destructive nature of the imperial state and of Chinese social institutions such as the patriarchal family. Anarchism offered a vision of human beings in society that was an alternative to the constricting Confucian framework against which these young individualistic intellectuals rebelled. The scientism of Kropotkin's anarchism assured Chinese radicals that his vision was not only desirable but the inevitable end of human evolution.[116] Chinese anarchists, in turn, articulated for themselves a vision of a new Chinese and international society built on anarchist principles. Qu, for example, envisaged a future society as controlled by "free associations" in each major sphere of industry. Such associations would cooperate with one another according to the principle of mutual aid, and although there would be a central organ of coordination or control, that organ would have no political power like that of the existing state. There would be laws, in Qu's view, but these would differ from imperial rule because they would be based on popular opinion as communicated in open plenary meetings of the entire(!) populace.[117]

Among the Paris anarchists, the affirmation of such a vision was coupled with uncompromising cultural iconoclasm. If anarchism represented a modern, scientistic appreciation of man and his capabilities, the whole of China's traditionalism was its antithesis. Chu penned a scathing indictment of the entire Chinese tradition in the pages of *Xin shiji*:

> I say that the reason why China had not been able to progress with the world had been due to its emphasis upon things ancient and its treatment of modern things lightly. . . . We Chinese also have a tendency to treat all Western things as things which China had long experienced or possessed. For example, we say that China . . . long ago realized nationalism under the Yellow Emperor . . . ; that Lao Tzu was the founder of anarchism; . . . and finally, that China long ago practiced communism under the name of the wellfield system. Alas! . . . New knowledge comes at the

appropriate time, when it has the potential of realization. . . . There are countless
things which even modern man cannot foresee. How much, then, can one expect of the
ancients?[118]

Modern anarchism was said to advocate values that were precisely the opposite of
those of ancient sages that had dominated and crippled China for centuries. The
individual, rather than the family or the clan, would comprise the "basic unit in
society," and society would be formed through voluntary associations among
individuals within villages, then among villages, and, finally, among countries[119]
instead of the historic practice of conquest that had brought the empire into being.

In thus repudiating the values and social practices of "the ancients," Chinese
anarchists in France offered to their compatriots a novel, expanded conception of
revolutionary change. They shared Western anarchism's disdain for the political
realm, contending that a mere change in political elites or the structure of the state
alone could not purge China of the ills that prevented men and women from
realizing their innate virtues. Thus, most Paris anarchists remained members of
Sun's Tongmenghui, but they rejected its narrow political revolutionism focusing
on the overthrow of the Manchus and the establishment of a republic for a more
comprehensive conception of thoroughgoing social revolution. Guided by Sun's
concept of *minsheng-zhuyi* (people's livelihood) as the Third People's Principle,
the Tongmenghui envisaged a powerful role for the Chinese state in providing for
economic growth and the equitable distribution of its fruits among the Chinese
people. As early as 1906, Tongmenghui member Feng Ziyou, who had been born
and raised in Japan, interpreted the minsheng principle as state socialism premised
on the "equalization of land rights as advocated by Henry George." This would
involve land nationalization, which Feng felt would occur more easily in China
than elsewhere "because in the past most of the forests, mines, and roads had been
government owned and there had been a large amount of official land."[120] The
commitment to some form of socialism, as Sun had learned of it by reading George
and Marx and through contact with Japanese socialists, was included in the
Tongmenghui's membership pledge and in its "Revolutionary Manifesto of the
Military Government of the Revolutionary Brotherhood" circa 1911.[121] Sun hoped
that an industrializing China could bypass Western-style capitalism with its attendant ills, including class conflict. Thus, he advocated "a form of state socialism, in
which the interventionist state would undertake the scientific planning which
would govern the socialistic collaboration of private and state capital in a comprehensive program of national industrial development and modernization."[122]

By contrast, the anarchists, eschewing merely political revolution, saw the
whole of Chinese society as the locus of revolutionary change.[123] The oppression
from which Chinese suffered lay not merely in the state, the power and scope of
which was, in any case, not nearly as extensive as those of the states of more
industrialized societies. The freedom they sought was personal freedom, not
merely civic freedom. Civic freedom—"the capacity of adult members of a community to participate in its life and governance"[124]—was inadequate for China's
anarchists both because it offered only a political right to participate in a political

structure and because it entailed a set of laws and mutual obligations. Both were onerous and repugnant. Indeed, in the anarchist view, civic freedom tended inevitably to evolve into a grasp for sovereignal, organic freedom, which aspired to wield power over others on the basis of social bond(age). Thus, they believed that a political revolution would only shuffle the powerholders or rearrange the accoutrements of authority. It would be a "revolution of the few." Only a broadly social revolution would encompass the whole of Chinese society and provide the basis for genuine liberation. Such a social revolution would envelop the real locus of values and mores, enabling Chinese to overcome "selfishness" and establish "public-mindedness" (*gongdao*).[125] To be sure, the state remained a major object of attack for the anarchists qua anarchists, but (calling to mind Japan's Ōsugi) Chinese anarchists saw the major impediments to the realization of individual freedom to lie in nonpolitical social institutions and in culture itself. As in Rousseau, man had been born free and virtuous and had been corrupted in society by authoritarian institutions and practices. This treatment did not, of course, account for the origins of these oppressive elements, which were difficult to explain if men were born good, with consciences. Yet this perspective would contribute to a view of revolution as a cultural and educational process, and once it was melded with a Marxian materialist interpretation of history, the reverberations of this view would be felt in Mao's call for a "cultural revolution," a revolution in the superstructure—not merely the state, but all social institutions—as early as 1940.[126]

The protestations of the Paris anarchists notwithstanding, the content of these views and their unacknowledged inspiration by traditional Chinese humanistic perspectives created a dynamic tension in these young revolutionists with respect to nationality and patriotism. Removed from mainland China itself and alienated from their native culture, the founders of the Chinese anarchist movement in Paris could not react to the national dilemmas posed by anarchism predictably, given the intensity of China's domestic and international troubles. The increasingly ineffectual Qing court was not as absolutist nor as directly repressive as was the tsarist state with its omnipresent secret police force. Neither nationalism as a political force from below nor stateness—the identification of nation with state—had emerged in China as it had by the 1880s in Meiji Japan. One would expect that the lack of an effective state would have left aspiring Chinese anarchists without a suitable object of attack. China's humiliation in the international sphere—under alien rulers who forced their subjects to proclaim the ignominy of their subjugation by wearing the queue—should have aroused in Chinese intellectuals patriotic sentiments and out of that a determination to build a powerful state to liberate and protect the minzu. In such circumstances, if anarchism could be reconciled with nationalism as it was in Japan, it should have been even more likely to occur in China. Yet, culturally speaking, the first Chinese anarchists were committed not to "China" but to the West, and even in the absence of an analogue to the *kokutai* thought that bound nation and state into an organic whole, many Chinese anarchists felt compelled to reject nationalism along with statism. In this sense, it would be tempting to regard these anarchists as mere imitators of the West in the fullest sense, ignoring the implications of their convictions for the fate of their own countrymen and women. Indeed, even a cursory glance at the contents of the *Xin shiji* suggested that the anarchists were uniformly and cavalierly "anti-religion, anti-traditionalist, anti-family, anti-libertine, anti-elitist, anti-government, anti-militarist, and anti-nationalist."[127]

Yet the relationship of the Paris anarchists to Western civilization and to their own native culture was not so unproblematic. As for the West, they repudiated industrial capitalism, presumably the most highly developed form of Western civilization, and what it brought to China whether its people were receptive or not. As the anarchist group in Canton would later declare, capitalism was based on the system of private property, which "is the source of all evils and the starting point of all conflicts and miseries in society."[128] Observing its impact on European society, they concluded that it had produced the "poison of economic monopoly," which, in turn, spawned a steadily increasing gap between rich and poor. Thus, they were critical of those who would accept the political institutions of Western republicanism and constitutional democracy because those did not provide freedom for the poor, nor did they provide economic justice.[129] Capitalist society, in short, could not fulfill their ideals of absolute freedom and socioeconomic equality.[130]

Thus, the cosmopolitanism of the Paris anarchists did not dictate an unqualified acceptance of Western modernity. Nor was it unaffected by Chinese nationalism. Here the anarchist position was permeated with inconsistencies. Their participation in the revolutionary movement itself was strongly motivated by a fervent desire to help China, and this patriotism impelled many, such as Li Shizeng and Chu Minyi, to accept republican revolution against the Manchus as a positive first step toward the anarchist social revolution they advocated[131] even as they rejected republicanism as the ultimate political goal of their own activity. Such anguished patriotism was particularly pronounced in Wu, who had been an ardent nationalist from his days as a radical student in Tokyo in 1901 and 1902. In 1902, he had returned to Shanghai where he founded the Aiguo Xueshe (Patriotic Scholarly Society) and its organ *Subao*. While Wu helped to found Shijie-she (The World Association) in Paris with Li and Zhang and became an anarchist, his weltanshauung remained heavily imbued with virulent nationalistic anti-Manchu sentiment. Li and Chu moderated their patriotism, repudiating the anti-Manchu racism of many in the Tongmenghui as a perspective that "served to reinforce boundaries between different peoples, which obstructed evolution toward a better society."[132] By contrast, Wu regularly referred to the Qing as "the Manchu barbarians" and the "Manchu dogs" and contended that although the Chinese had generously accepted them as a part of the Chinese people, the Manchus were a minority that had no mandate to rule in China.[133] Historic figures such as Zeng Guofan, who had been widely respected for their efforts to initiate reforms in the Tongzhi Restoration, Wu condemned as traitors. They had betrayed the Confucian sages, who "had cautioned the Chinese not to confuse the distinction between the Chinese and the barbarians."[134] Finally, Wu assailed the Qing for their inability, even their lack of will, to repel the Western powers: "Did not Empress Dowager Tzu-hsi say that [s]he would rather give China to the foreigners than to the Chinese whom she called domestic slaves?"[135] Thus, Wu contended, China's revolution would not immediately be an anarchist revolution but would proceed through two stages: a nationalistic revolution (*minzu geming*), which would be based on what he saw as the Chinese people's deeply rooted racial consciousness, and a republican revolution that would constitute the prelude to the achievement of the anarchist revolution that would realize the Great Harmony (*datong geming*)—the ultimate universal harmony to be achieved by all humankind—that was envisaged by so many Chinese reformists and revolutionaries from Kang Youwei to Mao Zedong.[136]

As Wu's reference to the notion of datong indicates, the affirmative attachment to China went far beyond the emotional rejection of the Qing "barbarians." Although they explicitly rejected Chinese learning as backward, averring that Western culture was the basis of science, and they identified with Darwinist progressivism, Wu and other Paris anarchists were deeply inspired in their anarchism by Confucian and Daoist traditions. This was evident in their conception of humanity, in their view that anarchism was appropriate for the Chinese context, and most importantly, in their conviction that the coming revolution must be a revolution in modes of thought and morality along with economic revolution. All three of these themes would receive still more emphasis in the work of Chinese anarchists in Japan.

To be sure, if Confucianism as state philosophy and as the ideological support of institutions such as the family system earned the repudiation of the anarchists, in crucial respects, it and other strains in premodern Chinese thought were congenial to the anarchist vision. Confucianism itself embraced a humanism that would influence profoundly Wu's anarchism, for example. Kropotkin's view of men and women in society resonated with the Mencian view of human nature as naturally good and men and women having desires that led them into morality and harmonious association with others. "Men all have the heart that cannot bear the suffering of others," Mencius wrote. "The heart of commiseration is the beginning of humanity; the heart of shame is the beginning of righteousness; the heart of keeping oneself back in order to make way for others is the beginning of observing ritual; the heart of right and wrong is the beginning of wisdom."[137] These elements of basic morality were innate in human beings, according to Mencius, and they must be cultivated through moral education. This educational process amounted to "awaken[ing] them to the realization that they have got it within themselves."[138]

Significantly, Wu, and the Paris anarchists in general, saw their anarchist revolution as a moral quest, a process of educating men and women to change their psychology from one in which selfishness (*si*) and partial interests were primary to one oriented to *gong*, public spiritedness, or universal human interests.[139] Prefiguring Mao's espousal of a continuous cultural revolution against the norms and mores of class society, Wu asserted that this process of education would be continuous, as would the revolution itself:

Education continues every day; so does revolution. Education that brings about minor changes in social custom is a minor revolution. This is what people today call "reform" or "social reform," not revolution. Education that stirs up the vigor of all people and results in the change of all old habits and customs of all people is then a major revolution. . . . In the judgement of the anarchists, there is no such notion that revolution will be completed some day. Truth and justice advance uninterruptedly day after day, therefore education will not cease for a moment. This is to say that revolution will never come to an end.[140]

Much later, Mao was hostile both to traditional Chinese intellectuals and to formal education based on the written word. He espoused a form of education based on the essence of the daily life of the worker, as carried out through what he saw as a dialectical interaction between ordinary persons and the political leadership. This education would involve returning to man's true nature as creative laborer. There was a difference in emphasis, then, in Mao's espousal of continuous revolution from what was advocated by Wu, but Wu's contestation of traditional education as morally corruptive would come to be shared by Mao.[141]

Like Mencius, Wu regarded men and women as innately good, but he rejected the moral strictures of sages such as Mencius and the social institutions that they supported as "pseudomorality." Contemporary social institutions and ideology itself represented and served partial interests, the alienation of the self from others in society that was contrary to the "organic structure" (*jiti zhi jiegou*) of man's natural existence.[142] Through a process of education,[143] these were to be replaced by a socialist morality that embraced the values of the great French Revolution— liberty, equality, and fraternity—as well as gong.[144] This positive educational process would complement the violent, negative aspect of the revolution destined to destroy the institutions of violence supporting the existing order.[145]

These moral perspectives, so deeply influenced by Confucianism, were coupled with the strong attraction to Western scientism that motivated other Paris anarchists. Wu shared, for example, the Marxian appreciation of industrialism as the basis of communism, and science was to comprise 70 to 80 percent of education in the postrevolutionary society (moral education would constitute the remaining 20 to 30 percent). Here Wu differed from what Mao would advocate later when, in the late 1950s, he turned away from the orthodox Marxian valorization of industrialism. Wu explicitly distinguished scientific knowledge, which he stressed as necessary for Chinese progress, from the so-called "national essence" (*guocui*), which many traditionalists were promoting as deserving of preservation and protection from the inroads of Western philosophical perspectives. The latter, Wu argued, was not progressive, but suited to a bygone age, and would necessarily be supplanted by practical scientific Western knowledge.[146] It was this point that distinguished Wu and his comrades in the Western-oriented anarchosocialist movement in France from their anarchist compatriots in Tokyo, who had launched their movement at approximately the same time. Wu and others criticized Liu Shipei as utopianist for seeking the actual roots of his anarchism in Chinese anarchist traditions outside Confucianism.[147]

Chinese Anarchism in Tokyo

Xin shiji reported regularly on the Chinese anarchist movement in Tokyo, which had emerged under the influence of the Japanese radical left-wing movement. Indeed, the Japanese movement gradually became a major source of literature on

Western socialism and anarchism for Chinese students there.[148] By 1905, Zhang Ji, one of the first overseas Chinese students in Japan and a major editor of the reformist republican *Minbao*, fell under the influence of Japanese socialists (particularly in the Kin'yōkai) who attended lectures organized by the Chinese students on socialism. Nationalism, however, quickly became a major issue among those attracted to the anarchist program. Zhang Binglin, the highly nationalist Tongmenghui leader, drew close to anarchism briefly when he discovered that the state was a product of human artifice, rather than something of noble or "heavenly" derivation. Subsequently, his nationalism prompted him to turn against anarchism, asserting that anarchists "overlook the urgent problems of today and indulge themselves in seeking vain tickets for the distant future."[149] Out of this conflict, arising in part from such ideological issues and in part out of interpersonal tensions, emerged the Chinese anarchist movement in Tokyo. The birth of the movement was marked by the founding of the journal *Tianyi* (Natural Justice), edited by Liu Shipei and his wife He Zhen in June 1907, and then by the founding of the Shehui-zhuyi Jiangxihui (Institute for the Study of Socialism) late in August of the same year. Liu quickly emerged as the leading theorist of the movement. It is in his thought that one finds the most pronounced influence of premodern Chinese strains of thought on contemporary Chinese anarchism.

Before fleeing to exile in Japan early in 1907, Liu, like many revolutionaries, had failed the higher national civil service examination in 1902. En route home from the examination, Liu had encountered Zhang Binglin, Cai Yuanpei, and others associated with the Aiguo Xueshe (Patriotic Scholarly Society) and promptly joined the revolutionists. At this point, Liu's nationalist inclinations were markedly strong, prompting him to change his hame to Guanghan to reflect his fervent desire to eject the Manchus and restore the Han Chinese to power in their own land. Within the next year, Liu had written two books, one (*Rangshu*) on nationalism, drawing a sharp distinction between the Chinese cultural community and barbarians, and the other (*Zhongguo minyue jingyi* [An exposition of the idea of the social contract in China]) seeking to apply Rousseau's social contract theory to the quest for popular sovereignty in China. Once in Japan, Liu began to approach anarchism through contact with Japanese socialists (Kōtoku Shūsui and the national socialist Kita Ikki) established by Zhang Ji.[150] The young institute remained in contact with the anarchists of the Kin'yōkai, including Kōtoku, Sakai, Yamakawa, and Ōsugi, who spoke at the first, second, fourth, and fifth meetings of the institute respectively.[151] Although the new *Tianyi bao* lasted only one year, it may have had an even greater impact on Chinese revolutionists than the *Xin shiji* in Paris, given its greater proximity to China and the larger number of overseas Chinese students in Japan.[152] In 1908, the *Tianyi bao* was succeeded by *Hengbao* (The Balance), a journal that, like its predecessor, published excerpts from Western works, many of which had already been published in the *Xin shiji* in Paris. Although the new journal was predominantly anarchistic in tone, under the editorship of Liu it offered one of the first introductions of Marxism in Chinese when it published excerpts from the *Manifesto*.[153] At the same time, the new journal published pieces, most notably on Kropotkin's thought and on rural economics,[154] which helped to highlight the emerging discord between the anarchism of the Paris anarchists and those in Tokyo.

The dissension between the two branches of the young Chinese anarchist movement emanated from disparate understandings of what anarchism meant as well as from competing assessments of the relative value of Eastern and Western philosophical and cultural traditions for the anarchist vision. Chinese anarchists in Tokyo were fundamentally less iconoclastic than their counterparts in Paris, and they tended to be less enamored of Western civilization. Like their compatriots in Paris, the Tokyo anarchists aspired to "overthrow all rule of man over man" and to realize this human freedom in "internationalism, abolishing all national and racial distinctions."[155] This common internationalism extended to the enthusiastic promotion of Esperanto as the universal language that could help to render existing national and racial distinctions obsolete.[156] Nevertheless, the fundamental liberalism of their anarchism notwithstanding, like Kōtoku, Ōsugi, and others in the Japanese socialist movement, Chinese anarchists in Tokyo were more critical than the Paris group of the culture that accompanied industrial capitalism in the West. They inveighed, for example, against the high costs of individualism or "egoism," to borrow Kawakami Hajime's terms, in the West. They "tended to find individualism, liberalism, competition, and 'the law of the jungle' both frightening and immoral. The results they had produced in the West were not altogether attractive and there was no parallel to them in the Chinese tradition." By contrast, "[a]narchism not only resembled the Taoist rural idyll" but evoked an idyll long associated with certain strata of the Chinese peasantry, whose "longing for a pure, frugal, and egalitarian" society had been expressed historically in recurrent peasant uprisings.[157] Like the Paris group, the Tokyo anarchists valued absolute equality but stressed the importance of the organic ties among men and women in society over the absolute freedom of the individual. Whereas Tolstoy exercised little appeal for their counterparts in the Paris movement, for the Chinese anarchists in Tokyo, Tolstoy's anarchism, harkening back to a precapitalist past, drew closer to their ideal than Kropotkin's vision, even with the latter's emphasis on social ties concretized in the practice of mutual aid.[158]

A major axis of discord between the two groups lay precisely in the Tokyo group's appeal to anarchist currents in classical Chinese philosophy. A classical scholar, Liu Shipei was prominent among those who advocated the preservation of the *guocui* that the Paris anarchists repudiated with disdain.[159] Liu, then, was acutely aware of forebears in the Chinese philosophical tradition who had not served the Confucian hierarchy enforced by the imperial throne. As Xiao Gongquan has illustrated, the roots of Chinese anarchism may, indeed, be traced back to the Daoist writings of Laozi and Zhuangzi. Advocating the virtues of nonaction (*wuwei*), the two philosophers laid the groundwork for an anarchist perspective when they asserted that the government that governs least governs best. Zhuangzi and, later, Wu Nengzi in the Tang period went much further than Laozi, positing an idyllic state of nature like that portrayed by Rousseau in which men and women lived in harmony, equality, and freedom in accordance with a natural morality. In this view, natural morality, the *dao* and *de*, were destroyed by the sages in their

effort to impose rites and ceremonies of pseudomorality.[160] Other Daoist philosophers elaborated further on this theme. The "civilization" urged on society by the
so-called "sages" had introduced "artificial modes of life," wrote the third-century
philosopher Yuan Ji. The "culture" devised by the sages, Yuan argued, made
invidious "[d]istinctions between the noble and the lowly, the rich and the poor, the
ruler and the ruled, [and] spread their evil influences in all directions, bringing
injustice, conflict and hatred in their wake. The misery which government brought
forth was the greatest." In short, " 'When kings were instituted, oppression arose;
when officials were appointed, robbery began'."[161] The philosopher Bao Jingyan,
of the early fourth century, wrote likewise, "Government arose as an inevitable
consequence of . . . decadence." Wu was even more contemptuous of what the
sages had wrought:

> Alas! Nature . . . made us all animals, but we were humanized against Nature. Arbi-
> trary modes of life tantalized our desires; arbitrary distinctions intensified our conflicts;
> arbritrary culture polluted our integrity; punishments and punitive wars endangered
> our lives; and all these artificialities served no better purpose than to make us forget our
> original nature, disturb the balance of our emotions, and bring ruin to life itself, in a
> mad pursuit of extraneous trivialities! Men have lived and died in all ages without
> being able to recover from this delusion. This is the fault of the so-called sage.[162]

The result, Wu lamented, was that humankind found itself in something like the
state of nature as Thomas Hobbes later depicted human life *without* the *Leviathan*.
" 'The so-called sages regretted what they had done and, as a last resort, enacted
laws, instituted punishments and organized armies to keep the people in
check. . . . Man's life was destitute, miserable, and short. And there was no end
to this state of affairs'!"[163]

In Tokyo at the turn of the twentieth century, Liu Shipei certainly drew liberally
on Western anarchist thought: He endorsed, for example, Kropotkin's rebuttal of
Darwin.[164] Nevertheless, with this rich vein of anarchist thought in the Chinese
classics in mind, Liu and other Tokyo anarchists saw China's philosophical tradition as much closer to anarchist principles than those of other societies.[165] Laozi
appeared as the father of Chinese rural anarchism in the fifth number of *Tianyi
bao*,[166] and Liu praised Bao as having gone well beyond Laozi and Zhuangzi in
advocating the complete realization of human freedom in anarchy.[167] Indeed,
while Liu criticized certain Confucian sages for contributing to the rule of men
over men,[168] he also asserted that even Confucianism had advocated limited
government involvement in the lives of the people. Confucius and Mencius had
shared the anarchists' optimistic view of human nature, believing that men and
women found morality within themselves and could draw on its resources.[169] " 'If
only Chinese could be purged of their habits of obedience'" to corrupting political
and social institutions, then, Liu was convinced, " 'anarchism could be achieved in
China in the very near future'."[170]

A key aspect of Liu's attraction to his classical predecessors lay in their appreciation of the moral superiority of the unspoiled bucolic stage of human life. As in
Rousseau, centuries later, for most of Liu's Chinese anarchist forefathers, such an

adoration of the original state of humankind led to a certain despair, a resignation that the original pristine circumstances of humankind could never be restored.[171] There was a sense in which Liu's agreement with their longing for the past reflected a pride in China before the advent of the industrialism and commercialism that were most intimately associated with the West. As Dirlik has noted, "Tolstoy's idealization of rural life and manual labor, and opposition to the commercial economy confirmed ideas that Liu found in Chinese thinkers." Liu contended, "The monetary economy had led to the strengthening of despotism: the commercial economy had led to the impoverishment of many in the population, which had prompted government efforts under Wang Mang to establish control over land." The encroachment of Western imperialism intensified these effects as they weakened China's rural economy. Treaty port cities, teeming with nefarious Western influences, represented the nadir of human morality, the point of man's greatest departure from his natural, moral origins.[172]

If ancient philosophers concluded their etiologies of government on a most pessimistic note, however, Liu also found in his native philosophical heritage a basis for a positive vision of the society for which he yearned. The third-century B.C. agrarian utopianist Xu Hang, who had tried to realize an ideal society in which all, including the emperor himself, would participate equally in manual labor, Liu regarded as "'most akin to the anarchists of the West'."[173] Liu drew from Xu's work to develop his own theory of "balanced abilities" (*renli junli-shuo*). Rather than people specializing in one form of labor or another, which implied the emergence of classes in Liu's view,[174] he advocated that in his ideal (rural) society, each person change his or her occupation—study, construction, metallurgy and manufacturing, clothing production, food preparation, transportation, medicine, and, finally, nurturing of children—in accordance with his or her age, with the result that he or she would acquire diverse kinds of knowledge and expertise over a lifetime.[175] This arrangement would enable all people to engage in both mental and manual labor, eliminating the traditional gap between the two that other leading Chinese revolutionists from Li Dazhao to Mao Zedong would also repudiate.

Liu did not specify how these provisions would be maintained and enforced, if necessary, but he did stipulate that his ideal society would comprise villages of about one thousand residents each. Each community would provide homes to care for children under the age of five and adults over the age of fifty. This arrangement would supplant existing political and national boundaries.[176] Ultimately, Liu aspired to achieve something akin to Kang Youwei's datong, which applied the Confucian notion of a harmonious society by extending it to embrace the entire world.[177] A major difference between the utopias of Liu and Kang, however, lay in Liu's firm repudiation of the role of government. As an uncompromising anarchist, Liu even questioned the position of the *Xin shiji* anarchists who accepted the possibility of the institution of a republican regime as a positive step in the path to socialism. Ironically, Liu averred that even the old monarchy was preferable to a republican system, which he argued had increased social inequality in the West.[178]

Here, the antinomies of Liu's thought with respect to the national question become manifest. Liu took great pride in the fact that indigenous Chinese sources of anarchism predated the Western anarchism of Proudhon, Bakunin, and Kropotkin. Yet, at the same time, Liu asserted firmly that the anti-Manchu movement must be founded not on racially based Han Chinese pride but on resistance to authoritarianism, which he viewed as "another [superior?] phase of nationalism." The Manchus were to be resisted because they were in power and exercised dominion over others, and on this basis even Chinese emperors were to be resisted for their violation of the principles of human freedom and equality.[179] Thus, Liu also repudiated anti-imperialism as a political movement because it seemed to accept the domination of one's people by native instead of alien rulers.[180] These views placed him in conflict with his colleagues in the Tongmenghui as well as with many in the Paris movement. The ambivalence toward Chinese nationalism that they reflected presaged Liu's subsequent volte-face from anarchism to support of the late-Qing state and then the statist program of the Guomindang. Liu returned to Shanghai late in 1908 with his wife and served the governor of Jiangsu and Jiangnan as an agent provocateur pursuing his erstwhile colleagues in the revolutionary movement. After the 1911 revolution, he reemerged as one of China's most zealous cultural and political conservatives and concluded his career as an ardent nationalist activist.[181]

The Emergence of an Anarchist Movement in China

At approximately the same time that Liu moved from Tokyo back to China, Zhang Ji too returned to China, and the Chinese anarchist movement in Tokyo fell silent. The *Xin shiji* continued to be published in Paris, however, and although it could not be imported directly into China,[182] it exerted a decisive influence among worker-students abroad. Despite repeated attempts to repress the movement, it gradually began to flourish in China proper as a result of the efforts of the overseas activists. On the eve of the 1911 revolution, many of the Chinese worker-students who had become anarchists in Paris, including Wu and Li, returned to China where they rapidly invigorated the movement there. Li became vice-president of the Beijing-Tianjin section of the Tongmenghui in December 1911. The same year, Zhang Ji, Wang Jingwei, and Wu founded the Jindehui (Society to Promote Morality), an anarchist society that advocated a long list of moral prohibitions on personal behavior, including injunctions against prostitution, gambling, drinking alcohol and eating meat, and participation in government and politics.[183]

Meanwhile, as individual provinces declared their independence from the empire in October 1911, Jiang Kanghu launched the Zhongguo Shehuidang (Chinese Socialist party) with an eight-point platform. At the party's congress just one year later, a split emerged between the anarchist and state socialist factions. Jiang himself, convinced that the socialist party was becoming an instrument of political power rather than eschewing politics, asked that a firm commitment be made to the pursuit of "pure" anarchosocialism untainted by political involvements. When Jiang's perspective was rejected, he suggested a split, and a group of anarchists seceded to form the Shehuidang (Socialist party).[184] The new party urged a system of communism based on respect for the individual, equality of education, and the elimination of national boundaries, the family, and religion. Yet, despite their shared dedication to the principle of noninvolvement in politics, Jiang's own ideas concerning the future order brought him into political conflict with those who would become the leading figures in the anarchist movement in China, particularly Liu Shifu. Influenced by Western liberalism and social democracy, Jiang accepted individualism and emphasized the need for a competitive spirit. His program advocated republican government, basic education for all in society, the levy of rents only on land, and legislation to protect privacy. Finally, recognizing the potential for conflict between the competing values of freedom and equality, Jiang offered a singularly uninspiring and mechanistic solution to the dilemma: men and women would simply be equal in the first half of their lives and free in the latter half.[185] His new party lasted barely one month when it was banned by Yuan Shikai. The following year, the Zhongguo Shehuidang was also dissolved by the Yuan regime. Shortly thereafter a group in Shanghai founded the Wuzhengfu Gongchan-zhuyi Tongzhi-she (Society of Anarcho-Communist Comrades), and another in Nanjing founded the Wuzhengfu-zhuyi Taolun-hui (Anarchist Discussion Group).[186] Jiang's ideas were abandoned rapidly as these and other new anarchist associations found inspiration in other leaders newly returned from Japan and France.

In these years, many who had first embraced anarchism in Paris once again fled to France to escape the repression of the Yuan Shikai government. Yet the movement in China thrived, under the stimulation of those who had first launched the movements in France and Japan. Li, Wu, and Cai had had the foresight to establish associations for "Diligent Work and Economical Study" to send students abroad to study once again, as well as schools in Esperanto, which published translations of anarchist literature. Thus, from 1912, when the government agreed to subsidize the program to support Chinese students in France (perhaps to lessen pressures at home) until the end of World War I, the Chinese anarchist movement flourished both in France and at home.[187] In France, there were two centers of anarchist activity—Paris, where the journals *Ziyou* (Freedom)[188] and *Laodong* (Labor) were published and the short-lived French-Chinese University in Lyon for Chinese worker-students. The movement flourished until the end of the war when Chinese workers were no longer needed in great numbers and the French-Chinese University in Lyon was closed despite vigorous protests from Chinese worker-students. In China proper, the movement achieved its fastest growth in 1915–1916, particularly among disgruntled high school and college students who lived in very poor conditions. After Liu Shipei established the first Esperanto school in Shanghai in 1907, these and other anarchist activists opened similar schools to teach and promote Esperanto and to raise popular revolutionary consciousness. Anarchist organizations and magazines proliferated rapidly in this decade following the 1911 revolution. Wuzhengfu-zhuyi Chuanbo-she (The Society for the Propagation of Anarchism), Shi-she (The Truth Society) (at Beijing University), Fendou-she (The Struggle Society), the Annaqi Tongzhi-she (United Society of Anarchists), and the Wuzhengfu-zhuyizhe Tongmeng (Anarchists' League) were all founded during these years, and they published such magazines as *Renqun* (The Masses), *Annaqi zayan* (Free Writings), *Fendou* (Struggle), *Guofeng ribao* (National Customs Daily), and *Shehui yundong* (The Social Movement). The new anarchist groups clustered around two poles: those that advocated struggle and class conflict as essential to human development, on the one hand, and advocates of mutual aid, after Kropotkin, on the other. For the first group, it was particularly important for the revolution to destroy old forms of production and respond to the demands of the heart to raise human beings to a higher spiritual level. These anarchists advocated subjectivity over the significance of objective or scientific truth. By contrast, proponents of mutual aid focused less on revolutionary struggle than on efforts to create their utopias in practice. Two experiments in mutual aid, an agricultural commune in the mountains called "the New Settlement" and "Work and Study," an effort among Beida students to put an end to the gap between mental and physical labor, failed quickly.[189]

Yet the anarchists remained a potent force just after the Bolshevik Revolution, particularly in southeast China. When the warlord Chen Qiongming was firmly ensconced in Guangdong and Fujian provinces in 1918, he enlisted the anarchist Liang Bingxuan to facilitate the project of bringing China into modernity. Qu Shengbai was among those who returned from France after the war, settled in Canton, and founded the journal *Mingzhong* there. Similarly, anarchosyndicalists launched a newspaper called *Laodong* (Labor), edited by Wu Zhihui in Shanghai, but they, like the anarchists in general during this period, were strongest in Guangdong Province, where they operated under the protection of warlord Chen. By 1918 through 1920, the syndicalists had achieved sufficient prominence that workers were often spontaneously using their slogans in labor actions. The movement reached a peak in Hunan in the early-1920s, when the Society of Labor demonstrated against the Washington Naval Conference and denounced the Treaty of Versailles. The group's journal, called *Laogong zhoukan* (Work), published articles written by workers expressing primarily economic demands with respect to wages, hours, and other working conditions.[190] In addition, both the anarchist and the anarchosyndicalist movements in China were stimulated by those who had returned to France. In August 1916, Chinese in France launched the *Lüou zazhi* (Traveling in Europe Magazine), which was succeeded by the *Lüou zhoukan* (Traveling in Europe Weekly) in 1919. This was the official organ of the Hua-Fa Jiaoyu Hui Société Franco-Chinoise d'Education (Sino-French Educational Association) but it published the anarchist views of its editor, Chu Minyi, and other contributors, including Cai Yuanpei, Li Shizeng, Wang Jingwei, and Wang Shijie. Li, Cai, and others who lectured in a workers' school also publicized their views in the *Huagong zazhi* (Chinese Laborer's Journal), which was launched in January 1917.[191]

On the mainland, by far the most influential anarchist organization was the Shanghai group led by Liu Shifu (originally named Liu Sifu). Inspired by the narodnik example while studying in Japan circa 1904, Liu became a founding member of Sun's Tongmenghui in 1905. He returned to Canton where he was imprisoned for two years for his involvement in an assassination plot. During his imprisonment, Liu learned of anarchism through reports from the Tokyo and Paris groups and made a decisive shift from syndicalism to the anarchism of Kropotkin and Reclus. In 1912, Liu, with others who had led the Xiangjun army in the 1911 revolution, organized the Xin-she (Conscience Society), which required its members to live in accordance with strict moral injunctions, apparently influenced by the example of the sacred vows taken by Buddhist monks and laypersons. Liu and his associates also began to propagate anarchism through the written word. Liu, himself, founded the Huiming Xueshe in 1912 to propagate anarchism, and thereupon launched the *Huiminglu* (Record of the Huiming Xueshe, or Cockcrow Society), which was also titled *Pingmin zhi sheng* (Voice of the People).[192] Beginning in 1913, the journal was published under the title *Minsheng* (*La Vôco de la Popolo* in Esperanto) and had its headquarters in the international concession in Shanghai.[193] Meanwhile, Wu Zhihui, Li Shizeng, and Zhang Ji, recently returned from France and Japan, founded the Jindehui. These anarchists, known for their pioneering work in the overseas movements, pledged to eschew politics, but, like Liu Shipei, each gradually became involved in national politics. Thus, Liu Shifu soon became the only Chinese anarchist leader who was faithful to the anarchist repudiation of politics. It was, perhaps, for this reason that Liu acted as the spiritual leader of the anarchist movement in both Shanghai and Guangdong during his short career until he fell ill with tuberculosis and died in March 1915 at the age of 30.[194]

Liu was converted to anarchism through the influence of the Paris-based *Xin shiji* in 1909–1910, and the inspiration of the Paris group was deeply engraved in his thought. Nevertheless, having also studied in Japan and been exposed to the Chinese and Japanese anarchist movements there, he also exhibited some of the tendencies observed previously in the latter, specifically the influence of indigenous Chinese philosophical traditions. Like the Paris anarchists, Liu's anarchism drew heavily from the thought of Bakunin and Kropotkin.[195] Citing Kropotkin and the scientific anarchism of Benjamin Tucker, Liu explained, "Anarchists argue that men are completely free, accept no government, and abolish heads and institutions to which [men] accord authority." In short, the essence of anarchism was its rejection of the notion that might makes right.[196] Liu and his associates at the *Minsheng* were careful to distinguish their socialist views from those of Sun Yat-sen and their colleagues in Jiang Kanghu's Shehuidang. Liu sharply criticized Sun and Jiang for their lack of understanding of the role of economic arrangements in creating the ideal socialist society. In elaborating his Third People's Principle of Minsheng (people's livelihood, popularly understood to mean socialism), Sun had proposed an even larger role for the state, under whose auspices railroads and factories would be nationalized, and he compromised with private landownership by recommending a straight rental system to weaken landowners. Jiang, too, had maintained private property and a republican state in his prospectus, failing to come to terms with the need to bring an end to the distinction between rich and poor. In Liu's view, both these formulations were inadequate because true socialism necessarily required the eradication of private property. Sun and Jiang, in short, had failed to grasp a true comprehension of the nature of capital such as they would have gained from a systematic study of Marxism. Sun, Liu argued, did not realize that land was included in the definition of capital as a means of production; nor would Sun's notion of collectivization in terms of nationalization place land and other capital in the hands of the workers as true collectivization must do. For Liu, both the state and the holders of private capital together were responsible for the inequality in Chinese society, and true anarchocommunism must realize the elimination of both.

Noteworthy here is the role that Marxism played in Liu's anarchism. Liu combined the Marxian treatment of the state in relation to private property with indigenous Chinese philosophical traditions to support his anarchist vision. The ambivalence toward Chinese tradition that he shared with Liu Shipei together with his conviction that the success of anarchism in China was contingent on socialist revolution in the West brought the national question to the fore and helps elucidate why ultimately Marxism in its Leninist form would prevail over anarchism in China's socialist movement. Shifu was one of the first in China to define capital in Marxian terms and to stress the role of economic factors in the socialist revolution. His stature in the movement, in turn, kindled the interest of his fellow anarchists in Marxism as "scientific" socialism. As for Liu's own anarchist vision, he advocated the establishment of true workers' collectives, the elimination of the military, prisons, national boundaries, and other accoutrements of state power, and the universal adoption of Esperanto. Like Shipei in Tokyo, Shifu envisaged a society in which life would be planned according to life stages: Children would be required to attend school until the age of twenty or twenty-five, and adults would work until the age of forty-five or fifty, when they would rest at homes for the aged. Shifu, however, acknowledged that it was unlikely that China could achieve such a society immediately. That would await the realization of the anarchist revolution in Western Europe. In the meantime, Chinese revolutionists would prepare the groundwork by educating young men and women in their vision.[197]

The role of education in Liu's anarchism is of particular interest because it underscores the significance of moralism in his thought. For Liu, moralism was an essential characteristic of socialism that could not be sacrificed. Here Liu appears to have been influenced by Marx's criticisms of "utopian socialists" as well as by his forebears in Daoism and Buddhism.[198] Liu rejected Saint-Simon's socialism, for example, in favor of that of Louis Blanc, arguing that products must be distributed in accordance with human needs. The assessment of people's work on the basis of their individual capabilities and the distribution of the product as compensation for their labor was a procedure that was inherently unjust in his view. The very notion of "compensation", Liu argued, came from capitalist economics and rewarded those who were naturally endowed with greater strength than others: "Does not this sacrifice the principle of social equality? Is this appropriate for a standard of high moral virtue?"[199] Following Kropotkin, Liu argued that "economic freedom" from the shackles imposed by capitalism, "political freedom" from the burdens of coercive authority, and moral freedom were all required. The attainment of a society in which human relations would be experienced on the basis of Kropotkin's mutual aid Liu reinterpreted as the achievement of "*moral freedom.*"[200] In terms strikingly similar to those used by Daoist philosophers to characterize their repudiation of politics, Liu concluded that anarchism amounted to "three *wu*'s (no's)": no religion, no family, and no government.[201] These three obstacles to moral freedom were all to be eliminated in the anarchists' revolution. Liu dismissed readily the objections of those who feared anarchism: "People have become so accustomed to government, that they assume that if there is *zhu* [rule], there is *zhi* [peace and order], and if there is no *zhu*, there is *luan* [chaos]. Thus, they see anarchists as virtual thieves and arsonists seeking to destroy the existing order." His concept of anarchism as the realm of moral freedom allowed him to offer a confident riposte. The strictures of the false moralities of the family, religion, and government were obstacles to attaining genuine moral freedom, he argued. Like Liu Shipei, Shifu drew on a rich indigenous tradition of faith that humankind inherently shared a natural morality that could be cultivated through education. As in the program of French anarchosyndicalists, the syndicats would serve the Chinese movement not only to represent labor in the struggle against capital but also as vehicles for restoring this natural morality through education.[202] The Esperanto schools that the anarchosyndicalists instituted so widely after 1911 to propagate anarchism would serve the same moral purpose.[203]

The movement in China suffered a major shock when Shifu died suddenly in 1915. Without warning, China's struggling mainland anarchists were deprived of the youthful, vital spiritual leadership of one of the few who was not seduced away from anarchism by the rewards promised by participation in the new republic. Liu's journal *Minsheng* was closed down by the government briefly before resuming publication as a weekly. The anarchosyndicalist group in Shanghai, founded just eight months before Liu's death, also encountered official harassment and as a result of it sought association with another leading anarchist group, the Beijing Shi-she (Truth Society).[204] In the resurrected *Minsheng*, anarchists in the two groups wrote with the same quiet confidence that Liu had felt concerning the anarchist future of humankind.[205] Reflecting the increasing influence of scientism in China's New Cultural movement, however, their conviction was articulated more in terms of a Western-inspired faith in the scientific truth of evolutionism. This faith was simply reaffirmed by the victory of Marxism-Leninism—as scientific socialism—in Russia, a semi-Western society that had appeared hopelessly backward when the ephemeral victories of 1905 evaporated. Life was a contest not just between mankind and nature in its pristine state, but between human beings and the oppressive social and political institutions that they had crafted to serve themselves in that struggle. "Man, just like other creatures, must be dominated by the laws of nature," the anarchists believed, "but unlike other creatures that evolved then stopped, man never ceases to evolve, and while other creatures blindingly and absolutely are dominated by the laws of nature, man is only relatively, and with understanding, so dominated." Progress—and the assurance that China could at long last be saved—were secured by an appreciation of the rational capacities of man that has recurred in Western thought since ancient Greece.[206] The relationship of humanity to the natural world was problematized here in a manner that echoed the discourse of the Hellenist philosophers Plato and Euripides on the tension between law and (human) nature.[207] Was "nature" innately good? That depended on which "nature" one was discussing. Here there was great ambiguity. Human nature was viewed as progressive, whereas "[w]hatever is not progressive, not understanding, is man's animal nature." Yet, the Shanghai anarchists, echoing Liu and Kropotkin, affirmed the fundamental goodness of *human* nature ipso facto. "Man's thievery is something that evolved in his psyche over time, and if his environment were to be changed," they contended, "then his behavior would revert to its normal [moral] state."[208] Here, the views of Kropotkin and those drawing on Chinese perspectives on humankind were mutually supportive. Despite the ills people suffered under capitalism and various forms of repressive government, "[h]istorically, there is no record of any place where we do not find men moving from lack of comprehension to understanding and from non-evolution to evolution." The elements of man's animal nature, of "bestiality," that had been inculcated by nefarious environmental factors such as the state, then, would ultimately be overwhelmed by man's innate goodness, and thus by his innate "righteousness" once those negative institutions were eliminated.[209] Of course, it remained to be explained for China's anarchists, as for Kropotkin, how evil institutions and practices had accumulated so heavily as a result of the actions of fundamentally good men.

The antipathy of mainland anarchists toward the artifice of the state was complete, but did they not fear for the fate of the nation? Did nationalism have no effect on these anarchists who faced the miseries of China's malaise daily? Did not the historical evidence of China's subjugation by the advanced capitalist powers of the industrialized West indicate that their vision might be unduly optimistic, even dangerous, for China? China's anarchists were unmoved by such objections. Lacking a state would not be detrimental to China for two reasons. First, anarchism was an international movement that sought the union of all peoples and races in a single free and egalitarian society that transcended national boundaries. The *Minsheng* and other journals were published internationally in several different languages, including Esperanto, and the Chinese anarchists actively sought to cooperate with anarchists in other countries. Their hope was that, in attacking their own capitalist economies and state powers, their comrades in other anarchist movements would help to bring an end to the powers' ill-treatment of China.[210] In addition, the anarchists denied that they or their comrades elsewhere sought to create the luan that their critics feared. As in the Confucian and Buddhist philosophical frameworks, luan, they argued, arose out of human evil, and the anarchists sought to rid society of its sources outside man. Anarchism's quest to reform society required restoring individuals to their natural morality "because if human morality is not good then it is not possible to establish anarchism."[211] Conversely, once that morality had been made good in the anarchist world, China would no longer be threatened by the existing luan of its victimization by imperialism. Finally, the anarchists noted pointedly, China had a state at present, but that government was betraying the interests of its people by selling off Chinese assets in mines, railroads, and other resources to foreign powers rather than protecting and cultivating them. In any event, inasmuch as anarchism was the dominant trend internationally, there was no real need to fear for a Chinese nation bereft of state power.[212]

Nevertheless, even the anarchists in Paris who were most vehemently iconoclastic and internationalistic shared the national pride of anarchists in Tokyo and China proper in the natural compatibility between their anarchist vision and their own indigenous philosophical traditions. Western scholars had characterized the Chinese as passive, "modest," and harmonious in spirit and concluded that these traits had hindered the development of material civilization, a certain Taipu observed. But citing Bertrand Russell on the distinction between the human impulse to creativity and that toward possessiveness, he argued that modesty or a lack of aggressiveness vis-à-vis the latter did not necessarily imply a want of creativity. Taipu went on to claim that anarchism was peculiarly appropriate for China because the very notion of state or government was alien to China. Certainly, China had had an emperor and a bureaucracy, "a parasitic economic class," but "it goes without saying that China had no government," and the laws of the empire could not be regarded as *law* in the twentieth-century concept thereof. Although Chinese students studying in Japan had brought back the terms *zhengfu* (government) and *falü* (law) with them from Japan at the end of the Qing period, these concepts remained unknown among China's ordinary people. "They do not even know what the word 'police' means: If they see a policeman, they think he is a soldier," Taipu contended. "As for government, there is still none that has anything to do with the people except to collect money from them every year."[213] Such convictions concerning the "suitability" of anarchism for China posed a paradoxical counterpoint to the equally strongly held belief among Chinese anarchists that it was China's own traditions—in the family, in religion, and in the state—that were to be attacked, destroyed, and transcended in the anarchist revolution. However attracted they might have been by Western strains of anarchism and the philosophical heritage that supported them, then, ultimately many were as profoundly influenced by the very traditions they sought to escape.

If it were just a question of distinguishing between the natural morality of the Chinese people as opposed to the false morality of the Confucian sages, as Liu Shipei and others contended, the matter would be simple enough. But this was not the whole of the matter. Deeply driven by a nationalistic desire to save their nation, the anarchists' repudiation of the national state left the fate of China's anarchist revolution at the mercy of the Western powers. Some, like Taipu, seemed to claim that China's authoritarian structures had arisen out of external forces, that the West was the source of the evils afflicting China. Yet they turned to the West as the source of the good, of effective prescriptions to save China. Still more, many among these early socialist revolutionaries vehemently repudiated the Chinese philosophical past, and yet they relied on its logic—especially that of the Confucian component they rejected most strenuously—to articulate a comprehensive solution to China's problem. This paradox would recur throughout the history of China's socialist revolutionary movement.

These conflicting attitudes concerning China and the nation were widely evident among China's anarchists. By 1920, those who had remained in or returned to

China were enthusiastic participants in Marxist study groups led by Chen Duxiu and Li Dazhao, future Communist party founders. Indeed, many, if not most, such early Marxian socialists began their careers as populist anarchists.[214] In this sense, although interest in anarchism declined dramatically between 1921 and 1923 during the heated debate with the Bolshevists, the anarchist movement played a critical role in the birth and maturation of Marxism-Leninism in China.[215] By 1921, all three Chinese Marxist study groups in Beijing, Shanghai, and Canton were splintered by the debate over issues of centralized authority in the movement and the dictatorship of the proletariat raised by the Bolshevik revolution of 1917. Although many of the newly converted Marxists accepted and adhered to anarchist notions concerning the desirability of direct action and the general strike, the conflict within these groups intensified until the Marxists expelled the anarchists on the eve of the first CCP Congress of July 1921.[216]

This schism did not occur, however, before nationalism fused with populism to encourage the growth of Marxism-Leninism from within the anarchist movement itself. As the anarchist movements in China and Japan flourished after 1906–1907, the dilemmas of the national question inherent in this doctrine became increasingly clear. This was particularly so because, as in Russia, Chinese and Japanese anarchism tended to be linked with populist instincts to go "to the people," who were ultimately the Russian, Chinese, or Japanese nation. Kōtoku's direct action strategy was an effort to devolve the leading role in the revolution from the intellectuals, who had dominated the movement in small elite associations, to the masses, who showed themselves increasingly ready for an activist role through recurrent outbursts of violence in 1905 and 1906. Ōsugi took this populist idea a step further through his subjectivist doctrine in 1915 and 1916. In an article entitled "Rōdō undō to kojin-shugi" (The labor movement and individualism), "Ōsugi presented the corollary anti-intellectual position which his new found faith in the workers implied. He refuted the contention that the workers were unaware of any meaning in their acts by making the point that their 'uncorrupted' ignorance was a virtue and their knowledge a result of pure experience."[217] This conviction was comparable to Kropotkin's having been "more impressed by the faith of the workers in their movement than by any kind of organization or political ideal."[218] Such a high valuation of the intuitive wisdom of the Japanese people drawn from their life experience signified a certain faith in the values embodied in the life experience of the Japanese moral community. Kawakami Hajime, early in his career, looked back with nostalgia on the values and mores of preindustrial Japan. His nōhon-shugi (agrarianism) was directly linked to the belief that the Japanese peasants were ultimately the basis of true loyalty and patriotism and, thus, were the essential strength of the Japanese nation: "farmers were frugal, patriotic, obedient, and healthy. They made the best soldiers and the most loyal citizenry."[219] Similarly, as already noted, in his own first impulses toward socialism, Kōtoku not only saw no fundamental contradiction between socialism and the kokutai, but also placed its Confucian and Shintō values at the center of his anarcho-communism.

As discussed here, analogous loyalties to traditional Chinese philosophical values were manifested in the populism of early Chinese socialists and anarchists.

Much as Russian narodniki saw in the mir the basis of a socialism that would allow Russia to avoid the evils of Western industrial capitalism, Liu Shipei, Liu Shifu, and Taipu all saw anarchocommunism as somehow especially suited to the continuing predominance of the agricultural sphere in contemporary China. Such appeals to traditional socioeconomic forms invoked national pride and asserted the value of national uniqueness. More importantly, as the doctrine became less abstract in turning "to the people," humanitarian concerns elicited nationalistic impulses to protect the people against foreign encroachment and depredations. It is here that the destructive urges of anarchism (as evidenced in Bakunin, Ōsugi, and the Chinese anarchists in Paris) came into acute conflict with its constructive impulses to build a new society (as evidenced in Kropotkin, Kōtoku, and the Tokyo Chinese anarchist group).[220] While the destructive urge required the demise of impediments to human freedom in the existing society and the state, the constructive impulse sought a new and better society ensuring human freedom on the basis of "free association" and "mutual aid." Anarchism mandated the demise of the state, but without a defensive centralized power structure, how could such community be maintained? Indeed, in a country like China under siege by powers that accepted the doctrine of "might makes right," how could "the people" be truly liberated if the nation were not to be liberated by the power of some kind of indigenous state?

As Marxism strengthened its appeal after the October Revolution, these implications of the national question began to engage Asian anarchists more and more intensely, particularly in China. Li Dazhao, as the founder of the first Marxist study groups, is the exemplar of this emerging tendency. Li, like most other Chinese anarchists, was deeply influenced by Kropotkin's notion of mutual aid, and this influence and that of the Russian narodniki were powerfully evident in Li's thought even after he had become a Marxist.[221] Li's effort to resolve the national question recalled Bakunin's cryptic observation concerning the revolutions of 1848 that social revolutions and movements of national liberation were mutually dependent. Bakunin had written:

> Two great questions were posed from the first days of the spring [of 1848]: the social question and that of the independence of all nations, the emancipation of peoples internally and externally at once. The whole world understood that liberty was only a lie where the great majority of the population is condemned to lead a poverty-stricken existence and where, deprived of education, of leisure and of bread, it is destined to serve as a stepping-stone for the powerful and rich. Thus the social revolution presented itself as a natural and necessary consequence of the political revolution. At the same time, it was felt that while there is a single persecuted nation in Europe the complete and decisive triumph of democracy will be possible nowhere. . . . We must first of all purify our atmosphere and transform completely the surroundings in which we live, for they corrupt our instincts and our wills, they constrict our hearts and our intelligences. Therefore the social question appears first of all as the overthrow of society.[222]

Li, too, endeavored to resolve the national question in the manner of Bakunin: his nationalistic concern for the fate of China supported his demand for social revolution within China itself while he realized that without freedom from foreign domination, internal revolution would be to no avail. Moreover, Li never shared the extreme cultural iconoclasm of the Paris anarchist circle. He candidly valued certain aspects of Chinese tradition and wished to build upon them in creating a new social order. It was this nationalistic impulse that would subsequently prompt Li to respond so positively to the Bolshevik revolution. Unlike many of the Paris anarchists who eschewed nationalism completely or who embraced it in reaction against Bolshevism, Li sought to strengthen his ties with what he regarded as the "real" China—the peasantry—in the manner of the Russian narodniki. Kropotkin's moral ideal of mutual aid was appealing to Li, who, like Kōtoku and Kawakami, asserted that revolution necessitated spiritual as well as material or political change. Like Kawakami and Kropotkin, Li also deplored the increasing separation of the city from the countryside. In an article entitled "Qingnian yu nongcun" (Youth and the village) (February 1919), Li emphasized the importance of the countryside as the heartland of China and urged Chinese youth to abandon cities that had been corrupted by evil Western influences and return to the villages of their forebears. There the youth would live with the peasants, absorb their customs, and help to make the hamlet the seat of true democracy.[223]

Unlike the narodniki and Liu Shipei earlier in Tokyo, however, Li did not see a virtue in the ignorance and backwardness of Chinese peasants. Intellectuals from the cities would play a necessary educative and organizational role in preparing for the revolution. "Only if the intellectuals enter labor organizations will the laborers' organizations become enlightened," he wrote. "[O]nly if more and more youth return to the villages, will there be any hope of reforming village life; and only if village life feels the effects of reform will there be progress in social organization." But this role could be played only by intellectuals who simplified their own manner of life and participated in labor alongside the peasantry.[224] Here, like Bakunin, Li found room for nationalism in his populist anarchism: National liberation was part of individual liberation, and the populist desire to create that revolution through "the people" was the means for the accommodation of Li's nationalism with his anarchism. The dilemma would become much more complex, however, when the victory of Bolshevism over the Allied intervention coincided with the upsurge of nationalist sentiment directed against the Western powers and Japan in China. The focus of the national question was thereupon shifted to authority and statism, and a rupture between anarchism and Bolshevism would become unavoidable.

CONCLUSIONS: FROM ANARCHISM TOWARD MARXISM

The differences between the initial Chinese and Japanese impulses toward anarchism, notwithstanding, a key similarity in its appeal over Marxism from 1906 through 1917 lay in its voluntarism. Bakunin had differed with Marx on many points, but he was particularly averse to the notion that revolution had to await the maturation of certain objective conditions as Marx maintained. In the words of Paul Avrich, "Bakunin's was a dream of immediate and universal destruction, the leveling of all existing values and institutions, and the creation of a new libertarian society on their ashes."[225] Struggling against a repressive imperial regime, by which he would be executed on probably fabricated charges of treason, Kōtoku was impatient with the failure of the socialist movement to make any progress against the detested bureaucratic government. Likewise, struggling in the "winter period," Ōsugi had recourse to few legal avenues for achieving significant political change in any case, and he was anxious to employ his energies as an individual in social revolution. Anarchism satisfied that need. Chinese anarchists, too, were frustrated at the inability of progressives and reformers to revive the decaying Qing regime since the midnineteenth century, and anarchism proffered a ready weapon. The Russian Revolution of 1905 confirmed for both Chinese and Japanese revolutionists the notion that anarchism offered a viable means to oppose authoritarianism.

If anarchism gained predominance in the two socialist movements after 1906, it was not very carefully differentiated from Marxist thought in either case. This enabled anarchists and Marxists to cooperate with one another for a time even after the Bolshevik revolution. Nevertheless, when the contours of the Bolshevik movement and the new Soviet state became clear and the Soviet Union began to assert authority over the international socialist movement through the Comintern, by 1921, the decisive differences between anarchism and Marxism-Leninism became manifest. Of course, by this time, conditions had changed considerably in China and Japan. The Bolshevik victory, the rice riots in Japan after World War I, and the May Fourth movement all demonstrated that new opportunities for political action abounded and that its prospects were most promising. The leavening of anarchist voluntarism with Marxian determinism became more attractive as socialists now sought assurances that their movement would indeed culminate in successful revolution. The efficacy of the Marxian model had now been demonstrated in the society that Marx and Engels themselves had viewed as the most backward in Europe. The idealism and moralism of anarchism could be supplemented comfortably with the materialism of Marxism. Finally, the traumatic civil war in which the new Bolshevik revolutionary regime was attacked by more advanced capitalist powers demonstrated conclusively the need for some centralized state power to defend the revolution. To have argued against a strong Bolshevik state under war communism would have been tantamount to repudiating the revolution itself.

Indeed, the arrival of Bolshevik advisors in the East brought the more profound dimensions of the national question to the forefront. Some of these tensions had already existed in China in the emergence of the New Culture movement on the eve of May Fourth. Whether one espoused positive or negative freedom bore significant implications for the relationship one would come to have with Marxism-Leninism or with other at least temporarily statist varieties of socialism. For Kōtoku and Ōsugi and for most of the Chinese anarchist circle in Paris, the freedom to which they aspired was a negative freedom; they maintained a concept of freedom from restraints imposed by the state or by social institutions such as the family and organized religion rather than a positive "freedom to" act in any particular way.[226] Nevertheless, some among the Paris circle, Liu Shipei in Tokyo, and Liu Shifu on the mainland all appeared to adhere to a notion of positive freedom. The moral freedom to which the two Liu's aspired, for example, certainly involved a liberation from constrictive social and political institutions, but the purpose of this liberation was to achieve a freedom to act in accordance with mankind's innate moral proclivities. Some of those for whom the nationalist impulse to eject the Manchus was a major element of their anarchist revolutionism —such as Wu Zhihui and Cai Yuanpei—it will be recalled, had also founded the moralistic Jindehui. They aspired to a freedom to act to realize a moralistic program that was in accordance with the interests of the Chinese and their indigenous philosophical wisdom. Imperial and imperialistic domination by the Manchus, Westerners, and Japanese prevented them from realizing such a program. Their espousal of positive as opposed to negative freedom might have inclined these anarchists to embrace the mission of the nationalistic Guomindang in China. As for Li Dazhao, his anarchopopulism also espoused a positive freedom, but its content would incline him toward the Bolshevist variety of "statist" socialism.

These were the predominant outcomes of the activities of Chinese anarchists of the New Culture movement. As Dirlik notes, "concern for China's destiny as a nation was an important element in many intellectuals' advocacy of a cultural revolution during this period. This was obviously at odds with anarchist antinationalism and, on occasion, created hostility to the anarchists."[227] But how were China's anarchists to invoke indigenous traditions to achieve a radical national reconstruction? In Japan, the argument rested on the conviction that the Restoration, while claiming to restore indigenous traditions, had abandoned Japan's true cultural essence to the oppressive accoutrements of the West's industrial capitalism. The aversion to the West coincided, for Japan's early anarchosocialists, with their rejection of a state that had mistaken Westernization for modernization and industrialization. In China this was simply not the case. The supreme irony was that neither the Qing nor the anarchists could appeal to Daoism along with other indigenous perspectives to rebuild China on the basis of nationalist appeal. The alien status of the Qing aside, there was the fact that Daoism, Legalism, and Confucianism had become an amalgam of mutually supportive elements of the imperial regime. In the time the ancient Daoists wrote expressing the anarchist views cited by Liu Shipei and others, they might well have constituted real challenges to the orthodoxy of "the sages." But by the time Liu and others invoked their writings, these had become an integral part of the official ideological corpus. The appeal to Daoist roots, then, could offer only *wuwei* as a prescription. Over the generations such a prescription had reinforced the hold of the Confucian and Legalist components of state orthodoxy by providing a basis for criticism within the same philosophical system rather than a positive program of action. This withdrawal from politics in the Daoist scheme served to undercut anarchism, the role that Chinese anarchism could play as an ideal that dissented from the amalgam. At best, historically, Daoism simply provided a convenient rationale for the native scholar's withdrawal from the political realm altogether when China was under alien rule.

Clearly, this could not be an effective prescription for Chinese revolutionists who partook of any spirit of nationalism. Indigenously based anarchism could only work in China if the amalgam of which it had become a part was supplanted by a unitary weltanschauung that was uncompromised by Manchu rule and prescribed concrete action directed against the very official orthodoxy that enveloped Daoism as a component for nearly two millennia. Only then could Chinese radicals claim an effective tool with which to save China. To put it another way, if saving China meant destroying the status quo both intellectually and materially, an anarchism grounded in traditions that enshrouded that status quo simply could not prevail over the alternatives. As nationalism matured and deepened in China within the May Fourth incident, this truth would prove to be the Achilles' heel of Chinese anarchism. Those whose anarchopopulism had long ago been reconciled with nationalism, such as Li and Wu, would be inclined to accept the Bolshevik or Sunist alternative.

On this point, the comparison with developments in Japan is most instructive. There the outcome would be less clear cut. Those, like Ōsugi, whose anarchism was based on uncompromising individualism and whose zeal for the Japanese polity had been all but destroyed by his witness to the state's execution of Kōtoku, the Bolshevik example would be less convincing. As fellow anarchist and subsequent JCP leader Arahata Kanson noted, "Ōsugi never ceased to repudiate Soviet power after the Russian Revolution, stubbornly upholding the anarchist principles of opposition to central authority."[228] As Ōsugi's posture would suggest, those who had not reflected carefully on the national question before 1917 might accept Soviet authority with deep-seated reservations that might subsequently prompt them to secede from a party under Comintern domination. This would, indeed, be the case in Japan, as Yamakawa, Arahata, and Sakai, whether out of an anarchistic rejection of centralized authority or nationalistic pride, seceded from the JCP and formed the dissident Rōnō-ha just five years after they supported the bolshevists against Ōsugi. On that occasion, Japanese socialism seemed to come full circle, returning, in a manner of speaking, to Kōtoku's original accommodation of anarchism with nationalism. Thus, in China as well as in Japan, the national question would prompt revolutionists to adopt stances contrary to the orthodoxies of anarchism and Marxism-Leninism as well.

Nationalism and the Path to Bolshevism

"Nationalism" aspires to "the attainment and maintenance of self-government and independence on behalf of a group [at least] some of whose members conceive it to constitute an actual or potential 'nation' like others." Revolutionary nationalism differs from simple nationalism in its concern with the integration of conationals into a homogeneous unit, i.e., by its effort to forge a politically integrated nation-state. The basis of that homogeneity is conceived to be some sort of ethnic or cultural individuality which turns on a "myth of origin" and a "myth of historic mission." The defense of that ethnic or cultural individualism, and of the historic mission, demands of revolutionary nationalists an effort to enhance the international status and prestige of the national community by mobilizing human and material resources for a drive toward maximal economic autarky and self-sustaining economic and industrial growth. All of that necessitates a renovation and a regeneration of the cultural and social fabric of the nation through substantial institutional and social changes.[1]

"Revolutionary nationalism" found a place within both Chinese and Japanese Marxist thought in the first half of the twentieth century. Whether identified with the political Left or Right, it laid the foundation for the resolution of the national question in Marxism in both countries. Differing contexts—the political and economic positions of the two countries in the international system, their levels of economic development, and their indigenous modes of political thought—determined that the marriage of "revolutionary nationalism" with West European socialism would take distinct forms in the two societies. Nevertheless, because of their common experience as Asian societies subjected to pressures from more economically advanced West European nation-states, the tension between international socialist ideals envisaging the demise of the state and the quest for a strong national state based on cultural uniqueness was resolved predominantly in favor of the enterprise of state building to different degrees in China and Japan.

The 1917 Bolshevik revolution and Lenin's call for national liberation movements to protect that revolution brought the national question into sharp focus for both Chinese and Japanese Marxists. Several dimensions of the national question were illuminated dramatically by the creation of the new Soviet state in 1917. One dimension concerned the nature of the modern state and its relationship to economic change. In Marxist thought, the state apparatus was commonly identified as part of the "superstructure," its character determined by the economic base of society. Yet Marxists have historically associated the emergence of the modern national state with the growth of capitalism, its very purpose to provide a secure framework for the prosperity of the native bourgeoisie.[2] "The centralised state power, with its ubiquitous organs of standing army, police, bureaucracy, clergy, and judicature," wrote Marx, "originates from the days of absolute monarchy, serving nascent middle-class society as a mighty weapon in its struggles against feudalism." Eventually, "[a]t the same pace at which the progress of modern industry developed, widened, intensified the class antagonism between capital and labour, the State power assumed more and more the character of the national power of capital over labour, of a public force organised for social enslavement, of an engine of class despotism. After every revolution marking a progressive phase in the class struggle, the purely repressive character of the State power stands out in bolder and bolder relief."[3]

This perspective suggested that the state could be an actor in, rather than merely a reflection of, human historical development. The notion of the "potential autonomy of the state"[4] suggests that the state has always been more than just a passive superstructural element molded by a dynamic economic material base. It has a life of its own, affecting the development of the economic base itself. As Leon Trotsky once observed, this phenomenon has been particularly apparent in the role of states in such later-industrializing countries as tsarist Russia, Bismarckian Germany, and Meiji Japan in initiating revolutions from above to accelerate the transition from agrarian to modern industrial society.[5] If the state could be an active participant in the revolutionary transition to capitalist society in Western Europe and, particularly, in more backward societies, could not the state also perform an analogous role in a socialist revolution?

Erupting in a society far less industrialized than the European societies expected to be the first sites of the maturation of Marxian socialism, the Bolshevik revolution brought this issue to the fore. Having suffered an ignominious defeat by the much smaller Japan in 1905, Russia was not perceived to be a particularly advanced capitalist society, especially among early Japanese socialists.[6] Lenin's Bolsheviks had split with George Plekhanov's Mensheviks on the very issue of whether a proletarian-socialist revolution was premature and ill-conceived in such a predominantly agrarian and industrially weak setting. Lenin's decision to forge ahead in October raised a new issue: What would become of the state after the revolution? Because Marx's schema argued that socialism could emerge only where the productive forces of industrial capitalism had developed fully, before socialism could be realized in Russia, the new state would need first to complete the tasks of industrialization left unfinished by the weak prerevolutionary bourgeoisie. Hence, the proletarian dictatorship could not merely suppress counterrevolution by destroying the remnants of the bourgeoisie and managing the new society's day-to-day functions as Lenin's *State and Revolution* supposed.[7] Indeed, the very notion that the state should wither away along with class divisions after the revolution was brought into serious question by the desperate economic realities of postrevolutionary Russia. Thus, Soviet leaders engaged in prolonged debate on precisely how the revolutionary regime could perform its unexpectedly more extensive economic functions without resurrecting or perpetuating capitalism.[8]

The Bolsheviks quickly found that virtually all aspects of their initial intentions concerning the new state had to be compromised if their revolution was to survive. In "The Civil War in France," Marx had written, "the working class cannot simply lay hold of the ready-made state machinery and wield it for its own purposes."[9] Yet a serious shortage of skilled manpower meant that factories and state institutions could not be staffed by the illiterate workers and peasants that had swept the Bolsheviks into power, and the new leaders were soon forced to recruit former tsarist bureaucrats to the new state apparatus. The perceived need for the state, complete with its oppressive apparatus of army, police, and bureaucracy, was reinforced by the Siberian intervention of the advanced capitalist powers against the October Revolution. This experience left the new Soviet leaders in constant fear of "hostile capitalist encirclement" and justified the maintenance of a powerful military machine[10] and a strong state. In short, the experience of the Bolshevik revolution seemed to prove what the demise of the Second International in 1914 had strongly suggested: Marx's writings on the role of the nation-state during and after the revolution were at best incomplete and probably in need of revision. These issues were not lost to Chinese and Japanese Marxist observers writing to defend the Bolshevik revolution and the new revolutionary state.[11]

The demise of the Second International had occurred in response to a second aspect of the national question: the fate of the nation in revolution. During World War I, it had been simple enough to conclude, as had Lenin, that there was simply a lack of heartfelt commitment to the ideal of international socialism among its national leaders. After the Bolshevik victory in October, the Comintern's encouragement of movements of national liberation to support the struggling socialist state clouded the issue by reversing Lenin's World War I position and aligning nationalism with socialism. The nexus between this nationalist and the statist aspects of the national question lay in the notion of "socialism in one country." The Bolsheviks believed, as had Marx and Engels before them, that a socialist revolution in Russia could succeed and survive only with the support of ensuing proletarian revolutions in the more advanced capitalist societies of Western Europe.[12] But the collapse of the German revolution in 1919 soon dashed these hopes, and it was clear that Soviet Russia would remain the sole proletarian state for some time. Thus, socialism in one country, embracing multiple nationalities under a single revolutionary state, became a reality by 1920.

In the new circumstances, Lenin recognized the revolutionary potential in nationalist movements among colonial peoples, something he had anticipated several years earlier when he penned *Imperialism, the Highest Stage of Capitalism*. Now Lenin pressed for the successor to the Second International—destroyed by first-world nationalism in the West—to promote revolutionary nationalism in "colonial wars" in the East.[13] Such wars of national liberation would threaten the smooth operation of international imperialism. The seeds of a conflict between this prescription and the national aspirations of non-European revolutionaries, however, lay embedded in the very formulation of the new Comintern policy. Lenin never believed that in colonial and semicolonial societies such as India and China, where native bourgeoisies and proletariats were tiny and weak, socialist revolutions could be expected to triumph. Rather, Lenin's objective was to use national liberation movements in the East only to destabilize international capitalism, thereby fomenting revolution among the huge proletariats of Europe.

In short, Lenin's faith and that of Comintern leaders after him remained firmly vested in the urban centers of Europe.[14] The peasant masses of the East would occupy a decidedly subordinate role in their smychka (alliance) with the proletariat of the industrialized West.[15] This instrumentalist approach to revolution in the East became painfully apparent in Stalin's willingness to subordinate the Chinese Communist party (CCP) to Sun Yat-sen's Guomindang (GMD) in 1924, and in the disastrous outcome of that policy in 1927.[16] The Shanghai coup inevitably aroused serious questions in the minds of both Chinese and Japanese Marxists: How far could or should any native communist party sacrifice the interests of its own national revolution for those of the international revolution, or of its fatherland, the Soviet Union? If the Soviet Union was acting in its own narrow national interests, cleverly cloaked in the mantle of world revolution, perhaps the Bolshevik path— which Karl Radek correctly identified as Menshevik policy—was not a valid Chinese or Japanese path to socialism at all.[17] Before 1927, this issue already lurked beneath the surface, and after the tragedy of the Shanghai coup, such doubts strengthened the marriage of Marxism with nationalism in both China and Japan. In Japan, it afforded a major excuse for the secession of the Rōnō-ha from the Japanese Communist party (JCP) in 1927 and for the *tenkō* of JCP leaders Sano Manabu and Nabeyama Sadachika in 1933 (see chaps. 6 and 8 this volume). In China, it sanctioned Mao's pursuit of a revolution that was at once nationalistic and socialistic, in isolation from the Comintern to whose often contradictory policies he merely paid lip service.

In a world of imperialism and capitalist nation-states, where even the world's lone proletarian state was constrained to pursue socialism-in-one-country domestically and narrow national interests abroad, Chinese and Japanese Marxists had to wonder if the enterprise of state building realistically could be abandoned without committing national (*minzoku-teki* or *minzu-de*) suicide. Without the cultural entity, what would be the soil in which native Marxist revolutionaries would nurture socialism? And would not national or ethnic differences persist even if socialist revolutions were victorious throughout the world? As R. N. Berki has noted, nations are unequal in a way that human beings are not: they are endowed with far more disparate levels and kinds of resources.[18] Amid such inequalities warfare would, doubtless, continue. Perhaps the state could not be permitted to wither away if its military might would be needed to defend newly socialist cultures within their own national bounds.

Chinese and Japanese Marxists responded in similar ways to these challenges as they were posed by the Russian revolution. In both countries, before 1917, socialism had been a heterogeneous mixture of utopian, Christian, anarchist, populist, and Marxian socialist ideas. By raising these issues concerning the legitimacy of nationalism and statism, the October Revolution catalyzed new schisms in socialist movements within which disparate strands of socialism had hitherto coexisted.

This is not to say that no tensions involving nationalism existed in these movements before the October Revolution. In Japan, the Russo-Japanese War forced Meiji socialists to confront the contradiction between their pacifist aspirations to universal human harmony and the aggressive imperialist maneuvers of their own *kokutai*.[19] At the same time, Chinese socialists, even those who felt acutely the humiliation of China in the 1894–1895 Sino-Japanese War, looked to Japan for an example of successful nation and state building. Accordingly, racialism and pan-Asianism became conjoined with the call for minsheng-zhuyi (people's livelihood-ism, or socialism) among many followers of Sun Yat-sen.[20] In both China and Japan, then, a problematic relationship among nationalism, racialism, and pan-Asianism flourished even before the Bolshevik triumph. But the October Revolution exacerbated the conflict between Marxian socialism, on the one hand, and indigenous attachments to the nation and the state on the other. In Japan, this conflict took the form of the so-called *ana-boru* (anarchist-Bolshevik) debate. This vehement struggle split hard-core anarchists around Ōsugi Sakae from many former anarchosyndicalists such as Arahata Kanson and Yamakawa Hitoshi, who joined Sakai Toshihiko to follow the Bolshevik line of Marxist revolution under Comintern leadership. In the Chinese left-wing movement, a similar conflict occurred among early socialists, many of whom were overseas students heavily influenced by West European anarchism and Japanese socialism. Again, in China, the October Revolution forced a choice between anarchist and Bolshevik paths to revolution. With the rising tide of nationalism in China's May Fourth movement, the 1920s saw the triumph of Bolshevism over anarchist socialism in China as in Japan. Bolshevist Marxists quickly founded communist parties to follow the Comintern lead in international revolution.

In this turbulent period, some who had been pioneers in the introduction of Marxism into their respective countries began to transform Marxism into national socialist doctrines. In Japan, Takabatake Motoyuki, who produced the first complete Japanese translation of *Das Kapital* and played the leading role in reporting the Bolshevik revolution to the Japanese public, conceived a Marxist-Leninist theory of national socialism. Takabatake and the anarchist Ōsugi agreed that the Russian revolution had been nationalist and statist in impulse and outcome, but their shared interpretation reinforced their diametrically opposing tendencies toward statism, on the one hand, and anarchism, on the other.[21] In China, Dai Jitao, who had pioneered the introduction of Marxism into China, responded to the new Soviet state by constructing a national socialism on the basis of Sun Yat-sen's Three People's Principles.[22] Although Takabatake maintained his claim to be Marxist in formulating his new doctrine and Dai's adaptation of national socialism was coupled with vehement opposition to Bolshevism, both formulations endeavored to resolve dimensions of the national question raised by the October Revolution. As advocates of national socialism, these thinkers were in the minority in the left-wing movements in both China and Japan. Their responses to Bolshevism, however, reflected much broader tendencies in the two movements. In neither case would anarchism triumph, precisely because anarchism could not respond adequately to the national question. Those who would create viable socialist movements in either country could not triumph without affirming the nation and the state. Thus, Dai's and Takabatake's national socialist formulations foreshadowed the way in which the national question would be resolved in the two Marxist movements by World War II. Li Dazhao's nationalism prevailed over Chen Duxiu's internationalism and heralded the emergence of an effective nationalistic Chinese socialist movement under Mao, and Takabatake's national socialism portended the collapse of Japan's Communist party in *tenkō* and the articulation of other Marxian national socialist doctrines in Japan in the late-1920s and 1930s. In both cases, anarchism was abandoned for Bolshevism as many of China's and Japan's socialists concluded that in the threatening international arena of the early twentieth century, to abandon nation building and state building would be suicidal for their peoples and for their movements.

NATIONALISM AND EARLY SOCIALISM IN CHINA AND JAPAN

It is not surprising that Chinese and Japanese Marxists should have reached such a conclusion given the context in which early Marxian socialism evolved in the two countries. Nationalistic responses to the pressures of the international arena were common among early socialists in both countries. Beginning in the midnineteenth century, political elites in China and Japan, reacting to Western encroachments, formulated policies designed to secure the political integrity of their respective regimes. China was first to be affected by Western expansion in the opium wars of the 1840s, but it was Japan that first developed an effective response that could be labeled self-consciously nationalistic. Meiji liberals and socialists in turn challenged the elite nationalism of the Meiji leadership to structure movements— embracing an element of populist nationalism—that opposed the repressive domestic and internationally expansionist policies of an ever more powerful state. This occurred decades before such recognition that the West had violated the territorial integrity of the vaguely defined Middle Kingdom appeared among Chinese intellectuals in the May Fourth movement.[23] How the ruling elite resolved the national crisis precipitated by the Western powers contributed to the pattern of thought among dissidents in each society. In Japan, young Meiji socialists (like the liberal activists in the jiyū minken undō [civil rights movement]) operated within a nationalistic consensus endowed with a sense of internal and international historical mission.[24] Reformers and revolutionaries may have objected to certain aspects of the *kokutai* framework, but they saw the new orthodoxy as formulated by the Meiji oligarchs as being positively related to the political rejuvenation of the Meiji Restoration.[25] By contrast, in China the task of formulating a new political orthodoxy incorporating nationalism fell entirely to reformers and to revolutionaries inspired by the Japanese example from whose ranks the first socialists emerged.[26]

This difference between the Chinese and Japanese experiences is attributable partly to the universalism that permeated traditional Chinese Confucian political theory, on the one hand, and the rejection of the universalist elements of this Chinese philosophy that accompanied the demise of the Tokugawa shogunate, on the other.[27] In both cases, the inability of the governing elites to eject the offensive foreigners accelerated internal tendencies toward political collapse, resulting in the demise of the Tokugawa shogunate and then of the Qing dynasty. In Japan, however, late in the Edo period, the Kokugaku and Mito intellectual schools had already launched a reaction against the wholesale adoption of Chinese thought in Japan and spearheaded a philosophical endeavor to return to things Japanese.[28] These Japanist ideas were employed purposefully by the Meiji leaders to create the *kokutai* orthodoxy in support of the state. In combination with ideas borrowed from German *Staatsrecht* theory, these indigenous elements drawing on Shintō, Buddhist, and Confucian tenets formed a framework for political thought and action that was at once nationalist and statist.[29]

At the same time, racialism inspired pan-Asianism in both China and Japan. Racism was of only temporary utility for the 1911 Chinese revolution, but it was far more deeply rooted in Japanese official and dissident nationalist thought. The *kokutai* embraced only the Japanese minzoku. Many Japanese progressives and radicals, including the anarchist Kōtoku Shūsui,[30] saw in the 1894–1895 Sino-Japanese War a chance for Japan's superior and unique race to defeat the "decadent past" and save all Asian peoples from further encroachments by the West.[31] Kōtoku argued that special characteristics had enabled Japan's minzoku to form the first powerful nation-state in Asia. The Japanese "possessed lofty ideals." Through even such disparate slogans as "revere the emperor, expel the barbarians" and "popular rights and freedom," there was a "common thread" in the aspiration to found "a great civilized nation in East Asia."[32] That Japanese "offered themselves gladly for the sake of humanity and justice, and thought lightly of death for the cause of loyalty and devotion," Kōtoku continued, was "one of the reasons we can be proud to be a country of superior men [*chün-tsu*]."[33] Such racialist sentiment remained for Meiji socialists "a force for change and progress," "a liberating force that cut through the fetters of tradition and particularistic relationships of the former feudal society."[34] Until the Russo-Japanese War, then, Japanese socialists did not question the relationship between nationalism and socialism, but the war split the movement between those who felt it necessary to engage in imperialism to defend the *kokutai* and those who did not. Statist socialists like Yamaji Aizan became alienated from those who were repulsed by the Meiji state's imitation of Prussia's aggressive military posture.[35] Yet pan-Asian inclinations remained in evidence in both Chinese and Japanese socialist circles at least until the October Revolution.

These currents in the early socialist movements conditioned Chinese and Japanese responses to the Russian revolution. When the October Revolution urged upon them the national question in all its Marxist dimensions, Japan's socialists were far less likely than their Chinese counterparts to make the dispassionate analytical distinction between state and nation that Marxist theory required. Kōtoku's ability to accomplish this in reaction to the Sino-Japanese War was an anomaly. Japan had already succeeded in building a strong state, but as long as nationalism remained important, state building would not be abandoned by Japanese socialists. Before the Bolshevik victory and the Comintern's repudiation of Japanese expansionism and Japan's imperial institution, Japanese socialists could ignore this issue. But October 1917 marked a watershed: the socialists were forced to deal with Japan's participation in the Siberian intervention. In the years to follow, Marxists from Takabatake Motoyuki to Yamakawa Hitoshi to Takahashi Kamekichi would insist that Japanese expansionism was inoffensive to Marxian interests. Unlike Chinese revolutionaries struggling to build a state in the vacuum left by the fall of the Qing, this attachment to the *kokutai* made Japanese Marxists who retained nationalist and statist inclinations conservative even in their revolutionism. Understanding these outcomes requires a more detailed analysis of the role of nationalism in the nascent socialist movements in China and Japan.

Meiji Socialists and the Kokutai

The *kokutai* consensus enabled Meiji socialists to link their reformism with the spirit of nationalism aroused by the Western intrusion. The pervasiveness of this doctrine as an ideology of national rejuvenation had powerful implications. It imposed firm limitations on the aspirations of the short-lived liberal civil rights movement of the 1870s, and it would prove to have the same effects on the Marxian socialist movement by the 1930s.

In Japan, the native Japanist elements that had become supreme in the *kokutai* notion were invoked by liberal and socialist opposition movements as a basis of legitimacy for their cause. Liberal ideas imported from France and England allowed them to repudiate as alien and unbefitting the Japanese nation the Prussian Staatsrecht tenets used by the Meiji oligarchy to assert the rights of the state vis-à-vis the citizen and to quash dissent.[36] Interestingly, the oppositionists often rejected Prussian statism as not reflective of the true essence of the uniquely Japanese *kokutai* because it did not rest on an appreciation of the uniqueness of the Japanese minzoku. Here was a parochial philosophical nationalism operating even among liberal and radical groups agitating for universalist humanitarian causes.

Among socialists this nationalistic desire to preserve what was uniquely Japanese was reflected in their view that Meiji industrialization had brought tremendous costs. Founded on Western individualism, the importation of capitalism in Japan introduced an unpleasant atomism and competitiveness into what had been (ideally, at least) a harmonious, organic society. In short, capitalism and its attendant social ills threatened the fabric of the *kokutai* while socialism, with its emphasis on men and women in society rather than individual self-interest, could restore a newly modernized Japan to its accustomed harmonious and peaceful order.[37] (These views echoed Russian Slavophiles' repudiation of capitalism a century earlier, but because of Russia's relative "backwardness," Russian populists did not influence Japan's socialists until after the 1905 Russian revolution.)[38] The impact of the *kokutai* consensus on Japan's socialist movement, however, was such that it made any effort to distinguish state from nation problematic. Until about 1880, liberal leaders of the civil rights movement such as Ueki Emori (1857–1892), who were concerned with the conflict between Staatsrecht (*kokken*) and civil rights (*minken*),[39] repudiated the monarch as "rational" and even tried to deny the very existence of the mikado (emperor). Thereafter, however, liberal agitators accepted the legitimacy of the imperial system, which, in turn, became the premise of their call for "constitutional democracy."[40] Similarly, the liberal labor movement led by Yoshino Sakuzō in the Taishō period arose out of Fukuzawa Yukichi's advocacy of "'liberation of the individual for the sake of national (*kokka-teki*) independence'."[41] Meiji civil rights activists did, however, try to oppose the elevation of the prerogatives of the state over the rights of citizens that seemed to be justified by German Staatsrecht theory. When Itagaki Taisuke (1827–1919) demanded an elective assembly, the civil rights movement led by Ueki and Nakae Chōmin (1847–1901) cited French revolutionary ideas concerning the rights of man. The economic crisis of 1881–1885 facilitated their task by causing a split between more radicalized peasants and the increasingly conservative landlords that had been the sources of support of the nascent civil rights movement. Accentuating the differences in the interests of the two groups, the crisis recalled the schisms that had supported political radicalism in revolutionary France.[42] But the liberal movement finally collapsed after dissent was suppressed under the 1875 Press Regulations and 1880 Regulations of Assembly and the government's promise in 1881 that economic crisis would give way to the granting of a constitution and the formation of a parliament by the end of the decade. In practice, of course, the 1889 Constitution granted far fewer rights than liberal leaders had demanded, and the Diet established in 1890 had very limited power.[43]

As the liberal civil rights movement faded, two other trends emerged. Socialist ideas were being introduced into Japan while popular publicists proselytized among the masses the nationalist sentiment that had motivated the Meiji elite. The Kokusui-ha (National Essence School) promoted both nationalism and socialism. Convinced that nationalism must have a strong popular base, Kuga Katsunan (1857–1907), Tokutomi Sohō (1863–1957), and Miyake Setsurei (1860–1945) launched the newspaper *Nihon* (Japan) and the magazines *Kokumin no tomo* (The Nation's Friend) (1887–1898) and *Nihonjin* (The Japanese) (1887), respectively. Miyake's *Nihonjin* advocated Japanism in opposition to the Westernizing policies of the Meiji government, and *Kokumin no tomo* (inspired by the American publication, the *Nation*) was associated with the left wing of the Liberal party and advocated *heimin-shugi* (social democracy, or "commonerism").[44] According to future JCP leader Sakai Toshihiko, aged nineteen when *Nihonjin* was launched, these publications were regarded as required reading for youth of his generation because of their "new ideas."[45] Indeed, although the term *socialism* had been used first by enlightenment thinker Katō Hiroyuki in the 1870s, socialism was popularized as *shakai-shugi* in 1887 when *Kokumin no tomo* serialized selected writings of Henry George.[46]

The early bond between heimin-shugi and Japanist nationalism would persist into the early twentieth century. It was reflected in the agrarianism (*nōhon shisō*) of Marxist pioneer Kawakami Hajime, for example. Writing in 1904, Kawakami idealized the rural sector, the nonindustrialized, non-Westernized part of Japanese society, as the ultimate source of the nation's strength, to be preserved at all costs.[47] Similarly, Kōtoku shared the fear of many Meiji socialists that non-Japanese elements imported in the Meiji's aggressive Westernizing effort would ultimately bring ruin to Japan. Kōtoku, then, applauded efforts by civil rights leaders and *Nihonjin* contributors to separate statism from nationalism; and he defended his coupling of socialism with populist nationalism by arguing that "socialism was merely the reform of economic organization, and had nothing to do with the kokutai or the seitai (form of state): It attacked neither."[48] The notion of socialism was contrasted to capitalist "individualism"; and even as an opposition movement, in the view of Kōtoku and others, socialism did not threaten Japan's communitarian *kokutai*. On the contrary, before the Russo-Japanese War, early socialists saw the threat to the *kokutai* and the Japanese national essence in Western capitalism and its structure of economic exploitation. Their aim, therefore, was not to alter the *kokutai* but to initiate radical changes in the structure of economic activity.[49] This determination to resolve Japan's social problems to restore harmony to their rapidly changing society was imbued with a powerful and nativist moral impulse. Young men and women of this generation had been schooled in Confucian ethics, and many had received training in Christianity and learned of French and British socialist thinkers through seminary or church activities.[50] Christian socialists associated with the Hongō Unitarian Church near Tokyo Imperial University joined left-wing Liberal party members to found the Shakai-shugi Kenkyūkai (Society for the Study of Socialism) in 1898. Numbering Katayama Sen among its first members, the group discussed the writings of Western socialists such as Claude Henri Saint-Simon, Charles Fourier, and Pierre Joseph Proudhon, as well as Karl Marx. Members of this group formed the more activist Shakai-shugi Kyōkai (Socialist Association) two years later; all but one (Kōtoku Shūsui) of the new group's six leaders were Christians.[51] A year after this group was dissolved by the Home Ministry, Katayama, Kōtoku, and Abe Isoo then founded the similarly short-lived Shakai Minshutō (Social Democratic party) in May 1901.[52]

If there was no inherent conflict between nationalism and socialism in the view of these early socialists, the Meiji leadership, threatened by any reformist aspiration, especially when inspired by Western liberal ideals, repressed liberals and socialists alike. The Russo-Japanese War brought the official and dissident nativisms into conflict by forcing Japan's socialists to confront nationalism in the form of imperialism. The socialist Heimin-sha (Commoners' Society), founded in 1903 by Kōtoku and Sakai, urged its newspaper's readers to oppose the war.[53] During the short life of the Heimin-sha, diversity grew within its ranks. The progress of the war finally caused the movement to splinter into five groups: (1) Christian socialists led by Kinoshita, Abe, and Ishikawa Sanshirō, who launched the magazine *Shin kigen* (New Era); (2) antiparliamentarian syndicalists around Kōtoku; (3) the parliamentarist faction around Katayama and Tazoe Tetsuji (1873–1908); (4) a compromise faction led by Sakai; and (5) national-socialists, led by Yamaji Aizan.[54] The last group formed when Yamaji Aizan and Shiba Teikichi (1869–1939) founded the Kokka Shakaitō (National/State Socialist party) in August 1905.[55]

Yamaji's group is the most significant from the perspective of the national question. Yamaji's nationalistic reaction to Japan's international position presaged the national socialism of Takabatake, Takahashi, and the tenkōsha of the 1930s. Yamaji, like Takabatake, an unorthodox "Christian influenced by Confucianism and historical materialism," believed that the state stood above society as a "supra-class entity."[56] Even before he announced himself to be a nationalist advocate of Japanese imperialism in 1904, Yamaji's writings portrayed an appreciation of the role of the state that conflicted with the views of orthodox Marxists. In an 1893 article, "The Reason I Believe in Christianity," Yamaji firmly rejected the "cool contracturalism" and "cold individualism" of the Western liberal view of the state.[57] Yamaji's conviction that the issue of the survival of the state was more fundamental than individual rights and individual freedoms predisposed him toward his subsequent national socialism.

The turning point for Yamaji was the perception of a changed international context after the Sino-Japanese War. The American annexation of Hawaii in 1897, the German leasing of the Shandong Peninsula, the Russian leasing of Dalian, the U.S. occupation of the Philippines in 1898, and France's leasing of Canton Bay and the outbreak of the Boxer Rebellion in the following year—this succession of events dramatically underscored to Yamaji the significance of Japan's war with Russia. Just as early Meiji liberal Fukuzawa Yukichi had deepened his appreciation of the Imperial Household and the need for military activism to defend Japan in the late 1870s and 1880s,[58] Yamaji determined that the Japanese *kokutai* and the Imperial Household at its center were precious treasures to the Japanese people and must not be allowed to perish in an international arena that was more threatening than ever.[59] Essays that Yamaji penned during the decade after 1904, the height of his career, stressed his attachment to what he saw as unique qualities of Japan that rendered it intractable to the requirements of Marxian analysis of the imperial state. Indeed, it was this view that convinced Yamaji that Marxism in Japan was a "foreign" socialism imported from an alien context; it criticized Japan through "the eyes of Marx," a German perspective. His state socialism was an independent thought system that grew organically out of the study of Japanese history and that appreciated the uniqueness of Japan as a society that "especially valued the *kokutai* and human emotions."[60] Yamaji's nativist perspective revealed to him that the Japanese state was not simply a product of "class conflict." Rather, Japan comprised three so-called classes, or categories: the state and its institutions that held sovereignty, nobility, and the common people. The imperial institution was sovereign and could cooperate or conflict with the other two "classes," depending on internal and external conditions. But it was precisely the nature of relations among these "classes" that distinguished Japan's sacred *kokutai* from other states. Japan's Imperial House was one with its people (*kunmin ikke*), unlike monarchies in Western societies.[61] Thus, the program of Yamaji's National/State Socialist party (Kokka Shakaitō) not only called for universal suffrage, welfare protection for workers and the unemployed, and other progressive social policies; it also explicitly endorsed the "unity of monarch and people in the single family of the Japanese *kokutai*" and advocated the "peaceful expansion of the state."[62] As Yamaji's critics were quick to note, "the inclusion of the word 'peaceful' [made] the meaning [of this last article] vague," and the advocacy of the protection of industry under the tutelage of the state did not seem revolutionary. After all, wrote the same critic, "since he who manages industry directly is a capitalist, doesn't this amount to protecting capitalists in the name of the people?"[63] But however much Yamaji's critics might have wished to discredit his national socialism, Yamaji's conviction of Japan's exceptionalism would be echoed among many Japanese Marxists for several decades to come. Indeed, when the October Revolution brought to a close the winter period following Kōtoku's death, with it the national question erupted anew, producing new schisms among anarchists, Bolshevists, and national socialists that went far deeper than those of 1905.

Nationalism and Socialism in Pre-1917 China

In Japan, an effective nationalistic response to Western encroachments emerged from opponents of the shogunate who became the new Meiji leaders. Just as the key to Japan's recourse to *kokutai* thought lay in its cultural antecedents so, too, can the explanation for the ineffectiveness of the Chinese elite be found in its intellectual past. As Joseph Levenson once noted, "The dilemma posed by intellectual alienation from tradition and emotional ties to it still existed" in the last half century of the ailing alien dynasty. "But the nationalist dispensed with the effort to end the dilemma by somehow justifying Chinese tradition. He still hoped to establish the cultural equivalence of China with the West; but his ingenious way of accomplishing this was to deny that culture was the proper unit of comparison. That unit was the nation."[64]

Thus, in Qing China, a certain kind of nationalism had already found a place in certain antiestablishment groups. Secret societies such as "the *Tian-ti hui*, the *Pai-lien hui*, and the *Tien-li chiao*, for example, sought the establishment of a sovereign nation free of foreign domination."[65] Whatever its limitations, such nationalist sentiment was more likely to be harbored by associations holding heretical religious or mystical beliefs because Chinese Confucian orthodoxy could not easily accommodate it. As Levenson has argued, "the intellectual history of modern China has been the process of making *kuo-chia* of *t'ien-hsia*."[66] Tianxia (all under heaven) was the universal category of Chinese Confucian statesmen who believed government to reside in the sphere of morality; and embedded in it was the assumption of China's moral superiority for China was at the core of tianxia. To this must be contrasted the view of Italian Renaissance political theorist Niccolò Machiavelli, whose *Prince* placed raison d'état firmly beyond the moral realm, or at least recognized frankly that without the exercise of power, the morality defined by the state could not be preserved. The two conceptions of politics clashed violently when the Western powers pursued unsavory ends with amoral means (the opium trade) in China and refused to abandon their enterprise in the face of Chinese imperial resistance. Qing resistance was premised initially not on a claim to exclusive national sovereignty as per the dictates of Western international law.[67] Rather, reflecting the Confucian view of government as a moral enterprise, their objection was to the immorality of the opium trade corrupting its officials and commoners.[68]

The difficulties of the Qing elite, then, were in large part a product of its stubborn adherence to the notion of tianxia in the face of invasion by the attributes of guo. As Levenson explains, "*T'ien-hsia* signifies 'the (Chinese) Empire—alternatively, 'the world'; as *t'ien-hsia*, China *is* the world. And *kuo* is a local political unit, a part of 'the Empire' in classical times, and in the modern world, 'the nation.' In the earlier time it was its contrast with *kuo*, the regime of power, which defined the *t'ien-hsia* as the regime of value."[69] It is precisely because there was no guo limitation on tianxia that there could be no equation between morality and the Chinese nation. Within the context of tianxia, Qing statesmen retained their holistic, absolute belief in Chinese values. Thus, they were constrained to rely on the partial and inadequate solution embodied in the *tiyong* formula of change within tradition—retaining Chinese essence while adopting Western technology. Under the leadership of Zeng Guofan, Li Hongzhang, and Zhang Zhidong, gentry who had proved themselves in suppressing the Taiping rebellion, the self-strengthening movement of the Tongzhi Restoration (1862–1874) sought to industrialize and fortify the empire while bolstering Confucian traditions in statecraft.

The successes of China's Tongzhi Restoration were many and impressive,[70] but its limitations inhered in its initial conception. Having pacified the Taipings, government would be restored to its uncorrupted just and benevolent form. Prosperity would follow directly upon the restoration of domestic harmony. This backward- and inward-directed approach accepted the utility of Western arms but preferred that the empire rest, as it always had, on moral rectitude and not on force. In short, the ideal continued to be minsheng—people's livelihood based on agriculture and minimal intervention by the state—and government by elite "men of talent" imbued with Confucian tenets and supplied by an examination system dating back to the Tang dynasty. This approach contrasted sharply with the Meiji oligarchy's importation of elements of the political thought of the West along with its industrial capitalism. The Meiji's synthesis of Western and indigenous Japanese ideas in the effective *kokutai* myth could not be undertaken in China. Chinese Confucianism had established a dichotomy between tianxia as a moral entity and the political unit (guo) characterized by its basis in and protection by military force. As Confucian statesmen (*junzi*, virtuous men), the leaders of China's Restoration pursued the moral ideal. The merely political, such as the resort to force to suppress rebellion, could be only a temporary diversion from the Way of moral statesmanship. In Levenson's words, "The civilization, not the nation, ha[d] a moral claim on man's allegiance."[71]

Meiji leaders were hampered by no such dichotomy. As it was finally formalized late in the nineteenth century, the *kokutai* notion embraced nation and culture or state and nation, incorporating ethnicity as well in a land believed to be more ethnically homogeneous than China. In addition, historically, Japan's political development before the Meiji Restoration had culminated in the centralized feudalism of the Edo period. The Tokugawa shogunate ratified an historical importance and legitimacy of military power as the provenance of government in Japan. This was not the case in China, where the junzi preparing for government service cultivated himself intellectually rather than physically in keeping with Confucian views on the use of force. (Mao would struggle against this predisposition toward mental over physical labor among Chinese elites, urging physical training on those who would serve the national cause in the Sino-Japanese War.)[72] But in Japan, the supremacy of the Tokugawa shogun, a military "generalissimo," had firmly established a legitimate role for force on which the Meiji oligarchs could draw, even as they "restored" power to the emperor and ostensibly reduced the role of military personnel in favor of civil bureaucrats. The Meiji *kokutai* sublated the Chinese Confucian dichotomy between the realm of morality and the realm of power by combining the two under the sovereignty (tōchiken) of the emperor. Given the reality of alien dynastic rule and the normative constraints imposed by Confucianism, this solution was not available to Chinese nationalists; it failed for those who tried it. It was an artificial and alien conception: not only could China not claim a single indigenous imperial line of ten thousand generations on which to base it,[73] but when a dynasty fell in revolution, it was always the emperor who was ultimately at fault. In Japan, by contrast, the myth of the emperor as the font of political legitimacy was maintained by the persistent use of his authority to justify official actions of staff and bureaucrats.

The consequences of the Chinese dichotomy between tianxia and guo reached beyond the Tongzhi Restoration and the aborted 1898 Reform movement, to affect the manner in which nationalism finally emerged in the mainstream in China. This occurred outside the ranks of Qing officialdom among scholars such as Yan Fu, Liang Qichao, and Zhang Binglin, who were educated in Western as well as traditional Chinese thought.[74] Nationalism evolved first in the quest for the kind of "wealth and power" (fuqiang) that Japan had achieved. Yan Fu, who produced translations and commentaries on writings of Adam Smith, John Stuart Mill, Thomas Huxley, Herbert Spencer, and Baron Charles de Montesquieu, drew heavily on Charles Darwin's evolutionism. The notion of the "survival of the fittest" aptly reflected the cruel realities of nineteenth-century China in its confrontation with the West. For Yan and his followers Liang and Zhang, China's challenge was to equip itself with the spiritual and material resources to survive in the West's zero-sum game of international relations.[75]

This was not the only view of China's mission among its new nationalists. A dualism emerged in Chinese nationalist thought, whereby social Darwinism was admittedly the law according to which international relations among guo operated but the traditional ideas of a moral utopia remained intact. Kang Youwei, initially his student Liang, and others, including Tongmenghui revolutionist Hu Hanmin, envisaged China leading the way to a universal moral order of harmony and justice (datong) analogous to what was to have prevailed in the Confucian tianxia.[76] Such a traditional Confucian perspective also infused the new nationalists' concern for the welfare of the Chinese people. The reformist Liang called for the renewal of the people (*xinmin*),[77] as revolutionist Sun Yat-sen advocated a minsheng-zhuyi (people's livelihoodism) that resounded with traditional Confucian morality when he coupled nationalism with socialism in his Three People's Principles. Thus, like Meiji socialists concerned with the public good threatened by rapid industrialization, Chinese nationalists never fully abandoned the Confucian view of politics as a sphere of morality, however much they attacked it as a useful guiding philosophy for a new China. As Confucian philosophers believed, "the gauge of the *t'ien-hsia*'s peace or chaos is the joy or sorrow of its myriad people, not the rise or fall of its ruling house."[78]

The Russian revolution gave added impetus to the coupling of the desire to raise China's international position with the aspiration to throw off the imperial yoke and enable Chinese to enjoy the blessings of government more widely than ever before. Although Japanese tended to see Russia as less developed than Japan after the 1905 war, Chinese dissident intellectuals hearing of the activities of Russian narodniks saw Russia as relatively advanced. The initiation of reforms after the 1905 Russian revolution seemed to portend similar events in China. Thus, the 1905 revolution had a far greater impact in China than in Japan; it reinforced both Liang's reformism and the revolutionists' commitment to secure broader political participation for all Chinese.[79]

The state played an important role in early Chinese "revolutionary nationalism," which some date from the founding of Sun's Xingzhonghui (Society to Revive China) in 1894.[80] There was a fragile interplay here, as for the anarchists, between the newfound appreciation of the West and the posture one assumed vis-à-vis China's problematic past. Sun's revolutionists combined both the nation and state elements of the Western notion of the nation-state in their applications of his principles of nationalism (*minzu-zhuyi*) and socialism (minsheng-zhuyi). The Chinese state would not only be strong in order to compete internationally, but it would also have a more activist role than government had ever played in Chinese history, for Sun's socialism advocating the equalization of land rights was clearly state socialism. The radicalism of this concept was tempered by the nationalism enmeshed in Sun's notion of socialism. Huang Xing pridefully sought in China's past the roots for the advocacy of Western-style socialism: He proposed that the Tongmenghui flag be designed after the character *jing* to symbolize the idealized ancient well-field system of landholding.[81] Chinese nationalist revolutionaries around Sun, then, were intent on building a socialism with a strong state, but before 1911, their nationalism was also heavily imbued with a narrow social content that could be transferred to pan-Asianism when their animus was shifted from the alien Manchu dynasty to Western Caucasians after 1911. Their initial emphasis on anti-Manchu sentiment seemed to emerge directly out of the conflict between tianxia and guo. Although reformers such as Kang Youwei were "never anti-dynastic, and . . . blamed Chinese for distortion of the genuine Chinese tradition," anti-dynastic revolutionism seemed logically to go hand-in-hand with censuring the Manchus for China's ills. "If it had to be acknowledged that the contemporary West, intellectually and politically, was far in advance of China, the blame could be heaped on the Manchus and the Chinese spared."[82] This solution enabled the revolutionist to believe that the Chinese people could support a newly prosperous republican regime after the fall of the Qing dynasty.[83] Anti-Manchu racism gave the revolutionists "a straw to clutch at, something to keep them from sweeping along to either cold iconoclasm or arid traditionalism." As Levenson stresses, China's nationalist revolutionaries "re-issued, as supposedly nationalistic fare, seventeenth century, long-outmoded culturalistic invectives against the Manchus."[84]

The revival of the anti-Manchu rhetoric of Ming restorationists, however, attracted a huge following among radical Chinese students on the mainland and in Japan. The overseas Chinese student community in Japan increased almost fourfold to one thousand between 1901 and 1903 and peaked in 1905–1906 in response to the Qing government's encouragement of study abroad.[85] Such overseas Chinese student communities became hotbeds of anti-Manchu nationalism on which Zhang and Sun drew support for their revolutionism.[86] As public opposition to the Russian presence in Manchuria grew, revolutionary organizations proliferated among the student community. Almost all such groups, revolutionist and reformist, were anti-Manchu.[87] Sun's minzu-zhuyi articulated for them a view of national unity based on "a putative shared biological or ethnic identity that allowed every Chinese to recognize his fellow nationals immediately."[88] This racial imagery excluded Manchus from the Chinese national community. On the eve of the 1911 revolution, Sun wrote, "The Manchus have done us enough cruelty. Now is the time to raise an army and overthrow the Manchu government and regain the sovereignty of our country."[89]

After 1911, however, Sun reinterpreted his minzu-zhuyi to include all ethnic groups in China, including the Manchu, equally in a unified nation, and this new interpretation was symbolized in the Republic's early "five-barred flag."[90] As the young Republic quickly degenerated into a new monarchism under Yuan Shikai, a Chinese who kowtowed before the foreigner as the Manchus had, it was clear that the larger task envisaged by Liang's notion of "the new people" (xinmin) still lay ahead. As Lu Xun wrote in *Kuangren riji* (Diary of a madman), those "cannibalizing" Chinese society had not been Manchus alone. It fell to post-1911 iconoclasts like Chen Duxiu and Li Dazhao to specify how the Chinese people might restore control over their own destiny in a world in which they were still the prey of Western imperialism. The outcome at Versailles and the ensuing May Fourth movement assured that revolutionary nationalism would now be redirected against the Caucasian races of Europe. At the same time, Japan's Twenty-One Demands and Lenin's renunciation of tsarist encroachments in China after October 1917 turned post-1911 revolutionaries away from pan-Asianism and the Japanese model toward the anti-imperialist revolution in Russia.[91] Once again, socialism and nationalism would be conjoined, but it would not be in the expansionist, statist, or nascent pattern of imperial Japan or of Dai Jitao's state socialism. The predominant response would be formulated theoretically by Li and Chen as a Chinese Bolshevism and adopted organizationally by Sun Yat-sen's Guomindang as well as by the Chinese Communist party with the help of Bolshevik advisors.

NATIONALISM, STATENESS, AND MARXISM-LENINISM

If nationalism and socialism were compatible to early Chinese and Japanese socialists, the October Revolution illuminated the dilemmas inherent in combining nationalism with specifically Marxian socialism. The disintegration of the young Chinese Republic under Yuan Shikai's duplicity, in contrast to Japan's embarkment on new imperialist ventures, meant that the Bolshevik victory would occasion a far more violent reaction in Japan. There it splintered the socialist movement into a Marxian national-socialist party, a weak anarchist movement, and a struggling new Communist party, many of whose members seemed not fully informed of, nor persuaded by, Bolshevism. In China, such a dramatic schism did not occur, but the overall outcome was similar. Chinese anarchists faded into oblivion with the birth of the CCP, and the state socialist thought formulated by Dai was developed outside the bounds of Comintern leadership in sharp reaction against what Dai saw as a threat of domination by the new Soviet regime.

Yet the contrast between Japan's dramatic ana-boru debate and the relatively smooth acceptance of Lenin's concept of national liberation movements by Chinese Marxists (including Dai) offers a clue to the subsequent return of most Japanese Marxists to the *kokutai*, on the one hand, and Mao's pursuit of nationalism within the constraints of Marxism-Leninism, on the other. Stateness had been the self-conscious aim of the Meiji oligarchs, and Japan's Marxists fell victim to its ideology. In China, the problem was a lack of stateness; there was no state to which Chinese had become wedded. Living in a virtually stateless China after the demise of the Qing, Chinese Marxists could more easily conceive a China that had stood up (*zhan qi lai le*) as a nation without abandoning the Marxian goal of a stateless socialism.

The Ana-Boru *Debate*

The split in the Japanese socialist movement after the October Revolution was the culmination of constant tension over revolutionary means. Kōtoku's advocacy of "direct action" was challenged by Katayama's and Tazoe's promotion of legalist parliamentary means. Sakai, claiming to follow the Second International "orthodoxy" of Karl Kautsky and August Bebel, represented a compromise between these two groups. His compromise position, supported by Kōtoku, Yamakawa, and Arahata, emerged victorious from the Nihon Shakaitō (Japanese Socialist party) Second Congress in 1907. With both union activity and organized political activism illegal in Japan, Sakai's position was purely theoretical, muddling the distinction between Marxism and anarchism by claiming elements of both. His victory was a triumph for neither side.[92] The ideological conflict continued to simmer after this party was dissolved the same year until the JCP was established fifteen years later.

This controversy echoed the conflict between political action and economism in the early Russian socialist movement. As historian Samuel Baron notes, the populists, "prior to the formation of 'The People's Will,' did not regard theirs as a political fight. As anarchists, they were opposed to political struggle, since such a struggle signified to them the acceptance of the state principle . . . [when t]hey sought an end to all states." The populists of "Land and Liberty" and "the General Redivision" devoted themselves instead to "agitation among the masses, revolving around their *economic* needs." This "direct action" they believed would precipitate the collapse of the state and the emergence of the new anarchosocialist order.[93] The compromise position that won over the Nihon Shakaitō Second Congress was actually closer to Kōtoku's direct action (chokusetsu-kōdō ron) strategy and testified to the overwhelming influence of anarchosyndicalism in the left-wing movement in this period.[94] This predominance of the ideas of Bakunin and Kropotkin over Marxism was reinforced by the successes of the 1905 Russian Revolution.[95]

Anarchism continued to dominate Japan's socialist movement until World War I. The war, the October Revolution stimulating renewed growth in Japan's labor union movement, and the unprecedented rice riots in 1918 finally brought to an end the so-called *winter period*.[96] The dawn of this new era brought renewed interest in Marxism, and it was the Marxist Takabatake Motoyuki, not the anarchosyndicalists described here, who became the center of socialist activism. Takabatake, who like Yamaji was a Christian as a young man (and studied briefly at Dōshisha seminary), responded to the Russo-Japanese War as Yamaji had, opposing the pacifism of Christian socialists. After the war, Takabatake abandoned Christianity and joined the so-called "materialist" (non-Christian) faction to study Marxism. After reading Marx's *Capital* during a short period in prison, Takabatake fell in line with the entire socialist movement behind Kōtoku's "direct action" doctrine from 1907 to 1911.[97] After Kōtoku's death, Takabatake joined Sakai and Yamakawa to lead the underground movement in the Baibun-sha, which published such organs as *Hechima no hana* (The Gourd-flower). Takabatake studied Marx's economic theory during this period, and by the time the Bolshevik revolution erupted, he was a firm Marxist. His argument that the outcome of the Russian revolution demonstrated that Marxism was properly "statist" in both theory and practice caused a break with Yamakawa, Sakai, and other socialist leaders in 1918 and 1919.[98] Takabatake's formulation of his own national socialist variety of Marxism caused him to remain alienated from them for the remainder of his life. Nevertheless, as a translator of Kautsky's commentary on *Capital* and a major chronicler of the details of the Russian revolutionary movement in the successor to *Hechima no hana*,[99] Takabatake played a crucial role in molding Japanese interpretations of the Russian events and in stimulating the debates that culminated in yet another rupture of the left-wing movement between 1918 and 1923.

Because most Japanese viewed Russia as extremely backward economically and politically, the socialist community reacted to the February and October revolutions with shock. It seemed extraordinary that "the absolute autocratic monarchy would crumble in Russia, the 'headquarters' of European reactionary forces." In response to the February Revolution, Japanese socialists secretly published a congratulatory message to the new Russian provisional government in Russian and other newspapers abroad.[100] The ensuing confusion among Japanese socialists concerning the revolution was the product of their lack of familiarity with most of its leading figures. Although certain names—George Plekhanov, Vera Zasulich— were well known among Japanese socialists, they knew nothing of Lenin and the Bolsheviks.[101] In mid-1917 and even as late as 1920, Sakai assumed Lenin was an anarchist and remarked that Bolshevism " 'somewhat resembled syndicalism' ,"[102] and in debate with Takabatake in 1918, Ōsugi claimed that "Bolshevik tactics are the tactics of anarchism."[103] Such interpretations of events in Russia reflected preexisting ideological tendencies.

Takabatake's detailed reports on the revolution in his "International Notes" column, beginning in June 1917 helped to dispel much of this confusion. Recognizing the crucial role of the workers', peasants', and soldiers' soviets, Takabatake correctly saw the February Revolution as but the first step of a far more thoroughgoing upheaval.[104] More importantly, his stress on the emergence of a strong Soviet state after October presented Japan's predominantly anarchist movement with a reality that did not fit its preconceived notions of socialist revolution.[105] Takabatake boldly exposed these realities in his column in *Shin shakai* (New society), precipitating a debate with Yamakawa by 1919 that prefigured the permanent anarchist-bolshevist rupture of 1922–1923. Takabatake's analysis of the Bolshevik revolution laid the groundwork for his critique of the orthodox Marxist view of the state and for his alternative strategy for the left-wing movement. Ironically, Takabatake agreed with the anarchist Ōsugi that the new Soviet dictatorship of the proletariat demonstrated that Marxism was fundamentally statist. This conclusion enabled Takabatake to continue to accept Marxism and transcend the direct action versus parliamentarism controversy in the movement, while it led Ōsugi to reject Marxism entirely. The impact of October 1917 on Yamakawa, however, was to change his position through a protracted debate with Takabatake on the correct analysis of the Bolshevik experience. From this shift in Yamakawa's position would emerge his hōkō tenkan ron (change of direction theory) on which the new JCP was built.[106]

Takabatake's effort to destroy the dichotomy between political parliamentarist and economic direct action strategies, then, became the focal point of the ana-boru debate. In Takabatake's view, this dilemma posited a dangerous separation of political activity from the economic movement, and the triumph of the anarchist strain from 1907 to 1917 had signaled that Japanese socialists had abandoned the state and political activism. Takabatake's ill-fated support of Sakai in the thirteenth general election in 1917 had been premised on the belief, encouraged by Russia's February Revolution, that practical revolutionary political activity was now possible and would render obsolete the abstract dichotomy between direct action and parliamentary politics. He saw in the Bolsheviks a revolutionary party that had succeeded precisely because it transcended this dichotomy. Yamakawa claimed that Takabatake had set up a "straw man," that the movement had never intended that political action and economic activism should be taken in isolation from each other.[107] But Takabatake insisted that the Bolshevik revolution had demonstrated conclusively that the question of political authority had to play a much larger role in the Japanese socialist movement. Lenin had shown that economic activity must be combined with an attack on the old bourgeois state to make a successful revolution, and after the revolution, a new state power, such as the Soviet dictatorship of the proletariat, would have to be established to implement the socialist program. "Marxism is originally statism," Takabatake contended, even if Lenin had failed to realize this and had fallen into anarchistic utopianism in writing *State and Revolution*. "To centralize production, and thus to operate a general economy under this vast integrated organization of production," Takabatake continued, "is

utterly inconceivable without assuming statism and a highly centralized authority."[108] Unable to convince his colleagues of the validity of his national socialism,
Takabatake finally left the Baibun-sha. He was impatient with Sakai's inability to
seize the initiative when the rice riots erupted; and he detested the individualistic
antisocial and antistatist attitudes of Ōsugi and his anarchist followers.

Despite the rupture of his relationships with other leading socialists, Takabatake's contestation of the conventional understanding of the Bolshevik revolution exerted an important impact on the movement, contributing to the formation
of the JCP in 1922. Shortly after his debate with Takabatake ended in 1918,
Yamakawa began to reconsider his own position. Seeing the Hara Kei cabinet as
representative of bourgeois political power, he called for the creation of a proletarian political party—a demand he would repeat in subsequent years as Rōnō-ha
leader.[109] After joining Arahata to organize a study group "to criticize Marxism"
and to spread anarchosyndicalist views through the magazine *Aofuku* (Blue Uniform), Yamakawa gradually reconciled himself with the statist elements of Bolshevism. In December 1919, Yamakawa wrote a defense of the Soviet dictatorship
of the proletariat, arguing that a strong state was required to defend the lone
socialist country against more economically advanced forces of reaction.[110] Finally, in 1922, Yamakawa abandoned anarchosyndicalism and adopted many of
Takabatake's own counterarguments with his "Change of direction" article in the
July-August *Zen'ei* (Vanguard).[111] The strategy outlined in this piece, in turn,
became the basis for policy and tactics of the nascent Communist party.

The years 1922 and 1923, then, marked the peak of the ana-boru debate.
Between the Takabatake-Yamakawa debate and 1922, however, continued "confusion over the nature of the Russian revolution . . . enabled Japanese anarchosyndicalists and Bolsheviks to work together."[112] In December 1920, Sakai founded the Nihon Shakai-shugi Dōmei (Japanese Socialist League), which included
anarchosyndicalists, bolshevists, and national socialists (except Takabatake). Together Sakai, Yamakawa, and Kawakami edited the journals *Shin shakai* (New
Society), *Shakai-shugi kenkyū* (Studies in Socialism), and *Shakai mondai kenkyū*
(Studies on Social Problems) to introduce Marxism into Japan in greater detail. As
the Comintern began to show interest in Japan as the sole imperialist power in
Asia, Japan's Marxists reciprocated by publishing pieces about the Comintern.[113]
Ironically, it was the anarchist Ōsugi who made the first contact with the Com-
intern. Offered ten thousand yen to support Japan's socialist movement by Gregory
Voitinsky at the October 1920 conference of Far Eastern socialists in Shanghai,
Ōsugi accepted the funds at a time when Sakai and Yamakawa were hesitant to
establish relations with the Comintern.

Nevertheless, the celebrated split between the bolshevists, now prepared to
submit to Comintern authority, and the anarchists was not long in coming. Even
before the Japanese Socialist League was banned in 1922, ideological antagonisms
between the two groups intensified, peaking with the founding of the Rōdō Kumiai
Sōrengō (General Association of Labor Unions) in September 1922.[114] With
Yamakawa's *Zen'ei* (Vanguard) (launched in January 1922) engaged in an ideological struggle against Ōsugi's anarchist *Rōdō undō* (The Labor movement), league
members aligned with one faction or the other. The bolshevists, attracting former

anarchists such as Arahata, gained momentum, culminating in the establishment of the JCP in 1922.[115] Some former anarchists, such as Arahata, would continue to oppose certain Comintern proposals, but by 1923, the anarchist movement had "lost its mass support in the debate with the Bolshevik faction."[116] If only for a while, former anarchists such as Arahata and Yamakawa suppressed their anarchist and nationalist instincts resisting Comintern authority. When the Comintern produced analyses of the "Japan problem" that did not accord with these leaders' views, however, earlier anarchist and nationalist instincts would reemerge to lead them out of the party as the Rōnō-ha in 1927–1928.

The ana-boru debate reveals profound concerns among Japanese socialists concerning the role of the state in revolution. The first schism, Takabatake's break with the Baibun-sha, occurred when he interpreted the October Revolution to affirm the possibility of developing socialism within the bounds of a single country. Sakai, Yamakawa, Ōsugi, Arahata, and others were still struggling to reconcile the nationalist and anarchosyndicalist inclinations in their early socialism with the potentially threatening new Soviet state. The second breach occurred when Ōsugi completely rejected the statist impulse of Marxism-Leninism while Sakai, Yamakawa, and Arahata gradually came to terms with the Bolshevik state and Comintern authority. As nationals of an imperialist power, they had to abandon any latent nationalistic sentiments toward the *kokutai* to support the Comintern line against Japanese expansionism. A tension between nationalism and Marxism-Leninism would remain dormant in Japan through the 1920s, to reemerge on occasions such as the debate on the Comintern order to eliminate the imperial system. With no such organic notion of a powerful state in China, Chinese Marxists could more easily reconcile nationalism with Marxism-Leninism. Where the goal of promoting the well-being of Chinese seemed to require a strong state, anarchism quickly became virtually a nonissue.

Chen Duxiu and Li Dazhao: Nationalism and Internationalism in Chinese Marxism

The dilemma of China's self-strengtheners demonstrates how even a reluctant, defensive quest for "modernity" among intellectuals in non-European societies confronts them with fundamental questions concerning the relative worth of indigenous culture and values and those of the Western societies they are seeking to emulate. As Maxime Rodinson phrased it, "How far is it necessary to go . . . in order to achieve the enviable prosperity of the industrialized countries? Must one go so far as to sacrifice values that are especially cherished, those that constitute the particularity, the individuality, the identity of the peoples concerned? And what if those values (or some of them at least) are precisely the factor responsible for the backwardness" that they are trying to overcome?[117] This dilemma between particularity and universality in human development was at the core of the national question as it appeared in the 1910s and 1920s, when the socialist movements in China and Japan turned from anarchism to Bolshevism. And it was as evident in China's self-strengtheners and subsequent reformers and revolutionaries as it was in the aspiration of Meiji socialists to reclaim indigenous values such as community that they felt were sacrificed in the drive for rapid industrialization. Stunned by the collapse of the Qing and the political and cultural vacuum left by the rapid disintegration of the republic,[118] May Fourth intellectuals discerned in the Bolshevik revolution an alternative to the Western model for China's development.[119] With it, the Bolshevik revolution brought new dimensions of the national question concerning the role of nationality and the state in a Marxian-inspired revolution.

Yet the impact of the October Revolution was not nearly as immediate or dramatic in China as it was in Japan. Japan had a socialist movement that had begun to confront the national question during the Russo-Japanese War, but in China, interest in socialism clustered around Sun's minsheng-zhuyi did not command as much attention or inspire the concerted organizational and journalistic activity of Japanese socialists.[120] More compelling than Marxian socialism in China were the philosophies of Darwin, Mill, Huxley, and Spencer, which seemed better able to account for the developmental gap between Western Europe and China. If the predominant intellectual problem after 1911 remained how to "save China," these doctrines explained the mechanics of the international struggle to which China had become hostage and how China might be pulled out of its stagnancy and into the international system on an equal basis.

Hence, there was relatively little interest in Marxism in China until after 1917, and then it gained a wide audience only with the spread of the May Fourth movement in 1919.[121] The coincidence of the May Fourth movement, the first truly nationalistic movement in China, with the increased interest in the doctrine underscores the significance of the national question in making Marxism in its Leninist incarnation appealing in China. There are many reasons for the delayed Chinese response. Their eyes focused on Western Europe and the United States as sources of advanced ideas and "progress," Chinese intellectuals were not inclined to look toward Russia for new progressive ideas.[122] Moreover, after the disaster of Yuan's rule, intellectuals such as Chen and Lu Xun were more convinced than ever that a fundamental cultural change was required for China, crippled by its cannibalistic values, to attain a respected place in the world. Nevertheless, there was no social-democratic movement as cohesive as that in pre-1917 Japan to analyze and integrate the implications of the Bolshevik victory for a changing China.[123] At best, China had a broadly "progressive" movement in which socialism played a role that was clearly secondary to and separate from what was considered the first order of business—saving China from the Western powers and from natives such as Yuan who were prepared to exploit China's national crisis for personal gain. When the emotional tide of the May Fourth movement finally prompted Chinese intellectuals to turn away from the West, they confronted the national question in all its dimensions. Now their confrontation with the national question as posed by the Bolshevik revolution helped to create Marxist-Leninists out of many who had been only vaguely attracted to revolutionary socialism before.

Although their conversion to Marxism-Leninism led Chinese intellectuals like Chen Duxiu to defend the new Soviet state against anarchist criticism,[124] there was no protracted ana-boru debate. Nevertheless, the national question was no less significant in the development of Chinese than of Japanese Marxism. Neither Li nor Chen converted to Marxism until after 1917, and Chen did so more reluctantly than Li. Their approaches both to the Bolshevik revolution and to the aspects of the national question it raised with respect to China are best explained in light of their pre-1917 intellectual inclinations. From before the October Revolution through the 1920s, Li and Chen were in conflict with one another on the nationalist aspect of the national question at almost every point. Before 1917, Chen, as a professor of history at Peking University, distinguished himself as the cosmopolitan editor of the journal *Xin qingnian* (New Youth). Suspicious of patriotism and nationalism and concerned that China could not be saved unless its decrepit Confucian traditions were discarded in toto, Chen sought a Chinese enlightenment from Western political philosophies. He echoed Lu Xun's faith in China's youth as the key to intellectual salvation:[125] the old had clung to China's traditions long after the demise of the Qing dynasty had proved them useless; the young, however, might be educated in a progressive Western outlook. In this early *Xin qingnian* period, Western conceptions of modernity and Chinese philosophical and cultural traditions collided in Chen's conflicted psyche, reflecting the contradiction between the modern Western guojia and the Chinese paradigm of tianxia identified earlier. A cultural iconoclast, Chen feared that any remnants of the old, such as those resurrected by Yuan, would contaminate a new China and prohibit its emergence as a powerful modern nation-state.[126]

Li, however, did not share Chen's faith that complete Westernization was the path to China's salvation. He maintained a certain nationalistic pride in China and a conviction that in its two-thousand-year intellectual tradition remained elements of value to the West as well as to China. Like Chen, Li was concerned with the differences between the East and the West, although ultimately his approach reaffirmed indigenous values rather than repudiating them. His depiction of "The Basic Differences between Eastern and Western Civilizations" (written in either 1918 or 1920), like Chen's earlier articles on the subject,[127] depicted the East as spiritualistic, passive, naturalistic, and conservative, in contrast to the energetic, progressive, scientific, and materialistic West. These assessments of the weaknesses of Oriental civilization closely resembled the views of Hegel and Marx: the East was stagnant, lacking an appreciation of individualism, tending toward superstition, and supporting despotic government. Chen, therefore, concluded that the whole of the Chinese tradition must be swept aside[128] and in its place adopted the philosophical bases of Western strength. Overlooking Japan's recent success in relying on the traditional Oriental emphasis on family in his highly emotional renunciation of the Chinese past,[129] Chen concluded that China's familism must be abandoned for Western-style individualism.[130]

Li's conclusion was different, however:

> Oriental and Occidental civilizations really are the two great pivots of world progress, and just as the cart must have two wheels and the bird two wings, it is impossible for one to be lacking. Moreover, these two great spirits will themselves gradually harmonize and fuse to create unlimited progress and a new life. Oriental civilization has

become stagnant and Western civilization is weary under the burden of materialism; the crisis of the world cannot be overcome unless a new, third civilization emerges. [131]

Li argued that Russia, geographically and culturally situated at the intersection of Europe and Asia, was the only country which could undertake "[t]he creation of a new civilization in the world that simultaneously retains the special features of Eastern and Western civilizations, and the talents of the European and Asian peoples." [132] In this view, the characteristics of East and West were complementary rather than antithetical. While Chen's treatment of the East as hopelessly backward was consonant with the Hegelian imagery of a world history that had left the East far behind, [133] Li's view was more akin to Bolshevik Leon Trotsky's treatment of geography and human progress. Trotsky's notions of "uneven and combined development" and "permanent revolution" suggested that although tsarist Russia's 'Oriental' characteristics were deplorable, its backwardness held a special potential to produce proletarian socialism before its fruition in the West. [134] This view echoed the narodnik faith in the peasant masses and their primitive institutions, such as the village commune (mir), although as a Marxist, Trotsky believed in the socialist potential of the proletariat rather than that of the peasantry. Both Li and, subsequently, Mao emphasized, as had advocates of Sun's minsheng-zhuyi based on the legendary well-field system, the advantages inherent in China's backwardness for its development of socialism. Here in Li's thought was a theme that would resonate with the Japanese national socialism of Sano Manabu (see chap. 8 this volume). This was the notion that China required spiritual regeneration, a process that would spring from China's old as well as from the new. [135] Li's perspective fit neatly with nationalistic proclivities and would further the effort to inject Chinese national essence into Marxist thought. Indeed, this became the thrust of Mao's argument for the integration of theory and practice against his Russian-Returned-Student "dogmatist" rivals for CCP leadership in the 1930s and early 1940s. [136]

By contrast, Chen's perspective led him to adopt another strain in Trotsky's thought—the devotion to Marxian internationalism coupled with a fundamental distrust of patriotic and nationalistic impulses. If the Comintern's subsequent condemnation of Chen as a Trotskyist was valid that early in Chen's career, it was in this perspective. [137] For Li and others, nationalism grew out of a stubborn pride in certain aspects of Chinese culture and offered a defense mechanism against the wholesale philosophical encroachment by the West along with its humiliating physical presence. [138] Chen, however, viewed such nationalistic sentiment as dangerous: it threatened to "let tradition in by the back door" [139] so that China would never be free from the morass of Western oppression. [140] Chen's internationalism also reflected a need to be thoroughly consistent intellectually: he could not accommodate his negative assessment of the implications of Chinese culture easily with Li's nationalism. Thus, although Chen experienced a brief nationalist phase at the height of the May Fourth movement, his primary commitment was to an internationalism that could salvage the Chinese nation. His "Call to Youth," which appeared in the first issue of *Xin qingnian* (New Youth), urged advocates of the New Culture movement, "Be cosmopolitan, not isolationist."

Such sentiment was never expressed by Li, who even as a Marxist, Meisner concludes, "never really abandoned Chinese nationalism for Marxist internationalism."[141] This was certainly not surprising in view of the profundity of the dilemmas with regard to nationalism and cultural pride with which China's reformists and revolutionists had been afflicted for several generations as they confronted the challenges posed by the Western powers. Nevertheless, the relationship between nationalism and internationalism in Li was highly nuanced. In responding to the Bolshevik revolution, for example, Li's delayed reaction in mid-1918 was couched in universalist terms.[142] At that time, before the disillusionment of the Treaty of Versailles, most Chinese intellectuals still faced West, and it was months before the immediate reports of the Russian revolution in the Chinese press made an impact on their community.[143] Li took the lead here, proclaiming that like the French Revolution, the Bolshevik revolution was of world-historical significance. Li's appreciation of the importance of nationalism as a world-historical force was evident here in his reference to the French Revolution. As for Li himself, his own nationalism was evident in his projecting for China a central role in reconstructing world civilization through the medium of a Russia that incorporated Eastern and Western elements.[144] More importantly, however, his appeal on the significance of the Russian revolution rested on the cosmopolitanism that would govern his conversion to Marxism the following year. Li fully appreciated the universalism of the themes of the French Revolution, but the Russian revolution, in his view, was even more advanced than the French precisely because of its explicitly internationalist appeal. Li saw the emerging revolutionary order in Russia as the wave of the future, a surge in which China and other oppressed societies would follow. He then became a Marxist out of the same politically activist impulse that had governed his intellectual stance since 1911.[145]

Nevertheless, it was also characteristic of Li's nationalism that he should have grasped the importance of the Russian example for China and gradually adopted the internationalist Marxian philosophy that guided the Bolsheviks. Li had studied Marxism in 1916 at Japan's Waseda University, where he learned Marx's economic theory, studied Hegel, and fell under the influence of the Japanese socialist Abe Isoo.[146] This acquaintance with Marxism, however, was not reflected in his writings until after the October Revolution. Nevertheless, it was undeniable that Li was moved by nationalist concerns when he finally did address Marxism in conjunction with the revolution in Russia. Even then, it was clear that his attraction to Marxism was more emotional and pragmatic than intellectual. In his essay "Wo de Makesi-zhuyi guan" (My Marxist Views) (May 1919), Li criticized the labor theory of value—the cornerstone of Marxism as science to those who sought in it intellectual truth—and echoed Kawakami Hajime's criticism of Marx's relative neglect of the role of human will and other spiritual elements in history.[147] Conversely, Li was most impressed with the theory of class struggle and the related notion of class consciousness because of their implications for the primacy of human activity as the motor force of history.[148] Li had always emphasized the human role in China's regeneration, but after October 1917, Marxism provided a focal point for this motive force in (proletarian) self-consciousness, at the level of the individual and at the level of the nation as community.[149]

Chen's response to the October Revolution was both more protracted and more intellectual than Li's although it was the excitement of the May Fourth movement that finally drew Chen's attention to the Russian revolution's implications for China. Having closely identified with the Allied cause during World War I[150] and believing deeply in Western "science and democracy," the internationalist Chen was more resistant to a doctrine that was so critical of Western civilization, and he hesitated to ally with a faction that advocated a separate peace with Germany. Thus, it was not until the Versailles treaty shattered his faith in Western commitments to international equality and democracy that Chen was drawn to the Bolshevik example. As a fervent nationalist, albeit briefly, Chen was now unreceptive to Marxism because it was a Western doctrine. Yet, interestingly, by mid-1920, Chen had abandoned his blanket denunciation of "states"[151] and was defending the new Soviet state against anarchist critics.[152] When Chen finally adopted Marxism upon his release from prison in December 1919, he approached it as a "scientific socialism"[153] and restored his intellectual consistency by shedding the brief emotional nationalistic impulses he had held in 1919 and returning to the internationalism that he would maintain through the 1930s. Now the Chinese revolution could only be understood as part of the struggle of "the oppressed classes and oppressed peoples and states, against international imperialism."[154]

Ultimately, both Chen and Li responded to the Bolshevik revolution by cofounding the CCP, and in so doing, they found themselves in conflict with Chinese anarchists who had been a major force in China's socialist movement at home and abroad. In China's version of the ana-boru debate from 1920 through 1922, Zhou Enlai as a young student in Paris engaged anarchists Cai Yuanpei, Li Shizeng, and Wu Zhihui while in China proper, Chen and Li Da debated anarchist Qu Shengbai.[155] Having formed the CCP secretly in May 1920,[156] founding members Chen, Zhou Fohai, Li Ji, Li Da, Li Hanjun, Shi Cuntong, and Xu Xinkai wrote furiously to defend their Bolshevism against anarchists whose views remained unchanged in the face of the October Revolution. The conflicts between Chinese anarchists and bolshevists were the same that inspired the conflict between Bakunin and Marx, Russia's populists and Bolsheviks, and Japan's anarchists and bolshevists: the issue of political organization for revolutionary activity, the notion of the dictatorship of the proletariat, and the conception of revolution itself. Central to all these concerns was the question of political authority, but almost as important was each group's conception of "modernity," of China's future in a world dominated by the Western powers. In this sense, the national question was at least as crucial in China's anarchist-bolshevist debate as it was in Japan's.

Qu was the major participant in the controversy on the anarchist side. His position was straightforward. Drawing from the work of Bakunin and Kropotkin, Qu argued that the goal of the revolution was the realization of man's freedom as an individual in society through free association. All institutionalized power and law and any state—including a "dictatorship of the proletariat"—were conducive to unbridled oppression. The anarchists maintained faith that men and women were fundamentally good, and they were convinced that syndicalist organizations—not Lenin's elitist vanguard party—could destroy the artificial instruments with which man oppressed man.[157] Thus, China's anarchists, like those of Japan, conflicted with the new bolshevists over the issue of authority both in the revolutionary party and the postrevolutionary state. Finally, like Russia's narodniks, China's anarchists had serious doubts about the desirability of industrialization. Their idealized view of the noble peasant as the basis for an ideal anarchist future, like that of the narodniks, came under fire from China's bolshevists.

The anarchists were disadvantaged in this controversy from the very outset. Bereft of their spiritual leader Liu Shifu in 1915,[158] the anarchists found themselves in conflict with the bolshevists precisely when the national question, emerging in the wake of China's humiliation at Versailles, made it essential that they be most prepared to respond. The bolshevist critique was effective because it was based on political realism concerning human nature (compare Takabatake's critique later) and China's plight in particular. On a theoretical level, Chen, Li Da, and other bolshevists, like Takabatake, rejected the anarchists' optimism about human nature and about the ability of the untutored masses to accomplish desired social change. Much as China's philosophical Legalists challenged the Mencian view, they argued that such change was not possible unless evils inherent in human beings were eliminated or controlled, and such control required political organization.[159] Indeed, Chen doubted that human nature could be made "entirely good" at all, even with effective political and economic institutions.[160] The bolshevists asserted that at the very least, proletarian dictatorship would be necessary, as it was in the Soviet Union, to prevent "old [political] forces" from undermining essential social reforms.[161] Here the key issue became the consolidation of the revolution itself, although the anarchists pointedly refused to conceptualize it in terms of a consolidation of power, which connoted authority. By contrast, the bolshevists viewed the issue in terms of the consolidation of power by the formerly subordinate classes over their erstwhile oppressors. For them, the Bolshevik experience of the civil war and the failure of China's own 1911 revolution had demonstrated the need for new institutions to be effective in consolidating a revolutionary regime. Not only was anarchism incapable of furnishing such institutions, but if Kropotkin's "free federation" were established instead of proletarian dictatorship, the anarchist approach would permit capitalists to regain power and exercise it oppressively.[162] In Chen's view, if truly effective social reforms were ever to be implemented in China, the seizure of state power and wielding it as an instrument of social revolution were essential.[163] Indeed, Chen, the cultural iconoclast, argued that the bane of China in the past had been its anarchist tradition embodied in the Daoist philosophies of Laozi and Zhuangzi.[164] Such philosophical perspectives could only obstruct Chinese efforts to build a strong and effective revolutionary state power.

Finally, the October Revolution demonstrated to Chen, Zhou, and others drawn to the CCP the importance of a powerful state in helping specifically later-industrializing societies leap to the forefront of world history. Even if anarchism had once been suited to primitive tribal society, its notion of free association was no asset to an underdeveloped country. That anarchism flourished most in later-industrializing agrarian societies such as China, Russia, and Southern Europe was, Chen contended, attributable to the fact that anarchism was "a utopian, emotional" philosophy that grew naturally in such societies. Chinese anarchists "talk[ed] loftily of 'truth,' 'good,' and beauty, but when you discuss the actual [problem] of the means of developing industry, I'm afraid," wrote Zhou, "that, except for shaking and destroying large-scale production and opposing centralization, in the final analysis they have nothing concrete to propose."[165] As a basis for developing China's economy, anarchism offered no central institutions to balance supply and demand. To Chinese bolshevists who now had no faith in the effectiveness and equity of Adam Smith's "invisible hand," anarchism was likely to produce the same negative economic consequences as capitalism.[166] Now that China, like the new Soviet Union,[167] was seeking to develop independence and its own industry while avoiding the capitalist path, Chen pointed out, anarchists, who "have never recognized the realities of the economics of contemporary society," were ill-equipped to lead the country. Chen like Zhou, then, pressed for Marx's "scientific," objective, nonutopian socialism as the key to resolve China's socio-economic crisis.[168]

It is important to note that for some bolshevists the potential role that the state might play in China's economic development was an important factor recommending the example of Russia's Bolshevism, which was now, it must be recalled, in its highly state-centric period of war communism. Zhou, for example, stressed that only Marx's communism proposed a revolution in economic production, which was the only way to resolve China's economic malaise. Here Zhou cited advocates of state socialism to argue that using the state instead of bourgeois competition was the most efficient way to an industrialized and socialist China.[169] Moreover, the bolshevists argued, the increasingly dense concentrations of population that would accompany the inevitable industrialization that the anarchists refused to recognize could not accommodate anarchism: they required a complex social organization of the sort that had been unnecessary in more primitive times.[170] As Zhou insightfully noted, China's anarchist leaders seemed to appreciate this fact, because when Cai Yuanpei, Li Shizeng, and Wu Zhihui did confront China's concrete problems, the solutions they devised were contrary to anarchism. All three, in fact, would conclude their careers as leaders of the nationalist right wing of the Guomindang.[171] The realities of China's situation—"where industry does not prosper, economic power is held by foreigners, and the workers are ignorant"—dictated that the anarchosyndicalist vision of popular self-rule could not possibly be realized.[172] Thus, like Takabatake in Japan, Zhou defended the need for authority in the form of the proletarian dictatorship in the Soviet Union as a practical necessity as a stage of a revolution that would take a long time to complete.[173] If the anarchist message was destruction, destruction of the past had already occurred in China, but now it was time to rebuild a strong new China in place of the old. The impact of the October Revolution was to convince even the internationalist Chen to resolve the national question in a statist direction.[174]

For Li, Chen, and Zhou, then, the confrontation with the national question prompted their turn toward Bolshevism. As in Japan, the realities of the international context pressed upon the socialist community a social Darwinist orientation that saw that the chains of tradition must be cast aside if the Chinese were to survive as a people.[175] Before the October Revolution produced the anarchist-bolshevist conflict, the less iconoclastic Li had found Darwinism too deterministic; and to its emphasis on struggle as humankind's primary instinct, Li preferred Kropotkin's vision of mutual aid, based on man's inherent tendency toward cooperation within the national community.[176] After 1922, however, Li's nationalism led him to apply Marx's notion of class struggle to conflict among nations and races. This analogy moderated the importance of class conflict within China for the sake of a national cause. Li's new depiction of the entire Chinese nation as part of the world proletariat[177] helped to justify the CCP's subsequent restraint on class struggle in the interests of the anti-Japanese resistance.[178] The potential conflict between Marxian proletarianism and Chinese backwardness and nationalism was, thus, essentially resolved by a notion of telescoped national-democratic and proletarian revolutions akin to Trotsky's and Lenin's notion of permanent or uninterrupted revolution. As CCP leader Qu Qiubai wrote in 1926, the aim of the Chinese revolution was to "attain China's independence, to attain the political power of the common people," and "to establish a citizens' government of the entire nation." For China's bolshevists, Lenin's contribution to Marxism on imperialism and wars of national liberation created the crucial link between the quest for China's national salvation and world proletarian revolution.[179]

Racialism and pan-Asianism also found their way into Li's and Chen's resolution of the national question. This concerned Chen only during his brief nationalist phase, but racialism had occupied a prominent position in Li's thought before 1917. Li called for all Asian peoples to unite in a "New Asianism" (*xin Yashiya-zhuyi*) against the white races of Western Europe (although this view did not blind him to Japan's use of pan-Asianism to justify the victimization of other Asian peoples).[180] Li's "New Asianism" simply expanded his nationalism to embrace a larger fold of oppressed masses.[181] Li's pan-Asian nationalism and Chen's internationalism could both be accommodated within Leninist orthodoxy. In Japan, a nation well on the imperialist path and where stateness in all respects was well developed, however, this solution was less feasible, and a tension between the two strains remained latent in Japanese Bolshevism long after Yamaji Aizan and Takabatake Motoyuki had left the fold.

The National Dilemma under Comintern Leadership

The impetus to create national communist parties in China and Japan initially came from the new Soviet government's almost desperate interest in Eastern peoples. Their own revolution only one year old, Soviet leaders convened the first Congress of Communist Organizations of the East in Moscow in November 1918. At the Second Congress, one year later, Lenin called for an alliance between the proletariat of the advanced capitalist countries "and the toiling and exploited masses of the East." By mid-1921, Comintern representative Maring (Sneevliet) had become involved in the establishment of the CCP.[182] This strategy was affirmed at the Comintern's Second Congress in August 1920 and the Baku Congress of Eastern Nations the following month. Finally, representatives from China, Japan, Korea,

Mongolia, and other Asian countries gathered in Moscow in January 1922 at the First Congress of the Toilers of the Far East.[183] It was here, now one or two years after the CCP had been formed, that the Comintern ordered the establishment of a Japanese Communist party.[184]

The creation of Communist parties in both China and Japan did not resolve the national question for their Marxists, however. On the contrary, the relationship between the Comintern and the new indigenous parties would prove to be a constant irritant, a forum for continual conflict between nationalism and internationalism and for the constant tension between the universal and the particular as an intellectual problem inherent in Marxism itself. Chinese and Japanese Marxists were compelled to emphasize the universalistic elements of Marxism to demonstrate that the patterns of development exhibited by their own societies were compatible with Marx's model. Only thus could it be argued that proletarian revolution was the historical necessity in China and Japan that Marx claimed it to be in Europe. The fact that the two parties were led by the Soviet-dominated Comintern placed an additional premium on universalism, for Comintern strategy for each movement was always couched carefully in terms of the interests of the international revolution. This problem became the national question when native Marxists chafed under Comintern control and found themselves in disagreement with its analyses and prescriptions. Yet, dependent psychologically on Soviet guidance and financial support, national Communist leaders hesitated to abandon the Comintern even after the disastrous Shanghai coup in 1927 and repeated failure in Japan. It was not mere coincidence that the tragedy in China and Mao's effort to forge a new path occurred at the same time that the 1927 Theses triggered the secession of the Rōnō-ha from the JCP. The national question presented itself fully at the same time in both instances, and Japan's dissidents derived support from the calamitous outcome of blind obedience to the Comintern in China.

Thus was the national question posed in Marxian terms in China and Japan as it had never been before by the October Revolution. There were those in both societies, however, who cut the Gordian knot of their dilemma by devising immediate, simpler nationalistic solutions in the form of national socialist doctrines.

BEYOND THE OCTOBER REVOLUTION: BOLSHEVISM AND NATIONAL (OR STATE) SOCIALISM

The Kokka Shakai-shugi of Takabatake Motoyuki

A leader in the introduction of Marxism into Japan, Takabatake Motoyuki was among the first Japanese Marxists whose reflections on the Russian experience and its implications led them to reinterpret Marxism as a Japanist national socialism. As a result of Takabatake's efforts in the wake of October 1917, Japan's socialist movement split not into only two factions, the anarchist and the bolshevist, but into three. Takabatake's kokka shakai-shugi formed a third current, offering a view that transcended the contradictions in Lenin's pronouncements on the need for the Soviet dictatorship of the proletariat and its "withering away," so uncritically accepted by those who formed the JCP. Takabatake's theory exposed the contradictions of Marx's original formulation, which he did not abandon entirely but instead criticized as flawed with utopian anarchist tendencies. In the emergence of the new Soviet state, Takabatake saw realistically the development of the very strengthening of the militaristic state that Nikolai Bukharin feared would characterize the capitalist state in the age of imperialism.[185] Takabatake's affirmation of the continuing significance of the national state in the era of proletarian socialism would be echoed in the two decades to follow among many other Japanese Marxist-influenced radicals. Retaining their faith in the Japanese nation and state, Kita Ikki, Akamatsu Katsumaro, and Abe Isoo all saw in the new Soviet regime affirmation of the increased role of the militarized state in the international arena. Even Kawakami, who never joined the majority of his peers in abandoning Communism in the 1930s and 1940s, saw the Soviet state as "a leader in the transition from 'laissez-faire economics to state planning'." As Bernstein has noted, "The real message of the revolution . . . was the possibility of achieving socialism, whatever its meaning in the Japanese context, without destroying the nation."[186]

Takabatake was a pioneer in this movement to transform Marxism into national socialism. His eclecticism led him to expand his interpretation of the October Revolution for a Japanese audience into a full reappraisal of Marxism-Leninism on the national question. Well schooled in the history of Western European and Eastern philosophy, Takabatake was not prepared to accept Marx's ideas uncritically, unlike most of his peers among Japanese bolshevists. While Takabatake accepted the Marxian analysis of capitalist society, by 1919 he entertained serious doubts about the validity of (historical) materialism, and he concluded that Marx and Engels had simply been wrong concerning the nature of the state.

Takabatake's kokka shakai-shugi,[187] however, was not formulated only in response to purely theoretical concerns. Rather, the addition of statism and nationalism to his Marxism was also a response to practical concerns, many of which related to Japan's international position. For Takabatake, Marxism in its original form could not respond to Japan's needs during the Taishō period. After World War I, Japan faced mounting international criticism for trying to maintain its economic growth through expansion abroad. Meanwhile, its troops remained in the Soviet Union well after other Allied participants in the intervention against the Bolshevik revolution had withdrawn, and the postrevolutionary regime in the Russia with which Japan had had hostile relations in the past showed no sign of simply "withering away." Takabatake concluded that a powerful national state would still be required in Japan as well, even after the Marxian socialist revolution, to guarantee the security of the Japanese people against the hostility of both capitalist and "proletarian" states.

Takabatake's eclecticism was unusual at a time when fellow Marxists such as Kushida Tamizō and Kawakami concentrated on clarifying such basic Marxian concepts as "surplus value." The combination of Takabatake's German-language ability and his broad background in Western European philosophy equipped him well to understand Marx's conception of the state, complete with its Hegelian and liberal roots. Takabatake's writings cited not only the most widely disseminated classics, *Das Kapital* and the *Communist Manifesto*, but they also drew on less readily available works, including "Preface to a Critique of Political Economy," "The Poverty of Philosophy," *Anti-Dühring*, and *Origin of the Family, Private Property, and the State*.[188] He also drew on events and philosophical trends in the European socialist movement, noting anarchist and statist elements in the ideas of Proudhon, Lenin, and Eduard Bernstein. His study of the concepts of the state found in the work of Thomas Hobbes, Jean-Jacques Rousseau, and G. W. F. Hegel enabled Takabatake to appreciate the contributions of his predecessors in state socialism, such as Ferdinand Lassalle, without blindly imitating them. Lassalle's thought was based on "ethical statism," which drew heavily on the value-laden Hegelian conception of the state and was non-Marxist. Takabatake's theory of state socialism, premised on a "functional statism," was his own original contribution to Marxist thought.[189]

Before he addressed the national question in terms of Japan's domestic and international contexts, Takabatake offered a trenchant critique of Marx's theory of the state. Takabatake could accept Marx's economic theory at the same time that he repudiated Marx's notion of the withering away of the state because he believed that Marx had erred fundamentally in his conception of the class state. Marx, Takabatake argued, was Janus-faced. Marx's socialism was scientific, based on a careful analysis of the dynamics of capitalism, but there was also a utopian and emotional Marx whose internationalism and anarchism permeated the *Communist Manifesto* and other writings. Marx's notion that the state would wither away after a socialist revolution was unscientific, for it ignored the fact that human nature, as Hobbes had suggested, was fundamentally evil. Men and women were egotistical and needed to be dominated or ruled, even in a socialist society, Takabatake argued, for human nature would not change despite the most radical transformation in the relations of production.[190]

The fallacy of Marx's class conception of the state was evident to Takabatake in the many self-contradictions in the notion of a "proletarian state," in the very idea of a "dictatorship of the proletariat" that would gradually wither away. According to Engels's *Anti-Dühring*, the proletariat destroys the bourgeois state, takes state power into its own hands, and uses that power to nationalize the means of production. Thereby, the proletariat abolishes the state. Later in the same work, however, Engels maintains that the state is not abolished (*aufgehoben*), that it simply withers away (*abschaffen*). The passage on the withering away of the state was used by Bernstein and other German Social Democrats to oppose revolution in favor of "evolutionary socialism." Lenin repudiated this "opportunism" by arguing that the proletarian revolution destroys the real state, the bourgeois state. The proletarian dictatorship was not a true state that perpetuated class conflict and oppression in Lenin's interpretation; rather it was to be a semi-state, only the vestige of the true state. But Takabatake maintained that Lenin had failed to resolve the contradiction in Engels's argument. Because Engels described the proletarian state as exercising class domination over the bourgeoisie, in fact, it was the state qua state that would wither away. Marx appeared to concede this point by using the term "proletarian state." The conception necessarily remained muddled, however, because of the "huge contradiction between the non-Marxist reality that [in Soviet Russia] the state does not disappear even though exploitation disappears and the Marxist theory that the state is the embodiment of exploitation[-based] domination."[191] Reality required a new theory.

Takabatake claimed that the essence of the state does not lie in class exploitation. Rather, "The essence of the state lies in control (domination). Control (*tōsei*) precedes exploitation." The ruling function was necessary in all societies[192] as the product of people's conflicting desire and need for social cohesion to protect themselves and further their development, on the one hand, and their antisocial egoism, which had the capacity to destroy social unity if not brought under control, on the other. The ruling function then developed naturally and spontaneously, not through an artificially contrived social contract as described by Hobbes and Rousseau. Once the ruling function was established in society, it began to be differentiated and assigned to a specific class when victorious peoples in tribal wars took slaves and ruled the vanquished tribes. When the ruling function fell to a specific class, the state was born. Thus "both conceptually and historically, the functions of rule and control preceded the establishment of classes and became its premise," rather than the inverse, as Marx had argued.[193] The conflict between exploiter and exploited did not precede the state, but followed it. This conflict meshed with the relationship between ruler and ruled when the exploiting class "used the functions and organs of the existing state to serve both the maintenance of exploitation and the repression of the exploiting class."[194]

To pursue socialism in a consistently scientific manner, Takabatake insisted, it was necessary to "abstract as purely as possible the state as a ruling function vis-à-vis man's evil nature." State socialism recognized the state as a "supraclass" and "suprahistorical" permanent institution in the service of humankind's best interests.[195] State socialism sought to remove the impure element of exploitation from the relation of "pure domination" that would still be necessary in post-revolutionary society. Thus, the state socialist program advocated the centralization of production and the abolition of individual capitalism as a means to this end. The state would continue to increase its powers of domination, and the ruling power would inevitably devolve again to a class composed of people who were superior in academics, art, or other fields.[196] This state socialism was still essentially Marxist because it invoked Marx's scientific interpretation of the state, and, hence, it diverged from Lassalle's ethical idealism. Finally, by acknowledging the practical necessity for "control" or "domination" in every stage of human society, Takabatake's state socialism avoided Marx's utopianism and the troublesome questions about the length of the "transition" period and the operability of "stateless" socialism that necessarily arose therefrom.[197]

Despite the strengths of these theoretical points, it is clear from Takabatake's political program that certain nationalistic considerations were also crucial. In his view, the revolutionary movement would purge itself of the anarchistic and anti-statist tendencies that had characterized it since 1907[198] and would then build a socialism tailored to the national needs of the Japanese people. Specifically, Takabatake advocated measures shared with Leninist Marxism: the abolition of capitalism, a centralized planned economy, state ownership of land and large capital, state management of large industries, political democracy, and socioeconomic equality. These measures would be pursued under the existing emperor system. "Japan's monarchy is the most appropriate form of state for the Japanese *kokumin* [people, or nation]," Takabatake declared. Takabatake thus reaffirmed the identity between the *kokutai* and the Marxist socialist community that early-Meiji socialists had assumed before the Russo-Japanese War ruptured it for most of them in 1904–1905. The postrevolutionary imperial state would protect and defend the Japanese people from external and internal threat by a system of universal mandatory military service. Internationally, it would seek cooperation with other "colored peoples" to end "the present oppression and exploitation of the colored peoples by white peoples."[199]

Observing Japan's international situation during the Taishō period, Takabatake found evidence that the state was necessary for the realization of socialism as well as evidence of threats against which a socialist Japan must be prepared to defend itself. The key to both points lay in his interpretation of the Russian revolution. In the aftermath of that revolution, Takabatake found support for the view that "Marxism was essentially statist" and that a powerful state would be required for the achievement of socialism. Indeed, it was this interpretation of the October Revolution that drew Takabatake into conflict with both anarchosyndicalists and Japanese bolshevists whose admiration of the Russian experience led them to found a Japanese Communist party.

Many Japanese socialists, such as future JCP leader Yamakawa Hitoshi, joined Takabatake in praising the Bolshevik revolution, but the new Japanese bolshevists rejected the argument that the proletarian state was necessarily a permanent fixture in Russia.[200] Moreover, these Marxists became devoted to the orthodox Comintern line repudiating Japanese nationalism, and through the 1920s, they were increasingly alienated by Takabatake's advocacy of state socialism as his commitment to the state became more and more unconditional. Over the decade, his call for "a powerful state for the sake of socialism" was transformed into advocacy of "socialism for the sake of the state."[201]

In large part, this change occurred because Takabatake's nationalistic attachment to the cause of state socialism was being reinforced by international tensions. This doctrine was peculiarly suited to Japan; it represented "an infusion of Marxist wisdom into 'Japanese spirit' (*Yamato damashii*)," hence its basis in the tennō-sei (emperor system).[202] Yamakawa was prepared to acknowledge that if national socialism merely implied socialism achieved within a national unit, then, yes, the Soviet Union was national socialist; its experience, however, could be accommodated within the bounds of "international socialism," which "does not necessarily ignore the natural unit of the kokumin." In the view of orthodox bolshevists, a separate doctrine of national socialism was not necessary.[203] Clearly, however, Takabatake was not concerned with the mere coincidence of a socialist system with national borders. His social Darwinist perspective convinced him of the ever-present danger of international hostility directed against Japan. Because it was not possible to explain warfare by economic motives alone, given that warfare derived fundamentally from man's egoism and will to power over others,[204] the danger of war would persist even after socialist revolutions. Thus nationalism would continue to be a valid object of value even after the attainment of socialism; without the Japanese nation, there would be no fruits of socialism to enjoy. Consequently, class struggle "must be affirmed only within the country." It would not extend abroad because in the event of war that would "amount to [socialists] fighting against their own country's capitalists, in concert with the workers of enemy countries."[205]

As discussed, Japan's socialists had confronted the national question before, at the time of the Russo-Japanese War, and the issue had split their movement. Takabatake, like Yamaji Aizan, refused to oppose the war. Again in the 1920s, Takabatake felt that Japan was gravely threatened by a powerful Russian state, even though that state was now socialist. Japan must guard against "workers' imperialism" on the part of the Soviets, for any state, whether capitalist or proletarian socialist, had a natural propensity to expand. Most Japanese bolshevists cried out for Japan's withdrawal from the Siberian intervention, but Takabatake argued that Russia should first release Siberia from the bondage forced on it by the tsarist regime.[206] Furthermore, the Comintern's encouragement of national liberation movements in Asia could be viewed as an effort on the part of "workers' and peasants' Russia" to lure Asian peoples into enslavement.[207] Given the realities of international power politics, it was necessary "to make one's state strong and wealthy." Asian revolutionaries should imitate Lenin's own patriotism lest, having escaped oppression by capitalist imperialism, they fall victim to "workers' and peasants' imperialism."[208]

Nor was the danger posed by the capitalist powers past. At a time when Europe and America were denouncing Japan for militarism and expansionism, Takabatake believed that the capitalist powers were preventing Japan from pursuing the same foreign-policy course that the powers themselves had used to increase their prestige. Late-industrializing countries such as China and India were beginning to threaten Japan's prosperity from below at the same time that the great powers were seeking to prevent Japan from taking the steps necessary to achieve the full fruition of Japanese capitalism (and, thus, the demise of capitalism). Takabatake was convinced that a powerful racial element operated here: the great powers claimed to want peace not out of a sincere desire for peace but to force Japan back into its former enslaved position with other Asian peoples. These intentions were evident in the iniquitous outcome of the Washington Naval Conference. In any event, because of its late start, Japan's expansionism was minuscule compared to that of England, Russia, France, and the United States.[209] Consequently, Takabatake argued, those Japanese Marxists who cited Lenin's theory of imperialism in order to attack their own country's expansionism were merely blind imitators of the West. Their antistatism endangered the Japanese people, and such Marxists deserved more severe punishment than the existing state had awarded them.[210] In Takabatake's mind there was no conflict between the quest for proletarian revolution and devotion to a powerful national state: both these elements were required for the improved welfare of the Japanese people. In the late 1920s, Japan was still a disadvantaged nation, and the pursuit of his state socialism, Takabatake argued, would both liberate and protect the kokumin.

Takabatake Motoyuki's Marxian kokka shakai-shugi is remarkable for its amalgamation of elements commonly associated with "leftist" radicalism and "rightist" extremism. Its distinctive combination of general observations about the nature of man, the state, and Marxism, along with a nationalistic attachment to peculiarly Japanese institutions such as the imperial institution, however, causes it to bear much broader implications for the nature of Japanese Marxism and for the kinds of choices that the October Revolution forced upon Chinese as well as Japanese Marxists. If Marxism was a logical response to Japan's domestic tensions during the Taishō era, Takabatake's addition of a nationalist or statist element to Marxism was a rational response to the changed, threatening conditions of Japan's international context. It would be all the more difficult for Marxists in the still more disadvantaged and later-industrializing China—even those who began their involvement in the socialist movement as anarchosocialists—to resist the temptation to resolve the national question in favor of nationalism and statism.

Dai Jitao: Anti-Communist National Socialism in Revolutionary China

The nationalism of Takabatake's response to the Bolshevik revolution reverberated still more deeply in China. When the humiliation at Versailles followed so soon after the October Revolution, the passionate nationalistic responses of Chen, Li, and other May Fourth intellectuals to China's repeated victimization by the Western powers and Japan coincided with the Comintern's call for national liberation movements in colonial and semi-colonial countries in the wake of Germany's abortive Spartacus uprising. In the years to follow, the new Chinese Communist party would blend this nationalism into its Marxism to lead a struggle that was as much for China's survival as a nation as for thoroughgoing socioeconomic revolution in the city and countryside.

Chen, Li, and their comrades in the CCP, however, did not articulate the only possible admixture of Chinese nationalism with Marxism. There were others whose nationalistic struggle to "save China" led them to question the notion that such a struggle could succeed in the framework of an alien revolutionary theory that envisaged the destruction of precisely the kind of strong, effective national state that China needed to survive after the miserable failure of the 1911 revolution. In their view, the problem was not to eliminate the state as a repressive apparatus but to create a viable national state that could protect and nurture a modernizing Chinese people. Thus, by the mid-1920s, many who had helped to launch the Chinese socialist movement as anarchists were rejecting the pursuit of socialist revolution under the auspices of the Soviet-dominated Comintern and now favored a nationalistic and statist revolution that brooked no compromise on the need for Chinese to make their own revolution in their own way. Under the banner of Sun Yat-sen's Three People's Principles, anarchist leaders Wu Zhihui, Li Shizeng, and Cai Yuanpei became three of the "Four Elders" of the right wing of the Guomindang. Together with Hu Hanmin, Zhu Zhixin, and others who had supported Sun in the days of the Tongmenghui, these former anarchosocialists endorsed Sun's vision of a socialist China after the revolution centered around a powerful state. The leading spokesman for their variety of national socialism was Dai Jitao (1882–1949).

Like Takabatake, Dai had impressive credentials as a leading Marxist-oriented socialist in the years before his formulation of national socialism. Dai was first exposed to socialist and other "progressive" Western intellectual currents in Japan, where he took a degree from the Nihon University in 1909.[211] Dai was in Japan just when a consensus was emerging among the Chinese student community there to back Sun's call for "men of determination" to overthrow the ineffective Qing dynasty.[212] Now, back in Shanghai late in 1911, Dai gathered colleagues from his days as an apprentice on the dissident *Tianduo bao* (Bell) in Tokyo to found his own newspaper, *Minquan bao* (People's Rights). The new daily immediately became the primary vehicle for the articulation of the Tongmenghui platform and Sun's aspirations for republican China. From the pages of the *Minquan bao*, Dai harshly castigated the corrupt presidency and imperial pretensions of Yuan Shikai.[213] Expressing sentiments that would resound with his celebration of Chinese tradition one decade later, Dai likewise sharply criticized the moral decadence of Shanghai. The city was for him a symbol of China's degradation at the hands of the West and of the nation's inability to nurture true republican ideals and morals into its people.[214] At this point, Dai was convinced that the 1911 revolution had failed because leaders such as Yuan could not inculcate the sort of national spirit that was essential to democracy, the absence of which reformer Liang Qichao and others had lamented before the revolution.[215] Despite his closeness to Sun, a Western-educated intellectual, here Dai's critique of revolutionary China reflected his deep roots in, and continuing affinity for, the Confucian philosophical tradition that saw government as a positive sphere of morality.

With the failure of the anti-Yuan "Second Revolution" of 1913, Dai and other republican leaders were forced back into exile in Japan. During this period, between 1913 and 1917, Dai drew close to Sun, as he would remain for the rest of Sun's life. As Mast and Saywell note, "A filial relationship emerged from [the] cooperation [between the two men], through which Tai *experienced* Sun's thought."[216] For the rest of his career, Dai would devote himself totally to the articulation of Sun's Three People's Principles as the only hope for China's survival. This thread would run consistently through his thought, from his first affiliation with the Tongmenghui on the eve of the 1911 revolution through the 1940s.

Many elements of Dai's intellectual system crystallized during this period of exile and close association with Sun. Both Japan's successful self-strengthening through industrialization and the bitter experience of Yuan's sabotage of the 1911 revolution convinced Dai (as Mao would conclude later) that without military power and leadership equipped to inculcate a daring revolutionary spirit in China's millions, the revolutionary movement was destined to fail.[217] When he finally returned to China from exile in 1918, a discouraged Dai briefly retreated from the evils he had seen in Shanghai and went to the countryside—the real China—and to

Buddhism. But returning to Shanghai in response to the May Fourth demonstrations in Beijing,[218] Dai was caught up in the movement's nationalistic fervor. Coupled with Russia's October Revolution two years earlier, May Fourth convinced Dai that the Russian revolution heralded the international role of China's national revolution against capitalist imperialism.[219] Like Li and Chen, Dai too was drawn to Marxism-Leninism. By September 1919, Dai distinguished himself as one of the first Chinese intellectuals to attempt a Marxian analysis of Chinese history. Li Dazhao's article, "Wo de Makesi-zhuyi guan" (My Marxist Views), antedated Dai's piece by several months; but having learned much more Marxian economic theory from Takabatake's translations of *Das Kapital* (Capital) and of Karl Kautsky's *Ökonomische Lehren* (Economic teachings),[220] Dai attempted what Li's work did not—the use of Marxist economic theory to analyze Chinese history. The article, entitled "The Sources of Dysfunction in China from an Economic Point of View," stressed several economic factors contributing to China's current political and social crisis. First, like so many who responded angrily to the Treaty of Versailles in 1919, Dai saw economic imperialism by advanced Western capitalist societies as a major cause of China's current distress.[221] Economic and social decline that were natural products of China's historical dialectic were worsened, he argued, by the economic dislocation caused by Western imperialism. Nevertheless, Dai concluded his hasty overview of China's situation on a positive note: the same historical dialectic that had brought China such misery over the previous fifty or sixty years also promised an upturn in China's fortunes in the 1920s. Echoing Chen's and Li's earlier faith in Western science in China's New Culture movement and Sun's *Jianguo fanlue* (Outline of national reconstruction), Dai sought to stir up optimism and enthusiastic support for China's revolutionary movement.[222] Like Li, Dai contended in succeeding essays that the October Revolution promised a new future for China and for other societies that had suffered from Western encroachment. China's revolution of national liberation would proceed as part of an inescapable wave of world revolution.[223]

Despite this sanguine view of the implications of Russia's revolution for China, just as Sun, whom Dai now served faithfully as secretary, turned to join hands with the Soviet leadership to advance the Chinese revolution, Dai dissociated himself from the Comintern's leadership and began to articulate his own brand of indigenous national socialism. Disenchanted by the politicking surrounding the Guomindang's 1924 Reorganization that admitted Communists into the party and suspicious of the wisdom of subjecting China's indigenous national revolutionary movement to outside guidance, Dai distanced himself from the Reorganization. He soon carved out a separate path that would serve as a rallying point for Guomindang rightists who never accepted Sun's decision to cooperate with the CCP and to allow what Dai and others saw as a disruptive emphasis on class struggle to influence Guomindang policies. Over the rest of the decade, Dai's suspicion of Russian chauvinism and its ill effects on the Chinese revolution deepened as he drew closer to Chiang Kai-shek after Sun's death in 1925.[224] By the middle of that year, Dai had already issued two pamphlets attacking the CCP and systematizing his own national socialism: *Sun Wen-zhuyi zhi zhexue de jichu* (The philosophical foundations of Sun Yat-senism) and *Guomin geming yu Zhongguo Guomindang* (The national revolution and the Chinese Guomindang). The two works, which took Sun's minsheng principle as the inspiration for an indigenous Chinese state socialism, were tremendously influential in drawing support to the Right Guomindang with which Dai remained identified for the remainder of his career.

Unlike Takabatake, Dai wrote explicitly to attack the CCP, but although Dai's national socialism was anti-Communist, like Takabatake's, it was not anti-Marxist. On the contrary, the Marxian tones that characterized Dai's work in the May Fourth movement continued to be evident in Dai's anti-Communist socialist vision. In *Guomin geming yu Zhongguo Guomindang* (The national revolution), Dai repeatedly drew on Marxist-Leninist conceptions such as the notion that imperialism is an outgrowth of capitalism, the extraction of surplus value as the fundamental mechanism of capitalism producing misery among the workers and class conflict, and even democratic centralism as the organizational principle of the Guomindang.[225] Nevertheless, Dai maintained two central tenets of Sun's thought that fundamentally conflicted with orthodox Marxism: (1) a commitment to revolutionary change coupled with an aversion to class struggle within a nation that was struggling for its very survival in a hostile international environment[226] and (2) a fundamental mistrust of mass movements as reliable agents of social change. The first point led Dai to channel his labor activism away from conflict (or "struggle" *fendou*) and toward a cooperative (*xiezuo*) approach that would not disrupt the mythical natural harmony of traditional Chinese society. The second point supported Sun's view that China needed military rule and then Guomindang tutelage for an indeterminate period on the path to republicanism. This view, which posited a single-party state (or party-state) to play the central role in China's state socialism, clashed with the Marxist vision of a stateless communism after the revolution, however consonant it was with Soviet reality.

The key to Dai's national socialism lay in his single-minded devotion to Sun's Three People's Principles and the Chinese essentialism that informed his view that the Principles constituted a new crystallization of Chinese traditional values. As Dai interpreted it, minsheng was at the core of these principles, and it held the key to both the nationalist and statist elements of Dai's national socialism. Dai's formulation was considerably more emotional and less theoretically rigorous than Takabatake's. His point of departure in the 1925 pamphlets was the distinction between Sun's thought, as an indigenous philosophical system, and Soviet-style "communism," which Dai portrayed as an insidious foreign ideology that threatened to destroy the natural and essential unity of the Chinese people. Dai's nationalism shared much with Confucian and neo-Confucian conservatives. His "nation" was a cultural conception, one that included on an equal basis Manchus, Mongols, Tibetans, and other minority peoples who had been "absorbed" culturally by the Han Chinese.[227] Thus, Dai brought forward into the twentieth century the cultural concept of China as tianxia that had prevailed in the previous century. China was culturally superior to other peoples and societies, in Dai's view. China's traditional philosophy, which Sun had now distilled in the form of the Three People's Principles, Dai characterized as "the quintessence of spiritual culture in the history of world civilization."[228] Dai, then, juxtaposed the internationalism of the CCP to the nationalism of the Guomindang and argued that China's national salvation could come only through the latter.

Here, recalling Sun's pan-Asianism, Dai drew lessons from Japan's success in building a modern nation-state. The Meiji oligarchs had certainly drawn on foreign ideas; but in Dai's view, the essential force behind the success of the Meiji Restoration had been a distinctively Japanese national spirit embodied in the *kokutai*.[229] China, too, needed not class consciousness but a national self-consciousness of its glorious past, a spirit of national self-confidence based on indigenous values.[230] The elements of Chinese tradition that could support a state socialism uniquely suited to China's own national context were to be found not in the internationalist ideology of the CCP, whatever its temporary concessions to nationalism, but in "People's Principles" that drew on traditional Chinese Confucian values.

The realities of China's international situation, which Dai saw in social Darwinist terms, made Marxian internationalism all the more inappropriate for Chinese revolutionaries. Armed with its faulty unidimensional materialist view of history, the CCP was incapable of inspiring the deep self-consciousness of the enduring importance of both the state and the nation that alone could supply the "revolutionary energy to carry out [China's] national revolution." As Mao would claim of his CCP rivals who had learned their Marxism only through "book-learning" in the Soviet Union, what was needed to inspire this "revolutionary energy" was a systematic study of Chinese realities.[231] In the absence of this study, Marxian internationalism was simply "an absurd illusion" pressed by Western theorists who did not share a fervent longing to save China.

> [T]o think that with the economic organization of the entire world changed, and capitalism eliminated, differences among peoples, the struggle for existence among peoples, will then come to an end, and that the entire world can then achieve everlasting peace is a kind of absurd illusion. . . . Certainly, the great majority of those who advocate socialism today are nationals of powerful countries and live in imperialist states. Their methods of analysis, their arguments are certainly necessary and appropriate [for them]. But what considerations do people who live in such weak nations as China have? Why must we intentionally shut our eyes and not see clearly the true reality? How can we insist on discarding the spirit of nationalism that we ourselves most need today and will require in the future as well and adopt instead an "incomplete theory" [created by] socialists of [other, more] powerful countries?[232]

By contrast, Sun's minsheng principle, which harkened back to traditional Confucian virtues,[233] offered the key to resolving not only China's problems but those of the world as well. The state was as critical as nationalist sentiment to the realization of Sun's concept of socialism. This had become clear in the early years of the Tongmenghui, when Sun first formulated his Three People's Principles. Having just returned from Western Europe a strong supporter of Henry George, Sun articulated his minsheng principle with Georgism in mind—particularly its policy of the equalization of land rights and its single tax system.[234] According to Feng Ziyou, Sun had previously advocated socialism using the Japanese term *shakai-shugi* but had switched to *minsheng-zhuyi* as a more inclusive term; and in *Minbao*, the Tongmenghui organ, *minsheng* was consistently used as a synonym for socialism in the Western sense.[235] But because occasionally Sun described measures that did not correspond to Georgism,[236] Sun remained ambiguous about the concrete provisions that his *minsheng-zhuyi* would entail. Thus, between 1905 and 1907, Feng Ziyou, Zhang Binglin, Hu Hanmin, and Zhu Zhixin published article after article in the pages of the *Minbao* in an effort to flesh out the concept. These essays played an important role in the debate between the revolutionists and reformers supporting Liang Qichao and his *Xinmin congbao*. Although they varied in their interpretations, all converged on the notion that at the very least *minsheng* meant socialism, and, probably, a socialism very close to the social policy school of Bismarckian reformers or the national socialism of Ferdinand Lassalle, even though all participants on the Tongmenghui side were also "decidedly influenced by [the] Marx" with whose work they had become familiar in Japan.[237] By the time Dai wrote as official interpreter of Sun's thought in the mid- and late-1920s, many of these original Tongmenghui members were leading supporters of the right wing of the Guomindang and of Dai's position.

Dai's rationalization of the need for a statist socialism was not as sophisticated as Takabatake's, which had been grounded in comparative Eastern and Western perspectives on the nature of humankind and society. Yet Dai did offer general philosophical arguments to support his position. In his view, the state was needed not to protect individuals from each other within the national community, as Takabatake's Hobbesian view would have it, because for Dai human nature was fundamentally good, ruled by the ancient Confucian notion of *ren'ai* (humanitarian love). The state was needed, however, to protect its citizens from dangers outside the national society. The state's support of the development of China's forces of production in both industry and agriculture was an important part of this mission. Thus, Dai's platform called for the equalization of land use rights on the basis of state landownership, state ownership of large industry and transportation facilities, and the state's encouragement of the free development of small-scale industry.[238] Certainly, much of this was compatible with what the Bolsheviks had undertaken under the rubric of war communism in the years of civil war immediately after October 1917. But the state Dai envisaged was to be a state of the "whole people," not just a single class.[239] Dai, then, firmly repudiated the notion of the dictatorship of the proletariat along with the notion of class struggle.

Lacking Takabatake's background in other national socialist doctrines, Dai's doctrine was hampered by his uncritical acceptance of Sun's rather vague People's Principles, and by his half-hearted effort to resurrect traditional elements of China's past that had already failed China miserably by 1911. Nevertheless, as the leading orthodox interpreter of Sun's thought in the 1920s and 1930s, Dai's work remains of substantial significance. In China, as in Japan, those who would make a socialist revolution had to address fundamental questions concerning the compatibility of a desire to assert the value of one's own culture in the threatening international environment, on the one hand, and a Marxian conception of revolutionary change that devalued the nation and the state that would be needed to protect it during and after the revolution, on the other. Despite its weaknesses, Dai's statist formulation offered an alternative that was attractive to the many who followed the Guomindang, even to some who had begun their socialist odyssey as anarchists.

CONCLUSIONS: THE RUSSIAN REVOLUTION AND EARLY RESPONSES TO THE NATIONAL QUESTION

The October Revolution and its immediate outcome in the emergence of a strong Soviet state at the forefront of the international communist movement by the early 1920s posed the national question clearly and boldly in all its dimensions to Chinese and Japanese socialists. The impact of the event was more immediate and dramatic in Japan. There, it exacerbated existing tensions within the socialist movement, culminating in the traumatic ana-boru schism and the creation of the JCP in 1922. In China, reaction was delayed because there was no socialist group as coherent and well organized as that in Japan. Yet again, the predominant response in China entailed the abrupt demise of its weak anarchist movement and the establishment of a Communist party under the sponsorship of the Soviet-dominated Comintern.

In both China and Japan, the Bolshevik revolution also occasioned the advent of new schools of national socialism. Both Takabatake Motoyuki and Dai Jitao believed deeply in the transformative capacities of the state and the creative energies of nationalism as an enduring force in the international system. The Bolshevik revolution and the emergence of a powerful Soviet state during the civil war confirmed both the nationalist and statist impulses motivating the two men's doctrines. Interestingly, however, in the one case—Takabatake in Japan—national socialism was pursued without abandoning Marxism-Leninism and on the basis of a "correct" reinterpretation of the Bolshevik experience. Meanwhile, in China, Dai Jitao found Leninist Marxism incompatible with the tenets he felt were essential to the indigenous thought of Sun Yat-sen, and where his Marxism had led him to be forward-looking in 1919, his reaffirmation of traditional Chinese values as the foundation for his state socialism drained his doctrine of its revolutionary content. In China, it was Li Dazhao's effort to resolve the national question, the contradiction between the universal and the particular within the context of Marxism-Leninism, that became the predominant Chinese response to the Russian revolution, as it would culminate in the synthesis of Mao Zedong's thought. In Japan, Takabatake emulated Yamaji Aizan but was well in the minority in 1919. Yet his statist and nationalist approach, if illegitimate to the Comintern, fore-shadowed the Imperial Household-centered socialisms of the Kaitō-ha and ten-kōsha Sano Manabu in the 1920s and 1930s. Takabatake's response would not succeed as a revolutionary doctrine, for, as Gail Bernstein has noted, "the Japanese government had already monopolized the symbols of Japanese nationalism and the coercive forces of the state."[240] Yet by the late 1920s, Takabatake's national socialism comprised the major tide in Japan's left-wing movement.

The international position of China and Japan vis-à-vis Russia, the West, and one another during and after the October Revolution, patterns of indigenous political philosophy, and the degrees of stateness of the two societies all contributed to these Chinese and Japanese responses to the Russian revolution and the national question by the mid-1920s. In the view of both Chinese and Japanese Marxian socialists, their societies had been relatively oppressed participants in an international system defined by the Western imperialist powers. The October Revolution in what had previously been among the world's most "backward" societies gave dramatic new hope to oppressed Asian peoples. As Yamakawa wrote in 1923, "The most important phenomenon in international relations since World War I has been the emergence of the exploited states and the decline in the power of international capitalist (exploiting) countries. Soviet Russia is the head of the alliance of exploited states (e.g., China) against Great Britain and the United States, the leading exploiter states." For Japanese Marxists, Japan had itself previously embarked on imperialist ventures, but its still relatively subordinate position vis-à-vis the West left it the "choice to ally with either side."[241] The Japanese bolshevists who formed the JCP determined that to ally with the Soviet Union would not sacrifice Japanese national pride: Japan would pursue a peaceful moral world order. And, if Russia had been backward relative to Japan before 1917, its new domestic and international posture made it a suitable model for Japanese behavior.

For Chinese Marxists, this aspect of the national question was far less ambiguous. For them to ally with the Soviet Union as Marxists did not require them to repudiate the behavior of an existing Chinese state, for there simply was no effective state in China. The pursuit of a Marxist program of internal revolution could only elevate China's international position. Thus, even Dai Jitao and Hu Hanmin readily envisaged an alliance among oppressed nations to oppose the alliance of imperialist states that was the League of Nations.[242] By contrast, Takabatake maintained that the alliance of proletarians could never be international if the Japanese *kokutai* were ever endangered by a proletarian state (the Soviet Union).

Yet pan-Asianism on both sides confused the issue. Japan had proved that it could succeed at the social Darwinian game of international relations; so pan-Asianism, for many Japanese, implied the expansion of Japanese influence throughout all Asia.[243] Conversely, Chinese revolutionaries around Sun who had begun to express sentiments for "racial-based solidarity" among Asian peoples against imperialism began to recognize the contradictions introduced into their pan-Asian sentiment by Japan's increasing participation in imperialist ventures in Asia. While Sun glorified the Russo-Japanese War as the first victory of yellow over white peoples, anti-Japanese sentiments among Chinese revolutionaries blossomed with Japan's presentation of the Twenty-One Demands to China in 1915. Then, Sun's and Li's pan-Asian ideals constituted pleas for Japan to reject the existing immoral order of interstate relations and its privileges.[244] But on the Japanese side, Takabatake was quite comfortably a realist who defended statism as necessary in the threatening international environment of the twentieth century.

Both his statism and his nationalism reflected unambiguously long-standing Japanese fears of Russian imperialism. Such sentiments would be echoed in the writings of the Rōnō-ha and of tenkōsha in the 1930s.

Aside from the international environment, prevalent views on the state and the level of stateness achieved in China and Japan also influenced Chinese and Japanese responses to Bolshevism. Takabatake and Li responded to the high degree of stateness achieved by Meiji Japan and the lack of an effective state in China. Both responses emerged as dominant, linking nationalism with Marxism, reflecting the conviction that consciousness and collective will as expressed in a nation-state (or aspiration thereto) were crucial. No Asian Marxist in this international context rejected the promise of the state's transformative capacities, motivated by collective national spiritual wills.[245] Yet JCP Marxists would be left in the awkward position of having to deny the importance of national(ist) consciousness for Japan while affirming the role of the national state as a positive, transformative force in the Soviet Union.

This created tensions beneath the surface of the Japanese movement, tensions that would be resolved by tenkōsha succumbing to the spirit of the *kokutai* thereafter. But neither Japanese nor Chinese Marxists could escape the essence of the Marxist national question in their relations with the Comintern. In both cases, there were indigenous analyses of the two states and proper strategies for the two movements. But in China, the lack of stateness allowed the nationalist impulse toward particularity to evolve in a Maoist-Marxist strategy that was indigenous, opposed to early Comintern prescriptions, and ultimately prevailed, culminating, paradoxically, in *practice* in a system that was ultimately state-centric, while the high degree of stateness in Japan determined that a similar impulse toward particularity be fused with open rebellion to the Comintern. Through the 1920s and the 1930s, Chinese Marxists would produce theoretical Marxist literature on Chinese society that was relatively unsophisticated while Mao worked out the most successful formula in the hinterland. In the same period, driven underground by government repression, indigenous Marxist debate on Japanese society produced a highly sophisticated academic literature, while Comintern revolutionary strategy carried out in a highly statized society permitted close scrutiny of the JCP by both the Japanese state and the Comintern. When Comintern strategy failed there, there was no room for particularity within the orthodox Marxist-Leninist movement, and the national question came to be resolved in Japan in the manner of Takabatake in 1919, first on the fringes of the movement and then exploding it. Where the *kokutai* myth was pervasive and the nation was undifferentiated from the state, a nationalist theoretical synthesis such as that of Li Dazhao and Mao Zedong— nationalistic but not statist in its theoretical incarnation—was not likely to emerge.

PART THREE

History, the State, and Revolutionary Change: Marxist Analyses of the Chinese and Japanese States

State, Nation, and the National Question in the Debate on Japanese Capitalism

The development of the world economic crisis is shaking the foundation of the entire capitalist order, and therefore also of Japan's capitalist system. . . . The resolution of the deadlock in economic development, the instability of political rule, and social unrest require a change . . .; and without investigating the inevitable basic contradictions, it is probably impossible even to grasp a clue to the resolution of the problem. To examine the history of the establishment of Japanese capitalism, to investigate the special nature of its development, which was full of contradictions, is therefore the key to the discovery of the path of the fundamental resolution of the problems confronting Japanese capitalism. This *Symposium* seeks to provide that key. . . . Our hope is not to interpret history but to change it.[1]

IN DECEMBER 1927, a group of Marxists led by Sakai Toshihiko and Yamakawa Hitoshi abruptly severed their ties with the struggling Japanese Communist party (JCP). Within weeks they had founded their own journal *Rōnō* (Labor-Farmer) and set out to popularize their own interpretation of the correct strategy for a socialist revolution in Japan. The Rōnō-ha (Labor-Farmer faction), as it came to be called after their new dissident publication, adamantly rejected the Comintern's views on the subject. The Comintern's 1927 Theses claimed that Japan lagged far enough behind Russia's own "backwardness" in February 1917 to require a two-stage (first bourgeois and then proletarian) revolution to achieve socialism; and it was this claim that prompted the Rōnō-ha's exit from a Communist party that willingly accepted the Comintern's view. The Rōnō-ha's efforts to refute the Comintern's strategy of two-stage revolution gave rise to the so-called debate on Japanese capitalism (*Nihon shihon-shugi ronsō*).[2] JCP loyalists defending the Comintern's strategy disputed Rōnō-ha arguments in scholarly journals, and in 1932 and 1933 they issued a vigorous riposte in painstakingly researched studies collected in the seven-volume *Nihon shihon-shugi hattatsu shi kōza* (Symposium on the history of the development of Japanese capitalism). The controversy between the *Rōnō* and *Kōza* factions raged for almost a decade until it was forcibly suppressed in the mid-1930s as the Special Higher Police (Tokkō) redoubled its efforts to crush dissent in the rising fervor to win the war on the Asian mainland.

Embracing Marxist and other left-leaning scholars in the nation's leading universities,[3] what began as a practical dispute over the strategy and tactics of the socialist revolutionary movement rapidly escalated into a sophisticated controversy over the interpretation of Japanese political and economic development since the Tokugawa era as the two sides endeavored to apply the Marxist paradigm to uncover the universal aspects and the peculiarities of Japan's recent experience. By the close of the debate in the prewar era, its participants had produced a voluminous literature of pioneering scholarly research into Japanese economic and political history. This impressive literature has exercised a powerful influence over Japanese Marxist and non-Marxist scholarship on Japan's political and economic history, and the controversy that gave rise to it continues to cast an imprint on Japanese politics—descendants of the prewar Kōza-ha lending support to the critical perspectives of the JCP on the shortcomings of contemporary Japanese democracy, on the one hand, and the successors of the Rōnō-ha comprising the theoretical leadership for the Japanese Socialist party's (JSP) conceptualization of social democracy, on the other.[4] Today, as in the prewar period, scholars directly or obliquely associated with the Kōza-ha and the Rōnō-ha have taken the lead in formulating critical theoretical perspectives on Japanese politics and economics,[5] and in most cases these are views that forcefully challenge the rigid orthodoxy of classic Marxist-Leninist thought.

As the foundation for these recent innovations, the work of the original Rōnō-ha and Kōza-ha transcended the arid, dogmatic formulations offered in official Comintern and JCP documents. Predictably, of course, Rōnō-ha Marxists, tenkōsha (apostates from the Communist party), and members of the so-called Dissolutionist faction (Kaitō-ha) as well as others opposed to the politics and policies of the JCP have routinely criticized Kōza-ha theorists as mere parrots of the party line pronounced from Moscow.[6] The view that Marxist leaders of all these factions followed a general tendency of the period "to import theory [directly] from Western society and not from the empirical facts" of Japanese existence, merely adopting and dogmatically propagating "Comintern orthodoxy," is a sentiment shared by many contemporary native scholars of Japanese Marxism as well.[7] But such an evaluation is more valid with reference to an earlier era, when the writings of leading Marxists appeared primarily as Communist party documents or as articles introducing the fundamental tenets of Marxism than to the studies produced by the debate on Japanese capitalism. In the period immediately after 1922, the party existed precariously under Comintern tutelage, and basic Marxist theory was still being absorbed in Japan. Aside from the national/state socialism of Takabatake Motoyuki, Marxist theoretical work that could merit the label "original" yielded only the dogmas of Yamakawaism and Fukumotoism—doctrines that represented opposite extremes of thought supporting the effort to build a Leninist party that was at once a vanguard party and a more broadly based coalition that could respond to the clarion call "To the Masses!" issued by the Third Comintern Congress of mid–1921.[8] These conflicting requirements for a mass communist party constructed to spearhead a bourgeois-democratic revolution that would explode rapidly into proletarian revolution were reiterated throughout subsequent Comintern theses on Japan.[9] Because the debate on Japanese capitalism initially grew out of a controversy on party strategy and tactics, the dilemmas of organizing a mass vanguard party remained to plague *Rōnō* and *Kōza* scholars. Nevertheless, the debate on Japanese capitalism itself generated scholarship by a wide range of party and nonparty scholars linking empirical research and theoretical work of such depth that the controversy marked a major watershed in the evolution of Marxism in Japan.

The wealth of scholarship produced in the debate was duly noted and used heavily in E. H. Norman's controversial study *Japan's Emergence as a Modern State* in the 1930s and 1940s.[10] If otherwise this literature was neglected in Western scholarly circles until very recently, its achievements as the first systematic effort to analyze Japanese political and economic development with a comparative perspective has justifiably enabled it to exercise a profound and continuing influence on Japanese scholarship in history, political science, and economics from the 1920s and 1930s to the present.[11]

Because the controversy occurred in "the era when [Japan] turned from 'the conditions of Taishō democracy' to an age of war and fascism,"[12] it is not surprising that the concerns associated with the national question should have figured prominently in the debate on Japanese capitalism. With reference to nationalism, national pride and questions concerning the universal and particular, or special, aspects of Japan's development experience were at the heart of the debate from the very outset. This was evidenced in the Rōnō-ha's refusal to accept an externally generated set of policy prescriptions that were based on the Comintern leadership's limited knowledge of Japanese realities. At the same time, even before the 1927 Theses precipitated the Rōnō-ha's secession from the JCP, Marxists who became leaders on both sides of the controversy were challenged to apply Marx's universalist schema to Japan to repudiate the unabashedly nationalistic application of Marxism by Takahashi Kamekichi in defense of Japanese expansionism.[13] Nationalism, then, played a role both as a positive irritant and as a negative factor in precipitating the debate.

The other aspect of the national question, the issue of the state—its nature and role in contemporary Japanese society and the implications of these for revolutionary strategy—played an even more critical role in the debate on Japanese capitalism. To be sure, the controversy addressed a broad range of issues concerning Japan's political and economic development, among them the relationship of a lagging agrarian sphere to an industrial sector in rapid transformation, the internal versus external sources of Japan's industrial revolution, and the positive or negative impact of Japan's "Asiatic" heritage. Yet, touching on all these concerns and central to the entire debate was the need to analyze the nature of the Japanese state. The character of the state—whether it was to be viewed as essentially feudal or bourgeois—would determine if the revolutionary transition to socialism in Japan required one stage or two. It was precisely in a state that had played a heavy role in Japan's industrialization, in apparent contradiction to the Marxian axiom that it was the economic base that determines the superstructure, that Japan's most notable peculiarities seemed to lie. This posed the greatest challenge to those seeking to apply Marx's universalist categories to Japan. Confronted by the coexistence of a highly developed, even imperialistic, form of finance capital and "trustification," on the one hand, and the absence of a strong, more broadly based bourgeoisie that could support the development of bourgeois democracy, on the other, the Comintern under Bukharin's leadership chose to argue in effect from the top down, that is, from the character of the superstructure to the base. The continued presence of authoritarian political institutions—the emperor, the Privy Council, the extralegal influence of the genrō, the Naidaijin [Lord Keeper of the Privy Seal], and the Imperial Household Minister[14]—was of special concern here. According to the JCP's Draft Program of 1922 and the so-called 1927 Theses, the existence of "feudal remnants" in the political superstructure indicated that the bourgeois revolution begun by the Meiji Restoration had not yet been completed by Japan's weak bourgeoisie. Instead of bourgeois democracy, a state power that was semi-feudal in character remained intact, its class basis a "bloc of a segment of the commercial bourgeoisie and large landlords."[15] This interpretation, adopted by the JCP and defended by the Kōza-ha, constituted the basis for the Comintern strategy of two-stage revolution. The proletariat would carry to fruition the bourgeois-democratic revolution that Japan's bourgeoisie had failed to complete. Only then could this first revolution move rapidly into the proletarian-socialist revolution. In this view, the bourgeois revolution was particularly urgent in the countryside where feudal rents and "extraeconomic coercion" (a hallmark of feudal landholding) remained; and the proletarian revolution could not proceed until the agrarian problem was resolved by the commercialization of the agricultural sector.

The alternative interpretation of the peculiarities of Japan's situation was that adopted by Yamakawa's Rōnō-ha. Arguing that the economic base was at the stage of highly developed finance capitalism, the *Rōnō* theorists asserted that the Meiji Restoration had, indeed, been a complete bourgeois-democratic revolution, hence, only a one-stage strategy of proletarian revolution was required. As for the countryside, land rents were capitalistic in nature, determined by free-market relations, and the situation was ripe for proletarian revolution.[16] Ironically, Rōnō-ha scholars, such as Columbia University-trained Inomata Tsunao, found themselves using Nikolai Bukharin's systematically maligned notions of state capitalist trust and state capitalism well after Bukharin's political demise, in order to stress Japan's high level of capitalist development and oppose the Comintern line of two-stage revolution formulated by Bukharin himself.

Both the Rōnō-ha and Kōza-ha interpretations could, as Yamakawa insisted,[17] be justified by the language of the 1927 Theses, and each interpretation rested on a particular view of the nature of the Japanese state. Here the question of the nature of the imperial institution was central: its existence and continued presence with other authoritarian institutions formed a complex, a tennō-sei—an emperor *system*—that signaled to Kōza-ha theorists that the state power born of the Meiji Restoration was not a bourgeois democracy. The tennō or mikado and the institutions that with it comprised the tennō-sei were remnants of a previous age that had to be eliminated before the tasks of bourgeois-democratic revolution begun by the Restoration could be deemed complete. *Kōza* theorists, thus, fully supported the demand to abolish the imperial system that had been written into the party's program, at Comintern insistence but only after protracted debate, in 1922. By contrast, for theorists of the *Rōnō* position, the presence of the emperor did not at all negate the democratic nature of the Meiji and Taishō state, as evidenced by the existence of the Diet, competitive political parties, cabinet rule, and constitutional government (as opposed to government by fiat). The revolution could proceed immediately to the proletarian stage. In effect, the imperial institution did not occupy a central position for Rōnō-ha Marxists. It was a "bourgeois monarchy," and its influence would gradually decline until the tennō-sei itself disappeared. If this did not occur until the state itself "withered away" after the socialist revolution, this would pose no theoretical problem for Rōnō-ha Marxists.[18] In short, for the Kōza-ha, the imperial institution, the tennō-sei, as they called it, was at the core of the entire state structure in Japan, the key to identifying its underlying class basis in semi-feudal agriculture; but for the Rōnō-ha, it was but a mere appendage of a state apparatus based on a highly capitalistic industrial sphere and commercialized agriculture.

But was the imperial institution truly so insignificant in the Rōnō-ha critique, or did the Rōnō-ha's opposition—along with that of the Kaitō-ha, Takabatake Motoyuki, and *tenkōsha* proponents of a Marxian national socialism—to the Comintern's call to abolish the emperor system signify a deeper subjective attachment to the imperial institution that Russian leaders in the Comintern could not possibly comprehend? Could this attachment explain what appeared to be a marked reluctance to treat the imperial institution in the objective general terms required by Marx's theory of the state and reject it in accordance with the demands of revolutionary theory? In the degree of importance attached to the imperial institution lies the key to the centrality of the national question to the debate on Japanese capitalism. Marxism required a detached, dispassionate treatment of the imperial institution, affection for the uniqueness of which was deeply inculcated into all Japanese who had come of age in the late Meiji and Taishō. The diffuse nationalism that Maruyama Masao has noted in Japanese intellectuals of this generation[19] thus made the analysis of the state at once the most critical and the most formidable task for participants in the controversy because it obfuscated and blurred state power and its class-power configurations.

Nevertheless, Marxism held a special attraction in Japan in part precisely because it was the first scientific and general political theory that allowed a critique of the official *kokutai* family-state (kazoku kokka) ideology premised on the uniqueness of the Japanese polity.[20] The conventions of Meiji and Taishō Japan, supported by the state's effective police network, prohibited direct discussion of the imperial system itself and discouraged speculation on the legitimate origins of government in abstract and universalist terms. Political theory as such could not exist in this context. Even the heated mainstream (non-Marxist) *kokka-gaku* (state studies) controversy between Uesugi Shinkichi's authoritarian tennō shuken ron (the doctrine that sovereignty resides in the tennō) and Minobe Tatsukichi's emperor-organ theory (*tennō kikan setsu*) based on the German orthodoxy of state sovereignty (*kokka shuken ron*) was conducted entirely in legalistic terms. This was not a controversy in political philosophy but rather a debate between broad and narrow constructions of Article 1 of the Meiji Constitution delineating the power of the throne. For both Uesugi and Minobe, the imperial institution was a given. Its legitimacy was not open to question or judgment by abstract general theories on the origins of government.[21] The German Staatsrecht thought of J. K. Bluntschli and Georg Jellinek had been foremost among Western theories contributing to the development of Japanese political thought at the outset of the Meiji period. This strand of German political theory and the less influential British constitutional theory, which supplied the theoretical basis of the Japanese party cabinet system and continued to be taught at Waseda University even after the promulgation of the Meiji Constitution in 1889, were combined with the *Kokugaku* school's sonnō (revere the emperor) thought of the Tokugawa era to form the emperor-centered official orthodoxy of Hozumi Yatsuka and his disciples at Tokyo Imperial University.[22] Apace with the consolidation of Meiji imperial power, these imported European theories were absorbed into Shintō and *kokutai* thought, and their abstract generality was gradually but steadily superseded by the special elements of native Japanese thought on the emperor. Thenceforth, these European bodies of thought on the state could no longer fulfill the role that Marxism would come to play in Japan as a universalist theory untainted by the mystification and particularism of the official family-state mythology.

Marxism, then, offered Japanese intellectuals of the third generation since the Restoration a tool with which to analyze critically and comprehensively politics in general. The abstract categories of Marxist thought could be applied systematically to study the relationship between state and society, concepts hitherto conflated or undifferentiated in indigenous pre-Marxist thought, in Japan as well as in China. The heretical implications of this bold theory linking political power with economic interests did not deter Marxists in Japan from working with it. For the repressive regime increasingly narrowed the range of permissible criticism to exclude any reformists so that liberals and eventually Marxists in general, whatever their actual writings on the state, fell victim to the vague injunctions of the Peace Preservation Law. Moreover, until preparation for the war effort began in earnest early in the 1930s, intellectuals working as university scholars were relatively free to dabble in the application of Marxist theory to Japan, for they tended to be treated less harshly by the regime than were revolutionary activists.[23]

The prerequisite for the application of Marxist political theory to the analysis of Japanese politics, however, was a firm grounding in the theory itself. It is in this respect that the emergence of the debate on Japanese capitalism signalled a turning point in the history of Marxism in Japan. Before 1925 this precondition was absent.[24] The appearance of Noro Eitarō's work at this time, which, in turn, inspired the seven-volume *Kōza*[25] marked a dramatic break with initially extremist responses to the Russian revolution in Japan—the anarchism of Ōsugi Sakae versus the state socialism of Takabatake Motoyuki and the progression from Yamakawa's advocacy of a mass united front proletarian political force[26] to Fukumoto Kazuo's dogmatic "division before unity" (*bunri ketsugō ron*) conception of an ideologically pure and tempered vanguard party.[27] Yamakawa and Fukumoto did "recognize the need for a guiding theory [for the JCP] to be based on an analysis of Japanese capitalist economics and politics." As Koyama Hirotake has noted, however, the two party leaders "only acknowledged this need . . . and did not perform any basic analysis of the special features of Japanese capitalism. Nor did they clarify the nature and role of the Japanese imperial system in tandem with a systematic analysis of Japanese capitalism." Yamakawa's and Fukumoto's unelaborated references to the state in terms of "absolutist forces" (*zettai-shugi seiryoku*), "absolutist institutions bequeathed from the past" (*zettai isei*), "autocratic forces" (*sensei seiryoku*), and "feudal remnants" (*hōken isei*), then, merely underscored "the low level of their theory of the state" to which many critics have attributed their errors in tactical and organizational theory.[28]

This state of affairs within the JCP on the eve of the debate on Japanese capitalism helps to account for the lack of interest among Western scholars in the extensive corpus that emerged from the debate. But in treating the imperial system and completing what was left undone by Yamakawa and Fukumoto, the works produced by the participants in the debate on Japanese capitalism undermine the implicit assumption that if Japanese Marxist theory had had any intrinsic merit, the movement would not have failed so miserably. Drawing on eminent Soviet and European theorists from Lenin to Gramsci, participants in the controversy treated the issues associated with the peculiarities of Japanese development in such a way that the debate contributed significantly to the understanding of Marxism and of political development in general. This scholarship illuminated certain theoretical difficulties and lacunae in Marxism as a whole by confronting the extreme disjuncture between the apparent nature of Japan's economic base, on the one hand, and that of its political superstructure, on the other. The achievement of such dramatic gains, however, awaited challenges that emerged both within and outside Japan by 1927.

THE THEORETICAL ASSIMILATION OF MARXISM IN JAPAN

The debate on Japanese capitalism marked a dramatic watershed in the development of Marxism in Japan, indicating that the basic tenets of Marxism had been sufficiently absorbed so that they could be applied to analyze the peculiarities of Japanese politics and economics. The deepening appreciation of all aspects of Marxist economic, philosophical, and political theory and the practical debate on Marxist revolutionary strategy and tactics, informed by Comintern pronouncements, together established the groundwork for the scholarly accomplishments of the participants in the debate on Japanese capitalism. Out of these developments emerged the two major impulses that combined to prompt the controversy. Internally, Takahashi Kamekichi's heretical theory of "petty imperialism" set a new standard for the innovative application of Marxism to analyze Japanese development. His work challenged those who would repudiate his defense of Japanese expansionism to produce their own interpretations supporting the Leninist view that there could be no legitimate place for nationalism among Marxists in capitalist Japan. At the same time, Comintern theses on the revolution in Japan resting on premises concerning Japanese development that were mutually contradictory aroused resistance among many in the JCP, reinforcing the need for Japan's Marxists to articulate compelling alternative analyses of Japanese development for themselves. Together, these internal and external forces stimulated the maturation of a modest dispute over revolutionary strategy and tactics into a theoretically sophisticated discussion of the universal and particular aspects of the Japanese experience.

Beyond the party lines of Yamakawaism and Fukumotoism within the JCP, the understanding of Marxism in Japan proceeded quickly throughout the 1920s. In response to the Russian revolution, young Marxists produced in rapid succession translations of Marx's works, secondary accounts of the same, and biographical essays on leading Marxists. The *Marukusu-den* (Biographies of Marx) (1920) compiled by Sakai and Yamakawa along with Yamakawa's *Reinin to Torotsuki* (Lenin and Trotsky) (1921) introduced Marxist figures to the Japanese public. Complementing Takabatake Motoyuki's translation of *Das Kapital* in 1919, these works helped to spread Marxism after the Russian revolution and rekindled the fervor for change that had lain cautiously dormant during the "winter period" (fuyu no jidai) following the execution of anarchist Kōtoku Shūsui. Japanese Marxists also took tentative steps to produce original works on Marxism. Sakai's *Yuibutsu shikan no tachiba kara* (From the perspective of historical materialism) (1919) and *Kyōfu, tōsō, kanki* (Fear, struggle, joy) (1920), as well as Yamakawa's *Shakai-shugisha no shakai kan* (The socialist's view of society) (1919) were representative works of this genre. These, however, did not yet involve "the study of the Japanese state and Japanese capitalism as a whole"[29] requisite to the formation of a truly Japanese brand of Marxism. Movement in this direction occurred only tentatively in response to the post–World War I distress in the Japanese economy. Japan had prospered during World War I as the country took over markets from Allied Powers preoccupied with the war in Europe. Thus, during the war, exports had driven the Japanese economy to double its industrial production and increase its overall range of products.[30] At the end of the war, intense speculation drove rice prices upward rapidly, to which the rice riots of 1918 were an impassioned response.[31] The ensuing recession fell most heavily upon the agrarian sector, worsened in 1922 to 1923, and, aggravated by growing over-population, threatened to escalate further thereafter.[32] The remainder of the 1920s were years of recurrent recessions and bank panics during which farmers continued to suffer disproportionately greater losses than others. From 1920 to 1925, private investment declined, and only a slight recovery occurred in 1927 before Japan joined the rest of the capitalist world in the Great Depression. A gross national product that had grown at the rate of 4.56 percent per year between 1912 and 1917 achieved only an average rate of growth of 2.75 percent between 1917 and 1931.[33] The economic slump resulted in an upsurge of unrest in the countryside. The incidence of tenants' strikes rose from fewer than 500 in 1917 to 11,136 between 1925 and 1929, and to 19,139 between 1930 and 1934.[34]

The sense of crisis engendered by these dramatic changes in Japan's economic situation was intensified by international trends that further threatened the Japanese economy. China was Japan's primary market for exports of cotton thread and cloth, which recorded steady growth from the turn of the century and peaked in 1922. As China began to experience a nationalist awakening with the May Fourth movement in 1919, however, Japanese fortunes in the China market were abruptly threatened. When Chinese began to establish their own indigenously managed textile enterprises and to deal with other Chinese rather than Japanese suppliers and merchants, Japanese exports to China fell sharply by as much as 20 percent from

1922 to 1927. Japan's textile merchants readily found new markets in the British and French East Indies and Africa, but this could only be a temporary solution to the problem, for China's nationalist awakening could be repeated elsewhere.[35] Thus, Japan would continue to be pressed for markets and raw materials abroad, and its capitalist economic development would be threatened. As a consequence of the deepening sense of economic crisis, Japanese Marxists became more deeply engaged in the study of Marx's economic theory to support the newly rekindled labor and agrarian movements. Under the influence of Bukharin's, Lenin's, and Rosa Luxemburg's theories of imperialism, from about 1922 to 1925 the study of Marx's economics came to focus on applying the concepts of monopoly capitalism and world capitalist breakdown to Japan's own political and economic structures.[36] This development established the basis for a conflict with the Comintern's problematical diagnosis of Japan as both alarmingly "imperialist" and too backward for socialist revolution.

These years, during which Marxist economic concepts were imported and debated in Japan, coincided with the establishment of economics as an independent discipline in the academic community. In April, 1919 the economics department became independent of the law faculty at Tokyo Imperial University, a precedent that was shortly followed at Kyoto Imperial University as well.[37] Almost immediately thereafter, beginning in 1922 and 1923, there was a virtual explosion in the study of the technical aspects of Marxist economics in Japanese academic circles. Yet politics remained the domain of the JCP leadership, and only late in the 1920s did individual Japanese Marxist scholars begin to integrate the philosophical and political with the economic aspects of Marxism.

The career of Kawakami Hajime, Kyoto Imperial University professor and a Marxist pioneer in Japan whose writings often appeared in translation in Chinese magazines as well, exemplified these trends.[38] Kawakami was first attracted to socialism by his concern with the social ills that resulted from Japan's rapid industrial growth during the Meiji period. The theme of human selfishness or egoism (*jiko-shugi*), which he associated with capitalism and its attendant poverty among the working class, pervaded his early writings on Western capitalist economics and on socialism. Kawakami's concern with human morality and economics prompted his brief flight to Itō Shōshin's *Muga En* (Garden of selflessness) in 1906 and inspired his popular *Shakai-shugi hyōron* (Critique of socialism) (1905) and *Binbō monogatari* (Tale of poverty) (1916).[39] Kawakami's consistent linkage of ethics with the scientific concerns of Marx's economics[40] drew harsh criticism from his student Kushida Tamizō (1885–1934) and others.[41] Many, including Kawakami himself, have credited Kushida's critique of the former's moralism with Kawakami's subsequent dedication to the study of Marxist economics and his role in the establishment of Marxism as academic subject matter in Japan.[42] At the urging of Kushida and others, Kawakami focused on economic theory and founded the journal *Shakai mondai kenkyū* (Studies on social problems) in 1919.[43] A major force in the study and dissemination of Marxism throughout its existence through October 1930, the journal carried articles on historical materialism as well as essays debating such basic concepts of Marxism as capital, wage labor, and surplus value.[44] In the meantime, Kawakami himself published a series of books on aspects of Marxian economics as well as translations of Marx's *Wage Labor and Capital* (1921) and *Wages, Profits and Value* (1921).[45] Subsequently, from 1927 to 1929, with Ōyama Ikuo, Kawakami produced *Marukusu-shugi kōza* (Symposium on Marxism), a series with articles on such basic subjects as the state and religion written from a Marxist perspective by Sano Manabu, Ōyama Ikuo, and others.[46] Among them appeared essays by Noro, "Nihon shihon-shugi hattatsu shi" (The History of the Development of Japanese Capitalism), and Hattori Shisō, "Meiji ishin shi" (The History of the Meiji Restoration), which went beyond the mere presentation of Marxist ideas on various aspects of politics and, thus, were precursors of the essays published in the *Nihon shihon-shugi hattatsu shi kōza*.[47] Together these scholarly works laid the groundwork for the systematic application of the Marxist theory of the state to Japan's imperial system.

During this period, certain scholars began to take that first crucial step toward the systematic application of Marxist theory to Japan's social and economic development that would be attained fully only in the *Rōnō-Kōza* debate. Sano Manabu (1892–1953), a lecturer in economic history at Waseda University and a Central Committee member of the newly established JCP, began to move in this direction as early as 1922. In that year, he published *Nihon shakai shi joron* (A preface to Japanese social history) and in the following year, *Nihon keizai shi gairon* (Outline of Japanese economic history).[48] These early studies were "not written from a thoroughly materialistic or Marxian point of view," Sano himself readily acknowledged.[49] Similarly, Honjō Eijirō (1888–1973), a Kyoto Imperial University professor of economics who had studied in Europe and the United States, wrote a series of books analyzing Japanese social and economic development in terms of Marxist categories albeit "from the liberal but not Marxian point of view."[50] At mid-decade, Honjō published three major works: *Nihon shakai shi* (Japanese social history) (1924); *Kinsei nōson mondai shiron* (Treatise on the modern agrarian problem) (1925); and *Nihon zaisei shi* (A history of Japanese finance) (1926).[51] Like Sano's work, Honjō's was a rudimentary effort to locate phenomena in Japanese social, political, and economic history to which Marxian concepts could be applied. These studies themselves could not by any means be regarded as comfortably within the Marxist tradition. Indeed, a significant theme that paralleled the ideas of early Chinese revolutionaries such as Sun Yat-sen[52] appeared in these writings and would be repeated in the wave of mass *tenkō* in the 1930s: the question, posed precisely as such, of the extent to which Marxist notions such as class struggle reflected any aspect of Japanese reality. Presaging Sano's post-*tenkō* formulation of a uniquely "Oriental" brand of Marxism that denied the applicability of the notion of class conflict to Japan's nonindividualistic society,[53] Honjō treated the concept of class struggle rather skeptically. His *Nihon shakai shi* essayed "an analysis of the pre-Meiji period to see whether this history is [manifested] in a class struggle or whether inter-class struggle is greater than intra-class struggle."[54] Meanwhile, Sano continued to publish on various aspects of Marxist political thought in such left-wing journals as *Marukusu-shugi* (Marxism), *Shakai kagaku* (Social Science), and *Musansha shinbun* (The Proletarian News) through 1930, but these essays were no more creative than his earlier efforts.[55]

Ironically, the most provocative and innovative work that emerged in the mid-1920s was Takahashi Kamekichi's thesis of *"puchi teikoku-shugi"* (petty imperialism). At a time when others were still struggling with fundamental Marxian concepts, Takahashi's theory exhibited a sophisticated mastery of such concepts and considerable imagination in their application to Japan. His analysis of Japanese expansionism, however, could only be regarded as an apologia for Japanese imperialism, and as such it helped to foment the debate on Japanese capitalism by drawing the fire of both Rōnō-ha dissidents and JCP loyalists. In addition, the Japanese exceptionalism that characterized Takahashi's application of Marxian categories to his own society's recent development placed the national question squarely at the center of the ensuing controversy on Japanese capitalism in three ways. First, it raised the key issue of the universality and particularity of Japan's historical experience and of the Marxist categories that Takahashi and his challengers would use to analyze it. Secondly, it problematized the issue of the legitimacy of Japanese nationalism in the age of imperialism at a time when most Japanese Marxists had placidly accepted the Comintern orthodoxy that decreed that they must oppose both Japan's imperial system and its expansionist foreign policy. This issue was, in turn, linked to the question of how one was to interpret the nature of the Japanese state and the fate of its elements in the course of a Marxian socialist revolution. That Takahashi's thesis highlighted these elements of the national question helps to explain the highly emotional reaction against it among his colleagues in the socialist movement and the impetus that it gave to their production of alternative Marxian accounts of the Japanese experience.

Takahashi Kamekichi (1891–1977) was an economist who wrote for the *Tōyō keizai shinpō-sha* (Oriental economic news agency) until 1926, when he became an independent economic historian. Educated at Waseda University, Takahashi was unable to pursue graduate work in economics or law because of financial difficulties. Thus, self-educated in Marxian economic theory, Takahashi became an avid observer of domestic and international economics during his years at the newspaper, and he cultivated a preference for empirical analysis and a healthy distrust of pure theory. He became involved in the Japanese social movement after meeting socialists Taguchi Unzō and Katayama Sen on a sojourn in the West in 1919 and 1920. On returning to Japan, he drew closer to Yamakawa and Sakai, became a founding member of the left-wing Seiji Kenkyūkai (Political Studies Association) in 1924, and was actively involved with the Nihon Nōmintō (Japanese Farmers' party), a group with both leftist and rightist leanings. After 1928, when he ran unsuccessfully for office as a Nōmintō candidate, Takahashi severed all ties with the social movement.[56] In any case, Takahashi was less influential for his political activism than for his extensive publications. He became a prolific writer, producing several dozen works on political economy by the end of World War II. In 1932, Takahashi founded his own economics institute and subsequently served as a consultant to the Japanese colonial administrations in Manchukuo and

Taiwan and as an advisor to the Japanese government in a variety of posts, most notably serving in the cabinet's War Planning Office.[57] During the war, Takahashi was also linked with more explicitly right-wing nationalist groups, such as the Shōwa Kenkyūkai, a research association that supported the government's military and economic policies in Asia.[58]

By 1927, Takahashi's pioneering scholarship on Japanese political economy had already earned him high regard among Marxist and non-Marxist scholars of economic development.[59] His thesis concerning the deadlock of the Japanese economy, the *yukizumari-ron*, was presented in his *Nihon shihon-shugi keizai no kenkyū* (Studies on the Japanese capitalist economy) in 1924 and quickly became influential in the left-wing movement. The yukizumari thesis nicely mirrored the distressing economic realities confronting Japan in the 1920s. Briefly, Takahashi argued that Japanese capitalism had become "deadlocked" before reaching its highest point of development. Unlike more advanced capitalist countries that had already reached the monopoly stage, then, Japan's deadlock could be broken by state policies designed to restore the conditions that had promoted Japan's economic growth from the middle to the end of the Meiji period. "The soil that has nurtured the development of our capitalism from its infancy to maturity has . . . become exhausted of its main nutritive elements; . . . many contradictions inherent in the development of capitalism have intensified, and thus it has become impossible for our economy to continue the capitalistic development [it has sustained] up to now."[60]

The ingredients of Japan's prior growth to which Takahashi referred were the following: (1) a growth in productive forces achieved by the importation and refinement of "modern science and technology" from Europe and the United States; (2) the effect of this growth in productive forces to render previously unexploited natural resources useful; and (3) a generous supply of cheap labor. These factors had enabled the Japanese economy to peak, but then it had begun to stagnate immediately after World War I. Mineral production figures testified amply to this stagnation. Copper production fell 44 percent from its peak in 1919 to 1927; silver production declined by 39 percent from 1917 to 1927; coal production dropped by 11 percent from 1919 to 1922, rising briefly but falling short of its 1919 level in 1927; oil production had slipped from its 1919 peak by 44 percent by 1927; and sulphur production in 1927 was less than half of its 1917 level. In the agrarian sector, the area of cultivated land peaked in 1922 at 6,090,000 chō (1 chō = 2.45 acres) and fell gradually to 6,081,000 chō in 1927. Takahashi attributed these trends to the disappearance of the aforementioned elements of earlier success combined with new impediments to the development of Japanese capitalism that had emerged domestically and internationally. Among these were rising wages resulting from the growth of unionism in the wake of the Bolshevik revolution, the undermining of supportive measures such as import duties, the intensification of competition from later-industrializing societies, and, most importantly, obstacles placed in the path of Japanese economic expansion by rising nationalism in less-industrialized societies, especially China.[61]

This work, offered by Takahashi to account for the abrupt downturn in Japan's economic fortunes after World War I, was methodologically and theoretically far superior to the earlier studies of Sano and Honjō, and it was satisfying and reassuring in its demonstration that Marxian economic categories could, indeed, help to interpret the pattern of Japan's development since the late-Tokugawa era. What Takahashi offered as the solution to Japan's economic impasse, however, was provocative and unsettling to his peers in the left-wing movement. This solution, elaborated in an article entitled "Nihon shihon-shugi no teikoku-shugi-teki chi'i" (The imperialistic position of Japanese capitalism), denied the applicability of Lenin's understanding of imperialism to Japan's international behavior and endorsed Japanese expansion onto the Asian mainland. Takahashi claimed that because of the peculiarities of capitalist development in Japan, Lenin's theory of imperialism was not fully applicable to it: Japanese capitalism had "not yet attained the stage of imperialism" in the Leninist sense. On the contrary, Takahashi asserted, Japan's relative backwardness by comparison with Western Europe and the United States, where finance and monopoly capital flourished, placed Japan "in the position of a country subject to imperialism." Japan, which remained a net capital-importing country, was not yet a society whose expansionist activities were powered by the needs of finance capital.

> Japan may be imperialistic; however, it is at the most an imperialistic country such as the petty bourgeoisie is to the *grande bourgeoisie*; if we can establish the category of petty [bourgeois] imperialism in the manner of the term petty bourgeoisie, then Japan is merely a *petty-imperialist country*. Thus, just as the interests of the petty bourgeoisie coincide with those of the proletariat rather than [those of] the *grande bourgeoisie*, the interests of petty imperialist countries coincide more with those of [countries] subject to imperialism than with those of large imperialist countries; consequently . . . if we consider Japan's international position, Japan is now in a position in which it is difficult [for it] to avoid inevitably bearing the hues of a nationalist [*kokumin-teki*] movement in the anti-imperialist movement.[62]

"While Japan has colonies in Korea, Taiwan, and Manchuria, these incursions do not necessarily signify what today's Left calls 'imperialism'," Takahashi declared. Japan's expansionism was absolutely essential "for the sake of Japan's independence and self-support." In short, in the international arena, Japan, like the societies of other Asian peoples, was an oppressed country exploited by the "international irrationality and immorality" of the "white races" of Europe and America. Japan's relatively advanced economic status among the peoples of Asia only destined Japan to take leadership in liberating the "yellow peoples" of the world from the yoke of the exploitation of the West.[63]

Much to the consternation of Takahashi's peers in the Marxist movement, his argument had a certain perverse logic, however unpalatable his conclusions. Takahashi's views helped to account for the unmistakable trend of increasingly expansionist Japanese militarism that coincided with the consolidation of the Meiji state. This militarism had been evident in the defeat of China in the 1894–1895 war, the 1905 triumph over Russia, the Twenty-One Demands presented to China in 1915, Japan's participation in and extension of the Siberian expedition against the new

Soviet regime, participation in World War I, and the preparations in the 1920s for the move into Manchuria. Yet the peculiarities of Japan's own pattern of development caused Takahashi to call into question the universality of Lenin's definition of imperialism as "the highest stage of capitalism." Noting the phenomenon of imperialism on the part of less-industrialized countries, Takahashi's analysis approached Takabatake Motoyuki's argument for state socialism premised on the possible dangers of "proletarian imperialism."[64] In addition, Takahashi asserted that because of Japan's status as a late-industrializer, there was a qualitative difference in the 1920s between Japan's expansionism and the imperialism of the advanced capitalist states, the United States, Great Britain, and Germany. Given its dearth of raw materials, Japan had never flourished as a heavy capital goods-producing country, and as a late-developer, it had been deprived of the benefits of free trade. Tariff barriers had already been erected and economic spheres of influence carved out in Asia and Africa by the time Japan entered the world market.[65] Moreover, Japanese imperialism would continue to differ from that of Western Europe and the United States in the future as it had in the past: it would continue to have to appeal to military rather than to economic expansion first, because Japan lacked the financial forces and industrial power that impelled the imperialistic development of the Western powers.[66] Thus, Takahashi's interpretation suggested what other Marxists dared not: that no later-industrializing society could be expected to duplicate the pattern of development of those that industrialized first because of the international conditions established by that earlier capitalist industrialization. At the same time, Takahashi's views managed to incorporate what would be the Rōnō-ha's emphasis on Japan's economic progress with the future Kōza-ha stress on Japan's underdevelopment relative to the earlier industrializers of the West. Finally, the entire argument was couched in terms of the Marxian ideal of proletarian socialist revolution. The reason that Japan must break the impasse in its capitalist development, Takahashi urged, was that if Japanese capitalism failed to reach its fullest potential, the proletarian socialist revolution so fervently desired by the Left would be postponed indefinitely.

The challenge to those on the left who would defend Lenin's anti-imperialist orthodoxy was clear: an alternative, equally rigorous and compelling, Marxist interpretation of Japanese development would have to be articulated. Either it would have to be demonstrated that Japanese capitalism was already highly developed enough to fit Lenin's five criteria for imperialism, as the Rōnō-ha (behind Inomata Tsunao) would do, or one would have to argue, as Noro and the Kōza-ha would, that Japan was indeed still very much a feudalistic society and that the impetus for Japanese military expansion came from an alliance of the ruling classes of the old feudal order with those of the rising capitalist structure.[67] In any case, the problem posed by Takahashi's work articulated the pivotal theoretical problem of the entire debate on Japanese capitalism: How could one analyze Japanese political and economic development so that it fit into the model provided by Marx and Lenin? How could the peculiarities of Japan's situation be accommodated to the Marxist-Leninist model without surrendering to those who would, like Takahashi, manipulate the Marxian framework to legitimate an ultra-rightist military policy that would bear an uncomfortable resemblance to the doctrine of the Greater East Asia Co-Prosperity Sphere? Finally, and most importantly, Takahashi's petty imperialism thesis exposed for all to see the inconsistencies of a Comintern position that called for a revolution against Japanese backwardness while denouncing Japan for nationalistic and "imperialist" designs that Lenin himself had claimed were characteristic only of advanced capitalist countries. The Comintern's insistence late in 1927 that Japan was even more backward than its leaders had believed in 1922 prompted the final rejection of this untenable position by the Rōnō-ha.

COMINTERN THESES AND THE CONTROVERSY ON REVOLUTIONARY STRATEGY AND TACTICS

As Marxist theory was being imported and assimilated in Japan during the 1920s, the authoritative source of guidance for Japan's Marxist revolutionary movement was the Soviet-led Communist International. The Comintern theses issued from Moscow in the 1920s and the 1930s established guidelines for the operation of the Japanese Communist party, and the first indigenous theoretical efforts, Yamakawa-ism and Fukumotoism, were formulated largely in response to these pronouncements. It was in reaction to the Comintern theses that the controversy on revolutionary strategy and tactics that later evolved into the debate on Japanese capitalism first arose. In many respects, then, the Comintern's directives stimulated, if they failed to constrain, the contributions made by participants in the debate on Japanese capitalism.

Four major Comintern directives shaped the controversy over revolutionary strategy and tactics:[68] the 1922 Draft Program of the JCP, the 1927 (July) Theses on the Japan Problem, the 1931 Draft Political Theses, and the 1932 Theses on the Situation in Japan and the Tasks of the Communist Party. Many factors affected the Comintern's recommendations, including Soviet perceptions of the changing international environment and responses to developments in Japan; indeed, at times, the theses reflected internal political conflicts within the Soviet Union of which JCP followers in Japan were only vaguely aware. Nevertheless, whatever their weaknesses and the circumstances that gave rise to them, the Comintern's theses offered applications of Marxist theory to contemporary Japan, however inconsistently, and to those, all who would offer such formulations themselves were compelled to respond. As a result, the Comintern's theses, particularly the 1927 Theses that precipitated the secession of the Rōnō-ha from the struggling party, were an essential catalyst of the debate on Japanese capitalism.

The Soviet leaders who formulated the Comintern's directives on Japan had the opportunity to consult with Japanese representatives to the Comintern such as Katayama Sen, but they themselves had almost no firsthand knowledge of Japan. Instead, they relied on implicit or explicit analogies between Japan's political and economic development and Russian conditions in the revolutions of 1905 and February and October of 1917. More importantly, as the headquarters of the international socialist movement, the Third International always formulated its theses on Japan in the context of the international movement. Thus, Japan strategy, like the strategy for the Chinese Communist party, was consistently conceived as part of the Comintern's general strategy for world revolution.

Throughout the 1920s and 1930s, this was a "united front" strategy. An outgrowth of the Russian revolutionary experience and the failure of the Russian revolution to kindle proletarian socialist revolutions in the more advanced capitalist countries of Western Europe, the united front strategy envisaged an international smychka (alliance) that would reproduce on an international scale the alliance between workers and peasants that had brought the Bolsheviks to power in Russia. This conception visualized a schematic alliance between the peasants of national liberation movements in the East and workers in advanced capitalist countries in the West: Wars of national liberation in countries subjected to imperialism would sever the essential link of imperialist domination that allowed the economies of advanced countries in the West to prosper, thereby provoking economic distress and proletarian socialist revolutions in the advanced capitalist societies of the West.[69]

Nevertheless, the peculiarities of Japan's situation made it difficult to apply this strategy to Japan. On the one hand, the fact that Japan's industrial sector was highly industrialized (and that Soviet leaders feared a renewal of Japanese militarism directed against their homeland) dictated that Japan be counted among the advanced capitalist societies of the West. This meant that nationalism could have no legitimate place in the strategy for the Japanese revolution. On the other hand, the so-called "dual structure" of the Japanese economy[70]—the persistence of a lagging agrarian sphere that had not yet undergone commercialization alongside an advanced industrialized urban sphere—called into question Japan's status as an advanced capitalist power. These peculiarities, underscored by an "Orientalist" predisposition[71] to see Japan and other Asian societies as consistently more backward than Russia, were accentuated by the presence of a system of imperial rule that was heavily imbued with a mystical religious cast. Thus, virtually all the Comintern's pronouncements on Japan between 1922 and 1932 stressed Japan's backwardness and insisted that socialist revolution could come to Japan only through two stages.

From the very outset, then, the dualism in Japan's political and economic situation—the coexistence of modern capitalism with aspects of the former order—forced the Comintern to emphasize one aspect or the other; and when the 1922 Draft Program of the JCP emphasized backwardness, there was the potential for conflict between the Comintern's diagnosis and the views of the future Rōnō-ha leader Yamakawa. The 1922 Draft Program, formulated by Bukharin as leader of the Comintern's Japan Commission,[72] clearly set forth the problematic "issue of the complex nature of class relations in capitalist Japan"[73] to which it would be difficult to apply either the strategies devised for the colonial peoples of the East or those proposed for the defunct movements in Western Europe. It was already clear in the early 1922 document that the continued existence of the imperial institution posed major theoretical difficulties in defining the current stage of Japan's political and economic development. Extensive debate on the provision that the party seek to abolish the institution hampered the JCP's deliberations on the draft, and some, including the subsequent leading tenkōsha Sano Manabu, remained unpersuaded and conceded the issue only with reluctance. At this point, a major concern for the party was pragmatic: Would it be prudent for the young, struggling party to risk alienating a population that was emotionally attached to the Imperial Household by advocating its elimination? Many felt that while the Draft Program correctly recognized the tremendous economic gains that Japan had made during World War I, "it ignored the general national[istic] sentiment that had emerged as a result." Instead, the program equated the Japanese emperor to the Russian tsar, thus drawing an analogy that was inaccurate as well as unpalatable to loyal believers in the uniqueness of the Japanese emperor.[74] At the same time, Japan was recognized as a special case in which the coexistence of feudal remnants alongside the bourgeoisie made the task of defining an appropriate revolutionary strategy unusually difficult. The document went on to describe the emperor in terms that evoked Marx's imagery of the Asian despot:

[T]oday Japanese capitalism still retains some traces of the feudal relations of the previous era. Most of the land is in the hands of large semi-feudal landlords; the greatest among those is the emperor (mikado) as the head of the Japanese government. . . . The remnants of feudalism still occupy a dominant position in the state structure today: the state organs are still held in the hands of a bloc comprised of a certain part of the commercial and industrial bourgeoisie and large landlords. The special semi-feudalistic nature of state power is expressed clearly by the major and guiding role that the *genrō* (note: read "nobility") have in the constitution. Under such conditions, the forces opposed to the existing state power not only arise from the working class, the peasants, and the petty bourgeoisie, but also arise from a broad segment of the so-called liberal bourgeoisie—they too are opposed to the existing government.[75]

The limits of Japan's capitalist development were, thus, evidenced economically by the power of Japan's large landholders, which constituted the power base of the imperial state. Thus, it was clear that Japan urgently required the completion of a bourgeois revolution that had only been begun by the Meiji Restoration. This was the necessary prerequisite for any future proletarian socialist revolution.

In short, although the 1922 Draft Program recognized the special characteristics of Japan's situation, Bukharin's emphasis on Japan's backwardness and his prescription of a bourgeois revolution amounted to applying to Japan virtually the same strategy that had been devised for the "semicolonial" countries of India and China, despite Japan's superior economic development. This tended to confirm the suspicion that in the absence of adequate concrete familiarity with Japan's realities, Comintern leaders simply classified Japan uncritically along with other later-industrializing Asian countries and formulated its revolutionary strategy accordingly. This would be difficult for many in Japan to accept, for Japanese intellectuals at the time tended to view tsarist Russia—to which 1922 Japan was being likened—as considerably backward in comparison with Taishō Japan.[76]

Even as the new Draft Program was being transported back to Japan and JCP members were deliberating on it, there were emerging already within the party elements of the doctrine of Yamakawaism that would subsequently support the Rōnō-ha's rejection of the Comintern strategy. There would be three basic tenets of the Rōnō-ha position: (1) that the JCP should be dissolved and replaced "with a social-democratic political party (a united front party)"; (2) the view that "feudal remnants in the village are not rooted in the land system, so a struggle over land is not of major importance" to the revolution; and (3) that "the emperor system since the Meiji period has been essentially a bourgeois monarchy, and absolutist structures are merely . . . remnants that are no longer of any significance. Thus a bourgeois-democratic struggle to overthrow the emperor system is not necessary."[77] Immediately after the formation of the JCP, some of these elements began to materialize as Yamakawa worked to devise a revolutionary strategy for the Japanese socialist movement. In August of that year, Yamakawa's article "Musan-kaikyū undō no hōkō tenkan" (A change of direction in the proletarian movement), responded to the Comintern's 1921 slogans "To the masses!" and "Advance toward political struggle" by advocating the "massification" (*taishū-ka*) of the JCP and a dramatic move out of the "winter period" through political struggle.[78] Subsequently, in 1924 and 1925, Yamakawa would elaborate on this theme by advocating a single united front political party. His essay "Tan'itsu musan-kaikyūtō ron" (On a single proletarian political party), maintained that the JCP had now made it possible for the proletariat to organize legally and openly and, thus, rejected Lenin's vanguard party concept as inappropriate to Japan. Although the proletariat would comprise the core of the new party, it would embrace "all organized and unorganized laborers, peasants, and lower levels of the middle class and all anti-capitalist movements and organization."[79] This vision drew censure as "Japanese-style legalism and dissolutionism," and many argued that Yamakawa's failure to take the imperial system into sufficient account made it impossible for him to support his repudiation of the vanguard party idea.[80]

Despite its divergences from orthodox Leninism, Yamakawa's views on the "massification" of the party were immediately adopted as JCP policy. But within one year, the intense police repression that kept the party from formally adopting its Draft Program led Yamakawa to advocate the party's dissolution. In his view, a party that had to operate in secret would become alienated from the masses and, thus, ineffective. As party leader, Yamakawa prevailed, and the party was dissolved in March 1924, less than two years after its birth. Between 1924 and 1926, Yamakawa found himself in agreement with the Comintern insomuch as he was advocating a united front. Moreover, in 1926, as the party was being reorganized, the Comintern temporarily altered its estimation of the situation in Japan in the "Moscow Theses," adopted at the Sixth Comintern Executive Committee Plenum. The new theses' claim that "the bloc political power of capitalists and landlords hitherto under the hegemony of the landlords now was completely under the hegemony of the bourgeoisie" and, thus, that a bourgeois revolution was no longer necessary, brought the Comintern closer to Yamakawa's position and introduced considerable confusion among Japan's Marxists.[81] This sense of disorientation was only relieved when the 1927 Theses returned to the Draft Program's emphasis on Japan's backwardness.

If Yamakawa was in temporary agreement with the Comintern on revolutionary strategy and tactics, he was in new conflict with his successor as leader of the reborn JCP, Fukumoto Kazuo. When the party was reorganized, many had been dissatisfied with Yamakawa's leadership and turned to the freshness of Fukumoto's mastery of Marxist theory and his stress on the need for a vanguard party.[82] Fukumoto's notion of a vanguard party based on theoretical expertise and ideological purity achieved through constant struggle within the Left emerged as the dominant force within the movement in the mid-1920s. Just before the Moscow Theses were issued, Fukumoto claimed that "Japan's bourgeoisie had still been unable to destroy the so-called absolutist-autocratic forces."[83] Thus, Fukumoto came into conflict with Yamakawa on both organizational theory and the analysis of the Japanese state. Fukumoto's ascendancy was shortlived, however. His personality, his pedantic manner, and his increasing influence among youth eventually alienated many within the left-wing movement.[84] Opposition crystallized during his trip to Moscow in March 1927. Comintern leaders also turned against him when they heard a report by Nabeyama Sadachika that criticized Fukumotoism and its potentially harmful effects on the movement.[85] The 1927 Theses roundly denounced Fukumoto for his "abstract" theory of organization that threatened to isolate the party from the masses but also denounced Yamakawaism for the opposite deviation.[86] More importantly, the new theses returned to the Draft Program's emphasis on Japan's backwardness, particularly in the countryside, as the basis for a policy of two-stage revolution. As the vanguard of the proletariat, the JCP would lead a united front of revolutionary workers, peasants, and "urban petty bourgeois" in completing the bourgeois-democratic revolution begun by the Meiji Restoration. The Comintern thus maintained the notion of a united front between the JCP and other progressive left-wing organizations, but now stressed that "the communist party absolutely must not lose its independence" and must "make no ideological concessions."[87] Clearly, the lessons of the disastrous Comintern "bloc-within" strategy subordinating the CCP to the Guomindang in China were not lost on the Comintern's Japan Committee.[88]

Despite the new theses' clear return to the premises of the 1922 Draft Program, however, there were ambiguities in its position on the state and its economic basis that helped to provoke the vigorous opposition of Yamakawa, Sakai, and Arahata. On the one hand, the Comintern underscored the semifeudal nature of state power and stressed the robust persistence of absolutism in the feudal elements of the state. On the other hand, however, confronted with "Japanese imperialism . . . on a rising curve of development," the Comintern was led to emphasize the high level of development of Japanese capitalism in the urban sphere to account for Japanese imperialism. Thus, the theses claimed that "the present Japanese government is in the hands of a bloc of the capitalists and landlords," but as the motivator of Japan's imperialist policies particularly in China, clearly the bourgeoisie was dominant. Thus, the emperor himself was dual in character: "The Mikado [emperor] is not only a big landowner, but also a very rich stockholder in many stock companies and combines; he also has his own bank, with assets of 100 million yen."[89] The state, then, was capitalistic but not yet a bourgeois-democratic state. The logical difficulties of the Comintern's effort to explain this circumstance are fully evident in the following paragraph:

The struggle for the democratization of the Japanese state, the abolition of the monarchy, and the removal of the present ruling cliques from the government in a country with such a high level of capital concentration will therefore inevitably change from a struggle against feudal survivals into a struggle against capitalism itself. The bourgeois-democratic revolution of Japan will rapidly grow into a socialist revolution precisely because the contemporary Japanese state, with all its feudal attributes and relics, is the most concentrated expression of Japanese capitalism, embodying a whole series of its most vital nerves; to strike at the state is to strike at the capitalist system as a whole.[90]

In short, the Comintern now called for a bourgeois revolution against a state that was dominated by the bourgeoisie.

Not surprisingly, then, Yamakawa and others claimed that the new theses actually supported a strategy of one-stage revolution.[91] They were, in fact, consistent with the claim of the 1926 Moscow Theses, which had asserted that capital had gained hegemony in the landlord-capitalist bloc ruling the Japanese state.[92] As Rōnō-ha sympathizer Tsushima Tadayuki has argued, "the establishment of bourgeois hegemony in state power and the holistic existence of absolutism cannot be reconciled."[93] In other words, in the 1927 Theses, the Comintern prescribed a revolutionary strategy that was inconsistent with its own interpretation of the political situation. Thus, even Kōza-ha sympathizers Koyama Hirotake and Kishimoto Eitarō have conceded that the 1927 Theses "reproduced in more obvious form the contradictions and confusion of the previous 1926 Moscow Theses."[94] Nevertheless, with a new Central Committee designated at the behest of the Comintern, the 1927 Theses became the JCP's official strategy. When the Rōnō-ha seceded from the party in December 1927, the conflict over strategy and tactics gathered momentum as the debate on Japanese capitalism.

The relief from the confusion of the 1926 Moscow Theses that Comintern loyalists in the JCP must have felt on hearing of the prescription for two-stage revolution in the 1927 Theses was temporary at best. Within four years—under new leadership after Bukharin's fall from power in late 1929—the Comintern had issued the 1931 Draft Political Theses. Here the Rōnō-ha found the most emphatic support it ever received from the Soviet leadership of the international Communist movement for its strategy of one-stage revolution. Perhaps as part of Stalin's effort to remove "Bukharinist" influences from Comintern policy,[95] perhaps in response to the new international depression that had descended in 1929,[96] or even in reaction to the suppression of the Hamaguchi cabinet,[97] the 1931 Theses called for intensified class struggle and an immediate one-step "proletarian revolution broadly embracing bourgeois-democratic responsibilities."[98] The new theses, formulated by the Comintern in late 1930, completely contradicted the analysis of the 1927 Theses, arguing that the Japanese state was dominated by monopoly capital.[99] The new policy would be implemented under a new JCP leadership headed by Kazama Jōkichi, who carried them by memory from the Fifth Profintern Congress of August 1930 in Moscow back to Japan. Nevertheless, like the party's original program, this document too remained a "draft," for it did not have the formal approval of the many high-level JCP officials who were in prison at the time.[100]

The presentation of a one-stage revolutionary strategy in the 1931 Draft Political Theses placed the JCP leadership in the awkward position of seeming to adopt wholesale the analysis of the Kaitō-ha and of the Rōnō-ha that had seceded from the party in dissent over the 1927 Theses. Party Central immediately endeavored, unconvincingly, to differentiate the Comintern's 1931 formula from those of the dissident factions by claiming that its version recognized "the bourgeois-democratic responsibilities to be embraced within the basic responsibilities of the socialist revolution." Because the Rōnō-ha did not believe that agriculture remained semifeudal, the "emperor system had already become but an ornament of the bourgeoisie without any real basis."[101] But by late-1932, such verbal subterfuge was no longer necessary, as the Comintern's 1932 Theses had already returned to its prescription of two-stage revolution. The 1931 Draft Political Theses were denounced as "Trotskyist," its author, the Asianist George Safarov, had been removed from the Comintern, and a new set of theses drafted by former Bukharin supporter Kuusinen invoked the Bukharinist analysis of the Japanese state to return to the revolutionary strategy of the 1922 Draft Program and the 1927 Theses.[102] Heightened Soviet fears of Japanese militarism on the Asian continent were reflected in the use of highly emotional language describing Japanese society as "barbaric," "backward," and "feudalistic." The connection between Japanese imperialism and the feudal elements in the emperor system and ruling military cliques was emphasized in the renewed call for a bourgeois-democratic revolution that must begin by overthrowing these feudalistic elements.[103]

The 1932 Theses were accepted as official JCP policy and published in Japanese in July 1932 with some discomfiture on the part of the Party Central that had been established to implement the conflicting 1931 Theses the previous year.[104] The new theses placed renewed emphasis on the imperial system as the " 'principal bulwark of the political reaction and of all the relics of feudalism in the country'."[105] The new theses produced a theory of the state that incorporated an analysis of the agrarian economic base with an interpretation of the superstructural emperor system as a unified whole. A pessimistic document indeed, the 1932 Theses posited a strategy for Japan that was based on a recognition of those troublesome and unique aspects of Japanese society that had plagued Bukharin and the JCP from the outset. The 1932 Theses combined an analysis of these Japanese peculiarities with an outlook that placed Japan at a stage of development on a par with that of prerevolutionary tsarist Russia, prescribing the workers', peasants', and soldiers' soviets that were familiar from the Russian revolution.[106]

Most fascinating was the 1932 Theses' interpretation of the Japanese state. Here again, the Comintern undertook the task of reconciling the contradictory elements of the 1927 Theses' analysis of the state as both the repository of semifeudal elements and the agent of imperialist maneuvers in Asia. This the Comintern endeavored to do by highlighting the symbiotic relationship between urban capitalist elements and feudalistic elements in the agrarian sector. Japan's absolutism, the theses maintained, was based on the combination of an industrially advanced bourgeoisie and "Asiatically backward semi-feudal rule in the villages that obstructs the development of Japan's agrarian forces of production and accelerates the deterioration of agriculture and impoverishment of the main masses of peasants." "Japan's emperor system . . . stands on a parasitic feudal class mainly as a landlord, and on the other hand, also stands on a rapacious bourgeoisie that is becoming wealthy rapidly." The upcoming revolution must complete the bourgeois-democratic tasks undertaken by the Meiji Restoration by destroying this absolutist state power—resting on a balance of class forces—which was oppressive within and militaristically expansive without.[107]

The 1932 Theses were the last systematic analysis of Japan presented by the Comintern. As the most complete and provocative interpretation of the Japanese state, it had a significant impact on the continued debate on Japanese capitalism that had begun with the 1927 Theses. The analysis of the imperial state, a major point discussed in the document, was in fact a primary axis of conflict between the Rōnō-ha and the Kōza-ha, and the debate escalated sharply on this issue until it was forcibly terminated in 1937.

Between 1927 and 1937, then, the controversy evolved in a manner that focused tremendous energy on the analysis of the Japanese state. Because the 1932 Theses offered the Comintern's most thorough depiction of the so-called emperor system (tennō-sei) to date, participants in the debate on Japanese capitalism, particularly on the Kōza-ha side, began to devote considerable effort to the rigorous analysis of the Japanese state. During these years, the controversy produced two distinct approaches with radically opposing assessments. The Rōnō-ha's relatively less subtle analysis, developed in immediate response to the 1927 Theses, reflected a straightforwardly instrumentalist interpretation of the state. By contrast, the Kōza-ha made a sustained effort to understand the Comintern's depiction of the tennō-sei as the core of an absolutist rather than a bourgeois state in the context of Japan's historical development since the late Tokugawa period (*bakumatsu*). This endeavor led the Kōza-ha to develop a more structuralist approach to the state and forced its scholars to deal with such issues as the concept of the Asiatic mode of production in their effort to account for the continuing centralized power of the Japanese state. The controversy over the nature of the state and the role of the Japanese "national character" in determining those qualities came to occupy a central place in that debate.

THE RŌNŌ-HA: AN INSTRUMENTALIST APPROACH TO THE JAPANESE STATE

Yamakawaism and the 1927 Theses

The Rōnō-ha's approach to the Japanese state was derived directly from the Yamakawaist strategy and tactics that had dominated the JCP at its inception. Yamakawaism had persisted as opposition to Fukumotoism in 1925 and 1926, and it took on new significance when the 1927 Theses appeared. The publication of the journal *Rōnō* in response to the theses marked the reemergence of Yamakawaism in the form of Rōnō-ha theory.[108]

National pride figured heavily in the Rōnō-ha's dramatic rejection of the 1927 Theses and the JCP under Comintern authority. The group immediately identified itself as a group of "non-Communist party Marxists,"[109] the first Japanese Marxists to accept Marxism but reject Leninism as a universal model of socialist revolution. Yamakawa wrote explicitly on the limitations of the Russian model of two-step revolution:

> That Bolshevism is a development of Marxism does not mean that it is the only [possible] development from Marx's basic theory . . . but means that it made Marx's basic theory develop within the practice of the revolutionary movement, in response to the special conditions of the Russian Revolution. In that sense, the revolutionary movements of individual countries must develop their own respective revolutionary theories. . . . It does not mean to imitate German Social-Democracy or Russian Communism (Bolshevism); but it is necessary to return to Marx and begin from there.[110]

Thus, the group around Yamakawa and Inomata did not accept the Comintern and JCP analogy between Russian and Japanese absolutism requiring a bourgeois revolution that would overthrow the imperial system.[111] In addition—and this was deeply resented by those in the Kōza-ha—the Rōnō-ha underscored its relatively less antagonistic position vis-à-vis the Japanese state when it sought to distinguish itself, in the eyes of the authorities, from orthodox members of the JCP who were loyal to the Comintern line. This move was directly linked to the March 15 (1928) government repression of the left-wing movement in which 1,568 persons were arrested, and the April 10 Incident in which the Nihon Rōdō Kumiai Hyōgikai (Japanese Council of Labor Unions), the Rōdō Nōmintō (Labor-Farmer Party), and the Musan Seinen Dōmei (Proletarian Youth League) were all banned.[112] Rejecting the label "social democrats" levied against them by labor activist Watanabe Masanosuke[113] and insisting that the Rōnō-ha was but a different school of Marxism, Yamakawa, Inomata, and Arahata issued a joint statement carefully distinguishing themselves from the more "extremist" and dangerous communist elements who rightly should be repressed.[114]

While the Rōnō-ha came into conflict with the Comintern, however, the dissidents were not unanimous in their attitudes toward Moscow. Yamakawa questioned "the very existence of the Comintern" and objected in principle to "the control and leadership over the [Japanese] movement by any international organ." By contrast, Inomata suggested that the dissidents try "to make the Comintern regard the Rōnō-ha as the orthodox form of Japanese Marxism, by proving the correctness of the Rōnō-ha's theory and practice."[115] Consequently, Inomata was more inclined to address seriously Noro's theoretical support for the strategy of two-stage revolution and eventually became less attached to the Yamakawa group. He developed a consistent approach to the Japanese state to accompany the economic interpretations of Japanese capitalism and the agrarian problem offered by Kushida Tamizō and Tsuchiya Takao. By contrast, Yamakawa wrote primarily with reference to the practical movement and, thus, developed only an analysis of the Japanese state to support the first of the three major elements of Rōnō-ha thought, the concept of a united front proletarian political party.

In his essay "Seiji-teki tōitsu sensen e!" (To a political united front!) in the premier issue of the journal *Rōnō*, Yamakawa laid the groundwork for Inomata's treatment of the Japanese state. Reviewing the historical course by which Japan had attained the "stage of monopoly finance capital," Yamakawa argued that the Meiji Restoration, as Japan's bourgeois revolution, had "proclaimed the transition from feudal society to capitalist society." He acknowledged that the revolution had been led not by Japan's "weak and immature" bourgeoisie but by "mainly lower-stratum *bushi*"; the latter, having lost their own economic basis, "could stand on the economic base of the rising bourgeoisie and represent that class's interests . . . as [their] only means of survival." Because political power did not fall into the hands of the bourgeoisie immediately, a transitional autocratic "hanbatsu" government emerged, and the completion of the tasks of bourgeois revolution required an additional half-century. The hanbatsu regime was a bureaucratic and military regime that itself lacked any economic basis and represented the interests of the still rising bourgeoisie. These "absolutist remnant forces" were gradually assimilated into the forces of the bourgeoisie during the development of capitalism through four processes: (1) the maturation and strengthening of the bourgeoisie; (2) the reduction of the dependence of state capital on private capital and the increased significance of the former; (3) the decline of the significance of agriculture and the transformation of landlords into capitalists; and (4) the deepening of the imperialist nature of Japanese capitalism, the expansion of the dominance of monopolistic finance capital, and the increase in the reaction of the bourgeoisie. Together these transformations demonstrated the growing power of bourgeois forces secured by the supportive association of the state with private capital. Over the decades that these changes occurred, Japan turned decisively from a transitional absolutist regime to one in which the bourgeoisie could rule effectively.

The final consolidation of the rule of the bourgeoisie, Yamakawa argued, was apparent in the birth of a party cabinet system. In 1928 and 1929, therefore, the proletariat confronted "an imperialistic, reactionary, bourgeois political power which [had] assimilated and strengthened the absolutist remnant forces." Therefore, there was no "fundamental opposition" between the remnant forces of the "nobility, bureaucracy, *gunbatsu* [military cliques], etc." and the bourgeoisie. At the same time, there was increased opposition to the bourgeoisie in the countryside among the non-landowning classes, because of the "impoverishment of peasants and the semi-serf semi-proletarian character of peasant farmers." This resulted in an alliance between the "imperialistic bourgeoisie" and rural landlords that was evident in economic concessions made by the former to the latter. Thus, the Comintern's interpretation that perceived a division between the Seiyūkai (Rikken Seiyūkai, Friends of Constitutional Government Association), as a landlord party, and the Kenseikai (Constitutional Association), as an urban commercial and industrial bourgeois party, was completely mistaken by 1928. Rather, the combination of the two forces, abetted by the extension of universal suffrage in 1925, had resulted in "the bourgeoisie and the proletariat . . . being the only two classes directly opposing each other." This situation paralleled the Russian case not on the eve of, but after, the February revolution and the end of the tsarist autocracy,[116] and

Yamakawa offered his anti-Fukumotoist organizational strategy of the united front political party to galvanize opposition to the "reactionary imperialist bourgeoisie." The new party would struggle not simply for the JCP's demand of "bourgeois democracy" against "absolutist autocracy" but for the democracy demanded by "the workers, peasants, and all other laboring and oppressed people" "against the rule of the imperialist bourgeoisie."[117]

There were, however, many problems with Yamakawa's concept of the united front. Yamakawa never really responded to the question of why the left-wing movement required a proletarian political party as a "special form of the united front." As of 1928, Yamakawa argued, Japan needed a merger of the four proletarian political parties.[118] But could this demand be met? Was a single proletarian political party a viable and defensible strategy under Japan's "special" conditions? To Inomata Tsunao fell the task of answering these questions with a detailed analysis of the contemporary Japanese state.

Inomata Tsunao and the Development of an Instrumentalist Approach to the Japanese State

The definitive presentation of the Rōnō-ha analysis of the Japanese state was offered by Inomata Tsunao's "Gendai Nihon burujoajii no seiji-teki chi'i" (The political position of the contemporary Japanese bourgeoisie), published in the November 1927 issue of *Taiyō* (The Sun). Inomata grounded his analysis in the 1927 Theses's stipulation that "the contemporary Japanese state, despite all its feudal appendages and remnants, is the most concentrated expression of Japanese capitalism and the embodiment of its entire central nervous system."[119] Inomata agreed with the 1927 Theses that "absolutism (*zettai-shugi*), as a feudal remnant in Japan, was physically represented in such institutions as the Privy Council, the House of Peers, the General Staff Headquarters, the *i' aku jōsō* [direct appeal to the throne by the military]," and in "feudalistic" ideology.[120] The burden of Inomata's analysis, then, was to demonstrate the extent to which rule by feudal autocratic forces had given way to a mature bourgeois state in Japan. In so doing, Inomata developed an instrumentalist approach to the Japanese state, showing how specific state activities could be traced to the interests of the newly empowered bourgeoisie.

Interestingly, Inomata applied Bukharin's observations on the nature of the advanced capitalist state to Japan.[121] Anxious to disprove the Comintern's thesis on the continued significance of "feudal autocratic" militaristic forces in Japan, however, Inomata confined his reliance on Bukharin to treat the more superficial indicators of the influence of the bourgeoisie in Japanese politics rather than drawing on Bukharin's observations on the increasing role of the military in the capitalist state in the age of imperialism. Fellow Rōnō-ha Marxist Okada Sōji (1902–1975) agreed with Bukharin that "what is 'militarist' today is not only Japanese capitalism, but is a characteristic common to all capitalist countries."[122] Nevertheless, Inomata maintained that the military was a feudal remnant, and as such it did not figure prominently in his conception of the Japanese capitalist state.

Like most other Rōnō-ha scholars, Inomata was anxious to categorize Japan as an advanced capitalist state, where the bourgeois revolution had already been completed, by submerging the particular in the general. By contrast, Kōza-ha theorists emphasized the particular features of Japan's feudalism over its general characteristics as a capitalist state. The emphasis of each faction on particularity or generality[123] tended to weaken its approach to the state. In Inomata's case, the illumination of the growth of finance capital and state monopoly capitalism was vitiated by his failure to address directly the imperial institution and the "feudalistic" military forces that supported and used it. Thus, Inomata's analysis could not provide an adequate justification for Yamakawa's united front proletarian political party strategy.

FEUDAL ABSOLUTIST FORCES AND THE JAPANESE CAPITALIST STATE

Whatever the weaknesses of his approach, Inomata may be credited with having confronted the problem of the role of the "so-called feudal absolutist forces" emphasized in Comintern depictions of the Japanese state. In *Gendai Nihon kenkyū*, a collection of articles published in late-1927 and 1928, Inomata took a historical perspective, conceding the impact of feudal remnants on the early development of the Meiji state. "The existence of our own civil and military state bureaucracy cannot be considered *first of all* apart from the [imperial] institutions" that he and the Comintern had identified as "absolutist remnant forces."[124] Inomata admitted that these feudal remnant forces had not been resisted and eliminated in Japan, presumably until the Taishō and Shōwa eras when the influence of the civilian and military state bureaucracy had declined, permitting the Japanese bourgeoisie finally to establish political supremacy. Yet it was the tenacity of these feudal remnant forces that was to be explained, and here Inomata was at pains to deny the peculiarity of the domestic and international conditions within which Japanese capitalism had developed. To account for these peculiarities and the eventual demise of feudal absolutism, therefore, Inomata returned to the Meiji period. The dilemma of the general versus the particular in Inomata—the need to explain the persistence of the imperial system and its accoutrements in their specific historical form and then to account for their sudden loss of significance in an advanced capitalist state—was evident, then, from the very outset of his treatment of feudal remnant forces.

The issue emerged immediately in Inomata's consideration of the material basis "of the still surprisingly great political power of the systematized feudal remnants, the civil and military bureaucracy."[125] This material basis Inomata found in the system of landownership, which was unlike the landownership systems of the Russian ancien régime and Germany, both of which produced large estates and powerful landlords. Japanese capitalist development had been distinctive because of a variety of "internal natural and social conditions and international circumstances."[126] As a result of these peculiar conditions, although feudal remnant institutions of the bakumatsu and the Meiji eras had long ago lost their material basis, they continued to exercise significant political power, particularly through the operation of their ideology, through the 1920s.[127]

Internationally, Inomata saw much in common with the controversial Takahashi Kamekichi's depiction of external constraints on Japanese development. Japan, a "resource poor" society, had begun to industrialize when world capitalism had already begun "to end the period of relatively peaceful, free competition and entered the period of monopoly imperialism." Japan itself was spurred on to imperialist expansion "based on military supremacy" early in its capitalist development because of the scarcity of its own resources, "the weaknesses of neighboring oriental countries, and the pressures of the imperialist countries on them." By World War I, Japan had established a solid position in the production of silk and other commodities and was itself exploiting colonies and semicolonies even while it remained a net importer of foreign capital.[128]

Domestically, Inomata contended, the Meiji regime had been founded by lower-level samurai and staffed by a bureaucracy that had lost its material basis and, therefore, could act on behalf of the bourgeoisie. In enabling the rapid development of capitalism in Japan, the state undertook two major measures. First, the Meiji government swept away what remained of the feudal agrarian land system, the material basis of feudal absolutism, and, thus, prevented the establishment of semifeudal large-scale landownership. On the positive side, "under high protective tariffs, trustification and cartelization evolved early in some industries, [and the regime] prepared [the conditions of] the monopoly stage with the development of state capital and large capital closely linked to it."[129]

This pattern of economic development before World War I had specific political consequences for Japan. First, because of the importance of warfare, there was "rapid growth in armaments, along with militarization and financial" burdens that helped the military maintain an important role long after the traditional bushi economic basis had disappeared. Similarly, the bourgeoisie, "able to achieve a decisive victory without a decisive struggle," became both more powerful and more reactionary in Japanese politics.[130] The Diet saw the gradual decline of landlord forces and their replacement by capitalist forces; and landlord parties, deprived of their old economic base, were themselves gradually transformed into capitalist forces. Because Japan lacked large landlords comparable to those in Russia and Germany,[131] the Japanese landlord class lacked the power to struggle effectively against the rising bourgeoisie, and at the same time the bourgeoisie became "cowardly, indecisive, and compromising." As a consequence, capitalism could mature only under the tutelage of the government of semifeudal bureaucrats and military cliques, the survival of which became extremely prolonged. When the war boom propelled Japan into the most advanced stage of capitalism, the absolutist elements could no longer act as an independent political force. The rule of the bourgeoisie was consolidated as Japan changed from a debtor country to a creditor country. But even as the bourgeoisie emerged supreme, it was already being intimidated by "the political upsurge of the proletariat." Itself having gained power "without receiving the baptism of 'liberty,'" the bourgeoisie, acting in collusion with feudal remnants, was reactionary almost from the outset.[132]

Yet the transformation of the bourgeoisie into a force of reaction combined with other factors to permit the continued influence of absolutist remnants in Japan.

Through the late-1870s, the Meiji government had required and wielded absolute power to suppress opposition to its efforts to open the way for capitalist development in Japan. Thus, the state repressed the *jiyū minken* (civil rights) movement, and the drive toward liberalism that was typically associated with the rise of the bourgeoisie in Western Europe was instead spearheaded by landlords mobilizing large numbers of peasants. Thus the bourgeoisie had always been linked with autocracy, rather than with democratizing forces, in Meiji Japan.[133] Moreover, the state's role in promoting capitalist development through "official enterprises" was indicative of the special, mutually dependent relationship between the bourgeoisie and autocratic state power in Japan.[134] The distinctive nonliberal elements of the contemporary state reflected this heritage. "Medieval absolutism," Inomata asserted, remained deeply rooted in "the ideology of absolutist domination and submission" propagated through Japan's educational system;[135] and "local self-government lacks substance and is under the direct control of local officials directly subordinate to the central government." The exercise of force by the old pillars of autocracy, the army and the police, was brutal and naked.[136]

It was at this point that the instrumentalism of Inomata's analysis entered. Despite the continued significance of absolutist remnant forces in the Japanese polity, Inomata insisted that "the *surprising* strength of the state bureaucrats is premised on our recognition of the real power of the bourgeoisie," not semifeudal forces. The bourgeoisie had finally come to "dominate Japanese politics because they control production," and as the concentration of capital increased so did the concentration of political power. According to Inomata, by 1923, 84 percent of all company capital came from a mere 8 percent of the existing joint-stock companies, and 2 percent of large companies controlled 61 percent of all capital. The state, then, was but "the 'central committee' of the Japanese industrial club, the public organ that determines and promulgates the high-level policies of Japanese monopoly capitalists."[137] Thus, Inomata claimed, although "the casing of the Japanese state is still embellished with many feudal remnants, its content is becoming bourgeois." The embourgeoisement of landlords, as they came to rely increasingly on income from capital rather than from rents on land, was key to the development of an increasing mutual dependency between bourgeoisie and landlords.[138] Together, absolutist remnant forces and the monopolistic bourgeoisie, Inomata argued, acted to extend the sphere of capitalist exploitation and to mitigate the intense contradictions that accompanied the rapid growth of Japanese capitalism.

With the concentration of capital in Japan had come a "lowering of the rate of profit, surplus capital, and surplus population" and, especially after World War I, poor business conditions that resulted in a dearth of markets for Japanese goods. Inomata offered the data in tables 1 and 2—showing growing production accompanied by declining exports—to elucidate the significance of the crisis occasioned by overproduction. Thus, Japan was increasingly dependent on other countries for markets as well as for supplies of raw materials and foodstuffs. Echoing Takahashi's analysis, Inomata stressed the pivotal position of China in this respect. In response to the burden of the new challenges to Japanese capitalism, he argued, the bourgeoisie turned to the "rationalization" of domestic industry with the support of

TABLE 6.1

Production Increases in Major Japanese Commodities

Year	Pig Iron (Thousands of Metric Tons)	Steel Materials (Thousands of Metric Tons)	Coal (Millions of Tons)	Raw Silk Thread (Millions of Kan)[a]	Cotton Thread (Millions of Kan)[a]	Paper Making (Millions of Sun)[b]	Cement (Millions of Barrels)
1914 (Prewar)	317	282	22	3.7	88	208	3.6
1919 (Wartime high)	595	552	31	6.3	93	942	6.6
1920	529	537	29	5.8	79	—	7.8
1921	480	561	26	6.2	84	—	9.0
1922	559	662	28	6.4	98	—	10.8
1923	599	619	29	6.7	91	873	13.0
1924	585	906	30	6.1	98	941	12.8
1925	685	1,102	31	—	109	1,079	14.5

Source: Inomata, Gendai Nihon kenkyū, (1934) pp. 24–25.
[a]kan = 8.33 lb.
[b]sun = .1 ft., 1.2 in.

TABLE 6.2
The Development of Japanese Import and Export Trade (in millions of yen)

Year	Exports	Imports	Total Trade Volume	Exports − Imports[a]
1914 (Prewar)	591	595	1,186	−4
1919 (Wartime high)	2,098	2,173	4,272	−74
1920	1,948	2,336	4,284	−387
1921	1,252	1,614	2,866	−361
1922	1,637	1,890	3,527	−253
1923	1,447	1,982	3,427	−534
1924	1,807	2,453	4,260	−646
1925	2,305	2,572	4,878	−267
1926	2,044	2,377	4,422	−322

Source: Inomota, *Gendai Nihon kenkyū,* (1934) p.26.
[a]Balance of trade.

the state: the fusion of weak enterprises, the disposal of surplus capital, the conclusion of price agreements, and the formation of cartels and syndicates. A clear "transformation of production relations" in Japan was occurring as a result: Japanese capitalism was moving into its final form, a "state capitalist trust" (*kokka shihon-shugi-teki torasuto*).[139] The Tanaka Gi'ichi cabinet's response to collapsing banks by extending loans from the Bank of Japan and instituting a three-week moratorium on bank payments illustrated the mechanics of the increasingly close relationship between the state and the bourgeoisie. This handling of the crisis firmly established the supremacy of the so-called five large banks (Mitsui, Mitsubishi, Sumitomo, Yasuda, and Dai'ichi), the core of the dominant finance capitalist zaibatsu, according to Inomata. In showing how this came about, Inomata stressed how individuals in the government agencies and parliamentary representatives of the "bourgeois political parties" effecting this "rationalization" could be associated with specific, highly influential capitalist concerns.[140] Yet, the bourgeoisie as a class, dependent in part on feudal absolutist forces, were unwilling or unable to eliminate them. This task, essential to the fruition of "bourgeois democracy in Japan," fell to the revolutionary proletariat.[141]

In this discussion of the persistence of feudal remnants in the Japanese state, the weaknesses of Inomata's reliance on an instrumentalist approach are readily apparent. Such an approach presupposes that those who are part of the state structure act to perpetuate their own interests, the interests of the dominant economic class. Yet bushi, or samurai, not bourgeois, carried out the Meiji bourgeois-democratic revolution. Absolutism seems to be "a product of bourgeois development," but "on what kind of [material] basis does [Inomata's] view that seemed to recognize the existence of absolutism in the feudal Tokugawa period rely?" Inomata argued that a landlord government never existed in the Meiji era, yet he also claimed that "in the early political parties, landlords were predominant."[142] Furthermore, absolutist remnants ruled in the 1920s without any class basis. Landlords in the state acted on behalf of capital, but "they do not themselves manage large agricultural enterprises." Their only link with capital lay in income received from interest and dividends.[143] This raised the question of whether the Rōnō-ha claim of the embourgeoisement of landlords was adequate to establish the shift to bourgeois dominance of the state apparatus. Inomata's reliance on an instrumentalist analysis of the relationship between class forces and government policy would support a view of the state as relatively autonomous that could account for the actions of the Meiji state in support of industrialization in the interests of the bourgeoisie. Here, Inomata's account, which saw a shift from absolutism to bourgeois dominance as having occurred later than Yamakawa would have, was a stronger position. But it, too, left the above questions unanswered. Finally, what was the economic basis of the imperial institution? If the state lacked an absolutist material and class basis, how did it continue to function so effectively in the modern Japanese capitalist state? Inomata's instrumentalism was far more cogent when he relied on Bukharin's theory of state monopoly capitalism than on his often self-contradictory treatment of feudal remnants.

STATE CAPITALIST TRUST

Nikolai Bukharin had developed a theory of the advanced capitalist state a decade before Inomata wrote. His lengthy article "K teorii imperialistichiskogo gosudarstva" [Toward a theory of the imperialist state], which developed further the ideas in his *Imperialism and World Economy*, was completed in July 1916 although it was not published until 1925.[144] Identifying what Rudolf Hilferding had seen as a mere tendency, Bukharin asserted that finance capital must necessarily pursue a policy of imperialism. Through the growth of monopolies and finance capital, he argued, all the advanced capitalist countries had become national trusts; and because "trustification had come to involve a merging of industrial interests with state power itself, he termed it a 'state capitalist trust.'"[145]

The most innovative aspect of Bukharin's ideas on advanced capitalism lay in his view of the role of the state. As finance capitalists tried to manage the inevitable contradictions of capitalism, the economy came to be completely organized and controlled by them. The state, as the "executive committee of the bourgeoisie," inevitably played a role in this process because it had to act in the interests of capital. The state thereby became an active participant in the economy, and thus the state in advanced capitalism differed from all previous states because of its "'colossal economic powers . . . placing all of economic life under the iron heel of the *militaristic* [imperialist] *state.*'" The state becomes "a New Leviathan, before which the fantasy of Thomas Hobbes seems child's play. And even more '*non est potentas super terram quae comparatur ei*' (there is no power on earth that can compare with it)."[146] As the contradictions of capitalism were overcome within a national framework, however, they were transferred to the international sphere, where they were manifested in wars among individual state capitalist trusts.[147] This argument had several unpleasant implications for Marxist revolutionaries in the 1920s. Because of the ability of the capitalist state to forestall crises and thereby maintain economic stability, proletarian revolution would be much less likely to occur in advanced capitalist societies, where all-powerful states could exercise repression effectively.[148] The perpetual need for capital to expand meant that the state had to be aggressive, therefore militaristic.[149]

These ideas were readily disseminated in Japan and China through translations of Bukharin's writings as well as through his speeches as head of the Comintern in 1926 and 1927. Inomata relied on them to place the Japanese state within the context of developments in world capitalism. As international capitalism experienced a temporary stabilization in the midst of its long-term decline,[150] Japan too, with the rising importance of the state in its economy, experienced alternating crises and stabilization. As the ruling bourgeoisie endeavored to manage crises by strengthening the role of the state in the economy, the further concentration of capital and development of monopoly capitalism were the result. "The whole effort of the finance capitalist bourgeoisie now," wrote Inomata, "is concentrated on the organizational construction" of "the final form of the transformation" Bukharin had described in 1916—a strong "state capitalist trust."[151]

Thus, the utility of Bukharin's theoretical work on the advanced capitalist state merely reinforced Inomata's instrumentalism. "The state is increasingly the organ of class rule, but it operates as the representative of the interests of about a handful of monopoly magnates rather than the executive organ of all the bourgeoisie." It was becoming a state capitalist trust. Not only specific political parties but individual names and economic interests could be associated with state policies in dealing with the recurrent crises that plagued Japan in the 1920s.[152] But in addition to adopting domestic measures to rationalize industry, the state also acted internationally. Thus, Inomata's application of Bukharin's work on state capitalism led him to a straightforward explanation of Japanese imperialism.[153]

JAPANESE IMPERIALISM

Initially writing in criticism of Rosa Luxemburg's theory of imperialism in 1926,[154] Inomata turned his full attention to the problem of Japanese imperialism in response to Takahashi's thesis of petty imperialism. In refuting Takahashi's argument, Inomata stressed the international context for the development of the imperialist state, arguing that Takahashi's theory was methodologically unsound because it endeavored to apply Lenin's five attributes of imperialism as a world system to the capitalist systems of individual states. The very notion of imperialism, Inomata stressed, "implies mutual competition among advanced capitalist countries, and means the subjugation and exploitation of semi-civilized peoples and uncivilized peoples by such competitive countries." Thus, Inomata argued that while Japanese capitalism had indeed been militaristic in character initially, Japan had already reached a sufficiently high level of capitalist development for its wars against China (1894–1895) and Russia (1904–1905) to be classified as imperialist ventures.[155] Yet because an imperialist country could only come into being in the context of imperialism as an international system, Inomata argued that "Japan established itself decisively as an imperialist country (in the modern sense) via the Sino-Japanese War."[156] Nevertheless, Japan's transition to a fully capitalist imperialism was realized only with the growth of finance capital in World War I. Before that time, Japanese imperialism had been a policy of monopoly capital, which, as Lenin argued, had to be supplemented by a monopoly on military power in the region. Only after the war did Japan pursue "typical policies of imperialism," namely "policies of finance capital."[157] Such policies then became the lifeblood of the Japanese state: "Clear tendencies of the stabilization and strengthening of socialist Russia and the progress of China's revolutionary capitalist development, in addition to the strengthening of the pressure toward the Orient of England, Germany, and France, which are strengthening their [own] stability, and especially of the United States overflowing with the power of capital, now ma[d]e the entire fate of Japan hang on the success or failure of its imperialist policies." The position of China was especially critical here. China was the site of 90 percent of Japan's foreign investment, and Japan was the most significant of the thirteen creditor countries making loans to China, holding 20 percent of all railroad loans, 90 percent of all telegraph loans, and 50 percent of all loans to local organizations. Thus, the revolution in China threatened to aggravate the existing contradiction between Japanese production forces and markets, to slow the rate of Japanese economic growth, and, thus, "to hasten the demise of Japanese capitalism."[158] With chilling foresight, Inomata went on to note that as the United States, also benefiting from World War I, advanced upon China, the danger to Japanese capitalism and the possibility of direct conflict between the United States and Japan increased steadily.[159] These uncomfortable possibilities had to be considered in developing a strategy of revolution for Japan's own oppressed proletariat. Here, however, Inomata parted with Rōnō-ha faction leader Yamakawa. Inomata claimed direct support from the 1927 Theses for his organizational strategy,[160] he was not averse to using the analogy of Russia between February and October 1917 to make his argument, and he espoused a strategy that clearly had a "step 1" and a "step 2." The key to his alternative to Yamakawaism lay in the analysis of the agrarian problem.

The Agrarian Problem

The agrarian problem was at once both central and peripheral to the debate on Japanese capitalism. According to the 1927 Theses, the agrarian problem was that a "lack of land and extreme poverty still prevail among the peasantry" while "large landowners continue to be an extremely important and independent element in Japanese political and economic life."[161] In determining the nature of the state, the question of whether the economic base was primarily feudalistic or capitalistic was crucial. Neither Yamakawa nor Inomata, however, devoted more than sparse attention to the problem, with the exception of Inomata's late work (1937) done after he had become alienated from the Rōnō-ha in the early 1930s. Thus, it fell to economists such as Kushida Tamizō to conduct abstruse and technical debates on the nature of agrarian rents. Their economic writings were never fully integrated into the Rōnō-ha's analysis of the Japanese state and revolutionary strategy. As time does not permit a detailed analysis of the debate on the agrarian problem here, the issue will be treated only insofar as it relates to the Rōnō-ha's analysis of the state.[162]

The 1922 Draft Program had declared that the semifeudal remnants of the Japanese state did, indeed, have a material basis in Japan's agrarian landownership system.[163] In the 1927 Theses, the Comintern recognized that a high degree of trustification had occurred as Japan evolved toward state capitalism, but large semifeudal landlords continued to figure prominently in the Japanese state. Power continued to be shared between large capitalists and landlords, and the Seiyūkai was identified with "the feudal elements, lords, and military cliques who play a large role in the government."[164] After the brief concession to the Rōnō-ha position in the 1931 Draft Political Theses, the 1932 Theses stressed once again the feudal features in the Japanese state, the most important element of which was the imperial system. Here, equal in importance to monopoly capital as the basis of the state, was Japan's "large landownership" system, the elimination of which was essential to the achievement of bourgeois democracy in Japan.[165] Thus, although the Comintern retreated somewhat from the language of the 1922 Draft Program, which depicted the emperor as the highest landlord in a manner akin to Marx's description of the Asiatic despot, the 1932 Theses still found Japanese agriculture to be "Asiatically backward" and, therefore, in need of a thorough revolution in the countryside. The problem for the Rōnō-ha, then, was this: in order to defend its strategy of one-stage revolution against an imperialist bourgeois state, it would have to prove that the economic base of that state was thoroughly capitalistic, in the agrarian as in the urban sector. Simply to show the existence of state capitalism was inadequate, for the Comintern had acknowledged its existence and still argued for a preliminary bourgeois revolution directed against feudal remnants that maintained a persistent economic basis in large landownership.

Inomata had taken the first step for the Rōnō-ha in stressing that Japan did not, in fact, share large landownership as it existed in Russia and Germany. To the extent that landlords were of political significance, he argued, they had been bourgeoisified, and other feudal remnants had lost their economic basis in the land when the Meiji Restoration's land tax reforms "*destroyed* . . . traditional relations of production—feudal landholding," "legalized private ownership," and opened "a new stage of the *development* of excessively small-scale agricultural *production*."[166] Nevertheless, one element here that separated Inomata from others in the Rōnō-ha was his concession that "[t]he development of capitalist production methods in agriculture has not progressed" and that a basic division persisted between the agrarian sector and the industrial sector ruled by finance capital.[167] The existence of such a split could be construed as support for the Comintern's view of a state in the hands of a bourgeois-feudal landlord bloc.

Rōnō-ha economists Sakisaka Itsurō, Tsuchiya Takao, and Kushida Tamizō were more insistent than Inomata that the old feudal agrarian landholding system had been replaced by a system of capitalist agricultural enterprise. For them, in the interest of theoretical consistency, "high agricultural rent, the low standard of living of the peasants, and low industrial wages would have to be explained by non-feudal elements such as competition among tenants and the insufficient expansion of industrial employment."[168] Thus, against Kōza-ha insistence that high agrarian rents remained feudalistic because of the persistence of "extra-economic coercion," Kushida asserted that even where such rents continued to be paid in kind, they were not feudalistic but "precapitalistic." Thus, even though payment of rents in kind "was a special characteristic of feudal government," rents in kind are not necessarily feudal ground rents. "Why? Because payment in kind itself is being conceptually converted into currency in the minds of landlords and tenants."[169] The key to the nature of the landlord-tenant relationship, then, lay not in the physical form in which rents were paid but in the nature of the personal relationship between the two parties. Rōnō-ha economists insisted that extra-economic coercion did not persist after the Meiji Restoration: "'No case [was] known in which a landowner . . . prohibited a change of occupation by a tenant for fear of the loss of rent'."[170] Feudal personalistic relations had been replaced by impersonal capitalist contracts; land prices and rents were now the product of supply and demand curves, not noneconomic means of coercion exercised by the feudal landlord. Japanese peasants were no longer serfs but free individuals acting in an open, competitive market.[171]

Naturally, in this view, the state that arose on the basis of the new order reflected the capitalist interests of the new ruling class in the countryside. Inomata stressed that "the old feudal lords and nobility who would be new landed nobility and the enjoyers of private large landownership . . . elected to be money capitalists rather than landed nobility."[172] Nevertheless, the Rōnō-ha was not entirely effective in contesting the Kōza-ha's assertions of the persistence of noneconomic coercion. Ogura Takekazu, for example, "found many examples of communal coercion to force peasants to pay rent." Even Kushida admitted that "the method of the determination of rent at the time of the land tax reform . . . in 1875 clearly followed from that prevailing in the Tokugawa period; . . . and now, more than half a century later . . . the remnants of the feudal system continue to exist."[173]

Inomata was no doubt aware of these limitations in the Rōnō-ha position as he distanced himself from Yamakawa and produced his large volume focusing on the special "Asiatic features" of Japanese agriculture in 1937. In this study, Inomata came close to transcending the problem of "dogmatism" raised by the effort of the Rōnō-ha and the Kōza-ha to fit Japan squarely into either the capitalist or feudal mode of production. By this time, he was prepared to recognize the coexistence of feudal elements with predominantly capitalist features as a general phenomenon, particularly in later-industrializing societies like Japan. "Even in England, the motherland of capitalism, [capitalism] also took a rather long time to destroy and transform the feudal mode of production. Even there . . . one still finds remnants of the old mode. Our Japanese captialism required only sixty or seventy years to achieve four hundred years of development. Thus, remnants are more numerous." The fact that Japan had relied on "Asiatic" wet-field cultivation for three thousand years further retarded this process of transition, Inomata argued.[174] Although he did not return to the controversy over the nature of the state, the implications of this new work on the agrarian problem drew Inomata closer to the Kōza-ha position on the nature of the state. The Kōza-ha approach to the state, however, would be dramatically different from Inomata's instrumentalist Rōnō-ha view of the state as a tool of the superordinate economic classes.

THE KŌZA-HA: A HISTORICAL AND STRUCTURAL APPROACH TO THE JAPANESE STATE

The Tennō-sei*: Arguing from Superstructure to Base*

> It is always the direct relationship of the owners of the conditions of production to the direct producers—a relation always naturally corresponding to a definite stage in the development of the methods of labour and thereby its social productivity—which reveals the innermost secret, the hidden basis, of the entire social structure, and with it the political form of the relation of sovereignty and dependence, in short the corresponding specific form of the state. (Karl Marx)[175]

In defending the Comintern line of two-stage revolution, Marxists loyal to the JCP argued that the persistence of the imperial institution in a form that sacrificed democratic rights to authoritarian rule indicated that Japan had yet to complete the bourgeois-democratic revolution set in motion by the Meiji Restoration. The strategic debate with the Rōnō-ha over the 1927 Theses was conducted energetically by labor leader Watanabe Masanosuke, and after his death in 1928, by Ichikawa Shōichi (1892–1945) and Takahashi Sadaki. The open controversy over revolutionary strategy and tactics drew to a close when their primary vehicle, the journal *Marukusu-shugi* (Marxism), ceased publication in April 1929 in the wake of the government repression of the preceding year.[176] The debate was resumed in theoretical and historical terms by Noro Eitarō and the group of scholars he assembled, which became known as the Kōza-ha.

Like the Rōnō-ha, when writing about the nature of the Japanese state, Kōza-ha scholars were responding to Takahashi Kamekichi's petty imperialism argument as well as to the 1927 and 1932 theses. The Rōnō-ha had generally responded to Takahashi's challenge simply by seeking to demonstrate that Japan had, indeed, developed to the stage of monopoly finance capitalism and, thus, conformed to Lenin's definition of imperialism. The task for the Kōza-ha was much more complex, however. Loyal to the Comintern's view that although Japan was indeed an advanced capitalist society in the urban sphere it was hampered by feudal backwardness in the agrarian sphere that was in turn reflected in the Japanese state, the Kōza-ha had first to locate the historical roots of Japan's continued backwardness and then explain the complex mechanisms that enabled the more-advanced and less-developed aspects of the society to operate as an integral whole.

In their writings, the Kōza-ha offered a systematic analysis of what they termed "the emperor system." The group used this term very deliberately to stress that it was a set of institutions that extended beyond the person of the emperor himself;

and they integrated this examination of the nature of the state with a historical study of changes in Japanese political, economic, and social structures since the late-Tokugawa period. To analyze the complex relationship between the old feudal forces they claimed continued to wield significant political power and the representatives of the new capitalist structure, the Rōnō-ha's instrumentalist approach, which neglected elements inconsistent with their thesis of advanced capitalism, was inadequate. Instead, the Kōza-ha relied on a "structural" (*kōzō-teki*) approach to the Japanese state and society, an approach that coincides both nominally and methodologically with what Western Marxists five decades later call a "structuralist" approach to the state.

As noted in chapter 2, structuralists reject the instrumentalist assumption that there is a self-conscious ruling class that shapes state policies to respond to its own class interests. Citing Marx's observations on the limitations on consciousness imposed by the material conditions in which men live,[177] structuralists argue that the instrumentalist view "leads one to expect the degree of rationality of politically implemented strategies certainly to be restricted and marked by 'false consciousness'."[178] Instead, structuralists claim that "the functions of the state are broadly determined by the structures of the society rather than [as in the instrumentalist approach] by the people who occupy the positions of state power."[179] It is not, then, consciousness or purposive rationality but the larger constraints of the socio-economic structure of the society that determine the activity of the state and its functionaries. Such constraints arise from "the systematic functional interrelationships among" "the concrete social institutions that make up a society."[180] Thus, while Inomata's analysis focused on linking state policies to specific individuals acting in the interest of Japan's "state capitalist trust," the Kōza-ha highlighted the structural relationship between Japan's dual economic base and its political superstructure.

Many scholars have identified the work of the Kōza-ha almost entirely with the Comintern's elaboration of the two-stage revolutionary strategy in the 1932 Theses. "Kōza-ha theory is the academic foundation of the '32 Theses," Rōnō-ha historian Tsushima Tadayuki once wrote. "The existence of serfdom in agrarian relations, absolutist rule in the state—academically [Koza-ha theory] provided a basis for these [points] and thus tried to make the correctness of the two-stage strategic theory [a] necessary [conclusion]."[181] This interpretation is misleading, however, given the actual chronology of the publication of the *Nihon shihon-shugi hattatsu shi kōza* (herafter referred to as the *Kōza*) and of the earlier works by Noro that were its inspiration. Noro had already published several essays in the thirteen-volume *Marukusu-shugi kōza*, edited by Ōyama Ikuo and Kawakami Hajime,[182] when, in mid-1931, shortly after the publication of the 1931 Draft Political Theses, Noro joined Iwata Yoshimichi (1898–1932) to plan a *kōza* (a published symposium). The collection of studies would offer "'the key to fundamental solutions of various immediate problems'" through a complete analysis of the "'conditions of the development of Japanese capitalism'."[183] Thus, even after the Draft Political Theses reversed the Comintern position to adopt a policy of one-stage revolution, Noro was planning to lay the intellectual groundwork to defend the need for a preliminary revolution that would complete the political tasks of the bourgeois-democratic revolution. For this effort, Noro gathered theorists and scholars from within and outside the party, particularly those already involved in two major cultural and research associations, the Puro-ka (Association for Research in Proletarian Science) and the Sangyō Rōdō Chōsajo (Industrial Labor Research Bureau).[184] As the *Kōza* was being prepared, the Japanese military was beginning to move into Manchuria and Mongolia, and repression of dissidents at home intensified. Many associated with the *Kōza* were arrested in the March 1932 roundup of Bunka Dōmei (Culture League) and Puro-ka members, and, thus, its contributors changed repeatedly. Eventually, Noro himself was arrested, and others moved underground. Despite these hazards, the seven-volume work was published between May 1932 and August 1935, undergoing repeated revisions because of censorship.[185]

By the time the 1932 Theses were promulgated, then, most contributions to the *Kōza* had already been completed. That there was so much agreement between the views expressed in the *Kōza* and the new theses was not fortuitous, of course. Kōza-ha scholars had been heavily influenced by the 1927 Theses, which the 1932 Theses supported, and Noro had persuaded the group not to alter writings already in progress when the 1931 Draft Political Theses were published.[186] Meanwhile, as the *Kōza* was being prepared, the controversy on revolutionary strategy with the Rōnō-ha had lost much of its intensity. Noro himself readily recognized, as did the 1927 Theses, the 1931 Draft Theses, and the 1932 Theses, that " 'today, when the capitalist mode of production has already long been the dominant [mode of] production, it goes without saying that those holding the hegemony of political rule are the bourgeoisie, especially the finance bourgeoisie'."[187] The question that the *Kōza* was to address, then, was how to "understand the basis and content of the democratic duties indicated within the basic responsibilities of the socialist revolution," "democratic duties" that should be fulfilled in a two-stage revolution. Was it the continued prevalence of "semi-feudal relations of production [that] remained dominant in agriculture" that still necessitated a bourgeois-democratic revolution? Were such "semi-feudal" relations of production the material basis of Japan's highly undemocratic "emperor system"?

Because Noro himself already recognized "bourgeois hegemony" as he was planning the *Kōza*, he developed its argument so that it did not cause internal inconsistency in the *Kōza* when the 1932 Theses became the basis for JCP strategy. The only new element introduced by the 1932 Theses was an emphasis on the emperor system that Kōza-ha Marxists such as Hattori Shisō had already developed as early as 1927 and that further encouraged Kōza-ha theorists to pursue in depth this institution that Rōnō-ha scholars had downplayed.[188] Through the efforts of the Kōza-ha, its more subtle, structuralist approach to the state gained a firm position in Japanese Marxism.[189] The Kōza-ha's structuralism was facilitated by its historical perspective on absolutism as a general phenomenon, for absolutism, as Marx and Engels had described it, was, like Bonapartism, based on a temporary balance of rising and declining economic classes. Therefore, the absolutist state could not be identified as the mere instrument of a single ruling economic class, as was required by a purely instrumentalist approach to the state.[190]

The 1932 Theses helped to support this development in Kōza-ha theory by arguing that the absence of a correct interpretation of the absolutist emperor system had "hampered the objective analysis of Japanese capitalism," had led to an incorrect depiction of Japan's state power, and therefore had aroused considerable confusion in the JCP's revolutionary strategy. Even if the state did link landlords to the upper strata bourgeoisie, it could not be regarded as a mere instrument of those two classes. Rather, the new theses argued, "Japan's emperor system has maintained its independent and relatively significant responsibilities and its absolutist nature, barely concealed by pseudo-constitutional forms." Japan's Marxists had to look beyond the surface of the state and consider the political party system in conjunction with the imperial institution if they were to find the true economic basis of a state that enjoyed considerable autonomy under the leadership of bureaucrats and the military. This economic basis was "landownership—Asiatically backward semi-feudal domination in the countryside" common among "the most backward colonial countries," which hindered the "development of the productive forces of Japanese agriculture." In this view, even Japan's admittedly powerful finance capital relied on feudal remnants and the emperor system to exercise its rule and could not be analyzed apart from the other two components.[191]

The burden of the Kōza-ha's argument rested on the claim that the economic basis of the Japanese state was not an advanced capitalistic economy, as the Rōnō-ha claimed but a countryside that remained semifeudal. In supporting this view, the Kōza-ha used a mode of argumentation that could raise serious methodological issues. Citing the passage from Marx's *Das Kapital* quoted previously, they argued from the nature of the political "superstructure," in somewhat circular fashion, to determine that the persistence of feudal production relations in the economic base in the countryside required the prescribed bourgeois-democratic revolution. Even if the emperor was acknowledged to be the head of an imperialist state, the Kōza-ha and the 1932 Theses characterized the emperor system as absolutist and feudalistic like the "militaristic imperialist tsarist state" and Germany under the Kaiser. Strictly speaking, absolutism was a state form of the last stage of feudalism: it arose where the bourgeois revolution had not yet been completed, and its "historical role lay in nurturing and promoting the development to a still higher state of a bourgeoisie which still had not developed to [the point of] being an independent force gathering political power."[192] In Hirano's words, "the relations that form the entire foundation of the special state form in this period of absolutism . . . are the exploitation of serfs, or rather, semi-serf peasants and independent small producers, and on this entire economic structure is established this political formation."[193] Thus, to accept the notion that the emperor system was absolutist was to assume that it reflected a feudalistic economic base.[194] The problem for the Kōza-ha was to prove the persistence of this base despite Japan's obvious success in becoming an expansionist capitalist state.

Therefore, Kōza-ha scholars stressed the peculiar aspects of the development of Japanese capitalism. Specifically, they argued not only that the Meiji Restoration left feudal remnants intact but also that their power expanded as the state itself benefited from the growth of capitalism and imperialist adventures.[195] Indeed, Kōza-ha scholars Hirano Yoshitarō and Yamada Moritarō claimed that the supreme paradox of Japanese capitalism was that these feudal remnants themselves were the basis for its development.[196] Proof of the existence of absolutism lay in agrarian relations: the land tax, which from the Meiji through the Shōwa periods was the "essential successor of feudal dues"; and the landlord-tenant relationship, which was not capitalist but was based on "semiserf tenant rent."[197] On the first point, Hirano wrote, " 'The Meiji government first built up its own unique structure of political rule on the basis of the payment of land taxes to the government which reorganized feudal dues and on the basis of the legal guarantee of tenant rent collection as the source of the land tax'." In short, " 'The "Land Tax Reform" of 1873 essentially perpetuated as they were the so-called *sozei* (old feudal dues) prescribed by the Prefectural Administration Regulations—with a change in form to cash—and merely unified them on a national scale'."[198]

Noro took this argument a step further, attributing to the special "Asiatic" features of Japan the autocratic tendencies of the modern Japanese state. This is a theme on which others, most notably Hani Gorō and Hirano Yoshitarō would elaborate further. Initially, Noro simply asserted that the state was the country's highest landlord, since it levied feudal type rents, in the form of taxes, on the direct producers (peasants). In Noro's words, "the land tax reform . . . did not immediately imply the abolition of feudal rents, but thereby, in reality, rents in kind (dues in kind) [paid] to feudal landowners now were merely changed into cash rents (cash land taxes) [rendered] to the state as the single highest monopolistic landowner."[199] Noro conceded Inomata's point that landownership was not predominantly large-scale landownership in Japan. But he went on to argue that this alone could not establish that there was no material basis for semifeudal absolutist forces. Inomata was wrong to assume that only feudal agrarian systems based on large-scale landownership such as those of Russia and Germany could support absolutism. Rather, as Hirano maintained, the true test lay not in the size of land units, but in the relationship of those who held it vis-à-vis the direct producers. In Japan, this relationship was not a capitalistic one in which farmers (or tenant farmers) hired wage labor in pursuit of profit; tenant farmers remained direct producers who used their own households' labor to produce a mere subsistence. Because the Meiji state relied on the same levies as feudal rents, the feudal character of the relationship between landowners and direct producers remained: now it was simply the state, rather than the feudal lord, that appropriated the surplus in the form of cash taxes. As a transitional absolutist state, the emperor-centered structure used this surplus to accomplish primitive capital accumulation. The resulting juxtaposition of semifeudal relations of production in agriculture with the growth of capitalism in the nation as a whole became " 'one of the most fundamental contradictions of Japanese capitalism'." This contradiction "could be resolved only by the sublation of the capitalist system itself" by the elimination of the emperor system, by agrarian revolution, and by the completion of a socialist revolution.[200]

Precisely because of this emphasis on continuity from Tokugawa to Shōwa, the Kōza-ha has been vulnerable to the charge that its analysis of the tennō-sei was static, that it did not allow for any change in the economic basis and its superstructure. This danger may have been inherent in the Kōza-ha's method of stipulating first the nature of the tennō-sei and then proceeding to determine the character of its economic base. In addition, the Kōza-ha's conviction that the tennō-sei was not comparable to the British monarchy could have reflected the more widely shared Japanese belief in the *kokutai* family-state ideology, in which Japan's emperor system was truly unique. Despite these alleged shortcomings, however, the Kōza-ha's contribution to an understanding of the dynamics of the development of capitalism and the Japanese state since the Tokugawa period is not to be underestimated. Its application of the notions of absolutism and oriental society to the analysis of the Japanese state held potentially greater flexibility and promise than the Rōnō-ha's explicitly instrumentalist perspective.

Absolutism and the Japanese State

In the Kōza-ha view, the Meiji Restoration was not the predominantly successful bourgeois revolution that the Rōnō-ha claimed it to be.[201] The Meiji Restoration had merely begun this revolution by undermining feudal political centers in 1869 through the abolition of the feudal domains (han) and establishment of the prefectures (*ken*) and transferring sovereignty from the multiple feudal states (kuni) to a single head, the emperor, on a national level. Furthermore, the new regime acted to facilitate the development of capitalism in Japan in a variety of ways: by lifting, in 1872, the ban on the purchase and sale of land imposed by the Tokugawa shogunate in 1643; by legalizing private landownership; and by permitting the redistribution and merger of lands by removing, in 1875, laws restricting landownership by individuals. Nevertheless, the Meiji reforms left intact an underlying system of agrarian relations that made the new Meiji state neither bourgeois nor entirely feudalistic.[202] It was at this point that Marx's and Engels's concept of absolutism proved to be most helpful to the Kōza-ha cause.

Noro summarized the Kōza-ha view on the incompleteness of the Meiji Restoration succinctly:

> *Pure feudal landholding relations* were abolished for a time, along with the restrictions that accompanied it, by the reforms of the Meiji Restoration. Even so, this fact does not imply that it, as [Inomata] says, "abolished the *land system* of feudal agriculture as the basis of feudal absolutism." It merely accomplished the removal of pure feudal landholding relations, i.e., abolished the relations of pure feudal landholding by the bakufu and three hundred daimyos, and in its place put unified land ownership under the sovereignty [*shuken*] of the absolute monarch. . . . In our country the state ["as

before"] is the highest landlord, and sovereignty is land ownership gathered on a national scale. Our country's land taxes, both in their traditional conception and in reality, could not differ essentially from the form of ground rent.[203]

If the Meiji state "did not deliberately try to advance the development of large landownership," "it clearly opened the path for the concentration" of landownership through its policies. Consequently, in the late-1920s, half of all arable land in Japan was held by tenants, and "we still do not see a marked development of capitalism in agriculture" even though the new state implemented protectionist measures for the benefit of the native bourgeoisie.[204] If the new Meiji state was neither bourgeois nor purely feudal any longer, it could be described as "absolutist."

The special role of this absolutist state and the limits of capitalist development in Japan were explained in Kōza-ha historical analyses of the origins of the imperial institution itself and of its development paralleling economic progress in the Tokugawa and Meiji periods. As in other feudal societies, Kōza-ha scholars argued, in Tokugawa feudalism lay the germinating seeds of capitalism in Japan and the source of its own demise in the Meiji Restoration. Capitalist enterprises developed in embryo form in the government production offices established by individual han, enabling merchants, usurers, and feudal daimyo themselves to accumulate capital in the form of currency. Manufacture, typically of textiles, cotton cloth, paper, wax, lacquerware and porcelain, as well as dyeing and weaving, sake brewing, mining and metallurgy developed under the putting-out (*toiya*) system, which brought cottage industry under the domination of commercial capital.[205] With the emergence of a network of internal water transport on the basis of the shogun's *sankin kōtai* (alternate attendance) system, these developments engendered commodity circulation on a national scale by the end of the Edo period. The commercial capital produced in this process could have been converted to industrial capital, if the "feudal fetters" were removed, if the domestic market were fully integrated to transcend han boundaries, and if other conditions of the capitalist mode of production (such as the importation of technology and participation in the world market) had been present.[206]

Indeed, several such conditions for the growth of Japanese capitalism had been encouraged by the shogunate. Recognizing the importance of commercial capital and commercial cities, "the bakufu . . . brought all such cities as Edo, Osaka, Sakai, Kyoto, and Nagasaki under its direct rule, made the Ikuno, Sado, and Ashio mines [its] direct jurisdiction, and made the power to coin money [its] exclusive jurisdiction." Promoting industries and reorganizing the armies, the state became engaged in "primitive accumulation." The bourgeoisie in the bakufu's own domain was weak, so the shogun granted to the bourgeoisie in commercial cities licensed (or chartered) monopolies. Thus, it became impossible for Japan to develop a form of state that would be comparable to those in Western Europe that employed bourgeois as supporters against feudal lords to establish a fully centralized regime. The conditions lacking for the shogun were also absent for other feudal lords as well, even though the latter encouraged "serf-commodity" production and circulation through government monopolies on rice and mining in their own domains. While the bakufu did play an important role in promoting capitalism, therefore, it did not immediately become a Western European-style absolutist state. The individual han developed relatively equally and in balance with one another so that a fully centralized transitional state was not conceived until the Meiji Restoration.[207]

Finally, because of "Asiatic" peculiarities in the "serf-agrarian" system in the countryside (discussed later in this chapter), the commercial capital that grew rapidly during the Tokugawa shogunate was not transformed into the industrial capital needed for the full fruition of the capitalist mode of production.[208] As commodity production and circulation swelled in the process described previously, the increases in *kokinonari* (miscellaneous exactions), *unjō* (taxes on those engaged in shipping, fishing, and hunting) and forced labor that financed development occasioned peasant uprisings in the closing years of the bakufu. Significantly, such disturbances were concentrated in areas that had undergone the greatest transformation to a commodity economy, most notably in han, such as the Tosa, Suō, Awa, Iyo, Satsuma, and Saga, where government-sponsored industries had developed. Kōza-ha scholars maintained that even with the growth of commercial capital, conditions in the countryside were such that when industrial capital emerged, it did so on the basis of essentially feudal economic organization. Japan's "Asiatic" serfdom was characterized by a "low level mode of agricultural production" on an extremely small and inefficient scale. As exactions on the peasantry increased, their ability to eke out a subsistence declined, and they turned to handicraft industries such as spinning and weaving to supplement their meager yields from the land. In these circumstances, aggravated by the shogunate's forcible isolation of Japan from the world market, the development of industry separate from agriculture was hindered, as was the conversion of commercial into industrial capital. Mercantile and usury capital remained in the villages where they led a "parasitic" existence on the serf system by lending money to feudal lords. Such capital could not accomplish the revolutionary transformation of Japan to capitalism on a national scale. Commercial centers such as Edo and Osaka, unlike 1640 London and 1777 Paris, were not based on industrial production but existed only to sustain feudal lords and their families. Thus, the feudal system that had developed by the late bakufu combined the tentative growth of commercial capital with the steady increase of feudal exploitation. Because it did not produce an industrial bourgeoisie, the system began to stagnate, to disintegrate from within. It finally collapsed abruptly, "as when a mummy hits the air," when it made contact with the dynamic system of world capitalism.[209]

The Kōza-ha argued, then, that the Tokugawa order had collapsed from a combination of internal and external factors. Internally, the emergence of capitalism on the basis of a semiserf agrarian economy produced antagonisms between the Imperial Court and the shogunate, peasants and feudal lords, han and the shogunate, lord and retainer. A major force in these antagonisms was the warrior class, which came to be separated from the land. Toyotomi Hideyoshi (1536–1598) had conducted land surveys and established separate areas of habitation for peasants and samurai, thus initiating the Tokugawa's strict policy of fixed social status. Living off rice stipends from bakufu and han granaries, the samurai had been transformed gradually into mere "parasitic holders of fief and stipend rights" in the early-1800s. They were easily swept aside by the Meiji Restoration's compulsory commutation of stipends (*kinroku kōsai*), initiated in 1876.[210]

A second cause of the demise of the bakufu was its conflict with feudal han, a conflict that was not resolved until those who established the Restoration government overthrew the shogun, abolished the han, and established prefectures. Finally, there were large samurai who stood in antagonism with the peasants. At the time of the Restoration, "there were 399,000 households of extremely large samurai who were able to exist only as parasites, by the cruel extortion of serfs on the basis of an Asiatic petty serf system." Lower-stratum samurai numbered 1.5 million of this group; exceedingly impoverished, they played a tremendously destructive role in bringing down the Tokugawa order. These political and economic antagonisms, abetted by the challenge of the Western powers, were finally resolved in the demise of the Tokugawa system. Yet, the system that replaced it was not a bourgeois but a transitional absolutist state with a dual character. As dramatic as its reforms were—and both Kōza-ha and Rōnō-ha agreed that the reforms were the most revolutionary element of the Meiji Restoration—they left much of the old feudal system intact in the form of "semifeudal" forces. As Hirano argued, "Not only was the traditional lord-vassal relationship retained, but as long as the general system of petty semi-serfs remained, it was possible for [the old feudal daimyo] to be made a political power supporting those forces that stood on that semi-serf system." One example of this phenomenon was the continuity of political power wielded by the Satsuma, Tosa, Chōshū, and Hizen han. The new government, the hanbatsu, "merely represented the four han and maintained a balance of power among them."[211]

An absolutist state destined to execute the full transition from feudalism to the capitalist mode of production, the Meiji regime faced a formidable task. The capitalism that it inherited was "chipped and distorted" by its origins in a semi-serf land system, and the new state had to complete the tasks of primitive capitalist accumulation that the indigenous bourgeoisie had been too weak and immature to accomplish on its own. Because of the coincidence of external military pressures and internal backwardness, this process was especially violent as the Meiji state sought to accomplish in fifty years what the British had required two centuries to achieve. The state was constrained to retain the semi-serf system that had nurtured nascent capitalism in Edo Japan, and as a result, the bourgeoisie that emerged after the Meiji reforms was a "serf-landlord bourgeoisie." This, in turn, had a negative impact on the achievement of the democratizing elements of the bourgeois revolution. "Since the nascent bourgeoisie itself was based on a serf system and reproduced it, it furthermore embossed the entire system with the form of semi-serf capitalism, and the entire basis of such an economic structure caused the political rule to be characterized in the same way."[212]

The Meiji state, then, could best be characterized as "a composite unified system of feudal possession" under the dictatorship of the hanbatsu. The bureaucracy, staffed by former samurai, opposed any possibility of bourgeois democracy, such as espoused by the *minken undō* (civil rights movement). Aspects of the ancient despotic system were recalled and old laws revived and copied into new legal codes, even as the political system of Emperor Friedrich II of Prussia (1740–1806) was adopted as the model for the new state. The revival of old forms was evident also in the means the new leadership used to accumulate capital: the use of "extra-economic coercion toward the peasantry and urban workers," reliance on forced labor, and strict regulation of slave labor. At the same time, the government established intimate relationships with commercial capitalists—such as the Mitsui and Shimada families, which had originated in the han industries and would combine to form zaibatsu in the succeeding decades. On these companies the state relied heavily for loans to help finance industrialization.[213]

Most importantly, the threat from abroad forced the Meiji state to accomplish industrialization rapidly and in such a manner as would strengthen the nation militarily. This, too, had important political implications. As Hirano noted, "the protection and nurturing of capitalist production, the importation of technology, and the transplantation of industry had to be conjoined with the official patriarchical organization of the Meiji government. Thus, it was no accident that this patriarchical tutorial protectionist bureaucratic organization (*bevormundende Bureaukratie*) structured the entire state system, as an indispensable framework for the establishment and development of capitalism."[214] Because of the international threat, the new state took on a militaristic character, as it promoted heavy industry and a huge military structure " = key industry system," financed by the semi-serf land system and sustained by a strong regular army and police network. It created the Tokyo and Osaka munitions factories and naval shipbuilding yards, many of which relied on formerly han structures. As a result, under the tutelage of the Meiji state, Japanese capitalism developed its heavy industry first and then its light consumer industries, although han-sponsored enterprises had given capitalism a head start in the latter category. The results were impressive. Whereas in 1872 the laying of the Tokyo-Yokohama railway line had found Japan heavily dependent on British aid, by the turn of the century, Japan had achieved self-sufficiency in the communications and transport network required for a powerful military structure.[215] In this pattern, Japan's development was comparable with German development from the early nineteenth century to the turn of the century.[216] In Germany, as in Japan, the external threat (the French Revolution, in the former case) was a powerful determinant of the manner in which the state promoted capitalist industrialization. Both cases diverged dramatically from the classic French pattern of bourgeois revolution from below.[217]

What emerged from this Kōza-ha analysis of Japanese capitalist development was a conclusion expressed succinctly by Yamada Moritarō: the distinctive feature of Japan's "militaristic semi-serf" capitalism was the "relationship of mutual regulation/adjustment between semi-serf petty cultivation and capitalism."[218] Capitalism had flourished on the basis of a semifeudal agrarian system in the Tokugawa era in such a way that it could not survive without that base. As capitalism flourished, feudal elements did not disappear but were strengthened,

and the concentration of power in the Meiji state merely reinforced these tendencies. Thus, feudal remnants were reflected in the political superstructure, even
while the regime's close ties to usury capital and commitment to build a large
military apparatus promoted the growth of finance and monopoly capital and
imperialism. That such a state was merely absolutist rather than bourgeois was
reflected in the emperor system.

On this point Kōza-ha scholars were in agreement. Yet they interpreted absolutism in various ways. Hattori followed Marx's and Karl Kautsky's interpretation
very closely, emphasizing the balance or equilibrium among class forces.[219] By
contrast, Hirano argued that there could be no equilibrium between bourgeoisie
and landed aristocracy where the bourgeoisie did not struggle. He stressed instead
semi-serfdom in large landownership and the concentration of power into a kind of
"state feudalism" under the Meiji state. This was not pure feudalism, but feudalism
in its final stages, hence absolutism. As for Noro, he acknowledged no large-scale
landownership but claimed that the Meiji state had promoted capitalism by further-
ing the concentration of land. All three scholars injected into their analyses of
Meiji absolutism some allusion to the Asiatic origins of the emperor system and its
consequences. Indeed, despite their precise references of absolutism as a transitional stage between feudalism and capitalism, Kōza-ha depictions of the Meiji
state as absolutist were consistently bound to the notion of Asiatic despotism as
Hirano, Noro, and Hattori took a cue from the Comintern theses and made some
mention of the state acting as Japan's highest landlord. In their view, only the
peculiarities inherited from Japan's Asiatic past—such as extremely small-scale
agriculture in isolated village communities—could cause Japan's transition to
capitalism to evolve in the distinctive manner that they described. Only such
factors could explain the continued autocratic character of the Japanese state well
after the transition to finance capital and imperialist adventurism driven by the
interests of capital had been achieved. The problem was that Noro, Hirano, and
others in the Kōza-ha firmly rejected Takahashi's view that Japanese expansionism
could be explained by anything other than Lenin's interpretation of imperialism
"as the highest stage of capitalism." Hence, Japan's status as an advanced capitalist
state stood in direct conflict with the incompleteness of the industrializing
bourgeois-democratic revolution that they alleged. The notion of "oriental society" helped the Kōza-ha to reconcile this apparent contradiction.

Oriental Society, the Asiatic Mode of Production, and the Development of Japanese Capitalism

The notion of oriental society played a dual role in Kōza-ha theory. First, it helped
to differentiate Japan from the Western European model on which Marx's and
Engels's work had been based, thereby highlighting and explaining the differences
between the two development experiences. At the same time, stress on Japan's
"Asiatic" characteristics allowed Kōza-ha scholars to differentiate Japan from
societies such as China and India that had been far less successful in their indige-

nous capitalist development. (Indeed, it is one of the less attractive chapters in the history of Japan's Marxism that many, especially Hirano and Sano, used the Asiatic mode of production idea after their *tenkō* to justify Japan's leadership in East Asia through the effort to build a Greater East Asia Co-Prosperity Sphere.)[220] Given the Kōza-ha's emphasis on the peculiarities of Japanese capitalism, it is not surprising that allusions to the Asiatic mode of production should have been copious in their work but not in Rōnō-ha writings.[221] These references occurred most often in efforts to periodize Japanese history in Marxian terms by scholars such as Hayakawa Jirō, Aikawa Haruki, and Akizawa Shūji. To what extent the concept of the Asiatic mode of production applied to Japanese history was such a significant issue that these scholars continued to draw on Soviet works on the subject even after Stalin's 1931 Leningrad Conference had removed it from the arena of acceptable scholarly study.[222] As an effort to apply Marxist categories to the full length and breadth of Japanese history, the controversy over the Asiatic mode of production and oriental society touched on a much wider range of issues than can be treated here.[223] Therefore, I consider the issue only as it related to the Kōza-ha's understanding of the relationship between Japan's economic development and the emperor-system state.

Treatment of this issue requires a clear distinction between the notion of "oriental society," on the one hand, and the Asiatic mode of production, on the other. Marx judged "oriental societies" normatively to be devoid of qualities of lasting humanistic value, and this judgment allowed him to legitimate the exercise of dominion and repression by the European imperialist powers over Asian societies. As discussed, Marx expressed this view unambiguously in his appraisal of British behavior in India: only the destruction of the "solid foundation of Oriental despotism" by the onslaught of Western imperialism could enable "mankind" to "fulfill its destiny."[224]

This highly emotional rejection of oriental society conflicted with Marx's claim to have produced a detached "scientific" analysis of all modes of production, including the "Asiatic mode of production."[225] For Marx, oriental society was the product of a special mode of production in which small-scale agriculture was carried out on the basis of production relations involving communal property ownership and cooperation. It was characterized by small, scattered agrarian communities, the absence of private property, and a despotic superstructure. Clearly, this concept could be problematic for Asian followers of Marx. What should have been a precise distinction between the Asiatic mode of production and oriental society was muddled because Marx had devised the concept of the Asiatic mode of production "to account for a type of society outside the mainline of Western development."[226] As a result, the apparent conflict between the notion of an allegedly static oriental society and the view that Marx's scientific schema of progressive modes of production was universal has aroused recurrent controversy among both Chinese and Japanese Marxists. (On the Chinese case, see chapter 7.) This controversy peaked in the 1930s as the Comintern tried to formulate a strategy of revolution for Asia in the face of world war, was revived after World War II, and reemerged in the 1970s and 1980s as Asian Marxists continued to be concerned with the persistent problem of the state and impediments to democratization in their societies.

In Japan in the 1920s and 1930s, the issue arose in the Kōza-ha's consideration of the limits of capitalist development in Japan's dual economic structure and the reasons for the special role of the Meiji absolutist state. Both Hirano and Hani saw a direct link between the lineage of an "oriental" past and the autocratic character of the emperor system state that they confronted in the 1920s. Both saw the emperor system as a form of rule that originally arose on the basis of the oriental society described by Marx and Engels, and its Asiatic character had a significant impact on all subsequent political and economic developments in Japan. According to Hani, "the imperial forces that originated in [Japan's] Asiatic ancient society and at one time were the highest political authority lost that power along with the maturation of feudalism. But, by adapting [that authority] to the feudal structure, they first avoided destruction early as manor-holders and subsequently as [holders] of imperial territories, dominions, and fiefs." The Asiatic character of the original emperor system made the feudalism that matured fully in the Tokugawa period distinctive because even under the bakufu, the Imperial court continued to be the "eternal head of the system Asiatically." This accounted for the duality of the Tokugawa regime as a centralized feudalism that differed from European feudalism:[227] it was feudalistic, but "it retained the dregs of Asiatic rule, and in the later period it exhibited a tendency towards absolutism."[228] Although Tokugawa feudalism was not based directly on "the ancient Asiatic mode of production itself, nevertheless," Hirano agreed, "it was tinged with the special characteristics of the Asiatic mode of exploitation."[229] It was the resulting distinctiveness of Tokugawa feudalism that effectively limited the extent and character of the development of capitalism in Japan.

But what did Kōza-ha scholars understand oriental society and the related notion of the "Asiatic mode of production" to be? As did Soviet scholars Mikhail Godes and Yevgeny S. Iolk, Hirano and Hani treated the Asiatic mode of production not as a fully developed mode of production but as a variant of the ancient or feudal modes of production. Unlike Greek and Roman antiquity wherein society was divided between free men and slaves, Hirano wrote, Asiatic society was characterized by total slavery. There was no class of free citizens. The only social division existed not among classes but between despot and slaves, state and society. The state was a creature of the emperor, who was the despot. The oriental despot owned all land and all means of production including slaves. In Hirano's perspective, Asiatic society was not a geographical but an analytical category invoked to distinguish a variant of slave society that did not produce for a market. In terms of Marx's enumeration of the progressive epochs of human history, slavery—whether classical Greek and Roman or Asiatic—could evolve into feudalism, capitalism, and, finally, socialism. There was, therefore, no contradiction between the notion of Japan as an "Asiatic" society and Japan as a society that evolved into a form of "pure" albeit "Asiatic" feudalism. Moreover, still other elements of Marx's notion of oriental society were incorporated into Hirano's conception: the social functions performed by the state, such as irrigation and flood control; the identity of land taxes with rents, indicating that the despot or emperor was the society's highest landlord; and the role of oriental despotism in hindering the development of capitalism, particularly in the agrarian sector. Feudalism had developed more readily in Japan than in China not because one was oriental while the other was not—both were oriental societies—but Japan's geographical features, its mountainous terrain, made it more amenable to feudalism, whereas China's highly centralized civil service system allowed a national bureaucratic elite, reduced centrifugal forces, and made it less so.[230]

Like Hirano, Hani drew on Marx's *Capital* as well as the work of Karl Wittfogel, Max Weber, and Soviet scholars. His approach, however, was to place the Meiji Restoration in the context of the "encounter between Asia and European and American capitalism."[231] Hani firmly rejected interpretations of the Asiatic mode of production based on water control, "conflict with nomadic peoples," and "surplus population." Instead, like Hirano, Hani argued that the Asiatic mode of production was "nothing other than *essentially* the *slave* or *serf mode of production*"[232] in which coercion and oppression are particularly cruel and could take the form of " 'unlimited ownership of the persons of the producers'."[233] In Hani's view, Asiatic society did not precede class divisions: its state was based on such antagonisms that were characteristic of late clan society and not only on the performance of common social functions. For Hani, as for Hirano, then, being an oriental society did not prevent the future development of feudalism and capitalism.[234]

In Japan, the characteristics of oriental society were manifested in its ancient *be* system of communal slave ownership. Because community ownership of land was also characteristic of this period, the development of private property, a requisite for feudalism and capitalism, was hindered. When private landownership appeared along with commodity production, it retained some characteristics of the old tribal or clan society so that land came to be concentrated on a "state scale." Similarly, the people were not serfs of private landowners but serfs of the state. These oriental characteristics of Japanese antiquity persisted into the era of feudalism when the state hindered the development of free economic activity among the populace at every point. This accounted for the peculiar form of Japanese feudalism and for the difficulty of transforming commercial capital gained from han granaries and production offices into industrial capital. The Asiatic remnants of Japanese feudalism also accounted for the failure of Tokugawa feudalism to produce an absolutist government immediately. The forces of world capitalism forced the demise of Tokugawa feudalism and the rapid ascent of Japanese capitalism to the imperialist stage even while Japan's Asiatic legacy made the completion of an indigenous bourgeois-democratic revolution impossible. Having lived under Asiatic despotism, the Japanese had lost all aspirations to individual freedom. "Feudal production relations . . . under the Asiatic form," Hani concluded pessimistically, "were now . . . continued, to repress the people under imperialism." Only the newly awakened proletariat could complete this bourgeois-democratic revolution so long after Japanese capitalism had advanced to the imperialist stage.[235]

These observations on oriental society in Japanese history had a far greater significance for the Kōza-ha than the brevity of references to it in Kōza-ha writings would indicate. On the one hand, they affirmed the position of Japan and other late-industrializing non-European societies in Marx's theory of social development and revolution. In Hani's words, "the so-called colonization of India, the semi-colonization of China, and the opening of ports and the Meiji Restoration in Japan are none other than the oriental historic expression of world-historical laws."[236] At the same time, the notion of oriental society helped to attest to the peculiarities of Japanese capitalism that required that it still undergo a bourgeois-*democratic* revolution as late as the 1920s and 1930s. The notion, thus, helped to fill some crucial gaps in the Kōza-ha treatment of the state. Once Japan was treated in an Asian context, the emperor system and its ideology could be recognized as a mere myth that was "common to Asia's monsoon belt."[237] Nevertheless, if it was enshrouded in myth, this emperor system was not harmless, for it maintained a powerful material basis in economic arrangements that remained tinged with "Asiatic" characteristics, especially in the agrarian sphere. If such Asiatic remnants of feudalism and absolutism were not destroyed through bourgeois-democratic revolution, the proletarian revolution advocated by Kōza-ha and Rōnō-ha alike simply could not materialize.

CONCLUSIONS: NATIONALISM, MARXISM, AND THE ANALYSIS OF THE JAPANESE STATE

The objective political conditions that had permitted the debate on Japanese capitalism to ascend to new theoretical heights rapidly became the cause of its demise. By 1937, the political repression that had forced the practical debate on strategy and tactics to take a more abstruse academic form brought it to a close until after the war. The so-called February 26 military incident occurred in 1936, closely followed by the censure of Minobe Tatsukichi and his emperor-organ theory for lèse majesté. In September of that year, a group of Kōza-ha theorists was arrested in the Communist Academy incident, and the Rōnō-ha was silenced by December 1937 with the Jinmin Sensen Jiken (Popular Front incident). By February 1938, Rōnō-ha theorists Yamakawa, Ōuchi Hyōe, Inomata, and Sakisaka Itsurō were all in prison.[238] Aside from the arrests themselves, the increasing pervasiveness of government repression after 1931 alienated participants on both sides from the practical concerns that had first spawned the debate.[239] Eventually, nearly all fell under the shadow of the mass *tenkō* (recantations) that enveloped the left-wing movement in the mid- to late-1930s and 1940s.

Despite its sudden demise, the debate on Japanese capitalism held enduring significance, particularly with respect to the national question. For the first time in the prewar period, learned Japanese scholars undertook to analyze the origins and legitimacy of the state that asserted dominion over them, and their efforts had a lasting impact on scholarship in the postwar period. When the war was over and the Left reemerged on the Japanese political scene, the controversy over the nature of Japanese capitalism and the prewar state was revived. On this occasion, the question of the nature of the imperial institution once again loomed large: What was to account for the turn to fascism and imperialism in the 1930s? Was it a state that was thoroughly capitalistic and bourgeois, or was it a "militaristic, feudalistic" state that had led Japan into the disaster of the Pacific War? In the aftermath of the experience, theorists such as Kamiyama Shigeo and Shiga Yoshio broached once again the issue that had helped to prompt the debate when raised by Takahashi Kamekichi in the 1920s.[240] In the postwar years, conflict between the renascent Japanese Communist party and a Japanese Socialist party descended from the prewar Rōnō-ha followed the same lines of division between the prewar Kōza-ha and Rōnō-ha, respectively. Today, with the passing of the Shōwa emperor (Hirohito), who was on the throne when the "emperor system" was at issue in the 1920s and 1930s, it is the descendants of the original participants in the debate on Japanese capitalism, particularly on the Kōza-ha side, who once again question the implications of the survival of the imperial institution for democratization in Japan. In the postwar period, the notion that the political superstructure might enjoy relative autonomy from its economic base and even affect it significantly is the direct product of the prewar endeavors of Noro, Hirano, and Yamada; on the other hand, Yamakawa and Inomata laid the groundwork for the development of the sort of indigenous path to social democracy that has been espoused by the Japanese Socialist party since 1984. But the difficulty of the analytical task as it affects the imperial system remains unabated. The view of the prewar Kōza-ha had coincided with constitutional scholar Minobe Tatsukichi's recognition that democratization would require the destruction of the emperor system (at least as an absolutist rather than genuinely parliamentarian system, in Minobe's case). At the same time, Minobe also agreed with the Rōnō-ha that parliamentarism in the Taishō era signaled the emergence of bourgeois democracy even as the Kōza-ha saw the same as pseudoconstitutionalism.[241]

Perhaps it is not surprising that Marx's generalizations about the state could not resolve the question of the nature of state power that was so central to the debate on Japanese capitalism. Marx readily acknowledged that a bourgeois state might assume a variety of forms,[242] and the two Japanese factions split on precisely this issue. In short, the debate on Japanese capitalism found the two factions contesting the fundamental issue of the generality and specificity of state forms. The Rōnō-ha clearly argued on the side of the uniformity or generality of state forms in capitalist society. The Kōza-ha also seemed to claim generality in arguing that if the Japanese state had been truly bourgeois and democratic, it would not have been burdened with its peculiar imperial institution. Both positions were problematic from the perspective of Japanese nationalism. The Rōnō-ha position, by dissolving the particular into the universal, seemed to signal a reluctance to tackle an extended critique of the imperial institution that was the focus of Japanese loyalties. Its instrumentalist emphasis on ties between individual Dietmembers and officials, on the one hand, and individual capitalist enterprises, on the other, seemed to divert attention from the manner in which the mystical elements associated with the Imperial House were manipulated in a manner that was quite at odds with the workings of politics in the bourgeois state as Marx and Engels had described it. In this respect, the Kōza-ha's structuralist approach was more productive, pointing to the mutual interaction of institutions, practices, and, especially, ideology bequeathed from the past with the new forms borrowed from the West that gave Japanese politics its unique flavor. Yet in arguing that the emperor system could not be compared with the British monarchy, the Kōza-ha was taking a position of Japanese exceptionalism that might be likened to Takahashi Kamekichi's unpalatable position. In each case, one's stance on the state bore implications for the legitimacy of one's nationalism and national identity as a Japanese. The debate pitted those who claimed that Japan was as much an advanced capitalist society as almost any Western European country against those whose attention to Japan's peculiarities led them to condemn Japan to a backwardness that required a continuing bourgeois revolution even as one contested the power of the Japanese bourgeoisie. Similar polarities concerning the general and the particular and the relative value of one's own society in Marx's world-historical schema were also immediately evident in efforts by Chinese Marxists to resolve the national question by analyzing their own society's past and present. It is to their efforts that I now turn.

National Identity and the State in the Controversy on Chinese Social History

The debate on Japanese capitalism generated a rich pioneering scholarly literature on the socioeconomic and political development of Japan from the late Tokugawa period through the troubled Shōwa years. Initially driven by questions concerning the nature and the future of Japanese revolution, the controversy gradually took on a life of its own and, despite the absence of a successful socialist revolution there, engendered the major contribution of Marxism to Japanese intellectual life. As observed here, the national question figured heavily in the controversy, directing special attention to questions concerning Japan's relationship to the whole of Asia and its position as an "oriental" society in the unfolding of the universal history of Marx's and Engels's schema. In China, too, the systematic historical analysis of the past in Marxian terms grew out of conflict among Marxists within and outside the Chinese Communist party concerning the proper strategy and tactics of the Chinese revolution. There, where a Marxist-inspired revolution swept to victory in 1949, the controversy on Chinese social history marked the decisive emergence of the Marxist historiography that would dominate the treatment of the Chinese past after the revolution.

It is not the purpose here to recapitulate in detail the findings of existing studies of the nascent Marxist historiography on China.[1] The point is, rather, to illuminate the central role that the national question played in arousing the controversy and in affecting the major trajectories of its resolution. As in Japan, Marx's commentaries on Asia and Soviet interpretations of the limited potential for revolution in China pressed upon indigenous Marxists the challenge of situating China firmly within the mainstream of Marx's framework of revolutionary change. This task would be considerably more formidable in China than it had been for Japan. As recalled from consideration of the twin issues of oriental society and the Asiatic mode of production in the context of the debate on Japanese capitalism, Marx had adopted an approbative stance on Western imperialism in the East. Characterizing India as a prototypical "Asiatic" society that had lost "all grandeur and historical energies," Marx had contended that it could be brought back into the flow of human history only by violent social revolution induced by the brutal ravages of British imperialism.[2] This position would be considerably more problematic for Marxists in a China that had suffered from Western depredations for almost one century than it had been in Japan. More importantly, Asia's standing in Marx's overall schema raised significant theoretical complications for nationalistic Chinese who were compelled to demonstrate that the Chinese revolution—as an ultimately socialist revolution—was necessitated by the terms of Marx's historical outline. The issues involved were of such great consequence for China's Marxists from the Left Guomindang, through the CCP itself, and even among its besieged Trotskyists that they merit more detailed consideration here.

As has been noted elsewhere,[3] there was an apparent contradiction between Marx's negative normative assessment of "oriental societies" and his claim to have analyzed what he called the Asiatic mode of production "scientifically." Marx remarked on oriental society and the phenomenon of "oriental despotism" in several works, most extensively in the *Grundrisse*,[4] but he never satisfactorily resolved the issue by presenting a systematic analysis of where the so-called Asiatic mode of production fit into his larger scientific schema of human history. In the preface to *A Contribution to the Critique of Political Economy* (1859), where Marx summarized his historical materialism, he asserted, "In broad outlines Asiatic, ancient, feudal, and modern bourgeois modes of production can be designated as progressive epochs in the economic formation of society."[5] Oriental society, then, was the product of a special mode of production, presumably the Asiatic, "in which small-scale agriculture was carried out on the basis of production relations involving communal property ownership and cooperation."[6] It was characterized by the dispersal of agricultural villages that lacked the institution of private property and supported a despotic political superstructure. Here, it appeared that Marx had devised his poorly elaborated notion of the Asiatic mode of production "to account for a type of society outside the mainline of Western development."[7] On the one hand, he seemed to proffer the construct of oriental society to describe an allegedly static kind of society that appeared to be geographically specific, and, on the other, his enumeration of the Asiatic among the ancient, feudal, and capitalist modes of production suggested a universal historical category without any necessary geographical referent. Not surprisingly, then, as Marxism moved from Western Europe eastward through Russia, the ambivalence embedded in Marx's position occasioned, first, speculation among Russia's earliest Marxists, including Lenin and Plekhanov, and, then, heated debate that reached a peak circa 1930 as Soviet Marxists associated with the Comintern sought to legitimate revolutionary strategy and tactics for Marxian revolutions farther to the east. The controversy was revived repeatedly after World War II, stimulated by the Chinese Communist victory, intensified by evidence that movements of national liberation from European imperialism were spreading elsewhere in Asia, Africa, and Latin America.[8]

When the Leningrad Conference was convened under the leadership of Joseph Stalin in 1931, Stalin's intent was to reject the Asiatic mode of production construct that had gained such currency among Soviet scholars during the 1920s. Yet, Stalinist critics neither resolved in an intellectually satisfactory fashion the difficulties noted previously nor successfully discouraged Chinese and Japanese Marxists from pursuing the implications of the notion for the place of their own societies in the Marxian paradigm. In the West, the notion of the Asiatic mode of production has met with a decidedly negative reception. Maurice Godelier's acceptance of the notion as a valid concept[9] constitutes a minority point of view in the face of a consensus expressed well by E. J. Hobsbawm's view that "in the field of the study of oriental societies," "Marx combines profound insight with mistaken assumptions, e.g., about the internal stability of some such societies."[10] Indeed, Perry Anderson has concluded that "Marx was both empirically and theoretically wrong in establishing this concept [of the Asiatic mode of production] and so are those Marxists who try to give it a new lease on life."[11]

For Chinese scholars discussing the concept, a major difficulty arises from the introduction of a historical perspective that is in conflict with certain indigenous Chinese perspectives concerning society and history. Marx's interpretation was premised on a Hegelian concept of universal history that had defined Asia as bypassed by history. In the view posited in Hegel's *Philosophy of History*, oriental civilization, having once been the most advanced in human society, had become passive and stagnant, yielding pliantly to the progressive dynamism of occidental society, and finally, unable any longer to play a world-historical role in human development, fell completely outside the flow of world history.[12] In Marxian terms, the sole salvation for defunct oriental societies lay in the shock precipitated by Western imperialism, as the bourgeoisie of the West, determined "to create a world after its own image,"[13] dissolved mercilessly the stagnant and oppressive institutions of these societies.

This view of the place of the East in human history clearly reflected the political (im)balance of power between East and West that had evolved by Hegel's and Marx's time. In the late-eighteenth and early-nineteenth centuries, European nation-states expanded steadily outward, easily bringing into their dominions less-centralized, less-industrialized, and less-militarized societies in Africa and Asia.[14] Reflecting this political and economic asymmetry between East and West, Marx's posture proclaimed the values of the European Enlightenment: the view of unilinear historical progress propelled by human knowledge or consciousness; the notion that men and women should seek mastery over the forces of nature; and the juxtaposition of religion, viewed as primitive superstition, against secular scientific truth as the hallmark of modernity. Such values have not been universally shared among all societies. In China, Confucianism embraced a cyclical notion of history, and Daoism maintained that humanity should live in harmony with, rather than in perpetual struggle to dominate, nature.[15]

As Asians whose societies had been victimized by Western imperialism, Chinese Marxists, even more so than Japanese leftists, should well have been troubled by the implications of the depiction of Asia in Marx's historical materialism. Nevertheless, several factors mitigated the impact of this concern in China. First, implicit in the adoption of Marxism itself was acceptance of certain Western notions concerning social change. As discussed, Chinese and Japanese progressives tended to conjoin a nationalist reaction against Western imperialism with a fervor for domestic social change. By the turn of the twentieth century, most such thinkers accepted the notion that the successful intrusions of the Western powers into the East were simply the product of their technological and military superiority and the values that supported it. This occurred first in Japan where there had been a long tradition of philosophical syncretism. Only subsequently did such a concession to Western values appear in China, which had maintained a prestigious dynastic system on the basis of a fairly stable set of indigenous Confucian, Daoist, and Buddhist principles.[16] Only after repeated failures to reform while retaining China's philosophical essence was it finally conceded that the ideas and values that were the foundation of Western societies were at least as important as military and industrial technology to their accretion of superior "wealth and power."[17] It was the product of this concession, particularly with the occurrence of the October Revolution, that Marxism became attractive to Chinese and Japanese radicals as an all-embracing philosophical system that stood at the forefront of Western scientific thought.

Moreover, by the late nineteenth century, the new Japanese state that emerged from the Meiji Restoration had shown itself to have "caught up" with the West in its development of industrial capitalism and modern military power. At this point, in China, Marxism had been less attractive than anarchism among adherents of Western socialism, and it would remain relatively unappealing to Chinese intellectuals until the nationalist May Fourth Movement of 1919. Then, when they finally encountered Marxism anew in its powerful Leninist formulation, it was a Marxism that repudiated the West with its imperialist designs and affirmed Chinese nationalism. Finally, it should be noted that in neither China nor Japan was there full exposure to Marx's pessimistic writings on the East nor to Soviet writings on the question of oriental society in particular until the mid-1920s and 1930s, when Marxism had already established strong roots in the two Communist parties. To be sure, there developed an intense scholarly interest in Marx's view of oriental society during the debate on Japanese capitalism, but much of the concern with the subject in Japan came to revolve around its comparative application to China. By then, Japan had exceeded the predictions of the oriental society construct and developed industrial capitalism, which Marx had asserted would be impossible in Asia where private property had never been permitted to exist under the despotic oriental state. More importantly, Japan's Marxists could cite Marx himself to claim that their own homeland exhibited a social formation in the Tokugawa period that coincided precisely with Marx's conception of feudalism.[18] Here was a clear breach between Marx's treatments of China and Japan. There was a basis upon which Japanese Marxists could treat the Asiatic mode of production as something that applied to Japan only in the distant past. Yet, the fact that Japan had successfully moved on from its oriental history to prototypical feudalism and then capitalism might have offered hope to China's Marxists for the future of their own society if they could locate in it as well signs of feudalism and indigenous "sprouts" of Western-style capitalism.

Here it is important to note that not everything that Marx wrote specifically on China was negative enough in tone to alienate prospective adherents in China. At the same time that he penned the piece quoted above on India, Marx published an article on "Revolution in China and Europe" for the *New York Daily Tribune* (June 14, 1853). There and in subsequent essays, Marx speculated that England had aroused revolution in China in the form of the Taiping Rebellion and that, consequently, the disruption in China might spark a revolutionary reaction in Europe. There, denouncing the evils of imperialism, Marx saw in the Taiping Rebellion the potential for a Chinese national revolution serving as a vanguard of worldwide progress.[19] The anti-imperialist rhetoric of these pieces, as in Lenin's *Imperialism: The Highest Stage of Capitalism*, was compelling for Chinese nationalists such as Li Dazhao. Li initially ignored the reference to China's Asiatic backwardness that was implicit in the fact that Marx's hope for China had been a bourgeois-democratic revolution culminating in capitalist society, rather than a proletarian revolution culminating in the socialism that Marx longed to see in Europe and to which Li aspired for China.[20] Significantly, by 1862, Marx's view of the Taiping movement had shifted to a negative one condemning "its semireligious garb and senseless destruction."[21]

Finally, there had also been ambiguities in Marx's and Engels's treatment of the notion of oriental society as it had applied to later-industrializing Russia. In his *Grundrisse*, Marx had treated the Russian agrarian commune (mir, or obshchina) in terms of the "Slavonic community." This was a form of property that lay developmentally between the "oriental community" and the modern "Germanic community," which had seen the emergence of the private property that was necessary for the emergence of feudalism and then industrial capitalism.[22] As Lenin noted in his study, *The Development of Capitalism in Russia* (1899), feudalism was strengthened in Russia even as it was on the decline in the West, and the traditional peasant commune had survived in Russia long after analogous forms had yielded to private property in the agricultural sphere in Western Europe. On several occasions, disappointed by the failure first of the revolutions of the 1840s in the West and then the collapse of the Paris Commune of 1871, Marx had acknowledged the possibility that in the remanence of the mir lay the fresh, new prospect of a rapid transition to socialist society without Russia having to experience the ills of capitalism. In the survival of the peasant commune, in short, lay the fascinating, albeit vaguely troubling, implication that there might be a separate, alternative path of development to the "form of economy which will ensure, together with the greatest expansion of the productive powers of social labour, the most complete development of man," and Marx reprimanded those such as the Russian narodnik N. K. Mikhailovsky, who "fe[lt] obliged to metamorphose my historical sketch of the genesis of capitalism in Western Europe into an historico-philosophical theory of the *marche générale* imposed by fate upon every people, whatever the historical circumstances in which it finds itself."[23]

Perhaps recognizing the danger of this reformulation to the integrity of Marxism itself—that, as Leszek Kolakowski has noted, "It might seem that the doctrine applied only to Western Europe and that capitalism itself was an accident"[24]— Engels assailed a similar narodnik belief that the commune offered the basis for a direct transition to a unique Russian communism.[25] Shortly thereafter Marx also qualified his earlier optimism. Writing in their 1882 preface to the second Russian edition of the *Manifesto*, Marx and Engels averred that only "[i]f the Russian Revolution becomes a signal for a proletarian revolution in the West, so that both complement each other, the present Russian common ownership of land may serve as the starting point for a communist development."[26] Once again, despite the implications of the oriental society construct to the contrary, Marx and Engels reaffirmed their historical schema as a unilinear one in which East would finally join West in achieving socialist revolution. Subsequently, both the former narodnik George Plekhanov and Lenin elaborated on the theme of the Asiatic characteristics that had impeded Russia's historical development.[27] By 1921, Chinese Marxists had access to the Japanese translation of Plekhanov's *Fundamental Problems of Marxism*,[28] which contended that differences in geographical environment had determined divergent paths of development in East and West. Nevertheless, for Marxists in China, the success of the October Revolution seemed to demonstrate conclusively that Russia indeed shared the same path to modernity in socialist revolution that Marx had described for Western Europe.

Together, these factors minimized the possibility that Marx's pessimism about Asia and his endorsement of the positive role of European imperialism would alienate potential Chinese and Japanese Marxist revolutionaries. Nonetheless, Marx's broad commitment to the notion of a universal history combined with his determination to see Asia as different from the West together imposed on Chinese Marxists with much greater gravity than on their Japanese counterparts a crucial aspect of the national question: the relationship between the universal and the particular in Marx's thought and its implications for the prospects of Marxian-inspired revolution in Asia. If one was drawn to Marxism for its scientific precision and for its universality as scientific truth, could one mitigate the rigidity of Marx's periodization of history without vitiating the power of the theory itself as a basis for revolutionary strategy? In other words, if one decided that part of Marx's holistic schema of human development was wrong—as the CCP appeared to do when it rejected completely the applicability of the notion of the Asiatic mode of production to contemporary China even before the Soviets denounced the theory at the authoritative Leningrad Conference of 1931[29]—or if one revised that schema through "reinterpretation," how could one still cite Marx's model to claim that the revolution was not merely desirable but inevitable? China's alleged backwardness required the utmost certainty of success in revolution offered by the deterministic elements in Marx's schema.

Given these concerns, it is not surprising, then, that the historical moment of the eruption of the debate on Japanese capitalism was shared by the outbreak of the controversy on Chinese social history (*Zhongguo shehui shi lunzhan*). Emerging from developments in the Chinese revolution, particularly the debacle of the Shanghai coup, the debate ultimately addressed all the broad theoretical issues raised here by Marx's writings. The most troublesome problems here were precisely those related to the national question, and these directly linked the Chinese to the Japanese controversy. As already noted, the Comintern's controversial judgments on Japan were heavily colored by its distress over developments in China.[30] Indeed, the Comintern's 1927 Theses, which had helped to precipitate the debate on Japanese capitalism, had prescribed for Japan precisely the same two-stage revolutionary strategy that it formulated for the economically lagging

China. Yet whereas Japan had an overwhelmingly powerful state, which exercised effective ideological hegemony over almost the whole of Japanese society and now threatened both China and revolutionary Russia, China had essentially no effective national state. The republic founded in 1911 bore no resemblance in 1927 either to feudal absolutism or to bourgeois democracy. The geographically uneven development of China's economic base—the concentration of industrial capital on the coast—complicated the matter still further. If Japan was quintessentially feudalistic and China an oriental or post-oriental class society in Marxist terms, where was the despotic state that had caused China's economic stagnation? Even if one was convinced that the appellation *despotic* applied to Qing or imperial China in general, certainly the feeble republic of the 1920s was not as despotic[31] as the "semi-Asiatic" tsarist state in Russia had been when Russian Marxists first assailed it at the turn of the twentieth century. More fundamentally, the key questions for the Marxist theoreticians and strategists of China were "first, is contemporary Chinese society after all a feudal society or a capitalist society? Secondly, was the Chinese Revolution, after experiencing the defeat of 1927, a bourgeois revolution or a proletarian revolution?"[32] Finally, there was the urgent concern for Chinese intellectuals not only in the 1920s and 1930s but in the late 1970s and 1980s as well: Could China build a new national state that was not despotic that could lead China to economic and political modernity?[33] Could China achieve a stateness that would enable Chinese to assert themselves in the international arena and support the task of industrialization effectively without jeopardizing the opportunity to realize the achievement of fundamental human political and economic rights? These issues were embedded in the terms in which the controversy on Chinese social history was conducted even when they were not articulated explicitly.

The nationalism that provoked these concerns was intimately tied up with the question of the legitimacy of class struggle in the Chinese revolution. Hu Hanmin and Dai Jitao, among the first to use Marxist categories to analyze Chinese affairs, both repudiated class struggle as a threat to Chinese national unity in their early writings in 1919 and 1920.[34] At that time, their protests aroused no significant opposition. But by 1927, the denial of the need for class struggle by many but not all Guomindang Marxists aroused considerable controversy. Indeed, as Dirlik notes, scholars of the Left Guomindang "were largely responsible for triggering the Social History Controversy,"[35] and the issue of class struggle rapidly emerged at the forefront of it. When Left Guomindang leader Chen Gongbo wrote in his critique of the Guomindang, *Zhongguo Guomindang suo daibiao shi shenme?* (What does the Chinese Guomindang represent?) that the Guomindang represented the petty bourgeoisie, peasantry, and laborers and not the (national) bourgeoisie,[36] a certain Jing Pu responded that there was no class conflict in China. Chen retorted that classes and class struggle existed in China whether Jing wished to acknowledge them or not, and the weakness of the Guomindang to date had been the product of its failure to achieve sufficient class consciousness to take a proper stand in this class struggle.[37] It was the abrupt change in the revolutionary situation in China in 1927—the sudden decline in the revolutionary fervor that had accompanied the Northern Expedition and Chiang Kai-shek's turn against the CCP and the Left Guomindang—that accounts for this change in the intellectual climate among non-CCP Marxists.

This shift in intellectual climate, in turn, established the basis for a systematic historical examination of the roots of China's current crisis in the distant and not-so-distant past. One could only make sense of the disaster of 1927 by looking backward to discern clearly the forces that had contributed to it. At this critical juncture in the revolutionary movement, Chinese Marxists on all sides felt compelled to make Marxism truly their own by fashioning an indigenous grasp of Chinese history based on this Western-inspired schema of social change. It would appear that the repression by Chiang's Guomindang itself contributed directly to the controversy: just as intensified state pressure in Japan drove the hitherto open debate on JCP strategy and tactics underground to assume a more scholarly form, the events of 1927 prompted intellectual Marxists in China to step back from the immediate crisis and analyze it in a more dispassionate academic manner so that the revolution might be revived.[38] Thus, the link between the intellectual controversy and the actual revolution was never severed. As historiographer He Ganzhi wrote, "To begin with contemporary China, to reach back from there to China before imperialist aggression, to trace the history of Chinese feudalism, from feudalism to go back to the slave system, and finally to reach the period of the Asiatic mode of production—[the purpose of] all this was to expurgate the demands of the past and present and to ascertain our future direction."[39]

As in Japan, this quest aroused and exposed tremendous diversity within Chinese Marxism. In addition to those associated with the CCP, factions within the Left Guomindang led by Chen Gongbo (whose organ was *Geming pinglun* [Revolutionary review]) and Gu Mengyu (who published *Qianjin* [Advance] in 1928–1929), and smaller groups around Wang Jingwei and Shi Cuntong developed competing perspectives on Chinese history and the revolution.[40] Most participants were critical of both the CCP and the Guomindang,[41] and in their critiques of the two party lines made a significant effort to come to grips with the difficulties of applying Marx's historical schema and theory of revolution to China. In so doing, they helped to expose some problems with respect to the national question identified here in Marxist thought as it moved from West to East: the tension between universality and particularity, the role of the pursuit of stateness (the unity of nationality with the state) in a national revolution designed to culminate in a stateless communist society, and, finally, whether the limits of Marx's knowledge of Asian societies, the sparseness of his work on precapitalist societies, and the rigidity of his overall framework undermined the legitimacy of the application of his allegedly universal theory to China. Unlike the Japanese debate, however, one notes that Chinese participants in the controversy on Chinese social history were unable to assemble new data and produce a volume of scholarship that was particularly illuminating about the course of Chinese history itself. Yet the controversy and the terms in which it was waged remain highly significant for what they reveal about the depth of the national question in Chinese Marxism. The determination of China's Marxist historians to impose Marxian historical categories on their nation's history constituted an assertion of national identity and cultural dignity. This was the underlying motivation for what might superficially appear to be a fruitless endeavor to append Marxian labels to Chinese dynastic periods. Ironically, proud of their nation's heritage and resolved to prove China's equivalency to the West, participants in the controversy would find themselves characterizing their nation's history in terms of long periods of near stasis during which the kind of social change that occurred in the West was said not to have occurred in China. In the rest of this chapter, I sketch how this paradoxical pattern first emerged in the controversy on the periodization of Chinese history and the Asiatic mode of production.

THE STIMULUS FROM WITHOUT: COMINTERN THESES AND SOVIET ANALYSES OF THE REVOLUTION IN CHINA

The controversy on Chinese social history arose from concrete problems in the practice of the Chinese revolution. The Chinese Communist party was theoretically, strategically, and financially dependent on the Third International, and Chinese Marxists who sought to understand the place of China's socioeconomic development in world history took as their point of departure analyses proffered by Comintern pronouncements and Soviet academic studies of China.

There were two stages in the evolution of the Chinese Communist movement before 1949. During the first stage, from its inception in 1920–1921[42] through the early-1930s, the party's policies and politics fell under the close domination of the Soviet-led Comintern. Thereafter, in the Jiangxi Soviet (1931–1934) and Yan'an periods, the movement experienced the steady emergence and articulation of an indigenous Chinese Communist strategy that would supplant the program of the Stalin-Bukharin and then exclusively Stalinist (after 1929) leadership that had yielded such bitter fruit for the revolutionaries in China. The Comintern's formulations were not internally consistent, nor were they the product of a consensus within the Soviet leadership, and, consequently, the seemingly endless series of pronouncements from the Soviet Union introduced more uncertainties into the effort to analyze the situation in China than they resolved. It is in large part because of the theoretical inadequacies and the unfortunate consequences of the Soviet analyses and prescriptions that Chinese scholars sought to investigate the nature and significance of China's socioeconomic history for themselves. Nevertheless, Soviet work on China established a basis for discussion for Chinese historians, and, thus, its inconsistencies and the incoherence of Comintern policy in China would also be reflected in their own contributions.

The point of departure for Comintern policy in China was Lenin's interpretation of *Imperialism, the Highest Stage of Capitalism* (1916). Addressing the Second All-Russia Congress of Communist Organizations of the Peoples of the East in November of 1919, Lenin articulated clearly the implications of this work for peoples that had been victimized by the Western powers: "The civil war of the working people against the imperialists and exploiters in all the advanced countries is beginning to be combined with national wars against international imperialism." "We know that in the East," he declared, "the masses will rise as independent participants, as builders of a new life, because hundreds of millions of the people belong to dependent, underprivileged nations, which until now have been objects of international imperialist policy, and have only existed as material to fertilise capitalist culture and civilisation." Lenin saw in China's 1911 revolution, as well as revolutionary movements in Turkey, Persia, and India, reverberations of Russia's own 1905 and the promise that as they were "becoming alive to the need for practical action," "all the Eastern peoples will participate in deciding the destiny of the whole world." Through the phenomenon of imperialist conquest, Lenin argued, these primarily agrarian peoples shared with the Russian and European proletariats the experience of oppression by world capitalism, and they would unite in alliance with them just as peasants and workers had united to bring about the victorious revolution of 1917 in Russia.[43]

Although Lenin continued his vehement denunciations of "petty bourgeois nationalism" of the sort that had destroyed the Second International, he vested nationalism in "the more backward states and nations, in which feudal or patriarchal and patriarchal-peasant relations predominate" with a new legitimacy. "All Communist parties," he urged in the Draft Theses for the Comintern's Second Congress, "must assist the bourgeois-democratic liberation movement in these countries."[44] Herein lay the critical distinction that the Comintern drew between China and Japan on the national question. As witnessed previously, inconsistencies were manifested in the Comintern's treatment of Japan, however. In the Comintern view, the dual structure of Japan's economic base was reflected in a political superstructure in which political power was shared by a bloc of landlords and bourgeois. On the one hand, the persistence of the imperial system with its supporting institutions and their roots in agrarian relations that remained semifeudal in the countryside determined the need for a two-stage revolution in Japan not only at the inception of the JCP in 1922 but even as late as 1932. At the same time, Japan's status as a highly advanced capitalist society, indicated by the concentration of capital and the appearance of finance capital in the urban industrial sector, disqualified Japanese nationalism from a legitimate place in the Japanese revolutionary movement.

The anomalies of the Comintern's position here and the challenges that its pronouncements throughout the 1920s and 1930s on revolution in the East posed for Marxists in China and Japan become fully evident only when one considers the Japanese case in light of the Soviet leadership's directives on China. In terms of revolutionary strategy and tactics, the Comintern position amounted to prescribing essentially the same strategy of two-stage revolution for the highly industrially developed Japan as it did for the revolutionists of economically lagging China. The Comintern position dictated—not without some irony—that Japan's revolution could only proceed with the completion of a bourgeois-democratic revolution against the hegemony of the bourgeoisie.[45] Yet while Leninist orthodoxy asserted the legitimacy of nationalism in the stage of the bourgeois-democratic revolution, all measures possible were to be taken to guard against expressions of Japanese nationalism as imperialism, particularly against the Chinese revolution.

Similar inconsistencies in the Comintern's position on the Chinese revolution were manifest almost from the very outset. The key to these incongruities lies in the initial formulation of the Comintern approach to the Chinese revolution as a fundamentally instrumentalist strategy and in the Soviets' low estimation of the potential for Chinese, or, indeed, any other Asian, revolutionaries to execute a revolution that would culminate in socialism. It was this combination of attitudes that precipitated the early conflict between Lenin's Eurocentrism and the Indian M. N. Roy's Asiocentrism at the Second Comintern Congress in 1920. Roy not only insisted that the revolution in Europe "depends entirely on the course of the revolution in the East" but also repudiated Lenin's advocacy of supporting indigenous nationalist movements that were "bourgeois-democratic" in character. Lenin invoked the example of the Russian revolution in which the Bolsheviks had found it expedient to cooperate with the liberal bourgeoisie when it was resolute in its opposition to tsarism; and he contested Roy's assertion that instructions appropriate to a socialist revolution made sense in a society in which "the proletariat . . . numbers 5 million and there are 37 million landless peasants, [and] the Indian communists have not yet succeeded in creating a Communist Party in their country."[46]

Lenin did make some minor concessions to Roy's sensibilities, by changing the wording of his "Theses on the National and Colonial Question" from "bourgeois-democratic liberation movement of the workers and peasants" to "revolutionary liberation movement." Nevertheless, the profound tension between the two perspectives remained, to be revealed again and again in tense exchanges between indigenous Asian Marxists and the Soviet Comintern leadership. The Baku Congress later in 1920 was witness to another such conflict between two positions on the revolution in the East. There were eight Chinese delegates among its 1,891 attendees, but most of those representing the East were Central Asian Muslims. The previous year, at the first Conference of Muslim Communists of Central Asia in May 1919, these Marxists had already begun to express disillusionment with what they perceived as chauvinistic attitudes among Russians, many of whom had served as colonists and functionaries in Turkestan. "'We were still obliged to endure a contemptuous attitude on the part of the former privileged classes towards the indigenous masses','" one such delegate lamented. "'This attitude is that of the communists, who retain a mentality of oppressors and regard the Muslims as their subjects'."[47]

As for the revolution in China, it is important to note that the earliest Comintern prescriptions for the CCP emerged just as the national question was beginning to pose a potent threat to the unity of the struggling young Soviet state. Even as the Chinese Communists were moving to found their own party under Comintern auspices, tensions between the Comintern and both George Safarov, the Turkic Communist who served as Lenin's representative in Central Asia, and Mirza Sultan-Galiev amply reflected the conflict that would afflict Comintern efforts to dictate satisfactory policies for the revolution in China. Safarov was heavily embroiled in conflicts within the CPSU over the national question as it affected Soviet Asia. He repeatedly repudiated Great Russian chauvinism, demanded nativization of local party and governmental bodies in Soviet Asia, and insisted on guarantees of "national-cultural autonomy" in such areas. His vocal expression of such demands led Stalin to condemn him as a "Bundist," "i.e., a follower of a Jewish autonomist heresy in Russia's labor movement, and, hence, one not to be trusted." Together with Turkic leader Mirza Sultan-Galiev, Safarov began to devise important strategies for mobilizing Moslem populations within the Soviet Union, proposals that aroused suspicions that led to the exclusion of these important Asian Marxists from Comintern deliberations and then their liquidation at Stalin's initiative.[48]

The position of Sultan-Galiev in this conflict between Soviet and indigenous native Communists is most instructive for an understanding of the dimensions of the national question as they intersected in Soviet domestic politics and Comintern policy on China. In the years immediately after the Russian revolution, Sultan-Galiev had become a protégé of Stalin, who in 1920 appointed him as one of the three members of the Small Collegium of the Commissariat of Nationalities and coeditor of the Commissariat's organ *Zhizn' natsional'nostei* (The life of nationalities). Sultan-Galiev may bear partial responsibility for Lenin's and the Comintern's turn to the East after 1919. In the fall of that year, in a series of articles published in *Zhizn' natsional'nostei*, Sultan-Galiev argued that the main emphasis of revolutionary activity should be not in Western Europe but in the East as "the weakest link in the capitalist chain" and, indeed, that "the failure of Communist revolutions abroad was directly attributable to the inadequacy of Soviet efforts in the Eastern borderlands." Such revolutionary effort in the East, however, needed to respond to special conditions there where no strong urban proletariat existed. The Communists should nurture indigenous Moslem Communists and be conciliatory toward Moslem religious and other cultural traditions, he urged.[49] At this time, as a Volga Tatar Communist, Sultan-Galiev was not advocating a separate autonomous Tatar state, and there was no conflict between Sultan-Galiev's views and the basic Bolshevik strategy of 1919–1920. Indeed, as Richard Pipes notes, their pan-Islamic tendencies enjoyed Kremlin backing as it sought support among Islamic populations. Their position did, however, stand in contrast to that of the so-called left Tatar movement, headed by Said Galiev, who opposed national autonomy and wished to maintain the "privileged position which the Russians and other Europeans enjoyed in the Kazan province."[50] The situation changed in November 1919 when Sultan-Galiev's group advocated a separate Volga Tatar republic. His group, however, was unable to contest effectively the power of the left Tatar movement, and a new Autonomous Tatar Socialist Soviet Republic, created in September 1920, fell under the leadership of the left-wing Said Galiev.[51]

Meanwhile, in the brief interval since the October Revolution, it had become clear to Sultan-Galiev that socialist revolution had not ended the national inequalities that had existed under the old order, and by 1919, he had begun to doubt that the proletariat would genuinely liberate colonial and semicolonial peoples. The initiation of the New Economic Policy reinforced this disillusionment when it "returned to positions of power the classes which he and other Moslem Communists had identified with the old colonial regime: Russian merchants and officials, as well as Moslem tradesmen and clergymen." True liberation and elimination of world inequality, Sultan-Galiev now concluded, would be achieved not by the victory of the proletariat but by a new hegemony of the colonial and semicolonial peoples over industrialized peoples. "The formula which offers the replacement of the world-wide dictatorship of one class of European society (the bourgeoisie) by its antipode (the proletariat), i.e., by another of its classes, will not bring about a major change in the social life of the oppressed segment of humanity," Sultan-Galiev asserted. It was the war against the imperialism of industrialized societies that held the key to universal human liberation.[52]

When Sultan-Galiev propounded these ideas in 1921, they drew no opposition from the Central Committee of the Soviet party. Sultan-Galiev's group was soon able to gain control of the Volga Tatar CP and state power, however, and Sultan-Galiev then began to urge the creation of a Colonial International uniting victims of imperialism that would counter the influence of the Third International. He also urged the resurrection of the Moslem Communist party that had been dissolved by the Russian party in 1918 as well as the creation of a separate Soviet Moslem or Turkic republic. Not surprisingly, these inclinations toward separatism finally drew a strong reaction from his former mentor, and Sultan-Galiev was arrested. His case was heard at a special conference of minorities held in Moscow in June 1923. Stalin now charged Sultan-Galiev with violating the bounds of the need to cooperate with Turkic Moslems and advocating treason. The latter confessed and repented but was, nevertheless, expelled from the party.[53]

In the meantime, the Comintern promulgated numerous pronouncements on the Chinese revolution that reflected the instrumentalism of its approach to the movements of national liberation that it urged in the East and its low expectations for the possibility of achieving socialism in China itself in the near term. Its lack of familiarity with circumstances in China was starkly apparent. Most important was a striking absence of the sort of detailed analysis of the course of Chinese socio-economic and political development to date that one could find in Comintern theses on Japan. The most detailed such effort that appeared in time to affect the first Chinese analyses in the controversy on Chinese social history was the 1928 Resolution on the Land Problem and the Resolution on the Peasant Problem of the Sixth Congress of the Chinese Communist Party (also 1928). As Benjamin Schwartz has noted, these resolutions were "much more detailed than any previous discussion of the Chinese agrarian problem, and echo[ed] within their pages a weighty discussion which had arisen among Soviet theoreticians concerning the nature of Chinese rural society."[54]

Certainly, Comintern representatives in China and pronouncements issuing from the Comintern itself exerted a heavy influence on the formulation of these resolutions, but it is important to note what was omitted here and from Comintern documents on China. In Japan, the point of departure for Comintern theses was always an analysis of the structure of the state and its relationship to underlying economic relations. In the diagnosis of the existing state lay the key to the prescription of a one-stage or two-stage revolutionary strategy for Japan. To be sure, part of the Comintern's problem was that there was almost no unified national Chinese state against which to direct the revolution. Its targets were foreign imperialism and warlords, alleged to be "agents of foreign capital . . . hostile to Soviet Russia," which together stood in a mutually supportive relationship with feudal relations in the countryside.[55] Yet nowhere did the Comintern's theses offer even a tentative coherent analysis of how these relationships had come into being, how they affected the political superstructure in China, and their implications for the revolutionary process. These omissions help to explain the miscalculations that contributed to the debacle in Shanghai in 1927. Coupled with the persistent failure of the CCP under Comintern guidance to make significant strides in the late 1920s, they provided an important catalyst for Chinese Marxists themselves to undertake a systematic inquiry into the nature of the society that they aspired to change through nationalist and socialist revolution.

From the outset, in Comintern treatments, the prospects for the Chinese revolution were submerged within the dream of a proletarian revolution in the West and the urgent need to protect the world's lone proletarian state. Thus, the First Congress of Communist and Revolutionary Organizations of the Far East in January 1922 contended simply that the Communist parties of the East "must win leadership of the national revolutionary movements,"[56] and "orient themselves towards Soviet Russia as the bastion of all the oppressed and exploited masses."[57] "The Chinese revolution is a link in the chain of world revolution[;] it will be a tremendously powerful factor in revolutionizing the entire East."[58] As late as March 1926, Gregory Zinoviev, who would soon fall from his position as head of the Comintern, even suggested that the nationalist revolutions in the East might turn immediately into socialist revolutions: "If they succeeded in winning the colonies for socialism before a strong native bourgeoisie had grown up, these countries could skip the capitalist stage of development."[59] Yet such a sanguine perspective ultimately was not to prevail under the Stalin-Bukharin leadership. Even during Zinoviev's leadership, the CCP failed to impress Comintern officials that it could prevail in China and provide security for the Soviet Union to the south. "The only serious national-revolutionary group in China is the Kuomintang," the Executive Committee of the Comintern (ECCI) declared in January 1923, "which is based partly on the liberal-democratic bourgeoisie and petty bourgeoisie, partly on the intelligentsia and workers." This observation, coupled with the recognition that "the working class is directly interested in the solution of this national-revolutionary problem, while still being insufficiently differentiated as a wholly independent social force," dictated the necessity for the CCP's subordination to the Guomindang.[60] Although the Seventh ECCI Plenum of December 1926 concluded that "the Chinese Communist Party has grown in a short time into a first-class political factor in the country," the plenum criticized the party for a tendency to "underestimat[e] . . . the present movement."[61] At the Fifteenth CPSU Conference two months earlier, "Bukharin said that the central task in China was the fight against foreign imperialism and therefore the national-revolutionary united front had to be maintained." Yet, as Leon Trotsky noted, the ECCI resolution did not even mention Chiang's Canton coup of March 1926.[62]

Ironically, even as the Stalin-Bukharin leadership struggled to distinguish itself clearly from Trotsky's prescriptions for the revolution in China, the Seventh ECCI Plenum acknowledged "the most important peculiarity of China's economic situation . . . [in] the variety of forms existing side by side in the Chinese economy, beginning with finance-capital and ending with patriarchal survivals."[63] This pronouncement closely resembled Trotsky's notion of uneven and combined development opening new possibilities for socialist revolution in later-industrializing societies. Thus, the Comintern suggested that although "the Chinese revolution is historically bourgeois-democratic in nature, it is bound to acquire a broader social character."[64] Nevertheless, even after Chiang's Guomindang had turned against the CCP violently in Shanghai in April 1927, the theses of the oppositionists encouraging the CCP to take the offensive in the agrarian and urban revolution were firmly rejected.[65] Once Stalin had begun to consolidate his power, the Comintern facilely dispensed with the opposition's concerns: "The characterization of the present stage of the Chinese revolution as one which is already a socialist revolution is false. Equally false is its characterization as a 'permanent' revolution[;] . . . [this] is a mistake similar to that made by Trotsky in 1905."[66] There was to be no question that the Chinese revolution was limited to achieving a bourgeois national state; if Chinese society still lingered at the stage Russia had reached by 1905, it was not possible now, nearly two decades later, that China could be on the threshold of socialism.

The bitter conflicts within the Soviet Union on the national question described here were intimately linked to the highly tentative analyses of the Asian societies in which the Soviets sought to stimulate nationalist revolutions. The determination of Soviet authorities to submerge the particular characteristics of Asian societies in the universal was evidenced in Safarov's eventual acquiescence to the view of Pavel Mif and others associated with the Institute for the Study of the China Problem that China's "Asiatic feudalism" was state feudalism, its main characteristic the identity of rents and taxes.[67] Many Soviet scholars were, however, intrigued with the characteristics of these societies that appeared to be specifically Asian and produced studies to analyze them in greater depth. Such thinking within the Soviet Union was stimulated in 1925 by the publication of an article by David B. Riazanov, head of the Marx-Engels Institute, entitled "Marx on India and China," which described Marx's writings on oriental society and the Asiatic mode of production.[68] Furthermore, the same year, Eugene S. Varga, a leading economist, "declared that government-controlled productive and protective water works were the basis of Chinese society and that the scholarly administrators, the *literati*, and not the representatives of private property such as the landowners, constituted China's ruling class."[69] In other words, in the past as in the present the Chinese economic elite was not a class that controlled private property, but one that dominated public property. At this point a small circle developed around Varga and his fellow Hungarian emigré economist Ludwig S. Mad'iar. The two men together studied Marx's views on oriental society and strongly endorsed the validity of his notion of the Asiatic mode of production. From 1927 to 1947, Varga would head the Soviet Institute for the Study of the World Economy and World Politics and was soon known as the leading Soviet authority on the world economic crisis. With this 1925 article, however, Varga also began to publish extensively on the Chinese economy and revolution,[70] and his subsequent writings went on to identify China explicitly as an Asiatic society that differed in fundamental respects from feudal society as commonly understood.[71]

Mad'iar, too, applied the Asiatic mode of production concept to China, but his views were based on his own experience working with Comintern advisor Mikhail M. Borodin in China in 1926–1927. China was Mad'iar's area of specialization, and he published a series of writings on its rural economy, boldly asserting that China in his own day remained dominated by the Asiatic mode of production.[72] Like Varga, Mad'iar viewed the Asiatic mode of production as a separate mode of production that differed from feudalism in its lack of feudal lords and property. Citing George Plekhanov, however, Mad'iar stressed the influence of geography after the primitive communal stage,[73] arguing that the need for water control to prevent floods and for artificial irrigation was the key to the formation of this mode of production. The need for such public works generated the establishment of a despotic state in ancient societies based on rural communities. The despot owned the land and the water in this formation, Mad'iar asserted. Nevertheless, he insisted that this was a specific class social formation, thus opposing those who saw in the despotic state a supraclass entity. Yet he agreed with Varga's position that the major contradiction or conflict lay between the peasants and the state.[74] Most importantly, China, like all precapitalist societies, had experienced the development of commercial and usury capital; indeed, commercial capital had appeared in China long before it emerged in the West. Yet commercial and usury capital were inadequate to revolutionize China in the direction of industrial capitalism because of the overwhelming power the despotic state wielded over production.[75] Such industrialization required the existence of private property, which was precluded by the despot's possession of the land.

Mad'iar's and Varga's position on the notion of the Asiatic mode of production seemed to be granted official validation in 1928 when the concept appeared to describe certain colonial countries in the Bukharin-drafted program of the Comintern's Sixth Congress.[76] Nonetheless, by 1930 an intense conflict had arisen between Mad'iar and Varga, on the one hand, and those who would prevail at the Leningrad Conference on the Asiatic Mode of Production in February 1931 on the other. Varga openly criticized Comintern official Yevgeny S. Iolk and others on the editorial board of *Problemy Kitaia* (Problems of China) who argued that the Asiatic mode of production was not a separate mode of production but merely a variant of feudalism. If this had been Marx's view, Varga wrote, " 'he would have said so'."[77] Accusing Iolk of having revised Marx on the subject, Varga contended that the time had come to convene a conference to settle the issue. At this time, Varga and Mad'iar confronted opponents who did not have established reputations as scholars of the Far East. Mikhail Godes and Iolk were joined by Sergei I. Kovalev, the historian of antiquity, in their attack on the view that the Asiatic mode of production constituted a separate mode of production. Iolk had served as a translator in China from 1925 to 1927, but neither he nor Godes had published extensively on the question of the Asiatic mode of production before 1930.[78] The evidence would suggest that they were emboldened in their attack on Mad'iar and Varga by the support of Joseph Stalin. By now Stalin had prevailed over both Bukharin, his final rival among the original Leninist Politburo for the succession and a major architect of Comintern policy in the East, and Gregory Zinoviev, who had also figured heavily in making Comintern policy in the East in the mid-1920s.

What links Soviet treatments of the issue of the Asiatic mode of production to the national question in China is the 1927 Shanghai Coup that was the immediate catalyst for the controversy over this hitherto neglected element of Marxist theory. Both Lenin and Plekhanov had referred liberally to the role of Asiatic characteristics associated with Marx's concept of oriental society in their discussions of Russia's own economic development. As a populist, Plekhanov had noted Russia's "vegetative, non-developmental character," its inability to promote change to new modes of production out of any internal dynamic.[79] Subsequently, as a Marxist, Plekhanov drew closer to Lenin's view that Russia's Asiatic past and continuing semi-Asiatic culture were responsible for its continuing tardiness in developing industrial capitalism[80] but that the Asiatic mode did not necessarily preclude further development along the typically Western path; Asiatic Russia had indeed evolved a form of feudalism.[81]

Nevertheless, in 1931, the issue was not Russian development but that of China, and the political motivation of the concerted attack launched by Godes's report at the Leningrad "Discussion on the Asiatic Mode of Production" was at best thinly disguised. Karl Wittfogel has suggested cogently that the Asiatic mode of production was so vehemently denounced because it might be applied to interpret Stalinism as an Asiatic "restoration" of bureaucratic class rule in Russia itself. Godes and Iolk, however, situated their attack on Mad'iar, Varga, Riazanov, and, by implication, the deposed Bukharin—none of whom was permitted to attend the discussion[82]—in terms of the situation in China:

> If we deem it possible to discuss the question of the "Asiatic mode of production," then it is primarily because we are concerned with the political conclusion to be drawn from the theory of the Asiatic mode of production.
>
> We are not here because, as Comrade Kokin said, we "need at last to study the history of the Orient and include it in world history." This is not the reason we are discussing the Asiatic mode of production, but in order to turn the practical history now being created by the heroic struggle of the exploited masses of China, Indo-China, and India, to the interests of the labouring masses by means of the correct method. . . .
>
> And so, if we approach things from this perspective, . . . then it is perfectly clear that the interpretation of individual statements by Marx and Engels on the Orient, presented to us in the guise of a superficially perfected theory about a particular Asiatic mode of production, is absolutely unacceptable from a political point of view.[83]

As the passage demonstrates, the Asiatic mode of production controversy was an integral part of the debate over China policy, which was itself enmeshed in the power struggle between Stalin and his erstwhile rivals to succeed Lenin: Trotsky and Bukharin. As Wittfogel indicates, the outcome of the Leningrad Conference stressed three major points: (1) that the notion that "a functional bureaucracy could be the ruling class"—a key component of the Asiatic mode of production idea— was "un-Marxist"; (2) that the "Asiatic-bureaucratic interpretation of the Chinese 'gentry' was invalid"; and (3) that "the theory of the Asiatic mode of production imperiled the work of the Communist International in the colonial and semi-colonial countries of Asia" by enabling Asian nationalists to challenge the "doctrinal authority" of the Comintern on the basis of the alleged uniqueness of their societies.[84] The seriousness with which Comintern leaders regarded this threat to their authority is not to be underestimated.

By the time of the Leningrad Conference, the radical nationalist challenge to the Comintern's Eurocentric approach to the revolution in the East had been defeated decisively. Shortly before Sultan-Galiev was rearrested and then disappeared entirely in 1929–1930,[85] M. N. Roy's confrontation with Lenin and his successors had been resolved. At its Sixth Congress of 1928, the Comintern denounced Roy for "rightist deviation" and then expelled him the following year.[86] As Iolk had written the previous year in *Problemy Kitaia*, individuals such as these and scholars who attributed validity to the notion of the Asiatic mode of production erred "in treating the colonial and semi-colonial nations as distinct from Europe in terms of Marxist theory." In this way, they "mystify Eastern studies,"[87] in short making the East as a whole less accessible to, and malleable by, the Comintern.

And the Chinese revolution was the most important Comintern concern in the East. Godes was unambiguous in stressing the centrality of the problem of the Chinese revolution to the entire discussion and the threat of nationalists such as the ill-fated Sultan-Galiev to the entire enterprise of the Leningrad Conference:

> The theory of the Asiatic mode of production, which emphasizes the exclusive specificities of oriental history, can easily play into the hands of nationalist elements in the Orient. They could hide under the veil of this exclusive nature and insist that the teachings of Marx and Lenin are inapplicable to the Orient [perhaps as Takahashi Kamekichi did with respect to Lenin on imperialism and Japan]. At the same time, this theory of exclusivity completely satisfies imperialism, since it is associated with the view that oriental society was stagnant and therefore that European capitalism played a messianic role.[88]

It is, perhaps, significant, in this respect, that shortly before the Leningrad Conference a historical conference was held in the Georgian capital of Tbilisi, which denied the utility of the Asiatic mode of production idea for Turkey and Persia.[89] The conclusions generated by the Leningrad Conference, of course, like those produced at Tbilisi, were the product of political pressures rather than rigorous academic treatment, and they could not lay to rest Chinese or Japanese Marxists' doubts that the notion of the Asiatic mode of production might retain some relevance to their own societies. Thus, even while they distorted the actual dynamics of Chinese society in applying the term *feudal* to it, they did help to expose some major theoretical difficulties that had arisen in the Soviet discourse on the Asiatic mode of production and in Comintern views of the Chinese revolution.

There was scant evidence that the term "feudalism" could really apply to a society that had neither serfs on land that could not be bought or sold nor lords with large fiefs. Yet, as early as 1926, Stalin had begun to stress the role of feudal remnants in Chinese society, and in 1928 the Chinese Communist party itself, at its Sixth National Congress in Moscow, yielded to Stalin's influence by emphasizing feudal relations in the Chinese countryside and rejecting the Mad'iar-Wittfogel view of China as an Asiatic society.[90] Although an earlier version of the resolutions passed at this Congress had relied on the concept of the Asiatic mode of production,[91] the final version stressed that " 'Chinese peasants suffer a combined feudal and capitalist mode of exploitation'."[92] As Schwartz notes, though the dominant elements in the Chinese countryside were said to be feudal, the word was not as well defined as it had been in Marx's and Engels's original usage, "and in China it was used to refer to all those economic and social phenomena which cannot be understood in terms of a Western system of Private Property. The phrase 'semifeudal' [was] used to indicate the fact that private property relations exist side by side with 'feudal relations'."[93] In retrospect, the vagueness of such new formulations concerning feudalism highlights the difficulties of the Asiatic mode of production concept as applied by Mad'iar to analyze China. Mad'iar had asserted that the "remnants" of the Asiatic mode of production coexisted alongside the "remnants" of feudalism: in other words, at some point, private property and feudalism had, in fact, emerged in China and elsewhere in the Orient.[94] Although it was conceivable that such a coexistence could occur, the Soviet discussion had posited the Asiatic mode of production and feudalism as alternative and mutually exclusive depictions of the current state of Chinese society. As originally presented by Marx, the rise of private property had been an impossibility under the despotism characteristic of the Asiatic mode of production, and the de facto existence of private property, in the form of a hereditary right to hold land and use serfs, was an essential component of feudalism. Therefore, Mad'iar's interpretation could only be sustained if he made some alteration in Marx's original portrayal of the stagnancy of oriental society.

Not surprisingly, given Marx's views on the impact of Western imperialism, Mad'iar argued that the confrontation between European imperialism and the Asiatic mode of production in India and China had presumably triggered the move from the Asiatic to feudal and capitalist relations of production. As Godes perceptively noted, this proposition posed a variety of theoretical problems: Did the Asiatic mode of production fall, and, if so, precisely how? In addition, Godes found other inconsistencies in Mad'iar's and Varga's interpretations of the history of the East.

> If the Asiatic mode of production ended in China in the Chou dynasty, then Mad'iar is incorrect in bringing it down to the nineteenth century. If Mad'iar is right when he considers that the European incursion found the Asiatic mode of production, then how

does he explain the economic and social structure of contemporary China? . . . If Mad'iar is right, and if the survivals of feudal relations predominate in China, then by what miracle, in an era of European intrusion, did the Asiatic mode of production evolve into the feudal mode of production? And if to the present day the survivals of the Asiatic mode of production dominate [as Varga asserted], then how do you connect this with the pronouncements of the [now Stalin-dominated] Communist International on the character of the Chinese revolution?

None of these issues, Godes insisted, could be resolved satisfactorily on the basis of the Asiatic mode of production concept elaborated by Varga and Mad'iar. More importantly, Iolk claimed that this theory "reflect[ed] well-defined foreign influences" (Germany's Wittfogel, perhaps, as well as the two Hungarian émigrés) and challenged the Stalinist view, thus constituting "the wet nurse for the theoretical position of Trotskyism."[95]

Godes proposed a solution that was purely semantic: "The Asiatic mode of production is nothing other than feudalism. The Orient, in a very unique fashion, went through the same stages of social development as Europe." Careful study, Godes argued, would lead one to discover in the East, as in the West, the essential characteristics of feudalism, which he defined as follows: "Landownership is the basis for the accumulation of the surplus product; the direct producer conducts his own independent economic operation; in the relations between the owner of the means of production and the direct producer, extra-economic compulsion prevails; [and] the hierarchy of landownership corresponds to the hierarchy of political power." Godes did not deny that the elements that Mad'iar and M. Kokin and G. Papaian identified as accoutrements of the Asiatic mode of production existed in the East.[96] He did, however, reject the notion that these characteristics could "either individually, or taken together, . . . fulfill the main requirements for the construction of a separate mode of production."[97] Thus, in practice the traditional Chinese gentry were to be considered not "Asiatic-bureaucratic" but feudalistic in character. Moreover, the notion that a state bureaucracy, based on public management rather than its private ownership of land and other means of production, could comprise a ruling class was denounced as un-Marxist. With a single stroke, Stalin's critics of the Asiatic mode of production theory thus relegated the peculiarities of Asian societies such as China to insignificance and allowed Comintern Marxists conveniently to ignore Marx's embarrassing remarks on the positive role of Western imperialism in the East.

Godes's formulation that the Asiatic mode of production was merely a variant of feudalism was not the sole Soviet resolution of the issues raised at the Leningrad meeting. Another critique of the Mad'iar-Varga understanding of oriental society was offered during the 1930s by the historian Sergei I. Kovalev of the University of Leningrad. Kovalev, best known for his 1935 work *Istoriia drevnego mira* (History of the ancient world), was the leading Soviet theorist on antiquity. Kovalev agreed with Godes that the Asiatic mode of production was but a variant of another mode of production—in Kovalev's case, a variant of the slave owner formation of antiquity. More important, however, for consideration here of the controversy on

Chinese social history, is that so influential was the notion of the Asiatic mode of production as applied to China by Varga and Mad'iar that other Soviet theorists—including Prigozhin, Grinovitch, and Struve—continued throughout the 1930s to seek in the feudal mode of production elements that had previously been identified by Varga and Mad'iar. Indeed, despite the attack on his work at Leningrad, Mad'iar was permitted to publish in the Comintern organ *International Press Correspondence*, later in 1931, an article, "Flood Disasters in China," that invoked the imagery of oriental despotism based on large-scale waterworks.[98] Similarly, through the 1930s, Wittfogel analyzed the history of Chinese economic development in terms of the evolution of a despotic "Asiatic" system based on large-scale waterworks.[99] Such writings became more accessible to Chinese scholars through translations into Japanese by the Kōza-ha Marxist Hirano Yoshitarō and others.[100] Moreover, the new interpretation of the Sixth CCP Congress, with its emphasis on a symbiotic relationship between feudalism and imperialism in China, was not entirely persuasive to those who would seek other interpretations of China's past and present. It is not surprising, then, that through the late 1920s and 1930s Chinese Marxist scholars should have determined to develop for themselves coherent interpretations of Chinese history as the CCP struggled to make a socialist—not merely bourgeois-democratic—revolution in a society that remained remote from the prototype of bourgeois-capitalist society in Marx's paradigm.

THE PERIODIZATION OF CHINESE HISTORY: THE DEVELOPMENT OF CAPITALISM IN CHINA

The Marxist paradigm of history defines revolution in terms of the transition from one mode of production to another through class conflict. Within this framework, participants in the controversy on Chinese social history from 1927 to 1937 endeavored to define China's place in Marx's schema of universal history in order to assure themselves that his depictions of bourgeois-democratic and then socialist revolution applied to their own society. The "backwardness" of Chinese society and Marx's views on the East, however, placed a special burden on these writers. Just as Lenin had penned *The Development of Capitalism in Russia* to counter the narodnik contention that Marxism was not applicable to Russia's past and future, Chinese Marxists, too, felt impelled, particularly after the painful setback of 1927, to demonstrate that their society's historical course had followed the path of Europe's development, whatever China's allegedly "oriental" characteristics. Moreover, like Japanese Marxists debating the issue of "manufacture" in the Tokugawa era, many felt obliged to establish that industrial capitalism had emerged in China independently and not merely as a result of the Western intrusion.

The controversy, then, came to revolve around what Joseph R. Levenson described as a "passion for equating Chinese history with the West's by periodization, and thus denying to China any highly individual character, . . . combined with insistence that all the transitions were internal to China."[101] It is ironic that this should have occurred just as Mao Zedong, reacting to the inadequacies of Comintern prescriptions, was taking the first tentative initiatives to devise his own strategy for a Marxian revolution. This he would do by modifying its universalities to accord with his own observations about China's peculiarities.[102] In so doing, Mao did not indulge in extensive speculation about Chinese social formations in the distant past. Rather, he addressed the problem of historical stages simply by adding the prefix "semi" to the Marxian term "feudal" to characterize contemporary China. This allowed him to legitimate agrarian revolution and, after the demise of the First United Front, a strictly conditional cooperation of the Guomindang during the Sino-Japanese War.

For those committed to systematic periodization of China's socioeconomic development in more rigorous terms, however, such an exercise alone could not suffice. The problem of equivalence would be a formidable one even for scholarly treatment. Benjamin Schwartz has depicted the intellectual dilemma of indigenous Marxist historians as follows:

> Since in terms of the values inherent in [the] Marxist view [of the transition from slavery to feudalism to capitalism], the dignity of any culture hinges precisely on its latent capacity to produce a modern industrial system—to deny this immanent capacity to China is to relegate China to an inferior historic position. . . .
>
>   Furthermore, if China's development is to be taken as a duplicate of Western development in Marxist terms, it must inevitably emerge as a defective duplicate. If . . . the emergence of a Chinese capitalism was inhibited by the aggressive intrusion of Western capitalist imperialism, the question remains—why did not Chinese capitalism emerge simultaneously with or even before Western capitalism? . . . If the maturation of the contradictory forces was inhibited by cultural or geographical factors, it must be admitted that factors outside of the mode of production played a dominant role in Chinese history. In any case, the duplicate remains defective.[103]

If this conclusion were denied, there was yet a third possibility—that Marx's was not a universal history at all but only a theory about events in Western Europe during a particular era and, thus, reflected only the values and power relations dominant in Marx's lifetime. Yet if this were the case, politically, China's Marxists would be powerless to claim a scientific basis on which to assert that the time was ripe for revolution in China.

Chinese Marxists were committed to the Marxian schema as a universal, coherent whole, and where it did not mesh neatly with Chinese realities, the proud nationalistic commitment to social revolution on the Marxian model required that the schema be slightly altered yet remain within the Marxian framework. Such efforts produced no fewer than thirty alternative periodizations of China's progression from primitive communist society to the "feudal," "semicolonial," "colonial," "capitalist," "precapitalist," or undefined contemporary period.[104] These conceptualizations were not merely a matter of scholarship. Like the debate on Japanese capitalism, the controversy emerged directly out of conflict over the proper strategy and tactics for the revolution in China. Although the debate proper did not begin until after the rupture of the First United Front, as early as 1924 some Chinese Marxists, frustrated with the Comintern's policy of alliance with the Guomindang, felt driven to "theoretical reflection." Such early efforts by Peng Shuzhi, Chen Duxiu, and others marked the first steps toward the periodization of Chinese history. Contemplating the reasons for the failure of the 1911 revolution, for example, Peng portrayed China as "a semicolonized country." For centuries, China had been dominated by "feudal production relations" that were radically disrupted by the ravages of imperialism. The turn of the twentieth century brought the emergence of a bourgeoisie, prompted by Western influence in the port cities.[105] Although Western imperialism brought wealth to some Chinese, the Western influence was pernicious in this account because it also brought with it the negative aspects of capitalism that were criticized in Marx's *Capital*.

Peng's analysis reflected a profound ambivalence concerning China and its position in human history. By characterizing China as a feudal society until the Western intrusion, Peng affirmed China as a society endowed with the internal dynamic necessary to develop capitalism on its own. Yet at the same time, he seemed to imply that China's capitalist development had depended on the intervention of the West. As a certain nationalistic impulse imbued all subsequent Chinese efforts to periodize Chinese history, their authors would share a similar ambivalence. Participants in the controversy were caught between the need to affirm China's place in a universal history and the need to recognize the undeniably special characteristics that had made their imprint on China's experience with the development of capitalism. Thus, ultimately, many would find themselves compelled at once to repudiate the exceptionalism implicit in the Asiatic mode of production construct and to postulate characteristics of Chinese development in containing many elements commonly identified with that construct.

The controversy itself was provoked by the publication of Left Guomindang literature by associates of Wang Jingwei after 1927. The new literature claimed that China was neither feudal nor capitalist but that the "ambiguity of the class structure had enabled parasitic political forces of a feudal nature to retain their power, with these forces, at the same time, serving the cause of imperialists."[106] This claim implied that although China needed a "national" revolution it did not require intense class struggle, and it provoked CCP partisans to bolster their own position—particularly on the need for agrarian revolution—by further inquiry into China's social history. As the debate evolved, those associated with the Left Guomindang emerged as one of three distinct currents. Left Guomindang theorists, including Tao Xisheng, Chen Gongbo (editor of *Geming pinglun* [Revolutionary review]), Gu Mengyu (editor of *Shuangshi* [Double ten]), and Zhou Gucheng, were also known as the *Xin shengming* (New life) faction because of their identification with the periodical of that name.[107] They contested the CCP view that "China was predominantly feudal, with imperialism supporting (or perpetuating) the feudal social structure in China." CCP participants, who published in *Bolshevik*, *Xin sichao* (New tide), and other magazines, included Guo Moruo, Li Lisan, Pan Dongzhou, Zhu Peiwo, Chen Boda, Xiong Deshan, and Qu Qiubai. Finally, the Trotskyist group, also known as the *Dongli* (*Der Motor*) faction after their journal, also published in *Dushu zazhi* (Reading magazine). Its contributors included Ren Shu, Yan Lingfeng, Liu Guang, Liu Jingyuan, and Li Ji.[108] The theoretical position assumed by each group was directly related to its revolutionary strategy because the ultimate purpose of the scholarly endeavor was to respond to the threat posed by the failures of 1927 to the legitimacy of Marxian revolution.

The Periodization of Chinese History within the Chinese Communist Party

The CCP position that feudalism was dominant in China and supported by imperialism was consistent with that of the Stalin-Bukharin Comintern leadership; Chinese society was feudalistic, more backward than Russia had been in 1905 in this view and, thus, could be expected to execute only a bourgeois-democratic revolution in the near term.[109] In 1928, in response to the Shanghai debacle (and to the failure of Comintern policy in England at the same time) the Comintern abandoned its United Front tactics in favor of vehement class struggle against social democracy, which it viewed as "becoming more bourgeois and imperialist, more and more an integral part of the bourgeois state." The Comintern thus launched the so-called "third period" of intense class struggle on the international front.[110]

W. Zhou	E. Zhou	Qin	Qing	Present
feudalism	transition	⟶	semifeudal society	⟶

In China, this policy was manifested in the short-lived Li Lisan line and the establishment of urban soviets such as the ill-fated Canton Commune. The periodization of Chinese history developed by Li before the dissolution of his leadership in 1931 reflected the changes in Comintern strategy. Li postulated a schema in which feudalism had developed in China as early as the Western Zhou period (1122–255 B.C.), had experienced a "transitional" period beginning in the Eastern Zhou (255–249 B.C.), and since the late imperial era had been "semifeudal" in character.[111] By the end of the 1920s, this developmental process had produced a China that was dominated economically and politically by both feudalism and imperialism, which were inextricably linked in mutual support.[112] As for Mao, Li's designation of contemporary Chinese society as "semifeudal" conceded the influence of the bourgeoisie in China and, thus, permitted the CCP to adopt an aggressive stance against the bourgeoisie (as represented by the Guomindang) without eliminating the possibility of a rapid progression to full proletarian socialist revolution, as a more rigid application of the Marxist category of feudalism to contemporary China would have done. The more flexible application of such categories by Li, as by Marxists in the other two factions, enabled them to show that China fit the universal categories required by the Marxian schema to justify their revolutionary activities.

Other Communist participants in the controversy produced variations on this theme. The most prominent of these was Guo Moruo, whose argument that China had experienced slave society was the basis for a "four-stage development" (*si-duan lun*) scheme that would be shared by many others. Guo's *Zhongguo gudai shehui yanjiu* (Studies on ancient Chinese society) (1930) was "the first significant effort to extend the analogy with European development over the whole of Chinese history." As such, it provoked intense controversy among contemporaries. Although it was more sanguine about China's ability to evolve fully into a capitalist mode of production than were most CCP treatments, Guo's schema did provide the historical premises for the current CCP line on the periodization of Chinese history.[113] Drawing on Lewis H. Morgan's *Ancient Society* and Friedrich Engels's *Origin of the Family, Private Property and the State* as well as evidence gleaned from bone inscriptions, Guo's work posited the following progression of historical stages in China: primitive gens society with "Asiatic" characteristics from pre-Yin (late-Shang) through the Yin dynasty; slave society like that of Greek and Roman antiquity in the Western Zhou; after a short transitional period in the Eastern Zhou, entry into the feudal stage in the Qin period (221–207 B.C.); and finally, after remaining feudalistic until the Opium Wars beginning in 1840, the transition to capitalist society by 1930.[114] Guo insisted that feudalism could not have collapsed immediately after the Qin dynasty because signs of it—in the presence of regional principalities, frontier forts, and regional generals—persisted well into the Qing period.[115]

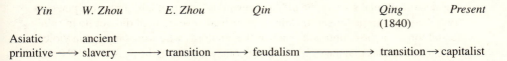

Yin	*W. Zhou*	*E. Zhou*	*Qin*	*Qing* (1840)	*Present*
Asiatic primitive ⟶	ancient slavery ⟶	transition ⟶	feudalism	⟶ transition ⟶	capitalist

Guo's schema appeared to address the issue of historical equivalence by embracing all the social formations enumerated by Marx. It is noteworthy, however, that feudalism in Guo's scheme lasted for two thousand years, and this raised precisely the theoretical difficulties identified by Schwartz. In addition, as Dirlik has noted, "while [Guo] eagerly accepted Marx's social formations as stages in a universal scheme of development, he ignored altogether Marx's formulation of the dynamics of historical progress in terms of the periodic contradiction between the mode [sic] and the relations of production." Technological innovation appeared in his work as "the unilateral motive force of historical evolution;"[116] "'the development of the economy of mankind [was] premised on the development of tools'," in Guo's view.[117] Thus, the reason that China had not spontaneously developed to the industrial capitalist stage, Guo argued, lay in its failure to invent the steam engine.[118] Thus, Guo avoided a systematic consideration of the specific relations of production in China that had come to act as "fetters" on the further development of forces of production, which, in turn, produced the transition to a new era. Thus, Guo also was unable to address the issue of precisely why the transition to feudalism and then feudalism itself had lasted so long in China. Nevertheless, despite this anomaly, Guo's scheme had two virtues that made it attractive to many of his peers. First, its close approximation to Marx's succession of the "Asiatic, ancient [slave], feudal, and modern bourgeois epochs" fit China neatly into Marx's universal history. Second, his contention that China was currently capitalistic satisfied the political desire to show that a socialist revolution was, indeed, possible in China.

The Left Guomindang versus the CCP on Capitalism in China's Past and Present

Other CCP contributors approached more closely the Comintern and Li Lisan view of the continuing power of feudal economic relations in contemporary China.[119] These interpretations were developed and refined largely in response to the work of Tao Xisheng, whose views ("Tao Xishengism") were widely cited as representative of the Left Guomindang perspective. Like CCP scholars, those associated with Tao Xishengism were adamant defenders of the left-wing critique of the Guomindang line. There were certainly a variety of views within the Left Guomindang camp, particularly concerning the continuing role of the CCP in the national revolution, but generally its political line could be found in the writings of its eminent advocate Chen Gongbo. After the collapse of the First United Front with the CCP, Chen developed an analysis of Chinese society that took issue with key points of CCP orthodoxy, which Chen now viewed as having "betrayed the national revolution in China." First, although Chen agreed with the CCP that China was a semicolonial society, he did not view it as "semifeudal." From his perspective, the major impediment to China's industrial development did not lie in semifeudal forces in the countryside such as the landlords who were targeted in violent land confiscations that the CCP was erroneously urging on the peasantry.[120] Chen, like other Left Guomindang authors, did acknowledge the continuing significance of "feudal forces" such as rural gentry, which were incompatible with the new bourgeoisie,[121] but in his view, the primary enemy of the Chinese national revolution was foreign imperialism, which actively manipulated the remanent feudal forces for its own gain.[122] Chen's colleague Ma Jun elaborated on this point. "In the normal process of the development of capitalism," Ma observed, "although petty handicraft industry and the agricultural economy decline in mutual response to one another, there are rising industry and commerce to replace them, which then gradually absorb the unemployed petty handicraftsmen and peasants. However, China's capitalist forces come from without, and in the incomplete development of commerce and industry under the original feudal society, petty handicraft industry and the rural economy have begun already to be shaken, causing petty handicraftsmen and peasants to lose their economic support. . . . The more severe the invasion of China by international capitalist imperialism, the more troubled the Chinese national economy and the more numerous the unemployed."[123] Notable here is how determined Ma was—like most other Marxists who had been drawn to the movement by the nationalistic impulse of the anti-imperialist Lenin—to assert that China's economic troubles were primarily the product of external rather than internal forces. A liberal argument that asserted the positive value of commercial activity with the West would be unpersuasive among those who were troubled by the dominance of the West in the relationship.

Hence, Chen observed a pivotal role for international imperialism in determining China's status as a semicolonial society. In Chen's view, this overwhelmingly negative foreign influence, evidenced even in economic distress in the rural hinterland, necessitated that Marx's views be revised in at least one respect—its emphasis on class struggle. Marx's projection that the middle strata would disappear and leave the bourgeoisie and the proletariat to struggle against one another simply did not apply to China, Chen asserted. This assumption had led the CCP to place primary stress on representing the proletariat, but its leaders failed to grasp the "true interests" of this class, which in any case was too miniscule to carry out a socialist revolution. In China, the industrial workers' wages gave them a standard of living and, thus, certain interests that were like those of the petty bourgeoisie, Chen averred.[124] Nor did China even truly have a bourgeoisie as such; it had only "wealthy individuals" who lacked political or economic organization. Thus, the single most influential and significant class in Chinese society was precisely the group that Marx had ignored in his conceptualization of society on the verge of socialist revolution—the collective middle strata that comprised neither bourgeoisie nor proletariat. In such a setting, class struggle became random conflict among many social strata, destroying nationalism, imperiling the national revolution, driving the petty bourgeoisie who were foremost among these middle strata from the revolutionary camp. The CCP's emphasis on class struggle, then, hindered the implementation of democracy by creating enmity among classes and obstructed production, thus making it difficult to create the state capital that—consistent with Sun Yat-sen's vision—Chen saw as necessary for the establishment of socialism.[125]

This last point was essential to Chen's argument. The achievement of national unity under a powerful state guided by progressive socialist values was the immediate objective of the Left Guomindang's national revolution.[126] The ultimate goal—that which drew them close to their fellow Marxists in the CCP despite the divergence in the means they espoused—was minsheng-zhuyi as proclaimed by Sun Yat-sen and interpreted as socialism implemented under the auspices of a progressive national state. The creation of an effective, unified state power dedicated to achieving that end would be both an end and a means for that revolution.[127] State capital ownership was, of course, not the only element of the minsheng-zhuyi program. Conditions in the countryside required that this socialism would also involve the equalization of landownership rights. The latter, however, like China's industrial development, would also be achieved through the leadership of an effective state power.[128] Here the Left Guomindang diverged from its Marxist comrades in the CCP in two major respects. First, even if the Soviet Union could be denounced for its inability to achieve true communism because of the "dictatorship of the communist party," China's Communist partisans of the Comintern line were "idealist anarchists"[129] because they failed to appreciate the value of the national state as an objective of the revolution and the means to the achievement of social justice in China, Chen asserted. Second, this value that the Left Guomindang attributed to the realization of effective state power in turn buttressed the group's insistence on the priority of nationalist unity over class conflict.[130]

	Yin	W. Zhou	E. Zhou	Qin	Qing	Present
gentile society		$\longrightarrow$ feudalism	transition commercial capital $\longrightarrow$	transitional period with gentry commercial capitalism $\longrightarrow$		

Thus, Left Guomindang Marxist historians developed analyses of China's socioeconomic history that minimized the role of "feudal forces" as an obstacle to China's current economic development. Tao Xisheng formulated at least three different periodizations of Chinese history. In 1929, Tao published two major works analyzing Chinese social history: *Zhongguo fengjian shehui shi* (History of Chinese feudal society) and *Zhongguo shehui zhi shi de fenxi* (An analysis of the history of Chinese society). There and in his *Zhongguo shehui yu Zhongguo geming* (Chinese society and the Chinese revolution) (1931), Tao argued that China had been in the stage of gentile society through the Yin (Shang) period, had attained the flowering of feudalism in the Western Zhou, the transitional phase of rising commerce in the Eastern Zhou, commercial capitalism under gentry (*shidaifu*) society during the imperial era from Qin to Qing, and was presently a semicolonial country where feudalism no longer existed in the economic base (as the CCP argued) but where "feudal forces" remained in the superstructure of Chinese society.[131] In this account, feudalism had begun to dissolve in the Spring and Autumn and Warring States periods to give way to a transitional stage by the Qin era. Significantly, Tao attributed the early demise of feudalism to internal factors, particularly to flourishing commercial capital and the spread of irrigation in agriculture, developments which in his view left no room for feudalism.[132] By 1932, Tao had altered this periodization to include slave society so that China proceeded from gentile or tribal society to slave society in the Eastern Zhou until the third century A.D., to feudal society in the imperial era, and precapitalist society from the Song to the present.[133] Both these early periodizations had the virtue of identifying elements of concrete Chinese realities that could be positioned in Marx's original schema. Finally, in 1935, Tao offered yet another periodization identifying only three stages: the ancient, from the fifth century B.C. to the third century A.D., the middle ages from the third through the ninth centuries A.D., and the modern age, from the tenth through the midnineteenth centuries. The latter roughly corresponded to what he had defined before as the precapitalist stage.[134]

	E. Zhou	Qin	Song	Qing	Present
gentile society	slavery	feudalism $\longrightarrow$	precapitalist society $\longrightarrow$		

Tao's views appeared to raise more difficulties than they resolved. Although all three of his formulations were consistent with the CCP position in that they all depicted contemporary China as a society that was not yet completely capitalistic, his efforts drew fire from CCP partisans on several points. First, the CCP rejected the view, articulated clearly by Tao and supported by most associated with the Left Guomindang, that "feudalism no longer exist[ed]" in China; only "feudal forces still exist[ed]."[135] In addition, Tao's efforts drew fire on two other specific points: (1) the implication in his work that the flourishing of commercial capital could account for the transition from one mode of production to another; and (2) the emphasis that he placed on the role of the shidaifu (scholar-gentry class). Although initially Tao was careful to note that "commercial capital alone could not change an old mode of production into a new one,"[136] this assertion was immediately undermined by a treatment of China's economic development over the past two millennia that was dominated by the attribution of a pivotal role to commercial capital. Tao ascribed the collapse of feudalism in China in the Spring and Autumn and Warring States periods to the growth of commercial capitalism, which was most salient in the state of Qi. Once Qi was able to dominate China, it provoked a succession of wars among feudal lords, the ultimate outcome of which was the centralized Qin state.[137] Throughout, commerce, Tao argued, encouraged the further development of the division of labor, which, in turn, contributed to the further growth of commerce. Thus, on the one hand, the flourishing of Chinese commercial capital since the Qin and Han periods had not been matched by the development of the "organization of production" in China; on the other, in commercial capital lay the key to understanding the centrifugal forces impeding the emergence of a unified national state and the superior prospects for such national unity in the 1930s. Finally, the precapitalist stage in which China found itself on the threshold of the 1930s was, Tao argued, distinguished precisely by the dominance of commerce over industry.[138]

Tao was supported in his emphasis on the role of commercial capital in the dissolution of feudalism and the establishment of modern industrial capitalism by Shi Jun[139] and *Dushu zazhi* editor Wang Lixi: "We believe that China's historical commercial capital can, according to the laws of history, spontaneously develop to industrial capitalism, if there is no external impediment."[140] More problematic, however, was Tao's concept of *xian-ziben-zhuyi* (precapitalism). Tao had offered five characteristics to identify this stage: (1) the existence of free labor; (2) the dispersion of land cultivation with land rents up to 50 percent of crop yields; (3) the existence of commerce and industry; (4) the flourishing of internal and international trade; and (5) the adoption of cash land rents. Tao posited his xian-ziben-zhuyi as a new historical stage, distinct from both feudalism and capitalism, but, his critics were quick to ask, could not all these phenomena be found in late-feudalism?[141] Most importantly, all three of Tao's periodizations specified an extremely long period of "transition" from feudalism to capitalism: three thousand years in his first effort, and approximately one thousand years in the latter two. These characterizations of Chinese development seemed to beg the central issue: if commercial capital was so significant to the transition to capitalism and had flourished for so long in China, then why had not China developed an industrial capitalist society autonomously? Why did China experience only *pre*capitalist society for such a long period? Why had it not experienced the sort of scientific and technological breakthrough that had nurtured industrial capitalism in Western Europe? Thus, what Tao seemed to give to the nationalist advocate of a socialist revolution in China with one hand he took away with the other. On the one hand, the impetus for the demise of feudalism and the transition to capitalism was internally generated, but on the other, it never culminated in the full fruition of a capitalist society in China. This suggested a certain Chinese exceptionalism, and such a posture was unacceptable among orthodox supporters of the CCP who accepted the Eurocentric universalist claims of Marx's schema.

Partisans of the CCP were quick to respond to the difficulties raised by Tao's interpretations. The CCP position reflected the Comintern's uneasiness with any effort to attribute special qualities to development in the East. "There is no special character to the laws of Chinese social development," wrote Lü Zhenyu.[142] Reminding the reader that "the immediate main task of the Chinese revolution is to eliminate feudal remnants," such as agrarian landlords, Zhu Peiwo penned an extensive critique of Tao's depiction of Chinese economic history. Zhu attacked Tao's positions on the gentry and commercial capital and then offered a periodization of his own. First, he argued that Tao had failed to establish an economic basis for the shidaifu. Tao's treatment seemed to place the shidaifu between bureaucrats and landlords—that is, without a secure economic basis of their own—and invoked the ascendancy of this group in accounting for the transition from feudalism to a period of bureaucratic government after the Qin and Han periods.[143] Such an account was problematic in appearing to attribute great power to a state that was not firmly grounded in the material conditions that Marxist orthodoxy posited as decisive. It, thus, also rendered more difficult the task of demonstrating the equivalency of the trajectory of China's socioeconomic development with that of the West. Second, Zhu argued that commercial capital—which his colleague Lü Zhenyu stressed had existed since antiquity[144]—could not bring about the transition from feudalism to industrial capitalism. Li Lisan had noted correctly that commercial capital could certainly disrupt the rural economy by inducing peasant households to produce for the unstable market and, thus, foment peasant wars arising out of the new uncertainties of producing for a market, but it could not cause the demise of feudalism.[145] Thus, citing Marx's *Poverty of Philosophy* and *Capital*, Zhu argued that only industrial, and not commercial, capital could play such a revolutionary role.[146]

Noteworthy here is the resemblance between this discussion and the post-World War II debate between the Western Marxists Maurice Dobb and Paul Sweezy. Here again the key issue was whether the transition from feudalism to capitalism in general was caused by factors internal or external to the feudal mode of production itself.[147] In China's case, however, the implications of the issue of external versus internal dynamics of the transition to capitalism reached far beyond those of the Dobb-Sweezy controversy. The possibility that capitalism had come to China only from without—which seemed to be the orthodox CCP position on the matter—immediately required that one answer the question of why that was the case because it certainly did not appear to have been, from the vantage point of Chinese Marxists in the 1920s and 1930s, for Europe—if one took European peculiarity as a universal norm. At the very least, the Soviet literature applying the Asiatic mode of production to China required serious consideration. Tao's emphasis on the shidaifu and the advent of bureaucratic government coupled with the long "transition" to something that never materialized underscored the potential significance of the exceptionalism of the oriental society model. There were troubling new possiblities here. Perhaps the Chinese state, bureaucratized and under the domination of the shidaifu, had prevented the full emergence of capitalism in China, as it did in the Asiatic mode of production construct, despite the dynamic presence of usury and commercial capital. Still more importantly, perhaps the legacy of such a past would continue to bode ill for China's chances of achieving an economically flourishing, more democratic and socialist society in the 1930s.

Yet in the aftermath of the Leningrad Conference, Zhu and other CCP advocates sought to avoid such troubling implications of the Asiatic mode of production construct entirely. The key to their advocacy of a socialist revolution in China lay in emphasizing China's historical commonalities with the West, not its divergences. Thus, following the lead of fellow Asian Communist Safarov, Chinese Communists attributed to China a succession of Marxian developmental stages that simply omitted all mention of the Asiatic mode of production.[148] The aforementioned Zhu, for example, espoused the basic CCP view that Western encroachment in the midnineteenth century had brought with it a disruption of the natural village economy by imported commodities.[149] This assertion, unlike Tao's periodizations, ignored evidence that rural China was marketized.[150] Yet Zhu stressed that "the basic principle of the feudal mode of exploitation (whereby nominal landlords used extraeconomic pressure to extract surplus labor from independent[151] producers [peasants])" persisted as (in accordance with Engels's writings on feudalism) had the "absolute supremacy of the natural economy" long after the Spring and Autumn and Warring States periods cited in one of Tao's periodizations as the demise of Chinese feudalism.[152] Indeed, Zhu further argued that feudal elements remained intact in the economic structure of Chinese society and not merely in the superstructure.[153] Like fellow historian Zhou Gucheng,[154] Zhu maintained that it was only in the late nineteenth century, when Western capitalism began to invade China with its own commodities, threatening the natural economy, that feudalism began to disintegrate.[155]

This demise of feudalism was still in its early stages as late as the 1930s, however, and, thus, the "immediate main task of the Chinese revolution [was] to eliminate feudal remnants."[156] In so arguing, Zhu lent support to the CCP view that a thoroughgoing revolution with intense class conflict was needed, whereas the Left Guomindang denied the need for class struggle in China. The Left Guomindang (like the Soviet leader Karl Radek, who had fallen alongside Bukharin), CCP supporters claimed, underestimated the continued significance of feudal forces in China because it overestimated the role that commercial capital could play without being transformed into industrial capital. In China, commercial capital had not been transformed into industrial capital[157] but through the agency of the gentry had become wedded to the land and simply intensified oppression and exploitation that remained essentially feudal in character.[158] Moreover, there was no evidence that the Chinese landlord class was now seeking embourgeoisement (transformation into bourgeois) as the now Trotskyist Chen Duxiu contended.[159]

This argument was, in turn, related to a second criticism by the CCP: the Left Guomindang failed to see continued evidence of feudalism in China's economic base because its understanding of feudal relations was fundamentally incorrect. Tao had spoken ambiguously of the "land system" as the main indicator of the feudal mode of production;[160] but Zhu insisted that the key to feudalism lay in the mode of exploitation and, specifically, in what Marx had identified in volume 3 of *Capital* as reliance on "extraeconomic coercion." Remnants of such "extra-economic coercion" persisted two thousand years after Tao claimed the feudal "land system" had disappeared as landlords (Tao's shidaifu) acted not as the "force of the demise of feudalism but as its pillar" and continued to do so until the Western encroachment in the 1840s. Such extraeconomic coercion had lingered for centuries in a variety of forms—the exaction of more than 50 percent (and up to 70 or 80 percent) of agricultural produce in taxes by the landlord from the peasant; the requirement that peasants make other mandatory payments besides rent to the landlord; the "corvée labor system"; "the right of landlords to exercise political domination over the peasants"; and the intimidation that was implicit in the class system itself. The form in which land rents were paid was also irrelevant, particularly because the payment of rents in kind was the prevalent practice in the entire imperial period, and not just until the Spring and Autumn Warring States period (722–484 B.C.), when Tao alleged Chinese feudalism ended.[161] Thus, Zhu's alternative periodization simply saw feudalism as antedating the Spring and Autumn and Warring States periods and extending into the nineteenth century when its demise began because of the external impetus of Western imperialism.[162] Such an argument, of course, asserted a certain stagnancy across a long period of Chinese history and did not attend to social developments that had hitherto been recorded in dynastic histories.

Finally, partisans of the CCP position assailed an element of Tao's argument that was highly important in terms of its own assessment of the character of the intellectual stratum that had formed the core of the now defunct imperial bureaucracy. The CCP position reflected considerable ambiguity on this group and its relationship to the defunct imperial state. CCP partisans criticized Tao's analysis of the role of the scholar-gentry (shidaifu) and the apparent separation therein between base and superstructure. At issue here was the universality of the aristocracy as a class and whether China had had an analogue to the aristocracies of Western Europe that had been so pivotal in Marx's depiction of feudalism and the transition to capitalism. Depending on the treatment of this pivotal group[163]—as an intellectual stratum, as a class with an economic basis in the land, or as a bureaucratic class whose power derived from control over public resources—one could interpret Chinese society in various periods as feudal or *Asiatic*, and the imperial state could be viewed as relatively weak and decentralized or highly bureaucratic and despotic. In Tao's view, after the Qin and Han periods, China moved from feudal to bureaucratic society, and political domination passed from the hands of the landed aristocratic class to the shidaifu.[164] Wang Lixi, Zhu Peiwo, Li Ji, and others opposed this view for its overemphasis on the political role of the gentry in Chinese history and for what they saw as carelessness in Tao's use of the notion of class.[165] Moreover, the CCP had to wage a consistent argument against the Left Guomindang's insistence that there were no longer any feudal elements in the economic base but only feudal elements in the current superstructure. This sort of uncoupling of base and superstructure would presumably bear implications for work concerning the imperial state, but CCP participants in the controversy did not pursue this point.

Yet criticism of Tao and the Left Guomindang position by CCP participants yielded several alternative schemes of periodization. Zhu was joined by Chen Boda and Xiong Deshan in his view that feudalism remained in Chinese society. Chen and Xiong both concluded that the Asiatic, as a variant of feudalism, was the dominant mode of production in China.[166] Lü Zhenyu produced a much more detailed demarcation of the stages of Chinese history in Marxian terms. Lü's account was more broadly and solidly based than that of Zhu, drawing both on what he viewed as Marxian classics in historical periodization that dated back to the origins of humankind and on other sources. Recalling that Marx's *Grundrisse* was not available to him at this point, one may note that Zhu drew liberally on Morgan's *Ancient Society*, Engels's *Origin of the Family*, Lenin's analysis of Russian development, and the writings of Japanese Marxists Yamakawa Hitoshi and Tanaka Tadao. Yet Zhu brought to bear on these precursers in Marxian historiography relatively recent evidence yielded by Shang oracle bones, as well as traditional Chinese historical sources such as the *Shiji* (Historical annals) and *Hanshu* (History of the Han dynasty). Like Zhu, Lü insisted that the key to feudalism lay elsewhere than in the land system, noting that the manorial system had not even been a universal characteristic of feudalism in Europe.[167] The key elements of feudalism lay rather, as Lenin had argued, in the prevalence of the natural economy, the basis of exploitation "in labor being subordinated to the land," and in the "extraeconomic coercion" of serfdom.[168] In its similarity to analogous claims made by Japanese contributors to the controversy on Japanese captialism, this contention enabled Lü both to associate Chinese feudalism more closely with what it was considered to be in Western Europe and to acknowledge change within China's feudalism from one period to another as many other historical schemas would not. Most notably, Lü distinguished the period of Zhou disunity from the "mutant form" of feudalism under the "externally unified state" of the Qin period. These, of course, were characteristics of the Chinese body politic that had been evidenced in traditional Chinese dynastic historiography, but now they could be comprehended in the more universal terms of a historical schema that allowed China's historiographers to identify important commonalities with patterns of Western history. Yet Lü still claimed that all three basic characteristics of feudalism persisted in the entire history of Chinese society from the Qin through the Qing to be disrupted only by the outbreak of the Opium War, the "invasion of capitalism," which resulted in China's present "semicolonial, semifeudal" status.[169]

Pre-Yin	*Shang/Yin*	*Spring-Autumn*	*Warring States*	*Qin* ←—— *Empire* ——→ *Qing*
	(1766 B.C.)	(722–481 B.C.)	(403–221 B.C.)	(221–206 B.C.) (1644–1911)

primitive
communal gens slavery   origin of feudalism —— feudal-serf economy ——————————→

Trotskyist Interpretations of China's Development

This interpretation could not be sanguine enough for Chinese Trotskyists, who had now, in the wake of their expulsion from the party in 1929, coalesced into a distinctive dissident strain within the Chinese Marxist movement. Where the CCP and its loyalists were compelled, formally at least, to adhere to the orthodoxy that their revolution was limited to the status of a bourgeois-democratic revolution of national liberation, the application of Trotsky's internationalist theory of world revolution to China stressed that the impact of "uneven development" had made the possibility of a permanent revolution culminating in socialism and communism possible in China, as it had been in Russia. "In capitalist society," Trotsky observed, "every real revolution, . . . more particularly now, in the imperialist epoch, tends to transform itself into a permanent revolution, in other words, not to come to a halt at any of the stages it reaches . . . up to the final abolition of class distinctions. . . . The Chinese revolution contains within itself the possibility of the conquest of power by the proletariat."[170] Thus, Trotsky and Chinese Trotskyists repudiated the Stalin-Bukharin policy in the pre-1927 period, which had been based on the assumption that foreign imperialism in China had welded all classes together into a single nationalistic anti-imperialist bloc. Instead, they stressed that "'The class struggle between the bourgeoisie and the masses of workers and peasants is not weakened but, on the contrary, it is sharpened by imperialist oppression'."[171] Chinese Trotskyist historiographers, then, were more likely to articulate periodizations that stressed the development of China as a capitalist society in its most recent generations and the implications of that economic growth for the prospects that the proletariat would take the lead in overthrowing imperialism and push on to a socialist revolution directed against the native bourgeoisie.[172]

Thus, Chinese Trotskyists were steadfast in their refusal to adhere to the Leninist-inspired orthodoxy that imperialism was necessarily deleterious to the development of capitalism in China. The paradox here is that it was through the internationalist conceptual lenses of Trotskyism that this group of Chinese historiographers was able to affirm, in nationalistic fashion, their identity as Chinese by asserting Chinese equivalency with the West as manifested where it mattered most—in the indigenous development of capitalism. Trotskyite historiographers contended almost uniformly that imperialism had "destroyed" not the sprouts of indigenous Chinese capitalism but "the economic basis of feudalism." Although initially, the influx of foreign commodities hurt China's rural economy, Yan Lingfeng argued, with the introduction of railroads and capitalist production techniques, particularly at the turn of the twentieth century, the development of capitalism in Chinese society was accelerated.[173] Beyond this contention, the Trotskyists themselves differed, with Yan taking a compromise position between Liu Jingyuan's insistence that the parasitic existence of the Chinese bourgeoisie rested on continued feudal exploitation, on the one hand, and Ren Shu's and Liu Guang's rejection of any role for feudal elements in China, on the other.[174] While affirming the primacy of capitalism in contemporary China, Yan conceded that Chinese capitalism was not "pure" capitalism: "In China, particularly in the countryside, it is extremely clear that there are remnants of many precapitalist relations and various other extremely complex feudal remnants." As in prerevolutionary Russia, new technologies coexisted with extremely old technologies, and remnants of precapitalist patriarchal and medieval social relations coexisted with new capitalist relations. Nevertheless, as of 1930, "China [was indeed] a capitalist society" in which the bourgeoisie was dominant even as, he dissented from many of his Trotskyist peers, it remained dependent on the international bourgeoisie.[175] This position lent itself to some controversial reinterpretations of the course of the Chinese revolution. Chen Duxiu argued, for example, that what had been a debacle for the CCP—the 1927 Shanghai Coup—reflected a victory for Chinese nationalism in the historical sense that it marked the victory of China's national bourgeoisie over other classes. The invasion of international capitalism and the penetration of commercial capital had also caused an essential change in the socioeconomic structure of the Chinese village. Left behind were mere feudal remnants, landed gentry, themselves seeking to become bourgeois through involvement in urban industry and commerce.[176]

This muting of the influence of feudalism in China in comparison with other Chinese historiographical treatments was most evident in the work of Li Ji, who offered the most comprehensive Trotskyist analysis of Chinese social history. Li's point of departure was his disputation of M. N. Roy's observation that many Marxists believed that China's historical development lacked a crucial link—feudalism. Li insisted that this might be true of non-Chinese Marxists, but it was certainly not true of his fellow Marxists in China, who seemed uniformly to describe nearly every age of China's history in terms of a feudalism of millennia in duration.[177] Li's own periodization depicted a much shorter duration for the feudal mode of production—nine hundred years. In his view, Chinese social history could be divided into five periods: primitive communism during the legendary period of the Age of Five Rulers; the Asiatic mode of production[178] in the Xia through the end of the Yin, feudalism beginning only in the Zhou dynasty, protocapitalism during the imperial era until the Opium Wars, and capitalism from the Opium Wars to the present. Drawing heavily on the research of Morgan, Li acknowledged the dearth of "direct" evidence to support his claims; it was necessary to rely on inference from such "indirect" substantiation as quotations from traditional Chinese histories and philosophical works of the respective periods. Such evidence as quotations from Mencius and observations in the *Beishan* chapter of the *Shijing* (Book of odes) were held to demonstrate the progression from gens communal society into the Asiatic mode of production and then to feudalism when the forebears of the Zhou conquered the late Yin kings.[179]

Feudalism and the transition to capitalism were at the core of Li's periodization in support of Trotskyist revolutionary strategy. Li treated feudalism much as Zhu did. Quoting Marx's *Capital* and then Lenin, Li argued that the major conditions of feudalism included the predominance of the natural economy in which all produced for a subsistence rather than for trade, the direct producers being attached to the land, and peasants, as serfs, being individually subordinated to the feudal lord. Li was able to truncate the duration of the period during which this mode of production was dominant by adding a new stage to the progression. Feudalism, he argued, persisted only until the Spring and Autumn and Warring States periods when feudalism collapsed and a new mode of production emerged, which he termed the protocapitalist mode of production (*qian-ziben-zhuyi*).[180] Finally, after two millennia in this stage, propelled by the importation of advanced technology from the West, capitalism emerged in China. True to his Trotskyist position, Li was adamant in his insistence that China since the Opium War had been capitalist in character.[181] "Although there are still remnants of the protocapitalist mode of production and other modes of production existing, the capitalist mode of production is clearly occupying the leading position," he insisted.[182] His periodization appeared as follows:

Pre-Yin Xia	*Shang/Yin*	*Zhou*	*Qin*	← *Empire* ──────→	*Qing*
(−2206 B.C.)	(2205–1135 B.C.)	(1135–247 B.C.)		(246 B.C.–1839)	(1840–)
primitive communism	Asiatic mode of production	→ feudalism──────→		*qian-ziben-zhuyi* (protocapitalist)	→ capitalist

Since the Opium Wars, Li contended, China's capitalism had prospered despite the substantial impediments posed by the imperialist powers and the power of warlords, particularly the Beiyang military clique. Indeed, Li argued, against those who would protest that he had dated the origins of capitalism in China too early, that, if anything, he had dated it too late. Although the production of industrial machinery did not emerge in China until the 1860s, he stressed that Marx had referred to sixteenth-century Europe as capitalistic although that period was a full century and a half before machine manufacture had emerged there. In China, industrial production for military purposes had begun in the 1860s, and in the 1880s, light industry had started to flourish under official sponsorship. The defeat by Japan in 1894 spurred the further development of Chinese capitalism, as private large-scale enterprises began to thrive. Finally, foreign capital began to be invested in factories in large coastal cities such as Shanghai, taking advantage of cheap Chinese raw materials. The growth of capitalism, in turn, produced China's bourgeois revolution in the form of the revolution of 1911. Now, as Li wrote after the partial success of the 1925–1927 revolution directed against "imperialism and warlords," "economically, the city controls the countryside, international imperialism governs China," and the Chinese revolution had reached a new stage.[183]

Li's periodization drew intense criticism on two points: (1) his characterization of the late Shang era as the Asiatic mode of production and (2) his notion of qian-ziben-zhuyi. The more remarkable aspect of Li's periodization was his application of the notion of "protocapitalist" (qian-ziben-zhuyi) society to characterize imperial China from Qin to Qing, culminating in the full flowering of capitalism after the Opium wars. Li's use of the term translated here as *protocapitalist* was misleading inasmuch as Marx had used the notion of *precapitalist* modes of production to refer to all social formations preceding capitalism. Yet Li was attempting to make a very specific point. Li believed China's development—except for its experiencing the Asiatic rather than the classic ancient mode of production—to be fundamentally equivalent to that of the West. Despite China's Asiatic past in his schema, Li emphatically repudiated those like Ren Shu who would suggest that the impetus for China's capitalist development had had to come from outside, that China lacked its own internal developmental dynamic toward capitalism.[184] It was important for him, as for others engaged in this controversy, to be able to identify within China's own history such an impulse to change. His qian-ziben-zhuyi, then, was conceived as a specific social formation that was a universal element rather than a peculiar characteristic of China. Nowhere, he argued, had feudalism yielded capitalism immediately. Instead, the demise of feudalism everywhere had produced a separate stage of development that was merely "transitional."[185] This period was characterized by several specific features: "(1) direct unity between petty agriculture and cottage industry; . . . (2) a heavy preponderance of usury capital and commercial capital; (3) commercial control of industry; (4) the existence of a landlord class and other upper classes; (5) the existence of independent producers in the form of handicrafts workers; (6) the existence of remnants of every kind of preceding mode of production; and (7) the bankruptcy of agricultural workers into impoverished people and the concentration of production tools" in the hands of the few. Li quoted passages from the *Shiji*, *Qian Han shu* (Book of the early Han), and other traditional historical sources to document the existence of these characteristics in imperial China from Qin to Qing.[186]

Li's critics were quick to assail his alternative to Tao's periodization. Chen Xiaojiang argued that it made no sense to speak of a period of more than two thousand years as a transitional period rather than as simply "unique." Moreover, the characteristics of Li's qian-ziben-zhuyi could be found in other modes of production and appeared to be simply a confused mixture of such traits.[187] Mo Dazhao attacked Li for being unable to attribute causation to any specific factor in his explanation of change from one mode of production to another and for exaggerating the significance of merchants in causing the transition from feudalism to capitalism. Mo also argued that Li failed to recognize that imperialism had not strengthened China's national bourgeoisie but had simply produced more compradors.[188] This was significant for the fate of China's nationalist revolution for two reasons. First, Li's Trotskyist interpretation threatened to overstate the extent to which capitalism had developed and feudalism had been abolished in China, just as it overestimated the extent to which, in the course of this transformation, China had evolved a reasonably integrated national capitalist economy. Moreover, an industrial capitalist class so dependent on, and subservient to, foreign capital would not be imbued with the nationalistic consciousness and independent commitment to the creation of a strong Chinese state necesssary to play a supportive role in the revolution. Finally, Mo leveled his strongest objection: If the qian-ziben-zhuyi society was a separate mode of production, how could it be described, as Li did at one point, as "the remnants of the Asiatic mode of production"? Could mere "remnants" be dominant elements determining a mode of production?[189] And, one might add, implicit but unelaborated by Li were the important implications of this depiction of protocapitalism, namely, (1) that it might, in fact, have been a geographically specific category rather than a universal experience and (2) that for those two crucial millennia a despotic Asiatic state that was peculiar to China as an oriental society had figured in the excruciatingly long Chinese transition to capitalism, a transition that had finally reached fruition only as a result of the impact of Western imperialism in the Opium War and after.

Li was anxious to distinguish his protocapitalist stage from Tao's precapitalism, which began only in the Song period, one century after the beginning of Li's. " 'His society of the precapitalist period is a feudal society, or at best a postfeudal [*hou-feng-chien*] society," Li claimed. "What we call proto-capitalist society is neither feudal nor postfeudal; rather it is a society where the proto-capitalist mode of production has taken hold following the demise of the feudal mode of production'."[190] In other words, Tao's precapitalism understated the potential for capitalist development in China, suggesting even the possibility of retrogression under the impact of remanent but still powerful feudal forces. By contrast, Li's was to be a universal, progressive stage through which it was necessary for any society to pass for capitalism to emerge.

Li's account was also important for its effort to situate the traditional Chinese gentry in Marxian terms. Here Li contested the emphasis that Tao placed on the separation between political and economic power in his discussion of the various roles played by the enigmatic shidaifu. Li consistently stressed the determining nature of changes in the economic base as reflected in class differentiation. It would not do, after all, for China alone to be found to have had a ruling class the material bases of which could not readily be located in China's economic structure, for this once again would suggest a Chinese exceptionalism that clashed with the determination to assert China's equivalency with the West. Finally, China had ultimately emerged as a capitalist society in Li's treatment, whereas it remained feudal in Tao's. This would not seem to be exceptional but for the fact that Comintern Marxists and others were determined to posit China as a society that was much less advanced economically than Russia had been on the eve of the October Revolution. Censured and unwelcome by orthodox Communists in any case, Chinese Trotskyists were free to explore the boundaries of the acute nationalist shame that so many manifested in associating China's backwardness with the feudal terms of Marxian discourse.

Nevertheless, it is significant that in Li's account, the transitional period that had lasted for only a few centuries in Europe endured for two thousand years in China. The same objection might be made to both Tao's precapitalist and Li's protocapitalist stages: as Chen argued, commercial capital simply could not both change China and keep it the same for two thousand years.[191] Yet Li's critics were no better able to overcome the weaknesses of Li's approach than others had been. Chen himself, for example, also resorted to a similar device—defining a new mode of production or historical stage—in accounting for the two thousand years from Qin to Qing. He argued that a "tenant hireling" system (*dianyongzhi*) had arisen after feudalism in China. This new stage was more advanced than feudalism, yet it was not a transitional precapitalist society. Chen was clearly uncomfortable with the implications of conceptualizing a new mode of production as something that was strictly "transitional." Nevertheless, Chen's own new social formation was not without its own difficulties. It was not clearly differentiated from feudalism,[192] and, thus, it too was imbued with the hues of a "transitional stage." Nor did it appear to be universal rather than peculiarly Chinese in character. Finally, as in Tao's portrayal, China once again appeared to be in stasis over a period of more than a dozen dynasties. This was precisely the sort of stagnation, so closely associated with the Asiatic mode of production, from which these Marxists were attempting to distance themselves in their endeavor to claim for China a dignified national identity as an autonomous actor in human history—like Western societies.

What, then, did Chinese historians accomplish through the periodization exercise? It would be difficult to argue that their efforts produced important new factual knowledge on the nature of Chinese history. Nevertheless, they did constitute first attempts to situate China's economic history within the universe of global historical experience in the organization of production at the same time that it located China's political experience in comparative terms that were not appropriate as long as China was treated within the context of the paradigm of the unique Middle Kingdom. Perhaps what is most striking about the entire discourse is precisely the new historians' determined repudiation of any claim to uniqueness. What had been a source of pride in the past—China's difference from the rest of the world—had suddenly become a source of shame now that the new contest between the Middle Kingdom and the Western state system had resulted in domination—political, economic, and cultural—over the former hegemonic power. It is only in these terms that the effort to periodize Chinese history can be appreciated in the fullness of its cultural significance. Periodizing Chinese history in Marxian terms constituted a scholarly means by which to validate China's national experience as equivalent in value to that of the West. In these histories, Chinese were autonomous subjects of the same human history that Westerners had made in their own societies despite evidence to the contrary that was deeply painful to those who had been accustomed to view their own society as constitutive of universal human values. In the final analysis, nearly all these periodizations simply superimposed Marxian categories on a history that remained demarcated in traditional dynastic terms. The compromises that this required were reflected in the invocation of long periods of "transition" or even new modes of production while Chinese historians struggled to avoid the negative implications of explicitly associating these phenomena with Marx's Asiatic mode of production. Other participants in the controversy on

Chinese social history were less intimidated by either the results of the Leningrad Conference or the implications of an Asiatic past for China's future, and they undertook to examine directly the components of the Asiatic mode of production concept for further clues to China's past and present.

THE PROBLEM OF THE ASIATIC MODE OF PRODUCTION IN CHINESE HISTORY

Western scholars have noted that the notion of the Asiatic mode of production "was not popular in China and the reactions to it were mostly negative" during the controversy on Chinese social history. Following the precedent of the Leningrad Conference, many who conceded that Chinese development was special viewed that specialness in terms of variations on the basic modes of production enumerated by Marx, such as feudalism or slavery.[193] To be sure, the notion of a separate oriental society that did not match the Western experience was unpalatable to most Chinese Marxists, and many either ignored or repudiated it.[194] As already observed, Chinese and Japanese Marxists were determined to demonstrate that their societies were part of the mainstream of Marx's universal history, did not require the Western intrusion to develop industrial capitalism, and, indeed, had important progressive roles to play in global human development.

Nevertheless, the twin concepts of oriental society and the Asiatic mode of production did exercise a significant impact on participants in the controversy on Chinese social history. As noted, Marx's remarks on Asia were something of an albatross about the neck of Marxists in China and Japan alike. In portraying his universal history, Marx had never insisted that all feudal elements would cease to exist immediately upon the rise of the bourgeoisie. Yet what he had written about the exceptionalism of the East, Lenin's and Plekhanov's observations on the "Asiatic" impediments to Russia's development, and Comintern pronouncements on the "Asiatic" backwardness of their societies together predisposed Chinese and Japanese Marxists to discern in relics of their pasts unwelcome indications that their societies lagged even further behind the West than the development of indigenous capitalist forms would suggest. As one assesses the continued significance of the notion of the Asiatic mode of production for the controversy in China, then, it is important that one not be led astray by the sophistry that characterized the resolution of the "problem" of the Asiatic mode of production at the Leningrad Conference. Even Iolk, Godes, and Kovalev continued to employ the analytical category of *Asia* even as they sought to deny its validity by conflating it with feudalism or slavery. Still more, in both the debate on Japanese capitalism and the controversy on Chinese social history, the difficulties posed by the implicit geographical referent in Marx's use of the term *Asiatic* were not easily overcome by those concerned that their own societies might not have duplicated Western Europe's developmental path. Wang Lixi noted in 1931 the difficulties here for China's Marxists:

> Chinese history is not easy to understand: From the beginning of history, one already continually grasps signs, some that [it] is the same as Europe's situation, and some that

the "struggle for a water supply" (*yushui douzheng*) should be written in the first page of China's history. Its development is also peculiar, [with] a long period of stagnancy and inability to develop to the stage of industrial capital by relying on the laws of history. Was this "long period" the period of feudalism? Or was it the period of commercial capital? What is the reason for this "stagnancy"? Can China reach the industrial capitalist stage without relying on external force? In other words, can China itself develop by relying on [universal] historical laws? These are problems that [we] are now debating and cannot resolve. Marx too could not fully understand these strange national institutions so he especially offered the term *oriental* for the social formation. This puzzling expression is now confusing many people.[195]

Guo Moruo spoke for many, then, when he protested, " 'Chinese are neither gods nor are they monkeys,' so of course nor can the development of China's social history fall outside the common law [of the dialectical development of human society] and take another path."[196] Nevertheless, the Asiatic mode of production—the validity of the concept given the universality of Marx's schema and the question of whether it had ever existed in China—was one of "the three greatest issues in Chinese historical research at this time [1927–1937]," wrote Lü Zhenyu.[197] Indeed, debate continues in both East and West today over the correct understanding of the notion. There are those who reject it as completely useless, an indicator of Marx's ignorance about the East;[198] and there are others who accept the concept as a potentially nongeographic-specific term applying to a social formation that need not always precede ancient slave society but may fit elsewhere in Marx's scheme. If the Chinese controversy is reconsidered in these terms, even when the notion of the Asiatic mode of production was reinterpreted as a variant of another mode of production, the concept asserted itself as a challenge to the periodization of Chinese history to duplicate the economic history of the West. If one did not reject the notion of oriental society and abandon the category *Asiatic* entirely, one might have "accepted" it in terms of a path of development that differed slightly from, but was parallel to, that of Europe and then subsequently converged with European development for a variety of reasons.[199] The highly respected Plekhanov strongly advocated the notion of oriental society as a geographic referent in the latter manner.[200]

Similarly, many participants in the controversy on Chinese social history, while repudiating the Asiatic mode of production as a formally separate, geographically specific, chronological stage in Chinese history, incorporated references to China's (negative) "Asiatic" characteristics in their periodizations. Others accepted key elements of Marx's description of oriental society in order to account for what appeared in Marxian terms to be long periods of minimal change in Chinese social history. Thus, the impact of the oriental society construct was, in fact, far greater than is indicated by the mere number of instances in which the Asiatic mode of production emerged as a distinct stage in indigenous Marxist periodizations of Chinese history. It is a measure of the anguish that Chinese Marxist historians experienced as they asserted equivalency with the West that the term *Asiatic* or *despotism,* or new modes of production outside Marx's list or long periods of "transition" that appeared suspiciously as periods during which

Chinese society was suspended in stasis emerged repeatedly in the controversy despite the enormous disincentives to grant the notion of oriental society and the stagnation associated with it any validity at all. As committed Marxists, these scholars did not question whether the blame for the apparent disjuncture between theory and reality might have lain in Marxism rather than in China. Rather, in addressing the issue of China's identity as an *Asian* society these historians sought to resolve both the nationalist and statist components of the national question through their historiography.

Why would these scholars have weighted so heavily such a vague and apparently unilluminating category as *Asiatic*, which dissolved China's positive and negative peculiarities in a sea of ill-defined traits held to characterize many disparate societies in the East? The key here is that their Marxist applications of the Asiatic mode of production and oriental society notions served as vehicles of trenchant cultural criticism of the Chinese past.[201] Within this framework, the term *Asiatic* functioned as a category that encompassed the negative attributes of the Chinese past, including a state held to be despotic, which could be blamed for inhibiting China's ability to evolve the economic and political mores and institutions that were associated with bourgeois modernity in the Marxian paradigm. The notion of a diffuse set of *Asiatic* characteristics, rather than the specifically ordered accoutrements of the Asiatic mode of production, informed many indigenous efforts to reinterpret Chinese history in Marxian terms. Armed with these indicators rather than the paradigm in its wholeness, these new historians—and succeeding generations chafing under authoritarian CCP rule[202]—could challenge the ideological, cultural, and political despotisms of the past and present, while affirming the possibility of China's achieving something much superior in the future. It also offered them a Marxian category that they found useful in analyzing China even though the actual existence of private property in imperial China would have signaled that Marx had been completely in error in singling out Asia as distinctive. In short, the invocation of the appellation *Asiatic* ironically enabled at once the affirmation of the Marxian claim to historical universality and a nationalistic assertion of Chinese identity that repudiated the despotic past while offering hope for the future.

This point illuminates a major challenge confronted by Chinese as well as Japanese Marxists in adapting Marxism to their own contexts while accommodating it to a measure of national pride. The issue of the state—particularly the role of the state in national economic development—was central here, because the despotic state was held to be a distinctive characteristic of oriental society. In this model, the superstructure, including the despot, was accorded an uncharacteristically large determinate role. In the despot lay the key to the inability of oriental societies to evolve of their own initiative into more economically advanced modes of production, because the despot's exclusive ownership of everything, including the population itself, was said to obstruct the development of private property, feudalism, and capitalism. Chinese, like Japanese, Marxists would seek in this alleged pattern an important clue to why the transition to capitalism and bourgeois democracy was so retarded in their societies. It also conveyed a disquieting suggestion that bureaucratic state power, having arisen out of geographical or other conditions, might exercise a continuing negative influence on their societies' socioeconomic and political maturation. A powerful state might, as it apparently had in Japan's Meiji Restoration, contribute to the rapid transformation to industrial capitalism. Yet again, as suggested by the severe limitations on democratic rights in Japan's Meiji, Taishō, and Shōwa eras, it might also impede the full realization of democratic socialism or stateless communism after their revolutions. In the Chinese controversy, as in the Japanese, then, the treatment of the state reflected concern over the determinative role the state might have played in China's history.

Chinese Marxists benefited from access to Soviet work on the Asiatic mode of production by the time the controversy on Chinese social history erupted in the late 1920s. Mad'iar's work on the Asiatic mode of production in China was translated and published in Chinese in 1928; articles by Mad'iar and Wittfogel on the subject were published in *Xin shengming* the following year, at the same time that Fan Zhongyun introduced the ideas of Varga.[203] The proceedings of the Leningrad Conference were also available in Japanese translation (by Kōza-ha Marxist Hayakawa Jirō) in 1933.[204] Before Chinese scholars began to draw on this work and consider it in their periodization of Chinese social history in 1931 and 1932, however, the Soviet literature had already begun to provoke debate in Japan on the application of the theory to both China and Japan. Rōnō-ha scholars emphasizing Japan's industrial modernity borrowed generously from Varga's work and generally limited their application of the notion to China.[205] By contrast, Kōza-ha Marxists such as Hani Gorō and Hirano Yoshitarō, who emphasized Japan's backwardness, found the concept useful with reference to Japan as well as China. Drawing on the writings of Mad'iar, Varga, Wittfogel, and Max Weber, Hani pointedly differentiated Japan's progress to feudalism and nascent capitalism from China's apparent inability to emerge from Asiatic "stagnancy."[206] Similarly, drawing on Noro Eitarō's writings of 1929 and 1930, Hirano found the notion of oriental society helpful in explaining why China and Japan had failed to duplicate the Western pattern of bourgeois revolution, particularly in the political sphere.

Hirano's application of the oriental society notion is most suggestive for understanding the varieties of interpretation to be found in the controversy on Chinese social history. He argued in effect for two parallel paths of development in Europe and Asia. Both kinds of societies began with primitive clan or tribal society and then moved into the slavery period. In classical Greek and Roman antiquity, the ownership of slaves was private. In other cases, however—and here Hirano did not use the term *Asiatic* in a geographical sense although those societies that had experienced this latter variant of slavery tended to be in the "Orient"—what arose was total slavery. In these societies slaves, land, and all means of production were owned not privately but by the state (the emperor or despot). From slave society, the two paths converged once again in feudalism, then capitalism, and socialism. Nevertheless, Hirano argued that the actual experience of "Asiatic despotism" had exercised a profound impact on all subsequent socioeconomic and political development in the East. The enormous role the state had played in production and public works had instilled in its people a profound passivity. As a result, in Japan, for example, the civil rights movement of the Meiji era (the jiyū minken undō) had had to struggle against deeply ingrained patterns of "Asiatic submissiveness" among the citizenry. In addition, the legacy of Asiatic despotism was a more centralized feudalism in Japan although geography also had had an impact there. Japan's natural divisions by sea and mountains had lessened tendencies toward centralization, Hirano maintained. Finally, the heritage of the despotic state could influence the development of commerce and industrial capitalism, depending on whether the state endeavored to encourage commerce as a participant or discourage it.[207]

Similar arguments were advanced by Japanese Marxists such as Hayakawa specifically with respect to China as the controversy in China proceeded and its literature was translated and published in Japan.[208] In China itself, it was Guo Moruo's pioneering study of ancient Chinese society that brought the issue of the Asiatic mode of production to the fore. Guo argued that the Asiatic mode of production constituted the ancient primitive communal society. " 'Broadly speaking', " he wrote, " 'before Western Chou [Chinese society] was a so-called 'Asiatic' primitive communist society. Western Chou corresponded to the slave society of Greece and Rome. With Eastern Chou, especially after Ch'in [255–206 B.C.], China truly entered the feudal period'."[209] In this treatment, Guo at once seemed to reject Marx's depiction of four successive modes of production as bases of class societies while mechanistically accepting literally the sequence itself. This analysis seemed to allow Guo to avoid Chinese exceptionalism. Yet, in fact, its substitution of a stage designated with what was apparently a geographical referent for something that Marx had depicted as classless and universal reintroduced the very same problem. Thus, his periodization would come under attack from fellow Chinese Marxists not only for its assertion of the existence of slavery in the Zhou period on the basis of scant evidence but also for its inclusion of a reinterpreted and highly problematic conceptualization of the Asiatic mode of production.[210]

Many participants in the controversy responded to Guo by attacking the concept of the Asiatic mode of production using the arguments employed by Iolk and S. M. Dubrovsky at the Leningrad Conference.[211] Others, however, replied by analyzing the concept independently and using it to explain aspects of China's social history—such as the lack of a classical slave social formation like that of Athens and Rome—that were otherwise difficult to situate in Marx's universal schema. Li Ji offered one of the most thoughtful applications of the Asiatic mode of production notion to China. This was probably because, as a Trotskyist who was in fundamental dissent with the Soviet leadership in the Comintern, Li felt more free than others might have to question Soviet orthodoxy on the matter. In Li's treatment, the Asiatic mode of production appeared immediately after primitive communism and before feudalism so that it supplanted classical slave society in much the same manner as it did in Hirano's paradigm. Drawing critically on a wide variety of Soviet treatments of the concept from Mad'iar to Iolk, Li concluded that from what Marx wrote on the Asiatic mode of production, its most significant distinguishing characteristic was state ownership of land, hence the identity of rents and taxes.

This was the first form of ownership rights that was described in Morgan's *Ancient Society*, Li asserted, and it corresponded to what had existed in the Yin period. The three books of Pan Geng, a ruler in the late-Shang period, "clearly tell us of private property, classes, and the state all appearing one after the other" in this period, Li wrote, and he concluded that gens communal society as described by Morgan and Engels had already collapsed in the time of Pan Geng's rule.[212] Other traditional historical sources such as the observation that " 'There is no land under heaven that is not owned by the king' " in the "Beishan" (Northern mountains) chapter of the *Book of Odes* provided further indirect evidence for Li's periodization. On the basis of such texts, Li concluded that from the era of Pan Geng to the end of the Yin was the Asiatic mode of production. Interestingly, Li emphatically did not adopt the view of Soviet historian Kovalev that the Asiatic mode of production was simply a variant of slavery. Nevertheless, it did supplant slavery in Li's periodization. According to Li, during the reigns of Pan Geng and Tai Wang, the Yin people were not surrounded by strong and hostile nomadic peoples that constrained them to engage in continual warfare. As a result, there were few captives taken as slaves to produce a classic slave mode of production. "Therefore," Li determined, "after the collapse of China's tribal society, the development of the mode of production did not take the form of Athens and Rome, but the Asiatic form."[213]

Li's interpretation drew vehement criticism on several grounds. Mo Dazhao offered an extraordinarily muddled critique, the most significant point of which was that if Li could argue that feudalism had grown out of an antiquity in which there was no distinction between the prince and the state, there was no reason that a similar argument could not be made of early feudal Europe. Li's argument was a "forced interpretation" based on "prejudgment," according to Mo.[214] In addition, Li's account took issue with that offered by Guo on the issue of whether slave society as it existed in Greece and Rome had ever existed in China. Interestingly, He Ganzhi reaffirmed Guo's position on slavery by placing the Asiatic mode at the beginning of his own periodization as if in agreement with Guo's view that Asiatic society constituted primitive communal society. He's own interpretation drew heavily on the Soviet and Japanese discussions of the issue, particularly the latter, which he found the more fruitful in their application of the notion of the Asiatic mode of production to the actual history of the East. He's discussion exhibited fully the ambivalence toward the Asiatic mode of production and oriental society concepts that was reflected in the controversy on Chinese social history as a whole. On the one hand, He seemed to deny the notion of any special Asian mode of production, arguing that what made China appear to be "peculiarly stagnant" in terms of the Marxian schema was merely the accumulation of remnants from previous modes of production.[215] At the same time, however, He found peculiarities in "oriental history" dating back to the period before the emergence of slavery. Indeed, he argued that the Orient never did develop the same fully mature slaveowner formation as did classical Rome and Greece: In China, the nascent slave system "stagnated."[216] He was careful to stress, throughout his treatment of the Asiatic mode of production, that the basic succession of historical stages in the East remained "progressive" in character, a fact that Iolk and other critics of the

Asiatic mode of production in the Soviet Union seemed to understate.[217] He found the arguments of Japanese Marxist Aikawa Haruki particularly helpful in achieving the proper balance among these factors. Aikawa, like He, objected to any scheme that omitted any of Marx's historical stages, and he had been critical of the interpretation of Hayakawa Jirō, who had implied that China had "skipped over" the slavery stage. As a Chinese historian, He may have been drawn to Aikawa's effort to minimize the peculiarities of Japan's own historical development, for Aikawa's treament implied that the Asiatic mode of production was simply a transitional era between primitive communal society and class society and as such could be considered a universal rather than a geographically specific category.[218] Aikawa did, however, identify certain special features of socioeconomic development in the East, a judgment that He found inescapable. Aikawa's solution was to define the Asiatic mode of production as a tributary system—in which a dominant tribal group was paid tribute by surrounding, subject clans—that preceded the emergence of slavery. The tributary system existed within the context of village communities or communes. The remnants of the tributary system were what, in turn, distinguished slavery and feudalism—"oriental feudalism"—in the East from the same in Western Europe.[219] It was the power of the state, "the Eastern monarch," He concluded, that distinguished the former from the latter. Thus, feudalism could be characterized either by the territorial division of power among a number of states, as in Western Europe, or by a centralized political organ "Asiatic style." Yet fundamentally the two systems were the same: socioeconomically, they both constituted the same feudal mode of production.[220]

Still others were even more flexible with the concept of the Asiatic mode of production, placing it later in Chinese history in part to account for what they saw as a prolonged period of economic stagnation. Indeed, although for neither Guo nor He was this a primary consideration in explicating the Asiatic mode of production in Chinese history, it was so for others. Xiong Deshan, for example, characterized all of imperial China from Qin to Qing as Asiatic, reinterpreting the term *Asiatic* to denote a variant of the feudal mode of production.[221] Xiong identified in Chinese feudalism at least two characteristics associated with Marx's oriental society model. Most importantly, Xiong agreed with Wang Zhicheng's early advocacy of an Asiatic mode of production that was distinguished most by its economic stagnation.[222] This economic stagnation had, in turn, rendered China vulnerable to, and unable to respond effectively to, attacks from surrounding nomadic tribes. The warfare and consequent conquest by such peoples as the Mongols and Liao, which typically enjoyed lower levels of culture, resulted, in turn, in the further reduction of opportunities for Chinese industrial advancement, Xiong argued.[223]

Xiong did not specify which aspect of the Asiatic mode of production caused the economic stagnation that was central to his conception, unlike Liu Xingtang, who subsequently identified as the source of the problem the village community (*gongtongti*, or *kyōdōtai* as it appeared in Japanese analyses of rural nondevelopment).[224] Yet the state did play a central role in Xiong's treatment, one that was similar to that depicted in Soviet accounts. "The state occupied a dominant position" in the agrarian society of imperial China with "waterworks its major responsibility." This role in the economy was pivotal to the state's political power. Interestingly, here Xiong was able to integrate his interpretation with the traditional Confucian notion of dynastic cycles. In the latter years of each dynasty, Xiong observed, the state became exhausted by expenditures such as repairs to dikes, dams, and irrigation ditches, which localities then had to assume. Local gentry, of course, were unable to undertake such onerous duties as effectively as the central government, and when they did, they often shifted the onus to those least able to pay, and floods and famine followed in quick succession. The great famine that afflicted China in the last sixty years of the Ming dynasty typified this phenomenon and helped to explain the hastening of the change in dynasties through peasant rebellions.[225] Dynastic change, however, did not constitute fundamental socioeconomic transformation in a society that remained stagnant economically throughout the imperial period in Xiong's account. This particular emphasis in Xiong's treatment was echoed elsewhere. The CCP's Chen Boda, for example, also characterized imperial China's two-thousand-year history as Asiatic in terms of a stagnant variation of feudalism. In his view, China had experienced feudalism in the Western Zhou and a period of transition to the new variant of feudalism in the Eastern Zhou.[226] Although both these scholars insisted on conflating the Asiatic mode of production with feudalism, they accepted the appellation *Asiatic* to stress the stasis that was peculiar to China's variety of feudalism. Significantly, in neither Xiong's nor Chen's interpretations had China ever emerged from this Asiatic system to experience a transition from feudalism to capitalism such as that which occurred in the West.

Western Zhou	*Eastern Zhou*	*Qin*	*Qing*	*Present*
feudalism	transition	Asiatic (feudal) ———————————————————————— - - - - ▶		

It is not surprising, then, that some of those who rejected the concept of oriental society out of hand were not particularly convincing inasmuch as their own schematizations of Chinese social history appeared to incorporate elements of that notion. Two such scholars are particularly worthy of note because of their attention to the problem of the state and the relationship between superstructure and base. Hu Qiuyuan and Wang Lixi, both editors of *Dushu zazhi*, denounced the oriental society notion. Together, they rejected the implication that geographical conditions could prevail over forces of production to elevate the particular over the universal in the Chinese or any other case. Instead, Hu and Wang chose to explain the troublesome two-millennium imperial period in China in terms that would permit full comparability with the West. They chose to designate this era as a transitional period of a special social formation between feudalism and capitalism—*zhuanzhi-zhuyi* (despotism).[227] It is possible that there was some confusion on Marx's own historiography here. What Hu and Wang were describing as feudal *zhuanzhi-zhuyi* was, in fact, Marx's and Engels's notion of the precapitalist stage of feudal absolutism, which was originally to be found in

Marx's *Eighteenth Brumaire* describing the interlude of falling feudal forces and rising capitalist forces and which Hu had seen Soviet historian M. N. Pokrovsky (*Russia in World History*) apply to Russian history.[228] Hu, like Tao, saw feudalism as having collapsed early in China.[229] Hu championed his own view in opposition to Wang Yichang's periodization: primitive communal society → gentile society → feudal society → despotic/Asiatic society → capitalist society (colonial/semicolonial capitalist society) → socialist society.[230] An important difficulty, however, arose in Hu's and Wang's terminology. Hu sought to differentiate his view from the notion of a despotic state that was specifically "oriental" in character by grounding his absolutist empire on the rising urban, commercial classes. The oriental despot, by contrast, stood alone above and autonomous from classless society. Hu then redefined the Asiatic mode of production as merely "an oriental version" of zhuanzheng-zhuyi (despotism).[231]

Pre-Yin	*Yin*	*Zhou*	*Warring States*	*Qin*	*Qing*	*Present*
primitive society	gentile (tribal) society	feudalism ⟶		despotic society ⟶		Opium Wars despotism/semi-colonialism

It is clear from Hu's discussion that he was aware that the correct term for "absolutism" as coined in Japan (whence most Chinese Marxist terminology came) was *zettai-shugi* (*juedui-zhuyi* in Chinese); and Hu was familiar with both this convention—a term that he saw stressing the concentration of power, undemocratic character, bureaucratism, and violent nature of the regime in question—and the debate then raging in Japan about Meiji absolutism.[232] Yet he chose instead a term that was associated with oriental society. Moreover, even as he sought to conflate it with Marx's and Engels's *absolutism*, as a phenomenon evident in all class societies, he stressed its relevance to Russian and then Chinese and Japanese history. Hu distinguished between two varieties of despotism: feudal despotism, such as that of Napoleon or Bismarck, which rested on a balance between nobility and bourgeois, and semicolonial despotism under the impact of imperialism. The latter, which Yuan Shikai's government was said to exemplify, opposed "precapitalist gentry and compradores and a portion of the national bourgeoisie to . . . oppressed peasants, workers . . . and all revolutionary petty bourgeois."[233] Although it would appear that the semicolonial form would have typified China, Hu drew on Pokrovsky's description of "despotism" as a postfeudal, precapitalist stage that had characterized the transition from feudalism to capitalism in Russia to analyze China's economic development. Hu and Wang, then, argued that the growth of commodity exchange had weakened feudal economic relations and the power of the landed nobility. This allowed power to be concentrated in the monarch,[234] which came to be bolstered by a massive bureaucracy and military power. As the state needed more and more resources to support its military and bureaucratic apparatus, it increased its exactions on a largely peasant population that occasionally rebelled, usually unsuccessfully. Finally, the rule of the despot resembled the Marxian notion of absolutism in that it was fundamentally antifeudal in character, although it did permit certain feudal relations to be sustained.[235] Indeed, it was in their stress on the class basis of this despotism in the nobility and rising merchant class that Wang and Hu sought to distinguish themselves from advocates of an Asiatic mode of production notion that saw only two classes in society: the despot and those he ruled. They rejected any interpretation that would have posited a state above and independent from social classes. In addition, their perspective stressed despotism as a dynamic social formation in transition rather than as a stagnant social formation lacking an internal dynamic moving it toward capitalism. Yet at the same time that Hu promoted this description as a universal stage in the transition from feudalism to capitalism, he also argued that China's despotism was "special" because landed feudal interests and those of the commercial bourgeoisie were not strongly opposed but rather easily linked to one another in China. He did not specify why this should have been the case. He did suggest, however, that despotism moderated conflict between these classes, thus perpetuating the now weakened feudal relations. Having been created by the corrosive effect of commercial capital on feudal relations of production, this was a form of state that was at once feudal and antifeudal, destined to ease the transition from feudalism while supporting feudal production relations as they were.[236]

It is evident from Hu's and Wang's accounts that while they repudiated the Asiatic mode of production theory in its original form and endeavored to articulate an alternative, universalist interpretation of the history of imperial China, in the content of their own formulations the two scholars failed to escape the negative implications of the oriental society model. They argued that during the entire two-thousand-year imperial period China was in the transitional despotic or absolutist stage. This was certainly a far longer period than the transition under absolutism that Marx had described in France, which was at most one or two centuries, and Hu and Wang, like Tao and so many others, were at a loss to account for the apparent lack of movement in Chinese social history during this long interlude between feudalism and capitalism. Moreover, although they situated their despotic society after the feudal stage, Hu's and Wang's emphasis on the impact of the political superstructure on subsequent economic development evoked images of a powerful oriental despot inhibiting the emergence of the requisites of feudalism and capitalism. In short, even for the most inventive critics of the oriental society model as presented by Mad'iar and Varga, the implications of many of Marx's original observations on Asiatic society remained to intrude on their application of Marxist sociohistorical theory and revolutionary strategy to China.

CONCLUSIONS: ORIENTALISM AND MARXISM

There were meaningful similarities between the controversy on Chinese social history and the debate on Japanese capitalism with reference to the national question. In Japan, the Kōza-ha, or orthodox Comintern-JCP, view of Japanese history bore a strong resemblance to certain indigenous views of China. In an important sense, the Kōza-ha position stood between the CCP position and that of the Left

GMD. On behalf of the Left GMD, Tao argued that "the superstructure could exist independently even though it must owe its origins to the appropriate economic basis; the surviving superstructure could even become an obstacle to the further development of the foundation itself."[237] This was very much akin to the Kōza-ha claim that feudal remnants continued to reside in the superstructure of Japanese society, particularly in the tennō-sei and its institutional supports, long after feudalism had given way in large part to capitalism in the economic base. Both arguments implied that a new kind of social formation had arisen in which feudal remnant forces and the bourgeoisie survived in a mutually parasitic relationship. The same kinds of data were brought to bear, however, not in the Kōza-ha and Left GMD but in the Kōza-ha and CCP arguments. Both CCP and Kōza-ha authors pointed to the forms of exploitation rather than to land rents and ownership to demonstrate the persistence of feudal forces in the two cases. "Extraeconomic coercion" was the key phrase here supporting the thesis that feudalism persisted, and the form of state—or the presence of warlords instead of centralized state power—was cited to support the thesis that Japan and China remained semifeudal in character. Argument was made, in effect, from superstructure to base; despite the significant differences between the two societies, economic development or nondevelopment could be explained in terms of superstructural features of Chinese or Japanese history. Finally, although the official condemnation of Trotsky in Moscow inhibited Marxists in the two societies from accepting the maligned theory of permanent revolution, the promise of flexibility in historical periodization contained in Trotsky's identification of uneven and combined development, of elements of old and new relations of production coexisting in contemporary society, was immensely attractive in China as in Japan. Thus, even as fundamental Marxian categories were invoked, Chinese as well as Japanese Marxists found it necessary to interpret the realities of their respective societies to account for special characteristics that might be attributed to earlier modes of production.

What is most notable here is that Chinese and Japanese Marxists, theorizing with some autonomy from the Comintern, were constantly haunted by the specter of "backwardness," which emerged just as persistently as it had been presented in the Comintern leadership's original formulas for the Chinese and Japanese revolutions. Even Rōnō-ha Marxists, particularly Inomata Tsunao, and many Chinese Trotskyites such as Li Ji, Hu Qiuyuan, and Wang Lixi, who were most optimistic about the development of capitalism and prospects for immediate proletarian revolution, acknowledged the powerful persistence of so-called feudal elements in their societies. As a result, they were hesitant about the extent to which they could expect to see the full realization even of bourgeois democracy with all its imperfections in their own societies and, if so, under what conditions. They exhibited profound suspicions that some bourgeois-democratic stage of revolution, however abbreviated, might be a prerequisite to successful socialist revolution in their societies. It would appear that the doubts about the past and future of Asian societies in Marx and his successors in the Soviet Union were transmitted effectively and unshakably to Chinese and Japanese Marxists despite their efforts to demonstrate equivalence to the West.

In his recent work on *Orientalism*, Edward W. Said insightfully recognized his subject as "a style of thought based on an ontological and epistemological distinction made between 'the Orient' and . . . 'the Occident'." This orientalism, he argued, "can be discussed and analyzed as the corporate institution for dealing with the Orient—dealing with it by making statements about it, authorizing views of it, describing it, by teaching it, settling it, ruling over it: in short, Orientalism is a Western style for dominating, restructuring, and having authority over the Orient."[238] It was the unfortunate circumstance of Chinese Marxists that the doctrine to which they were committed for the means to revolutionize Chinese society was "orientalist" in this sense. Marx's devotion to a universal world history notwithstanding, he himself was the product of an age in which the East was no longer conceived to be part of that history but something else. The notion of oriental society—vaguely defined to encompass huge expanses of undifferentiated space from Russia and China to Egypt—can be perceived justifiably as a reflection of this attitude in Marx and of his inability to supersede this perspective because of his tremendous lack of knowledge about "the East." Nor was this orientalism simply a value-free distinction between oneself and others. Rather, it was a normative distinction as well. If the East was once the seat of great civilizations, so be it; but compared with nineteenth-century Western Europe, it was a stagnant, valueless mass of barbarism and ignorance. The only hope for this pathetic Orient lay in its being ravaged cruelly, but ultimately for the well-being of all humankind, by the expansive capitalist West.

This perspective within Marxism itself posed a profound problem for Chinese Marxists who wished to demonstrate that China fit Marx's historical schema and, therefore, was ripe for proletarian-socialist revolution. Indeed, it could be argued that in a very real sense, in seeking to force Chinese history into the Marxian paradigm, these intellectuals were subjecting themselves to another kind of Western domination, to a domination of foreign values and concepts, having determined that their own indigenous values could not enable China to survive foreign encroachment nor to resolve its internal social problems. As participants in the controversy on China's social history struggled to squeeze China's long and rich history into Marx's allegedly universal categories, they continually found themselves confronting the troublesome premises of the Asiatic mode of production. In nearly all periodizations produced by participants in the controversy, the imperial age from Qin to Qing was depicted as a single unchanging entity. As Wang Lixi and Chen Xiaojiang both noted at the time, the central concern was always how to account for the period of two thousand years from the Qin through the Qing dynasties.[239] Perhaps this conundrum was unavoidable because of the very longevity of Chinese civilization in comparison with the span of European history treated by Marx and Engels: there simply were not enough stages in Marx's schema to periodize the imperial era into discrete two- or three-hundred-year segments to record changes within Chinese society. What could be accomplished under the purview of traditional Confucian dynastic histories—or some alternative indigenous paradigm—had to be abandoned under Marx's scheme. Chinese Marxists were left with the discomfiting task of explaining how, having claimed that China's history was part of universal human history, no significant social change had occurred for two thousand years without once again raising the specter of a separate history of an oriental society characterized by prolonged stagnancy and backwardness under a despotic state.

Nor did this problem pertain only to the past. As they looked from their nation's past toward its future, China's revolutionary Marxists had to be concerned with the implications of this pattern for the future of their revolution. What would be the legacy of a long imperial era, characterized by an unwieldy bureaucracy under the domination of the shidaifu stratum that they found so difficult to characterize in Marxian economic terms? The immense weight of this tradition could foreordain a continuing struggle against tendencies toward despotism and bureaucratism during the transition to the new society. Given the prominence of such concerns in the controversy on Chinese social history, it is not surprising that in the resolution of the national question that would emerge hegemonic in China—Mao's reformulation of the notion of the permanent revolution—the need for conscious, voluntarist struggle, a Promethean effort to push the revolution forward in opposition to deeply embedded cultural inclinations toward bureaucratism and statism, should have become so pronounced.

Many participants in the controversy on Chinese social history who repudiated the Asiatic mode of production and simply periodized Chinese history in terms of communal, ancient, feudal, and bourgeois society avoided these issues entirely. Yet as contemporary historians in the People's Republic of China continue their effort to understand Chinese history—and particularly the problem of the bureaucratic, despotic state, an issue that remains very much alive today—in Marxian terms, the issue of the Asiatic mode of production has been inescapable. Where the nature of the imperial system and the problem of the specifically *Chinese* state was and remains the most vexatious issue in the continuing debate on Chinese social history, the dilemma between universal history and oriental society was in the 1930s and persists today as the most problematic concern for scholars of the historiographical aspects of the national question in Chinese Marxism.

PART FOUR

Outcomes: The Reconciliation of Marxism with National Identity

Tenkō: Emperor, State, and Marxian National Socialism in Shōwa Japan

As OBSERVED here, the national question figured heavily in the debate on Japanese capitalism and the controversy on Chinese social history. Intellectuals in both societies had been attracted to Marxism-Leninism along with other strands of "progressive" Western thought in a nationalistic desire to "modernize" in order to resist the perceived encroachments of more advanced societies. But how could the internationalist and stateless ideals of Marxian socialism be reconciled with the nationalistic concerns that had prompted the turn to Marxism at the outset? In the 1920s, when these controversies first erupted, the primary challenge that the national question posed to Asia's Marxists was how they could demonstrate the applicability of Marx's political and economic theory to their non-European contexts. Their efforts to periodize and interpret Chinese and Japanese history in terms of Marx's paradigm were driven by the need to show that China and Japan were indeed ripe for socialist revolution, in one stage or two. Analyzing the character of the existing state in Marxian terms was an essential step in articulating and defending revolutionary strategy. The history and nature of state power in the Chinese and Japanese pasts provided valuable clues to the challenges of the present, and the exploration of these histories in terms of the Asiatic mode of production and oriental despotism promised to reveal the roots of negative patterns of authoritarian political rule that would have to be overcome in bourgeois-democratic and socialist revolutions. Certainly, the peculiarities of (Asian) national characteristics were set against the universalist claims of Marxist theory in these discourses.

Nevertheless, with the outbreak of hostilities on the Asian mainland in 1931 and their intensification to full-scale war in 1937, Chinese and Japanese Marxists were drawn into the maelstrom of nationalistic fervor in support of, or in resistance to, Japanese expansionism. The war, then, forced Chinese and Japanese Marxists to confront the national question in a different form. Suddenly, war threatened the very survival of those for whom Chinese and Japanese Marxist revolutionaries proposed to build socialism. Now it was not so easy to sacrifice the state or nationalistic sentiments on the altar of Marxism's stateless internationalism. Initially, how Chinese and Japanese Marxists would approach nationalism and the state in their renewed importance in the changed international context differed on the basis of Comintern instructions to the two Communist parties. When the two parties were formed in 1921 and 1922, Comintern leaders, stressing Japan's "backwardness," prescribed the same two-stage revolutionary strategy for Japan that it established for China, and even as it recognized Japan's tremendous capitalistic economic growth, the Comintern essentially maintained the same strategy for

Japan through 1932, when it issued its final set of theses on Japan. As Soviets with strong recollections of Japan's defeat of Russia in 1905 and Japan's protracted role in the Siberian expedition against the Bolshevik Revolution, however, Comintern leaders chose to stress Japan's advanced level of industrial development when they considered the appropriate role for nationalistic sentiment in Japan's revolution. Affirming the role of Chinese nationalism in a bourgeois revolution to achieve national unity and the expulsion of the imperialist powers, Bukharin and his colleagues adamantly rejected Japanese nationalism as a bourgeois, counter-revolutionary force. The party's Draft Platform and subsequent Comintern theses called for the overthrow of the very symbol of the Japanese nation, the emperor, and his supporting institutions, as "feudal remnants," and the successive theses intensified their opposition to Japanese nationalism as the enemy of China's rising revolution in the 1920s.

It will be recalled that even before the JCP was born in 1922, there were those who would not accept the Comintern's judgment on Japanese nationalism. Takabatake Motoyuki and his followers (see chap. 5) asserted that Lenin, the father of Bolshevism, had been a statist, even if he did not realize it. Seeing the continuing need for a strong Japanese state after the revolution to protect the Japanese people from internal and external threats (such as "proletarian imperialism") and confirming his sentimental attachment to the imperial symbol of Japan's people (or nation, minzoku), Takabatake's Marxian national socialism established a precedent for those who would have second thoughts about the Comintern's dim view of nationalism in Japan. As Japan's economic and political crisis deepened in the mid- and late 1920s, many who had subscribed to Marxism-Leninism began to experience such doubts as well. Takahashi Kamekichi's resistance to the application of Lenin's understanding of imperialism gave voice to these doubts. By 1930, others, this time within the struggling Japanese Communist party itself, revealed that their attachment to the imperial institution and to other things Japanese overwhelmed the Marxist-Leninist call to take on the existing structure of power in their nation. This tension between Marxian internationalism and sentimental nationalism peaked when Japanese aggression in the 1931 Manchurian incident brought war to the Asian mainland. In the succeeding years, hundreds upon hundreds of Japanese Marxists, imprisoned under the broadened proscriptions of the 1925 Peace Preservation Law, chose to recant (*tenkō suru*) their ties to the JCP and reaffirm their commitment to the Japanese emperor and nation in their vision of Japan's future.

Considered in isolation, the *tenkō* phenomenon, that is, mass recantation of imprisoned JCP and non-JCP Marxists, could be attributed to the privations of imprisonment. Certainly, the extremely poor prison conditions, the psychological and physical hazards of imprisonment, including the use of torture, and the determination of the authorities to induce *tenkō* against the threat to social unity that these dissidents represented contributed to the desire to mitigate one's punishment through *tenkō*.[1] But there is something much more than the prison phenomenon here, a remarkable pattern in which leading Japanese radical thinkers who were not subjected to these pressures resolved the tension between Marxist internationalism and Japanese national identity by fashioning of their Marxism indigenized systems of socialism that did not challenge either the Japanese emperor or Japanese expansionism. These thinkers included Takabatake, Takahashi Kamekichi, Kita Ikki, who is commonly cited as the inspiration for the right-wing February 26 incident,[2] and Akamatsu Katsumaro, whose national socialist doctrine experienced several incarnations.[3] They, like leading tenkōsha Sano Manabu, articulated "Japanist" (*Nihon-teki*) doctrines of Marxian national socialism that confound the conventional distinction between the left and right ends of the political spectrum. This pattern is of sufficient moment to the Japanese left-wing movement to merit detailed scrutiny.

In this chapter I focus on the case of Sano—and through him the Kaitō-ha that he first repudiated and then emulated—as a leading Japanese Communist party member who struggled with the need to affirm Japanese national identity while remaining a committed Marxist. He resolved the nationalist/internationalist tension by combining indigenous philosophical values and perspectives with his Marxism to formulate a doctrine of national/state socialism based on the existing imperial system. Although most of the hundreds of Japanese who *tenkō*ed in the 1930s may not have subscribed to Sano's particular variety of Marxian national socialism, the conflict that Sano experienced and his effort to resolve it was widely shared in the form of *tenkō*. It is argued that taken together with positive theoretical endeavors such as those of Sano, Takabatake, and the Kaitō-ha, *tenkō* became the predominant means by which prewar Japanese Marxists sought to reconcile the conflicting demands of Marxism and nationalism. The predominance of this nationalistic and statist reconciliation of Marxism with the promotion of Japanese national identity can then be compared and contrasted with the marriage of Marxism with nationalism in revolutionary China.

TENKŌ AND ITS HISTORICAL SIGNIFICANCE

On June 8, 1933, Sano Manabu and Nabeyama Sadachika, imprisoned JCP leaders, issued a public proclamation repudiating the JCP and all other Communist affiliations. This action, to which they themselves referred as *tenkō*, sent shock waves throughout the Japanese left-wing movement. Their joint conversion triggered a wave of mass *tenkō* by fellow Marxists and developed into a movement that finally destroyed the long-beleaguered Japanese Communist party. This phenomenon reveals the importance of Japanese Marxist efforts to adapt the nineteenth-century European philosophy of Marxism to their non-European, twentieth-century context.

Tenkō demonstrates how Marxism, like political theory in general,[4] is transformed as it moves from one milieu to another. Most often, in Marxism, this adaptation revolves around the national question. Throughout the existence of the JCP, Japan's Marxists confronted the national dilemma on two levels. In practical terms, the Comintern theses' injunction that the JCP seek to abolish the imperial institution and reject Japanese nationalism in toto made the kind of resolution of the issue achieved in China—the Leninist fusion of a national liberation movement with Marxian socialism—far more difficult in Japan. More fundamentally (as in China as well), the very acceptance of Marxism-Leninism could appear as subordination to European cultural imperialism. In Japan, such a conflict between national identity and submission to the Soviet formula of Marxism-Leninism challenged Japanese Marxists to produce indigenous variants of socialist thought that could accommodate Japan's national needs. The particularism of the nationalist socialism that emerged as a result in prewar Japan poses a dramatic contrast with the nationalistic, but antistatist, marriage of Marxist thought with national identity in the Chinese revolution.

Tenkōsha leaders Sano and Nabeyama had had long and impressive careers as Marxists. Sano (1892–1953), a graduate of Tokyo Imperial University, taught economics at Waseda University in 1920, joined the JCP in 1922 and its Central Committee the following year, attended the Fifth Comintern Congress, and helped to draft the Shanghai Theses in 1924.[5] Nabeyama (1901–1979), a laborer with only an elementary school education, helped to establish an Osaka branch of the young JCP, led the effort to revive the party after official repression had forced its dissolution in 1924, and rose to become a member of the Comintern's Central Committee in 1928. By the summer of 1929, both he and Sano were in prison. In 1931 and 1932, they advocated using the public trial of JCP members as a forum for propaganda and continued political struggle. Partly because of their leadership in this maneuver, they were sentenced to life imprisonment in October 1932. When they made their *tenkō* "Proclamation to Fellow Defendants" eight months later, both men were immediately expelled from the party.[6] In the ensuing months and years, a near flood of *tenkō*s by imprisoned JCP members followed, culminating in organized *tenkō*s by entire left-wing groups. Beginning in 1937, with the full outbreak of war with China, Japanese government authorities adopted and encouraged *tenkō* as a way of reintegrating leftists into Japanese society and mobilizing the entire society in nationalistic fervor to support the war.[7]

The first tenkōsha were among the thousands arrested during the 1920s and 1930s under the Peace Preservation Law of 1925, which forbade participation in associations seeking to repudiate or change the national polity (*kokutai*). As the police gathered more information on the party from early arrestees, they captured the party's core membership. From June 1931 to October 1932, 200 leading members of the JCP were jointly tried in Tokyo District Court. Of these, 187 were convicted and sentenced to terms from two years to life imprisonment.[8] The following year, many younger party officials in prison followed Sano and Nabeyama.[9] Within one month of the latter's joint *tenkō* statement, 548 others formally renounced their party affiliations. As Steinhoff has noted, continued arrests and mass defections "brought about the complete destruction of the Communist movement in Japan."[10] By 1940, nearly all JCP members had *tenkō*ed, including many who had once condemned Sano's and Nabeyama's action. Most of the exceptions, such as Yamakawa Hitoshi, were associated with the Rōnō-ha, which, having left the JCP, was more secure from police pressures until 1936.

Group, or organizational, *tenkō* reached a peak in 1942 when almost all existing political parties and labor organizations merged to form the Taisei Yokusansai

(Imperial Rule Assistance Association).[11] The left-wing socialist movement was now but a ghost of its former self. Radical Marxist intellectuals such as Hirano Yoshitarō, who had made innovative contributions to Marxist literature concerning Japanese capitalism, began to reflect their *tenkō* in new nationalistic writings that they hastened to denounce after the war. For many such Marxists, *tenkō* proved to be a disgrace, atonement for which motivated much of their scholarship after Japan's defeat.

Marxism as a Threat to Japanese National Identity

The *tenkō* of Sano and Nabeyama was not remarkable per se, for similar individual and group recantations of Communism had occurred in Italy, France, and Germany in the 1920s.[12] A widespread simultaneous recantation across several countries had occurred as early as 1914 with the demise of the Second International over the issue of national loyalties in World War I. In many such cases, particularly in Germany, the decision to rally to the support of the homeland explicitly involved the rejection of Marx's claim that the workingman had no country.[13] These German recanters were succeeded by advocates of National Bolshevism during the Weimar Republic—"a rapprochement between German nationalism and Russian Communism"[14]—but they also rejected the fundamental Marxian tenet of attaining socialism through domestic class conflict.

Two features distinguished Japan's *tenkō* movement from these other instances. First, a great number not only of individuals but groups *tenkō*ed. Here the sheer efficiency of the Japanese police was an important factor. But one must also consider the dynamics of relations among Japanese Marxists as well as the pattern of relations between these Marxists and Japanese society at large. Steinhoff notes that "*tenkō* helped solve the crucial problem of maintaining the integration of Japanese society during the dual crisis of political modernization and impending war."[15] In attempting to explain the phenomenon, Japanese authorities themselves classified *tenkō* into the three categories of "political, citizen ['common-man'], and religious ['spiritual']" *tenkō*s. "A political (*seiji-teki*) *tenkō* was one based on political differences of opinion with the Communist Party, as in the Sano-Nabeyama prototype. Citizen (*shimin-teki*) *tenkō* involved a desire to return to normal life as a good Japanese citizen. In religious (*shūkyō-teki*) *tenkō*, one gave up Communist ideology because of a new belief in something else, though not necessarily an organized religion."[16]

These three elements in the official classification—political, civic, and spiritual—should not be regarded as autonomous or mutually exclusive: They were mingled and made interdependent in the mystical emperor-centered notion of the *kokutai*. According to the pervasive family-state ideology formulated in the Meiji period, membership in the Japanese national polity, or *kokutai*, and, hence, one's relationship to the emperor, provided the basis for one's individual identity.[17] Membership in this group, or any group in Japan, remained in the 1920s and 1930s the crucial referent for one's individual identity.[18] Because Marxism-Leninism demanded allegiance to the Soviet-dominated Comintern and disruption of the *kokutai*, it placed believers firmly beyond the pale of their traditional political, civic, and spiritual frame of reference. Japan's Marxist-Leninists, then, felt even more intensely the agony that commonly afflicts members of a vanguard revolutionary party as described by Michael Walzer:

> Vanguard consciousness is the work of intellectuals somehow cut loose from the constraints of the old order—or of intellectuals who cut themselves loose: These are people, usually young people, who respond to the decadence of their world by withdrawing. They give up conventional modes of existence, conventional families and jobs; they choose marginality; they endure persecution; they go into exile. They are receptive to radical and, as their opponents rightly say, to foreign ideas: Calvinism in sixteenth- and seventeenth-century France, Marxism in Russia and China.[19]

Marxists who joined the JCP in the 1920s possessed this kind of vanguard consciousness. Although most were privileged intellectuals associated with Tokyo Imperial University, they abandoned the mundane concerns that V. I. Lenin claimed inhibited revolutionary consciousness. They left the bounds of traditional Japanese consensus on society and polity, and they became "marginal" when they adopted alien radical ideas to change their own society.

Walzer's observations on the nature of relations among individuals within a vanguard group help to explain certain aspects of *tenkō*. As Walzer notes, vanguard groups "are closed and exclusive. Joining the vanguard is a matter of choice, but it requires also the acceptance of new members by the old. And the old have, through choices of their own, established certain criteria."[20] It should be understood, however, that although the Japanese Communists may have been alienated from their native environment, they shared numerous patterns of behavior characteristic of Japanese society at large. The Soviet or Comintern model of orthodox Marxist-Leninist behavior, to the extent that it had become influential in Japan, lost appeal as arrestees were insulated from foreign contact during imprisonment. The prison experience strained their vanguard consciousness. They had support neither from their traditional social ties nor from a Leninist party. More "conventional," indigenous Japanese modes of group interaction might then be expected to resurface even among JCP loyalists, and the revival of these modes would explain the massive dimensions of *tenkō*. The traditional group orientation with its system of mutual obligations governing Japanese interpersonal relations from the most intimate family level to that of the emperor is well known.[21] The political, civic, and spiritual ties that bound all Japanese into the single *kokutai* family were, doubtless, operative to some extent from the outset in Marxist circles (as they are known to be even among outlaw gangsters).[22] But they would appear to have grown more potent, more compelling, as imprisoned Japanese Marxists lost contact with their only alternative model of behavior.

The privations suffered by the imprisoned leftists may have had a role in inducing some of the recantations. But the testimonies of many tenkōsha indicate that prison life strengthened their traditional sentiments of solidarity not only with fellow Marxists as a group but also with the larger Japanese minzoku [race/people/nation]. Consider, for instance, the strength of group orientation, inherent in the mythology of the *kokutai*, in the following testimony by tenkōsha Sumida Moribei:

> The pleading of the authorities, family love, the great change in the political leadership of Asia centering on the fatherland Japan after the Manchurian Incident, the rapid progress of our fatherland Japan as revealed in the inroads of Japanese goods menacing world markets, my internal reflections on myself, etc., can all be considered various necessary conditions for my *tenkō*. But the most basic one, I am convinced, was being able to experience great, limitless *on* (grateful, dutiful love) toward the country, being able to perceive great Imperial Japan as the fountainhead of benevolence itself—in other words, being able to recognize myself as His Majesty's child (subject). The very fact that I could place myself in this self-consciousness was completely due to the strength of the nation, and no matter what I did I couldn't think of it as my own strength. I perceived the arrest, imprisonment, and interrogation completely as instruments of benevolence, and became grateful.[23]

Similarly, Nabeyama felt guilty for his inability to accept the special favors he received from prison guards (often at risk to themselves for violating prison rules) as "simple human kindness." But eventually he came to see his guards as fellow Japanese and his *tenkō* as a reflection of this insight.[24] For Nabeyama, as for Kobayashi Morito, another "political" tenkōsha, *tenkō* meant "being reborn [spiritually] as a member of the Japanese people (kokumin)."[25] Takabatake Michitoshi has noted yet another aspect of this sense of group identity: "What dominated group *tenkō* even among positive followers [of Sano] was the spirit of emotional submission to the leader rather than the adoption of new principles [of national socialism]."[26] This recurrent theme in the accounts of the so-called political, civic, and religious tenkōsha suggests that the group orientation prevalent in prewar Japanese society is by far the most cogent explanation for the proportions and dynamics of the *tenkō* phenomenon. *Tenkō* reflected both solidarity with the *kokutai* and solidarity with the subgroup of fellow JCP Marxists.

It is also apparent that the so-called political *tenkō* did not result merely from disapproval of JCP activities or Comintern policies. It was heavily imbued with sentiments of strong positive attachment to family as well as to nation and with the spiritual elements—the combination of Confucianism, Buddhism, and indigenous Japanese Shintō (which may fairly be characterized as worship of the Japanese minzoku)—underpinning the family-nation concept of *kokutai*. The fact that the Japanese have traditionally taken these *ninjō* (literally, "human feelings") to be "a much more specific constellation of feeling and . . . specifically . . . Japanese,"[27] underscores the peculiarity of the *tenkō* phenomenon and its perception by tenkōsha as a return to things Japanese.

It is not reasonable to argue, then, as some do, that *tenkō* was simply the product of separate decisions by individuals who saw, upon study, the deficiencies of Marxism, or concluded that Japan needed a political system like that of Germany or Italy to overcome internal disorder, or declared their acceptance of the ideology of the *kokutai* without really believing in it.[28] Such explanations could not account for the massive movement that embraced several thousand leftists in individual and group *tenkō* in the short period of six to ten years. It would be a mistake to disregard the group dynamics that were so peculiarly powerful in Japan or to overlook the internal and international political contexts within which the tenkōsha acted. These considerations help to identify the universal versus the particular elements of *tenkō* in Japan and the factors that encouraged or impeded the emergence of a similar phenomenon in revolutionary China.

Explaining Tenkō*: Japanese Marxism and the National Question in Comparative Historical Perspective*

A second feature of *tenkō* lies in its historical position in the linear development of Japanese Marxist thought. Not only was it distinguished by its range and momentum but it also differed from other cases (except, significantly, the German case), in that it represented but one in a long series of occasions on which Japanese socialists—beginning with the earliest forerunners of the JCP, the Meiji Christian socialists—developed theories of national or state socialism. As noted, there is continuity, an unmistakable pattern, in the advocacy of Marxian national socialism and Japanese expansionism from Takabatake Motoyuki to Akamatsu Katsumaro to Takahashi Kamekichi to members of the "dissolutionist faction" (Kaitō-ha) to Sano Manabu's elaboration of an Oriental "socialism in one country" after *tenkō*.[29] That Japan was the aggressor and China the victim during the Sino-Japanese War is not a sufficient explanation of why Marxism in China was fused with nationalism in a Leninist revolutionary tradition, while this reconciliation turned to national socialism based on the existing imperial system in Japan. Advocates of Marxian national socialism in Japan were not always imprisoned, and there was not always a "clear and present danger" in the form of impending war when these successive forms of Japanese national socialism were conceived. Furthermore, during the 1930s, Communists in Europe surrendered to their national fascisms en masse only reluctantly, following Joseph Stalin's declaration that social democracy was a greater evil than national socialism. In Japan, this occurred readily and in opposition to the Comintern's stance on the war.

These considerations suggest that the potential for the mass *tenkō* of the 1930s was inherent in the manner in which Marxian socialism was absorbed and assimilated in Japan from the outset. The striking similarities with German Marxist tendencies to evolve anti-Western national-socialist ideologies also suggest a more general problématique posed by the national question for the adaptation of Marxism in later-industrializing states. Comparing Japan (and Germany) with China, one finds that this dilemma was inherent in Marxism itself at its original formulation. Although China and Japan had achieved different levels of industrial development by the 1930s, both were late-industrializing societies that began their capitalist industrialization in adverse international conditions late in the nineteenth century. Marxists in both countries exhibited a tendency to draw on nationalism and to downplay internal class conflict. As seen in chapter 5, Li Dazhao, co-founder of the Chinese Communist party, for example, extended the analogy of domestic class struggle to the international arena much as Lenin did.[30] This tendency intensified as Marxism traveled farther afield from its birthplace and as the expansion of the world capitalist economy increasingly divided the world into wealthier capitalist states and exploited societies, and the relationship between classes and states became even more problematic.

As R. N. Berki has noted, in the original doctrine of Marxism, class conflict is stressed as the motor force of human history, yet international relations remain important for two reasons: the persistence of conflict among nation-states in the capitalist world economy and the likelihood that national and ethnic divisions will continue to produce conflict among postrevolutionary socialist "nations" even after the "state," the internal organ of class domination, has disappeared. In both cases, the essential problem is "that whether or not the ultimate goal is the complete unity of mankind, the separateness of nations is *given*, and as long as this separateness lasts, for instance, in the form of linguistic diversity and separate identities, a demand for unification is tantamount to a demand that small nations be absorbed into, and ruled over by, big ones."[31]

As nineteenth-century imperialism tended to cause class and national divisions to coincide, it evoked a response characteristic of both Marxists and non- or anti-Marxists—to extract the social-Darwinist elements of Marx's analysis of domestic class struggle and apply them to the international sphere. Lenin accomplished this most skillfully by elevating class struggle to the international arena through his theory of imperialism. Appealing to Asian peoples after 1917, he laid the groundwork for Li Dazhao's reference to the imperialist powers as the world bourgeoisie and the laboring and oppressed masses of the East as the proletariat of the world.[32] Lenin's formula did not require the negation of internal class struggle. But from 1921 on, Comintern policy endorsed united front strategies, including not only proletarians and peasants but all anti-imperialist bourgeois forces in societies embroiled in movements of national liberation. At the other end of the political spectrum, Adolf Hitler rejected Marx's notion of domestic class struggle as alien to the German Geist (spirit). He argued that individuals were oppressed only insofar as the people (Volk) of which they were a part was oppressed. The Marxian emphasis on class struggle would subvert the urgent German effort to build "a State which would not be a piece of mechanism alien to our people, constituted for economic purposes and interests, but an organism created from the soul of the people themselves."[33] Between these two extremes, one can locate the endeavors of Japanese (and German) Marxists to evolve doctrines of national or state socialism, premised on organic ethnic unity that class struggle must not be permitted to disrupt. In Japan, as in Germany, national socialism (in China, anti-imperialism) was designed to fuel the crusade to fulfill the national destiny in a threatening international environment. In general, nationalism motivated defections from Communist parties in more advanced Western countries, reflecting displeasure with Stalinism or Soviet domination. But Marxist thinkers in Japan and Germany were notable for their positive efforts to aggrandize their own states by fashioning ideologies that combined nationalism with socialism.

During the late nineteenth and early twentieth centuries, Japanese observers were inclined to perceive the international sphere as threatening, and German thinkers had similar perceptions in the eighteenth and nineteenth centuries. Both Germany and Japan had lagged considerably behind France and England in the formation of strong, centralized nation-states, and the impetus for state-building was provided by external threats.[34] In one case, this situation produced the "German problem"—the quest to unify all people of German ethnic origin, accompanied by an antiliberal mode of political thought resulting from both the historical origins of German nationalism and Bismarck's rapid industrial revolution from above that left many traditional social forms intact.[35] It may be recalled that German nationalism first arose in response to the French revolution and Napoleon's expansionist wars. It was from the outset (except for the brief revolutions of 1848) antiliberal—conservative. Similarly, when Japanese nationalism was aroused by the Western threat, it was harnessed by the political and economic forces that made the Meiji Restoration, borrowing extensively from German institutions and thought. As such, Japanese nationalism, too, bore an intensely antiliberal hue.[36]

In Germany, these developments generated a state-centric political theory. Hegel went so far as to exalt the state as the highest form of, and a necessary condition for, human existence. His schema set the Germanic people apart from their Western European neighbors as well as from the distant Asians, a theme that became explicit in Hitler's thought. Both men rejected the liberal state—one based on a social contract and a set of contrived mutual obligations between ruler and ruled, a state with limited powers and limited ends—as alien to the German spirit. These tendencies in German thought yielded political theories of state, not popular, sovereignty (as in, e.g., J. K. Bluntschli) and provided the intellectual context for the national-socialist doctrines of German Marxists in the twentieth century.

Such German Marxists shared a number of common characteristics. They suspected that, as embodied in the expansive regimes of Britain and France, liberalism and capitalism were hostile to German national aspirations. Thus, emerging directly out of the humiliation of World War I, "National Bolshevism was based on a psychology of resentment toward the West and an intense love-hate relationship with the East."[37] Its advocates' antipathy toward capitalism resulted from their concern that it stood to destroy their traditional values. The social-Darwinist elements of their early Marxism were drawn to provide a racialist basis for their national-socialist doctrines, and for class struggle was substituted racial conflict among the peoples of the world. These points appeared in the thought of Ludwig Woltmann, for example, as early as 1900.[38]

Many such elements were also evident in Japanese Marxist efforts to evolve national-socialist doctrines from the late Meiji through the *tenkō* period. A perception of modern industrial capitalism as an alien and destructive force had been a major impetus propelling the first Meiji socialists toward Marxism. Kawakami Hajime's attraction to Marxism, for example, had grown out of his "absolute repudiation of [the] egoistic activity" on which capitalist economics was based.[39] Moreover, as the Japanese encountered socialism they understood it in terms of their own prevailing political thought—the official family-state *kokutai* ideology—which, in the late Meiji period, performed a role not unlike that of German

Staatsrecht theory. The *kokutai* ideology buttressed the Meiji government's revolution from above by invoking traditional family-centered Shintō beliefs and ancient mythology concerning the emperor. Many Japanese saw the individualism of capitalism as destructive of valuable elements in the Japanese tradition. They opposed capitalism because they wished to preserve the values that centered around the family and the state. In the words of Japanese scholar Tanaka Masato:

> With respect to the state [*kokka*], particularly the emperor system state, "socialism" was taken to be the opposite of "individualism," as something that was not antagonistic to Japan's *kokutai*. It is the structure of exploitation of the capitalist economy that is anti-*kokutai* thought, that endangers the state [*kokka*], it was argued. . . . Because of such [reasoning], up to the Russo-Japanese War, Meiji socialists possessed no consciousness of themselves as outsiders vis-à-vis the state at all; and they themselves did not expect that their opposition to the Russo-Japanese War would make them heretical.[40]

Japan's status as a late-developing industrial nation-state also prompted Japanese intellectuals to share a social-Darwinist perspective on international relations. The fact that Japan, too, had been a "victim" in the world's uneven process of political and economic development engendered a "Japanese problem" analogous to the German problem. It called for a powerful national state that could protect the livelihood of—give ample living space to—the allegedly superior Japanese minzoku (people). The Japanese military attempted desperately to resolve this "problem" through the so-called Greater East Asian Co-Prosperity Sphere and by a violent thrust onto the Asian mainland in the 1930s.[41] This nationalist drive was fueled by the same sort of racialism that was characteristic of German national socialists. Fearing that the United States and Great Britain acted from racist motivations to curtail Japanese expansion, Japanese political leaders saw imperialism as an urgent necessity. Their "national" socialism would not be confined within the narrow national bounds imposed by the Western powers; it would comprise all territories necessary and predestined to afford adequate living space and resources for the superior Japanese people. Thus, tenkōsha Sano Manabu's national socialism, for example, would embrace Taiwan, Korea, Manchuria, and, eventually, the entire Asian mainland.[42]

Capitalism, individualism, and an artificial state based on a social contract—ideas in the mainstream of Western liberalism, and perceived as such—were all rejected as alien by Japanese and German national socialists. Instead, they favored socialism, corporatism, and an organic state founded on ethnic unity and rooted in an indigenous national spirit. In Japan, *kokutai* thought provided the indigenous framework for the national socialism produced by Marxist thinkers. But because Marxism itself had emerged in response to Western liberal political thought,[43] Japanese Marxist theorists confronted yet another dilemma as they endeavored to preserve national identity in their quest for socialism. How much of Marxism could be retained without sacrificing an appreciation of Japanese uniqueness? How many modifications could one make in Marx's scheme to accommodate national peculiarities without sacrificing the essential core of Marxist theory? Was not such a socialism a regression to pre-Marxian "utopian" socialism? Or, in George L. Mosse's words on the dilemma in Germany, "[W]as it not a contradiction to believe simultaneously in a revolutionary yet conservative change?"[44]

This dilemma remains the most profound manifestation of the national question for Marxist thinkers in the Third World in the 1990s.[45] It was precisely this problem that tenkōsha such as Sano Manabu, who continued to claim allegiance to Marxist principles, attempted to resolve in prewar and wartime Japan.

The Kokutai, *The "Emperor System," and Japanese National Identity*

That the national question lay at the heart of *tenkō* is evident in the role of *kokutai* as a referent for individual identity in motivating "citizen" and "religious," as well as "political" tenkō. As political tenkōsha, Sano and Nabeyama sought to return to indigenous Japanese political values following their isolation from Soviet-dominated activist revolutionary politics. Their experience suggests that Marxism, with its objective theory of the class state, not only challenged the conventional, more emotional, Japanese loyalty to native political institutions; inasmuch as it required the destruction of the emperor system, the Marxism-Leninism of the Comintern and the JCP also ultimately posed a serious threat to Japanese national identity, creating an intellectual, psychological, and social conflict that all Japanese Marxists were at pains to resolve.

The counterexamples of reluctant or non-tenkōsha, such as Kawakami Hajime, support this interpretation. It appears that Kawakami's prolonged and anguished adoption of Marxism allowed him to confront the Marxist worldview in terms of his conventional manner of thinking about the imperial institution, shaped as it had been by the official mythology of the Meiji state. By contrast, Marxists of the younger generation of Sano and Nabeyama had never directly addressed the contradictions between these two disparate modes of political thought. When imprisoned and stripped of their organizational support, they readily fell back on the traditional Japanese attachment to the *kokutai* that they themselves had never scrutinized and from which Kawakami had labored so hard to extricate himself.[46]

Thus, *tenkō* may be viewed in terms of a struggle between indigenous and alien modes of political thought. According to Fujita Shōzō:

> when [one] called "*tenkō*" [the case of] a person who had forgotten the orthodox national philosophy [*kokumin tetsugaku*] in the Japanese system and had been "seduced by foreign ideas" that are in fact "to be regarded as wholly impossible, as vain dreams" (words of Minister of Justice Hara [Yoshimichi] . . . on June 27, 1928, concerning the Communist Party arrests), *tenkō* was born as a unique fundamental category in the history of contemporary Japanese thought. It meant subjectively to cease "antinationalist [*kokumin-teki*] behavior" and positively to follow faithfully with respect to the situation of emperor-system Japan.[47]

This was the usage that Sano and Nabeyama applied to their own action. For Sano, *tenkō* was an emotional return to being Japanese, and the spiritual nature of this transformation was evident in the religious imagery of his words.

[T]rue *"tenkō"* must be a purification that we, having c‍‍
motherland, perform with resolve to die foremost in o‍
[it] must mean the condition of a purified *kokoro* [h‍
    True *tenkō* does not imply a change in thought acc‍
operation or a retreat from the social movement. It m‍
their own evil sins and have committed painful self-a‍
faith by the power of purification and are reborn into comp‍
premise, by all means there must be repentance that could lead t‍
struggle of self-repudiation.[48]

What makes Sano's *tenkō* of particular note is his determination to m‍
nativism *into* his Marxism, rather than merely to supplant one with the other. San‍
sought to justify his *tenkō* on grounds that would permit him to incorporate elements of his original Marxism into a uniquely Japanese socialism. He and
Nabeyama argued that they were turning away from a Communist party that had
come to be dominated by "a minority of barbaric petty-bourgeois intellectuals . . . and was losing its essential strong worker mentality."[49] They were
returning to the laboring Japanese masses from whom the party had become
increasingly alienated in its submission to Soviet direction. Depending on one's
political perspective, then, the Sano-Nabeyama *tenkō* was either a shift from
proletarian internationalism to petty-bourgeois nationalism or the rejection of a
bourgeoisified vanguard party for the true proletarianism of the Japanese masses.
    In either case, *tenkō* implied a contradiction between the Marxism of the JCP
and indigenous Japanese political values. This tension is best understood with
reference to intellectual developments in Taishō and Shōwa Japan. During the
period of Taishō democracy (1912–1925), many Western ideas, including liberalism and Marxism, were adopted in Japan albeit without an adequate appreciation
of the premises on which these systems of thought were originally based. New
Western concepts floated about then without roots in an uneasy coexistence with
indigenous modes of political thought. As Fujita has pointed out, "Japanese political thinkers could have no notion of abstract right. One consequence of this was
that during the Taishō period [Japanese leaders of the movement] understood
[u]niversal suffrage as the 'demand of the age' rather than as a 'right'." When the
suffrage was won, this understanding redounded to the advantage of the imperial
political system rather than undercutting it, for "our people rejoice in being treated
as concrete personalities with human emotions rather than [in terms of] abstract
right."[50]
    Such a positioning of the proud and allegedly unique personalism of Japanese
political society against the abstractions of Western political thought became a
prominent theme of the *tenkō* movement. Marxism, with its all-embracing view of
progress through violent class struggle and its theory of the oppressive class state,
could not easily be accommodated (as was the single measure of universal suffrage) to the concept of the *kokutai*. Sano and Nabeyama had initially accepted
Marx's theory of the state uncritically. Indeed, in the late 1920s, Sano had written
extensively to introduce Marxist thought on the state in leading publications such

· *CHAPTER EIGHT* ·

arukusu-shugi kōza (Symposium on Marxism), *Marukusu-shugi* (Marx-
hakai kagaku (Social science), and *Musansha shinbun* (Proletarian news).[51]
tenkō, Sano and Nabeyama "pointed out the true sterility of a theory that
scended Japanese society; [they] returned to the true feelings of the living
panese workers, farmers, and masses, and, without making any change in the
national philosophy (*kokumin tetsugaku*) of the Japanese people (*minzoku*), reaffirmed it positively 'such as it was' and, furthermore, endeavored to theorize it."[52]

After the Manchurian incident, the requirement that the JCP actually implement the resolution of the 1928 Sixth Comintern Congress to oppose Japanese
imperialism in order to defend the fatherland of socialism, the Soviet Union,
served as a catalyst in this volte-face to national socialism. As early as 1922, the
Comintern had pressed the JCP to oppose Japanese imperialism and to call for the
abolition of the emperor system.[53] The party accepted these instructions with
considerable reluctance (with Sano leading the opposition).[54] But the Manchurian
incident of 1931 marked a push toward open war with China, and the subject of
nationalism could no longer be avoided. Nabeyama wrote: "[Previously] we [the
JCP] had considered the crisis brought on the fatherland by war and the tragic
impact therein on the working masses; and we had fought to the utmost of our
abilities to hinder war [by opposing Japanese imperialism in China]. [But] the
situation which I had . . . imagined and feared then arose . . . [in the form of]
the Manchurian Incident. No longer was [war] a theoretical issue; [now] we had to
confront war [with China] before our very eyes as a question of life and death."
Nabeyama also believed that, since Stalin's accession to power, the Soviet Union
was "handl[ing] foreign relations on the basis of its own state interests. If there was
the need, it would form a state alliance with any country[,] even if that country's
Communist Party was fighting that government for its life."[55] If the Soviet Union,
the fatherland of socialism, could act in this fashion, how could Japanese Marxists
legitimately turn their backs on their own proletarian compatriots?

In this context, the difficulty of reconciling the *kokutai* with a Marxian theory of
the state became quite clear. Sano's pronouncements on the state at the time of his
trial[56] manifested considerable confusion on the nature of the state, indicating an
underlying problem that had not been resolved in the minds of most JCP members
by 1931. The *kokutai* and, by implication, the emperor system at its core, had been
presumed to be unique. Yet in his legal defense, Sano argued that the *kokutai*
would remain intact even if the Japanese monarchy were abolished. One would
have thought that if the emperor system were uniquely Japanese, it would have had
to be included in a Japanese socialism. The Japanese Communists were initially
inclined to repudiate this connection. But they were shaken by the Comintern's
1931 Draft Political Theses, which argued that Japan was not so semifeudal as to
require a bourgeois-democratic revolution to destroy the monarchy before undertaking a proletarian revolution. This position seemed to yield to the Rōnō-ha,
which Sano had been denouncing as monarchist,[57] and it suggested that the emperor system might be made compatible even with revolutionary Marxist assumptions about state power.

The Sino-Japanese War reinforced this effect when it called into question Soviet motivations for the abrupt changes in Comintern policy that occurred in 1931 and 1932. The growing threat to the homeland led Sano and Nabeyama to ask why they should seek to abolish the *kokutai* precisely when it was most threatened.[58] Because the *kokutai* embraced not only the state but also the nation, not only Nihon (Japan) but Nihonjin (Japanese), no socialism was conceivable without it. Without the *kokutai*, there was no Nihon in which to build socialism and no Nihonjin to partake of its blessings. A Marxist perspective on the state that demanded its destruction, then, constituted a threat to Japanese national identity itself. If the party had become "non-Japanist" under Comintern domination, it had to be abandoned. For Communists such as Sano, even if it might reasonably be argued that all cultures possess multiple potentials, the imperial institution was so intimately bound to Japanese identity that within the context of the indigenous political, social, and religious conception of Japaneseness the two could not be extricated readily. Thus, Sano wrote, "[I] felt painfully the negation of becoming a Japanese who had forgotten being Japanese."[59] This was indeed an identity crisis and the ultimate motivation for Sano's and Nabeyama's *tenkō*.

Kokutai thought also supplied both the "excuse" and "acceptance" of the two leaders' *tenkō*. Developments within the JCP were held to demonstrate values repugnant to the Japanese tradition. The party, composed now of intellectuals rather than workers, was unable to respond properly to right-wing terrorist attacks on economic leaders, the assassination of Premier Inukai Tsuyoshi, and the attempted military coup of 1932. The "gang incident"—an armed bank robbery in which JCP members were allegedly involved—and mutual charges of espionage within the party were alarming to men like Nabeyama trying to uphold party ideals under the stress of prison life. These were signs of "sickness" within the party that offended Nabeyama's traditional morality based on group loyalty and solidarity.[60] Sano concluded that the decline of solidarity binding the minzoku together resulted from the party's class orientation. "A movement of classism becomes something cold, of sadness and gloom because it encourages selfishness." The orthodox Marxian emphasis on class, in this view, had led Communists to despise all morality.[61] These observations confirmed the suspicion that perhaps all of Communism, as represented in the JCP, was inhuman, alien to Japan, and unacceptable. This "excuse" for *tenkō* was reinforced by the assessment that the Communist party had no prospects for success. Sano, explaining his *tenkō* to Kawakami Hajime, pointed to the failures of communist parties in Germany and China as well as in Japan.[62] The final element of *tenkō*, the "acceptance" of a new worldview, also lay in the myth of the *kokutai*, which in this case provided a ready-made alternative to Marxism-Leninism.

In the actual text of the Sano-Nabeyama *tenkō* proclamation, these roles of *kokutai* thought as motivation, excuse, and acceptance of *tenkō* are easily discernible. The document contained nine sections denouncing the JCP for its petty-bourgeois nature and its overreliance on the Comintern; criticizing the Comintern and the policy errors it had made in ignorance of Japan's unique characteristics; arguing that each country must develop its own socialism on the basis of its own national culture; repudiating the demand for the abolition of the emperor system and affirming its representation of Japan's proper course of historical development; rejecting pacifist slogans; opposing colonial independence movements directed against Japan; advocating a single socialist state embracing Japan, Korea, Taiwan, Manchuria, and China; supporting the demand to secede from the Comintern, noting that it would probably collapse during the war in any case; and retaining previous positions on workers' benefits and the need for agrarian revolution. The idea of proletarian socialism remained intact as the proclamation urged the formation of a legal vanguard to guide the workers in revolution. But Sano and Nabeyama called for the positive recognition, rather than the rejection, of the continued importance of the state and minzoku in revolutionary Japan.[63]

The Imperial Household, the core of the *kokutai*, was profoundly influential in inspiring and sustaining *tenkō*, from its initial rejection of Comintern leadership to a reasoned abandonment of Marx's theory of the impersonal class state. But even more importantly, the notion of *kokutai* combined racialism, mysticism, and familism to produce a concept of a patriarchal Japanese state viewed as an organic entity. "Without denying the concept of class struggle, [the tenkōsha] could claim that the Japanese people were unique in class unity before the Emperor, and therefore workers and managers alike should support national endeavors."[64] The place of the emperor as both head of the state and father by blood kinship of the extended family of the entire Japanese people precluded the separation of nation from state in Japanese political thought. When the war forced Japanese Marxists to reconsider the notion of the state, upon reflection they found that the traditional Japanese attachment to the Imperial Household and its accoutrements made it almost impossible for them to accept Marxian thought on the matter. This aspect of Marxism came to be regarded as alien and illegitimate and to be replaced by a racialist and particularistic view of the state that could accommodate Japan's *kokutai*. This became the basis for Sano's new socialism in one country, or national socialism.

SANO MANABU AND THE TRANSFORMATION OF MARXISM INTO NATIONAL SOCIALISM

As one of the struggling JCP's top leaders, Sano Manabu drew hundreds of others along with him in *tenkō* within a month after he made his joint *tenkō* proclamation with fellow leader Nabeyama. Unlike most of his fellow tenkōsha, however, Sano ventured beyond the mere renunciation of his Communist ties to evolve formally his own Marxian doctrine of socialism-in-one-country (*ikkoku shakai-shugi*). Professing a return to what he considered the essence of Japaneseness, Sano offered his national socialist doctrine as a superior version of socialism, one that was based on traditional "oriental" (*tōyō-teki*) perspectives on mankind and society yet retained certain orthodox Marxist tenets concerning socioeconomic change.[65]

After World War II, Sano elaborated these ideas as the basis for a new vanguard socialist party and established his own Nihon Seiji Keizai Kenkyūjo (Japan Institute for the Study of Politics and Economics) to disseminate them. Persistent efforts to promote his "oriental" brand of Marxian socialism failed to arouse widespread popular support, however. When the wartime surge of intense nationalism had subsided and Occupation policies permitted Japanese Marxists to participate freely in politics, Sano's efforts to propagate his socialism-in-one-country were but a painful reminder of what for most Marxists had been a shameful submission to state power. Nevertheless, Sano's thought remains significant because it was part of a larger pattern in which prewar Japanese Marxists articulated national socialist ideas and founded organizations to realize them. Sano's extensive writings chronicle his odyssey from being a staunch leader of the JCP who attacked the earlier heresies of Marxian national socialists to his call for an indigenous Japanese path to socialism and advocacy of his own national(ist) adaptation of Marxism. Sano's reevaluation of Eastern philosophical traditions, his critique of the orthodox Marxist-Leninist theory of the state that was echoed by other tenkōsha, and the articulation of his national socialist thought offer valuable clues to the understanding of the dynamics of the transformation of Marxism to national socialism in prewar Japan.

As Sano's case indicates, not all tenkōsha jettisoned Marxism along with their Communist ties. Indeed, as the previous discussion suggests, one may distinguish between tenkōsha who repudiated the JCP, particularly in opposition to its subordination to Soviet leadership in the Comintern, on the one hand, and those who abandoned the Marxian framework as well in order to return to an indigenous philosophical or spiritual tradition such as Buddhism or orthodox Japanese thought on the *kokutai*, on the other.[66] Sano belonged to the first category, yet he also appealed to the values of spiritualism and harmony in traditional "oriental" perspectives to criticize the narrowness of historical materialism, the vision of violent revolution, and other aspects of the Marxism-Leninism of the JCP while he retained Marxian categories of the analysis of economic change from one mode of production to another.

In this respect, Sano can be compared with others who, as observed here, adapted Marxism to Japan by transforming it into a nationalist and statist variety of Marxian philosophy. More than one decade before Sano's *tenkō*, Takabatake Motoyuki formulated his Marxian national socialism, and later, in the 1920s, Takahashi's petty imperialism thesis eschewed the orthodox Leninist denunciation of Japanese expansionism and sought to legitimate that very expansionism in Marxist terms. In 1929, two years after Takahashi scandalized his fellow Marxists with this "petty imperialism" thesis, yet another tide of nationalism swept the struggling Japanese movement. A group of imprisoned JCP members led by Mizuno Shigeo (which came to be called the Kaitō-ha, or "Dissolutionist Faction") prefigured the *tenkō* of Sano and Nabeyama when they abandoned the JCP, denounced its alien domination by the Comintern, argued for the dissolution of the party, and advocated an indigenous system of socialism based on the Imperial Household.[67] Finally, after the Manchurian incident, socialist activist Akamatsu Katsumaro, too, adopted an explicitly national socialist program. The outbreak of war with China underscored Akamatsu's fear that the international environment was becoming more brutally competitive, with "ever more defensive national economies striving for survival, independence, and self-sufficiency." Convinced that Marxian internationalism was futile idealism, Akamatsu formulated a variety of Marxian national socialism that supported Japanese expansionism and reflected even stronger, deeper, sentimental ties to the Japanese national community and its emperor than had Takabatake's.[68] Among these thinkers, only the Kaitō-ha and Akamatsu joined Sano in explicitly couching their positions in terms of a return to Japanese "national character." Neither the continually vacillating Akamatsu—who changed his position at least three times from 1923 to 1955[69]—nor the considerably junior Kaitō-ha wielded the authority of Sano in his capacity as leader of the JCP's prison Central Committee, nor did they write as prolifically as did Sano on the roots of their national socialism.[70] The Kaitō-ha's program, however, closely approximated that of Sano. Indeed, according to Kobayashi Morito—a former JCP member who headed the thought section of the Teikoku Kōshinkai (Imperial Renewal Association), the official agency for rehabilitation of tenkōsha—the Sano-Nabeyama *tenkō* "was a [direct] development of the thought of these Kaitō-ha tenkōsha."[71]

When Sano's national socialism is considered alongside that of the Kaitō-ha and other nationalistic socialists of prewar Japan, it strongly suggests that the key to this pattern of Marxian national socialism lay in the interplay between two factors: one external and the other internal. First, the increasingly critical economic and political conditions of the late Taishō and early Shōwa eras were both originally induced and then aggravated by Japan's position as a later-industrializing society.[72] Even though Japan had made rapid economic progress under state-led industrialization from the 1870s through the end of World War I, increasing economic distress accompanied the imbalanced industrial and agrarian growth that had resulted in the emergence of Japan's "dual economy."[73] It will be recalled that when the war boom ended, Japan fell into an economic slump and experienced recurrent bank panics and severe recessions in the agrarian sphere. By the mid-1920s, Takahashi's thesis that Japan was experiencing an economic deadlock (*yukizumari*) was widely accepted among Japanese economists, and one of the important aspects of Takahashi's interpretation lay in his emphasis on the continuing disadvantages that plagued Japan as a result of its status as a tiny resource-poor late-industrializing country seeking economic growth in a world dominated by the advanced industrialized West European powers and the United States. Takahashi contended that Japan's upward path of capitalistic industrial development had been interrupted as Japan found itself besieged by pressures from above and below in a hierarchical international system. The division of resource- and market-rich Asia and Africa into exclusive spheres of influence by the more advanced capitalist states of the West by the turn of the twentieth century now challenged Japan's ability to sustain rapid economic growth by similar strategies of economic expansion. At the same time, in areas where Japan had managed to gain a foothold, such as China, its position was threatened by a rising tide of nationalistic intellectual, proletarian, and peasant movements. China's nationalist revolution, resulting in the boycott of Japanese goods and forcing Japan to seek new markets elsewhere, portended similar national liberation movements threatening Japan's economic expansion throughout Asia.[74]

This international setting pressed Japanese Marxists such as Sano, Takabatake, and Takahashi to view the Marxian vision of a stateless internationalist socialism as utopian. If such a vision had ever made sense for socialists in advanced capitalist societies, they concluded, it certainly could not apply to those in later-industrializing societies subjected to nationalist pressures from above and below in the world order. Sandwiched between these twin forces, how could Japanese Marxists who critically evaluated Marx's thought on nation and state negate nationalism and stateness and expect to achieve the capitalist development necessary (in Marx's schema) to establish a socialist society? How could an antistatist antinationalist position gain the popular support essential for a socialist revolution, particularly where the populace shared such a powerful sentimental identification with the emperor? Finally, how could the security of the new socialist society be guaranteed after the revolution if there were to be no state power to defend it? The validity of these concerns was underscored by increasing evidence that nationalism and statism were the wave of the future in other later-industrializing societies—Italy under Benito Mussolini, Germany under Adolf Hitler, and even Chiang Kai-shek's Guomindang in revolutionary China.[75] As the specter of war in the Pacific loomed closer, Japanese Marxists, like European socialists in 1914, were increasingly pressured by the Special Higher (Thought) Police and began to feel that the stateless vision of Marx promoted by the chauvinistic Stalin was untenable. At the very least, the JCP's repudiation of nationalism and the Imperial Household could not appeal to Japan's masses. If Marxism was to remain the basis for Japan's revolutionary movement, it would have to be dramatically reinterpreted to legitimate revolutionary nationalism for Japan as well as for the Soviet Union and China.

The indigenous attachment to the emperor system, discussed here as a vital element of the *tenkō* phenomenon in general, thus constituted the second major factor shaping the emergence of Marxian national socialism in interwar Japan. *Kokutai* thought provided a ready fabric from which these thinkers could fashion a new interpretation of Marxism that could respond effectively to the exigencies of the international environment. A socialism constructed under the mikado (emperor) could protect and nurture the Japanese people; and old values such as social harmony, which many felt had been compromised by the rapid growth of industrial capitalism,[76] could be preserved without abandoning the progressive dream of Marxian socialism. Thus, one finds in Sano and the Kaitō-ha—as in Takahashi and Takabatake, who were not in prison at the time they undertook their formulations—positive efforts to adapt Marxism to Japan by injecting nationalism and statism into it.

The Thought of the Kaitō-ha and Sano's Critique

In the years before his *tenkō*, Sano Manabu's credentials as a loyal JCP Marxist were impressive. Although he assumed a position of party leadership almost immediately, Sano also founded *Musansha shinbun* (Proletarian news) and wrote extensively to introduce Marxism into Japan. As early as 1922, he was one of the first to attempt a systematic application of Marxist theory to Japanese social and economic history,[77] and by the end of the decade he was widely published in leading Marxist journals.[78] Although Sano had been among those who yielded only reluctantly to the Comintern's requirement that the JCP seek to eliminate the Japanese monarchy, by 1931 it was evident that Sano's acceptance of the Marxist-Leninist view of the state and nationalism was complete. He appealed to that perspective in his defense of the JCP in its public trial, and from his prison cell, he harshly attacked the Kaitō-ha for its illusions about the true class character of the imperial state.

Nevertheless, the Kaitō-ha offered a model for precisely the sort of creative intertwining of orthodox Japanese perspectives on nation and emperor that Sano himself would undertake only two years later. The group was led by Mizuno Shigeo (1899–1972), an activist intellectual, whose prison statement (*jōshinsho*) of May 1929 advocated the immediate dissolution of the existing JCP and independence for Japan's socialist revolutionaries from the foreign leadership of the Comintern. The group included Toyoda Tadashi (1900–1981), Asano Akira (1901–1990), Murao Satsuo (1902–1970), and Kadoya Hiroshi (1901–), all of whom were barely thirty years old at the time of their *tenkō* in support of Mizuno's stance. The slightly older Minami Ki'ichi, a graduate of Waseda, had been a lesser figure in the left-wing movement and remained on the fringes of the group.[79]

The careers of the men of the Kaitō-ha were remarkably similar. All, except Minami, had attended Tokyo Imperial University where they were members of the progressive Shinjinkai (New Men's Association). All had entered left-wing politics through the labor movement, serving in the Sōdōmei (Japanese Labor Federation) and then the radical splinterist Hyōgikai (Council of Japanese Labor Unions). They participated in Communist party activities only after the first JCP had been dissolved and became influential after 1927 because of their participation in efforts to revive the party in 1925 and 1926. All were arrested in the March 15 (1928) incident or in April 1929 and had been in prison for barely one year when they advocated the demise of the JCP they had helped to rebuild. After their *tenkō*, the JCP expelled the group, dubbing it the "Dissolutionist Faction" in September 1929. In June 1940, the group adopted the name Nihon Kyōsantō Rōdōsha-ha (Japanese Communist party, Workers' Faction). In March 1931, on release from prison, the group established its own Central Committee, which issued draft theses criticizing the JCP for "blindly following the Comintern and advocating abolition of the emperor system" and calling for a one-stage revolution for socialism-in-one-country under the Imperial Household. The group cleverly published its own organ called *Akahata* (Red flag), which was also the name of an official JCP organ. They were heavily criticized both within and outside the JCP, however, and, failing to gain any widespread mass support, the faction was dissolved in July 1932.[80]

As did Sano and Nabeyama subsequently, those who formed the Kaitō-ha *tenkō*ed because of a new "recognition" of and appreciation for the "uniqueness" of Japan and the Japanese people.[81] This was something to which they had accorded scant attention while absorbed in the abstract methodology of Marx's historical materialism during Fukumoto Kazuo's leadership of the JCP.[82] In Kobayashi's description of the group's *tenkō*, it is clear that the unity of state and nation maintained in the concept of the *kokutai* played a major role in the conversion of the Kaitō-ha.

The sentiment that the Imperial Household is our head family is confirmed by us as one big family in which the emperor and his subjects are one [*kunmin ittai*]. Consequently, it is extremely natural that the slogan of the abolition of the emperor system that the Communist Party espoused should be repudiated. Only by coming into contact with real things, concrete things, could we know the bankruptcy of Marxist formulistic theory. In other words, hitherto the methodology had been structured by agonizing over how to make both the history and current situation of Japan accord with the formulas of Marxism. . . . Indeed this was the concrete social basis on which the so-called Kaitō-ha developed within the camp of the Japanese Communist Party in April 1930.[83]

The security of the *kokutai* perspective clashed dramatically with the repeated failures and repression that these idealistic young Marxists encountered in the JCP. Such "realities" as the rise of fascism and national socialism elsewhere and the prospect of war in the Pacific would become more compelling after the Manchurian incident than they were in 1929. As Kobayashi has noted, "at the time of their proclamation, the influence of the JCP was not waning," a factor that helps to account for the limited impact of the Kaitō-ha's *tenkō*.[84] Nevertheless, the newly revived JCP was plagued by police roundups, and the policies conceived by Soviet leaders ignorant of Japanese conditions did not appreciably strengthen the party.[85]

Mizuno and his followers turned away from the revolution promoted in Moscow to demand "the realization of a socialism based on the Imperial Household." In their prison statements, the group made the following demands:

1. Dissolution of, or break with, the existing JCP;

2. Withdrawal from the Comintern as the only possible means by which to abandon the slogan calling for the abolition of the emperor system. Minami further asserted that Japanese did not need the support and cooperation of foreign laborers to carry out their own revolution;

3. Monarchism and the replacement of the JCP slogan calling for the abolition of the emperor system by the slogan "democratization of politics";

4. The creation of a legal revolutionary socialist party to replace the JCP after it had been dissolved.[86]

In addition, the Kaitō-ha challenged the Comintern's view of the nature of the Japanese revolution. It will be recalled that with the exception of shortlived deviations in the 1926 Moscow Theses and the 1931 Draft Political Theses, from 1922 to 1932[87] the Comintern insisted that the imperial rule reflected a feudal backwardness that required a revolution in two stages. Throughout the period, the Comintern remained consistent in repudiating both the monarchy and Japanese imperialism, and both these points were unacceptable to the proud nationalists of the Kaitō-ha. Echoing Takahashi on Japan's dependence on economic expansion in Asia, the Kaitō-ha called for the exploitation of colonies like Korea and Taiwan; this was absolutely essential to the livelihood of the Japanese people, they claimed. Hence, the JCP's Leninist slogan calling for colonial independence would have to be replaced by a moderate demand for colonial self-government. Similarly, Mizuno and his followers rejected any domestic policy that endangered the integrity of the *kokutai* or the well-being of its emperor. There would be no agrarian revolution that involved the confiscation of palace, court, temple, shrine, and landlords' lands, as the JCP advocated. Asano argued that such policies were unnecessary because feudal agrarian relations no longer existed in Japan, and the emperor was not a large feudalistic landlord, as the 1927 Theses had maintained. Finally, the new socialist party would be legal because there must be no violent revolution that would tear asunder the treasured fabric of the *kokutai*. Violent revolution through class struggle was an unfortunate abstract conceptual obsession in Japan that had gained ground under the influence of the Chinese revolution. Socialism could be attained on the basis of the existing emperor system, Murao asserted, through peaceful parliamentary means.[88]

What unified these elements of the Kaitō-ha program was the conviction that the uniqueness of Japan's *kokutai* rendered Communist slogans based on universal abstract notions of class and state inapplicable. Takahashi Kamekichi's exceptionalism had been grounded in a Marxian economic analysis of Japan's position in an international system that had changed since Marx's time. By contrast, the Kaitō-ha's exceptionalism lay in a rediscovery of Japan's unique essence, so unappreciated by the JCP and its Soviet mentors.

> [T]he Japanese Communist Party is virtually ignorant about the realities of Japanese society. It has paid no attention to it, nor has it done anything at all in order to know it. . . . [In the Communist] movement, we have felt as if it were ultra-nationalistic [*kokusui-shugi*] or reactionary even to mention Japan's peculiarities. Even giving consideration to popular consciousness has been derogated as tailism vis-à-vis the masses. But how can one establish correct policies without knowing peculiarities? How can one formulate appropriate slogans without understanding the national character? . . . We cannot [any longer] deny . . . the blood that flows in our bodies.[89]

For the Kaitō-ha, Japan's uniqueness was manifested in the imperial institution, which they regarded as the unitary center of the *kokutai*, suprahistorical, permanent, and unchanging.[90] According to Kobayashi, these men felt that "our country's Imperial Household was not a class phenomenon, [but] was the center of the holistic unified expression of the whole people. [It was the] characteristic sentiment of the Japanese people to believe in the Imperial Household as the head family." Murao emphasized four aspects of Japan's emperor system: "(1) the historical fact of the 2,500-year continuous imperial line"; (2) its longstanding role as an object of popular "faith" in the Shintō religion; (3) its historical isolation from political and economic forces; and (4) the relationship between its Restoration in 1868 and the extraordinary achievements of Meiji Japan.[91]

These factors the Kaitō-ha cited to refute Comintern-JCP policies targeting the abolition of the emperor system. But in February 1931, in defense of the JCP, Sano reasserted the need to abolish the emperor system by appealing to the economic analyses of Japanese society found in the 1922 Draft JCP Program and the 1927 Theses. Sano repudiated the notion that Japan's imperial system transcended classes and could defy the universal laws of human social development as described by Marx and Engels. The emperor system was not unchanging but had experienced many transformations since antiquity in response to varying socio-economic bases, from ancient communal society to the bourgeois-landlord alliance dominating contemporary Japanese society. In short, Sano asserted, Japan's imperial institution had to be analyzed in terms of socioeconomic change in the same manner as the state structures of societies like England and France. Although the duration of Japan's continuous imperial line was extraordinary indeed, it was not unique, and its peculiarities did not suffice to invalidate the Marxist view of the state. Rather, this revolutionary historical perspective ultimately required the destruction of the emperor system as the most important task of the proletarian revolution in Japan.[92]

In making this argument, Sano confronted a key issue of the Marxist debate on Japanese capitalism then raging outside prison walls: the question of the basic nature of the Japanese state and the role of the imperial institution as an organ of state power. Confronted with the coexistence of what appeared in Marixan terms to be bourgeois and feudal forms in Japanese society, Sano argued uneasily that the emperor system represented both. On the one hand, he asserted that the emperor "acted as the executor of grand bourgeois policies at home and abroad." Yet the emperor system also had a "landlord character and acted for the benefit of landlords" that the Comintern characterized as feudal. Japanese imperialism was a bourgeois-landlord imperialism then, for the landlord class continued to be an independent ruling element even though the bourgeoisie had maintained political and economic hegemony since the Meiji Restoration and had promoted the growth of state capitalism. Thus, unlike the British crown, the Japanese monarchy was a "semifeudal political form" lagging far behind the most advanced form of bourgeois rule, the republic. It performed a variety of functions antithetical to the revolutionary purposes of the JCP: it governed the bureaucratic and military cliques, suppressed workers' and peasants' movements, supported the continued power of such feudal remnants as the genrō and the Privy Council, and took the lead in colonial policy, particularly in efforts to quash revolutionary movements elsewhere in Asia (especially China). Finally, Sano noted, the myth of creation buttressing the position of the Imperial Household was common to "all uncivilized peoples," including the Eskimos of Alaska and the aborigines of Taiwan. The current mythology surrounding the emperor system, he argued, had been created deliberately to support the bourgeois revolution at the time of the Meiji Restoration. The bourgeoisie simply continued to employ this myth to legitimate the power of the state by mystifying the bourgeois-landlord political system. The primitive character of this myth ultimately exposed the reactionary rather than progressive nature of the emperor system, Sano averred. Such a system could only hinder Japan's development to an advanced form of socialism. Hence, it had to be swept away, along with all other remnants of feudal and bourgeois society.[93]

Sano concluded that the Kaitō-ha's advocacy of an emperor-based socialism marked them as "social democrats" (a derogatory term) who differed only slightly from the dissident Rōnō-ha. Their philosophy went a step beyond the "social democracy" of the latter to form a new doctrine of "social fascism." This, Sano asserted, was "an international tendency within social democracy that [was] un-folding rapidly in the so-called third period—the time of mounting crises in world capitalism. It [was] a union of social democracy with a fascist state organ, a [form of] social democracy with fascist theory." Social fascists endeavored to split the "proletarian front," often using violence against Communist party demonstrations; they "advocated the interests of capital"; they were imbued with a "bourgeois statist xenophobia and narrow nationalism"; they supported "aggression in foreign policy," for "imperialist war, and for the exploitation of colonies and semi-colonies"; and they "supported reactionary political organizations," especially monarchies. Sano concluded that only the increased Bolshevization of the Japa-nese Communist party could effectively counter those aspects of social fascism that were evident in the Kaitō-ha.[94]

Ironically, the courtroom propaganda strategy in which these arguments were made seems to have facilitated the *tenkō* phenomenon by providing an arena for the direct confrontation of Marxism with *kokutai* thought. Like most JCP members, Sano had accepted Marxism without contemplating critically its conflicts with indigenous orthodoxy on nation and state.[95] The courtroom propaganda strategy forced JCP members to apply the Marxist theory of the state systematically and articulately, and, consequently, it exposed their confusions on the issue. In court, the JCP pleaded not guilty to the charge of violating the Peace Preservation Law by plotting to change the *kokutai*. Its defense rested on the distinction between the notions of *kokutai* (national polity) and seitai (form of government). The party argued that its desire to abolish the monarchy implied a change in the seitai, but not a change in the *kokutai*. In Sano's words, "What we consider to be the problem is not the Imperial Household but monarchy as a political form (or "bourgeois" dictatorship). Even if the monarch alone were to disappear, it would be impossible for the workers and peasants to be liberated; our basic aim is nothing other than to eliminate "bourgeois" dictatorship and proclaim a "proletarian" dictatorship."[96] It is evident that even in the mind of Sano himself, who "occupied the position of the party's theoretical leader as the best expositor of the 1927 Theses,"[97] this alleged distinction was not clear. Sano made an equally vain effort to explain it in his critique of the Kaitō-ha: "The monarchy and the Imperial House do not mean the same thing, but the two are inseparable," he wrote weakly.[98] Sano's argument did not preclude the possibility of a proletarian dictatorship under the emperor-led *kokutai*; therein lay the potential for a socialist revolution without opposition to the emperor system.

The confusion manifested in Sano's statements indicates an important underly-ing problem that had not been resolved by JCP Marxists as late as 1931.[99] If the *kokutai* and the emperor system at its core were unique, as they were presumed to be, they could not be rejected out of hand but would have to be accepted and, perhaps, accommodated with socialism in Japan. This implication was strength-ened by the threat of war and the resulting reappraisal of the Marxian position on nationalism. The emergence of a concrete threat to the homeland led Marxists like Sano and Nabeyama to ask why they should seek to abolish the *kokutai* precisely when it seemed most in peril.[100] Having forcibly confronted these issues in the courtroom, only two years later, Sano assumed the stance of the Dissolutionist Faction that he had just denounced as social fascist.

Tenkō *and the East-West Dichotomy: Marxism as Alien Ideology*

As observed here, *tenkō* demonstrated clearly the emotional appeal of the ideology of the emperor system over the non-Japanese mode of thought that was Marxism-Leninism. Under the combination of increasingly hostile international conditions and domestic conditions adverse to the JCP, the alternative social science framework that had originally promoted Marxism as a basis for criticism and radical change became a major liability.[101] Marxism had appealed to young Japanese intellectuals because its claim to scientific truth and universality empowered their critique of their own society from without. Marxism's interpretation of politics and economics both helped to explain many of the unfortunate realities of Taishō and Shōwa politics and enabled Japanese activists to step outside the dominant *kokutai* framework in order to criticize the separate components of Japanese society fully. Yet Sano's *tenkō* and its massive impact on the left-wing movement indicate how the status of Marxism as an imported philosophical system rendered it suspect for Japanese Marxists themselves under the changing conditions of the early 1930s. In its Soviet incarnation as Marxism-Leninism, when it appeared that the JCP's solutions to Japan's social problems were repeatedly ineffective in the Japanese context, Marxism's alien character became starkly evident.[102] Conceived on the basis of the Western European experience, where different values and customs had defined the context of social change, its historical schema might or might not be applicable to Japan. Might not the Japanese intellectual who, nevertheless, attempted to use the Marxian framework to criticize Japanese society be subjecting himself and Japan to "cultural imperialism"? Might not some indigenously conceived theory of social change be more applicable to Japanese realities and, therefore, be preferable to Marxism as a basis for planning radical change?

Sano's conversion reflected the strength of such doubts in the atmosphere of rising crisis in the early 1930s. Immediately after his *tenkō*, Sano reviewed Marxism along with major Chinese and Japanese classics to systematize his critique of Marx's historical materialism and to explicate a socialist thought that could reconcile the culturophilosophical conflicts that prompted him to *tenkō*. In Sano's view, differences between Eastern and Western ethics and philosophy made orthodox Marxism inappropriate as a blueprint for social revolution in an Eastern environment. He reflected, "We are Orientals, Japanese. Our socialism must be something appropriate to the Oriental, Japanese environment. No matter how cosmopolitan a character Western Europe's socialism has, it is something that West European peoples had created in conformance with their special social environment, so it is unreasonable to try to transfer it wholesale as it is. To Orientalize, to Japanize West European socialist principles is most important of all."[103]

Sano felt that his character as an Asian was crucial to his repudiation of Soviet-style Marxism in *tenkō* and that his reawakening to "oriental" culture was the key to his critique of Marxism as an alien ideology. In his prison diary, Sano asserted:

I believe that a deep concern for Asia was a correct element that I have continued to maintain since the time of *tenkō*. The specialness of Asian society and culture; [the view] that the elimination of the conservatism of India and China are conditions for the progress of world history; the necessity that Asia be liberated from the capitalism of Europe, America, and Japan; [the conviction] that the formation of a socialist league of Japan, China, and Korea first, rather than a vague internationalism, is a possible, and furthermore, a necessary aim have been [my] beliefs since that time. In prison, I endeavored to study [anew] the history, social structure, and culture of the Orient and to raise my self-consciousness as an Oriental man.[104]

On the basis of his new "oriental" consciousness, Sano found that fundamental aspects of Marxian thought conflicted with traditional Oriental approaches to man and society. First among these was an epistemological issue: Looking back to the turn of the century, Sano observed that in accepting Marx's theory of revolution uncritically, intellectuals of his generation had fallen victim to a superficial "intellectualism." Since the Meiji period, in the defensive quest for Western knowledge, young Japanese had not only accepted Western ideas that were contrary to oriental traditions but also despised their own homeland for its lack of comparable wisdom. Sano discovered, however, that "Western knowledge is knowledge of phenomena, knowledge of cause and effect, mere recognition alienated from volition and sentiment." By contrast, "Oriental knowledge is intuitive knowledge, essential knowledge [gained] by the operation of intelligence fused harmoniously with volition and sentiment; instead of looking at an object from without, [it] grasps it from within as something linked with oneself. Thus, [in the East] intellect is fused with deed, faith, and love."[105] The cold intellectualism of an "objectivist view of history [such as one found in Marxism] could not lead man to true self-consciousness and joy," Sano declared.[106]

Thus, it was unfortunate that young Japanese intellectuals in the Meiji and Taishō periods had been seduced by Western-style abstract knowledge estranged from the Japanese national experience. "Alienated from its own people's life and instinct, [Marxist thought] naturally became formula without creativity," reflecting Western and not Eastern realities.[107] Notwithstanding the abstract principles of socialism, its "real form varies its pattern depending on the *minzoku* (race/people). Formulaic internationalism implies becoming a spiritual slave."[108] Egoism and individualism were the products of this wholesale importation of Western-style learning, of which Sano himself had partaken, and Marxism was part of this package of Western learning. Distant from the real needs of the Japanese people, Marxism taught materialism, "a non-spiritualistic fatalistic view of history that erases mankind's creative will and activity, a mechanistic schematism in the theory of the base and superstructure of society, and a conceptual game." It offered an atomistic view of individual men, the hedonistic pursuit of comfortable clothing, food, and lodging as the highest ideals, antinationalism, suprastate internationalism, a preoccupation with the specter of socioeconomic classes in constant conflict, the denial of the role of great men in history, and a violent but utopian theory of social revolution.[109] Indeed, Sano came very close to asserting what Takabatake had suggested earlier about Marxism as ideology in the Marxian sense, meaning "false consciousness": like the ideologies of Hobbes, Locke, and Hegel, Marxism, particularly in those aspects that were alien to the East, reflected the values of the Western bourgeois-capitalist society in which it had been born.[110]

At the core of Marx's thought, for example, was the theme of class struggle, an emphasis that Sano rejected as excessive and inapplicable to oriental society. The manner in which Marx had treated the subject served to underscore its incompatibility with the "oriental experience." As John M. Maguire has pointed out, "Marx present[s] class relations . . . as merely alienated individual activity."[111] This individualism or egoism was precisely the element of capitalism that was most repugnant to Meiji socialists such as Kawakami, as well as to Sano and Nabeyama.[112] Indeed, the Marxian stress on individualism and the pursuit of profit as the bases of capitalism buttressed Sano's conviction that capitalism was alien to the Orient as well as that orthodox Marxism, as a response to Western capitalism, was not directly applicable in the East. Nonetheless, Sano was optimistic that a socialism might be formulated combining elements of both East and West: "In the Orient, cooperative social characteristics based on natural spontaneous human love are stronger than profit or intellect [as motivations for human behavior]. . . . If we adopt the self-consciousness of the Western European individual and reintegrate it into this, then we can show to the world a new social form that West Europeans too must consider."[113] Thus, Sano endeavored to define an Oriental socialism that would contain important lessons for Western socialists as well.

Sano was convinced that, despite its deficiencies vis-à-vis the West, "there are aspects of Oriental civilization in philosophy and religion that are superior to Western Europe." Ironically, in many respects, Sano's evaluation of the Orient shared much in common with Marx's pessimistic and often derogatory views.[114] As did Hegel and Marx, Sano observed that "the ancient civilization of the world began from the Orient, and until the middle ages, the Orient also frequently dominated the West." Since the sixteenth century, however, the Orient had "lagged behind Western Europe in social organization and culture," and European imperialism had placed the Orient in danger of losing its few remaining spheres of superiority. As did Marx, Sano saw Asia as dominated by "small-scale irrigated agriculture," "a fatalistic ideology" that caused "the freedom of spirit to be curtailed and [the attainment of] fresh, lively knowledge about nature and humanity to be hindered," and "a despotic political order [that] rules and restricts the freedom of the individual."[115]

Nevertheless, Sano placed far greater weight on the superior aspects of Eastern culture that he discovered by immersing himself in Eastern classics. Over a two- to three-year period, Sano "read and learned thoroughly" Japanese classics including the ancient historical chronicles of the *Kojiki* and the *Nihon shoki*, *norito* (Shintō ritual prayer), the first poetry anthology *Man'yōshū*, *senmyō* (ancient imperial proclamations), and other works from the ninth through the nineteenth centuries. He found in these admittedly "simple, crude" works essential philosophical characteristics of Japan: an "affirmation of life," "pantheism," a creative spirit that saw "stagnation as death," activism based on the perceived "unity between nature and man," and a realism that stressed the present. The classics also revealed that "[i]n the ancient state, there had been none of the private ownership or class divisions that existed in later ages, nor consequently, the anxiety and pessimism that arose therefrom."[116] Similarly, in Chinese classics such as the *Lunyü* (Analects), *Zhongyong* (Doctrine of the mean), and novels such as the *Hongloumeng* (Dream of the red chamber) Sano found the Japanese themes of pantheism and "unity of thought and action" echoed, as well as additional elements of the notion of government by morality, led by philosophers who emphasized "democracy and regarded making the people's livelihood secure as paramount," and the concept of self-denial (*kokuji*).[117]

These aspects of Eastern heritage offered Sano an important corrective to facets of Marxism that tenkōsha like himself found offensive. Marx's and Lenin's depiction of the state as a mere instrument of exploitation was unacceptable to those who saw the state (whether viewed in Confucian, Buddhist, or *kokutai* terms) as a locus of positive moral value. Marx's notion of the state, like that of Western political theorists from Machiavelli to Hegel, had been authoritarian and (with the exception of Hegel) amoral, Sano asserted.[118] This authoritarian core of Marxism—as of Western thought as a whole, in his view—involved assumptions that contradicted indigenous Japanese beliefs about state and society. Marx's notion of authority was based on violence: its content was armies, prisons, and other organs of violence. As a result, Marx had overlooked the purely nonviolent leadership and organizational functions of the state and failed to see the potential for nonviolent revolution. In addition, Marx and Lenin had analyzed the state "exclusively from a class perspective," but, in Sano's view, such an interpretation was too simple. Ancient Japanese history demonstrated that the state did not, in fact, exist only because of classes. Consequently, "to say that in a socialist society, with the disappearance of classes, the state will experience a natural death cannot be but an elegant illusion. The state as the organization of power cultivating mankind will probably continue to exist for a long time."[119] The hope of the "withering away of the state" ignored the fact that "the state is the most realistic condition of human society. Civilized man cannot live apart from the state," Sano asserted.[120]

It was because Marxism had been derived from an analysis of Western capitalist society that Marx had identified the state so fully with class exploitation. Having returned to his Eastern philosophical roots, Sano found that "because capitalism became predominant, elements such as egoism, profit-ism, materialism, and class-ism became powerful, the public leadership character that formed the essence of [state] authority became weak, and the danger that [state] authority would be above and removed from social life became more serious than in any previous age."[121] For Sano, as for Takabatake, the state was not inherently exploitative and oppressive but became so only with the development of capitalism in the West.

Marx had also emphasized classes and material or economic causation to the neglect of any appreciation of the minzoku. "Politics, economics, and culture" interacted mutually to form human society; historical materialism, with its notions of surplus value and class differentiation, was incorrect in its single-minded emphasis on economic factors.[122] The absolutization of economics, the exaltation of the role of economic classes in human history, rendered Marxism a mechanistic theory by which economics conditioned politics.[123] Sano argued that his previous obsession with materialistic Western philosophy, including Marxism, had obscured an essential aspect of socialist revolution that was readily apparent from the perspective of Eastern philosophy—the need for a spiritual revolution as well as a radical change in the economic institutions of society. Here Sano found inspiration in Buddhism, as a spiritual basis for resolving social problems. "Buddhism," he argued, "is not content only with a superficial institutional resolution [of the problem of exploitation], as is ordinary socialism, but endeavors to resolve [it] in relation to a revolution in human nature." The struggle for socialism was above all a moral struggle between good and evil, and a socialist society in which the state provided the essential conditions not for exploitation but for "cooperative labor" was possible only on the basis of a "spiritual revolution."[124] Drawing on Confucian and Buddhist thought, Sano saw that in such a revolution men and women would constantly strive for kokuji (self-denial) to achieve a true resolution of the social problems plaguing Japanese society.

This call for spiritual revolution bears comparison to the ideas of Li Dazhao and Mao Zedong in China, both of whom argued that reforms directed at socioeconomic arrangements alone were not sufficient to realize meaningful social change. For both men, a spiritual and cultural revolutionary process was essential. For Sano, as for Mao and Li, Confucian conceptions concerning spiritual self-cultivation and moral regeneration became essential components of the adaptation of Marxism to the East Asian context.[125] All three moderated Marx's espousal of class conflict in favor of a notion of national salvation. Li and Mao were determined that internal cleavage should not jeopardize China's ability to resist foreign encroachments in the critical early decades of the twentieth century. Sano, too, felt that Marxism's emphasis on class was not only divisive in the wars of national liberation that were essential to the survival of Asia but was also antithetical to the presumption of natural harmony that was characteristic of "oriental philosophy". Sano argued that as an ideology of liberation, Marxism failed to value the minzoku, even as international imperialism increasingly made minzoku and economic class coincide. It was here, in the discussion of Marx's neglect of ethnicity and nationalism, that Sano moved beyond the critique of Marx to articulate his own positive notion of socialism-in-one-country.

Ikkoku Shakai-shugi: *Toward an "Oriental Socialism"*

Despite the attention Sano devoted to East-West differences, his view of Japan as unique inspired both his *tenkō* and his vision of socialism in Japan. As he wrote in his prison diary, "That it was necessary to open up a unique path to socialism with our own national strength was the first reason for my *tenkō*."[126] Sano believed that the inability of Marxism in its Comintern-JCP form to respond to Japan's realities was one of the major reasons that Marxian socialism had encountered such resistance in Japan.[127]

As Sano formulated his own alternative socialist doctrine, the emotional content of his *tenkō* was reflected in his treatment of the tension between the alleged universalism of Marxism as formulated in Western Europe and the particular characteristics of the individual Japanese minzoku to which any vision of socialism in Japan must be adapted. Marx's assertion that he had derived his schema on the basis of a "scientific" analysis of the historical laws governing socioeconomic development implied a claim to its universal applicability. But Sano and his fellow imprisoned Marxists suddenly recognized that even the epistemological and methodological bases of Marx's schema came into conflict with the intuitive foundations of Eastern and, especially, Japanese culture and philosophy. By following the Comintern's line on violent revolution against the imperial institution, they felt, they were committing treason against the *kokutai*.[128] Once awakened to love for the minzoku in prison—to the realization that "the *minzoku* is not only something sentimental, but . . . a concrete reality, an active, living political force and a deep moral force"[129]—Sano was able to cast aside the alien premises of Marxism and return to oriental first principles.

For Sano, the minzoku had a far greater historical role than Marx had attributed to it when he proclaimed that in the era of socialist revolution class superseded nationality. Contrary to Marx's view, the minzoku and the state would play crucial roles in the liberation of human beings through socialism. "Mutual love" was the basis for the nation, which in turn formed the foundation for the cooperative society that was socialism. "Patriotism is the emotion of loving one's own country, . . . loving one's own *minzoku* through the medium of the form of the state." Sano asserted, as had Takabatake before him, that Lenin was such a patriot. Finally, "[p]atriotism forms the spiritual energy of socialist construction."[130] Yet Sano felt that the conflict between his view of the primacy of the minzoku and Marx's emphasis on classes could be reconciled, for "the core of the *minzoku* is laborers." Moreover, the nation and nationalism would be the essential vehicle by which the conflict between "haves" and "have nots" in the international sphere would result in the socialist liberation of the East from the yoke of Western imperialism.[131] More importantly, Sano stressed the inherent superiority of the Japanese minzoku, a superiority that not only would enable it to achieve stateness and thereby socialism but would also enable it to be the leader of national liberation through socialist revolution for all of Asia.

The peculiar virtues of the Japanese held for Sano the key to a dissenting view of Marx's theory of the state. Unlike the Western state, the Japanese state was, he argued, a cooperative community and not the product of intense class conflict.[132] Here Sano stressed elements of Japan's orthodox *kokutai* thought. He envisaged a socialism premised on an imperial institution which, through spiritual revolution, returned to the noble traditions of the Meiji state under which the *kokutai* concept had been systematized as state orthodoxy. On the basis of that *kokutai*, Sano's Japanese socialism, centered around the emperor system, would be unique and superior to any other form of socialism. "In the countries of other minzoku, state and society are in antagonism, and God and the state are not compatible; by contrast, in Japan, God, state, and society form a complete union. To die for one's country is the greatest service to God, the greatest loyalty to the emperor, and also the highest way of life as social man. The subjects of His Majesty regard dying for one's country as the greatest joy."[133]

Nevertheless, Sano's national socialist vision was not designed for realization within the existing bounds of the Japanese state. In his view, these bounds and, indeed, the very notion of the nation-state itself were, like Marx's theory of the state, imposed from without by the West. Sano believed that the superiority of the Japanese lay in their independence, their "capability as rulers," and their "accumulation of the essence and purity of Oriental culture."[134] Thus, as a Japanese thinker, he could formulate for Japan, Taiwan, and Korea (which he regarded as part of Japan),[135] as well as Manchuria and China what thinkers of these other Asian countries could not formulate for themselves. It was his express hope that the Pacific war, the war for the Greater East Asian Co-Prosperity Sphere, would evolve into a war of national liberation for all the peoples of the Orient under Japanese leadership.[136] Presumably, the national peculiarities of Korea, Taiwan, Manchuria, and China—"the amount of population, geographic position, national resources, the extent of the development of the forces of production, the form of culture, historical traditions, and differences of temperament, etc."[137]—were not of such significance that these societies should be permitted to develop their own indigenous national forms of socialism.

Japan would play a special role in Sano's transformation of Marxism to national socialism because it alone, of all societies of the Orient, shared both Western and oriental characteristics. Its emperor system was evidence that Japan's special characteristics had enabled it to build a strong nation and state.[138] These qualities made Japan uniquely capable of developing socialism indigenously, for Japan alone had "pass[ed] through the same feudal system as Western Europe's middle ages," and "cultivate[d] Western European social life and thought through the importation of capitalism since the Meiji."[139]

Early in the Pacific war, Sano saw proof of Japan's potential to lead the rest of Asia in this enterprise. As the defeatism of the JCP perished with the party in *tenkō*, "the glorious future of [the Japanese empire as] an absolutely invincible and leading country in the world [became] apparent."[140] Sano's socialism-in-one-country, like Takahashi's "petty imperialism" notion, accommodated the military vision of a Greater East Asian Co-Prosperity Sphere to a revolutionary ideal that maintained some Marxian elements: industrialism, proletarianism, and socialism. But unlike the Marxism of the JCP, Sano's vision shared the determination of Japan's military leaders to resolve Japan's social and economic crisis on the basis of its unique and unchanging *kokutai*.

CONCLUSIONS

Although Sano Manabu went a step further than most *tenkōsha* in formulating a systematic theory of national socialism, nearly all of them shared an alternative worldview in the *kokutai* that was central to the national socialism of Sano and the Kaitō-ha.[141] As noted here, this theme in the thought of Sano and the Kaitō-ha echoed strongly the ideas of other Marxian national socialists in prewar Japan. The emphasis on nationalism in a hostile international environment, the conviction that the state had been and would continue to be essential to social development, and the desire to retain the imperial system as an essential element of a socialism that would be truly Japanese in character—these ideas were shared by Takabatake, Takahashi, Akamatsu, the Kaitō-ha, and many tenkōsha of the 1930s. Sano's writings, with their stress on the East-West dichotomy and Japanese exceptionalism, help to illuminate why these kinds of revisions were made and why the JCP—which permitted no nationalistic deviation from the orthodoxy of Soviet Marxism—collapsed under police pressure but without significant resistance from the Japanese people.

Two factors emphasized in this chapter help to account for this pattern. The first factor was Japan's position in the international system and the changes in the 1930s that made that position more precarious. The resonance between the thought of Sano and the Kaitō-ha with the transformation of Marxism to national socialism in Italy and Germany during the same period highlights the significance of this factor. Early in the twentieth century, Marxists in such later-industrializing societies found that while their countries continued to be disadvantaged internationally the Marxism of Lenin could not accommodate their nationalisms. In colonies or semicolonies such as China or India, backwardness was heralded as a virtue, and nationalism was held to be an agent of historical progress that could be welded to Marxism legitimately. In the view of Sano, Takahashi, and others, Japan shared many of the disadvantages from which other Asian societies suffered at the hands of countries that had industrialized first. By the 1920s, Japan, which fit neatly into the category of neither advanced capitalist power nor colonial or semicolonial state, could not pursue economic expansion along the same path pioneered by the Western European powers. Having carved out exclusive spheres of influence, the powers now changed the "rules of the game" of world politics at the London and Washington Naval conferences precisely when Japan was prepared to participate as an equal in the international sphere. This difficulty was of concern not only to Japan's capitalists but also to its believers in Marx's theory of revolution as well. As Takahashi observed, socialism could not come to fruition as long as Japan's capitalist development remained deadlocked. Because orthodox Leninist Marxism would not accommodate nationalism in such a country, that orthodoxy had to be changed, militantly, by Marxists who perceived their country's dilemma and responded to it nationalistically.

The existence of a powerful statist orthodoxy christened in the early-Meiji period to support state-led industrialization was the crucial second internal factor that shaped the particular form that the transformation of Marxism into national socialism assumed in prewar Japan. *Kokutai* thought, if in a revised form, provided a convenient tool for Marxists like Sano, the Kaitō-ha, Takabatake, and others to replace the apparently inapplicable and culturally unpalatable aspects of orthodox Marxism-Leninism with notions more acceptable to Japanese sensibilities. Their transformation of Marxism into a doctrine of indigenized national socialism could respond not only to Japan's international dilemma, but also to the need for an indigenous socialist doctrine that could be a source of national pride. For Sano and other tenkōsha, the repeated failures of the JCP and impending war clearly exposed the deficiencies of Marxist orthodoxy as applied to Japan by the Comintern. *Kokutai* thought was a compelling alternative in the face of these weaknesses, and it both helped to compel *tenkō* and inspired alternative, indigenous formulations of socialism for modern Japan. Much like Chinese Marxists from Li to Mao and African Marxists such as Julius Nyerere and Amilcar Cabral, Sano and others felt the need to transform Marxism into a doctrine that could respond to aspirations of their national peoples that were rooted in their own philosophical traditions. Adapting Marxism to Africa, both Nyerere and Cabral felt an urgent need to reaffirm traditional values indigenous to their societies. Nyerere, for example, found in *ujamaa*, the "familyhood" of the cooperative agrarian community of Tanzania's own cultural history, a model for building a uniquely African socialism. Similarly, Cabral called on his fellow citizens to "Return to the Source" to rediscover traditional values to be reaffirmed in postcolonial socialist Guinea-Bissau.[142] For Sano and his fellow Japanese tenkōsha, the *kokutai* and loyalty to the Imperial Household that lay at its core gave the nationalistic adaptation of Marxism in prewar Japan its uniquely Japanese content. This crucial role of the *kokutai* in turning Marxists into Japanese nationalists is the basis for the argument here that *tenkō* represented the predominant means by which Japanese Marxists endeavored to resolve the national question in the prewar era.

The work of Western and Japanese scholars who have commented on the nature of Japanese nationalism supports this conclusion. Certain characteristics of this nationalism made Marxism, especially its universalism, alien and fragile in the Japanese context. Robert Bellah has argued that whereas nationalism in the West supplanted the particularism of earlier feudal society, "Japanese nationalism remained peculiarly particularistic due to its focus on the imperial family, reigning for ages eternal, the main family of which all Japanese families are branch families." Where Christianity served as a universalistic religion, Shintō, incorporated into the new *kokutai* idea in the Meiji period, remained particularistic.[143]

This persistence of particularism helps to explain why the conflict between nationalism and Marxism was especially bitter and ultimately biased in favor of nationalism in prewar Japan. It also suggests why the most natural path for the tenkōsha was to support Japanese expansion onto the Asian mainland. Japanese policy was said to have the goal of "liberating the oppressed peoples of Asia."[144] But the racialism inherent in Japan's nationalism made its "liberation movement" an imperialist, rather than an anti-imperialist, enterprise. Imperialism became the common denominator of ultranationalist militarists and Marxists trying to regain a secure sense of national identity. In the process, the *kokutai*, the ultimate referent for Japanese identity, made the general national question in Marxism a psychological as well as an intellectual dilemma for Japanese Marxists.

As the comparisons drawn with Germany and Italy demonstrate, Japan's Marxists faced the same national question that Marxists in other later-industrializing states must resolve. In Japan, however, because of the peculiarities of indigenous modes of thought on nation and polity, the conflict was not merely nationalism versus internationalism, as it would be in China, the Soviet Union, and other settings, but Marxism versus national identity, Marxism versus Japaneseness itself. Imprisonment, the trial, and war forced Marxists who had previously skirted the problem to confront it directly. *Tenkō* and the reformulation of Marxism as a uniquely Japanese national socialism were the result.

Mao and the Chinese Synthesis of Nationalism, Stateness, and Marxism

THE NATIONAL QUESTION IN THE CHINESE REVOLUTION: MARXISM AS A STRATEGY OF NATIONAL DEVELOPMENT

The twenty years of the Communist Party of China have been twenty years in which the universal truth of Marxism-Leninism has become more and more integrated with the concrete practice of the Chinese revolution. . . . For a hundred years, the finest sons and daughters of the disaster-ridden Chinese nation fought and sacrificed their lives, one stepping into the breach as another fell, in quest of the truth that would save the country and the people. . . . But it was only after World War I and the October Revolution in Russia that we found Marxism-Leninism, the best of the truths, the best of weapons for liberating our nation. And the Communist Party of China has been the initiator, propagandist and organizer of the wielding of this weapon. As soon as it was linked with the concrete practice of the Chinese revolution, the universal truth of Marxism-Leninism gave an entirely new complexion to the Chinese revolution. Since the outbreak of the War of Resistance Against Japan, our Party, basing itself on the universal truth of Marxism-Leninism, has taken a further step in its study of the concrete practice of this war and in its study of China in the world today, and has also made a beginning in the study of Chinese history. These are all very good signs.[1]

Thus, in 1941, Mao Zedong assessed the success with which the Chinese Communist party had adapted the nineteenth-century European theory of Marxism to the twentieth-century context of an agrarian Asian society victimized by Western and Japanese military might. As was the case among Japanese Marxists, the outbreak of hostilities in 1931 and, then, full-scale war in 1937 intensified the tensions over the national question for Chinese Marxists. When China was humiliated by the 1919 Versailles treaty, the national question was already very much in evidence. Young intellectual leaders such as Chen Duxiu and Li Dazhao turned eagerly toward Marxism in its Leninist incarnation blending an anti-imperialism that supported the nationalist drive to build a strong China with Marx's ultimate ideal of stateless communism. They found in this complex formulation a tool with which to end the national disunity that perpetuated China's humiliation. Late in the 1920s, the national question reemerged when participants in the controversy on Chinese social history tried to reconcile the peculiarities of China's historical development with Marx's universalist schema. In the 1930s and 1940s, not merely China's national pride but the survival of its people and its very existence as an independent national unit were at stake. In the midst of this crisis, Mao Zedong devised a revolutionary strategy that enabled the CCP to take the lead in the national resistance to Japan while building a solid basis of support that would carry it to victory over the Guomindang when the war ended.

This process at once resolved certain issues associated with nationalism and state building and raised others. On the one hand, because China, unlike Japan, was a less-industrialized society suffering under economic and military pressure from the advanced industrialized powers, Comintern leaders viewed Chinese nationalism as having a legitimate and positive role to play in the Chinese revolution. Thus, with respect to nationalism, the situation of Chinese Marxists was fundamentally different from that of their Japanese counterparts: Before and after the Manchurian incident, with their own nation the victim and Japan the aggressor, Chinese Marxists did not have to place themselves in direct opposition to the leadership of the Comintern to articulate a vision of socialism that affirmed their nationalist sentiments. On the other hand, this did not mean that the indigenization of Marxism as theory and as revolutionary strategy in China could proceed entirely under and in accordance with Comintern direction. On the contrary, the more intense the efforts of CCP leaders, most notably Mao and his colleague Chen Boda,[2] to "sinify" Marxism-Leninism, the greater became the divergence between their own ideas concerning the kind of revolution China should have and how it should be achieved and those of the Comintern leadership. Thus, the tensions over the national question—and of leading a local Communist party that was not subservient to Moscow—came to be manifested in this period in a schism of sorts within the party and between its rising leaders and its Comintern supporters. Even after the disaster of the Shanghai coup in 1927 deprived the CCP of its ability to challenge Guomindang power in the cities, the Comintern persisted in instructing the CCP to subordinate itself to the Guomindang, to pursue an urban strategy, and to sacrifice radical activism among the peasantry. A succession of unfortunate CCP leaders obediently followed the Comintern's instructions to no avail and were ousted and scapegoated for their failure. During these years, Mao's stormy relationship with the party's central leadership reflected the emerging schism over an urban strategy that was based on the universalist expectations of Marx's schema of proletarian socialist revolution and a rural strategy that celebrated the role of peasant uprisings in China's remarkable history of dynastic change. Early conflicts with Party Central and Mao's subsequent espousal of a military strategy and radical land policies that transgressed the bounds established by Comintern orders led to Mao's estrangement from Party Central through the 1920s and early 1930s.[3] In the countryside, first in his native Hunan Province, then in Jiangxi, Mao and Zhu De laid the groundwork for a rural strategy that would take adequate account of China's own special characteristics.

When Mao finally achieved dominance in the party after the 1935 Zunyi conference during the Long March, this schism gave way to new tensions. As the CCP struggled to establish its own "alternative hegemony" in the remote base areas,[4] the national question took a new form in Mao's indigenized Marxism-Leninism. With the nationalistic drive to resist Japan firmly at the center of CCP policy, particularly after the outbreak of full-scale war in 1937,[5] the CCP adopted a united front strategy, seeking the cooperation of social groups it had previously attacked.

The national question now concerned the issue of stateness as well as the question of who comprised the nation in the party's vision of China's future. In the CCP's rural base areas, Mao and his colleagues had the opportunity to develop not only strategy and tactics for taking power but also methods for exercising power after the revolution. At one and the same time, then, the CCP sought to establish a state power that would engineer revolutionary change in Chinese society and to develop methods of leadership that would prevent that power from being institutionalized as the same sort of bureaucratic, intellectual, elite leadership remote from China's millions of common people that had characterized previous Chinese states. Certainly, this was the same national question that was posed in the Soviet Union just after October 1917. Nonetheless, China's underdevelopment—even relative to the considerably backward Russia of 1917—and the circumstances of its tardy industrialization compelled China's Marxists to confront the issue in still more fundamental terms. The association of industrialization with the Western influence of the coastal treaty port cities that Mao and other nationalistic Chinese viewed as pernicious rendered suspect even the "petty-bourgeois" intellectuals who comprised the main reservoir of CCP membership in the early years. Coupled with Mao's dissident insistence on the potential of the peasantry to play the leading role in China's revolution, this meant that one might well question that aspect of Marxism that assumed that the liberation of humankind "presuppose(d) the entire economic history of mankind up through capitalism."[6] Moreover, Mao accentuated a theme that echoed Li Dazhao's writings before and after his conversion to Marxism: the need for spiritual transformation, the transformation of human souls, as well as revolutionary change in the social and economic organization of society.[7] Mao contended that the Japanese sought to plunder the Chinese people spiritually as well as materially. They were "working to destroy the national consciousness of the Chinese people," forbidding them "to show the slightest trace of Chinese national spirit."[8] Thus, the cultivation of such "national consciousness" became an essential part of the Chinese Communist party's revolutionary strategy. With the injection of these new elements, in Mao, Chinese Marxism became a strategy of national development, but in its new form it was pregnant with doubts as to what the endpoint of that development should be. At issue was no longer revolutionary strategy alone, a Chinese path to socialism, but a Chinese kind of socialism as well. Here both components of the notion of "national development" itself came into question. Who comprised the nation when the theory and practice of the CCP before and after 1949 excluded so many, on the basis of class origins, from membership in *the people* (*renmin*)? What was the desideratum of "development"? Was it to be primarily political or economic in character? Chinese revolutionary leaders from the time of Sun Yat-sen had called into question the desirability of accepting a Western definition of modernity that was premised on industrial capitalism. In this sense, the new way that Mao addressed the national question in the 1930s and 1940s portended the split with the Soviet party two decades later over Mao's articulation of an alternative vision that repudiated the Soviet model and that Soviet leaders, in turn, saw as anarchistic, populistic, and not genuinely Marxist.[9]

The notion that what Mao achieved in these years was the *sinification* of Marxism, its adaptation to China's national context for practical strategic purposes, has long comprised a major theme of Western work on Mao.[10] This paradigm has been very helpful in illuminating the new elements of Mao's thought, particularly as they reflect the influence of traditional Chinese perspectives on man and society.[11] Nevertheless, this paradigm does not permit a full appreciation of the subtleties of the national question as he treated them. More importantly, the particularism of the notion of sinification has inhibited potentially fruitful comparisons of themes in Chinese Marxism with the thought of Western thinkers with respect to such universally significant issues as bureaucracy, cultural change, and the dilemmas inherent in the effort to institutionalize revolutionary change.[12] The approach taken here seeks to illuminate Mao's thought on such issues as they concerned the national question, drawing comparisons where possible.

Treating Mao's resolution of the national question in China does impose difficulties that did not arise in analyzing Japanese Marxism. Japan's Communist party under Comintern domination found itself unable to compete successfully with the domination and hegemony of the Shōwa state, and its Marxists finally succumbed to the power of the state and its ideological framework in *tenkō*. In China, by contrast, the CCP succeeded in taking power first in isolated base areas and then in the country as a whole, and, thus, one has a corpus of both theory and practice to take into account. The painful realities of events such as the Great Leap Forward and the Cultural Revolution, the tragic dimensions of which became fully evident only in revelations after Mao's death, must not deter one from treating the ideas that inspired the practice on their own terms. Only such an approach can allow one to appreciate the true enormity of the problem of the state in the nineteenth and twentieth centuries, the dual-edged character of the appeal to national identity and the construction of an institutional edifice to protect it. In practice, Mao's solution to the national question issued, as in Japan, in the triumph of statism, but it must be recognized that in both its theoretical formulation and in aspects of its actual practice it was highly anarchistic. An important task of what follows is to show how this disjuncture could have emerged. As Michel Foucault once observed, "most of the time, the state is envisioned as a kind of political power which ignores individuals, looking only at the interests of the totality, or . . . of a class or a group among the citizens. [But] the state's power (and that's one of the reasons for its strength) is both an individualizing and a totalizing form of power. Never, . . . in the history of human societies—even in the old Chinese society—has there been such a tricky combination in the same political structures of individualization techniques, and of totalization procedures."[13] Indeed, it is precisely in what Foucault referred to as the "individualizing," the atomizing aspects of the process of nation and state building—some of which are conceived theoretically in the thought examined here—that the totalizing process finds its strength as it breaks down the familial and other traditional social ties on which people have relied in the past to enhance the power that they as individuals might wield vis-à-vis the political structures of the national state.

The point of departure for Mao's formulation of these elements lay precisely in his assertion of a vibrant and dynamic Chinese national identity, and it is here that the antinomies of both his thought and his practice originate. Mao exhibited considerable ambivalence concerning the social and philosophical legacies of both China and the West. Marxism provided him an effective tool with which to criticize both. Mao militantly rejected traditional "feudalistic" China—it was primarily to this that he referred when he criticized the "old"—but he was also hostile to much of the new "West." He was especially disdainful of capitalism and Western assumptions about the nature of modernity as these were reflected in the Western drive to dominate China. He rejected the primacy of abstract reason and intellect unleavened by intuition, and he was particularly skeptical of those (such as Max Weber) who would claim that the supremacy of the "rationality" glorified in the Enlightenment was embodied in the bureaucracy of the modern state. Indeed, it was this point that would decisively separate Mao from his more urban-oriented colleague Liu Shaoqi. The two were at one in criticizing the legacy of old China,[14] but Liu, who operated much more than Mao in the urban sector and had absorbed its influences, was not as anxious to challenge Western notions of modernity that were embedded in Marxist thought.[15]

When treating the problem of bureaucratic authority and other issues related to this broadened sense of the national question, Mao was caught between two conflicting imperatives: the need to identify China's historical experience within the universal pattern of human history stressed in Marx's schema in order to legitimate China's revolution, on the one hand, and the view that China's historical and cultural peculiarities required adjustment—one hesitates to use the ideologically charged term *revision*—of the orthodoxy of Marxism-Leninism to accord with the requirements of Chinese conditions, on the other. Mao's professed hostility to the bureaucratism of the institutionalized modern state would appear to have distinguished Mao's adaptation of Marxism from those in Japan who fashioned of Marxism national- or state-socialist doctrines. Paradoxically, however, his attitudes concerning the particular and universal elements of China drew him close to Japanese Marxian national socialists such as Sano Manabu, who also questioned certain key Western Enlightenment assumptions of Marxism concerning modernity. Like Sano and Takabatake, moreover, Mao's revolutionary nationalism was not so parochial as to preclude the application of his theory and practice to other Asian societies and in the West.[16] Thus, as the following discussion demonstrates, even in treating the national question nationalistically, Mao ventured well beyond sinification to advance questions and responses of significance well beyond Chinese borders.

Yet Mao himself encouraged the dominance of the sinification paradigm as the framework of his thought. This was precisely the framework within which he found political advantage in attacking rivals who had learned their Marxism—in theory and practice—in the Soviet Union. Even before he adopted the phrase *sinification of Marxism* as his own in 1938,[17] writing "On Practice" in 1937, Mao recognized the power of the appeal to Chinese national identity. There he stressed two related points: that genuine knowledge arose out of practical experience and that without the concrete experience of participating in the Chinese revolution, the theory of Marxism-Leninism was incomplete and invalid in China and ultimately useless to the Chinese people.

> From the Marxist viewpoint, theory is important, and its importance is fully expressed in Lenin's statement, 'Without revolutionary theory there can be no revolutionary movement.' But Marxism emphasizes the importance of theory precisely and only because it can guide action. If we have a correct theory but merely prate about it, pigeonhole it and do not put it into practice, then that theory, however good, is of no significance. Knowledge begins with practice, and theoretical knowledge is acquired through practice and must then return to practice.[18]

Herein lay a major defect in the CCP, Mao argued. "Many Party members are still in a fog about Chinese history. . . . There are many Marxist-Leninist scholars who cannot open their mouths without citing ancient Greece; but as for their own ancestors [and their concrete, historical praxis]—sorry, they have been forgotten."[19] Mao proposed to redress this error by pressing his own application of Marxism-Leninism to Chinese practice. Here Mao appealed to nationalist sentiment, to the greatness of China's "thousands of years of" "glorious revolutionary tradition and . . . splendid historical heritage." In this heritage Mao found a national myth with which to galvanize support for his vision of the Chinese revolution. "The history of the Han people [and of '(a)ll the nationalities of China']," he claimed, "demonstrates that the Chinese never submit to tyrannical rule but invariably use revolutionary means to overthrow or change it."[20] Effective resistance to Japan and the quest for socialist revolution required the "unity of theory and practice" in this specifically Chinese setting. Thus, while Chinese academic Marxists in the coastal cities engaged in the highly abstract controversy on Chinese social history, Mao and others in the hinterland devised the practical application of Marxism-Leninism as revolutionary strategy to the war-torn rural sphere that dominated the Chinese context.

Distance from the Comintern in both a literal and symbolic sense facilitated Mao's resolution of the national question in this manner. As in Japan, this solution was predictable by the 1920s, when the theoretical father of Chinese Marxism, Li Dazhao, carefully mingled elements of nationalism into his Marxism. In Japan, the analogous response was prefigured by Takabatake's national socialism and by the Rōnō-ha's exit from the JCP in 1927. This response, culminating in *tenkō* in the 1930s, constituted a surrender of Japan's Marxists to an existing state power whose effective national myth preempted and nullified appeals to nationalism from the Left. In China, however, the sole rival of the CCP's combination of nationalism with Marxian social revolution was the ineffectual Guomindang, which commanded little such loyalty from its citizens. The contrast between these Chinese and Japanese responses to the national question may be attributable to the high degree of stateness —the identification of nation with state[21]—in Japan and the near lack thereof in the absence of effective state power in China. Yet in both cases, the nationalist dedication to the mission of building a powerful and purified national state triumphed and did so with indifference, if not direct opposition, to Comintern authority.

This posture vis-à-vis the Comintern was significant in at least two ways. First, the Comintern was the symbol of Marxism's internationalist orientation, and the overwhelming response of Chinese and Japanese Marxists by the 1940s was to favor nationalism over internationalism. The fact that Chinese nationalism was legitimate in Moscow as Japanese nationalism was not enabled Mao to claim, without Comintern disapproval, that Chinese "patriotism is applied international-ism."[22] Secondly, the pursuit of nationalist ends implied the acceptance of "social-ism in one country" in principle and not merely out of necessity as in the Soviet case. Theoretically, as an advocate of Marxian communism, the Comintern stood for the achievement of socialism as a supranational and antistatist necessity, even though in reality the Comintern increasingly conflated the interests of the interna-tional Communist movement with those of the Soviet state so that the Comintern became a mere extension of the Soviet foreign policy machinery. It is not surpris-ing, then, that Chinese and Japanese Marxists clung desperately to the goal of a strong national state even if it was to be merely a temporary phenomenon. The Comintern had conceived revolution in the East—in terms of national liberation movements against the Western imperialist powers—as an instrument to transform the hostile international enviroment by fomenting socialist revolution among Western societies.[23] By contrast, indigenous revolutionaries in China as well as in Japan aspired to achieve socialism itself in their own countries whether in the form of state socialism (Marxian or otherwise) or Marxist, ultimately stateless, communism.

The year 1927 marked a turning point in the relations of both Chinese and Japanese Marxists with the Comintern and in the resolution of these issues. It was in December of that year that Yamakawa Hitoshi led the Rōnō-ha out of the Japan's Communist party. In China, April of the same year had marked the disastrous Shanghai Coup, which decimated the CCP's urban membership and affiliated labor leaders in the coastal city. The tragedy in China clearly resulted from views of Comintern leaders that diverged from those of the CCP, but it did not immediately prompt the CCP to defy Comintern authority. On the contrary, the emergence of a nativist revolutionary Marxism-Leninism in the form of Mao's thought occurred only gradually. After 1927, and particularly after the demise of the Li Lisan line in 1931, the Comintern became less and less effectively interventionist in China. As Benjamin Schwartz has noted, the success of the de facto rural strategy around the Jiangxi Soviet accompanied the conspicuous collapse of the Comintern's prole-tarian strategy of urban insurrection.[24] Direct Comintern influence on the Chinese revolution abated in the ensuing years as "the Chinese Communist movement completed its historic shift from the cities to the countryside."[25] The Comintern's withdrawal from close supervision of the revolution in China enabled Mao and other CCP leaders to develop their own ideas on revolutionary strategy, most of which were at variance with the Comintern's directives, while paying lip-service to its authority. Yet the CCP's reliance on the Soviet Union lingered even when its relations with the Comintern changed. Stalin, as Lenin's successor, for example, continued to be a major conduit of legitimacy for the party leadership's Marxist credentials.[26] Even Mao, as he sought to establish his own authority as the party's leading theorist, could ill-afford to deny himself the mantle of ideological descen-dance in a direct line from Marx and Engels to Lenin to Stalin. It was not until after de-Stalinization was underway in the Soviet Union in the late 1950s that Mao would openly challenge Stalin's monopoly on leadership, concluding that Stalin had been only 70 percent a Marxist.[27]

This transition in Chinese-Soviet relations was protracted, but the significance of the 1927 Shanghai coup for the subsequent evolution of "sinified" Marxism is indisputable. As Raymond F. Wylie has noted in his study of Chen Boda, Mao's political secretary, the "search for the 'correct' relationship between Soviet Marxist-Leninist theory and Chinese revolutionary practice became a key *leitmotiv* of the entire Chinese Communist movement in the years after 1927."[28] Just as the October Revolution of 1917 had done, the 1927 coup illuminated the national question in Marxism in all its dimensions. The notion of "sinification" helps to bring one particular issue to the forefront—the role of nationalism in a Marxian-inspired revolution. The internationalist posture of Marx's, Engels's, and Lenin's Marxism and its acceptance in China as a "scientific truth" valid universally implied that there was no legitimate role for nationalist sentiment once a society had reached the stage of proletarian-socialist revolution. Lenin's and Nikolai Bukharin's imagery of a smychka (alliance) between national liberation movements in the East and the revolutionary proletariats of the West had been the cornerstone of the Comintern's Eastern strategy since 1920, but nationalism was valid in China because it was a progressive force in the bourgeois-democratic revolutionary stage. Moreover, in the Comintern view, national liberation movements in the less-industrialized countries of Asia would always be subordinate to the leadership of the world's first and sole proletarian nation, the Soviet Union. Because the Soviet Union was the only existing dictatorship of the proletariat, to serve its interests was to serve the cause of international revolution. Leaders of less world-historically progressive national liberation movements would lack the international vision of the Soviet-dominated Comintern leadership and should willingly submit to the judgments of the latter in matters of theory and strategy.

Chinese Marxists accepted these premises at least through 1927, and their faith was reflected in psychological, as well as military and financial, dependence on the Comintern. One measure of this dependence was the reluctance with which the notion of the need to "sinify" Marxism was accepted when Mao proposed it to the CCP leadership late in 1938. In Wylie's words,

> In calling for the Sinification of Marxism, Mao was clearly moving into uncharted theoretical terrain. A lack of enthusiasm within the Party for the concept is suggested by the omission in the Sixth Plenum's political resolution of any mention of the need to Sinify Marxism-Leninism. Many Party Leaders probably feared that the Sinification of Marxism-Leninism would deprive it of the prestige and authority associated with its two famous European exponents, and would isolate Communists in China from the mainstream of the international communist movement. Also, the concept would possibly antagonize Stalin and the Comintern, who might see in the Sinification of Marxism the unhealthy influence of Chinese petty bourgeois nationalism in the CCP.[29]

Chinese Marxist scholars participating in the controversy on Chinese social history endeavored to place China firmly within the purview of Marx's universal history so that the revolution in China could be legitimated as historically valid and inevitable. Yet Mao's and Chen's call for sinification seemed to elevate the particular at least to the same level as the universal. Would not such a process ultimately threaten the validity of the application of Marxist thought to China at all? On the other hand—although CCP leaders resisted this suggestion—might not the debacle of April 1927 demonstrate that the Comintern held no irrefutable monopoly of wisdom on the course of the international communist movement in each of its national settings?

Linked with the nationalist issues illuminated by the 1927 coup were statist elements of the national question. The nexus of the two problems lay in the notion of "socialism in one country." The 1927 debacle demonstrated irrefutably the ultimate isolation of the CCP in its battle against the Guomindang and the need for an effective military strategy. Whatever the mythology of the international Communist movement, the incident suggested that the Chinese party did, indeed, have interests apart from those of the Comintern and that the CCP could not rely on Comintern expertise or willingness to intervene on behalf of the Chinese party when its guidelines failed. Nor was there reason to expect that this divergence of national interests would vanish after the revolution. Like the CPSU, the CCP would, doubtless, be pressed to build a powerful state to defend its victory and consolidate its "dictatorship of the proletariat" after the revolution, and without the further spread of socialism, in a world of hostile capitalist states the party could expect to proceed with "building socialism in one country" in a manner that would assure China's survival in the face of foreign threat. Clearly, that task would have to be undertaken on the basis of internal Chinese conditions, and, again, the notion of a Chinese "dictatorship of the proletariat" emerging as an effective unit in a supportive international socialist community was chimerical.

Finally, the need to pursue "socialism in one country" in a hostile international environment mandated the construction of socialism under the aegis of a powerful state buttressed by a strong military apparatus based on a robust industrial infrastructure. The backwardness of the Chinese economy seemed to require, even more so than in the Soviet Union, that the state undertake many more functions than those envisioned by Marx's original notion of proletarian dictatorship or in Lenin's *State and Revolution*.[30] At the very least, it seemed to fall to the state to accomplish what China's weak and immature bourgeoisie had not: complete the economic modernization that Marxism-Leninism claimed was the prerequisite for achieving socialism and communism. The urgency of these requirements was heightened by the powerful nationalist impulse of the Chinese people, and they threatened the orthodox Marxist dream of a stateless socialist society. Mao's endeavor tackled all these dilemmas.

Mao as Revolutionary Strategist: The Marriage of Revolutionary Nationalism with Marxism

"Continuous Revolution": National Liberation as Revolutionary Strategy

For many years we Communists have struggled for a cultural revolution as well as for a political and economic revolution, and our aim is to build a new society and a new state for the Chinese nation. That new society and new state will have not only a new politics and a new economy but a new culture. In other words, not only do we want to change a China that is politically oppressed and economically exploited into a China that is politically free and economically prosperous, we also want to change the China which is being kept ignorant and backward under the sway of the old culture into an enlightened and progressive China under the sway of a new culture. In short, we want to build a new China. Our aim in the cultural sphere is to build a new Chinese national culture.[31]

Revolutionary nationalism—a nationalism that aspired to remake the Chinese nation—was at the core of the adaptations that Mao Zedong made in Marxism-Leninism. Where other CCP leaders humbly and gratefully accepted the Comintern's often misguided policies, Mao's view that with his consciousness of the lessons of China's past he was far better equipped to direct the Chinese revolution than the Comintern's remote and poorly informed leadership emboldened him to develop strategies and doctrines that conflicted sharply with those of the Comintern. His nationalism exacerbated these conflicts with the Comintern leadership because it prevented him from accepting the Comintern's view that China was so much more backward than 1917 Russia that Lenin's and Trotsky's strategy of permanent revolution could not apply in China. Instead, the Stalin-Bukharin leadership maintained for China's revolutionaries a strict demarcation between the bourgeois-democratic and the proletarian-socialist revolutions; there would be no telescoping of revolutionary stages in China as there had been in Russia. To be sure, Mao paid lip-service to the two-stage Stalinist strategy. But, relatively insulated from Comintern pressures deep in China's hinterland, in "On New Democracy," penned in 1940 to consolidate his position as the party's theoretical leader, Mao outlined a radical new program to prepare for socialist revolution in the bourgeois-national revolutionary stage.

The CCP's material and psychological dependency on the Comintern leadership made the emergence of this reformulation of Marxism-Leninism a long and tortuous process. From the very outset of the collaboration between the Comintern and China's Marxists, there had been a major discrepancy between Soviet expectations for revolution in China and those of CCP leaders. The Leninist conception that inspired the Comintern's united front strategy for China placed the Chinese revolution in the category of a bourgeois-democratic revolution focused on the consolidation of a national state, led by the national bourgeoisie, and directed against Western imperialism. If Lenin had envisaged a proletarian socialist revolution in China, it was to be far into the future. Lenin's hope was that nationalist resistance to imperialism in the East would promote economic crisis and proletarian revolutions in the West. Lenin and his successors were less, if at all, concerned to realize proletarian socialism in the colonial and semicolonial nations of the East, whose proletariats were negligible. In short, although Lenin's united front strategy was a response to twentieth-century events around him—and specifically to the failure of a socialist revolution to materialize in Germany—his instrumentalist treatment of the East echoed Marx's nineteenth-century estimation of the East as fundamentally backward. Nevertheless, in his desperation to achieve international support for his new "proletarian" state, Lenin adopted a much more positive assessment of the future potential of the East. It was this optimism that drew nationalist Chinese intellectuals to Marxism in the form of Marxism-Leninism.

Needless to say, Marx's bald apology for British imperialism in the East as the hope of worldwide social revolution could scarcely have appealed to Chinese intellectuals enveloped in the nationalist fervor of the May Fourth movement. Li Dazhao had been much more impressed by Marx's subsequent, fleetingly more sanguine articles suggesting that the Taiping rebellion would bring revolution to fruition in China, ending its long-standing stagnation, thrusting it into modernity, and enabling its people to cast off the yoke of imperialism. It was this anti-imperialist imagery, which Lenin reinforced, that drew Li to Marxism. In 1922, Li wrote excitedly of China's new prospects:

> Among the classes it is the proletariat that suffers from the oppression of capitalism, and internationally it is the weak peoples. In the past century, the Chinese people have been trampled under the iron hoofs of the armed aggressive imperialism of the mature capitalist states, and thus have sunk to a weak and defeated position. We laboring masses, suffering under manifold oppression, suddenly heard the October Revolution's call to "overthrow world capitalism," "overthrow world imperialism"; such a sound in our ears was exceptionally weighty, exceptionally momentous, exceptionally significant. . . . [Because of] the October Revolution, which has such great historical significance, . . . all peoples of oppressed nation-states like China should become deeply conscious of their own responsibilities, and should hasten without hesitation to ally [in] a "democratic united front," establish a people's government, and resist international capitalism—this must be counted as part of the world revolution.[32]

With his imagery of China as a proletarian nation vis-à-vis the imperialist capitalist countries, Li envisaged that China too would achieve a Marxian socialist revolution.

Yet Marx and Lenin had spoken not of the achievement of proletarian socialism in China but of a nationalist revolution that would allow China to attain bourgeois democracy under Western-style capitalism. Their view of "oriental" societies as backward and stagnant prohibited both Marx and Lenin from expecting of Asia the same economic and political developments experienced in the West. When Marx wrote of "'the effect the Chinese revolution seems likely to exercise upon the civilized world',"[33] he was borrowing the Hegelian interpretation of world history that juxtaposed the once great and now defunct "Orient" with the "civilized" world of Western Europe. In his analysis, *The Development of Capitalism in Russia*, Lenin felt compelled to demonstrate that Russia had been sufficiently Westernized to follow the West European path of development despite the onus of *Asiatic* features that had seemed likely to doom Russia to permanent stagnancy.[34]

Lenin's limited expectations for a bourgeois-democratic revolution in China governed Comintern policies in China from 1921 to 1931. This brought the founders of the CCP, who aspired to a socialist revolution, into conflict with the international organization at the outset. As Maurice Meisner has pointed out, "on one point both Li and Ch'en were agreed—China would follow a noncapitalist path to socialism. In 1921 in discussing the question of how China was to be industrialized, the two founding fathers of the [CCP] . . . had both explicitly denied the necessity of a capitalist phase of development. Neither spoke of even the possibility of an intervening bourgeois-democratic revolution for both in their different ways anticipated a direct and rapid transition to socialism."[35] Here, Chen and Li sought to avoid what they saw as the costs of capitalist industrialization in the West, although their acceptance of the Marxian periodization would seem to suggest that they might have been repudiating political democratization—also the task of the bourgeoisie in Marx's paradigm—as well as the institution of private property in the means of production. Nevertheless, in 1922, the Comintern destroyed Chen's and Li's hopes for a rapid transition to socialism when it supported Sun Yat-sen's Guomindang as the bourgeois-led party to be the vanguard of China's national revolution. Within two years, these contacts culminated in the subordination of the fledgling CCP to Sun's party. In China, "where there was no labour movement of any size or significance to which overtures for a united front could be made," Comintern leaders were convinced "that the KMT [Guomindang] was not primarily a class party, but a party of all anti-imperialist groups and classes."[36] All aspirations to mobilize a radical mass-based labor and peasant movement, a task at which the CCP had already become quite adept by the birth of the First United Front in 1924, were to be quashed lest the broad anti-imperialist national front led by the Guomindang be disrupted. This policy of restraint remained the keynote of the Comintern policy of the "bloc within" for the CCP through the 1927 Shanghai Coup.[37]

The Comintern was hampered by the rigidity of its application of Marx's historical schema to China. This inflexibility and its detriment to the CCP were revealed fully throughout the Comintern's close supervision of the Chinese revolution. There were, of course, considerations of Realpolitik that moved Stalin to ally with the Guomindang: he wanted to back the party most likely to emerge victorious so that he could control events in China.[38] Just as important, however, were the doctrinal concerns set out previously. A socialist revolution was to be executed under "proletarian hegemony," and because China had but a tiny working class, a socialist revolution was impossible. Instead, despite indications that the Guomindang, increasingly dominated by Chiang Kai-shek, was closely tied to the old land-based gentry and the mores of warlord politics, the Comintern insisted on seeing it as a genuine "national bourgeoisie,"[39] with disastrous results. When the united front collapsed with open and violent conflict between the Guomindang and the CCP, the Comintern steadfastly maintained a policy of "adventurist" urban uprisings under Li Lisan even while the proletariat was still tiny and urban centers were policed by the armed Guomindang.[40] Not surprisingly, the Comintern's call for urban rather than rural soviets resulted in the tragic Canton Commune and a succession of other dismal losses.[41]

Despite their divergence from the Comintern in aspiring to immediate socialist revolution, Chen and Li were also bound by a very literal interpretation of Marx. Their quest for socialism was, like that of the Comintern, premised on "proletarian hegemony" in a society with no highly developed and cohesive proletariat. Chen denied a leading role in the revolution to China's peasantry, and although Li was enthusiastic about peasant revolution, he felt that he needed to stress China's proletarian international status to legitimate the CCP's socialist revolution.[42] Both Chen *and* Li were Trotskyist in a sense:[43] Both envisaged the kind of uninterrupted or permanent revolution that Russia had experienced as desribed by Trotsky in 1905,[44] yet both were also bound by Trotsky's own rigidities about Marxism. Trotsky's interpretation of the Russian revolution (which Lenin later adopted) implied precisely what Li and Chen desired—an immediate progression to socialist revolution, avoiding a long period of the maturation of capitalism and its attendant evils. Trotsky's and Lenin's prescription for Russia also addressed Chen's and Li's disillusionment with the model offered by the Western powers in the wake of the Versailles treaty: The appalling conduct of the Western powers called into question for them the desirability of institutions and guarantees associated with what Lenin disparaged as the fundamentally flawed and fraudulent parliamentarism of "bourgeois democracy."[45] Yet Trotsky, like Lenin, had remained wedded to the notion that socialist revolution could occur only in urban centers under proletarian leadership. Trotsky's "theory of uneven development" allowed the possibility of permanent revolution even where the proletariat was tiny and weak. But his argument was that the importation of foreign technologies and the growth of capitalism under state sponsorship had promoted disproportionate strength in the proletariat so that the bourgeoise remained weak, undeveloped, and unable to crush the proletariat's revolutionary impulse. Thus, the Trotskyist/Leninist revolutionary scenario was also premised on urban insurrection. Even if it had not been executed in the same flawed manner as was the Comintern's so-called Li Lisan Line, its call for the formation of urban soviets seemed equally doomed to failure by the military power of the Guomindang and warlords.[46]

China's Trotskyists have consistently condemned Mao's pre-1949 revolutionary peasant-centered rural strategy as essentially petty-bourgeois, as a "Stalinist challenge to the permanent revolution" of Trotsky.[47] Yet Mao's strategy—in practice if not always in theory—shared much with that of Trotsky in that it repudiated the strictures of what the Comintern claimed was Marxist-Leninist orthodoxy. After Chen Duxiu's ignominious expulsion from the CCP as a Trotskyist, Mao was always careful in his writings not to allow himself to be associated with "Trotskyism." Thus, in "On New Democracy," Mao spoke scrupulously in terms of the Stalinist "stages" that figured so prominently in the Comintern's restriction of China to bourgeois-democratic revolution. Examined closely, however, the substance of Mao's argument indicated clearly that his strategy was one of continuous or permanent revolution. Mao stressed the critical differences between "old bourgeois democracy" and the "new democracy" made possible by the changed international environment occasioned by the outbreak of World War I and the October Revolution. As had his mentor Li two decades earlier, Mao strongly emphasized that China's revolution would follow in the footsteps of Russia's; regardless of China's economic "backwardness" relative to the West, its path to socialism would not embrace the institutions of the bourgeois stage, wait for decades or centuries for the maturation of capitalism and the rule of "old" bourgeois democracy, and then proceed to the revolution culminating in the dictatorship of the proletariat.

> Although the Chinese revolution in this first stage (with its many sub-stages) is a new type of bourgeois-democratic revolution and is not yet itself a proletarian-socialist revolution in its social character, it has long become a part of the proletarian-socialist world revolution and is now even a very important part and a great ally of this world revolution. The first step or stage in our revolution is definitely not, and cannot be, the establishment of a capitalist society under the dictatorship of the Chinese bourgeoisie, but will result in the establishment of a new-democratic society under the joint dictatorship of all the revolutionary classes of China headed by the Chinese proletariat. The revolution will then be carried forward to the second stage, in which a socialist society will be established in China.[48]

Here Mao rebelled against Trotskyist as well as Comintern interpretations of the appropriate revolutionary strategy for China in two ways. First, there was a powerful populist current in Mao's thought that took Lenin's notion of a smychka between proletariat and peasantry[49] a step further. Recognizing that the peasantry would remain a major political force in China for some time, Mao abandoned Marx's and Lenin's misgivings about the potential of the peasantry to play a leading role in socialist revolution, and, repudiating the importance of the cities[50] and omitting the "temporary" element from Lenin's provisional alliance between the proletariat and the (to Lenin, unalterably "petty bourgeois") peasantry, Mao erased any firm demarcation between the bourgeois-democratic and the socialist stages of revolution as it concerned the role of the peasantry. Secondly, Mao did essentially the same for the role of nationalist sentiment by permitting the marriage between nationalism and *socialist* revolution that the Comintern's united front strategy denied. As a result, by a curious twist, Mao reconciled what was in conflict elsewhere in the international socialist movement. In the Soviet Union, the slogan "socialism in one country" served as Stalin's tool with which to repudiate Trotsky for his internationalism, for his permanent revolution thesis, and for other notions associated with him. By contrast, under Mao's leadership, "socialism in one country" and "permanent revolution" came to be conjoined in the CCP's nationalistic quest for "new democracy" leading directly into socialist revolution.

The Populist Current: Marxist Revolution on a Peasant Base

Initially, Mao undertook this melding of nationalism with socialism from a perspective that took issue with orthodox Marxism-Leninism. Having participated in Marxist study groups in Beijing, Mao retreated to his native countryside in 1925 to seek repose from his conflicts with Party Central. By this time, Peng Pai, a CCP member from a landlord family, had already achieved considerable success in organizing the peasantry in part of Guangdong Province. This Peng accomplished, although in deference to the views of then CCP leader Chen he had deprecated any role for the peasantry more expansive than its collaboration in subordination to the proletariat. Returning to his native Hunan, Mao discovered considerable agitation among the peasants partly in response to the antiforeign May Thirtieth movement, which the CCP had helped to organize. As he related to Edgar Snow, " 'Formerly I had not fully realized the degree of class struggle among the peasantry, but after the May 30th Incident . . . and during the great wave of political activity which followed it, the Hunanese peasantry became very militant. I left my home, where I had been resting, and began a rural organizational campaign'."[51]

The written product of these efforts was Mao's "Report on an Investigation of the Peasant Movement in Hunan," published in March 1927 in *Xiangdao zhoubao* (Guide weekly). The article made almost no immediate impact on CCP strategy, but it was the point of departure for the development of Mao's thought on the role of the peasantry in the Chinese revolution. As Schwartz has noted, the document "is almost completely bare of Marxist trappings."[52] Unlike the uninspired "Analysis of the Classes in Chinese Society," penned one year earlier, the report was a highly emotional piece, written out of intense hostility to foreign and internal oppression and the excitement Mao felt when he discovered in his native province political fervor that had been absent among the peasantry since the May Fourth movement. Writing authoritatively on the basis of his direct extended experience,[53] Mao concluded that the peasantry would be the main force in China's revolution. Comparing the relative importance of city and countryside in China, Mao now stood much closer to the Russian narodnik (populist) tradition than to the urban orientation of orthodox Marxism-Leninism. "If we were to compute the relative accomplishments of various elements in the democratic revolution on a percentage basis, the urban dwellers and military would not rate more than thirty percent, while the remaining seventy percent would have to be allotted to the accomplishments of the peasants in the countryside," he declared.[54]

Here, Mao shared with the Paris and Tokyo Chinese anarchists an important populist theme as he envisioned the historic Confucian utopia of datong[55] in terms of a rural society unblemished by what he viewed as the repressive institutions of property.[56] Nevertheless, Mao's posture on China's rural past was highly problematic. Unlike Russia's narodniks, he was not devising a peasant-based revolutionary strategy that sought to build socialism on the basis of old indigenous institutions such as the peasant commune (mir, or obschina) but one that would destroy such traditional institutions as the family, which he, like many radical Chinese of his generation, viewed as oppressive.[57] How could his organizing of peasant discontent mobilize the overthrow of traditional society when previous successful peasant rebellions had achieved virtue by reestablishing age-old virtuous systems of rule? Here Mao's Marxism collided directly with his populist identification with the "real," rural China. As a Marxist, Mao appeared to accept both industrialization as China's fate and the Western Enlightenment view that was its premise, one that envisioned humankind seeking to conquer nature. Mao's emphasis on the role of consciousness in enabling Chinese to prevail over limitations apparently imposed by nature—as reflected in his advocacy of a leading revolutionary role for China's peasantry as well as in his celebration of voluntarism, "The Foolish Old Man Who Removed the Mountains," in 1945 and again during the Great Leap Forward[58]—eschewed the traditional Confucian perspective that stressed harmony between humanity and nature.[59] At the same time, however, Mao harkened back to a traditional antiurban impulse, one which saw cities as pernicious areas "where man disregarded nature, truth was clouded [and virtue] weakened."[60] Whereas the Russian narodniki had felt compelled to go into the countryside to raise revolutionary consciousness where none existed, Mao responded to what he believed to be an overwhelming torrent of energy arising from the peasants themselves. This energy needed only to be organized and directed, not created. The peasants, especially the poorest among them, were a tide that would sweep aside even the CCP, unless the party allied with them. What would be the party's response? "There are three alternatives," Mao contended. "To march at their head and lead them? To trail behind them, gesticulating and criticizing? Or to stand in their way and oppose them? Every Chinese is free to choose, but events will force you to make the choice quickly."[61] Lenin had believed the peasants' perspective to be limited to their own small world of the mir (in Russian, *mir* means both "world" and "peace" and refers to the traditional commune), and allowed them to be organized successfully by the Social Revolutionaries (SRs). By contrast, given the spirited response to the nationalistic May Thirtieth movement in China's countryside, Mao attributed to the peasant the ability to act in larger, national interests. Here Mao was inspired by the enthusiast's understanding of the historic role of peasant uprisings in bringing down defunct Chinese dynasties and installing their successors.[62] He would draw further on this faith that the peasant could act on behalf of the larger national community throughout the Yan'an period, when the CCP organized peasants to resist Japan, and after 1949 when he mobilized them to fulfill his goals for China.

Mao was not the first Chinese Marxist to appreciate the significance of the peasantry to China's future. Li, who influenced Mao heavily on the issue,[63] wrote consistently on the centrality of the countryside to China's national regeneration. In 1919, Li had called upon Chinese youth to go to the villages and work alongside the peasants, helping them to better their lot and to govern themselves while learning from them as well.[64] In late 1925 and 1926, after becoming disaffected with conservative tendencies in the Guomindang, Li was removed from a leading position by the Guomindang's Central Executive Committee. Increasingly concerned about the isolation of revolutionary intellectuals from the mass peasant base, Li once again stressed the central role of the peasantry in the revolution. "'In economically backward and semi-colonial China," Li wrote, "the peasantry constitutes more than seventy per cent of the population; among the whole population they occupy the principal position, and agriculture is still the basis of the national economy. Therefore, when we estimate the forces of the revolution, we must emphasize that the peasantry is the important part'."[65] As Mao would do later, Li drew on China's rich folklore of peasant uprisings bringing about dynastic change, but he was also influenced by Peter Kropotkin's stress on the spontaneous impulse of the peasantry toward cooperation. Li deeply admired the peasantry's spontaneous organizational endeavors, but, like Russia's narodniki, he was also convinced that if they were to fulfill their role in the national revolution, they needed an intellectual vanguard from outside the village to heighten peasant consciousness and direct peasant energies.

The voluntarism in this emphasis on the need for revolutionary consciousness also subsequently emerged in the thought of Mao.[66] Although Li echoed orthodox Marxism-Leninism's stress on "proletarianism," he stressed this in China's international rather than in its domestic environment. Indeed, he approached Mao's eventual position when he argued that China's peasant masses were no impediment to socialist revolution. Li and Mao both argued—in a manner consonant with the Confucian faith in the need for continual self-cultivation (*xiuyang*)[67]—that one could attain socialist revolutionary consciousness without necessarily being a proletarian in China's domestic context. If being determined consciousness, as Marx had claimed, consciousness could also determine being. This voluntarism became the key to the first step in Mao's approach to the national question—his confrontation with the fact that China's national characteristics did not fit the universal criteria for Marx's socialist revolution.[68] Mao's combination of populist faith in China's vast peasantry to possess the revolutionary consciousness to play a leading role in social revolution cum national liberation in the Sino-Japanese War would enable this fusion of anti-imperialist nationalism with the opening of the path to socialist revolution in wartime China.

Having asserted the compatibility of Marxian socialism with Chinese nationalism, however, it was less clear how in practice the two orientations would be reconciled. Marxism posited that human history progressed within individual national societies by means of class struggle. This thesis would seem to conflict with the need to temper class conflict in order to project the national unity of the Second United Front between the Guomindang and CCP directed against Japanese aggression. On the other hand, nationalism and socialism were compatible in that they shared an appreciation of community—in the case of the CCP, class-based community achieved through individualization as other bases of community, such as the family, were repudiated—and both required a high degree of consciousness of the positive attributes of that community and its objectives. As a proud Chinese revolutionary leader insistent on the possibility of achieving socialism as well as national independence for China in the short term, Mao perceived a major challenge in the national question. There was a need to reconcile those aspects of the Marxian quest for socialism—particularly the notion of class struggle between peasant and landlord, proletarian and bourgeois—that needed to be present for the longer-range goal with the shorter-range imperative of maintaining national unity for the task of nation- and state-building that was the prerequisite of socialist revolution in China.

Characteristically, of course, Mao insisted that there was no conflict between Chinese nationalism and the quest for internationalist socialism. "In wars of national liberation patriotism is applied internationalism," he claimed.[69] Nevertheless, just as there were tensions in Mao's effort to advocate "permanent revolution" without provoking denunciations of "Trotskyism," the "contradictions," to borrow one of Mao's favorite expressions, inherent in his endeavor were evident in his own pronouncements during the Sino-Japanese War:

We are exponents of the theory of the transition of the revolution ["and not of the Trotskyite theory of 'permanent revolution'"] and we are for the transition of the democratic revolution in the direction of socialism. The democratic revolution will develop through several stages, all under the slogan of a democratic republic. The change from the predominance of the bourgeoisie to that of the proletariat is a long process of struggle, of struggle for leadership in which success depends on the work of the Communist Party in raising the level of political consciousness and organization both of the proletariat and of the peasantry and the urban petty bourgeoisie.[70]

Although Mao successfully avoided any association with Trotsky, his adoption of the Bolshevik strategy of continuous or permanent revolution for China ratified Mao's stress on the significance of the role of China's peasantry in a revolution that would be both nationalist and socialist. Where Lenin and his successors had limited the revolutionary role of the peasantry to a temporary expedient in the first, bourgeois-democratic, stage of the Russian revolution, however, Mao recognized that China's socialist revolution could not be waged without them. The slogan of mass democracy—although it would always be limited by the primacy of the party and its supreme leader—Mao saw as the CCP's primary tool in forging effective resistance to Japan and achieving revolutionary victory over the Guomindang. Such an invocation of democracy would have been meaningless if it excluded the peasantry, some 80 percent of China's population, from an active role in preparing the stage for socialist revolution. During the Yan'an period, in his "On New Democracy," Mao proclaimed both the orthodoxy and the originality of his vision. Mao declared that the new international circumstances of the twentieth century enabled China's revolution to repudiate bourgeois democracy and assume its "new democratic" character embracing nationalistic peasants in social revolution.[71] Nevertheless, the project of the new democratic revolution also entailed the creation of a new, effective Chinese national state, which brought up the second, statist, aspect of the national question. During the Yan'an period, state building from the bottom up was accepted as a necessary measure for China's revolutionary peasants to counter effectively the rule of the Guomindang, warlords, and Japanese invaders.

The Sino-Japanese conflict was not the first occasion on which national sentiment was aroused among Chinese peasants; the May Thirtieth movement had been one such earlier occasion, impelling peasants in Mao's own home province to express the antiforeign sentiment that so inspired Mao about the revolutionary potential of the peasantry. This sentiment had its positive as well as negative aspects. As Chalmers Johnson has pointed out, "During the war, the peasants began to hear and use such terms as *han-chien* (Chinese traitor), *wei-chün* (bogus army, i.e., the puppet forces), *wan-chün* (reactionary army, i.e., the KMT forces as seen by Yenan), and *Rih-kou* (Japanese bandits). The intrusion of these terms into the peasants' vocabulary signified the spread of a force that hitherto was prevalent only among the intelligentsia and city-bred people—namely, nationalism."[72] With this consciousness of the enemy came also a new consciousness of "China" and of "Chinese nationality." Even if, as Mark Selden has noted, "it was not nationalistic rhetoric but agrarian revolution . . . that initially won widespread support and paved the way for the increasingly effective military and political participation of the rural population" in the CCP base areas,[73] nationalism played a vital role in mobilizing support for the antiwar resistance and the campaign for democracy and then socialism waged by the CCP. The invocation of the broad notion of the "people," incorporating peasants into the national struggle for socialism, however, also provided a virulent weapon with which to assail those who had arisen from the wrong class or exhibited behavior that was not in solidarity with what was determined to be appropriate by the party and its leadership.

The key point here is that as Mao understood it, the mobilization of China's peasant masses for nationalist and ultimately socialist ends required "democracy" on a mass scale such as Chinese had never before experienced. In both Mao's thought and CCP practice, this "democracy" meant mass participation, mass mobilization for ends defined by and under the leadership of the party. The multiplicity of challenges to CCP power forced the party to recognize that, as Foucault has argued, "power relations are rooted deep in the social nexus, not reconstituted 'above society' "; power exists in all social relations.[74] Thus, effective mass mobilization meant the penetration of the power of CCP leadership to the very bases of Chinese society. This realization bore important implications for the role of "stateness" in the Chinese revolution. Without stateness—effective control over territory, the availability of potent military force, and the ability to invoke and implement sanctions against those who would violate the law—China's masses would have no effective national unit within which to build socialism. Thus, for the first time, Chinese living in the CCP's base areas would have a state whose power would extend to the lowest levels of Chinese society. Along with the abatement of class struggle during the resistance effort,[75] the Maoist vision of "new democracy," then, laid the groundwork for a revolutionary socialist party-state, one that would be strengthened rather than wither away after the revolution as the original Marxist formula envisioned.

MARXISM AND STATENESS: "SOCIALISM IN ONE COUNTRY"

The Quest for Stateness versus Stateless Communism

The question then arises: what transformation will the state undergo in communist society? In other words, what social functions will remain in existence there that are analogous to present functions of the state? This question can only be answered scientifically, and one does not get a flea-hop nearer to the problem by a thousand-fold combination of the word people with the word state.

Between capitalist and communist societies lies the period of the revolutionary transformation of the one into the other. There corresponds to this also a political transformation period in which the state can be nothing but *the revolutionary dictatorship of the proletariat.*[76]

Mao's coupling of nationalism and populism with the determination to build "socialism in one country" bore serious implications for the question of the role of the state during and after China's revolution. Mao repeatedly stressed that "[t]he

Chinese revolution has become a very important part of the world revolution," and in that sense, his Marxism was internationalist. Nevertheless, his emphasis on the need to appreciate China's peculiar characteristics through praxis demonstrated that the framework within which he aspired to build socialism was not merely an international community vaguely defined, but China, a nation with a distinguished two-thousand-year history. Mao appealed openly to Chinese national pride when he explained why "New Democracy" and socialist revolution would be required in China instead of the "old democracy" that had flourished historically in capitalist societies. "[T]he history of modern China is a history of imperialist aggression, of imperialist opposition to China's independence and to her development of capitalism. Earlier revolutions failed in China because imperialism strangled them, and innumerable revolutionary martyrs died, bitterly lamenting the non-fulfillment of their mission."[77] If the Chinese people, as a nation, were now to resist foreign encroachment and achieve socialism in their own homeland, they would require a state powerful enough to defend them and take the lead in providing the industrial prerequisites for socialism. Much of what Mao wrote in "On New Democracy," then, was devoted to describing the politics and economics of this new state. The difficulty was that the essence of this "new democratic" state lay in its mission to prepare the way to socialism and communism, to a society in which, in Marx's formulation, classes would disappear and the state itself would become superfluous. Even if the Chinese revolution in the 1930s and 1940s was in an earlier stage than Russia's October Revolution, the problem of revolutionary statebuilding was essentially the same in the parts of China under CCP control as it had been for the Bolsheviks: How was one to build a state the ultimate purpose of which was to prepare the groundwork for its own demise?

Despite this fundamental similarity between the Russian and Chinese revolutions, in 1930s and 1940s China, the issue of the nature of the state during and after the revolution was much more complex. It was not merely a matter of the dictatorship of the proletariat and the transition to stateless communism. Two factors, both of which issued from China's underdevelopment relative to the experiences of Russia and Western Europe, complicated matters for China's Marxist revolutionaries. First, building state power where no effective state power existed would mark the achievement of a primary aspect of the bourgeois-democratic revolution. Second, although Marx's schema of proletarian socialist revolution envisaged that a postrevolutionary state would exist for a short period primarily to eliminate counterrevolutionary class forces, the perceived need to give the state greater economic and political powers to accomplish the economic development that the immature bourgeoisie had left undone came into direct conflict with the Marxist assumption that a transitional state with little to do but suppress the bourgeoisie could easily wither away. Mao's treatment of this and related problems exposed major weaknesses in Marx's and Engels's initial conceptualization of the dictatorship of the proletariat and the withering away of the state. It also helped to explain the highly bureaucratic and brutal Stalinist outcome in the Soviet Union that Mao was loathe to acknowledge before the world's two great socialist powers came into conflict in the late-1950s.

Marx had asserted emphatically the need for the "revolutionary dictatorship of the proletariat" after a socialist revolution, but this was not the brutal state machinery that Stalin created. Unfortunately, however, Marx wrote very little on the transitional state. Much of what he did write, like the passage from the "Critique of the Gotha Program" cited here, did little more than highlight the difficulties intrinsic to the notion of a transitional revolutionary state. Marx did comment at length on the Paris Commune (1871), which Engels would later remark "was the Dictatorship of the Proletariat," but two decades after the commune, Engels even more strongly than Marx stressed the dangers inherent in the use of a conspiratorial vanguard party to govern the revolutionary regime such as the Blanquists had formed in the commune, and Marx directly attacked the Blanquists. Blanqui was arrested just before the proclamation of the commune, which threw off "the opposing power of the former centralized government, army, political police, bureaucracy, which Napoleon had created in 1798 and which since then had been taken over by every new government as a welcome instrument and used against its opponents." The commune recognized the need to abolish the old state: "[T]he working class, once come to power, could not go on managing with the old state machine." In short, the commune exposed fully what was unacceptable about the old state: "What had been the characteristic attribute of the former state? Society had created its own organs to look after its common interests, originally through simple division of labour. But these organs, at whose head was the state power, had in the course of time, in pursuance of their own special interests, transformed themselves from the servants of society into the masters of society."[78]

This observation on the French ancien régime raised more questions than it answered concerning the nature of the transitional revolutionary state power. What would guarantee that the new postrevolutionary state power, which would be like the former state in its exercise of class dictatorship, would not itself assume a life of its own? Marx's response included universal suffrage and elections of officials subject to recall,[79] but what would become of the powers turned over to the military and the police in the name of suppressing the opposition of the formerly dominating class? Engels's writings describing the transition to communism exposed fully the contradictions between the espousal of the dictatorship of the proletariat and the claim that the state would ultimately wither away. At the highest point of the development of capitalism, Engels claimed, crises became so profound that "the official representative of capitalist society, the state, is constrained to take over their management." At this stage, the "capitalist relationship" between bourgeois and proletarians "is not abolished; it is rather pushed to an extreme." "But at this extreme," Engels continued, "it is transformed into its opposite. State ownership of the productive forces is not the solution of the conflict, but it contains within itself the formal means, the key to the solution." The solution itself lay in "society . . . taking possession of the productive forces which have outgrown all control other than that of society itself." Marx was silent as to how this would occur, but Engels advocated that the victorious proletariat, now in possession of state power, appropriate the means of production and "transform [them] into state property." Clearly, if the state were going to hold these means of production, it would have to manage them. Yet it remained unclear in both Marx's and Engels's writings by what organizational means society would take and exercise power over these means of production without constructing a fatally flawed state of the same ilk as the prerevolutionary state. Furthermore, as the Russian revolution demonstrated, the mere "administration of things and the direction of the processes of production" would not be an insignificant but a weighty and challenging responsibility that would require the expertise of individuals highly trained in carrying out industrial production on a mass scale. This consideration would certainly appear all the more compelling the more technologically advanced an industrial (or postindustrial) a society might be. Nevertheless, the reliance in less-industrialized China and Soviet Russia on state power to push further ahead the technological level of their societies—the forces of production—in order to establish the minimum economic conditions to provide plenty for all in an egalitarian society compelled Marxist leaders in their societies to confront this same problem in a slightly different form. Mao's treatment of political authority and the problem of bureaucracy as discussed later accentuates the weaknesses of Marx's and Engels's formulation concerning the end of the state. In light of the concrete challenges of directing production in a technologically advanced industrial society or guiding a less-industrialized society to such a higher technical level, the logic of the orthodox argument as formulated by Engels seems mere sophistry.

> The first act in which the state really comes forward as the representative of society as a whole—the taking possession of the means of production in the name of society—is at the same time its last independent act as a state. . . . [I]n doing this, [the proletariat] puts an end to itself as the proletariat, it puts an end to all class differences and class antagonisms, it puts an end also to the state as the state. . . . When ultimately it becomes really representative of society as a whole, it makes itself superfluous. As soon as there is no longer any class of society to be held in subjection, . . . there is nothing more to be repressed which would make a special repressive force, a state, necessary. . . . The state is not "abolished," *it withers away*.[80]

Yet, despite the way that the terms *class*, *state*, and *administration* were manipulated in these passages, they did not resolve the concrete difficulties the CPSU and the CCP confronted concerning the utility and the fate of state power during and after the revolution.

The leadership of an elite Leninist vanguard party, with so many of the traits to which Marx had objected in the Blanquists, made these issues still more pressing a half-century later in China. Marx and Engels had repudiated the revolutionary party's assumption of the instruments of the former state in the Paris Commune. There, in the terms of their schema, human socioeconomic and political development had been at the forefront of world history in an advanced capitalist West European society. The conditions of a twentieth-century Asian society like China, victimized by foreign encroachment and still predominantly an agrarian society where industrialization was minimal, were quite different. For the CCP, many issues concerning the revolutionary state resulting from such circumstances had already become manifest in the Bolshevik experience. After the October Revolution, Lenin's new regime immediately perceived a need to build a powerful state to defend the fragile revolution from the hostile capitalist powers that intervened in support of White Russian resistance. Lenin had stressed the need to smash completely the existing state power in *The State and Revolution* just months before the October Revolution.[81] Nevertheless, although the Bolsheviks had claimed, against the old regime, that the workers themselves would be able to handle all necessary political and economic managerial tasks, they soon felt themselves compelled to borrow the apparatus of the old tsarist state, even the much reviled bureaucracy, to survive internal and external threat. Where the vast majority of the population was illiterate and untrained in essential skills, what was left of the former tsarist elite became managers of the factories, served as officers in the army, and assumed official positions in the bureaucracy under the Bolsheviks.[82] Moreover, as a later-industrializing society that had not developed industrial capitalism to a great extent before its socialist revolution, Russia required a powerful state not only to defend the revolution against hostile advanced industrialized powers in the West but also to assume positive economic functions, well beyond the minimum necessity of repressing hostile class forces. The new Soviet state could not merely ease the transition from bourgeois to socialist society by repressing the bourgeoisie but would first have to finish doing what the bourgeoisie had been unable to do: create a highly industrialized society that could meet the basic needs of a hungry population and provide the infrastructure for a unified national economy. As a result, during the first decade after the revolution, unexpectedly bereft of Lenin's charismatic leadership in 1922, the Bolsheviks debated intensely how the new regime could accomplish these more ambitious tasks without betraying the socialist ideal of a state that would quickly wither away.[83] What was not central to this debate, although it was subsequently treated separately by Nikolai Bukharin and Leon Trotsky, was an important underlying theme: What would be the implications for the "withering away of the state" of a powerful interventionist "dictatorship of the proletariat" endeavoring to effect an economic "revolution from above" that was far more extensive than anything Marx had imagined? Following on the heels of the revolutions of 1905 and 1917, Stalin's Third Revolution—forced collectivization, rapid industrialization, and the Great Purges from 1929 through 1938—marked the apex of the aggrandization of the new state power.[84] The disillusioned old Bolsheviks Bukharin and Trotsky, themselves victimized by the new state, lamented the betrayal of the revolution in the creation of a new privileged bureaucratic class.[85]

There were good reasons that this problem should have aroused more concern among Chinese Marxists at an early stage of the revolution than it had among the Bolsheviks. First, although the peasantry also comprised 80 percent of its population, prerevolutionary Russia had undergone sufficient industrialization to permit the Bolsheviks to ride to power on the basis of a much larger core of urban support by workers and soldiers. This factor—the fact that Russian society was imbued with more of the characteristics of the industrial modernity of Marx's paradigm—gave the Bolsheviks greater reason to be sanguine about their ability to achieve stateless communism after the revolution. Second, opposition to the tsarist regime's disastrous participation in World War I had mobilized mass support for the Bolsheviks. Although Russia experienced considerable foreign ownership in its industrial sector, Russia itself had not been victimized by foreign encroachment as had China for a century. The search for a formula to "save China" from such encroachment helped to make the nationalistic quest for "stateness" a very large part of the Chinese revolution, particularly during the Sino-Japanese War. More-over, Chinese society, lacking even the Bolsheviks' industrial proletarian base, demanded an even greater role for the state in promoting a level of industrialization that could presumably bring an end to the long-standing cycles of famine and flood among China's vast and rapidly increasing population. Finally, even as late as 1949, when the CCP established its own state power nationwide, there was no evidence that twentieth-century international conditions requiring a powerful de-fensive state would change significantly. Socialist revolution had begun to show signs of spreading, but it was not likely to conquer the advanced capitalist nation-states of Europe and North America that had so threatened China in the past. As the Korean War would demonstrate just two years after the CCP's conquest of state power, such international circumstances threatened to make it necessary to justify the permanent existence of a "transitional" state as the party endeavored to build "socialism in one country." Finally, as the Shanghai Coup in 1927 had already demonstrated, there were limits to the reliability of Soviet pledges to protect China. Because Lenin's formula for national liberation movements acknowledged that nationalism was acceptable as long as it was revolutionary, could not both the Soviet Union and a new Chinese socialist state continue to justify separate nation-alisms at the expense of Marxian internationalism? Japanese Marxist Takabatake, suspicious of Soviet designs in the Far East shortly after 1917, had even suggested the possibility of "proletarian imperialism." In Takabatake's view, imperialism did not derive from impulses solely characteristic of capitalist states, as Lenin's theory suggested, but arose out of a militaristic nationalism that could characterize any national state, whether "bourgeois" or "proletarian."[86] Such a prospect must have been even more threatening to leaders of the much more vulnerable and impotent China.

Ideology and Consciousness: Stateness and the Path to Stateless Communism in China

In the 1920s, 1930s, and 1940s, Mao's immediate concern was with survival—the survival of the party and the survival of his hard-won leadership within the party—and this meant state building in defense against the existing Japanese threat, although much of what Mao wrote on leadership during this period would subse-quently be applied to postrevolutionary circumstances as well. What is most remarkable about Mao's writings on these issues is his stress on the importance of ideological work. It will be recalled that Mao regarded the creation of nationalistic élan among his fellow citizens as one of the CCP's most urgent tasks. As the CCP successfully exploited such nationalism in areas it brought under its control during the war, the party needed to construct its own state within a state, so to speak. Mao argued that there were three forms of state: (1) the bourgeois state, "the old European-American form of capitalist republic under bourgeois dictatorship, which is the old democratic form and already out of date"; (2) "the socialist republic of the Soviet type under the dictatorship of the proletariat"; and (3) "a third form of state [that] must be adopted in the revolutions of all colonial and semi-colonial countries, namely, the new-democratic republic." With both old bourgeois democracy and proletarian socialism inappropriate for China's socio-economic conditions, Mao prescribed the creation of a "new democratic republic" in the liberated areas. Mao's "new democracy" was distinguished, theoretically, from old democracy in at least two respects. First, it was the laboring masses, including the peasantry (under the leadership of the proletariat) that exercised domination in the "new democracy." Second, and most importantly, the purpose of this "new democracy" was to lay the groundwork for a socialist revolution. Here Mao was emphatically not concerned with establishing a more vigorous capitalism or a democratic political system endowed with the accoutrements associated with "bourgeois democracy" in China. Rather, the new state, the new-democratic republic, would play a major role in encouraging what the CCP termed "cooperative" production and boosting the peasant economy. The new-democratic republic would "own the big banks and the big industrial and commercial enterprises," Mao wrote. Such "state enterprises will be of a socialist character and will constitute the leading force in the whole national economy," he claimed. In this transitional stage, "the republic [would] neither confiscate capitalist private property in general nor forbid the development of such capitalist production as does not 'dominate the livelihood of the people.' " Nevertheless, as Sun Yat-sen, Li Dazhao, and Chen Duxiu had before him, Mao vowed that "we must never establish a capitalist society of the European-American type or allow the old semi-feudal society to survive."[87]

For Mao, the struggle against capitalism and feudalism was as much a cultural struggle, an ideological struggle, as a battle in the realm of socioeconomic organization. In advocating socialist revolution in a China that had not yet freed itself from feudal institutions and had developed a badly crippled capitalist economy dominated by foreign powers, Mao asserted that intellectuals, peasants, and those of other class origins—including bourgeois and petty-bourgeois—were capable of attaining socialist revolutionary consciousness. Here, the whole notion of *class* became very fluid in Mao's thought. Distinctions among the various subaltern classes in Chinese society were attenuated by both Mao's resolve to build a socialism that could embrace the whole Chinese *nation*[88] and his uncoupling of objective class position from the capability to develop "proletarian", socialist consciousness. (The term *proletarian* thus came to be used almost synonymously with the notion of *socialist*.) Two key elements should be stressed here concerning the roles that class and nation played in Mao's thought in this New Democracy period. First, as the category of those who were engaged positively in the enterprise of building Chinese socialism was broadened, the animus against those who could not be trusted to give their full cooperation to this process was intensified. Secondly, by embracing the peasantry—historically viewed as the "real" China—

as a central force in this protosocialist category of the renmin (people), Mao was able to conflate the nationalist mission of saving China with building socialism in one country. Here in Mao the Chinese revolution as a nationalist movement nearly eclipsed socialist internationalism: Mao spoke of internationalism almost only in terms of Soviet support for socialist revolution in and beyond China.

Here, too, Mao's contribution to the Marxist discourse on the potential of the peasantry is not to be underestimated. To be sure, in accordance with Lenin's formulation of the notion of continuous revolution, Mao always insisted that although the peasantry might participate in the early stages of the revolution, it would do so only under the leadership of the Communist party acting, it claimed, in the interest of the proletariat that was alleged to be in the vanguard of the socialist revolution.[89] Mao, like Lenin, also saw the importance of the role of intellectuals in the Chinese revolution. "China's entire revolutionary movement originated from the initiative of young students and intellectuals who had been awakened," Mao declared on the twentieth anniversary of the May Fourth movement.[90] Intellectuals were capable, he maintained, of cultivating proletarian class consciousness and supporting the work of China's new democratic and then socialist revolution. In both cases, ideological consciousness was said to have some independence, or autonomy, from class origins.[91] Nevertheless, Mao diverged dramatically from Lenin in at least two respects. First, as a CCP leader who had not had the benefit of as much higher education in China and abroad as others in the party, Mao did not share Lenin's trust in and enthusiasm for the intelligentsia fully. Lenin regularly derided "petty-bourgeois" intellectuals, but as one of them, and particularly as one who shared family ties to the nineteenth-century intellectual narodnik movement,[92] he had great faith in their leadership of the revolutionary movement. "Without revolutionary theory there can be no revolutionary movement," Lenin declared. Russia's radical intelligentsia would bring this revolutionary theory and the revolutionary consciousness it nurtured to the masses. Endowed with a broad view of the production process and uninhibited by the worker's lack of time, perspective, and intellectual ability to view the process of production as a whole, intellectuals, Lenin argued, were the true purveyors of revolutionary proletarian consciousness. "[T]here can be no talk of an independent ideology formulated by the working masses themselves in the process of their movement."[93]

By contrast, Mao returned to Marx's pronouncement that consciousness emerged out of participation, or praxis, in the production process and in the revolution itself, and this Mao used to support his instinctive antipathy to China's intellectuals. Mao was suspicious of the enormous breach between mental and physical labor in traditional China. Thus, Mao qualified his praise of the role intellectuals played in China's revolution with the injunction that only if "the millions of students unite with the tens of millions of worker and peasant youth could China have a powerful youth movement."[94] "In the final analysis, the dividing line between revolutionary intellectuals and non-revolutionary or counterrevolutionary intellectuals is whether or not they are willing to integrate themselves with the workers and peasants and actually do so."[95] Exclusive attention to mental cultivation may have endowed traditional intellectuals with a profound understanding of the Confucian classics, but it alienated them from the real China, the China of the peasantry. After all, in Chinese folklore it had always been the peasantry whose rebellious instincts had revealed the lack of virtue in imperial rule and had brought about the transition from one dynasty to another. The heroes in this historical drama were always peasant heroes, and their contribution to the flow of Chinese history, as Mao saw it, was duly recorded in *Shuihuzhuan* (The water margin) and other historical novels and fables that Mao cited in support of his own revolutionary endeavors. This position bolstered Mao's increasing antipathy to those (intellectuals) whom he viewed as unable to appreciate his own contribution to China's revolution. Unlike Lenin, Mao did not believe that mental cultivation alone could produce proletarian revolutionary consciousness, and he was deeply suspicious of those who had come from an intellectual background that was commonly viewed as superior to his own rural upbringing, and, conversely, true revolutionary consciousness could only come from the laboring masses directly involved in the concrete, if soiled, praxis of manual labor.

> I came to feel that compared with the workers and peasants the unremoulded intellectuals were not clean and that, in the last analysis, the workers and peasants were the cleanest people and, even though their hands were soiled and their feet smeared with cow-dung, they were really cleaner than the bourgeois and petty-bourgeois intellectuals. That is what is meant by a change in feelings, a change from one class to another. If our writers and artists who come from the intelligentsia want their works to be well received by the masses, they must change and remould their thinking and their feelings. Without such a change, without such remoulding, they can do nothing well and will be misfits.[96]

Mao, himself from a middle-peasant background, had much greater faith in the peasantry as a revolutionary force than had Lenin.[97] To be sure, Lenin envisaged a major role for the peasantry in Russia's equivalent of Mao's "new democratic" stage, but, at the same time, he predicted that the smychka (alliance) between workers and peasants would come to an abrupt end once Russia moved to appropriate peasant property in the interest of what the Bolsheviks believed to be socialist revolution. Peasants were unalterably petty-bourgeois, in his view, and once land had been expropriated from the expropriators, their sole aspiration would remain a petty-bourgeois quest for individual small-scale landownership, however "unproductive" and "unprogressive" such landownership might be.[98] By contrast, in Mao's China, the peasantry, not just intellectuals, had the capacity for proletarian consciousness; this was implied by Mao's and Liu's advocacy of self-cultivation and remolding. Indeed, in speaking of the need to develop theoretical knowledge of Marxism-Leninism alongside their concrete experience in the making of one's daily livelihood as well as revolution, Mao drew no distinction between the capacities of workers and peasants to be "good communists."[99] Peasants were fully capable of achieving "proletarian" socialist consciousness, and as the main pillar of CCP support, they would have a full and essential role to play in the socialist stage of China's revolution—especially its proletarian dictatorship—not just in the "old" democratic or "new" democratic stage.

This is not to say that there was unmitigated support for this position within the CCP itself. There were apparent differences between Mao and Liu Shaoqi on this issue, for example. Liu, speaking during the Zhengfeng (Rectification) Campaign in 1941, traced the rise of all negative tendencies within the party to "non-proletarian influences," including the peasantry.[100] Such influences, in his view, threatened the proletarian consciousness that was at the core of the party.[101] Mao was certainly concerned about petty bourgeois influences as well, but in his view those that were most harmful to the leadership of the party were more likely to come from intellectuals.[102] Ultimately, the true measure of the suitability of a party member lay in his consciousness, in his ability to blend the theory of Marxism-Leninism with Chinese practice, or at least to accept the party leadership's interpretation of what that meant. Working class origin alone could not guarantee that; and less desirable class roots would not preclude it.[103]

The centrality of consciousness to Mao's vision of the Chinese revolution calls to mind Italian Marxist Antonio Gramsci's distinction between *domination* and *hegemony*. For Gramsci, domination was leadership exercised by force or the threat of resort thereto. By contrast, hegemony constituted leadership exercised by persuasion and the creation of an ideological consensus based on shared values. Gramsci argued that as societies progressed toward capitalism and the emergence of a bourgeois state, leadership was exercised less and less by domination and more and more by hegemony. Consequently, in advanced capitalist societies, support for the status quo existed as much beyond the formal bounds of the state, in civil society, as in the state structure itself. Institutions such as the church, schools, and informal civic organizations embraced the dominant value system and propagated it, often quite subtly, through their activities. This observation had important implications for the prospects for revolution in advanced capitalist societies. "The same thing happens in the art of politics as happens in military art," Gramsci wrote: "war of movement increasingly becomes war of position. The massive structures of the modern democracies, both as State organisations, and as complexes of associations in civil society, constitute for the art of politics as it were the 'trenches' and the permanent fortifications of the front in the war of position; they render merely 'partial' the element of movement which before used to be 'the whole' of war, etc."[104] Thus, socialist revolutions in societies such as Russia, where capitalism and political democracy were less developed, could prevail simply by crushing the coercive apparatus of the state; but in more highly industrialized capitalist societies, where the state was based on less coercive power but the ruling class was armed with a stubborn and deeply rooted hegemony over civil society, such "wars of manoeuvre" against state power would not succeed. Rather, Communist parties would have to rely on protracted "wars of position" in which socialist revolution was preceded by the creation of an alternative hegemony of proletarian values and cultural norms. Only when the majority had been won over to the alternative hegemony of the working class—or, alternatively, to the CCP's dictatorship in the name of the proletariat—could the state be smashed and a new political and economic order built.[105]

Gramsci's stress on the need for the party, "the New Prince," to engage in prolonged ideological work, building proletarian socialist consciousness through a protracted war of position, was directed specifically at socialist parties in advanced capitalist societies. Nevertheless, his insights resonate with Mao's views concerning what was needed to achieve socialist revolution in China. In China, where there was almost no effective state power to rule by domination, the CCP needed, in effect, to construct an "alternative hegemony" in the external form of anti-imperialist nationalism to support the transition from new-democratic to proletarian socialist revolution. It is significant that in the absence of any acquaintance with the works of the young Marx, Mao should have shared not only with Gramsci but also with the reformist Liang and the anarchist pioneers of the Marxist movement in China an appreciation of the role of consciousness and thought in building a revolutionary China. The object of the revolution lay not merely in the organization of labor or in the destruction of the authoritative apparatus of the existing power structure but went much deeper into the fabric of Chinese society itself. Immersed in the military struggle against the Japanese invaders, Mao, like Gramsci, used military terms to link human will and conscious action to the success of the revolutionary movement. In his early years of dissension from Party Central, as Mao struggled with Zhu De and others to fashion a new rural strategy premised on guerilla warfare, Mao criticized Lin Biao for his "overestimation of the importance of objective forces and underestimation of subjective forces."[106] Mao elaborated on this theme subsequently. "Conscious activity is the special characteristic of mankind, and still more is it a special characteristic of man in war. . . . Victory and defeat in war on the one hand is determined by the military, political, economic, geographical conditions, the nature of the war and the international support of the two sides; but it is not only these. . . . If one is to decide victory and defeat, one must add subjective efforts, the conscious activities of the war, of leading and waging the war."[107] Neither war nor the class struggle that comprised social revolution could be waged successfully, in Mao's view, without the subjective prerequisite of consciousness.

The emphasis on study, on the cultivation of proper revolutionary consciousness, and on "ideological work" within the CCP that one finds as a consistent motif in Mao's writings from the 1930s through the 1960s arise directly out of this expanded appreciation of the problem of "subjective conditions." To be sure, Lenin had identified this problem and attempted to resolve it by postulating the need for a vanguard party built on intellectuals who would bring revolutionary proletarian consciousness to the workers "from without." Mao's reformulation not only took issue with Lenin on the locus and roots of revolutionary consciousness, it also took Lenin's argument on the need to cultivate subjective conditions of revolution a step further. To return to Gramsci's terms, Mao's emphasis on ideological work constituted an effort to create an alternative hegemony, a new people, a new popular consciousness and new social mores in the CCP's base areas. Here Mao, as well as Liu Shaoqi (who would in the Cultural Revolution two decades later be destroyed by Mao over the acceptability of the Soviet model and of certain Western notions concerning modernity) applied Confucian notions concerning the need for the junzi's (virtuous man's) constant self-cultivation in virtue, to urge the cultivation of proletarian revolutionary consciousness among Chinese intellectuals and peasants who aspired to participate in the CCP's socialist revolution. Liu's classic work, written for the Rectification Campaign of the early 1940s, made copious references to Confucius and Mencius on the cultivation of virtue.

> [S]ubjective effort and self-cultivation in the course of revolutionary struggle are absolutely essential, indeed indispensable, for a revolutionary in remoulding himself and raising his own level. . . .
>
> Mencius . . . said that no one had fulfilled "a great mission" and played a role in history without first undergoing a hard process of tempering. . . . Still more so must Communists give attention to tempering and cultivating themselves in revolutionary struggles, since they have the historically unprecedented "great mission" of changing the world.[108]

In the view of Mao, whose own rural background and experiences at Beijing University encouraged a deep distrust of intellectuals who historically disdained manual labor, those most likely to gain proletarian revolutionary consciousness were those closest to manual labor. Thus, Mao at once appeared to divorce ideological consciousness from class origin even more than had Lenin even while he restored Marx's emphasis on the role of active participation in the production process in creating revolutionary consciousness. Mao's faith in the ability of not only the proletariat but China's nationalistic intellectuals—drawn to the CCP by its passionate opposition to Japanese imperialism—and vast peasantry as well to achieve socialist revolutionary consciousness formed the basis for Mao's belief that China's revolution would culminate in socialism and communism. His "people's democratic dictatorship" would lead to a "dictatorship of the proletariat" that would embrace all who had the proper consciousness if not the most desirable class origins.

Socialist Revolution from Above and Below: Elitism Democracy, and the "Mass Line"

Mao's use of the term *democracy* is worthy of note here, for it touches on the relationship between political leader and those led that is so central to his approach to the revolutionary and postrevolutionary state. Indeed, much of the emphasis that Mao and Liu placed on self-cultivation applied specifically to the leadership of the CCP. The class origin of intellectual recruits into the party was clearly a major reason for this emphasis on the need for continual self-cultivation. But this was not the only reason for the launching of the Zhengfeng (Rectification) Campaign in the early 1940s.[109] Mao, Liu, and others appeared to discern in political power itself the ability to corrupt its holders, thus, potentially creating a bureaucratic structure with interests apart from and opposed to those of the people the power of the party itself was established to serve. For Mao, democracy—interpreted as a means to mobilize mass participation in political activities for ends defined by the leadership of the party—served as a critical means to avoid this corruption of those in power. Only with democracy and "democratic methods," Mao asserted, could the party's anti-Japanese resistance campaign succeed. This was an instrumentalist approach to democracy: "[D]emocracy is the most essential thing for resistance to Japan, and to work for democracy is to work for resistance to Japan. Resistance and democracy are interdependent, just as are resistance and internal peace, democracy and internal peace. Democracy is the guarantee of resistance, while resistance can provide favourable conditions for developing the movement for democracy. . . . Actual events have . . . shown that to define the new stage and to set the winning of democracy as our task, is to move a step closer to resistance."[110]

The mass line that Mao articulated during these years was a Chinese version of democratic centralism, a theme that was emphasized constantly in Mao's writings in the Yan'an period.[111] This was not a concept that involved any of the accoutrements of bourgeois democracy, such as due process of law, the independence of the judiciary, checks and balances among different governmental branches, or guarantees of basic civil liberties. Rather the concept of leadership could be seen as consistent with the traditional Confucian belief that the acceptance or rejection of an imperial leadership by the "real" China, China's peasantry, uncorrupted by the West, pronounced judgment on that leadership. Thus, in Mao's view, democracy was a process—not a set of institutions—that would enable the party to have constant input from the peasants in order to "establish a good line."[112] It would, thus, protect the party from being deserted suddenly by its base in the countryside as had been so many imperial Chinese regimes in the past. Democracy would assure the party of the constant availability of China's peasantry to be mobilized by the leadership of the party. "[T]he people must be free to support it and have every opportunity of influencing its policies. This is the meaning of democracy," Mao wrote. "On the other hand, the centralization of administrative power is also necessary, and once the policy measures demanded by the people are transmitted to their own elected government through their representative body, the government will carry them out and will certainly be able to do so smoothly, so long as it does not go against the policy adopted in accordance with the people's will."[113]

As these comments indicate, to the extent that Mao held a concept of democracy, that conception was severely limited by his notion of leadership. This is evident even in his generous description of the mass line in terms of a two-way relationship between leaders (the CCP) and the masses.

> In all the practical work of our Party, all correct leadership is necessarily "from the masses, to the masses." This means: take the ideas of the masses (scattered and unsystematic ideas) and concentrate them (through study turn them into concentrated and systematic ideas), then go to the masses and propagate and explain these ideas until the masses embrace them as their own, hold fast to them and translate them into action, and test the correctness of these ideas in such action. Then once again concentrate ideas from the masses and once again go to the masses so that the ideas are persevered in and carried through.[114]

The mass line has been a paradoxical element of Chinese Marxism: Like Rousseau's *Social Contract*, it has both democratic and nondemocratic elements. On the one hand, the mass line conception prescribed a revolutionary process relying on a certain faith in the simple wisdom of the common person engaged in the concrete practice of production and revolution, in opposition to the abstract theory of intellectual knowledge. Here it bears a closer resemblance to Marx's distrust of Blanquist intellectual leadership than to Lenin's elitist and dictatorial notion of the vanguard party, based on a deeply rooted mistrust of mass spontaneity.[115] Mao distrusted and disliked intellectuals of the sort who had made him feel inferior when he, handicapped by a middle peasant background and a heavy Hunanese accent, was doing menial work as an assistant librarian at Beijing University in 1918–1919.[116] In some writings, such as "On Practice," Mao stressed that it was in experience, particularly in production and class struggle, that true knowledge originated,[117] and this treatment privileged the experience, the practice, of the direct producers. At the same time, Mao's concept of leadership was highly elitist in its own way. The ideas of the masses were inherently "scattered" and "unsystematic," just as the citizens in Rousseau's polity could discern only partial interests and articulate "particular wills." Ordinary women and men required the leadership of a party of persons with true revolutionary consciousness that could discern the true interests of all Chinese or, at least, of Chinese with a proper class perspective.[118] Moreover, the Rectification Campaign was needed because even the party itself could be crippled by those of inadequate consciousness or corrupted by power. The ultimate implication of this reasoning—fully realized only decades later in the Cultural Revolution when Mao had lost hope in the ability of the party to reform itself from within—was that the party required a visionary leader specially gifted to discern the Way. In arguing thus, Mao, now seeking despite his humble origins to establish himself as the party's theoretical leader, was not prepared to relinquish for himself the traditional mantle of leadership worn by China's emperors even while he himself was suspicious of and threatened by his Soviet-educated rivals as he sought to consolidate his leadership of the party. The loosening of the link between class origin and consciousness reinforced this role of the leader because class origin and direct experience as a peasant or a worker did not guarantee that one would have "proper" ideas, and it was necessary to have one who could discern this correctness serve as arbiter. The charge that one was against "the people" could be—and was, both in the first Rectification Campaign and in subsequent mass movements—wielded against those who simply disagreed on strategy or tactics with the supreme leader.

The CCP's overall approach to party leadership derived from two strains in Mao's own thought: (1) the notion of the party-state as formulated in China first by Sun Yat-sen[119] and realized in the Soviet Union and (2) the populist current, encompassing certain tenets of Confucian thought. In fact, the first concept, the party-state, also derived indirectly from the Chinese Confucian political philosophical tradition. Historically, the notion of political party (dang), often translated as "faction," was associated with the pursuit of private, selfish rather than public aims.[120] Political associations in the late imperial era were, thus, implicit, if not explicit, threats to the ruling imperial authorities, and they remained illegitimate where "harmonious familiastic images . . . sustained the state by making dissent a sign of selfish factionalism."[121] Sun's vision of a single-party state in which the Guomindang would rule in a period of tutelage to prepare the Chinese to rule themselves enabled the contradiction between public and private interests to be overcome in the concept of dang. The party would represent the whole national interest because it would be one with the state. This is a perspective that does not view interests arising out of civil society—especially insofar as that concept is associated with capitalist forces in contestation with the state—as legitimate.[122] Similarly, the mass line, with its appeal to the importance of mass participation in politics, helped to assure that Mao's vanguard party would not be construed as the representative of a narrow set of interests apart from and above those of the Chinese nation as a whole. It helped to vest the CCP with popular legitimacy while it reflected the traditional distinction between public and private interest in Chinese thought. As John Bryan Starr has noted, "[A]uthority misused to further one's own personal interests, is, in Mao's view, the principal cause of the creation of new class enemies—of the process of embourgeoisement—in a socialist society. It is the goal of organizational reform and cultural revolution to minimize this corrupting misuse of authority."[123]

A second element in the mass line idea is a populism that draws on the Confucian-Mencian view of benevolent government as a moral enterprise directed at enhancing the welfare of the people. "Serve the People"[124] was a CCP maxim during the Yan'an period and, as a basis for the legitimacy of CCP leadership in the base areas, was invoked to contrast the treatment of commoners in these areas with that of people under Guomindang rule. The significance of the ambivalence of traditional Confucian perspectives on the peasantry is underscored by the absence of any similar mandate for the CPSU in Russia. The CCP's distinctive revolution was to build socialism from both above and from below, ending the artificial division between the Western-influenced coast and the countryside of the "real" China and terminating the elevation of mental over manual labor. This populism at once coincided with nationalistic impulses while it conflicted with the partial definition of the "people" on the basis of consciousness. The latter could—and would—exclude many segments of Chinese from the preferred category.

The Rectification Campaign of the early 1940s presaged the new conception of permanent revolution that would prescribe the Cultural Revolution in the early 1960s. The issue was no longer simply the need for a continuous revolution from the bourgeois-democratic stage to the proletarian socialist stage as envisaged by Trotsky. Instead, the concern was the need for a constant reliance on mass mobilization to purge those in political power of the corrupt nature that appeared to have come upon them either through the influences of their class background or by corrupting effects of elitism arising out of their effective wielding of political power over people of lesser social status. In many essays penned for the Zhengfeng Campaign, Mao deplored the tendency for those in authority in the Party to fall into "sectarianism," "dogmatism," "commandism," and "bureaucratism."[125] In this campaign, waged in part to establish firmly Mao's authority as the party's undisputed theoretical leader, both Mao and Liu associated these negative tendencies in the party with both "bourgeois" and "semi-feudal" influences, but the corrupting influence of the successes achieved in the exercise of political power itself was even more important. Liu attributed the tendency for party cadre to become alienated from the masses in the 1940s less to the "restoration of [a] capitalism" that had never been dominant in China than to the self-corruptive nature of political power itself. "Some members of our Party," Liu asserted, "cannot withstand the plaudits of success and victory; they let victories turn their heads, become brazen, arrogant and bureaucratic and may even vacillate, degenerate and become corrupted, completely losing their original revolutionary quality."[126] Thus, both Liu and Mao saw the continual cultivation of virtue, including the destruction of earlier conceptions thereof, as essential to socialist revolution because it would guard against and remedy such degeneration. Yet, as in the case of Rousseau's legislator, appointing the party or the state as the guardian of revolutionary virtue was not without its difficulties. Even a temporary state power threatened to degenerate into the same kind of "chains" that had bound men and women under the old state power.[127] Mao and Liu proposed self-cultivation and periodic purges, in which the masses themselves, under the direction of the charismatic leader, would criticize the party, as the solution to this problem.[128] Nevertheless, the central difficulty remained: given the corruptive nature of political power and the need for the "particular wills" (to use Rousseau's term) of the people to be "reinterpreted" so that they accorded with what was best for all China, who was to determine when a new rectification campaign was necessary? Mao's solution seemed to require a sort of equivalent to Rousseau's legislator, yet more powerful, someone who was superhuman, whose wisdom transcended the normal bounds of class-based perspectives, one who was neither subject to the weaknesses and partial perspectives of the masses nor shared the susceptibility of others in the party to corruption by the experience of being in power.[129] Whence would such a person come, and who would assure that he or she would be in a position to enforce his or her will on the party?[130]

This dilemma in Mao's concept of leadership helps to highlight an important polarity within Marxism as a whole—the ambivalence of Marxism as a system of thought concerning Western Enlightenment assumptions on the nature and meaning of modernity. On the one hand, Marxism sees capitalism and its accoutrements, including the modern state, as progressive; yet they were severely defective from a moral point of view, and, thus, they were to be superseded by still more progressive forms in the process of socialist revolution.[131] Socialist revolution at once would develop what people had become in industrial modernity still further while it would repudiate certain aspects of that modernity. In Mao one finds the affirmation of only one side of this polarity. To be sure, Mao embraced the goal of economic growth through industrialization as the prerequisite of a socialist order explicitly and enthusiastically, at least through the early years of the People's Republic. Mao adopted the vocabulary of Marxist-Leninist orthodoxy in seeing China as "backward" economically and acknowledging that "to build a strong, highly industrialized socialist country will require several decades of hard work, say fifty years, or the entire second half of the present century."[132] Yet, as Schram has noted, "one may legitimately ask whether his broader vision of the Chinese revolution, even as he entertained it in 1949, would ultimately prove compatible with such technical modernization."[133] Mao never adopted the development of a vigorous industrial capitalism as a goal for China,[134] and he repudiated the Western identification of bureaucracy as an essential and positive aspect of human development. On the contrary, his notion of leadership, incorporating the mass line and continual mobilization of the masses against those who had been corrupted, constituted a vehement rejection of the Weberian category of legal "rational" bureaucratic authority[135] for a vision that must rely ultimately on charismatic authority, on a leader with special powers.[136] Moreover, Mao, like Sun, Li, and Chen, saw the party-state as an essential tool for positive revolutionary change in China, yet Mao also exhibited a profound antipathy to institutionalized political authority even in the party itself that could only be remedied by an individual endowed with special powers, like Rousseau's legislator. This, of course, was at the heart of the dilemma of the Chinese revolution itself. How could revolution and the charisma of its leadership be institutionalized without undermining what they represented? Or, in terms of the national question, how could a revolution that required the effective use of state power wield that power without undermining its own goals, which in theory, at least, required the dissolution of the state in classless society?

Reflecting precisely these dilemmas, Mao's solution to the problem of limiting party and state power was at once anarchistic and potentially authoritarian. Like those involved in the controversy on Chinese social history who were drawn to the concept of "Asiatic" society, Mao was mindful of the Confucian bureaucratic tradition in "feudal" China. Perhaps because of this historical legacy, China's new leaders were more likely than those in the West to "transform themselves from the servants of society into the masters of society."[137] Thus, while Mao emphasized the danger of bourgeois influences, he suggested that it was not merely the return of a bourgeoisie that had never wielded significant power in China but the persistence of certain cultural attitudes toward power—which he conveniently subsumed under the rubric of "feudalism"—that was the source of the threat described by Marx and Engels. A revolutionary desire to "serve the people" had to supersede the impersonal self-serving politics of bureaucracy in order for the CCP to retain its popularity and legitimacy.[138] Mao, then, saw the threat as well as the promise in the "potential autonomy" of the party-state from social class. This recognition underscored the antinomy between anarchism and statism in his thought. "Democracy is . . . democracy under centralized leadership, not the democracy of anarchism. Anarchism is not what the people want," he declared in his famous speech to the Supreme State Conference in February 1957.[139] Yet, maintaining an anarchist bent with respect to state power, he concluded that "[t]he ultimate instrument of socialist transformation was to be struggle, not the state."[140] "'To rebel is justified!'" Mao had written in 1939. In launching the Cultural Revolution, Mao revived this rhetoric. "'Revolutionaries are Monkey Kings. . . . We wield our golden rods, display our supernatural powers, and use our magic to turn the old world upside down, smash it to pieces, pulverize it and create chaos—the greater the confusion the better! We are bent on . . . hewing out a proletarian new world!'"[141] Given the role of the supreme charismatic leader, this meant that the state, and the party that was mandated to control it, both were subject to the judgment of the leader, and if the leader mandated "class struggle" as necessary, state power and the power of the institutionalized party could both collapse. This, of course, is precisely what occurred during the Cultural Revolution in the 1960s. In both the Rectification Campaign in the 1940s and the Cultural Revolution two decades later, Mao set the masses of the Chinese people against those in the apparatus of party leadership who were said to be enemies of both the "people" and the leader. Although Mao himself would become alarmed at the extent to which private grievances drove the movement to unanticipated excesses and seek to rein it in, the movement reaffirmed Marx's conviction that class struggle—after as well as during the revolution[142]—was the motor force of history. Nevertheless, the relationship of the masses to the party and the state was always to be mediated by the insight of the visionary leader, who alone, incorruptible, could recognize the impending threat of those who had been corrupted and lead the purifying assault against them. Because he alone could determine when the need for struggle had passed, in the role of the leader lay the statist corrective for the anarchist moment.

One final aspect of Mao's stress on the importance of ideological work marked a significant departure from the manner in which Marxists had previously conceptualized the relationship between base and superstructure. To be sure, Mao was careful to reiterate in his writings the orthodox position on the relationship between economics, on the one hand, and politics and culture, on the other. "A given culture is the ideological reflection of the politics and economics of a given society," he wrote in "On New Democracy." China's domination by both "an imperialist culture" and "a semifeudal culture" reflected "imperialist rule, or partial rule" over China's economy and China's "semifeudal politics and economy." This "reactionary culture," Mao declared, "must be swept away." Conversely, "[t]here are socialist elements in our politics and our economy, and hence these socialist elements are reflected in our national culture; but taking our society as a whole, we do not have a socialist politics and a socialist economy yet, so that there cannot be a wholly socialist national culture."[143] But how was the transformation from the old to the new culture to occur? The orthodox Marxist formulation suggested that as a society made the transition from one mode of production to another, the change in the superstructural realm of politics and culture would occur automatically in response to changes in economic forces and relations in the economic base. It might take some period of transition, but new socioeconomic arrangements would themselves engender appropriate political and cultural forms. Mao's and Liu's stress on the need for constant spiritual cultivation, however, suggested that they did not believe that this would be the case. Their treatment of ideological and cultural change instead altered the connection between the so-called base and superstructure. Cultural change, ideological change, in their view, required special, separate attention in a separate revolutionary process. Even an industrial worker needed to cultivate his or her consciousness continually to attain the correct perspective.

This loosening of the connection between base and superstructure had both positive and negative aspects. In a positive sense, the CCP was less tightly constrained by the limitations of China's lagging economic base in waging its struggle. As observed here, this enabled the CCP to build a revolutionary movement that claimed to be proletarian in outlook even while the party membership itself was heavily intellectual and peasant in class origin. This perspective also suggested, however, that change in socioeconomic institutions alone would not be sufficient to produce China's new socialist national culture. Most importantly, Mao explicitly articulated a point that Engels had tentatively suggested in a controversial passage in *Anti-Dühring*[144]—that it was entirely possible for the organized political power of the state to have a causal effect on the economic development of a society. This had been the case, in Marx's view, in so-called "oriental" societies where the presence of the despot had prevented the emergence of private property and the spontaneous development of industrial capitalism.[145] In the 1930s, Mao had come to share the conviction of many May Fourth intellectuals and their predecessors that the key to saving China lay in changing the way in which Chinese thought about politics.[146] In Marxian terms, the cultural and political superstructure was inhibiting China's economic development[147] and was responsible for China's miserable position vis-à-vis the great powers. Mao was emphatic on this point and boldly defended its consistency with orthodox Marxism:

> When the superstructure (politics, culture, etc.) obstructs the development of the economic base, political and cultural changes become principal and decisive. Are we going against materialism when we say this? No. The reason is that while we recognize that in the general development of history the material determines the mental and social being determines social consciousness, we also—and indeed must—recognize the reaction of mental on material things, of social consciousness on social being and of the superstructure on the economic base. This does not go against materialism; on the contrary, it avoids mechanical materialism and firmly upholds dialectical materialism.[148]

In this concept, a cultural revolution—a revolution in the realm of culture and not just in production relations—was a prerequisite for, an essential part of, the achievement of China's bourgeois-democratic and proletarian socialist revolutions.

This claim was intimately linked to the policy of ideological remolding, while it carried with it at once all the liberating and absolutizing tendencies that inhered in Mao's treatment of leadership and political authority. In February 1957, Mao acknowledged that an excessive number of people had been killed as "counterrevolutionaries" in the early years of the People's Republic. But he proudly distinguished China's record from that of Stalin, who, he had evidently learned from Nikita Khrushchev's Secret Speech, had had 20 percent of Seventeenth Party Congress (1934) delegates and 20 percent of Central Committee members killed.[149] To this practice Mao contrasted the CCP's policy of requiring individuals to undergo the "self-transformation" of remolding. This approach avoided the wasteful, vitiating, and demoralizing impact on the minzu of policies that discarded those with wrong ideas. The alternative, reaching out to offenders to bring them back into the national fold, promised to strengthen the minzu by achieving its integration (*yiyuan-hua*). One is reminded here of the Japanese state's highly successful exploitation of the *tenkō* impulse to achieve maximum integration of the Japanese minzoku, to strengthen their resolve in wartime and in opposition to the internal threat posed by the left-wing movement. The comparison illuminates the importance of the identification of a threat to the success of this maneuver. Thus, in China, even as ideological remolding was held up as a more humane, patient approach to the problem of political dissent, it was consistently recognized that a hard core of counterrevolutionaries remained whose presence demanded uncompromising measures by a state exercising dictatorship in the name of the whole people. If the state was ineffective in transforming those willing to undergo reeducation and in repressing those who were not, the entire enterprise of building socialism was in jeopardy. In short, it appeared that superstructure—state and consciousness—and not "objective conditions" played the determinative role, and in the early 1960s as Mao grew increasingly impatient in his pursuit of socialism, the line distinguishing the treatment of those who were cooperative with the revolutionary leadership and those beyond the pale grew increasingly blurred.[150] Now, Mao was convinced, class conflict in the form of the revolution in the superstructure would have to continue well after the transfer of political power to the CCP. In stressing self-cultivation as the key tool of this cultural revolution, Mao, borrowing on the very Confucian "ideology" that he denounced as "feudalistic," was offering a Chinese solution to the issues concerning nationalism and the state in the Chinese revolution. Nevertheless, although it was conceived in the particularity of China's indigenous intellectual tradition and historical circumstances, Mao's notion of a cultural revolution in permanence held universal implications for Marx's theory of revolution.

Maoism and the Chinese Solution to the National Question

From the Rectification Campaign of the 1940s through the Great Proletarian Cultural Revolution, the reassessment of Mao's contribution in 1981,[151] and the massacre at Tiananmen Square on June 4, 1989, the tension between nationalist statism versus stateless international socialism in Chinese Marxism has continued to be evident in Chinese Communist thought and practice. Under Mao's leadership in the 1940s, the party had embarked on the construction of a revolutionary party-state that could satisfy the nationalistic aspirations of the Chinese people and fulfill the dream of a socialist alternative to capitalist industrialization. At the same time, lacking a commitment to a preexisting national state, Chinese Marxists in the pre-1949 period, unlike Japan's, seemed to be able to respond to the national question by conjoining nationalism with Marxism within the CCP/Comintern framework without yielding to statism. In the call for continuous remolding and self-cultivation and in their advocacy of the mass line, Mao, Liu, and others tried to establish a foundation of procedures that would assure the dissolution of this state in accordance with Marx's ideal of stateless communism. Marxian socialism also called for internationalism, but the pursuit of China's national interests had constituted the CCP's most potent basis of legitimacy because the party claimed to lead a revolution that had begun as a movement of national liberation. The survival of the national state and the threat to China posed by more highly industrialized and militarily superior capitalist nation-states effectively prohibited the abandonment of stateness. Once China, like the Soviet Union, had become, in the view of the CCP, an essential link in the world socialist revolution, to sacrifice China would mean to sacrifice the international socialist revolution itself.

The dilemma of these postures on the two aspects of the national question suggests major issues in realizing a genuinely socialist revolution that Marx and Engels had never anticipated in their environment. What would be the impact of the new characteristics of the international system in the twentieth century? Specifically, did not the increasing interconnectedness between the state and the industry that supports its military endeavors—even in the capitalist society that professed the most hostility to certain kinds of state involvement in the economy, the United States—suggest that there was no longer a sanguine prospect for the stateless communism that Marx and Engels envisaged? Perhaps the tortured history of post-1949 China's vacillation between the pursuit of ideologically pure socialism and economic "modernization" showed that the two tasks could not be undertaken simultaneously. Did this not demonstrate the truth of the founders' conviction that the skipping of stages could not result in a successful socialist revolution?

As observed here, Mao's endeavors to respond to the national question by sinifying Marxism produced important new problems concerning political authority and socialist revolution, and these tensions deepened with the dialectic between theory and practice after 1949. As the CCP drove to victory in 1949, Mao had demonstrated a full appreciation of the Marxist emphasis on the urban sector and advanced technology as the arena for building socialism: "The centre of gravity of the Party's work has shifted from the village to the city."[152] Accordingly, the Soviet stress on the imperative of urban-oriented industrialization was adopted as the model for the CCP's First Five-Year Plan after 1949. Subsequently, however, Mao's quest for the continued sinification of Marxism, animated increasingly by indigenous philosophical traditions more than by Leninist orthodoxy, led him to a utopianism that celebrated the spirit and rural focus of Yan'an and the backwardness of the Chinese people while it rejected the Soviet model of industrialization.[153] Praising the example of the emperor Qin Shihuang, whom he invoked as a heroic national symbol,[154] Mao asserted the primacy of will and consciousness over material limitations. The fact that Mao, who was not to be deterred by his fundamental ignorance in the realm of economics, was able to see these views realized in the disastrous policies of the Great Leap Forward resulted in the starvation of millions of the Chinese people he had urged the party to serve.[155] The notion of "uninterrupted revolution" (*buduan geming*) that Mao developed in his rejection of the Soviet model in turn provided for a still greater emphasis on continuing class conflict within socialist society in what he came to call "continuous revolution" (*jixu geming*).[156] When this notion was implemented in the launching of the Cultural Revolution, the antinomies of Mao's thought concerning the national question reached a zenith in yet another mortal chapter for the Chinese nation as the anarchist and statist components of Mao's thought collided. Now

Mao came to see the power not only of the state but of the party as well as an impediment to the forces of class struggle that he viewed as necessary for the further development of his revolution.[157] He launched an attack on both that unleashed a firestorm as it provided a vehicle for the vehement expression of personal grievances against adversaries who could be labeled as class enemies in the name of the revolution.[158] Moreover, in calling for a revolution that was specifically cultural in character, the Mao who advocated the injection of an appreciation of Chinese realities into Marxism-Leninism instigated what his most severe critics have called a war on Chinese culture itself.[159] Finally, Mao's attack on the party and the bureaucracy, coupled with his glorification as the charismatic supreme leader during this period, laid the basis for the statist practice of his successors even as they have disavowed Mao's "mistakes."[160]

Thus, the Maoist claim to repudiate statism through the endorsement of perpetual class struggle under the leadership of a visionary leader made the choice between anarchy and statism less clearly defined. Ultimately, the issue at the nexus of the nationalist and statist aspects of the national question concerned the difficult issue of political authority.[161] As it has been treated in Western philosophical discourse, authority is conceptualized primarily either (1) in terms of a consensus of values shared among members of a society or (2) in terms of social cohesion established or maintained by coercion or by the threat of recourse to force.[162] Weber's distinction among three ideal types or bases of authority—traditional, charismatic, and "rational-legal"—posited the latter as characteristic of "modern" industrial societies; and this proposition has provided the foundation for the flourishing of formal-procedural approaches to authority in contemporary Western political science.[163]

There is a consistency within modern Western political thought on the nature of authority that reflects a certain unity between the two conceptualizations distinguished here. Thomas Hobbes, John Locke, Rousseau, Marx, Weber, and Gramsci all recognized the importance of (the threat of) force in creating and maintaining political authority even if the role of coercion was often masked or gradually attenuated by the appearance of a societal consensus of values. These dominant values are, in turn, reflected in rules and procedures and institutionalized in the "rule of law"; the law itself articulates and enforces values and carries the threat of punitive sanctions. Mao's concept of leadership or authority shared very little with these understandings in Western discourse. In rejecting rational-legal authority and deriding rules and the routinization of authority as the enemies of his revolution, Mao was setting forth an alternative understanding of political leadership and authority. His concept of politics as a moral sphere—where morality was ultimately judged by the supreme leader who alone was imbued with the power to discern true virtue—is scarcely comprehensible in terms of the rationalist assumptions that guide even the most cogent Western Marxian critics of bourgeois rule, such as Herbert Marcuse and Jürgen Habermas.[164] Mao's invocation of political authority in terms of the cultivation of revolutionary virtue owes much to the Confucian understanding of politics in terms of moral authority. Thus, his perspective shares more in common with the nondeontological substantive-purposive understandings of authority held by ancient and medieval Western thinkers such as Plato and Saint Thomas Aquinas. This approach is less conducive to an unambiguous option for anarchism or statism. As in formal-procedural interpretations of authority, leadership is always assumed to be necessary, but institutions and the rules by which they are to operate—in short, the bureaucratic accoutrements of authority that customarily adorn the modern Western nation-state—are not seen as essential to the legitimate exercise of political power. In the absence of such institutions, authority is most easily exercised by none or by the arbitrary will of one, acting in the name of the state.

Although Marx and Engels had bemoaned the shortcomings of bourgeois democracy, they had seen its endorsement of personal rights and liberties and their guarantee through institutional arrangements as progressive moments in human history. Presumably, the experience of bourgeois democracy in advanced capitalist societies would leave its imprint on the social democracy that would emerge after a proletarian socialist revolution. The legacy of bourgeois democracy would be a set of norms and procedures that would provide the basis for an even broader application of democracy that would extend to the economic realm. In China, however, as in Russia, there was no such historical legacy of the bourgeois state. Nor did Mao's understanding of leadership incline him to accept rules and institutions that, even if initially designed to accord with the revolutionary vision, could be turned to obstruct the exercise of visionary leadership when it was required. Like Lenin, Mao eschewed institutionalized guarantees against the abuse of power by a supreme leader in revolutionary and postrevolutionary China. Lenin recognized too late the dangers of relying on the good faith of devoted Bolshevik leaders, and under Stalin emerged a repressive and murderous combination of the "cult of the personality" around charismatic leadership and bureaucratic privilege with tragic consequences for the Soviet people.

What have been the implications of Mao's concept of leadership for the fate of social democracy in postrevolutionary China? To be sure, during the Sino-Japanese conflict, popular participation understood in terms of mass mobilization was a key element for the CCP. But such participation served as part of a revolutionary strategy, as a means to a higher end, to achieve popular support for national liberation from the grip of Western imperialism and the Japanese invasion and to prevail over the Guomindang. During the war years, democracy meant less the rule of law and procedural guarantees than a claim to represent the national will.[165] Here, Rousseau's legislator's precarious perch straddling rational-legal authority (as the law-giver) and charismatic authority is the key to the ambiguity concerning authority in his social contract. In Mao as in Rousseau the priority of substantive virtue over institutional and procedural arrangements attached little importance to particular interests and the right of individuals to express and act on them politically. Unless a democratic culture could be created that would prize rights as much as obligations, the tension between the option for chaos versus the perils of institutionalized power, on the one hand, and the need for a strong and visionary leader, on the other, could well resolve itself—and would—in a larger measure of stateness and statism than China enjoyed in the prerevolutionary era.

Marxism, Nationalism, and Late Industrialization: Conclusions and Epilogue

Conclusions: Liberation, Nationalism, and the Problem of the State

The history of Marxism in China and Japan in the interwar years is the chronicle of a dynamic transformative discourse. On one side, was a distinctively West European Enlightenment philosophical system and, on the other, were radical intellectuals of a dramatically disparate cultural heritage operating in national and international contexts that differed substantially from that in which Marxism was born. Chinese and Japanese scholar-activists were, nevertheless, anxious to wield Western ideas and ideals to revolutionize their own societies. Their radicalism at once embraced a political philosophy that was rooted in an alien West European setting while it contested the political and economic imperialism that had come to constitute Western Europe's posture—even the position of Marxism itself—toward their native societies. Indeed, it was the predicament in which Chinese intellectuals found their society and the unfortunate example it posed for Japanese observers in the late nineteenth and early twentieth centuries that gave rise to the national question most broadly conceived in Asia.

Radical thinkers in both China and Japan were drawn to Marxism by its claim to be scientific and by its radical critique of Western capitalist society. Marxism was a modern Western philosophical system that would serve as a medium for the liberation of their peoples from their painful subordination to the West as well as from domestic sources of oppression, including the capitalist growth urged by the Western model. In this same attraction to Marxism, however, also lay the foundation of their disquiet in the face of the national question. As it had been defined in nineteenth-century Europe to pertain to the role of nationalism in the Marxist movement, the national question ultimately concerned the very survival of the peoples these revolutionaries aspired to liberate by means of a socialist revolution. In the face of an increasingly violent and hostile international system, they could ill-afford to indulge in a facile resolution of the issue. They could not yield unreflectively to an orthodoxy dictated by other, Western, Marxist thinkers in other, more favorable, circumstances by means of a wholesale repudiation of nationhood and stateness.

Lenin's acknowledgment of the hierarchical character of the international system and his embellishment on the thought of the founders appeared to open new possibilities for the resolution of the matter beyond the frontiers of orthodoxy and heterodoxy that had been drawn in the heated debate around World War I. Yet there was another dimension of the dilemma of Asian Marxists that Lenin's rearticulation of the issue could not resolve. Intrinsic to Marxism, as well as to social Darwinism, liberalism, and other strands of West European thought imported into the East were views on humanity, nature, and society that were fundamentally alien to those nurtured in the Confucian, Daoist, and Buddhist traditions of China and Japan. Among the new Western perspectives were a view of history as a secular rather than a cyclical process,[1] a conviction that humankind was destined to be master over nature rather than to live in idyllic harmony with it, and a vision of the political as a domain that was not inherently a sphere of moral value. Consequently, the discourse with Marxism in its West European orientation itself cast Chinese and Japanese theorists into a deeply problematic relationship with their own native cultures. If they accepted the terms of the Marxist account of human history, if they undertook to reinterpret and reassess their own social histories in those terms, would they not be succumbing to Western cultural imperialism? Would not their own societies always be found wanting in some important universal dimension of human experience according to such a yardstick of "modernity"? The Asiatic mode of production notion certainly suggested as much as Chinese and Japanese forays into the concept, particularly with respect to Chinese social history, amply demonstrated. Why should not these scholar-activists generate indigenous models of social and political development to accord with the historical experiences of their own peoples? If this were done, however, they could no longer assume with confidence the necessity of the revolutionary change that was promised by the Marxist scientific model.

In the final analysis, issues such as these brought Chinese and Japanese revolutionists face to face with the most fundamental questions concerning their own identities and the nature of the liberation they sought to achieve through a Marxian socialist revolution. The challenge was to resolve these questions so as to affirm their identities without vitiating the Marxian framework. To be sure, they perceived revolutionary change as a vehicle by which to achieve liberation, but liberation of *whom—from* what—*to* what? If the point was to liberate oneself and one's people from the past, this implied the repudiation of one's own cultural heritage. Such a posture was problematic for the nationalist. Joseph Levenson explicated this problem compellingly in his study of the crisis of Confucianism in late imperial China. "[Traditionalism] must exist in nationalism. . . . The sense of community which is essential to nationalism depends on people's acknowledgment of a common past. And the common past must be prized if a man is to let it forge a bond between himself and his fellow-nationals." As a result, the Chinese nationalist found himself in an acute dilemma. "He was to have a special sympathy for the Chinese past, and he was to review the Chinese past with a disinterested critical honesty."[2]

The situation of the Japanese radical vis-à-vis his past was less tortured than that of the Chinese. In late nineteenth-century China, it finally appeared that the Confucian tradition was no longer serving the nation but constituted a major factor in its demise. It was incontrovertible that an intellectual and political tradition that exalted moral cultivation and evaluated scholarly expertise as the primary criterion for service to the state while—in principle at least—it despised the exercise of military force could only collapse in the engagement with the West. This was not because of any inherent moral superiority of Western ideals and values. It was, rather, the product of the fact that the values of industrial capitalism gave the Western powers legitimate recourse to military force, to the relentless pursuit of technological innovation with the support of the state, and to competitiveness based on the economic and military power of the national state that Chinese had traditionally eschewed. Hence, "progress" in a manner that would allow China to survive Western encroachment intact seemed to require that the Confucian tradition be jettisoned to embrace a vision of modernity that was defined empirically and normatively by the Western historical experience. By contrast, such agonizing over identity, over the meaning of being Japanese, did not prevent Japanese thinkers and political leaders from taking radical and decisive action to defend Japan in the face of the Western intrusion. The Tokugawa shogunate's own legitimacy had been based on its military supremacy, and the regime lost that legitimacy when it could not respond effectively to the demands of U.S. Commodore Matthew Perry. Those from the outer domains of Chōshū, Satsuma, Tosa, and Hizen who overthrew the shogunate under the slogan "expel the barbarians and revere the emperor" established a new regime that seemed to hearken back to Japanese tradition by restoring power to the emperor. With their authority now buttressed by this myth of imperial "restoration," the Meiji oligarchs thereupon launched a radical industrializing revolution that would enhance Japan's position in the international hierarchy.

For Japan's leaders, national pride abetted rather than hindered the course of reform and revolution. There was no urgent compulsion at the outset to distinguish between the need to adopt Western technology for its utility (yong), on the one hand, and the imperative to preserve the essence (ti) of what was Chinese, or Japanese, on the other.[3] It had long been part of the Japanese cultural practice to borrow elements from abroad and integrate them into Japanese society and culture. This tradition facilitated the Japanese appropriation of Western technology, political arrangements, and even theoretical elements to produce a new, improved amalgam. Moreover, it was possible for Japanese leaders to adopt key elements of the Western state system—most notably its hierarchy premised on military power—without experiencing a fundamental dissonance with Japan's own historic philosophical values and practices. The competitive military hierarchy of the Tokugawa's centralized feudalism could simply be transposed to the international arena with the new Meiji kokka, or national state, replacing the feudal kuni (states) of the internal Tokugawa order.

Nevertheless, despite these important differences, Japan did not prove to be entirely immune from the difficulties that beset China in its cultural confrontation with the West. The convulsions that Japan experienced in the late 1920s and 1930s evidenced a belated intellectual crisis of precisely the sort that had afflicted Chinese intellectuals in the late-nineteenth century. Shōwa Restorationists lamented that the essence of the Japanese body politic promised by the Meiji Restoration had been sacrificed in the reckless adoption of the accoutrements of Western "modernity." The social problems that had arisen pari passu with the Meiji Restoration's crash industrialization and the multidimensional movement for Taishō democracy reflected the erosion of an essence that was incarnate in the emperor, an essence that could only be recovered with a new restoration in the Shōwa era.[4] Radical nationalist and statist ideas emerged among intellectual leaders of the Shōwa era such as Miki Kiyoshi and Ryū Shintarō, who sought a new political model that would be more appropriate for Japan's special characteristics than imported Western ideas.[5] All these evinced a deferred crisis of national identity. The *tenkō* phenomenon and the repeated transmutation of Marxism from an internationalist, antistatist philosophical system into a national statist one exalting the traditional Japanese imperial system also reveal the profundity of this intellectual crisis in the 1930s.

The radicalism of Marxism itself exacerbated the elements of such crisis. At the heart of the doctrine lay an appeal for an ideal of human emancipation that necessarily imported a sense of identity in terms of one's humanity, nation, kinship, or individuality for those who would adopt it. Chinese and Japanese Marxists could no more escape the implications concerning liberation and identity than could any other Marxist thinker. The issue would be that much more profound and significant for them in their non-European cultural and intellectual context. What was the essence of who they were, and whence came the motivation for the revolutionary struggle? Were they engaged in the revolution as individuals who directly bore the burdens of oppression domestically and internationally? In most cases, the Marxists under examination here were intellectuals. To borrow Mao's terms, they were mental, not manual, laborers. In working for the revolution, however, they identified themselves as one with those who labored with their hands in city and countryside. As Marx observed, even the social strata that were relatively privileged in class societies were victimized by man's alienation from himself and his fellow human beings through the division of labor. For radical Chinese and Japanese scholar-revolutionaries, then, the struggle for social and political liberation could be intensely personal, just as it was for the worker or the peasant. This, too, was evidenced in the tensions that resulted in *tenkō* as well as in the determination of CCP members to remold themselves spiritually.

As it evolved in this new Asian setting, however, the national question entailed an added set of concerns bearing on the relationship between identity and revolutionary change. In what capacity and by what means would men and women achieve the true human emancipation of which Marx had written? The altered international circumstances that conditioned Lenin's reformulation of the issue in 1919 suggested that one could not achieve true emancipation if one's people could not move within the mainstream of human history. In this view, national self-determination constituted at once an effort to liberate a nation and an endeavor of individuals to affirm their self-worth as members of the larger Chinese or Japanese community. Yet Lenin's solution seemed to raise more difficulties than it solved. As applied by Comintern leaders in the 1920s and 1930s, it legitimated nationalist struggle for China as a later-industrializing society victimized by the Western capitalist powers. Yet such a vehicle of self-affirmation was denied to Japanese, whose nation was not colonized or semicolonial, but, nevertheless, was a late industrializer that experienced real vulnerabilities in an international hierarchy, the highest ranks of which appeared (to Chinese and Japanese as to many non-Europeans, at least) to be allocated on a basis of racial exclusivism. Furthermore, Marx himself had denigrated the value of oriental culture and what it had to offer to universal human civilization as a whole. In his view, Western imperialism was not harmful, but salutary. Its subjugation and transformation of the "traditional," "stagnant" societies of the East held the sole hope not only for the reentry of Asia into the mainstream of world history but, indeed, for the progress of the history of the world as a whole.[6] Was it possible, then, to affirm oneself as Chinese or Japanese, to find any value worth preserving in one's own Asian cultural past even in the midst of revolutionary change without denying something essential to Marxism? Conversely, was it logically possible to subscribe to Marx's historical schema as a scientifically sound account of man in the world without repudiating one's past and, perhaps, the very foundation of one's identity? Could one assert one's self-worth fully without predicating the human relations, the primary ascriptive ties of family, kinship, and extended community that help individuals to recognize and define their humanity?

As the breadth and depth of these concerns attest, the dialogue between Marxism and its Asian interlocutors "caused a profound shock. Nor did Marxism itself," Carrère d'Encausse and Schram observe, "escape unchanged from the encounter."[7] It would be more accurate to remark that neither Marxism nor Asia itself emerged unaltered from the experience. In general terms, the Chinese adaptation of Marxism provided the opportunity for the rise of a nationalistic revolutionary movement that surpassed the bounds of the Comintern's initial prescription for national-bourgeois revolution to seek to become a socialist and then fully communist regime. After a protracted struggle and an agonizing process of adaptation and accommodation in the midst of violent revolution and civil war, Marxism in its Maoist incarnation achieved preeminence over all other rivals for national power in China within a few short years after World War II. In Japan, by contrast, even before full-scale war had erupted, the political, economic, and intellectual crisis that helped to lead Japan to what was known as the Pacific War[8] resulted in a resounding triumph of Japanese nationalism over socialism[9] that crushed the internationalist Marxist movement. Marxists there were crippled by the Japanese Communist party's submission to Comintern insistence that the very focus of Japanese national identity, the Imperial Household, be destroyed, and they found themselves unable to counter effectively the prior appropriation of the powerful symbols of legitimacy and identity in *kokutai* by the imperial state.

In previous chapters I have traced the emergence of these outcomes. Chinese and Japanese Marxists shared a common point of departure for the discourse, with Japanese Marxists exercising considerable influence over the content of what the Chinese came to know as Marxism through their movement and their translations of key writings. Japanese influence was strikingly evident in the Chinese anarchist movement, particularly in the anarchist group based in Tokyo. The circumstances of Chinese and Japanese anarchists differed strikingly, particularly the degrees of stateness manifested by the powerful late Meiji and early Taishō state, on the one hand, and the tottering Qing, on the other. Nevertheless, China had a vital and energetic anarchist movement, one that recognized, like Japan's Ōsugi, that human bondage could arise as much from social institutions and practices as in the form of the state. Nevertheless, in neither China nor Japan could the anarchist movement prevail when it met its rival in the potent, statist form of Marxism-Leninism. Anarchism's radical rejection not only of the state but of the nation, not only of the patriarchal family but also of other deeply rooted communal values, and not only of structures of the state but of organizational structures for its own movement left it powerless to contest Marxism-Leninism with its tightly knit organizational structure, its frank recognition of the need for a temporary state after the revolution in the form of the dictatorship of the proletariat, and its consecration of nationalism in bourgeois-democratic movements for national liberation. In China and Japan, many of those—such as Takabatake, Dai, Cai, and Wu—who resisted the appeal of Marxism in its new incarnation turned to an even more avidly nationalist and statist doctrine. In both societies, of course, certain anarchist strains would resurface as the native parties chafed under the Comintern's close supervision. It was no mere coincidence that those who exited from the JCP in 1927 to form the Rōnō-ha—Yamakawa, Sakai, and Arahata—had had strong backgrounds as anarchists, and resistance to Comintern guidance as well as to the strictures of the old "feudal" ideology and customs of Confucianism came to be manifested in Mao as well. But in the Rōnō-ha and in Mao's thought, the anarchist current always remained in dynamic tension with the urge to defend what was the Japanese or Chinese national community by creating and maintaining a viable state. Thus, Rōnō-ha activists succumbed just as surely as did the Kōza-ha to the nationalistic impulses that accompanied the outbreak of war with China. Under pressure from the Comintern to push for the abolition of the imperial system—the focal point of Japanese national identity—Japan's Marxists accepted the injunction only reluctantly and protected themselves from its implications for themselves individually and collectively through the alternative group identification provided by the party and the international Communist movement. Once removed from that alternative community and forced by imprisonment and the trial to confront directly the conflict between their adherence to Communism and their identity as Japanese, the alternative identification could not sustain them. By contrast, because the Comintern had always encouraged nationalism for China's bourgeois-democratic movement of national liberation, Chinese Marxists were spared this conflict. Yet their quest for a powerful national state to protect Chinese and defend what they insisted would be a fully socialist revolution did bring them into conflict with the official orthodoxy of the quest for stateless communism. As a result, in the Chinese adaptation of Marxism an uneasy tension remained between anarchism and stateness, between the impulse to build China into a strong national state and the urge to struggle against the onerous legacy of the imperial bureaucratic state and patriarchal Confucian social relations. These tensions and the resulting ambiguities were embedded in Mao's call to build a new Chinese national culture through continuous revolution.

This, in rough outline, recapitulates the overall outcome of the discourse on the

Asian landscape in the interwar years, but what were its consequences for Marxism itself? The breadth of the concerns noted here have compelled an analysis of Chinese and Japanese Marxism with respect to the national question in two interrelated senses. First, most broadly, the national question concerned the problem of adaptation itself. Emerging first when Russian revolutionaries endeavored to apply Marxism to their own country—"backward" and on the fringes of the doctrine's birthplace—the terms of the national dilemma were recast when the effort was made to transplant it to Japan and China, the first sites in which the new Soviet regime endeavored to foment revolution after the collapse of Spartacus in 1919. In its broadest possible terms, then, the national question concerned the contradiction between the universality of Marx's historical schema and theory of revolution and the particularity of the disparate national contexts to which that theory of revolution was applied. This became particularly problematic as Marxism expanded from its original European setting. Marx himself knew little about Asia, and this weakness was reflected in his problematic treatment of oriental society and the Asiatic mode of production, notions that in their implied geographic specificity suggested that Marx's allegedly universal history was never, in fact, universal even in the eyes of Marx himself. Such a challenge to the universal validity of Marx's history constituted, in turn, a contestation of the universal applicability of his entire theory of revolution inasmuch as revolution through class struggle formed the linchpin of Marx's holistic conception of world history.

Second, more specifically, the national question involves the related issues of nationalism and stateness. What links the two levels of concern together is the issue of individual and group identity. This linkage, observed in the analysis of the evolution of the Chinese and Japanese movements, can be seen in a slightly different way in the debate on Japanese capitalism and the controversy on Chinese social history. The scholars and activists examined here were of the world of "the people without history," to invoke Eric Wolf's penetrating analysis criticizing the sort of unilinear view of history that Marx's schema implies.[10] The notions of oriental society and the Asiatic mode of production implied that even Marx and Engels doubted that history unfolded in unilinear fashion and at the same time reaffirmed the orientalist conviction that the peoples of China and Japan, as all Asian peoples, had somehow been left behind by the dynamic of world history. Thus, Chinese and Japanese Marxists had to confront the issue of the place of Asia in human history and the question of the situations of their own societies within Asia. Nationalism, a fundamental pride in one's own being as Chinese, Japanese, or Asian, demanded the affirmation of the role of Asia in human history. Somehow, Asian Marxists had to accommodate their aspirations for their own societies to Marx's and Engels's historical schema, which echoed Hegel's *Philosophy of History* in seeing the maturation of humankind in the movement of consciousness from East to West. This could not be simply a negative accommodation, however, if nationalist sentiment was to be affirmed. In the Asian—as opposed to the European—context, this became the core of the national question. The issue was no longer simply one of the determination of national borders to conform to the aspirations of minority peoples in the collapsing empires of nineteenth-century Europe. It was one of the affirmation of the very being of these peoples and the value of their own experiences to the universal truths that were to be encompassed by Marxism as a universal doctrine.

This was the impulse behind both the debate on Japanese capitalism and the controversy on Chinese social history. It is also the reason that the Asiatic mode of production absorbed so much attention during the courses of both controversies even though the Leningrad Conference was supposed to have removed the subject from the range of acceptable discussion. Related to this was the problem of the historical state in the two societies, for it was the presence of the oriental despot, in Marx's view, that prevented the evolution of oriental societies through feudalism to capitalism. Needless to say, the subject was less troublesome in Japan because Marx had cast Japan as a prototypical feudal society. Nevertheless, the subject still absorbed the energies of those, particularly in the Kōza-ha, who sought explanations for Japan's nonequivalence to the West in terms of political development to accompany the spectacular gains made in the Meiji period. In the Asiatic mode of production, Hirano and Hani found an explanation for what they saw as the passivity of Japan's common people, and other scholars quite consciously conflated the absolutism of the Meiji state with oriental despotism as they sought to account for the antidemocratic turn of the Meiji regime. Finally, Marxists in both the Rōnō-ha and the Kōza-ha found the construct of the state in oriental society very suggestive in trying to understand the Meiji revolution from above. Here was the key to the startling autonomy of the Meiji state from social classes in Japanese society.

Such implications of the Asiatic mode of production idea would be much more disquieting for China's Marxist historians, however. Whereas it was unquestionable whether Japan had moved beyond feudalism to experience a high level of capitalist development, in China, even feudalism was in question. Had China experienced a slave formation of the type of ancient Greece or Rome? If not, what had it experienced? What was its impact on China's subsequent development? Here was the key that could unlock the secret of the Chinese revolution, but here, too, was a dangerous instrument that could destroy that revolution by denying its legitimacy in Marxian terms. Few Chinese—in their endeavor to assert China's dignity through equivalence with the West—actually used the Asiatic mode of production label in their paradigms. Yet historian after historian found himself denying to China the dynamic of change that had propelled Western societies forward from slavery to feudalism to capitalism. In their effort to assert their dignity as Chinese, Marxist historians, nonetheless, fell victim to this trap, unavoidably perhaps as they sought to adjust several millenia of Chinese history to fit Marx's European-based paradigm.

Here, then, in the two controversies the nationalism issue was an extension of the tension between the particularity and the universality of the European experience embodied in Marxism. The doctrine of Marxism itself would prove to be useless if it could not be adapted as revolutionary theory to respond to the requirements of one's own national context. In its most extreme embodiment, this kind of intellectual nationalism could threaten the integrity of Marxism itself as a philosophy justifying revolutionary change on the basis of universal historical forces. Conversely, nationality and nationalism brought into focus the related issue of how much Marxism might be altered while being adapted to the particularities of a new national context and still be identifiable as Marxism. In short, the issue of what constituted the essence of Marxism was posed as the profound problem of whether one could ever truly appropriate and adapt as ideology a philosophy with such universalist pretensions to a national context so disparate from that in which the doctrine was originally conceived.

Mao's interpretation of Marxism as having both general and particular elements offered one solution to the dilemma of the nationalist Marxist. Mao's response was such that it enabled his Chinese adaptation to profess a universalist essence even as its claim to legitimacy in the Chinese national context rested on its accurate discernment of the requirements of revolutionary change in China. Yet, in Mao's view, there was an essential unity between the particularity and the universality of things, including Marxism itself. This unity would enable Mao's reformulation of Marxism—as it would presumably permit Japanese national adaptations of the same—to offer claims to universality that could rival those of his predecessors in Marx, Engels, and Lenin. Raymond F. Wylie has taken note of the full, radical ramifications of Mao's claim.

> Given Mao's belief that the general and the particular character of a thing cannot be separated, the implication is that Leninism as a theory of revolution cannot be separated from its societal background. In other words, . . . Leninism is nothing more or less than the union of Marxist theory and practice; it is "Russianized" Marxism. . . . Nevertheless, Mao does affirm the applicability of Leninism to China, but in a new form, by pointing out that general character represents "universal truth for all times and all countries, which admits of no exception," while individual character "exists conditionally and temporarily, and hence is relative." This would mean that Leninism's general character (its Marxian-ness) would be valid for China because it represents "universal truth." As for Leninism's particular character (its Russian-ness), it could be dispensed with because it is merely "relative." The implication is that once transplanted to China, Leninism would have to shed its Russian particular character and adopt a Chinese universal character. Thus, the integral combination of Marxist general character and Chinese particular character would be "Sinified" Marxism; as such it could not be referred to as Leninism, for Leninism is "Russianized" Marxism containing both universal and particular character.[11]

In Mao's reformulated, sinified Marxism would also inhere certain universal elements enriched by insights gained from China's own historical experience in revolution. Mao's observations concerning praxis as the root of true knowledge and understanding of the world supported the claim that Chinese Marxism had something of universal value to offer to the world. Such an assertion was animated as much by pride in Mao's identity as Chinese as by the practical requirements of the Chinese revolution, and after the CCP victory, they would support the Chinese claim to international leadership of the Communist movement. There was a dialectic or contradiction, then, to borrow Mao's term, between the claim to universality and the particularity of the cultural context that gave rise to that assertion. Mao, like Sano, Takabatake, and other nationalistic Marxists in Japan, at once claimed to espouse Marxism in all the internationalism expressed in the "Communist Manifesto" call to workers of all countries to unite and at the same time professed to articulate a new version of the doctrine with universalist elements. Like Marxism in its original European incarnation, Chinese and Japanese Marxism would offer insights, not simply strategies of revolution, that promised to be applicable well beyond the cultural bounds in which they were conceived.

The patriotism, or nationalism, that inhered in such claims was validated in part by Lenin's encouragement of movements of national liberation outside the European metropolis. It is significant that the ascension and expansion of the influence of Marxist thought should have coincided with the emergence of nationalism as a powerful new force in the East. It is suggestive for the analysis here that this was also an era that saw the dramatic rise of competitive nationalistic sentiment in Western and Central Europe. As insightful inquiries into French radical nationalism and German conservatism in this era have demonstrated,[12] in the West, the radical nationalisms[13] of the late-nineteenth century were associated philosophically with an intense reaction against the rationalist, republican traditions of the Enlightenment. The philosophical positions adopted by Georges Sorel[14] and Friedrich Nietzsche[15] reflected a profound disenchantment with the hegemonic Enlightenment conceptualization of man in society. These men contested what they perceived to be the Enlightenment's excessive faith in human reason, its overvaluation of rationality, its attribution of greater esteem to what was created by human beings by rational artifice over what was animated by spontaneous *volonté*, and its promotion of associations among people that were the outgrowth of reasoned design rather than the product of what was natural and organic.

These tendencies flourished in fin de siècle Europe, but their patterns also bore implications for the nationalisms encountered in China and Japan, not least because of direct influences exercised by the European example. In France, where large numbers of Chinese students flocked to study just when the nationalistic components of this irrationalism were being articulated by Georges Sorel, these perspectives stood in problematic relation to what Chinese and Japanese students encountered in the political structure there. The views of Sorel and others of the increasingly vocal nexus between Left and Right rejected the politics of republican democracy and reflected an intense yearning for the symbols of distinctive national identity and organic political unity that had predated the destructiveness of the French Revolution.[16] If one queries why such a powerful movement should have emerged in France and not in England, one might hypothesize that the violence of the destruction of the French monarchical polity coupled with the incompleteness and unevenness of the industrial transformation in France[17] were critical determinants. The aftermath of the Revolution left intact enough of the previous social formation to encourage a sense of nostalgia for the restoration of its social relations. Thus, the French Revolution left in its wake a strong restorationism that was unrivaled in the aftermath of England's Glorious Revolution—or, indeed, in the immediate wake of Japan's Meiji Restoration, in which great efforts were made to assure Japanese that nothing had changed.[18] Well over one century after the event, powerful forces lingered on both sides of the question as to whether the 1789 Revolution had, after all, been for the good of France.[19] The radical nationalism of Maurice Barrès, Paul Déroulède, and their followers, then, articulated a profound sense of alienation from what was supposed to be France's destiny in Enlightenment modernity.[20]

In Germany, as a later-industrializing society, this sort of radical nationalism was echoed but evolved through a distinctive series of phases. The social bases of this impulse expanded and changed from the late nineteenth through the early twentieth centuries to embrace larger segments of the petite bourgeoisie.[21] Without overstating the continuities between Imperial Germany and the Germany of the Third Reich,[22] one might note among those who formulated the basis for the radical nationalist impulse a pronounced consistency in the repudiation of the assumptions that had come to define the dominant Western Enlightenment conception of modernity.[23] The articulation of their radically conservative views reflected a profound intellectual reorientation in this direction throughout Europe at the end of the nineteenth century—in France, Germany, Russia, Austro-Hungary, and Italy.[24] There was a sense in which even among those societies that might be viewed as Western, even among those whose societies underwent industrialization well before China and Japan, prevailing Western notions of what constituted modernity proved to be profoundly problematic. There was something in the experience of late industrialization (or partial industrialization) itself that seemed to catalyze this ambivalence, even hostility, toward modernity in the Enlightenment mold.

In both Germany and France, these views tended to be associated with the emergence of nationalistic yearnings, as the disillusionment with a notion of "modernity" based on the primacy of the rational and the man-made metamorphosed into a search for spiritual roots, thus drawing men and women back towards organic *gemeinschaftliche* ties. The work of Sorel invoked fruitfully and provocatively this antirationalist impulse and attracted many youthful Marxists to radical nationalism, particularly in Italy, where such radical young men and women had grown disenchanted with the promises held forth by Western industrial modernity and even by orthodox and revisionist Marxism.[25] If Marxism had fallen into crisis as scientific socialism, this offered hope for the true essence of Marxism as the basis for liberation through the operation of political myth.[26] In the radical nationalism of Sorel and his followers within and outside France, the myth of the nation played a pivotal role. As Hobsbawm has noted, "[p]olitical nationalism is revolutionary in its [very] origins": despite its appeal to primary ties based on kinship, for example, it is "particularly effective in disrupting traditional hierarchies and ties of dependence." "[A]ctual kinship plays only the most subordinate or marginal role in radical nationalist movements," Hobsbawm continues. "Yet it is the persistent, one might almost say the basic, theme of nationalist rhetoric."[27] This was evident in German and French radical nationalism at the end of the nineteenth century, and it would become strikingly evident in Chinese anti-Manchu racialism and then radical nationalism both within and beyond the bounds of Meiji and then Taishō and Shōwa orthodoxy.

If nationalism itself was politically radical in its genesis, what was it, then, that imbued it with its distinctive coloration at the end of the nineteenth and the early twentieth centuries? These nationalisms were not radical in their rejection of primary ties but rather in their affirmation of them against new, often contractual ties devised by the rational thinkers of the Enlightenment. To understand the link between the European radical nationalisms identified here and the nationalisms of Chinese and Japanese radical intellectuals and the implications of the latter for their relationship to Marxist orthodoxy, several matters must be clarified. It has been noted in studies of smaller national groupings that what constitutes the nation is more than simply shared kinship ties; what matters is a sense of a shared "state of mind," what might be termed national consciousness.[28] What is of primary significance, in other words, is not that individuals share certain ethnic characteristics but that they see themselves as sharing something unique as members of a given national group. In addition, as both Geoff Eley and Hans Kohn have argued, nationalism could be constituted in at least two ways. Although it may be an exaggeration to argue that the one is associated historically with Western nationalisms while the other is manifested in nationalisms of the East,[29] their observations do suggest bases for contemplating the quality of the nationalisms encountered among Chinese and Japanese Marxists. Eley notes that there has been an important "distinction between a political or voluntarist conception of nationality and an irrational or organic one." The first he identifies with "the great constructive experience of the French Revolution and is linked to notions of citizenship and popular sovereignty, where the nation signifies a political category of freely associating individuals." The second, conventionally associated with Johann Gottfried von "Herder and the German romantics," is what Eley describes as the "organic version." This, as observed in Friedrich Nietzsche, Sorel, and others, is opposed to the French revolutionary conception and "insists on the inherited, historicist character of national identity." In its rejection of the French Revolution, "it is thought to be deeply antipathetic to the ideals of liberal democracy usually derived from the first conception."[30] As A. D. Smith describes it, in the organic concept of the nation the following elements are involved:

> The individual has no meaning apart from the community of birth. Individuality is predicated of the group. The individual can realize himself through it alone. It has a life history, it is self-generating and self-sufficient, a seamless, mystic entity, ascertainable through objective characteristics—of history, religion, language and customs. Nations are "natural" wholes, they constitute the sole historical realities. Therefore the individual is primarily distinguishable in terms of his nationality, and only secondarily by social and personal traits. To opt out of the community is to risk the loss of a man's individuality.[31]

Inasmuch as it is alleged to be linked with the East, this second concept is the more interesting and provocative for the study of the link between Marxism and radical nationalism as discovered here in the marriage between nationalism and Marxism in China and Japan.

Nationalisms of the late nineteenth century might have appealed to either conception of the nation, but all nationalisms as ideologies seek to stress the uniqueness of the unity that they sanctify and imbue it with an immanent substantiality. Nevertheless, despite such claims, recent histories of the nationalisms of small nations—Rumanians, Greeks, and, indeed, Italians, as well as others—reflect the "artificial or manufactured character of the nineteenth-century nationalities."[32] Eley, thus, has attempted to draw a "threefold distinction in the overall periodization of nationalism: between structural processes of state-formation [or 'nation building'], located mainly in the countries of Western and Northern Europe between the fifteenth and late-eighteenth centuries; the emergence of nationalism as a specific ideology in the period of the French Revolution, leading to processes of ideological and cultural innovation, particularly amongst peoples aspiring to a measure of political independence; and finally processes of cultural unification, extending over several generations and owing much to the widening penetration of a centralizing government (classically in the three areas of railway-building, schooling and conscription)." "On this basis," Eley concludes, "nationalism becomes a clear instance of historical contingency, linked to political intervention, new ideologies and cultural change, and expressing a transformation of social identity, initially on the part of individuals but eventually for whole populations."[33]

Behind Eley's efforts lies an endeavor to demystify the essence of nationality, to strip away the veil of organicism in which nationalism as ideology seeks to cloak itself, and to reveal the purposeful manipulations that lie behind the making of nations. As for his periodization of stages of national building, if it applies accurately to the European context (and that judgment lies beyond the scope of the present work), what has been witnessed in China and Japan raises significant doubt as to its applicability to those examined here. In late-nineteenth and early-twentieth century China and Japan, certainly one can identify a process of cultural penetration by established governments. Efforts that would qualify for such a description were manifested both in the Qing China of the Tongzhi Restoration and Meiji Japan. Nevertheless, what seems to be missing from the analysis of the genesis of European nationalisms, a new catalyst of nationalism and then radical nationalism, cannot be omitted here—the impact of the intrusion of new actors in the form of states in quest of political, economic, military, even cultural domination over host peoples. The responses that this elicited were of at least two varieties. First, there were responses by the Chinese and Japanese states. Both the Meiji and the Tongzhi Restoration leaderships embarked on the kind of activities that Eley described as "processes of cultural unification" in which through the adoption of advanced Western technologies, particularly in communications and transportation, the state was able to extend its penetration into the society. Nevertheless, the state-initiated reforms in the two societies appear to have differed substantially from one another and from what Eley has described in his periodization of nationalisms in the West. First, only the Meiji Restoration appears to have been self-consciously nation building as well as state building in character. The status of the Manchus as an alien dynasty might not have been problematic within the context of the concept of China as a cultural entity up to this point, but with the weakness of the Qing in the face of the Western intrusion, it began to be of consequence for the constitution of a national state that could effectively contest the West on its own grounds. Thus, what the Manchus initiated could be described as state building and—in its invocation of Confucian philosophical norms to support its endeavors—cultural unification as well, but it was not nation building. This task was left for those frustrated with the mixed results of Tongzhi, for more radically reformist intellectuals such as Liang Qichao, who recognized the need for a cultural reconstitution of the Chinese as a nation, and for Zhang Binglin, Sun Yat-sen, and other revolutionists who in their racialism redefined China to exclude the Manchu rulers. To this Chinese experience in and after the Tongzhi Restoration, for example, in the Revolution of Meiji—for, indeed, it was revolutionary in its undertaking[34]—is counterposed an official effort to construct not only a state but a nation as well. The *kokutai* myth that supported the revolution of the Meiji oligarchy comprised the elements that Eley identified as the constituents of the organic notion of nationality and that Kohn associated with nationalisms of the East. During the middle and late years of the Meiji era, liberal Japanese intellectuals impressed with the message of the French Revolution—thinkers such as Fukuzawa Yukichi and Nakae Chōmin—folded into this organic nationalism elements of the radical French concept of nationality as citizenship.[35]

It was into this eddy of nationalities and nationalisms in formation in China and Japan that Marxist ideas were introduced. Because of the challenges posed by the dialectic between universality and particularity within Marxism itself and the dramatic cultural differences between the host societies and the birthplace of the doctrine, the relationship between the nationalism that radical intellectuals in China and Japan exhibited in this period and the Marxian ideal of universal internationalist revolution was highly problematic. Just as there were important differences in the circumstances of their societies early in the twentieth century, Chinese and Japanese radical intellectuals likewise exhibited important differences in the patterns of their efforts to resolve the national questions with respect to culture and nationality. The collapse of the 1898 Reform movement in China marked the disintegration of faith in Confucian norms, and those seeking revolutionary change were characteristically cultural iconoclasts. In this early stage of the Chinese revolutionary movement, nationalism was still very much in the making as racialism was directed against the Manchus, rather than embracing a consciousness of nationality in contradistinction to other nationalities and other cultures of the broader international environment. This second notion of nationalism would only come to full fruition on the occasion of the May Fourth movement in reaction to the humiliation of the Treaty of Versailles in 1919. By contrast, in Japan, encouraged by the Meiji state's mobilization of nationalist sentiment, even early Meiji socialists, untroubled by the need to deny what was Japanese to pursue modernity, also embraced many of the symbols of Japanese nationality. Except for principled opposition to expansionist wars against China and Russia at the turn of the twentieth century, many of these Meiji socialists stood in unity with the Meiji state's promotion of the values of the sacred *kokutai*. Yet even the banner of cultural iconoclasm did not prevent young Chinese radicals from finding themselves in problematic relationship to their culture and their identity as Chinese. As observed here, even among Chinese anarchists who targeted structures of authority in traditional philosophical perspectives and social practices, the destructiveness of anarchism did not necessarily entail a wholesale rejection of one's Chineseness. Indeed, the denouement of the anarchist episode in the conversion of many of its early apostles to the statist nationalism of the 1920s and 1930s Right Guomindang confirms the complexity of the predicament of the anarchosocialist in early twentieth-century China.

The rise and maturation of Marxism in the Chinese setting underscores the eclipse of anarchism by a stance that could affirm Chinese nationalism. When it was no longer native Chinese questioning the value of their own cultural traditions but a matter of the Western powers threatening their very physical existence, cultural iconoclasm gave way to an effort to define and appreciate what was distinctively Chinese while seeking a formula that would empower the Chinese to resolve their own internal and external problems. In this respect, the coincidence of the momentous May Fourth movement with the articulation of Lenin's affirmation of nationalism as a progressive force among colonial and semicolonial peoples was the key catalyst for the rise of a Marxist revolutionary movement in China. Marxism in its Leninist incarnation offered a means by which to accept the legitimacy of the quest for modernity while enjoying the satisfaction of its pursuit being in opposition to terms defined by the Western powers. It is fortunate for the fate of Marxism in China that thinkers such as Li Dazhao remained comfortably unaware of Marx's paeans to the progressiveness of Western imperialism. He, Mao and other thinker-strategists of the Chinese revolution—unlike the historians concerned with the Asiatic mode of production in the controversy on Chinese social history—could set aside issues concerning the relative values of Eastern and Western civilizations to build their movement on a comfortable synthesis of universal elements in Marxism-Leninism with what was particular and potentially of universal value in Chinese revolutionary experience. Through the 1920s and 1930s in China, nationalism came into ascendancy as a positive, identity-affirming force and reemerged as a powerful negative impetus in the second Sino-Japanese War of the 1940s. Through an often tense confrontation in these years between Chinese initiative and prescriptions of the Soviet-dominated Communist International, there gradually emerged a new synthesis of Chinese Marxism that reflected successful marriage of Chinese nationalism with Marxist internationalism.

In Japan, such a marriage would materialize only in a repudiation of orthodox Marxism-Leninism on the question of Japanese nationalism. Indeed, nationalism would not even prove to be at issue between the anarchist Ōsugi and the Marxian state socialist Takabatake Motoyuki. For all his flouting of Japanese convention, Ōsugi's psyche remained firmly wedded to his sense of his Japaneseness even to the point of approving—with Takabatake—Japan's position in the divisive Russo-Japanese War. By the time he had published Japan's first complete translation of Marx's *Capital*, Takabatake was leading his own national socialist movement, and Ōsugi was reacting with alarm to the growth of the new postrevolutionary Soviet state and with caution at the prospect of a Japanese Communist party that would be under the domination of the Soviet Union. Affirmations of Japanese national identity continued to surface after the founding of the JCP in 1922. It was only after heated debate and pronounced discomfort that the young party accepted the terms of the program drafted by Bukharin that called for the overthrow of the symbol of Japanese national identity, the Imperial Household. Within only five years, the party had splintered over the issue of accepting the Comintern's authority on the proper revolutionary sequence for Japan. At issue, in large part, was the status of Japan's Imperial House, whether in its mystical peculiarity it signaled that Japan was too backward for a proletarian-socialist revolution. The Rōnō-ha's abrupt exit from the party was as much a proud repudiation of the Comintern's diagnosis that Japan was less "modern" than Russia had been on the eve of October 1917 as it was a rejection of the specific two-step revolutionary process dictated by the Soviet-dominated Comintern.

The circumstances here were not without their ambiguities. When the two JCP factions engaged in the debate on Japanese capitalism, they did so in angry reaction against the nationalistic apologia for Japanese imperialism offered by Takahashi Kamekichi's heretical application of Marxism to repudiate the Leninist-inspired Comintern position in opposition to Japanese nationalism. This concerted response did not lay to rest the contradictions between the natural impulse to affirm Japaneseness and the demands by the Comintern to repudiate their nation and its symbols. Within another three years, as the JCP struggled to combat the repressive measures adopted against it by the Shōwa state, nationalism had cut further into the heart of the movement with the pre-*tenkō tenkō* of Mizuno Shigeo and his followers in the so-called Kaitō-ha. Their advocacy of an Imperial Household-centered socialism in Japan was not premised on the same functionalist statism of Takabatake, but they shared the latter's enthusiasm for the Imperial Household as the repository of Japanese national identity. The outbreak of war with China in 1931 heightened the urgency of resolving the national question in Japan, and it fueled the cascade of *tenkō* launched by the joint proclamation of Sano Manabu and Nabeyama Sadachika. Sano, in turn, echoed the sentiments of the Kaitō-ha, if not their precise reformulation of Marxism for the Japanese national context.

Japanese who married Marxism with nationalism tended to appeal to an organic sense of the nation in which the myth of nationality born of kinship weighed heavily. Those of the Kaitō-ha and Sano Manabu all borrowed heavily on the elements of the *kokutai* myth of the nation to maintain a powerful role for the state in their assimilation of Marxism to Japanese nationalism. There was no such statist pattern among the Chinese Communist party leaders. They valued highly their identities as Chinese, but their adaptations of Marxism to China's particular circumstances did not involve the reformulation of the doctrine of Marxism itself to accommodate radical nationalism as it did in Japan. Indeed, on closer examination, their nationalist agenda appears to have been profoundly different from that which animated the transformation of Marxism into Japanese national socialism. In this sense, the nationalism observed in Japanese Marxian national socialists is of a piece with the radical nationalism noted among the national socialists of turn-of-the-century France and Germany. It exalted irrationalism; it turned against conceptions of the nation and of the state as the products of human artifice; and it questioned the accoutrements of modernity that Japan had adopted tout ensemble in the revolution of Meiji. Ultimately, it drew very near to what would come to be seen as a variety of fascism akin to that espoused by those who claimed to follow Sorel, Nietzsche and other fin de siècle irrationalist nationalists. With the worship of the organic nation came an elevation of the organic state as the sine qua non for the existence of the nation. Into the new radical Marxian vision was incorporated the remanence of values that had almost been lost, sacrificed at the altar of modernity by Meiji oligarchs overly eager to accept Western culture in place of indigenous Japanese cultural norms. No such organic notion of the Chinese nation or view of the state as constitutive thereof pervaded the writings of Mao Zedong, Chen Boda, Liu Shaoqi, or others seeking to sinify Marxism. It was on this question of the national state, then, that one finds the definitive difference between the Chinese and Japanese Marxist responses to the national question as the war between the two countries ended and the Chinese Communist party rose to power.[36]

Lenin's perspective had reformulated the national question for the Asian and African contexts, but it would not allow it to transcend the issue of the state as it had been raised in Europe and as it was reinforced by the specter of the rise of a state that promised to be more formidable than any in the capitalist West—the Bolsheviks' own dictatorship of the proletariat. As conceived by Marx and Engels, the goal of communism embraced a vision of a society without a state, without the oppressive, coercive mechanisms that had characterized all previous eras in human history save the primitive communal society that inspired Marx's vision of postcapitalist communism. The state would wither away after the proletarian revolution but not before a temporary dictatorship of the proletariat arose to supervise the transition from capitalism to socialism. There were at least three separate issues that emerged here concerning the state for Marxists in Asia: (1) the nature of the state as a desideratum of revolutionary change in movements of national liberation; (2) the role of the state in socialist revolution and, thus, the question of whether the notion of a proletarian dictatorship was at all sensible given the goal of stateless communism; and (3) the question of whether the goal of statelessness was at all reasonable not only in general but particularly in societies that had seen socioeconomic formations in which the state was alleged to have been more repressive and oppressive than anything in the history of the West.

The Marxists in China and Japan who treated these concerns were acutely aware that the dictatorship of the proletariat in the world's first socialist state did not merely flourish but swelled alarmingly in the civil war period, producing an expansive bureaucratic and police structure that showed no signs of allowing any of the state's structure to "wither away." This spectacle profoundly affected the radical movements in the East that had sprouted under the influence of anarchism. On the one hand, among a small minority in Japan led by Ōsugi Sakae, it dispelled the illusion that the Marxism of the Bolsheviks held much in common with their own anarchism and, thus, reinforced their repudiation of the structures of state power. To both Chinese and Japanese the Bolshevik experience demonstrated, however, the futility of the rejection of the state given the international realities of the early-twentieth century. This Russian experience, coupled with China's continued humiliation by the powerful capitalist states of the West, even crippled as they were by World War I, contributed to the volte-face of radical Chinese anarchists to the side of the statist right wing of the Guomindang by the early 1920s. Indeed, the fortitude of the new Bolshevik state in the face of the Western powers encouraged the growth of bolshevism in both China and Japan in the 1920s precisely because it seemed to demonstrate that Marxism-Leninism was a thought system that promised to empower those who were not of the West to resist those who were. It was but a short step to draw from the Bolshevik experience not merely inspiration from the example of proletarian socialist revolution but also the encouragement to revise Marxism-Leninism itself to accord with the realities exhibited in the Soviet Union. Thus, Takabatake would contend, only a utopian socialist who ignored the realities of the nature of men and women and of current international politics could contemplate Marx's and Engels's assertions about the withering away of the state without revising them.

By the late 1920s, signs were omnipresent that the world was being engulfed by a wave of statism. Stalin had secured his dictatorial powers over the Soviet state by the 1930s. Fascism had overtaken Marxists in Italy from within the Marxist movement itself.[37] As in late nineteenth-century France and Germany, what lay behind the new statism was the nationalism that Lenin would address first during World War I immediately after the October Revolution. These realities reinforced the need for leaders of Marxist movements in China and Japan to address the issue of the state from a slightly different angle. A nationalistic movement against Western imperialism, as advocated in Lenin's call for movements of national liberation, embraced the advocacy of a bourgeois-democratic revolution. In Marx's original schema, such a revolution called for the building of a nation-state to protect the nationality from foreign encroachment and to defend and nurture indigenous capitalism. Both Chinese and Japanese Marxists were compelled to confront the issue in precisely these terms despite the substantial differences between their national circumstances. It will be recalled that although the Russian-dominated Comintern deeply feared the specter of Japanese imperialism, Comintern leaders also prescribed a two-stage revolution for Japan, just as they did for China. There is no question that the strategy was problematic; if the Japanese state was dominated by a bloc of landlords and capitalists under the hegemony of the bourgeoisie, then Japan's Marxists were being asked to wage bourgeois revolution against the bourgeoisie. More importantly, a key part of the mission of the bourgeois revolution was to create an effective, centralized national state, yet Japan's Marxists were urged to destroy that very state.

Even if these complications had not existed for Japanese Marxists, how could Marxian nationalists in either society in pursuit of bourgeois-democratic revolution be expected to agitate for nationalism and stateness—the union of the nation with the state—without jeopardizing the Marxian ideal of stateless socialism? Yet how could such socialism be achieved and maintained without the strong national state—particularly where the forces of production had allegedly not matured sufficiently to permit it—in an international environment in which the imperialist powers had demonstrated with arms wielded against the Soviet state their hostility to socialism? These became particularly thorny issues for Chinese and Japanese Marxists for two reasons. First, Marx's oriental society notion implied that for cultural and geographical reasons, Asian societies were more likely to develop powerful states standing autonomous above society. Second, Chinese and Japanese Marxists never accepted the notion that their revolutions should encourage simply bourgeois-democratic development in the short term. Proletarian socialism was their aim even in the less industrially developed China, and this required that a stateless society be kept firmly in mind as the ultimate goal of the revolution.

The national question was resolved in precisely the opposite of the direction of the ideal of stateless communism in Japan by the 1940s. By contrast, as early as the Yan'an era, Chinese Communist leaders exhibited a profound concern with preventing the emergence of negative characteristics associated with statism. The formula of "New Democracy"—which insisted on embedding the elements necessary for the transition to socialism in the very process of democratic revolution itself—endorsed the application of measures designed to stem the elements of stateness even as they were coming into being. Bureaucratic power, attitudes and practices of political leadership that might tend to the arrogation of autonomous interests and power by the state in opposition to those of ordinary Chinese were targeted by the periodic rectification campaigns launched by the CCP beginning in the 1940s. It is important to note that in attacking the accoutrements of statism, the CCP also targeted customs and perspectives that they perceived to have been inherited from its own Chinese past and not just in "bourgeois" customs and attitudes learned from the West. This recreated in Chinese Marxists a certain ambivalence toward things Chinese. This might have proved to be a healthier posture toward one's own identity than the choices that seemed to be available to Japan's Marxists. Either they avoided the issue entirely by accepting in toto a Comintern prescription or they indulged in the sort of radical Japanese nationalism that yielded the national-statist reformulations found from Takabatake to Sano. The evidence indicates that most Japanese Marxists, indeed, endeavored to do the first, and as internal socioeconomic crisis mounted in Japan, they succumbed to the second.[38] It would appear that Marxists in China were able to avoid this trauma, in part because China had not experienced the extent of Japan's remolding in the Western image and in part because they were not schooled in a powerful new statist orthodoxy like Japan's *kokutai*.[39] In Japan, the vague recollection of a harmonious past intensified nationalist passions as the crises of Taishō and Shōwa demonstrated that the revolution of Meiji had destroyed the legendary harmony of the very *kokutai* whose interests it pledged itself to fulfill. Such sentiment was not merely the ideology of a few intellectuals within and outside the Marxist movement but reverberated through the national community with enough breadth to sustain a desperate war effort for eight years. Circumstances contrasted starkly in China. There, the remanence of the past was not to be celebrated but to be lamented, and behind Mao and Liu, Chinese radicals sought in Marxian universalism a philosophical system transcendent of national differences that could save the national entity that was China.

EPILOGUE: NATIONALISM AND STATISM IN POSTWAR CHINA AND JAPAN

In the years following Japan's defeat in World War II and the victory of the CCP in 1949, the national question continued to be of singular significance to the Marxist movements in the two societies. The fundamental issues would continue to concern the tension between the universality of Marxism and the requirement of its adaptation to the peculiarities of a new cultural setting, and nationalism and the role and fate of the state would continue to conflict with the ultimate vision of stateless international socialism. As they had in the interwar years, the Chinese and Japanese Marxist movements would continue to share much in their struggles to resolve the national question while remaining, as much as possible, within the bounds of Marxist-Leninist orthodoxy. In particular, the two movements would come to converge on the problématique of the state both in the terms in which it had surfaced in the interwar years and in new ways in response to new issues that emerged in the two societies.

With the CCP's victory in 1949, the New Democratic stage was to continue until China was ready for the transition to socialism, and so, too, was the quest for a viable Chinese national state. To be sure, with the defeat of Japan in 1945 and with the CCP's ascent to national power four years later, China had at long last "stood up" (*zhan qi lai le*).[40] In the immediate years thereafter, however, the CCP was compelled to struggle to extend its effective national control beyond that limited range over which the GMD had actually exercised effective rule to territories that had been the strongholds of hostile landlord and business interests in rural and urban areas, respectively, particularly in South China and into Tibet. Nor did the challenge from the more advanced capitalist societies of the West abate immediately. China once more found itself embroiled in full-scale war in the Korean conflict in the early 1950s, even before the Communists had successfully brought pockets of resistance under control.

Thus, the remanence of this aspect of the national question in the post-1949 period—the period of continuing the revolution rather than the "postrevolutionary era," if one follows the theory and practice of post-1949 Chinese communism under Mao—led ineluctably to the problem of the state. Mao and his colleagues rejected democracy in the Western bourgeois mold for China. "There are bourgeois republics in foreign lands, but China cannot have a bourgeois republic," Mao argued, "because she is a country suffering under imperialist oppression. The only way is through a people's republic led by the working class."[41] Marx's perspective on democratic politics under socialism and then communism, however, had been conditioned by the experience of bourgeois democracy in the West. What, then, would become of the democratic aspects of the revolution the CCP aspired to make if the model that had comprised the basis for their doctrine was cast aside?

The issue of what to do with national minorities would pose a major challenge to this aspect of the CCP's revolutionary position. Despite Mao's acknowledgment of the problem of "Han chauvinism" and his recognition that the Soviet example was not to be emulated on the nationalities question,[42] however, the issue has not been resolved satisfactorily in terms of concrete policies, particularly with respect to the status of Tibet. To a large extent, this has been a product of the party's strict adherence to the orthodoxy that socialism and communism can be realized "only by unflaggingly fighting the vestigial thought of bourgeois nationalism."[43] Only limited concessions have been made to the nationalist sentiment of minorities: With minorities granted "autonomy" in some areas, the constitutions since 1949 have not recognized their right to self-determination.[44] Not surprisingly, then, the call for greater recognition of political and cultural rights of national minorities has become an integral part of China's struggling human rights movement.[45] Nevertheless, the failure to resolve this issue in the Marxist polity four decades after the CCP came to power and three decades after it claimed to have achieved the communist stage is of much greater significance than the tiny 6 percent proportion of the total population comprised by national minorities would suggest.[46] As in the Soviet Union—and, indeed, as in Marxism itself—the effort to dissolve the particularities of the less powerful into universalities defined by those who wield greater power may appear no different than the assertion of the primacy of the particularity of the greater power. This is the core of the national question in its broadest possible terms, not only as it is posed within the terms of Marxist thought but as it confronts the non-Western world as a whole in the received mandate to achieve "modernity."

Nationalism and the Problem of the State from Prewar to Postwar Japan

In Japan, too, the persistence of the problem of nationalism has continued to be linked intimately to the question of the nature and role of the state during and after the revolution. Of course, in Japan revolutionary change had not been achieved by the indigenous Marxist movement, nor had the movement itself managed to extricate itself from the predicament of the national question during the turbulent years of the second Sino-Japanese War. After the war, when those who had been held political prisoners under the old regime were released, the problem of Japanese nationalism resurfaced to rivet the attention of Marxists who had been involved in the prewar movement. The ignominious demise of the Japanese Communist party in the massiveness of *tenkō* in the 1930s and 1940s had to be overcome by earnest and harshly critical analyses of the shortcomings of the prewar regime. These would be launched, however, within the context of schisms within the Marxist movement that grew directly out of the contours of prewar factionalism.[47] The JCP was revived from among the survivors of the Kōza-ha in 1945. In an essential continuity with the prewar party, the resurrected party continued to embrace the Comintern formula of a two-stage revolution, its immediate goals remaining "to eliminate the emperor system, democratize Japan, and carry out land reform."[48] Meanwhile, under the leadership of Suzuki Mosaburō, the Nihon Shakaitō (Japanese Socialist party) was born in the same year, its left wing coinciding with the prewar Rōnō-ha. Like the Communist party, the new Socialist party advocated democratization and the establishment of socialism in Japan but also embraced an evolutionary, peaceful transition to socialism (*heiwa kakumei*) in accordance with prewar Rōnō-ha leader Yamakawa Hitoshi's invocation of Marx's, Engels's, and Lenin's view that socialism could be attained by such means.[49]

As in post-1949 China, the issue of nationalism reemerged almost immediately in the postwar controversies over the origins of the imperialism and fascism that had led Japan into the disastrous war. There was also the question of the status of Japan under the occupation of U.S. troops. Because the reforms initiated under Supreme Commander of Allied Forces in the Pacific (SCAP) were reversed in midstream, their legacy was sufficiently ambiguous to incite vehement debate among the postwar Marxist factions. Japanese nationalism was at the center of the controversy, inasmuch as the debate concerned the role and significance of Japanese in making or completing their own bourgeois-democratic revolution.

The inconsistencies in SCAP policies derived from the reemergence of the cold war with the articulation of the Truman Doctrine in 1947. Immediately after the war, General Douglas MacArthur had launched sweeping initiatives intended to democratize and demilitarize Japanese political and economic life. Aside from measures that directly attacked the structure of Japan's military, such as the demobilization of Japan's military forces, the dissolution of paramilitary organizations, and the purging of the top wartime political leadership, the Allied reforms also targeted other, less direct, sources of support for the prewar militaristic political system. A major element included the disestablishment of Shintō as the state religion and the emperor's declaration that he was no longer to be considered divine. Other critical measures included the weakening and decentralization of the oppressive police apparatus; so-called zaibatsu-busting, the dismantling of the huge financial cliques that had dominated the prewar economy and provided the foundation for Japan's military infrastructure; and, notably, a sweeping program of land reform, premised on the belief—shared, curiously, with the prewar Comintern and Kōza-ha—that "the social and economic condition of the Japanese countryside was a powerful causal factor in bringing about Japan's aggressive policies in Asia."[50]

The latter element, land reform, was of central importance to Marxists concerned with the analysis of the Japanese nation and state in the postwar era. Under the Allied land reform program, although the results varied by locale, by 1950, land tenancy had declined from almost 50 percent to only 10 percent of arable land, while rent controls mitigated the pressures of high rents on agrarian households.[51] This achievement was matched in the urban sector by the dissolution of eighty-three zaibatsu holding companies and the passage of significant antimonopoly legislation.[52] These latter achievements, however, were brought into question by the sudden reversal of the emphasis of Occupation policy from dismantling of Japanese military industrial capability to the strengthening of Japan as the bastion of support for America's containment of the Soviet Union in the Pacific. This new emphasis was reinforced by the prospect and then the reality of the Communist victory in China. Both the successes and the limitations of SCAP policy bore significant implications for Japan's Marxists, but in their ambiguity lay the seeds of ambivalence and discord. Within the context of the debate on Japanese capitalism as it extended into the postwar era, the descendants of the two prewar factions

launched a vigorous controversy on the nature of the Occupation and the significance of its reforms for understanding Japan's development experience.

Interestingly, the two factions were in agreement on the fundamentally progressive character of the SCAP reforms. The Rōnō-ha stance in this respect was the
more consistent because the JSP maintained that faction's advocacy of a single-
stage proletarian socialist revolution. Rōnō-ha scholars argued that the SCAP
reforms had rationalized Japanese capitalism and made it into a more stable form of
"state monopoly capitalism."[53] They had finally eliminated the remnants of semifeudal agriculture that had hampered the efficiency of Japanese capitalism in the
prewar era.[54] What was important from the Rōnō-ha perspective was that what had
remained of a semifeudal character in the countryside had been in the superstructural realm, in the sphere of "feudalistic thought, sentiments, and habits."[55] The
elimination of such elements in the reforms represented a progressive, democratizing element in Japanese history, but this was but a superficial contribution. As part
of an endeavor to strengthen Japan as a monopoly capitalistic society, Rōnō-ha
scholars argued, the SCAP reforms could not be salutary in the final analysis. At
the same time that they mitigated undemocratic elements associated with feudalism in the countryside, the overall effect of the reforms was to reinforce nondemocratic bourgeois elements of the Japanese state.[56] Compared to the Kōza-ha
perspective, this interpretation of the SCAP reforms was relatively straightforward, yet it still placed the descendants of the prewar Rōnō-ha in problematic
relation to Japanese culture just as the Kōza-ha view would. Rōnō-ha scholars
were, after all, praising the SCAP reforms for their destruction of traditional
Japanese norms and mores in the countryside and for completing a bourgeois-
democratic revolution that Japanese apparently lacked the capacity to achieve for
themselves.

This dilemma, in a much more pronounced form, was also at the heart of Kōza-
ha interpretations of the same events. As early as the JCP's Fifth Party Congress of
February 1946, the Kōza-ha began to incorporate the Occupation reforms into the
view of Japanese "backwardness" that was the foundation of its two-stage revolutionary strategy. The congress made two major changes of significance to the
national question. First, while the JCP would adhere to the prewar two-stage
revolutionary strategy, the Occupation reforms were to be viewed as a progressive,
liberating force. Ultimately, of course, as the leading capitalist power in the West,
the United States remained the enemy of the advocates of socialist revolution, but
in the immediate term, the Kōza-ha concurred with the Rōnō-ha that the Occupation was salutary in contributing to the democratization and demilitarization of
Japan.[57] Second, JCP leader Nosaka Sanzō embarked on an effort to Japanize
Marxism in a manner that would draw the JCP close to its rivals in the Rōnō-ha.
Nosaka contended that the changed conditions of occupied Japan made the call for
violent revolutionary change on the Bolshevik model advocated by the 1932
Theses no longer necessary. Now that the JCP could operate openly as a competitive political party, Nosaka argued, the party should emulate the Chinese example
and seek a broad base of support from workers, peasants, intellectuals, and other
progressive elements, including the new JSP.[58] Because, at this early stage, it was

yet unclear how radical the SCAP reforms would actually be, the party still advocated the effort to complete the bourgeois democratic revolution begun by the Meiji Restoration and abetted by the new reforms. Accordingly, the party continued to call for land reform, the dissolution of the imperial system, and further democratization.

Once the true extent of SCAP intentions became evident, particularly in the area of land reform, however, Kōza-ha scholars became convinced that they were even more revolutionary than the Meiji Restoration had been in achieving the tasks of the bourgeois-democratic revolution. The leading Kōza-ha economic scholar, Yamada Moritarō, for example, contended that the land reforms of SCAP had "opened a new path liberating Japanese agriculture" from its backward basis, thus making possible the reconstruction of the semifeudal Japanese economy as a whole.[59] This view was profoundly problematic. In this rather sanguine early interpretation of the Occupation reforms, the United States, allegedly a reactionary and imperialistic power, appeared as the agent of a liberating revolution from above that was far more radical than what Japanese had been able to accomplish for themselves in the Meiji Restoration. Where was Japanese initiative in this process? Why had an external agency been necessary at all? Was this a sign that Japan, like China, and, indeed, like oriental societies in general in the Marxian view, were endowed with no internal dynamics of change of their own but required external stimuli if they were to achieve the change that would allow them to rejoin humankind in modernity?

To some extent these doubts were mitigated by the Occupation's shift in policies and the impact of that change on the Kōza-ha's interpretation of the reforms. Although the view that the postwar reforms formed part of Japan's bourgeois-democratic revolution would be resurrected later in the decade, now that SCAP was turning against the Japanese Left, the overall American influence on postwar Japan would be viewed with deepening suspicion. Nosaka argued that the Occupation reforms had been inadequate and had left intact the three pillars of the prewar emperor system: its economic basis in the landed elite in the countryside, the bureaucracy, and monopoly capitalism. In addition, with the sudden increase of pressures by the state on the Left, Nosaka argued that once again violent revolution might be necessary to overthrow a state that continued to be fundamentally repressive.[60]

This negative valuation of American influence was strengthened under the Soviet Union's overwhelming influence on the party. Pressured to adopt a much harsher assessment of the American influence, the JCP accepted the 1951 Theses. This new program asserted that the United States had brought Japan not democratization but "only chains and slavery" and argued that the basis of the absolutist emperor system in semifeudal landownership persisted in Japan as a result of the inadequacy of SCAP's land reform efforts.[61] The adoption of these theses marked a turning point for the postwar JCP with respect to the national question. From this point on, a major theme of JCP literature would be nationalistic opposition to Japan's subordination to the United States. As in the prewar era, the new position would be supported by rigorous scholarly research, in the form of a new *Kōza* published in 1953. Asserting that the SCAP reforms had merely "reorganized, in a subordinating manner, a semi-feudalistic Japanese monopoly capitalism,"[62] the new *Kōza* depicted the relationship between the United States and Japan as an imperialistic one, formed of the American desire to dominate the world economy, as reflected in the Truman Doctrine and its anti-Chinese role in the Korean War. The reforms, then, were not liberating or democratizing, but rather, as "the abortion of democratic revolution in Japan," they comprised "the foundation of American imperialism toward Japan."[63] The current postwar Japanese state, in this view, did not constitute a significant improvement over that of the prewar era. It comprised the same basic constellation of forces as the prewar state except that these elements were now reactionary in a new fashion in their direct subordination to the United States. "The Yoshida [Shigeru] government represented the reactionary interests" of "the emperor, the old reactionary military cliques, especially privileged bureaucrats, parasitic landlords, and monopoly capitalists," the new *Kōza* scholars wrote. Their class basis was preserved in the remanence of "the semi-feudal relations of the emperor system, landlord landownership, etc." left behind by the Occupation's dismally incomplete land reforms.[64] The reforms had required former tenants to purchase land; they had allowed tenancy and high rents to persist; and farmers continued to be squeezed by the twin pressures of heavy taxes and rice prices limited by the state.[65]

The full terms of this Kōza-ha treatment of the Occupation reforms lie beyond the scope of the present work. It is sufficient to note here that relatively positive and negative assessments of the impact of the Occupation reforms struggled for supremacy within the JCP in the 1950s and the 1960s. In 1958, a compromise position emerged in the form of a report by Miyamoto Kenji to the Seventh Party Congress. The compromise recognized the salutary impact of the reforms without vitiating the argument for a two-stage revolutionary strategy and articulated a fiercely nationalistic posture vis-à-vis American domination over Japan in the postwar era. Thus, Miyamoto acknowledged that as a result of the reforms, "along with the loss of the emperor's absolute right, the structure that made the military, the Naimushō, the Privy Council, the Upper House, and the bureaucracy relatively independent political forces has been dissolved, . . . and the Diet has been accorded the position of the highest organ of national sovereignty." Politically, the outcome of these changes was to accord monopoly capitalism a greater role in the Japanese state than ever before. Economically, the result was that the primary contradiction between peasants and landlords that had dominated Japan's "backward" countryside was replaced by the conflict between peasants and "their exploitation and usurpation by American imperialism and the [Japanese] monopoly capitalism that is subordinate to it."[66] The stress that Miyamoto placed on the subordination of Japanese monopoly capitalism became the new linchpin of the JCP argument for a strategy of two-stage revolution because it helped to account for the incompleteness of Japan's bourgeois-democratic structure despite the highly advanced stage of its capitalist development.[67] As articulated by Miyamoto, this argument became the basis for the program adopted at the JCP's Eighth Party Congress of early-1961, and it has shaped the party's position to the present.

This is not to say that the new position precluded the emergence of related controversies, such as that over the extent to which the United States had succeeded in its efforts to reduce Japan to quasi-colonial status.[68] As has been noted elsewhere, a major contradiction was embedded in this Kōza-ha position. "If the United States had tried to limit the complete democratization of Japan . . . then SCAP's putative bourgeois-democratic revolution did not occur, and thus the postwar reforms did not really constitute a revolution at all. If this revolution did occur despite U.S. efforts to obstruct it, this contradicted the JCP's claim that American power over Japan was sufficiently great as to impair Japan's national independence."[69]

Throughout this controversy on the Occupation and Japan's relationship to the United States in the postwar era, Japanese Marxists were compelled to contend with the issue of the autonomy of Japanese political and economic development. Japanese nationalist impulses to self-determination and the problem of the character of the state before and after the war were, of course, at issue. The nature of the prewar state cast a heavy shadow over those who endeavored to effect full democratization in postwar Japan, and, perhaps for that reason, a debate rivaling in significance the controversy over the Occupation reforms arose concerning the origins of Japanese "fascism" and imperialism in the 1930s and 1940s. Did the rise of Japanese militarism in these years indeed constitute a fascism of the same basic type as the polities of Nazi Germany and Mussolini's Italy? If so, how was one to account for it in terms of the Marxist periodization of human history? To return to the issue as it had been posed by Takahashi Kamekichi in 1927, How could Japanese expansionism and ultra-nationalism be explicated in Marxian terms?

The primary difficulty here was rooted in the Comintern's problematical analysis of the nature of the Japanese political economy in the prewar era. The same theses that had given rise to the split between Rōnō-ha and Kōza-ha in the late 1920s and early 1930s expressed the central dilemma that Japanese, indeed Chinese and Japanese Marxist scholars together, confronted in attempting to apply the Marxian historical schema to their societies. What they discerned in their native societies did not seem to fit precisely any of the specific modes of production described by Marx. Characteristically, Marxists on both sides of the East China Sea had long tended to take as their point of departure a fundamental misconstruction of Marx's paradigm, an error that was in part attributable to Marx's own manner of formulating it. Although Marx had never intended that his schema of human development through progressive modes of production be taken to denote that every society must pass through a uniform sequence of historical stages clearly delineated one from another, in fact, it was precisely in this sense that his paradigm tended to be applied both by Soviet scholars and by Chinese and Japanese Marxist theoreticians.

Thus, in the immediate aftermath of the disastrous Pacific War, Marxists in Japan yearned to find in the Marxian schema some explanation for the rapid crescendo of ultranationalist sentiment centered around the imperial system that led their country into imperialist war.[70] Here the issues of nationalism and statism were inextricably linked. The cause of the dispute lay in the Comintern's internally inconsistent treatments of the Japanese state in the 1927 and 1932 theses. There, the state's behavior had been overdetermined by both "semifeudal" landlord elements and advanced monopoly capitalist forces. There was no problem here for Rōnō-ha scholars, who rejected what they saw as the Comintern's unwarranted emphasis on the allegedly "backward" elements of Japan's society and state. Within the Kōza-ha, however, there was considerable uneasiness about the Comintern's interpretation even if it did inspire Yamada Moritarō's classic description of Japanese expansionism as a "militaristic semi-feudal imperialism."[71] By 1946, as soon as the JCP had reconstituted itself, the controversy over Japanese imperialism was revived within the Kōza-ha, with Shiga Yoshio and Kamiyama Shigeo the leading participants.

In a sense, Kamiyama's view reconciled the Rōnō-ha and Kōza-ha positions. He argued that Japan's had been a "dual imperialism" (*nijū no teikoku-shugi*), issuing from both advanced capitalist development of the sort described by Lenin and by an imperial institution that remained absolutist. The period after the Manchurian incident, in this view, represented not the emergence of fascism in Japan but a strengthening of the reactionary elements of the emperor system.[72] In opposition to this interpretation, Shiga drew even closer to the Rōnō-ha position, asserting that during the 1930s and 1940s, Japanese capitalism had achieved substantial development beyond its level at the time the 1927 and 1932 theses were drafted. The result was that the emperor system was no longer simply absolutist but imperialistic in the classic capitalist sense. During the war years, this state was compelled by militarist and bureaucratic forces to act in a fascist fashion, thus earning it the label "military fascism."[73] The effect of Shiga's argument was to graft onto an economic base that he saw as highly "modern" a political superstructure that he characterized as "feudalistic-militaristic" even while using the term *fascism* to refer to this phenomenon.[74] Such a treatment was not only problematic on a theoretical level; it was also infelicitous as it impinged on the implications of the analysis for an appreciation of the national question. Suddenly, Japan seemed to have had a state that was incomparable not only to the bourgeois democracies of Britain and the United States but also to fellow late industrializers Italy and Germany. What remained of distinctively Japanese traditional attributes seemed to disqualify Japan even for the straightforward use of an appellation (fascism) that referred to the perversities of modern capitalist development. Ultimately, the significance of this was that, as in China, without a cultural revolution, a reformation of what was Japanese, or Chinese, to something modern as defined on the Western model, the Chinese or Japanese societies or states could not be characterized in the universalizing terms of the Marxist model. In the prewar period, those who had dared to call into question these implications of being a Marxist had become Marxists of quite a different sort; they became Marxian national socialists. After the war, it was in China that such daring questioning of the implications of the Marxian notion of modernity occurred, not in a Japan whose Marxists felt deeply stung by the humiliation of the *tenkō* experience.[75]

Thus, the debate on Japanese fascism proceeded in postwar Japan without questioning in a fundamental way the premise of the need for a two-stage revolution in Japan that the Comintern and JCP had advocated before the war. The Rōnō-ha, characteristically stressing the advanced features of Japanese capitalism, analyzed the prewar state as a fascist power supported by "the combination of the military, bureaucracy, and zaibatsu." In the view of scholars such as Yamakawa Hitoshi, Ōuchi, and Sakisaka Itsurō, the rise of fascism marked the decisive shift of the bourgeoisie to a reactionary mode in which it acted in the interests of finance capital. At the same time, the Rōnō-ha was able to incorporate into its analysis the semifeudal elements such as the military and the bureaucracy that made such mischief in Kōza-ha interpretations. What was for the Rōnō-ha classic fascism was for Kamiyama "absolutist reaction" and for Shiga an "emperor system" operating with great independence yet being forced to execute fascist tasks. There were a great many difficulties here, particularly in Shiga's interpretation. If the state enjoyed such structural autonomy, presumably it had come from the pattern of its development as a capitalist state, yet Shiga denied himself that recourse by claiming that the emperor system state had remained absolutist and, thus, had not yet enjoyed a high level of capitalist development. Perhaps because he recognized these difficulties, Shiga modified his position to claim the higher development of Japanese capitalism in the 1930s and 1940s that would allow him to approach more closely the Rōnō-ha position.[76] While others, including Hattori Shisō, also drew close to the Rōnō-ha position in interpreting fascism,[77] still others within the Kōza-ha argued that although a transformation had occurred in the 1930s and 1940s, the imperial state had never lost its absolutist, semifeudal character.[78]

Through all these treatments, there is a sense that there was something particular to the Japanese body politic as reflected in the character of the imperial institution. It would appear that even in the harsh light of the postwar era, it was difficult for Kōza-ha Marxists to free themselves of the mystical aspects of the imperial institution that they rejected so vehemently. Even now, almost half a century after the Japanese defeat and the desacralization of the emperor, the Imperial Household remains at the center of questions concerning the limitations of Japanese democracy. The death of Emperor Hirohito in 1989 simply intensified this debate. Despite the substantial differences between the fates of the revolutionary movements in the two societies, it is important to note that this focus on the problem of democracy has drawn Japanese Marxism close to Chinese thought in the postrevolutionary period. The two movements have converged in the centrality of components of the national question concerning the state to contemporary Marxist controversies on the development of the two societies. Ultimately, in short, the political theory of Chinese and Japanese Marxism became absorbed in the problem of realizing and then transcending Western forms of state power.

The controversies in postwar Japan detailed here were not merely arid scholarly debates without practical consequences. They have informed policy debates within and between the Communist and Socialist parties. Today, the JCP and JSP consistently promote their agendas as guarantors of full democratization in Japan and vehemently contest any action—such as joint ministerial worship at Yasukuni shrine, the revision of textbooks to exclude negative references to the Sino-Japanese War, or the dispatch of Self-Defense Forces to participate in the Gulf War—that might be taken to revive Shintō as state religion, inspire ultranationalism and militarism, or restore the prewar reverence for the emperor.[79] Their campaigns, however, have not surmounted the complex set of issues involved in the national question in Marxism. These may be appreciated more fully in light of postrevolutionary developments in China, for despite the fact that the Marxist revolutionary movement in China issued in a dramatic victory while that in Japan suffered a traumatic and equally dramatic failure, the dimensions of the national question confronted by the two movements continue to exhibit important commonalities as they did in the interwar years when the two movements often exercised direct influence on one another.

The Permanent Revolution and the Problem of the State in Post-1949 China

In China, the national question was apparently resolved by Marxists led by Mao Zedong as early as the Yan'an era, but it continued to reverberate in the postrevolutionary era. Here the nationalist element was closely intertwined with questions concerning the nature and the role of the state in revolutionary change after the revolutionary party has acceded to power. As observed here, a key aspect of Mao's sinification of Marx lay in his claim that Marxism-Leninism, like all Marxism, comprised both particular and universal elements. Within the dialectic between the universal and the particular lay a profound cultural ambivalence toward both Chinese culture and that of the West. This had already become evident in Mao's theoretical work "On Practice" as well as in the implementation of rectification campaigns beginning in the Yan'an era, and it was expressed explicitly both in Mao's thought and in Liu Shaoqi's explanation of why rectification was necessary at all. In *How to Be a Good Communist*, Liu argued that it was necessary to attack the vestiges of the old society,[80] and he assailed both the so-called "feudalistic" elements of Chinese tradition and habits and attitudes associated with bourgeois society that had been learned from the West. At this point, there was no fundamental divergence between the positions of Mao and Liu.[81] By the late 1950s it had become clear that the dialectic between the universal and the particular within Marxism as a whole, as Mao had described it in 1937, was being reproduced in the simultaneous effort to proclaim the discovery of a specifically Chinese path to socialism/communism, on the one hand, and the alleged universality of the Chinese revolutionary model, on the other.

Not surprisingly, given the significance of the scale and strategic position of the revolutionary triumph of Marxism in China, the world was compelled to wait only a short time before this tension became apparent. The sinification of Marxism had proven its validity in the success of the revolution, and Mao did not hesitate to expand his claims to the universal elements of his new formulation. Indeed, as early as 1945 and 1949, Liu was broadly alluding to the applicability of Mao's strategy for the Chinese revolution to "national liberation movements" in "similar conditions in other lands of Southeast Asia."[82] In succeeding years, these claims would be bolstered by the death of Joseph Stalin and Mao's struggle against the "revisionism" of Nikita Khrushchev.[83] Mao was at once repulsed by Khrushchev's revelation of Stalin's crimes in his "Secret Speech"[84] and encouraged by Khrushchev's introduction of the notion of "multiple paths to socialism" at the Twentieth Party Congress of the Communist party of the Soviet Union.[85] By 1957, there were signs that tensions between Khrushchev and Mao increasingly involved Mao's assertion that the Chinese Communist party was the rightful leader of Communist movements in the Third World. As Schwartz notes, on this occasion Mao's vehement insistence against Khrushchev's promotion of polycentrism in the movement[86]—that " 'the socialist camp must have a head' "—signified "new pretensions to authority on the part of the Chinese Communist Party."[87] Thus, as early as autumn 1956, Mao spoke to leaders of Latin American communist parties of the lessons of the Chinese revolution in its setting of peasant masses "oppressed by imperialism and feudalism."[88] There is also evidence that in this period, the nationalism that supported such Chinese claims was further inflamed by a Soviet proposal that the Chinese leadership allow the Soviet Union to build submarine bases along the Chinese coast. This proposition bore an uncomfortable resemblance to the institution of the treaty ports created on the demand of the Western powers a century earlier, for they would be under foreign rather than Chinese control.[89] In the ensuing years, with the legitimacy of each party's leadership threatened by the conflicting claims of the other,[90] open conflict between the two national parties finally erupted. The publication of such polemical pieces as "On Khrushchev's Phoney Communism" in the early 1960s further intensified the Chinese effort to offer to communist parties in other later-industrializing societies the Chinese adaptation of Marxism as a universally applicable model of socialist revolution.

The dismissal of Marshal Peng Dehuai as Minister of Defense in 1959 marked the apogee of Sino-Soviet tensions in the period before they became public. These tensions help to illuminate the full dimensions that the national question would come to assume in post-1949 China. During a visit to the Soviet Union from April through June that year, Peng openly criticized Mao Zedong's Great Leap Forward policies.[91] At the time of Peng's trip, it had already become evident that there were those in the Chinese leadership, including Mao, who were prepared to allow Sino-Soviet relations to deteriorate just when Chinese leaders had secured from the Soviet Union vital agreements for aid in the fortification and professionalization of the Chinese military.[92] Subsequently, on the eve of the Central Committee Plenum at Lushan late that summer, Peng circulated a "Letter of Opinion" among prominent party leaders condemning the dramatic failures of the Great Leap Forward. Peng's subsequent dismissal in September 1959, his replacement by Marshal Lin Biao, the purge of other military leaders who had spoken in support of Peng at the Plenum, and the launching of an Anti-Rightist Campaign in 1959–1960 marked a turning point of sorts in the articulation of the national question in revolutionary China.[93]

In the new circumstances, the national question would involve considerably more than just competition among petty nationalisms to claim leadership of the international Communist movement and much more than the question of the nature and role of the state in revolution. It, like the national question in latter-day Japanese Marxism as well, would come to contest the terms of the Western construction of modernity of which the Marxism of Marx, Engels, and Lenin partook fully. In China, as in Japan, historians and scholar-activists seeking to apply the Marxian historical schema to their native societies had, for the most part, accepted the model in its entirety along with all its assumptions concerning the nature of men and women in society. Here there are important contrasts to be noted between Chinese Marxists under Mao's leadership and those in Japan. Within the context of orthodoxy, there were two ways in which the national question as it concerned identity and meaning was resolved in Japan. The Rōnō-ha had chosen to dissolve the particular into the general and, thus, neglected whatever implications might have been borne by the peculiarities of Japan's imperial state and other aspects of Japanese society that would have been considered part of its superstructure. Nevertheless, Rōnō-ha scholars concurred with Kōza-ha theorists that Japan's bourgeois-democratic revolution had been incomplete and that what remained that could be described as "semifeudal," as some remanence of Japanese tradition, was the antithesis of modernity and had to be extirpated for the bourgeois-democratic revolution to be deemed complete. There were those, however, who did not accept this verdict upon things Japanese, but Takabatake, Sano, and others who dared to be more accepting of what was Japanese had to defy orthodoxy to make of Marxism something that could accommodate what they valued of the Japanese past. Mao's sinification of Marxism shares much in common with the latter response yet does not take recourse to statist thought even as it resulted in statist practice. This might well be the most significant, provocative, and intellectually challenging aspect of the Maoist contribution to Marxism.

In the early years of the People's Republic, of course, Chinese leaders were content to adopt the Soviet model in order to achieve rapid industrialization. As in the Soviet Union, this was undertaken in order to fulfill the criteria of industrial modernity that were presumed to be requisite for the full flowering of Marxian socialism and then communism. By the time the First Five-Year Plan gave way to the Great Leap Forward in the late 1950s, however, Marxist notions of development were being reformulated in China. This reformulation posed a fundamental challenge not only to the Soviet example—hence the Soviet role in the domestic Chinese conflict over Peng Dehuai—but also to the understanding of Western modernity that is embodied in the Marxian historical schema. The subsequent launching of the Cultural Revolution in turn introduced new elements into the confrontation between what was Chinese and what Marxism-Leninism took to be modern. Finally, in the post-Mao period, the issue has endured through the introduction of the strategy of the "Four Modernizations" and in the contestation of the Deng Xiaoping leadership's prioritization of economic change by advocates of a "fifth modernization," democratization.[94]

In the early years of its power, the Chinese leadership implemented the Soviet (or Stalinist) model of rapid industrialization and collectivization. Although collectivization in China was carried out more gradually, with significant departures from the traumatic Soviet experience,[95] fundamentally, the Chinese Communists accepted the Soviet model, which assumed that modern socialism and communism required that an agrarian economy be transformed into an urban one; that heavy industry prevail over light, consumer-oriented industry so that full-scale industrialization could be achieved; and that the interests and preferences of urban labor take precedence over those of rural peasantry. Rapid industrialization on this model also seemed to require other accoutrements of "modernity": a technocratic elite, a rational-legal bureaucracy of the sort that Max Weber had identified with modern society, and a certain measure of the continued division of labor between manual and mental labor. All these elements were built into a First Five-Year Plan for China that achieved impressive results.

There were two major difficulties in this approach. First, it prescribed a devaluation of precisely that sector of Chinese society that the CCP had found most indispensable to its rise to power despite the party's repeated insistence that its peasantry was also under the "leadership" of the proletarian vanguard. Mao at once argued that the CCP represented the political leadership of the proletariat,[96] and that the Chinese peasantry had historically been the fount of revolutionary, democratizing change,[97] while he also asserted that in this century as in the past, the leadership of the revolutionary movement, even the CCP itself, had come directly out of the agrarian revolution in China.[98] In addition, like the interwar Marxist analyses stressing the need to destroy completely all vestiges of "backwardness" remaining in capitalist Japan, the Soviet strategy targeted those elements that were not only indigenously Chinese and associated with Chinese tradition but also were identified by the CCP under Mao as the "real China," the key to the Chinese revolution, for elimination in favor of the adoption of standards of modernity defined in the West.[99] To be sure, the formula of the "people's revolutionary dictatorship" adopted during and after the revolution in lieu of *dictatorship of the proletariat* represented an attempt to mitigate the difficulty of apparently excluding the peasantry. The dilemma remained, however, of how to pursue modernity in a sense that did not imply the slavish imitation of Western bourgeois society simply stripped putatively of its exploitative elements.

This was not a simple matter. Mao had already demonstrated some appreciation of its intricacies when he proposed the creation of a new Chinese culture as early as the Yan'an era. Then, in calling for a cultural revolution in China, Mao articulated a concept of modernity that he shared with May Fourth intellectuals. Scientific and democratic, the new culture that would provide the basis for China's new socialist society would have to be nurtured by "assimilat[ing] a good deal of foreign progressive culture, not enough of which was done in the past." This assimilation process would be undertaken in a critical fashion: "[W]e should not gulp any of this foreign material down uncritically," Mao admonished, "but must treat it as we do our food—first chewing it, then submitting it to the working of the stomach and intestines with their juices and secretions, and separating it into nutriment to be absorbed and waste matter to be discarded—before it can nourish us." A similar attitude would have to apply to the treatment of China's feudal past. "A splendid old culture was created during the long period of Chinese feudal society. . . . It is imperative to separate the fine old culture of the people which had a more or less democratic and revolutionary character from all the decadence of the old feudal ruling class."[100]

As Starr has noted insightfully, through the 1960s, Mao seems to have been able to apply this reasoning judiciously to the treatment of Confucius. Where Confucius was deemed to have been representative of the feudal classes and, thus, his thought was to be viewed as inappropriate for "new democratic" and "socialist" China, he could, nevertheless, be assessed positively in a historicist perspective as one who was progressive in making a positive contribution to the articulation of the feudal mode of production.[101] Yet such reasoning seems to have led to different conclusions in the subsequent anti-Confucius anti-Lin Biao campaign. There, Confucius was portrayed as one who was not even progressive for the feudal era, and, thus, his contributions to world civilization appeared to be negated in their entirety.[102] This shift in the appraisal of Confucius would seem to have marked a significant change. It is important to note, however, that even the historicist reading that was favorable to Confucius lent itself to a negative evaluation of Confucianism and of the traditional social practices associated with it vis-à-vis Western culture. After all, it was Confucianism's fundamental perspective on the relationship between humanity and nature and among men and women in society that Mao's and Liu's emphasis on the need for (disciplined) struggle in "the continuing revolution" (jixu geming) rejected, beginning in the Yan'an period.[103] In the new era, struggle and conflict were "the source of truth and progress."[104] Thus, even a historicist perspective on Confucianism failed to address the most fundamental questions concerning the relative value of Chinese civilization. Why should Chinese have been concerned with the struggle against feudalism and against Confucianism as part of that struggle as late as the late twentieth century, long after feudal social formations had disappeared from Western Europe? Why was it that what was Western was to be viewed as so much more advanced than what was Chinese in the realm of culture? Why was it that Western civilization was so much more "progressive" in Mao's view than that of China at the outset?

In fact, Mao himself appeared to pose such questions when he formulated his program of the Great Leap Forward. Yet, significantly, even here, he seemed conflicted in his assessment of the relative value of Chinese and Western civilizations. On the one hand, Mao's goal was to match the achievements of the Western capitalist industrialized societies such as Great Britain and the United States. Thus, he accepted as the criteria of success the standard measures applied in the West to estimate the relative levels of industrial development of various economies. At the same time, he repudiated the Soviet model of industrialization and specifically the Western industrial capitalist values that had been inherent in the Stalinist drive to complete the tasks left undone by Russia's native bourgeoisie.

Mao had begun to express doubts about the Stalinist model as early as 1956 when he spoke of the "Ten Major Relationships." There he asserted the need for a greater balance between the heavy industrial and light/consumer industrial sectors and between industry and agriculture.[105] Mao insisted that the Chinese leadership needed to respond to the most basic needs of its people for food and clothing. Indeed, this is properly viewed as the point of departure for Mao's new approach in the Great Leap Forward: the emphasis on China's massive millions as the true basis of China's politics and of its economic development as well. For what China lacked in qualitative terms (technology), it would compensate in quantitative terms (its population resources). Thus, the most significant point lay not primarily in Mao's objectives but in the means that he proposed to use to attain them. Although Mao may have accepted conventional Western measures of economic success in articulating the objectives of his campaign, he repudiated the conventional wisdom of modern Western economists—and those of the increasingly "bourgeois" Soviet Union as well[106]—concerning how to go about achieving them. The elevation of the agricultural sector as "the foundation" in the policy of "walking on two legs," the discovery of the key to economic progress not in the massive importation of foreign technologies and the erection of expansive large-scale factories but in the will and dedication of the Chinese people that had carried the CCP to victory in 1949—these marked dramatic departures from the Soviet model. Mao's view constituted a fundamental reworking of Marxism in accommodation to what Mao now insisted on seeing as the strengths of the distinctive Chinese context. In China's backwardness would no longer lie its weakness but its virtue. This was Mao's point in stressing that China was "poor and blank":[107] what it did not have in the accoutrements of Western-style capitalism would be less likely to hamper China's progress to socialism. Thus, Mao was both embracing and fundamentally contesting the notion of modernity as it was implicit in orthodox Marxism. In his promotion of backwardness as a virtue, he seemed to recall the position of Russian narodniki of the late-nineteenth century who saw in the peasant commune a shortcut to socialism. Hence, with the formation of people's communes within one decade after the revolution, Mao was able to proclaim that China was overtaking the Soviet Union and was realizing not merely socialism but communism.[108]

Coupled with this reformulation of a Chinese path to Communist modernity were certain elements that prefigured the launching of the Great Proletarian Cultural Revolution one decade later. Rejected with the Soviet model was the reliance on a large cadre of technocrats and the bureaucratic hierarchy that was characteristic of advanced capitalist societies and that the Soviet Union had reproduced under Stalin (although ironically Mao blamed this phenomenon on Khrushchev's "revisionism"). As much as two years before the launching of the Great Leap Forward, Mao endorsed "great democracy" as directed against bureaucrats as well as against other enemies of the people:

> If great democracy is now to be practised again, I am for it. You are afraid of the masses taking to the streets, I am not, not even if hundreds of thousands should do so. . . . The great democracy set in motion by the proletariat is directed against class enemies. . . . Great democracy can be directed against bureaucrats too. I just said that there would still be revolutions ten thousand years from now, so possibly great democracy will have to be practised then. If some people grow tired of life and so become bureaucratic, if, when meeting the masses, they have not a single kind word for them but only take them to task, and if they don't bother to solve any of the problems the masses may have, they are destined to be overthrown. Now this danger does exist. If you alienate yourself from the masses and fail to solve their problems, the peasants will wield their carrying-poles, the workers will demonstrate in the streets and the students will create distur-

bances. Whenever such things happen, they must in the first place be taken as good things.[109]

As this passage illustrates, at the core of Mao's concept of democracy was the notion of struggle as something that would produce the subjective requisites of socialism in China.[110] In Mao's view, the task of constructing socialism in China was as much an effort to construct an "alternative [socialist] hegemony" in the realm of ideas, to borrow Gramsci's terms, as it was to create the material conditions necessary for socialism and to change the relations of production. Indeed, as his concept of the Great Leap evolved, Mao became convinced that the immediate construction of his alternative hegemony was the key means to the creation of the material conditions and production relations of socialism as well, and it was on this point that he took issue with those such as Liu Shaoqi, who retained faith in the party's earlier commitment to "socialist industrialization" as a "step-by-step" process of "the socialist transformation of agriculture, handicrafts and capitalist industry and commerce over a fairly long period."[111] Mao feared that adhering to the longer time schedule and relying excessively on bureaucratic and technocratic features adapted from advanced capitalist societies to achieve economic development on the Western and Soviet model would produce precisely the opposite of the desired effects. This would strengthen "bourgeois" elements in Chinese society at the expense of socialist and socializing forces. Hence, the notion of the two roads[112] that had already appeared in Mao's writing on the occasion of the Anti-Rightist Campaign of 1957 lingered through his reluctant retreat from power in the wake of the collapse of the Great Leap to reemerge to center stage in the Cultural Revolution almost one decade later. Two important points are to be noted here: first, the centrality of the problem of the state to the distinction drawn between the two roads and, second, the fact that Mao's invocation of ideological or spiritual change[113] in the realm of politics as the requisite of China's modernization lies in essential continuity with the past and present. Mao's view links similar perspectives from the era of the Self-Strengthening movement to the current conflict between young dissidents and the Deng Xiaoping leadership over the issue of whether economic modernization can actually be achieved in China without a prior fundamental change in thinking and culture.

First, to address the problem of the state: Mao was concerned about the challenge of change in the realm of "superstructure." Here, his preoccupation with ideology and with consciousness offered an instrument with which to control the tendency for an oppressive state to arise. His treatment of bureaucracy, which attributed the appearance of its unwanted characteristics to "bourgeois" forces, was the centerpiece of his insistence on the need for a continuous or permanent revolution. Before launching the Great Leap Forward, the party had accepted the Leninist view that the path to socialist modernization passed through the experience of building "state capitalism," as "a peaceful means of transition" to socialism.[114] This state capitalism, as a means, was considered to be fundamentally consistent with the end, socialism, inasmuch as it existed "not chiefly to make profits for the capitalists but to meet the [mutually compatible] needs of the people and the state." Gradually, "this state-capitalist economy of a new type takes on a socialist character to a very great extent and benefits the workers and the state," Mao had written in 1953.[115] Yet, subsequently, Mao seems to have become convinced that "state capitalism" did nothing to negate the pernicious essence of either the state or capitalism and, thus, to rely on state capitalism implied strengthening elements of both these impediments to socialism. In particular, Mao recognized at this point that the very exercise of political power itself, the experience of being part of the state apparatus, was itself a source of evil and counterrevolution. "We must watch out lest we foster the bureaucratic style of work and grow into an aristocratic stratum divorced from the people," Mao cautioned. "The masses will have good reason to remove from office whoever practises bureaucracy, makes no effort to solve their problems, scolds them, tyrannizes over them and never tries to make amends. I say it is fine to remove such fellows, and they ought to be removed."[116]

In this respect, it is significant that as Mao waged the battle over the failings of the Great Leap Forward with highly critical comrades at the end of the 1950s and into the early-1960s, he placed a new emphasis on the need to continue class struggle after the revolution. In large part to justify the violent purges of his erstwhile Bolshevik comrades, Joseph Stalin had written that classes persisted in socialist society and, thus, that class struggle must continue to be waged after the revolution.[117] By 1962, Mao was recasting his discussion of the need for continuing struggle against the "enemies" of the "people" as he had described it in "The Correct Handling of Contradictions among the People" in class terms, in terms of *proletariat* and *bourgeoisie*. This was consistent with his understanding of the danger of bureaucratism to the revolution as arising chiefly out of the influence of the bourgeoisie. " 'The overthrown classes will attempt to stage a comeback and new bourgeoisie elements will emerge in the socialist society. There are classes and class struggle throughout the period of socialist society'." " 'Such class struggle is protracted, complicated and sometimes even violent'."[118]

The permanent revolution comprised, then, a struggle against these elements as they inevitably tended to take on lives of their own with their day-to-day activity. As Starr notes, this understanding of permanent revolution differed from the notion of "permanent" or "continuous" revolution as Leon Trotsky had formulated it to refer to the bourgeois-democratic revolution "growing over" into a socialist revolution in later-industrializing societies.[119] To be sure, Mao's concept of new democracy did share with Trotsky's view a notion of the revolution gradually moving from one stage to another so that a rigid delineation of stages was no longer possible despite Mao's anxious assurances that his notion of buduan geming (uninterrupted revolution) was fundamentally different from that of the vilified Trotsky.[120] Subsequently, however, in the late 1950s, it was clear that Mao had made shifts in his own thinking about the permanent revolution. Now, the term *jixu geming* (continuous revolution) replaced the former appellation, and the continuity referred not so much to the transition from one stage of the revolution to another as to the nature of change "*within* the period of the socialist transformation."[121] After the revolution, so to speak, the revolution would continue, as the characteristics of society said to belong to the superstructural realm would become the direct target of revolutionary activity in the form of campaigns and *yundong*, or mass movements. "If the superstructure (ideology and public opinion included) protects the kind of relations of production the people dislike, they will transform it," Mao asserted.[122]

This adjustment in Mao's thought marked an extension of his earlier determination that China should build a new culture. The cultural change would be a continuous process during the transition to communism, and it alone could assure that communism would, indeed, be realized. This broadening of the notion of cultural change to refer to the progress of the revolution after the revolution, so to speak, is comprehensible within the context of Mao's disillusionment caused by the vehement criticism to which his Great Leap Forward continued to be subjected. This he viewed in part as evidence of the inability of the party, heretofore regarded as the repository of revolutionary virtue, to maintain itself on the "socialist road."[123] Thus, Mao turned to other models, beginning with the People's Liberation Army in the Socialist Education Campaign in 1962–1964. By the time of the Cultural Revolution, it had become clear that the party necessarily "derive[d] its legitimacy from Mao Tse-tung," the leader who, as the "great helmsman" of the Chinese revolution, alone could preside over the cultivation and guardianship of revolutionary virtue in China.[124] Yet, the enforcement of that virtue would be in the hands of the masses, and particularly of Red Guards, the youth to whom Lu Xun had appealed so long ago (in "Diary of a Madman") as the source of China's salvation. This, as Mao viewed it, was the essence of the "tradition of democracy" in China under Communist leadership.[125]

The second point concerns the continuity with the past and present of Mao's views on the role of cultural and ideological change in the revolution. Since the failure of the Self-Strengthening movement at the end of the last century, Chinese intellectuals from Yan Fu, Liang Qichao, and Li Dazhao to Mao and Liu have voiced concern with the key role of thought in social development. Within the Self-Strengthening movement itself, such a perspective was reflected in the determination to restore "Confucian values and institutions" against the encroachments of the Taiping heresy and moral degeneration in general.[126] After Tongzhi, this position was recast to stress the need to change one's thinking, the philosophy and culture of the Chinese people, for desirable social change to occur. This view, of course, bears much in common with the Confucian emphasis on self-cultivation as evidenced by Liu Shaoqi's invocation of the authority of Mencius and Confucius on the matter in his *How to Be a Good Communist*. The cultivation of political virtue issues from the nurturing of a correct standpoint, a correct Weltanschauung, a correct consciousness, correct ideas. Today, it is important to note, this constitutes an important theme in the thought of Chinese dissidents involved in the democratic movement. To eliminate the Chinese people's "conceptual problem," the fact that "our people have such a low level of consciousness and such a low cultural standard," constitutes a major rationale for the role of the democratic movement in achieving China's modernization.[127] Without a reawakening (*xing*) in the spirit of the Chinese people, a rethinking of their relationship to nature and to one another, a kindling of a new "civil consciousness," there lies no hope for China, argue proponents of democratic reform.[128] Here, in attacking the problem of cultural change as a critical aspect of democratization, Chinese dissidents have raised important issues concerning national identity and the problem of the state in China's continuing quest for modernity. This concern they share with Japanese Marxists confronting the statist dimensions of the national question in Japan in the 1990s.

Identity, the State, and Democratization

Throughout this work, a continuous theme has been etched in the intimate linkage between the national question in Marxism and fundamental issues concerning national identity. In contemporary China and Japan, such issues concerning national identity have arisen within and on the fringes of the Marxist movement in the context of democratizing initiatives. In both societies, the treatment of the national question in conventional terms has given way to new formulations that reflect ambivalence concerning national identity as Chinese and Japanese thinkers endeavor to define what it is they seek in modernity. The ability of the Chinese and Japanese peoples to determine their own destinies through democratic politics has emerged as the focus of this quest.

In China, dissident leaders of the democratic movement from the late 1970s through the 1990s have shared with Mao a concern about the problem of bureaucratism. This was a major theme of Mao's writings, but Mao's analysis focusing on the problem of capitalist restoration cannot respond adequately to their concerns about the form that bureaucratism has taken in China. Despite his harsh attacks on Confucianism and its oppressive cultural legacy, Mao's treatment targeted these elements in their feudal, that is, universal, character rather than in their specific representation in Chinese history. At the same time that he condemned the separation of mental from manual labor, however, he attributed the problem of bureaucracy to the development of the capitalist mode of production. This approach skirted an issue that scholars involved in the controversy on Chinese social history in the 1930s ached to address through the notion of the Asiatic mode of production—the nature and role of China's historical legacy as an "oriental" or Asiatic society as they operated in the persistence of the problem of the bureaucratic state in China. Thus, the issue has reemerged at least twice in the years since the recovery from the Cultural Revolution and the launch of the "Four Modernizations", first in the late 1970s and early 1980s in both the official and dissident press and again among dissidents in the late 1980s.[129]

In the earlier wave, Wu Dakun made a plea for the reexamination of the Asiatic mode of production notion with respect to the concrete characteristics of Chinese society in order better to understand the impediments and opportunities confronting China as it embarked on the "Four Modernizations." Wu concluded that the legacy of the Asiatic mode of production in ancient China contributed to a deeply entrenched patriarchal, bureaucratic state structure that made its imprint on feudal China. Thus, although China made the transition to feudalism relatively early, Wu argued, the Asiatic characteristics of the prior Asiatic mode of production caused the delay of China's capitalist development.[130] The leading dissident Wei Jingsheng at this time did not share the respect that Wu, Su Shaozhi, and other official intellectuals continued to hold for Marxism as a doctrine that might prove to be the basis for a humanistic socialism; Marxism was a "direct inheritance from feudal philosophy at its peak—Classical German Philosophy," in Wei's view. Nevertheless, he shared the disillusionment with the authoritarian bureaucratism of Chinese society that has inspired renewed interest in the Asiatic mode of production. Wei argued that the current system in China was a system that "regards suppression of individuality as its basic condition of survival." The system was contrary to the natural order in which "people's individuality enjoys priority over their sociality, although both individuality and sociality are important constituents of human nature." Wei argued that such a system could not be the basis for true collectivism but had merely perverted individualism and collectivism into "'autocratic individualism and small group mentality'."[131] Interestingly, the terms within which Wei posited his argument were evocative of those found in the analyses of oriental societies by European and Marxist scholars—the existence of the single free autocratic individual, resting on the small, dispersed, communities.

The later wave of such treatments in the late 1980s and early 1990s has been concentrated among dissidents, who have deplored China's heritage as an Asian society, and, for their negative implications for the assessment of the present leadership, they have drawn vigorous official criticism. Their problematic relationship to the Chinese past was evident as early as 1987 in an interview Fang Lizhi gave to the Hong Kong-based *Zhengming*, remarks that have been taken to advocate "all-out Westernization."[132] More recently, Fang took issue with a nationalistic stance, arguing that a spirit of "global citizenship" was necessary. Patriotism, he wrote, "comes to mean that what you love is the nation-state," complete with its apparatus of "repression"—the "police, the courts, the prisons, and the army." A similar, albeit more radical, position was assumed by the provocative Liu Xiaobo, a Columbia-educated dissident. Liu argued that China required a colonial experience, which would constitute a means to the Westernization that is necessary if China is to achieve modernity.[133] These challenges to Chinese national identity itself in the pursuit of modernity understood as industrialism and democracy peaked late in 1988. In the latter half of that year, a six-part radical television documentary entitled "River Elegy" ("He shang") was shown in China. It and the slightly less-radical script deplored so-called "Yellow civilization"—the civilization of the Yellow River—and exalted "blue civilization"—the civilization of "blue-eyed men" across the blue seas. Traditional symbols of Chinese national strength, such as the Yellow River and the Great Wall, were depicted as emblematic of the irrationality, introspective nature, and impotence of the Chinese people. Such characteristics were juxtaposed to the outward-oriented, competitive, and commercial culture of the West, and they were claimed to be responsible for preventing China's emergence as a modern society. The key to modernizing change now was said to lie—once again—in building a new Chinese national culture while assimilating Western culture. The notion of the Asiatic mode of production was clearly the inspiration for this piece although its authors and those who responded so favorably to it saw the Asiatic mode of production not in China's distant past but in its present.[134] Not surprisingly, Zhao Ziyang openly supported the documentary as a stimulus to illuminating debate. After the Tiananmen Square massacres of June 4, 1989, however, the authorities launched a severe attack on the series as "reactionary," no doubt recognizing fully its critical implications for the nature of the state in contemporary China.

Unquestionably, this dialogue reflects a profound disenchantment with the persistence of the powerful arbitrary, bureaucratic state into modern Chinese history despite the revolution and Mao's crusade to create a permanent revolution to prevent its resurgence and despite repeated campaigns against bureaucratism among both officials and dissidents since the fall of the Gang of Four. The tragic events of June 4, 1989, have reinforced this desperate disillusionment among China's dissident intellectuals. Although many of them have become anti-Marxist as well as anti-Maoist, perhaps, their reaction against China, against Asia, against that which they had assumed to be their own cultural identity in the past, also constitutes a reaction to the inadequacies of Marxism in theory and practice in China.

In searching for what has been missing from the recent and more distant Chinese path, radical Chinese thinkers today converge with Japanese Marxists in their treatment of the implications of the national question for the present and future of democracies in their societies. In Japan, too, for all the differences that separate the Socialist and the Communist parties, they agree in their opposition to a state that they see as oppressive. Both parties fear the lingering mythological or ideological influences of the oppressive prewar state based on an imperial system that they view as inherently authoritarian in character. Reflection on this issue in comparative historical perspective has yielded insightful work on both sides of the Rōnō-ha–Kōza-ha schism.

In the case of the Socialist party, as the party has extricated itself from the overwhelming influence of the extreme left-wing Shakai-shugi Kyōkai (Socialist Association), new theoretical work from two separate directions has undergirded the creation of a new party platform to herald a new age of democratization for Japan.[135] Informed by an appreciation of the unfortunate realities of politics in Eastern Europe and the prospects for reform there, in the late 1970s and early 1980s scholars associated with the Japanese Socialist party embarked on a reassessment of major issues having to do with the relationship between Marxism and the state. Under the leadership of economist Ōuchi Tsutomu (son of the prewar Rōnō-ha scholar Ōuchi Hyōe and likewise a professor of economics at the University of Tokyo), Lower House Dietman Hori Masao, Tokyo University economist Baba Hiroji, and others organized the Rōdōsha Jishu Kanri Kenkyū Kaigi (Workers' Self-Management Research Conference) in 1978 to address the need to specify a new concept of socialism for Japan. The group asserted that the Soviet-inspired *Nihon ni okeru shakai-shugi e no michi* (hereafter *Michi*), which had been drafted under the influence of prewar Rōnō-ha Marxist Sakisaka Itsurō's notion of peaceful revolution, was "unrealistic," and they undertook to articulate an alternative Marxian vision of socialism that could provide a basis for the strategy and tactics of a Japanese Socialist party seeking to open the Japanese political system to more democratic practices.[136] Shortly thereafter, also disenchanted with Sakisaka's Shakai-shugi Kyōkai, another group of scholars left the group under the leadership of Fukuda Yutaka of Hōsei University. Like the Ōuchi-Hori group, this splinter group has opposed the JSP's pro-Soviet orientation that supported authoritarian rule in Eastern Europe, rejected Marx's thesis of the progressive immiseration of the proletariat as "obsolete," and contested the Soviet model of postrevolutionary society. Finally, the two groups became concerned with a crucial issue that must confront a socialist party in any advanced industrialized society—how to make socialism more appealing in a context in which the objectives of democracy and social welfare have ostensibly already been attained.[137]

These theoretical developments were matched by the effort by Ishibashi Masashi, the new chair of the Socialist party, to move the party into a "pragmatic direction" that would enable it to exceed the 30 percent limit on the proportion of Diet seats it has been able to gain since 1955. This effort, which continued under the leadership of Japan's first female party leader Doi Takako from September 1986 through mid-1991, had a dual focus. First, the party endeavored to distance itself as much as possible from its Marxist roots and, thereby, from its historical association with the Soviet Union. Secondly, it has involved adopting more "pragmatic" policy stances, as evidenced in the party's moderation of its opposition to the existence of the Self-Defense Forces. The latter, which many constitutional scholars regard as unconstitutional,[138] had traditionally been repudiated by the JSP. After top JSP leaders paid a visit to Washington, D.C., to promote their image as a party capable of acting responsibly in power in the realm of foreign policy, the party also adopted Ishibashi's *iken gōhō ron* (unconstitutional but legal thesis). The compromise formula accepted the Self-Defense Forces as established in accordance with law (*gōhō*) although they were unconstitutional (*iken*). Moreover, Ishibashi, Mutō Sanji, another powerful leader of the party's right wing, and the party's "New Draft Manifesto" together urged the possibility of coalition with democratic forces that they have traditionally viewed as relatively "conservative," such as the Democratic Socialist party (which had seceded from the JSP), to break the LDP's monopoly on power.[139] In the meantime, in part to assure that such intentions to move in a "pragmatic" direction did not undermine the party's socialist commitment, those engaged in work such as that of the Workers' Self-Management group contributed to the 1983 document "Our New Conception of Socialism" produced by the party's Socialist Theory Center.[140] Such theoretical developments within the JSP have been made in connection with studies directed toward a better understanding of the nature of advanced capitalism, of the nature of the state in advanced capitalist society, and of the possibilities for alternative democratic socialist models.[141]

Still other perspectives that, like those of Chinese dissidents in the 1990s, are highly critical of the limitations of democracy in their society, have emerged on the side of the descendants of the prewar Kōza-ha. Since the late 1960s and early 1970s, these scholars have sought to understand why Japan achieved such exceptional economic growth during this period while the undemocratic elements of its polity appeared to survive unchanged. Operating within the context of the Koza-ha's adherence to the prewar analysis that Japan required a two-stage revolution, Uchida Yoshihiko (b. 1913) and Hirata Kiyoaki (b. 1922) have evolved an understanding of the relationship between Japanese contemporary economic and political development that has drawn adherents known as the "civil society school." The group's *shimin shakai-ron* (theory of civil society) offers an interpretation of what both the JSP and the JCP see as the shortcomings of democracy in Japan. As the school's appellation indicates, its point of departure is the notion of civil society, "a society in which men free themselves of feudal or premodern communities in order to become independent individuals and enjoy liberty and equality legally and morally." This is a society in which "the identity between labor and property" prevails, in other words, the existence of property is based on the labor of the individual.[142] In short, the central thesis of the civil society school is that in Japan, capitalism developed without Japan's ever having developed a thriving civil society. Building on Yamada Moritarō's depiction of the post-Meiji Restoration Japanese state and society, then, Uchida argues that Japanese capitalism retained and relied on feudal or premodern elements. After the war, as a result of the American Occupation, civil society did achieve "considerable" development, Uchida concedes, but, ironically, it was the continuing weakness of the elements of civil society in Japan that permitted the exceptionally rapid development of Japanese society in the 1960s. Herein lay the difference between Japanese development and the West European experience, Uchida argued. "In Europe, God created the rights of man and afterward, man created the rights of the State," he wrote, citing Kawakami Hajime. "On the contrary in Japan, God created first of all the rights of the State and then the State created the rights of man." Thus, in Japan, capital and the state flourished while civil society remained powerless, leaving behind a curious paradox in the "supermodernization" of capital as a result of the weakness of its civil society.[143]

Hirata has developed Uchida's observations in a slightly different direction to criticize even the economic formation of capitalism in postwar Japan. Hirata has pointed to the development of what he calls "cooperative capitalism" in Japan. Contrived to assure the development of capitalism in the face of the pressures of world capitalism, the model maintains "precapitalist social relations integrated within capitalism" itself. This is said to be evidenced not only in the reciprocal relations of ownership that characterize relations among large industrial groups in Japan (the *keiretsu*) but also in the relationship between MITI and similar "patronal organizations" that together constitute the "hegemonic power of civil society" and in enterprise-based unions, *ringi*, and other devices said to assure the passivity of labor vis-à-vis management. This arrangement in the economic realm is duplicated in politics in the practice whereby extensive consultation among interested economic groups on political measures precedes parliamentary consideration. This, Hirata argues, has contributed to the constitution of a variant of corporatism despite the appearances of a fully competitive parliamentary system. Such practices, Hirata implies, have impeded Japan's ability to evolve an authentic competitive party system in which alternation of the party in power is genuinely possible.[144]

These analyses of Japanese democracy by the descendants of the prewar Kōza-ha and Rōnō-ha are characteristically rejected out of hand by those of each opposing faction. Nevertheless, they do offer interesting and provocative insights on the nature of contemporary political and economic life in Japan. Like the critics of the state in China, these Japanese dissidents raise issues of great significance that lie at the heart of the national question as broadly construed. Here are matters concerning the assertion of group and individual identities, rights of self-determination, and duties to state power. Finally, but not least importantly, their concerns have to do with the fundamental notion of what constitutes modernity. For the civil society school, civil society is said to be a "methodological concept" rather than an historical category, and it is to be differentiated from simple capitalist society as it has existed historically in the West. Similarly, Fang Lizhi's call for "a truly global civilization"[145] is an effort to transcend narrow nationalisms, much in the same universalizing manner of the orthodox internationalist Marxist. Nevertheless, in comparing their own societies with the democracies of Western Europe and the United States, these scholar-dissidents address in the post-1949 and post–World War II era issues embedded within the national question that have, in fact, percolated beneath the surface of all the efforts to resolve it traced here since the interwar era. What is the content of the democracy, the self-determination, for which these activists struggle? What, after all, constitutes the modernity that Chinese and Japanese Marxists have sought in bourgeois-democratic and, then, Marxian socialist revolution? Is there any way of defining it so that it is not simply a description of realities based on the experiences of other peoples in other cultures, so that it does not require the negation of one's identity in the historical past, and so that one's own people might realistically aspire to achieve it? This problématique has confronted Marxist and non-Marxist activists not only in China and Japan, it is universal in character, and it is intrinsic to the aspiration to modernity beyond the Western world. In the hegemonic Western conception, modernity constitutes a form of the assertion of one's identity, but as soon as it is borrowed or imported to a non-Western setting, it appears that the path to modernity must pass through self-abnegation. Those seeking self-determination must define their democratizing quest in new terms, terms of their own, terms that transcend this dilemma. As another century draws to a close, struggles for modernization and democratization continue within and without the Marxist movements in China, Japan, and elsewhere, and the ultimate resolution to the national question, through revolution or through evolution, remains a momentous challenge.

• N O T E S •

INTRODUCTION

1. Marx, "Critique of Hegel's 'Philosophy of Right'," p. 142.

2. See Alter, *Nationalism*; Kohn, *Idea of Nationalism*; Kemiläinen, *Nationalism*; and Kamenka, *Nationalism*.

3. See, for example, Connor, "Ethnonationalism," pp. 196–220.

4. Just, "Triumph of the Ethnos," pp. 72–73.

5. The terms *nationality* and the *nation* are used almost interchangeably here and in other key sources. See, for example, Hobsbawm, *Nations and Nationalism*, pp. 8ff.

6. Stalin, "Marxism and the National Question," p. 8. Karl W. Deutsch's stress on social communication also privileges as nationalities those who live in close geographical proximity to one another. See Deutsch, *Nationalism and Social Communication*.

7. Interestingly, Lenin too, confronted with the realities of the nationality problem in postrevolutionary Russia, granted Jews, who, with Muslims had never been granted the status of *nationalities*, representation in the People's Commissariat for Nationalities (Narkomnats) as well as in the Bolshevik party. See later and Carrère d'Encausse, *Le grand défi*, pp. 125–126, 132, 190ff.

8. Marx, "Civil War in France," p. 629.

9. See Lenin, *State and Revolution*, pp. 311–398.

10. Gellner, *Nations and Nationalism*, p. 1.

11. Breuilly, *Nationalism and the State*.

12. Gellner, *Nations and Nationalism*, pp. 48–49.

13. Just, "Triumph of the Ethnos," pp. 85ff.

14. See Habermas, *Structural Transformation of the Public Sphere*, pp. 23–28.

15. See Marx, "German Ideology," pp. 176–186.

16. Marx and Engels, "Address to the Communist League," p. 506; Luxemburg, "Russian Revolution," pp. 47ff.; and Lenin, *Imperialism*, passim.

17. Marx, "German Ideology," p. 185.

18. Marx, "On the Jewish Question," p. 46.

19. See Marx and Engels, *Manifesto of the Communist Party*, pp. 346, 350; Marx, "Economic and Philosophic Manuscripts of 1844," pp. 60–67, 78–79; Marx and Engels, "German Ideology," pp. 124, 162, 164.

20. See the insightful treatment of Hayes, *Essays on Nationalism*.

21. See Schorske, *German Social Democracy*.

22. See the discussion later in this chapter.

23. Marx, "Critique of Hegel's 'Philosophy of Right,' pp. 141–142.

24. Compare Marx's comments on the same in Marx, "On the Jewish Question" and Marx, "German Ideology."

25. "Totality" as a pivotal concept of Western Marxism has a dual meaning. Substantively, it has to do with the dream of the restoration of man's wholeness from his fragmentation and alienation from himself by the mechanics of class society. (Totalization refers to the process by which men and women reappropriate their wholeness.) Methodologically, it has to do with the quest of the Marxist intellectual for a holistic view of man and the fullness of the human dilemma in society. For an exhaustive analysis of the place of this concept in Western Marxism, see Jay, *Marxism and Totality*.

26. Marx, "Critique of Hegel's 'Philosophy of Right'," p. 142.

27. I have borrowed this phraseology from the title of Mosala and Tlhagale, *Unquestionable Right to Be Free*.

28. See the insightful essay on Czech dissident intellectuals, including Havel, by Sartre, "Czechoslovakia," especially pp. 89–99 passim.

29. See the essays of Mihaly Vajda, a student of Georgy Lukács, collected in Vajda, *State and Socialism*, especially "The Crisis of the System in Eastern Europe and the Attitude of Hungarian Intellectuals," pp. 123–131.

30. For excellent treatments of the collapse of Communist rule in Poland that manifest the dual character of peaceful revolution there, see Ziemer, "Systemwandel in Polen: (I); and Systemwandel in Polen: (II)."

31. "It follows from what I have argued that the general will is always rightful and always tends to the public good; but it does not follow that the decisions of the people are always equally right. We always want what is advantageous but we do not always discern it. The people is never corrupted, but it is often misled; and only then does it seem to will what is bad." Rousseau, *Social Contract*, p. 72.

32. See Skocpol, "Bringing the State Back In," pp. 3–37.

33. I use the term *ideology* with caution to refer to a systematic set of ideas incorporating a program of action. It is not intended to bear the negative Marxist connotation of "false consciousness." Because of this and other negative connotations associated with the term, as noted below, I avoid it in this work, and use other terms, such as *political thought*, or *theory*, instead.

34. See Brzezinski and Huntington, *Political Power*, pp. 130, 134–139; Mills, *Power Elite*, pp. 400–404; Deutsch, *Nationalism and Social Communication*, pp. 32–37; and Lichtheim, "Concept of *Ideology*," pp. 3–46, especially 22–30 on positivism and the critique of ideology. I use the term *ideology* here cautiously only because it is widely used in the literature. It is taken here to refer to an overarching theoretical perspective on the world with implications for political action. (Cf. Hoffman, *Gulliver's Troubles*, p. 114.) It is not invoked here in the Marxian sense,—or even, it might be said, in the popular American sense—to mean "false consciousness."

35. Wolin, "Study of Revolution," pp. 345–346. This is particularly true, as Wolin notes, of the brief treatment of revolution in Talcott Parsons's theory of society (see p. 350), as well as of the equilibrium theory of Chalmers Johnson, in *Revolutionary Change*, pp. 166–172. It is noteworthy that both Marxist and structural-functionalist writers on the theory of revolution have thus tended to strip Marxism of its truly ideological components, thereby depicting revolution as a mechanical act of relatively unconscious individuals in the context of a social structure that is dominant to the extent that its equilibrium or disequilibrium determines human behavior. Thus, the Parsonian scheme, which reduced ideology to "values" divorced from conscious action (cf. Wolin, "Study of Revolution," p. 347) may be compared to the repeated reference to people as mere "agents" of larger socioeconomic forces in the writings of the structuralist Marxist Nicos Poulantzas, who has made one of the major recent contributions to the Marxist theory of the capitalist state. His work will be discussed in chapter 2. See his *Political Power and Social Classes*, pp. 187–224; and Bridges, "Nicos Poulantzas," pp. 180–182.

36. This is true of the two main varieties of academic social science theories of revolution that emerged in the postwar period: (1) the aggregate psychological, stressing the motivations of political violence in general (here, rebellion in general is not carefully distinguished from successful revolutions), for example, the frustration-aggression theory

in Gurr, *Why Men Rebel*; and (2) systems, or value-consensus theories, emphasizing revolution as a violent response to societal disequilibrium, for example, Parsons, *Social System*; Merton, *Social Theory and Social Structure*; Almond, "Functional Approach to Comparative Politics," pp. 3–64; Almond, "Political Systems and Political Change," pp. 28–42.

37. Wolin, "Study of Revolution," p. 349.

38. See Kuhn, *Structure of Scientific Revolutions*, pp. 92–94, 103. See also the treatment of "the highly efficient enforcement powers of the scientific community" with reference to political theory in Wolin, "Paradigms and Political Theories," pp. 143–144.

39. Cf. Wolin, "Study of Revolution," p. 352.

40. These tendencies have long been evident in the writings of Thomas Paine (*The Rights of Man*) and Edmund Burke (*Reflections on the Revolution in France*), for example.

41. Eckstein, "Perspective on Comparative Politics," p. 11.

42. Ibid., pp. 28, 27.

43. Wolin, "Study of Revolution," pp. 345, 346.

44. Skocpol, "Varieties of 'Historical Sociology'," pp. 6–7. Examples of this approach include Moore, *Social Origins of Dictatorship and Democracy*; Wallerstein, *Modern World System*; Skocpol, *States and Social Revolutions*; and C. Tilly, L. Tilly, and R. Tilly, *Rebellious Century*.

45. The work of Charles Tilly is an exception to this rule. His perspective contains an element of voluntarism in its emphasis on the goal of revolution—such as sovereignty—and his emphasis on mobilization as a prerequisite for successful revolution. In this respect, his approach, which arose in opposition to the frustration-aggression theory of Ted Gurr, has been termed "political-conflict" theory. See Skocpol, *States and Social Revolutions*, pp. 10–16; C. Tilly, "Revolutions and Collective Action," pp. 520–521; and C. Tilly, *From Mobilization to Revolution*, pp. 202–209.

46. Skocpol, *States and Social Revolutions*, p. 18. Cf. Wood, "American Revolution," p. 129. In categorizing these approaches, I have drawn heavily on Skocpol, "Explaining Revolutions," pp. 155–175.

47. Skocpol, *States and Social Revolutions*, pp. 15, 304n-305n. For an insightful analysis of the voluntaristic element in Mao's thought, see Wakeman, *History and Will*, especially chaps. 14 and 20.

48. On this tension in Marxism in general, see Kirkup, *History of Socialism*, especially pp. 48, 159; and Kolakowski, *Main Currents of Marxism*, 1:341. On Bolshevism, see Bauer, *New Soviet Man*, pp. 14–15; Ulam, *Bolsheviks*, p. 99; and Cohen, *Bukharin and the Bolshevik Revolution*, pp. 108–109, 129. On Mao and Marxism in general, see Starr, *Continuing the Revolution*, pp. 32–35; Wakeman, *History and Will*, pp. 218, 219, 224; and on the conflict in Marxism, Leninism, and Chinese communism, see Schwartz, *Rise of Mao*, p. 24; and Meisner, *Li Ta-chao*, (1977) especially chaps. 6 and 7. Exclusive emphasis on historical determinism is generally identified with "vulgar Marxism" and the "positivist" work of Engels after 1876–1878. See Hobsbawm, "Karl Marx's Contribution to History," p. 270; and Lichtheim, *Marxism*, pp. 238, 238n.

49. See Tucker, *Philosophy and Myth in Karl Marx*, p. 129, and chap. 8, especially pp. 129–132; and Kolakowski, *Main Currents of Marxism*, 1:341.

50. See Miliband, *State in Capitalistic Society*, and idem, "Marx and the State," pp. 128–150. The instrumentalist Marxist approach to the contemporary state is analyzed in contrast to the structuralist approach in chapter 2, in this volume.

51. Gold, Lo, and Wright, "Recent Developments" (October 1975), p. 39. Cf. the

discussion in Wolfe, "New Directions," p. 140, for a comparison of the Marxist structuralism of Nicos Poulantzas and his predecessor Louis Althusser with the structuralism of Talcott Parsons.

52. See, especially, Skocpol, *States and Social Revolutions*, pp. 19–33, 284–293; Skocpol, "Critical Review," pp. 30, 33; Trimberger, "State Power," p. 86; and idem, *Revolutions from Above*, chap. 1.

53. Skocpol, *States and Social Revolutions*, p. 18.

54. Collins, "Comparative Approach to Political Sociology," p. 52.

55. See, for example, Boulding, "National Images and International Systems," pp. 120–131; idem, *Image*; Steinbruner, *Cybernetic Theory of Decision*; de Rivera, *Psychological Dimension of Foreign Policy*; Jervis, "Hypotheses on Misperception," pp. 239–254; and idem, *Perception and Misperception*.

56. Skocpol, *States and Social Revolutions*, chap. 7 passim.

57. This suggestion is discounted as "too purposive" an understanding. Ibid., table 2, pp. 282–283, 298n.

58. See ibid., pp. 168–171.

59. Collins, *Conflict Sociology*, p. 391 (Collins's italics). On Weber's notion of legitimacy, see Bendix, *Max Weber*, pp. 290–297; Weber, (1958) *From Max Weber*, pp. 78–79, 294; and [Weber], *Max Weber*, pp. 124–132, 324–329.

60. [Weber], *Max Weber*, p. 367.

61. Walzer, "Theory of Revolution," pp. 30–32.

62. Lenin, *What Is to Be Done?* p. 25.

63. Kolakowski, *Main Currents of Marxism*, 1:341.

64. Wolin, "Study of Revolution," p. 347.

65. Lenin, " 'Left-Wing' Communism," p. 306 (Lenin's italics).

66. Lenin, " 'Left-Wing' Communism," p. 378, quoted in Anderson, *Considerations on Western Marxism*, p. 105. It is important to interject here a caveat necessitated precisely by the Marxist's insistence on the inseparability of theory and practice. I have argued here that revolutionary ideology is essential to an adequate understanding of the nature and consequences of revolutionary practice. In treating revolutionary thought as political thought, in this book I approach Marxism and its variants in China and Japan in much the same manner as it treats political liberalism or the thought of Plato and Socrates. In other words, although theory can be treated as ideology, as a guide to practical action, action itself must not be confused with theory. Thus, although thinkers who were also revolutionists, such as Lenin and Mao Zedong, are responsible for their individual behaviors in the political process, their actions should not be confused with their thought when their thought is treated, as is the thought of John Locke or Jean-Jacques Rousseau, qua political theory. In short, although ideology is treated as an important factor in the pattern of revolutionary change, such change is not to be confounded with the thought of the revolutionary as a political thinker.

67. See, for example, Schram, *Political Thought of Mao Tse-tung*, pp. 112–117; idem, *Mao Tse-tung*, p. 355; Wakeman, *History and Will*, chap. 15; and Wylie, "Sinification of Marxism'," pp. 447–480.

68. See Wagner, "Sano Manabu"; Hoston, "Transformation of Marxism," pp. 25–47; and idem, "Marxism and National Socialism," pp. 43–64. These examples are discussed in depth in chap. 8.)

69. Wylie, " 'Sinification of Marxism'," p. 455.

70. Almond, *Appeals of Communism*.

71. Matsuzawa, *Nihon shakai-shugi no shisō*, pp. 194–197.

72. See Li, *Introduction of Socialism into China*; and Bernal, *Chinese Socialism to 1907*.

1. See, for example, Connor, *National Question*; Haupt, "Les Marxistes," pp. 9–61; and Lowy, "Le problème de l'histoire," pp. 370–391, both in Haupt, Lowy, and Weill, *Les Marxistes et la question nationale*"; and Davis, *Nationalism and Socialism*.

2. For the ambiguities of Marx's position, see Szporluk, *Communism and Nationalism*, chap. 11 passim.

3. Marx and Engels, *Communist Manifesto*, p. 488.

4. Ibid., p. 482.

5. Marx, "Critique of Hegel's 'Philosophy of Right'," p. 141.

6. Dahrendorf, *Society and Democracy in Germany*, (1979) especially chaps. 1, 3, and 4; and Taylor, *Course of German History*, chap. 1.

7. See Szporluk, *Nationalism and Communism*, chaps. 2 and 3, passim.

8. See Hayes, *Historical Evolution of Modern Nationalism*, pp. 232–233, 237.

9. Szporluk, *Communism and Nationalism*, p. 10. On nationalism and industrialization, cf. Gerschenkron, "Economic Backwardness," p. 24.

10. Luxemburg's position may have reflected the peculiar difficulties of Jews in articulating those interests. The Zionists among them certainly saw themselves as a separate nationality, and those of other nationalities who targeted the diaspora for persecution saw them as a separate culture and would not allow them to forget that (see Sartre, *Anti-Semite and Jew*).

11. Luxemburg, "National Question and Autonomy," pp. 104–105.

12. Here Luxemburg was citing Karl Kautsky in *Die Neue Zeit, 1897–1898*, 1:517 (Luxemburg, "National Question and Autonomy, p. 159.)

13. Luxemburg, "National Question and Autonomy," p. 166 (Luxemburg's italics).

14. Ibid., p. 131.

15. Luxemburg, "Quousque tandem," quoted in Nettl, *Rosa Luxemburg*, 1:270.

16. Luxemburg, "National Question and Autonomy," pp. 110–111 (Luxemburg's italics).

17. Haupt, "Les Marxistes," pp. 40–45, 111–112.

18. Bauer, "National Character," pp. 270–271, 274–275.

19. Haupt, "Les Marxistes," pp. 45ff.

20. "'Bol'nye voprosy' nashei partii: 'Likvidatorskii' i 'natsional'ny' voprosy," in Lenin, *Polnoe sobranie sochinenii*, in Tucker, *Stalin as Revolutionary*, pp. 150–151, 23.

21. Lenin, *Polnoe sobranie sochinenii*, 27:252–266, cited in Carrère d'Encausse, *Le grand défi*, p. 42.

22. Carrère d'Encausse, *Le grand défi*, pp. 43–48.

23. Stalin, *Sochineniia*, 2:296–367.

24. Tucker, *Stalin as Revolutionary*, pp. 152–154; Carrère d'Encausse, *Le grand défi*, pp. 48–51.

25. Space does not allow a fuller discussion of the intricacies of Lenin's thought on the national question within Russia here. See Carrère d'Encausse, *Le grand défi*, pp. 54–59.

26. See Lenin, "Right of Nations," pp. 152–180.

27. See Knei-paz, *Leon Trotsky*, chaps. 3–4.

28. See Tucker, *Stalin as Revolutionary*, chap. 7 passim.

29. See Gregor, *Young Mussolini*; and Nolte, *Three Faces of Fascism*, pt. 3 passim.

30. See Schorske, *German Social-Democracy*.

31. Von Klemperer, *Germany's New Conservatism*, (1958) p. 139, chap. 4 passim; cf. Mosse, *Crisis of German Ideology*, pp. 280–281; Neumann, *Behemoth*, pp. 191–199; and Meinecke, *German Catastrophe*, (1963) especially chap. 2.

32. See Hitler, *Mein Kampf*, pp. 187, chap. 11 passim.

33. See Marx to the editor of the *Otyescestvenniye Zapisky*, (1975), p. 354.

34. Engels, "Social Relations in Russia," p. 666.

35. Lenin, "Right of Nations," p. 164.

36. Lenin, "National Pride," p. 198.

37. See especially the account in Chamberlin, *Russian Revolution*.

38. Tucker, *Stalin as Revolutionary*, p. 224.

39. G. Bandzeladze, *Etika: Opit izlozhenia systemy marksistskoi etiki* [Ethics: An attempt to systematize Marxist ethics], 2d ed. (Tblisi: Idatelstvo 'Sabchota Sakartvelo,' 1970), p. 367, quoted in Kubálková and Cruickshank, *Marxism-Leninism*, p. 228.

40. Schapiro, *Communist Party*, p. 225.

41. For a detailed account of the disintegration of the empire and the challenges the Bolsheviks confronted in piecing together the new union, see Pipes, *Formation of the Soviet Union*.

42. Carrère d'Encausse, *Le grand défi*, pp. 95–99 passim.

43. Ibid., pp. 98–101.

44. Ibid., p. 109.

45. Stalin, *Sochineniia*, 4: 408, quoted in Tucker, *Stalin as Revolutionary*, p. 230.

46. Carrère d'Encausse, *Le grand défi*, p. 127.

47. See Suny, *Baku Commune*.

48. Tucker, *Stalin as Revolutionary*, pp. 230–238.

49. Lenin, "Question of Nationalities," pp. 719–724.

50. Carrère d'Encausse, *Le grand défi*, p. 126.

51. Schapiro, *Communist Party*, pp. 230–232.

52. Tucker, *Stalin as Revolutionary*, pp. 244–250. See Lenin, "Against Great-Russian Chauvinism," pp. 659–660.

53. See Carrère d'Encausse, *Le grand défi*, pt. 4, chap. 3.

54. Lane, *Politics and Society in the USSR*, (1982) p. 439.

55. See the vivid account of this campaign in Massell, *Surrogate Proletariat*.

56. Schlesinger, *The Nationalities Problem and Soviet Administration* (1956), cited in Lane, *Politics and Society in the USSR*, p. 443.

57. Rigby, *Communist Party Membership*, pp. 366–367.

58. Lenin, "National and Colonial Questions," pp. 621–622.

59. The Poles, Latvians, and Armenians were represented by commissariats, whereas the Ukrainians had only a section.

60. Carrère d'Encausse, *Le grand défi*, pp. 131–133.

61. Ibid., pp. 125–126.

62. Carrère d'Encausse, *Le grand défi*, pp. 110, 111.

63. Lenin, "Right of Nations," p. 156.

64. Massell, *Surrogate Proletariat*, p. 6.

65. Ibid., p. 37 (Massell's italics).

66. Pipes, *Formation of the Soviet Union*, pp. 259–260.

67. Massell, *Surrogate Proletariat*, p. 397.

68. Ibid. passim.

69. Ibid., pp. 43ff.

70. Ibid., p. 49.

71. See Lenin, "National and Colonial Questions," pp. 620–621; and Cohen, *Bukharin and the Bolshevik Revolution* (1973), p. 149.

72. Lenin, "National and Colonial Questions," pp. 622–623.

73. Ibid., p. 623. "[T]he Communist International should support bourgeois-democratic national movements in colonial and backward countries only on condition that, in these countries, the elements of future proletarian parties, which will be communist not only in name, are brought together and trained to understand their special tasks, i.e., those of the struggle against the bourgeois-democratic movements within their own nations" (ibid., p. 624).

74. See Lenin, "Two Tactics of Social-Democracy," pp. 79–110.

75. Lenin, *Polnoë sobranie sochinenii*, 41:133, quoted in Lenin, "National and Colonial Questions," p. 619.

76. Ibid., p. 624.

77. Ibid., p. 623.

78. See Knei-paz, *Leon Trotsky*, chap. 4 passim.

79. Engels quoted in Lenin, *State and Revolution*, pp. 365, 386ff.

80. See Pipes, "Toward the Police State."

81. Cohen, *Bukharin and the Bolshevik Revolution*, pp. 206ff, 144ff. By the late 1930s, after Stalin's consolidation of power against his rivals, the expansion of the Soviet state had progressed to such an extent that the Italian Marxist Bruno Rizzi felt compelled to write in alarm of the bureaucratization of the world (see Rizzi, *Bureaucratization of the World*).

82. See Wright, *China in Revolution*, passim.

83. Hegel, *Philosophy of History*, pp. 174, 175, 18.

84. See Gregor and Chang, "*Nazionalfascismo*," pp. 21–37.

85. Such denunciations were found in the *Manifesto*, *Socialism: Utopian and Scientific*, and *The Poverty of Philosophy* (Marx's critique of Pierre-Joseph Proudhon's *Philosophy of Poverty*), all of which were translated early and widely read among Asian Marxists.

86. Bloom, *World of Nations*, p. 32.

87. Ibid., pp. 68–69.

CHAPTER 2

1. An overview of these indigenous pre-Marxian conceptions of the polity in China and Japan is presented in chapter 3.

2. See the classification of theories of the state in Clark and Dear, *State Apparatus*, p. 15.

3. Nettl, "State as a Conceptual Variable," pp. 562–565.

4. Tilly, "History of European State-Making," p. 32.

5. Nettl continues, "It is significant that the word *l'État* in French should be the only one normally beginning with a capital letter" ("State as a Conceptual Variable," p. 567).

6. Perry Anderson recently argued that Eastern Europe (including Russia), lacking the structural legacies of classical antiquity, consistently lagged behind Western Europe in its political development. Indeed, Anderson argues that when it finally did evolve, absolutism (a misnomer, for it is quite distinct, in this usage, from despotism or aristocracy) in Eastern Europe was a different, cruder variant than its Western European counterpart. See his *Lineages of the Absolutist State*, pp. 430–431.

7. Tilly, "History of European State-Making," p. 34.

8. Tilly, "Theories of Political Transformation," pp. 632–637. Compare Otto Hintze on

the need for both political and economic entrepreneurship in the simultaneous rise of capitalism and the modern state. See Hintze, "Economics and Politics in the Age of Modern Capitalism," pp. 428–431.

9. See Marx, "Economic and Philosophic Manuscripts," p. 67; and Joseph O'Malley, editor's introduction in Marx, *Hegel's "Philosophy of Right,"* pp. xiii–xiv. There is also a "Draft Plan for a Work on the Modern State" by Marx dated 1845 (in Marx and Engels, *German Ideology,* cited by Maguire, *Marx's Theory of Politics,* p. 8).

10. Tucker, "Political Theory of Classical Marxism," p. 80.

11. Alan Wolfe, "New Directions," p. 131.

12. V. I. Lenin, "State and Revolution," in *The Lenin Anthology,* ed. Tucker, p. 335.

13. Tilly, "Theories of Political Transformation," pp. 628–629; cf. Miliband, *State in Capitalistic Society,* pp. 6, 6n. Perry Anderson's work poses an important challenge to this generalization. See his *Passages from Antiquity to Feudalism* and *Lineages of the Absolutist State.*

14. See Weber, *Law in Economy and Society,* pp. 336–337; and Bendix, *Max Weber,* (1962) pp. 417, 418, 418n.

15. "The specific economic form, in which unpaid surplus labor is pumped out of direct producers, determines the relationship of rulers and ruled, as it grows directly out of production itself and, in turn, reacts upon it as a determining element. . . . It is always the direct relationship of the owners of the conditions of production to the direct producers . . . which reveals the innermost secret, the hidden basis of the entire social structure, and with it the political form of the relation of sovereignty and dependence, in short the corresponding specific form of the state. This does not prevent the same economic basis— the same from the standpoint of its main conditions—due to innumerable different empirical circumstances, natural environment, racial relations, external historical influences, etc., from showing infinite variations and gradations in appearance, which can be ascertained only by analysis of the empirically given circumstances" (Karl Marx, *Capital,* chap. 47, sec. 2, par. 2 [pp. 791–792]).

16. See Marx, "German Ideology," p. 128; cf. Marx, "Economic and Philosophic Manuscripts of 1844," p. 94.

17. Wolfe, "New Directions," p. 133; Tucker, "Political Theory of Classical Marxism," p. 59.

18. Wolfe, "New Directions," p. 134; cf. Miliband, *State in Capitalistic Society,* pp. 134–135.

19. Wolfe, "New Directions," p. 132; and Hyppolite, "Marxisme et philosophie," pp. 109–110.

20. Wolfe, "New Directions," p. 132.

21. Plamenatz, *Karl Marx's Philosophy of Man,* p. 209.

22. O'Malley, editor's introduction to Marx, *Hegel's "Philosophy of Right,"* pp. xlv–xlvii; and Löwith, *From Hegel to Nietzsche,* pt. 2, chap. 1.

23. O'Malley, Editor's introduction to Marx, *Hegel's "Philosophy of Right,"* p. xlvii; and Hegel, *Philosophy of Right,* par. 187. Cf. Marx, *Hegel's "Philosophy of Right"* (hereafter cited as *Critique*), pp. 72, 80; and Avineri, *Social and Political Thought of Karl Marx,* pp. 43–45; and Girardin, "Marxist Theory of the State," p. 193; and Marx, "German Ideology," p. 127.

24. Hegel, *Philosophy of Right,* par. 301, par. 301 Addition; cf. Kolakowski, *Main Currents of Marxism,* 1:125.

25. Löwith, *From Hegel to Nietzsche,* p. 235, quoted in O'Malley, Editor's introduction to Marx, *Hegel's "Philosophy of Right,"* p. xlv.

26. Hegel, *Philosophy of Right*, par. 302.

27. Marx, *Critique*, p. 69.

28. Ibid., pp. 77, 123; cf. Marx, "On the Jewish Question," pp. 31–32.

29. Marx, *Critique*, p. 47.

30. O'Malley, Editor's introduction to Marx, *Hegel's "Philosophy of Right,"* p. lii.

31. Marx, "Critique of Hegel's 'Philosophy of Right'," pp. 141–142.

32. Marx, *Critique*, p. 33.

33. Marx, "Critique of Hegel's 'Philosophy of Right'," p. 135; Hyppolite, "La conception Hegelienne de l'etat," p. 122.

34. Marx, *Critique*, p. 64; and Rubel, *Karl Marx*, pp. 72–74.

35. Wakeman, *History and Will*, (1975) p. 29.

36. Hegel, *Erstes Systemprogramm des deutschen Idealismus*, translated in Lichtheim, *Marxism*, p. 36, quoted in Wakeman, *History and Will*.

37. Hegel, *Philosophy of Right*, par. 258.

38. See Ralph Miliband's discussion of this point in "Marx and the State," in *Karl Marx*, pp. 130–132; and Dupré, *Philosophical Foundations of Marxism*, chap. 4 passim.

39. Marx, "A Contribution to the Critique of Hegels 'Philosophy of Right'," p. 132.

40. Plamenatz, *Karl Marx's Philosophy of Man*, pp. 295–296.

41. Kolakowski, *Main Currents of Marxism*, 1:125.

42. See Marx, *Critique*, pp. 30, 121. Cf. Hyppolite, "La conception Hegelienne de l'Etat," pp. 129–133.

43. Hook, *From Hegel to Marx*, pp. 249–250.

44. Marx, "On the Jewish Question," p. 30. Cf. Avineri, *Social and Political Thought of Karl Marx*, pp. 43–44; and Miliband, "Marx and the State," pp. 132–134.

45. Marx, "On the Jewish Question," p. 33; Marx and Engels, *Holy Family* passim; Kolakowski, *Main Currents of Marxism*, 1:150–151; Wakeman, *History and Will*, pp. 29–30; and Rubel, *Karl Marx*, pp. 81–87.

46. Avineri, *Social and Political Thought of Karl Marx*, p. 17.

47. Girardin, "Marxist theory of the State," p. 195.

48. "[A]t its highest point the political constitution is the constitution of private property" (Marx, *Critique*, p. 99). "This material, immediately *sensuous* private property is the material sensuous expression of *estranged human* life." "The positive transcendence of *private property* as the appropriation of human life is, therefore, the positive transcendence of all estrangement—that is to say, the return of man from religion, family, state, etc., to his *human*, i.e., *social* mode existence" (Marx, "Economic and Philosophical Manuscripts," pp. 70–71 [Marx's italics]).

49. Plamenatz, *Marx's Philosophy of Man*, pp. 209–210.

50. Ibid., p. 209.

51. Engels, *Herr Eugen Dühring's Revolution in Science*, [hereafter cited as *Anti-Dühring*], pp. 306–307; Lenin, "State and Revolution," pp. 335–350.

52. Lichtheim, *Marxism*, pp. 373–375.

53. Marx, "Critique of the Gotha Program," p. 395.

54. Karl Marx, "Civil War in France," p. 557. Cf. Wakeman, *History and Will*, pp. 29–30.

55. Plamenatz, *Karl Marx's Philosophy of Man*, p. 279; cf. Maguire, *Marx's Theory of Politics*, p. 13. Marx's notes on Lewis H. Morgan's *Ancient Society, or Researches in the Lines of Human Progress from Savagery, through Barbarism to Civilization* (London: Macmillan, 1877) were available to Engels and used extensively in the preparation of *Origin of the Family*. These notes can be found in Marx's abstract of *Ancient Society*, in

Marx Engels Archives (in Russian) 9 (1941): 1–192. See Engels, preface to the first edition in *Origin of the Family*, p. 71.

56. Engels, *Anti-Dühring*, p. 198; cf. Daniels, " 'Withering Away of the State'," p. 119.

57. Engels, *Anti-Dühring*, p. 165. Cf. the assertion in the same work that "the exercise of a social function was everywhere the basis of political supremacy" (p. 198).

58. Ibid. Cf. Plamenatz, *Karl Marx's Philosophy of Man*, pp. 280–281; and Maguire, *Marx's Theory of Politics*, p. 229. The state described by Engels as a structure arising purely for the performance of "social functions" was, thus, not Marx's "political state" (or state qua state) at all. Of course, the second phenomenon described by Engels might occur in class society as well and figures also in of the notion of the "potential autonomy" of the state from either the dominant socioeconomic class or from society as a whole, a notion that has become the object of intense debate among contemporaneous Marxist theorists. This issue will be pursued later. Solomon F. Bloom has noted a separate difficulty in the fact that "Marx used the term "state" habitually, though not exclusively, to denote the forms of government peculiar to class societies. He defined "politics" similarly as a function of the self-consciousness and conflict of classes" (*World of Nations*, p. 66).

59. Engels, *Origin of the Family*, p. 228; and Maguire, *Karl Marx's Theory of Politics*, p. 226.

60. Engels, *Origin of the Family*, pp. 229–230.

61. Ibid., pp. 224–226; cf. Kolakowski, *Main Currents of Marxism*, 1:358–359; Sanderson, "Marx and Engels on the State," p. 947; and Hobsbawm, "Karl Marx's Contribution to History," p. 280.

62. This was, however, considerably less emphasis on the role of private property than that of Morgan's original account. Leacock in the introduction to Engels, *Origin of the Family*, p. 46.

63. Engels, *Origin of the Family*, p. 170 (Engels's italics).

64. Karl Marx and Friedrich Engels, *Germany Ideology*, trans. R. Pascal, (New York: International Publishers, 1939) p. 77, quoted in Plamenatz, *Marx's Philosophy of Man*, p. 282.

65. See, for example, Marx, *Capital*, vol. 3, chap. 47, sec. 2, par. 2 (p. 79).

66. Tucker, "Political Theory of Classical Marxism," p. 66.

67. The most complete discussion of alienation appears in *German Ideology*, especially pp. 123–125. Here the division of labor is identified with private property, whereas in Engels's *Origin of the Family* it moves through several stages, beginning with a division of labor in communal society between "pastoral tribes" and "barbarians" (p. 218). On the "inevitable" "transformation of the state and organs of the state from servants of society into masters of society," see Marx, "Civil War in France," p. 536.

68. The most salient example of a state arising on community rather than private property is "oriental despotism," which "appears to lead to a legal absence of property." See Marx's discussion in the partial translation of the *Grundrisse* entitled *Pre-Capitalist Economic Formations*, p. 70; and Engels, *Anti-Dühring*, p. 200.

69. Moore, *Critique of Capitalist Democracy*, (1969) pp. 26–92.

70. Marx, *Capital*, vol. 3, chap. 47, sec. 2 (pp. 791–792); cf. Engels, "Marx's Contribution to the Critique of Political Economy," 1:363–364.

71. Tucker, "Political Theory of Classical Marxism," p. 76; cf. Marx, "Civil War in France," p. 252.

72. Marx, "Civil War in France," p. 552.

73. Kolakowski, *Main Currents of Marxism*, 1:360–363; Daniels, " 'Withering away of the State'," pp. 119–120; and Marx, "Eighteenth Brumaire," pp. 472–473.

74. Marx and Engels, *Communist Manifesto*, quoted in Miliband, "Marx and the State," pp. 134–135.

75. Sanderson, "Marx and Engels on the State," pp. 949–950. See Marx, "Parliamentary Debates" and "Elections in England."

76. Maguire, *Marx's Theory of Politics*, p. 13 (Maguire's italics).

77. See especially the writings of Nicos Poulantzas, *Political Power and Social Classes*; "The Problem of the Capitalist State," pp. 238–253; and *State, Power, Socialism*.

78. This view departs somewhat from the interpretation presented in Tucker, "Political Theory of Classical Marxism," pp. 59–60.

79. On the need for this ideological function of the bourgeois state, much has been written. A major contribution was made here by the Italian Marxist Antonio Gramsci in the 1920s. Gramsci saw many ideological functions of the state performed by institutions conventionally viewed as part of civil society, such as schools and churches. See Gramsci, *Selections from the Prison Notebooks*, pp. 5–23, 123–205, 206–276. Similarly, Louis Althusser draws a distinction between the ideological (ISAs) and repressive apparatuses of the capitalist state, a theme that is reflected in Poulantzas's work as well. See Althusser, "Ideology and Ideological State Apparatuses," pp. 142–152; and Poulantzas, *Political Power and Social Classes*, pp. 195–224. Cf. W. G. Runciman, "Karl Marx and Max Weber," pp. 46–47.

80. Engels, *Origin of the Family*, p. 231; cf. the analysis of Metternich's rule in Austria-Hungary on the basis of a political balance among forces of the bourgeoisie, nobility, and peasantry (in addition to racial factors), in Engels, "Hungary and Panslavism," pp. 58–59.

81. Sanderson, "Marx and Engels on the State," p. 951.

82. Tucker, "Political Theory of Classical Marxism," pp. 70–71.

83. Marx, "Eighteenth Brumaire," pp. 515–516.

84. Engels in the introduction (1891) to Marx, *Civil War in France*, p. 535.

85. Ibid., p. 536.

86. Maguire, *Marx's Theory of Politics*, pp. 19–20.

87. Marx, *Pre-Capitalist Economic Formations*, pp. 69–70; cf. Barry Hindess and Paul Q. Hirst, *Pre-Capitalist Modes of Production* (London and Boston, Mass.: Routledge and Kegan Paul, 1975), pp. 218–219.

88. Marx, *Pre-Capitalist Economic Formations*, p. 70.

89. See Skocpol and Trimberger, "Revolutions," pp. 103–113; Trimberger, *Revolutions from Above*; Moore, *Social Origins of Dictatorship and Democracy*; and Stepan, *State and Society*.

90. Engels, *Anti-Dühring*, pp. 202–204.

91. See Marx, "British Rule in India," pp. 381–382.

92. Engels, *Anti-Dühring*, pp. 303–305.

93. Tarschys, *Beyond the State*, p. 90.

94. Lichtheim, *Marxism*, pp. 323–324; and Tucker, "Political Theory of Classical Marxism," p. 64.

95. Lichtheim, *Marxism*, pp. 324, 349.

96. Tucker, "Political Theory of Classical Marxism," p. 64.

97. Engels in the introduction to Marx, *Civil War in France*, pp. 534–535.

98. Lichtheim, *Marxism*, pp. 127–129. Compare the usage of the term "the masses" in subsequent Soviet and Chinese formulations.

99. Trotsky, *Revolution Betrayed*, especially pp. 45–64; and Milovan Djilas, *New Class*.

100. One might suggest that such an effort to rebuild human psychology for socialist

production should have been less urgent in Russia, with its prolonged remanence of the rural commune (*mir* or *obshchina*) into the twentieth century, than in societies where the individualist privatism of capitalist society had matured more fully, supplanting earlier communal forms as in Western Europe. Marx tentatively suggested this possibility in a draft of a letter to Vera Zasulich, "Letter on the Russian Village Community," pp. 218–226. Cf. Engels, "Social Relations in Russia," pp. 594–597; and Marx and Engels, preface to the 1882 Russian edition of the *Communist Manifesto*, in ibid., pp. 333–334.

101. In this respect, this author rejects the judgment that "[l]ike most of the theoretical content of party ideology, the doctrine of the state remained substantially unchanged from the Revolution to 1929" (Daniels, "'Withering Away of the State,'" p. 122).

102. Daniels, "'Withering Away of the State'," pp. 113, 114, 120, 115–116. Cf. Cohen, *Bukharin and the Bolshevik Revolution* (1975) pp. 42–43; and Cohen, "Theoretical Foundations of Bolshevism," pp. 436–457.

103. The work was published in condensed form in 1916–1917 in *Jugend-Internationale*, *Arbeiterpolitik*, *Die Tribune*, *Klassekampen*, *Stormklokan*, and *Novy Mir*. It did not appear in full in its original form until 1925 when it was published in *Revoliutsiia prava* (Heitman, *Nikolai I. Bukharin*, p. 29). For Lenin's objections to Bukharin's work, see "Zametki na stat'iu N. I. Bukharina," pp. 329–330; and "Zamechaniia na stat'iu N. I. Bukharina," pp. 331–338. See also the correspondence between Bukharin and Lenin over Lenin's refusal to print Bukharin's article in "Iz materialov Instituta Marksa-Engel'sa-Lenina." These letters were probably released as part of Stalin's campaign to discredit Bukharin by demonstrating the latter's alleged consistent disagreement with Lenin.

104. Wolfe, "New Directions," p. 136. A complete list of references is to be found in Lenin, *Gosudarstvo i revoliutsiia*, pp. 430–431, 391–406.

105. Compare Bukharin's definition of the state in "The Theory of the Imperialist State:" "'From the point of view of Marxism, the state is nothing other than the greatest general organization of the ruling classes, the basic function of which consists of the preservation and extension of the exploitation of the oppressed classes.'" (In *Revoliutsiia prava*, I, 7, quoted in Daniels, "'Withering Away of the State,'" p. 117.)

106. Lenin, "State and Revolution."

107. Lenin, "State and Revolution," pp. 192, 203, 226 (Lenin's italics).

108. Ibid., pp. 227, 28, 228n., 229.

109. In Vienna, Bukharin studied the work of Austro-Marxists Rudolf Hilferding and Otto Bauer on monopoly capitalism and, drawing on their writings, completed his major work *Imperialism and World Economy* in 1915 (published in its entirety in 1918). Cohen, *Bukharin and the Bolshevik Revolution*, p. 14; and Heitman, "Between Lenin and Stalin," p. 88.

110. Bukharin, *Historical Materialism*, p. 246 (Bukharin's italics).

111. Cohen, *Bukharin and the Bolshevik Revolution*, p. 28.

112. Bukharin and Preobrazhensky, *ABC of Communism*, p. 239. Cf. Bukharin, "Rabochaia aristokratiia," p. 2.

113. Trotsky, *Revolution Betrayed*, pp. 248–252. See also Cohen, *Bukharin and the Bolshevik Revolution*, p. 157; and Lewin, *Political Undercurrents*, pp. 68–72.

114. Cohen, *Bukharin and the Bolshevik Revolution*, p. 206; Lewin, *Political Undercurrents*, p. 63; and Robert C. Tucker, "The Image of Dual Russia," (1972) pp. 121–122.

115. Bukharin, "Imperialism and World Economy," pp. 387, 390. These ideas also appear in Bukharin and Preobrazhensky, *ABC of Communism*, pp. 162–166. Bukharin did not appear, however, to share Lenin's acute perception of the continuing importance of nationality and nationalism in the imperialist period. See Cohen, *Bukharin and the Bol-*

shevik Revolution, pp. 35–36; and Nikolai Bukharin, *Imperialism and World Economy*, (1973), pp. 166–167.

116. Cohen, *Bukharin and the Bolshevik Revolution*, p. 253.

117. Ibid., pp. 215, 292–293; and Hammond, "Bukharin and the Chinese Revolution," (Review Essay on Cohen, *Bukharin and the Bolshevik Revolution, 1888–1938*), pp. 463–472.

118. Cohen, *Bukharin and the Bolshevik Revolution*, p. 292.

119. Ibid., pp. 255, 31; Bukharin, *Imperialism and World Economy*, chaps. 10, 11, 13; idem, "Teoriia 'organizovannoi beskhoziaisvennosti'," pp. 183–184.

120. Cohen, *Bukharin and the Bolshevik Revolution*, p. 174.

121. Erlich, *Soviet Industrialization Debates*, pp. 84–89; and Lewin, *Russian Peasants and Soviet Power*, chap. 6 passim.

122. Daniels, "'Withering Away of the State'," pp. 122–124.

123. Ibid., pp. 123–124. This speech is contained in Stalin, *Problems of Leninism*, pp. 656–663.

124. Tucker, Letter to the Editor, *Foreign Affairs* 58, no. 5 (Summer 1980): 1180.

125. See Heer, *Politics and History*, pp. 656–663.

126. Lenin, *What Is to Be Done?* p. 50 (Lenin's italics).

127. Gramsci, "Study of Philosophy," pp. 355, 360; idem, "Modern Prince," and idem, "Notes on Italian History," p. 113, all in Gramsci, *Selections from the Prison Notebooks*.

128. Gramsci, "Modern Prince," p. 161; and idem, "Intellectuals," in Gramsci, *Selections from the Prison Notebooks*, p. 12.

129. Gramsci, "State and Civil Society," pp. 229–239. See the exceptionally lucid presentation of Gramsci's thought in Adamson, *Hegemony and Revolution*, especially chaps. 6, 7; and Buci-Glucksmann, "Hegemony and Consent."

130. M. to R. [Karl Marx to Arnold Ruge], September 1843, in Tucker, *Marx-Engels Reader*, p. 8 (italics in original).

131. Jay, *Marxism and Totality*, p. 109.

132. See Lukács, *History and Class Consciousness*.

133. See Marcuse, *One-Dimensional Man*, pp. xi, xiv–xvi, 11, 168–169.

134. See Stojanović, *Between Ideals and Reality*, p. 5 (italics in original).

135. On the ambiguities of Habermas's position vis-à-vis Marx, see "Translator's Introduction," in Habermas, *Legitimation Crisis*, passim; and Jay, *Marxism and Totality*, pp. 463–483.

136. Marcuse, "Struggle against Liberalism"; Ollman, *Alienation*; and Avineri, *Social and Political Thought of Karl Marx*, cited in ibid., p. 40.

137. Althusser, "Ideology and Ideological State Apparatuses"; Poulantzas, *Political Power and Social Classes*, pp. 195–224. Offe is a student of Habermas and endeavors to prove the class character of the state that other scientific Marxists assume a priori. Offe's writings on the state include *Strukturprobleme des Kapitalischen Staates*; "Structural Problems," pp. 31–56; and "Theory of the Capitalist State," pp. 125–144. Offe's objective is to understand the "State . . . as a capitalist State—and not . . . merely a 'State in Capitalist Society'" (Offe, "Structural Problems," p. 31).

138. Althusser, *For Marx*, pp. 233–234.

139. Althusser, "Ideology and Ideological State Apparatuses," passim.

140. Althusser and Balibar, *Reading Capital*.

141. Gold, Lo, and Wright, "Recent Developments," pt. 1, pp. 31–32.

142. Poulantzas recognizes this problem explicitly in *Political Power and Social Classes*, pp. 24–25.

143. Gold, Lo, and Wright, "Recent Developments," pt. 1, p. 32 (italics in original). Some would argue that Miliband is neither an instrumentalist nor a structuralist, but I would place him firmly in this instrumentalist category. His work includes *The State in Capitalistic Society* and a number of articles in debate with the structuralist Nicos Poulantzas, such as "Capitalist State," pp. 53–60; and "Poulantzas and the Capitalist State," pp. 83–92.

144. Offe, "Structural Problems," pp. 31–32 (Offe's italics).

145. Gold, Lo, and Wright, "Recent Developments," pt. 1, pp. 32–33. Significant instrumentalist studies include Domhoff, *Who Rules America?*; Nichols, "Ruling Class"; Domhoff, *Higher Circles*; Kolko, *Triumph of Conservatism*; J. Kolko and G. Kolko, *Limits of Power*; Menshikov, *Millionaires and Managers*; and Weinstein, *Corporate Ideal*.

146. Gold, Lo, and Wright, "Recent Developments," pt. 1, p. 33.

147. Miliband, "Poulantzas and the Capitalist State," p. 85n; and idem, "Marx and the State," pp. 135–136.

148. Miliband, "Marx and the State," pp. 139, 137–138 (Miliband's italics); and Miliband, *State in Capitalistic Society*, pp. 93–94.

149. Miliband, *State in Capitalistic Society*, p. 5.

150. Ibid., p. 35. See, for example, Williams, "Marxist Cultural Theory"; and Poulantzas, "Problem of the Capitalist State," pp. 246–247.

151. See Block, "Ruling Class Does Not Rule," p. 8; and Krieger and Held, "Theory of the State?" pp. 189–207.

152. Marx, "German Ideology," pp. 112–139. To this extent, structuralists such as Offe, Althusser, and Poulantzas tend to be more effective in applying some of the aspects of the work of the early Marx pertaining to consciousness.

153. Offe, "Structural Problems," p. 34.

154. Ibid., pp. 32, 35 (Offe's italics); Poulantzas, "Problem of the Capitalist State," pp. 245–246.

155. Offe and Ronge, "Theory of the State," p. 36.

156. Gold, Lo, and Wright, "Recent Developments," pt. 1, p. 36; and Bridges, "Nicos Poulantzas," pp. 163–164.

157. Offe, "Structural Problems," p. 47 (Offe's italics); Poulantzas, *Political Power and Social Classes*, pp. 42, 44–45, 189.

158. Here Poulantzas seems to have drawn on Gramsci's ambiguous observations concerning the state and civil society although Miliband, too, sought support from Gramsci for his view of the role of the dominant classes in establishing and maintaining hegemony. See Miliband, *State in Capitalistic Society*, p. 183; Williams, "Gramsci's Concept of Egemonia," p. 587; and J. Merrington, "Gramsci's Marxism."

159. Poulantzas, *Political Power and Social Classes*, pp. 50, 44–55 passim. See Bridges, "Nicos Poulantzas," pp. 165–170. Cf. Offe, "Theory of the Capitalist State," pp. 128–133, 144.

160. Offe, "Structural Problems," p. 54 (Offe's italics).

161. Offe, "Theory of the Capitalist State," p. 133.

162. Block, "Ruling Class Does Not Rule," pp. 10, 11, 13, 15; Offe and Ronge, "Theory of the State," p. 140.

163. Poulantzas follows Gramsci's section of the *Modern Prince* entitled "Brief Notes on Machiavelli's Politics" (pp. 125–133) in arguing thus. Gold, Lo, and Wright, "Recent Developments," pt. 1, p. 38; cf. Poulantzas, *Political Power and Social Classes*, p. 21; and Offe and Ronge, "Theory of the State," p. 142.

164. See, for example, Poulantzas, *Political Power and Social Classes*, p. 20.

165. Gold, Lo, and Wright, "Recent Developments," pt. 1, p. 39.

166. Miliband, "Capitalist State," p. 57.

167. Gold, Lo, and Wright, "Recent Developments," pt. 1, pp. 38–39.

168. Offe, "Structural Problems," p. 47 and supra; cf. Gold, Lo, and Wright, "Recent Developments," pt. 1, p. 45. Similarly, Block reintroduces class consciousness and rationality threefold in the perspectives of the bourgeoisie, the proletariat, and the managers of the state apparatus. See Block, "Ruling Class Does Not Rule," pp. 7–8; cf. Krieger and Held, "Theory of the State?" passim.

169. Skocpol, "Critical Review," p. 18.

170. Hobsbawm, "Karl Marx's Contribution to History," p. 273.

171. I am here relying on Edward Said's powerful description of this phenomenon. "Orientalism" is "a style of thought based on an ontological and epistemological distinction made between 'the Orient' and (most of the time) 'the Occident'." It constitutes "a western style for dominating, restructuring, and having authority over the Orient" "by making statements about it, authorizing views of it, describing it, teaching it, settling it, ruling over it." Said correctly saw this same perspective in Marx's characterization of the East as a passive, unchanging, stagnant mass. See Said, *Orientalism*, (1979), pp. 2, 3, 153–156.

172. See Hegel, *Philosophy of History*.

173. Marx, "British Rule in India," pp. 581–582 (Marx's italics).

174. Marx, "History of His Opinions."

175. Bailey and Llobera, *Asiatic Mode of Production*, p. 1.

176. Others, including Karl Wittfogel, who systematized the notion of Asiatic despotism, have attributed the demise of the concept to its potential application to the Soviet regime. See his *Oriental Despotism*, pp. 380ff.; Lichtheim, *Marxism*, pp. 147, 147n.; and Shteppa, *Russian Historians and the Soviet State*, pp. 47–48.

177. Kolakowski, *Main Currents of Marxism*, 1:350.

178. Meisner, "Despotism of Concepts," pp. 103–104. "Japan, with its purely feudal organisation of landed property and its developed *petite culture*, gives a much truer picture of the European middle ages than all our history books," Marx wrote (Marx, *Capital*, 1:718n). See also Marx, *Capital*, 3:877; Marx, *Pre-Capitalist Economic Formations*, pp. 70, 88; and Godelier, "The 'Asian Mode of Production'," p. 39.

179. Lowe, *Function of "China,"* pp. 11–14.

180. Lichtheim, "Oriental Despotism," p. 67.

181. Friedrich Engels to Karl Marx, June 6, 1853, in Mark and Engels, *Selected Correspondence*, (1975) p. 66.

182. Engels, pp. 198ff.

183. Wittfogel, *Oriental Despotism*, p. 384; Engels, *Anti-Dühring*, pp. 198, 200, 165. Cf. Marx, *Capital*, 1:514, on the importance of natural conditions, such as the need for irrigation in the East for historical development.

184. Godelier, "Asian Mode of Production," p. 39.

185. Marx, *Capital*, 3:634; cf. ibid., 1:357; and Engels, *Anti-Dühring*, p. 195.

186. Karl Marx to Frederick Engels, June 2, 1853, in Marx and Engels, *Selected Correspondence*, p. 65 (Marx's italics).

187. Marx, *Capital*, 3:331; 1:357; 3:796; and 1:333.

188. Ibid., 3:791.

189. Ibid., 3:597.

190. Marx, "British Rule in India," pp. 581–582; Marx, "Future Results of British Rule in India," p. 583; Marx, *Capital*, 3:333–334; cf. Lowe, *Function of "China,"* p. 27.

191. Lichtheim, *Marxism*, p. 152. Cf. Hobsbawm, in the introduction to Marx, *Pre-Capitalist Economic Formations*, p. 38.

192. Marx to the editor of the *Otyescestvenniye Zapisky* [Notes on the fatherland] (End of 1877), in Marx and Engels, *Selected Correspondence*, p. 354.

193. Marx, *Pre-Capitalist Economic Formations*, p. 97; cf. Lichtheim, *Marxism*, pp. 148–152.

194. Lichtheim, *Marxism*, pp. 217–218; and Marx and Engels, *Communist Manifesto*, p. 334.

195. Baron, "Plekhanov's Russia," pp. 390, 392, 393; Baron, "Development of Soviet Historiography," p. 382; and Baron, *Plekhanov*, chap. 4.

196. Plekhanov, *Sochineniya* (Collected works), 10:154, and 20:12, quoted by Baron, "Development of Soviet Historiography," pp. 383, 384.

197. Baron, "Plekhanov's Russia," pp. 400, 396, 398, 399.

198. Baron, "Development of Soviet Historiography," pp. 382–385; Baron, "Plekhanov's Russia," p. 401.

199. Plekhanov's denunciation by Pokrovsky (even with Stalin's full support in 1929) did not, however, diminish his stature as the founder of Russian Marxism in China and Japan. *Fundamental Problems of Marxism* was one of the first works of Russian Marxism introduced into Japan after the October Revolution and was translated into Japanese and widely read by 1925. See Baron, "Development of Russian Historiography," pp. 393, 388; and Shteppa, *Russian Historians*, chap. 4 passim.

200. Plekhanov, *Fundamental Problems of Marxism*, pp. 49–55, 64, 57; He, *Zhongguo shehui shi wenti lunzhan*, pp. 5–6; cf. Lichtheim, *Marxism*, pp. 145–146.

201. Lenin, *Development of Capitalism in Russia*, pp. 176–177.

202. Baron, "Transition from Feudalism to Capitalism," p. 721.

203. Trotsky articulated this theory with reference to Russian development in *Results and Prospects* (1906) and in the essays of *1905*. See the comprehensive discussion in Knei-Paz, *Leon Trotsky*, chap. 3. On Russia as Asiatic, see *1905*, Eng. ed. pp. 3–8, 12–15, 38–39. Cf. Deutscher, *Prophet Armed*, pp. 148–154.

204. Baron, "Transition from Feudalism to Capitalism," p. 724.

205. Lenin, *Development of Capitalism in Russia*, pp. 195–197.

206. The following is an abbreviated treatment of the subject that focuses on the theme of the national question. For a more extended treatment, see Hoston, *Crisis of Development in Prewar Japan*, pp. 140–145.

207. Varga's (1879–1964) essays on China included: "Ekonomicheskie problemy revoliutsii v Kitae" [Economic problems of the revolution in China], *Planovoe khoziaistvo* [Planned economy], no. 12 (1925); "Osnovnyi problemy Kitaiskoi revoliutsii" [Fundamental problems of the Chinese revolution], *Bol'shevik*, no. 8 (1928); "Novaia nauchnaia literatura o Kitae" [The new scientific literature on China], *Pravda* [Truth], January 6, 1929; and "Perspektivy kitaiskoi revoliutsii: Zakluchitelnii vazdel" [Perspectives of the Chinese revolution: The final chapter), in Mad'iar, *Ocherki po ekonomike Kitaeia*. For a comprehensive bibliography of Soviet scholarship on China during this period, see Nikiforov, *Sovetskie istoriki o problemakh Kitaia*, pp. 368–397. Both Varga and Mad'iar (1891–1940) appear to have been close associates of Nikolai Bukharin, and the demise of their account of Asian society coincided with Bukharin's fall from power.

208. Riazanov (whose given name was David Borisovich Goldendach), who compiled the first edition of the twenty-seven volumes of the *Complete Works of Marx and Engels*, was accused of counterrevolutionary activities in 1931, was purged, and died (perhaps executed under Stalin) in 1938.

209. Wittfogel, *Oriental Despotism*, p. 401.

210. See Mad'iar, *Ekonomika sel'skogo khoziaistva v Kitae* (Moscow: Gosudarstvennoe

Izdatelstvo 1928); idem, *Ocherki po ekonomike Kitaia* (1930); idem, *Sovremennoe soso'tianie kitaiskoi revoliutsii* (1920); and idem, "Dve agrarnye programmy."

211. This portrayal may be contrasted with G. William Skinner's portrayal of Chinese peasant communities as bodies that alternated in being relatively "open" and closed, isolated "self-sufficient" communities. In his view, generally, the isolation of these communities tended to peak at times of foreign conquest. See his intriguing article, "Chinese Peasants and the Closed Community," pp. 270–281.

212. Mad'iar, "Legitimacy of the AMP," pp. 76–94.

B213. The only work by Godes listed in the Nikiforov bibliography is *Shto takoe kemalistiskii put' i bozmozhen li on v Kitae?* [What is the Kemalist road (of Kemal Ataturk) and is it possible in China?] (Leningrad, 1928). Iolk's major writings appeared only in 1930. These included: "K voprosy ob osnovakh obshchestvennovo stroia drevnova Kitaia"; *"O zadachakh Marksistsko-Leninskogo izucheniia"*; "Review of M. Kokin and G. Papaian, *'Tszintian': Agrarnii stroi drevnevo Kitaia"* ["Jingtian": The agrarian system of ancient China]; and "K voprosy ob 'Aziatskom' sposobe proizvodstva" [On the problem of the 'Asiatic' mode of production].

214. Wittfogel, *Oriental Despotism*, p. 402.

215. Iolk, "AMP and the Class Struggle," p. 97.

216. See Schwartz, *Rise of Mao*, pp. 122–123; and Wittfogel, *Oriental Despotism*, pp. 405, 405n.

217. Mad'iar, "Legitimacy of the AMP," pp. 93–94.

218. Godes, "Reaffirmation of Unlinealism," pp. 102, 104; and Iolk, "AMP and the Class Struggle," p. 98.

219. Godes, "Reaffirmation of Unilinealism," pp. 103–104.

220. See chapter 7 in this volume.

221. Moriya, *Nihon Marukusu-shugi*, pp. 42–43.

222. Lukács, *Lenin*, pp. 50, 59 (Lukács's italics).

223. Marx and Engels, *Communist Manifesto*, pp. 338–339.

CHAPTER 3

1. Bauer, "National Character," p. 275.

2. See, for example, the controversies on Maoism in the 1950s and 1970s: Wittfogel, "Legend of 'Maoism'," pt. 1, pp. 72–86, pt. 2, pp. 35–42; Pfeffer, "Mao and Marx," pp. 421–460; and Schwartz, "Essence of Marxism Revisited," pp. 461–472.

3. To cite an extreme example of this position, one scholar remarked in the mid-1970s that "it was hardly surprising that socialism in Japan should have been deformed from birth" because "there were elements in the cultural background of the early socialists in Japan which would prevent them from understanding socialism correctly anyway" (Crump, "False Start for Socialism," 1:3).

4. Georges Sorel is, of course, the most striking example of this tendency in the history of French Marxism, but in many other instances the French Left drew near to the French Right. See the excellent studies of Sternhell, *La droite révolutionnaire*, and idem, *Ni droite, ni gauche*.

5. See, for example, Neumann's *Behemoth*; Gregor and Chang, *"Nazionalfascismo,"* pp. 21–37.

6. See Dahrendorf, *Society and Democracy in Germany*, (1979) especially chaps. 1, 3, and 4; cf. Taylor, *Course of German History*, chap. 1.

7. See chapter 8, in this volume, for a more extended discussion of these tendencies in German thought in comparison with Japan.

8. For an extended and insightful discussion of the rise of irrationalism in France, see Sternhell, *La droite révolutionnaire*, chap. 1.

9. Marx, *Capital*, 1:341n.

10. Engels, *Anti-Dühring*, p. 299.

11. Rankin, *Early Chinese Revolutionaries*, pp. 26, 29–30, 71; and Scalapino, "Prelude to Marxism," pp. 196–197. See also Schwartz, *Wealth and Power*, chap. 4.

12. See Notehelfer, *Kōtoku Shūsui*, pp. 49, 56ff.

13. The notion of "traditional" political thought is used with due caution here, for in neither Japan nor China was there a single, uniform body of thought so easily labeled as such. In China, Legalist, Confucian, and Daoist perspectives coexisted with Buddhism and folk religion to produce a philosophical setting in which the relative influence of different elements varied from time to time. Similarly, in Japan, Confucianism and Chinese classical philosophy flourished alongside Shintō and Buddhism. Japan, however, more than China, exhibited a certain unity of political thought reflecting the more rigid political and social hierarchical organization of Japanese society. I speak here of late Tokugawa and Meiji thought in Japan and of late Qing and early Republican Chinese thought. For excellent treatments of Japanese thought during this period, see Bellah, *Tokugawa Religion*; Pittau, *Political Thought in Early Meiji Japan*; and Ishida *Meiji shisō shi kenkyū*, pp. 3–149 passim. In a 1985 study, Carol Gluck takes issue with the implication of Japanese historiography on *tennō-sei* thought (the orthodoxy legitimating the Meiji state on the basis of the divinity and sanctity of the imperial institution), but her account of the formation of that tennō-sei thought in willy-nilly fashion does not gainsay the fact that official efforts were made to systematize this orthodoxy, to disseminate it, and to wield it both to legitimate the Meiji state's industrializing activities and to counter its potentially destabilizing social effects. See Gluck, *Japan's Modern Myths*. For accounts of official and scholarly efforts to articulate and disseminate this *kokutai* thought, see Nakase, "Meiji kenpō" pp. 59–71; and Ukai, "Kenpō ni okeru tennō no chi'i," pp. 504–511. For an especially insightful analysis of the controversies among leading theorists of the various strands of ancient Chinese philosophy, see Schwartz, *World of Thought*.

14. See Wray, "Japanese Images of the *Kokutai*"; and Takeda, "Tennō-sei shisō no keisei" 3:270, 297–303.

15. Takeda, "Tennō-sei shisō no keisei," p. 269.

16. Pittau, *Political Thought in Early Meiji Japan*, p. 132; Takeda, "Tennō-sei shisō no keisei," pp. 273–274.

17. An, "Meiji shoki ni okeru Doitsu," (1976) pp. 121, 140–142.

18. Ibid., pp. 126, 127, 139.

19. Pittau, *Political Thought in Early Meiji Japan*, p. 145; Takeda, "Tennō-sei shisō no keisei," pp. 274–275; cf. Ishida, "Ideorogii to shite no tennō-sei," p. 39; and Ishida, "Kokka yūkitai setsu" passim. This position of the people in the body politic might be compared to their position in medieval Europe in the concept of the "divine right of kings."

20. See Armstrong, *Light from the East*, p. 3.

21. Pittau, *Political Thought in Early Meiji Japan*, p. 157; cf. Mingelberg, "Lorenz von Stein," p. 274.

22. See Suzuki, *Kenpō seitai to Roesler*, p. 142.

23. Pittau, *Political Thought in Early Meiji Japan*, p. 157.

24. Takeda, "Tennō-sei shisō no keisei," p. 284; cf. Ienaga, "Nihon ni okeru kyōwashugi" passim.

25. Hoston, "State, Modernity, and the Fate of Liberalism," pp. 287–316.

26. Fukuzawa, "Teishitsu ron," 5:464.

27. Fukuzawa, "Sonnō ron" 6:246–247, 267; and idem, "Teishitsu ron," p. 464. Cf. the discussion in Craig, "Fukuzawa Yukichi," pp. 99–148.

28. *Shakai kagaku daijiten*, s.v. *kokutai*, p. 632. Katō Hiroyuki, as a Meiji Enlightenment thinker, introduced this distinction in his 1874 work *A New Theory of the State*.

29. In passing the law, the Diet affirmed this conflation of state and nation by rendering *kokutai* a legal term. See the discussion in Mitchell, *Thought Control in Prewar Japan*, pp. 66ff.

30. The importance of the military element is evident in the following passage from *Kokutai no Hongi*:

Harmony as of our nation is not a mechanical concert of independent individuals of the same level that has its starting point in [cold] knowledge, but a great harmony that holds itself together by having the parts within the whole through the actions that fit the parts.

And then, this harmony is clearly seen also in our nation's martial spirit. Our nation is one that holds *bushidō* in high regard, and there are shrines deifying warlike spirits. Our martial spirit does not have for its objective the killing of men, but the giving of life to men. This martial spirit is that which tries to give life to all things, and is not that which destroys. War, in this sense, is not by any means intended for the destruction, overpowering, or subjugation of others; and it should be a thing for the bringing about of great harmony, that is peace, doing the work of creation by following the way. (Japan, Department of Education, *Kokutai no Hongi*, pp. 93–95 [insertion by Hall])

Cf. Pittau, *Political Thought of Early Meiji Japan*, p. 2.)

31. Bellah, *Tokugawa Religion*, pp. 19–20.

32. Dening, "Confucian Philosophy in Japan," pp. 136–140, 116, 119–120.

33. Ibid., 136–140, 116, 119–120.

34. Earl, *Emperor and Nation in Japan*, p. 216.

35. Matsumoto, "Atarashii seiji ishiki no hōga," pp. 7, 9–12.

36. Earl, *Emperor and Nation*, p. 32.

37. Matsumoto, "Atarashii seiji ishiki no hōga," pp. 10, 13.

38. Earl, *Emperor and Nation*, p. 67; Bellah, *Tokugawa Religion*, pp. 99–100.

39. Bellah, *Tokugawa Religion*, pp. 98–99; Matsumoto, "Atarashii seiji ishiki no hōga," p. 16; and Hori, "Meiji shoki no kokka ron," p. 722.

40. Bellah, *Tokugawa Religion*, p. 103.

41. Earl, *Emperor and Nation*, p. 221.

42. Cf. Sansom, *History of Japan*, 3:236; Earl, *Emperor and Nation*, pp. 222–224; Matsumoto, "Atarashii seiji ishiki no hōga," pp. 45–47; and Maruyama, *Nihon seiji shisō shi kenkyū*, chap. 3.

43. See Minobe, "Kunshu no kokuhō-jō no chi'i," pp. 1–6; idem, *Kenpō satsuyō*; cf. Miyazawa, *Tennō-kikan setsu jiken*, passim; Miller, *Minobe Tatsukichi*, p. 65; Nakase, "Meiji kenpō moto," pp. 59–71 passim; Nakase, "Tennō-kikan setsu kakuritsu katei," pp. 155–195; Nakase, "Tennō-kikan setsu no genryū"; and Ukai, "Minobe hakushi no shisō to gakusetsu," passim.

44. Interview with Ishida Takeshi, Tokyo, August 11, 1979. See, especially, Uesugi, *Kenpō jutsugi*; idem, *Kokutai kenpō oyobi kensei*, pt. 1; and idem, "Kokutai ni kansuru isetsu," pp. 3–13. Cf. Kakei, *Dai Nihon teikoku kenpō no konpon gi*, for tennō-centered

state theory following Hozumi Yatsuka and Uesugi. In the latter work is a color diagram depicting the Japanese polity with the *tennō* at the center.

45. Interview with Ukai Nobushige, Tokyo, July 23, 1979.

46. Interview with Fujita Shōzō, Tokyo, August 3, 1979. Cf. Fujita, *Tennō-sei kokka no shihai genri*, 2d ed. (Tokyo: Mirai-sha, 1978), pp. 5–114.

47. Ukai, "Kenpō ni okeru tennō no chi'i," pp. 504–506. For a treatment stressing the authoritarian elements as inherent in Meiji political thought from the outset, see Hori, "Meiji shoki no kokka ron," pp. 711–744 passim.

48. Wray, "Japanese Images of the *Kokutai*," p. 64; interview with Fujita Shōzō, Tokyo, August 3, 1979; interview with Ishimura Osamu, Tokyo, August 21, 1979.

49. See the memoir of Minobe's son, Minobe Ryōkichi, "Sore de mo tennō wa kikan de aru," pp. 61–96; cf. Miyazawa, "Kikan setsu jiken to Minobe Tatsukichi sensei," pp. 42–44.

50. Storry, *Double Patriots*, pp. 162–166.

51. Wray, "Japanese Images of the *Kokutai*," p. 103; Ishida, *Meiji seiji shisō shi kenkyū*, pp. 7–8; and idem, "Ideorogii to shite no tennō-sei," p. 39.

52. See Plato, *Republic*, par. 412b–416d. The remarkable congruity between the notion of the *kokutai* drawing on Shinto mythology concerning the origin of Japan and the emperor with the Sun Goddess, on the one hand, and Socrates's remarks to Glaucon, on the other, are underscored by Bloom's depiction of what the notion "noble lie" denoted.

This famous lie consists of two very diverse parts. According to the first part, all the members of the city, and particularly the warriors, were born from the earth and educated and equipped prior to emerging from it. If the citizens believe the tale, they will have a blood tie to the country; their relationship to it will have the same immediacy as does their relationship to the family. . . . It identifies city and regime with country, which is the object of the most primitive political loyalty.

The second part of the lie gives divine sanction to the natural hierarchy of human talents and virtues while enabling the regime to combine the political advantages of this hierarchy with those of mobility. The problem is to establish a regime in which the hierarchy established by law reflects the natural one, or in which virtue is the only title to membership in the ruling class. (Bloom, "Interpretive Essay," in *Republic*, pp. 366–367.)

53. See Maruyama, *Thought and Behavior*, chap. 3 passim.

54. Ishida, *Meiji seiji shisō shi kenkyū*, pp. 3–149.

55. Hall, *Kokutai no Hongi*, pp. 87, 89, 90 (Hall's interpolation).

56. Yoshida, *Shiki Shichisoku*, quoted in ibid., p. 90.

57. See chapter 4 in this volume.

58. See Bellah, *Tokugawa Religion*, pp. 13, 14.

59. Cf. Wilson, *Radical Nationalist in Japan*, p. 22.

60. Hall, *Kokutai no Hongi*, p. 176. *Tenkōsha* [apostate from the Japanese Communist party] Sano Manabu would echo this condemnation of Western individualism in the early 1930s. Mao Zedong, too, as Benjamin Schwartz has noted, rejected such Western-style individualism as well. This congruence may be notable if it reflects a more widely shared critical disposition concerning possible differences between Western and Eastern civilizations as they were debated vigorously in the May Fourth period in China. (On Sano and Mao, see Hoston, "*Ikkoku Shakai-shugi*"; Schwartz, "Filial Piety and Revolution," p. 577. For some representative views in the controversy on Eastern and Western civilizations, see

Chen Duxiu, "Jidujiao yu Zhongguoren," 1:417–422; and Chen Ruoshui, "Liang Shuming yu 'Dong-Xi wenhua ji qi zhexue'," pp. 217–223).

61. Kobayashi Morito, himself a tenkōsha, claimed that tenkōsha felt acutely that the disparity between the unity of nation and state in Japan, on the one hand, and the abstraction of the idea of the state from nation in the West was a significant indicator that the JCP itself "had been born not from within Japan but from without. In such a case as Japan, in particular, where *minzoku* [nation] and *kokka* were one and the same," the JCP and its Comintern-inspired slogans to destroy the state and its monarchy were cold and truly alien (see Kobayashi, *Tenkōsha no shisō to seikatsu*, pp. 7–8). See also chapter 8, in this volume, for a more detailed consideration of *tenkō* and the role of pre-Marxian Japanese perspectives in contributing to its emergence.

62. Suzanne Ogden has suggested that "the cultural-political dichotomy" as drawn in the work of John K. Fairbank is "a false one, since *tien hsia*, as commonly used, could refer to either the world, or to the *kuo-chia*, or both. And the concept of 'Empire' could certainly be seen as having 'political' characteristics, although for China the Chinese Empire was considered coterminous with 'civilization.' Even Fairbank, who popularized the dichotomy," Ogden goes on to argue, "hedges in his more recent works by making a distinction between 'culture' and 'power structure' and then merging the two" (see Fairbank, "Early Treaty," p. 273; Ogden, "Chinese Concepts of the Nation, State, and Sovereignty," pp. 32–33.) This argument is weakened by Ogden's own acknowledgment that Qing documents indicate that, despite their awareness of precise territorial boundaries, Chinese officials "did not inquire into the nature of the *kuo-chia*, the political state, until they became aware of Western political thought in the late 19th century" (p. 33). This, of course, came as the result of contact with the West's interstate system. (Ogden speaks primarily of the guojia as a unit of international relations in her work.) Before that time, the tributary system of China's "international relations" denied the existence of political states outside China with legitimate and equal claims on sovereignty. This remains the most important consideration.

63. See the insightful discussion of this confrontation in Schwartz, *Wealth and Power*, especially pp. 12–13.

64. Hoston, "'Theology' of Liberation?" pp. 170–171.

65. See Fung, *History of Chinese Philosophy*, 2:684–685; and Wing-Tsit, *Source Book in Chinese Philosophy*, chap. 39.

66. See Teng and Fairbank, *China's Response to the West*, pp. 147–164, 195.

67. Kung-chuan, *Modern China*, pp. 128–129.

68. Ibid., pp. 128–129.

69. On this important chapter in Chinese history and the emerging schism between the republican and revolutionary movements, see Li, *Political History of China*, (1967) chap. 7 passim. See also Dutt, "First Week of Revolution," pp. 384–385; and Chang, "Constitutionalists," pp. 143–160.

70. Liang, "Guojia yunming lun," 8:94–103.

71. Lin, *Crisis of Chinese Consciousness*, pp. 27, 6n.

72. See, especially, Liang, "Lixian zhengti yu zhengzhi daode," 8:52–56; and idem, "Xinmin shuo," in *Zhuanji* 4. This inclination in Liang's thought was strikingly evident in the evolving titles of his periodical in Japan. What began in November 1898 as *Qingyi bao* (Public Opinion) became *Xinmin congbao* (New People Magazine) in 1902 and then *Guofeng bao* (The National Spirit) beginning in 1910. See Li, *Political History of China*, p. 188. See also Levenson, *Mind of Modern China*, 2d. rev. ed.; and Chang, *Liang Ch'i-ch'ao*.

73. See Chang, *Chinese Intellectuals in Crisis*; and the studies collected in Furth, *Limits of Change*.

74. In addition to the works cited previously, see the following on this spectrum of intellectual responses to the West: Levenson, *Confucian China and its Modern Fate*, vol. 1, chaps. 6–9; Xiao, *Zhongguo zhengzhi sixiang shi*, 6th ed., vol. 2, chaps. 21–23; Schwartz, *Wealth and Power*, chap. 12; and Wang, *Chinese Intellectuals and the West*.

75. See Sabine, *History of Political Theory*, pp. 277, 512–514.

76. Xiao, "Zhongguo zhi zhengyuan lun," pp. 535—538.

77. See Lin, "Evolution," pp. 185–191.

78. See Locke, *Second Treatise on Government*, par. 211–229.

79. See Huang, *Ming-i tai-fang lu* (1663), pp. 1b-6, trans. in *China's Response to the West*, p. 8.

80. Legge, *Four Books*, pt. 2, chap. 14 (Mencius's italics).

81. *Mencius*, book 5, pt. 1, chap. 5. Schwartz notes, "The term *t'ien ming* is never used in the *Analects* in the sense of "the Mandate of Heaven." To this extent, the notion of the mandate of Heaven and the legitimacy of revolution as the change of the mandate (*geming*) is definitively Mencius's contribution to the Confucian tradition. See Schwartz, *World of Thought*, p. 110.

82. "'Some men labour with their minds, and some with their strength. Those who labour with their minds govern others; those who labour with their strength are governed by others. Those who are governed by others support them; those who govern others are supported by them.' This is a principle universally recognized" (*Mencius* book 3, pt. 1, chap. 4.) Compare Plato's assertion, "[L]et's now dare to say this: philosophers must be established as the most precise guardians. . . . Then bear in mind that you'll probably have but a few. For the parts of the nature that we described as a necessary condition for them are rarely willing to grow together in the same place; rather its many parts grow forcibly separated from each other" (*Republic*, book 6, par. 488b–489c, 502e–503b.)

83. *Mencius*, book 2, pt. 1, chap. 23; cf. *Analects* (also in *Four Books*), book 13, chap. 9.

84. *Mencius*, book 5, pt. 1, chap. 5.

85. Ibid., book 4, pt. 1, chap. 9 and book 1, pt. 2, chap. 10.

86. Ibid., book 1, pt. 2, chap. 8.

87. Yu-lan, "Traditional Chinese Society," p. 22, 25.

88. Ibid., pp. 29, 25.

89. Ibid., p. 30.

90. See Xiao, "Zhongguo zhi zhengyuan lun," p. 546. Note that "Xiaoyao you" is the title of the first chapter of *Zhuangzi*, the writings of the Daoist Zhuangei.

91. Hsiao, "Anarchism in Chinese Political Thought," p. 254.

92. Ibid., p. 252.

93. Quoted in ibid., p. 155. Cf. Hsiao, *History of Chinese Political Thought*, pp. 623–630.

94. Xiao, "Zhongguo zhi zhengyuan lun," pp. 547–548.

95. Hsiao, *History of Chinese Political Thought*, chap. 6 passim.

96. Xiao, "Zhongguo zhi zhengyuan lun," pp. 538–542; and Wakeman, *History and Will*, (1975), p. 49.

97. Schwartz, *World of Thought*, p. 295.

98. Hsün Tzu, "Man's Nature is Evil," p. 157.

99. Hobbes, "Leviathan," p. 143.

100. Schwartz, *World of Thought*, p. 295.

101. Lau, "Theories of Human Nature," pp. 551–552.

102. Ibid., pp. 555–557, 563.

103. Feizi, "Five Vermin," p. 102.

104. Ibid., pp. 102–103.

105. Wakeman, *History and Will*, p. 52.

106. Ogden, "Chinese Concepts of Nation, State and Sovereignty," p. 23.

107. Ibid., pp. 23–24.

108. Schrecker, *Imperialism and Chinese Nationalism*, pp. 45–47, 53–54, 251.

109. Schwartz, "Chinese Perception of World," p. 285.

110. See Li, *Introduction of Socialism into China*, passim.

111. Hoston, *"Ikkoku Shakai-shugi,"* p. 171.

112. As the example of Japanese tenkōsha would later demonstrate, adherence to Marxism itself—particularly under the conditions of Soviet domination of the Communist movement through the Comintern—would subsequently prove itself to be susceptible to the same charge. See ibid., p. 172.

113. On the basic similarity of the initial Chinese, Japanese, and Korean responses to the Western threat in this respect, see Watanuki, "State Formation in East Asia," p. 430.

114. On the factors contributing to this ultranationalism, see ibid., pp. 430–431; Hirai, "Ancestor Worship," pp. 41–42; Kosaka, *Japanese Thought in the Meiji Era*, 9:132, 82; and Brown, *Nationalism in Japan*, chap. 5 passim, especially pp. 91–93, 101. The best representation of the extremist statist and mythological elements in Japanese political thought is well articulated in the *Kokutai no Hongi*, quoted in the discussion of the *kokutai* previously. Horie Yasuzō has traced the origins of this process back beyond the Meiji into Confucian state theory in Tokugawa Japan. See his "Confucian Concept of State," pp. 26–38.

115. On the importance of the theory of the state to Chinese intellectuals, particularly in the 1920s and 1930s, see Chang, *Marxian Theory of the State*, p. viii. On the process of adaptation, see Wright, *Last Stand of Chinese Conservatism*, chap. 12; Schwartz, *Wealth and Power*, pp. 42–67, chap. 7; Huang, *Modern Chinese Liberalism*, chap. 4, p. 99; Xiao, *Zhongguo zhengzhi sixiang shi*, vol. 2, chap. 22, pp. 803–833, and 839–870; Levenson, *Confucian China and Its Modern Fate*, vol. 1, chap. 7; and Wang, *Chinese Intellectuals and the West*, chaps. 8, 10 passim. The idea of the party-state is discussed in chapter 7, this volume.

116. Although it might be assumed that the theory of imperialism was most widely disseminated and adopted in the Far East in its Leninist form in the wake of the Russian revolution, in fact, in Japan the works of Luxemburg, Hilferding, and Bukharin were more widely accepted as providing the theoretical account of "economic underpinning of imperialism" than was Lenin's *Imperialism: The Highest Stage of Capitalism* (1916). Lenin's work was translated into Japanese from the French in 1923 by Aono Suekichi and was widely read but was regarded by many Japanese Marxist theorists (e.g., Takahashi Kamekichi and Inomata Tsunao) as theoretically inadequate and inapplicable to Japanese capitalism, considered by many already to be in decline. See Inomata, *Teikoku-shugi kenkyū*, p. 20; Takahashi, "Nihon shihon-shugi," p. 2; Moriya, *Nihon Marukusu-shugi riron*, pp. 44–45; and chapter 5, this volume. Similarly, the implication that the growing importance of Marxism-Leninism in China was, in large part, attributable to "receptiveness to the anti-imperialist appeals of Lenin and Trotsky" is present in many works on the Chinese Communist movement as well as in Mao Zedong's writings. (See Meisner, *Li Tachao*, (1977), p. 97; Schwartz, *Rise of Mao*, pp. 20–21; and Mao, "People's Democratic Dictatorship," p. 375, 377–378; and Rong, "Xinhai geming qian," pp. 11–12.) There is little evidence, however, that Chinese Marxists were acquainted with and receptive to

Lenin's writings on imperialism; on the contrary, there is much to indicate that the most important writings of Lenin with which they were familiar were *State and Revolution* and works on national self-determination translated into Chinese in 1920 and 1921. Through that time and, perhaps, for as much as a decade afterward, most of what Chinese intellectuals such as Li Dazhao knew of imperialism was the term used in the "non-Leninist sense [that] had been introduced into China through Japanese as early as 1895" (See Chow, *May Fourth Movement*, pp. 354, 355n.) The Japanese works included Ukita Kazuomi's *Teikoku-shugi* (Imperialism), "translated into Chinese by the Ch'u-yang hsueh-sheng pien-chi-so in 1895, and Kōtoku Denjirō's [Shūsui] . . . *Imperialism, the Spectre of the Twentieth Century* (Nijū seiki no kaibutsu teikoku-shugi) (1901) was translated by Chao Pi-chen in 1902" (Chow, *May Fourth Movement*, p. 354n). I have found no evidence of a direct influence exercised by the works of Hilferding, Luxemburg, and Bukharin on the subject in China.

117. Tilly, "Theories of Political Transformation," p. 620.

118. Chang, "Neo-Confucian Moral Thought," p. 270; the reference to "transformative thought" comes from Metzger, *Escape from Predicament*. The same ideas, here described as adopted by Chinese intellectuals from the 1890s, were also adopted in Japan. See, for example, Bailey, "Popular Rights Movement of the 1880s," pp. 49–63; and Wilson, "Kita Ikki's Theory of Revolution," p. 90.

119. On Engels as a revisionist, see Avineri, *Social and Political Thought of Karl Marx*, chap. 6; Hodges, "Engels' Contribution to Marxism," pp. 297ff; Labedz, *Revisionism*, pp. 179–187, 344–346, and 349n; Lichtheim, *Marxism*, pp. 58–61, 234–258; Marcuse, *Soviet Marxism*, pp. 138, 142–145; Tucker, *Philosophy and Myth in Karl Marx*, 2d ed., p. 184; and Sartre, *Critique de la raison dialectique*, pp. 121–135. A defense of Engels's contribution is presented in Kolakowski, *Main Currents of Marxism*, 1:399–408. See also Luxemburg's critique of Lenin's reinterpretation of Marxism, in *Russian Revolution*. In contrast, Hodges sees Lenin's interpretation of "the contribution of dialectics" not as "the formulation of the most general interconnections in nature, society, and human thought" but in "the use of these formulas as guides towards further specialized investigations within these areas." Lenin, thus, returns "to the original context of Marx's thought" (p. 308).

120. Moriya, "Nihon ni okeru Marukusu-shugi no seiritsu," pp. 115–139.

121. Arahata Kanson [pseud. of Arahata Katsuzō], *Nihon shakai-shugi undō shi*, pp. 13–17. The *Kokumin no tomo* also published translations of Edward Carpenter, *Civilization: Its Cause and Its Cure* (1889) and a work rendered in Japanese, *Genji no shakai-shugi* (Present-day socialism). *The Kokumin no tomo*, subsequently, became the *Kokumin shinbun* (The People's Paper) and serialized Victor Hugo's *Les Misérables* (trans. Hara Hōitsuan) (Arahata, *Nihon shakai undō shi*, p. 16). Cf. Totten, *Social Democratic Movement in Prewar Japan*, p. 24.

122. Matsuzawa, *Nihon shakai-shugi no shisō*, p. 26.

123. The schism within the Meiji socialist movement between Christian socialists and the "materialist faction" (*yuibutsu-ha*), or Marxists, did not appear until circa 1906 when opposition to the Russo-Japanese war could no longer maintain the unity of this group, which espoused heterogeneous socialist ideas, from reformist to revolutionary, around a single goal. See Takeuchi, "Nihon no Marukusu-shugi," p. 12; and Arahata Katsuzō [Arahata Kanson], "Heimin-sha jidai."

124. This coincided with the emergence and maturation of progressive liberalism in England. See Stefan Collini, *Liberalism and Sociology*.

125. See chapter 5 this volume.

126. Formerly, when knowledge of Western European socialism was first introduced in Japan during the "enlightenment period," it was regarded as a threat, for it posed the spectre

of a state system that repudiated the free market economy. See, for example, Katō Hiroyuki's *Shinsei taigi* (The great duty of true government) and Nishi Amane's *Hyakugaku renkan* (The chain of a hundred schools). Matsuzawa, *Nihon shakai-shugi no shisō*, p. 35. On the theme of antistatism among Christian Socialists in Japan, see Bamba and Howe, *Pacifism in Japan; Christian and Socialist Tradition*; quotations here are taken from H. D. Harootunian's review of this book in *American Historical Review* 85, no. 3 (June 1980): 697.

127. Matsuzawa, *Nihon shakai-shugi no shisō*, p. 26; and Onabe, *Nijū seiki*, 4:465.

128. *Nihon shakai undō jinmei jiten* (Biographical dictionary of Japan's social movement) (Tokyo: Aoki Shoten, 1979), s.v. Abe Isoo. The link between Unitarianism and early Meiji Christian socialism was significant, but the reasons for it are unclear. Abe Isoo, Katayama Sen, and Murai Tomoyoshi, leaders of the Shakai-Shugi Kenkyūkai, all studied at universities in the United States that were affiliated with Congregationalism or Unitarianism. Both Abe and Murai were baptized into Christianity circa 1880 under educator Niijima Jō, a Japanese who studied at Amherst College, converted to Christianity, and founded Dōshisha University. Abe went to the United States in 1891 to study the value of the Bible as a historical resource and social problems. At Hartford Theological Seminary, where he studied for three years, he read Edward Bellamy's *Looking Backward* and was influenced to believe that socialism provided the solution to poverty. After studying at Berlin University and observing the socialist movement in Glasgow, Abe returned to Japan in 1895 as a Christian socialist. He subsequently became the head of the Shakai-shugi Kenkyūkai when, in 1900, its name was changed to the Shakai-shugi Kyōkai to mark its transformation to an activist group. Abe then cofounded, along with Katayama and Kōtoku, Japan's first socialist party in 1901, joined other Christian socialists to publish the *Shin kigen* (New Era) after the post-Russo-Japanese War split in the movement and in 1924 helped to found the Japan Fabian Society (*Nihon shakai undō jinmei jiten*, s.v. Abe Isoo). Similarly, Katayama studied at the Congregationalist Grinnell College and at Andover (also Congregationalist) and Yale seminaries before returning to Japan in 1895. Converting to Christianity while in the United States, Katayama was influenced by Richard Ely's work and a biography of Ferdinand Lassalle (ibid., s.v. Katayama Sen). Finally, Murai also studied at Andover Theological Seminary and, on returning to Japan, became a preacher at the socially oriented Unitarian Hongō Church (ibid., s.v. Murai Tomoyoshi). Except for Kōtoku, all members of the Shakai-shugi Kenkyūkai appear to have been Unitarians who became socialists unambiguously only after the Peace Police Law was implemented in 1900 ("Nihon no Marukusu-shugi," pp. 8–9). The link between Unitarianism and Japanese Christian socialism may be attributable to educational experiences in the United States where Unitarians had split from the Congregational church in the 1830s in Massachusetts. "Unitarian reformers focussed on social evils—that is the way people treat each other— rather than on the sins of personal behavior in relation to drink, dress, sexual relations and Sabbath activities. Having inherited the Puritan sense of the corporate community, Unitarians believed that governments must work actively to heal public ills. . . . [They] moved away from wealth and toward human rights; toward radical positions in social questions" Kelley, *Cultural Pattern in American Politics*, p. 204. See also Howe, *Unitarian Conscience*. A direct link to the church in Tokyo may be evident in the fact that in 1887 the Unitarian church dispatched its first missionary, A. M. Knapp, to Japan, and with the evangelical and Universalist churches, the Unitarian church became the central moving force of Japan's "free Christian" movement. In 1887, Knapp organized the Unitarian church in Japan. The new church "repudiated evangelism . . . [, and] its teachings gradually were absorbed into the socialist political movement and its church activities ceased" (*Kirisuto-*

kyō dai jiten [Encyclopedia of Christianity], rev. and enl. ed. [N.p.: Kyōbun-kan, n.d.], s.v. "Uniterian"; and Murakami, *Nihon shūkyō jiten*, p. 355; and Ukai Nobushige, personal letter, April 12, 1980. Cf. the mention of a Unitarian church in Shiba, Tokyo, as a meeting place for the Shakai-shugi Kenkyūkai and participation in that group by "a zealous advocate of the single tax of Henry George" Reverend Charles E. Garat, in Kublin, "Japanese Socialists and the Russo-Japanese War," p. 325.

129. The title of Ely's work was rendered in Japanese *Shakai-shugi to shakai kairyō* (Socialism and social reform). Other works included: *Shakai-shugi kōryō* (The socialist program), by Ishigaya Fūzō; *Saisei kigen* (Words of warning on social reform) by Jō Tsunetarō; *Shakaitō sabun* (Trivia on socialist parties) by Ishigaya Fūzō; *Kokka-shakai sei* (State socialism), by Dawson, trans. Mitsuyoshi Motojirō; *Kokka-shakai ron* (State social-ism), by Shiba Teikichi; and *Sai ankoku no Tōkyō* (Darkest Tokyo), by Matsubara Iwagorō (Arahata, *Nihon shakai-shugi undō shi*, p. 20).

130. Yamakawa and Sakisaka, *Yamakawa Hitoshi jiden*, p. 380.

131. Arahata, *Kanson jiden*, 1:99, 100.

132. *Nihon shakai undō jinmei jiten*, s.v. Kōtoku Shūsui; and Arahata, *Kanson jiden*, 1:111–113.

133. The two men were elected vice-presidents at the congress.

134. Arahata, *Kanson jiden*, pp. 111–113, 132–135. A financial report on the Second International published in *Chokugen* in early-1905 revealed that from 1900 to 1905, the contribution allotted to Japan was the smallest, one hundred francs, of which only seventy-five francs had actually been paid. The *Shakai-shugi hyōron* (Socialist review), published in Paris, was also an important vehicle of exposure to European Marxism at this time. See Arahata, *Nihon shakai-shugi undō shi*, pp. 107, 108.

135. Takeuchi, "Nihon no Marukusu-shugi," p. 13. According to another source, the translation of the *Manifesto* was a joint effort by Kōtoku and Sakai. Some minor disparities in translation that might have encouraged misinterpretation included the translation of *bourgeois* as *shinshi* (gentleman), *bourgeoisie* as *shinshi-batsu* (gentlemen's clique), and "proletariat" as *heimin* (commoner). Matsuzawa, *Nihon shakai-shugi no shisō*, p. 41.

136. *Nihon shakai undō jinmei jiten*, s.v. Sakai Toshihiko.

137. Arahata, *Nihon shakai-shugi undō shi*, p. 106. At that point, Abe Isoo was already working on a translation of *Capital*.

138. Takeuchi, "Nihon no Marukusu-shugi," p. 11; and Matsuzawa, *Nihon shakai-shugi no shisō*, p. 40. A third pioneering work, often cited along with these, was Sakai and Morichika, *Shakai-shugi kōryō* (The socialist program) (1907). All three works mistrans-lated the term *value* (*kachi*) as *kakaku*, which can be translated either as "value/worth" or "price," thus obscuring the meaning of the term "surplus value" in Marx's work. See Moriya, *Nihon Marukusu-shugi riron*, p. 13n.

139. Moriya, *Nihon Marukusu-shugi riron*, p. 12.

140. It has been argued that "a curious coalition of social-democrats and Leninists alike tried to de-emphasize the importance of Marx's early writings" (Avineri, *Marx's Socialism*, p. xii). See the essay by Fetscher, "Young and Old Marx," pp. 36–58 in the same volume. Cf. Tarschys, *Beyond the State*, pp. 90–91.

141. Takeuchi, "Nihon no Marukusu-shugi," pp. 11–12; and Matsuzawa, *Nihon shakai-shugi no shisō*, p. 40.

142. Takeuchi, "Nihon no Marukusu-shugi," p. 12. Cf. Matsuzawa, *Nihon shakai-shugi no shisō*, pp. 35, 36. The identification of Marxism with historical materialism is underscored by the conventional treatment of "the thought of the Japanese Communist Party as materialism" although Lenin's role in formulating this body of thought as adopted in

Japan is often overemphasized. See Kuno and Tsurumi, *Gendai Nihon no shisō* (1978), p. 33 and chap. 2 passim.

143. This was one of three translations begun in 1919, the others by Matsu(u)ra Kaname and Ikuta Chōkō (1881–1936). After five years, Takabatake finished the full three volumes. Moriya, *Nihon Marukusu-shugi riron*, p. 17; and idem, "Nihon ni okeru Marukusu-shugi no seiritsu," p. 125.

144. Inumaru, "Nihon Marukusu-shugi no genryū," 2:8. See also Arahata, *Kanson jiden*, 1:384; Yamakawa, *Jiden*, p. 369; Moriya, *Nihon Marukusu-shugi riron*, p. 11; and Koyama Hirotake, *Nihon Marukusu-shugi shi*, p. 20. "Russia no kakumei" was an excerpt from the introduction in the German text of Lenin's speech in Switzerland in March 1917 entitled "Roshia kakumei ni okeru Roshia shakai minshu rōdōtō no ninmu ni tsuite" (On the responsibilities of the Russian Social-Democratic Labor Party in the Russian Revolution). Moriya, *Nihon Marukusu-shugi*, p. 14.

145. Durkee, "Communist International and Japan," p. 27.

146. Moriya, *Nihon Marukusu-shugi riron*, p. 17. Lenin's work was not introduced as a separate volume until the September 1921 publication of Yamakawa Hitoshi and his wife Yamakawa Kikue's translation of *The Immediate Tasks of the Soviet Government* (April 1918) (Moriya, *Nihon Marukusu-shugi riron*, p. 15).

147. Bukharin was en route from exile in America to Russia. Moriya, *Nihon Marukusu-shugi riron*, pp. 52, 53. During Bukharin's leadership of the Comintern, Japanese Marxists often deferred readily to Bukharin's views as those of one who understood Japan better than his colleagues did. Thus, Bukharin is credited with the authorship of the original 1922 Draft Program of the Japanese Communist party and with the inspiration for the Comintern's 1927 Theses on Japan. See the following: Kondō Eizō, *Komuminterun no misshi*, p. 269; Uchida (and Wakano), *Nihon shihon-shugi ronsō*, pp. 47–48; interviews with Nakamura Takafusa, Tokyo, July 11, 1979 and July 17, 1979; Kazama, *Nihon Kyōsantō no rekishi* 1:1–5; Tateyama, *Nihon Kyōsantō kenkyo hishi*, pp. 220–222; Koyama, *Nihon Marukusu-shugi shi*, pp. 47–48. Cf. Durkee, "Communist International and Japan," pp. 41–46; and Swearingen, "Japanese Communist Party and the Comintern," pp. 50–51.

148. Moriya, *Nihon Marukusu-shugi riron*, p. 43; and interview with Arahata Kanson, Tokyo, August 17, 1979. The academic Marxist Ōuchi Hyōe, who belonged to the Rōnō-ha (Worker-Farmer faction, which repudiated Comintern authority and seceded from the Japanese Communist party in December 1927), complained in 1936 that in Japan "Marxism was translated Bukharinistically and adopted '*narodnik*-ly' particularly by the Kōza-ha (Ōuchi, "Kaihan no tame ni" [Introduction to the revised edition], in Inomata Tsunao, *Nōson mondai nyūmon* [Introduction to the agrarian problem] [Tokyo: Kōdo-sha, 1937]). To the extent that the Kōza-ha elaborated the interpretation of the Bukharinist 1927 Theses on Japan, this interpretation is justified. In fact, however, Bukharin's influence was most evident in Rōnō-ha work, especially in the application of his notion of state monopoly capitalism to Japan. See chapter 6 in this volume (interview with Nakamura Takafusa, Tokyo, July 17, 1979; interview with Taniuchi Yuzuru, Tokyo University Law School, Tokyo, August 3, 1979). Basic texts other than those described later include Stalin's *Foundations of Leninism, History of the Communist Party of the Soviet Union*, Soviet economist Yevgeny Varga's writings, and articles in the magazine *International* (1927–1933). Matsuzawa, *Nihon shihon-shugi no shisō*, p. 195.

149. There has been intense debate on the continuities and discontinuities in Marx's thought in light of the revelation of these works. See the volume edited by Avineri, *Marx's Socialism*, especially Avineri's introduction, p. ix. Although the year 1847 and the publication of *The Poverty of Philosophy* has been designated by some as the point of departure for

the analysis of mature Marxism (e.g., Poulantzas, *Political Power and Social Classes*) the French structuralist Marxist Louis Althusser has presented a more complex fourfold classification of Marx's writings: "1840–44: The Early Works; 1845: The Works of the Break; 1845–1857: The Transitional Works; 1857–1893: Mature Works" (Althusser, *For Marx*). See Bridges, "Nicos Poulantzas," p. 162n. I have labeled the *Grundrisse*, of which volume 1 of *Capital* is "an enlarged and revised version," transitional because it reflects the continuity in Marx's thought. See Fetscher, "Young and Old Marx," p. 48; and Hobsbawm's introduction to the English translation of this work by Marx, *Pre-Capitalist Economic Formations*, pp. 9–38.

150. Engels's *Origin of the Family* was translated into Japanese in 1920. Moriya, "Nihon ni okeru Marukusu-shugi no seiritsu," p. 125, and Moriya, *Nihon Marukusu-shugi*, p. 17. Pannekoek, like Lenin and Bukharin, emphasized "revolution as an act of smashing the state," but it is not clear whether Japanese Marxists were well exposed to this theme in his work. See Robert V. Daniels, "'Withering Away of the State'," p. 117.

151. Beginning in 1928, *Sutārin-Bukhārin chosakushū* and the Kozō-sha edition of *Marukusu-Engerusu zenshū* (Complete works of Marx and Engels) were published, just one year after Hakuyō-sha's publication of the ten-volume *Reinin chosakushū* (Collected works of Lenin). Moriya, *Nihon Marukusu-shugi riron*, pp. 42–43.

152. Moriya, "Nihon ni okeru Marukusu-shugi no seiritsu," pp. 127, 119. This Japanese interest in neo-Kantian philosophy may be compared to the revival of Kantian idealism in late-industrializing 1870s Germany. The revival had political implications because it stirred inquiry into issues left unresolved by the creation of the Bismarckian state, especially "the question [of] whether Germany was to evolve along Western lines or retain its famous 'uniqueness'" (Lichtheim, *Marxism*, p. 291). In respect to this issue, the revival was analogous to its counterpart in Japan and the endeavor to formulate a Japanist philosophy.

153. The foreword to *The ABC of Communism* declares, "Obviously, the older Marxist literature, such as *The Erfurt Programme* [1891] is largely inapplicable to present needs." (Bukharin and Preobrazhensky, *The ABC of Communism*, p. 57. The theoretical portion of this book is attributed to Bukharin [ibid., p. 28]).

154. See the excellent discussion on this point in Tarschys, *Beyond the State*, p. 90 and chap. 3.

155. See the analysis of the debate on Japanese capitalism in chapter 6 this volume.

156. See, for example, Sano, *Gokuchū-ki*, pp. 93–95; and Sano, *Minzoku to kaikyū*, pp. 15–17. These points will be treated in more detail in chapter 8 this volume.

157. "Thus, the concept of 'equality' . . . was a concept common to both the Unitarian faction—which held a kind of *jinmin-shugi* [Russian-style populism] and the left(-wing) *minken ron* [democracy, popular rights], represented by Nakae Chōmin citing the school of J. J. Rousseau." Takeuchi, "Nihon no Marukusu-shugi," pp. 10–11; and Matsuzawa, *Nihon shakai-shugi no shisō*, pp. 42–43.

158. Matsuzawa, *Nihon Shakai-shugi no shisō*, pp. 29–32. At the turn of the twentieth century, Katayama Sen deplored "the waning of patriotism in Japan at that time," arguing that "'patriotism is the highest current of thought in the people as a motivation of activity, even the livelihood and food of the state (*kokka*) and has the greatest impact on all prosperity or decay of health, rise and decline of civilization, and particularly in advancing moral concepts and raising character'" ("Eikoku konnichi no shakai" [English society today] (1897), in *Katayama Sen chosakushū* 1:221, quoted in Matsuzawa, *Nihon shakai-shugi no shisō*, p. 27.

159. Bernstein, "Early Japanese Socialists," p. 329.

160. Crowley, "Japan's Military Foreign Policies," p. 91; cf. Crowley, *Japan's Quest for Autonomy*; and Watanuki, "State Formation and Nation-Building," p. 432.

161. See, for example, Nakamura Takafusa, "Nihon shihon-shugi ronsō' ni tsuite," pp. 185–197; and my interview with Nakamura Takafusa, Tokyo, July 11, 1979.

162. Said, *Orientalism* (1979) pp. 2–3. It might be argued that this tendency has persisted to the present. On Soviet thought, for example, see Vitkin, *Vostok*. On the political difficulties of Soviet orientalists, see Pak, *Sovietskoë vostokovedenie*, especially pp. 5–7; and Massell, *Surrogate Proletariat*, p. xxxv.

163. Ishida Takeshi has noted immediate and delayed confrontations with this issue as a generational difference among Japanese Marxists that may help to explain the pattern of tenkō: "Kawakami Hajime ni okeru itan e no michi" pp. 1–18. In China, a fierce debate on the subject was launched by the publication of conservative Liang Souming's *Dongxi wenhua ji qi zhexue*, first published in 1921. Li Dazhao contributed to the subject earlier with an article entitled "Dongxi wenming genben zhi yidian." See the brief bibliography in the Chinese debate in Chun-jo Liu, *Controversies in Modern Chinese Intellectual History*, pp. 138–143.

164. An excellent example is provided in Hirano Yoshitarō, *Dai Ajia-shugi no rekishi-teki kiso*.

165. See his essay, "Shina kakumei gaishi" (Unofficial history of the Chinese revolution) (1915), in *Kita Ikki chosakushū*, vol. 2. Kita was a member of Sun Yat-sen's Tongmenghui, was close to Song Jiaoren, and was in China from immediately after the 1911 revolution until 1913 and again from 1916 to 1919. Tanaka Sōgorō, *Kita Ikki*, chaps. 3 and 4; and Wilson, *Radical Nationalist in Japan*, pp. 43–64.

166. Beckmann and Genji, *Japanese Communist Party*, pp. 114, 120, 144, 151.

167. See the excellent discussion of Chinese and Japanese work on the issue in He, *Zhongguo shehui shi wenti lunzhan*, 3:1–78 passim, and the discussion in chapters 5 and 6 in this volume.

168. Carrère d'Encausse and Schram, *Marxism and Asia*, p. 6. For an excellent treatment of the dilemma for the Moslem world, see Rodinson, *Islam and Capitalism*, pp. 1–3.

169. As it was argued in Zhu Zhixin [Xianjie], "Lun shehui geming dang yu zhengzhi geming bingxing," pp. 43–66.

170. Rong, "Xinhai geming qian," p. 10.

171. Li, *Introduction of Socialism*, p. 108. More conservative estimates place about eight thousand Chinese students in Japan between 1905 and 1907. Huang, *Liang Ch'i-ch'ao*, p. 37, fig. 1, and p. 41.

172. Huang, *Liang Ch'i-ch'ao*, pp. 36, 41. The publication of Chinese translations of Japanese books peaked in the early part of the first decade of the twentieth century at about 200 and, again, at about 120 circa 1930 (Huang, *Liang Ch'i-ch'ao*, p. 38).

173. Li, *Introduction to Socialism*, pp. 108, 109, 69; cf. Rong, "Xinhai geming qian," pp. 11–12.

174. Scalapino and Schiffrin, "Early Socialist Currents," pp. 321–322; Jansen, *Japanese and Sun Yat-sen*; Chang, *Intellectual Transition in China*, p. 132; and Schiffrin, *Origins of the Chinese Revolution*, pp. 255–299.

175. Li, *Introduction of Socialism*, p. 4; Bernal, *Chinese Socialism to 1907*, p. 59. See also the example of Chen, who asserted that socialism in Europe and Russia and, finally, in China was a universal response to the evils of capitalism and its fruition in imperialism. See Ch'en's semiautobiographical *Communist Movement in China* (1966) p. 63.

176. *Datong shu*, pp. 62 and 356, cited by Rong, "Xinhai geming qian," pp. 7, 5; cf. Xiao, *Zhongguo zhengzhi sixiang shi*, 2:691–699; Bernal, *Chinese Socialism to 1907*, chap. 1 passim; Li, *Introduction of Socialism*, p. 4; and Hsiao "In and Out of Utopia," pt. 2, p. 109.

177. Chang, *Intellectual Transition in China*, pp. 262–268; Rong, "Xinhai geming qian," pp. 8–9.

178. Li, *Introduction of Socialism*, pp. 8, 15–16.

179. Ding, *Liang Rengong* 1:94, and Sanetō, *Chūgokujin Nihon ryūgakushi*, p. 343, both cited in Li, *Introduction of Socialism*, p. 8.

180. Li, *Introduction of Socialism*, pp. 8, 46.

181. Liang cited Benjamin Kidd in this passage ("Biming Zhongguo zhi xinmin" [Pen name China's New Citizen] and "Jinhualun geming zhe Jide zhi xueshuo" [The theory of the evolutionary socialist Kidd], in *Xinmin congbao*, no. 18, cited in Rong, "Xinhai geming qian," p. 6.

182. Liang Qichao, "Zhongguo she shehui zhuyi" [Chinese socialism], *Xinmin congbao*, no. 46–48 (February 14, 1904), quoted by Li, *Introduction of Socialism*, p. 10.

183. Ibid.

184. Chang, *Intellectual Transition in China*, pp. 266–268; Scalapino and Schiffrin, "Early Socialist Currents," pp. 335–336.

185. Li, *Introduction of Socialism*, p. 12. Liang was writing an article entitled "Waizi shuru wenti" [The issue of the import of foreign capital], *Xinmin congbao*, no. 52 (September 10, 1904), no. 53 (September 24, 1904), no. 54 (October 9, 1904), and no. 56 (November 7, 1904); and Scalapino and Schiffrin, "Early Socialist Currents," p. 336.

186. Zhang, *Zhongguo jindai chuban shiliao*, 1:174; this date is given as 1902 in Chang, *Intellectual Transition in China*, p. 262.

187. Zhang, *Zhongguo jindai chuban shiliao*, 1:174; Rong, "Xinhai geming qian," pp. 5–6; Li, *Introduction of Socialism*, p. 13; and Bernal, *Chinese Socialism to 1907*, pp. 94–96.

188. Zhang, *Zhongguo jindai chuban shiliao*, 1:174; *Nihon shakai undō jinmei jiten*, s.v. Kōtoku Shūsui and Shimada Saburō; cf. Li, *Introduction of Socialism*, pp. 14–15.

189. Zhang, *Zhongguo xiandai chuban shiliao*, 1:390–391, cited in Li, *Introduction of Socialism*, p. 118n.

190. Zhu Zhixin, under the pen name Zheshen, *Minbao*, no. 2 (November 26, 1905) and no. 3 (April 5, 1906), cited in Rong, "Xinhai geming qian," pp. 6, 6n; and Li, *Introduction of Socialism*, pp. 24, 25. Zhu also made this point, describing Marx's socialism as "scientific" in his article entitled "Lun shehui geming dang yu zhengzhi geming bingxing" (Why social revolution should be carried out along with political revolution), which was published under the pen name Xianjie in no. 5 of the *Minbao* (Rong, "Xinhai geming qian," p. 6). Zhu's knowledge of socialism seems to have come from Japanese sources (Li, *Introduction of Socialism*, p. 26).

191. Rong, "Xinhai geming qian," pp. 6–7.

192. A speech by Zhang Taiyan on "Kokka-ron" (Theory of the state) given at one JSP organized meeting was published in the *Minbao*, no. 17 (October 1907) (ibid., p. 7).

193. These articles appeared in the *Minbao*, no. 2 (November 26, 1905) and no. 4 (May 1, 1906), respectively. Li, *Introduction of Socialism*, pp. 63–64; and Rong, "Xinhai geming qian," p. 7.

194. Sun, "Minbao shounian jinian yanshuo" (Speech commemorating the anniversary of the *Minbao*), cited by Rong, "Xinhai geming qian," p. 10.

195. Li, *Introduction of Socialism*, pp. 66–68; Rong, "Xinhai geming qian," pp. 9–10; and Scalapino and Schiffrin, "Early Socialist Currents," pp. 325–329.

196. *Minbao*, no. 4 (May 1, 1906). See Li, *Introduction of Socialism*, pp. 56–59; Scalapino and Schiffrin, "Early Socialist Currents," pp. 326–329; Schiffrin, "Sun Yat-sen's Early Land Policy," pp. 549–564. See Hu [Min Yi], "Gao feinan minsheng-zhuyizhe," pp. 45–155; and Zhu, "Tudi guoyou yu caizheng," pt. 1, pp. 67–99 and pt. 2, pp. 33–71.

197. Bernal, *Chinese Socialism to 1907*, p. 191, chap. 7 passim.

198. Li, *Introduction of Socialism*, p. 10.

199. Qu "confessed that he lacked a thorough grounding in Marx's writings." "Duoyu de hua," p. 18, cited in ibid., p. 109.

200. Mao Tse-tung, "Reform Our Study," in *Selected Works of Mao Tse-tung*, 3:19, 24.

201. Li, *Introduction of Socialism*, pp. 110, 124n.

202. Zhang, *Zhongguo jindai chuban shiliao*, 2:433.

203. Zhang, *Zhongguo xiandai chuban shiliao*, 1:68, 69. The Renmin Chuban-she was a CCP organ established September 1, 1921. In 1923, it merged with the Xin Qingnian-she and, again, later merged with the Shanghai Shudian and established the Pingmin Shushe in Canton. The Xin Qingnian-she had separated from the Qunyi Shushe in September, establishing itself in Shanghai's French concession. Closed down by the French concession in 1921, it moved to Canton (ibid., 1:74n, 75n).

204. Gao and Zhang, "Wusi yundong qijian Li Dazhao," pp. 6–7. Li's essay was published in *Xin qingnian* 6, no. 5 (May 1919): 521–537 and 6, no. 6 (November 1919): 612–624 and also appears in *Li Dazhao xuanji* (1962) pp. 173–212. The references given here refer to the text in *Li Dazhao xuanji*.

205. Zhang, *Zhongguo xiandai chuban shiliao*, 1:75n.

206. Li, "Wo de Makesi-zhuyi guan," pp. 181–185, especially p. 185. Full translations of the *Poverty of Philosophy* and the *Critique of Political Economy* did not appear in Japan until 1926 (Moriya, *Nihon Marukusu-shugi*, p. 42).

207. Zhang, *Zhongguo jindai chuban shiliao*, 1:68–69, 68n. The title of this work was *Zibenlun rumen* (Introduction to *Capital*), with the translator given as Li Shushi; it was published as part of the *Makesi quanshu* (Complete writings of [Karl] Marx).

208. Ibid., pp. 68–69, 76n.

209. Ibid., p. 70. The name of the author of the latter work is transliterated Guoliefu (V. I. Gorev, perhaps). Translated by Qu Qiubai, it included two early 1926 essays by Qu under the single title "Notes taken when studying the philosophy of materialism" (Yanjiu weiwulun zhexue shi suo chaolu de biji) (ibid., p. 76n).

210. The exception to this rule, of course, was in "Oriental society," a notion to which Chinese and Japanese Marxists were exposed relatively late. This was, no doubt, a major factor that stimulated Chinese and Japanese Marxists to pursue the notion of the Asiatic mode of production in depth. See chapters 6 and 7 in this volume.

211. Deutscher, *Stalin: A Political Biography*, p. 299n.

212. Girardin, "Marxist Theory of the State," p. 200.

213. Avineri, *Social and Political Thought of Karl Marx*, pp. 41, 37.

214. Ibid., pp. 36–38.

215. Lichtheim, *Marxism*, p. 246.

216. Ibid., p. 243.

217. Ibid., pp. 252–253, 255.

218. See such difficulties in the analyses of the Meiji Restoration offered in the debate on Japanese capitalism in Hoston, "Conceptualizing Bourgeois Revolution."

CHAPTER 4

1. Bakunin, "Statism and Anarchy" (1873), in *Bakunin on Anarchy*, pp. 341–342.

2. See Hegel, *Philosophy of History*; Marx, *Capital*, pp. 332–334; idem, "British Rule in India" (June 10, 1853), pp. 653–658; idem, "Future Results of British Rule in India" (July 2, 1853), pp. 659–664.

3. Scalapino and Yu, *The Chinese Anarchist Movement*, p. 1.

4. For an excellent description and analysis of the role of political murder in the history of tsarist Russia, see Carrère d'Encausse, *Le malheur russe*. On the impression the repressive tsarist state made on the narodnik movement, see Baron, "Development of Soviet Historiography," pp. 382–384; and Baron, "Plekhanov's Russia," pp. 396–400.

5. See Karl Marx to Vera Zasulich, "Letter on the Russian Village Community" (1881), pp. 218–226. When Marx and Engels reversed their initial agreement with the narodniki, they did so vehemently. See Engels, "Social Relations in Russia" (1875); and Marx and Engels, preface to the Russian edition of 1882 to the "Manifesto of the Communist Party," pp. 471–472.

6. Bakunin, "International and Karl Marx" (1872), pp. 310–311 (Bakunin's italics).

7. Bakunin, "Federalism, Socialism, Anti-Theologism" (1867), pp. 125–126 (Bakunin's italics).

8. Goldman, "Anarchism," p. 58.

9. Proudhon, "Economics and Justice," p. 51.

10. P. J. Proudhon, *What Is Property?* 1:38–39; and Dunbar, *Elisée Reclus*, p. 119. Reclus's linkage of scientism with anarchism was characteristic of anarchists at the end of the nineteenth century, and it was an important element appealing to Chinese and Japanese anarchists. See his *L'Homme et la terre*, *An Anarchist on Anarchy* (London: J. Tochatti, 1897), and *L'Evolution*.

11. Fernand Pelloutier, the French anarcho-syndicalist leader who was a major source of inspiration to Chinese worker-students in France, was a major force in this transformation of the syndicat from mere trade union to an instrument of revolutionary anarchism. See Kedward, *Anarchists*, p. 17, 61, 62.

12. Tucker, "Political Theory of Classical Marxism," p. 89.

13. Quoted in Kolakowski, *Main Currents of Marxism*, 1:249, 250.

14. Cf. Ansart, *Marx et l'anarchisme*, pp. 331–334.

15. Goldman, "Anarchism," p. 59.

16. Ibid., pp. 60–62.

17. Bakunin, "Federalism, Socialism, Anti-Theologism," p. 133 (Bakunin's italics).

18. Maitron, *Le Mouvement anarchiste en France*, 2:171, 172.

19. Bakunin, "Statism and Anarchy," p. 328.

20. Nevertheless, as Europe continues to strive for integration in the 1990s, and the independence-seeking Baltic republics and other national and subnational units seek inclusion into the Conference on Security and Cooperation in Europe (CSCE) process, perhaps Bakunin's vision is closer to being realized than one would expect.

21. Tucker, "Political Theory of Marxism," pp. 89–90.

22. Engels, *Ausgewählte Briefe*, 263, 341, quoted in Bloom, "'Withering Away' of the State," p. 115.

23. Lenin, *State and Revolution*, in 2:181, quoted in Tucker, "Political Theory of Marxism," p. 89.

24. Bloom, "'Withering Away' of the State," pp. 115–116.

25. Miliband, "Marx and the State," in *Karl Marx*, pp. 147–148; cf. Guillaume, "Mi-

chael Bakunin," pp. 45–46. Bakunin supported the Sonvilier Circular of 1871, which argued as follows: "The future society must be nothing else than the universalization of the organization that the International has formed for itself. We must therefore strive to make this organization as close as possible to our ideal. How can one expect an egalitarian society to emerge out of an authoritarian organization? It is impossible. The International, embryo of the future society, must from now on faithfully reflect our principles of federation and liberty, and must reject any principle tending toward authority and dictatorship" (Quoted in ibid., p. 45).

26. Bakunin, "International and Karl Marx," p. 295 (Bakunin's italics). On Kropotkin, see Woodcock, *Anarchism*, p. 196.

27. Kropotkin certainly accepted the possibility of violent revolution. See Kropotkin, *Conquest of Bread*, p. 27. Nevertheless, other writings suggest that the impulse to cooperation and mutual aid is so natural that violence would not be necessary (see Kropotkin, *Fields, Factories and Workshops*, conclusion.)

28. Kropotkin, *Fields, Factories, and Workshops*, pp. 214–216; see also idem, "Selections from Mutual Aid," p. 170.

29. See especially Bakunin, "Statism and Anarchy," pp. 336–337.

30. Cf. Goldman: "Thinking men and women the world over are beginning to realize that patriotism is too narrow and limited a conception to meet the necessities of our time" "Patriotism," p. 142.

31. Woodcock, *Anarchism*, p. 153. For more on the traditional populist imagery of dual Russia, see Tucker, *Soviet Political Mind*, (1972) chap. 6.

32. Bakunin, quoted in Venturi, *Roots of Revolution*, p. 433.

33. Michael Bakunin, quoted in Woodcock, *Anarchism*, p. 153 (Woodcock's interpolation).

34. Venturi, *Roots of Revolution*, p. 434.

35. Bakunin, "Federalism, Statism, Anti-Theologism," p. 106 (Bakunin's italics). Cf. Venturi, *Roots of Revolution*, p. 434.

36. Nettl, "State as a Conceptual Variable," pp. 571, 566.

37. *Mohan roppō* (Model six law codes), 1982 ed. (Tokyo: Sanseidō, 1981), s.v. Dai Nihonkoku kenpō. This translation is mine, not the official translation.

38. See Uesugi, *Kenpō jutsugi*; idem, *Kokutai kenpō oyobi kensei*; and Hozumi, "Waga kenpō no tokushitsu," pp. 493–609, and other essays in *Hozumi Yatsuka hakushi ronbun shū*.

39. Shinobu, *Taishō seiji shi*, p. 858.

40. Kato, "Taishō Democracy," p. 225.

41. Koyama, *Nihon Marukusu-shugi shi*, p. 12.

42. Ibid., p. 11; and Inumaru Gi'ichi, "Nihon Marukusu-shugi no genryū," 2:14–15.

43. Scalapino and Yü, *Chinese Anarchist Movement*, p. 6; cf. Price, *Roots of the Chinese Revolution*, pp. 121–124, 153–156.

44. Bernal, "Chinese Socialism before 1913," p. 66.

45. See Hsiao, "Anarchism in Chinese Political Thought," pp. 249–263. Specific aspects of this tradition will be discussed later.

46. Cf. Akiyama, *Nihon no hangyaku shisō*, p. 219.

47. This name appears variously as Qu Shengbai, Ou Shengbai, and Qu Shengbo in Western secondary sources. The character that appears in journal articles published under his name, however, is pronounced "Qu," and, therefore, that is the pronunciation that has been adopted here. On Qu's influence on Mao, see Chow, (1967) p. 75.

48. Here *hegemony* is used in the Gramscian sense to refer to the consent to or accep-

tance of the legitimating principles of a political system, in contrast to *domination*, which is rule resting on coercion or the threat thereof. See Gramsci, *Selections from the Prison Notebooks*, (1971) pp. 238–239, 243.

49. See Li Yü-ning, *The Introduction of Socialism into China*, passim; Bernal, "Chinese Socialism before 1913," pp. 68–69; and Price, *Roots of the Chinese Revolution*, p. 122.

50. Onabe, *Nijū seiki*, 4:464.

51. See Kōtoku, *Shakai-shugi shinzui*, p. 19 and passim.

52. Kōtoku, "Shakai-shugi to kokka," pp. 61–64.

53. *Konsaisu jinmei jiten*, s.v. Kemuyama Sentarō; and Notehelfer, *Kōtoku Shūsui*, p. 169. Miyashita and Kanno were executed along with Kōtoku in the *taigyaku jiken* (high treason incident) in 1911.

54. Ling-nan Yü-i nü-shih [pseud.], "Tung-Ou nü-hao chien," with commentary by T'an-hu-k'o [pseud.], in *Hsin hsiao-shuo hui pien* (Anthology of new fiction) Yokohama, n.d., pp. 8–9, quoted in Price, *Roots of the Chinese Revolution*, p. 125.

55. On the subtle complexities of the thought of Liu, see Staburova, *Anarkhizm v Kitae*, pp. 32–34, 39–43.

56. See chapter 2 this volume; Ishida, *Meiji seiji shisō shi kenkyū*, chap. 1; Pittau, *Political Thought in Early Meiji Japan*; and Gluck, *Japan's Modern Myths*.

57. The anarchism of Ōsugi was most idiosyncratic in his native context. He believed that the path to the anarchist revolution was dual-faceted, relying on a combination of (1) the expansion of the individual ego as a dynamic, creative force and the assertion of the conscious will of the worker; and (2) the cooperation of individuals in society through the syndicat. The psychological dimensions of Ōsugi's philosophy of the ego are beyond the scope of this book. For sustained analyses of this dimension of Ōsugi's thought and practice, see Stanley, *Ōsugi Sakae*, especially pp. 57–58, and chap. 2 passim; and Large, "Romance of Revolution," pp. 442, 452.

58. Needless to say, Ōsugi's radical individualism, certainly not a "traditional Japanese virtue", must be noted as an exception to this pattern. He was able to mediate the apparent conflict between his advocacy of the expansion of the individual ego with the communalism of anarchism by stressing the value of syndicalism in the anarchist struggle.

59. See Venturi, *Roots of Revolution*, p. x and passim.

60. See Maruyama, "Meiji kokka no shisō," pp. 213–215, 231–232; and idem, "Kuga Katsunan," pp. 291–295.

61. Bernstein, *Japanese Marxist*, p. 40.

62. Arahata, *Nihon shakai-shugi undō shi*, pp. 22–23.

63. Matsuzawa, *Nihon shakai-shugi no shisō*, p. 36.

64. Katayama, *Waga shakai-shugi*, p. 257, quoted in ibid., pp. 36, 37–40.

65. Kublin, *Asian Revolutionary*, pp. 70–71.

66. Notehelfer, *Kōtoku Shūsui*, pp. 49, 56–57, 66–75; and Nakamura, "Kōtoku Shūsui," pp. 22–23.

67. Kirkup, *Inquiry into Socialism* p. 41, quoted in Notehelfer, *Kōtoku Shūsui*, p. 77 (Notehelfer's italics).

68. On traditional Confucian perceptions of parties (*dang*), see Wakeman, "Price of Autonomy," pp. 35–70.

69. Kōtoku, "Genkon no seiji shakai to shakai shugi," p. 520, quoted in Notehelfer, "Kōtoku Shūsui and Nationalism," p. 35.

70. Notehelfer, "Kōtoku Shūsui and Nationalism," pp. 34–35.

71. Nakamura, "Kōtoku Shūsui," pp. 21–23; Notehelfer, *Kōtoku Shūsui*, pp. 76–78. See the bibliography given in Kōtoku, *Shakai-shugi shinzui*, p. 8.

72. Swift, "Yamakawa Hitoshi," p. 181; Notehelfer, *Kōtoku Shūsui*, p. 110. On the preeminence of ethics in Kropotkin, see Woodcock, *Anarchism*, chap. 7.

73. Notehelfer, "Kōtoku Shūsui and Nationalism," pp. 35–36.

74. Kōtoku, "Shakai-shugi to kokutai" pp. 73–74.

75. Kōtoku, "Shakai shugi to kokutai," 2:165. See also [Kōtoku Shūsui] *Teikoku shugi*, p. 34, quoted in Notehelfer, "Kōtoku Shūsui and Nationalism," p. 37.

76. See Tucker, *Soviet Political Mind*, (1972) chap. 6.

77. Nakamura, "Kōtoku Shūsui," p. 34.

78. Arahata, *Kanson jiden* 1:132–140. Cf. Bernstein, "Russian Revolution," pp. 328–329.

79. Notehelfer, *Kōtoku Shūsui*, pp. 118–135; and Nakamura, "Kōtoku Shūsui," p. 21.

80. Nakamura, "Chokusetsu kōdō-ron," pp. 38–39, 43; Takeuchi, "Nihon no Marukusu-shugi," pp. 13–14; Koyama and Kishimoto, *Nihon no hikyōsantō Marukusu-shugisha*, pp. 10–11. Cf. Kida, *Meiji no risō*, pp. 212–213; Swift, "Yamakawa Hitoshi," pp. 225, 225a; and Yamakawa, *Yamakawa Hitoshi jiden*, p. 295.

81. Notehelfer, *Kōtoku Shūsui*, p. 116.

82. Nakamura, "Chokusetsu kōdō-ron," pp. 54, 41–44.

83. Ibid., pp. 31–33, 40–41, 46–47; Matsuzawa, *Nihon shakai-shugi no shisō*, pp. 100–101; and Swift, "Yamakawa Hitoshi," pp. 195–196.

84. Moriya, *Nihon Marukusu-shugi riron*, pp. 13n–14n.

85. On Ōsugi's antimilitarism as a member of the Heimin-sha, see Akiyama, *Nihon no hangyaku shisō*, pp. 146–155.

86. Reclus had participated in the Paris Commune before forced to leave France to pursue his scholarship in geography and anarchist activities in Switzerland and Belgium. See Dunbar, *Élisée Reclus*.

87. Ōsugi's persistent efforts to impose his application of the philosophy of the expansion of the ego through free love upon his wife and mistresses was harmful to both his movement and his own physical well-being. Kamichika, frustrated with the emotional and financial strains of the four-way relationship, slashed his throat in November of 1916 and was sentenced to two years in prison for attempted murder. The resulting scandal caused the rupture of Ōsugi's ties to leading members of the left-wing movement, such as Sakai, Takabatake, and Yamakawa, who publicly reproached Ōsugi for his shortsightedness and selfishness in pursuing indiscriminate passion at the expense of the movement. Itō was murdered with Ōsugi after their arrest in the white terror that followed the great Kantō earthquake of September 1, 1923. See Stanley, *Ōsugi Sakae*, chaps. 7, 11; and Large, "Romance of Revolution."

88. See Stanley, *Ōsugi Sakae*, pp. 47–48, 62–64; and Ōsugi, "Sei no sōzō," p. 55.

89. Stanley, *Ōsugi Sakae*, p. 64; cf. Takeuchi, "Nihon no Marukusu-shugi," pp. 16–17; and Kida, *Meiji no risō*, pp. 215–216.

90. Sakai, *Nihon shakai undō shiwa*, 6:277–278.

91. Stanley, *Ōsugi Sakae*, p. 91.

92. Sakai, *Nihon shakai undō shiwa*, 4:277–286.

93. These were "Seifuku no jijitsu" (The reality of conquest), "Sei no kakujū" (The expansion of life), and "Sei no sōzō" (The creation of life), first published in *Kindai shisō* [Modern thought], 1, no. 9, (June 1913), 1, no. 10 (July 1913), and 2, no. 4 (January 1914), respectively. All appear in *Osugi Sakae zenshū*, vol. 2.

94. This view is in many respects comparable to Gramsci's view of civil society and its institutions as part of the oppressive apparatus of the state in advanced industrial society.

95. Here Ōsugi stressed much more than Kōtoku the attainment of human freedom through destruction, as Bakunin stressed. Cf. Simcock, "Anarcho-Syndicalist," p. 37–40.

96. Kida, *Meiji no risō*, pp. 215–216.

97. Stanley, *Ōsugi Sakae*, pp. 59–70.

98. Ōsugi, "Sei no sōzō," 2:55, quoted in Stanley, *Ōsugi Sakae*, p. 70.

99. Ōsugi, "Minzoku kokka-shugi no kyogi," 1:240–249.

100. Ōsugi, "Seifuku no jijitsu," pp. 26–27.

101. Ōsugi, "Minzoku kokka-shugi no kyogi," p. 249.

102. Here Ōsugi prefigured the work of both Gramsci and French structuralist Marxist Louis Althusser. (Especially see Ōsugi, "Minzoku-kokka-shugi no kyogi," pp. 245–249.) Cf. Gramsci's stress on the role of intellectuals of the institutions of civil society in exercising hegemony in support of the state's maintenance of the domination of the ruling over the subaltern classes. See Gramsci, *Selections from the Prison Notebooks*, especially pp. 5–23, 257–264; and Althusser, "Ideology and Ideological State Apparatuses."

103. Ōsugi, "Seifuku no jijitsu," p. 27.

104. See chapter 5 this volume.

105. Staburova, *Anarkhizm v Kitae*, p. 51.

106. Wang, "Wu Chih-hui," pp. 82–84.

107. Dirlik, "Vision and Revolution," p. 126.

108. *Dictionnaire biographique*, s.v. Li Shizeng, Wu Zhihui; and Staburova, *Anarkhizm v Kitae*, p. 52.

109. *Zhejian Chao*, 8:18, quoted in Bernal, *Chinese Socialism to 1907*, p. 100.

110. Price, *Roots of the Chinese Revolution*, p. 153.

111. This was doubtless the inspiration for the title *Xin shiji* (New century) with which the Paris anarchists christened their first journal.

112. Staburova, *Anarkhizm v Kitae*, p. 54.

113. Li Shizeng and Chen Minyi, and subsequently Huang Lingshuang, explained revolution as "re-evolution," "portraying revolution as the motive force of evolution" (Dirlik, "New Culture Movement," p. 278).

114. Dirlik, "New Culture Movement," p. 281.

115. Sanlian, *Wusi shiqi qikan jishao* 3:216–217, quoted in Dirlik, "New Culture Movement," p. 281.

116. See *Xin Shiji*, 5:1–2.

117. See Staburova, *Anarkhizm v Kitae*, pp. 153–154.

118. Chu, "Looking at the Past," p. 2, quoted in Scalapino and Yü, *Chinese Anarchist Movement*, pp. 8–9.

119. "A Letter to *Xin Shiji* from a certain Individual, with Answers," *Xin Shiji*, no. 8 (August 10, 1907): 2–3, cited by Scalapino and Yü, *Chinese Anarchist Movement*, p. 11.

120. Li, *Introduction of Socialism into China*, pp. 57–59.

121. Wilbur, *Sun Yat-sen*, p. 16; and Sharmon, *Sun Yat-sen*, (1968) pp. 58, 98–99, 116–119; Price, *Roots of the Chinese Revolution*, pp. 155–156, 158; and Bernal, *Chinese Socialism to 1907*, pp. 58–59. Sun's interpretation of *minsheng* subsequently became the basis of the national socialism advocated by Dai Jitao, who was the official spokesman for Sun after 1911.

122. Gregor and Chang, "*Nazionalfascismo*," p. 26, citing Sun Yat-sen, *International Development of China* (Shanghai: Commercial Press, 1920), pp. 1–3, 147.

123. Cf. Dirlik, "Vision and Revolution," p. 124.

124. See the discussion of these concepts of freedom in the West in relation to the master-slave relationship in Patterson, *Freedom*, 1:3–5.

125. See Li Shizeng, "Da pangguanzi" (Response to a bystander), *Xin shiji* (August 3, 1907).

126. See chapter 8 this volume.

127. Scalapino and Yü, *Chinese Anarchist Movement*, p. 7.

128. "Declaration of the Social Communist Revolutionary Group," *Minsheng*, no. 33 (July 15, 1921): 4.

129. See *Xin shiji*, no. 6: 4, no. 18: 2; no. 79: 4; no. 92: 5–8, quoted in Dirlik, "Vision and Revolution," p. 136. Cf. "Social Communist Revolutionary Group," p. 4.

130. See, for example, Yi, "Annaqi yu ziyou" (Anarchy and freedom), *Ziyou* (Freedom), no. 1 (December 1920): 2.

131. Dirlik, "Vision and Revolution," pp. 140–141.

132. Ibid., pp. 139–140.

133. Wu, "Wen Man-Han yijian yu gemingdang," pp. 3–4, quoted in Wang, "Wu Chih-hui," p. 92.

134. Wang, "Wu Chih-hui," p. 92.

135. Wu Zhihui, "Man li" pp. 3–4, quoted by Wang, "Wu Chih-hui," p. 93.

136. Wang, "Wu Chih-hui," p. 94.

137. *Mencius*, IIA. 6, J 3, pp. 14b–16a, quoted in Lau, "Theories of Human Nature," p. 547.

138. "Mencius said: 'The gentleman penetrates deep into the Way, for he wants to find it within himself. If he finds it within himself, then he can feel at home in it. If he can feel at home in it, he can draw greatly on its help. If he can draw greatly on its help, he can take from it left and right and always meet with its source. Hence the gentleman wants to find it within himself'" (*Mencius*, IVB. 14, J 8 p. 6a, quoted in Lau, "Theories of Human Nature," p. 564).

139. See Dirlik, "Vision and Revolution," p. 141.

140. Wu Zhihui, "Wuzhengfu-zhuyi yi jiaoyu wei geming shuo" (The anarchists regard education as revolution), *Xin shiji*, no. 58: 10–12, quoted in Wang, "Wu Chih-hui," p. 96.

141. See chapter 9 this volume.

142. See Dirlik, "Vision and Revolution," pp. 142, 143.

143. See Dirlik, "New Culture Movement," p. 277.

144. Wu Zhihui, "Shu mou jun youjian hou" (Written after reading the letter from a certain gentleman), in *Xin shiji*, no. 42: 2–3, quoted in Wang, "Wu Chih-hui," pp. 98–99.

145. See Dirlik, "New Culture Movement," pp. 278–279.

146. See "Kongzi geming," *Xin Shiji* (June 20, 1908): 4, quoted in Dirlik, "New Culture Movement," p. 275. Wu even rejected China's traditional character-based writing system as archaic and inferior to Western alphabet-based systems and called for its rejection in favor of Esperanto. See Wang, "Wu Chih-hui," pp. 112, 102–106.

147. Dirlik, "Vision and Revolution," p. 153. Yet Wu's own anarchist vision was fairly simple and bucolic: his would be a society without private property, and he envisaged houses with flowers in front, trees in back, and terraces with a view. See Wang, "Wu Chih-hui," p. 111.

148. Major works of Japanese socialists that were translated into Chinese included the following: Fukui Junzō (trans. Zhao Bizhen), *Kinsei shakai-shugi* (Modern socialism), published by Guangzhi Shuju as *Jinshi shehui-zhuiyi* in 1903; Murai Tomoyoshi's *Shakai-shugi* (Socialism), Shimada Saburō's *Shakai-shugi gaihyō* (Outline of socialism), Ōhara Shōichi's *Shakai mondai* (Social problems), and Nishikawa Kōjirō, *Shakaitō* (The socialist party). Chinese students in Japan also published the same year material about the Russian anarchist movement in *Jiangsu* and *Zhejiang chao* (see Zhang, *Zhongguo jindai chuban*

shiliao, 1:174, quoted in Onogawa, "Liu Shih-p'ei and Anarchism," pp. 78–79.) Of the Japanese authors mentioned, Murai and Nishikawa were both Christian socialists who subsequently split with "materialist" Marxian socialists.

149. Onogawa, "Liu Shih-p'ei and Anarchism," pp. 97–98.

150. According to one account, Liu's and Zhang's Institute for the Study of Socialism was founded on the recommendation of Kōtoku (Bernal, *Chinese Socialism to 1907*, pp. 204, 224).

151. Ibid., pp. 74–78, 87–89, 96; Staburova, *Anarkhizm v Kitae*, pp. 30–31, 47–48; and *Dictionnaire biographique*, s.v. Liu Shipei.

152. Dirlik, "Vision and Revolution," p. 127.

153. Onogawa, "Liu Shipei and Anarchism," pp. 98–99; Dirlik, "Vision and Revolution," p. 127.

154. See the essays collected in Ge Maochu et al., eds. *Wuzhengfu-zhuyi sixiang ziliao xuan*, vol. 1.

155. *Tianyi bao*, 8, 9, and 10 (combined) (October 30, 1907), quoted in Onogawa, "Liu Shih-p'ei and Anarchism," p. 92. This desire to abolish distinctions among human beings extended to gender differences as well. Liu and his wife He crusaded boldly for equality between the sexes. Besides those mentioned, see also 11 and 12 (November 30, 1907) of *Tianyi bao*.

156. Staburova, *Anarkhizm v Kitae*, p. 102.

157. Bernal, "Chinese Socialism before 1913," pp. 66–67.

158. The primacy of the influence of Bakunin and Kropotkin over Tolstoy for the Paris anarchists was evident in the content of the material they used to introduce Western anarchism to the readers of their journals. See, for example, the translation of chapter 2 of Bertrand Russell's *Roads to Freedom: Socialism, Anarchism, and Syndicalism*, which appeared as "Bakuning Bokunin [sic] yu wuzhengfu-zhuyi" (Bakunin and anarchism), trans. Ling Shuang, pp. 3–13. In this passage, Tolstoy's followers were dismissed as a small minority of the anarchist movement.

159. See Dirlik, "Vision and Revolution," p. 147. Liu wrote for the nationalistic *Guocui xuebao* published in Shanghai from 1905 through 1911 (Staburova, *Anarkhizm v Kitae*, p. 40; and *Inventaire des périodiques chinois*, p. 45.)

160. See Hsiao, "Anarchism in Chinese Political Thought," pp. 249–252, 256–257.

161. Ibid., pp. 254, 257, 258.

162. Ibid., p. 259. Unfortunately, no translation of the work of Wu, an unknown personage who assumed this curious pen name meaning "can do nothing" is available in Western languages (259n, 256).

163. Ibid., p. 260. For more detail on Bao's thought, see Hsiao, *History of Chinese Political Thought*, pp. 623–630.

164. Scalapino and Yü, *Chinese Anarchist Movement*, p. 30.

165. Martin Bernal notes that Liu and his close associate Zhang Binglin were both also influenced by Buddhism. See Bernal, "Liu Sifu," p. 3.

166. Staburova, *Anarkhizm v Kitae*, pp. 54–56; Dirlik, "Vision and Revolution," p. 148.

167. Shen Shu, "Baosheng xueshu fawei" (The decline of Bao-sheng's scholarship), *Tianyi bao*, 8, 9, 10, combined, p. 50, cited in Onogawa, "Liu Shih-p'ei and Anarchism," p. 95. Zhang Binglin also referred to Laozi, Zhuangzi, and Baosheng as anarchist philosophers of ancient China (Onogawa, "Liu Shih-p'ei and Anarchism," p. 95).

168. Onogawa, "Liu Shih-p'ei and Anarchism," p. 95.

169. See Lau, "Theories of Human Nature," pp. 564–565.

170. *Xin Shiji*, 22: 4, quoted in Dirlik, "Vision and Revolution," p. 148.

171. Rousseau's views on humanity in the state of nature are most eloquently expressed in his First Discourse on the influence of progress of the arts and sciences on human well-being and Second Discourse on the origin of human inquality.

172. Dirlik, "Vision and Revolution," pp. 148–149.

173. Onogawa, "Liu Shih-p'ei and Anarchism," p. 80.

174. See Liu Shipei, "Wuzhengfu-zhuyi zhi pingdeng-guan," *Tianyi bao*, 4 (July 25, 1907), 5 (August 10), and 7 (September 15).

175. See *Tianyi bao*, 3 (July 10, 1907); also included in *Xinhai geming-qian shinianjian relun xuanji*, vol. 2, pt. 2, cited by Onogawa, "Liu Shih-p'ei and Anarchims"; Staburova, *Anarkhizm v Kitae*, pp. 39–40; and Onogawa, "Liu Shih-p'ei and Anarchism," pp. 90–92.

176. Onogawa, "Liu Shih-p'ei and Anarchism," p. 90.

177. See Hsiao, *Modern China*, pp. 47–53. Formulated circa 1888, the outline of Kang's theory had been introduced by his student Liang Qichao in 1901 in "Nan Hai-kang xiansheng zhuan" (The life of Mr. Haikang Nan), *Qingyi bao*, no. 100 (November 11, 1901) (Onogawa, "Liu Shih-p'ei and Anarchism," p. 91.)

178. See Dirlik, "Vision and Revolution," pp. 149–150.

179. Wei Yi, "Bian Manchu fei Zhongguo zhi chenmin," (Arguing that the Manchus are not Chinese subjects), *Min bao* (The people's news), no. 18 (December 25, 1907): 22–23, cited by Onogawa, "Liu Shih-p'ei and Anarchism," p. 87; "Feibing feicai lun" (On disarmament and the abolition of property), *Tianyi bao*, 2 (June 25, 1907), and Liu Shipei and He Zhen, "Lun zhongzu geming yu wuzhengfu geming zhi deshi" (On the merits and demerits of the racial revolution and anarchist revolution), *Tianyi bao* 6 (September 1, 1907) and 7 (September 15, 1907), cited by Onogawa, "Liu Shih-p'ei and Anarchism," p. 93.

180. See Liu and He, "Lun zhongzu geming," Wei, "Bian Manren fei Zhongguo zhi zhenmin," and Shen Shu, "Ouzhou shehui-zhuyi yu wuzhengfu-zhuyi yitong kao" (A consideration of the similarities and differences between European socialism and anarchism), *Tianyi bao*, 6 (September 1, 1907), p. 24, cited by Onogawa, "Liu Shih-p'ei and Anarchism," p. 94.

181. Onogawa, "Liu Shih-p'ei and Anarchism," p. 99; and Dirlik, "Vision and Revolution," p. 127.

182. "Zhi wuzhengfudang wanguo dahui shu," pp. 4–5.

183. For those discouraged by the strict moral injunctions of the Jindehui, Li joined Cai Yuanpei to establish the Shehui Gailianghui (Social Reform Society), a group with similar aspirations but fewer moral strictures. The Jindehui, however, was considerably more moderate in its behavioral requirements than Liu Shifu's Xin-she (Conscience Society), on which it was patterned. See *Dictionnaire biographique*, s.v. Li Shizeng, and Staburova, *Anarkhizm v Kitae*, p. 53. On Liu Shifu's group, see later.

184. Staburova, *Anarkhizm v Kitae*, pp. 70–71.

185. Ibid., pp. 90–92.

186. "Zhi wuzhengfudang wanguo dahui shu," pp. 5–7.

187. Ibid., pp. 108–113.

188. *Inventaire des périodiques chinois dans les bibliothèques françaises* (Inventory of Chinese periodicals in French libraries), comp. Michel Cartier, *Documents et Inventaires* 3 (Paris: Centre de Recherches et de Documentation sur la Chine Contemporaine, Ecole des Hautes Etudes en Sciences Sociales et Institut des Hautes Etudes Chinoises, Collège de France, 1984), s.v. *Ziyou*.

189. Staburova, *Anarkhizm v Kitae*, pp. 102–103, 117–127; Xu Shanguang and

Liu Jianping, *Zhongguo wuzhengfu-zhuyishi* (N.p.: Hubei Renmin Chuban-she, 1989), pp. 89ff. and app.

190. Staburova, *Anarkhizm v Kitae*, pp. 132–138.

191. Dirlik, "New Culture Movement," pp. 272, 273; *Inventaire des périodiques chinois*, pp. 74, 109–110.

192. The journal had sections in Chinese and Esperanto and was entitled in Esperanto *La Vôco del' Popolo.*

193. *Dictionnaire biographique*, s.v. Liu Sifu; Staburova, *Anarkhizm v Kitae*, p. 119 ff.; Bernal, "Liu Sifu," pp. 1–2.

194. Bernal, "Liu Sifu," pp. 2–4; and Zhuan Fu, "Shifu-jun xinglue" pp. 1–3.

195. See the description of Bakunin and Proudhon as the founders of anarchism, followed by the translation of part of the first chapter of Kropotkin's *Conquest of Bread*, in [Liu] Shifu, "Wuzhengfu-zhuyi zhi yuanzu" pp. 1–3.

196. [Liu] Shifu, "Wuzhengfu-gongchan-zhuyi shiming," pp. 1–2.

197. Staburova, *Anarkhizm v Kitae*, pp. 78–80, 86–92.

198. Shifu, the name that Liu Sifu adopted, has a distinctly Buddhist flavor. *Shi* means teacher, and *fu* is a term that means renewal or restoration to one's original (moral) condition.

199. [Liu] Shifu, "Gongchan-zhuyi komunismo zhi yuanze," pp. 1–2.

200. Liu, "Kelupaotejin wuzhengfu-gongchan-zhuyi zhi yaoling," p. 8 (Liu's italics).

201. [Liu] Shifu, "Annaqi" p. 8.

202. [Liu Shifu] Shi Fu, *Shi Fu wencun*, [Liu] pp. 81–83, 56, cited by Dirlik, "New Culture Movement," p. 284. Again, compare Gramsci on education and the need to create a new *egemonia* in the revolutionary process. Compare also the role of education in the anarchism of the Paris anarchist group. See Li Shizeng, "Shehui Gexin zhi liang da yaosu," pp. 569–578.

203. Staburova, *Anarkhizm v Kitae*, pp. 96, 99.

204. Ibid., pp. 119ff.

205. See, for example, "Wuzhengfu Gongchan-zhuyi Tongzhi-she xuanyan shu—Declaracio de Anarhiist-Kommunista Groupa de Shanghai" (Declaration of the Anarcho-Communist Group of Shanghai), *Minsheng*, 16 (July 4, 1914): 1–3.

206. See Boas, *Rationalism in Greek Philosophy.*

207. See Patterson, *Freedom*, 1:178ff.

208. "Wuzhengfu gongchan-zhuyi zhi xinli-shang de jieshi" 30 (March 15, 1921):5–6; 31 (April 15, 1921); and 32 (May 15, 1921).

209. Ibid., 30:7–8. Cf. "Wuzhengfu Gongchan-zhuyi shu," pp. 2, 3, 5.

210. See Staburova, *Anarkhizm v Kitae*, pp. 101–104.

211. "Wuzhengfu Gongchan-zhuyi shu," pp. 2–3.

212. Taipu [pseud.], "Wuzhengfu-zhuyi yu Zhongguo," pp. 26–27.

213. Ibid., pp. 24–26.

214. See Staburova, *Anarkhizm v Kitae*, pp. 110–113, 145–146; *Dictionnaire biographique*, s.v. Wu Zhihui.

215. Cf. Dirlik, "New Culture Movement," p. 256.

216. Staburova, *Anarkhizm v Kitae*, pp. 146–150.

217. Simcock, "Anarcho-Syndicalist," p. 41.

218. Venturi, *Roots of Revolution*, p. 479.

219. Bernstein, *Japanese Marxist*, p. 59. See especially Kawakami, "Sonnō ron" (1905) (On the reverence for agriculture in Japan), in Kawakami, *Kawakami Hajime chosakushū*, 1:129–221.

220. This distinction is drawn with caution, of course: the two urges are present in all varieties of anarchist thought.

221. Maurice Meisner, *Li Ta-chao*, (1977) chap. 4.

222. Quoted in Woodcock, *Anarchism*, pp. 155–156.

223. Li Dazhao, "Qingnian yu nongcun" (Youth and the village) (February 1919), in Li, *Li Dazhao xuanji*, pp. 146–150. Cf. Shimamoto, "Go-shi ki no eikyō, Ri Taishō no shisō o tōshite," p. 32. Compare the policy of *xiafang* (sending down) under Mao after the revolution.

224. Li, "Qingnian yu nongcun," pp. 149–150.

225. Paul Avrich, preface to Dolgoff, *Bakunin on Anarchy*, pp. xix–xx.

226. See the discussions of these notions in the following: Isaiah Berlin, *Two Concepts of Liberty*; Benn and Weinstein, "Being Free to Act," pp. 194–211; and Connolly, *Terms of Political Discourse*.

227. Dirlik, "New Culture Movement," p. 290.

228. Arahata, "Heimin-sha jidai," p. 331. Ōsugi himself was arrested with other leftist activists and murdered by police of the state he despised in the aftermath of the great Tokyo earthquake of 1923.

CHAPTER 5

1. Gregor and Chang, *"Nazionalfascismo,"* pp. 23–24.

2. See Marx and Engels, "Manifesto of the Communist Party," pp. 474–483. Cf. Hintze, "Economics and Politics," pp. 422–452; Hintze, "State in Historical Perspective," 1968 ed., (1973), pp. 154–169; Tilly, "History of European State-Making," pp. 3–83; and idem, Tilly, "Theories of Political Transformation," pp. 601–638, passim.

3. Marx, "Civil War in France," pp. 629–630.

4. For the development of this notion, see Poulantzas, "Problem of the Capitalist State," pp. 246–247; and chapter 1 this volume.

5. See Knei-paz, *Leon Trotsky,* chap. 3 passim.

6. See Bernstein, "Early Japanese Socialists," pp. 328–329; and Yamakawa, "Sobieto seiji no tokushitsu to sono hihan," 2:386.

7. Lenin, "Gosudarstvo i revoliutsiia," vol. 33.

8. See Cohen, *Bukharin and the Bolshevik Revolution,* (1975), chaps. 5, 6; Erlich, *Soviet Industrialization Debates;* and Lewin, *Russian Peasants and Soviet Power,* chaps. 6, 7.

9. Marx, "Civil War in France," p. 629; cf. Friedrich Engels, Introduction, to Marx, "Civil War in France," p. 627.

10. The doctrine of hostile capitalist encirclement encouraged the "war scare" of 1927 (see Cohen, *Bukharin and the Bolshevik Revolution,* chap. 8) and was only repudiated by Nikita Khrushchev's attack on the notion of the "inevitability of war" at the Communist party of the Soviet Union (CPSU)'s Twentieth Party Congress in 1956. See Tucker, *Soviet Political Mind* (1972); Linden, *Khrushchev and the Soviet Leadership,* chap. 2; and Schapiro, *Communist Party,* 2d ed., chap. 30.

11. See Yamakawa, "Sobieto seiji," passim; and the discussion of Takabatake Motoyuki later in this chapter. Cf. Li Dazhao, "Pingmin zhengzhi yu gongren zhengzhi" (Democracy and ergatocracy) (July 1, 1922), pp. 397–398 (in collection hereafter cited as *Li Dazhao xuanji*).

12. See Cohen, *Bukharin and the Bolshevik Revolution,* chap. 5; and the 1882 preface to the Russian edition of the "Manifesto of the Communist Party," p. 334.

13. Lenin, *Sochineniia*, 3d ed., 19:324, quoted in Cohen, *Bukharin and the Bolshevik Revolution*, p. 36.

14. See North, *Moscow and Chinese Communists*, 1963 ed., chap. 6; and Lerner, *Karl Radek*, pp. 136–146.

15. See Cohen, *Bukharin and the Bolshevik Revolution*, pp. 148–154; and Hammond, "Bukharin and the Chinese Revolution," pp. 463–472.

16. For a cogent Trotskyist critique of Comintern policies stemming from this approach, see Isaacs, *The Tragedy of the Chinese Revolution*.

17. Lerner, *Karl Radek*, pp. 144–146.

18. Berki, "Marxian Thought," pp. 80–105.

19. See Tanaka, *Takabatake Motoyuki*, p. 3.

20. Jansen, *Japanese and Sun Yat-sen*, (1970) p. 201, and chap. 9 passim; and Wilbur, *Sun Yat-sen*, pp. 56–58; see also Wilson, *Radical Nationalist in Japan;* and Kita, *Kokutai-ron*, vol. 1.

21. Tanaka, *Takabatake Motoyuki*, pp. 111–113.

22. See Mast, *"Tai Chi-t'ao, Sunism and Marxism,"* pp. 227–249; Mast and Saywell, "Revolution out of Tradition," pp. 73–98; Saywell, "Thought of Tai Chi-t'ao," and Mast, "Intellectual Biography of Tai Chi-t'ao."

23. See Ogden, "Chinese Concepts of Nation, State, and Sovereignty," pp. 32–33; and Schrecker, *Imperialism and Chinese Nationalism*, chap. 2 passim.

24. Sakata, "Meiji zenhan-ki no kokka-shugi," p. 27 and passim; Maruyama, "Kuga Katsunan," pp. 291–295; and idem, "Meiji kokka no shisō," pp. 213–215, 231–232.

25. Notehelfer, "Kōtoku Shūsui and Nationalism," p. 33.

26. See Schwartz, *Wealth and Power;* Lin, *Crisis of Chinese Consciousness*, pp. 36–37; Hao, *Intellectual Transition in China*, pp. 95–111, 149–219; Huang, "Liberalism and Nationalism," pp. 521–536; Huang, *Modern Chinese Liberalism;* Liang, "Aiguo lun," vol. 2, chap. 3, pp. 65–77; Kondō, "'Minkoku' to Ri," pp. 287–288; Xiao, *Zhongguo zhengzhi sixiang shi* (1977), chaps. 21–24; and Wang, *Chinese Intellectuals and the West*, chaps. 8, 9, 10.

27. It must be noted that these generalizations concerning universality and particularity do not apply unproblematically to the religious sphere. Robert Bellah has argued that during the Tokugawa period, Japanese religion demonstrated a move toward a more universalist orientation in contrast to the particularism of Chinese beliefs. Nevertheless, the philosophical developments at the end of the period covered by Bellah that laid the groundwork for the assertion of the uniqueness of the Japanese emperor in the Restoration movement indicates the philosophical transition to the more particularistic posture that is described later. Indeed, see Bellah, *Tokugawa Religion* (1970) pp. 188–189.

28. Earl, *Emperor and Nation in Japan*, pp. 216, 221; Matsumoto, "Atarashii seiji ishiki no hōga," 1:10, 13; and Inoue, "Tōitsu kokka no jijon," 1:114–126.

29. See Pittau, *Political Thought in Early Meiji Japan*, pp. 132–157; Suzuki, *Kenpō seitai to Roseler*, p. 142; and Takeda, "Tennō-sei shisō no keisei," pp. 270, 273–274, 297–303.

30. Notehelfer, "Kōtoku Shūsui and Nationalism," p. 35.

31. Jansen, *Changing Japanese Attitudes towards Modernization*, p. 78; and idem, *Japanese and Sun Yat-sen*, pp. 51–53. Writing in the aftermath of the Twenty-One Demands, Li Dazhao, who himself had once espoused a sort of pan-Asianism, vehemently denounced Japanese "pan-Asianism" as racist chauvinism. See Li, "Da Yaxiya-zhuyi yu xin Yaxiya-zhuyi," pp. 127–129. See also Maruyama, "Ajia nashonarizumu," pp. 17–24.

32. [Kōtoku Shūsui], "Risō naki kokumin," *Kōtoku Shūsui senshū* (Selected works of Kōtoku Shūsui), 2:61, quoted in Notehelfer, "Kōtoku Shūsui and Nationalism," p. 32.

33. [Kōtoku Shūsui], "Kokumin no mahi," *Kōtoku Shūsui senshū* (Selected works of Kōtoku Shūsui), 2:62, quoted in Notehelfer, "Kōtoku Shūsui and Nationalism," p. 32.

34. Notehelfer, "Kōtoku Shūshui and Nationalism," p. 33.

35. Ibid., p. 37; and Arahata, "Heimin-sha jidai," pp. 1097–1107; cf. Kublin, "Japanese Socialists and the Russo-Japanese War," pp. 322–339; and Arahata, *Kanson jiden*, vol. 1, chap. 2.

36. See Ishida, "J. S. Mill 'Jiyū-ron'," pp. 1–46; and Hoston, "State, 'Modernity,' and the Fate of Liberalism in Prewar Japan."

37. Hoston, *Crisis of Development in Prewar Japan*, p. xiv; Bernstein, *Japanese Marxist,* chap. 6.

38. See Baron, "Plekhanov's Russia," pp. 388–404; and Venturi, *Roots of Revolution,* passim. On the impact of the 1905 revolution, see Tanaka, *Kōtoku Shūsui,* pp. 259–264. There is no mention of Russian influence before this in Totten, *Social Democratic Movement,* vol. 1, chap. 2. Cf. Arahata, *Kanson jiden,* pp. 132–140.

39. Tanaka, "Takabatake Motoyuki ron," p. 36.

40. Takeda, "Tennō-sei shisō no keisei," p. 284.

41. Takano Fusatarō, quoted by Tanaka, "Takabatake Motoyuki ron," p. 36; and Tsujino, "Reimei-ki rōdō kumiai undō"; Ishida, *Meiji seiji shisō shi kenkyū,* pp. 96–97; cf. Kawakami, "Socialism in Japan," p. 565.

42. Hirano, *Nihon shihon-shugi shakai no kikō,* p. 388.

43. Totten, *Social Democratic Movement,* pp. 18–19.

44. Ibid., p. 24; cf. Nakase, "Meiji kenpō moto," pp. 59–61.

45. Kida, *Meiji no risō,* pp. 155–156.

46. Totten, *Social Democratic Movement,* p. 24.

47. Sumiya, "Kaisetsu," 1:488–490.

48. Kida, *Meiji no risō,* pp. 204–205.

49. Tanaka, *Takabatake Motoyuki,* p. 3.

50. Totten, *Social Democratic Movement,* pp. 25–26; Kublin, *Asian Revolutionary,* pp. 130–131; and Tanaka, *Takabatake Motoyuki,* chap. 1.

51. These were Abe Isoo, Katayama, Kawakami Kiyoshi, Naoe Kinoshita, and Nishikawa Kōjirō.

52. Totten, *Social Democratic Movement,* pp. 25, 26.

53. Arahata, "Heimin-sha jidai," passim.

54. Kida, *Meiji no risō,* pp. 208–209.

55. See Yamaji, "Genji no shakai mondai," especially pp. 385–395.

56. Kida, *Meiji no risō,* p. 204.

57. Yamaji, "Yoga kidokyō o shinzuru yuen," vol. 2.

58. See Craig, "Fukuzawa Yukichi," in p. 135; and Fukuzawa, "Heiron," 5: 297.

59. See Oka, "Kaisetsu," 2:459–460; and Yamaji, "Shakai-shugi kanken," 2:195–197.

60. Yamaji, "Genji no shakai mondai," 21:394.

61. Yamaji, "Shakai-shugi kanken" 2:195–197. Yamaji's belief that the notion of class conflict did not apply to Japanese reality led him, in 1908, to protest that he was not a Marxist although he considered Marx with John Stuart Mill (curiously enough) to be the greatest modern Western thinkers. See Yamaji, "Genji no shakai mondai," p. 394.

62. Arahata, *Nihon shakai-shugi undō shi,* p. 114.

63. Ibid., pp. 114–115.

64. Levenson, *Confucian China and its Modern Fate,* 1:98.

65. Gregor and Chang, "Nazionalfascismo," p. 24. Gregor and Chang cite Feng Ziyou, *Geming ishi* (Anecdotes of the Chinese revolution) (Taipei: Taiwan Commercial Press,

1969), 1:1, Lilia Borokh, "Notes on the Early Role of Secret Societies in Sun Yat-sen's Republican Movement," pp. 135–144, Boris Novikov, "The Anti-Manchu Propaganda of the Triads, ca. 1800–1860," pp. 49–64, all in *Popular Movements and Secret Societies in China, 1840–1950* (Stanford, Calif.: Stanford University Press, 1972); and Davis, *Primitive Revolutionaries of China*. See also Chesneaux, *Peasant Revolts in China*.

66. Levenson, *Confucian China and Its Modern Fate*, 1:103.

67. Ogden, "Chinese Concepts of the Nation," pp. 23, 33, chap. 2 passim.

68. Fairbank, *United States and China*, pp. 162–165; and idem, *Trade and Diplomacy*.

69. Levenson, *Confucian China and Its Modern Fate*, 1:99 (Levenson's italics).

70. See Wright, *Last Stand of Chinese Conservatism;* and Teng and Fairbank, *China's Response to the West* (1979), chaps. 5–7.

71. Levenson, *Confucian China and Its Modern Fate*, 1:101–102.

72. Cf. Solomon, *Mao's Revolution*, (1972) pp. 171–173; Selden, *Yenan Way*, pp. 226–227; and Lee, "Hsia Fang System," pp. 40–62.

73. Cf. Levenson, *Confucian China and Its Modern Fate*, 2:136–139.

74. See Schwartz, *Wealth and Power*, chaps. 1, 2; Levenson, *Confucian China and Its Modern Fate*, 1:88–96. Cf. Price, *Russia and the Chinese Revolution*, chap. 5; and Rankin, *Early Chinese Revolutionaries*, pp. 64–88; and Wang, *Chinese Intellectuals and the West*, pp. 193–194. One might also include Sun Yat-sen among this group. Sun was not a "scholar" but was educated in Western missionary schools.

75. See Schwartz, *Wealth and Power*, chap. 12 and passim; Price, *Russia and the Chinese Revolution*, p. 126; Levenson, *Mind of Modern China*, pp. 115–121; Lin, *Crisis of Chinese Consciousness*, pp. 31–32, 36–37, 56–63; Chang, *Intellectual Transition in China*, passim; Wang, *Chinese Intellectuals and the West,* pp. 193–222; and Onogawa, "Shinmatsu no shisō," pp. 1–36.

76. Price, *Russia and the Chinese Revolution*, chap. 5, p. 164.

77. Ibid., p. 163; Wang, *Chinese Intellectuals and the West*, chap. 8; and Huang, "Liberalism and Nationalism," passim.

78. Levenson, *Confucian China and Its Modern Fate*, p. 101 (Levenson's italics).

79. Price, *Russia and the Chinese Revolution*, chap. 5.

80. Gregor and Chang, "*Nazionalfascismo*," p. 24.

81. See Liew, *Struggle for Democracy*, pp. 70–71; Hsüeh, *Huang Hsing and the Chinese Revolution*, pp. 50–56; and Song, "Wo zhi lishi," 1:319–320.

82. Levenson, *Confucian China and Its Modern Fate*, 1:88.

83. Sun reflected this anti-Manchu sentiment in his Nanjing Manifesto of January 5, 1912. See ibid., 1:191n.

84. Ibid., 1:88–94; cf. Onogawa, "Shinmatsu no shisō" and Wang, *Chinese Intellectuals and the West*, p. 19.

85. Price, *Russia and the Chinese Revolution*, p. 119; and Wang, *Chinese Intellectuals and the West*, p. 233.

86. Cheng, "T'ung-meng-hui," p. 67; Wang, *Chinese Intellectuals and the West*, p. 232.

87. Wang, *Chinese Intellectuals and the West*, p. 233. Liang, however, argued that "nationalism should be broadened to include the Manchus in a struggle against the foreign 'races,' that only enlightened despotism could achieve the supreme goal of strengthening China, and that economic progress in China depended far more upon industrial than agricultural productivity." See ibid., pp. 224–225, 248; Scalapino and Schiffrin, "Early Socialist Currents," pp. 321–342; and Levenson, *Confucian China and Its Modern Fate*, 1:97.

88. Gregor and Chang, "*Nazionalfascismo*," p. 24; Schiffrin, *Origins of the Chinese*

Revolution, pp. 42–44; Sharmon, *Sun Yat-sen* (1968), pp. 74–79; and Sun Yat-sen, *Guofu quanji,* 1:A174–175.

89. Sharmon, *Sun Yat-sen,* pp. 87–88.

90. Ibid., pp. 118, 286.

91. See Lin, *Crisis of Chinese Consciousness,* chap. 2; Chow, *May Fourth Movement* (1967), chap. 1; Kondō, "'Minkoku' to Ri," p. 289; and Maruyama, "Ajia nashonarizumu," p. 17.

92. Koyama, *Nihon Marukusu-shugi shi,* pp. 15–16; Sakai, *Nihon shakai-shugi undō shiwa,* 6:284; Kublin, *Asian Revolutionary,* pp. 194–196; and Notehelfer, *Kōtoku Shūsui,* chap. 6.

93. Baron, "Origins of Russian Marxism," p. 47 (Baron's italics).

94. Arahata, *Kanson jiden,* pp. 242–243; Sakai, *Nihon shakai-shugi undō shiwa,* 6:284.

95. Sakai, *Nihon shakai-shugi undō shiwa,* 6:285; and Arahata, *Kanson jiden,* pp. 132–148. Koyama argues that this anarchist influence accounted for "the inconclusiveness of the 'Bolshevik' standpoint" of Sakai, Yamakawa, and Arahata (Koyama, *Nihon Marukusu-shugi shi,* pp. 16–18). Notably, all three subsequently seceded from the JCP in defiance of Comintern authority to form the dissident Rōnō-ha in 1927–1928. (See chapter 6 this volume.) One effect of this anarchist influence was to relegate the study of Marxian economics to academics outside the socialist movement, such as Kawakami Hajime.

96. Koyama, *Nihon Marukusu-shugi shi,* pp. 18–19.

97. Tanaka, *Takabatake Motoyuki,* pp. 57–60. Yet shortly after the Bolshevik revolution, Takabatake maintained that he had always opposed, or at least resisted, the dominance of anarchism within the movement. He argued that the anarchist tendency mistakenly "saw the state, authority, and, furthermore, politics in general, all in the sense of being the morality, or rather the organ of the bourgeoisie," and, therefore, it turned socialists and workers away from political activity (Takabatake Motoyuki, "Kokka shakai-shugi no hitsuzen-sei," pp. 178–179).

98. Tanaka, *Takabatake Motoyuki,* chaps. 3–5; and Tanaka, "Takabatake Motoyuki ron," pp. 41–44.

99. Tanaka, "Takabatake Motoyuki ron," p. 38; Kikuchi, *Roshiya kakumei,* p. 261.

100. Arahata, "Roshiya kakumei no koro," p. 181; Bernstein, "Early Japanese Socialists," pp. 330–331; and Arahata, *Kanson jiden,* p. 384.

101. Arahata, *Kanson jiden,* p. 384; Arahata, "Roshiya kakumei," p. 180; Inumaru, "Nihon Marukusu-shugi no genryū," 2:8; Arahata, *Nihon shakai-shugi undō shi,* p. 113; and Takeuchi, "Nihon no Marukusu-shugi," pp. 17–18.

102. Kazama, *Nihon Kyōsantō no rekishi,* 1:22, quoted in Durkee, "Communist International and Japan," p. 12; and Inumaru, "Nihon Marukusu-shugi no genryū," p. 8; and Bernstein, "Early Japanese Socialists," pp. 333–335.

103. Quoted in Kikuchi, "Roshiya kakumei," p. 269; and Kondō, *Ichi museifu-shugisha no kaisō,* p. 79.

104. Tanaka, "Takabatake Motoyuki ron," pp. 39–40; Arahata, *Kanson jiden,* pp. 384–385; cf. Bernstein, "Russian Revolution," pp. 331–332.

105. Takabatake found the discomfort of Japan's anarchists "rather gratifying" (Takabatake, "Kokka shakai-shugi no hitsuzen-sei," p. 125).

106. Sakai, *Nihon shakai-shugi undō shiwa,* p. 289.

107. Tanaka, "Takabatake Motoyuki ron," pp. 38–39, 44–45; and Tanaka, *Takabatake Motoyuki,* p. 120.

108. Takabatake, "Kokka shakai-shugi no hitsuzen-sei," pp. 175, 178–180; Tanaka, "Takabatake Motoyuki ron," pp. 41–44.

109. Tanaka, *Takabatake Motoyuki*, pp. 121–123, 142.

110. Bernstein, "Early Japanese Socialists," p. 333. Yamakawa, "Roshiya no shihai kaikyū," 5:249–53; Yamakawa, "Sobieto seiji no tokushitsu to sono hihan," 2:386, 389–390, 393–396; and Koyama, *Nihon Marukusu-shugi shi*, p. 20; and Inumaru, "Nihon Marukusu-shugi no genryū," pp. 11–12.

111. Tanaka, "Takabatake Motoyuki ron," p. 46; cf. Arahata, "Yamakawa Hitoshi ron."

112. Bernstein, "Early Japanese Socialists," p. 335.

113. Takeuchi, "Nihon no Marukusu-shugi," p. 18; Koyama, *Nihon Marukusu-shugi shi*, p. 19; Moriya, *Nihon Marukusu-shugi*, p. 14n.; Inumaru, "Nihon Marukusu-shugi no genrū," pp. 9–11; Sakai, *Nihon shakai-shugi undō shiwa*, p. 281; and Yamakawa, "Dai-san Intanashonaru" 3:236–239.

114. Moriya, *Nihon Marukusu-shugi riron*, p. 15; Takeuchi, "Nihon no Marukusu-shugi," p. 18; Sakai, *Nihon shakai-shugi undō shiwa*, p. 288; and Koyama, *Nihon Marukusu-shugi shi*, pp. 22–23.

115. Moriya, *Nihon Marukusu-shi shugi riron*, pp. 15–16; Inumaru, "Nihon Marukusu-shugi no genrū," p. 30; and Koyama, *Nihon Marukusu-shugi shi*, p. 23.

116. Durkee, "Communist International and Japan," pp. 47–48; and Tateyama, *Nihon Kyōsantō kenkyo hishi* p. 199.

117. Rodinson, *Islam and Capitalism*, p. 1.

118. See Levenson, *Confucian China and Its Modern Fate*, vol. 2, chap. 9; Satoi, "Ri Taishō no shuppatsu," pp. 15–18; and Shimamoto, "Go-shi ki no eikyō," p. 27; cf. Kondō, "'Minkoku' to Ri," p. 20.

119. Shimamoto, "Go-shi ki no eikyō," p. 26.

120. Meisner, *Li Ta-chao* (1977), p. 99.

121. Ibid., p. 61.

122. Nomura, "Chūgoku ni okeru Marukusu-shugi," p. 1653.

123. Meisner, *Li Ta-chao*, p. 60.

124. Ibid., p. 113.

125. On Lu Xun's iconoclasm, see Lin, *Crisis of Chinese Consciousness*, chap. 6.

126. See ibid., chap. 4.

127. See Li, "Dong-Xi wenming genben zhi yidian," first published in the July 1918 issue of *Yanzhi jikan* (Political review), and contained in [Li Dazhao], *Shouchang wenji* (Collected works of [Li] Shou-chang), pp. 37–48. Chen's article treating this subject most directly was "Dong-Xi minzu," 1:35–40. See also Chen, "Wuren zuihou zhi juewu," 1:49–56 passim; and idem, "Jinri Zhongguo zhi zhengzhi wenti," 1:224–225.

128. See Chen, "Xianfu yu kongjiao," 2:103–111; and idem, "Zai lun kongjiao wenti," 1:129–134.

129. This is not to underestimate the important differences between familial structures in China and Japan. Among other key variations, as noted in chapter 3 this volume, in Japan filial piety reinforced loyalty to the state. See also the illuminating Japanese treatment of the Chinese family in comparative historical perspective in Shiga Shūzō, *Chūgoku kazoku hō no genri* (Principles of Chinese family law) (Tokyo: Sōbun-sha, 1967).

130. Chen, "Dong-Xi minzu," 1:37–38; cf. Chen, "Rensheng zhenyi," 1:183–184. Those who rejected the West, such as neo-Confucian Liang Sou-ming, Chen alleged, were simply ignorant of Western civilization. Cf. Chen Ruoshui, "Liang Souming yu *Dong-Xi wenhua*," 1:217–225.

131. Li, "Dong-Xi wenming," quoted in Meisner, *Li Ta-chao*, pp. 46–47; and Li, "Xinjiu sichao zhi jizhan," pp. 155–157. See also Kondō, "'Minkoku' to Ri," pp. 291–292 (19–20); and Peng, "Wusi shiqi," pp. 50–51.

132. Li, "Fa O koming chih pichiao kuan," quoted in Meisner, *Li Ta-chao,* p. 64.

133. See Hegel, *Philosophy of History.*

134. See Knei-paz, *Leon Trotsky,* chaps. 3, 4.

135. See Li, "Qingchun," pp. 65–76; Li, "Jin," pp. 93–96; Li, "Xinde! Jiude!" pp. 97–100; and Li, "Qingnian yu laoren," pp. 1–4. Cf. Nomura, "'Go-shi' jidai no shikō," pp. 292–293; and Maruyama, "Ri Taishō no shisō," pp. 53–54.

136. See Mao, "On Practice," pp. 65–84; and idem, "Reform Our Study," pp. 198–208.

137. A follower of Chen, Wang Fanxi, contends that it was not until after Chen was removed as CCP leader that he gained any true familiarity with Trotsky's writings. See Wang, "Chen Duxiu," pp. 163–164; cf. Kuo, *Ch'en Tu-hsiu,* p. 210.

138. Cf. Meisner, *Li Ta-chao,* pp. 47–48.

139. Levenson, *Confucian China and Its Modern Fate,* 1:125; Schwartz, *Rise of Mao,* pp. 17–18. See especially Chen, "Jiu sixiang yu guoti wenti," 1:147–149.

140. Peng, "Wusi shiqi," p. 48.

141. Meisner, *Li Ta-chao,* p. 37.

142. Nomura, "'Go-shi' jidai no shikō," pp. 21–22; Li, "Bolshevism de shengli," pp. 112–118.

143. Peng, "Wusi shiqi," pp. 52–53.

144. See Li, "Fa-E geming zhi bijiao guan," pp. 101–104. Li had also interpreted the February revolution in terms of a world tide of democratic change in Li, "Eguo da geming zhi yingxiang," pp. 81–82. See Shimamoto, "Go-shi ki no eikyō," pp. 28–29; and Nomura, "Kindai Chūgoku no shisōka," p. 181. Chen had made a similar effort. See Chen, "Eluosi geming," 1:144–145.

145. This is to be contrasted with Chen's early view that one should abstain from politics in the interest of pursuing cultural transformation first. Meisner, *Li Ta-chao,* pp. 91–95, 150–154; Zhang, *Li Dazhao tongzhi geming sixiang,* p. 28; and Maruyama, "Ri Taishō no shisō," pp. 48–49.

146. Ibid., p. 49.

147. Li, "Wo de Makesi-zhuyi guan," pp. 173–211; Zhang, *Li Dazhao tongzhi geming sixiang,* p. 38. Li's concern with the spiritual dimension was most pronounced in his "Jingshen jiefang," p. 309. For a more detailed discussion of this point in both Li's and Chen's thought, see Hoston, " 'Theology' of Liberation?" pp. 169–197.

148. Li, "Wo de Makesi-zhuyi guan," pp. 189–195. Cf. Nomura, "Kindai Chūgoku no shisōka," pp. 27–29, 31–32; and Kondō, "'Minkoku' to Ri," pp. 22–23.

149. Cf. Gao and Zhang, "Wusi yundong," p. 10.

150. Chen, "Eluosi geming," pp. 144–145.

151. See Chen's critique of the reification of states in Chen, "Ouxiang" 1:229; cf. Peng, "Wusi shiqi," p. 57.

152. Nomura, "Chūgoku ni okeru Marukusu-shugi," p. 1653; and Kuo, *Ch'en Tu-hsiu,* p. 81.

153. Nomura, "Chūgoku ni okeru Marukusu-shugi," p. 1653; and Peng, "Wusi shiqi," p. 60.

154. Chen, "Shiyue geming yu Zhongguo minzu jiefang yundong," p. 1234.

155. Many of Chen's articles are collected in *Shehui-zhuyi taolun ji.* See Scalapino and Yü, *Chinese Anarchist Movement,* pp. 55–59.

156. This date is in conflict; the party's official founding date is July 1921. See Chow, *May Fourth Movement,* p. 248.

157. See [Qu], "Qu Shengbai da Chen Duxiu shu," pp. 109–119; and "Qu Shengbai zai da Chen Duxiu shu," pp. 125–127.

158. *Dictionnaire biographique*, s.v. Liu Sifu and Li Shizeng.

159. See Chen, "Shehui-zhuyi piping," pp. 74–96; [Chen] "Chen Duxiu zai da Qu Shengbai shu," *Shehui-zhuyi taolun ji*, pp. 119, 124; [Chen,] "Chen Duxiu san da Qu Shengbai shu," pp. 137–138; [Jiang], "Wuzhengfu-zhuyi zhi jiepou," p. 14ff., reprinted in *Shehui-zhuyi taolun ji*, pp. 219–237.

160. Chen, "Shehui-zhuyi ruhe zai Zhongguo kaishi jinxing," p. 89.

161. Wu, "Women weishenme zhuzhang gongchan-zhuyi," pp. 23–30; idem, "Duoqu zhengquan," pp. 3–9; and C. T. [pseud. of Li Da?], "Women yao zenyang gan shehui geming," pp. 9–27.

162. Chen, "Tan zhengzhi," pp. 1–15.

163. Wu, "Duoqu zhengquan," passim; C. T., "Women yao zenmeyang gan shehui geming," pp. 9, 27; and Li [Jiang], "Shehui geming de shangque," p. 6.

164. Chen, "Chinese Style Anarchism," *Xin qingnian* (New youth) 9, no. 1 (May 1, 1921): 5–6, cited by Scalapino and Yü, *Chinese Anarchist Movement*, p. 57. Cf. Nii, "Museifu-shugi ron," 7:1.

165. Zhou, "Gongchan-zhuyi yu Zhongguo," p. 8.

166. Li [Jiang], "Shehui geming de shangque," pp. 4–5; and Wu, "Women weishenme zhuzhang gongchan-zhuyi," passim.

167. See Zhou [Wu], "Shiyue geming," pp. 1–8.

168. Chen, "Shehui-zhuyi piping," pt. 1, pp. 74–77, pt. 2, pp. 78–86, passim; Chen, "Women xiangxin hezhong shehui-zhuyi," pp. 19–20; and Chen, "Shehui-zhuyi ruhe zai Zhongguo kaishi jinxing," passim.

169. Zhou [Wu], "Gongchan-zhuyi yu Zhongguo," p. 8.

170. "Chen Duxiu san da Qu Shengbai shu," pp. 140–141.

171. *Dictionnaire biographique*, s.v. Li Shizeng, Wu Zhihui.

172. Zhou [Wu], "Gongchan-zhuyi yu Zhongguo," p. 8.

173. Zhou [Wu], "Eguo geming shi shibai le me?" p. 21.

174. Subsequently, as Chen became more and more deeply involved in Trotskyism and the critique of Stalinism, he might have wished to retract his earlier emphasis on the need for strong centralized political and economic institutions after a socialist revolution. Writing to Chinese students abroad in 1940, he identified Stalinism more closely with fascism. See Chen, "Gei xiliu de xin," pp. 68–77, and the conclusion to chapter 5 this volume.

175. Peng, "Wusi shiqi," p. 47; compare Chen's vision of China's national revolution as part of a tide of world revolution in "Shehui-zhuyi ruhe zai Zhongguo kaishi jinxing."

176. Li, "Jieji jingzheng yu huzhu," pp. 222–225.

177. Li, "You jingji-shang jieshi," pp. 295–302.

178. See Selden, *Yenan Way*, chap. 4, especially pp. 124–125.

179. Qu Qiubai, "Liening-zhuyi yu Zhongguo de guomin geming," 1300 and passim; cf. Meisner, *Li Da-chao*, pp. 65–70.

180. Li, "Da Yaxiya-zhuyi yu xin Yaxiya-zhuyi," pp. 127–129; Li "Zai lun xin Yaxiya-zhuyi," pp. 278–282; cf. Li "Pan . . . ism zhi shibai yu Democracy zhi shengli," pp. 105–108; and Li "Yaxiya qingnian de guangming yundong," pp. 327–329; Kondō, "'Minkoku' to Ri," p. 23; and Peng, "Wusi shiqi," p. 56.

181. Shimamoto, "Go-shi ki ni okeru," pp. 31–32.

182. North, *Moscow and Chinese Communists*, p. 56.

183. Swearingen, "Japanese Communist Party and the Comintern," pp. 14–17, 24–25; Durkee, "Communist International and Japan," pp. 27–31; and Inumaru, "Nihon Marukusu-shugi no genryū," pp. 12–13.

184. Inumaru, "Nihon Marukusu-shugi no genryū," p. 30.

185. See Bukharin, "K teorii imperialisticheskogo gosudarstva."

186. Bernstein, "Early Japanese Socialists," pp. 342–344.

187. "State socialism" and "national socialism" are used interchangeably here as translations of *kokka shakai-shugi*. The nationalist and statist components of Takabatake's thought were so closely intertwined that neither translation alone is adequate.

188. Takabatake, *Marukusu-gaku kaisetsu,* pp. 85–98.

189. Takabatake, "'Puroretaria kokka' no ronri-teki hatan," p. 106. Lassalle's concept of state socialism was a program of evolutionary socialism achieved on the basis of the existing Prussian state. He tried to influence Chancellor Otto von Bismarck to adopt his 1862 Arbeiter Programm (workers' program) of universal suffrage and workers' cooperatives. Lassalle could justify socialism within the context of the state, because, like Hegel, he believed that only the state could "help the development of the human race toward freedom" (see Russell, *German Social Democracy,* p. 54; Footman, *Ferdinand Lassalle,* and Kolakowski, *Main Currents of Marxism,* pp. 238–244).

190. Takabatake, *Jiko o kataru,* pp. 75–76; Tanaka, "Takabatake Motoyuki ron," p. 56; and Takeda "Kakumei shisō to tennō-sei," pp. 272–276.

191. Takabatake, "'Puroretaria kokka' no ronri-teki hatan," pp. 86–92.

192. Ibid., p. 95.

193. Takabatake, "Kokka shakai-shugi no hitsuzen-sei," pp. 199, 190–200.

194. Takabatake, "'Puroretaria kokka' no riron-teki hatan," pp. 95–96; Takabatake, "Shakai-shugi bunrui-jō no ichi kōsatsu," p. 104.

195. Tanaka, "Takabatake Motoyuki ron," pp. 50–54.

196. Takabatake, "Kokka shakai-shugi no hitsuzen-sei," p. 202.

197. Takabatake, "Shakai-shugi bunri-jō no ichi kōsatsu," pp. 109–110.

198. Takabatake, "Kokka shakai-shugi no seisaku," pp. 214–218.

199. Takabatake, *Kokka shakai-shugi taigi,* pp. 21–22; idem, "Kokka shakai-shugi no seisaku," pp. 219–225.

200. Yamakawa, "Kokka shakai-shugi to rōdō mondai," 2:275–285; and Yamakawa, "Sobieto seiji no tokushitsu," 2:386–408.

201. Tanaka, "Takabatake Motoyuki ron," pp. 51, 58, 84n.

202. Ibid., p. 50; and Takeda, "Kakumei shisō to tennō-sei," pp. 282–285.

203. Yamakawa, "Kokka shakai-shugi to rōdō mondai," 2:276.

204. Takabatake, "Teikoku-shugi no hatten,", pp. 270–273; and Takabatake, "Gunkoku-shugi," pp. 247–248.

205. Takabatake, *Kokka shakai-shugi taigi,* p. 2.

206. Takabatake, "Gunkoku-shugi," pp. 250–252.

207. Tanaka, "Takabatake Motoyuki ron," p. 60; and Takeda, "Kakumei shisō to tennō-sei," pp. 279–281.

208. Tanaka, "Takabatake Motoyuki ron," p. 60.

209. Takabatake, "Gunkoku-shugi," pp. 253–259.

210. Ibid., pp. 247–248; and Takabatake, "Kokka shakai-shugi no seisaku," pp. 216–219.

211. *Konsaisu jinmei jiten,* s.v. Dai Jitao; and Mast, "Tai Chi-t'ao, Sunism and Marxism," p. 228.

212. See Schiffrin, "Enigma of Sun Yat-sen," pp. 465–466.

213. See Dai [Dai Jitao], "Jinri zhi zhengzhiguan," pp. 83–86. (Dai Tianchou is the name Dai was given at birth.) For additional details on Dai's activities during this period, see Bernal, "Tzu-yu-tang and Tai Chi-t'ao."

214. Dai [Dai Jitao], "Dushi zui'e lun," sec. 2.

215. See Dai [Dai Jitao], "Bingli zhuanzhi zhong zhi zhenghaichao," 2:119–122, and "Bingli zhuanzhi zhi da chenggong," 2:123–125. See also the insightful discussion in Mast and Saywell, "Revolution Out of Tradition," pp. 75–76.

216. Mast and Saywell, "Revolution Out of Tradition," p. 77 (Mast's and Saywell's italics).

217. Dai [Dai Jitao], *Riben lun,* pp. 166ff; Lukin, "Ideologiia Kitaiskovo natsionalizma," p. 174.

218. Mast, "Tai Chi-t'ao, Sunism, and Marxism," pp. 229–233.

219. See Dai [Dai Jitao], "Dongfang wenti yu shije wenti," 4:1729–1745.

220. This essay, entitled "Cong jingji-shang guan Zhongguo de luan yuan," was published in *Gaizao* (Construction) in September 1919. See the discussion in Mast, "Tai Chi-t'ao, Sunism, and Marxism," pp. 239–240.

221. Although Mast's account asserts the contrary (Mast, "Tai Chi-t'ao, Sunism, and Marxism," p. 241), Dai, indeed, cited "imperialism" as such a major factor in the difficulties of Eastern societies in China's position in the early 1920s. See, for example, his 1924 "Dongfang wenti yu shijie wenti."

222. See Mast, "Tai Chi-t'ao, Sunism, and Marxism," pp. 241–245.

223. Dai, "Dongfang wenti yu shijie wenti."

224. See Mast and Saywell, "Revolution Out of Tradition," pp. 84–87.

225. Dai [Dai Jitao], "Guomin geming yu Zhongguo Guomindang," pp. 425, 427–428.

226. Cf. Li's application of the notion of class struggle to the international arena. Meisner, *Li Ta-chao,* p. 145.

227. Dai drew a very confusing distinction between "statism" (*guojia-zhuyi*) and "nationalism" (*minzu-zhuyi,* Sun's first People's Principle). Statism, he argued, was based on military power, whereas the nation was based on culture. He maintained that he was not a statist, inasmuch as he held an inclusive notion of "China" as including minority peoples and repudiated a "statism" that was based on the military supremacy of a single "nationality" and endeavored to invade other nationalities' countries. See Dai [Dai Jitao], "Sanmin-zhuyi de guojia-guan," pp. 53, 60–62. Of course, as the discussion to follow demonstrates, Dai was certainly statist in the sense that he affirmed a powerful national state for China.

228. Lukin, "Ideologiia kitaiskovo natsionalizma," p. 169.

229. Dai [Dai Jitao], *Riben lun,* pp. 10–11, 79–82.

230. Ibid., 165–166, 170. Dai, "Guomin geming yu Zhongguo Guomindang," pp. 448, 426. Note that Dai's emphasis on the importance of how Chinese think about their problems to their ability to resolve them resonates with Lin Yü-sheng's observations on this as a general intellectual tendency among late-Qing and early-Republican Chinese intellectuals (Lin, *Crisis of Chinese Consciousness*).

231. Dai [Dai Jitao], "Guomin geming yu Zhongguo Guomindang," pp. 450–452.

232. Ibid., p. 448.

233. See Sun [Yat-sen], *"Three Principles,"* pp. 248, 252. Cf. Chang, "'Fascism' and Modern China," p. 559.

234. Sun saw "George's single tax system and the appropriation of the unearned increment" as "a painless method of financing the industrial revolution—riches for all, poverty for none" (Scalapino and Schiffrin, "Early Socialist Currents," p. 325). On George's influence on Sun's thinking concerning land rights equalization, see Bernal, *Chinese Socialism to 1907;* and Schiffrin, "Sun Yat-sen's Early Land Policy," pp. 549–564.

235. Feng, *Geming ishi* 3:216, cited by Scalapino and Schiffrin, "Early Socialist Currents," pp. 324–325.

236. Bernal, *Chinese Socialism to 1907,* pp. 72–73.

237. Scalapino and Schiffrin, "Early Socialist Currents," pp. 327–330.
238. Dai[Dai Jitao], "Guomin geming yu Zhongguo Guomindang," p. 449.
239. Dai[Dai Jitao], "Sanmin-zhuyi zhi guojia-guan," p. 67.
240. Bernstein, "Early Japanese Socialists," p. 347.
241. Yamakawa, "Sakushu kuni to hisakushu kuni," 5:239.
242. Mast suggests that one motivation for this proposal by Dai was a preference for a broader alliance over one solely with the Soviet Union in which inhered the possibility of Soviet domination (see Mast, "An Intellectual Biography of Tai Chi-t'ao," pp. 231–233).
243. Kida, *Meiji no risō*, p. 131.
244. Maruyama, "Ajia nashonarizumu," pp. 19–21.
245. Cf. Kawakami Hajime's view that the state was not merely "the superstructure standing atop an economic structure" but "form[ed] one part of the economic structure as the basis of the society" (Kawakami, *Marukusu-shugi no tetsugaku-teki kiso*, p. 271.)

CHAPTER 6

1. *Nihon shihon-shugi hattatsu shi kōza*, 1:1.
2. For a full-length study of the debate on Japanese capitalism (*Nihon shihon-shugi ronsō*) in English, see Hoston, *Crisis of Development in Prewar Japan*. Almost all works on the debate in Japanese are written from the perspective of one of the two factions. Among the many excellent studies from the Kōza-ha and Rōnō-ha perspectives, respectively, see Koyama, *Nihon shihon-shugi ronsō shi* (History of the debate on Japanese capitalism); and Kojima, *Nihon shihon-shugi ronsō shi*.
3. Many of its contributions were imported into China and were to influence the Controversy on Chinese Social History (*Zhongguo shehui shi lunzhan*). See chapter 7 in this volume.
4. See Hoston, *Crisis of Development in Prewar Japan*, chap. 9; and idem, "Between Theory and Practice," pp. 175–207.
5. The most influential scholars descended from associates of the prewar Rōnō-ha belong to the economic school of Uno Kōzō (1897–1977) and his student Ōuchi Tsutomu (1918–), son of prewar Rōnō-ha scholar Ōuchi Hyōe. Uno scholar Itoh Makoto has estimated that "there are probably around two hundred professional scholars who could be classified as Uno theorists—or about one-fifth of the total of Japanese Marxist economists" (Itoh, *Value and Crisis*, p. 38). The Uno school has focused on three areas: the development of the pure theory of capitalism, the stage theory of the development of world capitalism, and the analysis of the economics of advanced capitalism. For overviews of the Uno school, see Mawatari, "Uno School"; Itō, *Gendai no Marukusu keizaigaku*, pp. 114–131; and Sekine, "Uno-riron." In the Kōza-ha tradition, the most significant and promising theoretical developments have been made by the *shimin shakai ron* (Civil Society) School led by Uchida Yoshihiko and Hirata Kiyoaki. This school posits the centrality of civil society—a society that has been liberated of the hierarchical and oppressive bonds of premodern communities and in which individuality is affirmed—as a key concept for criticizing contemporary Japanese capitalist society. I am indebted to Yamada Toshio for introducing me to the Civil Society School. See Yamada, Masaki, and Shirogane, "Japanese Marxism Today," pp. 78–85; Yamada, "Shimin shakai no genzai," pp. 95–115; and Yamada, "Les tendances du marxisme japonais," pp. 38–41.
6. See, for example, Tsuchiya, *Nihon shihon-shugi shi ronshū*, p. 6; Tsushima, *"Nihon shihon-shugi ronsō" shiron*, p. 6; Sano, "Sano Manabu jōshinsho—Kaitō-ha ni tsuite" (Sano Manabu's written statement: On the Dissolutionist Faction), handwritten, February

1931, pt. 1 passim; Sano, "Gokuchū-ki," pp. 94–95; and Kobayashi, *Tenkōsha no shisō to seikatsu,* pp. 7–8.

7. Interview with Fukushima Shingo, Tokyo, July 30, 1979; and Kuno and Tsurumi, *Gendai Nihon no shisō,* (1978) pp. 36–37.

8. Inumaru, "Nihon Marukusu-shugi no genryū," 2:18.

9. The 1927 Theses called for an "ideologically tempered, trained Leninist centralized mass communist party with resolute faith" ("Nihon mondai ni kansuru ketsugi [ni-nana nen teize]," p. 45); cf., the discussion of the party's role in the 1932 Theses. See "Nihon ni okeru jōsei (san-ni teize)," passim, especially pp. 95–98, 101.

10. Norman, *Japan's Emergence.*

11. In scholarly circles, the Kōza-ha's influence has always been particularly pronounced in comparative history and political science. The Rōnō-ha influence has been greater in studies of the dynamics of advanced capitalist economics. Interview with Onabe Teruhiko, Tokyo, August 1, 1979; interview with Minobe Ryōkichi, Tokyo, July 30, 1979. Cf. the discussion of Marxist influence on Japanese academia in *Japanese Studies of Modern China,* pp. xvii-xix.

12. Ōishi, "Kaisetsu," p. 10.

13. For more complete treatments of Takahashi's role in precipitating the debate on Japanese capitalism, see Hoston, *Crisis of Development in Prewar Japan,* chap. 4; and idem, "Marxism and Japanese Expansionism," pp. 1–30.

14. These were identified as peculiarities of the Japanese state both in Comintern documents and scholarship by nonparticipants in the debate beginning with the founding of the JCP in 1922. See "Nihon kokka kikō-zu no kaisetsu," 4:369–379, especially pp. 371–372. Cf. "Nihon Kyōsantō kōryō sōan," p. 5; Voichinsukii [Voitinsky], "Nihon ni okeru kaikyūsen," p. 10; and "Nihon ni kansuru ketsugi (ni-nana nen teize)" pp. 30–33, all in *Kominterun Nihon ni kansuru teize shū.* Authorship of both the 1922 Draft Program and the 1927 Theses is generally attributed to Nikolai Bukharin.

15. "Nihon Kyōsantō kōryō sōan," p. 5.

16. For an examination of the debate on the economic issues of land rents and agrarian relations, see Hoston, *Crisis of Development in Prewar Japan,* chap. 8; Yasuba, "Debate on Japanese Capitalism," pp. 63–82; and Beckmann, "Japanese Adaptations," 3:103–114.

17. See Yamakawa, "Seiji-teki sensen e!" 19:174–218.

18. Interview with Arahata Kanson, Takahashi Masao, and Watanabe Fumitarō, Tokyo, August 17, 1979; quotation from Uchida and Nakano, *Nihon shihon-shugi ronsō,* (1952), p. 33.

19. Maruyama, "Kuga Katsunan," pp. 291–295, and Maruyama, "Meiji kokka no shisō," pp. 213–215, 231–232.

20. On the family state concept, see Ishida, *Meiji seiji shisō shi kenkyū,* pt. 1, especially chap. 1, sec. 2, and also chapter 1 of this volume.

21. Interview with Ishida Takeshi, Tokyo, August 11, 1979; interview with Ukai Nobushige, Tokyo, July 23, 1979.

22. See Hori, "Meiji shoki no kokkaron," pp. 711–744 passim. Hozumi studied German public law at Heidelberg, Berlin, and Strausburg universities in Germany from 1884–1888. British constitutional theory is more often identified with the progressive constitutional monarchic movement and the party movement. Although Hozumi's orthodoxy on the Meiji constitution was heavily influenced by his work in Germany, his emperor-centered concept of the Japanese state was firmly vested in the late Tokugawa *kokutai* idea. See Nakase, "Meiji kenpō moto," pp. 62, 66; Ishida, *Nihon kindai shisō shi,* p. 166; and Suzuki, *Nihon kenpōgaku shi kenkyū,* pt. 1.

23. Kawakami Hajime noted that although university professors were often regarded as advocates of dangerous ideas in the 1920s, and their publications were often banned, for the most part censorship was desultory; thus, university professors enjoyed a broad range of freedom in their work. This circumstance reflected "the authority/prestige that Japanese professors enjoyed in society despite the rule of a militaristic police-type imperial regime." See Kawakami, *Omoide*, pp. 213–214.

24. Kawakami Hajime asserted in his autobiography, "It was not until at least the beginning of the Shōwa era that Marxism was truly understood in Japan," (*Jijōden*, 1:197).

25. Noro, along with publisher Iwata Yoshimichi, conceived the *Kōza* but was arrested in November 1933 and died the following year at age thirty-four of illness under the strain of interrogation. See Koyama, *Nihon Marukusu-shugi shi*, pp. 66–68.

26. Yamakawa's organization theory lacked any "notion of a vanguard party." See Inumaru, "Nihon Marukusu-shugi no genryū," pp. 56–58; see Yamakawa, "Musan-kaikyū undō no hōkō tenkan," pp. 71–81; and Yamakawa, "Nihon ni okeru demokurashii," pp. 105–135. Cf. Yamazaki, "'Shakai-shugi e no michi'," 1:85; and Koyama and Kishimoto, *Nihon no hi-kyōsantō Marukusu-shugisha*, pp. 137–138.

27. See Nakaura, "Nihon Marukusu-shugi no shisō hōhō," especially 1:80–82; and for a description of Fukumotoism as a combination of Lenin's organization theory with Lukács's emphasis on consciousness, see Takeuchi, "Nihon no Marukusu-shugi," pp. 28–29. Cf. Koyama, *Nihon Marukusu-shugi shi*, pp. 30–31; Watanabe, "Fukumoto Kazuo," 1:145–201; and Nagaoka, *Nihon shihon-shugi ronsō no gunzō*, pp. 12–18.

28. Koyama, *Nihon Marukusu-shugi shi*, pp. 33–34.

29. Koyama and Kishimoto, *Nihon no hikyōsantō Marukusu-shugisha*, pp. 11–12.

30. Kato, "Taishō Democracy," p. 218.

31. Yamamura, "Japanese Economy," p. 309.

32. Ohkawa and Rosovsky, *Japanese Economic Growth*, pp. 96, 98.

33. Ohkawa and Rosovsky, *Japanese Economic Growth*, p. 33, table 2.3, and p. 25, table 2.1.

34. Lockwood, *Economic Development of Japan*, pp. 56–57.

35. Takabatake, "Teikoku-shugi no kisū," pp. 286–290.

36. Moriya, *Nihon Marukusu-shugi*, p. 21; Shakai Keizai Rōdō Kenkyūjo, *Nihon shihon-shugi ronsō shi*, p. 6; and interview with Nakamura Takafusa, Tokyo, July 11, 1979.

37. Matsushima, "Nihon ni okeru Marukishizumu no tenkai," p. 9.

38. For a biography that treats the private and psychological aspects of Kawakami's life more than the themes of his Marxism as part of these general trends in Japanese Marxism, see Bernstein, *Japanese Marxist*. The bibliography by Amano Keitarō helps to illuminate some of these themes: *Kawakami Hajime hakushi bunkenshi*. Two other essays that are helpful in this respect are Fujita, "Aru Marukusu-shugisha," pp. 64–87; and Ishida, "Kawakami Hajime ni okeru itan e no michi," pp. 1–18.

39. Kawakami, *Jijōden*, 1:153–157; Bernstein, *Japanese Marxist*, chap. 3 passim.

40. This may be likened to Chinese Marxist Li Dazhao's notion of "the dual-faceted reconstruction of body and soul," the need for spiritual change to accompany Marxist prescriptions for change in social organization. For an extended interpretation of the significance of this similarity between Chinese and Japanese Marxism, see Hoston, "'Theology' of Liberation?" pp. 165–221. In both Li's and Kawakami's humanitarianism may be found the influence of Leo Tolstoy. Itō Shōshin's philosophy was "an amalgam of Buddhism, Christianity, and Tolstoyan humanism—Itō had also [like Kawakami himself] read Tolstoy's *My Religion*" (Bernstein, *Japanese Marxist*, p. 46). Li seems to have been influ-

enced by Tolstoy's ideas concerning the reconstruction of rural life. See Li's "Qingnian yu nongcun," pp. 146–150; and Shimamoto, "Goshi-ki no eikyō," pp. 32–35.

41. Kushida later became embroiled in the economic aspects of the debate on Japanese capitalism on the side of the Rōnō-ha. At this time, he had already immersed himself in the study of Marxism and would come to produce a translation of *The Poverty of Philosophy* (Kawakami Hajime to Kushida Tamizō, June 24, 1923, Kawakami Hajime, *Kawakami Hajime yori Kushida Tamizō e no tegami*, pp. 117–118). Fukumoto Kazuo was among those who took Kawakami to task for his emphasis on morality. Not known for his skills in interpersonal relations, Fukumoto's attack was so harsh and abrasive that it merely alienated Kawakami (Kawakami, *Jijōden*, 1:195; cf. 1:188).

42. Fujita, "Aru Marukusu-shugisha," p. 84; Kawakami, *Jijōden*, 4:123.

43. Kawakami did endeavor to rid himself of these idealist trends in his thought. In the first issue of *Shakai mondai kenkyū* (January 1919), Kawakami wrote of the thought of Robert Owens, repudiating Owens's "humanitarian thought" (Kawakami, *Jijōden*, 1:159). On the founding of *Shakai mondai kenkyū*, see Kawakami, *Jijōden*, 1:221–222.

44. Amano, *Kawakami Hajime hakushi bunkenshi*, pp. 193, 195, 197–198, 200–202.

45. Kawakami, *Jijōden*, 1:159–160.

46. See Moriya, *Nihon Marukusu-shugi riron*, p. 63; and Uyehara, *Leftwing Social Movements in Japan*, pp. 141–142.

47. The essay by Noro was published in three parts, in volumes 5 (1928), 7 (1928), and 13 (1929). Hattori Shisō's article appeared in two parts, published in volumes 4 (1928) and 5 (1928). (Uyehara, *Leftwing Social Movements in Japan*, pp. 141–142.)

48. Shakai Keizai Rōdō Kenkyūjo, *Nihon minshu kakumei ronsō shi*, p. 6.

49. Uyehara, *Leftwing Social Movements in Japan*, p. 144.

50. Ibid., p. 140.

51. Shakai Keizai Rōdō Kenkyūjo, *Nihon minshu kakumei ronsō shi*, pp. 6–7. Uyehara gives the date of publication of *Nihon shakai shi* as 1926 (Tokyo: Kaizō-sha) (*Leftwing Social Movements in Japan*, p. 140).

52. See Li, *The Introduction of Socialism into China*, pp. 66–68; Rong, "Xinhai geming-qian," pp. 5–12; and Scalapino and Schiffrin, "Early Socialist Currents," pp. 321–342.

53. See, especially, Sano, *Minzoku to kaikyū;* Hoston, "Transformation of Marxism," pp. 25–47; and idem, "*Ikkoku shakai-shugi.*"

54. Uyehara, *Leftwing Social Movements in Japan*, p. 140.

55. Many of these articles, dated 1927 through 1930, are collected in Sano, *Seiji-ron.*

56. Takahashi, *Takahashi keizai riron*, 1:57–65, 108–111.

57. Ibid., 2:9–12.

58. Shōwa, *Burokku keizai ni kansuru kenkyū*, p. 2 (preface).

59. His postwar three-volume study of Japanese development is still very highly regarded and heavily cited even among Japanese Socialists who dispute Takahashi's Marxist credentials. See Takahashi, *Taishō-Shōwa zaikai no hendō*. Interview with Moriya Fumio, Tokyo, June 5, 1982; interview with Sakisaka Itsurō, Tokyo, June 7, 1982; interview with Takahashi Masao, Tokyo, June 4, 1982.

60. Takahashi, *Nihon shihon-shugi hattatsu shi*, p. 332; and Takahashi, *Nihon keizai no yukizumari*, pp. 17–21.

61. Takahashi, *Nihon shihon-shugi hattatsu shi*, pp. 332–338; and Takahashi, *Nihon keizai no yukizumari*, pp. 22–25, 36–37.

62. Takahashi, "Nihon shihon-shugi no teikoku-shugi–teki chi'i," *Taiyō* (The Sun)

(April 1927), pp. 5–6, quoted in Moriya, *Nihon Marukusu-shugi*, p. 76 (Moriya's italics); cf. Moriya, *Nihon Marukusu-shugi no rekishi to hansei*, p. 58.

63. Takahashi, "Nihon shihon-shugi," pp. 39, 45–47, 61–62, 91–92; Takahashi, *Nihon shihon-shugi hattatsu shi*, pp. 272–275, 371–373. Cf. the observations on the negative effects of Japan's temporary excess of international credits on the Japanese economy in Horie, "Foreign Capital and Japanese Capitalism," pp. 39–41; and Ohkawa and Rosovsky, *Japanese Economic Growth*, pp. 298–299.

64. Takabatake claimed that Lenin was a nationalist, if unconsciously so, and that the need for Japan to fear Russian imperialism did not vanish with the new Soviet regime. Citing Hobbes on the potential for war preceding the birth of the state and paralleling Bukharin's analysis of new possibilities for postcapitalist developments of the state unforeseen by Marx, Takabatake combined both premises in constructing his Japanese Marxist national socialism. See Hoston, "Marxism and National Socialism," p. 57; Tanaka, "Takabatake Motoyuki ron," pp. 33–86; Takeda, "Kakumei shisō to tennō-sei"; and Tanaka, *Takabatake Motoyuki*, passim.

65. Instead of heavy industry, fully 73 percent of Japan's exports were textiles from 1921 to 1925. This reflected the fact that no room remained in the international market for the expansion of Japanese heavy industry (Takahashi, "Nihon shihon-shugi no chi'i," pp. 53–66).

66. Takahashi, *Nihon shihon-shugi hattatsu shi*, pp. 371–373.

67. For Inomata's critiques, see Inomata, *Teikoku-shugi kenkyū;* and for Noro's, see Noro, *Puchi-teikoku-shugi ron hihan.* For summaries of these critiques, see Hoston, *Crisis of Development in Postwar Japan,* pp. 89–94; Baba, "Taigai kankei," pp. 96–99; and Kojima, *Nihon shihon-shugi ronsō shi,* pp. 140–146. Takahashi's intent to provoke the leadership of the Left was indicated in the title of the book in which his "petty imperialism" essays were reprinted: *Sayoku undō no riron-teki hōkai—Uyoku undō no riron-teki konkyo* (The theoretical collapse of the left-wing movement—The theoretical basis of the right-wing movement). After the furious storm that his petty imperialism essays aroused, Takahashi could no longer publish in *Marukusu-shugi, Shakai-kagaku,* or at his former publishing house, the left-wing Hakuyō-sha (Takahashi, *Takahashi keizai riron,* p. 114).

68. These, of course, were not the only Comintern pronouncements made during this decade. Others, such as the 1928 Moscow Theses, also stimulated discussion among Japan's Marxists, but space does not permit detailed discussion of all these directives and their impact here. For a more detailed discussion of the four theses treated here, see Hoston, *Crisis of Development in Prewar Japan,* chap. 3. In the mid-1980s additional Comintern documents concerning Japan have also been discovered and collected. See the important collection assembled by Murata, *Shiryōshū.*

69. See Cohen, *Bukharin and the Bolshevik Revolution*, pp. 25–43.

70. See Ohkawa and Rosovsky, *Japanese Economic Growth,* pp. 37–38; and Watanabe, "Industrialization," (1968) pp. 110–134.

71. See Said, *Orientalism,* especially pp. 153–156.

72. There are conflicting accounts of the drafting of the platform, but most agree on Bukharin's authorship. The first JCP meeting at Shakujii in November 1922 discussed the program, but the program was never formally adopted because the first large-scale arrests of JCP members occurred on June 5, 1923, before the party could complete its deliberations. See Nabeyama, *Watakushi wa kyōsantō o suteta,* pp. 61–62; Kazama, *Nihon Kyōsantō no rekishi,* pp. 1–4, 86–87.

73. Uchida and Nakano, *Nihon shihon-shugi ronsō,* p. 47.

74. Kazama, *Nihon Kyōsantō no rekishi,* pp. 89–90.

75. "Nihon Kyōsantō kōryō sōan," p. 5; cf. Uchida and Nakano, *Nihon shihon-shugi ronsō,* p. 48.

76. See Bernstein, "Early Japanese Socialists," p. 329.

77. Uchida and Nakano, *Nihon shihon-shugi ronsō,* p. 33.

78. See Yamakawa, "Musan-kaikyū undō no hōkō tenkan." Yamakawa and Arahata Kanson claimed that the "change in direction" occurred independently of the Comintern, but the Comintern influence is difficult to deny. See Beckmann and Okubo, *Japanese Communist Party,* p. 52.

79. Koyama, *Nihon Marukusu-shugi shi,* p. 27; and Yamakawa, *Yamakawa Hitoshi jiden,* p. 433.

80. Koyama, *Nihon Marukusu-shugi shi,* pp. 25–28; and Koyama and Kishimoto, *Nihon no hikyōsantō Marukusu-shughisha,* pp. 13–14, 138.

81. Nabeyama, *Watakushi wa kyōsantō o suteta,* pp. 117–119.

82. See Kazama, *Nihon Kyōsantō no rekishi,* pp. 164–165. According to one analysis, Fukumotoism was a combination of Lenin's organizational theory and Lukács's dialectical materialism as set forth in *History and Class Consciousness.* See Takeuchi, "Nihon no Marukusu-shugi," pp. 28–29.

83. Fukumoto, "Rōnō seitō to rōdō kumiai" (The workers' and farmers' political party and labor unions), *Marukusu-shugi* (Marxism) (January 1926): 10–13, quoted in Koyama and Kishimoto, *Nihon no hikyōsantō Marukusu-shughisha no rekishi,* pp. 1119–1120.

84. Kawakami, *Jijōden,* 1:196–197.

85. Kazama, *Nihon kyōsantō no rekishi,* p. 175.

86. "Nihon mondai ni kansuru ketsugi (ni-nana nen teize)" (Resolution on Japan [The 1927 Theses]), in *Kominterun Nihon ni kansuru teize shū* pp. 40–41, 43; and Swearingen, "Japanese Communist Party and the Comintern," p. 51.

87. "Nihon mondai ni kansuru ketsugi," p. 43.

88. See Degras, "United Front Tactics," pp. 15–18. Cf. Brandt, *Stalin's Failure in China,* (1966) chap. 6; and North, *Moscow and Chinese Communists,* chaps. 6, 7.

89. The "1927 Theses," in Beckmann and Okubo, *Japanese Communist Party,* p. 297.

90. Ibid., p. 298.

91. Yamakawa, "Shōnin shinsei."

92. Durkee, "The Communist International and Japan," pp. 95–96; and Koyama and Kishimoto, *Nihon no hikyōsantō Marukusu-shugisha,* pp. 141–142.

93. Tsushima, *"Nihon shihon-shugi ronso" shiron,* pp. 29–30.

94. Koyama and Kishimoto, *Nihon no hikyōsantō Marukusu-shugisha,* p. 142; cf. Koyama, *Nihon Marukusu-shugi shi,* pp. 43–44.

95. See Durkee, "Communist International and Japan," p. 152; and Uchida and Nakano, *Nihon shihon-shugi ronsō,* p. 24n.

96. The new theses began with an analysis of the crisis confronting world capitalism and its implications for Japan. See "Nihon Kyōsantō seiji teize sōan," pp. 46–49.

97. See Sano, "Mosukō to Nihon Kyōsantō no kankei shi," p. 101.

98. Tsushima, *"Nihon shihon-shugi ronsō" shiron,* p. 7.

99. Sano, "Mosukō to Nihon Kyōsantō no kankei shi," p. 101; and Beckmann, "Japanese Adaptations," p. 107.

100. Durkee, "Communist International and Japan," pp. 155–158, 178; and Beckmann and Okubo, *Japanese Communist Party,* pp. 196–205.

101. Koyama, *Nihon Marukusu-shugi shi,* p. 61.

102. Kuusinen had also penned a report on "Japanese Imperialism and the Nature of the Japanese Revolution." See "Nihon teikoku-shugi to Nihon kakumei," pp. 102–119.

103. Sano, "Mosukō to Nihon Kyōsantō no kankei shi," p. 102.

104. See Koyama, *Nihon Marukusu-shugi shi,* pp. 62–63; and "Shin teize happyō ni saishi dōshi shokun ni tsugu," p. 120, 121, 127.

105. Koyama, *Nihon Marukusu-shugi shi,* p. 57.

106. See "Nihon ni okeru jōsei to Nihon Kyōsantō (san-ni teize)," pp. 81–85.

107. Ibid.

108. Koyama, *Nihon Marukusu-shugi shi,* pp. 45–46. It should be stressed that Fukumotoism experienced no such revival partly because its themes did not resonate with the key concerns about the state and revolution that dominated the debate on Japanese capitalism.

109. Koyama and Kishimoto, *Nihon no hikyōsantō Marukusu-shugisha,* p. 132; Uchida and Nakano, *Nihon shihon-shugi ronsō,* pp. 79–81. Cf. Yamakawa, *Yamakawa Hitoshi jiden,* p. 429.

110. Yamakawa, *Yamakawa Hitoshi jiden,* pp. 428–429.

111. Ibid., p. 430.

112. Koyama and Kishimoto, *Nihon no hikyōsantō Marukusu-shugisha,* p. 143.

113. See Watanabe Masanosuke, "Nihon Kyōsantō kenkyo"; Uchida and Nakano, *Nihon shihon-shugi ronsō,* p. 103; Koyama, *Nihon Marukusu-shugi shi,* p. 46; and Koyama and Kishimoto, *Nihon no hikyōsantō Marukusu-shugisha,* p. 140.

114. The statement, which appeared in the May 1928 issue of *Rōnō,* outraged JCP loyalists and the Comintern. In response, having had the JCP expel the Rōnō-ha formally from the party, the Comintern rejected the notion of a workers' and peasants' political party outside the JCP (see the Comintern's "Theses on the Revolutionary Movements of Colonies and Semi-colonies"; Uchida and Nakano, *Nihon shihon-shugi ronsō,* p. 102; and Koyama and Kishimoto, *Nihon no hikyōsantō Marukusu-shugisha,* p. 148).

115. Koyama and Kishimoto, *Nihon no hikyōsantō Marukusu-shugisha,* pp. 148–149. Rōnō-ha sympathizer Tsushima Tadayuki has asserted that Inomata's view was not even a strictly one-stage revolutionary theory but almost a "compromise between the single-stage strategic doctrine and two-stage strategic theory" (*"Nihon shihon-shugi ronsō" shiron,* p. 8).

116. Yamakawa here objected to the interpretation offered by Yevgeny Varga in his essay "Nihon shihon-shugi no busshitsu to sono seisaku" (The basis of Japanese capitalism and its policies), *International* (November 1927). See Yamakawa, "Seiji-teki tōitsu sensen e!" pp. 174–183.

117. Yamakawa, "Seiji-teki tōitsu sensen e!", pp. 183–201.

118. Ibid., pp. 215n., 216n., 217–218.

119. Tsushima, *"Nihon shihon-shugi ronsō" shiron,* pp. 13–14; cf. Uchida and Nakano, *Nihon shihon-shugi ronsō,* p. 45.

120. Uchida and Nakano, *Nihon shihon-shugi ronsō,* p. 19; Inomata, *Gendai Nihon kenkyū,* pp. 113, 157, 168.

121. Inomata's 1932 work on monopoly capitalism in Japan contained a chapter entitled "Kokka shihon-shugi" (State capitalism), which indicates the heavy influence of Bukharin's formulations. See Inomata, *Nihon no dokusen shihon-shugi,* chap. 7, pp. 107–135.

122. Okada Sōji, "Nihon shihon-shugi no kiso mondai" (Basic problems of Japanese capitalism), *Kaizō* (August 1934): 21, cited by Uchida and Nakano, *Nihon shihon-shugi ronsō,* pp. 244–245.

123. In this respect a meaningful comparison might be drawn with the narodnik-Marxist debates in turn-of-the-century Russia.

124. Inomata, *Gendai Nihon kenkyū,* p. 113 (Inomata's italics).

125. Ibid., pp. 113–144; Uchida and Nakano, *Nihon shihon-shugi ronsō*, pp. 19–20.

126. Inomata Tsunao [Niijima Issaku, pseud.], "Teize," (1) 1:13.

127. Inomata, *Gendai Nihon kenkyū*, p. 157.

128. Inomata [Niijima], "Teize," 1:12–13.

129. Ibid., p. 13; Inomata, *Gendai Nihon kenkyū*, p. 158.

130. Inomata [Niijima], "Teize," 1:13.

131. According to Inomata, in 1907, in Germany 52 percent of all arable land comprised fields of more than 100 ha, whereas, in 1924 Japan, only 7 percent of all arable land was held by owners of fields of 50 ha or more.

132. Inomata [Niijima], "Teize," 1:13–14; Inomata, *Gendai Nihon kenkyū*, pp. 146–148, 162–166; and Inomata [Niijima], "Teize," 2:24.

133. Inomata, *Gendai Nihon kenkyū*, pp. 148–149, 152–154, 158–159, 161; and Inomata, "Teize," 2:13–14.

134. Inomata [Niijima], "Teize," 1:14–15.

135. Inomata, *Gendai Nihon kenkyū*, pp. 167–168.

136. Inomata [Niijima], "Teize," 2:25.

137. Inomata, *Gendai Nihon kenkyū*, pp. 114–115, 135–136, 141 (Inomata's italics).

138. Inomata [Niijima], "Teize," 2:25–27; and Inomata, *Gendai Nihon kenkyū*, p. 144.

139. Inomata, *Gendai Nihon kenkyū,*, pp. 25–27, 44–50, 115–117; and Inomata [Niijima], "Teize," 2:27.

140. See Inomata, *Nihon no dokusen shihon-shugi*, pp. 111–112.

141. Inomata, *Gendai Nihon kenkyū*, pp. 109–114; Tsushima, *"Nihon shihon-shugi ronsō" shiron*, pp. 56–57; and Inomata [Niijima], "Teize," 2:25–26.

142. Tsushima, *"Nihon shihon-shugi ronsō" shiron*, pp. 62–63.

143. Inomata [Niijima], "Teize," 2:25.

144. It finally appeared in full, although without its lost conclusion, in *Revoliutsiia pravda, sbornik pervyi* (Moscow, 1925): 5–32. See Cohen, "Theoretical Foundations of Bolshevism," pp. 441, 441n.

145. "Theoretical Foundations of Bolshevism," pp. 438–441; and Heitman, "Between Lenin and Stalin," pp. 81–82.

146. "K teorii imperialistichiskogo gosudarstva," pp. 15–18, 21–22, 25, 27, and 18, 28, 30, quoted in Cohen, "Theoretical Foundations of Bolshevism," pp. 441–443.

147. See Bukharin, "Imperialism and World Economy," pp. 387–388.

148. Heitman, "Between Lenin and Stalin," pp. 82–86.

149. See Cohen, *Bukharin and the Bolshevik Revolution*, (1975) pp. 14, 174–175, 254–255; and Bukharin, "Organized Mismanagement," pp. 396–397.

150. Here Inomata cites a piece by Bukharin entitled "Shihon-shugi no antei to musan-kaikyū no kakumei" (The stability of capitalism and the proletarian revolution). Inomata, *Gendai Nihon kenkyū*, pp. 18–23; and Inomata [Niijima], "Teize," 1:11–12; and Inomata, *Kyoku-Tō ni okeru teikoku-shugi*.

151. Inomata [Niijima], "Teize," 1:17–18; Inomata, *Gendai Nihon kenkyū*, pp. 117–120; and idem, *Nihon no dokusen shihon-shugi*, p. 110.

152. Inomata, *Nihon no dokusen shihon-shugi*, pp. 111–112; and idem, *Kyoku-Tō ni okeru teikoku-shugi*, pp. 374–375.

153. Inomata, *Kyoku-tō ni okeru teikoku-shugi*, pp. 389–391, 395; idem, *Nihon no dokusen shihon-shugi*, pp. 132–133.

154. See Inomata, "Shihon-shugi hōkai no riron-teki konkyo" [The theoretical basis of the collapse of capitalism], *Kaizō* (January 1926).

155. Inomata, "Shihon-shugi Nihon," pp. 123–124, 146–147, 149.

156. Inomata, "Doronuma ni kanbotsu shita," pp. 307–308; and idem, "Nihon teikoku-shugi," pp. 198, 206.

157. Inomata, "Shihon-shugi Nihon," p. 149; idem, "Nihon teikoku-shugi," pp. 194–197.

158. Inomata, *Gendai Nihon kenkyū*, pp. 94–97, 102–105.

159. Inomata [Niijima], "Teize," pp. 21–23.

160. Tsushima, *"Nihon shihon-shugi ronsō" shiron*, pp. 106, 111, 114–127.

161. "Nihon mondai ni kansuru ketsugi (ni-nana nen teize)," p. 32.

162. A detailed examination of the agrarian problem in the debate on Japanese capitalism is provided in Hoston, *Crisis of Japanese Development in Prewar Japan*, chap. 8.

163. "Nihon Kyōsantō kōryō sōan," p. 5.

164. "Nihon mondai ni kansuru ketsugi (ni-nana nen teize)," p. 33.

165. "Nihon ni okeru jōsei to Nihon Kyōsantō," pp. 81–85.

166. Inomata, "Tochi mondai to hōken isei," pp. 148–149 (Inomata's italics).

167. See Inomata, *Nōson mondai nyūmon*, chap. 3; and idem, "Tochi mondai to hōken isei," pp. 144–147.

168. Yasuba, "Debate on Japanese Capitalism," pp. 64, 69.

169. Uchida and Nakano, *Nihon shihon-shugi ronsō*, p. 145.

170. Kushida Tamizō, *Nōgyō mondai, Kushida Tamizō zenshū*, (Kaizō-sha, 1935), 3:333. Published initially as "Wagakuni kosakuryō no tokushitsu ni tsuite," *Ōhara shakai mondai kenkyusho zasshi*, vol. 8, no. 1 (June 1931), quoted by Yasuba, "Debate on Japanese Capitalism," p. 68.

171. Uchida and Nakano, *Nihon shihon-shugi ronsō*, pp. 145–148, 246–249.

172. Inomata, "Tochi mondai to hōken isei," p. 149.

173. Yasuba, "Debate on Japanese Capitalism," pp. 69–70.

174. Inomata, *Nōson mondai nyūmon*, pp. 4, 29–64.

175. Marx, *Capital*, 3: chap. 47, sec. 2, par. 2 (pp. 791–792).

176. Koyama, *Nihon Marukusu-shugi shi*, pp. 48–49.

177. Marx and Engels, "German Ideology," pp. 112–139.

178. Offe, "Structural Problems," p. 34.

179. Gold, Lo, and Wright, "Recent Developments," p. 36.

180. Ibid. Cf. Bridges, "Nicos Poulantzas," pp. 163–164.

181. Tsushima, *"Nihon shihon-shugi ronsō" shiron*, p. 151.

182. Under the collective title "Nihon shihon-shugi hattatsu no rekishi-teki jōken" (The historical conditions of the development of Japanese capitalism), Noro's work appeared in three parts published in March and June 1928 and March 1929 (vols. 5, 7, 13).

183. Noro, "Nihon shihon-shugi hattatsu shi kōza: Shui sho" (A symposium on the history of the development of Japanese capitalism: Letter of intent), quoted in Koyama, *Nihon Marukusu-shugi shi*, p. 66.

184. Koyama, *Nihon Marukusu-shugi shi*, pp. 66–67.

185. Several essays in the *Kōza* were subsequently rewritten, combined, and published separately as in the case of Yamada, *Bunseki* and Hirano, *Nihon shihon-shugi shakai no kikō*. Ibid., pp. 67–68.

186. Hani, "Kōza gojū shūnen ni yosete," p. 31; interview with Ikumi Takuichi, Tokyo, June 17, 1982; and Kazahaya, "'Nihon shihon-shugi hattatsu shi kōza'," pp. 196–197.

187. Noro, *Nihon shihon-shugi hattatsu shi*, p. 284, quoted in Tsushima, *"Nihon shihon-shugi ronsō" shiron*, pp. 83–84.

188. Koyama, *Nihon Marukusu-shugi shi*, p. 68. Hattori, a graduate of Tokyo Imperial University's sociology department and participant in the Sanro and Puro-ka who is more

noted for his work in the debate on manufacture (see Hoston, *Crisis of Development in Prewar Japan,* chap. 5), published a volume on *Zettai-shugi ron* (The theory of absolutism). As early as 1928, Hattori had published the article "Zettai-shugi ron: Marukishizumu ni okeru zettai-shugi no gainen" (The theory of absolutism: The concept of absolutism in Marxism), in *Marukusu-shugi kōza,* vol. 9. It is reprinted in *Marukishizumu* 1:381–410.

189. Besides Hattori and Noro, Hirano Yoshitarō wrote the most on the nature of the emperor system as an absolutist state. See Hirano, *Burujoa minshu-shugi kakumei;* and idem, *Nihon shihon-shugi no kōzō,* a collection of the essays he published in the original *Kōza.* For summaries of the Kōza-ha view of the state from a Kōza-ha perspective, see Moriya, *Tennō-sei kenkyū,* idem, "Tennō-sei no busshitsu-teki," pp. 24–34.

190. See Engels, *Origin of the Family,* p. 231; cf. Marx, "Eighteenth Brumaire," pp. 515–516.

191. "Nihon ni okeru jōsei to Nihon Kyōsantō," p. 83; cf. Kuusinen [Kūshinen], "Nihon teikoku-shugi to Nihon kakumei no seishitsu" pp. 114–115.

192. Moriya, *Tennō-sei kenkyū,* p. 137; and Hattori, "Zettai-shugi ron," pp. 384, 389.

193. Hirano, *Burujoa minshu-shugi kakumei,* pp. 58–59.

194. Moriya, "Tennō-sei no busshitsu-teki kiso," p. 26.

195. Ibid., p. 27; cf. Kuusinen [Kūshinen], "Nihon teikoku-shugi to Nihon kakumei no seishitsu," pp. 104–105; Hirano, *Nihon shihon-shugi kikō,* p. 273; and the critique in Tsushima, *"Nihon shihon-shugi ronsō" shiron,* pp. 151–152.

196. Yamada, *Nihon shihon-shugi bunseki,* (1949) pp. 13–29, 183–215; and Hirano, *Nihon shihon-shugi shakai no kikō,* p. 273.

197. Moriya, "Tennō-sei no busshitsu-teki kiso," p. 27; and Hirano, *Nihon shihon-shugi shakai no kikō,* p. 277.

198. Hirano, *Nihon shihon-shugi shakai no kikō,* p. 273, quoted in Moriya, "Tennō-sei no busshitsu-teki kiso," p. 24.

199. Noro, *Nihon shihon-shugi hattatsu shi,* (1954) p. 162; cf. Noro, "Nihon ni okeru tochi shoyū kankei," pp. 47–55 passim.

200. Noro, *Nihon shihon-shugi hattatsu shi,* especially pp. 121–136, 271–280; and Noro "Nihon ni okeru tochi shoyū kankei," p. 201. Cf. Uchida and Nakano, *Nihon shihon-shugi ronsō,* pp. 23–25; Koyama, *Nihon Marukusu-shugi shi,* pp. 69–70.

201. For a fuller account of the debate over the Meiji Restoration as bourgeois revolution, with reference to the French Revolution as a model of bourgeois revolution, see Hoston, "Conceptualizing Bourgeois Revolution," pp. 539–581.

202. Noro, "Nihon ni okeru tochi shoyū kankei," p. 205.

203. Ibid., p. 303 (Noro's italics); cf. Hirano, "Ishin seiji," 1:23–24.

204. Ibid., pp. 53–55 (205–207).

205. According to Maurice Dobb, a Marxist scholar of early English capitalism, the putting-out system was common in "the early period of capitalism." In this system, the merchant capitalist purchased raw materials and supplied them to individual craftsmen, who processed the materials with handicraft work methods in exchange for compensation (wages). The merchant then sold the finished products on the market. See Dobb, *Development of Capitalism,* (1963) pp. 17, 17n. In the putting-out system, the merchants' "buying-up capital appeared as intermediary between the producers and the laborers to the extent of paying processing wages" (Ara, Uchida, and Fukuoka, *Keizai jiten,* s.v. *toiya-sei kanai kōgyō*).

206. Hirano, "Ishin seiji," pp. 4–5; Hirano, *Nihon shihon-shugi shakai no kikō,* (1959) p. 266.

207. Hirano, "Ishin seiji," p. 6n, 11–12n.

208. This is a point on which not all Kōza-ha scholars could agree. Beginning in 1933, Hattori Shisō stressed the extent to which significant indigenous development of industrial capitalism had occurred in the late-Edo period. This assertion prompted the so-called "manufacture debate," which found fellow Kōza-ha scholars Hirano and Yamada Shōjirō joining Rōnō-ha critic Tsuchiya Takao in rejecting Hattori's claim. See Hattori, "Ishin shi hōhō-jō no sho mondai," (1960) 1:91–194; Hattori, "Meiji ishin no kakumei oyobi han-kakumei"; vol. 1; Hattori, "Ma'nyufakuchua ronsō ni tsuite no shokan," 1:269–336; Hirano, "Jiyū minken," pp. 2–22; and Yamada Shōjirō, "Nōgyō ni okeru shihon-shugi no hattatsu," *Kōza*, 7:12, cited by Shakai Keizai Rōdō Kenkyūjo, *Nihon shihon-shugi ronsō shi*, p. 49. For an extended discussion of this controversy in English, see Hoston, *Crisis of Development in Prewar Japan*, chap. 5.

209. Hirano, "Ishin seiji"; and Uchida and Nakano, *Nihon shihon-shugi ronsō*, p. 188. This was precisely the point on which Hattori disagreed with the mainstream of the Kōza-ha. His contention was that substantial industrial capitalist development had occurred before the arrival of the "black ships" in the 1850s. Japan, unlike other Asiatic societies, did not require an external impetus to have an industrial revolution. See Hoston, *Crisis of Development in Prewar Japan*, chap. 5.

210. Cf. Beasley, *The Meiji Restoration*, pp. 337ff., 382–383.

211. Hirano, "Ishin seiji," pp. 5–6, 13–16. Cf. Hani, "Bakumatsu seiji-teki shihai," 1:38–39, 45–46; cf. Yamada, *Bunseki*, p. 216.

212. Hirano, "Ishin seiji," pp. 9–10; and Hirano, *Nihon shakai no kikō*, pp. 2–4.

213. Hirano, "Ishin seiji," pp. 10, 16–19, 56n.; and Hirano, *Nihon shihon-shugi shakai no kikō*, pp. 263–267.

214. Hirano, "Ishin seiji," 1:57; cf. Uchida and Nakano, *Nihon shihon-shugi ronsō*, pp. 188–189.

215. Uchida and Nakano, *Nihon shihon-shugi ronsō*, pp. 200–201, 217–221, 243–244; Yamada, *Bunseki*, pp. 74–75, 205.

216. Hirano, "Ishin seiji," 1:58–59n.

217. See Hirano's comparison of the two cases in Hirano, "Ishin seiji," 1:59n.

218. Yamada, *Bunseki*, p. 173.

219. See Hattori, "Zettai-shugi ron."

220. See, for example, Sano, *Minzoku to kaikyū*, pp. 11–13; cf. Hirano, *Dai Ajia-shugi no rekishi-teki kiso*.

221. The sole exception to this generalization was Inomata Tsunao, but his treatment of the subject occurred in his studies of the agrarian problem after he split with Yamakawa and others in the Rōnō-ha.

222. At the Leningrad Conference, Mikhail Godes, Yevgeny S. Iolk, and Sergei I. Kovalev, maintained that the Asiatic mode of production was not a separate mode of production at all but merely a variant of some other more fundamental mode of production. They prevailed over Ludwig S. Mad'iar and Eugene S. Varga, who espoused the Asiatic mode of production and saw it as of continuing significance in contemporary China. See Wittfogel, *Oriental Despotism*, (1981) pp. 401–402; and Hoston, *Crisis of Development in Prewar Japan*, pp. 140–145.

223. For a detailed treatment of the Asiatic mode of production as treated in the debate on Japanese capitalism, see Hoston, *Crisis of Development in Prewar Japan*, chap. 6.

224. Marx, "British Rule in India," pp. 653–658.

225. Marx, "History of His Opinions," p. 5.

226. Bailey and Llobera, *The Asiatic Mode of Production*, p. 1.

227. Hani, "Bakumatsu ni okeru seiji-teki shihai keitai," 1:31–38.

228. Ibid., pp. 37–38.

229. Hirano, "Ishin seiji," pp. 3–4, 4n.

230. Interview with Hirano Yoshitarō, Tokyo, July 27, 1979.

231. Takeuchi, "Nihon no Marukusu-shugi," p. 37.

232. Hani, "Tōyō ni okeru shihon-shugi no keisei," pp. 64–65.

233. A. [sic] Iolk, " 'Ajia-teki' seisan yōshiki no mondai ni yosete," (On the problem of the "Asiatic" mode of production), Russian ed., in *Marukusu-shugi no hata no moto ni* (Under the banner of Marxism), Japanese ed., no. 3 (October and December 1931), p. 80, quoted in Hani, "Tōyō ni okeru shihon-shugi no keisei," pp. 60–61, 55.

234. China had developed such a feudal system with Asiatic characteristics, Hani argued, but this "feudal despotic structure" was forcibly dissolved by the intrusion of foreign capitalism. Hani, "Tōyō ni okeru shihon-shugi no keisei," pp. 96–114 passim.

235. Ibid., pp. 118–150.

236. Ibid., p. 21.

237. Shiga, *Kokka-ron*, p. 110.

238. Uchida and Nakano, *Nihon shihon-shugi ronsō*, pp. 283, 285, 290; and Tsushima, *"Nihon shihon-shugi ronsō" shiron*, pp. 15–16.

239. Shakai Keizai Rōdō Kenkyūjo, *Nihon shihon-shugi ronsō shi*, p. 5.

240. See Kamiyama, *Tennō-sei ni kansuru riron-teki sho mondai* (1956); Shiga, *Sekai to Nihon;* Shiga, *Kokka-ron;* and Hoston, *Crisis of Development in Prewar Japan*, pp. 256–264.

241. Interview with Fujita Shōzō, Tokyo, August 3, 1979; interview with Minobe Ryōkichi, Tokyo, July 30, 1979.

242. See Maguire, *Marx's Theory of Politics*, pp. 202–204.

CHAPTER 7

1. A full account in English is offered in Dirlik, *Revolution and History;* see also the deeply insightful analyses of Schwartz in "Marxist Controversy on China," pp. 143–153; and "Stereotypes in Periodization," pp. 219–230.

2. Marx, "British Rule in India," pp. 581–582 (Marx's italics).

3. See chapter 2 in this volume and Hoston, *Crisis of Development in Prewar Japan,* pp. 127–135.

4. The portions of the *Grundrisse* that treat oriental society most directly are to be found in the English translation, Marx, *Pre-Capitalist Economic Formations.*

5. Karl Marx, preface to *Critique of Political Economy,* p. 5.

6. Hoston, *Crisis of Development in Prewar Japan,* p. 128.

7. Bailey and Llobera, *Asiatic Mode of Production,* p. 1.

8. It was also stimulated by the publication of Wittfogel's *Oriental Despotism* in 1957. See Chesneaux, "Le mode de production asiatique," pts. 1–3; Hobsbawm, introduction to Marx, *Pre-Capitalist Economic Formations;* and Hindess and Hirst, *Pre-Capitalist Modes of Production.* Among Asian Marxists, Japanese Marxist Hirano Yoshitarō, for example, examined Marx's writings on the subject especially closely (interview with Hirano Yoshitarō, Tokyo, July 27, 1979). More recently, the controversy has also been revived in both the Soviet Union and the People's Republic of China. See Menshikov, "Istorichieskogo razvitiia Kitaia'" and Ermachenko, "Kitaiskie istoriki"; Rapp, "China's Debate on the Asiatic Mode of Production," pp. 709–740; and idem, "China's Debate."

9. Godelier, " 'Asiatic Mode of Production'," pp. 209–257.

10. Hobsbawm, "Karl Marx's Contribution to History," p. 273.

11. Shanin, "Third Stage," p. 301. See the appendices to Anderson, *Lineages of the Absolutist State;* and Hindess and Hirst, *Pre-Capitalist Modes of Production*, pp. 213–214.

12. Hegel, *Philosophy of History*.

13. Marx and Engels, "Manifesto of the Communist Party," p. 339.

14. Cf. Said, *Orientalism*, p. 2.

15. See Fairbank, *The United States and China*, chaps. 3, 5. On Marx on the theme of consciousness and man's role in making history, George Lichtheim once wrote: "He took it for granted, though consciousness is conditioned by existence, it can also rise above existence and become a means for transcending the alienation that sets the historical process in motion" (Lichtheim, "Concept of Ideology," p. 21).

16. See the discussion in chapter 3; Xiao, "Zhongguo zhi zhengyuan lun," pp. 535–548; and Pittau, *Political Thought in Early Meiji Japan*.

17. For this emphasis, see Schwartz, *Wealth and Power;* cf. Beasley, *Meiji Restoration*.

18. For an insightful discussion of this point, see the appendix to Anderson, *Lineages of the Absolutist State*.

19. Meisner, *Li Ta-chao*, (1977) pp. 226–227; cf. Lowe, *Function of "China,"* pp. 17–23; and Torr, *Marx on China*.

20. Meisner, *Li Ta-chao*, pp. 228–229.

21. Lowe, *Function of "China,"* p. 22.

22. See Marx, *Pre-Capitalist Economic Formations*, passim.

23. Karl Marx to the editor of the *Otyescestvenniye Zapisky* (Notes on the Fatherland) (End of 1877), in Marx and Engels, *Selected Correspondence*, (1975), p. 354; cf. Maguire, *Marx's Theory of Politics*, pp. 217–218.

24. Kolakowski, *Main Currents of Marxism*, 1:350.

25. Engels, "Social Relations in Russia," pp. 665–675.

26. Marx and Engels, "Communist Manifesto," p. 472.

27. See Lenin, *Development of Capitalism in Russia*, pp. 195–197; Baron, "Development of Soviet Historiography," pp. 382–384; and Baron, "Plekhanov's Russia," pp. 396–400.

28. This was the first complete major work of Russian Marxism to be translated into Japanese and published between the October Revolution and 1921 (Fumio, *Nihon Marukusu-shugi riron*, p. 17.

29. This occurred at the CCP's Sixth Party Congress. See Schwartz, *Rise of Mao*, (1979) pp. 122ff; cf. Wittfogel, *Oriental Despotism*, p. 405.

30. Hoston, *Crisis of Development in Prewar Japan*, pp. 58–59.

31. Here the term *despotic* is taken to mean "arbitrary" and "autocratic."

32. Ma Yufu, quoted in Wang, "Zhongguo shehui shi lunzhan xumu," p. 2.

33. See Rapp, "Fate of Marxist Democrats," passim.

34. See Dai "Cong jingji-shang guan Zhongguo de luanyuan," pp. 1–19; cf. Mast, "Tai Chi-t'ao, Sunism and Marxism," pp. 227–249. See also Hu, "Zhongguo zhexue shi weiwu de yanjiu," pt. 1, pp. 513–543 and pt. 2, pp. 655–691.

35. Dirlik, *Revolution and History*, p. 33.

36. Chen, *Zhongguo Guomindang suo daibiao da shi shenme?*

37. Chen, "Da Jing Pu xiansheng," 1:111–119.

38. See Tao, *Zhongguo fengjian shehui shi*, p. 1; cf. Dirlik, *Revolution and History*, pp. 48–49.

39. He, *Zhongguo shehui shi wenti lunzhan*, p. 5. It might be noted that this effort is echoed in China in the 1980s and 1990s by archeological endeavors to establish the origins of humanity itself in China.

40. For an outline of these factions, see Yamada, *Chūgoku Kokumintō saha no kenkyū*. Other Left Guomindang periodicals included *Minyi* [People's Will] (March—May 1929), *Minxin* (1928–1929), and *Gongxian* [Contribution] (1927–), which carried articles by Wang and Chen. I am indebted to Yamada Tatsuo of Keiō University for his assistance in delineating these factions and locating materials.

41. Chen Gongbo, of the Left Guomindang, vested his hopes in a future reoriented GMD; the party's current platform coincided only slightly with the demands of the revolutionary situation, whereas the CCP's platform diverged from it entirely, he wrote in 1928. Chen, "Duiyu 'Ping guomin geming de weiji he women de cuowu' de huida," 1:69–71.

42. There is some confusion concerning the exact date of the surreptitious founding of the CCP. Schwartz reports the first signs of the existence of a party as evident in 1921, but Chen Bilan reports that Peng Shuze (Peng Shuzhi) joined the party in the autumn of 1920. See Schwartz, *Rise of Mao,* (1979) p. 34; and Pi-lan, "My Years with P'eng Shu-tse," p. 16.

43. Lenin, "Address to the Second All-Russia Congress," 1:246–247.

44. Lenin, "National and Colonial Questions," 1:376.

45. See Hoston, "Conceptualizing Bourgeois Revolution," pp. 539–581.

46. Carrére d'Encausse and Schram, *Marxism and Asia*, pp. 150–152.

47. G. Safarov, *Kolonial'naya Revoliutsiya. Opyt Turkestana* (Moscow, 1921), p. 97, quoted in ibid., p. 32.

48. Massell, *Surrogate Proletariat*, p. 56. See also Bennigsen and Quelquejay, *Les Muselmans de Russie*.

49. Mirza Sultan-Galiev, "Sotsial'naia revoliutsiia i Vostok," *Zhizn' natsional'nostei,* October 5, October 12, November 2, 1919, and idem, *Metody antireligioznoi propagandy sredi Musul'man* (Moscow, 1922), cited in Pipes, *Formation of the Soviet Union,* pp. 167–168.

50. Pipes, *Formation of the Soviet Union,* p. 168.

51. Ibid., pp. 170–172.

52. Sultan-Galiev, quoted in A. Arsharuni and Kh. Gabidullin, *Ocherki panislamizma i pantiukizma v Rossii* ([Moscow], 1931), pp. 78–79, quoted in Pipes, *Formation of the Soviet Union,* pp. 261–262.

53. In 1929, Sultan-Galiev was arrested once again and disappeared. Pipes, *Formation of the Soviet Union,* pp. 262, 262n., 263n.

54. Schwartz, *Rise of Mao,* p. 122.

55. See "Extracts from ECCI Instructions to the Third Congress of the CCP" (May 1923), 2:25–26, and cf. "Extracts from the Resolution of the Seventh ECCI Plenum on the Chinese Situation" (December 16, 1926), in Degras, *Communist International,* (1971) 2:342.

56. "First Congress of Communist and Revolutionary Organizations of the Far East, Moscow" (January 1922), in Degras, *Communist International,* (1971), 1:286.

57. Ibid., p. 391.

58. "Extracts from the ECCI Agitprop Department's Theses for Propagandists on the Second Anniversary of Lenin's Death" (January 1926), in Degras, *Communist International,* (1971), 2:240.

59. "The Sixth Enlarged Plenum of the ECCI" (February 17–March 15, 1926), in Degras, *Communist International,* (1971), 2:247.

60. "ECCI Resolution on the Relations between the CCP and KMT" (January 12, 1923), 2:5–6, and "Extracts from the Resolution of the Sixth ECCI Plenum on the Chinese Question" (March 13, 1926), 2:277, both in Degras, *Communist International* (1971).

61. "Extracts from the Theses of the Seventh ECCI Plenum on the International Situa-

tion and the Tasks of the Communist International" (December 13, 1926), in Degras, *Communist International,* (1971), 2:326.

62. "Extracts from the Resolution of the Seventh ECCI Plenum on the Chinese Situation" (December 16, 1926), in Degras, *Communist International,* (1971), 2:336, 338.

63. Ibid., pp. 338, 340. Cf. Knei-paz, *Leon Trotsky,* chap. 3 passim.

64. "Extracts from the Resolution of the Seventh ECCI Plenum on the Chinese Situation" (December 16, 1926), in Degras, *Communist International,* (1971), 2:342.

65. The Trotskyists contended, "[T]o continue the alliance with the bourgeoisie while holding back the workers and peasants would extinguish the revolutionary spirit of the masses; it meant abandoning the possibility of the socialist revolution." ("Extracts from the Resolution of the Eighth ECCI Plenum on the Chinese Question" (May 30, 1927), in Degras, *Communist International,* (1971), 2:382.

66. "Extracts from the Resolution of the Ninth ECCI Plenum on the Chinese Question" (February 25, 1928), in Degras, *Communist International,* (1971), 2:437.

67. Hoston, *Crisis of Development in Prewar Japan,* p. 168.

68. Riazanov (1870–1938) was another victim of Stalin's purges. He had compiled the first edition of the twenty-seven volume *Complete Works of Marx and Engels.*

69. Wittfogel, *Oriental Despotism,* p. 401.

70. These works included the following: "Ekonomicheskie problemy revoliutsii v Kitae" (Economic problems of the revolution in China), *Planovoe khoziaistvo* (Planned Economy) 12 (1925); "Osnovnie problemi Kitaiskoi revoliutsii" (Fundamental problems of the Chinese revolution), *Bol'shevik* 8 (1928); and "Novaia nauchnaia literatura o Kitae" (The new scientific literature on China), *Pravda* [Truth], January 6, 1929, and "Perspektivy kitaiskoi revoliutsii: Zakluchitelnii vazdel" (Perspectives of the Chinese revolution: The final chapter), in Mad'iar, *Ocherki po ekonomike Kitaia.* For a comprehensive bibliography of Soviet scholarship on China during this period, see Nikiforov, *Sovetskie istoriki o problemakh Kitaia,* pp. 368–397. Both Varga (1879–1964) and the more junior Mad'iar (1891–1940) appear to have been close associates of CPSU leader Nikolai Bukharin at this time. It is important to note that the rejection of the Asiatic mode of production notion espoused by N. S. Riazanov, Varga, and Mad'iar occurred at the same time as Bukharin's fall from power in 1929. See Cohen, *Bukharin and the Bolshevik Revolution,* (1975) chap. 9.

71. Wittfogel, *Oriental Despotism,* p. 401.

72. See his *Ekonomika sel'skogo khoziaistva v Kitae* (1928); *Ocherki po economike Kitaia* (1930); *Sovremennoe sosto'ianie kitaiskoi revoliutsii* (1929); and "Dve agrarnye programmy."

73. Mad'iar, *Ekonomika sel'skogo khoziaistva v Kitae,* pp. 11ff.

74. See Mad'iar, "Legitimacy of the AMP [Asiatic Mode of Production]," pp. 76–94.

75. Mad'iar, *Ekonomika sel'skogo khoziaistva v Kitae,* pp. 8–9, 13.

76. Carrère d'Encausse and Schram, *Marxism and Asia,* pp. 236–237.

77. *Problemy Kitaia,* nos. 4–5 (1930): 223, quoted by Wittfogel, *Oriental Despotism,* p. 401.

78. The only work by Godes that appears in the authoritative Nikiforov bibliography is *Shto takoe kemalistiskii put' i bozmozhen li on v Kitae?* (What is the Kemalist road [Kemal Ataturk] and is it possible in China?) (Leningrad, 1928). Iolk's writings began to appear only in 1930: "K voprosy ob osnovakh obshchestvennogo stroia drevnova Kitaia"; "O zadachakh Marksistsko-Leninskogo izucheniia kolonial'nikh i polukolonial'nikh stran"; Review of M. Kokin and G. Papaian, *"Tszintian" : Agrarnii stroi drevenego Kitaia* ("Jing-

tian": The agrarian system of ancient China), and "K voprosy ob 'Aziatskom' sposobe proizvodstva" (On the problem of the 'Asiatic' mode of production).

79. Baron, "Plekhanov's Russia," pp. 396–400.

80. See, for example, his *History of Russian Social Thought* begun in 1909 and published in 1914–1917 (Baron, "Development of Soviet Historiography," pp. 383, 384.

81. Lenin, *Development of Capitalism in Russia*, pp. 176–177; and Baron, "Transition from Feudalism to Capitalism," p. 721.

82. Wittfogel, *Oriental Despotism*, p. 402.

83. Iolk, "AMP and the Class Struggle," p. 97.

84. Wittfogel, *Oriental Despotism*, pp. 402, 402n.

85. See note 53 in this chapter.

86. P'eng [Peng Shuzhi], *Chinese Communist Party in Power*, p. 485.

87. Yevgeny Iolk [E. I.], "O zadachakh marksistsko-leninskogo izucheniia," p. 23.

88. Godes, "Reaffirmation of Unilinealism," p. 104.

89. Editor's introduction to part 2, in Bailey and Llobera, *Asiatic mode of Production*, p. 52.

90. See Schwartz, *Rise of Mao*, (1979) pp. 122–123.

91. Wittfogel, *Oriental Despotism*, p. 405.

92. Diliuci dahui guanyu tudi wenti de jueyian (Resolution of the Sixth Congress on the land problem) (Moscow, 1928), p. 7, quoted in Schwartz, *Rise of Mao*, (1979) p. 123.

93. Schwartz, *Rise of Mao*, (1979) p. 123.

94. Mad'iar, "Legitimacy of the AMP," pp. 93–94.

95. Godes, "Reaffirmation of Unilinealism," pp. 102, 104; Iolk, "AMP and the Class Struggle," p. 98. This last charge was not without irony, because the Resolutions of the Sixth CCP Congress also rejected the view that they claimed to be Trotskyist that "capitalist relations have already extended into the village economy." Schwartz, *Rise of Mao* (1979), p. 122.

96. See, for example, the emphasis that Kokin places on "the conclusion that every bureaucrat was a member of the ruling class in Asiatic society," in Kokin, "Asiatic Bureaucracy as a Class," pp. 95–96.

97. Godes, "Reaffirmation of Unilinealism," pp. 103–104.

98. Wittfogel, *Oriental Despotism*, pp. 405–406.

99. See, for example, Wittfogel, "Stages of Development," pp. 113–140.

100. Interview with Hirano Yoshitarō, Tokyo, July 27, 1979; see also the references to Wittfogel's work in Hirano, *Nihon shihon-shugi shakai no kikō*, pp. 309 ff. (This is a collection of studies that originally appeared in the *Nihon shihon-shugi hattatsu shi kōza*.)

101. Levenson, *Confucian China and its Modern Fate*, 3:48.

102. See Wylie, "'Sinification' of Marxism," pp. 447–480, and chapter 9 in this volume.

103. Schwartz, "Stereotypes in Periodization," pp. 219–230; cf. Schwartz, "Marxist Controversy on China," pp. 143–153.

104. See the chart in Dirlik, *Revolution and History*, pp. 187–190. It should be noted that in several cases, most notably in the descriptions of the periodizations of Zhu Peiwo and Tao Xisheng, this author's interpretations differ slightly from those of Dirlik.

105. Cadart and Cheng, *Mémoires de Peng Shuzhi*, pp. 443–445. At this point, Peng had not yet heard of Trotsky's theory of permanent revolution (p. 451), but from his description of Chinese society as imbued with characteristics that Trotsky would have described in terms of "uneven and combined development," it is evident why he should have been so strongly attracted to Trotsky's ideas.

106. Dirlik, *Revolution and History,* p. 72.

107. They also published in *Dongfang zazhi* (Eastern miscellany), *Geming Pinglun* (Revolutionary review), *Shuangshi* (Double ten), and *Qianjin* (Advance).

108. Dirlik, *Revolution and History,* pp. 69–72; Wang, "Zhongguo shehui shi lunzhan xumu," p. 9; and interview with Yamada Tatsuo, Keiō University, Tokyo, August 1979.

109. ·North, *Moscow and Chinese Communists,* (1963) chap. 6; and Lerner, *Karl Radek,* pp. 136–146.

110. Degras, "United Front Tactics," pp. 21–22.

111. See Li, "Zhongguo geming de genben wenti."

112. Ibid., p. 42.

113. Dirlik, *Revolution and History,* p. 139, chap. 5 passim.

114. See Guo, *Zhongguo gudai shehui Yanjiu,* especially pp. 176–177.

115. Chen Xiaojiang, "Fengjian shehui hechu qu?" p. 44.

116. Dirlik, *Revolution and History,* p. 141.

117. Guo, *Yanjiu,* p. 176, quoted in ibid. (Dirlik's interpretation).

118. Wang, "Zhongguo shehui shi lunzhan xumu," pp. 11–15.

119. See, for example, Pan, "Shina keizai no seishitsu," pp. 3–22.

120. See Chen, *Guomin geming de weiji,* pp. 14–15; and Chen, "Zai lun di-san dang," p. 2.

121. Chen, "Jinhou de Guomindang," pp. 4–5.

122. T. S. S., "Wo duiyu Zhongguo geming," pt. 1, p. 35.

123. Ma, "Zhongguo geming zhi jinri," p. 179.

124. Cf. Chen, *Zhongguo Guomindang suo daibiao de shi shenme?* (1928) pp. 110 ff. Compare also Frantz Fanon's observation that the circumstances in colonized societies renders it problematic to try to apply orthodox Marxist class categories to the social strata in such societies (see Fanon, *Wretched of the Earth*).

125. Chen, *Guomin geming de weiji,* pp. 3–9; cf. Ma, "Zhongguo geming zhi jinri," p. 22.

126. See Tao, "Tongyi yu shengchan," p. 13.

127. Chen, "Muqian zenyang jianshe guojia ziben?" pt. 1, pp. 2–4; idem, "Muqian zenyang jianshe guojia ziben?" pt. 2, p. 24; and idem, "Muqian zenyang jianshe guojia ziben?" pt. 4, pp. 9–14.

128. Chen, "Muqian zenyang jianshe guojia ziben?" pt. 1, pp. 2–4.

129. Chen, *Guomin geming de weiji,* pp. 4–5, 10.

130. See Shi, "Minzu yu jieji," pp. 3ff.

131. See Tao, *Zhongguo fengjian shehui shi,* passim; idem, *Zhongguo shehui zhi shi de fenxi;* idem, *Zhongguo shehui yu Zhongguo geming,* (1931) especially chaps. 4, 5; and the exposition in Zhu Peiwo [Zhu Xinfan, pseud.], "Fengjianxing de taolun," pp. 1–3.

132. Tao, *Zhongguo shehui yu Zhongguo geming,* pp. 96, 199.

133. He, *Zhongguo shehui shi wenti lunzhan,* 3:211–219; cf. Chen, "Fengjian shehui hechu qu?" p. 47.

134. He, *Zhongguo shehui shi wenti lunzhan,* 3:217–219.

135. Tao Xisheng, "Zhongguo shehui daodi shi shenme shehui?" p. 4. Interestingly, particularly in the wake of the Tiananmen Square massacre of June 4, 1989, this issue persists in intellectual debate in China in the 1990s.

136. Tao, "Tongyi yu shengchan," pp. 2–3; cf. Deliusin, "Tao Sishchen o kharaktere," pp. 6–8.

137. Tao, "Zhongguo shehui daodi shi shenme shehui?" pp. 8–9.

138. Ibid., pp. 3–4, 10. Here Tao shared fellow Left KMT Marxists' emphasis on

imperialism as the main impediment of the transition from precapitalism to capitalism (p. 13).

139. Shi, "Minzu yu jieji," p. 4.

140. Wang, "Zhongguo shehui shi lunzhan xumu," p. 15.

141. Ibid., pp. 215–216.

142. Lü, *Shiqianqi Zhongguo,* reprint of 1961 ed., p. 32.

143. Zhu, "Fengjianxing de taolun," pp. 34–38; cf. Wang, "Zhongguo shehui shi lunzhan xumu," p. 16.

144. Lü, *Shiqianqi Zhongguo,* pp. 27–28.

145. Li, "Zhongguo geming de genben wenti," pt. 2, pp. 52–53, 71.

146. Zhu, "Fengjianxing de taolun," pp. 19–21.

147. See Dobb, *Development of Capitalism;* (1963); and the essays collected in Paul Sweezy et al., *Transition from Feudalism to Capitalism.* Cf. the discussion of the "manufacture" thesis of Hattori Shisō in Hoston, *Crisis of Development in Prewar Japan,* chap. 5.

148. Chen, "Fengjian shehui hechu qu?" p. 47.

149. Zhu, "Fengjianxing de taolun," pp. 39–42. Here Zhu took issue with Left GMD member Gu Mengyu's argument (allegedly based on Bukharin's views) that the Chinese economy experienced no fundamental economic change with the invasion of the West.

150. See the classic piece on this aspect of imperial China, Skinner, "Marketing and Social Structure in Rural China," pt. 1, pp. 3–43; pt. 2, pp. 195–228; and pt. 3, pp. 363–399. See also Skinner, "Chinese Peasants and the Closed Community," pp. 270–281.

151. It is interesting that Zhu chose the word *independent* rather than *dependent* to describe direct producers in a mode of production that is usually categorized by the presence of serfs, who are dependent on lords for access to the land on which they produce.

152. Zhu, "Fengjianxing de taolun," p. 23; cf. Wang, "Zhongguo shehui shi lunzhan xumu," p. 15.

153. Zhu, "Fengjianxing de taolun," pp. 53–54.

154. See Zhou, *Zhongguo shehui zhi jiegou,* especially p. 292.

155. Ibid., pp. 39–42.

156. Ibid.

157. Compare Tao's assertion that over the previous century China's commercial capital had come under the domination of foreign commercial capital under the impact of imperialism. Tao, "Changqi heping zhi zhenduan," p. 2.

158. Ibid., pp. 14–30. Lü Zhenyu makes a similar point on the basis of volume 3 of *Capital.* See Lü, *Shiqianqi Zhongguo,* pp. 27–31.

159. Ibid., pp. 43–53. Zhu argued that this would be impossible in any case because China's large cities were dominated by foreign imperialist capital. The objects of his criticism were Chen Duxiu, "Zhi Zhonggong zhongyang de gongkai xin" (An open letter to the Central [Committee] of the Chinese Communist party) (1929) and Karl Radek (pp. 18–19).

160. Tao, "Zhongguo shehui daodi shi shenme shehui?" p. 6.

161. Zhu, "Fengjianxing de taolun," pp. 4–18, 29–34.

162. Ibid., pp. 18, 29–34.

163. Chen, "Fengjian shehui," p. 45.

164. Tao's position on the shidaifu was, indeed, full of inconsistencies. See the treatments in Tao, *Zhongguo shehui yu Zhongguo geming,* especially chap. 4; and Tao, *Zhongguo shehui zhi shi de fenxi,* pp. 38, 83–105; and Tao, "Zhongguo shehui daodi shi shenme shehui?" pp. 5, 9.

165. Zhu, "Fengjianxing de taolun," pp. 37–53; "Wang Zhongguo shehui shi," pp. 11–13, 16.

166. Dirlik, *Revolution and History,* pp. 187–188.

167. Lü, *Shiqianqi Zhongguo,* pp. 49–50.

168. Ibid., pp. 52–53.

169. Ibid., pp. 32–60.

170. Trotsky, *Problems of the Chinese Revolution,* pp. 127, 157.

171. Quoted in Degras, "United Front Tactics," pp. 17–18.

172. See Knei-paz, *Leon Trotsky,* chap. 4.

173. Yan, "Shina keizai mondai kenkyū," pp. 77–79. This essay comprised two essays originally published in the Trotskyist journal *Dongli,* nos. 1 and 2, and an unpublished essay critiquing the CCP position. Cf. Ren Shu, *Zhongguo jingji yanjiu xulun* (Introduction to the examination of the Chinese economy) (Shanghai, 1932), cited by Dirlik, *Revolution and History,* p. 85.

174. Dirlik, *Revolution and History,* pp. 85–90.

175. Ibid., pp. 73, 60.

176. Zhu, "Fengjianxing de taolun," pp. 42–43.

177. Li, "Gongxian yu pipong," *Dushu zazhi* 2, nos. 2–3 (March 1932): 2–3.

178. In his early work, Li included Shang/Yin society within the primitive communist mode of production and limited the Asiatic mode of production to include only the Yin/Shang era but subsequently expanded the Asiatic mode of production period to include Xia and Yin. See Li, "Gongxian yu piping," pp. 14, 15; and Li, *Zhongguo shehui shi lunzhan pipan,* 1936 ed., pp. 17, 53.

179. Li, "Gongxian yu piping," pp. 16–23.

180. Note that Li is using terminology in Chinese that is different from the *xian-ziben-zhuyi* postulated by Tao Xisheng. For the sake of clarity, I have translated Tao's term as *precapitalism* and Li's as *protocapitalism.*

181. Li, "Gongxian yu piping," pp. 39–45, 54–56.

182. Li, "Gongxian yu piping," p. 59.

183. Ibid., p. 57.

184. Here Li cited Ren, *Zhongguo jingji yanjiu xulun* (ibid., p. 54).

185. Li, *Zhongguo shehui shi lunzhan pipan,* (1936) passim; He, *Zhongguo shehui shi wenti lunzhan,* 3:202–209; and Dirlik, *Revolution and History,* pp. 200–207.

186. Dirlik, *Revolution and History,* pp. 51 ff.

187. Chen, "Fengjian shehui hechu qu?" p. 46.

188. Mo, *"Zhongguo shehui shi lunzhan pipan* de pipan," pp. 29–39.

189. Ibid., p. 20.

190. "Kung-hsien yu p'i-p'ing," *Tu-shu tsa-chi,* 2, nos. 7–8:48, quoted by Dirlik, *Revolution and History,* p. 205.

191. Chen, "Fengjian shehui hechu qu?" p. 45.

192. Mo, "Lun dianyongzhi ji xunhuan," pp. 352–53.

193. Dirlik, *Revolution and History,* p. 101; cf. Schwartz, "Marxist Controversy on China," p. 145.

194. See the critique of the concept in Mad'iar, for example, in Lü, *Shiqianqi Zhongguo,* pp. 14–21.

195. Wang, "Zhongguo shehui shi lunzhan xumu," p. 9.

196. Lü, *Shiqianqi Zhongguo,* p. 6.

197. Ibid., p. 12.

198. See, for example, Hindess and Hirst, *Pre-Capitalist Modes of Production.*

199. See Hobsbawm, Introduction to Marx, *Pre-Capitalist Economic Formations.*

200. See Baron, "Plekhanov's Russia," passim.

201. It was, of course, precisely this negative valuation of all associated with the Asian past that also limited Marxism's ability to function as a vehicle of cultural criticism in societies (such as Japan) whose Marxists were more self-confident about their own cultural histories. See Hoston, *"Ikkoku Shakai-shugi,* pp. 168–186.

202. See Rapp, "Fate of Marxist Democrats," passim.

203. He, *Zhongguo shehui shi wenti lunzhan,* pp. 10–15; and Dirlik, *Revolution and History,* p. 191.

204. See *Ajia-teki seisan yōshiki ni tsuite.*

205. See Inomata, *Gendai Nihon kenkyū,* pp. 5, 71–93, 164–177; and idem, *Kyokutō ni okeru teikoku-shugi,* pp. 201–202. Tsushima Tadayuki completely rejected Noro Eitarō's application of the notion of the "state as the highest landlord"—an element of Marx's model of oriental society—to Japan. See his *"Nihon shihon-shugi ronsō" shiron,* pp. 100–102.

206. Hani Gorō, "Tōyō ni okeru shihon-shugi no keisei," pp. 100–102.

207. Interview with Hirano Yoshitarō, Tokyo, July 27, 1979.

208. See He, *Zhongguo shehui shi wenti lunzhan,* pp. 120–136.

209. Guo, *Yanjiu,* p. 176, quoted by Dirlik, *Revolution and History,* p. 146 (Dirlik's interpretation).

210. For criticisms of Guo's views see Dirlik, *Revolution and History,* pp. 158–171.

211. Dubrovsky, *On the Question of an "Asiatic" Mode of Production, Feudalism, Serfdom, and Merchant Capital,* published in 1929, had laid the groundwork for the systematic attack on the Asiatic mode of production concept at the Leningrad Conference. Dubrovsky, director of the Agrarian Institute of the Communist Academy, exercised significant influence over many participants on the controversy on Chinese social history. He himself was not entirely orthodox in his treatment of Marx's and Engels's depiction of the progressive evolution of human society and described a total of ten modes of production. See Shteppa, *Russian Historians,* pp. 67–80.

212. Li, "Gongxian yu piping," pp. 25–26.

213. Ibid., p. 41.

214. Mo, "Zhongguo shehui shi lunzhan pipan de pipan," pp. 29–30, 168.

215. This is the part of He's argument that is stressed in Dirlik, *Revolution and History,* p. 220.

216. He, *Zhongguo shehui shi wenti lunzhan,* pp. 41–42.

217. Ibid., p. 42.

218. Aikawa, "Nihon dorei-sei ni kansuru kiso ronten," pp. 336–338.

219. Ibid., pp. 56–58.

220. Ibid., pp. 158–161.

221. See Xiong, "Zhongguo nongmin wenti zhi shi de xushu," pt. 1, pp. 1–27 and pt. 2, pp. 1–44.

222. Cf. Wang, "Zhongguo geming yu nongye wenti."

223. Xiong, "Zhongguo nongmin wenti zhi shi de xushu," pt. 2, pp. 11–12.

224. Cf. Liu Xingtang, "Zhongguo shehui fazhan xingshi zhi tanxian" (An investigation of the contours of the development of Chinese society), *Shi huo* (Food and Commodities) 2, no. 9 (October 1, 1935): 1–27, cited in Dirlik, *Revolution and History.* The kyōdōtai figured heavily in Japanese discussions of the Asiatic mode of production in the debate on Japanese capitalism. See Hoston, *Crisis of Development in Prewar Japan,* chap. 6.

225. Hoston, *Crisis of Development in Prewar Japan,* p. 39.

226. See Chen, "Zhongguo shehui tingzhi zhuangtai de jichu," pp. 1–21.

227. See Wang, "Zhongguo shehui xingtai fazhan-shi," pp. 1–39; and Hu, "Yaxiya

shengchan fangshi," pp. 1–23. Cf. He Ganzhi's summary and critique of Wang's and Hu's views in He, *Zhongguo shehui shi wenti lunzhan*, pp. 219–227.

228. Hu, "Yaxiya shengchan fangshi," pp. 15–22.

229. See Hu, "Zhongguo shehui–wenhua fazhan caoshu," pt. 1, p. 2.

230. Hu, "Zhuanzhi-zhuyi," p. 4.

231. Ibid.

232. Ibid., pp. 9, 12.

233. Ibid., p. 12.

234. Wang, "Zhongguo shehui xingtai fazhan-shi," p. 22.

235. See Hu, "Zhuanzhi-zhuyi;" and Hu, "Yaxiya shengchan fangshi," p. 14.

236. Hu, "Zhuanzhi-zhuyi," pp. 19–22.

237. Dirlik, *Revolution and History*, p. 96.

238. Said, *Orientalism*, pp. 2–3.

239. See Chen, "Fengjian shehui hechu qu?" pp. 43–44; and Wang, "*Zhongguo shehui shi lunzhan pipan* de pipan," p. 166.

CHAPTER 8

1. Steinhoff, "*Tenkō.*" Steinhoff treats *tenkō* primarily as a instrument used by the police. Prisoners were led to believe that they would receive early release or parole if they recanted, and the police and prison authorities widely publicized *tenkō*s to induce others to follow suit.

2. Kita is not treated in detail here. See Wilson, *Radical Nationalist in Japan*.

3. Strictly speaking, because they were not members of the Communist party, Takabatake, Kita, Takahashi, and Akamatsu are not regarded as tenkōsha although they were committed Marxists.

4. This generalization includes liberalism as well as Marxism. See Hoston, "State, Modernity, and the Fate of Liberalism."

5. *Nihon shakai undō jinmei jiten*, s.v. Sano Manabu; and Steinhoff, "*Tenkō,*" p. 4.

6. See Nabeyama, "Kokoro no sokuseki," pp. 16–25.

7. Steinhoff, "*Tenkō,*" pp. 252–253; cf. Mitchell, *Thought Control in Prewar Japan*, chap. 5 passim.

8. Steinhoff, "*Tenkō,*" pp. 3–5.

9. Takabatake, "Ikkoku shakai-shugisha," (1959) 1:168, 193n.

10. Steinhoff, "*Tenkō,*" pp. 6, 10n. Cf. Kuno and Tsurumi, *Gendai Nihon no shisō*, (1978) pp. 53–54.

11. Steinhoff, "*Tenkō,*" pp. 254–255.

12. See Gregor, *Young Mussolini*; and Nolte, *Three Faces of Fascism*, pt. 3 passim.

13. See Schorske, *German Social Democracy*.

14. Von Klemperer, *Germany's New Conservatism*, (1958) passim; cf. Mosse, *Crisis of German Ideology*, pp. 280–281; Neumann, *Behemoth*, pp. 191–199; and Meinecke, *German Catastrophe*, (1963) especially chap. 2.

15. Steinhoff, "*Tenkō,*" p. 7.

16. Ibid., p. 159.

17. See Ishida, *Meiji seiji shisō shi kenkyū*, pp. 3–149.

18. The difficulty of separating "religious" factors is suggested by Joseph Spae's observation that in Japan "there is no psychological room for compartmentalization between the sacred and the profane, and physical and the spiritual" (see Spae, "Sociology of Religion for Japan," pp. 5–6). Cf. Maruyama Masao's observation that Japanese defendants at the Tokyo

war crimes trials lacked any sense of individual responsibility for their wartime behavior. As members of the *kokutai* they acted not on individual initiative but to fulfill the "imperial will" (the will of the emperor and his ancestors). See Maruyama, *Thought and Behavior*, pp. 100–103.

19. Walzer, "Theory of Revolution," p. 32.

20. Ibid., p. 33.

21. Benedict, *Chrysanthemum and the Sword*, (1974) p. 116, chap. 6 passim.

22. Ibid., pp. 118–119; Kawashima, *Ideorogii to shite no kazoku seido*; idem, *Nihon shakai no kazoku-teki kōsei*. Cf. De Vos and Mizushima, "Japanese Gangs," pp. 289–325. Group orientation may have lost some of its force in postwar Japan, but its primacy in the interwar period is generally conceded. In this connection, see Frager, "Conformity and Anticonformity in Japan," pp. 203, 208; Fukutake, *Man and Society in Japan*; and Caudill and Scarr, "Japanese Value Orientation," pp. 53–91.

23. Quoted in Steinhoff, *"Tenkō,"* pp. 173–174.

24. See Nabeyama, *Watakushi wa kyōsantō o suteta*, pp. 132–133.

25. Kobayashi Morito, comp., *Tenkōsha no shisō to seikatsu*, pp. 4–5.

26. Takabatake, "Ikkoku shakai-shugisha," 1:183.

27. Takeo, "Giri-Ninjo," p. 329.

28. Onabe Teruhiko, personal letter, January 16, 1982.

29. Takabatake's thought is treated in chapter 5, and Takahashi's in chapter 6. Akamatsu, the Kaitō-ha, and Sano Manabu are treated later in this chapter.

30. See Meisner, *Li Ta-chao*, 1977 ed., pp. 188–191.

31. Berki, "Marxian Thought," pp. 81, 85 (Berki's italics).

32. See Lenin, "Imperialism,"; and Meisner, *Li Ta-chao*, (1979) pp. 145ff.

33. Hitler, *Mein Kampf*, p. 187, chaps. 11 and 12 passim.

34. See Tilly, "History of European State-Making," pp. 3–83 passim.

35. See Dahrendorf, *Society and Democracy in Germany*, (1979) especially chaps. 1, 3, and 4; cf. Taylor, *Course of German History*, chap. 1.

36. Cf. Sannosuke, "Significance of Nationalism," pp. 50–53.

37. Von Klemperer, *Germany's New Conservatism*, p. 139.

38. Ibid., pp. 99–100.

39. See Kawakami, *Jijōden*, 1:204–206; cf. Bernstein, *Japanese Marxist*, chap. 6. Cf. Nabeyama, "Kokoro no sokuseki," pp. 16–18.

40. Tanaka, *Takabatake Motoyuki*, p. 3.

41. See Crowley, "New Deal," pp. 235–264 passim; idem, *Japan's Quest for Autonomy*; and Takeuchi, "Ajia-shugi no tenbō," pp. 7–63 passim.

42. See Sano and Nabeyama, "Kyōdō hikoku dōshi ni tsuguru sho," 1:18; and Kobayashi, *Tenkōsha no shisō to seikatsu*, p. 23.

43. See Sano's rejection of Marx's theory of the state as the descendant of Western European "authoritarian" political thought in "Marukusu kokka-ron to sono hihan," 1: 523–588 passim; and the discussion later in this chapter.

44. Mosse, *Crisis of German Ideology*, pp. 281, 280.

45. See Nyerere, *Ujamaa*, and Cabral, *Return to the Source*, for this theme.

46. Ishida, "Kawakami Hajime ni okeru itan e no michi," pp. 1–18; cf. Fujita, "Aru Marukusu-shugisha," pp. 64–87.

47. Fujita, *Tenkō no shisō shi-teki kenkyū*, pp. 3–4.

48. [Sano], *Waga gokuchū no shisō henreki*, pp. 16–17.

49. Nabeyama, "Kokoro no sokuseki," p. 66.

50. Fujita, *Tenkō no shisō shi-teki kenkyū*, pp. 11–12.

51. See Sano, "Kokka-ron," 5:1–74; the articles published from 1927–1930 collected in Sano, *Seiji-ron*; and the essays included in Sano, *Kokka-ron/Sensō-ron*, especially the essay entitled "Kenryoku no shizen shi," pp. 335–345.

52. Fujita, *Tenkō no shisō shi-teki kenkyū*, p. 4.

53. Steinhoff, *"Tenkō,"* pp. 169–170.

54. Kazama, *Nihon Kyōsantō no rekishi*, 1:89–90; and Sano, "Mosukō to Nihon Kyōsantō no kankei shi," p. 99.

55. Needless to say, this is precisely what had happened in China. Nabeyama, "Kokoro no sokuseki," pp. 59, 64–65. Koyama Hirotake has argued that the war aroused a wave of xenophobia in Japan, and *tenkō* was a manifestation of that tide. See Koyama, *Nihon Marukusu-shugi shi*, pp. 72–73.

56. "Sano Manabu yoshin jinmon chōsho," quoted in Takabatake, "Ikkoku shakai-shugisha," 1:172–173.

57. Takabatake, "Ikkoku shakai-shugisha," 1:172–173.

58. See Nabeyama, "Kokoro no sokuseki," pp. 41–43; idem, *Watakushi wa kyōsantō o suteta*, pp. 151–153, 173–174; and Fujita, *Tenkō no shisō shi-teki kenkyū*, pp. 44, 45, 48.

59. Sano, "Gokuchū-ki," pp. 87–89.

60. Nabeyama, *Watakushi wa kyōsantō o suteta*, pp. 145–151; cf. Sano, "Gokuchū-ki," pp. 93–94; and Arahata, *Hidari no menmen*, pp. 91–93. Arahata, like many others, felt Nabeyama was more sincere in his humanist motivations toward *tenkō* (p. 89).

61. Sano, "Gokuchū-ki," pp. 91–92; Nabeyama, "Kokoro no sokuseki," pp. 11–14.

62. Kawakami, *Jijōden*, 3: 158–159.

63. Kobayashi, *Tenkōsha no shisō to seikatsu*, pp. 21–26.

64. Steinhoff, *"Tenkō,"* p. 175.

65. Nabeyama joined Sano in calling for "socialism-in-one-country" in their joint *tenkō* proclamation but did not systematically articulate such a doctrine during the years after their *tenkō*. See Sano and Nabeyama, "Kyōdō hikoku dōshi ni tsuguru sho," 1:3–20.

66. Takahashi Masao, personal letter, April 4, 1984. According to Takahashi, a Marxist economist who was affiliated with the prewar Rōnō-ha, even among members of the dissident Rōnō-ha, there was a split between those who accepted the validity of the October Revolution as a true socialist revolution and those who rejected it as "utopian" and "non-Marxist" (interview with Takahashi Masao, Tokyo, Japan, May 5, 1984).

67. In addition to these examples, Takabatake Michitoshi has named fifteen figures who espoused some form of national socialism after *tenkō*. See Naimushō Keihō-kyoku (Ministry of Home Affairs, Bureau of Criminal Law), *Shakai undō no jōkyō* (The state of the social movement), 1935 and 1942 eds., cited by Takabatake, "Ikkoku shakai-shugisha," p. 193n.

68. Totten, "National Socialism of Akamatsu Katsumaro," pp. 6–10; and Totten, "Akamatsu Katsumaro."

69. See Wagner, "Sano Manabu," p. 164.

70. Only two years before his own *tenkō*, Sano had denounced the Kaitō-ha as "social fascists" and reasserted the official Comintern-JCP line on the need to abolish the emperor system. This critique, which is addressed in detail later, is contained in Sano, "Sano Manabu jōshinsho," pt. 1, pp. 5–7, 10–13.

71. Kobayashi, *Tenkōsha*, p. 11. *Nihon shakai undō jinmei jiten*, s.v. Kobayashi Morito.

72. For a detailed analysis of this political and economic crisis, see Hoston, "Marxism and National Socialism," pp. 43–64; and Hoston, *Crisis of Development in Prewar Japan*, chap. 1.

73. See chapter 6 in this volume.

74. Takahashi, *Nihon keizai no yukizumari*, pp. 17–25, 36–37; idem, *Nihon shihon-*

shugi hattatsu shi, (1929) pp. 332–338, 358; and Hoston, "Marxism and Japanese Expansionism," pp. 16–18.

75. The failure of the communist/socialist parties in Germany and China and the rise of fascism during the 1920s in Italy and Germany made strong impressions on Sano and Takabatake. See Sano's explanation of his *tenkō* to Kawakami in Kawakami, *Jijōden*, 3:158–159; and Tanaka, *Takabatake Motoyuki*, pp. 200–201, 233.

76. This was particularly pronounced in the case of Kawakami Hajime. See Bernstein, *Japanese Marxist*, chaps. 4, 6.

77. These included *Nihon shakai shi joron* (A preface to Japanese social history) (1922) and *Nihon keizai shi gairon* (Outline of Japanese economic history) (1923). Shakai Keizai Rōdō Kenkyūjo, *Nihon minshu kakumei ronsō shi*, p. 6.

78. These publications included an attack on Takahashi's "petty imperialism" thesis. See Sano, "Waga haigai-shugisha," pp. 1–31.

79. Nakamura Yoshiaki (1899–) later joined this group, as did many others. Sano also lists Nakamura, Kikuchi Zengorō (1897–), Kawai Etsuzō (1903–1966), and Kore'eda Kyōji as members of this group (Sano, "Jōshinsho," pt. 1, pp. 5, 47). Kore'eda did *tenkō* but retracted his recantation immediately (*Nihon shakai undō jinmei jiten*, s.v. Kore'eda Kyōji). Several years after his *tenkō*, Nakamura published a text designed to encourage other "red" youth to return to their Japanese roots through *tenkō*. See Nakamura, *Kyōsantō bō hikoku no tenkō kiroku*.

80. *Nihon shakai undō jinmei jiten*, s.v. Asano Akira, Kadoya Hiroshi, Minami Ki'ichi, Murao Satsuo, Mizuno Shigeo, and Toyoda Tadashi.

81. Kobayashi, *Tenkōsha no shisō to seikatsu*, pp. 9–10.

82. See chapter 6.

83. Kobayashi, *Tenkōsha no shigō to seikatsu*, pp. 8–9.

84. Ibid., p. 11.

85. As described in chapter 6, the dissident Rōnō-ha had split from the JCP in December 1927 in opposition to the Comintern's 1927 Theses, and they, too, felt that it was a mistake for the party's leaders blindly to accept the erroneous direction of Soviet leaders. Perhaps because of this kinship in the Rōnō-ha and Kaitō-ha positions on the relationship between the JCP and the Comintern, the term "Dissolutionist Faction" was also applied to the Rōnō-ha by JCP loyalists.

86. Sano, "Jōshinsho," pt. 1, pp. 45–46, 5–10.

87. See chapter 6.

88. Sano, "Jōshinsho," pt. 1, pp. 45–46, 5–10.

89. Memorandum by K [Kadoya Hiroshi?], quoted in Kobayashi, *Tenkōsha no shigō to seikatsu*, pp. 11–12.

90. Sano, "Jōshinsho," pt. 1, p. 47.

91. Kobayashi, *Tenkōsha no shigō to seikatsu*, pp. 12–13.

92. Sano, "Jōshinsho," pt. 1, pp. 47–53, 59–60, pt. 2, pp. 1–9.

93. Ibid., pt. 1, pp. 53–59.

94. Ibid., pt. 1, pp. 5–7, 10–13.

95. By contrast, Kawakami Hajime, who never did *tenkō*, became a firm Marxist and JCP activist only very late in life after resolving the conflicts he perceived between Marxism and indigenous values and perspectives. See Ishida, "Kawakami Hajime ni okeru itan e no michi," pp. 1–18 passim.

96. [Sano], "Sano Manabu yoshin jinmon chōsho," quoted in Takabatake, "Ikkoku shakai-shugisha," pp. 172–173.

97. Takabatake, "Ikkoku shakai-shugisha," p. 171.

98. Sano, "Jōshinsho," pt. 1, p. 57.

99. The Comintern 1931 Theses added confusion to the JCP's position on the nature of state power in Japan. The 1931 Theses did not find in the emperor system evidence of extreme backwardness and, thus, seemed to support the view of the Rōnō-ha, which Sano had been denouncing as monarchist. See chapter 6, this volume, and Takabatake, "Ikkoku shakai-shugisha," pp. 172–173.

100. See Nabeyama, "Kokoro no sokuseki," pp. 41–43; Nabeyama, *Watakushi wa kyōsantō o suteta*, pp. 151–153, 173–174; and Fujita, *Tenkō no shisō shi-teki kenkyū*, pp. 44, 45, 48.

101. Sano's philosophical critique of Marxism as an alien ideology is analyzed in greater detail in Hoston, "*Ikkoku Shakai-shugi*," pp. 168–186.

102. Sano's nephew made this charge explicitly. See Sano, "Kakumeika Sano Manabu," pp. 111–127.

103. Sano, *Minzoku to kaikyū* p. 10.

104. Sano, "Gokuchū-ki," p. 97 (italics mine).

105. [Sano], *Waga gokuchū no shisō henreki*, pp. 12–15.

106. Sano, "Atarashii shakai-shugi no sekai-kan," 2:965.

107. Sano, *Waga gokuchū no shisō henreki*, pp. 12–15.

108. Sano, *Minzoku to kaikyū*, p. 9.

109. Sano, *Waga gokuchū no shisō henreki*, pp. 6–7; cf. Kobayashi, *Tenkōsha no shigō to seikatsu*, pp. 7–8.

110. See Takabatake, *Marukusu-gaku kenkyū*, pp. 79, 82.

111. Maguire, *Marx's Theory of Politics*, p. 17.

112. See Kawakami, *Jijōden*, 1:204–206; and Nabeyama's view that capitalism had caused a degeneration of morality, in Nabeyama, "Kokoro no sokuseki," pp. 16–18.

113. Sano, *Minzoku to kaikyū*, pp. 15–17.

114. These were best expressed in Marx, "British Rule in India" pp. 653–658.

115. Sano, *Minzoku to kaikyū*, pp. 11–13.

116. Sano, "Gokuchū-ki," pp. 111–113.

117. Ibid., pp. 115–118.

118. Sano, "Marukusu kokka-ron to sono hihan," 1:543–569; cf. Sano, "Gokuchū-ki," pp. 121–122.

119. Sano, "Marukusu kokka-ron to sono hihan," 1:570–573; and Sano, "Gokuchū-ki," pp. 120–121.

120. Sano, "Marukusu kokka-ron to sono hihan," 1:525. Takabatake had made a similar argument in "Kokka shakai-shugi no hitsuzen-sei," p. 175, and idem, " 'Puroretaria kokka' no ronri-teki hatan," pp. 109–110.

121. Sano, "Kenryoku to rōdō," 2:1001.

122. Sano, "Marukusu kokka-ron to sono hihan," 1:576; and Sano, "Gokuchū-ki," pp. 119–120.

123. Sano, "Marukusu kokka-ron to sono hihan," 1:573, 575. And on classes, compare Takabatake, *Marukusu-gaku kenkyū*, p. 82.

124. Sano, "Bukkyō to shakai-shugi," 3:732.

125. Ibid. passim. See Li, "Jingshen jiefang," p. 309; cf. Meisner, *Li Ta-chao*, especially chaps. 5, 6. This was also a major theme of Mao Tse-tung, *On New Democracy*, passim. See the extended discussion of this theme in Hoston, " 'Theology' of Liberation?" pp. 165–221. This very important issue is also the subject of the author's book-length work entitled "Faith, Will, and Revolutionary Change: Modernity and Liberation in the Non-Western World," Princeton University Press, forthcoming.

126. Sano, "Gokuchū-ki," pp. 87–89.

127. Sano, "Bukkyō to shakai-shugi," pp. 735–736.

128. Sano, *Waga gokuchū no shisō henreki*, pp. 6–7.

129. Sano, "Gokuchū-ki," pp. 96–97.

130. Sano, *Minzoku to kaikyū*, p. 336; and Sano, "Marukusu kokka-ron to sono hihan," 1:571–572.

131. Sano, *Minzoku to kaikyū*, pp. 21–29, 31–34.

132. Sano, *Waga gokuchū no shisō henreki*, pp. 19–20.

133. Ibid., p. 100.

134. Kobayashi, *Tenkōsha no shisō to seikatsu*, pp. 24–25; cf. Sano, "Gokuchū-ki," p. 97.

135. Sano, *Waga gokuchū no shisō henreki*, p. 25; and Sano and Nabeyama, "Kyōdō hikoku dōshi ni tsuguru sho," 1:16.

136. Sano and Nabeyama, "Kyōdō nikoku dōshi nitsuguru sho," 1:14. Sano subsequently felt that his support of the war had been "a kind of adventuristic opportunism" ("Gokuchū-ki," pp. 142–144), and after the war urged the reformation of the "militaristic" and "class"-based imperial system into a truly democratic basis for his national socialism (see Sano, "Tennō-sei to shakai-shugi" 2:381).

137. Sano, *Minzoku to kaikyū*, pp. 10, 9.

138. Kobayashi, *Tenkōsha no shisō to seikatsu*, pp. 24–25.

139. Sano, *Minzoku to kaikyū*, p. 13.

140. Sano, *Waga gokuchū no shisō no henreki*, pp. 3–4.

141. Patricia Steinhoff has asserted that "most of the people involved in *tenkō* did not share their leaders' preoccupation with ideology" and, thus, that the deliberations of Sano and Nabeyama on the issues discussed were irrelevant to the motivations of most *tenkōsha* (Steinhoff, "Tenkō and Thought Control," p. 87). This assertion misses the crucial point made here that the *tenkō* of Sano and Nabeyama was not a matter of mere "ideology" either but one of the assertion of individual identity through the medium of the Japanese minzoku. It is critical not to allow a predisposition, characteristic of much American literature in comparative politics, to dismiss "ideology" as irrelevant to actual behavior to blind one to the dimension of individual and group identity. On the latter tendency in American social science, see Brzezenski and Huntington, *Political Power*, pp. 17, 19; Hartz, *Liberal Tradition in America*, p. 10; and Hoffman, *Gulliver's Troubles*, pp. 114, 143–148.

142. See Nyerere, "Ujamaa," pp. 1–12; Cabral, *Return to the Source*; and Luke, "Cabral's Marxism," pp. 311–312.

143. Bellah, *Tokugawa Religion*, (1970) p. 181.

144. Peter Duus, "In Search of a National Mission: Nagai Ryūtarō," quoted in Matsumoto, "Significance of Nationalism," p. 55.

CHAPTER 9

1. Mao Tse-tung, "Reform Our Study" 3:17–18.

2. On the centrality of Chen Boda's role in the formulation of Mao's "sinification" of Marxism, see the excellent work by Raymond F. Wylie, "'Sinification' of Marxism," pp. 447–480; and idem, *Emergence of Maoism*, chap. 4.

3. Rue, *Mao Tse-tung in Opposition*, pp. 37–66, and passim.

4. The term *alternative hegemony* is borrowed from Italian Marxist Antonio Gramsci. Gramsci drew a distinction between "domination," that is, power based on the exercise of force, and "hegemony," which relied on ideological persuasion. Gramsci argued that in

advanced capitalist societies, the role of hegemony was much greater than that of domination and, thus, that it was not sufficient for a socialist party simply to seek to overthrow the existing state. The underlying ideological apparatus, conceptualized by those in power in terms of "consent," would remain intact and, thus, present stubborn resistance to any effort to establish a new socialist order. Thus, Gramsci argued that it was essential for socialist parties in advanced industrialized societies to engage in a prolonged "war of position" (as opposed to a direct attack on state power as in a "war of maneuver") in which they would seek first to establish an "alternative hegemony" of consensus in support of socialist values before they attacked state power. See Gramsci, *Selections from the Prison Notebooks*, pp. 56n., 57, 242–243; the masterful exposition in Adamson, *Hegemony and Revolution*, chaps. 6, 7; and Buci-Glucksmann, "Hegemony and Consent," pp. 116–126. Although Gramsci intended his view of the need for a war of position to apply to advanced capitalist societies, the CCP's experience in the base areas during the Yan'an seems to reflect the successful application of this strategy in a later-industrializing, peasant society.

5. See the classic work on this subject by Johnson, *Peasant Nationalism*. Although this author does not accept Johnson's view that "peasant nationalism" was the primary reason for the CCP's ultimate victory, his work effectively chronicles the appeal of the CCP's nationalist slogans in the face of Japanese aggression.

6. Schwartz, "Essence of Marxism Revisited," p. 469.

7. See Li, "Fengsu," cited in Maruyama, "Ri Taishō no shisō," pp. 47–48; Li, "Bolshevism de shengli," pp. 117–118; idem, "Pan . . . ism zhi shibai yu Democracy zhi shengli," pp. 107–108; idem, "Shumin de shengli," pp. 101–111; and Germaine A. Hoston, "'Theology' of Liberation?" pp. 179–181.

8. Mao, "On Protracted War," 2:129; cf. Mao, "Foolish Old Man," 3:271–272. For a more extended discussion, see Hoston, "'Theology' of Liberation," pp. 181–190. This issue is the subject of a much more detailed analysis in idem, *Faith, Will, and Revolutionary Change*.

9. See, for example, Rumyantsef, "Maoism," p. 243; and Krivtsov and Sidikhmenov, *Mao Tse-tung's Theoretical Conceptions*, p. 64.

10. The heated controversy of the "Symposium on Mao and Marx" that appeared in four issues of *Modern China* in 1976–1977 disputed how much "genuinely" Marxist (as opposed to peculiarly Chinese) content infused Mao's thought within the context of this paradigm. See also, for example, Schram, *Mao Tse-tung*; idem, *Political Thought of Mao Tse-tung*; Wylie, *Emergence of Maoism*; and Starr, "Sinification of Marxism," pp. 149–157.

11. For a definitive treatment of such influences, see Wakeman, *History and Will*.

12. There are notable exceptions, including the following: Dirlik, "Marxist Revolutionary Consciousness," pp. 182–211; Hoston, "'Theology' of Revolution"; Schwartz, "China and the West"; 1:365–379; idem, "Reign of Virtue."

13. Foucault, "Subject and Power," p. 213.

14. See the discussion of cultural revolution later in this chapter.

15. On the questioning of Western assumptions concerning modernity in Mao's thought, see Hoston, "'Theology' of Liberation," pp. 219–220. On the opposition between Liu and Mao, see Tsou, *Cultural Revolution and Post-Mao Reforms*, pp. 76ff; and Dittmer, *Liu Shao-ch'i*.

16. See Hoston, "Transformation of Marxism," p. 44.

17. See Schram, *Thought of Mao Tse-tung*, p. 70.

18. Mao, "On Practice," 1:304, 300.

19. Mao, "Reform Our Study," 3:19.

20. Mao, "Chinese Revolution," 2:306.

21. Nettl, "State as a Conceptual Variable," 559–592 passim.

22. Mao Tse-tung, "Role in the National War," 2:196.

23. See North, *Moscow and Chinese Communists*, 1963 ed., chap. 6; Lerner, *Karl Radek*, pp. 136–146; Cohen, *Bukharin and the Bolshevik Revolution*, (1975) pp. 148–154; and Hammond, "Bukharin and the Chinese Revolution," pp. 463–472.

24. Schwartz, *Rise of Mao*, p. 183.

25. Harrison, *Long March to Power*, p. 189.

26. When Mao celebrated his final victory over the Russian returned students (Wang Ming et al.) and launched the rectification (*zhengfeng*) campaign, he recommended as texts for the study of Marxism the *History of the Communist Party of the Soviet Union (Bolsheviks), Short Course* (a Stalinist product) and cited J. V. Stalin, "The Foundations of Leninism," *Problems of Leninism*, Russian ed. (Moscow, 1952) (Mao, "Reform Our Study," 3:24, 25n).

27. Mao, "Ten Major Relationships," 5:304. On Mao's problematic relationship with Stalin, see Schram, *Thought of Mao Tse-tung*, pp. 61, 136–137. Schram points out that the long passage in the current version of "On Contradiction" celebrating Stalin's analysis of the roots of Leninism as "a model for understanding the particularity and the universality of contradiction and their interconnection" was not present in the original 1937 version. Mao instead appealed to, as a Chinese source, Su Tongpo's poem, "The Red Cliff," to support his argument (p. 67, 68n).

28. Wylie, " 'Sinification' of Marxism," pp. 448–449. Wylie suggests that Mao borrowed the notion of the sinification of Marxism from Chen, "who first used it in an essay of May 1938, several months before it was adopted by Mao in his important report to the CCP's Sixth Plenum in October of that year" (p. 463).

29. Ibid., p. 477.

30. See Marx, "Civil War in France," p. 630; Engels, introduction to Marx, "Civil War in France," p. 627; and Lenin, "Gosudarstvo i revoliutsiia," 5th ed., vol. 33.

31. Mao, *Selected Works*, 2:340.

32. Shouchang [Li Dazhao], "Shi-yue geming yu Zhongguo renmin" (November 7, 1922), in Li Dazhao, *Li Dazhao xuanji*, p. 401.

33. Marx, "Revolution in China and Europe," *New York Tribune*, June 14, 1853, quoted in Meisner, *Li Ta-chao*, (1979), p. 226.

34. See Lenin, *Development of Capitalism in Russia*, cf. Baron, "Plekhanov's Russia," pp. 388–404. Interestingly, even with his nationalist zeal, Mao shared Lenin's view of China as backward, but he would not allow that perspective to vitiate his zeal for a socialist revolution in his own society.

35. Meisner, *Li Ta-chao*, (1979) pp. 217–218; cf. Schwartz, *Rise of Mao*, pp. 28–29.

36. Degras, "United Front Tactics," pp. 15–18.

37. Schwartz, *Rise of Mao*, p. 77. Cf. Brandt, Schwartz, and Fairbank, *Documentary History of Chinese Communism*, (1966) pp. 65–97.

38. Ibid., pp. 78–79.

39. Ibid., p. 69. Cf. Hammond, "Bukharin and the Chinese Revolution," passim.

40. Degras, "United Front Tactics," pp. 21–22; Brandt, Schwartz, and Fairbank, *Documentary History of Chinese Communism*, (1966) pp. 89–216.

41. Harrison, *Long March to Power*, pp. 137–140.

42. Schram, *Mao Tse-tung*; and Meisner, *Li Ta-chao*, (1979) chap. 1, p. 217.

43. Chen wrote, " 'In the Soviet Union the republic overthrew the feudal system only to be replaced by socialism a half year later. This is clear proof that there need not be any long interim period between feudalism and socialism' " ("Kuo-ch'ing chi-nien ti chia-chih" [The

value of celebrating the founding of the republic], *Hsin Ch'ing-nien*, vol. 8, no. 3 [November 1920], quoted in Schwartz, *Rise of Mao*, p. 29). Schwartz goes on to point out that in arguing thus, Chen was "a Trotskyist by instinct before Trotskyism had emerged as a distinct phenomenon and without Trotsky's ingenious theoretical rationalization" (Schwartz, *Rise of Mao*, p. 29).

44. See Knei-paz, *Leon Trotsky*, chap. 4. It remains unclear whether Li and Chen had, in fact, read Trotsky's writings on this subject and were influenced by them, but the similarity in logic remains compelling.

45. Lenin, "State and Revolution," pp. 341–344; and Lenin, "Left-Wing Communism," pp. 579–586.

46. See Trotsky, *Problems of the Chinese Revolution*; and the final chapter of Isaacs, *Tragedy of the Chinese Revolution*.

47. See P'eng Shu-tse (Peng Shuzhi), "Victory of the CCP," especially pp. 78–79, 92. The antipathy between Mao and the Trotskyists was mutual. Many Trotskyists were imprisoned after 1949 or fled into exile in Vietnam and then in France where Peng wrote his memoirs.

48. Mao, "On New Democracy," p. 347.

49. See Lenin, "Two Tactics of Social Democracy," pp. 79–110.

50. Mao Zedong, "Guomin geming yu nongmin yundong," 1:175–179. Cf. Schram, *Thought of Mao Tse-tung*, pp. 39ff.

51. Snow, *Red Star Over China*, p. 157, quoted in Schram, *Mao Tse-tung*, p. 82.

52. Schwartz, *Rise of Mao*, pp. 74–75; cf. Wakeman, *History and Will*, p. 222.

53. Brantly Womack, *Mao Zedong's Political Thought*, pp. 70–71.

54. "Hunan nung-min yün-tung kao-ch'a pao-kao" (A report on an investigation of the agrarian movement in Hunan) from *Mao Tse-tung Hsüan-chi* (Selected Works of Mao Tse-tung), p. 22, quoted in Schwartz, *Rise of Mao*, p. 75.

55. See Zarrow, *Anarchism and Chinese Political Culture*, Studies of the East Asian Institute, pp. 83, 112, 117, 121, 128.

56. See the discussion in Meisner, "Utopian Socialist Themes in Maoism."

57. On narodnik politics, see Venturi, *Roots of Revolution*, especially chap. 18.

58. Mao, "Foolish Old Man," 3:271–274.

59. See the discussion in Murphey, "Man and Nature in China," pp. 313–333.

60. Murphey, "City and Countryside," pp. 253–254.

61. Mao Tse-tung, "Peasant Movement in Hunan," 1:23–24.

62. See Wakeman, *History and Will*, pp. 90–91.

63. See Meisner, "Leninism and Maoism," pp. 2–36.

64. Li, "Qingnian yü nongcun," pp. 146–150. Cf. Shimamoto, "Go-shi ki no eikyō," p. 32.

65. Li, "T'u-ti yü nung-min," in *HC* (*Li Ta-chao hsuen-chi*), pp. 525, 535, quoted in Meisner, *Li Ta-chao*, (1979) p. 239. This article was published in six parts between December 1925 and February 1926.

66. Cf. Meisner, *Li Ta-chao*, (1979) p. 255.

67. See Wakeman, *History and Will*, chap. 16. Note the reference to the Confucian term *xiuyang* in the Chinese title of Liu Shaoqi's classic *How to Be a Good Communist* (1939, *Lun gongchandang-yuan de xiuyang*), pp. 7–76). Dittmer notes that it was Chen, Mao's secretary and collaborator in sinifying Marxism, who updated and revised *How to Be a Good Communist* in the early-1960s (Dittmer, "Death and Transfiguration," p. 472). Mao himself supported Liu's perspective in several essays before and after 1949. See, for example, Mao, "Party's Style of Work," 3:50. As this applied to dealing with those who had

erred in the party, however, there was a tension between the espousal of a long process of cultivation and Mao's advocacy of "shock therapy" as in his "Oppose Stereotyped Party Writing," 3:56. See the insightful discussion of this point in Dittmer, *China's Continuous Revolution*, pp. 69ff.

68. Cf. Meisner, *Li Ta-chao*, (1979) p. 255.

69. Mao, "Role in the National War," p. 196.

70. Mao, "Win the Masses," 1:290.

71. Mao, "On New Democracy," 2:343.

72. Johnson, *Peasant Nationalism*, p. 5.

73. Selden, *Yenan Way*, p. 79.

74. Foucault, "Subject and Power," pp. 222–224.

75. See Mao, "Tasks of the Chinese Communist Party," 1:263–283.

76. Marx, "Critique of the Gotha Program," p. 395 (Marx's italics).

77. Mao, "On New Democracy," p. 354.

78. Engels, Introduction to Marx, "Civil War in France," p. 535.

79. Marx, "Civil War in France," p. 632.

80. Engels, *Anti-Dühring*, pp. 304–307.

81. Lenin, "State and Revolution," p. 331.

82. See Ulam, *Bolsheviks*, (1968) pp. 457–469.

83. See Cohen, *Bukharin and the Bolshevik Revolution* (1975); and Erlich, *Soviet Industrialization Debates*, pt. 1.

84. See Cohen, *Bukharin and the Bolshevik Revolution*, (1975) chap. 10.

85. See Trotsky, *Revolution Betrayed*; Trotsky, "Stalinism and Bolshevism," (1976) pp. 359–369; and Bukharin, "Organized Mismanagement in Modern Society," pp. 394–403.

86. Since 1949 and through the emergence of the Sino-Soviet split in the late 1950s, the CCP has circumvented the issues for Marxist theory raised by Takabatake's suggestion simply by denying the socialist character of the Soviet Union and calling it "state capitalist."

> Compared with that of the capitalist-imperialist countries, the state monopoly capitalism of the Soviet Union is more monopolistic, more concentrated and more tightly controlled. All its economic lifelines including the war industry are directly controlled by the Soviet revisionist renegade clique which takes firm hold of the state machine. . . . To grab maximum profits, the Soviet revisionist bureaucrat-monopoly capitalist class steps up its aggression and expansion abroad, annexes new territories, plunders cheap raw materials and unloads its commodities abroad, exports capital and shifts its crises onto others. (*Daily Report: China*, October 7, 1975, p. A18, quoted in Bedeski, *Fragile Entente*, p. 58)

87. Mao, "On New Democracy," p. 353.

88. In Mao's mature thought, the achievement of socialism as a nationalist mission would only be realized through continual class struggle within the Chinese nation. Roots of this idea could be found in the Yan'an era, but the strength of Mao's conviction that this class struggle must recur continually after the revolution appears to have arisen out of disillusionment with the intellectuals and with the party itself after 1949.

89. Lenin, "Two Tactics of Social Democracy," pp. 99–107.

90. Mao, "Wusi yundong ershi zhounian" (May 4, 1939) (Speech at Yan'an commemorating the twentieth anniversary of the May Fourth movement), in *Mao Tse-tung ji*, 6:331.

91. In fact, Lenin's formulation went much further than this. In *What Is to Be Done?* Lenin maintained that the distance of "petty-bourgeois" intellectuals from the actual situa-

tion of the working class was *necessary* for the emergence of revolutionary "proletarian" consciousness. Quoting Karl Kautsky:

> Of course, socialism as a doctrine, has its roots in modern economic relationships just as the class struggle of the proletariat has, and, like the latter, emerges from the struggle against the capitalist-created poverty and misery of the masses. . . . Modern socialist consciousness can arise only on the basis of profound scientific knowledge. Indeed, modern economic science is as much a condition for socialist production as, say modern technology, and the proletariat can create neither the one nor the other, no matter how much it may desire to do so; both arise out of the modern social progress. (Lenin, "What Is to Be Done?" p. 28)

92. Lenin's brother Alexander Ulyanov was executed in 1887 for participating in an unsuccessful terrorist attack on Tsar Alexander III that year. See the account of this affair and its impact on Lenin in Ulam, *Bolsheviks*, (1968) pp. 9–18.

93. Ibid., p. 45.

94. Mao, "Wusi yundong ershi zhounian," 6:331.

95. Mao, "May 4th Movement," 2:238. Note that the official text, published in 1957, as the Hundred Flowers Campaign gave way to the Anti-Rightist Campaign, omitted the attribution of the "entire revolutionary movement" to intellectuals.

96. Mao, "Talks at the Yenan Forum," 3:73.

97. See the biography of Schram, *Mao Tse-tung*, chaps. 2–4.

98. Lenin, "Two Tactics of Social Democracy," pp. 79, and passim.

99. See Mao Tse-tung, "Party's Style of Work," 3:41.

100. Liu, "Intra-Party Struggle," p. 189.

101. Liu, "Training the Communist Party Member," in ibid., p. 112.

102. This is evident throughout Mao's writings during the Rectification Campaign, but it is most apparent in his "Talks at the Yenan Forum," passim.

103. Mao, "Party's Style of Work," p. 41. Compare the statement to this effect by Chen Yun: "[T]he Communist Party is not a 'labor party,' but 'an organized vanguard of the proletariat, the most advanced form of its class organization.' Therefore, not all workers can join the Party, but only those superior elements who are most conscious, active, and faithful to the working class mission" (Ch'en Yün, "How to Be a Party Member," p. 93).

104. Gramsci, "State and Civil Society," p. 243.

105. See Gramsci, "State and Civil Society," pp. 235–239; and Adamson, *Hegemony and Revolution*, especially chaps. 6, 7.

106. Mao, "Gei Lin Biao tongzhi de xin," 2:130.

107. Mao, "Lun chijiu zhan," 6:98.

108. Liu, *How to Be a Good Communist*, pp. 5–6.

109. Much of the literature on the subject stresses Mao's need to consolidate his power as a major factor in the launching of the Rectification Campaign. (See particularly, the translator's introduction to *Mao's China*, and Wylie, *Emergence of Maoism*.) Although the author of this study does not take fundamental issue with the importance of consolidating Mao's victory over the Russian returned students in the Rectification Campaign, other sources, such as Hinton, *Fanshen*, Selden, *Yenan Way*, and Oksenberg, "Getting Ahead and Along," on the circumstances leading to the launching of the Cultural Revolution, indicate that the heavily intellectual origins of the CCP did, in fact, lead to estrangement from and conflicts with the masses of peasants that had to form the CCP's peasant base during the revolutionary period.

110. Mao, "Win the Masses," 1:288–289.

111. See, for example, Mao Tse-tung, "Interview with James Bertram," 2:97; and Liu, "Intra-Party Struggle," p. 196.

112. Mao, "Talk at Central Work Conference," p. 164.

113. Mao, "Interview with James Bertram," p. 97.

114. Mao, "Methods of Leadership," 3:117, 119. Cf. Selden, *Yenan Way*, pp. 274–278; Lewis, *Leadership in Communist China*, pp. 70–100; and Townsend, *Political Participation in Communist China*, pp. 57, 72–74, 94–95, 101–102.

115. For this strain in Marx, see Engels, introduction, to Marx, "Civil War in France," p. 535. For Lenin's concept of the vanguard party, see Lenin, "What Is to Be Done?" especially pp. 50ff. and 67ff.

116. See Schram, *Mao Tse-tung*, p. 48.

117. Mao, "On Practice," 1:295ff; cf. idem, "Where Do Correct Ideas Come From?" pp. 502–504.

118. Cf. Schram, "Party in Chinese Communist Ideology," p. 8.

119. See Friedman, *Backward toward Revolution*, especially chap. 2.

120. This is not unique, of course. A similar usage of the "party" idea occurs in *Federalist* no. 5. In a society with little or no tradition of participatory and competitive politics, however, this assumption had a crippling effect on the development of a democratic polity in China.

121. See Wakeman, "Price of Autonomy," pp. 41, 54.

122. One might usefully compare the attitude that undergirded the dissolution of competing parties into a single overarching "party" in Japan in the 1930s.

123. Starr, *Continuing the Revolution*, p. 85.

124. Mao, "Serve the People," 3:177–178.

125. See, for example, Mao, "Reform Our Study," 317–325; idem, "Oppose Stereotyped Party Writing" 3:53–68 passim; idem, "Opposition to Party Formalism," pp. 33–53 passim.

126. Liu, *How to Be a Good Communist*, pp. 7–8.

127. See Rousseau, "Origins of Inequality"; and idem, *Social Contract*, p. 49.

128. Liu, *How to Be a Good Communist*, p. 86.

129. For other stimulating perspectives comparing Mao and Rousseau, see Schwartz, "Reign of Virtue," pp. 166–169.

130. The analogy here between Mao and Rousseau's legislator is admittedly an imperfect one. There is no indication in Rousseau that the legislator was meant to stay in a position of vigilant leadership once the laws had been formulated. Nevertheless, the analogy here holds for the purpose of highlighting the tensions among different concepts of leadership and their inherent problems in those of Mao and Rousseau.

131. See Schwartz, "China and the West," pp. 368–370.

132. Mao, "Speeches at the National Conference," 5:155.

133. Schram, *Thought of Mao Tse-tung*, p. 111.

134. For an excellent discussion of Mao's notion of development that correctly finds the roots of his rejection of the Soviet model in the Yan'an period, see Gray, "Two Roads," especially pp. 123–127.

135. See the excellent critique of the notion of rationality in Weber's (and Lenin's) in Hearn, "Rationality and Bureaucracy," pp. 37–54.

136. On this point, cf. Dittmer, *China's Continuous Revolution*, which also adopts this perspective. Mao's treatment of bureaucracy was extraordinarily complex and fraught with inconsistencies, the full range of which lie beyond the scope of the current work.

137. Engels, introduction to Marx, *Civil War in France*, p. 535.

138. See Starr, *Continuing the Revolution*, p. 89.

139. Mao, "On the Correct Handling," (Speaking Notes) p. 133.

140. Wakeman, *History and Will*, p. 27.

141. *Renmin ribao*, August 24, 1966, translated in *Peking Review* 37 (1966): 2–21, quoted in Schram, *Thought of Mao Tse-tung*, p. 172.

142. Here it should be noted that it was Stalin, seeking to justify his assault on old Bolsheviks in the Great Purges, who introduced the notion that class struggle would continue after the revolution (see Schram, "Mao Tse-tung and Permanent Revolution," p. 240; and Topper, "Commune to Cultural Revolution," pp. 174–175. Mao introduced this notion in China in 1957:

> In China, although in the main socialist transformation has been completed with respect to the system of ownership, and although the large-scale and turbulent class struggles of the masses characteristic of the previous revolutionary periods have in the main come to an end, there are still remnants of the overthrown landlord and comprador classes, there is still a bourgeoisie, and the remoulding of the petty bourgeoisie has only just started. The class struggle is by no means over. The class struggle between the proletariat and the bourgeoisie, the class struggle between the different political forces, and the class struggle in the ideological field between the proletariat and the bourgeoisie will continue to be long and tortuous and at times will even become very acute. (Mao, "Correct Handling of Contradictions," pp. 463–464)

143. Mao, "On New Democracy," p. 379.

144. In *Anti-Dühring*, Engels had noted the possibility that the state could attain some autonomy from the economic base and could encourage or retard economic development. In the final analysis, however, Engels opted for consistency and declared that any effort by the state to arrest the "normal" course of economic development was destined to fail. In short, superstructure could be somewhat autonomous of the economic base but could not disrupt the "normal" historical progression. See Engels, *Anti-Dühring*, pp. 202–204.

145. See Marx, *Pre-Capitalist Economic Formations*, pp. 69–70.

146. See Lin, *Crisis of Chinese Consciousness*.

147. Cf. Hearn, "Rationality and Bureaucracy," p. 49; Whyte, "Bureaucracy and Modernization in China," p. 151; and Schwartz, "Thoughts of Mao Tse-tung," p. 26.

148. Mao Tsetung, "On Contradiction," p. 116.

149. These figures are given as 80 percent and 50 percent in another version of this speech. See Mao, "On the Correct Handling" (Speaking Notes), p. 142.

150. See, for example, Mao's remarks in *Mao Tse-tung ssu-hsiang wan-sui* (1969), p. 426, quoted in Schram, *Thought of Mao Tse-tung*, p. 165.

151. See [Chinese Communist party], "Resolution on Certain Questions," pp. 1–86.

152. Mao, "Report to the Second Plenary Session," 4:363.

153. Schram, *Thought of Mao Tse-tung*, p. 128.

154. Ibid., p. 144. Subsequently, Mao was criticized for his resemblance to the autocratic character of Qin Shihuang. See ibid., p. 189; and Sullivan, "Analysis of 'Despotism,'" pp. 806–807.

155. See Bernstein, "Stalinism, Famine, and Chinese Peasants," pp. 343–344. Bernstein's account clarifies that Mao did not abandon materialist concern for raising Chinese standards of living. Indeed, in 1959, it was he who criticized officials in counties and communes for expropriation of peasant assets that resulted in starvation. Rather, the key point is that he elevated factors in the "superstructure" of society over the limitations imposed by the base.

156. For a developmental analysis of these two notions in Mao's thought and the relationship of the first to Mao's repudiation of the Soviet model, see Young and Woodward, "From Contradictions to Class Struggle," pp. 912–922. This interpretation takes issue with those offered by Schram and Starr.

157. As early as 1958, Mao had lamented the effect of the regulations imposed by state power in inhibiting class conflict. See ibid., p. 923.

158. Cf. Kraus, *Conflict in Chinese Socialism*, p. 109.

159. Simon Leys goes further, asserting that Maoism destroyed civilization itself and created a "spiritual desert." See Pierre Ryckmans [Simon Leys], *Chinese Shadows*, p. 24; and Meisner, "Marxism and Chinese Values," p. 106.

160. *Resolution on CPC History* and the discussion in Tsou, *Cultural Revolution and Post-Mao Reforms*, pp. 221–222.

161. For an authoritative discussion of the subject and an assessment of the many approaches to it in Western political philosophy, see Flathman, *Practice of Political Authority*.

162. Kelly, *Hegel's Retreat from Eleusis*, p. 204. Gramsci's insights on the nature of hegemony, described herein, offered an important corrective to the orthodox Marxist-Leninist treatment of authority in the latter terms.

163. Flathman draws a distinction between substantive-purposive theories of authority that understand authority in "functional or other teleological terms," on the one hand, and formal-procedural theories that conceptualize authority "as an attribute of rules, procedures, and offices." See Flathman, *Practice of Political Authority*, pp. 4–5.

164. See, in particular, Habermas, *Legitimation Crisis*; and Marcuse, *One-Dimensional Man*.

165. Mao, "Interview with James Bertram," p. 57. A suggestive comparison might be made with the claim to articulate the Imperial Will among Japanese military branches in the same period. See Titus, *Palace and Politics in Prewar Japan*.

CHAPTER 10

1. Graham Peck opens his insightful study of Republican China by noting this difference between Chinese and Western views of time. See *Two Kinds of Time*.

2. See Joseph R. Levenson's insightful study of *Confucian China and its Modern Fate*, vol. 1, pt. 2, pp. 59–79, 108–109.

3. There was some compulsion to restore a sense of Japanese national essence in the 1880s, but the point here is that agonizing over this did not prevent Japanese political leaders from undertaking necessary political and economic reforms, including the importation of Western knowledge and political ideas. See Gluck, *Japan's Modern Myths*, especially chap. 5.

4. See Shillony, *Revolt in Japan*; Smethurst, *Social Basis for Japanese Militarism*, pp. 163–165.

5. This analysis is supported by key elements of Fletcher, *Search for a New Order*.

6. Marx, "British Rule in India," pp. 657–658.

7. Carrère d'Encausse and Schram, *Marxism and Asia*, p. 4.

8. For an analysis that reinterprets prewar Japanese history in these terms, see Hoston, *Crisis of Development in Prewar Japan*.

9. See Ishida, "Socialism and National Consciousness," 167ff.

10. See Wolf, *Europe and People without History*.

11. Wylie, "'Sinification' of Marxism," pp. 455–456.

12. See Sternhell, *La droite révolutionnaire*, especially chaps. 1, 2; and von Klemperer, *Germany's New Conservatism*, (1968) especially pp. 36ff.

13. The focus of von Klemperer's study is German conservatism, but as the views of the Japanese and Chinese Marxian national socialist theorists treated here amply demonstrate, the distinction between the political Left and the Right, between radicalism and conservatism, becomes problematic when one is contemplating potently nationalistic views that advocate the resurrection of elements of the past to supplant the status quo. This is evident in the diverse treatments of Nietzsche, for example, treating him variously as conservative and radical. See, for example, von Klemperer, *Germany's New Conservatism*, pp. 36–39; Thomas Mann, "Nietzsches Philosophie im Lichte unserer Erfahrung" (Nietzsche's philosophy in the light of our experience), *Die Neue Rundschau* (The New Review) (Achtes Heft, Fall 1947); and Georg Brandes, "Aristokratischer Radicalismus. Eine Abhandlung über Friedrich Nietzsche" (Aristocratic radicalism: A treatise on Friedrich Nietzsche), *Deutsche Rundschau* [German Review], 63 (1890): 52–89.

14. See especially Sorel, *Reflections on Violence*, chap. 4.

15. See Nietzsche, *Beyond Good and Evil*, especially pp. 49, 191ff; and idem, "The Will to Power," *Works*, 3d ed. (New York and London, n.p., n.d.) 15:394.

16. On Sorel's views of the French Revolution, see his *Reflections on Violence*, pp. 119ff; and Juillard, "Sorel, Rousseau et la revolution française," pp. 10–14.

17. Bryan S. Turner has noted that while the French Revolution destroyed the old absolutist monarchy, it also elevated "the political and economic significance of the peasantry by the legislation of smallholdings," and the "post-revolutionary structure of rural France had the consequence of delaying capitalist development in the first half of the nineteenth century" (*Marx and the End of Orientalism*, p. 72).

18. Compare the advice offered in Machiavelli, *Discourses*, pp. 176–177.

19. Such sentiments have been evident in the scholarly debate over the proper interpretation of the French Revolution in the postwar era. See the Marxist interpretation that was predominant until the 1970s in Soboul, *La Révolution française*; and the contrary views reflected in Cobban, *Myth of the French Revolution*; and idem, *Social Interpretation of the French Revolution*; Furet and Richet, *La révolution française*; and Furet, *Interpreting the French Revolution*.

20. See Sternhell, *Maurice Barrès*; idem, "National Socialism and Anti-Semitism"; cf. Talmon, *Myth of the Nation*, especially pt. 8.

21. Eley, "Wilhelmine Right," pp. 123–131.

22. Ibid., p. 115.

23. See Mosse, *Crisis of German Ideology*, (1964), chaps. 1, 2. Von Klemperer, *Germany's New Conservatism*, (1968) chap. 2.

24. Sternhell, *Maurice Barrès*, p. 7. See also Masur, *Prophets of Yesterday*; Hughes, *Consciousness and Society*; and Sternhell, "Fascist Ideology," pp. 320ff.

25. Although it is weak on some accounts, the study by Jack J. Roth effectively depicts this influence. See his *Cult of Violence*, especially chap. 6. See also Gregor, *Young Mussolini*, especially pp. 25–28, 119–123.

26. See Georges Sorel, "La crise du socialisme" (The crisis of socialism), *Revue politique et parlementaire* 18 (1898): 611–612, quoted in Juillard, "Sorel, sessant'anni dopo," pp. 92–93.

27. Hobsbawm, "Reflections on Nationalism," pp. 388–389.

28. See Paul Robert Magosci, *The Shaping of a National Identity: Subcarpathian Rus', 1848–1914* (Cambridge: Harvard University Press, 1978), p. 2, quoted in Eley, "Nationalism and Social History," p. 94.

29. This is the association drawn by Hans Kohn in his *Idea of Nationalism*.

30. Eley, "Nationalism and Social History," p. 85.

31. Smith, *Theories of Nationalism*, p. 198.

32. Eley, "Nationalism and Social History," p. 90; see the books under review by Eley here: Keith Hitchens, *Orthodoxy and Nationality: Andrieu Sagun and the Rumanians of Transylvania, 1846–1873* (Cambridge: Harvard University Press, 1977); Gerasimos Augustinos, *Consciousness and History: Nationalist Critics of Greek Society 1897–1914* (New York: Columbia University Press, 1977); Magosci, *Shaping of a National Identity*, and Hans Mommsen, *Arbeiterbewegung und Nationale Frage: Ausgewählte Aufsätze* (The labor movement and selected essays) (Vendenhoeck and Rupprecht, DM 78, 1979), as well as T. de Mauro, *Storia linguistic dell'Italia unita* (A linguistic history of united Italy) (Bari, 1972).

33. Eley, "Nationalism and Social History," p. 93.

34. On the Japanese Marxist debate on the revolutionary character of the Meiji Restoration, see Hoston, "Conceptualizing Bourgeois Revolution."

35. See Hoston, "State, Modernity, and the Fate of Liberalism."

36. Although it overstates the significance of nationalism in the Chinese Communist victory, the definitive work on the issue of nationalism in the Communist revolution remains Johnson, *Peasant Nationalism*.

37. See Gregor, *Young Mussolini*.

38. Cf. the suggestions concerning the genesis of national-socialism in Germany, in Eley, "What Produces Fascism," pp. 71ff.

39. Thomas Nairn, *The Break-Up of Britain: Crisis and Neo-Nationalism* (London, 1977), cited in Eley, "State Formation," p. 288.

40. Mao, "Chinese People Have Stood Up!" 5:15–18.

41. See Mao, "People's Democratic Dictatorship," p. 375.

42. Mao, "Criticize Han Chauvinism," 5:87–88; Mao, "Ten Major Relationships," 5:295–296; and the brief discussion of liberating the Dalai Lama in Mao, "Speech at the Second Session," 5:346.

43. Wang, "Our Nationalities Policy," pp. 562–571.

44. See Nathan, *Chinese Democracy*, (1986) p. 109.

45. See the "Nineteen Points" of the Human Rights League, pp. 83–84, and "Kang Sheng," p. 189, both in Seymour, *Fifth Modernization*, pp. 83–84.

46. Mao made this claim in "Correct Handling of Contradictions," 5:406.

47. A detailed treatment of this factionalism and the underlying theoretical issues surrounding it is offered in Hoston, *Crisis of Development in Prewar Japan*, chap. 9.

48. Beckmann and Okubo, *Japanese Communist Party*, p. 275.

49. *Shakai-shugi Kyōkai teize*, p. 9; and "Nihon Shakaitō kōryō (kettō-ji)," p. 21.

50. Dore, *Land Reform in Japan*, p. 115.

51. Ibid., chaps. 6–8, especially p. 175, table 8.

52. Nakamura, *Postwar Japanese Economy*, pp. 23–25.

53. Kajinishi et al., *Nihon shihon-shugi no hattatsu*, 5:1470–1471.

54. Ibid., 5:1472–1473.

55. Ibid., 5:1449–1450, 1451n; Uno, "Wagakuni nōson no hōken-sei"; and Ōuchi, "Nōson minshuka no michi chikakarazu."

56. Kajinishi et al., *Nihon ni okeru shihon-shugi no hattatsu*, 5:1471–1472.

57. See Scalapino, *Japanese Communist Movement*, pp. 54–56.

58. Nihon Kyōsantō, *Nihon Kyōsantō no rokujū nen*, 1:154–171, and Scalapino, *Japanese Communist Movement*, pp. 56–57.

59. Yamada, "Nōchi kaikaku no rekishi-teki igi" (The historical significance of the land reforms), cited by Shibagaki and Saeki, "Sengo Nihon keizai no kihon mondai," pp. 50–51.

60. Scalapino, *Japanese Communist Movement*, pp. 59–60.

61. Ibid., pp. 60–63, 80–81; Kojima, *Nihon shihon-shugi ronsō shi* p. 214.

62. *Nihon shihon-shugi kōza* (Symposium on Japanese capitalism), 1:338, cited by Shibagaki and Saeki, "Sengo Nihon keizai no kihon mondai," p. 50.

63. Nihon Kyōsantō, *Nihon Kyōsantō no rokujū nen*, 1:176.

64. "'Nihon shihon-shugi kōza' no shuppatsu no tame ni" (For the beginning of the symposium on Japanese capitalism), in *Nihon shihon-shugi kōza*, vol. 1, cited by Kojima, *Nihon shihon-shugi ronsō shi*, pp. 208–209.

65. See Inoue Kiyoshi and Kondō Yasuo et al., "Nōchi kaikaku to han-hōken sei" (The land reforms and semi-feudalism), in *Nihon shihon-shugi kōza*, vol. 5; and Yamada Shōjirō et al., "Nōmin shūdatsu to nōgyō kiki" (The exploitation of peasants and agricultural crisis), in *Nihon shihon-shugi kōza*, vol. 6, both cited in Kojima, *Nihon shihon-shugi ronsō shi*, p. 212n.

66. Miyamoto Kenji, report on the party program to the Seventh Party Congress, quoted in Kojima, *Nihon shihon-shugi ronsō shi*, pp. 215–216.

67. Moriya, "Gendai Nihon no seiji kikō," 1:129.

68. See Kojima, *Nihon shihon-shugi ronsō shi*, pp. 251–265; and Takauchi, *Gendai Nihon shihon-shugi ronsō*, chaps. 2–5.

69. Hoston, *Crisis of Development in Prewar Japan*, p. 272.

70. Again, space does not permit a full discussion of the controversies on these issues. See Hoston, *Crisis of Development in Prewar Japan*, pp. 256–264.

71. See Yamada, *Bunseki*. (1934).

72. See Kamiyama, "Nihon teikoku-shugi no seikaku," pp. 200–215; Kojima, *Nihon shihon-shugi ronsō shi*, pp. 148–153.

73. Shiga, "Gunji-teki hōken-teki 'teikoku-shugi' ni tsuite," pp. 39–57.

74. See Kojima, *Nihon shihon-shugi ronsō shi*, pp. 153–154.

75. This is not to say that there were no Marxian national socialists in the postwar era in Japan. Sano Manabu certainly continued his work, but the weak following he drew was typical of those who took this path in the postwar era.

76. Shiga, *Sekai to Nihon*, pp. 47–48, cited by Kojima, *Nihon shihon-shugi ronsō shi*, p. 176; and Shiga, *Kokka-ron*, pp. 149–150, 157–159.

77. Hattori, "Dai Nihon teikoku-shugi," in *Hattori Shisō chosaku-shū*, p. 239, cited by Kojima, *Nihon shihon-shugi ronsōshi*, p. 178.

78. Hoston, *Crisis of Development in Prewar Japan*, pp. 263–264.

79. For detailed analysis of the relationship between Marxist theory and political practice in postwar Japanese politics, see ibid., pp. 264–291; and Hoston, "Between Theory and Practice," pp. 175–207.

80. Liu, *Liu Shaoqi xuanji*, especially pp. 60–61.

81. See Dittmer, *Liu Shao-ch'i*, pp. 22–25.

82. Strong, "Thought of Mao Tse-tung," pp. 161–174, and Liu Shao-ch'i, *Collected Works*, 3 vols. (Hong Kong, 1969), 2: 183–189, both cited in Dittmer, *Liu Shao-ch'i*, p. 25.

83. See Linden, *Khrushchev and the Soviet Leadership*, pp. 32–36

84. Schram, *Mao Tse-tung*, pp. 286ff. The Chinese official response was contained in the article "On the Historical Experience of the Dictatorship of the Proletariat." See Mao, "Speech at Second Session," pp. 341–342.

85. Schwartz, "Sino-Soviet Relations," (1970) pp. 143–144; and the early polemics

contained in Zagoria, *Sino-Soviet Conflict*, p. 39; and Gittings, *Sino-Soviet Dispute*, pp. 59–63.

86. See Keesing's Research Report no.3, *Sino-Soviet Dispute*, p. 7; and Linden, *Khrushchev and the Soviet Leadership*.

87. Schwartz, "Sino-Soviet Relations," p. 146.

88. Mao Tsetung, "Experiences in Our Party's History," 5:324–329.

89. Interview with Jiang Yuanchun, International Department of *Renmin ribao* (People's Daily), Williamsburg, Va., January 1981. Although this proposal is not mentioned in Gurtov's and Hwang's analysis of Sino-Soviet military relations in this period, the news of such a proposal helps to account for the antagonisms that they describe. See Gurtov, *China under Threat*, pp. 70–72.

90. Donald C. Heldman, "Sino-Soviet Split," pp. 51–58.

91. Charles, "Dismissal of Marshal P'eng Teh-huai," pp. 66–67; and idem, *Case of P'eng Teh-huai*.

92. Just one week after Peng's return to China in mid-June, the Soviets canceled an agreement committing new technology for the improvement of China's defense capability. This might have been the product of Peng's revelations, or it might have been a situation in which Soviet leaders simply used Peng's criticisms of domestic Chinese developments as a pretext for canceling aid. See Solomon, *Mao's Revolution*, (1971) p. 391.

93. See Ahn, "Great Leap Forward," p. 262.

94. See Nathan, *Chinese Democracy*, p. 104.

95. See Bernstein, "Leadership and Mass Mobilization," pp. 1–47; and Shue, *Peasant China in Transition*.

96. Mao, "Tasks of the Chinese Communist Party," 1:274; Mao, "Chinese Revolution," 2:330.

97. Ibid., 2:306–307.

98. Mao, "Strategy in China's Revolutionary War," 1:198.

99. Mao, "Peasant Movement in Hunan," 1:23–59.

100. Mao, "On New Democracy," 2:380–381.

101. Starr, *Continuing the Revolution*, pp. 267–272.

102. See the analyses by Wang, "*Past and Present in China Today*," pp. 1–24; Goldman, "China's Anti-Confucian Campaign," pp. 435–462; and Starr, "Weeding through the Old" pp. 1–12, as well as the selections from the campaign that appear in *Selected Articles Criticizing Lin Piao and Confucius*.

103. This emphasis was particularly strong in Liu's "Lun gongchandangyuan de xiuyang" (How to be a good Communist), and Liu, "On the Intra-Party Struggle," p. 208; and in Mao's "Struggle in the Chingkang Mountains," 1:92–93; idem, "Our Study," 3:163–176. See also the insightful discussion in Wright, "Struggle versus Harmony: pp. 589–602; and Solomon, *Mao's Revolution*, (1972) especially chaps. 11, 13.

104. Schram, "Mao Tse-tung and Permanent Revolution," p. 225.

105. Mao, "Ten Major Relationships," pp. 285–286.

106. Mao blamed the "restoration of capitalism" in the Soviet Union on Khrushchev, but, of course, it was under Stalin that the creation of the Soviet Union's "state capitalism" and massive bureaucracy occurred. This is an inconsistency in Mao that can only be explained by his dependence on the lineage from the founders through Stalin for his legitimacy as the Communist movement's authoritative leader.

107. Mao, "Ten Major Relationships," p. 306.

108. On the claims made vis-à-vis the Soviet Union, see Zagoria, *Sino-Soviet Conflict*, chap. 3.

109. Mao, "Speech at Second Session," p. 344.

110. See especially Mao, "Be Activists," 5:492–495.

111. See "Political Report of the Central Committee of the Communist Party of China" delivered by Liu Shaoqi, p. 167.

112. See the superb treatment of the theory and practice of the "two roads" in Gray, "Two Roads," pp. 109–157.

113. The stress in Mao's thought on spiritual or cultural change was also to be found in the thought of Chinese anarchists, in his mentor Li Dazhao, in Liu Shaoqi, as well as in Japanese anarchists and Marxists, and their commonalities are shared as well with theoreticians of Latin American Marxism and liberation theology and African black theology. The relationships among these thought systems suggested by this shared feature are the subject of a separate study, Hoston, *Faith, Will, and Revolutionary Change: Modernity and Liberation in the Non-Western World*, also to be published by Princeton University Press.

114. See Liu, "Political Report of the Central Committee," p. 173.

115. Mao, "On State Capitalism," p. 101 (author's interpolation).

116. Mao, "Speech at Second Session," p. 345.

117. See the insightful discussion on this point of continuity between Stalin and Mao in Topper, "Commune to Cultural Revolution."

118. "A Talk on the Question of Democratic Centralism" (January 30, 1962), in *Current Background* 891 (October 8, 1969), p. 39, quoted in Starr, "Conceptual Foundations," p. 622.

119. On Trotsky's concept, see Knei-paz, *Leon Trotsky*, chap. 4. On the relationship between Mao's and Trotsky's concepts, see also Schram, "Mao Tse-tung and Permanent Revolution," p. 222.

120. See Mao, "Tactics against Japanese Imperialism," 1:169; Mao, "Chinese Revolution," 2:330–331; and Mao, "On New Democracy," 2:358–360.

121. Starr, "Conceptual Foundations," p. 613.

122. Mao, "Second Session," p. 338.

123. Cf. the discussions in Schram, "Party in Chinese Communist Ideology," p. 18ff; and Solomon, *Mao's Revolution*, (1972) pp. 402–409, 432–452.

124. See the superb elaboration of this point in several theoretical dimensions, in Schwartz, "Reign of Virtue," p. 5. Cf. the treatment of Mao as a charismatic leader, in Schram, "Mao Tse-tung as a Charismatic Leader," pp. 383–388.

125. Mao, "Be Activists," 5:483–484.

126. Wright, *Last Stand of Chinese Conservatism,"* pp. 60–63.

127. See, for example, "Democracy and National Construction," pp. 157–158; "Thaw Manifesto," p. 78; "On Human Rights," p. 117; Xiao, "The Cultural Revolution and Class Struggle," pp. 136–137, and other pieces in Seymour, *Fifth Modernization*.

128. See the insightful study by Barmé, "Confession, Redemption, and Death," especially pp. 68–69, 72–73, 76–80; and Kelly, "Chinese Intellectuals in the 1989 Democracy Movement," in ibid., p. 46.

129. See, for example, *Shijie Shangu shigang* Bianxiezu (*An Outline History of the ancient World* Writing Group) "Yaxiya shengchan-fangshi"; Song, "'Yaxiya shengchan-fangshi—yiwen zhiyi," pp. 17–25; Pang, "Zhong-Xi fengjian huanzhi zhidu," pp. 3–13. See also the general allusions to China's "Asiatic character" in "On Human Rights," p. 117; and Wei Jingsheng, "Fifth Modernization," both in Seymour, *Fifth Modernization*.

130. See Wu, "Asiatic Mode of Production in History," pp. 53–77.

131. Quoted in Benton, "China's Oppositions," p. 75.

132. See "Conversation of Fang Lizhi with Wen Hui, Ming Lei," *Zhengming* 117 (July

1987): 17–36. The official critiques appear in *Renmin ribao* (People's Daily) (January 20, 1987) and *Hongqi* (Red Flag) (March–April 1987). Perry Link argues that Fang does not advocate "all-out Westernization," that this is an accusation made by the official press to arouse xenophobic sentiments against Fang's views, and that, in fact, Fang tends to avoid discussions of East versus West (Link, "Thought and Spirit of Fang Lizhi") Nevertheless, the problematic relationship to the Chinese past remains evident in Fang's views.

133. See "Liu Xiaobo, the 'Dark Horse' on the Literary Front," *Jiefang yuebao* (Liberation Monthly) no. 12 (1988), and "The Tragedy of the Enlightenment: Critique of the May Fourth Movement," *Huaren shijie* (Chinese World), no. 3 (1989). For similar total abnegations of Chinese traditional culture and even the Chinese as a race, see "Crisis! The Crisis faced by Literature in the New Era," in *Shengzheng qingnian bao* (October 3, 1986); and "Conversation with Li Zhehou: The Emotional, the Individual, and My Choice," *Zhongguo* no. 10 (1986). I am indebted to Yan Sun for introducing me to this literature.

134. The series was produced by Su Xiaokang, now in exile in Princeton, N.J., and Wang Luxiang. *He shang* (River elegy) (Beijing: Xiandai Chuban-she, 1988). Official criticism of the series was particularly vehement after the Tiananmen Square Massacre of June 4, 1989. See *Renmin ribao*, October 26, 1989.

135. A much more detailed treatment of these developments is contained in Hoston, "Between Theory and Practice," pp. 175–207.

136. Interview with Ōuchi Tsutomu, Tokyo, April 27, 1984. For a sustained critique of the *Michi* undertaken within the Workers' Self-Management Research Conference, see Baba, "'Nihon ni okeru shakai-shugi e no michi' hihan," pp. 8–107.

137. Others who left the Kyōkai with Fukuda include Kamakura Takai (Saitama University), Misono Hitoshi (Tokyo Keizai Daigaku), Nagasaka Satoshi (Ōita Daigakuin, Kyū-shū), Isayama Tadashi (Niigata University), and Yoshida Shintarō (Tōhoku University) (interview with Ōuchi Tsutomu, Tokyo, April 27, 1984); and Hayano and Inaka, "Sayoku riron"). In the meantime, another long-time critic of Sakisaka who had helped, with Sakisaka, to found the JSP after the war, Takahashi Masao, has also been involved in a similar critical enterprise with another group of scholars (interview with Takahashi Masao, Tokyo, May 5, 1984).

138. I am indebted to the late Ukai Nobushige for insights into the constitutional issues posed by the Jieitai. See also the brief reference to these issues in Ukai, *Kenpō*, (1981) pp. 69n–70n, and the longer discussion in Fukushima, *Nihon no "bōei" seisaku*, especially chap. 9, app.

139. See *Asahi shinbun* (Tokyo), June 26, 1985; and Mutō, *Hadaka no kakushin seiken ron*, pp. 49–52.

140. Interviews with Ōuchi Tsutomu, April 27, 1984; Hori Masao, May 4, 1984; and Minobe Ryōkichi, May 7, 1984.

141. The Uno school has grown up around the scholarship of Uno Kōzō (1897–1977), who claimed to belong to neither prewar faction but, in fact, was very close to the Rōnō-ha. See Hoston, *Crisis of Development in Prewar Japan*, pp. 284–287; and Hoston, "Between Theory and Practice," pp. 198–203.

142. Yamada, "Les tendances du marxisme japonais contemporain," p. 39.

143. Ibid., pp. 39–40. On Max Weber and the history of modern Japanese thought, see Uchida, *Nihon shihon-shugi no shisōzō* (also in *Uchida Yoshihiko chosakushū*, vol. 5). On the formation of civil society, see Uchida, *Sakuhin to shite no shakai kagaku*; and idem, *Dokusho to shakai kagaku*.

144. See Hirata, "La société civile japonaise contemporaine," pp. 66–69.

145. Fang, "Prologue," p. xxiv.

FOREIGN LANGUAGE SOURCES

Books

Ajia-teki seisan yōshiki ni tsuite [On the Asiatic mode of production]. Compiled by Soveito/Maukusu-shugi Tōyō Gakusha Kyōkai and translated by Hayakawa Jirō. Tokyo: Hakuyō-sha, 1933, 1948.

Akamatsu Katsumaro. *Nihon shakai undō shi* [History of Japan's social movements]. Tokyo: Tsūshin Kyōiku Shinkōkai, 1949.

Akiyama Kiyoshi. *Nihon no hangyaku shisō: Museifu-shugi undō shōshi* [Opposition thought in Japan: A brief history of the anarchist movement]. Tokyo: Gendai Shichō-sha, 1960; Tokyo: San'ichi Shobō, 1977.

Amano Keitarō. *Kawakami Hajime hakushi bunkenshi* [Bibliography of the writings of Kawakami Hajime]. Tokyo: Nihon Hyōron Shinsha, 1956.

Ansart, Pierre. *Marx et l'anarchisme: Essai sur les sociologies de Saint-Simon, Proudhon et Marx* [Marx and anarchism: Essay on the sociologies of Saint-Simon, Proudhon and Marx]. Paris: Presses Universitaires de France, 1969.

Ara Kenjirō, Uchida Tadao, and Fukuoka Masao, comps. *Keizai jiten* [Dictionary of economics]. Tokyo: Kōdan-sha Gakujutsu Bunko, 1980.

Arahata Katsuzō [Arahata Kanson]. *Hidari no menmen: Jinbutsu ron* [All of the left: Character sketches]. Tokyo: Hayakawa Shobō, 1951.

————. *Kanson jiden* [Autobiography of (Arahata) Kanson]. 2 vols. N.p.: Itagaki Shoten, 1948; Tokyo: Iwanami Shoten, Iwanami bunko, 1975.

————. *Nihon shakai-shugi undō shi* [History of the Japanese socialist movement]. Tokyo: Mainichi Shinbun-sha, 1948.

————. *Roshia ni hairu* [Going to Russia]. Tokyo: Kibō-kaku, 1924.

Bennigsen, A., and Ch. Quelquejay. *Les mouvements nationaux chez les Muselmans de Russie—le "Sultan-Galievism" au Tatarstan* [The national movements among Russian Moslems: "Sultan-Galievism" in Tatarstan]. Paris and The Hague: N.p., 1960.

Cadart, Claude, and Yingxiang Cheng. *Mémoirs de Peng Shuzhi: L'envol du communisme en Chine* [Memoirs of Peng Shuzhi: The takeoff of communism in China]. Paris: Gallimard, 1983.

Carrère d'Encausse, Hélène. *Le grand défi: Bolcheviks et nations 1917–1930* [The great challenge: Bolsheviks and nations 1917–1930]. [Paris]: Flammarion, Nouvelle bibliothèque scientifique, 1987.

————. *Le malheur russe: Essai sur le meurtre politique* [The Russian malady: Essay on political murder]. Paris: Fayard, 1988.

Cartier, Michel, comp. *Inventaire des périodiques chinois dans les bibliothèques françaises* [Inventory of Chinese periodicals in French libraries]. Documents et inventaires [Documents and inventories], no. 3. Paris: Centre de Recherches et de Documentation sur la Chine Contemporaine, Ecole des Hautes Etudes en Sciences Sociales et Institut des Hautes Etudes Chinoises, Collège de France, 1984.

Central Committee of the Communist Party (Bolshevik) (Vsesoiuznaia kommunisticheskaia partiia [bol'shevikov] Tsentral'nyi komitet). *History of the Communist Party of the So-*

viet Union (Bolehviks) Short Course (Istoriia Vsesoiuznoi Kommunisticheskoi partii [bol'shevikov]). New York: International Publishers, 1939.

Chen Duxiu. *Chen Duxiu xiansheng jiangyan lu* [Record of speeches of Chen Duxiu]. Shanghai: Xin Qingnian-she, 1924.

―――. *Chen Duxiu zuihou duiyu minzhu zhengzhi de jianjie* [Chen Duxiu's last brief explanation of democratic government]. Hong Kong: Zhongguo Chuban-she, 1950.

―――. *Duxiu wencun* [Collected writings of (Chen) Duxiu]. 2 vols. Hong Kong: Yuandong Tushu Gongsi, 1965.

Chen Gongbo. *Chen Gongbo xiansheng wenji* [Collected works of Chen Gongbo]. 2 vols. Kowloon, Hong Kong: Yuandong Tushu Gongsi, 1967.

―――. *Guomin geming de weiji he women de cuowu* [The crisis of the national revolution and our mistakes]. Shanghai: Fudan Shudian, 1928.

―――. *Zhongguo Guomindang suo daibiao de shi shenme?* [What does the Chinese Guomindang represent?]. Shanghai: Fudan Shudian, 1928.

Dai Jitao. *Dai Jitao xiansheng wencun* [Collected writings of Dai Jitao]. 4 vols. Taibei: Zhongguo Guomindang Zhongyang Weiyuanhui, 1959.

―――. *Dai Jitao xiansheng wencun zaixubian* [Dai Jitao's collected works, 2d suppl.]. Edited by Chen Tianxi. 2 vols. Taibei: N.p., 1968.

―――. *Dai Tianchou wenji* [Collected writings of Dai Tianchou]. Zhongguo Gendai Shiliao Congshu [Collected historial materials on contemporary China]. Shanghai: N.p., 1921; Taipei: N.p., 1962.

―――. *Riben lun* [On Japan]. Shanghai: Minzhi Shuju, 1928.

Deliusin. *Tao Sishchen o kharaktere i evoliutsii kitaiskogo obshchestva* [Tao Xisheng on the character and evolution of Chinese society]. Moscow: Institut Vostokovedeniia Akademiia Nauk SSSR, 1981.

Dictionnaire biographique du mouvement ouvrier international [Biographical dictionary of the international labor movement]. General editor Jean Maitron. *La Chine* [China]. Edited by Lucien Bianco and Yves Chevrier. Paris: Les Editions Ouvrières et Presses de la Fondation Nationale des Sciences Politiques, 1985.

Fujita Shōzō. *Tenkō no shisō shi-teki kenkyū: Sono ichi sokumen* [An intellectual historical study of tenkō: One aspect]. Tokyo: Iwanami Shoten, 1975.

―――. *Tennō-sei kokka no shihai genri* [The ruling principles of the emperor-system state]. 2d ed. Tokyo: Mirai-sha, 1978.

Fukushima Shingo. *Nihon no "bōei" seisaku* [Japan's "defense"policy]. Tokyo: Tōkyō Daigaku Shuppan-kai, 1978.

Furet, François, and Denis Richet. *La Revolution française* [The French revolution]. 2 vols. Paris: N.p., 1965–1966.

Ge Maochu et al., eds. *Wuzhengfu-zhuyi sixiang ziliao xuan* [Selected materials on anarchist thought]. Pt. 1. Beijing: Beijing University Press, 1984.

Guo Moruo. *Zhongguo gudai shehui yanjiu* [Research on ancient Chinese society]. Shanghai: N.p., 1930.

Hashikawa Bunzō, and Matsumoto Sannosuke, eds. *Kindai Nihon seiji shisō shi* [History of modern Japanese political thought]. Kindai Nihon shisō shi taikei [Outline of the history of modern Japanese thought]. nos. 3 and 4. Edited by Miyazawa Toshiyoshi and Ōkouchi Kazuo. 2 vols. Tokyo: Yūhikaku, 1971.

Haupt, Georges, Michael Lowy, and Claudie Weill. *Les Marxistes et la question nationale, 1848–1914: Etudes et textes* [The Marxists and the national question 1848–1914: Studies and texts]. Paris: François Maspero, 1974.

He Ganzhi. *Zhongguo shehui shi wenti lunzhan* [Controversy on problems in Chinese social history]. Qingnian zixue congshu [Youth self-study series]. vol. 3. Shanghai: Shenghuo Shudian, 1937.

Heimin shinbun ronsetsu shū [Collected articles of the *Heimin shinbun*]. Compiled by Hayashi Shigeru and Nishida Taketoshi. Tokyo: Iwanami Shoten, Iwanami bunko, 1961.

Hirano Yoshitarō. *Burujoa minshu-shugi kakumei: Sono shi-teki hatten* [The bourgeois-democratic revolution: Its historical development]. Hirano Yoshitarō ronbun shū [Collected works of Hirano Yoshitarō], no. 1 Tokyo: Nihon Hyōron-sha, 1948.

———. *Dai Ajia-shugi no rekishi-teki kiso* [The historical basis of Pan-Asianism]. Tokyo: Kawade Shobō, 1945.

———. *Nihon shihon-shugi no kōzō* [The structure of Japanese capitalism]. Hirano Yoshitarō ronbun shū [Collected writings of Hirano Yoshitarō], no. 3. Tokyo: Nihon Hyōron-sha, 1949.

———. *Nihon shihon-shugi shakai no kikō* [The structure of Japanese capitalist society]. Tokyo: Iwanami Shoten, 1934.

Hozumi Yatsuka. *Hozumi Yatsuka hakushi ronbun shū* [Collected essays of Hozumi Yatsuka]. Tokyo: Nissei Insatsu, 1913.

Ikumi Takuichi et al., eds. *Gendai no ideorogii* [Contemporary ideology]. 6 vols. Tokyo: San'ichi Shobō, 1961.

Imai Seiichi, comp. *Taishō shisō shū I* [Collected writings in Taishō thought]. Kindai Nihon shisō taikei [Outline of modern Japanese thought], no. 33. Tokyo: Chikuma Shobō, 1978.

Inomata Tsunao. *Gendai Nihon burujoajii no seiji-teki chi'i: Marukishizumu no tachiba yori* [The political position of the contemporary Japanese bourgeoisie: From a Marxist perspective]. N.p.: Nansō Shoin, 1927; Tokyo: Kaizō-sha, 1934.

———. *Gendai Nihon kenkyū: Marukishizumu no tachiba yori* [Studies on contemporary Japan: From a Marxist perspective]. Tokyo: Kaizō-sha, 1929, 1934.

———. *Kin'yū shihon ron* [The theory of finance capital]. Tokyo: Shōkō Shoin, 1948.

———. *Kyokutō ni okeru teikoku-shugi* [Imperialism in the Far East]. Keizaigaku zenshū [Complete economic studies], no. 24. Tokyo: Kaizō-sha, 1932.

———. *Nihon musan-kaikyū undō no hihan: Kominterun no hihan o yomite* [Critique of the Japanese proletarian movement: Reading the Comintern's criticism]. N.p.: Musan-sha, 1928.

———. *Nihon no dokusen shihon-shugi: Kin'yū shihon no kyōkō taisaku* [Japan's monopoly cpaitalism: Finance capital's policies toward the panic]. Tokyo: Nanboku Shoin, 1932.

———. *Nihon puroretariaato no senryaku to senjutsu: Zasshi Rōnō keisai ronbun shū* [The stategy and tactics of the Japanese proletariat: Articles published in the magazine *Labor-Farmer*]. Tokyo: Tosho Shinbun-sha, 1973.

———. *Nōson mondai nyūmon* [Introduction to the agrarian problem]. [Tokyo]: Kōdo-sha, 1948.

———. *Teikoku-shugi kenkyū* [Studies on imperialism]. Tokyo: Kaizō-sha, 1928.

Ishida Takeshi. *Meiji seiji shisō shi kenkyū* [Studies on the history of Meiji political thought]. Tokyo: Mirai-sha, 1954.

———. *Nihon kindai shisō shi ni okeru hō to seiji* [Law and politics in the history of modern Japanese thought]. Tokyo: Iwanami Shoten, 1976.

Ishidō Kiyotomo. *Kominterun Nihon ni kansuru teize shū* [Collected Comintern theses on Japan]. Tokyo: Aoki Shoten, Aoki bunko, 1961.

Itō Makoto. *Gendai no Marukusu keizaigaku* [Contemporary Marxist economics]. Tokyo: T. B. S. Buritanika (Brittanica), 1982.

Juillard, J. *Fernand Pelloutier et les origines du syndicalisme d'action direct* [Fernand Pelloutier and the origins of direct action syndicalism]. Paris: Editions du Seuil, 1971.

Kajinishi Mitsuhaya, Ōshima Kiyoshi, Katō Toshihiko, and Ōuchi Tsutomu. *Nihon ni okeru shihon-shugi no hattatsu* [The development of capitalism in Japan]. 13 vols. Vol. 5, *Nihon shihon-shugi no botsuraku* [The decline of Japanese capitalism]. Tokyo: Tōkyō Daigaku Shuppan-kai, 1977.

Kakei Katsuhiko. *Dai Nihon teikoku kenpō no konpon gi* [The basic meaning of the Greater Japanese Imperial Constitution]. N.p., n.d.

——. *Kokka no kenkyū* [Studies on the state]. N.p., n.d.

Kamiyama Shigeo. *Tennō-sei ni kansuru riron-teki sho mondai* [Theoretical problems concerning the emperor system]. Tokyo: Minshu Hyōron-sha, 1947. Rev. and enl. ed., Tokyo: Minshu Hyōron-sha, 1956.

Kawakami Hajime. *Jijōden* [Autobiography]. 5 vols. Tokyo: Iwanami Shoten, 1952.

——. *Kawakami Hajime chosakushū* [Collected works of Kawakami Hajime]. 12 vols. Tokyo: Chikuma Shobō, 1964–1965.

——. *Kawakami Hajime yori Kushida Tamizō e no tegami* [Letters from Kawakami Hajime to Kushida Tamizō]. Compiled by Ōuchi Hyōe and Ōshima Kiyoshi. Tokyo: Hōsei Daigaku Shuppan-kyoku, 1974.

——. *Marukusu-shugi no tetsugaku-teki kiso* [The philosophical foundations of Marxism]. Tokyo: Kōdo-sha, 1949.

——. *Omoide* [Recollections]. N.p.: Nihon Minshu-shugi Bunka Renmei, 1946.

——. *Yuibutsu-shikan kenkyū* [Studies in historical materialism]. Tokyo: Kōbundō Shobō, 1922.

Kawakami Hajime, and Ōyama Ikuo. *Marukusu-shugi kōza* [Symposium on Marxism]. 13 vols. N.p.: Seiji Hihan-sha, 1927–1929.

Kawashima Takeyoshi. *Ideorogii to shite no kazoku seido* [The family system as ideology]. Tokyo: Iwanami Shoten, 1957.

——. *Nihon shakai no kazoku-teki kōsei* [The familistic organization of Japanese society]. Tokyo: Nihon Hyōron-sha, 1950.

Kazama Jōkichi. *Mosukō to tsunagaru Nihon kyōsantō no rekishi* [The history of the Japanese Communist party in relation to Moscow]. Edited by Sano Manabu and Nabeyama Sadachika. Vol. 1. Tokyo: Fuman-sha, 1951.

Kida Jun'ichirō. *Meiji no risō* [Ideals of the Meiji period]. Tokyo: San'ichi Shobō, 1965.

Kikuchi Masanori. *Roshiya kakumei to Nihonjin* [The Russian Revolution and the Japanese]. Tokyo: Chikuma Shobō, 1973.

Kimura Tokio. *Nihon nashonarizumu shiron* [Historical treatise on Japanese nationalism]. Tokyo: Waseda University Press, 1973.

Kinoshita Hanji. *Nihon kokka-shugi undō shi* [History of the Japanese nationalism movement]. 2 vols. Tokyo: Fukumura Shuppan Kabushiki Kaisha, 1971.

Kita Ikki. *Kita Ikki chosakushū* [Collected works of Kita Ikki]. Tokyo: Misuzu Shobō, 1959–1972.

Kobayashi Morito. *Tenkōsha no shisō to seikatsu* [The thought and lives of *tenkōsha*]. Tokyo: Daidō-sha, 1935.

Kobayashi Ryōsei. *Ajia-teki seisan yōshiki kenkyū* [Studies on the Asiatic mode of production]. Tokyo: Ōtsuki Shoten, 1975, 1976.

——. *Nihon shihon-shugi ronsō no kaikan* [Recollections of the debate on Japanese capitalism]. Tokyo: Shiroishi Shoten, 1976.

Kojima Hinehisa. *Nihon shihon-shugi ronsō shi* [History of the debate on Japanese capitalism]. Tokyo: Arisue, 1976.

Kondō Eizō. *Komuminterun no misshi: Nihon kyōsantō sōsei hiwa* [Secret agent of the Comintern: Secret history of the Japanese Communist party]. Tokyo: Bunka Hyōron-sha, 1949.

————. *Kondō Eizō jiden* [Autobiography of Kondō Eizō]. Kyoto: Hiei Shobō, 1970.

Kondō Kenji. *Ichi museifu-shugisha no kaisō* [Memoirs of an anarchist]. Tokyo: Heibon-sha, 1965.

Konsaisu jinmei jiten: Nihon hen [Concise biographical dictionary: Japan edition]. Tokyo: Sanseido, 1976.

Kōtoku Shūsui. *Kōtoku Shūsui senshū* [Selected works of Kōtoku Shūsui]. Edited by Hirano Yoshitarō. 3 vols. Tokyo: N.p., 1949–1950.

————. *Shakai-shugi shinzui* [The essence of socialism]. Tokyo: Iwanami Shoten, Iwanami bunko, 1953.

Koyama Hirotake. *Nihon Marukusu-shugi shi* [History of Japanese Marxism]. Tokyo: Aoki Shoten, 1956.

————. *Nihon shihon-shugi ronsō shi* [History of the debate on Japanese capitalism]. 2 vols. Tokyo: Aoki Shoten, 1953.

Koyama Hirotake, and Kishimoto Eitarō. *Nihon no hikyōsantō Marukusu-shugisha: Yamakawa Hitoshi no shōgai to shisō* [Japanese non-Communist party Marxist: The life and thought of Yamakawa Hitoshi]. Tokyo: San'ichi Shobō, 1962.

Kuno Osamu, and Tsurumi Shunsuke. *Gendai Nihon no shisō: Sono itsutsu no uzu(maki)* [Contemporary Japanese thought: Five whirlpools]. Tokyo: Iwanami Shoten, 1956; Tokyo: Iwanami Shinsho, 1978.

Kushida Tamizō. *Kushida Tamizō zenshū* [Complete writings of Kushida Tamizō]. 5 vols. N.p.: N.p., 1935.

Li Dazhao. *Li Dazhao xuanji* [Selected works of Li Dazhao]. Beijing: Renmin Chuban-she, 1962.

Li Ji. *Zhongguo shehui shi lunzhan pipan* [Critique of the controversy on Chinese social history]. Shanghai: Shenzhou Guoguang-she, 1936.

Li Shengyu. *Guoji gongfa lun* [On international law]. Shanghai: Shangwu Yinshuguan, 1934.

Liang Souming. *Dongxi wenhua ji qi zhexue* [Culture and philosophy of the Orient and the West]. Taipei: Wenxue Chuban-she, 1977.

Liu Shaoqi. *Liu Shaoqi xuanji* [Selected works of Liu Shaoqi]. Tokyo: Zhonghua Wenhua Fuwu Chuban-she, 1967.

Lü Zhenyu. *Shiqianqi Zhongguo shehui yanjiu* [A study on prehistoric Chinese society]. Zhongguo shehui shi gang [Outline of Chinese social history], no. 1. Beijing: Renwen Shudian, 1934. Reprint of 1961 ed. Beijing: Shenghuo Dushu Xinzhi Sanlian Shudian, n.d.

————. *Zhongguo zhengzhi sixiang shi* [History of Chinese political thought]. Reprint of 1955 ed. Hong Kong: N.p., n.d.

Mad'iar, Ludwig. *Ekonomika sels'kogo khoziaistva v Kitae* [The economics of agriculture in China]. Moscow: Gosudarstvennoe Izdatelstvo, 1928.

————. *Ocherki po ekonomike Kitaia* [Works on China's economy]. Moscow: N.p., 1930.

————. *Sovremennoe sosto'ianie kitaiskoi revolutsii: Diskussiia v Kommunisticheskoi Akademii* [The current status of the Chinese revolution: A discussion at the Communist Academy]. Moscow: N.p., 1929.

Maitron, Jean. *Le Mouvement anarchiste en France* [The anarchist movement in France]. 2 vols. Paris: François Maspero, 1975.

Mao Tse-tung. *Mao Tse-tung ji* [Collected Writings of Mao Tse-tung]. 10 vols. 2d ed. Tokyo: Sōsō-sha, 1983.

Maruyama Masao. *Nihon seiji shisō shi kenkyū* [Studies in the history of Japanese political thought]. Tokyo: Tokyo Daigaku Shuppan-kai, 1952.

Maruyama Matsuyuki. *Chūgoku kindai no kakumei shisō* [Modern Chinese revolutionary thought]. Tokyo: Yamamoto Shoten, Kenbun Shuppan, 1982.

Matsuzawa Hiroaki. *Nihon shakai-shugi no shisō* [Japanese Socialist thought]. Tokyo: Chikuma Shobō, 1973.

Miyazawa Toshiyoshi. *Tennō kikan-setsu jiken: Shiryo wa kataru* [The emperor-organ theory: Historical documents narrate]. 2 vols. Tokyo: Yūhikaku, 1970.

Moriya Fumio. *Nihon Marukusu-shugi no rekishi to hansei* [The history of and reflections on Japanese Marxism]. Tokyo: Gōdō Shuppan, 1980.

―――. *Nihon Marukusu-shugi riron no keisei to hatten* [The formation and development of Japanese Marxist theory]. Tokyo: Aoki Shoten, 1967.

―――. *Tennō-sei kenkyū* [Studies on the emperor system]. Tokyo: Aoki Shoten, 1979.

Moriya Katsumi. *Shina shakai keizai shi* [History of Chinese society and economy]. Tokyo: Shōka-sha, 1934.

Murakami Shigeyoshi. *Nihon shūkyō jiten* [Encyclopedia of Japanese religion]. Tokyo: Kodan-sha, 1978.

Mutō Sanji. *Hadaka no kakushin seiken ron* [The theory of reformist political power laid bare]. Tokyo: Nihon Hyōron-sha, 1983.

Nabeyama Sadachika. *Tenkō jūgo nen* [Fifteen years since *tenkō*]. Rōdō minshu shiriizu [Labor democracy series], no. 7. N.p.: Rōdō Shuppan-bu, 1949.

―――. *Watakushi wa kyōsantō o suteta: Jiyū to sokoku o motomete* [I abandoned the Communist party: Seeking freedom and the fatherland]. Tokyo: Daitō Shuppan-sha, 1949.

Nagaoka Shinkichi. *Nihon shihon-shugi ronsō no gunzō* [Images of the debate on Japanese capitalism]. Kyoto: Mineruva Shobō, 1984.

Nakamura Yoshiaki. *Kyōsantō bō hikoku no tenkō kiroku: Sekishoku seinen kyōka tokuhon* [Record of the *tenkō* of a certain Communist party defendant: A reader for the enlightenment of Communist youth]. Osaka: Kōmin Ishiki Shinkō-kai, 1934.

Nihon Kyōsantō. *Nihon Kyōsantō no rokujū nen* [Sixty years of the Japanese Communist party]. 2 vols. and supplemental chronology. Vol. 1. Tokyo: Shin Nihon Bunko, 1983.

Nihon shakai undō jinmei jiten [Biographical dictionary of Japan's social movement]. Tokyo: Aoki Shoten, 1979.

Nihon Shakaitō kōryō bunken shū [Collected documents of the program of the Japanese Socialist party]. Tokyo: Nihon Shakaitō Chūō Honbu Kikan-kyoku, 1978.

Nihon shi jiten [Encyclopedia of Japanese history]. 3d ed. Tokyo: Ōbun-sha, 1979.

Nihon shihon-shugi hattatsu shi kōza [Symposium on the history of the development of Japanese capitalism]. 7 vols. Reissued on fiftieth anniversary of publication in 1932–1935 with suppl. Tokyo: Iwanami Shoten, 1982.

Nikiforov, V. N. *Sovetskie istoriki o problemakh Kitaia* [Soviet historians on problems of China]. Moscow: "Nauka," 1970.

Noro Eitarō. *Nihon shihon-shugi hattatsu shi* [History of the development of Japanese capitalism]. Tokyo: Tettō Shoin, 1930; Tokyo: Iwanami bunko, 1954.

Onabe Teruhiko. *Nijū seiki* [The twentieth century]. 16 vols. Vol. 4, *Meiji no hikari to kage* [Light and shadows of the Meiji]. Tokyo: Chūō Kōron-sha, 1978.

Ōsawa Masamichi. *Ōsugi Sakae kenkyū* [Studies on Ōsugi Sakae]. Tokyo: Hōsei Daigaku Shuppan-kyoku, 1971.

Ōsugi Sakae. *Jijōden* [Autobiography]. Tokyo: Nagasaki Shuppan-kan, 1979.

Ōsugi Sakae zenshū [Complete works of Ōsugi Sakae]. Edited by Ōsawa Masamichi et al. 14 vols. Vol. 2. Tokyo: Gendai Shichō, 1963.

Ōuchi Hideaki, Kamakura Takao, Hayashi Takehisa, and Saeki Naomi. *Uno Kōzō: Chosaku to shisō* [Uno Kōzō: (His) works and thought]. Tokyo: Yūhikaku shinsho, 1979.

Ōuchi Hyōe, Sakisaka Itsurō, Tsuchiya Takao, and Takahashi Masao. *Nihon shihon-shugi no kenkyū* [Studies in Japanese capitalism]. 2 vols. Tokyo: Kōdo-sha, 1948.

Ōzawa Masamichi. *Ōsugi Sakae sen: Museifu-shugi no tetsugaku* [Selected writings of Ōsugi Sakae: The philosophy of anarchism]. Pt. 1. Tokyo: Gendai Shichō-sha, 1976.

Pak, M. N. *Sovietskoe vostokovedenie* [Soviet oriental studies]. Moscow: N.p., 1965.

Peng Shuzhi. *Peng Shuzhi xuanji* [Selected writings of Peng Shuzhi]. 3 vols. Hong Kong: Shiyue Chubanshe, 1982–1984.

Qinghua, ed. *Fufa qingong jianxue yundong shiliao* [Historical materials on the (Chinese) worker-student movement in France]. 4 vols. Beijing: Beijing Chubanshe, 1979.

Reclus, Elisée. *L'Evolution, la révolution et l'ideal anarchique* [Evolution, revolution, and the anarchist ideal]. Paris: P-V Stock, 1898.

————. *L'Homme et la terre* [Man and the earth]. 2 vols. Paris: F. Maspero, 1982.

Rōnō [Labor-Farmer]. 12 vols. plus supplemental vol. Reprint ed. Tokyo: Hōsei University, 1975–1982.

Rubel, Maximilien. *Karl Marx: Essai de biographie intellectuelle* [Karl Marx: An intellectual biography]. Paris: Marcel Rivière et Cie., 1957.

Saeki Naomi, and Shibagaki Kazuo. *Nihon keizai kenkyū nyūmon* [Introduction to Japanese economic studies]. Tokyo: Tōkyō Daigaku Shuppankai, 1972.

Sakai Toshihiko. *Sakai Toshihiko zenshū* [Complete works of Sakai Toshihiko]. 6 vols. Tokyo: Chūō Kōron-sha, 1933.

Sakisaka Itsurō. *Nihon shihon-shugi no sho mondai* [Some problems of Japanese capitalism]. Tokyo: Kōdo-sha, 1947; N.p.: Shakai-shugi Kyōkai Shuppan-kyoku, 1976.

Sano Manabu. *Kokka-ron/Sensō-ron* [Theory of the state, Theory of war]. Tokyo: Kibō-kaku, 1930.

————. *Minzoku to kaikyū* [Race and class]. Minshu shiriizu [Democracy series], no. 3. Tokyo: Kinrō Jihō-sha, 1949.

————. *Sano Manabu chosaku-shū* [Collected works of Sano Manabu]. 5 vols. Tokyo: Sano Manabu Chosakushū Kankōkai, 1957–1958.

————. *Seiji-ron* [On politics]. Sano Manabu shū [Collected writings of Sano Manabu], no. 4. Tokyo: Kibō-kaku, 1930.

————. *Tōsō ni yorite kaihō e* [To liberation through struggle]. N.p.: Taibun-sha, 1923.

————. *Yuibutsu shikan hihan* [A critique of historical materialism]. Tokyo: Daiyamondo-sha, 1948.

Sano Manabu, and Nabeyama Sadachika. *Nihon Kyōsantō oyobi Komintaan hihan* [The Japanese Communist party and Comintern criticism]. N.p.: Musan-sha, 1934.

Sartre, Jean-Paul. *Critique de la raison dialectique, précedé de Question de méthode* [Critique of dialectical reason, preceded by a question of method]. Bibliothèque des idées [Library of ideas]. Paris: Gallimard, 1960.

Schram, Stuart R. *Documents sur la théorie de la "révolution permanente" en Chine* [Documents on the theory of "permanent revolution" in China]. Paris: Mouton, 1963.

Shakai Keizai Rōdō Kenkyūjo, ed. *Nihon minshu kakumei ronsō shi* [History of the debate on the Japanese democratic revolution]. Tokyo: Itō Shoten, 1947.

————. *Nihon shihon-shugi ronsō shi* [History of the debate on Japanese capitalism]. Tokyo: Itō Shoten, 1947.

Shakai mondai kenkyū [Research on social problems]. Edited by Kawakami Hajime. Kyoto: Kōbundō and Tokyo: Iwanami Shoten, 1919–1930.

Shakai mondai kōza [Symposium on social problems]. 13 vols. March 1926–June 1927.

Shakai-shugi Kyōkai teize [Theses of the Socialist Association]. Tokyo: Shakai-shugi Kyōkai, 1971.

Shehui-zhuyi taolun ji [Collected discussions on socialism]. Xin Qingnian Congshu [New youth series], no. 2. [Canton]: Xin Qingnian-she, 1922.

Shiga Shūzō. *Chūgoku kazoku hō no genri* [Principles of Chinese family law]. Tokyo: Sōbun-sha, n.d.

Shiga Yoshio. *Kokka-ron* [The theory of the state]. Nauka kōza [Nauka symposium], no. 10. N.p.: Nauka-sha, 1949.

————. *Sekai to Nihon* [The world and Japan]. N.p.: Gyōmyō-sha, 1948.

Shihōshō Keijikyoku [Ministry of Justice. Criminal Investigation Bureau]. *Shisō kenkyū shiryō* [Materials on the study of thought], no. 27. marked secret, Tokyo, April 1933.

Shinobu Seizaburō. *Taishō seiji shi* [History of Taishō politics]. Tokyo: Kawade Shobō, 1951; Tokyo Keisō Shobō, 1968.

Shioda Shōbee. *Nihon shakai undō jinmei jiten* [Biographical dictionary of Japan's social movement]. Tokyo: Aoki Shoten, 1979.

Shiryōshū: Kominterun to Nihon [Collected materials: The Comintern and Japan]. Compiled and translated by Murata Yōichi. Tokyo: Ōtsuki Shoten, 1987–1988.

Shisō Kagaku Kenkyū-kai. *Tenkō* [*Tenkō*]. 3 vols. Tokyo: Heibon-sha, 1959–1965.

Shōwa Kenkyū-kai. *Burokku keizai ni kansuru kenkyū* [Studies on the bloc economy]. Tokyo: Seikatsu-sha, 1939.

Soboul, Albert. *La Révolution française* [The French Revolution]. 2 vols. Paris: Gallimard, 1962.

Staburova, E. Yu. *Anarkhizm v Kitae 1900–1921* [Anarchism in China 1900–1921]. Moscow: Nauka under the auspices of the Academiia Nauk SSSR, 1983.

Sternhell, Zeev. *La Droite révolutionnaire 1885–1914: Les origines françaises du fascisme* [The revolutionary right 1885–1914: The French origins of fascism]. Paris: Editions du Seuil, 1978.

————. *Maurice Barrès et le nationalisme française* [Maurice Barrès and French nationalism]. Cahiers de la Fondation nationale des sciences politiques [Journal of the National Foundation of political sciences]. Paris: A. Colin, 1972.

————. *Ni droite, ni gauche* [Neither right nor left]. Paris: Editions du Seuil, 1983.

Suzuki Yasuzō. *Kenpō seitai to Roesler* [Roesler and the framing of the constitution]. Tokyo: N.p., n.d.

————. *Nihon kenpōgaku shi kenkyū* [Studies in the history of Japanese constitutional law]. Tokyo: Keisō Shobō, 1975.

Takabatake Motoyuki. *Hihan Marukusu-shugi* [Criticizing Marxism]. Tokyo: Nihon Hyōron-sha, 1934.

————. *Jiko o kataru* [On myself]. Tokyo: Jinbunkai Shuppan-bu, 1926.

————. *Kokka shakai-shugi* [State socialism]. Nihon Shakai-shugi Kenkyūjo panfuretto tokushū [Pamphlets of the Institute on Japanese Socialism, special collection]. Tokyo: Nihon Shakai-shugi Kenkyujo, 1932.

————. *Kokka shakai-shugi taigi* [Outline of state socialism]. Nihon Shakai-shugi Kenkyūjo panfuretto tokushū [Pamphlets of the Institute on Japanese Socialism, special issue]. Tokyo: Nihon Shakai-shugi Kenkyūjo, 1932.

———. *Marukishizumu to kokka-shugi* [Marxism and statism]. Tokyo: Kaizō-sha, 1927.

———. *Marukusu-gaku kaisetsu* [An explanation of Marxism]. Tokyo: Kaizō-sha, 1928.

———. *Marukusu-gaku kenkyū* [Studies on Marxism]. Tokyo: Daitō-kaku, 1919.

———. *Shakai-shugi-teki sho kenkyū* [Studies on socialism]. Tokyo: Taishū-sha, 1920.

Takahashi Kamekichi. *Gendai Nhon keizai no kenkyū (I)* [Studies on the contemporary Japanese economy, I]. Tokyo: Kaizō-sha, 1927.

———. *Meiji Taishō nōson keizai no hensen* [Changes in the Meiji and Taishō rural economy]. Tokyo: Tōyō Keizai Shinpō-sha, 1926.

———. *Nihon keizai no yukizumari to musan-kaikyū no taisaku* [The deadlock of the Japanese economy and the countermeasures of the proletariat]. Tokyo: Hakuyō-sha, 1926.

———. *Nihon shihon-shugi hattatsu shi* [History of the development of Japanese capitalism]. Rev. and enl. ed. Tokyo: Nihon Hyōron-sha, 1929.

———. *Nihon shihon-shugi keizai no kenkyū* [Studies on the Japanese capitalist economy]. Tokyo: Hakuyō-sha, 1924.

———. *Sayoku undō no riron-teki hōkai—uyoku undō no riron-teki konkyo* [The theoretical collapse of the left-wing movement: The theoretical basis of the right-wing movement]. Tokyo: Hakuyō-sha, 1927.

———. *Taishō-Shōwa zaikai no hendō* [Economic fluctuations in the Taishō and Shōwa periods]. Tokyo: Keizai Shinpō-sha, 1954–1955.

———. *Takahashi keizai riron keisei no rokujū nen: Nihon keizai gekidō no jidai to watakushi no jinsei* [Sixty years in the formation of Takahashi's economic theory: The era of Japanese economic turmoil and my life]. Tokyo: Tōshi Keizai-sha, 1976.

Takauchi Shun'ichi. *Gendai Nihon shihon-shugi ronsō* [The contemporary debate on Japanese capitalism]. Tokyo: San'ichi Shobō, 1973.

Takimura Ōdō. *Ajia-teki kokka to kakumei* [The Asiatic state and revolution]. Tokyo: San'ichi Shobō, 1978.

Tanaka Masato. *Takabatake Motoyuki: Nihon no kokka shakai-shugi* [Takabatake Motoyuki: Japanese national socialism]. Tokyo: Gendai Hyōron-sha, 1978.

Tanaka Sōgorō. *Kita Ikki: Nihon-teki fashisuto no shōchō* [Kita Ikki: Symbol of Japanese fascism]. Rev. and enl. ed. Tokyo: San'ichi Shobō, 1975.

———. *Kōtoku Shūsui: Ikkakumeika no shisō to shōgai* [Kōtoku Shūsui: The life and thought of one revolutionary]. Tokyo: Riron-sha, 1955.

———. *Tennō no kenkyū* [Studies on the emperor]. Tokyo: San'ichi Shobō, 1974.

Tao Xisheng. *Zhongguo fengjian shehui shi* [The history of Chinese feudal society]. Shanghai: N.p., 1929.

———. *Zhongguo shehui yu Zhongguo geming* [Chinese society and the Chinese revolution]. 3d ed. Shanghai: Xin Shengming Shuju, 1931.

———. *Zhongguo shehui zhi shi de fenxi* [Analysis of the history of Chinese society]. Shanghai: N.p., 1929.

Tateyama Takaaki. *Nihon kyōsantō kenkyo hishi* [Secret history of the arrests of the Japanese Communist party]. Tokyo: Bukyō-sha, 1929.

Toda Shintarō. *Tennō-sei no keizai-teki kiso bunseki* [Analysis of the economic basis of the emperor system]. Tokyo: San'ichi Shobō, 1947.

Tosaka Jun. *Nihon ideorogii-ron: Gendai Nihon ni okeru Nihon-shugi, fashizumu, jiyū-shugi, shisō no hihan* [On Japanese ideology: Critique of Japanist, fascist, and liberal thought in contemporary Japan]. Tokyo: Iwanami Shoten, Iwanami bunko, 1977.

Toyoda Shirō. *Nihon shihon-shugi ronsō hihan* [Critique of the debate on Japanese capitalism]. 3 vols. N.p.: Tōyō Keizai Shinpō-sha, 1958–1959.

Tsuchiya Takao. *Nihon shihon-shugi shi ronshū* [Collected essays on the history of Japanese capitalism]. Tokyo: Ikusei-sha, 1937.

Tsuchiya Takao, and Okazaki Saburō. *Nihon shihon-shugi hattatsu shi gaisetsu* [Outline of the history of the development of Japanese capitalism]. 2d. ed. Tokyo: Yūhikaku, 1948.

Tsushima Tadayuki. *Nihon ni okeru Marukusu-shugi: Futatsu no henkō ni taisuru tōsō*, rev. ed. [Marxism in Japan: Struggles against two tendencies]. Tokyo: Sangen-sha, 1949, 1952.

————. *"Nihon shihon-shugi ronsō" shiron* [Treatise on the "debate on Japanese capitalism"]. Tokyo: Kōdo-sha, 1947.

Uchida Jōkichi, and Nakano Jirō. *Nihon shihon-shugi ronsō* [The debate on Japanese capitalism]. Reprint of 2-vol. ed., rev. and enl. Tokyo: Shinkō Shuppan-sha, 1952.

Uchida Yoshihiko. *Dokusho to shakai kagaku* [Reading and the social sciences]. Tokyo: Iwanami Shinsho, 1985.

————. *Nihon shihon-shugi no shisōzō* [Images of Japanese capitalism through thought]. Tokyo: Iwanami Shoten, 1967.

————. *Sakuhin to shite no shakai kagaku* [Social science as a work]. Tokyo: Iwanami Shoten, 1981.

————. *Uchida Yoshihiko chosakushū* [Collected works of Uchida Yoshihiko]. 10 vols. Tokyo: Iwanami Shoten, 1988–1989.

Uesugi Shinkichi. *Kenpō jutsugi* [Explanation of the constitution]. Tokyo: Yūhikaku, 1913.

————. *Kokutai kenpō oyobi kensei* [The *kokutai* constitution and constitutional government]. Tokyo: Yūhikaku Shobō, 1916.

Ukai Nobushige. *Kenpō* [The constitution]. Tokyo: Iwanami Shoten, Iwanami Shinsho, 1956, 1981.

Uno Kōzō. *Keizai seisaku-ron* [Theory of economic policy]. 3d ed. [Tokyo]: Kōbundō Shobō, 1936, 1948.

Wusi shiqi qikan jieshao [Introduction to periodicals of the May Fourth Movement]. 3 vols. Peking: Renmin Chuban-she, 1958–1959.

Xiao Gongquan. *Zhongguo zhengzhi sixiang shi* [History of Chinese political thought]. Xiandai guomin jiben zhishi congshu [Collection of basic knowledge on the contemporary nation], no. 2. 2 vols. 6th ed. Taipei: Zhonghua Wenhua Chuban Shiye Weiyuanhui, 1964, 1977.

Xin Qingnian-she, ed. *Shehui-zhuyi taolun ji* [Collected discussions about socialism]. Canton: Xin Qingnian-she, 1922.

Xu Shanguang, and Liu Jianping. *Zhongguo wuzhengfu-zhuyi shi* [History of Chinese anarchism]. N.p.: Hubei Renmin Chuban-she, 1989.

Yamada Moritarō. *Nihon shihon-shugi bunseki: Nihon shihon-shugi ni okeru saiseisan katei ha' aku* [An analysis of Japanese capitalism: A grasp of the process of reproduction in Japanese capitalism]. Rev. ed. Tokyo: Iwanami Shoten, 1934; Tokyo: Iwanami Shoten, 1949.

Yamada Tatsuo. *Chūgoku kokumintō saha no kenkyū* [A study of the left wing of the Chinese Guomindang]. Tokyo: Keiō Tsūshin, 1980.

Yamakawa Hitoshi. *Yamakawa Hitoshi jiden* [Autobiography of Yamakawa Hitoshi]. Edited by Yamakawa Kikue and Sakisaka Itsurō. Tokyo: Iwanami Shoten, 1961.

————. *Yamakawa Hitoshi shū* [Collected works of Yamakawa Hitoshi]. Compiled by Takabatake Michitoshi. Kindai Nihon shisō taikei [Outline of modern Japanese thought], no. 19. Tokyo: Chikuma Shobō, 1976.

———. *Yamakawa Hitoshi zenshū* [Complete works of Yamakawa Hitoshi]. Tokyo: Keisō Shobō, 1966.

Yan Lingfeng. *Zhongguo jingji wenti yanjiu* [Study on Chinese economic problems]. Shanghai: Xin Shengming Shuju, 1931.

Zhang Jinglu, comp. *Zhongguo jindai chuban shiliao* [Materials on the history of modern Chinese publications]. 2 vols. Shanghai: Qunlian Chuban-she, 1954.

Zhang Jingru. *Li Dazhao tongzhi geming sixiang de fazhan* [The development of comrade Li Dazhao's revolutionary thought]. Wuhan: Hubei Renmin Chuban-she, 1957.

Zheng Xuejia. *'Shehui shi lunzhan' de qiyin he neirong* [Origins and content of the "controversy on social history"]. Taipei: Zhonghua zazhi-she, 1965.

Zhongguo xiandai chuban shiliao [Historical materials on contemporary publications in China]. Compiled by Zhang Jinglu. 4 vols. and suppl. Shanghai: Zhonghua Shuju, 1954.

Zhou Gucheng. *Zhongguo shehui zhi jiegou* [The structure of Chinese society]. Shanghai: Xin Shengming Shuju, 1930.

Zoku: Nihon shakai undō shi kenkyū shiron: Sono bunken to kenkyū no genjō [Continued: Historical discussion of studies in the history of Japanese social movements: The current state of documents and research]. Compiled by Koyama Hirotake. Tokyo: Shinsen-sha, 1979.

Articles

Aikawa Haruki. "'Ajia-teki seisan yōshiki' to Nihon hōken-sei ni kansuru ronsō (I)" [The "Asiatic mode of production" and the debate on Japanese feudalism]. *Rekishi kagaku* [Historical science] 2, no. 8 (October 1933): 57–69.

———. "Nihon dorei-sei ni kansuru kiso ronten—Awasete dorei-sei no 'tōyō-teki keitai' hihan" [Basic points at issue concerning Japanese slavery: With a critique of the 'oriental form' of slavery]. In Aikawa Haruki, *Rekishi kagaku no hōhōron* [The methodology of historical science], pp. 329–352. Tokyo: Hakuyō-sha, 1935.

Akamatsu Katsumaro. "Kyōsantō kōzai ron" [On the merits and demerits of the Communist Party]. *Chūō kōron* [Central review] (June 1934): 17–34.

An S. "Meiji shoki ni okeru Doitsu kokka shisō no jūyō ni kansuru ichi kōsatsu: Burunchuri to Katō Hiroyuki o chūshin to shite" ["The reception of J. C. Bluntschli's theory of the state by Hiroyuki Katō in early Meiji Japan"]. Nihon seijigaku nenpō, 1975: Nihon ni okeru Sei-Ou seiji shisō [Annals of the Japanese Political Science Association "Western Political Thoughts in Japan"] 1975: 113–156.

"Anarchist Activities 1907–1920" *Minsheng* [Voice of the people] no. 30 (March 21, 1921): 5–6.

Arahata Katsuzō [Arahata Kanson]. "Heimin-sha jidai" [The era of the Heimin-sha]. *Chūō kōron* [Central review] (Tokyo) nos. 1097–1107 (August 1978–July 1979).

———. "Roshiya kakumei no koro" [At the time of the Russian revolution]. *Sekai* [World] 265 (December 1967): 177–182.

———. "Yamakawa Hitoshi ron" [On Yamakawa Hitoshi]. *Kaizō* [Reconstruction] (January 1931).

Awaji Tokusaburō. "Dokusai seiji ron" [On dictatorial politics]. In *Marukusu-shugi kōza* [Symposium on Marxism], compiled by Kawakami Hajime and Ōyama Ikuo, 4:119–190. N.p.: Seiji Hihan-sha, 1927–1929.

Baba Hiroji. "'Nihon ni okeru shakai-shugi e no michi' hihan" [A critique of "The path to socialism in Japan"]. *Rōdōsha jishu kanri kenkyū* [Studies in workers' self-management] 5 (August 1979): 8–107.

———. "Taigai kankei" [Foreign relations]. In *Nihon keizai kenkyū nyūmon* [Introduction to Japanese economic studies], edited by Saeki Naomi and Shibagaki Kazuo, pp. 87–107. Tokyo: Tōkyō Daigaku Shuppan-kai, 1972.

———. "Uno riron to gendai shihon-shugi ron" [Uno theory and the theory of contemporary capitalism]. *Shakai kagaku kenkyū* [Studies in social science] 34, no. 1 (July 1982): 171–197.

"Bakuning Bokunin yu wuzhengfu-zhuyi" [Bakunin and anarchism]. Translated by Ling Shuang. *Ziyou* [Freedom] (Paris) no. 1 (December 1920): 3–13.

Bukharin, Nikolai I. "K teorii imperialisticheskogo gosudarstva" [Toward a theory of the imperialist state (1916)]. In *Revoliutsiia pravda, sbornik pervyi* [Revolutionary truth, part 1], pp. 5–32. Moscow: Kommunisticheskaia Akademiia, 1925.

———. "Rabochaia aristokratiia ili splochenie rabochikh mass?" [A labor aristocracy or a unity of laboring masses?]. *Pravda* [Truth], no. 204 (September 14, 1919).

———. "Teoriia 'organizovannoi beskhoziaisvennosti'" [The theory of "organized mismanagement"]. In *"Organizovannyi kapitalizm": Diskussiia v Komakademii* ["Organized capitalism": A discussion at the Communist Academy], pp. 183–199. 2d ed. N.p.: Moscow, 1930.

[Bukharin, Nikolai I., and Lenin, V. I.] "Iz materialov Instituta Marksa-Engel'sa-Lenina" [From materials of the Marx-Engels-Lenin Institute]. *Bol'shevik* [Bolshevik] 22 (November 30, 1932).

C. T. [pseud.] "Women yao zenmeyang gan shehui geming?" [How do we want to make social revolution?]. *Gongchandang* [The Communist party] no. 5 (June 7, 1921): 9–32.

Chao Lin. "Shiyue geming, liening-zhuyi he ruoxiao minzu de jiefang yundong" [The October Revolution, Leninism, and the liberation movement of weak peoples]. *Xiangdao zhoubao* [The Guide Weekly] 135 (November 7, 1925): 1235–1238.

Chen Boda. "Muqian zenyang jianshe guojia ziben?" [Now how do we build state capital?]. 3 pts. *Geming pinglun (quanji)* [Revolutionary review] pt. 1, no. 7 (1928): 1–4; pt. 2, no. 8 (1928): 22–26; pt. 3, no. 12 (1928): 16–18.

———. "Zhongguo shehui tingzhi zhuangtai de jichu" [The basis of the stagnancy of Chinese society]. *Wenshi* [Literature and history] 1, no. 4 (December 1934): 1–21.

[Chen Duxiu]. "Chen Duxiu san da Qu Shengbai shu" [Chen Duxiu's third reply to Qu Shengbai]. In *Shehui-zhuyi taolun ji*, edited by Xin Qingnian-she, pp. 137–155. Canton: Xin Qingnian-she, 1922.

[———.] "Chen Duxiu zai da Qu Shengbai shu" [Another reply from Chen Duxiu to Qu Shengbai]. In *Shehui-zhuyi taolun ji* [Collected discussions on socialism], edited by Xin Qingnian-she, pp. 119–124. Canton: Xin Qingnian-she, 1922.

———. "Dong-Xi minzu genben sixiang zhi cha'i" [The difference in the basic thought of Eastern and Western peoples]. In *Duxiu wencun* [Collected works of (Chen) Duxiu], 1:35–40. 2 vols. Hong Kong: Yuandong Tushu Gongsi, 1965.

———. "Eluosi geming yu wo guomin zhi juewu" [The Russian Revolution and our people's awakening]. *Xin qingnian* [New youth] 3, no. 2 (April 1, 1917): 99–101.

———. "Gei xiliu de xin" [Letter to students abroad]. In Chen Duxiu, *Chen Duxiu zuihou duiyu minzhu zhengzhi de jianjie* [Chen Duxiu's last brief explanation of democratic government], pp. 18–24. Hong Kong: Zhongguo Chuban-she, 1950.

———. "Geming de Shanghai" [Revolutionary Shanghai]. *Xiangdao zhoubao* [The Guide Weekly] 160 (June 30, 1926): 1568–1569.

———. "Jidujiao yu Zhongguoren" [Christianity and the Chinese], (February 1, 1920). In Chen Duxiu, *Duxiu wencun* [Collected works of (Chen) Duxiu], 1:417–422. 3 vols. Hong Kong: Yuandong Tushu Gongsi, 1965.

———. "Jinri Zhongguo zhi zhengzhi wenti" [China's present political problems (July 15,

1918)]. In *Duxiu wencun* [Collected works of (Chen) Duxiu]. Vol. 1 of 2 vols. Hong Kong: Yuandong Tushu Gongsi, 1965.

———. "Jiu sixiang yu guoti wenti—Zai Beijing Shenzhou Xuehui jiangyan" [Old thought and the question of the national polity—A lecture at the Peking Shenzhou Learned Society (May 1, 1917)]. In *Duxiu wencun* [Collected works of (Chen) Duxiu], 1:147–151. 2 vols. Hong Kong: Yuandong Tushu Gongsi, 1965.

———. "Ouxiang pohuai lun" [On the destruction of idols (August 15, 1918)]. In *Duxiu wencun* [Collected writings of (Chen) Duxiu], 1:227–230. 2 vols. Hong Kong: Yuandong Tushu Gongsi, 1965.

———. "Rensheng zhenyi" [The true meaning of human life]. In *Duxiu wencun* [Collected writings of (Chen) Duxiu], 1:181–185. 2 vols. Hong Kong: Yuandong Tushu Gongsi, 1965.

———. "Shehui-zhuyi piping" [Critique of socialism]. In *Shehui-zhuyi taolun ji* [Collected discussions on socialism], edited by Xin Qingnian-she, pp. 74–96. Canton: Xin Qingnian-she, 1922.

———. "Shehui-zhuyi ruhe zai Zhongguo kaishi jinxing" [How socialism is beginning to advance in China (June 20, 1923)]. In *Chen Duxiu xiansheng jiangyan lu* [Record of speeches of Chen Duxiu], pp. 21–36. Shanghai: Xin Qingnian-she, 1924.

———. "Shiyue geming yu Dongfang" [The October Revolution and the East]. *Xiangdao zhoubao* [The Guide Weekly] 178 (November 15, 1926): 1849–1850.

———. "Shiyue geming yu Zhongguo minzu jiefang yundong" [The October Revolution and the liberation movement of the Chinese people]. *Xiangdao zhoubao* [The Guide Weekly] 135 (November 1925): 1233–1235.

———. "Tan zhengzhi" [On politics]. In *Shehui-zhuyi taolun ji*, edited by Xin Qingnian-she, pp. 1–15. Canton: Xin Qingnian-she, 1922.

———. "Women weishenme xiangxin shehui-zhuyi?" [Why do we believe in socialism?]. In *Chen Duxiu xiansheng jiangyan lu* [Record of speeches by Chen Duxiu], pp. 1–12. Shanghai: Xin Qingnian-she, 1924.

———. "Women xiangxin hezhong shehui-zhuyi" [What kind of socialism do we believe? (June 1923)]. In *Chen Duxiu xiansheng jiangyan lu* [Record of speeches of Chen Duxiu], pp. 13–20. Shanghai: Xin Qingnian-she, 1924.

———. "Women xianzai weishenme zhengdou?" [Why do we struggle now?]. *Xiangdao zhoubao* [The Guide Weekly] 172 (September 25, 1926): 1752–1754.

———. "Wuren zuihou zhi juewu" [Our final awakening]. In *Duxiu wencun* [Collected writings of (Chen) Duxiu], 1:49–56. 2 vols. Hong Kong: Yuandong Tushu Gongsi, 1965.

———. "Xianfa yu kongjiao" [The constitution and Confucianism (November 1, 1916)]. In *Duxiu wencun* [Collected writings of (Chen) Duxiu]. 2:129–134. 2 vols. Hong Kong: Yuandong Tushu Gongsi, 1965.

———. "Zai lun kongjiao wenti" [More on the problem of Confucianism (January 1, 1917)]. In *Duxiu wencun* [Collected writings of (Chen) Duxiu]. Vol. 1 of 2 vols. Hong Kong: Yuandong Tushu Gongsi, 1965.

Chen Gongbo. "Da Jing Pu xiansheng lun Guomindang daibiao shenme" [A response to Jing Pu on what the Guomindang represents]. In *Chen Gongbo xiansheng wenji* [Collected works of Cheng Gongbo], 1:111–119. 2 vols. Kowloon, Hong Kong: Yuandong Tushu Gongsi, 1967.

———. "Duiyu 'Ping guomin geming de weiji he women de cuowu' de huida" [A response to the "Critique of the crisis of the national revolution and our mistakes" (June 3, 1928)]. In *Chen Gongbo xiansheng wenji* [Collected works of Cheng Gongbo], 1:66–80. 2 vols. Kowloon: Yuandong Tushu Gongsi, 1967.

Chen Gongbo. "Jinhou de Guomindang" [The Guomindang henceforth]. *Geming pinglun (quanji)* [Revolutionary review] no. 1 (1928): 1–14.

―――. "Muqian zenyang jianshe guojia ziben? (II)" [Now how do we build state capital?] *Geming pinglun (quanji)* [Revolutionary review] no. 8 (1928): 22–26.

―――. "Muqian zenyang jianshe guojia ziben? (IV)" [Now how do we build state capital?]. *Geming pinglun (quanji)* [Revolutionary review] no. 12 (1928): 9–14.

―――. "Zai lun di-san dang" [More on a third party]. *Geming pinglun (quanji)* [Revolutionary review] no. 8 (1928).

Chen Ruoshui. "Liang Shuming yu 'Dong-Xi wenhua ji qi zhexue.'" [Liang Shuming and *Eastern and Western cultures and their philosophies*]. In Liang Shuming. *Dong-Xi wenhua ji qi zhexue*, app. 1, pp. 217–225. Taipei: Wenxue Chuban-she, 1977.

Chen Xiaojiang. "Fengjian shehui bengkui-hou Zhongguo lishi wang hechu qu?" [Where did Chinese history go after the disintegration of feudal society?]. *Xiandai shixue* [Contemporary historiography] 2, no. 3 (1934): 43–81.

―――. "Wei xunqiu Zhongguo lishi heyi zoubushang ziben-zhuyi zhi lu zhe jin yijie" [Toward an understanding of the reasons why Chinese history was unable to take the path of capitalism]. *Xiandai shixue* [Contemporary historiography] 2, no. 1/2 (1934): 136–148.

Chesneaux, Jean. "Où en est la discussion sur le mode de production Asiatique" [What has become of the discussion on the Asiatic mode of production]. *La pensée* [Thought] 114 (April 1964); 122 (July–August 1965); 129 (October 1966); 128 (April 1968).

Chevrier, Yves. "De l'occidentalisme à la solitude: Chen Duxiu et l'invention de la modernité chinoise" [From Westernism to solitude: Chen Duxiu and the invention of Chinese modernity]. *Etudes chinoises* [Chinese studies] no. 3 (1984): 7–34.

[Dai Jitao]. "Cong jingji-shang guan Zhongguo de luanyuan" [The sources of disorder in China from an economic perspective]. *Jianshe zazhi* [Construction] (Shanghai) 1, no. 2 (September 1919).

Dai Tianchou [Dai Jitao]. "Bingli zhuanzhi zhi da chengong" [The great victory of the military dictatorship]. In *Dai Tianchou wenji* [Collected writings of Dai Tianchou]. Xiandai Zhongguo Shiliao Congshu [Collected historical materials on contemporary China]. Taipei: N.p., 1962.

―――. "Bingli zhuanzhi zhong zhi zhengzhichao" [Political currents in the military dictatorship]. In *Dai Tianchou wenji* [Collected writings of Dai Tianchou]. Zhongguo Xiandai Shiliao Congshu [Collected historical materials on contemporary China]. Taipei: N.p., 1962.

―――. "Dongfang wenti yu shijie wenti" [The Eastern problem and world problems]. In Dai Jitao, *Dai Jitao xiansheng wencun* [Collected works of Dai Jitao], edited by Chen Tianxi. "Buyi" [app.] 4:1729–1745. 4 vols. Taipei: Zhongguo Guomindang Zhongyang Weiyuanhui, 1959.

―――. "Dushi zui'i lun" [On the evils of cities]. In *Dai Tianchou wenji* [Collected writings of Dai Tianchou]. Zhongguo Xiandai Shiliao Congshu [Collected historical materials on contemporary China], section 2. Taipei: N.p., 1962.

―――. "Guomin geming yu Zhongguo Guomindang" (1925) [The national revolution and the Chinese Guomindang]. In *Dai Jitao xiansheng wencun zai shubian* [Dai Jitao's collected works, 2d suppl.], pp. 424–459. Taipei: N.p., 1968.

―――. "Jinri zhi zhengzhiguan" [My views on politics today]. In *Dai Tianchou wenji* [Collected writings of Dai Tianchou]. Zhongguo Xiandai Shiliao Congshu [Collected historical materials on contemporary China]. Taipei: N.p., 1962.

―――. "Sanmin-zhuyi de guojia-guan" [The view of the state in the Three People's

Principles]. In *Dai Jitao zuijin yanlun ji* [Collected recent speeches of Dai Jitao], pp. 51–70. Shanghai: Datong Shuju, 1929.

Dai Xingyao. "Zhongguo guanliao zhengzhi de moluo" [The downfall of China's bureaucratic government]. *Dushu zazhi* [Reading magazine] 1, no. 4/5 (August 1931): 1–39.

"Declaration of the Social Communist Revolutionary Group." *Minsheng* [Voice of the people] no. 33 (July 15, 1921): 4–5.

E. I. [Yevgeny Iolk]. "O zadachakh Marksistsko-Leninskogo izucheniia kolonial'nykh i polukolonial'nykh stran" [On problems of the Marxist-Leninist study of colonial and semicolonial countries]. *Problemy Kitaia* [Problems of China] 2 (1930): 23–27.

Ermachenko, I. C. "Kitaiskie istoriki o periodizatsii novoi istorii Kitaia (po materialam nauchnoi literatury KNR 1979–1982 gg) [Chinese historians on the periodization of a new history of China (According to materials of scientific literature of the People's Republic of China 1979–1982)]. In Institut Informatsii po Obshchestvennyi Naukam [Institute of Scientific Information on Social Sciences], Trinadtsatsaia nauchnaia konferentsiia po Kitae, chast' tri [Thirteenth Scientific Conference on China, pt. 3]. Moscow: Akademiia Nauk SSSR, 1983.

Fetscher, Iring. "Das Verhaltnis des Marxismus zu Hegel" [The relationship of Marxism to Hegel]. *Marxismusstudien* [Studies on Marxism] (Tübingen) 3/4 (1960–1962): 67–169.

Fu Yiling. "Zhongguo dianyongzhi pinglun: Guanyu dianyong shehui-shuo zhi yijian" [A critical discussion of China's farm servant system: Views on the theory of *dianyong* society]. *Xiandai shixue* [Contemporary historiography] 2, no. 1/2 (1934): 348–352.

Fujita Shōzō. "Aru Marukusu-shugisha: Kawakami Hajime" [A Marxist: Kawakami Hajime]. In Fujita Shōzō, *Tenkō no shisō shi-teki kenkyū: Sono ichi sokumen* [The intellectual historical study of *tenkō*: One aspect], pp. 64–87. Tokyo: Iwanami Shoten, 1975.

Fukuzawa Yukichi. "Heiron" [On warfare]. In *Fukuzawa Yukichi zenshū* [Complete writings of Fukuzawa (Yukichi)]. 5:297–348. 10 vols. Tokyo: Iwanami Shoten, 1959.

———. "Sonnō ron" [On revering the emperor] (1888). In Fukuzawa Yukichi, *Fukuzawa zenshū* [Complete writings of Fukuzawa (Yukichi)], 6:237–268. 10 vols. Tokyo: Kokumin Tosho, 1926.

———. "Teishitsu ron" [On the Imperial Household] (1881). In Fukuzawa Yukichi, *Fukuzawa zenshū* [Complete writings of Fukuzawa (Yukichi)]. 5:437–480. 10 vols. Tokyo: Kokumin Tosho, 1926.

Gao Quanpu, and Zhang Qizhi. "Wusi yundong qijian Li Dazhao de Makesi-zhuyi xuanchuan yundong" [Li Dazhao's propagation of Marxism during the period of the May Fourth movement]. *Lishi jiaoxue* [Historical education] (May 1959): 5–10.

Gao Yihan. "Riben jindai laodong zuzhi zhi yundong" [The recent labor organizations movement in Japan]. *Xin qingnian* [New youth] 7, no. 6 (May 1920): 1–14.

Goldendach, David Borisovich [Riazanov, David]. "Introduction to Marx über China und Idien" [Introduction to *Marx on China and India*]. *Unter dem Banner des Marxismus* 1, no. 2:370–378.

Gu Chaoxiong. "Makesi xueshuo" [The philosophy of Marx]. *Xin qingnian* [New youth] 6, no. 5 (May 1919): 450–465.

Hani Gorō. "Bakumatsu ni okeru seiji-teki shihai keitai" [The form of political rule in the late-Tokugawa period]. In *Nihon shihon-shugi hattatsu shi kōza* [Symposium on the history of the development of Japanese capitalism]. Vol. 1 of 7 vols. Tokyo: Iwanami Shoten, 1932–1933.

———. "Nihon shihon-shugi hattatsu shi kōza gojū shūnen ni yosete" [On the fiftieth anniversary of the symposium on the history of the development of Japanese capitalism]. *Tosho* [Books] no. 394 (June 1982): 26–37.

———. "Tōyō ni okeru shihon-shugi no keisei" [The formation of capitalism in the East]. In Hani Gorō, *Meiji ishin shi kenkyū* [Studies in the history of the Meiji Restoration], pp. 13–150. Tokyo: Iwanami Shoten, Iwanami bunko, 1978.

Harada Katsumasa. "Ajia rentai-shugi ni tsuite no kenkyū nōto: Nisshin sensō ni itaru dankai ni okeru" [A research note on the idea of Asian cooperation in the phase up to the Sino-Japanese War]. *Rekishi hyōron* [Historical review] 102 (February 1959): 28–37.

Hattori Shisō. "Ishin shi hōhō-jō no sho mondai" (April–June 1933)[Methodological problems in the history of the Restoration]. In *Hattori Shisō chosakushū* [Collected works of Hattori Shisō], 1:91–194. Tokyo: Riron-sha, 1955, 1960.

———. "Ma'nyufakuchua ronsō ni tsuite no shokan" [Thoughts on the manufacture debate (July 1952)]. In *Hattori Shisō chosakushū* [Collected works of Hattori Shisō], 1:269–336. Tokyo: Riron-sha, 1955, 1960.

———. "Meiji ishin no kakumei oyobi hankakumei" [Revolution and counter-revolution in the Meiji Restoration (February 1933)]. In *Nihon shihon-shugi hattatsu shi kōza* [Symposium on the history of the development of Japanese capitalism]. Vol. 1 of 7 vols. Reprint ed. Tokyo: Iwanami Shoten, 1932–1933, 1982.

———. "Zettai-shugi ron" [On absolutism]. In *Marukishizumu* (I) [Marxism I], compiled by Uchida Yoshihiko, Ōtsuka Hisao, and Matsushima Ei'ichi, pp. 381–410. Gendai Nihon shisō taikei [Outline of contemporary Japanese thought], no. 20. Tokyo: Chikuma Shobō, 1966.

Haupt, Georges. "Les Marxistes face à la question nationale: Histoire du problème" [The Marxists confronting the national question: History of the problem]. In *Les Marxistes et la question nationale 1848–1914: Etudes et textes* [The Marxists and the national question 1848–1914: Studies and texts], pp. 9–61. Paris: François Maspero, 1974.

Hayano Tōru, and Inaka Yoshiaki. "Sayoku riron, kenji ka tenkan ka, Nyū-Shakaitō ni hamon: Shakai-shugi Kyōkai 'Bunretsu' ikkagetsu'" [Left-wing theory, firm adherence or change, ripples in the New Socialist party: One month since the 'split' in the Socialist Association]. *Asahi shinbun* [The morning news], May 15, 1984.

He Siyuan. "Buersaiweike-zhuyi" [Bolshevism]. *Xinchao* [The new tide] 3, no. 2 (March 1922): 105–112.

Hirano Yoshitarō. "Jiyū minken: Sono seishitsu/undō no gendo/naibu-teki kihon tairitsu no kiso kōsatsu" [Civil rights: An examination of their character, the limits of the movement, and the basis of its fundamental internal contradictions]. *Kaizō* [Reconstruction] December 1933: 2–22.

———. "Meiji ishin ni okeru seiji-teki shihai keitai" [The form of political rule in the Meiji Restoration]. In *Nihon shihon-shugi hattatsu shi kōza* [Symposium on the history of the development of Japanese capitalism]. Vol. 1 of 7 vols. Tokyo: Iwanami Shoten, 1932–1935.

Hirata Kiyoaki. "La société civile japonaise contemporaine" [Contemporary Japanese civil society]. *Actuel Marx* [Marx today] (Paris) no. 2 (1987).

Hori Makoto. "Meiji shoki no kokka ron" [A look at the reception of German state thought in the early-Meiji era: Bluntschli and Katō Hiroyuki]. In *Kokka gakkai gojū shūnen kinen kokkagaku ronshū* [Commemoration of the fiftieth anniversary of the Kokka Gakkai: Collected essays on the theory of the state], pp. 711–744. Tokyo: Yūhikaku, 1937.

Hozumi Yatsuka. "Waga kenpō no tokushitsu" [Special characteristics of our constitution]. In Hozumi Yatsuka, *Hozumi Yatsuka hakushi ronbun shū* [Collected essays of Dr. Yatsuka Hozumi]. Tokyo: Nissei Insatsu, 1913.

Hu Hanmin [Min Yi]. "Gao feinan minsheng-zhuyizhe" [To those who denounce the principle of *minsheng*]. *Minbao* [The people's journal] no. 12 (March 1907): 45–155.

————. "Guojia bu-tongyi-de tongku" [The pain of the country's disunity]. In Hu Hanmin, *Geming lilun yu geming gongzuo* [Revolutionary theory and revolutionary work], 7:1391–1394. Shanghai: Minzhi Shuju, n.d.

————. "Jieji yu daode xueshuo" [Classes and theories of morality]. *Jianshe* [Reconstruction] 1, no. 6 (January 1920): 1175–1190.

————. "Zhongguo zhexue shi weiwu de yanjiu" [A materialist study of Chinese philosophy]. *Jianshe zazhi* [Reconstruction magazine] 1, no. 3 (October 1, 1919): 513–543; 1, no. 4 (November 1, 1919): 655–691.

Hu Qiuyuan. "Lüefu Sun Zhuozhang jun bing lüe lun Zhongguo shehui zhi xingzhi: A Memorandum" [A brief consideration of Sun Zhuozhang and a brief discussion of the nature of Chinese society]. *Dushu zazhi* [Reading magazine] 2, no. 2/3 (March 1932): 1–46.

————. "Yaxiya shengchan fangshi yu zhuanzhi-zhuyi" [The Asiatic mode of production and despotism]. *Dushu zazhi* [Reading magazine] 2, no. 7/8 (August 1932): 1–23.

————. "Zhongguo shehui–wenhua fazhan caoshu" [Draft on the development of Chinese society/culture]. *Dushu zazhi* [Reading magazine] Pt. 1, 3, no. 3/4 (April 1936): 1–96.

————. "Zhuanzhi-zhuyi: Zhuanzhi-zhuyi lilun yu Zhongguo zhuanzhi-zhuyi zhi shiji" [Despotism: The theory of despotism and the reality of despotism in China]. *Dushu zazhi* [Reading magazine] 2, no. 11/12 (December 1932): 1–53.

Hua Tiansheng. "Riben laodong yundong-zhong zuoyou liangpai zhi douzheng" [The struggle of the Left and Right factions within the Japanese labor movement]. *Xiangdao zhoubao* [The Guide Weekly] 115 (1925): 164–166.

————. "Riben puxuan yu wuchan-jieji" [Japan's universal suffrage and the proletariat]. *Xiangdao zhoubao* [The Guide Weekly] 108 (1925): 993–994.

Hyppolite, Jean. "La conception hégélienne de l'état et sa critique par Karl Marx" [The Hegelian conception of the state and the critique of it by Karl Marx]. In Jean Hyppolite, *Etudes sur Marx et Hegel* [Studies on Marx and Hegel], pp. 120–141. 2d ed. Bibliothèque philosophique Paris: Editions Marcel Rivière et Cie., 1965.

————. "Marxisme et philosophie" [Marxism and philosophy]. In Jean Hyppolite, *Etudes sur Marx et Hegel* [Studies on Marx and Hegel], pp. 105–119. 2d ed. Bibliothèque philosophique [Philosophical library]. Paris: Editions Marcel Rivière et Cie., 1965.

Imai Sei'ichi. "Kaisetsu" [Commentary]. In *Taishō shisō shū (I)* [Collected writings of Taishō thought], edited and with an introduction by Imai Sei'ichi. Kindai Nihon shisō taikei [Outline of modern Japanese thought], no. 33. pp. 457–490. Tokyo: Chikuma Shobō, 1978.

Ienaga Saburō. "Nihon ni okeru kyōwa-shugi no dentō" [The tradition of republicanism in Japan]. *Shisō* [Thought] (August 1958).

Inomata Tsunao. "Buhaarin" [Bukharin]. *Kaizō* [Reconstruction] (February 1929): 48–58.

————. "Doronuma ni kanbotsu shita 'puchi-teikoku-shugi'-sha (zokkō)" [A "petty imperialist" who has fallen into the quagmire (sequel) (October 1927)]. In Inomata Tsunao, *Teikoku-shugi kenkyū* [Studies on imperialism], pp. 247–402. Tokyo: Kaizō-sha, 1928.

————. "Hiyorimi-shugi-teki senryaku ka 'senryaku-teki' hiyorimi-shugi ka" [Opportunistic strategy or "strategic" opportunism? (March 1928)]. In Inomata Tsunao, *Nihon puroretariaato no senryaku to senjutsu: Zasshi Rōnō keisai ronbun shū* [The strategy and tactics of the Japanese proletariat: Collected essays published in the magazine *Labor-Farmer*]. pp. 47–84. Tokyo: Tosho Shinbun-sha, 1973.

————. "Nihon musan kaikyū no ippan senryaku" [The general strategy of the Japanese proletariat (November 10, 1927)]. In Inomata Tsunao, *Nihon puroretariaato no senryaku to senjutsu: Zasshi Rōnō keisai ronbun shū* [The strategy and tactics of the Japanese proletariat: Collected essays published in the magazine *Labor-Farmer*]. Tokyo: Tosho Shinbun-sha, 1973.

Inomata Tsunao [Niijima Issaku, pseud.]. "Nihon musan kaikyū undō ni kansuru teize: (I) Nihon shihon-shugi no gensei" [Theses on the Japanese proletarian movement: (I) The current situation of Japanese capitalism (1927–1928)]. In Inomata Tsunao, *Nihon puroretariaato no senryaku to senjutsu: Zasshi Rōnō ni keisai ronbun shū* [The strategy and tactics of the Japanese proletariat: Collected essays published in the magazine *Labor-Farmer*], pp. 11–23. Tokyo: Tosho Shinbun-sha, 1973.

————. "Nihon musan kaikyū undō ni kansuru teize: (II) Seiji jōsei" [Theses on the Japanese proletarian movement: (II) Political circumstances (1927–1928)]. In Inomata Tsunao, *Nihon puroretariaato no senryaku to senjutsu: Zasshi Rōnō ni keisai ronbun shū* [The strategy and tactics of the Japanese proletariat: Collected essays published in the magazine *Labor-Farmer*], pp. 24–27. Tokyo: Tosho Shinbun-sha, 1973.

————. "Nihon teikoku-shugi no shin dankai no mondai" [The problem of the new stage of Japanese imperialism (August 1927)]. In Inomata Tsunao, *Teikoku-shugi kenkyū* [Studies on imperialism], pp. 165–211. Tokyo: Kaizō-sha, 1928.

————. "Shihon-shugi Nihon no teikoku-shugi" [The imperialism of capitalist Japan (June 1927)]. In Inomata Tsunao, *Teikoku-shugi kenkyū* [Studies on imperialism], pp. 113–163. Tokyo: Kaizō-sha, 1928.

————. "Tochi mondai to hōken isei" [The land problem and feudal remnants (December 7, 1929)]. In Inomata Tsunao, *Nihon musan kaikyū no senryaku to senjutsu: Zasshi Rōnō ni keisai ronbun shū* [The strategy and tactics of the Japanese proletariat: Collected essays published in the magazine *Labor-Farmer*], pp. 137–162. Tokyo: Tosho Shinbun-sha, 1973.

————. "Waga senryaku ni okeru burujoa minshu-shugi-teki tōsō no yakuwari" [The role of the bourgeois-democratic struggle in our strategy (September 1928)]. In Inomata Tsunao, *Nihon puroretariaato no senryaku to senjutsu: Zasshi Rōnō ni keisai ronbun shū* [The strategy and tactics of the Japanese proletariat: Collected essays published in the magazine *Labor-Farmer*], pp. 85–107. Tokyo: Tosho Shinbun-sha, 1973.

Inoue Isao. "Tōitsu kokka no vijon" [The vision of a unified state]. In *Kindai Nihon seiji shisō shi* [History of modern Japanese political thought]. Kindai Nihon shisō shi taikei [Outline of the history of modern Japanese thought], edited by Miyazawa Toshiyoshi and Ōkouchi Kazuo, 1:111–150. 2 vols. Tokyo: Yūhikaku, 1971.

Inumaru Giichi. "Nihon Marukusu-shugi no genryū" [The origins of Japanese Marxism]. In *Gendai no ideorogii* (I) Vol. 2, *Nihon no Marukusu-shugi* [Japanese Marxism], edited by Ikumi Takuichi, pp. 7–63. 6 vols. Tokyo: San'ichi Shobō, 1961.

Iolk, Yevgeny S. "K voprosy ob 'Aziatskom' sposobe proizvodstva" [On the problem of the "Asiatic" mode of production]. *Pod znamenem marksizma* [Under the banner of Marxism], no. 3 (1931).

————. "K voprosy ob osnovakh obshchestvennovo stroia drevnova Kitai" [On the problem of the fundamental social order of ancient China]. *Problemy Kitaia* [Problems of China], no. 2 (1930).

————. "O zadachakh Marksistsko-Leninskogo izucheniia kolonial'nikh i polukolonial'nikh stran" [On problems of the Marxist-Leninist study of colonial and semi-colonial countries]. *Problemy Kitaia* [Problems of China], no. 2 (1930).

————. "Review of M. Kokin and G. Papaian, "Tszintian": Agrarnii stroi proizvodsta" ["Jingtian": The agrarian system of ancient China]. *Problemy Kitaia* [Problems of China], no. 4/5 (1930).

Ishida Takeshi. "Ideorogii to shite no tennō-sei" [The emperor system as ideology]. *Shisō* [Thought] 336 (June 1952): 32–43.

———. "J. S. Mill 'Jiyū-ron' to Nakamura Kei'u oyobi Gen Fuku" [J. S. Mill's "On Liberty" and Nakamura Kei'u and Yan Fu]. In Ishida Takeshi, *Nihon kindai shisō shi ni okeru hō to seiji* [Law and politics in the history of modern Japanese thought], pp. 1–46. Tokyo: Iwanami Shoten, 1976.

———. "Kawakami Hajime ni okeru itan e no michi" [The path to heresy in Kawakami Hajime]. *Shisō* [Thought] (October 1979): 1–18.

———. "Kokka yūkitai-setsu" [The state organ theory]. In *Kōza: Nihon kindai hō hattatsu shi* [Symposium: History of the development of modern Japanese law]. Vol. 2. Tokyo: Keisō Shobō, 1958.

Ishimuda Shō. "Kōtoku Shūsui to Chūgoku" [Kōtoku Shūsui and China]. In *Ajia-shugi* [Asianism], edited by Takeuchi Yoshimi. Gendai Nihon shisō taikei [Outline of contemporary Japanese thought] no. 9. Tokyo: Chikuma Shobō, 1963.

"Iz materialov Instituta Marksa-Engel'sa-Lenina" [From materials of the Marx-Engels-Lenin Institute]. *Bol'shevik* [Bolshevik], no. 22 (November 30, 1932).

Ji Lei. "Makesi de shehui xingshi lun" [Marx's theory of social forms]. *Dushu zazhi* [Reading magazine] 3, no. 3/4 (April 1936): 1–71.

Jisheng. "Gao laobingnong" [To workers, soldiers, and peasants]. *Gongchandang* [The Communist party] no. 4 (May 7, 1921): 5–13.

Juillard, Jacques. "Sorel, Rousseau et la revolution française" [Sorel, Rousseau, and the French Revolution]. *Cahiers Georges Sorel* [The Georges Sorel journal]. (Paris: Société d'études soreliennes) 3 (1985): 5–15.

———. "Sorel, sessant'anni dopo" [Sorel, sixty years later], *Mondo operaio* [Worker world] 35, no. 7/8 (July–August 1982): 90–97.

Kamiyama Shigeo. "Nihon teikoku-shugi no seikaku no mondai ni yosete: 'Gunji-teki teikoku-shugi' no gainen ni tsuite" [On the problem of the nature of Japanese imperialism: On the concept of 'militaristic imperialism']. In Kamiyama Shigeo, *Tennō-sei ni kansuru riron-teki sho mondai* [Theoretical problems concernng the emperor system], pp. 200–215. Rev. and enl. ed. Tokyo: Minshu Hyōron-sha, 1955, 1960.

Kano Masanao. "Kokka-shugi no taitō" [The emergence of statism]. In *Kindai Nihon seiji shisō shi* [History of Modern Japanese political thought], edited by Hashikawa Bunzō and Matsumoto Sannosuke. 2 vols. Kindai Nihon shisō shi taikei [Outline of the history of modern Japanese thought] no. 3, edited by Miyazawa Toshiyoshi and Ōkouchi Kazuo, 1:287–305. Tokyo: Yūhikaku, 1971.

Kawakami Hajime. "Kokka shakai-shugi no riron-teki kentō" [A theoretical examination of state socialism]. *Chūō kōron* [Central review] 47, no. 6 (June 1932): 2–36.

———. "Nihon dokutoku no kokka-shugi" [Japan's unique statism (March 1911)]. In Kawakami Hajime, *Keizai to jinsei* [Economics and humanity]. Tokyo: Jitsugyō no Nihon-sha, 1911.

———. "Nihon sonnō-ron" [Japanese agrarianism]. In Kawakami Hajime, *Kawakami Hajime chosakushū* [Collected works of Kawakami Hajime], 1:129–221. 12 vols. Tokyo: Chikuma Shobō, 1964–1965.

———. "Roshia kakumei to shakai-shugi kakumei" [The Russian revolution and socialist revolution (1922)]. In Kawakami Hajime, *Kawakami Hajime chosakushū* [Collected works of Kawakami Hajime], 10:226–250. 12 vols. Tokyo: Chikuma Shobō, 1964–1965.

———. "Seitai to kokutai" [The form of government and the national polity (1911)]. In Kawakami Hajime, *Keizai to jinsei* [Economics and humanity]. Tokyo Jitsugyō no Nihon-sha, 1911.

————. "'Shihon' ni arawareru yuibutsu shikan no danpen" [Fragments of historical materialism manifested in *Capital*]. In Kawakami Hajime, *Yuibutsu shikan kenkyū* [Studies in historical materialism]. Tokyo: Kōbundō, 1922.

————. "Sonnō ron" [On the reverence for agriculture in Japan] (1905). In Kawakami Hajime, *Kawakami Hajime chosakushū* [Collected works of Kawakami Hajime], 1:129–221. 12 vols. Tokyo: Chikuma Shobō, 1964.

————. "Yuibutsu shikan ni kansuru jiko seisan" [Self-adjustment concerning historical materialism]. *Shakai mondai kenkyū* [Studies on social problems] (Tokyo) 77 (February 1927): 2655–2673.

————. "Yuibutsu shikan to risō-shugi" [Historical materialism and idealism]. *Shakai mondai kenkyū* [Studies on social problems] (Tokyo) 11 (December 1919): 365–376.

Kazahaya Yasoji. "'Nihon shihon-shugi hattatsu shi kōza' hakkan gojū nen: Sono rekishi-teki igi to konnichi-teki igi" [Fifty years since the publication of the *Symposium on the history of the development of Japanese capitalism*: Its historical significance and its present significance]. *Keizai* [Economics] (June 1982): 188–199.

Kita Ikki. "Kokutai-ron oyobi junsei shakai-shugi" [The theory of the 'national polity' and pure socialism]. In Kita Ikki, *Kita Ikki chosakushū* [Collected works of Kita Ikki]. Vol. 1 of 3 vols. Tokyo: Misuzu Shobō, 1959.

Kōtoku Shūsui. "Shakai-shugi to kokka" [Socialism and the state (1902)]. In Kōtoku Shūsui, *Shakai-shugi shinzui* [The essence of socialism], pp. 61–64. Tokyo: Iwanami Shoten, Iwanami bunko, 1953.

————. "Shakai-shugi to kokutai" [Socialism and the national polity (1902)]. In Kōtoku Shūsui, *Shakai-shugi shinzui* [The essence of socialism], pp. 70–74. Tokyo: Iwanami Shoten, Iwanami bunko, 1953.

Koizumi Sakutarō. "Sakai-kun to Kōtoku Shūsui o kataru" [On Sakai and Kōtoku Shūsui]. *Chūō kōron* [Central review] 46, no. 10 (October 1931): 171–187.

Kondō Kuniyasu. "'Minkoku' to Ri Taishō no chi'i: Shingai kakumei kara go-shi undō e" [The "Republic" and the position of Li Dazhao: From the 1911 Revolution to the May Fourth movement]. *Shisō* [Thought] 477 (March 1964): 287–298.

Kuusinen [Kūshinen]. "Nihon teikoku-shugi to Nihon kakumei no seishitsu" [Japanese imperialism and the nature of the Japanese revolution (1932)]. In *Kominterun Nihon ni kansuru teize shū* [Collected Comintern theses on Japan], compiled by Ishidō Kiyotomo and Yamabe Kentarō, pp. 102–119. Tokyo: Aoki Shoten, Aoki bunko, 1961.

Lenin, V. I. "Gosudarstvo i revoliutsiia" [State and revolution]. In V. I. Lenin, *Polnoë sobranie sochinenii* [Complete works]. Vol. 30 of 55 vols. 5th ed. Moscow: N.p., 1958–.

————. "Zamechaniia na stat'iu N. I. Bukharina 'Imperialisticheskoë razboinich'e gosudarstvo'" [Remarks on N. I. Bukharin's article "The imperialist robber state"], in V. I. Lenin, *Polnoë sobranie sochinenii* [Complete works], vol. 33: *Gosudarstvo i revoliutsiia* [The state and revolution], 5th ed. Moscow: Gosudarstvennoë izdatel'stvo politicheskoi literatury, 1962.

————. "Zametki na stat'iu N. I. Bukharina, 'K teorii imperialisticheskogo gosudarstva'" [Notes on N. I. Bukharin's article, "Toward a theory of the imperialist state], in V. I. Lenin, *Polnoë sobranie sochinenii* [Complete works], vol. 33: *Gosudarstvo i revoliutsiia* [The state and revolution], 5th ed. Moscow: Gosudarstvennoë izdatel'stvo politicheskoi literatury, 1962.

Li Da. "Makesi-pai shehui-zhuyi" [Marxian socialism]. *Xin qingnian* [New youth] 9, no. 2 (June 1921): 1–11.

Li Da [Jiang Chun]. "Shehui geming de shangque" [A consideration of social revolution]. *Gongchandang* [The Communist party] no. 2 (December 7, 1920): 2–9.

Li Da. "Taolun shehui-zhuyi bing zhi Liang Rengong" [Discussion on socialism and questioning Liang Rengong]. *Xin qingnian* [New youth] 9, no. 1 (May 1921): 1–15.

Li Da? (C. T.). "Women yao zenyang gan shehui geming" [How are we going to make a social revolution?]. *Gongchandang* [The Communist party] no. 5 (June 7, 1921): 9–32.

Li Da [Jiang Chun]. "Wuzhengfu-zhuyi zhi jiepou" [An analysis of anarchism]. *Gongchandang* [The Communist party] no. 4 (May 7, 1921): 14–23.

Li Dazhao. "Bolshevism de shengli" [The victory of Bolshevism]. In *Li Dazhao xuanji* [Selected works of Li Dazhao]. Pp. 112–18. Beijing: Renmin Chuban-she, 1962.

Li Dazhao. "Da Yaxiya-zhuyi yu xin Yaxiya-zhuyi" [Great Asianism and new Asianism]. In *Li Dazhao xuanji* [Selected works of Li Dazhao], pp. 127–129. Beijing: Renmin Chuban-she, 1962.

––––––. "Dong-Xi wenming genben zhi yidian" [Fundamental differences between Eastern and Western civilizations] (July 1918). In *Shouchang wenji* [Collected works of (Li) Shou-chang]. Shanghai: N.p., 1951.

––––––. "Eguo da geming zhi yingxiang" [The influence of the great Russian Revolution]. In *Li Dazhao xuanji* [Selected works of Li Dazhao], pp. 81–82. Beijing: Renmin Chuban-she, 1962.

––––––. "Eluosi geming de guoqu he xianzai" [The past and present of the Russian Revolution]. *Xin qingnian* [New youth] 9, no. 3 (July 1, 1921): 1–20.

––––––. "Fa-E geming zhi bijiao-guan" [A comparative perspective on the French and Russian revolutions]. In *Li Dazhao xuanji* [Selected works of Li Dazhao], pp. 101–104. Beijing: Renmin Chuban-she, 1962.

––––––. "Jieji jingzheng yu huzhu" [Class struggle and mutual aid (July 6, 1919)]. In *Li Dazhao xuanji* [Selected works of Li Dazhao] pp. 222–225. Beijing: Renmin Chuban-she, 1962.

––––––. "Jin" [Now]. In *Li Dazhao xuanji* [Selected works of Li Dazhao], pp. 93–96. Beijing: Renmin Chuban-she, 1962.

––––––. "Jingshen jiefang" [Spiritual liberation (February 8, 1920)]. In *Li Dazhao xuanji* [Selected works of Li Dazhao], p. 309. Beijing: Renmin Chuban-she, 1962.

––––––. "Pan . . . ism zhi shibai yu democracy zhi shengli" (July 15, 1918) [The defeat of Pan . . . ism and the victory of democracy]. In *Li Dazhao xuanji* [Selected works of Li Dazhao], pp. 105–108. Beijing: Renmin Chuban-she, 1962.

––––––. "Pingmin zhengzhi yu gongren zhengzhi" ["Democracy and ergatocracy"]. In *Li Dazhao xuanji* [Selected works of Li Dazhao], pp. 395–400. Beijing: Renmin Chuban-she, 1962.

––––––. "Qingchun" [Spring (September 1, 1916)]. In *Li Dazhao xuanji* [Selected works of Li Dazhao], pp. 65–76. Beijing: Renmin Chuban-she, 1962.

––––––. "Qingnian yu laoren" [Youth and old people]. *Xin qingnian* [New youth] 3, no. 2 (April 1, 1917): 1–4.

––––––. "Qingnian yu nongcun" [Youth and the countryside (February 1919)]. In *Li Dazhao xuanji* [Selected works of Li Dazhao], pp. 146–150. Beijing: Renmin Chuban-she, 1962.

Li Dazhao [Shouchang]. "Shiyue geming yu Zhongguo renmin" [The October Revolution and the Chinese people] (November 7, 1922). In *Li Dazhao xuanji* [Selected works of Li Dazhao], pp. 401–402. Beijing: Renmin Chuban-she, 1962.

Li Dazhao. "Shumin de shengli" [The victory of the masses] (November 15, 1918). In *Li*

Dazhao xuanji [Collected works of Li Dazhao], pp. 109–111. Beijing: Renmin Chuban-she, 1962.

———. "Wo de Makesi-zhuyi guan" [My Marxist views (May 1919)]. In *Li Dazhao xuanji* [Selected works of Li Dazhao], pp. 173–211. Beijing: Renmin Chuban-she, 1962.

———. "Xinde! Jiude!" [The new! The old! (May 15, 1918)]. In *Li Dazhao xuanji* [Selected works of Li Dazhao], pp. 97–100. Beijing: Renmin Chuban-she, 1962.

———. "Xinjiu sichao zhi jizhan" [The battle between new and old currents of thought (March 9, 1919)]. In *Li Dazhao xuanji* [Selected works of Li Dazhao]. Beijing: Renmin Chuban-she, 1962.

———. "Yaxiya qingnian de guangming yundong" [The bright movement of Asian youth (April 30, 1920)]. In *Li Dazhao xuanji* [Collected works of Li Dazhao], pp. 327–329. Beijing: Renmin Chuban-she, 1962.

———. "You jingji-shang jieshi Zhongguo jindai sixiang biandong de yuanyin" [An economic interpretation of the causes of changes in modern Chinese thought (January 1, 1920)]. In *Li Dazhao xuanji* [Selected works of Li Dazhao]. Beijing: Renmin Chuban-she, 1962.

———. "Zai lun xin Yaxiya-zhuyi" (December 12, 1919) [More on new Asianism]. In *Li Dazhao xuanji* [Selected works of Li Dazhao], pp. 278–282. Beijing: Renmin Chuban-she, 1962.

Li Ji. "Duiyu Zhongguo shehui-shi lunzhan de gongxian yu piping" [Contribution and a critique of the controversy on Chinese social history]. *Dushu zazhi* [Reading magazine] 2, no. 2/3 (March 1932): 1–150; 2, no. 7/8 (August 1932): 1–62.

(Li) Lisan. "Qipian laodong jieji de quan-Yaxiya laodong huiyi" [The Pan-Asian workers' conference that deceives the proletariat]. *Xiangdao zhoubao* [The Guide Weekly] 148 (1926): 1383–1385.

———. "Zhongguo geming de genben wenti" [Fundamental problems of the Chinese revolution]. *Buersaiweike* [The Bolshevik] 3, no. 2/3 (March 15, 1930).

Li Longmu. "Li Dazhao tongzhi he wusi shiqi makesi-zhuyi sixiang de xuanchuan" [Comrade Li Dazhao and the propagation of Marxism during the May Fourth period]. *Lishi yanjiu* [Historical research] no. 5 (1957): 1–18.

Li Maimai. "Lun minzu yundong zhi lishi yiyi yu Zhongguo minzu yundong" [On the historical significance of national movements and the Chinese national movement]. *Wenhua jianshe yuekan* [Cultural reconstruction monthly] 3, no. 1 (October 1936): 67–76.

———. "Zhongguo fengjian zhidu zhi bengkui yu zhuanzhi junzhuzhi zhi wancheng" [The collapse of Chinese feudalism and the completion of the monarchy]. *Dushu zazhi* [Reading magazine] 2, no. 11/12 (December 1932): 1–64.

Li Shizeng. "Da pangguanzi" [Response to a bystander]. *Xin shiji* (August 3, 1907).

———. "Shehui gexin zhi liang da yaosu" [Two major elements of social reform]. *Jianshe* [Reconstruction] 2, no. 3 (April 1920): 569–578.

Liang Qichao. "Aiguo lun" [On patriotism] (1899). In Liang Rengong [Liang Qichao], *Yinbingshi heji* [Collected works of the ice-drinker's studio], compiled by Lin Zhijun. 40 vols. *Wenji*, vol. 2, chap. 3, pp. 65–77. Shanghai: N.p., 1936.

Liang Rengong [Liang Qichao]. "Guojia yunming lun" [On the fate of the state]. In Liang Rengong [Liang Qichao], *Yinbingshi heji* [Collected writings from the ice-drinker's studio], compiled by Lin Zhijun, 40 vols. *Wenji* no. 22 (vol. 8) pp. 94–103. Shanghai: N.p., 1936.

———. "Lixian zhengti yu zhengzhi daode" [Constitutional government and political morality]. In Liang Rengong [Liang Qichao], *Yinbingshi heji* [Collected writings from the ice-drinker's studio]. compiled by Lin Zhijun. 40 vols. *Wenji* 8, no. 23, pp. 52–56. Shanghai: N.p., 1936.

———. "Xinmin shuo" [A theory of a new people]. In Liang Rengong [Liang Qichao], *Yinbingshi heji* [Collected writings from the ice-drinker's studio], compiled by Lin Zhijun. 40 vols. *Zhuanji 4*. Shanghai: N.p., 1936.

Lin Yungai. "Shehui-zhuyi guojia zhi jianshe gailue" [Outline of construction in socialist countries]. *Jianshe* [Reconstruction] 2, no. 1 (February 1920): 69–86.

[Liu] Shifu. "Annaqi" [Anarchy]. *Minsheng* [Voice of the people] no. 17 (N.d.): 7–8 (199–200).

———. "Gongchan-zhuyi komunismo zhi yuanze" [The principles of communism]. *Minsheng* [Voice of the people] no. 11 (May 23, 1914): 1–2.

———. "Kelupaotejin wuzhengfu-gongchan-zhuyi zhi yaoling" [Outline of Kropotkin's anarcho-communism]. *Minsheng* [Voice of the people] no. 17 (N.d.): 8 (200).

———. "Wuzhengfu-gongchan-zhuyi shiming" [A clarification of anarcho-communism]. *Minsheng* [Voice of the people] no. 5 (April 11, 1914): 1–5 (48–53).

———. "Wuzhengfu-zhuyi zhi yuanzu" [The founders of anarchism]. *Minsheng* [Voice of the people] no. 13 (June 6, 1914): 1–3 (145–147).

Liu, Shipei. "Wuzhengfu-zhuyi zhi pingdeng guan" [The anarchist view of equality]. *Tianyi bao* [Natural justice] no. 4 (July 25, 1907); no. 5 (August 10, 1907); no. 7 (September 15, 1907).

Lukin, A. V. "Ideologiia kitaiskogo natsionalizma v rabotakh Tai Tsitao o Iaponii" [The ideology of Chinese nationalism in the works of Dai Jitao on Japan]. In *Semnadtsataia nauchnaia konferentsiia: "obshchestvo i gosudarstvo v Kitae"* [Seventeenth scientific conference: "Society and the state in China"]. Moscow: Nauka, 1986.

Ma En. "Guoji diguo-zhuyi yu dongfang bei yapo de guojia" [International imperialism and the oppressed countries of the East]. *Xiangdao zhoubao* [The Guide Weekly]. 176 (October 19, 1927): 1820–1822.

Ma Jun. "Zhongguo geming zhi jinri he mingbai" [The present and future of the Chinese revolution]. *Geming pinglun* [Revolutionary review] no. 1 (1928): 15–26.

Mad'iar, Ludwig S. "Dve agrarnye programmy v kitaiskoi revoliutsii" [Two agrarian programs in the Chinese Revolution]. *Problemy Kitaia* [Problems of China] no. 4–5 (1930).

Mao Tse-tung. "Gei Lin Biao tongzhi de xin" [Letter to Comrade Lin Biao] (January 5, 1930). In *Mao Tse-tung ji* [Collected writings of Mao Tse-tung]. Compiled by Takeuchi Minoru. Vol. 1 of 10 vols. 2d ed. Tokyo: Sōsō-sha, 1983.

———. "Guomin geming yu nongmin yundong" [The national revolution and the peasant movement]. In *Mao Tse-tung ji* [Collected writings of Mao Tse-tung], compiled by Takeuchi Minoru. Vol. 1 of 10 vols. 2d ed. Tokyo: Sōsō-sha, 1983.

———. "Lun chijiu zhan" [On protracted war (May 1938)]. In *Mao Tse-tung ji* [Collected writings of Mao Tse-tung], compiled by Takeuchi Minoru. Vol. 6 of 10 vols. 2d ed. Tokyo: Sōsō-sha, 1983.

———. "Zai Yan'an wusi yundong ershi zhounian dahui de yanjiang" [Speech at Yan'an commemorating the twentieth anniversary of the May Fourth movement]. In *Mao Tse-tung ji(* [Collected Writings of Mao Tse-tung] (May 4, 1939). Vol. 6 of 10 vols. 2d ed. Tokyo: Sōsō-sha, 1983.

Maruyama Masao. "Kuga Katsunan: Hito to shisō" [Kuga Katsunan: The man and his thought (1947)]. In Maruyama Masao, *Senchū to sengo no aida, 1936–1957* [Between wartime and postwar, 1936–1957], pp. 281–296. Tokyo: Misuzu Shobō, 1976.

———. "Meiji kokka no shisō" [The thought of the Meiji state (1946)]. In Maruyama

Masao, *Senchū to sengo no aida, 1936–1957* [Between wartime and postwar, 1936–1957], pp. 202–250. Tokyo: Misuzu Shobō, 1976.

Maruyama Matsuyuki. "Ajia nashonarizumu no ichi-genkei, Ri Tai-shō no Ajia-ron ni tsuite" [A model of Asian nationalism: On Li Dazhao's view of Asia]. *Rekishi hyōron* [Historical review] 113 (January 1960): 17–24.

————. "Ri Taishō no shisō to sono haikei: Shisō to taikeika to jissen to no kankei ni tsuite" [Li Dazhao's thought and its background: On the relationship between the systematization of thought and practice]. *Rekishi hyōron* [Historical review] 87 (August 1957): 40–61.

Matsuda Michio. "Yamakawa Hitoshi" [Yamakawa Hitoshi]. In *Nihon no Marukusu-shugi* [Japan's Marxism], edited by Suzuki Tadashi. Nagoya: Fūbai-sha, 1969.

Matsumoto Sannosuke, "Atarashii seiji ishiki no hōga: Sono shikaku to mondai" [The germination of a new political consciousness: Its viewpoints and problems]. In *Kindai Nihon seiji shisō shi* [History of modern Japanese political thought], edited by Hashikawa Bunzō and Matsumoto Sannosuke, 1:3–32. 2 vols. Kindai Nihon shisō shi taikei, no. 3 [Outline of modern Japanese thought], edited by Miyazawa Toshiyoshi and Ōkouchi Kazuo. Tokyo: Yūhikaku, 1971.

————. "Kenpō shisō no tenkai" [The unfolding of enlightenment thought]. In *Kindai Nihon seiji shisō shi* [History of modern Japanese political thought], edited by Hashikawa Bunzō and Matsumoto Sannosuke, 1:151–179. 2 vols. Kindai Nihon shisō shi taikei, no. 3 [Outline of the history of modern Japanese thought], edited by Miyazawa Toshiyoshi and Ōkouchi Kazuo. Tokyo: Yūhikaku, 1971.

Matsunaga Shōzō. "Jiyū minken shisō" [Thoughts on civil rights]. In *Kindai Nihon seiji shisō shi* [History of modern Japanese political thought], edited by Hashikawa Bunzō and Matsumoto Sannosuke, 1:180–205. 2 vols. Kindai Nihon shisō shi taikei, no. 3 [Outline of the history of modern Japanese thought]. Tokyo: Yūhikaku, 1971.

Matsushima Eiichi. "Nihon ni okeru Marukishizumu no tenkai: 'Nihon shihon-shugi' 'Meiji ishin' kenkyū to shakai kagaku no kakuritsu" [The development of Marxism in Japan: Studies of "Japanese capitalism" and "the Meiji Restoration" and the establishment of social science]. In *Marukishizumu (I)* [Marxism], compiled by Uchida Yoshihiko, Ōtsuka Hisao, and Matsushita Eiichi. Gendai Nihon shisō taikei, no. 20 [Outline of modern Japanese thought], pp. 7–72. Tokyo: Chikuma Shobō, 1966.

Menshikov, V. B. "K probleme svoeobraziia istoricheskogo razvitiia kitaia" [On the problem of the peculiar historical development of China]. In *Kitaia: Gosudarstvo i obshestvo. Akademiia Nauk SSSR. Institut Vostokovedeniia* [China: State and society. USSR Academy of Sciences. Institute of Oriental Studies]. Moscow: Nauka, 1977.

Minobe Ryōkichi. "Sore de mo tennō wa kikan de aru: Aru kenpō gakusha no shōsai" [Even so, the emperor is an organ: The life of a constitutional scholar]. In Minobe Ryōkichi, *Kumon suru demokurashii* [Democracy in anguish], pp. 61–96. Tokyo: Bungei Shunjū Shinsha, 1959.

Minobe Tatsukichi. "Kunshu no kokuhō-jō no chi'i" [The position of the monarch in state law]. *Hōgaku shirin* [Legal annals] 50 (November 15, 1903): 1–6.

Miyazawa Toshiyoshi. "Kikan-setsu jiken to Minobe Tatsukichi sensei" [Professor Minobe Tatsukichi and the organ theory affair]. *Hōritsu jihō* [Law bulletin] 20 (August 1948): 42–44.

Mo Dazhao. "Lun dianyong zhi ji xunhuan" [On the tenant-hireling system and circulation]. *Xiandai shixue* [Contemporary historiography] 2, no. 1/2 (1934): 352–361.

————. "Zhongguo shehui shi lunzhan pipan de pipan" [Critique of *A critique of the controversy on Chinese social history*]. *Xiandai shixue* [Contemporary historiography] (1934): 29–39.

Moriya Fumio. "Gendai Nihon no seiji kikō" [The political structure of contemporary Japan]. In *Kōza Gendai Nihon to Marukusu-shugi* [Symposium: Contemporary Japan and Marxism], vol. 1:101–162. 4 vols. Tokyo: Aoki Shoten, 1966.

———. "Nihon ni okeru Marukusu-shugi no seiritsu" [The establishment of Marxism in Japan]. *Gendai to shisō* [Modern times and thought] no. 39 (March 1980): 115–139.

———. "Tennō-sei no busshitsu-teki oyobi shakai-teki kiso ni tsuite" [On the material and social bases of the emperor system]. *Rekishigaku kenkyū* [Journal of historical studies] no. 167 (January 1954): 24–34.

Motoyama Yukihiko. "Meiji nijū nendai no seiron ni arawareta nashonarizumu" [Nationalism manifested in political discourse in the Meiji '20s]. In *Meiji zenhan-ki no nashonarizumu* [Nationalism in the early-Meiji period], compiled by Sakata Yoshio, pp. 37–84. Tokyo: Mirai-sha, 1958.

Nabeyama Sadachika. "Kokoro no sokuseki" [The footprints of my mind]. In Nabeyama Sadachika, and Sano Manabu, *Tenkō jūgo nen* [Fifteen years since *tenkō*], pp. 1–78. Rōdō minshu shiriizu, no. 7 [Labor democracy series]. Tokyo: Rōdō Shuppan-bu, 1949.

Nakajima Satoru. "Tenkō to hitenkō" [*Tenkō* and non-*tenkō*]. In *Gendai no ideorogii* [Contemporary ideology], edited by Ikumi Takuichi et al. 6 vols. Vol. 2, *Nihon no Marukusu-shugi sono 2* [Japanese Marxism (II)], pp. 131–168. Tokyo: San'ichi Shobō, 1961.

Nakamura Katsunori. "Chokusetsu kōdō ron no taitō: Kōtoku Shūsui no riron o megutte" [The emergence of the doctrine of direct action: On the theory of Kōtoku Shūsui]. *Hōgaku kenkyū* [Legal studies] 31, no. 10 (October 1958): 35–58.

———. "Kōtoku Shūsui no shōgai to shisō" [The life and thought of Kōtoku Shūsui]. *Hōgaku kenkyū* [Legal studies] 30, no. 11 (November 1957): 19–47.

Nakamura Takafusa. "'Nihon shihon-shugi ronsō' ni tsuite" [On the "debate on Japanese capitalism"]. *Shisō* [Thought] no. 624 (June 1976): 185–197.

Nakase Juichi. "Meiji kenpō moto ni okeru tennō kikan-setsu no keisei" [The formation of the emperor-organ theory under the Meiji Constitution]. *Hōritsu jihō* [Law bulletin] 34, no. 4 (April 1962): 59–71.

———. "Tennō kikan-setsu kakuritsu katei ni okeru Minobe riron no tokushitsu" [The special character of Minobe's theory in the process of the establishment of the emperor-organ theory]. *Dōshisha hōgaku* [Dōshisha law] 72 (June 1962): 155–195.

———. "Tennō kikan-setsu no genryū" [Origins of the emperor-organ theory]. *Rekishi hyōron* [Historical review] (February–August 1962).

Nakaura Masamitsu. "Nihon Marukusu-shugi no shisō hōhō no ichi tokushitsu: Fukumotoizumu no shisō shi-teki igi o megutte" [One characteristic of the methodology of Japanese Marxist thought: On the intellectual historical significance of Fukumotoism]. In *Gendai no ideorogii* [Contemporary ideology], edited by Ikumi Takuichi et al. 6 vols. Vol. 2, *Nihon no Marukusu-shugi (II)* [Japanese Marxism II], pp. 65–130. Tokyo: San'ichi Shobō, 1961.

"Nihon kokka kikō-zu no kaisetsu" [An explanation of the structural plan of the Japanese state]. In *Marukusu-shugi kōza* [Symposium on Marxism], compiled by Kawakami Hajime and Ōyama Ikuo. 4:369–379. *1928*. 13 vols. N.p.: Seiji Hihan-sha, 1927–1929.

"Nihon kyōsantō kōryō sōan" (1922) [Draft program of the Japanese Communist party]. In *Kominterun Nihon ni kansuru teize shū* [Collected Comintern theses on Japan], compiled by Ishidō Kiyotomo and Yamabe Kentarō, pp. 5–9. Tokyo: Aoki Shoten, Aoki bunko, 1961.

"Nihon kyōsantō seiji teize sōan" [Draft political theses of the Japanese Communist party (1931)]. In *Kominterun Nihon ni kansuru teize shū* [Collected Comintern theses on

Japan], compiled by Ishidō Kiyotomo and Yamabe Kentarō, pp. 46–75. Tokyo: Aoki Shoten, Aoki bunko, 1961.

"Nihon mondai ni kansuru shin teize happyō ni saishi dōshi shokun ni tsugu" [To all comrades on the occasion of the new theses on the Japan problem (1932)]. In *Kominterun Nihon ni kansuru teize shū* [Collected Comintern theses on Japan], compiled by Ishidō Kiyotomo and Yamabe Kentarō, pp. 120–128. Tokyo: Aoki Shoten, Aoki bunko, 1961.

"Nihon mondai ni kansuru ketsugi (ni-nana nen teize)" [Resolution on Japan (1927 theses)]. In *Kominterun Nihon ni kansuru teize shū* [Collected Comintern theses on Japan], compiled by Ishidō Kiyotomo and Yamabe Kentarō, pp. 28–45. Tokyo: Aoki Shoten, Aoki bunko, 1961.

"Nihon ni okeru jōsei to Nihon Kyōsantō no ninmu ni kansuru teize (san-ni teize)" [The situation in Japan and the responsibilities of the Japanese Communist party (1932 theses)]. In *Komintern Nihon ni kansuru teize shū* [Collected Comintern theses on Japan], compiled by Ishidō Kiyotomo and Yamabe Kentarō, pp. 76–147. Tokyo: Aoki Shoten, Aoki bunko, 1961.

"Nihon Shakaitō kōryō (kettō-ji)" [Program of the Japanese Socialist party (at the time of its founding)]. In *Nihon Shakaitō kōryō bunken shū* [Collected documents on the program of the Japanese Socialist party], compiled by Katsumata Sei'ichi and Kitayama Yoshio, p. 21. Tokyo: Nihon Shakaitō Kikanshi-kyoku, 1978.

"Nihon Shakaitō no shin sengen (sōan)" [The new manifesto of the Japanese Socialist party (draft)]. *Shakai-shugi* [Socialism]. Special number: Shakaitō "Shin sengen (sōan)" hihan (June 25, 1985): 34–44.

Nihon Shakaitō Shakai-shugi Riron I'inkai. "Nihon ni okeru shakai-shugi e no michi" [The path to socialism in Japan (1964)]. In *Nihon shakaitō kōyō bunken shū* [Collected documents on the program of the Japanese Socialist party], compiled by Katsumata Sei'ichi and Kitayama Yoshio, pp. 65–246. Tokyo: Nihon Shakaitō Chūō Honbu Kikanshi-kyoku, 1978.

Nii Itaru. "Museifu-shugi ron" [Anarchism]. In *Shakai kagaku kōza* [Social science symposium], edited by Kimura Tsuyoshi, 7:1–38. 15 vols. Tokyo: Seibundō, 1931–1932.

Nomura Kōkichi. "Chūgoku ni okeru Marukusu-shugi (jō): Sono keisei katei ni tsuite no nōto" [Marxism in China (I): Notes on its process of development]. *Shisō* [Thought] 486 (December 1964): 1652–1661.

———. "'Go-shi' jidai no nashonaru na shikō: Ri Tai-shō ni tsuite" [Nationalistic thinking during the May Fourth period, with reference to Li Dazhao]. *Shisō* [Thought] no. 453 (March 1963): 285–294.

———. "Kindai Chūgoku no shisōka: Ri Tai-shō to Marukusu-shugi" [A thinker in modern China: Li Dazhao and Marxism]. *Shisō* [Thought] no. 464 (February 1963): 19–33 [179–193].

Noro Eitarō. "Nihon ni okeru tochi shoyū kankei ni tsuite: Nakanzuku iwayuru 'hōken-teki zettai-shugi seiryoku no kaikyū-teki busshitsu-teki kiso' no mondai o chūshin to shite" [On landownership relations in Japan: With particular attention to the problem of the "class and material basis of the so-called feudal absolutist forces"]. *Shisō* [Thought] no. 84 (May, June 1929): 47–55 (199–207).

———. "Puchi-teikoku-shugi ron hihan" [Critique of the theory of petty imperialism]. In *Noro Eitarō zenshū* [Complete works of Noro Eitarō], 1:113–157. 2 vols. Tokyo: Shin Nihon Shuppan-kai, 1965.

Ōishi Ka'ichirō. "Kaisetsu: 'Nihon shihon-shugi hattatsu shi kōza' kankō jijō" [Commentary: The circumstances of the publication of the "Symposium on the history of the development of Japanese capitalism"]. In *Nihon shihon-shugi hattatsu shi kōza* [Symposium on the history of the development of Japanese capitalism]. 7 vols. and suppl. Tokyo: Iwanami Shoten, 1982.

Oka Toshirō. "Kaisetsu" [Commentary]. In Yamaji Aizan, *Yamaji Aizan shū* [Collected writings of Yamaji Aizan], edited with commentary by Oka Toshirō, pp. 455–461. Vol. 2 Min'yū-sha shisō bungaku shūsho [Collected works of the thought and literature of the Man'yū-sha], vol. 3. Tokyo: San'ichi Shobō, 1985.

Okazaki Tadao. "Kōtoku Shūsui ni okeru tōhō mondai" [The problem of the East in Kōtoku Shūsui]. *Rekishi-gaku kenkyū* [Historical studies] 145.

Ono Yoshihiko. "Nihon shihon-shugi ronsō" [The debate on Japanese capitalism]. In *Shakai kagaku daijiten* [Encyclopedia of social science], 14:305–307. N.p.: N.p., 1970.

Onogawa Hidemi. "Shinmatsu no shisō to shinka-ron" [Late-Qing thought and the theory of evolution]. *Tōhō gakuhō* [Journal of Oriental studies] 21 (March 1952): 1–36.

Ōshima Kiyoshi. "Inomata Tsunao no nōgyō-ron/senryaku-ron" [The agricultural theory and strategic theory of Inomata Tsunao]. *Shisō* [Thought] 595 (January 1974): 18–33; 596(February 1974): 78–102.

Ōsugi Sakae. "Sei no sōzō" [The creation of life]. In *Ōsugi Sakae sen, museifu-shugi no tetsugaku (I)* [Selected writings of Ōsugi Sakae, the philosophy of anarchism], compiled by Ōsawa Masamichi, pp. 53–62. Tokyo: Gendai Shichō-sha, 1976.

———. "Minzoku kokka-shugi no kyogi" [The fallacy of nationalism]. In *Ōsugi Sakae sen, museifu-shugi no tetsugaku (I)* [Selected writings of Ōsugi Sakae, the philosophy of anarchism], compiled by Ōsawa Masamichi, pp. 239–240. Tokyo: Gendai Shichō-sha, 1976.

———. "Seifuku no jijitsu" [The reality of conquest]. In *Ōsugi Sakae sen, museifu-shugi no tetsugaku (I)* [Selected writings of Ōsugi Sakae, the philosophy of anarchism], compiled by Ōsawa Masamichi, pp. 21–28. Tokyo: Gendai Shichō-sha, 1976.

Ōuchi Hyōe. "Nōson minshuka no michi chikakarazu" [The path of democratization of the agricultural village is not at hand]. *Sekai* [The world] (August 1946).

Ōuchi Tsutomu. "Kaihan no tame ni" [Introduction to the revised edition]. In Inomata Tsunao, *Nōson mondai nyūmon* [Introduction to the agrarian problem]. Tokyo: Kōdo-sha, 1937.

Pan Dongzhou. "Shina keizai no seishitsu" [The nature of the Chinese economy]. In *Shina keizai ron* [On the Chinese economy], translated and compiled by Tanaka Tadao, pp. 3–22. Tokyo: Chūō Kōron-sha, 1932.

Pang Zhuoheng. "Zhong-Xi fengjian zhuanzhi zhidu de bijiao yanjiu" [A comparative study of feudal autocracy in China and the West]. *Lishi yanjiu* [Historical research], no. 2 (1981): 3–13.

Peng Ming. "Wusi shiqi de Li Dazhao he Chen Duxiu" [Li Dazhao and Chen Duxiu in the May Fourth period]. *Lishi yanjiu* [Historical research] no. 6 (1962): 47–68.

Peng Shuzhi. "Liening-zhuyi shifou bushihe Zhongguo de suowei 'guoqing'?" [Is it true that Leninism is unsuitable for the 'state of the nation' of China?]. *Xiangdao zhoubao* [The Guide Weekly] 184 (January 21, 1927): 1948–1952.

[Peng] Shuzhi. "Shiyue geming dijiu zhounian de Su'e zhi jingji zhengzhi de jinbu" [The economic and political progress of the Soviet Union on the ninth anniversary of the October revolution]. *Xiangdao zhoubao* [The Guide Weekly] 178 (November 15, 1926): 1854–1857.

Peng Shuzhi. "Zhongguo zhengju da biandong zhi qianri yu minzhong zhi zeren" [The eve of a major change in China's political situation and the role of the masses]. *Xiangdao zhoubao* [The Guide Weekly] 167 (August 15, 1926): 1672–1675.

"Ping pingmin de duzai zhengzhi" [Critique of the dictatorship of the proletariat]. *Minsheng* [Voice of the people] no. 31 (April 15, 1921): 1–5 (407–411).

Polevoi, Yuri. "G. V. Plekhanov o vostochnom despotizme" [G. V. Plekhanov on oriental despotism]. *Narody Azii i Afriki* [Peoples of Asia and Africa] no. 2 (1967): 73–80.

Qu Qiubai. "Liening-zhuyi yu Zhongguo de guomin geming" [Leninism and China's national revolution]. *Xiangdao zhoubao* [The Guide Weekly] 143 (January 1926): 1300–1303.

———. "Lun Guomindang gaizupai" [On the Reorganization faction of the Guomindang]. In Qu Qiubai, *Fan Guomindang gaizupai* [Against the Reorganization faction of the Guomindang]. [Berlin]: N.p., 1929.

———. "Xiandai wenming de wenti yu shehui-zhuyi" [Problems of modern civilization and socialism]. *Dongfang zazhi* [Eastern miscellany] 21, no. 1 (January 1924): 1–11.

———. "Zhengzhi yundong yu zhishi-jieji" [The political movement and the intellectual class]. *Xiangdao zhoubao* [The Guide Weekly] 18 (January 1923): 147–148.

[Qu Shengbai]. "Qu Shengbai da Chen Duxiu shu" [Letter from Qu Shengbai in response to Chen Duxiu]. *Minsheng* [Voice of the people] no. 30 (April 5, 1921): 6–12.

———. "Qu Shengbai zhi Chen Duxiu shu" [Letter from Qu Shengbai to Chen Duxiu]. *Minsheng* [Voice of the people], no. 30 (April 5, 1921): 4–6 (370–372).

Qu Shiying. "Guojia-zhuyi yu guoji-zhuyi" [Nationalism and internationalism]. *Dongfang zazhi* [Eastern miscellany] 21, no. 1 (January 10, 1924): C54–61.

R [pseud.] "Hu Shi deng zhi zhengzhi zhuzhang yu women" [The political beliefs of Hu Shi et al. and us]. *Shaonian* [La Jeunesse] (Paris) no. 2 (1922): 51–53.

Rong Mengyuan. "Xinhai geming-qian Zhongguo shukan-shang dui makesi-zhuyi" [The introduction of Marxism in Chinese periodicals before the 1911 revolution]. *Xin jianshe* [New reconstruction], no. 3 (1953): 5–12.

Sa Mengwu. "Diyi tongyi, di'er shengchan" [First unity, then production]. *Xin shengming yuekan* [New life monthly] 3, no. 5 (May 1930): 1–4.

———. "Geming yu tongyi" [Revolution and unity]. *Xin shengming yuekan* [New life monthly] 3, no. 6 (June 1930): 1–4.

———. "Guomin geming yu shehui geming" [National revolution and social revolution]. *Xin shengming yuekan* [New life monthly] 1, no. 8 (August 1928).

Sakai Toshihiko. "Nihon shakai-shugi undō ni okeru museifu-shugi no yakuwari" [The role of anarchism in the Japanese socialist movement (1928–1929)]. In Sakai Toshihiko, *Sakai Toshihiko zenshū* [Complete works of Sakai Toshihiko]. 6:443–488. 6 vols. Tokyo: Chūō Kōron-sha, 1933.

———. "Nihon shakai-shugi undō shiwa" [Historical narrative of the Japanese socialist movement]. In Sakai Toshihiko, *Sakai Toshihiko zenshū* [Complete works of Sakai Toshihiko], 6:209–314. 6 vols. Tokyo: Chūō Kōron-sha, 1933.

Sakata Yoshio. "Meiji zenhan-ki ni okeru seifu no kokka-shugi" [The statism of the government in the early-Meiji period]. In *Meiji zenhan-ki no nashonarizumu* [Nationalism in the early-Meiji period], compiled by Sakata Yoshio, pp. 5–35. Tokyo: Mirai-sha, 1958.

Saku Tatsuo. "Yaxiya shengchan-fangfa lun" [The theory of the Asiatic mode of production], translated by Liu Gang. *Wenhua pipan* [Cultural criticism] 1, no. 4/5 (September 15, 1934): 196–217.

Sano Hiroshi. "Kakumeika Sano Manabu" [Sano Manabu, revolutionary]. *Kokumin hyōron* [National review] (June 1953): 111–127.

———. "Mosukō to Nihon Kyōsantō no kankei shi" [A history of relations between Moscow and the Japanese Communist party]. *Chūō kōron* [Central review] 65, no. 3 (March 1950): 96–103.

Sano Manabu. "Atarashii shakai-shugi no sekai-kan" [The worldview of a new socialism].

In Sano Manabu, *Sano Manabu chosakushū* [Collected works of Sano Manabu], 2:955–993. 5 vols. Tokyo: Sano Manabu Chosakushū Kankōkai, 1957–1958.

―――. "Atarashii zen'ei no tō no arikata" [How the new vanguard party ought to be]. In Sano Manabu, *Sano Manabu chosakushū* [Collected works of Sano Manabu], 5:962–965. 5 vols. Tokyo: Sano Manabu Chosakushū Kankōkai, 1957–1958.

―――. "Bukkyō to shakai-shugi" [Buddhism and socialism]. In Sano Manabu, *Sano Manabu chosakushū* [Collected works of Sano Manabu], 3:710–780. 5 vols. Tokyo: Sano Manabu Chosakushū Kankōkai, 1957–1958.

―――. "Gokuchū-ki" [Prison diary]. In Nabeyama Sadachika, and Sano Manabu, *Tenkō jūgo nen* [Fifteen years since *tenkō*], pp. 81–153. Rōdō Minshu Shiriizu, no. 7 [Labor democracy series]. Tokyo: Rōdō Shuppan-bu, 1949.

―――. "Kenryoku no shizen shi: Musansha kokka ni okeru kenryoku no mondai" [The natural death of the state: Problems of power in the proletarian state]. In Sano Manabu, *Kokka-ron/Sensō-ron* [Theory of the state/Theory of war], pp. 335–345. Tokyo: Kibōkaku, 1930.

―――. "Kenryoku to rōdō" [Authority and labor]. In Sano Manabu, *Sano Manabu chosakushū* [Collected works of Sano Manabu], 2:998–1008. 5 vols. Tokyo: Sano Manabu Chosakushū Kankōkai, 1957–1958.

―――. "Kokka-ron" [The theory of the state]. In *Marukusu-shugi kōza* [Symposium on Marxism], compiled by Kawakami Hajime and Ōyama Ikuo, 5:1–74. 5 vols. N.p.: Seiji Hihan-sha, 1927–1929.

―――. "Marukusu kokka-ron to seiji hihan no hōhōron" [The Marxist theory of the state and the methodology of political criticism]. In Sano Manabu, *Kokka-ron/Sensō-ron* [Theory of the state/Theory of war], pp. 147–184. Tokyo: Kibōkaku, 1930.

―――. "Marukusu kokka-ron to sono hihan" [Marx's theory of the state and its critique]. In Sano Manabu, *Sano Manabu chosakushū* [Collected works of Sano Manabu], 1:523–588. 5 vols. Tokyo: Sano Manabu Chosakushū Kankōkai, 1957–1958.

―――. "Minzoku mondai sho shō" [Some chapters on the national problem]. In Sano Manabu, *Kokka-ron/Sensō-ron* [Theory of the state/Theory of war], pp. 347–395. Tokyo: Kibōkaku, 1930.

―――. "Nihon minzoku no yūshūsei o ronzu" [The superiority of the Japanese people] (Letter to his sister dated August 10, 1933). In Sano Manabu, *Sano Manabu chosakushū* [Collected works of Sano Manabu], 5:945–961. 5 vols. Tokyo: Sano Manabu Chosakushū Kankōkai, 1957–1958.

―――. "Nikka Sensō no kiki o mae ni shite" [With the crisis of the Sino-Japanese war ahead] (Letter to his sister dated August 14, 1933). In Sano Manabu, *Sano Manabu chosakushū* [Collected works of Sano Manabu], 5:966–969. 5 vols. Tokyo: Sano Manabu Chosakushū Kankōkai, 1958.

―――. "Roshia kakumei/Reinin-shugi/kyōsantō" [The Russian Revolution, Leninism, and the Communist party]. In Sano Manabu, *Sano Manabu chosakushū* [Collected works of Sano Manabu]. 1:589–622. 5 vols. Tokyo: Sano Manabu Chosakushū Kankōkai, 1957–1958.

[Sano Manabu]. "Sano Manabu yoshin jinmon chōsho" [Preliminary statement of Sano Manabu]. In *Gendai shi shiryō* [Materials on contemporary Japan]. Vol. 20, *Shakai-shugi undō (7)* [The Socialist movement], pp. 185–298. Tokyo: Misuzu Shobō, 1968.

Sano Manabu. "Sei-Ou-teki sekai-kan to Tōyō-teki sekai-kan" [The West European worldview and the Eastern worldview]. In Sano Manabu, *Sano Manabu chosakushū* [Collected works of Sano Manabu], 2:931–949. 5 vols. Tokyo: Sano Manabu Chosakushū kankōkai, 1957–1958.

————. "Sensō-ron" [The theory of war]. In *Marukusu-shugi kōza* [Symposium on Marxism], compiled by Kawakami Hajime and Ōyama Ikuo. Vol. 2 (1927) of 13 vols.: 1–83 (86–169). Tokyo: Seiji Hihan-sha, 1927–1929.

————. "Tennō-sei to shakai-shugi" [The emperor and socialism]. In Sano Manabu, *Sano Manabu chosakushū* [Collected works of Sano Manabu]. 2:379–471. 5 vols. Tokyo: Sano Manabu Chosakushū Kankōkai, 1957–1958.

————. "Tōyō-teki sekai-kan to shakai-shugi" [The Eastern world view and socialism]. In Sano Manabu, *Sano Manabu chosakushū* [Collected works of Sano Manabu], 2:950–954. 5 vols. Tokyo: Sano Manabu Chosakushū Kankōkai, 1957–1958.

————. "Waga haigai-shugisha no teikoku-shugi sensō ron" [The theory of imperialist war of our chauvinists]. *Marukusu-shugi* [Marxism] 37 (May 1927): 1–31.

————. "Watakushi wa nani o yonda ka" [What did I read?]. In Sano Manabu, *Sano Manabu chosakushū* [Collected works of Sano Manabu], 5:893–896. 5 vols. Tokyo: Sano Manabu Chosakushū Kankōkai, 1957–1958.

————. "Yo wa naze ni kyōsantō o satta ka" [Why did I leave the Communist party?]. In Sano Manabu, *Sano Manabu Chosakushū* [Collected works of Sano Manabu], 1:1–37. 5 vols. Tokyo: Sano Manabu Chosakushū Kankōkai, 1957–1958.

————. "Yuibutsu shikan hihan" [Critique of historical materialism]. In Sano Manabu, *Sano Manabu chosakushū* [Collected works of Sano Manabu], 1:125–476. 5 vols. Tokyo: Sano Manabu Chosakushū Kankōkai, 1957–1958.

Sano Manabu and Nabeyama Sadachika. "Kyōdō hikoku dōshi ni tsuguru sho" [Letter of proclamation to fellow defendants (June 8, 1933)]. In Sano Manabu, *Sano Manabu chosakushū* [Collected works of Sano Manabu], 1:3–20. 5 vols. Tokyo: Sano Manabu Chosakushū Kankōkai, 1957–1958.

Satō Noboru. "Gendai Nihon Marukusu-shugi no mittsu no chōryū" [Three currents of contemporary Japanese Marxism]. In *Gendai no ideorogii* [Contemporary ideology], edited by Ikumi Takuichi et al. Nihon no Marukusu-shugi (I) [Japanese Marxism], 1:7–45. 6 vols. Tokyo: San'ichi Shobō, 1961.

Satoi Hikoshichirō. "Ri Tai-shō no shuppatsu: 'Gen-chi' ki no seiron o chūshin ni" ["Recommencement of Li Ta-chao: Mainly on his political arguments in the 'Statesmanship' (Yen-chih) period"]. *Shirin* [The Shirin or the Journal of History] 40, no. 3 (May 1957): 177–215.

Shanghai Wuzhengfu-gongchan-zhuyi Tongzhi-she. "Wuzhengfu-gongchandang zhi mudi yu shouduan" [The ends and means of the anarcho-Communist party]. *Minsheng* [Voice of the people], no. 19 (N.d.): 6–9 (222–225).

Shi [pseud.] "Zen jiande women buyao guojia?" [How to see that we do not want a state?]. *Xiangdao zhoubao* [The Guide Weekly] 187 (February 7, 1927): 1995.

[Shi] Cuntong. "Lixiang-zhong de yidang zhi guo" [Ideal party rule]. *Geming pinglun* [Revolutionary review] no. 16 (1928): 7–10.

Shi Jun. "Minzu yu jieji" [Nation and classes]. *Xin shengming* [New life] 3, no. 6 (June 1930): 1–11.

Shibagaki Kazuo. "'Nihon keizai kenkyū' ni okeru senzen to sengo" [Prewar and postwar in the study of the Japanese economy]. In *Nihon keizai kenkyū nyūmon* [Introduction to Japanese economic studies], edited by Saeki Naomi and Shibagaki Kazuo, pp. 15–35. Tokyo: Tōkyō Daigaku Shuppankai, 1972.

Shibagaki Kazuo, and Saeki Naomi. "Sengo Nihon keizai no kihon mondai" [Basic problems of the Japanese economy]. In *Nihon keizai kenkyū nyūmon* [Introduction to Japanese economic studies], edited by Saeki Naomi and Shibagaki Kazuo, pp. 36–84. Tokyo: Tōkyō Daigaku Shuppan-kai, 1972.

Shiga Yoshio. "Gunji-teki hōken-teki 'teikoku-shugi' ni tsuite" [On militaristic feudalistic "imperialism"]. In *Sekai to Nihon* [The world and Japan], pp. 39–57. N.p.: Gyōmyō-sha, 1948.

Shijie shanggu shigang Bianxiezu [*An outline history of the ancient world* writing group]. "Yaxiya shengchan-fangshi—Bucheng qiwei wenti de wenti" [The concept of the Asiatic mode of production—A question clear by itself]. *Lishi yanjiu* [Historical research], no. 2 (1980): 3–24.

Shimamoto Nobuko. "Goshi ki ni okeru Jūgatsu kakumei no eikyō: Ri Tai-shō no shisō o tōshite" [The influence of the October Revolution on the May Fourth Movement: Ideas of Li Ta-chao]. *Shiron* [Historica] 14/15 (March 1966): 25–47.

"Shin teize happyō ni saishi dōshi shokun ni tsugu" [We announce to our comrades the new theses on the Japan problem]. In *Kominterun Nihon ni kansuru teize shū* [Collected Comintern theses on Japan] (1932), pp. 120–128. Compiled by Ishidō Kiyotomo and Yamabe Kentarō. Tokyo: Aoki Shoten, Aoki bunko, 1961.

Shioda Shobee. "Nihon shakaitō no rekishi-teki seikaku" [The historical character of the Japanese Socialist party]. *Keizai hyōron* [Economic review] (June 1953): 2–10.

Song Jiaoren. "Wo zhi lishi" [My diary]. In *Zhongguo xiandai shiliao congshu* [Series of materials on contemporary Chinese history], edited by Wu Xiangxiang. Vol. 1, *Jianli minguo* [The establishment of the Republic]. Taipei: Wenxing Shudian Yinhang, 1962.

Song Min. "'Yaxiya shengchan-fangshi—bucheng qiwei wenti de wenti' yiwen zhiyi" ["The Asiatic mode of production—the problem of its not becoming an issue"—an inquiry]. *Lishi yanjiu* [Historical research] no. 5 (1980): 17–25.

Sumiya Etsuji. "Kaisetsu" [Commentary]. In Kawakami Hajime, *Kawakami Hajime cho-sakushū* [Collected works of Kawakami Hajime], 1:483–500. 12 vols. Tokyo: Chikuma Shobō, 1964–1965.

T. S. S. [pseud.] "Wo duiyu Zhongguo geming (I)" [My views on the Chinese Revolution]. *Geming pinglun (quanji)* [Revolutionary review] no. 6 (1928): 35–39, no. 8(1928): 27–31.

Taipu [pseud.] "Wuzhengfu-zhuyi yu Zhongguo" [Anarchism and China]. *Ziyou* [Freedom] no. 1 (December 1920): 22–26.

Takabatake Michitoshi. "Ikkoku shakai-shugisha: Sano Manabu/Nabeyama Sadachika" [Advocates of socialism-in-one-country: Sano Manabu and Nabeyama Sadachika]. In *Tenkō [Tenkō]*, edited by Shakai Kagaku Kenkyūkai, 1:164–200. 3 vols. Tokyo: Heibon-sha, 1959.

Takabatake Motoyuki. "Gunkoku-shugi" [Militarism]. In Takabatake Motoyuki, *Hihan Marukusu-shugi* [Criticizing Marxism]. Tokyo: Nihon Hyōron-sha, 1934.

———. "Kokka shakai-shugi no seisaku" [The policies of state socialism]. In Takabatake Motoyuki, *Hihan Marukusu-shugi* [Criticizing Marxism], pp. 213–226. Tokyo: Nihon Hyōron-sha, 1934.

———. "Kokka shakai-shugi no hitsuzen-sei" [The necessity of state socialism]. In Takabatake Motoyuki, *Hihan Marukusu-shugi* [Criticizing Marxism], pp. 173–202. Tokyo: Hihan Hyōron-sha, 1934.

———. "'Puroretaria kokka' no ronri-teki hatan" [The logical bankruptcy of the 'proletarian state']. In Takabatake Motoyuki, *Hihan Marukusu-shugi* [Criticizing Marxism], pp. 84–96. Tokyo: Nihon Hyōron-sha, 1934.

———. "Rōdō teikoku-shugi no kyoku-Tō shinshutsu" [The Far Eastern advance of workers' imperialism]. *Kaizō* [Reconstruction] (February 1927).

———. "Shakai-shugi bunrui-jō no ichi kōsatsu" [A look at varieties of socialism]. In

Takabatake Motoyuki, *Hihan Marukusu-shugi* [Criticizing Marxism], pp. 97–110. Tokyo: Nihon Hyōron-sha, 1934.

———. "Teikoku-shugi no hatten" [The development of imperialism]. In Takabatake Motoyuki, *Hihan Marukusu-shugi* [Criticizing Marxism], pp. 261–280. Tokyo: Nihon Hyōron-sha, 1934.

———. "Teikoku-shugi no kisū" [The outcome of imperialism]. In Takabatake Motoyuki, *Hihan Marukusu-shugi* [Criticizing Marxism]. Tokyo: Nihon Hyōron-sha, 1934.

Takahashi Kamekichi. "Gunshuku teigi no teikoku-shugi-teki imi to Nihon no tachiba" [The imperialist implications of disarmament proposals and Japan's position]. In Takahashi Kamekichi, *Sayoku undō no riron-teki hōkai: Uyoku undō no riron-teki konkyo* [The theoretical collapse of the left-wing movement: The theoretical basis of the right-wing movement], pp. 93–104. Tokyo: Hakuyō-sha, 1927.

———. "Makki ni okeru teikoku-shugi no henshitsu" [The deterioration of imperialism in the last stage]. In Takahashi Kamekichi, *Sayoku undō no riron-teki hōkai: Uyoku undō no riron-teki konkyo* [The theoretical collapse of the left-wing movement: The theoretical basis of the right-wing movement], pp. 1–38. Tokyo: Hakuyō-sha, 1927.

———. "Nihon shihon-shugi no teikoku-shugi-teki chi'i" [The imperialistic position of Japanese capitalism]. In Takahashi Kamekichi, *Sayoku undō no riron-teki hōkai: Uyoku undō no riron-teki konkyo* [The theoretical collapse of the left-wing movement: The theoretical basis of the right-wing movement], pp. 39–92. Tokyo: Hakuyō-sha, 1927.

Takeda Kiyoko. "Kakumei shisō to tennō-sei: Takabatake Motoyuki no kokka shakai-shugi o chūshin ni" [Revolutionary thought and the emperor system: On the state socialism of Takabatake Motoyuki]. In *Kindai Nihon seiji shisō shi (II)* [History of modern Japanese political thought II], compiled by Hashikawa Bunzō and Matsumoto Sannosuke, pp. 252–300. Kindai Nihon shisō shi taikei, no. 4 [Outline of the history of modern Japanese thought]. Tokyo: Yūhikaku, 1970.

———. "Tennō-sei shisō no keisei" [The formation of emperor system thought]. In *Iwanami kōza: Nihon rekishi* [Iwanami symposium: Japanese history]. Vol. 16: *Kindai 3* [Modern times], 267–311. 21 vols. Tokyo: Iwanami Shoten, 1962.

Takeuchi Yoshimi. "Ajia-shugi no tenbō" [The outlook of Asianism]. In *Ajia-shugi* [Asianism], edited by Takeuchi Yoshimi, pp. 7–63. Gendai Nihon shisō taikei, no. 9 [Outline of contemporary Japanese thought]. Tokyo: Chikuma Shobō, 1963.

Takeuchi Yoshitomo. "Nihon no Marukusu-shugi" [Japanese Marxism]. In *Marukishizumu (II)* [Marxism], edited by Takeuchi Yoshitomo, pp. 7–58. Gendai Nihon shisō taikei, no. 21 [Outline of contemporary Japanese thought]. Tokyo: Chikuma Shobō, 1965.

Tamaki Hideo. "Chūgoku nōson shakai keizai no gendankai narabi ni sono kenkyū hōhōron-jō no ronsō o miru" [A look at the current stage of the economy of Chinese rural society and some methodological controversies in research on it]. *Keizai hyōron* [Economic review] (April 1936): 130–146; (May 1936): 103–121; (June 1936): 74–90.

Tanaka Masato. "Takabatake Motoyuki ron: Taishō shakai-shugi no bunka" [On Takabatake Motoyuki: The differentiation of Taishō socialism]. *Shirin* [The Shirin or the Journal of History] 53, no. 2 (March 1970): 33–86.

Tanaka Tadao. "Zhongguo shehui-shi yanjiu-shang zhi jige lilun wenti" [Some theoretical problems in the study of Chinese social history]. *Dushu zazhi* [Reading magazine] 2, no. 2/3 (March 1932): 1–29.

Tao Xisheng. "Changqi heping zhi zhenduan" [Diagnosis of a long period of peace]. *Xin shengming yuekan* [New life monthly] 3, no. 11 (November 1930): 1–5.

———. "Tongyi yu shengchan" [Unity and production]. *Xin shengming yuekan* [New life monthly] 3, no. 4 (April 1930): 1–13.

————. "Zhongguo shehui daodi shi shenme shehui" [What kind of society is Chinese society?]. *Xin shengming* [New life] 1, no. 10 (October 1, 1928): 1–14.

Tong Wen. "Zenyang dao le xianzai?" [How did we arrive at today?]. *Qianjin* [Advance] 1, no. 1 (June 1, 1928): 54–60.

Toyoda, T. "Révolution française et révolution de Meiji: Etude critique des interpretations de Kōsa et Rōnō" [The French Revolution and the Meiji Revolution: Critical study of the Kōza and Rōnō interpretations]. *Annales historiques de la révolution française* [Historical annals of the French revolution] 35 (1963): 16–24.

Tsuchiya Takao. "Bakumatsu ma'nyufakuchua no sho ronten" [Some points at issue in bakumatsu manufacture (January 1934)]. In Tsuchiya Takao, *Nihon shihon-shugi shi ronshū* [Collected essays on the history of Japanese capitalism], pp. 162–178. Tokyo: Ikusei-sha, 1937.

————. "Ishin shi kenkyū no chūshin ronten: Bakumatsu ma'nyufakuchua no sho mondai" [Central points at issue in the study of Restoration history: Some problems of late-Tokugawa manufacture]. *Kaizō* [Reconstruction] (January 1934).

————. "Tokugawa jidai no ma'nyufakuchua" [Manufacture in the Tokugawa era (September 1933)]. In Tsuchiya Takao, *Nihon shihon-shugi shi ronshū* [Collected essays on the history of Japanese capitalism], pp. 137–161. Tokyo: Ikusei-sha, 1937.

Tsujino Tsutomu. "Reimei-ki rōdō kumiai undō ni okeru nashonaru na keiki" [The national moment in the labor union movement in the Reimei era]. *Dōshisha hōgaku*, no. 87.

Uesugi Shinkichi. "Kokutai ni kansuru isetsu" [Different views concerning the *kokutai*]. In *Taishō seiji shisō shū* [Collected writings on Taishō thought], compiled by Imai Sei'ichi, pp. 3–13. Kindai Nihon shisō taikei, no. 33 [Outline of modern Japanese thought]. Tokyo: Chikuma Shobō, 1978.

Ukai Nobushige. "Kenpō ni okeru tennō no chi'i: Kikan to shite no tennō to shōchō to shite no tennō" [The position of the emperor in the constitution: The emperor as an organ and the emperor as a symbol]. *Shisō* [Thought] no. 336 (June 1952): 504–511.

————. "Minobe hakushi no shisō to gakusetsu: Sono rekishi no igi" [The thought and theory of Dr. Minobe: Its historical significance]. *Hōritsu jihō* [Law bulletin] 20 (August 1948): 45–49.

Uno Kōzō. "Waga nōson no hōken-sei" [The feudal nature of our agricultural villages]. In *Nōgyō mondai joron* [Preface to the agrarian problem]. Tokyo: Kaizō-sha, 1947.

Varga, Eugene S. "Ekonomichiskie problemy revoliutsiv Kitae" [Economic problems of the revolution in China]. *Planovoe khoziaistvo* [Planned economy], no. 12 (1925).

————. "Novaia nauchnaia literatura o Kitae" [The new scientific literature on China]. *Pravda*, January 6, 1929.

————. "Osnovnyi problemy Kitaiskoi revoliutsii" [Fundamental problems of the Chinese revolution]. *Bol'shevik* [Bolshevik], no. 8 (1928).

————. "Perspektivy kitaiskoi revoliutsii: Zakluchitelnii vazdel [Perspectives of the Chinese revolution: The final chapter]. In L. Mad'iar, *Ocherki po ekonomike Kitaia* [Works on the economy of China]. Moscow: N.p., 1930.

Voichinsukii, G. (G. Voitinsky). "Nihon ni okeru kaikyūsen (Sankō ronbun)" [Class struggle in Japan (Reference paper) (1922)]. In *Kominterun Nihon ni kansuru teize shū* [Collected Comintern theses on Japan], compiled by Ishidō Kiyotomo and Yamabe Kentarō, pp. 10–27. Tokyo: Aoki Shoten, Aoki bunko, 1961.

Wang Lixi. "Zhongguo shehui shi lunzhan xumu" [Introduction to the controversy on Chinese social history]. *Dushu zazhi* [Reading magazine] 1, no. 4/5 (August 1931).

————. "Zhongguo shehui xingtai fazhan-shi zhong zhi mi de shidai" [The puzzle period in the history of the development of social formations in China]. *Dushu zazhi* [Reading magazine]. 2, no. 7/8 (August 1932): 1–39.

Wang Xingrui. "Zhongguo shehui shi xifenpai de pipan" [Critique of the faction that periodizes Chinese social history]. *Xiandai shixue* [Contemporary historiography] 2, 1/2 (1934): 165–208.

Wang Zhicheng. "Zhongguo geming yu nongye wenti" [The Chinese revolution and the peasant problem]. *Xin shengming* [New life] 1, no. 10 (October 1928).

"Wanguo Wuzhengfudang xuanyan" [Proclamation of the Anarchist International], translated by Yao Rong. *Minsheng* [Voice of the people] no. 24 (1915): 3–5 (279–281).

Watanabe Hiroshi. "Fukumoto Kazuo" [Fukumoto Kazuo]. In *Nihon no Marukusu keizaigaku: Sono rekishi to ronri* [Japan's Marxist economics: Its history and logic], 1:145–201. 2 vols. Tokyo: Aoki Shoten, 1967.

Watanabe Masanosuke. "Nihon Kyōsantō kenkyo to shakai minshu-shugisha no demagōgu" [The arrests of the Japanese Communist party and the demagoguery of the social-democrats]. *Marukusu-shugi* [Marxism] (May–June 1928).

Wu Baoding. "Gaizu Guomindang yu guomin geming zhi qiantu" [Reorganizing the Guomindang and the future of the national revolution]. *Geming pinglun* [Revolutionary review] no. 18 (1928): 41–45.

Wu Jialin. "Li Dazhao he Zhongguo de Makesi-zhuyi shixue" [Li Dazhao and China's Marxist historiography]. *Xuexi yu yanjiu* [Studies and research] 1 (1981): 54–58.

Wu Xie [pseud.]. "Duoqu zhengquan" [Take political power]. *Gongchandang* [The Communist party], no. 5 (June 7, 1921): 3–9.

———. "Women weishenme zhuzhang gongchan-zhuyi?" [Why do we advocate communism?]. *Gongchandang* [The Communist party], no. 4 (February 1921): 23–30.

"Wuzhengfu-gongchan-pai yu jichanpai zhi qidian" [Points of difference between the anarcho-Communist faction and the collectivist faction]. *Minsheng* [Voice of the people] no. 30 (March 15, 1921): 11–12 (361–362).

"Wuzhengfu Gongchan-zhuyi Tongzhi-she xuanyan shu" [Declaration of the anarcho-Communist group of Shanghai]. *Minsheng* [Voice of the people] no. 16 (July 4, 1914): 1–3 (193–195).

"Wuzhengfu-gongchan-zhuyi zhi xinli-shang de jieshi" [A psychological interpretation of anarcho-communism]. *Minsheng* [Voice of the people] no. 30 (March 15, 1921): 4–8 (354–358); no. 31 (April 15, 1921): 7–9 (399–401); no. 32 (May 15, 1921): 5–8 (411–414).

"Wuzhengfu-zhuyizhe duiyu tongleipai de zhenzheng taidu" [The attitude of the anarchists toward factions of the same type]. *Minsheng* [Voice of the people] no. 30 (April 5, 1921): 1–4 (367–370).

"Wuzhengfudang 1882 nian Rineiwa dahui xuanyanshu" [Text of the Declaration of the 1882 Geneva Congress of the Anarchist party], translated by Ruan Shengjie. *Minsheng* [Voice of the people] no. 5:5.

Xiao Gongquan. "Zhongguo zhengzhi sixiang-zhong zhi zhengyuan lun" [Theories of the origins of government in Chinese political thought]. *Qinghua xuebao* [Qinghua bulletin]. 9, no. 3 (1934): 535–548.

Xiong Deshan. "Zhongguo nongmin wenti zhi shi de xushu" [A historical narrative of the peasant question in China]. *Dushu zazhi* [Reading magazine] 1, 4–5 (March 1932): 1–27; 3, no. 3/4(April 1936): 1–44.

Y. K. [pseud.]. "Yige wuzhengfudangren he yige gongchandangren de tanhua" [A conversation between an Anarchist and a Communist]. *Shaonian* [La Jeunesse] (Paris) no. 10 (July 1, 1923): 21, 34.

Yamada Toshio. "Les tendances du marxisme japonais contemporain" [Trends in contemporary Japanese Marxism]. *Actuel Marx* [Marx today] no. 2 (1987): 34–44.

———. "Shimin shakai no genzai" [Civil society today]. In *Gendai shimin shakai no senkai* [The gyrations of contemporary civil society], edited by Hirata Kiyoaki, Yagi Ki'ichirō, and Yamada Toshio, pp. 95–115. Kyoto: Shōwa-dō, 1987.

Yamada Toshio, Masaki Hachirō, and Shirogane Hisanori. "Japanese Marxism Today" *Keizaigaku zasshi* [Journal of economics] (Osaka) 9 (1987): 68–93.

Yamaji Aizan. "Genji no shakai mondai oyobi shakai-shugisha" [Contemporary social problems and Socialists (1908)]. In *Meiji bunka zenshū* [Complete works of Meiji culture], 21:373–395. 24 vols. Tokyo: N.p., 1929.

———. "Shakai-shugi kanken" [My personal view of socialism (1906)]. In *Yamaji Aizan shū* [Collected works of Yamaji Aizan], edited with a commentary by Oka Toshirō. 2:147–214. 3 vols. Tokyo: San'ichi Shobō, 1985.

———. "Yoga kirisutokyō o shinzuru yuen" [The reason I believe in Christianity]. In *Yamaji Aizan shū* [Collected works of Yamaji Aizan], edited with a commentary by Oka Toshirō. Vol. 2, *Min'yū-sha Shisō Bungaku Shūsho* [Collected works of the thought and literature of the Min'yū-sha]. Tokyo: San'ichi Shobō, 1985.

Yamakawa Hitoshi. "Dai-san Intanashonaru" [The Third International (April 1921)]. In *Yamakawa Hitoshi zenshū* [Complete works of Yamakawa], 3:236–239. Tokyo: Keisō Shobō, 1966.

———. "Kokka shakai-shugi to rōdō mondai" [State socialism and the labor problem (September 13, 1919)]. In Yamakawa Hitoshi, *Yamakawa Hitoshi zenshū* [Complete works of Yamakawa Hitoshi], Vol. 2, June 1918 to April 1920, pp. 275–285. Tokyo: Keisō Shobō, 1966.

———. "Musan-kaikyū undō no hōkō tenkan" [A change of direction of the proletarian movement (1922)]. In *Yamakawa Hitoshi shū* [Collected works of Yamakawa Hitoshi], edited and with a commentary by Takabatake Michitoshi. Kindai Nihon Shisō Taikei, no. 19 [Outline of modern Japanese thought], pp. 71–81. Tokyo: Chikuma Shobō, 1976.

———. "Nihon ni okeru demokurashii no hattatsu to musan-kaikyū no seiji undō" [The development of democracy in Japan and the political movement of the proletariat (November 1923–April 1924)]. In Yamakawa Hitoshi, *Yamakawa Hitoshi shū* [Collected works of Yamakawa Hitoshi], edited wth a commentary by Takabatake Michitoshi. Kindai Nihon Shisō Taikei, no. 19 [Outline of modern Japanese thought], pp. 71–81. Tokyo: Chikuma Shobō, 1976. Tokyo: Chikuma Shobō, 1976.

———. "Roshiya no shihai kaikyū" [Russia's ruling class (July 1923)]. In Yamakawa Hitoshi, *Yamakawa Hitoshi zenshū* [Complete works of Yamakawa Hitoshi]. 5:248–255. Tokyo: Keisō Shobō, 1966.

———. "Sakushu kuni to hisakushu kuni" [Exploiting countries and exploited countries (July 1923)]. In Yamakawa Hitoshi, *Yamakawa Hitoshi zenshū* [Complete works of Yamakawa Hitoshi], 5:238–239. Tokyo: Keisō Shobō, 1966.

———. "Seiji-teki tōitsu sensen e! Musan seitō gōdō-ron no konkyo" (November 10, 1927) [To a political united front! The basis of the argument for the merger of proletarian political parties]. In Yamakawa Hitoshi, *Yamakawa Hitoshi shū* [Collected works of Yamakawa Hitoshi], edited with a commentary by Takabatake Michitoshi. Kindai Nihon shisō taikei [Outline of modern Japanese thought], no. 19, pp. 174–218. Tokyo: Chikuma Shobō, 1976.

———. "Shakai-shugi to minzoku tōsō" [Socialism and national struggle (December 1921)]. In Yamakawa Hitoshi, *Yamakawa Hitoshi zenshū* [Complete works of Yamakawa Hitoshi], 4:84–87. Tokyo: Keisō Shobō, 1976.

————. "Sobieto seiji no tokushitsu to sono hihan: Puroretarian/dikuteitaashippu to demokurashii" [The characteristics of the Soviet government and the critique of it: Proletarian dictatorship and democracy (December 1919)]. In Yamakawa Hitoshi, *Yamakawa Hitoshi zenshū* [Complete works of Yamakawa Hitoshi], 2:386–408. Tokyo: Keisō Shobō, 1966.

Yamamizu [pseud.]. "Riben zuijin zhengchao de kaizhan (shi-er yue wuri dongjing tongxin)" [Recent political developments in Japan (a letter from Tokyo dated December 5)]. *Xiangdao zhoubao* [The Guide Weekly] 181 (January 6, 1927): 1906–1909.

Yamazaki Shunsei. "'Shakai-shugi e no michi' to Yamakawa Hitoshi" ["The road to socialism" and Yamakawa Hitoshi]. In *Gendai no ideorogii* [Contemporary ideology], edited by Ikumi Takuichi et al., 1:81–106. 6 vols. Tokyo: San'ichi Shobō, 1961.

Yan Lingfeng. "Shina keizai mondai kenkyū" [Studies on China's economic problems]. In *Shina keizai ron* [On the Chinese economy], translated and compiled by Tanaka Tadao, pp. 53–117. Tokyo: Chūō Kōron-sha, 1932.

"Yaxiya shengchan-fangshi—Bucheng qiwei wenti de wenti" [The Asiatic mode of production: The problem of why it has not become an issue]. *Lishi yanjiu* [Historical research] no. 2 (1980).

Yi Hen [pseud.]. "Annaqi yu ziyou" [Anarchy and freedom] *Ziyou* [Freedom]. (Paris) no. 1 (December 1920): 2.

Zhang Heng. "Ping Tao Xisheng de lishi fangfa-lun" [Critique of Tao Xisheng's historical methodology]. *Dushu zazhi* [Reading magazine] 2, no. 2/3 (March 1932).

"Zhi wuzhengfudang wanguo dahui shu" [Open letter to the international congress of anarchist parties]. *Minsheng* [Voice of the people] no. 16 (June 27, 1914): 4–8 (184–188).

Zhou Enlai [Wu Hao]. "Eguo geming shi shibai le me?" [Has the Russian revolution failed?]. *Shaonian* [La Jeunesse]. (Paris) no. 6 (1922): 19–25.

————. "Geming jiuguo lun" [On revolution to save the country]. *Chiguang* [The red light] (Paris) no. 2 (February 15, 1924): 2–4.

————. "Gongchan-zhuyi yu Zhongguo" [Communism and China]. *Shaonian* [La Jeunesse] (Paris) no. 2 (August 1922): 6–11.

————. "Shiyue geming" [The October Revolution]. *Shaonian* [La Jeunesse] (Paris) no. 5 (December 1922): 1–8.

Zhou Fuhai. "Shixing shehui-zhuyi yu fazhan shiye" [The practice of socialism and the development of industry]. *Xin qingnian* [New youth] 8, no. 5 (January 1, 1921).

Zhu Peiwo [Zhu Xinfan]. "Guanyu Zhongguo shehui zhi fengjianxing de taolun" [A discussion of the feudal nature of Chinese society]. *Dushu zazhi* [Reading magazine] 1, no. 4/5 (November 1931): 1–54.

Zhu Qihua. "Dongli-pai de Zhongguo shehui-guan de pipan" [Critique of the Dongli faction's view of Chinese history]. *Dushu zazhi* [Reading magazine] 2, no. 2/3 (March 1932): 1–56.

Zhu Zhixin. "Tudi guoyou yu caizheng" [Land nationalization and finance]. *Minbao* [The people's journal] no. 15 (July 1907): 67–99.

Zhu Zhixin [Xianzhe]. "Lun shehui geming dang yu zhengzhi geming bingxing" [Why the social revolution should be carried out simultaneously with the political revolution]. *Minbao* [The people's journal] no. 5 (June 26, 1906): 43–66.

Zhuan Fu. "Shifu-jun xinglue" [Brief autobiography of (Liu) Shifu]. *Minsheng* [Voice of the people] no. 23 (May 5, 1915): 1–3 (265–267).

Zhuo Xuan. "Guoji-jian youchan-jieji zhuanzheng yu wuchan-jieji geming de xin qingshi" [The dictatorship of the bourgeoisie internationally and the new situation of the proletarian revolution]. *Shaonian* [La Jeunesse] (Paris) no. 12 (October 4, 1923): 40–47.

———. "Shenme shi wuzhengudangren de daode" [What is the morality of anarchist party members?]. *Shaonian* [La Jeunesse] (Paris) no. 11 (1923): 34–39; no. 12(1923): 29–40.

———. "Zhongguo de diwei yu gaizao" [China's position and reform]. *Shaonian* [La Jeunesse] (Paris) no. 10 (July 1, 1923): 13–21, 34.

Ziemer, Klaus. "Auf dem Weg zum Systemwandel in Polen: (I) Politische Reformen und Reformversuche 1980 bis 1988" [On the way to a change in the system in Poland: (I) Political reforms and reform efforts 1980 to 1988]. *Osteuropa* [Eastern Europe] (September 1989): 791–805.

———. "Auf dem Weg zum Systemwandel in Polen: (II) Vom 'Runden Tisch' zur 'IV. Republik'?" [On the way to a change in the system in Poland: (II) From the "Round Table" to "The Fourth Republic"?]. *Osteuropa* [Eastern Europe] (November–December 1989): 957–980.

Unpublished Sources

Arahata Katsuzō (Arahata Kanson). Interview, Tokyo, August 17, 1979.

Cheng, Shelley Hsien. "The T'ung-meng-hui: Its Organization, Leadership and Finances, 1905–1912." Ph.D. diss., University of Washington, 1962.

Doi Takako. Interview, Tokyo, June 25, 1982.

Durkee, Travers Edgar. "The Communist International and Japan, 1919–1932." Ph.D. diss., Stanford University, 1954.

Fujita Shōzō. Interview, Tokyo, August 3, 1979.

Fukuda Yutaka. Interview, Tokyo, July 3, 1985.

Fukushima Shingo. Interview, Tokyo, July 30, 1979.

Hayashi Takehisa. Interview, Tokyo, June 16, 1982.

Hirano Yoshitarō. Interview, Tokyo, July 27, 1979.

Hori Masao. Interviews, Tokyo, May 4, 1984, June 25, 1985.

Ikumi Takuichi. Interview, Tokyo, June 17, 1982.

Inomata Tsunao. "Inomata Tsunao-shi jōshinsho." [Written statement of Inomata Tsunao.] Prepared for Tōkyō chihō saibansho [Tokyo District Court], handwritten, March 3, 1941, March 15, 1941.

Ishida Takeshi. Interview, Tokyo, August 11, 1979.

Ishimura Osamu. Interview, Tokyo, August 21, 1979.

Itō Makoto. Interviews, Tokyo, June 11, 1982, May 7, 1984.

Jiang Yuanchun. International Department of *Renmin ribao* [*People's Daily*]. Interview, Williamsburg, Virginia, January 1981.

Kawasaki Kanji. Interview, Tokyo, July 10, 1985.

Krebs, Edward. "Liu Ssu-fu and Chinese Anarchism, 1905–1915." Ph.D. diss., University of Washington, 1977.

Kuwabara Takeo. Interview, Kyoto, April 19, 1984.

Levine, Marilyn. "The Found Generation: Chinese Communism in Europe, 1919–1925." Ph.D. diss., University of Chicago, 1985.

Maruyama Masao. Interviews, Tokyo, June 17, 1982; Tokyo, May 4, 1984; Tokyo, May 8, 1984.

All interviews were conducted by the author unless otherwise noted.

Mast, Herman William, III. "An Intellectual Biography of Tai Chi-t'ao from 1891 to 1928." Ph.D. diss., University of Illinois, 1970.

Minobe Ryōkichi. Interviews, Tokyo, July 30, 1979, May 7, 1984.

Mizuno Shigeo. "Jōshinsho: Nyūtō zengo yori 'San/ichi-go' ni itaru kikan ni okeru 'shisō no sui'i' ni tsuite." [Prison statement: On the 'shift in thought' in the period from about the time (I) entered the party to the March 15(th incident).] Handwritten, January 28, 1929.

―――. "Kansō (I): Dōshi K. ni atetaru keishiki ni oite." [Thoughts: in the form of addressing Comrade K.]. Pt. 1. Tōkyō chihō saibansho kenji-kyoku shisō-bu [Tokyo District Court prosecutor's office, Thought Bureau transcription], June 27, 1929.

―――. "Kansō (III) Mizuno Shigeo shuki: Tōkyō chihō saibansho kenji-kyoku shisō-bu sha. Dōshi M. K. ni atetaru keishiki ni te." [Thoughts, notes of Mizuno Shigeo: Transcription of the Tokyo District Court prosecutor's office, Thought Bureau, in the form of addressing Comrade M. K.]. Pt. 3. March 26, 1929.

Moriya Fumio. Interviews, Tokyo, August 6, 1979; Tokyo, June 5, 1982.

Mutō Sanji. Interview, Tokyo, July 10, 1985.

Nakamura Takafusa. Interviews, Tokyo, July 11, 1979, July 17, 1979.

Nitta Shunzō. Interview, Tokyo, June 1, 1985.

Ōishi Ka'ichirō. Interview, Tokyo, June 23, 1982.

Onabe Teruhiko. Interview, Tokyo, August 1, 1979.

Ōuchi Hideaki. Interview, Tokyo, June 29, 1985.

Ōuchi Hyōe. "Jōshinsho." [Written statement.] Handwritten manuscript, September 1941.

Ōuchi Tsutomu. Interviews, Tokyo, June 11, 1982; April 27, 1984; June 28, 1985.

Ogden, Suzanne Peckham. "Chinese Concepts of the Nation, State, and Sovereignty." Ph.D. diss., Brown University, 1975.

Roux, Alain. "Le mouvement ouvrier à Shanghai de 1928 à 1930." [The labor movement in Shanghai from 1928 to 1930.] Thèse du 3e cycle, The Sorbonne, 1970.

Sakisaka Itsurō. Interviews, Tokyo, June 7, 1982; June 14, 1982.

[Sano Manabu]. Shihō-shō, Keisei-kyoku [Ministry of Justice, Penal Office]. "Waga gokuchū no shisō henreki" [The course of my thoughts while in prison]. Marked confidential, August 1944.

Sano Manabu. "Sano Manabu jōshinsho: Kaitō-ha ni tsuite" [Sano Manabu's written statement: On the Dissolutionist faction], February 1931.

Satō Tsuneaki. Interview, Tokyo, July 3, 1985.

Saywell, William G. B. "The Thought of Tai Chi-t'ao, 1912–1928." Ph.D. diss., University of Toronto, 1968.

Shibagaki Kazuo. Interview, Tokyo, June 23, 1982.

Skocpol, Theda. "Varieties of 'Historical Sociology.'" Harvard University, September 14, 1977. Mimeograph.

Steinhoff, Patricia Golden. "*Tenkō*: Ideology and Social Integration in Prewar Japan." Ph.D. diss., Harvard University, 1969.

Swearingen, Rodger. "The Japanese Communist Party and the Comintern, 1919–1943: A Study of the Relationship between the Japanese Party and Moscow and the Success of the Japanese Special Higher Police (Thought Police) in Combating Communism in Japan." Ph.D. diss., Harvard University, 1953.

Swift, Thomas Duane. "Yamakawa Hitoshi and the Dawn of Japanese Socialism." Ph.D. diss., University of California, Berkeley, 1970.

Takahashi Masao. Personal letter, April 4, 1984.

———. Interviews, Tokyo, August 17, 1979; June 4, 1982; May 5, 1984; July 8, 1985.

Taniuchi Yuzuru. Interview, Tokyo University Law School, Tokyo, August 3, 1979.

Topper, Henry. "From the Commune to the Cultural Revolution: A Discussion of Party Leadership and Democracy in Lenin and Mao." Ph.D. diss., Johns Hopkins University, 1990.

Totten, George O. "The National Socialism of Akamatsu Katsumaro." Paper prepared for presentation at the Annual Meeting of the American Political Science Association, Washington, D.C., August 30–September 2, 1984.

Ukai Nobushige. Interview, Tokyo, July 23, 1979.

Wagner, Jeffrey Paul. "Sano Manabu and the Japanese Adaptation of Socialism." Ph.D. diss., University of Arizona, 1978.

Wang, Richard Tze-yang. "Wu Chih-hui: An Intellectual and Political Biography." Ph.D. diss., University of Virginia, 1976.

Watanabe Fumitarō. Interview, Tokyo, August 17, 1979.

Watanabe Yōzō. Interview, Tokyo, April 3, 1984.

Wray, Harold Joseph. "Changes and Continuity in Japanese Images of the Kokutai and Attitudes and Roles toward the Outside World: A Content Analysis of Japanese Textbooks, 1903–1945." Ph.D. diss., University of Hawaii, 1971.

Yamada Tatsuo. Interview, Tokyo, August 1979.

Yamafuji Akira. Interview, Tokyo, June 14, 1982.

Yamakawa Hitoshi. "Shōnin shinsei" [Witness's summons]. Handwritten manuscript, May 30, 1944, Ōhara Shakai Mondai Kenkyūjo. Hōsei University, Tokyo.

Yamamoto Masahiro. Interviews, Tokyo, June 21, 1982; July 10, 1985.

ENGLISH LANGUAGE SOURCES

Books

Adamson, Walter. *Hegemony and Revolution*. Berkeley and Los Angeles: University of California Press, 1980.

Alitto, Guy S. *The Last Confucian: Liang Shuming and the Chinese Dilemma of Modernity*. Berkeley: University of California Press, 1979.

Almond, Gabriel. *The Appeals of Communism*. N.p.: N.p., 1945.

Alter, Peter. *Nationalism*. London: Edward Arnold, 1989.

Althusser, Louis. *For Marx*. Translated by Ben Brewster. New York: Vintage Books, 1970.

———. *Lenin and Philosophy, and Other Essays*. New York: Monthly Review Press, 1972.

Althusser, Louis, and Balibar, Etienne. *Reading Capital*. Translated by Ben Brewster. London: Verso, 1979.

Anderson, Perry. *Considerations on Western Marxism*. London: New Left Books, 1976.

———. *Lineages of the Absolutist State*. London: Verso, 1974.

———. *Passages from Antiquity to Feudalism*. London: New Left Books, 1974.

Armstrong, Robert Cornell. *Light from the East: Studies in Japanese Confucianism*. Toronto: University of Toronto, 1914.

Avineri, Shlomo. *The Social and Political Thought of Karl Marx*. Cambridge Studies in the History and Theory of Politics. Cambridge: Cambridge University Press, 1968.

Bailey, Anne M., and Llobera, Josep R., eds. *The Asiatic Mode of Production: Science and Politics*. London: Routledge and Kegan Paul, 1981.

Bakunin, Mikhail. *Bakunin on Anarchy: Selected Works by the Activist Founder of World Anarchism*. Edited by Sam Dolgoff and translated with an introduction and preface by Paul Avrich. New York: Alfred A. Knopf, 1972.

Balazs, Etienne. *Chinese Civilization and Bureaucracy: Variations on a Theme*. Edited and with an introduction by Arthur F. Wright and translated by H. M. Wright. New Haven, Conn.: Yale University Press, 1964.

Bamba, Nobuya, and Howe, John F., eds. *Pacifism in Japan: The Christian and Socialist Tradition*. With a foreword by Robert N. Bellah. Vancouver: University of British Columbia Press, 1978.

Baron, Samuel H. *Plekhanov: The Father of Russian Marxism*. Stanford, Calif.: Stanford University Press, 1963.

Barshay, Andrew E. *State and Intellectual in Imperial Japan: The Public Man in Crisis*. Berkeley: University of California Press, 1989.

Basic Writings of Mo Tzu, Hsün Tzu, and Han Fei Tzu. Translated by Burton Watson. New York: Columbia University Press, 1967.

Bauer, Raymond A. *The New Soviet Man in Soviet Psychology*. Cambridge, Mass.: N.p., 1952.

Beasley, William. *The Meiji Restoration*. Stanford, Calif., Stanford University Press, 1972.

Beckmann, George. *The Making of the Meiji Constitution*. Lawrence: University of Kansas Press, 1957.

Beckmann, George M., and Okubo Genji. *The Japanese Communist Party, 1922–1945*. Stanford, Calif.: Stanford University Press, 1969.

Bedeski, Robert E. *The Fragile Entente: The 1978 Japan-China Peace Treaty in a Global Context*. Boulder, Colo.: Westview Press, 1983.

Bellah, Robert N. *Tokugawa Religion: The Values of Pre-Industrial Japan*. Glencoe, Ill.: Free Press, 1957; Boston: Beacon Press, Beacon Paperback, 1970.

Bendix, Reinhard. *Max Weber: An Intellectual Portrait*. Garden City, N.Y.: Doubleday, Anchor Books, 1962.

Benedict, Ruth. *The Chrysanthemum and the Sword: Patterns of Japanese Culture*. New York: New American Library, Meridian Books, 1946, 1974.

Berlin, Isaiah. *Two Concepts of Liberty*. Oxford: Clarendon Press, 1958.

Bernal, Martin. *Chinese Socialism to 1907*. Ithaca, N.Y: Cornell University Press, 1976.

Bernstein, Gail Lee. *Japanese Marxist: A Portrait of Kawakami Hajime, 1879–1946*. Harvard East Asian Series, no. 86. Cambridge: Harvard University Press, 1976.

Bloom, Solomon F. *The World of Nations: A Study of the National Implications in the Work of Marx*. New York: Columbia University Press, 1941.

Boas, George. *Rationalism in Greek Philosophy*. Baltimore, Md.: Johns Hopkins University, 1961.

Bose, Atindranath. *History of Anarchism*. Calcutta: World Press, 1967.

Boulding, Kenneth E. *The Image*. Ann Arbor: University of Michigan Press, 1956.

Brandt, Conrad. *Stalin's Failure in China, 1924–1927*. Cambridge, Mass.: Harvard University Press, 1958; New York: W. W. Norton, Norton Library, 1966.

Brandt, Conrad, Benjamin Schwartz, and John K. Fairbank. *A Documentary History of Chinese Communism*. Reprint. Cambridge, Mass.: Harvard University Press, 1952; New York: Atheneum, College ed., 1966.

Breuilly, John. *Nationalism and the State*. Chicago: University of Chicago Press, 1985.

The Broken Mirror: China after Tiananmen. Chicago: St. James Press, 1990.

Brown, Delmer M. *Nationalism in Japan: An Introductory Historical Analysis*. Berkeley: University of California Press, 1955.

Brugger, Bill. *Chinese Marxism in Flux 1978–1984*. Beckinham: Croom Helm, 1985.

Brzezinski, Zbigniew, and Samuel P. Huntington. *Political Power: USA/USSR*. New York: Viking Press, Penguin Books, 1964.

Bukharin, Nikolai. *Historical Materialism: A System of Sociology* (Teoriia istorichekogo materializma: populiarnyi uchebnik marksistskoi sotsiologii, 1925). New York: International Publishers, 1925.

———. *Imperialism and World Economy* (Mirovoe khoziaistvoi imperializm, 1918). With an introduction by V. I. Lenin. New York: International Publishers, 1929; New York: Monthly Review Press, Modern Reader paperback, 1973.

Bukharin, Nikolai, and Yevgeny Preograzhensky. *The ABC of Communism*. Edited and with an Introduction by E. H. Carr. Harmondsworth: Pelican Books, Pelican Classics, 1969.

Cabral, Amilcar. *Return to the Source: Selected Speeches of Amilcar Cabral*. Edited by African Information Service. New York: Monthly Review Press, 1973.

Carnoy, Martin. *The State and Political Theory*. Princeton, N.J.: Princeton University Press, 1984.

Carrère d'Encausse, Hélène Schram, and Stuart R. Schram. *Marxism and Asia: An Introduction with Readings*. London: Allen Lane, Penguin Press, 1969.

The Case of P'eng Teh-huai, 1959–1968. Hong Kong: Union Research Institute, 1968.

Cassirer, Ernst. *The Myth of the State*. New Haven, Conn.: Yale University Press, 1946.

Chang, Hao. *Chinese Intellectuals in Crisis: Search for Order and Meaning (1890–1911)*. Berkeley: University of California Press, 1987.

Ch'en, Jerome. *Mao and the Chinese Revolution*. New York: Oxford University Press, 1965.

Ch'en, Kung-po. *The Communist Movement in China*. Edited and with an introduction by C. Martin Wilbur. New York: Octagon Books; reprint. for the East Asian Institute, 1966.

Chamberlin, William H. *The Russian Revolution, 1917–1921*. 2 vols. New York: Macmillan, 1952.

Chan, Wing-tsit, trans. and comp. *A Source Book in Chinese Philosophy*. Princeton, N.J.: Princeton University Press, 1963.

Chang, Hao. *Liang Ch'i-ch'ao and Intellectual Transition in China, 1890–1907*. Harvard East Asian Series, no. 64. Cambridge, Mass.: Harvard University Press, 1971.

Chang, Kuo-t'ao. *The Rise of the Chinese Communist Party, 1921–1927*. Lawrence: University of Kansas Press, 1971.

Chang, Sherman, H. M. *The Marxian Theory of the State*. With an introduction by John R. Commons. Philadelphia: John Spencer, 1931.

Chesneaux, Jean. *Peasant Revolts in China, 1840–1949*. Translated by C. A. Curwen. London: Thames and Hudson, 1973.

———, ed. *Popular Movements and Secret Societies in China, 1840–1950*. Stanford, Calif.: Stanford University Press, 1972.

Chow, Tse-tsung. *The May Fourth Movement: Intellectual Revolution in Modern China*. Cambridge, Mass.: Harvard University Press, 1960; Stanford, Calif.: Stanford University Press, 1967.

Clark, G. L., and J. M. Dear. *State Apparatus: Structures and Language of Legitimacy.* Hemel Hempstead, Herts: George Allen and Unwin, 1984.

Cobban, Alfred. *The Myth of the French Revolution: An Inaugural Lecture.* London: H. K. Lewis, 1955.

———. *The Social Interpretation of the French Revolution.* Cambridge: Cambridge University Press, 1964.

Cohen, Stephen F. *Bukharin and the Bolshevik Revolution: A Political Biography, 1888–1938.* New York: Alfred A. Knopf, 1973; New York: Random House, Vintage Books, 1975.

Collini, Stefan. *Liberalism and Sociology: L. T. Hobhouse and Liberal Argument in England, 1880–1914.* Cambridge: Cambridge University Press, 1979.

Collins, Randall. *Conflict Sociology: Toward an Explanatory Science.* New York: Academic Press, 1975.

Compton, Boyd, ed. *Mao's China; Party Reform Documents, 1942–1944.* Seattle: University of Washington Press, 1952.

Connolly, William E. *The Terms of Political Discourse.* 2d ed. Princeton, N.J.: Princeton University Press, 1983.

Connor, Walker. *The National Question in Marxist-Leninist Theory and Strategy.* Princeton, N.J.: Princeton University Press, 1984.

Crowley, James Buckley. *Japan's Quest for Autonomy: National Security and Foreign Policy, 1930–1938.* Princeton, N.J.: Princeton University Press, 1966.

Dahrendorf, Ralf. *Society and Democracy in Germany.* Reprint. New York: Doubleday, 1967; New York: W. W. Norton, 1979.

Davis, Fei-ling. *Primitive Revolutionaries of China.* Honolulu: University of Hawaii Press, 1971.

Davis, Horace. *Nationalism and Socialism: Marxist and Labor Theories of Nationalism to 1917.* New York: Monthly Review Press, 1967.

de Rivera, Joseph H. *The Psychological Dimension of Foreign Policy.* Columbus, Ohio: Charles E. Merrill Publishing, 1968.

Degras, J., ed. *The Communist International, 1919–1943, Documents.* 3 vols. London: Oxford University Press, 1956.

Deutsch, Karl W. *Nationalism and Social Communication: An Inquiry into the Foundations of Nationality.* 2d ed. Cambridge, Mass.: MIT Press; and New York: Wiley, 1953, 1966.

Deutscher, Isaac. *The Prophet Armed: Trotsky, 1879–1921.* New York: N.p., 1954.

———. *Stalin: A Political Biography.* New York: Oxford University Press, 1949.

Dirlik, Arif. *Anarchism in the Chinese Revolution.* Berkeley: University of California Press, 1991.

———. *Revolution and History: Origins of Marxist Historiography in China, 1919–1937.* Berkeley: University of California Press, 1978.

———. *The Origins of Chinese Communism.* New York: Oxford University Press, 1989.

Dirlik, Arif, and Maurice Meisner, eds. *Marxism and the Chinese Experience: Issues in Contemporary Chinese Socialism.* Armonk, N.Y: M. E. Sharpe, 1989.

Dittmer, Lowell. *China's Continuous Revolution: The Post-Liberation Epoch 1949–1981.* Berkeley: University of California Press, 1987.

———. *Liu Shao-ch'i and the Chinese Cultural Revolution: The Politics of Mass Criticism.* Berkeley: University of California Press, 1974.

Djilas, Milovan. *The New Class.* N.p.: N.p., 1966.

Dobb, Maurice. *Studies in the Development of Capitalism*. Rev. ed. New York: International Publishers, 1963.

Dolgoff, Sam, ed. *Bakunin on Anarchy: Selected Works by the Activist-Founder of World Anarchism*. New York: Alfred A. Knopf, 1972.

Domhoff, G. William. *The Higher Circles*. New York: Vintage Books, 1970.

————. *Who Rules America?* Englewood Cliffs, N.J.: Prentice-Hall, 1967.

Dore, Ronald P. *Land Reform in Japan*. London: Oxford University Press, 1959.

Dunbar, Gary S. *Elisée Reclus; Historian of Nature*. Hamden, Conn.: Archon Books, 1978.

Dupré, Louis. *The Philosophical Foundations of Marxism*. New York: Harcourt, Grace and World, 1966.

Duus, Peter. *Party Rivalry and Political Change in Taishō Japan*. Harvard East Asian Series, no. 35. Cambridge, Mass.: Harvard University Press, 1968.

Earl, David Magarey. *Emperor and Nation in Japan: Political Thinkers of the Tokugawa Period*. Seattle: University of Washington Press, 1964.

Engels, Friedrich. *Germany: Revolution and Counter-Revolution*. The Marxist Library. Vol. 13. New York: International Publishers, 1933.

————. *Herr Eugen Dühring's Revolution in Science*. Translated by Emile Burns and edited by C. P. Dutt. New York: International Publishers, New World Paperbacks, 1939. [Cited as *Anti-Dühring*.]

————. *Origin of the Family, Private Property and the State: In Light of the Researches of Lewis H. Morgan*. Edited with an introduction by Eleanor Burke Leacock. New York: International Publishers, New World Paperbacks, 1972.

————. *Socialism, Utopian and Scientific*. London: S. Sonnenschein, and New York: C. Scribner's Sons, 1892.

Erlich, Alexander. *The Soviet Industrialization Debates, 1924–1928*. Cambridge, Mass.: Harvard University Press, 1960.

Fairbank, John King. *Trade and Diplomacy on the China Coast: The Opening of the Treaty Ports, 1842–1854*. Harvard Historical Studies. Cambridge, Mass.: Harvard University Press, 1953.

————. *The United States and China*. 4th ed. Cambridge, Mass.: Harvard University Press, 1979.

Fanon, Frantz. *Wretched of the Earth*. New York: Grove Press, 1968.

Flathman, Richard E. *The Practice of Political Authority*. Chicago: University of Chicago Press, 1980.

Fletcher, William Miles III. *The Search for a New Order: Intellectuals and Fascism in Prewar Japan*. Chapel Hill: University of North Carolina Press, 1982.

Fogel, Joshua A. *Ai Ssu-ch'i's Contribution to the Development of Chinese Marxism*. Harvard Contemporary China Series, no. 4. Cambridge, Mass.: Harvard University, Council on East Asian Studies, 1987.

Footman, David. *Ferdinand Lassalle: Romantic Revolutionary*. New Haven, Conn.: Yale University Press, 1947.

Friedman, Edward. *Backward toward Revolution: The Chinese Revolutionary Party*. Berkeley: University of California Press, 1974.

Friedman, Edward, Paul G. Pickowicz, and Marx Selden, with Kay Ann Johnson. *Chinese Village, Socialist State*. New Haven, Conn.: Yale University Press, 1991.

Fukutake, T. *Man and Society in Japan*. Tokyo: University of Tokyo Press, 1962.

Fung, Yu-lan. *A History of Chinese Philosophy*. Translated by Derk Bodde. Vol. 2, *The*

Period of Classical Learning (from the Second Century B.C. to the Twentieth Century A.D.). 2 vols. Princeton, N.J.: Princeton University Press, 1953.

Furet, François. *Interpreting the French Revolution.* Translated by Elborg Forster. Cambridge: Cambridge University Press, and Paris: Editions de la Maison des Sciences de l'Homme, 1981.

Furth, Charlotte, ed. *The Limits of Change: Essays on Conservative Alternatives in Republican China.* Harvard East Asian Series, no. 84. Cambridge, Mass.: Harvard University Press, 1976.

Gardner, Charles S. *Chinese Traditional Historiography.* Cambridge, Mass.: Harvard University Press, 1938.

Gellner, Ernest. *Nations and Nationalism.* Oxford: B. Blackwell, 1983.

Gerschenkron, Alexander. *Economic Backwardness in Historical Perspective: A Book of Essays.* Cambridge, Mass.: Harvard University Press, Belknap Press, 1962.

Gittings, John. *Survey of the Sino-Soviet Dispute: A Commentary and Extracts from the Recent Polemics, 1963–1967.* London: Oxford University Press for the Royal Institute of International Affairs, 1968.

Gluck, Carol. *Japan's Modern Myths: Ideology in the Late Meiji Period.* Princeton, N.J.: Princeton University Press, 1985.

Goldman, Emma. *Anarchism and Other Essays.* Toronto: Dover Publications, 1969.

Goldman, Merle. *China's Intellectuals: Advise and Dissent.* Cambridge, Mass.: Harvard University Press, 1981.

Gramsci, Antonio. *Selections from the Prison Notebooks.* Edited and translated by Quinton Hoare and Geoffrey Nowell Smith. New York: International Publishers, New World Paperbacks, and London: Lawrence and Wishart, 1971.

Gregor, A. James. *Young Mussolini and the Intellectual Origins of Fascism.* Berkeley: University of California Press for the Institute of International Studies, 1979.

Gurr, Ted Robert. *Why Men Rebel.* Princeton, N.J.: Princeton University Press, 1971.

Gurtov, Melvin. *China under Threat: The Politics of Strategy and Diplomacy.* Baltimore: Johns Hopkins University Press, 1980.

Habermas, Jürgen. *Legitimation Crisis.* Translated by Thomas McCarthy. Boston: Beacon Press, 1975.

————. *The Structural Transformation of the Public Sphere: An Inquiry into a Category of Bourgeois Society.* Translated by Thomas Burger. Cambridge, Mass.: MIT Press, 1989.

Hall, Robert King, ed. *Kokutai no Hongi: Cardinal Principles of the National Entity of Japan.* Cambridge, Mass.: Harvard University Press, 1949.

Harding, Harry. *Organizing China: The Problem of Bureaucracy, 1949–1976.* Stanford, Calif.: Stanford University Press, 1981.

Harrison, James Pinckney. *The Long March to Power: A History of the Chinese Communist Party, 1921–1972.* Praeger Library of Chinese Affairs. New York: Praeger, 1972.

Hartz, Louis. *The Liberal Tradition in America.* New York: Harcourt, Brace and World, Harvest Books, 1955.

Havens, Thomas R. H. *Farm and Nation in Modern Japan: Agrarian Nationalism, 1870–1940.* Princeton, N.J.: Princeton University Press, 1974.

Hayes, Carlton J. H. *Essays on Nationalism.* New York: Macmillan, 1928.

Hayes, Carlton J. H. *The Historical Evolution of Modern Nationalism.* New York: Macmillan, 1950.

Heer, Nancy Whittier. *Politics and History in the Soviet Union.* Cambridge: MIT Press, 1940.

Hegel, Georg Wilhelm Friedrich. *The Philosophy of History*. Translated by J. Sibree and with an introduction by C. J. Friedrich. New York: Dover Publications, 1956.

————. *Hegel's Philosophy of Right*. Translated and with notes by T. M. Knox. Reprint. New York: Oxford University Press, paperback, 1967.

Heitman, Sidney, comp. and ed. *Nikolai I. Bukharin: A Bibliography*. Hoover Institution Bibliographical Series, vol. 37. Stanford, Calif.: Hoover Institution on War, Revolution, and Peace, Stanford University, 1969.

Hilferding, Rudolf. *Finance Capital: A Study of the Latest Phase of Capitalist Development* [Das Finanzkapital, 1910]. Edited and with an Introduction by Tom Bottomore and translated by Morris Watnick and Sam Gordon. London: Routledge and Kegan Paul, 1981.

Hindess, Barry and Hirst, Paul Q. *Pre-Capitalist Modes of Production*. London: Routledge and Kegan Paul, 1975.

Hinton, William. *Fanshen: A Documentary of Revolution in a Chinese Village*. New York: Alfred A. Knopf, and Random House, Vintage Books, 1966.

Hintze, Otto. *The Historical Essays of Otto Hintze*. Edited by Felix Gilbert. New York: Oxford University Press, 1975.

Hitler, Adolf. *Mein Kampf*. Translated by James Murphy. London: Hurst and Blackett, 1939.

Hobsbawm, E. J. *Nations and Nationalism since 1780: Programme, Myth, Reality*. Cambridge: Cambridge University Press, 1990.

Hoffman, Stanley. *Gulliver's Troubles, Or the Setting of American Foreign Policy*. Atlantic Policy Studies. New York: McGraw Hill for the Council on Foreign Relations, 1968.

Hofheinz, Roy, Jr. *The Broken Wave: The Chinese Communist Peasant Movement, 1922–1928*. Harvard East Asian Series, no. 90. Cambridge, Mass.: Harvard University Press, 1977.

Hook, Sidney. *From Hegel to Marx: Studies in the Intellectual Development of Karl Marx*. New York: Humanities Press, 1950.

Hoston, Germaine A. *Faith, Will, and Revolutionary Change: Modernity and Liberation in the Non-Western World*. Princeton, N.J.: Princeton University Press, forthcoming.

————. *Marxism and the Crisis of Development in Prewar Japan*. Princeton, N.J.: Princeton University Press, 1986.

Howe, David Walker. *The Unitarian Conscience: Harvard Moral Philosophy, 1805–1861*. Cambridge, Mass.: Harvard University Press, 1970.

Hsiao, Kung-ch'üan. *A Modern China and a New World: K'ang Yu-wei, Reformer and Utopian, 1858–1927*. Seattle: University of Washington Press, 1975.

Hsiao, Kung-chuan. *A History of Chinese Political Thought*. Translated by F. W. Mote. Princeton Library of Asian Translations. Vol. 1, *From the Beginnings to the Sixth Century A.D.* 2 vols. Princeton, N.J.: Princeton University Press, 1979.

Hsiao, Tso-liang. *The Land Revolution in China, 1930–1934: A Study of Documents*. Far Eastern and Russian Institute Publications on Asia, no. 18. Seattle: University of Washington Press, 1969.

Hsüeh, Chün-tu. *Huang Hsing and the Chinese Revolution*. Stanford, Calif.: Stanford University Press, 1961.

Huang, Philip C. *Liang Ch'i-ch'ao and Modern Chinese Liberalism*. Publications on Asia of the Institute for Comparative and Foreign Area Studies, no. 22. Seattle: University of Washington Press, 1972.

Hughes, H. Stuart. *Consciousness and Society: The Reorientation of European Social Thought 1890–1930*. New York: Alfred A. Knopf, 1961.

580

Isaacs, Harold R. *The Tragedy of the Chinese Revolution*. Stanford, Calif.: Stanford University Press, 1951.

Itoh, Makoto. *Value and Crisis: Essays on Marxian Economics in Japan*. New York: Monthly Review Press, 1980.

Jansen, Marius B. *The Japanese and Sun Yat-sen*. Cambridge, Mass.: Harvard University Press, 1954; Stanford, Calif.: Stanford University Press, paper, 1970.

———, ed. *Changing Japanese Attitudes toward Modernization*. Princeton, N.J.: Princeton University Press, 1965.

Japan. Department of Education. *Kokutai no Hongi: Cardinal Principles of the National Entity of Japan*. Translated by John Owen Gauntlett. Edited and with an introduction by Robert King Hall. Cambridge, Mass.: Harvard University Press, 1949.

Jay, Martin. *Marxism and Totality: The Adentures of a Concept from Lukacs to Habermas*. Berkeley: University of California, 1984.

Jervis, Robert. *Perception and Misperception in International Politics*. Princeton, N.J.: Princeton University Press, 1976.

Johnson, Chalmers. *MITI and the Japanese Miracle: The Growth of Industrial Policy 1925–1975*. Stanford, Calif.: Stanford University Press, 1982.

———. *Peasant Nationalism and Communist Power: The Emergence of Revolutionary China, 1937–1945*. Stanford, Calif.: Stanford University Press, 1962.

———. *Revolutionary Change*. Boston: N.p., 1966.

Kamachi, Noriko, John K. Fairbank, and Ichiko Chūzō, comps. *Japanese Studies of Modern China since 1953: A Bibliographical Guide to Historical and Social Science Research on the Nineteenth and Twentieth Centuries, Supplementary Volume for 1953–1969*. Cambridge, Mass.: Harvard University Press for the East Asian Research Center, 1975.

Kamenka, Eugene, ed. *Nationalism: The Nature and Evolution of an Idea*. London: N.p., 1976.

Kedward, Roderick. *The Anarchists: The Men Who Shocked an Era*. London: Macdonald Unit 75; New York: American Heritage Press, 1971.

Keesing's Research Report no. 3. *The Sino-Soviet Dispute*. New York: Charles Scribner, 1969.

Kelley, Robert. *The Cultural Pattern in American Politics: The First Century*. New York: Alfred A. Knopf, Borzoi Books, 1979.

Kelly, George Armstrong. *Hegel's Retreat from Eleusis: Studies in Political Thought*. Princeton, N.J.: Princeton University Press, 1978.

Kemilainen, Aira. *Nationalism: Problems Concerning the Word, the Concept, and Classification*. Jyvaskyla, N.p., 1964.

Kirkup, Thomas. *A History of Socialism*. London: Adam and Charles Black, 1913.

Knei-paz, Baruch. *The Social and Political Thought of Leon Trotsky*. Oxford: Oxford University Press, Clarendon Press, 1978.

Kohn, Hans. *The Idea of Nationalism: A Study in its Origins and Background*. New York: Macmillan, 1967.

Kolakowski, Leszek. *Main Currents of Marxism: Its Rise, Growth, and Dissolution*. Vol. 1, *The Founders*. 3 vols. Oxford: Oxford University Press, Clarendon Press, 1978.

Kolko, Gabriel. *The Triumph of Conservatism*. Chicago, Ill.: Quadrangle, 1963.

Kolko, Joyce, and Gabriel Kolko. *The Limits of Power*. New York: Harper and Row, 1972.

Kosaka Masaaki. *Japanese Thought in the Meiji Era*. Translated David Abosch. Tokyo: Pan-Pacific Press, 1958.

Kraus, Richard Curt. *Class Conflict in Chinese Socialism*. New York: Columbia University Press, 1981.

Krivtsov, V. A., and V. Y. Sidikhmenov, eds. *A Critique of Mao Tse-tung's Theoretical Conceptions*. Translated by Yuri Sdobnikov. Moscow: Progress Publishers, 1972.

Kropotkin, Peter. *The Conquest of Bread*. New York: Vanguard Press, 1927.

———. *Fields, Factories and Workshops or Industry Combined with Agriculture and Brain Work with Manual Work*. Rev. and enl. ed. New York: Benjamin Blom, 1913.

Kubálková, V., and A. A. Cruickshank. *Marxism-Leninism and Theory of International Relations*. London: Routledge and Kegan Paul, 1980.

Kublin, Hyman. *Asian Revolutionary: The Life of Sen Katayama*. Princeton, N.J.: Princeton University Press, 1964.

Kuhn, Thomas S. *The Structure of Scientific Revolutions*. Foundations of the Unity of Science, vol. 2. 2d ed., enl. Chicago: University of Chicago Press, 1970.

Kuo, Thomas C. *Ch'en Tu-hsiu (1879–1942) and the Chinese Communist Movement*. South Orange, N.J.: Seton Hall University Press, 1975.

Labedz, Leopold, ed. *Revisionism: Essays on the History of Marxist Ideas*. New York: Praeger, 1962.

Lane, David. *Politics and Society in the USSR*. Rev. ed. New York: New York University Press, 1982.

Lawrance, Alan. *Mao Zedong: A Bibliography*. New York: Greenwood Press, 1991.

Lee, Feigon. *Chen Duxiu: Founder of the Chinese Communist Party*. Princeton, N.J.: Princeton University Press, 1983.

Legge, James, comp. and trans. *The Four Books*. Reprint. Taipei: Ch'eng-wen Publishing, 1971.

Lenin, V. I. *The Development of Capitalism in Russia: The Process of the Formation of a Home Market for Large-Scale Industry*. 2d rev. ed. Moscow: Progress Publishers, 1964.

———. *Imperialism, the Highest Stage of Capitalism*. Peking: Foreign Languages Press, n.d.

———. *The Lenin Anthology*. Edited by Robert C. Tucker. New York: W. W. Norton, 1975.

———. *Lenin on Politics and Revolution: Selected Writings*. Edited with an introduction by James E. Connor. Indianapolis, Ind.: Bobbs-Merrill, Pegasus; New York: Webster Publishing, 1968.

Lerner, Warren. *Karl Radek: The Last Internationalist*. Stanford, Calif.: Stanford University Press, 1970.

Levenson, Joseph R. *Confucian China and Its Modern Fate: A Trilogy*. 3 vols. Berkeley and Los Angeles: University of California Press, Campus Books, 1958, 1964, 1965.

———. *Liang Ch'i-ch'ao and the Mind of Modern China*. Cambridge, Mass.: Harvard University Press, 1953.

Lewin, Moshe. *Political Undercurrents in Soviet Economic Debates: From Bukharin to the Modern Reformers*. Princeton, N.J.: Princeton University Press, 1974.

———. *Russian Peasants and Soviet Power: A Study of Collectivization*. Translated by Irene Nove and with a preface by Alec Nove. New York: W. W. Norton, Norton Library, 1975.

Li, Chien-nung. *The Political History of China, 1840–1928*. Translated and edited by Ssu-yu Teng and Jeremy Ingalls. N.p.: D. Van Nostrand, 1956. Stanford, Calif.: Stanford University Press, 1967.

Li, Yü-ning. *The Introduction of Socialism into China*. Occasional Papers of the Asian Institute, Columbia University. New York: Columbia University Press, 1971.

Lichtheim, George. *Marxism: An Historical and Critical Study*. New York: Praeger, 1961.

Liew, K. S. *Struggle for Democracy: Sung Chiao-jen and the 1911 Chinese Revolution*. Berkeley: University of California Press, 1971.

Lin, Yü-sheng. *The Crisis of Chinese Consciousness: Radical Anti-Traditionalism in the May Fourth Era*. With a foreword by Benjamin I. Schwartz. Madison: University of Wisconsin Press, 1979.

Linden, Carl A. *Khrushchev and the Soviet Leadership, 1957–1964*. Baltimore, Md.: Johns Hopkins University Press, 1966.

Liu, Chun-jo. *Controversies in Modern Chinese Intellectual History: An Analytic Bibliography of Periodical Articles, Mainly of the May Fourth and Post-May Fourth Era*. Cambridge, Mass.: East Asian Research Center, Harvard University, 1973.

Liu, Shao-chi. *How to Be a Good Communist (Lectures Delivered at the Institute of Marxism-Leninism in Yenan, July 1939)*. Boulder, Colo.: Panther Publications, 1958.

Locke, John. *The Second Treatise on Government*. Edited and with an introduction by Thomas P. Peardon. Indianapolis, Ind.: Bobbs-Merrill, 1952, 1980.

Lockwood, William. *The Economic Development of Japan: Growth and Structural Change, 1868–1938*. Princeton, N.J.: Princeton University Press, 1954.

———, ed. *The State and Economic Enterprise in Japan: Essays in the Political Economy of Growth*. Studies in the Modernization of Japan. Princeton, N.J.: Princeton University Press, 1965.

Lowe, Donald M. *The Function of "China" in Marx, Lenin, and Mao*. Berkeley: University of California Press, 1966.

Löwith, Karl. *From Hegel to Nietzsche*. Translated by David E. Green. New York: N.p., 1967.

Lukács, Georg. *History and Class Consciousness: Studies in Marxist Dialectics*. Translated by Rodney Livingstone. Cambridge, Mass.: MIT Press, 1971.

———. *Lenin: A Study in the Unity of His Thought*. Translated by Nicholas Jacobs. Cambridge, Mass.: The MIT Press, 1971.

Luxemburg, Rosa. *The Russian Revolution: Leninism or Marxism?* With an introduction by Bertram D. Wolfe. Ann Arbor: University of Michigan Press, Ann Arbor Paperbacks, 1970.

MacFarquhar, Robert. *The Origins of the Cultural Revolution*. 2 vols. New York: Columbia University Press, 1987.

MacFarquhar, Roderick, Timothy Cheek, and Eugene Wu, eds. *The Secret Speeches of Chairman Mao: From the Hundred Flowers to the Great Leap Forward*. Harvard Contemporary China Series, no. 6. Cambridge, Mass.: Council on East Asian Studies, Harvard University, 1989.

Machiavelli, Niccolò. *The Discourses*. Edited by Bernard Crick. Harmondsworth: Penguin Books, Ltd., 1970.

Maguire, John M. *Marx's Theory of Politics*. Cambridge: Cambridge University Press, 1979.

Mao Tse-tung. *Mao Tse-tung Unrehearsed: Talks and Letters, 1956–1971*. Translated by John Chinnery and Tieyun. Edited and with an introduction by Stuart R. Schram. Harmondsworth: Penguin, 1974.

———. *On New Democracy*. Peking: Foreign Languages Press, 1967.

———. *Selected Works of Mao Tse-tung*. 5 vols. Peking: Foreign Languages Press, 1967, 1977.

Mao Zedong. *The Writings of Mao Zedong, 1949–1976*. Edited by Michael Y. M. Kau and John K. Leung. Vol. 1: *September 1949–December 1955*. Armonk, N.Y.: M. E. Sharpe, 1986.

Marcuse, Herbert. *One-Dimensional Man: Studies in the Ideology of Advanced Industrial Societies*. Boston: Beacon Press, 1964.

————. *Soviet Marxism: A Critical Analysis.* New York: Columbia University Press, 1958.

Maruyama, Masao. *Thought and Behavior in Modern Japanese Politics.* Translated by Ivan Morris. Expanded ed. Oxford: Oxford University Press, 1969.

Marx, Karl. *Capital.* Edited by Frederick Engels and translated by Samuel Moore and Edward Aveling. Vol. 1, *A Critical Analysis of Capitalist Production.* 3 vols. New York, International Publishers, New World Paperbacks, 1967.

————. *Capital.* Edited by Friedrich Engels. Vol. 3, *The Process of Capitalist Production as a Whole.* 3 vols. New York: International Publishers, New World Paperbacks, 1967.

————. *Critique of Hegel's "Philosophy of Right."* Edited and with an introduction by Joseph O'Malley and translated by Annette Jolin and Joseph O'Malley. Cambridge Studies in the History and Theory of Politics. Cambridge: Cambridge University Press, paperback ed., 1977.

————. *The Poverty of Philosophy.* With an introduction by Friedrich Engels. New York: International Publishers, New World Paperbacks, 1963.

————. *Pre-Capitalist Economic Formations.* Translated by Jack Cohen and with an introduction by Eric J. Hobsbawm. New York: International Publishers, New World Paperbacks, 1965.

Marx, Karl, and Friedrich Engels. *The Holy Family, or, Critique of Critical Criticism.* In *The Marx-Engels Reader* (Die heilige Familie), translated by Richard Dixon and Clemens Dutt. 2d ed., rev. Moscow: Progress Publishers, 1975.

————. *Selected Correspondence.* Translated by Dona Torr. Marxist Library, vol. 29. New York: International Publishers, 1942. Reprint. Westport, Conn.: Greenwood Press, 1975.

Massell, Gregory J. *The Surrogate Proletariat: Moslem Women and Revolutionary Strategies in Soviet Central Asia, 1919–1929.* Princeton, N.J.: Princeton University Press, 1974.

Masur, Gerhard. *Prophets of Yesterday: Studies in European Culture 1890–1914.* New York: Harper and Row, 1966.

Meinecke, Friedrich. *The German Catastrophe: The Social and Historical Influences which Led to the Rise and Ruin of Hitler and Germany.* Translated and with a preface by Sidney B. Fay. Reprint. Cambridge, Mass.: Harvard University Press, 1950; Boston: Beacon Press, Beacon Paperbacks, 1963.

Meisner, Maurice. *Li Ta-chao and the Origins of Chinese Marxism.* Cambridge, Mass.: Harvard University Press, 1967; New York: Atheneum, 1979.

————. *Marxism, Maoism and Utopianism.* Madison: University of Wisconsin, 1982.

Menshikov, S. *Millionaires and Managers.* Moscow: Progress Publishers, 1969.

Merton, R. K. *Social Theory and Social Structure.* N.p.: N.p., 1949.

Metzger, Thomas A. *Escape from Predicament: Neo-Confucianism and China's Evolving Political Culture.* New York: Columbia University Press, 1977.

Miliband, Ralph. *The State in Capitalistic Society.* New York: Basic Books, 1969.

Miller, Frank O. *Minobe Tatsukichi: Interpreter of Constitutionalism in Japan.* Berkeley: University of California Press, 1965.

Mills, C. Wright. *The Power Elite.* New York: Oxford University Press, Galaxy Books, 1956, 1959.

Mitchell, Richard H. *Thought Control in Prewar Japan.* Ithaca, N.Y.: Cornell University Press, 1976.

Moore, Barrington. *Social Origins of Dictatorship and Democracy: Lord and Peasant in the Making of the Modern World.* Boston: Beacon Press, 1966.

Moore, Stanley W. *The Critique of Capitalist Democracy: An Introduction to the Theory of the State in Marx, Engels, and Lenin*. Reprint. New York: Paine-Whitman Publishers, 1957; New York: Augustus M. Kelley, 1969.

Morley, James W., ed. *Dilemmas of Growth in Prewar Japan*. Princeton, N.J.: Princeton University Press, 1971.

Mosala, Itumeleng J., and Buti Tlhagale. *The Unquestionable Right to Be Free: Black Theology from South Africa*. Maryknoll, N.Y.: Orbis Books, 1986.

Mosse, George L. *The Crisis of German Ideology: The Intellectual Origins of the Third Reich*. New York: Grosset and Dunlap, 1964.

Nakamura, Takafusa. *The Postwar Japanese Economy: Its Development and Structure*. Translated by Jacqueline Kaminski. Tokyo: University of Tokyo Press, 1981.

Nakane, Chie. *Japanese Society*. Berkeley: University of California under the auspices of the Center for Japanese and Korean Studies, 1970.

Nathan, Andrew J. *Chinese Democracy*. Berkeley: University of California Press, 1985, paperback ed., 1986.

Nettl, J. P. *Rosa Luxemburg*. 2 vols. London: Oxford University Press, 1966.

Neumann, Franz. *Behemoth: The Structure and Practice of National Socialism, 1933–1944*. New York: Oxford University Press, 1941; reprint, New York: Octagon Books, n.d.

Nietsche, Friedrich. *Beyond Good and Evil: Prelude to a Philosophy of the Future*. Translated and with commentary by Walter Kaufmann. New York: Random House, Vintage Books, 1966.

Nolte, Ernst. *Three Faces of Fascism: Action Française, Italian Fascism, National Socialism*. Translated by Leila Vannewitz. New York: Holt, Rinehart and Winston, 1966.

Norman, E. Herbert. *Japan's Emergence as a Modern State: Political and Economic Problems of the Meiji Period*. Westport, Conn.: Greenwood Press, 1973.

North, Robert C. *Moscow and Chinese Communists*. 2d ed. Stanford, Calif.: Stanford University Press, 1953, 1963.

Notehelfer, F. G. *Kōtoku Shūsui: Portrait of a Japanese Radical*. Cambridge: Cambridge University Press, 1971.

Nyerere, Julius K. *Ujamaa: Essays on Socialism*. Oxford: Oxford University Press, 1968.

Ohkawa, Kazushi, and Henry Rosovsky. *Japanese Economic Growth: Trend Acceleration in the Twentieth Century*. Studies of Economic Growth in Industrialized Countries. Stanford, Calif.: Stanford University Press, 1973.

Ollman, Bertell. *Alienation: Marx's Conception of Man in Capitalist Society*. New York: Cambridge University Press, 1971.

Parsons, Talcott. *The Social System*. New York: Free Press of Glencoe, 1951, 1964.

Patterson, Orlando. *Freedom*. Vol. 1, *Freedom in the Making of Western Culture*. N.p.: Basic Books, 1991.

Peck, Graham. *Two Kinds of Time*. 2d ed., rev. and enl. Boston: Houghton Mifflin, 1967.

P'eng Shu-tse [Peng Shuzhi]. *The Chinese Communist Party in Power*. Edited by Leslie Evans. New York: Monad Press, 1980.

Pipes, Richard. *The Formation of the Soviet Union: Communism and Nationalism, 1917–1923*. Rev. ed. New York: N.p., 1968.

Pittau, Joseph, S.J. *Political Thought in Early Meiji Japan, 1866–1889*. Harvard East Asian Series, no. 24. Cambridge, Mass.: Harvard University Press, 1967.

Plamenatz, John. *Karl Marx's Philosophy of Man*. Oxford: Oxford University Press, 1978.

Plato. *The Republic*. Translated by Allan Bloom. New York: Basic Books, 1968.

Plekhanov, George V. *Fundamental Problems of Marxism*. New York: International Publishers, 1969.

Poulantzas, Nicos. *Political Power and Social Classes*. London: New Left Books and Sheed and Ward, 1973.

———. *State, Power, Socialism*. London: N.p., 1978.

Poulantzas, Nicos, and François Maspero. *Political Power and Social Classes*. London. New Left Books and Sheed and Ward, 1973, 1975.

Price, Don C. *Russia and the Roots of the Chinese Revolution, 1896–1911*. Harvard East Asian Series, no. 79. Cambridge, Mass.: Harvard University Press, 1974.

Proudhon, P. J. *What is Property? An Inquiry into the Principle of Right and of Government*. Translated by Benjamin R. Tucker. 2 vols. London: William Reeves, 1902.

Rankin, Mary Backus. *Early Chinese Revolutionaries: Radical Intellectuals in Shanghai and Chekiang, 1902–1911*. Harvard East Asian Series, no. 46. Cambridge, Mass.: Harvard University Press, 1971.

Reclus, Elisée. *An Anarchist on Anarchy*. London: J. Tochatti, 1897.

Resolution on CPC History (1949–1981). Beijing, Foreign Languages Press, 1981.

Rigby, T. H. *Communist Party Membership in the U.S.S.R., 1917–1967*. Princeton, N.J.: Princeton University Press, 1968.

Rizzi, Bruno. *The Bureaucratization of the World*. Translated and with an introduction by Adam Westoby. New York: Macmillan, Free Press, 1985.

Rodinson, Maxime. *Islam and Capitalism*. Translated by Brian Pearce. New York: Random House, Pantheon Books, 1973.

Roth, Jack J. *The Cult of Violence: Sorel and the Sorelians*. Berkeley: University of California Press, 1980.

Rousseau, Jean-Jacques. *The Social Contract*. Translated and with an introduction by Maurice Cranston. Harmondsworth: Penguin Books, 1968.

Rue, John E. *Mao Tse-tung in Opposition: 1927–1935*. Stanford, Calif.: Stanford University Press, 1966.

Russell, Bertrand. *German Social Democracy*. New York: Simon and Schuster, 1965.

Ryckmans, Pierre (Leys, Simon). *Chinese Shadows*. New York: Viking Press, 1977.

Sabine, George H. *A History of Political Theory*. 3d ed. New York: Holt, Rinehart and Winston, 1961.

Said, Edward W. *Orientalism*. New York: Random House, Vintage Books, 1978, 1979.

Sansom, George. *A History of Japan*. Vol. 3, *1615–1867*. 3 vols. Stanford, Calif.: Stanford University Press, 1963.

Sartre, Jean-Paul. *Anti-Semite and Jew*. N.p.: N.p., 1946.

Scalapino, Robert A. *Democracy and the Party Movement in Prewar Japan*. Berkeley: University of California Press, 1953.

———. *The Japanese Communist Movement, 1920–1966*. Berkeley: University of California Press, 1967.

Scalapino, Robert A., and G. T. Yu. *The Chinese Anarchist Movement*. Berkeley: University of California Press, 1961.

Schapiro, Leonard. *The Communist Party of the Soviet Union*. 2d ed., rev. and enl. London: Eyre and Spottiswoode, 1960; New York: Random House, Vintage Books, 1971.

Schiffrin, Harold Z. *Sun Yat-sen and Origins of the Chinese Revolution*. Berkeley: University of California Press, 1968.

Schorske, Carl. *German Social Democracy, 1905–1917: The Development of the Great Schism*. New York: J. Wiley, 1955, 1965.

Schram, Stuart. *Mao Tse-tung*. Harmondsworth: Penguin Books, 1966.

———. *The Thought of Mao Tse-tung*. Contemporary China Institute Publications. Cambridge: Cambridge University Press, 1989.

————, ed. *The Political Thought of Mao Tse-tung*. Rev. and enl. ed. New York: Praeger, 1969.

Schrecker, John. *Imperialism and Chinese Nationalism: Germany in Shantung*. Cambridge, Mass.: Harvard University Press, 1971.

Schurmann, Franz. *Ideology and Organization in Communist China*. Berkeley: University of California Press, 1968.

Schwartz, Benjamin I. *Chinese Communism and the Rise of Mao*. Cambridge, Mass.: Harvard University Press, 1951, 1979.

————. *In Search of Wealth and Power: Yen Fu and the West*. Cambridge, Mass.: Harvard University Press, Belknap Press, 1964.

————. *The World of Thought in Ancient China*. Cambridge, Mass.: Harvard University Press, 1985.

————, ed. *Reflections on the May Fourth Movement: A Symposium*. Harvard East Asian Series, no. 44. Cambridge, Mass.: Harvard University Press, 1972.

Selden, Mark. *The Yenan Way in Revolutionary China*. Harvard East Asian Series, no. 62. Cambridge, Mass.: Harvard University Press, 1971.

Selected Articles Criticizing Lin Piao and Confucius. Beijing: Foreign Languages Press, 1974.

Seymour, James D., ed. *The Fifth Modernization: China's Human Rights Movement 1978–1979*. With an introduction by Mab Huang and James D. Seymour. Stanfordville, N.Y.: Earl M. Coleman Enterprises, Human Rights Publishing Group, 1980.

Sharmon, Lyon. *Sun Yat-sen: His Life and Its Meaning*. With an introduction by Lyman P. Van Slyke. N.p.: Johns Day Company, Stanford, Calif.: Stanford University Press, 1968.

Shillony, Ben-Ami. *Politics and Culture in Wartime Japan*. Oxford: Oxford University Press, 1981.

————. *Revolt in Japan: The Young Officers and the February 26, 1936 Incident*. Princeton, N.J.: Princeton University Press, 1973.

Shteppa, Konstantin F. *Russian Historians and the Soviet State*. New Brunswick, N.J.: Rutgers University Press, 1962.

Shue, Vivienne. *Peasant China in Transition: The Dynamics of Development towards Socialism, 1949–1956*. Berkeley: University of California Press, 1980.

————. *The Reach of the State: Sketches of the Chinese Body Politic*. Stanford, Calif. Stanford University Press, 1988.

Silberman, Bernard S., and H. D. Harootunian, eds. *Japan in Crisis: Essays on Taishō Democracy*. Princeton, N.J.: Princeton University Press, 1974.

Skocpol, Theda. *States and Social Revolutions: A Comparative Analysis of France, Russia, and China*. Cambridge: Cambridge University Press, 1979.

Smethurst, Richard J. *A Social Basis for Prewar Japanese Militarism: The Army and the Rural Community*. Berkeley: University of California Press, 1974.

Smith, Anthony D. *Theories of Nationalism*. New York: Harper and Rowe, 1971.

Smith, Thomas C. *Agrarian Origins of Modern Japan*. Stanford, Calif.: Stanford University Press, 1959.

Snow, Edgar. *Red Star Over China*. New York: Random House, 1938.

Solomon, Richard H. *Mao's Revolution and the Chinese Political Culture*. Michigan Studies on China. Berkeley: University of California Press, 1971, 1972.

Somerville, John, and Ronald E. Santoni. *Social and Political Philosophy*. New York: Doubleday, Anchor Books, 1963.

Sorel, Georges. *Reflections on Violence*. Translated by T. E. Hulme. New York: Peter Smith, 1941.

Stalin, Joseph. *Problems of Leninism*. Moscow, N.p., 1940.

Stanley, Thomas A. *Ōsugi Sakae, Anarchist in Taishō Japan: The Creativity of the Ego*. Cambridge, Mass.: Council on East Asian Studies, Harvard University, 1982.

Starr, John Bryan. *Continuing the Revolution: The Political Thought of Mao*. Princeton, N.J.: Princeton University Press, 1979.

Steinbruner, John D. *The Cybernetic Theory of Decision: New Dimensions of Political Analysis*. Princeton, N.J.: Princeton University Press, 1974.

Stepan, Alfred. *The State and Society: Peru in Comparative Perspective*. Princeton, N.J.: Princeton University Press, 1978.

Stojanović, Svetozar. *Between Ideals and Reality: A Critique of Socialism and Its Future*. Translated by Gerson S. Sher. New York: Oxford University Press, 1973.

Storry, Richard. *The Double Patriots: A Study of Japanese Nationalism*. Boston: Houghton Mifflin, and Cambridge: Riverside Press, 1957.

Su Shaozhi. *Democracy and Socialism in China*. Nottingham, England: Spokesman, 1982.

Sun, Yat-sen. *Sun Yat-sen: His Political and Social Ideals*. Compiled, translated, and edited by Leonard Shihlien Hsu. Los Angeles: University of Southern California Press, 1933.

Suny, Ronald Grigor. *The Baku Commune 1917–1918: Class and Nationality in the Russian Revolution*. Princeton, N.J.: Princeton University Press, 1972.

Swearingen, Rodger, and Paul Langer. *Red Flag in Japan: International Communism in Action, 1919–1951*. Cambridge, Mass.: Harvard University Press, 1952.

Sweezy, Paul et al. *The Transition from Feudalism to Capitalism*. With an introduction by Rodney Hilton. London: New Left Books and Atlantic Highlands, N.J.: Humanities Press, 1976.

Szporluk, Roman. *Communism and Nationalism: Karl Marx versus Friedrich List*. New York: Oxford University Press, 1988.

Talmon, J. L. *The Myth of the Nation and the Vision of Revolution: The Origins of Ideological Polarisation in the Twentieth Century*. London: Secker and Warburg, and Berkeley: University of California Press, 1980.

Tarschys, Daniel. *Beyond the State: The Future Polity in Classical and Soviet Marxism*. Swedish Studies in International Relations, no. 3. Stockholm: Laromedelsförlagen, Scandinavian University Books, 1972.

Taylor, A. J. P. *The Course of German History*. 2d ed. London: N.p., 1945.

Teng, S. Y. and Fairbank, J. K. *China's Response to the West: A Documentary Survey, 1839–1923*. Cambridge, Mass.: Harvard University Press, 1954.

Thornton, Richard C. *The Comintern and the Chinese Communists, 1928–1931*. Seattle: University of Washington Press, 1969.

Tilly, Charles. *The Formation of National States in Western Europe*. Studies in Political Development, no. 8. Princeton, N.J.: Princeton University Press, 1975.

———. *From Mobilization to Revolution*. Reading, Mass.: Addison-Wesley, 1978.

Tilly, Charles, Louise Tilly, and Richard Tilly. *The Rebellious Century, 1830–1930*. Cambridge, Mass.: Harvard University Press, 1975.

Titus, David Anson. *Palace and Politics in Prewar Japan*. New York: Columbia University Press, 1974.

Torr, Dona. *Marx on China 1853–60*. London: Lawrence and Wishart, 1951.

Totten, George Oakley III. *The Social Democratic Movement in Prewar Japan*. Studies on Japan's Social Democratic Parties, no. 1. New Haven, Conn.: Yale University Press, 1966.

Townsend, James R. *Political Participation in Communist China*. Berkeley: University of California Press, 1967.

Tönnies, Ferdinand. *Community and Society*. Translated and edited by Charles P. Loomis. East Lansing: Michigan State University Press, 1957.

Trimberger, Ellen Kay. *Revolutions from Above: Military Bureaucrats and Modernization in Japan, Turkey, Egypt, and Peru*. New Brunswick, N.J.: Transaction Books, 1978.

————. *The Permanent Revolution, and Results and Prospects* (Permanentnaia revoliutsiia). New York: Merit Publishers, 1969.

————. *Problems of the Chinese Revolution*. Translated and with a foreword by Max Schachtman. Reprint. Ann Arbor: University of Michigan Press, Ann Arbor Paperbacks, 1967.

————. *The Revolution Betrayed: What Is the Soviet Union and Where Is It Going?* New York: Pathfinder Press, 1972.

————. *1905*. (Tsyiacha deviatsot piatyi). Translated by Anya Bostock. New York: Random House, 1971.

Tsou, Tang. *The Cultural Revolution and Post-Mao Reforms: A Historical Perspective*. Chicago: University of Chicago Press, 1986.

Tucker, Robert C. *The Marxian Revolutionary Idea*. New York: W. W. Norton, 1970.

————. *Philosophy and Myth in Karl Marx*. 2d ed. London: Cambridge University Press, 1972.

————. *The Soviet Political Mind*. Rev. ed. New York: W. W. Norton, 1971, Norton Library, 1972.

————. *Stalin as Revolutionary, 1879–1929: A Study in History and Personality*. New York: W. W. Norton, Norton Library, 1973.

————, ed. *The Lenin Anthology*. New York: W. W. Norton, 1975.

————, ed. *The Marx-Engels Reader*. New York: W. W. Norton, 1972; rev. ed., 1978.

Turner, Bryan S. *Marx and the End of Orientalism*. Controversies in Sociology, no. 7. London: George Allen and Unwin, 1978.

Ulam, Adam B. *The Bolsheviks: The Intellectual, Personal and Political History of the Triumph of Communism in Russia*. New York: Macmillan, 1965; New York: Collier Books, 1968.

Uyehara, Cecil H. *Leftwing Social Movements in Japan: An Annotated Bibliography*. Tokyo: Charles E. Tuttle, 1959.

Vajda, Mihaly. *The State and Socialism: Political Essays*. London: Allison and Busby, 1981.

Venturi, Franco. *Roots of Revolution: A History of the Populist and Socialist Movements in Nineteenth Century Russia*. With an introduction by Isaiah Berlin and translated by Francis Haskell. New York: Grosset and Dunlap, Universal Library, 1966.

von Klemperer, Klemens. *Germany's New Conservatism: Its History and Dilemma in the Twentieth Century*. With a foreword by Sigmund Neumann. Princeton, N.J.: Princeton University Press, 1957, 1968.

Wakeman, Frederic, Jr. *History and Will: Philosophical Perspectives of Mao Tse-tung's Thought*. Berkeley: University of California Press, 1973, Campus Books, 1975.

Wallerstein, Immanuel. *The Modern World-System: Capitalist Agriculture and the Origins of the European World-Economy in the Sixteenth Century*. New York: Academic Press, 1974.

Wang, Ming. *Mao's Betrayal*. Translated by Vic Schneierson. Moscow: Progress Publishers, 1979.

Wang, Y. C. *Chinese Intellectuals and the West, 1872–1949*. Chapel Hill: University of North Carolina Press, 1966.

Ward, Robert E., ed. *Political Development in Modern Japan*. Princeton, N.J.: Princeton University Press, 1968.

Watkins, F. M. *The State as a Concept of Political Science*. Studies in Systematic Political Science and Comparative Government, no. 3. New York and London: Harper and Brothers, 1934.

Weber, Max. *From Max Weber: Essays in Sociology*. Translated and edited by H. H. Gerth and C. Wright Mills. New York: Oxford University Press, 1946, paperback, 1958.

———. *Max Weber on Law in Economy and Society* (*Wirtschaft und Gesellschaft*, 1925). Translated by Edward Shils and Max Rheinstein. 2d ed. Cambridge, Mass.: Harvard University Press, 1954.

[Weber, Max]. *Max Weber: The Theory of Social and Economic Organization*. Edited by Talcott Parsons and translated by A. M. Henderson and Talcott Parsons. New York: Oxford University Press, 1947; New York: Macmillan Publishing, Free Press, 1964.

Weinstein, James. *The Corporate Ideal in the Liberal State*. Boston: Beacon Press, 1968.

Widor, Claude, ed. *Documents on the Chinese Democratic Movement, 1978–1980: Unofficial Magazines and Wall Posters*. Vol. 1. Paris: Ecole des Hautes Etudes en Sciences Sociales and Hong Kong; Observer Publishers, 1981.

Wilbur, C. Martin. *Sun Yat-sen: Frustrated Patriot*. New York: Columbia University Press, 1976.

Wilson, George M. *Radical Nationalist in Japan: Kita Ikki, 1883–1937*. Cambridge, Mass.: Harvard University Press, 1969.

Wittfogel, Karl A. *Oriental Despotism: A Comparative Study of Total Power*. New Haven, Conn.: Yale University Press, 1957.

Wolf, Eric R. *Europe and the People without History*. Berkeley: University of California Press, 1982.

Womack, Brantly. *The Foundations of Mao Zedong's Political Thought, 1917–1935*. Honolulu: University Press of Hawaii, 1982.

Woodcock, George. *Anarchism: A History of Libertarian Ideas and Movements*. Cleveland, Ohio: World Publishing, Meridian Books, 1962.

Wright, Mary Clabaugh. *The Last Stand of Chinese Conservatism: The T'ung-chih Restoration, 1862–1874*. Stanford, Calif.: Stanford University Press, 1957.

———, ed. *China in Revolution: The First Phase, 1900–1913*. New York: Yale University Press, 1968.

Wylie, Raymond. *The Emergence of Maoism: Mao Tse-tung, Ch'en Po-ta and the Search for Chinese Theory, 1935–1945*. Stanford, Calif.: Stanford University Press, 1980.

Zagoria, Donald S. *The Sino-Sovet Conflict, 1956–1961*. Princeton, N.J.: Princeton University Press, 1962.

Zarrow, Peter G. *Anarchism and Chinese Political Culture*. Studies of the East Asian Institute. New York: Columbia University Press, 1990.

Articles

Ahn, Byung-Joon. "Adjustments in the Great Leap Forward and Their Ideological Legacy, 1959–1962." In *Ideology and Politics in Contemporary China*, edited by Chalmers Johnson, pp. 257–300. Seattle: University of Washington Press, 1973.

Almond, Gabriel A. "Introduction: A Functional Approach to Comparative Politics." In *The Politics of the Developing Areas*. Edited by Gabriel A. Almond and James S. Coleman, pp. 3–64. Princeton, N.J.: Princeton University Press, 1960.

———. "Political Systems and Political Change." In *State and Society: A Reader in*

Comparative Sociology, edited by Reinhard Bendix in collaboration with Conrad Brand et al., pp. 28–42. Boston: Little, Brown and Company, 1968; Berkeley: University of California Press, Campus Books, 1973.

Althusser, Louis. "Ideology and Ideological State Apparatuses." In Louis Althusser, *Lenin and Philosophy, and Other Essays*, translated by Ben Brewster, pp. 127–186. New York: Monthly Review Press, 1971.

Anesaki, Masaharu. "Review of Robert Cornell Armstrong, *Light from the East*; Studies in Japanese Confucianism." *Harvard Theological Review* 8 (1915): 563–571.

Avineri, Shlomo. "The Hegelian Origins of Marx's Political Thought." In *Marx's Socialism*, edited by Shlomo Avineri, pp. 1–18. New York: Lieber-Atherton, 1972.

———. "Introduction." In *Marx's Socialism*, edited by Shlomo Avineri, pp. ix–xiii. New York: Lieber-Atherton, 1972.

Bailey, Jackson H. "Prince Saionji and the Popular Rights Movement of the 1880s." *Journal of Asian Studies* 21 (November 1961): 49–63.

Bakunin, Michael. "Federalism, Socialism, Anti-Theologism." (1867) In *Bakunin on Anarchy: Selected Works by the Activist-Founder of World Anarchism*, edited by Sam Dolgoff, translated and with an introduction and preface by Paul Avrich, pp. 102–147. New York: Alfred A. Knopf, 1972.

———. "The International and Karl Marx." (1872) In *Bakunin on Anarchy: Selected Works by the Activist-Founder of World Anarchism*, edited by Sam Dolgoff, translated and with an introduction and preface by Paul Avrich. New York: Alfred A. Knopf, 1972.

———. "Statism and Anarchy" (1873). In *Bakunin on Anarchy: Selected Works by the Activist Founder of World Anarchism*, edited by Sam Dolgoff and translated with an introduction and preface by Paul Avrich, pp. 323–353. New York: Alfred A. Knopf, 1972.

Balibar, Etienne. "Marx, Engels, and the Revolutionary Party," translated by Elizabeth Fox-Genovese. *Marxist Perspectives* 1, no. 4 (Winter 1978): 124–143.

Barmé, Geremie. "Confession, Redemption, and Death: Liu Xiaobo and the Protest Movement of 1989." In *The Broken Mirror: China after Tiananmen*. Chicago: St. James Press, 1990.

Baron, S. H. "Plekhanov, Trotsky, and the Development of Soviet Historiography." *Soviet Studies* 24, no. 3 (July 1974): 380–395.

Baron, Samuel H. "Plekhanov and the Origins of Russian Marxism." *Russian Review* 13, no. 1 (January 1954): 38–51.

———. "Plekhanov's Russia: The Impact of the West upon an 'Oriental' Society." *Journal of the History of Ideas* 19, no. 3 (June 1958): 388–404.

———. "The Transition from Feudalism to Capitalism in Russia: A Major Soviet Historical Controversy." *American Historical Review* 77, no. 3 (June 1972): 715–729.

Bauer, Otto. "National Character and the Idea of the Nation." Translated by I. A. Langnas. In *Essential Works of Socialism*, edited by Irving Howe, pp. 267–275. New Haven: Yale University Press, 1976.

Beckmann, George. "Japanese Adaptations of Marx-Leninism." In *Studies on the Modernization of Japan by Western Scholars*, pp. 103–114. Asian Cultural Studies, no. 3. Tokyo: International Christian University, 1962.

Beckmann, George. "The Radical Left and the Failure of Communism." In *Dilemmas of Growth in Prewar Japan*, edited by James W. Morley, pp. 139–178. Princeton, N.J.: Princeton University Press, 1971.

Bendix, Reinhard. "Tradition and Modernity Reconsidered." *Comparative Studies in Society and History* 9, no. 3 (April 1967): 292–346.

Benn, Stanley, and William Weinstein. "Being Free to Act, and Being a Free Man." *Mind* (April 1971): 194–211.

Benton, Gregor. "China's Oppositions." *New Left Review* 122 (July–August 1980): 59–78.

Berki, R. N. "On Marxian Thought and the Problem of International Relations." *World Politics* 24, no. 1 (October 1971): 80–105.

Bernal, Martin. "Chinese Socialism before 1913." In *Modern China's Search for a Political Form*, edited by Jack Grey, pp. 66–95. London: Oxford University Press, 1969.

———. "Liu Sifu and Anarchism in China." *Minsheng* [Voice of the people]. Reprint. Hong Kong: Longmen Shudian, 1967.

———. "The Triumph of Anarchism over Marxism, 1906–1907." In *China in Revolution: The First Phase, 1900–1913*, edited and with an introduction by Mary Clabaugh Wright. New Haven, Conn.: Yale University Press, 1971.

———. "The Tzu-yu-tang and Tai Chi-t'ao, 1912–1913." *Modern Asian Studies* 1, no. 2 (April 1967).

Bernstein, Gail. "Kawakami Hajime: A Japanese Marxist in Search of the Way." In *Japan in Crisis: Essays on Taishō Democracy*, edited by Bernard S. Silberman and H. D. Harootunian, pp. 86–109. Princeton, N.J.: Princeton University Press, 1974.

———. "The Russian Revolution, the Early Japanese Socialists, and the Problem of Dogmatism." *Studies in Comparative Communism* 9, no. 4 (Winter 1976): 327–348.

Bernstein, Thomas. "Leadership and Mass Mobilization in the Soviet and Chinese Collectivization Campaigns of 1929–1930 and 1955–1956: A Comparison." *China Quarterly* 31 (July–September 1967): 1–47.

———. "Stalinism, Famine, and Chinese Peasants: Grain Procurements during the Great Leap Forward." *Theory and Society* 13, no. 3 (May 1984): 339–377.

Bing, Don. "Sneevliet and the Early Years of the CCP." *China Quarterly* 48 (October–December 1971): 677–697.

Block, Fred. "The Ruling Class Does Not Rule: Notes on the Marxist Theory of the State." *Socialist Revolution* 33 (May–June 1977): 6–28.

Bloom, Solomon F. "The 'Withering Away' of the State." *Journal of the History of Ideas* 7, no. 1 (January 1946): 113–121.

Boulding, Kenneth E. "National Images and International Systems." *Journal of Conflict Resolution* 3 (June 1959): 120–131.

Bridges, Amy Beth. "Nicos Poulantzas and the Marxist Theory of the State." *Politics and Society* 4, no. 2 (Winter 1974): 161–190.

Brugger, Bill. "From 'Revisionism' to 'Alienation,' from Great Leaps to 'Third Wave'" *China Quarterly* 108 (December 1986): 643–651.

Buci-Glucksmann, Christine. "Hegemony and Consent." In *Approaches to Gramsci*, edited by Anne Showstack Sassoon, pp. 116–126. London: Writers and Readers Publishing Cooperative, 1982.

Bukharin, Nikolai. "Imperialism and World Economy." In *Essential Works of Socialism*, edited by Irving Howe, pp. 383–393. New Haven: Yale University Press, 1976.

———. "Organized Mismanagement in Modern Society." Translated by Valerie Rosen. In *Essential Works of Socialism*, edited by Irving Howe, pp. 394–403. New Haven, Conn.: Yale University Press, 1976.

Burks, Ardath W. "The Politics of Japan's Modernization: The Autonomy of Choice." In *Political Development in Modern Japan*, edited by Robert E. Ward, pp. 537–576. Studies in the Modernization of Japan, no. 4. Princeton, N.J.: Princeton University Press, 1968, paperback, 1973.

Caudill, W. and Scarr, H. A. "Japanese Value Orientation and Culture Change." *Ethnology* 1 (1962): 53–91.

Chang, Hao. "Neo-Confucian Moral Thought and Its Modern Legacy." *Journal of Asian Studies* 39, no. 2 (February 1980): 259–290.

Chang, Maria Hsia. "'Fascism' and Modern China." *China Quarterly* 79 (September 1979): 553–567.

Chang, P'eng-yüan. "The Constitutionalists." In *China in Revolution: The First Phase, 1900–1913*, edited and with an introduction by Mary Clabaugh Wright, pp. 143–160. New Haven, Conn.: Yale University Press, 1968.

Charles, David A. "The Dismissal of Marshall P'eng Teh-huai." *China Quarterly* 8 (October–December 1961): 65–74.

[Chinese Communist Party]. "Resolution on Certain Questions in the History of Our Party since the Founding of the People's Republic of China (Adopted by the Sixth Plenary Session of the Eleventh Central Committee of the Communist Party of China on June 27, 1981)." In *Resolution on CPC History (1949–1981)*, pp. 1–86. Beijing: Foreign Languages Press, 1981.

Ch'en, Pi-lan. "Looking Back over My Years with P'eng Shu-tse." In P'eng Shu-tse, *The Chinese Communist Party in Power*, pp. 13–47. New York: Monad Press, 1980.

Ch'en, Yün. "How to Be a Communist Party Member." (May 30, 1939) In *Mao's China: Party Reform Documents, 1942–1944*, translated and with an introduction by Boyd Compton, pp. 88–107. Seattle: University of Washington Press, 1952.

Cohen, Stephen. "Bukharin, Lenin and the Theoretical Foundations of Bolshevism." *Soviet Studies* 21, no. 4 (April 1970): 436–457.

Collins, Randall. "A Comparative Approach to Political Sociology." In *State and Society: A Reader in Comparative Political Sociology*, edited by Reinhard Bendix et al., pp. 42–67. Berkeley: University of California Press, 1973.

Connor, Walker. "Ethnonationalism." In *Understanding Political Development: An Analytic Study*, edited by Myron Weiner and Samuel P. Huntington, pp. 196–220. Boston: Little, Brown and Company, 1987.

"Conversation of Fang Lizhi with Wen Hui, Ming Lei." *Zhengming* [Contention] 117 (July 1987): 17–36.

Craig, Albert M. "Fukuzawa Yukichi: The Philosophical Foundations of Meiji Nationalism." In *Political Development in Modern Japan*, edited by Robert E. Ward, pp. 99–148. Princeton, N.J.: Princeton University Press, 1968.

Crowley, James B. "A New Asian Order: Some Notes on Prewar Japanese Nationalism." In *Japan in Crisis: Essays on Taishō Democracy*, edited by Bernard S. Silberman and H. D. Harootunian, pp. 270–298. Princeton, N.J.: Princeton University Press, 1974.

———. "A New Deal for Japan and Asia: One Road to Pearl Harbor." In *Modern East Asia: Essays in Interpretation*, edited by James B. Crowley, pp. 235–264. New York: Harcourt, Brace and World, 1970.

———. "Japan's Military Foreign Policy." In *Japan's Foreign Policy, 1868–1944: A Research Guide*. New York: Columbia University Press, 1974.

Crump, John. "False Start for Socialism in Japan: Socialist Thought to 1905." *Proceedings of the British Association for Japanese Studies* (Sheffield), pt. 2, 1 (1976): 1–25.

Daniels, Robert V. "The 'Withering Away of the State' in Theory and Practice." In *Soviet Society: A Book of Readings*, edited by Alex Inkeles and Kent Geiger, pp. 113–126. Boston: Houghton Mifflin, 1961.

Degras, Jane. "United Front Tactics in the Comintern 1921–1928." In *St. Antony's Papers*, no. 9, *International Communism*, edited by David Footman, pp. 9–22 Carbondale, Ill.: Southern Illinois University Press, 1960.

Dening, Walter. "Confucian Philosophy in Japan. Reviews of Dr. Tstsujirō Inoue's Three Volumes on This Philosophy." *Transactions of the Asiatic Society of Japan* (Tokyo), pt. 2, 36 (1908): 101–152.

DeVos, George A., and Keiichi Mizushima. "Organization and Social Function of Japanese Gangs: Historical Development and Modern Parallels." In *Aspects of Social Change in Modern Japan*, edited by R. P. Dore, pp. 289–325. Studies in the Modernization of Japan. Princeton, N.J.: Princeton University Press, Princeton Paperbacks, 1971.

Dirlik, Arif. "National Development and Social Revolution in Early Chinese Marxist Thought." *China Quarterly* 58 (April–May 1974): 286–309.

———. "The New Culture Movement Revisited: Anarchism and the Idea of Social Revolution in New Culture Thinking." *Modern China* 11, no. 3 (July 1985): 251–300.

———. "The Predicament of Marxist Revolutionary Consciousness: Mao Zedong, Antonio Gramsci, and the Reformulation of Marxist Revolutionary Theory." *Modern China* 9, no. 2 (April 1983): 182–211.

———. "Vision and Revolution: Anarchism in Chinese Revolutionary Thought on the Eve of the 1911 Revolution." *Modern China* 12, no. 2 (April 1986): 123–165.

Dirlik, Arif, and Edward S. Krebs. "Socialism and Anarchism in Early Republican China." *Modern China* 7, no. 2 (April 1981): 117–151.

Dittmer, Lowell. "Death and Transfiguration: Liu Shaoqi's Rehabilitation and Contemporary Chinese Politics." *Journal of Asian Studies* 40, no. 3 (May 1981): 455–479.

Doi, L. Takeo. "Giri-Ninjō: An Interpretation." In *Aspects of Social Change in Modern Japan*, edited by R. P. Dore, pp. 327–334. Studies in the Modernization of Japan. Princeton, N.J.: Princeton University Press, 1971.

Dutt, Vidya Prakash. "The First Week of Revolution: The Wuchang Revolution." In *China in Revolution: The First Phase, 1900–1913*, edited and with an introduction by Mary Clabaught Wright, pp. 383–416. New Haven, Conn.: Yale University Press, 1968.

Eckstein, Harry. "A Perspective on Comparative Politics, Past and Present." In *Comparative Politics: A Reader*, edited by Harry Eckstein and David E. Apter. New York: Free Press, 1963.

Ehrenreich, John. "The Dictatorship of the Proletariat in China." *Monthly Review* 27 (1975): 16–28.

Eisenstadt, S. N. "Socialism and Tradition." In *Socialism and Tradition*, edited by S. N. Eisenstadt and Yael Azmon, pp. 1–18. The Van Leer Jerusalem Foundation Series. Atlantic Highlands, N.J.: Humanities Press, 1975.

Ely, Geoff. "Nationalism and Social History." *Social History* 6 (1981): 83–107.

———. "State Formation, Nationalism and Political Culture in Nineteenth-Century Germany." In *Culture, Ideology and Politics: Essays for Eric Hobsbawm*, edited by R. Samuel and G. Stedman Jones, pp. 277–301. London: Routledge and Kegan Paul, 1983.

———. "What Produces Fascism: Preindustrial Traditions or a Crisis of a Capitalist State." *Politics and Society* 12, no. 1 (1983): 53–82.

———. "The Wilhelmine Right: How It Changed." In *Society and Politics in Wilhelmine Germany,* edited by Richard J. Evans, pp. 112–135. London: Croom Helm, 1978.

Engels, Friedrich. "Hungary and Panslavism" (1849). In Karl Marx, and Friedrich Engels, *The Russian Menace to Europe*, edited by Paul W. Blackstone and Bert F. Hoselitz. Glencoe, Ill.: Free Press, 1952.

———. "On Karl Marx's Contribution to the Critique of Political Economy." (1859) In

Karl Marx, *Selected Works*, edited by C. P. Dutt. Vol. 1. of 2 vols. New York: International Publishers, n.d.

———. "On Social Relations in Russia." In *The Marx-Engels Reader*, edited by Robert C. Tucker, pp. 665–675. 2d ed. New York: W. W. Norton, 1978.

Fairbank, John K. "The Early Treaty in the Chinese World Order." In *The Chinese World Order*, edited by John K. Fairbank. Cambridge, Mass.: Harvard University Press, 1968.

Fang Lizhi. "Prologue: On Patriotism and Global Citizenship." In *The Broken Mirror: China after Tiananmen*, pp. xxi–xxv. Chicago: St. James Press, 1990.

Fetscher, Iring. "The Young and the Old Marx." In *Marx's Socialism*, edited by Shlomo Avineri, pp. 36–58. New York: Lieber-Atherton, 1972.

Fletcher, Miles. "Intellectuals and Fascism in Early Shōwa Japan." *Journal of Asian Studies* 39, no. 1 (November 1979): 39–63.

Foucault, Michel. "The Subject and Power." In *Michel Foucault: Beyond Structuralism and Hermeneutics*, edited by Hubert L. Dreyfus and Paul Rabinow, pp. 208–226. Chicago: University of Chicago Press, 1983.

Frager, Robert. "Conformity and Anticonformity in Japan." *Journal of Personality and Social Psychology* 15, no. 3 (1970): 203–210.

Friedman, Edward. "Three Leninist Paths within a Socialist Conundrum." In *Three Visions of Chinese Socialism*, edited by Dorothy J. Solinger, pp. 11–45. Boulder, Colo.: Westview Press, 1984.

Fung, Yu-lan. "The Philosophy at the Basis of Traditional Chinese Society." In *Ideological Differences and World Order: Studies in the Philosophy and Science of the World's Cultures*, edited by F. S. C. Northrup. New Haven, Conn.: Yale University Press, 1949.

Gerschenkron, Alexander. "Economic Backwardness in Historical Perspective." In *Economic Backwardness in Historical Perspective*. Reprint. Cambridge, Mass.: Harvard University Press, 1966, 1979.

Girardin, Jean-Claude. "On the Marxist Theory of the State." Translated by Alan Wolfe and Amy Bridges. *Politics and Society* 4, no. 2 (Winter 1974): 193–223.

Godelier, Maurice. "The Concept of the 'Asiatic Mode of Production' and Marxist Modes of Social Evolution." In *Relations of Production: Marxist Approaches to Economic Anthropology*, edited by David Seddon and translated by Helen Lackner, pp. 209–257. London: Frank Cass and Company, 1978.

———. "The Concept of the Asian Mode of Production and the Marxist Model of Social Development." *Soviet Anthropology and Archeology* 4, no. 2 (1965): 39–41.

Godes, M. "The Reaffirmation of Unilinealism." In *The Asiatic Mode of Production*, edited by Anne M. Bailey and Josep Llobera. London: Routledge and Kegan Paul, 1981.

Gold, David A., Clarence Y. H. Lo, and Erik Olin Wright. "Recent Developments in Marxist Theories of the Capitalist State." *Monthly Review*, pt. 7, 27, no. 5 (October 1975): 29–43; pt. 2, 27, 6 (November 1975): 36–51.

Goldman, Emma. "Anarchism." In Emma Goldman *Anarchism and Other Essays*, with an introduction by Richard Drinnon, pp. 47–67. Toronto: Dover Publications, 1969.

———. "Patriotism: A Menace to Liberty." In Emma Goldman, *Anarchism and Other Essays*. with an introduction by Richard Drinnon, pp. 127–144. Toronto: Dover Publications, n.d.

Goldman, Merle. "China's Anti-Confucian Campaign, 1973–1974." *China Quarterly* 63 (1975): 435–462.

Gramsci, Antonio. "The Modern Prince." In Antonio Gramsci, *Selections from the Prison Notebooks*, edited and translated by Quintin Hoare and Geoffrey Nowell Smith, pp. 123–205. New York: International Publishers, 1971.

————. "Notes on Italian History." In Antonio Gramsci, *Selections from the Prison Notebooks*, edited and translated by Quintin Hoare and Geoffrey Nowell Smith, pp. 44–120. New York: International Publishers, 1971.

————. "State and Civil Society." In *Selections from the Prison Notebooks*, edited and translated by Quintin Hoare and Geoffrey Nowell Smith, pp. 206–276. New York: International Publishers, 1971.

————. "The Study of Philosophy." In Antonio Gramsci, *Selections from the Prison Notebooks*, edited and translated by Quintin Hoare and Geoffrey Nowell Smith, pp. 321–377. New York: International Publishers, 1971.

Gray, Jack. "Politics in Command: The Maoist Theory of Social Change and Economic Growth." *Political Quarterly* 45 (1974): 26–48.

————. "The Two Roads: Alternative Strategies of Social Change and Economic Growth in China." In *Authority, Participation and Cultural Change in China*, edited by Stuart R. Schram. Cambridge: Cambridge University Press, 1973.

Gregor, A. James, and Maria Hsia Chang. "Maoism and Marxism in Comparative Perspective." *Review of Politics* 40, no. 3 (July 1978): 307–327.

————. "*Nazionalfascismo* and the Revolutionary Nationalism of Sun Yat-sen." *Journal of Asian Studies* 39, no. 1 (November 1979): 21–37.

Grieder, Jerome. "Communism, Nationalism, and Democracy: The Chinese Intelligentsia and the Chinese Revolution in the 1920s and 1930s." In *Modern East Asia: Essays in Interpretation*, edited by James B. Crowley, pp. 207–234. New York: Harcourt, Brace and World, 1970.

Guillaume, James. "Michael Bakunin: A Biographical Sketch." In *Bakunin on Anarchy: Selected Works by the Activist-Founder of World Anarchism*, edited by Sam Dolgoff and translated with an introduction and preface by Paul Avrich, pp. 22–32. New York: Alfred A. Knopf, 1972.

Gurley, John. "The Formation of Mao's Economic Strategy, 1927–1949." *Monthly Review* 27 (1975): 58–132.

Hall, John W. "Feudalism in Japan: A Reassessment." *Comparative Studies in Society and History* 5 (1962): 15–51.

Hammond, Edward. "Bukharin and the Chinese Revolution." *Modern China* 1, no. 4 (October 1975): 463–472.

————. "Marxism and the Mass Line." *Modern China* 4, no. 1 (January 1978): 3–25.

Han, Feizi. "The Five Vermin." In *Basic Writings of Mo Tzu, Hsün Tzu, and Han Fei Tzu*, translated by Burton Watson, pp. 96–117. New York: Columbia University Press, 1967.

Hearn, Francis. "Rationality and Bureaucracy: Maoist Contributions to a Marxist Theory of Bureaucracy." *The Sociological Quarterly* 19 (Winter 1978): 37–54.

Heitman, Sidney. "Between Lenin and Stalin: Nikolai Bukharin." In *Revisionism: Essays on the History of Marxist Ideas*, edited by Leopold Labedz, pp. 77–90. New York: Praeger, 1962.

Heldman, Donald C. "The Sino-Soviet Split and Party Legitimacy." *Survey* 77 (Fall 1970): 51–58.

Hintze, Otto. "Economics and Politics in the Age of Modern Capitalism." In *The Historical Essays of Otto Hintze*, edited and with an introduction by Felix Gilbert, pp. 422–452. New York: Oxford University Press, 1975.

Hintze, Otto. "The State in Historical Perspective." In *State and Society: A Reader in Comparative Political Sociology*, edited by Reinhard Bendix et al., pp. 154–169. Boston: Little, Brown, 1968; Berkeley: University of California Press, paper, 1973.

Hirai, Atsuko. "Ancestor Worship in Yatsuka Hozumi's State and Constitutional Theory."

In *Japan's Modern Century*, edited by Edmund Skrzypczak, pp. 41–50. Tokyo: Sophia University, and Charles E. Tuttle, 1968.

Hobbes, Thomas. "Leviathan." In *Social and Political Philosophy*, edited by John Somerville and Ronald E. Santoni. New York: Doubleday, Anchor Books, 1963.

Hobsbawm, E. J. "Karl Marx's Contribution to History." In *Ideology in Social Science: Readings in Critical Social Theory*, edited by Robin Blackburn, pp. 265–283. New York: Random House, Vintage Books, 1973.

Hobsbawm, Eric. "Some Reflections on Nationalism." In *Imagination and Precision in the Social Sciences*, edited by T. J. Nossiter, S. Rokkan, and A. H. Hanson, pp. 385–486. London: N.p, 1972.

Hodges, Donald C. "Engels' Contribution to Marxism." *Socialist Register* (London) 1965: 297–310.

Horie, Yasuzō. "The Confucian Concept of State in Tokugawa Japan." *Kyoto University Economic Review* 32, no. 2 (October 1962): 26–38.

———. "Foreign Capital and the Japanese Capitalism after the World War I." *Kyoto University Economic Review* 20, no. 1 (April 1950): 38–59.

———. "Modern Entrepreneurship in Meiji Japan." In *The State and Economic Enterprise in Japan: Essays in the Political Economy of Growth*, edited by William W. Lockwood, pp. 183–208. Studies in the Modernization of Japan. Princeton, N.J.: Princeton University Press, 1965.

Hoston, Germaine A. "Between Theory and Practice: Marxist Thought and the Politics of the Japanese Socialist Party." *Studies in Comparative Communism* 20, no. 2 (Summer 1987): 175–207.

———. "Conceptualizing Bourgeois Revolution: The Prewar Japanese Left and the Meiji Restoration." *Comparative Studies in Society and History* 33, no. 3 (July 1991): 539–581.

———. "Emperor, Nation, and the Transformation of Marxism to National Socialism in Prewar Japan: The Case of Sano Manabu." *Studies in Comparative Communism* 18, no. 1 (Spring 1985): 25–47.

———. "*Ikkoku Shakai-shugi*: Sano Manabu and the Limits of Marxism as Cultural Criticism." In *Culture and Identity: Japanese Intellectuals during the Interwar Years*, edited by J. Thomas Rimer, pp. 168–186. Princeton, N.J.: Princeton University Press, 1990.

———. "Marxism and Japanese Expansionism: Takahashi Kamekichi and the Theory of 'Petty Imperialism'" *Journal of Japanese Studies* 10, no. 1 (Winter 1984): 1–30.

———. "Marxism and National Socialism in Taishō Japan: The Thought of Takabatake Motoyuki." *Journal of Asian Studies* 44, no. 1 (November 1984): 43–64.

———. "The State, Modernity, and the Fate of Liberalism in Prewar Japan." *Journal of Asian Studies* 51, no. 2 (May 1992): 287–316.

———. "A 'Theology of Liberation?' Socialist Revolution and Spiritual Regeneration in Chinese and Japanese Marxism." In *Ideas across Cultures: Essays on Chinese Thought in Honor of Benjamin I. Schwartz*, edited by Paul A. Cohen and Merle Goldman, pp. 169–221. Cambridge, Mass.: Harvard University Press, under the auspices of the Council on East Asian Studies, 1990.

Hsiao, K. C. "Anarchism in Chinese Political Thought." *T'ien-hsia Monthly* 3, no. 3 (1936): 249–263.

———. "In and Out of Utopia: K'ang Yu-wei's Social Thought, II. Road to Utopia." *Chung-chi Journal* 7, no. 2 (May 1968).

Hsün Tzu. "Man's Nature Is Evil." In *Basic Writings of Mo Tzu Hsün Tzu, and Han Fei Tzu*, translated by Burton Watson. New York: Columbia University Press, 1967.

Huang, Philip. "Liberalism and Nationalism in Liang Ch'i-ch'ao's Thought." *Monumenta Serica* 29 (1970–1971): 521–536.

Iolk, E. S. "The AMP and the Class Struggle." In *The Asiatic Mode of Production*, edited by Anne M. Bailey and Josep R. Llobera. London: Routledge and Kegan Paul, 1981.

Ishida, Takeshi. "Popular Attitudes toward the Japanese Emperor." *Asian Survey* 2, no. 2 (April 1962): 29–39.

―――. "Socialism and National Consciousness: The Case of Japan in the Periods before and after World War Two." *Chiba Daigaku hōgaku ronshū* 2, no. 2 (February 26, 1988): 158–168.

Jervis, Robert. "Hypotheses on Misperception." In *International Politics and Foreign Policy*, edited by James N. Rosenau, pp. 239–254. Rev. ed. New York: Free Press, 1969.

Just, Roger. "Triumph of the Ethnos." In *History and Ethnicity*, edited by Elizabeth Tonkin, Maryon McDonald, and Malcolm Chapman. ASA Monographs, no. 27. London and New York: Routledge and Kegan Paul, 1989.

Kato, Shuichi. "Taishō Democracy as the Pre-Stage for Japanese Militarism." In *Japan in Crisis: Essays on Taishō Democracy*, edited by Bernard S. Silberman and H. D. Harootunian, pp. 217–236. Princeton, N.J.: Princeton University Press, 1974.

Kawakami, Kiyoshi. "Socialism in Japan." *The International Socialist Review* 2, no. 8 (February 1902): 561–569.

Kelly, David. "Chinese Intellectuals in the 1989 Democracy Movement. In *The Broken Mirror: China after Tiananmen*, pp. 24–51. Chicago: St. James Press, 1990.

Kokin, M. D. "The Asiatic Bureaucracy as a Class." In *The Asiatic Mode of Production*, edited by Anne M. Bailey and Josep R. Llobera. London: Routledge and Kegan Paul, 1981.

Krieger, Joel, and David Held. "A Theory of the State? A Comment on Block's 'The Ruling Class Does Not Rule'" *Socialist Review* 40/41 (1978): 189–207.

Kropotkin, Peter. "Selections from Mutual Aid." In Peter Kropotkin, *The Essential Kropotkin*, edited by Emile Capouya and Keitha Tompkins, pp. 170–207. Tokyo: Liveright, 1975.

Kublin, Hyman. "The Japanese Socialists and the Russo-Japanese War." *Journal of Modern History* 22, no. 4 (December 1950): 322–339.

Landes, David S. "Japan and Europe: Contrasts in Industrialization." In *The State and Economic Enterprise in Japan: Essays in the Political Economy of Growth*, edited by William W. Lockwood, pp. 93–182. Studies in the Modernization of Japan. Princeton, N.J.: Princeton University Press, 1965.

Large, Stephen S. "The Romance of Revolution in Japanese Anarchism and Communism during the Taishō Period." *Modern Asian Studies* 11, no. 3 (1977): 441–467.

Lau, D. C. "Theories of Human Nature in Mencius and Shyuntzyy." *Bulletin of the School of Oriental and African Studies* 15 (1953): 541–565.

Lee, Renssalaer W. "The Hsia Fang System: Marxism and Modernization." *China Quarterly* (October–December 1966): 40–62.

Lenin, V. I. "Address to the Second All-Russia Congress of Communist Organisations of the Peoples of the East" (November 22, 1919). In *Lenin: Selected Works*. Vol. 1 of 3 vols. Moscow: Progress Publishers, 1975.

Lenin, V. I. "Against Great-Russian Chauvinism." In *The Latin Anthology*, edited by Robert C. Tucker, pp. 659–660. New York: W. W. Norton, 1975.

―――. "Imperialism, the Highest Stage of Capitalism." In *The Lenin Anthology*, edited by Robert C. Tucker. New York: W. W. Norton, 1975.

―――. "'Left-Wing' Communism, An Infantile Disorder," (April–May 1920). In *The*

Lenin Anthology, edited by Robert C. Tucker, pp. 550–618. New York: W. W. Norton, 1975.

————. "On the National Pride of the Great Russians." In *The Lenin Anthology*, edited by Robert C. Tucker. New York: W. W. Norton, 1975.

————. "Preliminary Draft Theses on the National and Colonial Questions for the Second Congress of the Communist International," (June 5, 1920). In *Lenin: Selected Works*. Vol. 1 of 3 vols. Moscow: Progress Publishers, 1975.

————. "The Question of Nationalities or 'Autonomisation.'" In *The Lenin Anthology*, edited by Robert C. Tucker. New York: W. W. Norton, 1975.

————. "The Right of Nations to Self-Determination." In *The Lenin Anthology*, edited by Robert C. Tucker, pp. 152–180. New York: W. W. Norton, the Norton Library, 1975.

Lenin, V. I. "State and Revolution: The Marxist Theory of the State and the Tasks of the Proletariat in the Revolution (August–September 1917)." In V. I. Lenin, *Lenin on Politics and Revolution: Selected Writings*, edited and with an introduction by James E. Connor. Indianapolis, Ind.: Bobbs-Merrill, Pegasus; New York: Webster Publishing, 1968.

————. "State and Revolution." In *The Lenin Anthology*, edited by Robert C. Tucker. New York: W. W. Norton, 1975.

————. "Communism and the East: Theses on the National and Colonial Questions." In *The Lenin Anthology*, edited by Robert C. Tucker. New York: W. W. Norton, 1978.

————. "Two Tactics of Social-Democracy in the Democratic Revolution" (1905). In *Lenin on Politics and Revolution: Selected Writings*, edited and with an introduction by James E. Connor. Indianapolis: Bobbs-Merrill, Pegasus, 1968.

————. "What Is to Be Done?" In *The Lenin Anthology*, edited by Robert C. Tucker, pp. 12–114. New York: W. W. Norton, 1975.

Li, Yizhe. "Concerning Socialist Democracy and the Legal System." *Issues and Studies*, no. 1 (1976): 110–148.

Lichtheim, George. "The Concept of Ideology." In George Lichtheim, *The Concept of Ideology and Other Essays*. pp. 3–46. New York: Random House, Vintage, 1967.

————. "Oriental Despotism." In George Lichtheim, *The Concept of Ideology and Other Essays*, pp. 62–93. New York: Random House, Vintage, 1967.

Lin, Yü-sheng. "The Evolution of the Pre-Confucian Meaning of *Jen* and the Confucian Concept of Moral Autonomy." *Monumenta Serica* 31 (1974–1975): 185–191.

Link, Perry. "The Thought and Spirit of Fang Lizhi." In *The Broken Mirror: China after Tiananmen*, pp. 100–114. Chicago: St. James Press, 1990.

Liu, Shao-ch'i. "On the Intra-Party Struggle." In *Mao's China: Party Reform Documents, 1942–1944*, translated and with an introduction by Boyd Compton. Seattle: University of Washington Press, 1952.

————. "Training of the Communist Party Member." In *Mao's China: Party Reform Documents, 1942–1944*, translated and with an introduction by Boyd Compton. Seattle: University of Washington Press, 1952.

Liu, Shaoqi. "Political Report of the Central Committee of the Communist Party of China" (September 15, 1956). In *Communist China 1955–1959: Policy Documents with Analysis*, with a foreword by Robert R. Bowie and John K. Fairbank. Cambridge, Mass.: Harvard University Press, 1962.

Luke, Timothy W. "Cabral's Marxism: An African Strategy for Socialist Development." *Studies in Comparative Communism* 14, no. 4 (Winter 1981): 307–330.

Luxemburg, Rosa. "The National Question and Autonomy." In *The National Question:*

Selected Writings of Rosa Luxemburg, edited and with an introduction by Horace B. Davis. New York: Monthly Review Press, 1976.

―――. "The Russian Revolution." In Rosa Luxemburg, *The Russian Revolution and Leninism or Marxism?* pp. 25–80. Ann Arbor: University of Michigan Press, Ann Arbor Paperbacks, 1961.

Mad'iar, L. I. "The Legitimacy of the AMP." In *The Asiatic Mode of Production*, edited by Anne M. Bailey and Josep R. Llobera, pp. 76–94. London: Routledge and Kegan Paul, 1981.

Mao Tse-tung. "Be Activists in Promoting the Revolution" (October 9, 1957). In *Selected Works of Mao Tse-tung*. Vol. 5. 483–497. 5 vols. Peking: Foreign Languages Press, 1977.

―――. "The Chinese People Have Stood Up!" (September 21, 1949). In *Selected Works of Mao Tsetung*. 5:15–18. 5 vols. Peking: Foreign Languages Press, 1977.

―――. "The Chinese Revolution and the Chinese Communist Party" (December 1939). In *Selected Works of Mao Tse-tung*. 2:305–334. 5 vols. Peking: Foreign Languages Press, 1967.

―――. "Criticize Han Chauvinism." In *Selected Works of Mao Tse-tung*. 5:87–88. 5 vols. Peking: Foreign Languages Press, 1977.

―――. "The Foolish Old Man Who Removed the Mountains" (June 11, 1945). In *Selected Works of Mao Tse-tung*, 3:271–274. 5 vols. Peking: Foreign Languages Press, 1967.

―――. "In Opposition to Party Formalism." In *Mao's China: Party Reform Documents, 1942–1944*, translated and with an introduction by Boyd Compton. Seattle: University of Washington Press, 1952.

―――. "Interview with the British Journalist James Bertram" (October 25, 1937). In *Selected Works of Mao Tse-tung*. 2:47–59. 5 vols. Peking: Foreign Languages Press, 1967.

―――. "The May 4th Movement" (May 1939). In *Selected Works of Mao Tse-tung*, 2:237–239. 5 vols. Peking: Foreign Languages Press, 1967.

―――. "On Contradiction" (August 1937). In *Selected Readings from the Works of Mao Tsetung*, pp. 85–133. Peking: Foreign Languages Press, 1971.

―――. "On New Democracy" (January 1940). In *Selected Works of Mao Tse-tung*. 2:339–384. 5 vols. Peking: Foreign Languages Press, 1967.

―――. "On Practice: On the Relation between Knowledge and Practice, between Knowing and Doing." (July 1937). In *Selected Readings from the Works of Mao Tsetung*, pp. 65–84. Peking: Foreign Languages Press, 1971.

―――. "On Protracted War" (May 1938). In *Selected Works of Mao Tse-tung*, 2:113–194. 5 vols. Peking: Foreign Languages Press, 1967.

―――. "On State Capitalism" (July 9, 1953), 5:101. 5 vols. Peking: Foreign Languages Press, 1977.

―――. "On Tactics against Japanese Imperialism" (December 27, 1955). In *Selected Works of Mao Tse-tung*, 1:153–178. 5 vols. Peking: Foreign Languages Press, 1967.

―――. "On the Correct Handling of Contradictions among the People" (February 27, 1957). In *Selected Readings from the Works of Mao Tsetung*, pp 432–479. Peking: Foreign Languages Press, 1971.

―――. "On the Correct Handling of Contradictions among the People (Speaking notes)" (February 27, 1957). In *The Secret Speeches of Chairman Mao: From the Hundred Flowers to the Great Leap Forward* edited by Roderick MacFarquhar, Timothy Cheek, and Eugene Wu. Harvard Contemporary China Series, no. 6, pp. 131–189. Cambridge, Mass.: Council on East Asian Studies, Harvard University, 1989.

————. "On the People's Democratic Dictatorship" (June 30, 1949). In *Selected Readings from the Works of Mao Tse-tung*, pp. 371–388. Peking: Foreign Languages Press, 1971.

————. "On the Ten Major Relationships." In *Selected Works of Mao Tse-tung*. 5:284–307. 5 vols. Peking: Foreign Languages Press, 1977.

————. "Oppose Stereotyped Party Writing" (February 8, 1942). In *Selected Works of Mao Tse-tung*, 3:53–68. 5 vols. Peking: Foreign Languages Press, 1967.

————. "Our Study and the Current Situation." (April 12, 1944) In *Selected Works of Mao Tse-tung*. 3:163–176. 5 vols. Peking: Foreign Languages Press, 1967.

————. "Problems of Strategy in China's Revolutionary War" (December 1936). In *Selected Works of Mao Tse-tung*, 1:179–254. 5 vols. Peking: Foreign Languages Press, 1967.

————. "Rectify the Party's Style of Work" (February 1, 1942). In *Selected Works of Mao Tse-tung*, 3:35–51. 5 vols. Peking: Foreign Languages Press, 1967.

————. "Reform Our Study" (May 1941). In *Selected Works of Mao Tse-tung*, 3:17–25. 5 vols. Peking: Foreign Languages Press, 1967.

————. "Report on an Investigation of the Peasant Movement in Hunan" (March 1927). In *Selected Works of Mao Tse-tung*, 1:23–59. 5 vols. Peking: Foreign Languages Press, 1967.

————. "Report to the Second Plenary Session of the Seventh Central Committee of the Communist Party of China" (March 5, 1949). In *Selected Works of Mao Tse-tung*, 4:361–375. Peking: Foreign Languages Press, 1967.

————. "The Role of the Chinese Communist Party in the National War" (October 1938). In *Selected Works of Mao Tse-tung*, 2:195–211. 5 vols. Peking: Foreign Languages Press, 1967.

————. "Serve the People" (September 8, 1944). In *Selected Works of Mao Tse-tung*, 3:177–178. 5 vols. Peking: Foreign Languages Press, 1967.

————. "Some Experiences in Our Party's History." September 25, 1956. In *Selected Works of Mao Tse-tung*. Vol. 5 of 5 vols. pp. 324–329. Peking: Foreign Languages Press, 1977.

————. "Some Questions Concerning Methods of Leadership" (June 1, 1943). In *Selected Works of Mao Tse-tung*, 3:117–122. 5 vols. Peking: Foreign Languages Press, 1967.

————. "Speech at the Second Plenary Session of the Eighth Central Committee of the Communist Party of China" November 15, 1956. In *Selected Works of Mao Tse-tung*. Vol. 5 of 5 vols. pp. 332–349. Peking: Foreign Languages Press, 1977.

————. "Speeches at the National Conference of the Communist Party of China" (March 1955). In *Selected Works of Mao Tse-tung*, 5:154–171. 5 vols. Peking: Foreign Languages Press, 1977.

————. "The Struggle in the Chingkang Mountains" (November 25, 1928). In *Selected Works of Mao Tse-tung*. 1:73–104. 5 vols. Peking: Foreign Languages Press, 1967.

————. "Talk at an Enlarged Central Work Conference" (January 30, 1962). In *Mao Tse-tung Unrehearsed, Talks and Lectures: 1956–1971*, edited by Stuart Schram, pp. 158–187. Harmondsworth: Penguin, 1974.

————. "Talks at the Yenan Forum on Literature and Art" (May 1942). In *Selected Works of Mao Tse-tung*. 3:69–98. 5 vols. Peking: Foreign Languages Press, 1967.

————. "The Tasks of the Chinese Communist Party in the Period of Resistance to Japan" (May 3, 1937). In *Selected Works of Mao Tse-tung*, 5 vols. 1:263–283. Peking: Foreign Languages Press, 1967.

————. "Where Do Correct Ideas Come from?" (May 1963). In *Selected Readings in the Works of Mao Tsetung*, pp. 502–504. Peking: Foreign Languages Press, 1971.

————. "Win the Masses in their Millions for the Anti-Japanese National United Front" (May 7, 1937). *Selected Works of Mao Tse-tung*, 1:285–294. 5 vols. Peking: Foreign Languages Press, 1967.

Marcuse, Herbert, "The Struggle against Liberalism in the Totalitarian View of the State." In *Negations*. Boston, Mass.: Beacon Press, 1969.

Marx, Karl. "The British Rule in India." In *The Marx-Engels Reader*, edited by Robert C. Tucker, pp. 653–658. New York: W. W. Norton, 1978.

————. "The Civil War in France" (1871). In *The Marx-Engels Reader*, edited by Robert C. Tucker, pp. 526–576, 618–652, 2d ed. New York: W. W. Norton, 1978.

————. "A Contribution to the Critique of Hegel's 'Philosophy of Right': Introduction." In Karl Marx, *Critique of Hegel's "Philosophy of Right,"* (in German), edited and with an introduction by Joseph O'Malley, pp. 129–151. Cambridge: Cambridge University Press, 1977.

————. "Critique of the Gotha Program." In *The Marx-Engels Reader*, edited by Robert C. Tucker, pp. 525–541. New York: W. W. Norton, 1978.

————. "The Economic and Philosophic Manuscripts of 1844." In *The Marx-Engels Reader*, edited by Robert C. Tucker. pp. 66–125. Rev. ed. New York: W. W. Norton, 1978.

————. "The Eighteenth Brumaire of Louis Bonaparte" (1852). In *The Marx-Engels Reader*, edited by Robert C. Tucker, pp. 594–617. New York: W. W. Norton, 1978.

————. "The Elections in England—'Tories and Whigs'." In Karl Marx and Friedrich Engels, *On Britain*. N.p.: N.p., 1953.

————. "The Future Results of British Rule in India." In *The Marx-Engels Reader*, edited by Robert C. Tucker, pp. 659–664. New York: W. W. Norton, 1978.

————. "The German Ideology: Part I." In *The Marx-Engels Reader*, edited by Robert C. Tucker. 2d ed., pp. 146–200. New York: W. W. Norton, 1978.

[Marx, Karl]. Karl Marx to the Editor of *Otyescesvenniye Zapisky* [Notes on the fatherland] (end of 1877). In Karl Marx and Friedrich Engels, *Selected Correspondence*, translated by Dona Torr. Marxist Library, vol. 29. New York: International Publishers, 1942. Reprint, Westport, Conn.: Greenwood Press, 1975.

Marx, Karl. "Letter on the Russian Village Community" (1881). In Karl Marx, and Friedrich Engels, *The Russian Menace to Europe*, edited by Paul W. Blackstone and Bert F. Hoselitz, pp. 218–226. Glencoe, Ill.: Free Press, 1952.

————. "Marx on the History of His Opinions." In *The Marx-Engels Reader*, edited by Robert C. Tucker, pp. 3–6. New York: W. W. Norton, 1978.

————. "On the Jewish Question." In *The Marx-Engels Reader*, edited by Robert C. Tucker, pp. 26–52. 2d ed. Tucker, New York: W. W. Norton, 1978.

————. "Parliamentary Debates." In Karl Marx, and Friedrich Engels, *On Britain*. N.p.: N.p., 1953.

————. Preface to Karl Marx, *A Contribution to the Critique of Political Economy*. In *The Marx-Engels Reader*, edited by Robert C. Tucker, pp. 3–6. 2d ed. New York: W. W. Norton, 1978.

————. "Theses on Feuerbach." In *The Marx-Engels Reader*, edited by Robert C. Tucker. 2d ed. New York: W. W. Norton, 1978.

Marx, Karl, and Friedrich Engels. "Address of the Central Committee to the Communist League." In *The Marx-Engels Reader*, edited by Robert C. Tucker, pp. 501–511. 2d ed. New York: W. W. Norton, 1978.

————. "Manifesto of the Communist Party." In *The Marx-Engels Reader*, edited by Robert C. Tucker, pp. 469–500. Rev. ed. New York: W. W. Norton, 1978.

Mast, Herman III. "Tai Chi-t'ao, Sunism and Marxism during the May Fourth Movement in Shanghai." *Modern Asian Studies* 5, no. 3 (1971): 227–249.

Mast, Herman III, and William G. Saywell. "Revolution Out of Tradition: The Political Ideology of Tai Chi-t'ao." *Journal of Asian Studies* 34, no. 1 (November 1974): 73–98.

Matsumoto, Sannosuke. "The Significance of Nationalism in Modern Japanese Thought: Some Theoretical Problems." *Journal of Asian Studies* 31, no. 1 (November 1971): 49–56.

Mawatari, Shōken. "The Uno School: A Marxian Approach in Japan." *History of Political Economy* 17, no. 3 (1985): 403–418.

Meisner, Maurice. "The Despotism of Concepts: Wittfogel and Marx on China." *China Quarterly* 16 (October–December 1963): 99–111.

———. "Leninism and Maoism: Some Populist Perspectives on Marxism-Leninism in China." *China Quarterly* 45:2–36.

———. "Marxism and Chinese Values." In *The China Difference*, edited by Ross Terrill, pp. 99–116. New York: Harper and Row, 1979.

———. "Utopian Socialist Themes in Maoism." In *Peasant Rebellion and Communist Revolution in Asia*, edited by John Wilson Lewis, pp. 207–252. Stanford, Calif.: Stanford University Press, 1974.

Merrington, J. "Theory and Practice in Gramsci's Marxism." *The Socialist Register* (London) (1968): 145–176.

Miliband, Ralph. "The Capitalist State: A Reply to Nicos Poulantzas." *New Left Review* 59 (January 1970): 53–60.

———. "Marx and the State." In *Karl Marx*, edited by Tom Bottomore, pp. 128–150. Englewood Cliffs, N.J.: Prentice-Hall, 1973.

———. "Poulantzas and the Capitalist State." *New Left Review* 82 (November–December 1973): 83–92.

Mingelberg, Kaethe. "Lorenz von Stein and His Contribution to Historical Sociology." *Journal of the History of Ideas* 22 (1961).

Muramatsu, Y. "Some Themes in Chinese Rebel Ideologies." In *The Confucian Persuasion*, edited by A. F. Wright, pp. 241–267. Stanford, Calif.: Stanford University Press, 1960.

Murphey, Rhoads. "City and Countryside as Ideological Issues: India and China." *Comparative Studies in Society and History* 14, no. 3 (June 1972).

———. "Man and Nature in China." *Modern Asian Studies* 1, no. 4 (January 1967): 313–333.

Nettl, J. P. "The State as a Conceptual Variable." *World Politics* 20, no. 4 (July 1968): 559–592.

Nichols, David. "The Ruling Class as a Scientific Concept." *Review of Radical Political Economics* 4, no. 5 (1972).

North, Robert C. "The Revolution in Asia: M. N. Roy." In *Revisionism: Essays on the History of Marxist Ideas*, edited by Leopold Labedz, pp. 91–100. New York: Praeger, 1962.

Notehelfer, Fred G. "Kōtoku Shūsui and Nationalism." *Journal of Asian Studies* 31, no. 1 (November 1971): 31–39.

Nyerere, Julius K. "Ujamaa—The Basis of African Socialism." In *Ujamaa: Essays on Socialism*, pp. 1–12. New York: Oxford University Press, Galaxy Books.

Offe, Claus. "Structural Problems of the Capitalist State." *German Political Studies* 1 (1974): 31–56.

———. "The Theory of the Capitalist State and the Problem of Policy Formation." In *Stress* and *Contradiction in Modern Capitalism*, edited by Leon N. Lindberg et al., pp. 125–144. Lexington, Mass.: D. C. Heath, Lexington Books, 1975.

Offe, Claus, and Volker Ronge. "Theses on the Theory of the State." *New German Critique* 6 (Fall 1975): 137–147.

Ohkawa, Kazushi, and Henry Rosovsky. "A Century of Japanese Economic Growth." In *The State and Economic Enterprise in Japan: Essays in the Political Economy of Growth*, edited by William W. Lockwood, pp. 47–92. Studies in the Modernization of Japan. Princeton, N.J.: Princeton University Press, 1965.

Oksenberg, Michel. "Getting Ahead and Along in Communist China: The Ladder of Success on the Eve of the Cultural Revolution." In *Party Leadership and Revolutionary Power in China*, edited by John Wilson Lewis. Contemporary China Institute Publications. Cambridge: Cambridge University Press, 1970.

"On Human Rights." In *The Fifth Modernization: China's Human Rights Movement 1978–1979*, edited by James D. Seymour and with an introduction by Mab Huang and James D. Seymour, pp. 111–127. Stanfordville, N.Y.: Earl Coleman Enterprises, Human Rights Publishing Group, 1980.

Onogawa Hidemi. "Liu Shih-p'ei and Anarchism." *Acta Asiatica* (Tokyo) no. 2 (1967): 70–99.

Pelzel, John C. "Japanese Kinship: A Comparison." In *Family and Kinship in Chinese Society*, edited by Maurice Freedman. Palo Alto, Calif.: Stanford University Press, 1970.

P'eng, Shu-tse. "The Causes of the Victory of the CCP." In P'eng Shu-tse, *The Chinese Communist Party in Power*, pp. 71–137. New York: Monad Press, 1980.

Pfeffer, Richard M. "Mao and Marx in the Marxist-Leninist Tradition." *Modern China* 2, no. 4 (October 1976): 421–460.

Pipes, Richard. "Towards the Police State." In Richard Pipes, *Russia Under the Old Regime*, pp. 281–318. New York: Scribner, 1974.

Poulantzas, Nicos. "The Problem of the Capitalist State." In *Ideology in Social Science: Readings in Critical Social Science Theory*, edited by Robin Blackburn, pp. 238–253. New York: Random House, Vintage Books, 1973.

Proudhon, Pierre-Joseph. "Economics and Justice." In *Selected Works of Pierre-Joseph Proudhon*, edited and with an introduction by Stewart Edwards and translated by Elizabeth Fraser, pp. 48–56. Garden City, N.Y.: Doubleday, Anchor Books, 1969.

Pyle, Kenneth B. "A Symposium on Japanese Nationalism, Introduction: Some Recent Approaches to Japanese Nationalism." *Journal of Asian Studies* 31, no. 1 (November 1971): 5–16.

Rapp, John A. "China's Debate on the Asiatic Mode of Production: The Fate of Marxist Democrats in Leninist Party States." *Theory and Society* 16 (1987): 709–740.

———, ed. "China's Debate on the Asiatic Mode of Production." *Chinese Law and Government* 2, no. 2 (Summer 1989).

Rohlen, Thomas P. "The Company Work Group." In *Modern Japanese Organization and Decision-Making*, edited by Ezra F. Vogel, pp. 185–209. Berkeley: University of California Press, 1975.

Rousseau, Jean-Jacques. "Discourse on the Origin and Foundations of Inequality (Second Discourse)." In Jean-Jacques Rousseau, *The First and Second Discourses*, edited and with an introduction and notes by Roger D. Masters and translated by Roger D. and Judith R. Masters, pp. 101–181. New York: St. Martin's Press, 1964.

Rumyantsef, A. "Maoism and the Anti-Marxist Essence of its Philosophy." *Kommunist* 2 (169). *Studies in Comparative Communism*. 2.3/4 (July–October 1969).

Runciman, W. G. "Karl Marx and Max Weber." In *Social Science and Political Theory*, pp. 43–63. Cambridge: Cambridge University Press, 1969.

Sanderson, John. "Marx and Engels on the State." *Western Political Quarterly* 16, no. 4 (December 1963): 946–955.

Sartre, Jean-Paul. "Czechoslovakia: The Socialism that Came in from the Cold." In Jean-Paul Sartre, *Between Existentialism and Marxism: Sartre on Philosophy, Politics, Psychology, and the Arts*, translated by John Mathews, pp. 84–117. London: New Left Books, and New York: Random House, Pantheon Books, 1974.

Scalapino, Robert A. "Prelude to Marxism: The Chinese Student Movement in Japan, 1900–1910." In *Approaches to Modern Chinese History*, edited by Albert Feuerwerker, Rhoads Murphey, and Mary C. Wright. Berkeley: University of California Press, 1967.

Scalapino, Robert A., and Harold Schiffrin. "Early Socialist Currents in the Chinese Revolutionary Movement: Sun Yat-sen versus Liang Ch'i-ch'ao." *Journal of Asian Studies* 18, no. 3 (May 1959): 321–342.

Schiffrin, Harold. "The Enigma of Sun Yat-sen." In *China in Revolution: The First Phase, 1900–1913*, edited by Mary Clabaugh Wright. New Haven, Conn.: Yale University Press, 1968.

———. "Sun Yat-sen's Early Land Policy: The Origin and Meaning of Equalization of Land Rights." *Journal of Asian Studies* 16 (August 1957): 549–564.

Schram, Stuart R. "From the 'Great Union of the Popular Masses' to the 'Great Alliance'" *China Quarterly* 49 (1972): 88–105.

———. "The Limits of Cataclysmic Change: Reflections on the Place of the 'Great Proletarian Cultural Revolution' in the Political Development of the People's Republic of China." *China Quarterly* 108 (December 1986): 613–624.

———. "Mao Tse-tung as a Charismatic Leader." *Asian Survey* 7, no. 6 (June 1967): 383–388.

———. "Mao Tse-tung and the Theory of Permanent Revolution 1958–1969." *China Quarterly* 46 (April–June 1971): 221–244.

———. "The Party in Chinese Communist Ideology." *China Quarterly* 38 (April–June 1969): 1–26.

Schwartz, Benjamin I. "Ch'en Tu-hsiu and the Acceptance of the Modern West." *Journal of the History of Ideas* 12, no. 1 (January 1951): 61–74.

Schwartz, Benjamin I. "China and the West in the 'Thought of Mao Tse-tung'." In *China in Crisis*, edited by Ping-ti Ho and Tang Tsou and with a foreword by Charles U. Daley, pp. 1:365–379. 2 vols. Chicago: University of Chicago Press, 1968.

———. "The Chinese Perception of World, Past and Present." *The Chinese World Order: Traditional China's Foreign Relations*, edited by John King Fairbank, pp. 276–288. Cambridge, Mass.: Harvard University Press, 1964.

———. "The Essence of Marxism Revisited: A Response." *Modern China* 2, no. 4 (October 1976): 461–472.

———. "The Legend of 'The Legend of Maoism.'" *China Quarterly* 2 (April–June 1960): 35–42.

———. "A Marxist Controversy on China." *Far Eastern Quarterly* 13, no. 2 (February 1954): 143–153.

———. "On Filial Piety and Revolution: China." *Journal of Interdisciplinary History* 3, no. 3 (Winter 1973): 569–580.

———. "The Reign of Virtue: Some Broad Perspectives on Leader and Party in the Cultural Revolution," *China Quarterly* 35 (July–September 1968): 1–17.

———. "Sino-Soviet Relations: The Question of Authority" (1963). In Benjamin

I. Schwartz, *Communism and China: Ideology in Flux*, pp. 130–148 (1970 ed.). Cambridge, Mass.: Harvard University Press, 1968; New York: Atheneum, 1970.

———. "Some Polarities in Confucian Thought." In *Confucianism in Action*, edited by D. S. Nivison and A. F. Wright. Stanford, Calif.: Stanford University Press, 1959.

———. "Some Stereotypes in the Periodization of Chinese History." *The Philosophical Forum*, n.s., 1, no. 2 (Winter 1968): 219–230.

———. "Thoughts of Mao Tse-tung." *New York Review of Books* 20 (1973): 26–31.

Sekine, T. "Uno-riron: A Japanese Conribution to Marxian Political Economy." *Journal of Economic Literature* 13, no. 3 (1975): 847–877.

Shanin, T. "The Third Stage: Marxist Social Theory and the Origins of Our Time." *Journal of Contemporary Asia* 6, no. 3 (1976): 289–308.

Shibagaki, Kazuo. "Dissolution of Zaibatsu and Decentralization of Economic Power." *Annals of the Institute of Social Science* no. 2 (1979): 1–60.

———. "The Early History of the Zaibatsu." *The Developing Economies* 4, no. 4 (December 1966): 535–566.

Shils, Edward. "Political Development in the New States." *Comparative Studies in Society and History* 2, no. 3 (April 1960): 265–292.

Simcock, Bradford L. "The Anarcho-Syndicalist Thought and Activity of Osugi Sakae, 1885–1923." *Harvard University East Asian Research Center, Papers on Japan* 5 (1970): 31–54.

Skinner, G. William. "Chinese Peasants and the Closed Community: An Open and Shut Case." *Comparative Studies in Society and History* 13, no. 3 (July 1971): 270–281.

———. "Marketing and Social Structure in Rural China." *Journal of Asian Studies* 24, no. 1 (November 1964): 3–43; 24, no. 2 (February 1965): 195–228; 24, no. 3 (May 1965): 363–399.

Skocpol, Theda. "Bringing the State Back In: Strategies of Analysis in Current Research." In *Bringing the State Back In*, edited by Peter B. Evans, Dietrich Rueschemeyer, and Theda Skocpol, pp. 3–37. Cambridge: Cambridge University Press, 1985.

———. "A Critical Review of Barrington Moore's Social Origins of Dictatorship and Democracy." *Politics and Society* 4, no. 1 (Fall 1973): 1–34.

———. "Explaining Revolutions: In Quest of a Socio-Structural Approach." In *The Uses of Controversy in Sociology*, edited by Lewis A. Coser and Otto N. Larsen, pp. 155–175. New York: Free Press, 1976.

———. "Wallerstein's World Capitalist System: A Theoretical and Historical Critique." *American Journal of Sociology* 82, no. 5 (March 1977): 1075–1090.

Skocpol, Theda, and Trimberger, Ellen Kay. "Revolutions and the World-Historical Development of Capitalism." *Berkeley Journal of Sociology* 22 (1977–1978): 101–113.

Spae, Joseph F. "Towards a Sociology of Religion for Japan." *The Japan Missionary Bulletin* 20 (1966): 1–22.

Stalin, Joseph. "Marxism and the National Question" (1912). In *Marxism and the National and Colonial Question*. New York: International Publishers, 1935.

Starr, John Bryan. "Conceptual Foundations of Mao Tse-tung's Theory of Continuous Revolution." *Asian Survey* 11, no. 6 (June 1971): 610–628.

———. "Mao Tse-tung and the Sinification of Marxism: Theory, Ideology, and Phylactery." *Studies in Comparative Communism* 3, no. 2 (April 1970): 149–157.

———. "Weeding Through the Old to Bring Forth the New." *Asian Survey* 15, no. 1 (1975): 1–12.

Steinhoff, Patricia G. "Tenkō and Thought Control." In *Japan and the World: Essays in*

Japanese History and Politics, edited by Gail Lee Bernstein and Haruhiro Fukui, pp. 78–94. New York: St. Martin's Press, 1988.

Sternhell, Zeev. "Fascist Ideology." *Fascism: A Reader's Guide, Analyses, Interpretations, Bibliography*, edited by Walter Laqueur. Berkeley: University of California Press, 1976.

———. "National Socialism and Anti-Semitism: The Case of Maurice Barrès." *Journal of Contemporary History* 8, no. 4 (October 1973).

Strong, Anna Louise. "The Thought of Mao Tse-tung." *Amerasia* 11, no. 6 (June 1947): 161–174.

Sullivan, Lawrence R. "The Analysis of 'Despotism' in the CCP, 1978–1982." *Asian Survey* 27, no. 7 (1987): 800–821.

Therborn, Göran. "The Rule of Capital and the Rise of Democracy." *New Left Review* no. 103 (May–June 1977): 3–41.

Tilly, Charles. "Reflections on the History of European State-Making." In *The Formation of National States in Western Europe*, edited by Charles Tilly, pp. 3–83. Studies in Political Development, no. 8. Princeton, N.J.: Princeton University Press, 1975.

———. "Revolutions and Collective Violence." In *Handbook of Political Science*, edited by Fred I. Greenstein and Nelson W. Polsby. Vol. 3, *Macropolitical Theory*, pp. 483–555. Reading, Mass.: Addison-Wesley, 1975.

———. "Western State-Making and Theories of Political Transformation." In *The Formation of National States in Western Europe*, edited by Charles Tilly, pp. 601–638. Studies in Political Development, no. 8. Princeton, N.J.: Princeton University Press, 1975.

Todd, Nigel. "Ideological Superstructure in Gramsci and Mao Tse-tung." *Journal of the History of Ideas* 35, no. 1 (January–March 1974): 148–156.

Totten, George O. "Akamatsu Katsumaro: Political Activist and Ideologue." In *The Russian Impact on Japan: Literature and Social Thought*, translated and edited by E. Peter Berton, Paul F. Langer, and George O. Totten, pp. 73–86. Los Angeles: University of Southern California Press, 1981.

Trimberger, Ellen Kay. "State Power and Modes of Production: Implications of the Japanese Transition to Capitalism." *The Insurgent Sociologist* 7 (Spring 1977): 85–98.

Trotsky, Leon. "Stalinism and Bolshevism" (1937). In *Essential Works of Socialism*, edited by Irving Howe, pp. 359–369. New Haven, Conn.: Yale University Press, 1976.

———. "Three Concepts of the Russian Revolution" (1946), translated by Charles Malamuth. In *Essential Works of Socialism*, edited by Irving Howe, pp. 340–358. New Haven, Conn.: Yale University Press, 1976.

Tucker, Robert C. "The Image of Dual Russia." In Robert C. Tucker, *The Soviet Political Mind: Stalinism and Post-Stalin Change*, pp. 121–142. Rev. ed., New York: W. W. Norton, 1971.

———. Letter to the Editor. *Foreign Affairs* 58, no. 5 (Summer 1980): 1180.

———. "The Political Theory of Classical Marxism." In Robert C. Tucker, *The Marxian Revolutionary Idea*, pp. 54–91. New York: W. W. Norton, 1970.

van Wolferen, Karel G. "The Japan Problem." *Foreign Affairs* 65, no. 2 (Winter 1986–1987): 288–303.

Vilar, Pierre. "On Nations and Nationalism," translated by Elizabeth Fox-Genovese. *Marxist Perspectives* 5 (Spring 1979): 8–29.

Wakeman, Frederic, Jr. "The Price of Autonomy: Intellectuals in Ming and Ch'ing Politics." *Daedalus* 101 (Spring 1972): 35–70.

Wallerstein, Immanuel. "A World-System Perspective on the Social Sciences." *British Journal of Sociology* 27 (1976): 343–352.

Walzer, Michael. "A Theory of Revolution." *Marxist Perspectives* 2, no. 1 (Spring 1979): 30–44.

Wang, Fanxi. "Chen Duxiu, Father of Chinese Communism." In *Wild Lilies, Poisonous Weeds: Dissident Voices from People's China*, edited by Gregor Benton, pp. 157–167. London: Pluto Press, 1982.

Wang, Feng. "The Great Victory in Our Nationalities Policy" (September 27, 1959). In *Communist China 1955–1959: Policy Documents with Analysis*, with a foreword by Robert R. Bowie and John K. Fairbank, pp. 562–571. Cambridge, Mass.: Harvard University Press, 1962.

Wang, Gungwu. "Juxtaposing the Past and Present in China Today." *China Quarterly* 51 (1975): 1–24.

Watanabe, Tsunehiko. "Industrialization, Technological Progress, and Dual Structure." In *Economic Growth: The Japanese Experience Since the Meiji Era*, edited by Lawrence Klein and Kazushi Ohkawa, pp. 110–134. Homewood, Ill.: Richard D. Irwin, and Nobleton, Ontario: Irwin-Dorsey Limited, 1968.

Watanuki, Joji. "State Formation and Nation-Building in East Asia." *International Social Sciences Journal* 23, no. 3 (1971): 421–434.

Whyte, Martin King. "Bureaucracy and Modernization in China: The Maoist Critique." *American Sociological Review* 38 (1973): 149–163.

Wilbur, C. Martin. "The Influence of the Past: How the Early Years Helped to Shape the Future of the Chinese Communist Party." *China Quarterly* 36 (October–December 1968): 23–44.

Williams, Gwyn A. "The Concept of 'Egemonia' in the Thought of Antonio Gramsci: Some Notes on Interpretation." *Journal of the History of Ideas* 21, no. 4 (1960): 586–599.

Williams, Raymond. "Base and Superstructure in Marxist Cultural Theory." *New Left Review* 82 (November–December 1973): 3–16.

Wilson, George. "Kita Ikki's Theory of Revolution." *Journal of Asian Studies* 26, no. 1 (November 1966): 89–99.

Wittfogel, K. A. "The Legend of 'Maoism'." *China Quarterly* 1 (January–March 1960): 72–86; 2 (April–June 1960): 16–34.

Wittfogel, Karl. "The Stages of Development in Chinese Economic and Social History." In *The Asiatic Mode of Production*, edited by Anne M. Bailey and Josep R. Llobera, pp. 113–140. London: Routledge and Kegan Paul, 1981.

Wolfe, Alan. "New Directions in the Marxist Theory of Politics." *Politics and Society* 4, no. 2 (Winter 1974): 131–159.

Wolin, Sheldon S. "Paradigms and Political Theories." In *Politics and Experience: Essays Presented to Professor Michael Oakeshott on the Occasion of his Retirement*, edited by Preston King and B. C. Parekh. Cambridge: Cambridge University Press, 1968.

———. "The Politics of the Study of Revolution." *Comparative Politics* 5, no. 3 (April 1973): 343–358.

Wood, Gordon. "The American Revolution." In *Revolutions: A Comparative Study*, edited by Lawrence Kaplan, pp. 113–148. New York: Vintage Books, 1973.

Wright, Arthur F. "Struggle versus Harmony: Symbols of Competing Values in Modern China." In *Thirteenth Symposium of Science, Philosophy, and Religion*. New York: Harper and Row, 1954.

Wu, Dakun. "The Asiatic Mode of Production in History as Viewed by Political Economy in Its Broad Sense." In *Marxism in China*, edited by Su Shaozhi et al., with a foreword by Ken Coates, pp. 53–77. Nottingham: Spokesman, 1983.

Wylie, Raymond F. "Mao Tse-tung, Ch'en Po-ta and the 'Sinification' of Marxism, 1936–1938." *China Quarterly* 79 (September 1979): 447–480.

Xiao Gongquan. "K'ang Yu-wei and Confucianism." *Monumenta Serica* 18 (1959).

Yamada, Toshio, Hachirō Masaki, and Hisanori Shirogane. "Japanese Marxism Today." *Keizaigaku zasshi* (Osaka) 9 (1987): 68–93.

Yamamura, Kozo. "The Japanese Economy, 1911–1930: Concentration, Conflicts, and Crises." In *Japan in Crisis: Essays on Taishō Democracy*, edited by Bernard S. Silberman and H. D. Harootunian, pp. 299–328. Princeton, N.J.: Princeton University Press, 1974.

Yasuba Yasukichi. "Anatomy of the Debate on Japanese Capitalism." *Journal of Japanese Studies* 2, no. 1 (Fall 1973): 63–82.

Young, G., and D. Woodward. "From Contradictions among the People to Class Struggle: The Theories of Uninterrupted Revolution and Continuous Revolution." *Asian Survey* 18, no. 9 (1978): 912–933.

388; on political power, 390, 394; on self-cultivation, 387, 390, 393–94, 396

Liu Shifu. *See* Liu Sifu

Liu Shipei, 138, 149, 157, 158–62, 164–66, 170, 172–73, 201, 484n. 198

Liu Sifu (Liu Shifu), 163–70, 172, 483n. 183

Liu Xingtang, 318

Locke, John, 37, 102, 353, 400, 448n. 66

London Naval Conference, 358

Lowe, Donald, 77

loyalty, 93

Lu Xun, 190, 196, 197, 438

Lü Zhenyu, 302, 305, 313

luan (disorder, chaos), 96, 98, 166

Lukács, Georgy, 67, 68, 111, 166, 446n. 29

Luo Pu, 138

Lüou zazhi (Traveling in Europe Magazine), 163

Lushan Plenum, 431

Luxemburg, Rosa, 5, 18, 20, 21, 24, 82, 106, 229, 252, 449n. 10

Ma Jun, 298

Machiavelli, Niccolò, 45, 104, 186, 354

Mad'iar, Ludwig S., 80, 81, 287, 288, 291–93, 316, 460n. 207

Malatesta, Enrico, 145, 150

Malthus, T. R., 131

Manchuria, 337, 342, 357

Manchurian Incident (1931), 327, 328, 333, 340, 343, 361, 362, 417, 428

mandate of Heaven, 97, 99, 100, 102, 104, 466n. 81

manufacture debate, 293

Mao Zedong, 11, 13, 41, 113, 118, 123, 180, 204, 216, 359, 385, 398, 418, 421, 430, 438, 448, 464n. 60; anarchism and, 137, 153, 155, 364, 375, 395, 396; on backwardness, 198, 394; on bureaucracy, 390, 395, 400–401, 436, 441; Chinese tradition and, 153, 375–76, 393, 400; on class struggle, 392, 396, 398, 400; Comintern and, 294, 363, 365–66, 374, 407; Confucianism and, 155, 375, 377, 391, 393, 395, 400, 407, 434; on consciousness, 375, 385, 392, 396, 436; on continuous revolution (*jixu geming*), 407, 437; on corruptive nature of political power, 390; on cultivation of revolutionary virtue, 377, 394, 398, 400; on cultural revolution, 155, 385, 396, 398, 400, 407; on democracy, 390–91, 401, 421, 435–38; feudalism and, 294, 365, 434; Gramsci and, 389; ideology and, 384–85, 387, 389, 396–97, 436; on imperialism, 380, 467n.

116; industrialization and, 211, 365, 375, 385, 394–95, 433, 435; on intellectuals, 156, 188, 376, 386, 387, 392, 405, 439; on leadership, 382, 390–93, 395–96, 400; Liu Shaoqi and, 365; on mass line, 391, 395; nationalism in, 178, 191, 214, 218, 365, 374, 377–80, 386, 399, 410–11; on New Democracy, 380, 385, 437; oriental society and, 82; on peasantry, 362, 374–76, 378, 393; on permanent revolution, 324, 441; on practice, 366, 385–88; *renmin* and, 363; sinification of Marxism by, 16, 361–62, 363–66, 368, 399, 410, 416, 420, 430; on spiritual transformation, 355, 363, 396; statism and antistatism in, 10, 364, 395–97, 400, 432; on transitional state, 385; Trotsky and, 373–74, 378; on uninterrupted revolution, *see* continuous revolution (*jixu geming*) (Mao); on vanguard party, 392; voluntarism in thought of, 389

Marcuse, Herbert, 67, 68, 400

Marukusu-shugi (Marxism), 256

Marukusu-shugi kōza (Symposium on Marxism), 257

Maruyama Masao, 225

Marx, Karl, 9, 21, 38, 39, 49, 74, 76, 108, 118, 138, 147, 184, 206, 275–76, 308, 309, 349; on absolutism, 261, 266, 319, 320; on alienation, 48, 50, 65; anarchism and, 51, 127; on Asia, 41, 275, 278, 312, 370, 406, 408; on Asiatic mode of production, 40, 316, 323, 408; on authority, 400; on bureaucracy, 382; on class struggle, 299, 396; on consciousness, 50, 386; critique of Hegel on the state, 48–50, 56, 58, 62; on democracy, 50, 421; on dictatorship of proletariat, 381; early writings of, 55, 69, 107, 110, 119, 121–22, 389, 470–71; on Germany, 7, 8; Hegelian influence on, 39, 48, 128, 371; on imperialism, 81, 273, 278, 371; influence of, in China, 215; on Japan, 234, 276, 409; later writings of, 55, 107, 119; on nationalism, 3, 5–6, 18, 45, 83, 128; on oriental despotism, 58, 237, 254, 291, 397; on oriental society, 77, 78, 80, 197, 266, 267, 276, 289, 313, 323, 371, 397, 406, 408, 420, 459n. 171; on Paris Commune, 59; on peasantry, 198, 374; on Russia, 25, 38, 79, 128, 177, 456n. 100, 476n. 5; on the state, 4, 10, 48, 54, 56, 61, 62, 83, 177, 206, 257, 382, 395, 397, 399, 452n. 15; and vanguard party, 381

Marxism, 8, 9; anarchism and, 165, 276; Eastern philosophical traditions and, 403; Hegelian and liberal roots of, 45, 405; as historical materialism, 68, 121, 229; as ideol-